Famous Americans

A Directory of Museums, Historic Sites, and Memorials

Victor J. Danilov

The Scarecrow Press, Inc.
Lanham • Toronto • Plymouth, UK
2013

Published by Scarecrow Press, Inc.
A wholly owned subsidary of The Rowman & Littlefield Publishing Group, Inc.
4501 Forbes Boulevard, Suite 200, Lanham, Maryland 20706
www.rowman.com

10 Thornbury Road, Plymouth PL6 7PP, United Kingdom

British Library Cataloguing in Publication Information Available

Library of Congress Cataloging-in-Publication Data

Danilov, Victor J.
  Famous Americans : a directory of museums, historic sites, and memorials / Victor J. Danilov.
      pages cm.
  Includes bibliographical references and index.
  ISBN 978-0-8108-9185-2 (cloth : alk. paper) — ISBN 978-0-8108-9186-9 (ebook)
  1. Historic sites—United States—Directories. 2. Museums—United States—Directories. 3. Memorials—United States—Directories. 4. Celebrities—United States—Directories. 5. United States—Biography—Directories. I. Title.
  E159.D35 2013
  973.025—dc23   2013011098

✄ ™ The paper used in this publication meets the minimum requirements of American National Standard for Information Sciences—Permanence of Paper for Printed Library Materials, ANSI/NISO Z39.48-1992.

Printed in the United States of America.

Contents

Preface

Every country has people who are considered "famous"—people who are known for their achievements, positions, beauty, or other attributes or failings. Some deserve it, others do not. Many seek fame, but only a few attain or reject it. And even less have museums, historic sites, or memorials devoted to their lives, careers, and accomplishments.

Most "famous" people are celebrated because they have made significant contributions to a nation or region. Others have made advances to humankind or a particular field or endeavor. A few people become famous because of other actions, which were not always of a favorable nature. These stories are told at many museum-like sites across the nation.

This study describes 472 museums, historic sites, and memorials of 407 Americans and a few people from other countries with museums in the United States who are regarded as "famous." It tells about their lives, achievements, and the events that influenced their becoming famous. The descriptions are divided into 26 categories—ranging from actors, artists, authors, musicians, and scientists to business, military, and political figures, with presidents of the United States being the largest category.

The nation has 129 museums, libraries, historic sites, and memorials devoted to American presidents. Abraham Lincoln has the greatest number of sites—21. Other categories with large numbers of famous people are authors/writers, 62; public officials/political figures, 36; musicians/singers/composers, 33; and social activists, 28.

The "famous" movement in the United States began in the early 1800s, with monuments honoring George Washington in the District of Columbia, Baltimore, and Virginia. They were followed by preserving George Washington's home at Mount Vernon, Virginia, and the historic houses of such presidents as James A. Garfield in Ohio and Andrew Jackson in Tennessee. The greatest growth occurred in the 1900s when the "famous" recognition movement spread to other fields and took other forms.

Famous people now are honored in museums and libraries dedicated to them; houses where they lived, were born, or once lived; parks, campuses, tombs, and sites of significant events; and such memorials as statues, towers, and obelisks. The State of New York has the most such famous tributes with 42, followed by Pennsylvania, 36; Massachusetts, 34; and Illinois, 29. The city with the greatest number of sites honoring famous people is Washington in the District of Columbia with 14. Next are Baltimore and Springfield, Illinois, with six sites and New York City and Concord, Massachusetts, with five.

Washington memorials have the highest annual attendances. The Lincoln Memorial attracts 5.5 million visitors annually, while the Franklin Delano Roosevelt Memorial has 2.8 million and the Jefferson Memorial 2.3 million. Other major attendance sites are Mount Rushmore National Memorial in Keystone, South Dakota, 2.7 million; Jefferson National Expansion Memorial, St. Louis, 2.5 million; Crazy Horse Memorial, Crazy Horse, South Dakota, 1 million; and Martin Luther King Jr. National Historic Site and Martin Luther King Jr. Center for Nonviolent Social Change, Atlanta, over 900,000.

Not all the "famous" museums, historic sites, and memorials are large or have high attendances. But they perform an invaluable public educational service with their exhibits, artifacts, and programs that have influenced the history and other aspects of the nation.

I want to thank all the "famous" museums, historic sites, and memorials, as well as *The Official Museum Directory*, Wikipedia, and other reference sources, for their assistance in this study.

Introduction

The museum world is filled with art, history, science, and other types of museums, historic sites, and museum-like institutions relating to "famous" people. They contain exhibits, objects, or programs relating to the lives and achievements of exceptional individuals.

Famous people usually are identified by their deeds—and sometimes their heritage or reputation. They also are called renowned, illustrious, eminent, celebrated, distinguished, acclaimed, noted, and even notorious. Many honorees are historical figures, but they can also be found in many other fields.

This study contains descriptions of the lives and accomplishments of 409 "famous" people at 472 museums, historic sites, and related facilities devoted to them in the United States. The museum-like institutions and sites take many different forms, including historic house museums, cultural centers, historic sites, and memorials, statues, and tombs that contain descriptive materials. Statues, tombs, and monuments without exhibits or information about those honored generally are not included. The museums are largely housed where the famed were born or once lived.

The descriptions are grouped in 26 categories, including actors, architects, artists/sculptors, athletes, authors/writers, aviators/astronauts, business/industrial/financial figures, educators, entertainers, explorers, first ladies, frontiersmen, journalists/publishers, medical innovators, military figures, musicians/singers/composers, outlaws, patriotic figures, playwrights, poets, presidents, public officials/political figures, religious leaders, scientists/engineers/inventors, social activists, and socialites.

Most of the famous people museums and sites were founded in the 1900s, but many are devoted to leaders in the 1700s and 1800s. George Washington was the earliest "famous person" to be honored in the United States. The first such attempt was made in 1783 when the Continental Congress voted to honor Washington with an equestrian statue at the place where the Congress is located. But the proposal never was implemented. The next attempt at a Washington memorial was made 10 days after his death in 1799. A Congressional committee recommended that a tomb be erected within the Capitol. However, lack of funds, disagreement over the type of memorial, and the Washington family's reluctance to move his body prevented progress on the proposal, and it was shelved in 1801 when the Democratic-Republican Party took over Congress from the Federalist Party.

Finally in 1832, the Washington National Memorial Society was founded to raise the funds and build the Washington Monument, the huge obelisk that now stands on the National Mall in Washington. Construction began in 1848 but was halted from 1854 to 1877 because of opposition from the Know-Nothing Party, lack of funds, and the Civil War. The monument finally was finished in 1884 and opened to the public in 1888. It is still the world's tallest stone structure and obelisk, standing 555 feet, 5¼ inches.

Meanwhile, during the Washington Monument's construction and delays, a number of other Washington memorials were developed. The first was a 30-foot monument erected by the residents of Boonsboro, Virginia, in 1827 (which later became the Washington Monument State Park in Middletown, Maryland). It was followed in 1829 by the 178-foot Washington Monument in Baltimore; Washington's home, which was purchased by a women's group in 1854 and made into the Mount Vernon historic estate; and Washington Headquarters State Historic Site in Newburgh, New York, in 1884—the nation's first publicly operated historic site.

It wasn't long before memorials for other famous people were being established. The home of James A. Garfield, the 20th president, was converted into the Garfield Memorial Library in Mentor Ohio in 1886 and later became the James A. Garfield National Historic Site; and "The Hermitage," the 1836 home of Andrew Jackson, the seventh President, in Hermitage, Tennessee, was opened as a historic house museum in 1889.

LINCOLN: THE MOST HONORED

Today, the greatest number of museums, historic sites, and related facilities dedicated to famous people in the United States are for the nation's presidents. There are 129 museums, memorials, monuments, tombs, and other historic sites honoring 43 presidents (actually 42 different people since Grover Cleveland was elected twice at different times—1885–1889 and 1893–1897). Every president has at least one site in his honor. Abraham Lincoln has the greatest number, 21, followed by George Washington with 14. Franklin Delano Roosevelt has seven; Ulysses S. Grant, six; and four presidents—Thomas Jefferson, Theodore Roosevelt, Harry S. Truman, and Lyndon Baines Johnson—have five places.

Authors and writers have the greatest number of museums and historic sites in the specialized fields with 62. Those with the most facilities are Edgar Allan Poe and Laura Ingalls Wilder with four, and Mark Twain (Samuel Langhorne Clemens), Ernest Hemingway, Robert Louis Stevenson, and Harriet Beecher Stowe with three.

Public officials and political figures rank next with 36 places dedicated to famous people. Jefferson Davis and Daniel Webster account for three, and Benjamin Franklin, Sam Houston, and Sam Rayburn have two sites. Social activists are the focus of 28 places, with six devoted to John Brown, five to Frederick Douglass, and three to Harriet Tubman. Musicians, singers, and composers have 33 honorees, with Paul Robeson having four sites; Elvis Presley and Lawrence Welk, three; and Marian Anderson and Stephen Foster, two.

Among the other famous people who have multiple museums and historic sites are inventor Thomas Edison and explorers Meriwether Lewis and William Clark, each with six; entertainer Buffalo Bill Cody, five; artist John James Audubon and frontiersman Davy Crockett, four; and lawyer/statesman Daniel Webster, religious leader Joseph Smith, scientist George Washington Carver, outlaw Jesse James, poets Henry Wadsworth Longfellow and Robert Frost, aviation pioneers Wilbur and Orville Wright, and entertainers Walt Disney and Will Rogers, three.

The most museums, historic sites, and memorials of famous people are located in the state of New York with 42 such facilities, followed by Pennsylvania with 36; Massachusetts, 34; Illinois, 29; Virginia, 28; California and Ohio, 27; and Missouri and Texas, 22. Cities with the largest number of "famous" tributes are Washington, DC, 14; Baltimore and Springfield, Illinois, 6; New York City and Concord, Massachusetts, 5; and Atlanta, Boston, Dayton, and Hyde Park, New York, 4.

HISTORIC HOUSES ARE THE MOST NUMEROUS

The largest number of famous people sites are historic house museums where the person was born or once lived. They include such places as the Thomas Edison Birthplace Museum in Milan, Ohio; the Mark Twain Boyhood Home and Museum in Hannibal, Missouri; and Graceland in Memphis, where singer/actor Elvis Presley lived. Many other museums are located where famous people once lived, including the Ernest Hemingway House Museum, Key West, Florida; Georgia O'Keeffe Home and Studio, Abiquiu, New Mexico; Susan B. Anthony Museum and House, Rochester, New York; and Brigham Young Winter Home, St. George, Utah.

Some historic homes are national or state historic sites, such as the Longfellow National Historic Site, Cambridge, Massachusetts; Frederick Law Olmsted National Historic Site, Brookline, Massachusetts; Eleanor Roosevelt National Historic Site, Hyde Park, New York; Willa Cather State Historic Site, Red Cloud, Nebraska; Scott Joplin House State Historic Site, St. Louis; William Allen White State Historic Site, Emporia, Kansas; and Jefferson Davis State Historic Site, Fairview, Kentucky.

A number of museums honoring famous people are devoted primarily to their work, rather than their lives. They include such art museums as the Andrew Warhol Museum, Pittsburgh; Frederic Remington Art Museum, Ogdensburg, New York; and Norman Rockwell Museum, Stockbridge, Massachusetts. Sometimes the work takes other forms, as occurs at Frank Lloyd Wright's buildings at Taliesin (his home which he designed) in Spring Green, Wisconsin, and Eleuthére Irénée du Pont's Hagley Museum and Library (an industrial museum site that includes the home of the Du Pont chemical company founder), Wilmington, Delaware.

Tributes also are made to famous people in many other ways. Some state parks are named for them and contain museums or interpretive centers about their lives and achievements, including the Will Rogers State Historic Park, Pacific Palisades, California; Davy Crockett Birthplace State Park, Limestone, Tennessee; and Buffalo Bill Ranch State Historical Park, North Platte, Nebraska. Libraries are part of some sites honoring famous people, as at the

Morgan Library and Museum, New York City; Senator Sam J. Erwin Jr. Library and Museum, Morganton, North Carolina; and Michael E. DeBakey Library and Museum, Baylor University, Houston.

Famous people are honored at such other types of sites as the Thurgood Marshall Center, Washington (cultural center); Stephen A. Douglas Tomb and Memorial, Chicago (tomb); Jim Bowie Display and Museum, Opelousas, Louisiana (city visitor center); Mary Pickford Museum, Cathedral City, California (theater); Hank Aaron Childhood Home and Museum, Mobile, Alabama (baseball field); Chanute Air Museum, Rantoul, Illinois (airfield); Hershey Story, Hershey, Pennsylvania (industrial plant); Perry's Victory and International Peace Memorial, Put-in-Bay, Ohio (column); and Mount Rushmore National Memorial, Keystone, South Dakota (mountainside).

Some museums celebrate the lives and work of foreigners who are honored with museums in the United States. They include the National Winston Churchill Museum and Winston Churchill Memorial and Library, Westminster College, Fulton, Missouri; Golda Meir House Museum, Denver; Folger Shakespeare Library, Amherst College, Washington; Thaddeus Kosciuszko National Memorial, Philadelphia; Robert Louis Stevenson Silverado Museum, St. Helena, California; Salvador Dali Museum, St. Petersburg, Florida; Rodin Museum, Philadelphia; Pablo Casals Museum, Old San Juan, Puerto Rico; Hans Christian Andersen Museum, Solvang, California; Pancho Villa State Park, Columbus, New Mexico; Father Marquette National Memorial, St. Ignace, Michigan; and museums of such early Spanish explorers as De Soto, Cabrillo, and Coronado.

A number of "famous" museums are devoted to two people who were related in their efforts, such as Meriwether Lewis and William Clark in their 1804–1806 exploratory expedition to the Pacific Coast (Lewis and Clark National Historical Park, Astoria, Oregon); Wilbur and Orville Wright, who jointly developed the first airplane in 1903 (Wright Brothers National Memorial, Kill Devil Hills, North Carolina); Jesse and Frank James, the most notorious outlaws of the nineteenth century (Jesse James Farm and Museum, Kearney, Missouri); and poets Robert and Elizabeth Browning (Armstrong Browning Library, Baylor University, Waco, Texas).

MEMORIALS LEAD IN ATTENDANCE

Memorial sites have the greatest attendances among those facilities honoring famous people. The Lincoln Memorial in Washington has the highest annual attendance with 5.5 million visitors. Other memorials with large attendances are the Franklin Delano Roosevelt Memorial, Washington, 2.8 million; Mount Rushmore National Memorial, Keystone, South Dakota, 2.7 million; Jefferson National Expansion Memorial, St. Louis, 2.5 million; Jefferson Memorial, Washington, 2.3 million; Crazy Horse Memorial, Crazy Horse, South Dakota, 1 million; Wright Brothers National Memorial, Kill Devil Hills, North Carolina, nearly 500,000; and Washington Monument, Washington, 460,000.

Among the "famous" museums and historic sites with the largest annual attendances are the Henry Ford, Dearborn, Michigan; J. Paul Getty Museum, Los Angeles; and Carnegie Museums of Pittsburgh, 1.6 million; Mount Vernon, George Washington's Estate and Gardens, Mount Vernon, Virginia, 1.1 million; Benjamin Franklin National Memorial, Philadelphia; and Ford Theater National Historic Site, Washington, 1 million; Martin Luther King Jr. National Historic Site and Martin Luther King Jr. Center for Nonviolent Social Change, Atlanta, and Biltmore Estate, Asheville, North Carolina, 900,000; Cabrillo National Monument, San Diego, 886,000; and Hearst Castle (home of William Randolph Hearst), San Simeon, California, 860,000.

Among the other museums honoring famous people with large attendances are Graceland (Elvis Presley's home), Memphis, and Abraham Lincoln Presidential Library and Museum, Springfield, Illinois, 600,000; Arlington House (Robert E. Lee), Arlington, Virginia, 500,000; George Washington Carver Museum, Tuskegee, Alabama, 490,000; Monticello, home of Thomas Jefferson, Charlottesville, Virginia, 450,000; and Lincoln's New Salem State Historic Site, Petersburg, Illinois, 400,000.

Others with substantial attendances include the Jean Lafitte National Historical Park and Preserve, New Orleans, 391,000; Autry National Center of the American West/Museum of the American West (Gene Autry), Los Angeles, 375,000; John and Mable Ringling Museum of Art (and Cá d'Zan home and Circus Museum), Sarasota, Florida, and Vanderbilt Mansion National Historic Site (home of Frederick W. Vanderbilt), Hyde Park, New York, 360,000; General George Patton Museum of Leadership, Fort Knox, Kentucky, 358,000; Washington Crossing Historical Park, Washington Crossing, Pennsylvania, and Malabar Farm State Park (author Louis Broomfield's home), Lucas, Ohio, 350,000; the Breakers (home of Cornelius Vanderbilt II), Newport, Rhode Island, 300,000.

Among the 13 sites in the federal museum system, the Ronald Reagan Presidential Library and Museum in Simi Valley, California, has the largest annual attendance with more than 300,000 visitors. The William J. Clinton Presidential Library and Museum in Little Rock, Arkansas, is second with an attendance of nearly 300,000. Ranking next are the LBJ Presidential Library in Austin, Texas, with 240,000, and John F. Kennedy Presidential Library and Museum in Boston, with 220,000.

Mount Rushmore National Memorial in Keystone, South Dakota, which honors four former presidents of the United States. Courtesy of the National Park Service and Mount Rushmore National Memorial; photograph by Ranger Ed Menard.

NEW AND CLOSED MUSEUMS AND HISTORIC SITES

New museums, historic sites, and memorials celebrating the lives and accomplishments of famous people continue to be founded and planned. Among those recently established include the George W. Bush Presidential Library and Museum, Dallas; Franklin D. Roosevelt Four Freedoms Park, New York City; Ulysses S. Grant Presidential Library, Starkville, Mississippi; Billy Graham Library, Charlotte, North Carolina; and Hank Aaron Childhood Home and Museum, Mobile, Alabama. The Dwight D. Eisenhower Memorial also is about to be added to the national memorials in the National Mall area of Washington.

Three new national monuments honoring individuals have been created by President Barack Obama in recent years. They include the César E. Chávez National Monument in Keene, California, in 2012, and two monuments in 2013—the Harriet Tubman Underground Railroad National Monument near Cambridge, Maryland, and the Charles Young Buffalo Soldier National Monument near Xenia, Ohio.

Many other tributes to famous people are in planning or fundraising stages for such famed figures as singer/dancer Michael Jackson in his hometown of Gary, Indiana, and at his Neverland Ranch near Santa Barbara, California; journalist and social critic H. L. Mencken in his former Baltimore home; abolitionist and writer Frederick Douglass in Rochester, New York, where he once lived; and former baseball stars Honus Wagner in Carnegie, Pennsylvania, Jackie Robinson in New York City, Mickey Mantle in Commerce, Oklahoma, and William Mays in San Francisco.

It has been difficult to find funding for new museums of all types during these difficult economic times. And some have not survived in recent years for financial or other reasons. Among those that have closed are the Frank Sinatra Museum, Hoboken, New York; Dolly Parton's "Rags to Riches" Museum, Pigeon Forge, Tennessee; Stonewall Jackson Museum at Hupp's Hill, Strasburg, Virginia; Wyatt Earp Museum, San Diego; Dizzy Dean Museum, Jackson, Mississippi; and Tom Mix Birthplace Park and Museum in Mix Run, Pennsylvania.

The Billy Sunday Collection in Winona Lake, Indiana, has been merged into the Reneker Museum of Winona History at Grace College, while the Joe Weatherly Stock Car Museum in Darlington, South Carolina, has become the Darlington Raceway Stock Car Museum. Others have not reopened after disasters, such as the Kate Chopin House, which was destroyed in a fire in Cloutierville, Louisiana, and the Douglas Fairbanks Sr. Museum in Austin, Texas, which was severely damaged in a flood.

Museums, historic sites, and memorials of famous people constitute a relatively small portion of the approximately 17,500 such facilities in the United States. But they are an important segment. They honor individuals who have had an impact in various aspects of the nation's history, culture, and life. They show us how we have evolved from a struggling frontier colony into a many-faceted modern society. And they inspire us with their stories of overcoming obstacles and their determination, creativity, and accomplishments.

THE PRESIDENTS

The nation's presidents dominate the list of museums, historic sites, and memorials of famous people in the United States with 119 facilities. More than a quarter of the tributes to famous people are dedicated to the 43 presidents from George Washington to George W. Bush. Thirteen are part of the federal system of presidential libraries and museums, and 106 others are operated by support groups, foundations, universities, and government agencies.

The presidential library system, as it is called, began in 1939 when President Franklin Delano Roosevelt donated his personal and presidential papers to the federal government and pledged part of his estate in Hyde Park, New York, to the United States. Friends of President Roosevelt formed a nonprofit corporation to raise funds for the construction of a library and museum to house the papers and exhibits. Roosevelt believed that presidential papers were an important part of the national heritage and should be accessible to the public. Roosevelt asked the National Archives to take custody of the papers and other historical materials and to administer the library/museum. It resulted in the founding of the Franklin Delano Roosevelt Presidential Library and Museum in 1940. It now has an annual attendance of 110,000.

When President Harry S. Truman also decided in 1950 to turn his papers and historical materials over to the government, it caused Congress to pass the Presidential Libraries Act of 1955, which established a system of privately financed and built and federally operated and maintained libraries and museums. Since then, nine other presidents have donated their buildings and historical materials to the government for presidential libraries and museums administered by the National Archives and Records Administration. The Harry S. Truman Library and Museum in Independence, Missouri, now has an annual attendance of 90,000.

A number of changes have been made since the federal system began in 1955. The Presidential Records Act of 1978 established that the presidential records that document the constitutional, statutory, and ceremonial duties of the office are the property of the government and not the presidents. When a president leaves office, the Archivist of the United States assumes custody of the records. The Presidential Libraries Act of 1986 required that private endowments linked to the size of a facility be made available to the National Archives and Records Administration to offset a portion of the facility's maintenance cost.

Two presidential library/museum facilities that were not part of the system have been added—the Herbert Hoover Presidential Library and Museum in West Branch, Iowa, in 1992, and the Richard Nixon Presidential Library and Museum in Yorba Linda, California, in 2007. The Hoover library and museum was picked up even though the Hoover presidency was before the federal library/museum system began, and the Richard Nixon Library and Birthplace was accepted into the program after being barred earlier because of Nixon's Watergate Scandal and resignation.

The 13 presidential libraries and museums contain more than 400 million pages of textual materials; nearly 10 million photographs; over 15 million feet of motion picture film; about 100,000 hours of disc, audiotape, and videotape recordings; and approximately 500,000 museum objects. The libraries/museums have such objects as family heirlooms, campaign memorabilia, awards, gifts from citizens and foreign dignitaries, and often reproductions of the Oval Office.

The Largest Presidential Library/Museum

The Ronald Reagan Presidential Library and Museum in Simi Valley, California, is the largest of the nation's presidential libraries. Founded in 1991, it covers 243,000 square feet, including a 90,000-square-foot pavilion that houses Air Force One, the Boeing 707 plane used by seven presidents from 1973 to 2001. The library houses 50 million pages of presidential documents, over 1.6 million photographs, 500,000 feet of motion picture film, and tens of thousands of audio and video tapes. It also contains Reagan's personal papers, including materials from when he was governor of California.

The museum features exhibits on Reagan's life and achievements, including his childhood, film career, military service, marriages, political career, and presidency. Among the objects displayed are Reagan's 1965 Ford Mustang car, his desk as governor, campaign materials, inauguration suit, table from the White House Situation Room, and a full-scale replica of the Oval Office. An F-14 Tomcat plane is located on the lawn, and Reagan's tomb memorial is near a section of the Berlin Wall. The annual attendance is over 300,000.

The William J. Clinton Presidential Library and Museum in Little Rock, Arkansas, occupies a 68,698-square-foot building on a 17-acre site that is part of the 30-acre Clinton Presidential Park. The park complex includes the Clinton Foundation, a restored historic train station that houses the University of Arkansas Clinton School of Public Service, and an arboretum, amphitheater, gardens, and children's play area.

The library has the largest archival collection of the federal presidential facilities administered by the National Archives and Records Administration. It includes 80 million documents, 21 million e-mail messages, 2 million

The Ronald Reagan Presidential Library and Museum in Simi Valley, California. Courtesy of the Ronald Reagan Library.

photographs, and 79 artifacts from the Clinton presidency. The museum has 20,000 square feet of exhibits that feature a 110-foot timeline of the Clinton presidency, 13 policy alcoves, a reconstruction of the Cabinet Room, and a full-size replica of the Oval Room.

Four presidential libraries and museums and one of the libraries are located on university campuses. The first was the LBJ Presidential Library (formerly the Lyndon Baines Johnson Library and Museum), which was dedicated in 1971 at the University of Texas in Austin. It is located on 14 acres adjacent to the LBJ School of Public Affairs and contains 45 million pages of historical documents, 15,000 volumes, and 3,900 serials in the library, and the museum collection consists of more than 54,000 objects. The exhibits range from the life and times of President Johnson to displays about the White House and Lady Bird Johnson. Annual attendance is 240,000.

The two Bush presidents also have located their presidential libraries and museums on university campuses in Texas. President George H. W. Bush founded his at Texas A&M University in College Station in 1997, while his son opened the George W. Bush Presidential Library and Museum at Southern Methodist University in Dallas in 2013. The library/museum at Texas A&M University attracts 138,000 visitors annually.

Gerald R. Ford is the only president to have a presidential library and museum at two different locations—the Gerald R. Ford Library was established in 1977 at the University of Michigan in Ann Arbor (which no longer is permitted by Congress), and the Gerald R. Ford Presidential Museum was opened in 1981 in his hometown of Grand Rapids, Michigan. The museum receives 204,000 visitors annually, while the library serves 750 a year.

Other federal presidential libraries and museums include the Dwight D. Eisenhower Presidential Library and Museum, Abilene, Kansas, which has an annual attendance of 160,000; John F. Kennedy Presidential Library and Museum, Boston, 220,000 annual attendance; Jimmy Carter Library and Museum, Atlanta, 82,000 annual attendance; and the two sites that were admitted later to the federal library/museum system by Congress—the Herbert Hoover Presidential Library-Museum in West Branch, Iowa, and the Richard Nixon Presidential Library and Museum in Yorba Linda, California—each with about 70,000 visitors annually.

Twenty-One Sites Honoring President Lincoln

Many other museums, historic sites, and memorials honor former presidents of the United States. They most often are located at houses were they were born or once lived. Others are national memorials, historic sites, state parks, tombs, and libraries and museums dedicated to their lives and achievements.

President Abraham Lincoln has the greatest number of sites—21 places—that honor his life and accomplishments. They range from the Lincoln Home National Historic Site, Abraham Lincoln Presidential Library and Museum, and Lincoln Tomb State Historic Site in Springfield, Illinois, to President Lincoln's Cottage, Ford Theatre National Historic Site, and Lincoln Memorial in Washington. The Lincoln Memorial has an annual attendance of 5.5 million, the largest annual attendance of all the facilities dedicated to the nation's famous people.

President George Washington ranks second in the number of dedicated famous sites with 14. The 555-foot, 5-and-a-quarter-inch Washington Monument obelisk in Washington, which was started in 1832 and completed in 1884, was the first famous person memorial. Despite its limited access, the tower has an annual attendance of 460,000 visitors. The monument, however, was closed for repairs in 2011 as a result of earthquake damage. Washington's home in Virginia—Mount Vernon—is one of the nation's most visited historic house museums with an annual attendance of over 1.1 million. Washington also is one of the four presidents (the others being Thomas Jefferson, Abraham Lincoln, and Theodore Roosevelt) who are sculpted in granite on the mountainside at the Mount Rushmore National Memorial in Keystone, South Dakota. The memorial has an annual attendance of 2.7 million.

In addition to being among the giant sculptures at Mount Rushmore, Lincoln is honored at 20 other sites. The Abraham Lincoln Presidential Library and Museum, which is not part of the federal library presidential system, is a state-operated site in Springfield, Illinois, with an annual attendance of 600,000. Five other historic sites in Springfield include Lincoln's home, law office, train departure for Washington, and tomb, as well as a memorial garden and nature center. The Lincoln Memorial on the National Mall in Washington has the highest attendance of any tribute to a famous person in the nation.

Jefferson is honored at four sites in addition to Mount Rushmore. The Jefferson Memorial in Washington has an annual attendance of 2.3 million, and the Jefferson National Expansion Memorial in St. Louis has 2.5 visitors a year. His historic home in Charlottesville, Virginia—Monticello—has an annual attendance of 450,000. Jefferson's one-time retreat in Forest, Virginia, now also is a historic house museum, known as Thomas Jefferson's Poplar Forest.

In addition to the Mount Rushmore memorial, Theodore Roosevelt is honored at four other sites—Theodore Roosevelt Birthplace National Historic Site, New York City, 40,000 annual attendance; Sagamore Hill National

The Abraham Lincoln Presidential Library and Museum in Springfield, Illinois. Courtesy of the Abraham Lincoln Presidential Library and Museum.

Historic Site, Oyster Bay, New York, 60,000 annual attendance; Theodore Roosevelt Inaugural National Historic Site, Buffalo, New York, 17,000 annual attendance; and Theodore Roosevelt Collection, Harvard College Library, Cambridge, Massachusetts.

Five sites, in addition to the Franklin D. Roosevelt Presidential Library and Museum in Hyde Park, New York, are devoted to FDR's life and accomplishments. They range from the Home of Franklin D. Roosevelt National Historic Site, which preserves his Hyde Park home, to the Franklin Delano Roosevelt Memorial, a national memorial in Washington. President Ulysses S. Grant is honored at six places, including the Ulysses S. Grant National Historic Site in St. Louis, where he was born; the Ulysses S. Grant Home State Historic Site in Galena, Illinois; and General Grant National Memorial in New York City. In addition to Jefferson, three other presidents are honored at five sites—Theodore Roosevelt, Harry S. Truman, and Lyndon B. Johnson.

Ten of the 13 presidents who are part of the federal library/museum system have chosen to be buried at their library/museum sites, including Franklin D. Roosevelt, who initiated the federal program. The exceptions are John F. Kennedy, who is buried at Arlington National Cemetery; Lyndon B. Johnson, interred at his Texas ranch; and Jimmy Carter, who plans to be buried near his home in Plains, Georgia. Gerald R. Ford chose his museum site in Grand Rapids, Michigan, as his burial site, rather than at his library in Ann Arbor, Michigan.

Presidential Museums before the Federal System

Many other museums, historic sites, and memorials honor presidents who served before the federal presidential library/museum system was initiated, including the first presidential library created in 1886 by the wife of President James A. Garfield. The 20th president was shot and killed in 1881 by a deranged political office seeker after only 200 days in office. Lucretia Garfield built an addition to their house in Mentor, Ohio, for his books and papers in 1886 and opened it to the public as the Garfield Memorial Library. In 2008 it became the James A. Garfield National Historic Site. It now also contains information about Garfield's life and career, early furnishings, memorabilia, and photographs, as well as his campaign office and horse barn.

The Adams National Historical Park in Quincy, Massachusetts, honors John Adams the nation's second president from 1797 to 1801, and his son, John Quincy Adams, the sixth president from 1825 to 1829. Annual attendance is 185,000. The former plantation of Andrew Jackson, who was known as "Old Hickory" because of his toughness and aggressive personality, now is the Hermitage in Hermitage, Tennessee, with an annual attendance of over 235,000.

Grover Cleveland is the only American president to serve two nonconsecutive terms. He was the 22nd and 24th presidents. He was president in 1885–1889, lost reelection, and became president again in 1893–1897. His birthplace in Caldwell, New York, is the site of the Grover Cleveland Birthplace. Woodrow Wilson Presidential Library and Museum in Staunton, Virginia, is devoted to the 28th president (1913–1921), who led the nation to victory in World War I but lost the battle to have the United States join the League of Nations, which he was instrumental in creating after the war.

Presidential museums, libraries, historic sites, and memorials have made an invaluable contribution to furthering public understanding and appreciation of the life and times of the nation's presidents. Such facilities are an important part of the national heritage and among the most popular historical sites in the nation.

Sites Honoring First Ladies

Seven of the first ladies also have made contributions with their historic houses and gardens. They include the wives of three early presidents and four of the more recent heads of the nation. The Abigail Adams Birthplace in Weymouth, Massachusetts, is where the wife of President John Adams and mother of President John Quincy Adams was born. Dolley Madison, whose husband was President James Madison, once lived at the restored Todd House, a historic house in Philadelphia. The Mary Todd Lincoln House in Lexington, Kentucky, is the family home of President Abraham Lincoln's wife.

Two of the more recent first lady sites are historic homes, and the other two are gardens. The Eleanor Roosevelt National Historic Site in Hyde Park, New York, was the private retreat and later home of the wife of President Franklin D. Roosevelt, and the Mamie Doud Eisenhower Birthplace in Boone, Iowa, was where President Dwight D. Eisenhower's wife was born. The gardens are the Lady Bird Johnson Wildflower Center founded in Austin, Texas, by the spouse of President Lyndon Baines Johnson, and the Betty Ford Alpine Gardens in Vail, Colorado, named for the wife of President Gerald R. Ford.

HISTORIC FIGURES

Every country has historical figures—people who have made important contributions to nation's development or have been recognized for other reasons. The Unites States has its share of people who have made significant historical contributions, but not all have achieved fame. And there are others who have become "famous" for other historical reasons—good and bad.

Among the historic figures have been explorers, frontiersmen, patriotic figures, public officials, politicians, military figures, entrepreneurs, religious leaders, social activists, socialites, and even outlaws. They have explored new territories, helped create a nation, fought wars, inspired a nation, started and operated companies, sought social change, and made other contributions.

The explorers with historic sites have ranged from early Spanish explorers and conquistadors and a French priest to the Lewis and Clark Expedition and Antarctica, Arctic, and Colorado River explorers. Hernando de Soto, a Spanish explorer, made the first extensive European exploration of the southeastern region of what later became part of the United States. He made landing in Tampa Bay with nine ships and over 600 soldiers in 1539. The De Soto National Memorial near Bradenton, Florida, commemorates the landing.

Francisco Vásquez de Coronado, a Spanish conquistador, was the first to organize an expedition into the American Southwest in 1540–1542. He is honored at the Coronado National Memorial near Sierra Vista, Arizona; Coronado State Monument in Bernalillo, New Mexico; and Coronado Quivira Museum in Lyons, Kansas. Another conquistador, Juan Rodríguez Cabrillo, led a 1542 Spanish exhibition that was the first European expedition to set foot on the West Coast. The Cabrillo National Monument is now located in San Diego, California, where he first came ashore.

The Father Marquette National Memorial in St. Ignace, Michigan, is dedicated to the French Jesuit missionary and explorer who traveled throughout the remote Great Lakes region in the 1660s and 1670s to open missions among the Indians—often accompanied by Louis Jolliet, a French Canadian fur trader and cartographer. Father Jacques Marquette also established a mission and village in 1671 in St. Ignace, now the location of the Marquette Mission Park, where a second mission was built.

Exploring and Mapping the West

The Lewis and Clark National Historical Park near Astoria, Oregon, is where Meriwether Lewis and William Clark and their Corps of Discovery camped in the winter of 1805 after reaching the Pacific Coast. Sacagawea, the Indian woman who served as interpreter and guide for the 1804–1806 Lewis and Clark Expedition, also is honored at the Sacajawea Interpretive Center near Pasco, Washington, and Sacajawea Interpretive, Cultural, and Educational Center in Salmon, Idaho.

John C. Frémont was known as "The Great Pathfinder" because of his early mapping exploits and later explorations in the American West. In addition, he became territorial governor of California and then Arizona, one of California's first two senators, an 1856 presidential candidate, and a Union general in the Civil War. The historic Frémont House, an 1875 Victorian-style house, is where he and his wife lived in 1878–1881 while he was territorial governor of Arizona. In 1972 the house was moved to the Sharlot Hall Museum in Prescott, where it is part of the historic house collection.

Another western mapper, surveyor, and explorer was John Wesley Powell. The John Wesley Powell Memorial Museum in Page, Arizona, and the John Wesley Powell River History Museum in Green River, Utah, are devoted to Powell, who made the first passage through the Grand Canyon, mapped and surveyed the Colorado and Green Rivers, and explored much of the Rocky Mountains in the mid-1800s. He later became director of the U.S. Geological Survey and the Smithsonian Institution's Bureau of Ethnology.

Two museums are devoted to Antarctica and Arctic explorers. The Captain Nathaniel B. Palmer House in Stonington, Connecticut, honors the sea captain who is credited with discovering Antarctica in 1820, and the Peary-Macmillan Arctic Museum at Bowdoin College in Brunswick, Maine, is named for two Bowdoin graduates, Robert E. Peary and Donald Baxter Macmillan, who explored the Arctic region.

The Frontiersmen and Their Exploits

The frontiersmen sometimes were explorers, but more often they were mountain men, hunters, settlers, Indian fighters, soldiers, or lawmen. They included such frontiersmen as Daniel Boone, Jim Beckwourth, Kit Carson, George Rogers Clark, Jim Bowie, Davy Crockett, and Wyatt Earp.

A replica of Lewis and Clark's Fort Clatsop, one of the historic attractions at the Lewis and Clark National Historical Park in Astoria, Washington. Courtesy of the National Park Service and Lewis and Clark National Historical Park.

Perhaps the most recognized frontiersman was Daniel Boone, who became known for his wilderness exploits and encounters with Indians during the 1700s and later his simulated adventures on television and in the movies. His life is the focus of the Daniel Boone Homestead, an open-air museum in Birdsboro, Pennsylvania, where he was born, and the Daniel Boone Home and Heritage Center in Defiance, Missouri, which contains his 1803–1810 home and a re-created pioneer village.

George Rogers Clark was a frontiersman who became a land surveyor and then a frontier military leader credited with winning the Old Northwest for the United States in the Revolutionary War. The George Rogers Clark National Historical Park in Vincennes, Indiana, is where he defeated the British and Indians in the 1778 Battle of Fort Sackville.

Jim Beckwourth was an African American mountain man who was a fur trader, explored the West, and lived with the Crow Indians for many years. He discovered the Beckwourth Pass through the Sierra Nevada Mountains during the Gold Rush years and later built a cabin and trading post in Portola, California, which now is the Jim Beckwourth Museum.

Kit Carson was a trapper, hunter, guide, scout, and Indian agent who became a military leader during the 1846–1848 Mexican-American War. After the war, he was a rancher, Indian agent, and brigadier general after his service during the Civil War. His home in Taos, New Mexico, is now the Kit Carson Home and Museum. The Kit Carson Memorial Chapel at Fort Lyon in Colorado, where he died, also is dedicated to Carson.

Jim Bowie and Davy Crockett were frontiersmen who died in the Battle of the Alamo in San Antonio, Texas, in 1836. Bowie, who was born in Kentucky and spent most of his life in Louisiana, migrated to Texas in 1830 when it was a state in the Mexican federation. He became a military leader in Texas when the colonists declared independence, and he was sent to the Alamo to retrieve the cannons and demolish the fort as the Mexican Army was marching to attack the former mission that had become a Texas fort.

After Bowie arrived, the occupants and Bowie decided to stay and defend the fort. They were joined by Davy Crockett and 30 volunteers from Tennessee, as well as a few others, increasing the fort defenders to several hundred against the 3,100 Mexican soldiers led by General Antonio López de Santa Anna. The Texans initially repelled the Mexican attacks but eventually were overwhelmed in the 13-day battle. Bowie and Crockett were among those killed, and the bodies of all the dead defenders were burned in a fire by General Santa Anna.

Bowie's life now is celebrated in the Jim Bowie Display and Museum in Opelousas, Louisiana. Crockett, who was a soldier, businessman, and politician in addition to frontiersman, is the subject of four tributes in Tennessee—Davy Crockett Birthplace State Park in Limestone; Crockett Museum, Lawrenceburg; David Crockett Cabin Museum, Rutherford; and Crockett Tavern Museum, Morristown.

Wyatt Earp was a frontier lawman in the late 1800s who became best known for his role in the so-called Gunfight at the O.K. Corral, in which three outlaw cowboys were killed in Tombstone, Arizona, in 1881. He served as sheriff, marshal, and other law enforcement capacities throughout the West before settling in Los Angeles, California, where he died in 1931. The house in which he was born in 1848 is now the Wyatt Earp Birthplace Home, a historic house museum in Monmouth, Illinois.

INSPIRATIONAL PATRIOTIC FIGURES

Some of America's best-known famous people are historic patriotic figures. They are known for giving speeches that urged resistance to British rule in the colonies, inspiring passion and sometimes action in writings and music, warning and taking action against enemy forces, producing patriotic symbols, and giving their lives for their country. Museums, historic sites, and memorials now honor such patriotic figures as Ethan Allen, Nathan Hale, Patrick Henry, Thomas Paine, Paul Revere, Betsy Ross, and John Philip Sousa.

Patrick Henry was a lawyer, legislator, and member of the Continental Congress who led the independence movement in Virginia. He headed the opposition to the Stamp Act of 1765 and is best known for his oratory and "Give Me Liberty, or Give Me Death" speech in 1775. He was considered one of the most influential exponents of the revolution and independence, along with Samuel Adams and Thomas Paine. He retired in 1790 to the Red Hill plantation near Brookneal, Virginia, which now is the Red Hill–Patrick Henry National Memorial.

Thomas Paine was a political philosopher and author who used the pen to fight the British in the American Revolutionary War. He wrote two of the most influential works during the revolutionary period—*Common Sense*, a widely read 1776 pamphlet that urged immediate declaration of independence, and the periodical, *Crisis*, a 1776–1783 series of 16 issues that upheld the colonial cause and rallied the Continental Army during the war. He also later wrote two of his most famous works—*The Rights of Man* and *The Age of Reason*. Two adjacent museums in his hometown of New Rochelle, New York, are now devoted to his life and career—the Thomas Paine Memorial Museum and the Thomas Paine Cottage.

Ethan Allen and his Green Mountain Boys were responsible for the first successful military action in the Revolutionary War. They captured Fort Ticonderoga in upstate New York from the British in 1775. Allen later became the founder of the state of Vermont. The Ethan Allen Homestead Museum in Burlington, Maine, now features his life. It also was in 1775 that silversmith Paul Revere made his famous midnight ride to alert the colonial militia of the approaching British forces before the battles of Lexington and Concord. His seventeenth-century home in Boston is now a historic house museum called the Paul Revere House. It has an annual attendance of nearly 265,000.

Another popular historic house site is the Betsy Ross House in Philadelphia, with an annual attendance of over 315,000. It is believed that Ross made the nation's first flag in the Georgian-style house in 1776. But there is still historical controversy as to where she made the first flag and whether it took place in that house since she lived in a number of houses during that period.

Among the many who died during the American Revolutionary War was Captain Nathan Hale, who was captured and hanged by the British while gathering information about British operations in 1776. Hale, who was on assignment for General George Washington, is remembered for his reported last words: "I only regret that I have but one life to lose for my country." The Nathan Hale Homestead Museum in Coventry, Connecticut, is now devoted to his life.

John Philip Sousa was called "The March King" for composing and playing military and patriotic marches during the late 1800s and early 1900s. He is best known for such march favorites as "The Washington Post," "Semper Fidelius" (official march of the U.S. Marie Corps), and "The Stars and Stripes Forever" (national march of the United States). Sousa served as director of the Marine Band for 12 years and of the Naval Reserve Band during World War I. He traveled throughout the nation giving military and patriotic band concerts for over 50 years. The Sousa Archives and Center for American Music at the University of Illinois at Champaign-Urbana is largely devoted to his life and works.

PUBLIC AND POLITICAL LEADERS

The contributions of many public officials and political leaders are often recognized in museums, historic sites, and memorials. They range from such early public officials as Benjamin Franklin, Alexander Hamilton, John Jay, Daniel Webster, John Marshall, John C. Calhoun, Henry Clay, Sam Houston, Stephen A. Douglas, and Jefferson Davis to more recent political leaders like Alben W. Barkley, Cordell Hull, James Nance Garner, Margaret Chase Smith, Samuel T. Rayburn, Thurgood Marshall, Jesse Helms, and Robert J. Dole. This category also includes a few foreign figures with American connections, such as Winston Churchill, Golda Meir, and Queen Emma.

Benjamin Franklin, one of the nation's Founding Fathers, was a politician, statesman, diplomat, scientist, and inventor who was also a printer, publisher, postmaster, philosopher, philanthropist, and active participant in many other fields. He now is honored at two Philadelphia sites—the Benjamin Franklin Memorial, located at the Franklin Institute, and the Franklin Court, part of the Independence National Historical Park, which has an underground Franklin museum in the neighborhood where he lived.

The homes of two other Founding Fathers—John Jay and Alexander Hamilton—have become historic house museums. Jay served as president of the Continental Congress in 1778–1770, was coauthor of the *Federalist Papers* in 1787, and served as the first chief justice of the U.S. Supreme Court in 1789–1795. His home is now the John Jay Homestead State Historic Site in Katonah, New York. Hamilton's 1802 home in New York City has become the Hamilton Grange National Memorial. Hamilton was the nation's first secretary of the treasury and the primary author of George Washington's economic policies. He died of a gunshot in a political duel with former vice president Aaron Burr in 1804.

The homes of three congressmen who were part of the "Great Triumvirate" in the first half of the 1800s—Henry Clay of Kentucky, John C. Calhoun of South Carolina, and Daniel Webster of Massachusetts—now also are historic house museums. Clay, who was considered one of nation's great orators, served three different terms as speaker of the House of Representatives, was secretary of state in 1825–1829, became a senator in 1831, and was an unsuccessful candidate for president in different parties three times (1824, 1832, and 1844). His Ashland plantation home in Lexington, Kentucky, is now preserved as Ashland, the Henry Clay Estate.

Calhoun was a politician, political theorist, and state's rights advocate who served as a congressman, senator, secretary of war, secretary of state, and vice president during the first half of the nineteenth century. Although he began his political career supporting a strong national government, he later defended slavery and the theory of minority rights in a democracy, and he was among the first to suggest that the only solution to North/South governing differences was secession from the Union. He resigned as vice president in 1832 in protest against a higher tariff and antislavery bills. His plantation and home, which he named Fort Hill for a nearby military fort, was later left by his heirs to the State of South Carolina for an agricultural college, which became Clemson University. The Calhoun home now is located on the university campus in Clemson, South Carolina.

Daniel Webster was a leading constitutional lawyer who became a senator, statesman, and cabinet member during his 40 years in national politics in the first half of the nineteenth century. He was one of the most famous orators and influential Whig political leaders in the period leading up to the Civil War. Webster participated in eight of the most important cases decided by the Supreme Court between 1801 and 1824 and served as a congressman, senator, and secretary of state under three presidents. It was said that he delivered the most eloquent speech given in Congress when he defended the Union and opposed the nullification efforts. He also ran for president unsuccessfully three times. Three historic sites now honor Webster—the Daniel Webster Birthplace State Historic Site in Franklin, New Hampshire, and the Daniel Webster Estate and Heritage Center and Daniel Webster Law Office and Library in Marshfield, Massachusetts.

Three historical sites are also dedicated to Jefferson Davis, president of the Confederacy in the Civil War, who was once a United States military officer, congressman, senator, secretary of war, and secretary of state. He believed each state was sovereign and had a right to succeed from the Union. The three tributes are Beauvoir, the Jefferson Davis Home and Presidential Library, Biloxi, Mississippi; Jefferson Davis State Historic Site, Fairview, Kentucky; and Jefferson Davis Memorial Historic Site, Fitzgerald, Georgia.

Sam T. Rayburn was a Texas Democratic congressman who was the most powerful and influential member of Congress in the twentieth century. He served in the U.S. House of Representative for nearly 49 years and was House speaker for a record 17 years. First elected in 1913, he served 24 terms as a congressman and was largely responsible for the passage of much of President Franklin D. Roosevelt's New Deal program in the 1930s. Two museums in Rayburn's hometown of Bonham, Texas, are dedicated to his life and career—the Samuel T. Rayburn House Museum and the Sam Rayburn Library and Museum.

Margaret Chase Smith of Maine was the first woman to serve in both the House of Representatives (1940–1949) and the Senate (1949–1973) and the first woman to be placed in nomination for president by a major party convention. She was a moderate Republican who was the first senator to denounce the scare tactics of Senator Joseph McCarthy in his communist witch hunt. The Margaret Chase Smith Library in Skowhegan, Maine, is devoted to her life and papers.

Robert J. Dole, a U.S. senator from Kansas from 1969 to 1996, holds the record as the longest serving Republican Senate majority leader. He led the party in the Senate from 1985 to 1996, when he was chosen as the Republican nominee for president. He now is a Washington lawyer. The University of Kansas has established the Robert J. Dole Institute of Politics in his honor on the Lawrence campus. It contains his papers and exhibits on his life and career, and seeks to promote political and civic participation and civil discourse in a bipartisan and balanced manner.

Westminster College in Fulton, Missouri, has a museum/library complex dedicated to Winston Churchill, the British prime minister who gave his famous "Sinews of Peace" address at the college in 1946. The address came to be known as the "Iron Curtain" speech because it marked the beginning of the Cold War. The Churchill tribute includes the National Winston Churchill Museum and the Winston Churchill Memorial and Library.

Two other sites preserve the houses of one-time foreign leaders. Golda Meir, prime minister of Israel in 1969–1974, grew up in America and once lived in Denver, where her former residence now is the Golda Meir House Museum. The Queen Emma Summer Palace in Honolulu, Hawaii, was the summer retreat of the queen consort of King Kamehameha IV of the Kingdom of Hawaii in 1856–1863, before Hawaii became a state.

MILITARY LEADERS AND HEROES

Military figures ranging from privates to generals are honored at museums, historic sites, and memorials for their valor and leadership on the battlefield or at sea. They include such military leaders as Nathanael Greene and John Paul Jones from the American Revolutionary War, Oliver Hazard Perry from the War of 1812, Ulysses S. Grant and Robert E. Lee from the Civil War, George Cook and Granville L. Dodge from the western frontier days, John J. Pershing from World War I, and George C. Marshall, Douglas MacArthur, and George Patton from World War II. Among those cited for heroism are servicemen Alvin C. York in World War I and Audie Murphy in World War II.

Nathaniel Greene was a Revolutionary War general whose battles in the Carolinas and Georgia so weakened the British Army under Lord Charles Cornwall that it helped make possible the surrender of the British at Yorktown. The house where he lived in 1770–1776 is now the General Nathanael Greene Homestead, a historic house museum in Coventry, Rhode Island. The John Paul Jones House Museum in Portsmouth, New Hampshire, is dedicated to the naval captain known for saying, "I have not yet begun to fight," in 1777 in response to a taunt about surrender from a British warship, which he later captured.

During the War of 1812, Commander Oliver Hazard Perry led American forces to a decisive naval victory over the British in the Battle of Lake Erie in 1813. It was the turning point in the battle for the American West. A memorial tower, called Perry's Victory and International Peace Memorial, is now located in Put-in-Bay, Ohio, near where the battle was fought. It has an observation deck at the 317-foot level and a visitor center with a film on the battle, the war, and tower construction, as well as living history demonstrations on weekends. The annual attendance is over 200,000.

Two Civil War Confederate generals have museums in their honor. The life and achievements of General Robert E. Lee are presented at his home, now Arlington House, the Robert E. Lee Memorial in Arlington, Virginia, and the Lee Chapel and Memorial at Washington and Lee University in Lexington, Virginia, where he was president after the war. Arlington House has an annual attendance of 500,000. Thomas Jonathan Jackson, who was known as General Stonewall Jackson, is the subject of the Stonewall Jackson House in Lexington and Stonewall Jackson's Headquarters in Winchester, Virginia.

Two historic house museums in the Omaha area celebrate the lives of two generals who had roles in the western frontier movement in the second half of the 1800s. The General Crook House Museum and Library/Archives Center in Omaha is named for Indian fighter George Crook, who was commander of the fort when it was built in 1879. The Historic General Dodge House, an 1869 Victorian home in nearby Council Bluffs, Iowa, was built by Grenville M. Dodge, a civil engineer who became an Army general and built the transcontinental and other railroads in the West and Midwest. World War I resulted in the establishment of the General John J. Pershing Boyhood Home State Historic Site in Laclede, Missouri, and the Sgt. Alvin C. York Historic Park in Pall Mall, Tennessee. Pershing was the commander-in-chief of the American Expeditionary Force in Europe during the war, and York achieved fame for attacking a German gun position, taking 32 machine guns, killing 28 enemy soldiers, and capturing 132 others during the war.

Among the World War II military figures with museums are General George C. Marshall, who built and directed the largest army in history and developed the postwar Marshall Plan to revitalize Europe (for which he received the Nobel Prize for Peace); General Douglas MacArthur, supreme commander of Allied forces in the Pacific theater; and General George S. Patton, commander of the Third Army. They are honored at such sites as the George C. Marshall Museum, Lexington, Virginia; George C. Marshall International Center at Dodona Manor, Leesburg, Virginia; General Douglas MacArthur Memorial, Norfolk, Virginia; MacArthur Museum of Arkansas Military History, Little Rock; General George Patton Museum of Leadership, Fort Knox, Kentucky; and General Patton Memorial Museum, Chiriaco Summit, California.

A celebrated World War II hero is honored at the Audie Murphy / American Cotton Museum in Greenville, Texas. Murphy was one of the most highly decorated soldiers of the war, receiving the Medal of Honor and 32 other American and foreign decorations for a series of heroic efforts, including cutting down a full squad of German infantry and directing artillery fire by telephone to destroy other units.

BUSINESS AND INDUSTRIAL LEADERS

Leaders of business and industry often have been recognized with museums and historic sites for starting or operating successful companies—and sometimes for their inventions or innovations. They include such leading figures as Eleuthére Irénée du Pont, John Deere, Thomas Alva Edison, George Eastman, Andrew Carnegie, R. J. Reynolds, John Pierpont Morgan, Henry Clay Frick, Henry Ford, William Randolph Hearst, Glenn C. Curtiss, Walter C. Chrysler, J. C. Penney, and Milton S. Hershey.

The Morgan Library and Museum in New York City. Courtesy of the Morgan Library and Museum; photograph by Graham S. Haber.

One of the earliest major companies was E. I. du Pont de Nemours and Company, now one or the largest chemical companies in the world. It began as a gunpowder manufacturer in Wilmington, Delaware, in 1802. It was founded by Eleuthére Irénée du Pont, a French immigrant whose historic house and 1802–1921 plant are now part of Hagley Museum and Library, founded in 1952 by a Du Pont foundation.

John Deere was a blacksmith who developed and manufactured the first cast-steel plow in 1837, which resulted in the founding of Deere & Company. It became the largest agricultural and construction equipment manufacturing company in the world. The John Deere Historic Site in Grand Detour, Illinois, preserves Deere's home and tells about the development of the plow and the company.

Thomas Ava Edison, who was America's most prolific inventor, established the nation's first industrial research laboratory, the first central power station, and 14 companies, including General Electric Company. He invented products ranging from light bulbs and the phonograph to the alkaline storage battery and the electric typewriter. Six museums and historic sites now honor Edison, including the Thomas Edison Birthplace Museum in Milan, Ohio, and the Thomas Edison National Historical Park in West Orange, New Jersey.

Andrew Carnegie was a Scottish immigrant who founded the American steel industry and became the world's richest man and one of its most important philanthropists in the late nineteen century. He sold his steel interests to financer-banker John Pierpont Morgan in 1901. Carnegie then gave away most of his fortune to support libraries, universities, museums, science, and world peace. He funded 2,507 libraries throughout the world and made major contributions to leading education and peace foundations and Pittsburgh educational and cultural organizations, including the Carnegie Mellon University and Carnegie Museums of Pittsburgh (which include art, natural history, science, and Warhol museums).

After Morgan bought Carnegie Steel Company's holdings, he merged them to form the United States Steel Company, the largest corporate enterprise in the world at that time. He also worked on funding and reorganizing railroads, electric, and other companies and was praised for helping to resolve the nation's 1893 and 1907 financial panics. He also was a collector of Old Master art and rare books that became the core of the Morgan Library and Museum in New York City.

Henry Clay Frick, a partner at Carnegie Steel who had great success in the coal, steel, and financial fields, also was an art collector. He began the Frick Collection in 1881 and opened it to the public as an art museum at his New York mansion in 1935. Frick's daughter, Helen, later founded the Frick Art and Historical Center where the family once lived in Pittsburgh. It focuses on the life and times of Henry Clay Frick.

Three family members of "Commodore" Cornelius Vanderbilt, founder of a steamboat, railroad, and financial dynasty, have historic house museums, including the largest privately owned home in the nation The 250-room French château Biltmore Estate, built in the 1890s in Asheville, North Carolina, was the home of George Washington Vanderbilt, who was named for his father's youngest brother and inherited great wealth. It has an annual attendance of 900,000. The other two historic houses are the Vanderbilt Museum National Historic Site, an 1896–1899 Beaux-Arts-style country home of grandson Frederick W. Vanderbilt, longtime director of the New York Central Railroad, in Hyde Park, New York, and the Breakers, a 70-room Italian Renaissance–style home built in 1893–1895 that was called a "summer cottage" by its owner, Cornelius Vanderbilt II. He succeeded his grandfather and father as president and then chairman of the New York Central and related railroads.

George Eastman, who established Eastman Kodak Company, is considered the founder of modern photography and the inventor of motion picture film. His 1905 Colonial Revival mansion in Rochester, New York, is now the home of the George Eastman House/International Museum of Photography and Film.

Another early founder of an industry was Washington Duke, a tobacco farmer who opened the first tobacco factory, leading to the 1890 establishment of the American Tobacco Company. The Duke farm is now the Duke Homestead State Historic Site in Durham, North Carolina. Another early tobacco giant was R. J. Reynolds, founder of the R. J. Reynolds Tobacco Company, whose birthplace is preserved at the Reynolds Homestead in Critz, Virginia; his home in Winston-Salem, North Carolina, now is the Reynolds House Museum of American Art.

Museums also honor three of the earliest leaders in the automobile industry—Henry Ford, Edsel Ford, and Walter P. Chrysler. Henry Ford, who founded Ford Motor Company in 1901, revolutionized automobile and industrial production with the use of modern assembly lines in the mass production of Model T Fords in 1908. He is now memorialized at his longtime home, Henry Ford Estate (Fair Lane), and the Henry Ford, the largest indoor/outdoor history museum complex in the nation, both in Dearborn, Michigan.

Ford's son, Edsel, who served as president of the Ford Motor Company from 1919 until his death in 1943, was responsible for replacing the aging Model T with new models and guiding the company's major expansion. His home, the Edsel and Eleanor Ford House in Gross Pointe Shores, Michigan, is now a historic house museum.

Chrysler was the founder of the Chrysler Corporation, ran the auto manufacturing company as president or chairman from 1925 to 1940, and financed the building of Chrysler Building, the world's tallest building in New

York City at the time. His life and career are featured at the Walter P. Chrysler Museum at the corporate headquarters in Auburn Hills, Michigan, and Walter P. Chrysler Boyhood Home and Museum in Ellis, Kansas.

In aviation, Wilbur and Orville Wright made the first successful sustained flight in an airplane in 1903. They formed an aeronautical company and sold their first plane to the U.S. Army in 1909. Wilbur died in 1912, and Orville sold their interest in the Wright aeronautical company in 1915 to Glenn H. Curtiss, another airplane builder. The role of the Wright brothers is described at three sites—Wright Brothers National Memorial, Kill Devil Hills, North Carolina; Dayton Aviation Heritage National Historical Park, Dayton, Ohio; and Wilbur Wright Birthplace and Interpretive Center, Hagerstown, Indiana.

Two other early aviation builders were Glenn H. Curtiss, who founded Curtiss Aeroplane and Motor Company, now part of Curtiss Wright Corporation, and Glenn L. Martin, who formed the Glenn L. Martin Aircraft Company in 1912 that became Lockheed Martin after several mergers. The Glenn H. Curtiss Museum in Hammondsport, New York, and the Glenn L. Martin Maryland Aviation Museum in Baltimore describe their flying and industrial careers.

Two leaders in the oil industry also have established museums—Frank Phillips, cofounder of Philips Petroleum Company in 1917, and J. Paul Getty, who founded the Getty Oil Company and became one of the richest men in the world. Phillips's home in Cherokee, Oklahoma, now is a historic home museum, and his ranch retreat near Bartlesville, Oklahoma, is the Woolarc Museum, devoted to art and history. Getty funded the J. Paul Getty Museum, a major Los Angeles art museum with an annual attendance of 1.6 million that also operates a branch museum at his former home, called the Getty Villa, in Pacific Palisades, California.

Among the editors and publishers who have museums on their lives and accomplishments are William Randolph Hearst, Robert R. McCormick, and William Allen White. Hearst, publisher of newspapers in New York, San Francisco, and some 30 other cities, was controversial and political. He was elected to the U.S. House of Representatives and ran unsuccessfully for mayor of New York City and governor and lieutenant governor of the state of New York. He built a huge 60,645-square-foot mansion on 250,000 acres near San Simon, California, in 1919–1947, which became a state historical park called Hearst Castle. It has an annual attendance of 860,000.

McCormick, the grandson of Joseph Medill, the legendary owner of the *Chicago Tribune* and mayor of Chicago, became president of the newspaper in 1911 and served as publisher and editor-in-chief from 1925 to 1955. He was a controversial and extremely conservative newspaper magnate who later also became owner of radio and television stations. His life and accomplishments now are presented at the Robert R. McCormick Museum at Cantigny, the 1896 country home of Medill in Wheaton, Illinois, which was enlarged by McCormick in 1932.

William Allen White was editor of the *Emporia Gazette* weekly newspaper in Emporia, Kansas. He became known nationally for his commonsense editorials and books and progressive movement political activities. He was called the "Sage of Emporia" and unofficial spokesman for Middle America in the early 1900s. White's home now is the William Allen White State Historic Site, and the newspaper is still published weekly and its building contains a small museum with White's old desk and other historical equipment and materials.

A number of business and industrial leaders in other fields are also honored in museums. The George Peabody House Museum in Peabody, Massachusetts, is the restored birthplace of the international merchant, financier, and benefactor of many universities and other causes. The J. C. Penney Museum in Hamilton, Missouri, and J. C. Penney Homestead in Kemmerer, Wyoming, honor the department store founder. The life and legacy of Milton S. Hershey, founder of the Hershey Company, are part of the firm's corporate museum—the Hershey Story: The Museum on Chocolate Avenue—in Hershey, Pennsylvania. And the Stan Hywet Hall and Gardens in Akron, Ohio, is located at the home of the founder of the Goodyear Tire & Rubber Company and Seiberling Rubber Company.

MEMORIALIZING RELIGIOUS FIGURES

More than a dozen museums and historic sites honor religious leaders who have founded religions, excelled in leadership, or are known primarily as social activists. They include theologian Roger Williams, an early proponent of religious freedom and separation of church and state; Joseph Smith, founder of the Church of Jesus Christ of Latter-day Saints; Mary Baker Eddy, who established the Church of Christ, Scientist; Brigham Young, early Mormon leader; Billy Graham, a leading evangelistic minister; and Martin Luther King Jr., the social activist who spearheaded the civil rights movement.

The Roger Williams National Memorial in Providence, Rhode Island, is a tribute to the English theologian who came to America in 1631 because he felt the Church of England was corrupt and that church and state should be separated. It also was a period when so-called Puritans or heretics were being burned at the stake. He founded a colony (which later became the state of Rhode Island) where refuges could come to worship as their conscience dictated.

Three historic sites honor Joseph Smith, who began the Latter-day Saints movement in 1830 with the publication of his *Book of Mormon*. He later established a large Mormon community in Nauvoo, Illinois, but was killed by a protesting mob in 1844. The historic sites are the Joseph Smith Birthplace Memorial, South Royalton, Vermont; Smith Family Farm, Palmyra, New York; and Joseph Smith Historic Site, Nauvoo, Illinois.

Smith was succeeded as head of the Mormon Church by Brigham Young, who led the pioneer followers to Utah after being driven out of Nauvoo. He established the church headquarters in Salt Lake City and guided its growth. Young is recognized for his leadership at his home in Salt Lake City, called the Beehive House, and at Brigham Young's Winter Home in St. George, Utah.

Mary Baker Eddy's system of prayer-based healing led to the founding of the Christian Science Church in 1879. She also authored *Science and Health with Key to the Scriptures*, which became the church's fundamental doctrinal textbook. The Longyear Museum in Chestnut Hill, Massachusetts, is devoted primarily to Eddy's life and accomplishments. The museum also offers guided tours of eight historic homes in the Boston area where she once lived. The Mary Baker Eddy Library, a library/museum in Boston, contains books and exhibits on Eddy's life, ideas, and achievements.

Two more recent church leaders with museums are Billy Graham and Martin Luther King Jr. Graham has attracted thousands with his evangelistic crusades around the nation and world, and many more with his radio and television programs, publications, and films. Two sites—the Billy Graham Center Museum at Wheaton College in Wheaten, Illinois, and the Billy Graham Library in Charlotte, North Carolina—tell of his life, achievements, and evangelic message.

Martin Luther King Jr. was an activist Baptist minister who played a major role in the 1950s–1960s African American civil rights movement. He was assassinated in 1968 by a racist. Two facilities in Atlanta now tell of his life and accomplishments at the site of his home and church—the Martin Luther King Jr. National Historic Site and the Martin Luther King Jr. Center for Nonviolent Social Change. Annual attendance is 900,000. His newest tribute is the outdoor Martin Luther King Jr. Memorial, which opened on the National Mall in Washington in 2011.

SOCIAL ACTIVISTS WHO SOUGHT CHANGES

Activists have brought many changes to the nation—in race relations, women's rights, social reforms, law, education, temperance, housing, and other fields. Among the well-known activists who now are celebrated in museums, historic sites, and memorials are Jane Addams, Susan B. Anthony, Frederick Douglass, Martin Luther King Jr., John Muir, Carry A. Nation, Rosa Parks, Elizabeth Cady Stanton, Harriet Tubman, and Booker T. Washington.

The greatest number of these figures relate to African American civil rights. This is where Martin Luther King Jr. probably has had the most impact in housing, education, voting, employment, and political action. His story is told at three museum-like sites described in the religion section. But there also are many others who have contributed to the progress.

Frederick Douglass was an escaped slave who became a social reformer, orator, writer, statesman, and leader in the abolitionist movement in the 1800s. His life and accomplishments are presented at five museums—Frederick Douglass National Historic Site, Washington; Frederick Douglass Museum and Caring Hall of Fame, Washington; Frederick Douglass Museum and Cultural Center, Highland Beach, Maryland; Frederick Douglass–Isaac Myers Maritime Park, Baltimore; and Banneker-Douglas Museum, Annapolis, Maryland.

Harriet Tubman was another former slave who became an activist in freeing other slaves via the Underground Railroad. She made 13 missions to free 70 slaves and guided an armed Union expedition that liberated over 700 slaves in South Carolina. Three museums bear her name—Harriet Tubman Home, Auburn, New York; Harriet Tubman Museum, Cambridge, Maryland; and Tubman African American Museum, Macon, Georgia. In 2013 a new national monument was created to honor Tubman—the Harriet Tubman Underground Railroad National Monument—at her birthplace near Cambridge, Maryland.

Three other sites relate to African American progress in the education field. Prudence Crandall, a white woman, opened New England's first academy for black girls in Canterbury, Connecticut, in 1833. A mob set fire to the school in 1834, but it reopened four years later when the "Black Law" was repealed and the school was opened to all students. The building is now the Prudence Crandall Museum.

Booker T. Washington was instrumental in providing higher education for black students. He was the first head of Tuskegee Normal and Industrial Institute (now Tuskegee University), founded in Alabama in 1881. It was the first college for African Americans. Washington, who became the foremost black educator in the nation and helped others start black colleges, remained with the school until his death in 1915. His campus home, "The Oaks," now is a historic house museum, and the Booker T. Washington National Monument is located near where he was born in Hardy, Virginia.

Another leading black educator and administrator was Mary McLeod Bethune, who founded a girls school, a college, and a national black women's organization and served as director of the Division of Negro Affairs of the National Youth Administration in 1938–1944 and advisor to President Franklin D. Roosevelt on racial matters. The Mary McLeod Bethune Home on the campus of Bethune-Cookman University, which she founded in Daytona Beach, Florida, and the Mary McLeod Bethune Council House National Historic Site, at her former townhouse in Washington, describe her contributions.

Among the others who have worked to advance African Americans and have museums dedicated to them are Rosa Parks, who is credited with starting the civil rights movement with her 1955 bus boycott (Rosa Parks Library and Museum, Troy University, Montgomery, Alabama); Thurgood Marshall, chief counsel of the National Association for the Advancement of Colored People who became the first African American justice of the U.S. Supreme Court (Thurgood Marshall Center, Washington); Ida B. Wells-Barnett, a journalist who was an early civil rights activist and suffragist who spearheaded an antilynching campaign and founded several women's organizations, (Ida B. Wells-Barnett Museum, Holly Springs, Mississippi); and John Brown, an obsessed abolitionist who was tried for treason and hanged for attempting an armed insurrection to eliminate slavery (Harpers Ferry National Historical Park, Harpers Ferry, West Virginia, and five other museum sites).

Many others have been social activists in other areas. Elizabeth Cady Stanton and Susan B. Anthony were leaders in the women's rights and suffrage movements in the second half of the nineteenth century. They started women's activist organizations, organized rallies, gave speeches throughout the nation, and worked to obtain passage of women's rights and voting legislation (which did not happen until after their deaths). The homes of Stanton in Seneca Falls, New York, and Anthony in Rochester, New York, are now historic house museums called the Elizabeth Cady Stanton House (which is part of the Women's Rights National Historical Park) and Susan B. Anthony Museum and House.

Two women who were involved in the temperance movement took entirely different approaches. Carrie A. Nation was a radical activist who used a hatchet to wreck saloons serving alcohol during the pre-prohibition days—sometimes while singing hymns and praying with another woman. She stopped only after being arrested and fined more than 30 times. Her house in Medicine Lodge, Kansas, is now the Carry A. Nation House Memorial (she sometimes spelled her first name differently).

Frances Willard was an educator, temperance reformer, and women suffragist who was one of the founders and longtime president of the Woman's Christian Temperance Union. She headed the national WCTU from 1879 until her death in 1898 and gave about 400 temperance lectures a year while traveling 30,000 miles annually. Her Evanston, Illinois, home, which served as the headquarters of the temperance organization, now is the Frances Willard House Museum.

Another early activist was Jane Addams, who was the cofounder of the nation's first settlement house, known as Hull-House, in Chicago in 1889. It was established in a restored mansion to primarily help recently arrived European women immigrants and their children. It gave housing to 25 women and served several thousand people a week. By 1911 Hull-House had 13 buildings and offered a night school for adults, kindergarten classes and clubs for older children and girls, and such facilities as a public kitchen, coffee shop, gym, bathhouse, book bindery, music school, drama group, library, playground, summer camp, art gallery, and labor museum.

Addams also was active in such other areas as education, politics, suffrage, and the peace movement, and she shared the Nobel Prize for Peace in 1931. Hull-House gradually was phased out as societal needs changed and the settlement house site was incorporated into its Chicago branch campus of the University of Illinois. The two remaining buildings are now part of the Jane Addams Hull-House Museum, which is devoted to her life and the settlement house.

Among the other activists honored in museums are John Muir, one of the nation's earliest and most influential naturalists and conservationists, who stimulated interest in conserving and protecting the environment and saved such wilderness areas as Yosemite Valley and Sequoia National Park (John Muir National Historic Site, Martinez, California); Helen Keller, the blind, deaf, and mute person who overcame her disabilities and became an activist for women's suffrage, labor rights, socialism, and other causes (Ivy Green, Birthplace of Helen Keller, Tuscumbia, Alabama); and John L. Lewis, a mining union leader who was one of the most effective, innovative, and controversial leaders in the history of labor (John L. Lewis Memorial Museum of Mining and Labor, Lucas, Iowa).

SOCIALITES

Isabella Stewart Gardner, Margaret Brown, Doris Duke, and Marjorie Merriweather were prominent socialites whose homes have become prized museums. Gardner, who was known for her stylish tastes and unconventional eccentricities, founded a major art museum in 1903 that evolved into the Isabella Stewart Gardener Museum in Boston. Margaret Tobin Brown became known as "The Unsinkable Molly Brown" because of her rescue efforts while surviving the 1912 sinking of the RMS *Titanic*. Her historic home in Denver now is the Molly Brown House Museum. Duke, who was known as the richest and most reluctant of celebrities at her time, built her "Shangri La" home in Honolulu in 1936–1938, which has the nation's most extensive collection of Islamic art and culture. In 1976 Merriweather converted her extensive home in Washington into the Hillwood Estate Museum and Gardens, which features eighteenth- and nineteenth-century French and Russian art, tapestries, furniture, and other works, including rare Fabergé Easter eggs.

REMEMBERING ATHLETES

Historical museums in the sports field are primarily about outstanding athletes, although several are devoted to coaches. Most tell about the careers of famous baseball players. Among those about the lives and performances of early players are the Ty Cobb Museum in Royston, Georgia; Shoeless Joe Jackson Museum and Baseball Library, Greenville, South Carolina; and Babe Ruth Museum, Baltimore.

The baseball careers of some more contemporary players are presented at the Bob Feller Museum, Van Meter, Iowa; Roger Maris Museum, Fargo, North Dakota; Roberto Clemente Museum, Pittsburgh; Ted Williams Museum and Hitters Hall of Fame, St. Petersburg, Florida; Hank Aaron Childhood Home and Museum, Mobile, Alabama; and Yogi Berra Museum and Learning Center at Montclair State University, Little Falls, New Jersey.

Outstanding athletes in such other fields as track, football, boxing, golf, and racing cars are also celebrated in museums. The life and career of Jim Thorpe, who excelled in track and football, can be seen at the Jim Thorpe Historical Home in Yale, Oklahoma. Another outstanding track performer is honored at the Jesse Owens Memorial Park Museum in Oakville, Alabama. In golf, the Jack Nicklaus Museum is located at Ohio State University in Columbus, and the Babe Didrikson Zaharias Museum and Visitor Center in Beaumont, Texas.

Two boxing greats are also featured at museums—the Jack Dempsey Museum and Park in Manassa, Colorado, and the Muhammad Ali Center in Louisville, Kentucky. In the racing car field, the Richard Petty Museum in Randleman, North Carolina, traces the career of one of the leading drivers and racing team operators. Two of the nation's most successful football coaches have museums at their universities—the Paul W. Bryant Museum at the University of Alabama in Tuscaloosa and the Eddie G. Robinson Museum at Grambling State University in Grambling, Louisiana.

INFAMOUS FIGURES

Some historical figures are early outlaws whose criminal lives are featured in museums, such as Jesse James and his brother, Frank; the Dalton Gang; and Billy the Kid. A national historical park and preserve in Louisiana also is named for Jean Lafitte, the French pirate and privateer who became an American ally during the War of 1812 with the British, and a state park marks a New Mexico raid by Pancho Villa, the Mexican bandit and revolutionary leaders.

The James brothers and four Younger brothers were members of the notorious James-Younger Gang that robbed banks, stagecoaches, and trains—and killed those who resisted—in the Midwest after the Civil War. Jesse James, who was the leader of the gang, was shot and killed by a gang member for a reward in 1882. Three museums now trace Jesse James's life and criminal career—the Jesse James Farm and Museum, Kearney, Missouri; Jesse James Home Museum, St. Joseph, Missouri; and Jesse James Bank Museum, Liberty, Missouri.

The Dalton Gang came later in the 1800s. It included three Dalton brothers (Grattan, Robert, and Emmet) and committed numerous railroad and bank robberies in the West before being killed or captured in 1892. Two museums deal with their lives and raids—Dalton Gang Hideout, Meade, Kansas, and Dalton Defenders Museum, Coffeyville, Kansas.

William H. Bonney was a young western gunman called Billy the Kid who was credited with killing 21 people in his brief criminal life in the second half of the 1800s. Although believed to be born in New York City, he lived in New Mexico from 1869 until shot to death by Sheriff Pat Barrett in 1881. He did most of his killings while a hired gunman in the 1878 "Lincoln County War" between New Mexico cattle barons. The Billy the Kid Museum in Fort Sumner, New Mexico, tells about his life.

The John Dillinger Museum in Hammond, Indiana, is devoted to the life and times of the 1930s bank robber known for his many bank robberies and daring jail escapes. Dillinger, who was called "Public Enemy No. 1" by the FBI, was killed by FBI agents in Chicago in 1934. Bonnie Parker and Clyde Barrow were a couple who robbed gas stations, stole cars, and killed policemen in the early 1930s. They eventually were killed in a shootout with sheriff's deputies on a country road near Gibsland, Louisiana, in 1934. The Bonnie and Clyde Ambush Museum in Gibsland now tells the story of their rise and fall.

The Jean Lafitte National Historical Park and Preserve, which consists of six physically separate sites in southeastern Louisiana, seeks to show the influence of the environment and history on a unique regional culture. It has an annual attendance of 391,000. Lafitte was a smuggler and a pirate who was captured and given a pardon for helping General Andrew Jackson defend New Orleans against the British in 1815—and then returned to piracy and was killed in a raid against Spanish vessels.

Villa was active in the 1909–1913 Mexican Revolution, became a regional governor, and then was driven out of office into Mexico's northern mountains and became a bandit. He crossed the American border in 1916 and raided Columbus, New Mexico, killing 16 persons and burning a military outpost and part of the town. The park is located at the former site of the frontier military post destroyed in the raid.

ADVANCING KNOWLEDGE

Educators, scientists, engineers, inventors, doctors, astronauts, and others who advance knowledge sometimes are honored at museums, historic sites, and memorials. Among those whose services, studies, discoveries, or innovations have made important educational, scientific, and technological contributions and have museum-like sites are William Holmes McGuffey, Benjamin Franklin, Noah Webster, Sequoyah, Mary McLeod Bethune, Booker T. Washington, Luther Burbank, Thomas Alva Edison, Samuel Morse, Eli Whitney, Rachel Carson, and Michael E. DeBakey.

Noah Webster, a prominent lexicographer, teacher, and author/editor in the late eighteenth and early nineteenth centuries, has been called the "Father of American Scholarship and Education." He published the first American dictionary in 1828 and spelling books that taught people to read. He also worked to make public education more secular and less religious. His West Hartford, Connecticut, house, built around 1748, is now a historic house museum called the Noah Webster House.

The William Holmes McGuffey Museum at Miami University in Oxford, Ohio, was the home of the developer of the *McGuffey Eclectic Readers*, an 1836–1837 series of four readers that millions used to learn to read. Sequoyah was an American Indian scholar who developed the Cherokee syllabary, which enabled the Cherokee to read and write. His 1829 one-room cabin in Sallisaw, Oklahoma, now is a historic site, called the Sequoyah Cabin.

The education of African Americans was advanced by Prudence Crandall, who opened the first academy for black girls in New England in 1833. It closed the next year after being set on fire, but reopened four years later after the passage of a state law that opened schooling to all children. The school is now the Prudence Crandall Museum in Canterbury, Connecticut. Mary McLeod Bethune opened a school for black girls in Daytona Beach, Florida, in 1904 that evolved into the Bethune-Cookman University. She also founded the National Council of Negro Women in 1935, served as director of the Division of Negro Affairs of the National Youth Administration in 1938–1944, and served as adviser to President Franklin D. Roosevelt on racial matters. Two museums now are dedicated to her— the Mary McLeod Bethune House on the Bethune-Cookman University campus and the Mary McLeod Bethune Council House National Historic Site in Washington.

Booker T. Washington probably had the greatest impact on African American education. He was the first head of the first black college in the nation—the Tuskegee Normal and Industrial Institute, which became Tuskegee University, in Alabama. The college was founded in 1881 and was such a success under Washington's leadership that other black colleges were established. He became a leading educator in the nation and the dominant figure in the African American community from 1890 to his death in 1915. The Booker T. Washington National Monument is located in Hardy, Virginia, where he was born, and the Oaks, his home on the Tuskegee campus, is a historic house museum.

Scientific and Technological Advances

The lives and advances of some of the nation's leading scientists, engineers, and medical and technical innovators are featured at museums, historic sites, and memorials in their honor. They include such figures as Benjamin Franklin, Samuel Morse, Robert Fulton, Joseph Priestley, Benjamin Thompson, Eli Whitney, Benjamin Banneker, Thomas Alva Edison, Luther Burbank, George Washington Carver, Wilbur and Orville Wright, Rachel Carson, Neil Armstrong, and Michael E. DeBakey.

In addition to being one of the nation's Founding Fathers, Benjamin Franklin was a man of many talents, including being a leading scientist and inventor. He made discoveries and theories in electricity, charted and codified the Gulf Stream, and invented the lighting rod, bifocals, Franklin stove, carriage odometer, medical catheter, and glass harmonica. His scientific and technological works are among the exhibits at the Benjamin Franklin National Memorial at the Franklin Institute and the underground museum at Franklin Court, the neighborhood historic site where his home was located, which is part of the Independence National Historical Park in Philadelphia.

Among the other early American scientific and engineering figures were Robert Fulton, Samuel F. B. Morse, Eli Whitney, Benjamin Banneker, Joseph Priestly, and Benjamin Thompson—all remembered in museums today. Fulton was an engineer and inventor best known for developing the first commercially successful steamboat in 1807. But he also designed the first practical submarine, the first steam-powered warship, and some of the earliest naval torpedoes. The Robert Fulton Birthplace in Quarryville, Pennsylvania, is now a historic house museum.

Morse was an artist who became the inventor of the telegraph in 1837 and Morse code, which became the primary language of telegraphy. His home in Poughkeepsie, New York, became a museum and nature center called Locust Grove, the Samuel Morse Historic Site. Whitney invented the cotton gin in 1793, which removed seeds from cotton and made it a profitable crop, and then he developed interchangeable parts that revolutionized manufacturing. The Eli Whitney Museum in Hamden, Connecticut, is devoted to his life and career.

Banneker was one of the nation's earliest African American scientists and inventors in the 1700s. He was an astronomer, mathematician, and surveyor, who was also an almanac author, farmer, and antislavery publicist. He made one of the first watches in America, predicted solar and lunar eclipses, helped survey the federal territory that became the District of Columbia, and produced some of the earliest farmers' almanacs. The Benjamin Banneker Park and Museum in Baltimore and the Banneker-Douglass Museum in Annapolis, Maryland, tell about his life and accomplishments.

Priestley was an English clergyman and chemist who discovered oxygen and several other gases and invented soda water. He emigrated to American in 1794 and continued his scientific investigations and religious activities (in the Unitarian Church) until his death a decade later. His home in Northumberland, Pennsylvania, is a historic house museum known as the Joseph Priestley House.

Thompson, who was also known as Count Rumford, was an American-born physicist and inventor who achieved fame in thermodynamics in Great Britain. A loyalist in the American Revolutionary War, he served in the British Army, left with British forces when they left Boston in 1776, and later was knighted for his military and scientific advances, such as developing what was called the mechanical equivalent of heat. His birthplace museum in North Woburn, Massachusetts, is known as the Benjamin Thompson House.

Among those who have made scientific and technological advances in the second half of the 1800s and early 1900s—and now have museums, historic sites, or memorials—are Thomas Alva Edison, Luther Burbank, George Washington Carver, Clara Barton, and Drs. Walter Reed, William Worrall Mayo, and Harvey W. Cushing.

Edison, who is regarded as America's greatest inventor, developed such advances as the practical light bulb, phonograph, motion picture camera, mimeograph, microphone, alkaline storage battery, electric typewriter, printing telegraph, and improved stock ticker tape. He also established the first industrial research laboratory and the first central power station. Edison received 1,093 American patents, and many others in Britain, France, and Germany, from 1869 and his death in 1931.

Six museums and historic sites honor Edison's life and many accomplishments: Thomas Edison National Historical Park, West Orange, New Jersey; Thomas Alva Edison Memorial Tower and Museum, Menlo Park, New Jersey; Thomas Edison Birthplace Museum, Milan, Ohio; Thomas Edison House, Louisville, Kentucky; Edison and Ford Winter Estates, Fort Myers, Florida; and Edison Museum, Beaumont, Texas.

Another prolific innovator was Luther Burbank, a horticulturalist and botanist who developed more than 800 strains and varieties of vegetables, fruits, flowers, grains, and grasses in a 55-year career. His home in Sana Rosa, California, where he lived from 1884 to 1906, is now the Luther Burbank Home and Gardens.

George Washington Carver was an African American botanist, educator, and inventor at Tuskegee Institute who produced more than 100 products made from peanuts for use in such fields as cosmetics, dyes, paints, plastics, gasoline, and nitroglycerin. He taught and conducted research at the black college from 1896 until his death in 1943. The George Washington Carver Museum on the campus in Tuskegee, Alabama, is devoted to his life and achievements. The George Washington Carver National Monument is located at his birthplace and boyhood home in Diamond, Missouri, and the George Washington Carver Memorial and Cultural Center is in Fulton, Missouri.

The Harvey Cushing/John Hay Whitney Medical Library at Yale University in New Haven, Connecticut, has a museum called the Cushing Center that honors Dr. Cushing, a turn-of-the-century neurosurgeon and pioneer in brain surgery who is known as the father of modern neurosurgery. In addition to exhibits about Cushing, the center displays more than 400 jars of patients' brain and tumor specimens from the university's medical archives collection.

Other physicians who have made medical advances and have museums describing their lives and work are Dr. William Worrall Mayo, who founded the Mayo Clinic, the first integrated group medical practice in 1890 (W. W. Mayo House, Le Sueur, Minnesota); Dr. Walter Reed, a U.S. Army physician who confirmed that yellow fever was transmitted by a particular mosquito species in 1900 (Walter Reed Birthplace, Gloucester County, Virginia); and Dr. Michael E. DeBakey, the first to perform a successful coronary artery bypass and insert a mechanical devise into the chest to assist the heart (Michael E. DeBakey Library and Museum, Baylor University Medical Center, Houston, Texas). Clara Barton, a teacher, nurse, and humanitarian who founded and served as first president of the American Red Cross in 1881, also is honored at two sites (Clara Barton Birthplace Museum, North Oxford, Massachusetts, and Clara Barton National Historic Site, Glenn Echo, Maryland).

Innovations in Aviation and Space

Far-reaching advances have been made in aviation and space since the Wright brothers' first flight in 1903. In addition to Wilbur and Orville Wright, others who have contributed to aeronautical progress and are celebrated in museums include Octave Chanute, Glenn H. Curtiss, Glenn L. Martin, Charles A. Lindbergh, and Amelia Earhart. In space exploits, museums honor astronauts Alan Shepard, John Glenn, Neil Armstrong, Virgil Grissom, Christa McAuliffe, and Ellison S. Onizuka.

Octave Chanute was an innovative railroad and bridge engineer who was one of America's earliest aviation pioneers. In the late nineteenth century, he developed early hand guilders in 1886–1897, invented the "strut-wire" braced wing structure of powered biplanes, and organized the 1893 International Conference on Aerial Navigation and the first written collection of aviation research in 1894. He also assisted Wilbur and Orville Wright in their initial flight efforts. The Chanute Air Museum in Rantoul, Illinois, contains exhibits on his life and career.

In 1903 the Wright brothers, who operated a bicycle shop in Dayton, Ohio, designed, built, and flew the world's first successful airplane. They made sustained flights for the first time in a motor-powered, heavier-than-air machine at Kill Devil Hills, near Kitty Hawk, North Carolina, where the Wright Brothers National Memorial is now located and attracts nearly 500,000 visitors annually. The Wright brothers also are honored at the Dayton Aviation Heritage National Historical Park in Dayton and the Wilbur Wright Birthplace and Interpretive Center in Hagerstown, Indiana.

Two early pilots and airplane builders were Glenn H. Curtiss and Glenn L. Martin. Curtiss built bicycles and motorcycles and set a motorcycle record of 136.36 miles per hour in 1907. He also became interested in flying and designed and flew his first airplane in 1908. He then won an international aviation meet in France, made the first long-distance flight in America, sold planes to the U.S. Navy, and acquired the Wright aeronautical company in 1915. The company, which became known for its early Curtiss Pusher, JN-4 Jenny, and NC-4 long-range flying boats, later became the Curtiss-Wright Corporation. The Glenn H. Curtiss Museum in Hammondsport, New York, is dedicated to his life and career.

Martin also was fascinated by the flying machine developed by the Wright brothers and built his own plane in 1909 at the age of 23. It was destroyed in its first flight, and he then made a short successful flight, which launched his long aviation career. In 1912 he built a seaplane that he flew in a record-setting round-trip from Newport Bay, California, to Avalon on Catalina Island. That launched the Glenn L. Martin Aircraft Company, which became Lockheed Martin in 1995 after several mergers. The Glenn L. Martin Maryland Aviation Museum in Baltimore is devoted to Martin's career and Maryland's aviation history.

Two of the nation's most famous aviators are Charles A. Lindbergh and Amelia Earhart. Lindbergh made aviation history in 1929 by flying nonstop from New York City to Paris in a single-engine monoplane called the *Spirit of St. Louis*. The 25-year-old former airmail and barnstorming pilot became a national hero who married an ambassador's daughter, Anne Morrow, who became a prominent aviator and author herself. They had an infant son who was kidnapped and murdered in 1932 in a sensational case in which the kidnapper was executed. Lindbergh's boyhood home in Little Falls, Minnesota, is now the Charles A. Lindbergh Historic Site, with exhibits about his life and achievements.

Earhart set numerous flying records in the late 1920s and early 1930s before she disappeared over the Pacific Ocean in 1937 while trying to be the first to fly around the world at the equator. She was the first woman to fly solo across the Atlantic Ocean in 1932 and set records flying from Hawaii to the mainland and Mexico City to New York in 1935. The Amelia Earhart Birthplace Museum in Atchison, Kansas, tells of her life and flying exploits.

Alan B. Shepard Jr. was the first American in space in 1961 and commander of the Apollo 14 space mission to the moon in 1971. His life and career are part of the McAuliffe-Shepard Discovery Center in Concord, New Hampshire. John Glenn was an astronaut who was the first American to orbit the Earth in 1962 and later served as a U.S. senator from Ohio from 1974 to 1999. While in the Senate in 1998, he also made a second space flight—participating in a nine-day research mission at the age of 77. The John and Annie Glenn Historic Site in New Concord, Ohio, honors Glenn and his wife, who helped improve programs for children, the elderly, and the handicapped. Neil Armstrong was the first person to set foot on the moon. He served as mission commander when the *Apollo 11* spaceship landed on the moon in 1969. He also was the command pilot for *Gemini 8*, which performed the first manned docking of two spacecraft. The Armstrong Air and Space Museum in Wapakoneta, Ohio, tells about his life and role in the space program.

Two space mission disasters also resulted in museums honoring three of the victims. In 1967 Virgil "Gus" Grissom and fellow astronauts Ed White and Robert Chaffee were killed during a training exercise and prelaunch test for the Apollo 1 mission. The State of Indiana established the Virgil Grissom Memorial Museum devoted to his life and achievements at the Spring Mill State Park near his hometown of Mitchell.

Astronaut Ellison S. Onizuka and Christa McAuliffe, the first teacher in space, died in the 1986 *Challenger* space shuttle disaster in which eight crew members and McAuliffe were killed when their spaceship's fuel tank ruptured and exploded after launch. The Astronaut Ellison S. Onizuka Space Center in Kailua-Kona, Hawaii, is dedicated to the memory of the state's first astronaut, and the McAuliffe-Shepard Discovery Center, an air and space museum in Concord, New Hampshire, honors McAuliffe and Alan Shepard, the first American astronaut in space from the state.

THE CREATIVE ARTS

One-third of the famous people in this study are in the arts. Most are authors and writers, but there are also musicians, composers, actors, poets, artists, sculptors, playwrights, entertainers, and architects. They produce the books, plays, movies, television shows, poems, artworks, concerts, buildings, and other creative works that we enjoy—and sometimes dislike.

Among the many famous arts figures honored with museums are such well-known people as artists Georgia O'Keeffe, Thomas Hart Benton, and Andy Warhol; sculptors Augustus Saint-Gaudens and Isamu Noguchi; poets Emily Dickenson, Robert Frost, and Walt Whitman; authors Louisa May Alcott, Edgar Allen Poe, and William Faulkner; playwrights Eugene O'Neill and Tennessee Williams; movie stars Clark Gable, Judy Garland, and Katharine Hepburn; singers/musicians Marian Anderson, Elvis Presley, and Louis Armstrong; and architects Frank Lloyd Wright and Frederick Law Olmsted.

Museums honoring early artists include the John James Audubon Center at Mill Grove in Audubon, Pennsylvania, and three other sites in Henderson, Kentucky; Francisville, Louisiana; and Key West, Florida; Gilbert Stuart Birthplace and Museum, Saunderstown, Rhode Island; Thomas Cole National Historic Site, Catskill, New York; and Whistler House Museum of Art, Lowell, Massachusetts.

Museums dedicated to artists of the late 1800s and early 1900s include the Frederick Remington Art Museum, Ogdensburg, New York; Edward Hooper House Art Center, Nyack, New Jersey; N. C. Wyeth House and Studio, Chadds Ford Township, Pennsylvania; Thomas Hart Benton Home and Studio Historic Site, Kansas City, Missouri; E. L. Blumenschein Home and Museum, Taos, New Mexico; and C. M. Russell Museum, Great Falls, Montana.

Museums on the lives and careers of twentieth-century artists include the Georgia O'Keeffe Museum in Santa Fe, New Mexico, and her home and studio in Abiquiu, New Mexico; Norman Rockwell museums located in Stockbridge, Massachusetts, and Rutland, Vermont; Andy Warhol Museum, Pittsburgh; and Charles M. Schulz Museum and Research Center, Santa Rosa, California.

Advances in Sculpture and Architecture

In the sculptor field, the Saint-Gaudens National Historic Site is located in Cornish, Connecticut; the Noguchi Museum in Long Island City, New York; and the Dr. Seuss National Memorial Sculpture Gardens (which depicts the stories of Dr. Theodore Seuss Geisel) in Springfield, Massachusetts. Two art museums are also devoted to a renowned foreign sculptor and a major foreign artist. The Rodin Museum in Philadelphia has the most extensive collection of works outside of Paris by sculptor Auguste Rodin of France, and the works of Salvador Dali, the noted Spanish surrealist artist, are featured at the Salvador Dali Museum in St. Petersburg, Florida.

In architecture, three outstanding architects are honored in museums. Frank Lloyd Wright is memorialized at three sites—the Frank Lloyd Wright Home and Studio in Oak Park, Illinois, and two places he designed and lived in—Taliesin in Spring Green, Wisconsin, and Taliesin West in Scottsdale, Arizona. The homes of two other innovative architects also are museums: the home and office of Frederick Law Olmsted, the founder of American landscape architecture, in Brookline and Lincoln, Massachusetts, and the home designed and built by Walter Gropius, founder and former director of the Bauhaus design school who fled Nazi Germany in 1934 to teach and practice in America.

Multiple Museums for Some Authors

Many authors are celebrated at multiple locations, usually where they were born or once lived. The lives and careers of Edgar Allan Poe and Laura Ingalls Wilder are each the focus of four museum sites. Poe, known for his tales of mystery and the macabre, is the subject of the Edgar Allen Poe National Historic Site in Philadelphia and museums in Baltimore; Richmond, Virginia; and Bronx, New York. Wilder, author of the popular Little House prairie family series, is honored at the Laura Ingalls Wilder Museum in her birth area of Pepin, Minnesota, and museums in Walnut Grove, Minnesota; Burr Oaks, Iowa; and Mansfield, Missouri.

Samuel Langhorne Clemens, better known by his Mark Twain pen name, has three museums devoted to his life and career—the Mark Twain House and Museum in Hartford, Connecticut, as well as museums at his birthplace in Stoutsville, Missouri, and boyhood home in Hannibal, Missouri. Other authors with three museums are Nathaniel Hawthorne (his birthplace in Salem, Massachusetts, and the Old Manse and Wayside in Concord, Massachusetts); Ernest Hemingway (Hemingway Museum and the Ernest Hemingway Birthplace in Oak Park, Illinois, and museums in Key West, Florida, and Piggott, Arkansas); and Harriet Beecher Stowe (museums at her center in Hartford, Connecticut, and in Cincinnati and Maysville, Kentucky).

Among the authors with two museums are Pearl S. Buck (home in Perkasaie, Pennsylvania, and birthplace in Hillsboro, West Virginia); John Steinbeck (National Steinbeck Center and a house museum in Salinas, California); Zane Grey (museums in Lackawaxen, Pennsylvania, and Norwich, Ohio); Washington Irving (Sunnyside home in Tarrytown, New York, and a museum in Ripley, Oklahoma); Sinclair Lewis (boyhood home and an interpretive center in Sauk Centre, Minnesota); William Sidney Porter, known as O. Henry (houses in Austin and San Antonio, Texas); and John Burroughs (a state historic site in Roxbury, New York, and a nature sanctuary, West Park, New York).

Other author museum sites include Louisa May Alcott's Orchard House, Ralph Waldo Emerson House, and Thoreau Farm, the birthplace of Henry David Thoreau, in Concord, Massachusetts; Jack London State Historic Park, Glen Ellen, California; Thomas Wolfe Memorial, Asheville, North Carolina; Herman Melville House, Pittsfield, Massachusetts; Willa Cather State Historic Site, Red Cloud, Nebraska; William Faulkner's home, Rowan Oak, Oxford, Mississippi; Margaret Mitchell House and Museum, Atlanta; the Mount, Edith Wharton's estate and gardens, Lenox, Massachusetts; Scott and Zelda Fitzgerald Museum, Montgomery, Alabama; Rachel Carson Homestead, Springdale, Pennsylvania; Alex Halley Museum and Interpretive Center, Henning, Tennessee; Eudora Welty House, Jackson, Mississippi; and Louis Bromfield's Malabar Farm State Park, Lucas, Ohio.

Some authors with museums also were poets, such as Ralph Waldo Emerson and Henry David Thoreau, who are remembered at historic sites in Concord, Massachusetts; Carl Sandburg, honored at his home, a national historic site in Flat Rock, North Carolina, and a state historic site in Galesburg, Illinois; and Robert Penn Warren at his birthplace museum in Guthrie, Kentucky.

Poets Robert Frost and Henry Wadsworth Longfellow have three museum sites—Robert Frost Farm, Derry, New Hampshire; the Frost Place, Franconia, New Hampshire; and Robert Frost Stone House Museum, Shaftsbury, Vermont; and Longfellow National Historic Site, Cambridge, Massachusetts; Wadsworth-Longfellow House, Portland, Maine; and Longfellow-Evangeline State Historic Site, St. Martinville, Louisiana.

Poets with two historic sites are William Cullen Bryant, homestead in Cummington, Massachusetts, and home in Roslyn Harbor, New York; James Whitcomb Riley, birthplace in Greenfield, Indiana, and home in Indianapolis; Walt Whitman, birthplace in Huntington, New York, and home in Camden, New Jersey; John Greenleaf Whittier, homestead in Haverhill, Massachusetts, and home in Amesbury, Massachusetts; and Paul Laurence Dunbar, with a state memorial and a Wright-Dunbar interpretive center in Dayton, Ohio.

Some Sites Honoring Foreign Authors and Poets

Some foreign authors and poets also are honored at museums in the United States. Three sites are devoted to Robert Louis Stevenson, the Scottish novelist, essayist, and poet who married an American woman in 1876 and lived here until 1890, when they moved to the Samoan Islands in the South Pacific. The museums are the Robert Louis Stevenson Silverado Museum, St. Helena, California; Robert Louis Stevenson House, Monterey, California; and Robert Louis Stevenson Memorial Cottage Museum, Saranac Lake, New York.

The Folger Shakespeare Library in Washington, DC. Courtesy of the Folger Shakespeare Library.

The D. H. Lawrence Ranch in San Cristobal, New Mexico, is where D. H. Lawrence, the English author, poet, playwright, and essayist, and his wife lived in 1924–1925. The life and works of Hans Christian Andersen, the Danish author and poet noted for his fairy tales, are the focus of the Hans Christian Andersen Museum in the Danish-oriented town of Solvang, California. The Armstrong Browning Library at Baylor University in Waco, Texas, is dedicated to the study and works of Robert and Elizabeth Browning, two of the most prominent English poets of the nineteen century.

Two museums honor playwright Eugene O'Neill (Eugene O'Neill National Historic Site, Danville, California, and Monte Cristo Cottage, New London, Connecticut). Other museums devoted to playwrights include the George Ade Memorial Association, Brook, Indiana; Arna Bontemps African American Museum, Alexandra, Louisiana; Tennessee Williams Birthplace/Home, Columbus, Mississippi; and August Wilson Center for African American Culture, Pittsburgh. The life and works of William Shakespeare are presented at the Folger Shakespeare Library, a library/museum operated by Amherst College in Washington.

Entertainment Museums

Birthplaces and former homes of some of the best-known movie, stage, and radio/television actors and Wild West show, circus, and theme park founders/operators now are historic house museums. They include the homes of such actors as the Clark Gable Birth Home and Museum, Cadiz, Ohio; Birthplace of John Wayne, Winterset, Iowa; Rosemary Clooney House, Augusta, Kentucky; Graceland (Elvis Presley's home), Memphis; William Hart Museum, Newhall, California; Ten Chimneys, the home of Alfred Lunt and Lynn Fontanne, Genesee Depot, Wisconsin; and three former homes of Will Rogers in Claremore and Oologah, Oklahoma, and Pacific Palisades, California.

Some hometowns also celebrate movie stars who were former residents with museums, such as Lucille Ball (with Desi Arnaz) in Jamestown, New York; James Dean, Fairmount, Indiana; Ava Gardner, Springfield, North Carolina; Jimmy Stewart, Indiana, Pennsylvania; and Judy Garland, Grand Rapids, Minnesota. Other museums are located at such sites as a movie theater (Mary Pickford), cultural center (Katharine Hepburn), and Western museum (Gene Autry). The latter has an annual attendance of 375,000.

Will Rogers was a cowboy, circus rider, trick roper who became a multifaceted entertainer. He was a comedian, humorist, social commentator, vaudeville performer, newspaper columnist, and movie actor. Rogers made 71 motion pictures and wrote more than 4,000 nationally syndicated newspaper columns. He died with noted aviator Wiley Post when their small plane crashed near Barrow, Alaska, in 1935. His life and career are presented at the Will Rogers Memorial Museum at his retirement home in Claremore, Oklahoma, as well as at his birth museum in Oologah, Oklahoma, and former home in the Pacific Palisades, California.

Wild West and Circus Performers

Five museums are devoted to the life and career of William C. Cody, better known as Buffalo Bill Cody. He was a Pony Express rider, frontier scout, buffalo hunter, showman, and operator of the traveling Buffalo Bill Wild West Show from 1892 to 1913. The museums are located where Cody was born, lived, and is buried. The Buffalo Bill Museum, with exhibits on his life and career, is one of five museums that compose the 237,000-square-foot Buffalo Bill Historical Center, founded in 1917 in Cody, Wyoming, in his memory. It now serves 200,000 visitors annually. The other Cody museums are where he was born in Le Claire, Iowa; his boyhood home in Princeton, Iowa; his ranch in North Platte, Nebraska; and his grave in Golden, Colorado.

Another early Wild West show performer and operator was Gordon W. "Pawnee Bill" Little, who worked in Wild West shows and then ran the Pawnee Bill's Historic Wild West Show on his ranch in Pawnee, Oklahoma, from 1888 until the early 1900s. Little's ranch is now the Pawnee Bill Ranch and Museum.

Traveling circuses were being founded at about the same time as the Wild West shows. Two of the circus pioneers were Phineas Taylor Barnum (known as P. T. Barnum) and John Ringling. Barnum started a small museum and then bought the American Museum in New York, Peale's Museum in Philadelphia, and other museums. He converted them into what he called the "P. T. Barnum Grand Traveling Museum, Menagerie, Caravan, and Hippodrome," which was destroyed in two fires in 1865 and 1868. He then merged with another circus in 1888 to form Barnum & Bailey Circus, only to die three years later. The circus evolved into the Ringling Bros. and Barnum & Bailey Circus in 1907 when purchased by John Ringling, one of five brothers who began the Ringling Bros. Circus in 1870.

Before his death, Barnum contracted to build a science and history museum in Bridgeport, Connecticut. The museum, which opened in 1893, went through several changes before reopening in 1989 as the Barnum Museum, a city-operated museum devoted to his life and the history of Bridgeport.

John Ringling was the surviving Ringling brother who took over the management of the Ringling Bros. and Barnum & Bailey Circus, purchased other circuses in 1929, and became the owner of every traveling circus in the nation. He also profited from various investments. Ringling and his wife, Mable, spent their winters in Sarasota, Florida, and made their home there after Sarasota became the winter quarters of the circus.

The Ringlings built a 56-room Venetian Gothic mansion, which they called Cà d'Zan (Venetian for House of John), in 1925 and the 21-gallery John and Mable Ringling Museum of Art in 1931 to house their large art collection. The restored mansion now features the Ringlings' original furnishings and art and the 30-room art museum contains paintings and sculptures by Old Masters. In 1948 the Circus Museum was added that traces the history of Ringling and other circuses and contains memorabilia and artifacts of the circus world.

Three museums honor Walt Disney, the innovative film and television producer and founder of Disneyland theme parks. He created animated cartoons that featured such characters as Oswald the Rabbit, Mickey Mouse, and Donald Duck; made movies like *Snow White and the Seven Dwarfs* and *Cinderella*; and created such popular television shows as the *Mickey Mouse Club* and *The Wonderful World of Disney*. His life and accomplishments are featured at the Walt Disney Family Museum in San Francisco and a museum in his hometown of Marceline, Missouri. His backyard miniature live steam railroad and barn have also been preserved and opened to the public as Walt Disney's Carolwood Barn in Griffith Park in Los Angeles.

Musical Museums

Musicians and singers are among the most popular entertainers. Many have museums founded in their honor that feature their lives, careers, and music. One of the most popular is Graceland, the home of Elvis Presley, the "King of Rock and Roll," in Memphis, which attracts 650,000 visitors annually.

Some of the musical performers have multiple museums, historic sites, or cultural centers honoring them. Four places have tributes to Paul Robeson, an international concert singer who also was a professional athlete, film and stage actor, and controversial activist. They include his home in Philadelphia and three cultural centers at two universities—Rutgers University campuses in Piscataway and Newark, New Jersey, and Pennsylvania State University in State College.

Three sites are devoted to Elvis Presley and Lawrence Welk. In addition to his home at Graceland, Presley's museums include his birthplace in Tupelo, Mississippi, and a museum in Pigeon Forge, Tennessee. Welk, the television band leader and impresario, has three museum sites—at his birthplace in Strasburg, North Dakota; retirement community in Escondido, California; and collection at North Dakota State University in Fargo.

Stephen Foster, the preeminent songwriter of the nineteenth century, and Marian Anderson, one of the most celebrated concert singers of the twentieth century—as well as Gene Autry, the singing cowboy—have two museums. Foster is honored at a memorial museum at the University of Pittsburgh and a folk culture state park and museum in White Springs, Florida; Anderson's birthplace/residence in Philadelphia and studio in Danbury, Connecticut, are now museums. And Autry has the Autry National Center of the American West in Los Angeles and a museum in Gene Autry, Oklahoma—a town named for him near the ranch he once owed.

Among the other singing movie stars with museums are Bing Crosby, known for his laid-back singing style, who is honored at the Crosby Museum at his alma mater, Gonzaga University in Spokane, Washington; Judy Garland, a dance and singing star, at a museum in her hometown of Grand Rapids, Minnesota; Rosemary Clooney, pop and jazz singer, at her house museum in Augusta, Kentucky; tenor Mario Lanza, who has a museum about his life and career at the Mario Lanza Institute in Philadelphia; and Rex Allen, a local cowboy who became a Western songwriter and singer, honored in a museum in Willcox, Arizona.

Pioneers in Music

A number of pioneers in different types of music are also remembered in museums. The W. C. Handy Museum and Library in Florence, Alabama, is dedicated to the African American musician and composer known as the father of the blues because he was the first to codify and publish songs of that genre. The Bessie Smith Cultural Center in Chattanooga, Tennessee, is named for the popular blues and jazz singer called the "Empress of the Blues." The Scott Joplin House State Historic Site in St. Louis honors composer and pianist Scott Joplin, who was called the "King of Ragtime." The life and career of Bill Monroe, who is credited with creating bluegrass music, is presented in a hometown museum in Rosine, Kentucky. Bandleader John Philip Sousa, who composed and played military and patriotic marches in the late 1800s and early 1900s, was called "The March King." The Sousa Archives and Center for American Museum at the University of Illinois at Urbana-Champaign pays tribute to his life and career. Fred Waring, a popular musician, bandleader, and radio and television personality for nearly 70 years, is known as "the man who taught America how to sing" because of his emphasis on choral music.

Many others who have excelled in music are honored at museums and historic sites. The home of Pablo Casals, the Spanish musician who is regarded as one of the greatest cellists of all time, is now a historic house museum in Old San Juan, Puerto Rico. The Eubie Blake National Jazz Institute and Cultural Center in Baltimore, Maryland, honors the composer, lyricist, and pianist of ragtime, jazz, and popular music. Hank Williams, who is featured in a museum in Montgomery, Alabama, was the leading country singer and songwriter in the first half of the twentieth century, and Jimmie Rodgers, known for his rhythmic yodeling, was one of the first country superstars and now has a museum in Meridian, Mississippi. The home of Louis Armstrong, the legendary trumpeter and singer known for his raspy singing voice and influence in jazz music, is the site of a house museum in Corona, New York.

The Woody Guthrie Archives in New York City is devoted to the folksinger, musician, and composer who wrote over 1,000 political, traditional, children's songs, ballads, and improvised works. The B. B. King Museum and Delta Interpretive Center in Indianola, Mississippi, traces the life and career of a leading blues guitarist, singer, and songwriter who gives about 250 performances a year and operates nine blues clubs. One of the largest collections of country music memorabilia is located at the Willie Nelson and Friends Museum and General Store in Nashville, Tennessee.

The Buddy Holly Center at Texas A&M University in Lubbock, Texas, honors the singer, songwriter, and rock and roll star who was killed in an airplane crash in 1959. Roger Miller, a musician, singer, and songwriter best known for his country/pops hits, is the focus of a museum in Erick, Oklahoma. Country singer and songwriter Loretta Lynn established a museum in the 1980s at her entertainment complex in Hurricane Mills, Tennessee. It is called the Coal Miner's Daughter Museum from the titles of her autobiography and the movie of her life.

The creative arts have had a great impact on life in America—and many of the famous artists, writers, musicians, and performers honored in museums, historic sites, and memorials have been at the forefront of the advances, innovations, and public enjoyment.

THE "FAMOUS" HAVE AFFECTED MANY FIELDS

In addition to the arts, people regarded as "famous" have affected many other fields, including government, education, science, business, industry, medicine, literature, religion, politics, civil rights, sports, and society. They usually have made positive contributions, although some have had a negative impact.

The "famed" have achieved their status largely because of their initiatives, knowledge, talents, foresight, or perseverance. Some have made major advances in their fields, while others have had relatively little societal impact.

In general, museums, historic sites, and memorials of famous people have become effective ways of honoring people who have accomplished much in their fields and the nation. These tributes tell us about the life, career, and achievements of presidents, patriotic figures, artists, performers, inventors, politicians, business leaders, athletes, activists, and others who have made significant contributions in the United States. And they enable us to have a better understanding and appreciation of the history and role of the nation.

Directory of Museums, Historic Sites, and Memorials of the "Famous"

ACTORS

Rex Allen

Rex Allen Arizona Cowboy Museum. The Rex Allen Arizona Cowboy Museum in Willcox, Arizona, honors a local cowboy who became a Western movie star, singer, and songwriter. After entering show business as a performer on radio programs, he began making successful country music albums in 1948 (which he continued doing until the 1970s). When singing cowboys became popular in American motion pictures in the late 1940s, Allen starred in 19 Hollywood Westerns. As the popularity of Western movies faded in the 1950s, he made the transition to television, cast as Dr. Bill Baxter in the *Frontier Doctor* weekly series and serving as a narrator on other television and motion picture programs. Over his career, he wrote and recorded many songs—some of which were featured in his films.

The Rex Allen Museum, founded in 1989, traces Allen's career and features an array of personal objects and memorabilia from his motion picture and television careers, such as the guitar case from his radio days and the buggy used in the *Frontier Doctor* television series. The museum also has a bronze statue of Allen, with his horse KoKo buried at the foot of the statue, and houses the Willcox Cowboy Hall of Fame. The major special event each year is "Rex Allen Days," which features a parade and a Western music and cowboy poetry festival.

Rex Allen Arizona Cowboy Museum, 150 N. Railroad Ave., Willcox, AZ 85643-2132. Phones: 520/384-2272 and 800/200-2272. E-mail: info@rexallenmuseum.org. Website: www.rexallenmuseum.org. Hours: 10–4 daily; closed New Year's Day, Thanksgiving, and Christmas. Admission: $2.

Gene Autry

Autry National Center of the American West. Gene Autry was the original "singing cowboy" of the movies, radio, and television. Beginning in the 1930s, he became the most popular Western film actor. During his long career, which spanned some 60 years, he starred in 93 motion pictures, 91 television productions, and many radio, live theater, and rodeo performances, and he wrote, sang, and recorded hundreds of songs. In addition to being inducted into the Country Music Hall of Fame and Songwriters Hall of Fame, he is the only celebrity to have five stars on the Hollywood Walk of Fame.

Autry began his radio career in 1928 and made his first recordings a year later. During his long career, Autry made 635 recordings, of which he wrote or cowrote more than 300, including *Back in the Saddle*, *Mexicali Rose*, and *The Last Round-Up*. He appeared in his first motion picture in 1934 as a dude ranch cowboy in Ken Maynard's film *Old Santa Fe*. The following year he starred in a Western movie serial, and by 1937 he was voted America's favorite cowboy. In addition to his recording and movie work, a weekly radio program was broadcast from Gene Autry's Melody Ranch from 1940 to 1956.

In 1950 Autry became one of the first major movie stars to move into television. In addition to producing and starring in *The Gene Autry Show* over the next five years, he produced other television programs. He retired from show business in 1964.

1

In 1961 Autry's great love for baseball resulted in his purchase of a major American League baseball team—the California Angeles (now the Anaheim Angels). This was followed by the founding of the Gene Autry Western Heritage Museum, which opened in 1988 and later became the Museum of the American West. It is now part of the Autry National Center of the American West, which also includes the Southwest Museum of the American Indian. The museum focuses on the history and culture of the American West, rather than on Autry. His career, however, is part of the exhibit on Western motion pictures and television. The annual attendance is 375,000.

Museum of the American West, Autry National Center of the American West, 4700 Western Heritage Way, Los Angeles, CA 90027-1462. Phone: 323/667-2000. Fax: 323/660-5721. Website: www.geneautry.com. Hours: Memorial Day–Labor Day—10–5 Tues.–Wed. and Fri.–Sun.; 10–8 Thurs.; remainder of year—10–5 Tues.–Sun.; closed Mon., New Year's Day, Independence Day, Labor Day, Columbus Day, Thanksgiving, and Christmas. Admission: adults, $9; seniors and students, $5; children 3–12, $3; children under 3, free.

Gene Autry Oklahoma Museum. The Gene Autry Oklahoma Museum is located in a small town in southern Oklahoma named for the Western movie star, who owned a ranch nearby. It is dedicated to the history and legacy of "singing cowboys," with exhibits on Autry, as well as Roy Rogers, Rex Allen, Tex Ritter, Eddie Dean, Ken Maynard, and others who appeared in Western motion pictures and on radio and television in the l930s–1950s. The museum, founded in 1990, contains photographs, movie posters, records, comic books, toys, and other Western collectibles of singing cowboys. It is the site of the annual Gene Autry Oklahoma Film and Music Festival. The annual attendance is 15,000.

Gene Autry Oklahoma Museum, 47 Prairie St., Autry, OK 73436 (postal address: PO Box 44, Autry, OK 73436-0044). Phone: 580/294-3047. Fax: 580/294-3454. E-mail: townofgeneautry@brightok.net. Website: www.geneautryokmuseum.com. Hours: 10–4 Mon.–Sat.; closed Sun., and Dec. 22–Jan. 6. Admission: free.

Lucille Ball and Desi Arnaz

Lucy-Desi Museum. The lives and careers of actress/comedian Lucille Ball and her first husband, actor Desi Arnaz, are presented at the museum portion of the Lucile Ball–Desi Arnaz Center in Lucy's hometown of Jamestown, New York. She was one of the most popular movie and television stars in a career that covered more than 40 years, and he was a musician and band leader best known for his role opposite his real-life wife in the classic television series *I Love Lucy*.

Ball began her career as a model and dancer in the late 1920s and received small parts in films before receiving her first featured role in *Go Chase Yourself* in 1938. She was appearing in other motion pictures the following year when she met Desi Arnaz, with whom she appeared in her next film and married in 1940. During their 20 years of marriage, they frequently worked together. It was during this period that they enjoyed their greatest success as the comical couple in the long-running *I Love Lucy* television series, which began in 1951.

The Lucy-Desi Museum, which opened in 1996 as part of the Lucille Ball–Desi Arnaz Center, is devoted to what became known as the "First Couple of Comedy." It contains exhibits about their lives and accomplishments and displays costumes, awards, photographs, and other memorabilia. It also has recordings of early radio programs, television videos, and interviews with some of Lucy's childhood friends.

Lucy-Desi Museum, Lucille Ball–Desi Arnaz Center, 300 N. Main St., Jamestown, NY 14701. Phone: 716/484-0800. Fax: 716/484-1018. E-mail: info@lucy-desi.com. Website: www.lucy-desi.com. Hours: 10–5 Mon.–Sat., 1–5 Sun.; closed New Year's Eve and Day, Easter, Thanksgiving, and Christmas Eve and Day. Admission: adults, $10; seniors, $9; children 6–18, $7; children under 6, free.

Rosemary Clooney

See Musicians/Singers/Composers section.

Bing Crosby

Crosby Museum. Harry Lillis "Bing" Crosby was a popular singer who successfully made the transition to radio, recording, and the movies to become a multimedia star. Known for his laid-back, intimate singing style, he became the one of the best-selling recording artists of the twentieth century with over a half billion records in circulations. He also won an Academy Award for best actor in 1944 for his role in *Going My Way*, received the first

Pictorial wall exhibit at the Lucy-Desi Museum, part of the Lucille Ball–Desi Arnaz Center in Jamestown, New York. Courtesy of the Lucille Ball–Desi Arnaz Center.

Grammy Global Achievement Award in 1963, and became one of the few actors to have three stars on the Hollywood Walk of Fame.

Crosby got his first big break in the 1920s as part of a vocal duo that became a trio known as the "Rhythm Boys." The trio was part of the touring band of Paul Whiteman, the nation's most famous bandleader at that time, and performed and recorded with such musicians as Tommy and Jimmy Dorsey, Bix Beiderbecke, Jack Teagarden, and Hoagy Carmichael. Crosby became the star attraction of the trio and recorded his first hit—a jazz-influenced rendition of "Ol' Man River"—with the Whiteman orchestra. After the group broke up, Crosby turned his attention to radio and motion pictures in the 1930s.

Crosby made his solo radio debut in 1931 and his first full-length movie in *The Big Broadcast* in 1932. This led to regular appearances on radio, best-selling recordings, and starring in motion pictures. He became the leading singer in the nation and one of the most popular movie actors. In 1936 he also replaced band leader Paul Whiteman as host of the *Kraft Music Hall* weekly radio program on NBC. It was in 1941 that Crosby made *White Christmas*, the biggest song hit of his career.

Crosby was instrumental in the development of the post–World War II recording industry as a radio and recording artist, as well as an investor in new recording equipment and techniques. He also continued to be featured in movies—appearing in 79 motion pictures during his career. He became the third most popular actor of all time in terms of tickets sold, ranking after Clark Gable and John Wayne.

Crosby was born in 1903 in Tacoma, Washington, but moved to Spokane with his parents three years later. His father built the family house at a site that later became part of the Gonzaga University campus. In 1957 he organized an Emmy-winning television program that raised funds for the construction of the Gonzaga library. The library building was later converted into the Crosby Student Center, which now houses the largest public collection of his memorabilia in the Crosby Museum. The museum, located in the Crosbyana Room, displays about 200 pieces of memorabilia from the historical collection.

Crosby Museum, Gonzaga University, Crosby Student Center, Crosbyana Room, Spokane, WA 99258. Phone: 509/313-1097. Website: www.gonzaga.edu. Hours: 7 a.m.–midnight Mon.–Fri., 11 a.m.–midnight Sat.–Sun.; closed major holidays. Admission: free.

James Dean

James Dean Memorial Gallery. Actor James Dean, who personified restless rebellious youth on the screen, is celebrated at the James Dean Memorial Gallery in Fairmount, Indiana, the actor's hometown and final resting place. The museum, which is housed in a restored 1890 Victorian home, tells of Dean's life and features thousands of memorabilia relating to his life and relatively brief acting career. Dean was born in 1931 and died at the age of 23 in a tragic automobile accident in 1955. He was killed when his car was hit by a passing motorist on his way to compete in a sports car race.

Although Dean made only seven films, he is best remembered for three of them, especially his role as a troubled high school rebel in the 1955 film *Rebel Without a Cause*. Two other motion pictures furthered his fame and popularity—as an awkward loner in *East of Eden* and a surly farmer in the *Giant*. The James Dean Gallery, which was established in 1988, contains over 1,000 photographs, original movie posters from the United States and other countries, publications devoted to Dean since the 1950s, tribute and novelty items related to Dean, and other items that help keep the memory of Dean alive.

James Dean Gallery, 425 N. Main St., PO Box 55, Fairmount, IN 46928. Phone: 765/948-3326. E-mail: di@jamesdeangallery.com. Website: www.jamesdeangallery.com. Hours: 9–6 daily; closed New Year's Day, Thanksgiving, and Christmas. Admission: free.

Katherine Dunham

See Social Activists section.

Clark Gable

Clark Gable Birth Home and Museum. Academy Award–winning actor Clark Gable was a leading actor in Hollywood motion pictures for a quarter of a century. He appeared in more than 70 films (67 talking pictures), usually portraying rough, masterful, romantic heroes. The Clark Gable Birth Home and Museum in Cadiz, Ohio, contains memorabilia and some of his belongings in the restored two-story house where he was born and lived until two years old. Among his personal items are a boyhood sled and his 1954 Cadillac.

Gable, who was known as the "King of Hollywood" in his heyday, began his movie career in the late 1920s. Among his early films were *Red Dust* in 1932 and *It Happened One Night* in 1934. He won an Oscar for *It Happened One Night* and later received critical acclaim for such movies as *Mutiny on the Bounty* (1935), *Gone with the Wind* (1939), and *The Hucksters* (1947). He continued making films until 1960, notably appearing in *Run Silent, Run Deep* (1958) and *The Misfits*, which was released in 1961—shortly after he died in 1960.

Clark Gable Birth Home and Museum, 138 Charleston St., Cadiz, OH 43907. Phone: 740/942-4989. Website: www.clarkgablefoundtion.com. Hours: Oct.–Apr.—10–4 Tues.–Fri.; closed Sat.–Mon.; May—10–4 Tues.–Sat.; closed Sun.–Mon.; June–Sept.—10–4 Tues.–Sat., 1:30–4 Sun.; closed Mon.; also closed major holidays. Admission: adults, $5.50; seniors, $4.75; children under 13, $3.

Ava Gardner

Ava Gardner Museum. Ava Gardner was one of Hollywood's leading actresses from the 1940s until her retirement in the early 1980s. She was known for her beauty and acting ability. She appeared in 60 motion pictures and was nominated by the Academy of Motion Pictures Arts and Sciences for an Oscar for best actress for her role in the 1953 film *Mogambo* and nominated three times by the British Academy of Films and Television Arts for other films.

Gardner was born in 1922 in the small rural community of Brogden, North Carolina, near Smithfield, where the Ava Gardner Museum is located. After being offered a movie contract in 1941, she appeared in the *Shadow of the Thin Man*. In the years that followed, she starred in such films as *Bhowani Junction*, *On the Beach*, and *The Night of the Iguana*. The Ava Gardner Museum is devoted to her life and movie career. It contains an extensive collection of memorabilia, including costumes, movie posters, awards, and such personal items as jewelry, clothing, china, and fine art, as well as 40 portraits of Gardner by artist Bert Pfeiffer.

Ava Gardner Museum, 325 E. Market St., Smithfield, NC 27577. Phone: 919/934-5830. Fax: 919/934-6998. Website: www.avagardner.org. Hours: 9–5 Mon.–Sat., 2–5 Sun.; closed Sun. from Nov. through Feb., Easter, Thanksgiving, and Christmas Eve and Day. Admission: adults, $6; seniors, military, and students, $5; children, $4.

Judy Garland

Judy Garland Museum. Judy Garland was an actress and singer almost from birth—her career spanning 45 of her 47 years. She became an international star in the movies, on the concert stage, and in the recording industry, receiving many honors. Garland was a childhood movie star who is best remembered for her role in *The Wizard of Oz*.

Garland was born Frances Ethel Gumm in Grand Rapids, Minnesota, in 1922. Her parents were vaudevillians who operated a movie theater that presented vaudeville acts, and she made her first appearance on the stage at the age of two and a half. She danced and sang Christmas songs with two older sisters on the family's theater stage. When the Gumms moved to California in 1926, the sisters made their film debut in a short subject film in 1926 and their final onscreen appearance together in 1935. During a performance in Chicago in 1934, actor George Jessel encouraged the Gumm sisters to change to a more appealing name. They became the Garland sisters, and Frances changed her first name to Judy. The Garland sisters broke up in 1935 when one of the sisters flew to Reno and got married.

At the age of 13, Judy received a contract from MGM. Her big break came when she was paired with Mickey Rooney in nine films. She then got the lead in the motion picture for which she became forever identified—*The Wizard of Oz*. This led to other well-received films, such as *Meet Me in St. Louis*, *Strike Up the Band*, and *Little Nellie Kelly*. These were followed by highly successful concerts and vaudeville-style performances, *A Star Is Born* and other films, appearances in television specials, and a weekly television series, *The Judy Garland Show*. In the 1960s she returned to the concert stage, but her health began to deteriorate and she died in 1969.

The life and times of Garland are depicted at the July Garland Museum, originally founded in 1975 and reorganized in 1994 in her hometown of Grand Rapids. The museum is located adjacent to the restored home where she was born and spent her early years, as well as the Children's Discovery Museum, a children's museum formerly named for Garland. The Judy Garland Museum contains a large collection of memorabilia from her career, including such objects as the carriage and other objects from *The Wizard of Oz* and the gold record she received for her song "Over the Rainbow."

Judy Garland Museum, 2727 U.S. Hwy. 169 S., Grand Rapids, MN 55744 (postal address: PO Box 724, Grand Rapids, MN 55744-0724). Phones: 218/327-9276 and 800/664-5839. Fax: 218/326-1934. Website: www.judygarlandmuseum.com. Hours: Jan.–Mar.—10–5 Fri.–Sat.; closed Sun.–Thurs. and New Year's Day; Apr.–Memorial Day—10–5 Mon.–Sat.; closed Sun. and Easter; Memorial Day–Sept.—10–5 daily; Oct.–Dec.—10–5 Fri.–Sat.; closed Sun.–Thurs., Thanksgiving, and Christmas. Admission (includes Children's Discovery Museum): $7 per person; children under 2, free.

William S. Hart

William S. Hart Museum. The 1927 Spanish colonial revival–style home of William S. Hart, a silent film cowboy star, is the site of the William S. Hart Museum on his former 265-acre ranch, which is now a Los Angeles County park named for him in Newhall, California. Hart, who began his movie career at the age of 49, made more than 65 silent films over 11 years, with his last being *Tumbleweeds* in 1925.

The museum, operated by the Natural History Museum of Los Anglers County, sits atop a hill within the park. Hart bought the ranch in 1921 and built the 22-room mansion six years later. He lived on what he called the Horseshoe Ranch for nearly 20 years before his death in 1946. Hart's former home now houses his original furnishings and collections of Western art, Indian artifacts, and early Hollywood memorabilia. Guided tours are offered of the museum. In addition, visitors can see the 1910 ranch house with period furniture, an assortment of barnyard animals, and a small herd of buffalo in the park. The annual attendance is 35,000.

William S. Hart Museum, William Hart County Park and Museum, 24151 Newhall Ave., Newhall, CA 91321. Phone: 661/254-4584. Fax: 661/254-6400. E-mail: information@hartmuseum.org. Website: www.hartmuseum.org. Hours: park—mid-June–Labor Day: 8–6 daily; remainder of year: 8–5 daily; museum—11–3:30 Wed.–Sun.; closed Mon.–Tues., New Year's Day, Thanksgiving, and Christmas. Admission: free.

Katharine Hepburn

Katharine Hepburn Museum. A small museum in the Katherine Hepburn Cultural Arts Center in Old Saybrook, Connecticut, honors the movie, stage, and television star and the community's most celebrated resident.

The museum, which is devoted to her life and career, is located adjacent to the main lobby of the center, a historic 1911 theater and town hall that has been renovated and renamed for Hepburn.

In 1999 Hepburn was ranked the greatest female star in the history of American cinema by the American Film Institute. She also holds the record for being selected the best female actress by the Academy of Motion Pictures Arts and Sciences. She won four Oscar Awards for such films as *Morning Glory* (1933), *Guess Who's Coming to Dinner* (1967), *The Lion in Winter* (1968), and *On Golden Pond* (1981). She also won an Emmy Award for her television role in *Love Among the Ruins* in 1976 and has received numerous other Oscar, Emmy, Tony, and Golden Globe award nominations.

In her long career, Hepburn made 52 motion pictures and television dramas. In addition to her Oscar-winning performances, she starred in such popular films as *Little Women, The Philadelphia Story, and The African Queen*. The museum contains memorabilia, photographs, and other materials related to her life and career.

Katharine Hepburn Museum, Katharine Hepburn Cultural Arts Center, 300 Main St., Old Saybrook, CT 06475. Phone: 860/510-0473. Website: www.katharineheburntheater.org. Hours: 11–5 Tues.–Fri.; closed Sat.–Mon. and major holidays. Admission: free.

Mario Lanza

See Musicians/Singers/Composers section.

Alfred Lunt and Lynn Fontanne

Ten Chimneys—Home of Alfred Lunt and Lynn Fontanne. Ten Chimneys was the longtime home of actors Alfred Lunt and Lynn Fontanne—considered to be the greatest husband-and-wife team in theater history. They married in 1922 and insisted that they only act together. They then starred in such productions as *The Guardsman* (1924), *Pygmalion* (1926), *Idiot's Delight* (1936), *O Mistress Mine* (1945), and *The Visit* (1958–1960). Their eclectic estate in Genesee Depot, Wisconsin, was a retreat from the stage, where they relaxed and rejuvenated.

Because the couple was so widely regarded, the leading figures in theater, arts, and literature came to Ten Chimneys to be with and work with the theater legends. In the process, the estate became an important place for artistic creation, discussion, and inspiration. Today, the site is a museum with historic furnishings, art, and diverse collections of Luntses and a living monument to theater and the arts.

Ten Chimneys is filled with memorabilia, photographs, and books. Among the historic items are notes from actor Laurence Olivier, mementoes from Helen Hayes and Noël Coward, inscribed first edition books from authors Edna Ferber and Alexander Woollcott, photos of the Luntses with the British Queen Mother, and remembrances from dozens of other intimates and luminaries. The estate is also the site of public programs and specialized theater, arts, and education programs for professionals. The annual attendance is 12,000.

Ten Chimneys—Home of Alfred Lunt and Lynn Fontanne, S43 W31575 Depot Rd., Genesee Depot, WI 53127 (postal address: PO Box 225, Genesee Depot, WI 53127-0225). Phone: 262/968-4110. Fax: 262/968-4267. Website: www.tenchimneys.org. Hours: office—9–5 Mon.–Fri.; closed Sat.–Sun. and major holidays; tours—May–mid-Nov.: Tues.–Sat.; closed Sun.–Mon, New York Eve and Day, Easter, Memorial Day, Independence Day, Labor Day, Thanksgiving and day after, and Christmas. Tour charges: adults, $28–$35; children under 12 not admitted.

Tom Mix

Tom Mix Museum. Tom Mix was a silent and talking picture Western cowboy star whose movie career spanned 26 years—from 1909 to 1935. During that period, he made 336 feature films, produced 88, wrote 71, and directed 117. Of this total, only nine movies and a 15-chapter serial (*The Miracle Rider*) were sound feature films. He was known for his quick action and daredevil stunts, with Mix and his horse, Tony, performing their own stunts.

Mix worked as a ranch hand before becoming a performer in various circuses, rodeos, and Wild West shows. He began making silent movies in 1909, and by the 1920s he was among the most popular and highest-paid film stars. Among his films were *In the Days of the Thundering Herd* (1914), *Riders of the Purple Sage* (1925), and *The Last Trail* (1927). He was married five times, led a lavish lifestyle, and was killed in a car accident in Arizona in 1940 when his speeding roadster went off the road at a bridge that was out over a dry wash and one of two large metal suitcases struck him in the head.

The Tom Mix Museum was founded in Dewey, Oklahoma, in 1968 and is now operated by the Oklahoma State Historical Society. It contains films and photographs of Mix as well as his personal collection of clothing, saddles, guns, and other belongings, including the two metal suitcases from the fatal accident. The annual attendance is 5,500.

Tom Mix Museum, 721 N. Delaware St., Dewey, OK 74029 (postal address: PO Box 190, Dewey, OK 74029-0190). Phone: 918/534-1555. E-mail: tommix@cableone.net. Website: www.tommixmuseum.com. Hours: 10:30–4:30 Tues.–Sat., 1–4:30 Sun.; open only Sat.–Sun. in Feb.; closed Mon., January, and major holidays. Admission: suggested donations—adults, $2; children, 50¢.

Mary Pickford

Mary Pickford Museum. Mary Pickford was called "America's Sweetheart" during the silent motion picture era. She was the most beloved and famous female movie star from 1909 to 1933. She had golden hair, a sweet face, and a childlike air of innocence on the screen. She made nearly 250 short and full-length silent movies and several talking pictures before retiring in 1934.

Pickford, whose birth name was Gladys Marie Smith, was born in Toronto, Canada, in 1893. She became a child actress at the age of five, appeared on the Broadway stage when 14, and became one of director D. W. Griffith's stock film players at 16. She first appeared in short films in 1909 and quickly advanced to full-length features. Among the popular motion pictures in which she starred were *Poor Little Rich Girl* and *Rebecca of Sunnybrook Farm* (1917), *Daddy Long Legs* (1919), *Pollyanna* (1920), *Little Lord Fauntleroy* (1921), and her last silent film, *My Best Girl*, in 1927. Among the few talking pictures she made was the 1929 *Coquette*, for which she won the Academy Award for best actress. She also received a Special Academy Award in 1976 for lifetime achievement.

The Mary Pickford Museum is a small museum inside the Mary Pickford Theater, a 14-screen complex in Cathedral City, California. The museum contains personal items contributed by family members, her 1976 Academy Award, a gown from one of her movies, and dinnerware from her "Pickfair" home. The museum also presents two biographical videos—one of which was produced by Pickford.

Mary Pickford Museum, 36-850 Pickfair St., Cathedral City, CA 92234. Phone: 760/328-7100. Hours: 10:30 a.m.– midnight daily. Admission: free.

Ronald Reagan

See Presidents section.

Burt Reynolds

Burt Reynolds and Friends Museum. The Burt Reynolds and Friends Museum in Jupiter, Florida, is a trip through memory lane. In addition to tracing the life and career of Reynolds, it includes his involvement with such other movie stars as Bette Davis, Jimmy Stewart, Dinah Shore, Henry Winkler, Darrin McGavin, Sally Field, and Adam Sadler in a Hollywood career that has spanned nearly 50 years.

Reynolds was a standout football player at Florida State University before being injured and turning to acting. He made the first of more than 100 motion pictures in 1961 with *Angel Baby*. Since then Reynolds has starred in such movies at *Deliverance* (1970), *The Longest Yard* (1974), *Starting Over* (1979), and three *Smoky and the Bandit* films (1976, 1980, and 1983)—and continues to make films.

The Burt Reynolds and Friends Museum is located in Jupiter, Florida, in an area where he grew up and his father once served as police chief in nearby Riviera Beach. The museum contains many Reynolds photographs, movie posters, awards, magazine covers, gifts, and some items from his films, such as the hat he wore in *Sam Whiskey* and a canoe from *Deliverance*. The museum also has a section featuring many of his Hollywood and other friends.

Burt Reynolds and Friends Museum, 100 N. U.S. Hwy. 1, Jupiter, FL 33468 (postal address: PO Box 264, Jupiter, FL 33468-0264). Phone: 561/743-9955. Fax: 561/743-9922. Website: www.burtreynoldsmuseum.org. Hours: 10–4 Fri.–Sun.; closed Mon.–Thurs. and major holidays. Admission: $3 donation.

Will Rogers

See Entertainers section.

Jimmy Stewart

Jimmy Stewart Museum. Actor Jimmy Stewart is remembered in his hometown of Indiana, Pennsylvania, at the Jimmy Stewart Museum on the third floor of the city's public library—near his boyhood home, family's old hardware store, and a bronze statue honoring him. He had a career of seven decades in the movies and on the stage and television, receiving an Academy Award for Best Actor and a Lifetime Achievement Award, American Film Institute Achievement Award, Golden Globe Award for Best Actor in a Dramatic Television Series, and other honors.

Stewart, who was known for his self-effacing persona, had his first stage experience while a student at the Mercersburg Academy prep school. He then participated in plays on campus and at a summer intercollegiate stock company on Cape Cod while attending Princeton University. After graduation in 1932, he joined the summer stock company again and then went to seek work on Broadway, where he roomed with aspiring actor Henry Fonda. He appeared in the *Goodbye Again* comedy on the New York stage and followed Fonda to Hollywood, where his first film was *The Murder Man* in 1935. Stewart made 100 movies, including such classics as *Mr. Smith Goes to Washington* (1939), *The Philadelphia Story* (1940), *Harvey* (1944), *Vertigo* (1958), and *It's a Wonderful Life* (1987).

He also had a long military career beginning in 1941. He was the first major actor to enlist in World War II. An experienced flyer, he served as a B-24 Liberator mission commander on bombing runs over German-controlled Europe. He was promoted to brigadier general in the U.S. Air Force Reserve in 1959.

The Jimmy Stewart Museum, which was founded in 1994, contains exhibits on his life, family history, and film, stage, radio, television, military, and civic careers. They feature personal and family items, movie posters, photographs, awards, movie props, military uniforms and medals, film clips, and a vintage theater. The museum has 7,500 visitors annually.

Jimmy Stewart Museum, 835 Philadelphia St., Indiana, PA 15701 (postal address: PO Box 1, Indiana, PA 0001). Phones: 724/349-6112 and 800/835-4669. Fax: 724/349-6140. E-mail: tharley@jimmy.org. Website: www.jimmy.org. Hours: 10–5 Mon.–Sat, 12–5 Sun.; closed New Year's Day, Easter, Thanksgiving, and Christmas. Admission: adults, $7; seniors, military, and students, $6; children 7–17, $5; children under 7, free.

John Wayne

Birthplace of John Wayne. The restored four-room frame house where movie star John Wayne was born in Winterset, Iowa, in 1907 is now a museum devoted to his life and career. The museum was founded in 1981 and has 40,000 visitors annually. It features a collection of memorabilia, including historical materials, photographs, letters from other prominent actors, and unusual items from his movies, such as the eye patch worn in *True Grit*, a hat from *Rio Lobo*, and a prop suitcase used in *Stagecoach*. Plans are underway to expand the museum to 8,500 square feet.

Wayne, who epitomized rugged masculinity, made 171 motion pictures—142 where he had the lead. After his parents moved the family to California, he played on the University of Southern California football team until an injury curtailed his athletic career. However, he appeared with USC teammates in several football films in the late 1920s and began working at local film studios after cowboy movie star Tom Mix got him a summer job working in the prop department in exchange for football tickets. He then began to appear in bit parts in films before being given major roles.

Born Marion Robert Morrison, he changed his name to John Wayne at the urging of the director of his first starring movie role in *The Big Trail* in 1930. During his long film career, he made such motion pictures as *Stagecoach* (1939), *The High and the Mighty* (1954), *The Searchers* (1956), *The Green Berets* (1968), *True Grit* (1969), and *The Shootist* (1976).

Birthplace of John Wayne, 216 S. 2nd St., Winterset, IA 50273. Phones: 515/462-1044 and 877/462-1044. Fax: 515/462-3289. E-mail: director@johnwaynebirthplace.org. Website: www.johnwaynebirthplace.org. Hours: 10–4:30 daily; closed New Year's Day, Easter, Thanksgiving, and Christmas. Admission: adults, $6; seniors, $5; children under 13, $2.

ARCHITECTS

Walter Gropius

Gropius House. Gropius House in Lincoln, Massachusetts, was something new in American architecture when built in 1938. It combined innovative materials such as glass blocks, acoustical plaster, and chrome banisters—rarely used in domestic settings at that time—with the traditional New England elements of wood, brick, and fieldstone. It had the usual New England post-and-beam wooden frame, but it looked and felt different with glass-block walls, vertical inside clapboards, and the latest technology in fixtures.

The house was designed by Walter Gropius, founder and director of the Bauhaus design school in Germany and one of the most influential architects of the twentieth century. He had come to teach at Harvard University's Graduate School of Design. Born in Berlin in 1883, he was able to leave Nazi Germany in 1934 with the help of an English architect on the pretext of making a temporary visit to Britain.

The modest house, which was the Gropius family residence until his death in 1969, now is a National Historic Landmark operated by Historic New England. It still contains many of the family possessions, including the furniture designed by architect Marcel Breuer and made in Bauhaus workshops and gift artworks by Josef Albers, Joan Miró, and Henry Moore.

Gropius, who designed many buildings in Germany and the United States, had a great impact on American architecture. He is considered, along with Ludwig Mies van der Rohe and Le Corbusier, among the forerunners of modern architecture. It now is possible to have a guided tour of the house and to attend various programs and lectures at the site, as well as see the Codman House, a historic eighteenth-century country estate two miles down the road. The annual attendance is 6,400.

Gropius House, 68 Baker Bridge Rd., Lincoln, MA 01773. Phone: 781/250-8098. Fax 781/259-9722. E-mail: gropiushouse@historicnewengland.org. Website: www.historicnewengland.org. Hours: June–Oct. 15—11–4 Wed.–Sun.; closed Mon.–Tues; Oct. 16–May—11–5 Sat.–Sun.; closed Mon–Fri. Admission: adults, $10; seniors, $9; children and students, $5.

Frederick Law Olmsted

Frederick Law Olmsted National Historic Site. The Frederick Law Olmsted National Historic Site in Brookline, Massachusetts, honors the architect recognized as the founder of American landscape architecture and the nation's foremost park maker. The historic site is located at Olmsted's 1883 home and office, which he called Fairsted. It was the world's first full-scale professional office for the practice of landscape design.

Olmsted, who was born in Hartford, Connecticut, in 1822, is noted for his designs of many public parks and landscapes, including intimate private gardens. He first received nationwide attention when he was appointed superintendent of New York City's Central Park in 1857 and then worked with Calvert Vaux in developing a new innovative design for the site.

Olmsted later designed such parks as Prospect Park in Brooklyn, South Park in Chicago, Belle Isle Park in Detroit, and the park systems in Boston, Buffalo, Seattle, and Louisville. He also designed landscapes for such places as the Capitol in Washington, Stanford University in California, and the Great Smoky Mountains and Acadia National Parks. In addition, he played an influential role in the creation of the National Park Service and Yosemite as a national reservation. Olmsted died in 1903, but his sons and successors expanded and perpetuated his design ideas, philosophy, and influence.

Nearly 1 million original design records relating to work on many of the Olmsted firm's landscapes are located at the historic site, established in 1979. It also contains the 1857–1980 Olmsted Archives and the Olmsted Center for Landscape Preservation. Ranger-led tours and programs are offered of the site, including the Fairsted home and office, as well as walks of Olmsted-designed landscapes in the Boston metropolitan area. The annual attendance is 4,500.

Frederick Law Olmsted National Historic Site, 99 Warren St., Brookline, MA 02445. Phone: 617/566-1689. Fax: 617/232-4073. Website: www.nps.gov/frla. Tour hours: 10–4 Fri.–Sun.; closed Mon.–Thurs. Admission: free.

Frank Lloyd Wright

Frank Lloyd Wright Home and Studio. A group of Midwestern architects inspired by Louis Sullivan and led by Franklin Lloyd Wright between 1890 and 1920 were known as the prairie school of architecture. It was primarily a residential architectural movement that emphasized a relationship to nature and the landscape, horizontal lines, natural materials, flowing interior spaces, and a reliance on handcrafting rather than mass production techniques. The structures usually were built of brick, wood, and plaster and had flat or hipped roofs with wide projecting eaves, stucco walls, and horizontal bands of casement windows. The movement got its name because the horizontal lines were thought to relate to the native prairie landscape.

During his long career, Wright designed 125 structures—many were in the prairie school style until it started to go out of favor in the 1920s. Among the early major works were the Larkin Building, Buffalo, New York (1904); Unity Temple, Oak Park (1906); and Robie House, Chicago (1909). His later designs included the Imperial Hotel,

Tokyo, Japan (1915–1922); Fallingwater, Mill Run, Pennsylvania (1936); S. C. Johnson & Son Inc., Racine, Wisconsin (1936–1942); and the Guggenheim Museum, New York City (1943–1959).

Wright, who was born in Richland Center, Wisconsin, in 1867, worked for Sullivan for six years and became the most gifted exponent of prairie school architecture. The home he built in 1889 in Oak Park, Illinois, is now a National Historic Landmark—known as the Frank Lloyd Wright Home and Studio. The home/studio served as his residence and workplace for 20 years.

In 1909 Wright left his family and home/studio and went to Europe. When he returned in 1911, he built Taliesin as his home and studio near Spring Green, Wisconsin, where he lived and worked until his death in 1959. In 1937 he added Taliesin West in Scottsdale, Arizona, as his winter home and school. Both of which now can be toured (see separate listings).

The home/studio in Oak Park was acquired in 1974 by the National Trust for Historic Preservation, which restored the site over 13 years and still owns the property. It is located in Oak Park's Frank Lloyd Wright–Prairie School of Architecture Historic District, which includes 27 Wright-designed structures and other historical and architecturally significant buildings. The home and studio now are operated as a museum by the Frank Lloyd Wright Preservation Trust. Guided tours are offered of the home and studio as well as the historic district. The historic home/studio has about 64,000 visitors annually.

Frank Lloyd Wright Home and Studio, 951 Chicago Ave., Oak Park, IL 60302 (postal address: 931 Chicago Ave., Oak Park, IL 60302). Phone: 708/848-1976. Fax: 708/848-1248. E-mail: info@gowright.org. Website: www.gowright. org. Hours: 10–5 daily; closed New Year's Day, Thanksgiving, and Christmas. Tours: adults, $15; seniors and children under 18, $12.

Taliesin. Taliesin, near Spring Green, Wisconsin, was the home of architect Frank Lloyd Wright from 1911 until his death in 1959. He built the home, which he used to explore his ideas about "organic" architecture, after leaving his first wife, spending 1909–1910 in Europe, and returning and resuming his American career in 1911. The hillside site is in a valley settled by his maternal family and where he spent many summers in his youth. He named the site for Welsh bard Taliesin, whose name means "shining brow" or "radiant brow," because the house was positioned on the "brow" of the hill.

The house, which was built from local limestone, had three wings (for living quarters, office, and farming). It was destroyed by fire twice. In 1914 a servant set fire to the living quarters and killed seven people with an ax. Wright rebuilt the house, only to see it destroyed again by fire in 1925. This time the cause is believed to have been an electrical surge during a lightning storm. The house was rebuilt and enlarged, and he later purchased the surrounding land to create an estate of 593 acres. Wright regarded Taliesin as an experiment and was continually changing it.

In 1939 Taliesin became Wright's summer home when he built Taliesin West in Arizona. The southwestern facility became his winter home and the main site of the Frank Lloyd Wright School of Architecture. Both sites are now owned by the Frank Lloyd Wright Foundation, with the Wisconsin location being operated by Taliesin Preservation Inc., a sister organization. Taliesin was the site of the Frank Lloyd Wright archive until 2012, when his architectural drawings, large-scale models, photographs, manuscripts, and correspondence were moved to the Museum of Modern Art and Columbia University's Avery Architectural and Fine Arts Library in New York City for greater accessibility.

The entire Taliesin estate was made a National Historic Landmark in 1982. It can be visited only through guided tours, with four options being offered May through October and weekend tours in April and November.

Taliesin, Taliesin Preservation Inc., 5607 City Rd. C, Spring Green, WI 53588. Phones: 608/588-7900 and 877/588-7900. E-mail: tours@taliesinpreservation.org. Website: www.taliesinpreservation.org. Hours: May–Oct.—varies with tours, but office 9–4:30 daily (also 10:30–1:30 Sat.–Sun. in Apr. and Nov.); remainder of year—office hours Mar.–Apr. and Nov.–Dec.: 9–4 Mon.–Fri.; Jan.–Feb.: 9–4 Mon.–Wed. Tour charges: varies with tours, ranging from $16 to $80 for adults; $14 to $75 for seniors, military, and students; free to $10 for children under 12 (but not permitted on some tours).

Taliesin West. Taliesin West in Scottsdale, Arizona, was the winter home and main site of the architecture school of Frank Lloyd Wright from 1937 until his death in 1959 at the age of 92. It was an extension of his original Taliesin home and workspace Wright established in 1911 near Spring Green, Wisconsin—and then became his summer home and school site. Both locations are now part of the Wright estate National Historic Landmark and owned by the Frank Lloyd Wright Foundation.

Taliesin West, which covers 640 acres, is a complex of low-rise buildings that house the Wright foundation, archives, and main campus of the Frank Lloyd Wright School of Architecture. They follow Wright's "organic" style of architecture with walls of cement embedded with desert stone found on the property. The buildings, located on a brow of the McDowell Mountains, include such structures as Wright's living quarters, office, main studio, school facilities, music pavilion, and theater, as well as a visitor center, garden room with Wright furniture, sculpture garden, and store. Seven types of guided tours of the buildings, grounds, and nearby desert area are offered at Taliesin West, with the three-hour behind-the-scenes tour being the longest and most expensive. The annual attendance at Taliesin West is 150,000.

Taliesin West, 12821 N. Frank Lloyd Wright Blvd., Scottsdale, AZ 85259. Phone: 480/860-2700. Website: www.franklloydwright.org. Hours: 9–4 daily, but varies with tours. Tour charges: general admission tours—$38 to $60; other tours—adults, $18 to $32; seniors, military, and students, $18 to $28; children over 12, $7 to $17; children 4–12, $7 to $17; children under 4, free.

ARTISTS

John James Audubon

John James Audubon Center at Mill Grove. Mill Grove, Pennsylvania, was the first American home of noted ornithologist, naturalist, and painter John James Audubon. It was there in the surrounding fields and woodlands that Audubon developed a passion for drawing and painting birds in 1803–1806. Today, the 175-acre site, a haven for birds and wildlife, remains largely as Audubon found it and serves as the educational center of the National Audubon Society and a National Historic Landmark.

Mill Grove, which has seven miles of trails, features the historic three-story stone farmhouse where Audubon lived. It now serves as a museum with original Audubon prints, oil paintings, and memorabilia. The center also exhibits and interprets a large collection of Audubon art, including his celebrated *Birds of America* with 435 life-size images of birds.

Audubon was born on a sugar plantation in Les Cayes, Saint-Domingue (now Haiti), in 1785—the illegitimate son of a French merchant/sea captain and a Creole chambermaid who died in a slave uprising. He was raised in the French countryside around Nantes, where he first developed an interest in birds and wildlife and began sketching. When he was 18, he was sent to America to avoid being conscripted into Napoleon's army and to manage the family's farm property at Mill Grove.

In the years that followed, Audubon sold the Mill Grove estate, married the daughter of an Englishman who owned an adjoining estate in 1808, and moved about the country at various tasks and painting birds and wildlife. In 1827–1838, he worked on *Birds of America*, resulting in double elephant folios with 435 hand-colored engravings and a smaller version. This was followed in 1845–1853 by *The Viviparous Quadrupeds of North America*, with 150 hand-colored lithographs of mammals in large and smaller editions, produced with John Bachman. Audubon spent his last years on an estate, now Audubon Park in New York City, where he died in 1851.

John James Audubon Center at Mill Grove, 1201 Pawlings Rd., Audubon, PA 19403. Phone: 610/666-5593. Fax: 610/630-2209. E-mail: millgove@audubon.org. Website: www.pa.audubon.org/centers_mill_grove.html. Hours: 10–4 Tues.–Sat., 1–4 Sun.; closed Mon. and major holidays. Admission: adults, $4; seniors, $3; children 5–17, $2; children under 5, free.

John James Audubon State Park and Museum. Artist John James Audubon came with his family to the frontier village of Henderson, Kentucky, in 1810 to operate a small mercantile business and study, sketch, and paint the birds and other wildlife in the surrounding wilderness. He had mixed success with the business, but he enjoyed exploring the nearby forests and sketching and painting the wildlife before leaving in 1819.

In 1898 the Henderson Audubon Society was formed to preserve the legacy of the great painter and naturalist. The society worked to establish a fitting memorial but was turned down for a federal grant for an Audubon museum in 1930 to house and display its large collection of Audubon materials. Local residents then began raising funds to buy land along the Ohio River that could be used for a state park and museum honoring Audubon. By 1934, 275 acres were acquired, and the state of Kentucky agreed to establish the park and began construction in 1938. The park now covers 700 acres and has campgrounds, cabins, gardens, shelter houses, picnic areas, trails, a lake, a 336-acre nature preserve, and the John James Audubon Museum.

The museum interprets Audubon's life and work within a time line of world events. It contains many of his oils and watercolors, including the double elephant folio of the *Birds of America*, as well as exhibits on Audubon's life and family personal belongings and furniture. The museum is said to have the largest collection of Audubon artifacts. A nature center also has a Wildlife Observation Room, Discovery Center with hands-on exhibits, and a

Learning Center where a naturalist and art educator present environmental and art programs. The museum's annual attendance is 12,000.

John James Audubon Museum, 3100 U.S. Hwy. 41 N., Henderson, KY 42420 (postal address: PO Box 576, Henderson, KY 42419-0576). Phone: 270/826-2247. Fax: 270/826-2286. E-mail: audubon@ky.gov. Website: www.parks. ky.gov/findparks/recpark/au. Hours: Mar.–Nov.—10–5 daily; Dec.–Feb.—8–4:30 Wed.–Sun.; closed Mon.–Tues., New Year's Eve and Day, Martin Luther King Day, Thanksgiving and day after, and a week during Christmas holiday. Admission: adults, $4; children 6–12, $2.50; children under 6, free.

Audubon State Historic Site. The Audubon State Historic Site in St. Francisville, Louisiana, preserves the ca. 1806 Oakley House and surrounding 100-acre forest where John James Audubon spent a brief stay in 1821. Audubon came upriver from New Orleans to teach drawing to the daughter of Mr. and Mrs. James Pirrie, owners of Oakley House, and to do bird illustrations. He was allowed to spend half his time in the woods working on his paintings. However, Audubon returned to New Orleans after four months following a misunderstanding with Mrs. Pirrie. During his stay, he completed or began 32 bird paintings. An interpretive center tells about the site and Audubon's visit, and guide tours and programs are offered.

Oakley House is a three-story, airy house that is an example of colonial architecture adapted to its climate and predates the relatively heavy details of classic revival in southern plantation homes. Its rooms have been restored in the style of the federal period (1790–1830)—reflecting the appearance when Audubon was there. Nearby are restored formal and kitchen gardens, a barn, and two slave cabins. Oakley House, which is on the National Register of Historic Places, receives 30,000 visitors a year.

Audubon State Historic Site, 11788 Hwy. 965, St. Francisville, LA 70775 (postal address: PO Box 546, St. Francisville, LA 70775-0546). Phones: 225/635-3739 and 888/677-2838. E-mail: audubon@crt.state.la.us. Website: www.crt. state.la.us/parks/iaudubon.aspx. Hours: 9–5 daily; closed New Year's Day, Thanksgiving, and Christmas. Admission: adults and children over 12, $2; seniors and children under 13, free.

Audubon House and Tropical Gardens. The Audubon House and Tropical Gardens in Key West, Florida, commemorates John James Audubon's 1832 visit to the city. It is believed that many of the 18 new birds he had sighted and drawn in Key West for his *Birds of America* folio were conceived in the Audubon House garden. The nineteenth-century house was built by Captain John H. Geiger, a harbor pilot and master wrecker who lived in the house with his wife and nine children. It was saved from demolition in 1958 by the Mitchell Wolfson Family Foundation, which now operates the historic house.

The house, a three-level structure built in the American classic revival architectural style, contains antique furnishings and 28 first-edition works of the famous naturalist/artist. The Audubon House Gallery, located separately from the main house, features a collection of original Audubon art and images. The tropical gardens cover an acre of orchids, bromeliads, and other tropical foliage, an herb garden, and an 1884-style nursery. The house/garden museum has an annual attendance of 40,000.

Audubon House and Tropical Gardens, 205 Whitehead St., Key West, FL 33040. Phone: 305/294-2116. Fax: 305/294-4513. E-mail: audubonhoue@audubonhouse.org. Website: www.audubonhouse.com. Hours: 9:30–5 daily. Admission: adults, $10; seniors, $8.50; students, $7.50; children 6–12, $6.50; children under 6, free.

Thomas Hart Benton

Thomas Hart Benton Home and Studio State Historic Site. The life and work of painter and muralist Thomas Hart Benton, one of the leaders of the regionalist art movement, can be seen at the Thomas Hart Benton Home and Studio State Historic Site in Kansas City, Missouri. Benton, who was known for his vibrant paintings and murals, lived in the late Victorian-style house of native quarried limestone and created many of his works in the converted carriage house that was his studio.

Many of Benton's artworks depict scenes of everyday life, largely in the Midwest. They often are paintings and murals, which frequently were controversial, and show the melancholy, desperation, and beauty of small-town life. One of Benton's greatest works is considered to be *A Social History of the State of Missouri* mural in the Missouri State Capitol.

Benton, who was born in Neosho, Missouri, in 1889, moved to Kansas City in 1935 after receiving art instruction in Chicago and Paris, serving in the navy, and teaching in New York City. The house and studio remain virtually as Benton left them. The house contains his simple furnishings and 13 of Benton's original artworks, while the studio

The studio of Thomas Hart Benton, part of the noted artist/muralist's state historic site in Kansas City, Missouri. Courtesy of the Thomas Hart Benton Home and Studio State Historic Site.

still has his coffee cans full of paint brushes, paints, and a stretched canvas ready to be converted into a painting. Benton died in the studio in 1975 while painting another of his many works. The annual site attendance is 5,700.

Thomas Hart Benton Home and Studio State Historic Site, 3616 Belleview, Kansas City, MO 64111. Phone: 816/931-5722. Fax: 816/931-5722. E-mail: benton.home.state.historic.site@dnr.mo.gov. Website: www.mostateparks.com/benton.htm. Hours: summer—10–4 Mon.–Sat., 12–5 Sun.; winter—10–4 Mon.–Sat., 11–4 Sun.; closed New Year's Day, Thanksgiving, and Christmas. Admission: adults, $2.50; children 6–12, $1.50; children under 6, free.

Ernest L. Blumenschein

E. L. Blumenschein Home and Museum. Ernest L. Blumenschein, who was known for his paintings of Native Americans and the Southwest, was cofounder of the Taos Art Colony and later one of the six charter members of the Taos Society of Artists in New Mexico. His home—furnished as it might have appeared when he lived there in 1898–1919—is now a historic house museum. The E. L. Blumenschein Home and Museum contains family art and possessions, works by other Taos artists, and fine European and Spanish colonial-style antiques.

The Taos Art Colony, which became a major school of American painting, consisted of a group of European-trained artists who were attracted to the visually beautiful environment of the region and settled near the ancient Taos Pueblo in northern New Mexico in the early twentieth century. The art colony began in 1898 after Blumenschein and Bert G. Phillips were delayed in Taos when their surrey broke down on the mountainous road north of Taos while on a sketching trip from Denver. They were impressed with the spectacular landscape and cultures of the area and decided to stay. A few years later, they were joined by such other artists as Joseph Henry Sharp,

W. Herbert Dunton, E. Irving Couse, and Oscar E. Berninghaus. The Taos Art Colony was different from other art "schools" that emerged at the turn of the century in that the Taos artists did not have a single aesthetic style. Yet the artists were inspired by the environment and produced works with vibrant colors and often scenes of Taos and the American Southwest.

The Blumenschein house/museum is one of two historic sites operated by Taos Historic Museums. The other site is the Hacienda de los Martinez, a 1800–1827 trading post. The museum's annual attendance is nearly 32,000.

E. L. Blumenschein Home and Museum, 222 Ledoux St., Taos, NM 87571 (postal address: PO Box 3409, Taos, NM 87571-3409). Phone: 575/758-0505. Fax: 75/758-0330. E-mail: director@taoshistoricmuseums.org. Website: www. taoshistoricmuseums.org. Hours: 10–5 Mon.–Sat., 12–5 Sun.; closed New Year's Day, Easter, Thanksgiving, and Christmas. Admission: adults, $8; children 5–15, $4; children under 5, free.

Thomas Cole

Thomas Cole National Historic Site. The Thomas Cole National Historic Site in Catskill, New York, honors the founder of the Hudson River school of American painting. The site, known as Cedar Grove, contains the restored home and furnished studio of the nineteenth-century artist, who is known as the father of American landscape painting.

Born in Bolton-le-Moors, England, Cole came to America in 1819 and settled in the Catskills in 1826. He first rented a room at Cedar Grove during one of his sketching trips in the late 1820s. In 1836 he married Maria Bartow, who occupied the house with her uncle, and then moved in permanently and lived there until his death at the age of 47 in 1848. It was at Cedar Grove where Cole painted some of his best-known works. He and the Hudson River school artists found inspiration in the scenery of the Hudson River Valley. Among his notable works were *Ox-Bow* and the *Course of Empire* and *Voyage of Life* series.

The federal-style 1815 Cedar Grove has been restored to reflect the years during which Cole lived there. The period rooms contain empire furnishings, some of which belonged to the artist, and several of his paintings. Other rooms contain exhibits on Cole's life, some of his oil sketches, and changing exhibitions on other major figures of the Hudson River school. The studio contains his easel and tools. The Cole family continued to occupy the house until 1965. It now is owned by the Greene County Historical Society. Guided tours are offered of the main house and studio.

Thomas Cole National Historic Site, 218 Spring St., Catskill, NY 12414. Phone: 518/943-7465. Website: www. thomascole.org. Hours: early May–late Oct.—10–4 Thurs.–Sun.; other times by appointment. Admission: grounds—free; house—adults, $8; seniors and students, $6.

Salvador Dali

Salvador Dali Museum. The Salvador Dali Museum in St. Petersburg, Florida, contains the most comprehensive collection of the works of Salvador Felipe Jacinto Dali I Domenech, the Spanish painter better known simply as Salvador Dali. The museum, which opened in 1982, was founded by two longtime collectors of Dali's artworks, industrialist A. Reynolds Morse and his wife, Eleanor, of Cleveland.

Dali was born in Figueres, Spain, in 1904 and later made his home in nearby Port Lligat. He had his first show in Barcelona in 1925 and attracted international attention with three paintings, including *The Basket of Bread*, at the Carnegie International Exhibition in Pittsburgh in 1928. He then became a surrealist and soon was the leader of the surrealist movement. It was during this period that he produced some of his best-known paintings, including *The Persistence of Memory*, featuring soft or melting watches.

In 1940 Dali escaped from Europe during World War II. He spent 1940–1948 in the United States, where the Museum of Modern Art in New York City gave him his first major retrospective exhibition. He then began to move away from surrealism and into his classical period, with an emphasis on scientific, historical, and religious themes. Among his best works during this period included *The Hallucinogenic Toreador* and *The Discovery of America by Christopher Columbus* (now in the museum's collection) and *The Sacrament of the Last Supper*. Dali opened a gallery in his hometown in 1974, but his health soon began to deteriorate and he was burned in a fire. He spent most of his last years in seclusion and died in 1984.

The Salvador Dali Museum, which has constructed a new larger complex, has 96 of Dali's oil paintings from the 1917–1970 period, as well as 100 watercolors and drawings, 1,300 graphics, sculptures, photographs, other objects of art, and an extensive archival library. The museum rotates the Dali collection and features it in special exhibitions. The annual attendance is over 200,000.

Salvador Dali Museum, 1000 3rd St. South, St. Petersburg, FL 33701-4901. Phone: 727/823-3767. Fax: 727/894-6068. Website: www.salvadordalimuseum.org. Hours: 10–5:30, Fri.–Wed., 10–8 Thurs.; closed Thanksgiving and Christmas. Admission: adults, $17; seniors, military, teachers, police, firefighters, $14.50; students over 9, $12; children 5–9, $4; children under 5, free.

Theodor Seuss Geisel (Dr. Seuss)

Dr. Seuss National Memorial Sculpture Garden. The Dr. Seuss National Memorial Sculpture Garden, part of the Springfield Museums complex in Springfield, Massachusetts, honors author and illustrator Theodor Seuss Geisel, creator of the popular Dr. Seuss books for children. He wrote and illustrated 44 children's books, which have been translated into more than 15 languages and sold over 200 million copies. They include such favorites as *The Cat in the Hat, Green Eggs and Ham, Fox in Socks, How the Grinch Stole Christmas,* and *Oh, the Places You'll Go!*

Geisel was born to German immigrants in Springfield in 1904. He attended Dartmouth College, where he was editor of the college's humor magazine, signing his works "Seuss," his middle name and his mother's maiden name (he credited her with his ability and desire to create the rhymes for which he later became famous).

Geisel then went to Oxford University in England but dropped out to tour Europe. When he returned to the United States, he became a cartoonist and had some of his work published in magazines. As World War II approached, he began contributing weekly political cartoons to *PM,* a liberal magazine, and then served in the U.S. Army Signal Corps, where he made training films, including a series of animated films featuring a trainee called "Private Snafu."

After the war, he contributed to such magazines as *Life, Vanity Fair,* and *Judge.* Viking Press then hired him to illustrate *Boners,* a collection of children's sayings. The illustrations received great reviews, and he was asked to write and illustrate his first book—*And to Think That I Saw It on Mulberry Street.* It was followed by *The Cat in the Hat* and other books that made "Dr. Seuss" the leading author and illustrator of children's books in the world. His books also were the basis of 11 children's television specials, a Broadway musical, and a feature-length motion picture.

The Springfield Library and Museums Association first proposed a monument to honor the local author and illustrator of children's books in 1986, but it was not until Geisel's death in 1991 that the Dr. Seuss National Memorial Sculpture Garden was developed. The $6.2 million garden is located with five museums—two art and history museums and a science museum—grouped around a quadrangle in downtown Springfield. The memorial garden features five large bronze sculptures of Dr. Seuss's whimsical creatures. One admission covers all the museums. The sculpture garden is free.

Dr. Seuss National Memorial Sculpture Garden, 21 Edward St., Springfield, MA 01103. Phones: 413/263-6800 and 800/625-7738. Fax: 413/263-6889. E-mail: info@sringfieldmuseums.org. Websites: www.springfieldmuseums.org and www.catinthehat.org. Hours: 9–5 daily; closed New Year's Day, Easter, Independence Day, Thanksgiving, and Christmas. Admission: free.

Edward Hopper

Edward Hopper House Art Center. The Edward Hopper House Art Center is housed in the birthplace and boyhood home of the realist painter in Nyack, New York. The historic house, listed on the National Register of Historic Places, influenced his art throughout his life, creating the moods in views from his childhood, the play of light in various rooms, and the nearby post-Victorian architecture.

Hopper is best known for his starkly realistic scenes of contemporary life. His oil paintings fall into two categories—common aspects of everyday life, such as interior and street scenes, and seascapes and rural landscapes. They often portray isolation and loneliness, and are characterized by a mastery of light. One of his most celebrated paintings is the 1942 *Nighthawks,* showing customers sitting at a counter in an all-night diner. Among his other popular works are *House by the Railroad* (1926), *Early Sunday Morning* (1930), *Sunlight in a Cafeteria* (1959), and *A Woman in the Sun* (1961).

Hopper, who was born in 1882, started commuting to New York City after graduating from high school to go to art school. He then taught drawing classes in the parlor of his Nyack home on Saturdays, made three trips to Paris, and moved to New York City in 1910. He lived in an apartment and studio in Greenwich Village from 1913 until his death in 1967. In 1924 he married Josephine Nivison, an artist who served as a model for many of his paintings.

Special exhibitions of Hopper's life and career are presented at the restored 1858 house, operated by the Edward Hopper Landmark Preservation Foundation. The historic house now functions as a multi-arts center and presents exhibitions featuring the work of emerging and established artists and juried theme events in all styles and media. It also has art, music, poetry, book, and photography programs and events. The annual attendance is 4,000.

Edward Hopper House Art Center, 82 N. Broadway, Nyack, NY 10960. Phone: 845/358-0774. Fax: 845/353-9856. E-mail: edwardhopperhouse@verizon.net. Website: www.hopperhouse.org. Hours: 1–5 Thurs.–Sun.; closed Mon.– Wed. and major holidays. Admission: $1 donation.

Samuel F. B. Morse

See Scientists/Engineers/Inventors section.

Isamu Noguchi

Noguchi Museum. The Noguchi Museum, which opened in 1985 in Long Island City, New York, is devoted to the life and sculpture of Isamu Noguchi. It is housed in the former factory studio of the noted artist, who was known for his sculpture and creations in public spaces. He also received praise for his design of theater sets, furniture, and lamps.

Noguchi, who was born in Los Angeles in 1904 and died in New York City in 1988, began his artistic career in 1918 as an apprentice with Gutzon Borglum, who later became best known as the creator of Mount Rushmore National Memorial. After attending the Leonardo da Vinci Art School in New York City, Noguchi had his first exhibit in 1924 and decided to pursue sculpture full-time. He initially specialized in portrait busts and then began to do public sculptures, theater sets, furniture, and lamps.

Noguchi's early work eventually led to large-scale works in many of the world's large cities. He was praised for earthy sculptures and meditative gardens that bridged the East and the West. Among his best-known works are *Red Cube* in New York City (1968), *Sky Gate* in Honolulu (1977), and the Billy Rose Sculpture Garden in Jerusalem (1960–1965).

The Noguchi Museum features a comprehensive collection of his works in stone, metal, wood, and clay in 13 galleries that encircle a garden with outdoor sculpture. One gallery is devoted to his interior design work. The museum also presents changing exhibitions and educational programs on his life and work and has extensive archives with Noguchi's records, correspondence, manuscripts, and photographs. The museum receives 26,000 visitors annually.

Noguchi Museum, 9-01 33rd Rd., Long Island City, NY 11106 (postal address: 32-37 Vernon Blvd., Long Island City, NY 11106). Phone: 718/204-7088. Fax: 718/278-2348. E-mail: info@noguchi.org. Website: www.noguchi.org. Hours: 10–5 Wed.–Fri., 11–6 Sat.–Sun.; closed Mon.–Tues. Admission: adults, $10; seniors and students, $5; children under 12, free.

Georgia O'Keeffe

Georgia O'Keeffe Museum. Georgia O'Keeffe was a major figure in American art from the 1920s until her death in 1986 at the age of 98. She was known for challenging the boundaries of modern American artistic style, as well as for her technical contributions. She painted flowers, rocks, shells, animals, bones, and landscapes—often transforming them into abstract images of color and light. She became part of the American modernism movement and was one of the few women to have professional influence in art at the time. Her life and works now are the subject of the Georgia O'Keeffe Museum in Santa Fe, New Mexico.

O'Keeffe was born in 1887 in Sun Prairie, Wisconsin, but found artistic inspiration in the desertlike prairies of the Southwest. After attending the School of the Art Institute in Chicago, she enrolled at the Art Students League in New York City. She won a prize for a still life but became discouraged with her early work and went into teaching. After resuming her painting, she met noted photographer Alfred Stieglitz in 1916 when some of her drawings were exhibited at his New York gallery. That was the beginning of a love affair that resulted in their marriage in 1924, the year she painted her first large-scale floral painting, *Petunia, No. 2*. Stieglitz also began photographing her, often in erotic naked poses that caused a public sensation. In addition, he presented many exhibitions of her paintings and handled much of her business affairs over the years.

During the 1920s, O'Keeffe changed from watercolors to oil painting and started to go on pack trips exploring the mountains and deserts of New Mexico and painting the region's distinctive architectural and landscape forms. Between 1929 and 1949, she spent part of nearly every year painting in the region. In 1934 she bought a house at Ghost Ranch after visiting the resort in northwestern New Mexico. It is where she was inspired to paint some of

The Georgia O'Keeffe Museum in Santa Fe, New Mexico. Courtesy of the Georgia O'Keeffe Museum; photograph by Robert Reck; copyright the Georgia O'Keeffe Museum.

her most successful landscapes, including *Summer Days*, featuring a cattle skull adorned with wildflowers against a desert background.

In 1945 O'Keeffe purchased an abandoned eighteenth-century hacienda in Abiquiu, New Mexico, renovated it, and made it into her home and studio, where she created many of her later works, such as *Ladder to the Moon* and *Above the Clouds I*. Stieglitz, from whom she had been separated for long periods over the years, died in 1946. O'Keeffe lived in Abiquiu until 1984, when she moved to Santa Fe two years before her death. The Abiquiu house/ studio now is a National Historic Landmark operated by the Georgia O'Keeffe Museum, which offers tours of the site (*see* separate listing).

The Georgia O'Keeffe Museum was opened in 1997 to perpetuate her artistic legacy. The museum, founded by philanthropists Anne and John Marion, has more than 2,000 of her works, including 1,149 paintings, drawings, and sculptures. Her works include abstractions, architecture, natural and still life, landscapes, trees, and other subjects.

The museum also has 1,770 photographs of O'Keeffe; important events in her life, her animals, and friends; such things as her library, clothes, and objects she collected and used in her paintings; 1,840 works by other artists; and a research center dedicated to the study of American modernism. The museum's collection is featured in changing exhibitions. The annual attendance is 100,000.

Georgia O'Keeffe Museum, 217 Johnson St., Santa Fe, NM 87501. Phone: 505/946-1000. Fax: 505/946-1091. E-mail: info@okeeffemuseum.org. Website: www.okeeffemuseum.org. Hours: 10–5 daily; closed Easter, Thanksgiving, and Christmas. Admission: adults, $10, but $5 for New Mexico residents; seniors and students over 17, $8; children and students under 18, free.

Georgia O'Keeffe Home and Studio. The Georgia O'Keefe Home and Studio in Abiquiu, New Mexico, is where the modernist artist lived and painted for much of her career. She bought the abandoned Spanish colonial-era hacienda in 1945, spent three years restoring the 5,000-square-foot structure, and moved from New York City permanently to live in the stunning landscape that inspired her art for 40 years.

O'Keeffe continued to use the house she bought in 1940 at nearby Ghost Ranch, where she previously spent part of each year beginning in the mid-1930s. Both sites later were purchased by the Georgia O'Keefe Museum in Santa Fe, but guided tours are given only at the Abiquiu home/studio, located approximately 50 miles northwest of Santa Fe.

After O'Keeffe's death in 1986, the Georgia O'Keeffe Foundation became owner and manager of the Abiquiu property. It preserved and maintained the house and its contents until bought by the Georgia O'Keeffe Museum. It now is possible to arrange for a tour of the house and studio and to see the surrounding landscape. O'Keeffe's longtime home still contains many of her furnishings and artworks.

Georgia O'Keeffe Home and Studio, Abiquiu, NM 87510 (postal address: PO Box 40, Abiquiu, NM 87510-0040). Tour office next to Abiquiu Inn on U.S. 84. Phone: 505/685-4539. Fax: 505/685-4551. E-mail: info@okeeffemuseum. org. Website: www.okeeffemuseum.org. Tour hours: mid-Mar.–late Nov.—9:30–3:30 Tues.–Fri.; closed Sat.–Mon.; June–Oct.—10–1:30 Sat. (with special tours at l on Thurs. mid-June–mid-Oct. with property manager who worked with O'Keeffe); closed remainder of week. Tour admission: $30–$40.

Frederic Remington

Frederic Remington Art Museum. Frederic Remington is best known for his paintings and sculptures of the American West frontier, with heroic and savage depictions of cowboys, soldiers, and Indians. But he also did impressionist landscape paintings of his beloved North Country of New York in his later life. Both can be found at the Frederic Remington Art Museum in Ogdensburg, New York.

Remington, who is considered with Charles M. Russell as one of the fathers of American Western art, was born in 1861 in nearby Canton, New York. At an early age, he demonstrated an interest in horses, military things, and art. After receiving his first formal training at Yale University and the Art Students League, he left college in search of adventure and excitement in the West. While on the frontier, he made sketches, took photographs, and gathered information that he later used at his home in New Rochelle, New York, to create popular paintings and bronzes of the frontier. Remington, who died in 1909, was credited with being the primary image maker of the glorified American West.

The Frederic Remington Museum, founded in 1923 and located in the 1810 former mansion of industrialist David Parish, contains the greatest collection of Remington paintings, drawings, and sculptures. It also has his library, notes, correspondence, annotated scrapbooks, working tools, sketchbooks, photographs, furniture, and even the cigars that were in his pocket before he died. The majority of the collection came from the estate of Remington's widow, Eva, who died in 1918. The museum's annual attendance is 10,000.

Frederic Remington Art Museum, 303 Washington St., Ogdensburg, NY 13669. Phone: 315/393-2425. Fax: 315/393-4464. E-mail: info@fredericregimington.org. Website: www.fredericremington.org. Hours: Nov.–Apr.— 11–5 Mon.–Sat., 1–5 Sun.; May–Oct.—10–5 Mon.–Sat., 1–5 Sun.; closed New Year's Day, Easter, Thanksgiving, and Christmas. Admission: adults, $9; seniors and students over 15, $8; military, $5; children under 16, free.

Norman Rockwell

Norman Rockwell Museum. The largest collection of paintings and illustrations by Norman Rockwell are located at the Norman Rockwell Museum, founded in 1969 in Stockbridge, Massachusetts. It has 574 original works by Rockwell, who is best known for his cover illustrations of everyday life created for the *Saturday Evening Post* over more than four decades. He was a prolific artist, producing over 4,000 works in his lifetime. Most of his paintings and illustrations, however, have been destroyed by fire or are in permanent collections.

Most of Rockwell's work was in illustrating magazine covers, books, calendars, posters, and other commercial products. Among his most popular works in the *Saturday Evening Post* were *The Four Freedoms* (1943), *Rosie the Riveter* (1943), *Saying Grace* (1951), and the *Willie Gillis* series, He is also known for his work for the Boy Scouts of America (*Boys' Life* magazine and calendars), illustrations for over 40 books (including *Tom Sawyer* and *Huckleberry Finn*), the *Four Seasons* calendar illustrations for Brown & Bigelow that were published for 17 years beginning in 1947, and many motion picture promotional posters.

Rockwell was born in New York City in 1894 and died in 1978 in Stockbridge, where he lived most of his adult life. He received his art education at the Chase Art School, National Academy of Design, and Art Students League. His first career breakthrough came in 1912 when he was asked to do a book illustration while only 18. He then became art editor of *Boys' Life* and started to do magazine covers. In 1916 he did the first of 321 covers for the *Sat-*

The Four Freedoms, *displayed at the Norman Rockwell Museum in Stockbridge, Massachusetts. Courtesy of Berkshire Visitors Bureau, all rights reserved.*

urday Evening Post. This led to covers for such other magazines as the *Literary Digest*, *The Country Gentleman*, *Leslie's Weekly*, *Judge*, and *Life*, as well as books, calendars, posters, and other illustrations.

The Norman Rockwell Museum contains the most significant public collection of Rockwell's work, as well as the artist's studio, art supplies, library, personal memorabilia, and archives with over 100,000 items, including papers, correspondence, photographs, publications, and other materials. In 1973 the Norman Rockwell Art Collection Trust bequeathed 367 of his works to the museum, including such illustrations as *The Four Freedoms*, *Main Street at Christmas*, and *Triple Self-Portrait*. The museum has an annual attendance of 140,000.

Norman Rockwell Museum, Rte. 183, 9 Glendale Rd., Stockbridge, MA 01262 (postal address: PO Box 308, Stockbridge, MA 01262-0308). Phone: 413/298-4100. Fax: 413/298-4142. E-mail: inforequest@nrm.org. Website: www.nrm. org. Hours: May–Oct.—10–5 daily; Nov.–Apr.—10–4 Mon.–Fri., 10–5 Sat.–Sun.; closed New Year's Day, Thanksgiving, and Christmas. Admission: adults, $15; seniors, $13; college students, $10; youth and children under 19, free.

Norman Rockwell Museum of Vermont. Norman Rockwell's years in Vermont are the focus of another museum—the Norman Rockwell Museum of Vermont—in Rutland. The artist, his wife, and three children lived in Arlington, Vermont, for 14 years (1939–1953) until his wife's illness prompted a move to Stockbridge, Massachusetts. The museum seeks to show the influences Vermont exerted on his artwork and career. During Rockwell's stay in the state, many neighbors served as models for his paintings.

The museum, originally founded in West Arlington in 1976 and moved to Rutland in 1978, contains 2,500 pieces of Rockwell's works, some of which span his 1911–1978 career. The museum's collection is presented in chronological order to show his development as an artist/illustrator and his connection and sensitivity to the nation's political, economic, and cultural history. The museum displays many of his illustrations for magazine covers, books, calendars, and advertisements.

Norman Rockwell Museum of Vermont, 654 Rte. 4 East, Rutland, VT 05701. Phones: 802/773-6095 and 877/773-6095. Fax: 802/775-2440. E-mail: cs@normanrockwellvt.com. Website: www.normanrockwellvt.com. Hours: 9–4 daily; closed major holidays. Admission: adults, $5.50; seniors, $5; children 8–17, $2.50; children under 8, free.

Auguste Rodin

Rodin Museum. The largest collection of works by renowned sculptor Auguste Rodin outside of Paris is located at the Rodin Museum in Philadelphia. The museum, which opened in 1928, was founded by movie theater magnate Jules Mastbaum, who began collected works by Rodin with the intent of enriching the lives of Americans by making the museum a gift to the city. Although Mastbaum died in 1926, his widow honored the commitment.

Rodin, who was born in France in 1840 and died in 1917, had a greater influence on the history of figurative sculpture than any sculptor since Michelangelo. He introduced a new era of artistic expression with lifelike figures that showed physical states ranging from inner turmoil to overwhelming joy. He was praised and criticized for such sculptures as *Age of Bronze*, *Monument to Honoré*, and *The Gates of Hell* (on which he worked from 1880 until his death). Rodin's *The Thinker* is considered one of the most famous sculptures in the world. He is also known for such outstanding works as *The Burghers of Calais*, *Eternal Springtime*, and *Apotheosis of Victor Hugo*.

In 1926 Mastbaum commissioned French architects Paul Cret and Jacques Gréber to design the Philadelphia museum's building and gardens. The museum now houses bronze castings, plaster studies, drawings, prints, letters, and books of Rodin. A cast of *The Thinker* sits outside in the entry courtyard, and a cast of the massive *The Gates of Hell* can be seen at the museum entrance. Visitors once entered the museum through the sculpture.

Inside the museum are casts of such sculptures as *The Kiss*, *Eternal Springtime*, *The Age of Bronze*, and the monumental *The Burghers of Calais*. The museum also has a copy of Rodin's ca. 1840 sketchbook from his student days, which can be seen on an interactive kiosk. The museum's annual attendance is over 50,000.

Rodin Museum, Benjamin Franklin Pkwy at 22nd St., Philadelphia, PA 19101 (postal address: PO Box 7646, Philadelphia, PA 19101-7646). Phone: 215/568-6026. Fax: 215/235-0050. Website: www.rodinmuseum.org. Hours: 10–5 Tues.–Sun.; closed Mon. and major holidays. Admission: $5 suggested donation.

Charles M. Russell

C. M. Russell Museum. Charles M. Russell was one of the leading artists who painted and sculptured cowboys, Indians, and landscapes of the Old West in the late 1800s and early 1900s. He was the first artist to create works about the Wild West who actually lived in the region, and he is regarded, with Frederic Remington, as one of the fathers of American Western art. During his long career, he produced nearly 4,000 paintings and bronzes. His home for 46 years was in Great Falls, Montana, now the site of the C. M. Russell Museum complex devoted to his life and artworks.

Russell, who was known as the "cowboy artist," was born in St. Louis in 1864 and dreamed about being a cowboy and living on the range. It was during this early period that he began doing sketches and making clay figures of animals. In 1860, at the age of 16, he came to the Judith Basin of Montana and worked, sketched, and painted as a cowboy and wrangler for 11 years before becoming a full-time artist. In 1896 Russell moved to Great Falls, where he spent the rest of his life and produced his greatest works, including *The Exalted Ruler*, *The Jerkline*, and *The Fireboat*. Russell died at his home in 1926.

The C. M. Russell Museum has exhibits about Russell and his artworks, displays about contemporaries and bison, an interactive gallery for families and children, and a research library. The complex also contains the 1900 Russell house with period furnishings and personal items and the 1903 studio with many of the materials he used to create his paintings and bronzes. The annual attendance is 60,000.

C. M. Russell Museum, 400 13th St. North, Great Falls, MT 59401. Phone: 406/727-8787. Fax: 406/727-2402. Website: www.cmrussell.org. Hours: Memorial Day–Labor Day—9–6 daily; remainder of year—10–5 Tues.–Sat., closed Sun.–Mon., New Year's Day, Easter, Thanksgiving, and Christmas. Admission: adults, $9; seniors and military, $7; students, $4; children under 6, free.

Augustus Saint-Gaudens

Saint-Gaudens National Historic Site. The 150-acre Saint-Gaudens National Historic Site in Cornish, New Hampshire, preserves the home, gardens, and studio of noted sculptor Augustus Saint-Gaudens, who was born in

Ireland but spent almost his entire life in the United States. He created over 150 imaginative works of art, ranging from exquisitely carved cameos to heroic-size public monuments in the late nineteenth century and early twentieth century. More than 100 of his works are exhibited in the galleries and on the grounds of the site, where guided tours originate at a visitor center.

Saint-Gaudens, who was considered the foremost American sculptor of the nineteenth century, was born to a French father and an Irish mother in 1848 in Dublin, Ireland, and came to American when his family immigrated when he was only six months old. He grew up in New York City and expressed interest in art when 13. He was apprenticed to a cameo cutter and took classes at Cooper Union and the National Academy of Design. He then studied at the École des Beaux-Arts in Paris and took classical art and architecture classes in Rome.

Saint-Gaudens received his first major commission in 1876—a monument to Civil War Admiral David Glasgow Farragut in New York in 1881. It was a departure from prior American sculpture, combining realism and allegory, and was a great success. It was followed by teaching and such distinctive public sculptures as the Adams Memorial, Peter Cooper Monument, John A. Logan Monument, and Shaw Memorial.

Saint-Gaudens first rented his home in Cornish in 1885 and then purchased it in 1891. He adapted what was a ca. 1800 inn to his needs and converted a hay barn into a studio. As his commissions and staff increased, he built a large studio where he did the concepts and initial models for his sculptures and assistants completed the projects. The studio was destroyed in a fire in 1904, and then a redesigned studio again burned in 1944. Other well-known artists followed Saint-Gaudens to Cornish to form an art colony, but it gradually dissipated after his death. The historic site has 40,000 visitors annually.

Saint-Gaudens National Historic Site, 139 Saint-Gaudens Rd., Cornish, NH 03745. Phone: 603/675-2175. Fax: 603/675-2701. E-mail: bj_dunn@nps.gov. Website: www.nps.gov/saga. Hours: Memorial Day–Oct.—9–4:30 daily and grounds till dark; Nov.–late May—only visitor center open 9–4:15 Mon.–Fri.; closed Sat.–Sun. Admission: adults, $5; children under 16, free.

Charles M. Schulz

Charles M. Schulz Museum and Research Center. The Charles M. Schulz Museum and Research Center in Santa Rosa, California, tells of the life and works of cartoonist Charles M. Schulz, known worldwide for his *Peanuts* comic strip and Charlie Brown and Snoopy characters. The comic strip ran for nearly 50 years (1950–2000) and appeared in more than 2,600 newspapers in 75 countries at its peak.

Schulz was born in Minneapolis in 1922, grew up in St. Paul, and began doing sketches at an early age. He later took correspondence art classes, served in the army during World War II, and taught art before beginning his cartoon career. Schulz had his first regular cartoon, *Li'l Folks*, published in the *St. Paul Pioneer Press* in 1947–1950. When the comic strip was dropped, the United Feature Syndicate agreed to syndicate *Peanuts*, where the principal characters were Charlie Brown and Snoopy and the story lines often were inspired by events in Schulz's own life. It proved to be highly popular, and Schulz drew the cartoon strip until his death in 2000.

The Charles M. Schulz Museum and Research Center opened in 2002 two blocks away from Schulz's former studio in Santa Rosa. It celebrates his life and the art of cartooning. The museum contains 6,000 drawings of the *Peanuts* comic strip, nearly 400 art pieces from other cartoonists commemorating his life, personal memorabilia, Schulz's studio, and various *Peanuts* displays. The museum also presents changing exhibitions, films, public programs, and art classes. The annual attendance is 50,000.

Charles M. Schulz Museum and Research Center, 2301 Hardies Lane, Santa Rosa, CA 95403. Phone: 707/579-4452. Fax: 707/579-4436. E-mail: inquiries@schulzmuseum.org. Website: www.charlesmschulzmuseum.org. Hours: Memorial Day–Labor Day—11–5 Mon.–Fri., 10–5 Sat.–Sun.; remainder of year—11–5 Mon. and Wed.–Fri.; 10–5 Sat.–Sun.; closed Tues., New Year's Day, Easter, Independence Day, Thanksgiving, and Christmas Eve and Day. Admission: adults, $8; seniors, college students, and children 4–18, $5; children under 4, free.

Gilbert Stuart

Gilbert Stuart Birthplace and Museum. Gilbert Stuart is considered one of America's finest portrait painters. During his career in the late 1700s and early 1800s, he did portraits of over 1,000 people, including the first six presidents of the United States. His best-known work is a portrait of George Washington, also known as the *Athenaeum* portrait, which he began in 1796 and never finished. However, he painted 130 reproductions of the original version and sold copies. It is the image of Washington that appears on the $1 bill. The *Athenaeum* portrait now is at the Boston Museum of Fine Arts. Another celebrated Stuart portrait is the large *Lansdowne* portrait that hangs in the East Room of the White House.

Stuart was born in Saunderstown, Rhode Island, in 1755 and moved to Newport at the age of seven. It is where he first showed great promise as a painter and where he was tutored by Cosmo Alexander, a Scottish painter. After going to Scotland with Alexander, he became a protégé of Benjamin West in England and exhibited at the Royal Academy in 1777.

Stuart returned to the United States in 1793 and two years later opened a studio in Germantown, now a part of Philadelphia. This is where he gained fame for his many portraits of important Americans of the period. In 1803 Stuart opened a studio in Washington and then moved to Boston in 1805. He continued to produce portraits of many political, social, and military leaders until his death in 1828.

Stuart, who suffered from financial problems during most of his life, initially was buried in an unmarked grave in the Boston Common. When his family recovered financially nearly a decade later, they planned to move his body to a family cemetery in Newport. But family members could not remember where he was buried, and the grave was never found.

The Gilbert Stuart Birthplace and Museum, founded in 1930 in Saunderstown, preserves the historic site where the noted portrait artist was born. The site, which was both a family home and a place of industry, has been restored and contains exhibits and reproductions of Stuart's artworks. The house was a workingman's home, and the industrial plant was the first snuff mill in America. Located in a wooded area along the banks of the Mattatuxet Brook, the site contains the Stuart home, herb gardens, the 1750 snuff mill, a partially restored 1662 gristmill, and a fish ladder, which features migrating herring, seeking to reach the pond above the mill dam in the spring. Guided tours are offered. The site has 5,400 visitors annually.

Gilbert Stuart Birthplace and Museum, 815 Gilbert Stuart Rd., Saundertown, RI 02874. Phone 401/294-3869. Fax: 401/294-3869. Website: www.gilbertstuartmuseum.com. Hours: early May–Sept.—11–4 Thurs.–Mon.; closed Tues.–Wed.; limited hours to mid-Oct.; closed remainder of year. Admission: adults, $6; children 6–12, $3; children under 6, free.

Andy Warhol

Andy Warhol Museum. The Andy Warhol Museum in Pittsburgh is dedicated to the life and works of the founder and leading exponent of "pop" art who also was a printmaker and avant-garde filmmaker. He transformed contemporary art by using mass production techniques to create his works and challenged preconceived notions about the nature of art, erasing traditional distinctions between fine art and popular culture.

The Andy Warhol Museum is located in the city where he was born in 1928. He showed early artistic talent and studied at the School of Fine Arts at the Carnegie Institute of Technology (which later became Carnegie Mellon University). In 1949 he moved to New York City and had a successful career in magazine illustration and advertising. He then began his pop art career by making paintings of iconic American products and silk-screened portraits of celebrities. His first one-man gallery exhibition was in Los Angeles in 1962, followed by an exhibition in New York. His controversial works rocked the art world.

It also was in the 1960s that Warhol began making underground films and founded the Factory, which became his studio and a gathering place of artists, writers, musicians, and underground celebrities. It was at the Factory that he was shot and seriously wounded by a disgruntled follower, but he recovered and continued to produce exceptional paintings, films, videos, and other works in the 1970s–1980s. He died at the age of 59 after surgery in 1987.

Opened in 1994, the Andy Warhol Museum is one of four museums known as the Carnegie Museums of Pittsburgh. It contains over 12,000 Warhol works in all media—paintings, drawings, prints, photographs, sculpture, films, videotapes, and installations from his creative life in the 1940s through the 1980s—as well as his archives. Among the works at the museum are some of Warhol's best-known pop art paintings, such as the portraits of *Marilyn, Liz,* and *Elvis;* works like *Campbell's Soup Cans, Brillo Boxes and Flowers,* and *Cow Wallpaper and Silver Clouds;* and such series as *Death in America, Maos, Skulls,* and *Rorschach.* Approximately 500 works from the museum's collection are displayed at any time. The annual attendance is 92,000.

Andy Warhol Museum, 117 Sandusky St., Pittsburgh, PA 15212-5890. Phone: 412/237-8300. Fax: 412/237-8340. E-mail: information@warhol.org. Website: www.warhol.org. Hours: 10–5 Tues.–Thurs. and Sat.–Sun., 10–10 Fri.; closed Mon., New Year's Day, Easter, Memorial Day, Independence Day, Thanksgiving, and Christmas. Admission: adults, $15; seniors, $9; students and children 3–18, $8; children under 3, free.

James McNeill Whistler

Whistler House Museum of Art. James McNeill Whistler was a noted nineteenth-century American painter and etcher who went to France to study in 1855 and never returned to the United States. He spent the rest of his life painting alternately in studios in Paris and London. He was a modernist painter with oils and etchings approaching the effects of French impressionism who was considered one of the most influential artists of the day and the finest etcher since Rembrandt.

Whistler's 1834 birthplace in Lowell, Massachusetts, now is the home of the Whistler House Museum of Art, which features etchings by Whistler and the works of nineteenth and twentieth century New England representational artists. They include such Whistler etchings as *Annie Seated* (1858), *The Poor* (1859), and *The Old Rag Woman* (1859). The house, which was the home of a number of leaders in the Industrial Revolution between 1823 and 1869, has served as the home of the Lowell Art Association since 1908. The museum's annual attendance is 7,000.

Whistler House Museum of Art, 243 Worthen St., Lowell, MA 01852, Phone: 978/452-7641. Fax: 978/454-2421. E-mail: mlally@whistlerhouse.org. Website: www.whistlerhouse.org. Hours: 11–4 Wed.–Sat.; closed Sun.–Tues. and major holidays. Admission: adults, $5; seniors and students 6–21, $4; children under 6, free.

N. C. Wyeth

N. C. Wyeth House and Studio. Newell Convers Wyeth, who went by N. C. Wyeth, was a celebrated illustrator and painter best known for his book and magazine illustrations, but who also did murals in major buildings in the first half of the twentieth century. He illustrated such books as *Treasure Island*, *The Last of the Mohicans*, and *Robin Hood*; produced art for magazines like the *Saturday Evening Post*, *Harper's*, and *Scribner's*; and created historical and allegorical murals for places such as the Boston Public Library, Missouri State Capital, and National Cathedral in Washington. His life and works are now honored at the N. C. Wyeth House and Studio, a branch of the Brandywine River Museum in Chadds Ford Township, Pennsylvania.

Wyeth was born in Needham, Massachusetts, in 1882 and received his early art training at the Massachusetts Normal Arts School, where he attended classes taught by illustrators Eric Pape and Charles W. Reed. In 1902–1904 he studied with the great illustrator Howard Pyle in Wilmington, Delaware. After his marriage in 1906, he settled in rural Chadds Ford Township. It was where Andrew Wyeth, who also became a prominent artist, was born and taught by his father. In 1911 N. C. Wyeth began his career as a book illustrator when he did the artwork for Robert Louis Stevenson's *Treasure Island*. Dozens of other books followed, as well as work for magazines and buildings.

Wyeth and a grandson died in 1945 when their car stalled while crossing railroad tracks. His wife and then daughter lived at the Chadds Ford home until 1994, when Brandywine River Museum took possession and began restoration of the property. In 1997 the house and studio were designated a National Historic Landmark. Tours are now given by Brandywine River Museum of the N. C. Wyeth House and Studio and on its 18-acre site. The Brandywine River Museum has Wyeth's archives and the largest collection of his artwork at its site in Chadds Ford.

N. C. Wyeth House and Studio, Murphy Rd., Chadds Ford Township, PA 19317 (postal address: Brandywine River Museum, U.S. Rte. 1 at Creek Rd., PO Box 141, Chadds Ford, PA 19317). Phone: 610/388-2700. Fax: 610/388-1197. E-mail: inquiries@brandywine.org. Website: www.brandywinemuseum.org. Hours: early Apr.–late Nov.— 10–3:30 Thurs.–Sun.; closed remainder of year. Admission: $5 in addition to Brandywine River Museum admission of $10 for adults and $6 for seniors, students, and children 6–12. Children under 6 are not permitted on tours.

ATHLETES

Hank Aaron

Hank Aaron Childhood Home and Museum. The life and achievements of Henry "Hank" Aaron, regarded as one of baseball's greatest players, are featured at a new museum in a park on the grounds of the Hank Aaron Stadium, home of the Mobile Bay Bears, a minor league team in his hometown of Mobile, Alabama.

The Hank Aaron Childhood Home and Museum, which opened in 2010, is housed in the home where Aaron lived as a child. It has been relocated and renovated to serve as the site of the museum. It contains exhibits, memorabilia, and photographs about his formative and professional years. The house was built by Aaron's father in 1942, and his mother lived there until shortly before her death in 2008.

Aaron hit 755 home runs during his 23-year major league career with the Milwaukee and Atlanta Braves in the National League and the Milwaukee Brewers in the American League. It was the record for 33 years before being surpassed by San Francisco Giants outfielder Barry Bonds in 2007. He was the first player to hit 500 home runs and reach 3,000 hits, and the only player to hit 30 or more home runs in a season at least 15 times. Aaron still holds the major league records for the most career runs batted in (2,297), most career extra base hits (1,477), and most career total bases (6,856).

Aaron was inducted into the Baseball Hall of Fame in 1982 and selected for the Major League Baseball All-Century Team in 1999. It also was in 1999 that Major League Baseball established the Hank Aaron Award to honor the best overall offensive player in the major leagues.

Hank Aaron Childhood Home and Museum, Hank Aaron Stadium, 755 Bolling Brothers Blvd., Mobile, AL 38606. Phone: 251/479-2327. Website: www.hankaaronstadium.com. Hours: 10–4 Mon.–Fri., 10–2 Sat.; closed Sun. and major holidays. Admission: adults, $5; seniors, military, and children under 13, $4.

Muhammad Ali

Muhammad Ali Center. The Muhammad Ali Center in Louisville, Kentucky, honors one of the nation's greatest boxers. He was a three-time world heavyweight champion who became known for his unorthodox "rope-a-dope" fighting style, as well as his "trash talk" against opponents. He called himself "The Greatest," and he was when he ruled the heavyweight ring in the 1960s–1970s. During his career, he had 56 wins (37 by knockouts) against only five losses. He retired in 1981, was diagnosed with Parkinson's syndrome three years later, and remains a popular and active public figure.

Born in Louisville in 1942, Ali originally was a black fighter known as Cassius Clay. He changed his name after joining the Nation of Islam in 1964. He became an amateur boxer as a teenager and went on to win six Kentucky Golden Glove titles, an Amateur Athletic Union national title, and the light heavyweight gold medal at the 1960 Summer Olympics in Rome. He turned professional in 1960 and in 1964 won the world heavyweight championship by beating Sonny Liston. He was stripped of the title in 1967 when he refused to serve in the army during the Vietnam War, saying he was a conscientious objector and that it was against his religious beliefs. He was convicted of refusing to serve, but it was later overturned.

Ali regained the heavyweight title in 1974 after defeating champion George Foreman, but lost it to Leon Spinks in 1978. He then captured the title for the third time by beating Spinks in a rematch in 1979.

The $60 million Muhammad Ali Center opened in downtown Louisville in 2005. The center, which has exhibits on Ali's life and displays his boxing memorabilia, is a cultural/educational center that also focuses on the themes of social responsibility, respect, personal growth, and peace. It also has historical, art, and interactive exhibits and a five-screen orientation theater. The annual attendance is 135,000.

Muhammad Ali Center, 1 Muhammad Ali Plaza, 144 N. 6th St., Louisville, KY 40202. Phone: 502/584-9254. Fax: 502/589-4905. E-mail: info@alicenter.org. Website: www.alicenter.org. Hours: 9:30–5 Tues.–Sat., 12–5 Sun.; closed Mon., New Year's Day, Easter, Independence Day, Thanksgiving, and Christmas. Admission: adults, $9; seniors, $8; military and students, $5; children 6–12, $4; children under 6, free.

Yogi Berra

Yogi Berra Museum and Learning Center. The Yogi Berra Museum and Learning Center on the campus of Montclair State University in Little Falls, New Jersey, is a sports education center with exhibits and programs about the former New York Yankees baseball star. The center was founded in 1998 "to preserve and promote the values of respect, sportsmanship, social justice, and excellence through inclusion, culturally diverse, sports-based educational programs and exhibits."

Berra was a three-time most valuable catcher who anchored the New York Yankees from the late 1940s to the early 1960s, a 15-time all-star player, and a member of 10 world championships teams (the most in baseball history). He also served as manager of both the New York Yankees and New York Mets and was the first person in over 40 years to win pennants in different leagues (Yankees in 1964 and Mets in 1973).

Lawrence Peter Berra, who got his nickname "Yogi" from a friend who said he resembled a yogi in a Hindu-themed movie, was born in 1925 in St. Louis. He left school after the eighth grade to help his family, working at menial jobs while playing American Legion baseball. He got his big league chance in 1943 when he was signed by the Yankees, but he then enlisted in the navy during World War II and survived when his rocket boat capsized during the D-day landing on Omaha Beach. In 1946 he was playing for the Yankees' farm team in Newark when he was called up to the majors and hit a home run in his first game. He became a star behind the plate and a master handler of pitchers—catching for three no-hitters. He also was a feared batter during a period when the Yankees had such sluggers as Joe DiMaggio and Mickey Mantle.

The Yogi Berra Museum traces his life and career and the history of baseball and the New York Yankees. It has exhibits featuring historic baseball equipment, photographs, and memorabilia, including Berra's 10 world championship rings. The museum also has an intimate ballparklike theater that shows films and serves as the site of public programs on such topics as character education, sportsmanship, peer leadership, sports ethics, women in sports, sports and social justice, and sports medicine and nutrition.

Yogi Berra Museum and Learning Center, Montclair State University, 8 Quarry Rd., Little Falls, NJ 07424. Phone: 973/655-2378. Fax: 973/655-6894. Website: www.yogiberramuseum.org. Hours: 12–5 Wed.–Sun.; closed Mon.–Tues. and major holidays. Admission: adults, $6; seniors, $5; children under 18, $4.

Paul W. Bryant

Paul W. Bryant Museum. The Paul W. Bryant Museum at the University of Alabama in Tuscaloosa honors both legendary Coach "Bear" Bryant and the history of football at the university. Bryant coached football at the university twice—as an assistant coach in 1936–1940 and as head coach in 1958–1983—and once held the record for winning more games than any other coach in big-time collegiate football. He had 25 winning seasons and won 323 games, 24 bowl games, and six national championships. He was national coach of the year three times and Southeastern Conference coach of the year eight times.

Bryant was born in Moro Bottoms, Arkansas, in 1913; earned his nickname by wrestling a bear in a theater in 1927; led his high school football team to a state championship in 1930; received a scholarship to the University of Alabama in 1931; and starred in football at Alabama in 1932–1935. He got his first coaching job at Union College in 1936 but left to be an assistant coach at Alabama. Bryant moved to Vanderbilt as assistant coach in 1940–1941, served in the navy during World War II, and became a successful head coach at Maryland in 1945–1946, Kentucky in 1946–1953, and Texas A&M in 1954–1958 before returning to Alabama. He announced his retirement in 1982 and died a few months later in 1983.

The Paul W. Bryant Museum, which opened in 1988, has exhibits, photographs, trophies, and memorabilia about the life and career of the famed coach and some of his former players and assistant coaches and the history of football at the university, which began in 1892. The museum also has a replica of Bryant's office, his trademark houndstooth hat, items from former players, special exhibitions, and an archive on football at the University of Alabama. The annual attendance is 40,000.

Paul W. Bryant Museum, University of Alabama, 300 Paul W. Bryant Dr., PO Box 870385, Tuscaloosa, AL 35487-0385. Phones: 205/348-4668 and 866/772-2327. Fax: 205/348-8883. E-mail: bryant-info@ua.edu. Website: www.bryantmuseum.ua.edu. Hours: 9–4 daily; closed major holidays. Admission: adults, $2; seniors and children 6–17, $1; children under 6, free.

Roberto Clemente

Roberto Clemente Museum. Roberto Clemente was a hall-of-fame right fielder who played for the Pittsburgh Pirates in 1955–1972 and died in a plane crash while en route to deliver aid to earthquake victims in Nicaragua in 1972. During his 18-year professional baseball career, he was the most valuable player in the National League in 1966, won 12 Gold Glove Awards, led the league in batting four seasons, and was selected to play in the all-star game 12 times. In 2007 the Robert Clemente Museum opened in Pittsburgh in his memory. It was started by photographer Duane Rieder, a Clemente fan, with the assistance of the Clemente family.

Clemente was born in Carolina, Puerto Rico, in 1934 and began his baseball career in the Puerto Rico Professional Baseball League. After accepting an offer to play with the Montreal Royals, he was drafted by the Pittsburgh Pirates in 1954. He was a popular player who was the first Hispanic to win a World Series as a starter in 1960 and the first Latin American to be elected to the Baseball Hall of Fame in 1973. Clemente also was involved in charity work in Puerto Rico and other Latin American countries. He often provided food and baseball equipment to needy people. His body never was recovered after the Nicaraguan mission.

The Roberto Clemente Museum is located in a former fire station in the Lawrenceville section of Pittsburgh. It contains exhibits about Clemente's life and career and has memorabilia, photographs, and such baseball equipment as uniforms, gloves, balls, and bats. It also has seats from the old Forbes Field, where Clemente played before the new ball field was constructed.

Roberto Clemente Museum, 3339 Penn Ave., Pittsburgh, PA 15201-1268. Phone: 412/621-1268. Hours: by appointment. Admission: adults, $20; children under 17, $10.

Ty Cobb

Ty Cobb Museum. Ty Cobb, considered by many to be the greatest baseball player of all time, is honored at the Ty Cobb Museum in Royston, Georgia. In his 22 years with the Detroit Tigers and two with the Philadelphia Athletics in 1905–1928, he set 90 records. He still holds the records for the highest career batting average (.337) and most career batting titles (12). Among the other career records he held for a half century before being surpassed were most hits (4,191), most runs scored (2,245), most games played (3,035), most at bats (11,434), and most stolen bases (892). He also batted over .300 for 23 years and was the first player to be inducted into the Baseball Hall of Fame (receiving 222 out of 226 possible votes).

Cobb, whose full name was Tyrus Raymond Cobb, was known as the "Georgia Peach." He was born in Narrows, Georgia, in 1886 and died in Atlanta in 1961. He was a right-handed outfielder for the Detroit Tigers from 1905 to 1926 (as well as manager in 1921–1926) and then spent two years with the Philadelphia Athletics before retiring in 1928. He played semipro ball and was sold to the Detroit Tigers by the Augusta Tourists for a reported $500 in 1905. In addition to his baseball talent, he was known for his aggressive playing style and surly temperament.

The Ty Cobb Museum, which was founded in 1998, seeks to foster education and understanding of baseball and its greatest hitter. In addition to exhibits on his life and career, the museum contains memorabilia, rare photographs, art, films, videos, and archives. Among the items on display is Cobb's 1907 medal for winning the American League batting title. The museum also houses the Franklin County Sports Hall of Fame.

Ty Cobb Museum, 461 Cook St., Royston, GA 30662-3903. Phone: 706/245-1825. Fax: 706/245-1831. Website: www.tycobbmuseum.org. Hours: 9–4 Mon.–Fri., 10–4 Sat.; closed Sun., New Year's Eve and Day, Independence Day, Labor Day, Thanksgiving, and Christmas Eve and Day. Admission: adults, $5; seniors, $4; students, $3; military and children under 5, free.

Jack Dempsey

Jack Dempsey Museum and Park. Jack Dempsey, who held the world heavyweight boxing title from 1919 to 1926, was one of the most popular boxers in history. He came from the mining town of Manassa, Colorado, and was known as "The Manassa Mauler" because of his aggressive style and punching power. The town now celebrates his life and career at the Jack Dempsey Museum and Park.

Dempsey, who grew up as William Harrison Dempsey in a poor family, dropped out of grade school to work and left home when 16 to find a better life. After traveling underneath trains and sleeping in hobo camps while seeking work, he found he had a talent for fighting and began training as a professional boxer. Many of his early fights were in mining camps. His exact fight record is not known because he sometimes boxed under another name, Kid Blackie. But he is credited with 66 wins, six losses, and one disqualification.

In 1919 he won the world's heavyweight championship by defeating defending champion Jess Willard. Dempsey is best remembered for his two fights with Gene Tunney, who beat him for the title before a record 120,557 crowd in Philadelphia in 1926 and again in a controversial rematch in Chicago a year later. Dempsey retired after the bout but made numerous exhibitions, appeared in firms, and opened a Broadway restaurant in New York City before his death in 1983.

The Jack Dempsey Museum and Park was dedicated by the City of Manassa in his honor in 1966. The museum is located in the cabin where he was born in 1895 and is surrounded by a small park. It contains memorabilia, photographs, and such objects as his boxing gloves.

Jack Dempsey Museum and Park, 412 Main St., PO Box 130, Manassa, CO 81141. Phone: 719/843-5207. Hours: Memorial Day weekend–Labor Day—9–5 Tues.–Sat.; closed Mon. and remainder of year. Admission: free.

Bob Feller

Bob Feller Museum. Bob Feller was a Cleveland Indians pitcher who was known for his fast ball and strikeouts. During his long career with the Indians, "Bullet Bob," as he was known, struck out 2,581 batters, compiled a pitching record of 266 wins and 162 losses, had three no-hitters, and was inducted into the Baseball Hall of Fame in 1962. His life and career are now presented at the Bob Feller Museum in his hometown of Van Meter, Iowa.

Feller was an Iowa farm boy born in 1918 who developed an interest in baseball at an early age. He learned to play in a ballpark that his father, Bill Feller, built on the farm. The park became the home field for the Van Meter Oakviews, with Bob Feller's father as the coach. Feller was a star pitcher for the Van Meter High School baseball team and later credited milking cows, picking corn, and baling hay with strengthening his arms and enabling him to throw his fastball.

Feller signed a baseball contract to play in the minor leagues for $1 and an autographed baseball. He played for Fargo-Moorhead and New Orleans teams before joining the Cleveland Indians in 1936. He was with the Indians for 18 years and was the first pitcher to win 20 or more games before the age of 21. He spent 1936–1941 with the Indians, served in the navy during World War II, and returned to pitch in 1945–1956. He led the American League in strikeouts seven times, was an all-star selection eight times, won the American League's pitching "Triple Crown" in 1940, and was pitcher of the year in the league in 1951. He was called "the greatest pitcher of his time" by the *Sporting News*.

The Bob Feller Museum, which opened in 1995, was designed by Feller's son, Stephen, an architect. It consists of two rooms and contains Feller's uniforms, trophies, photographs, newspaper stories, and a collection of balls and bats signed by Feller and other major league players. Special exhibitions and events also are presented, and the museum sponsors an annual Bob Feller Pitching Award Program that honors outstanding senior pitchers in Iowa high schools.

Bob Feller Museum, 310 Mill St., Van Meter, IA 50261 (postal address: PO Box 95, Van Meter, IA 50261-0095). Phones: 515/996-2806 and 866/996-2806. Fax: 515/996-2952. E-mail: info@bobfellermuseum.org. Website: www.bobfellermuseum.org. Hours: 10–4 Tues.–Sat., 12–4 Sun.; closed Mon. and major holidays. Admission: adults, $5; seniors and school-age children, $3; children under 6, free.

Shoeless Joe Jackson

Shoeless Joe Jackson Museum and Baseball Library. Shoeless Joe Jackson was an early twentieth-century baseball player who is remembered almost as much for his association with the conspiracy to fix the 1919 World Series as his performance as an outfielder and hitter. Although acquitted of being involved in the "Black Sox Scandal," Jackson was banned from playing after the 1920 season by Kenesaw Mountain Landis, the major leagues' first commissioner. His life and career now are depicted at the Shoeless Joe Jackson Museum and Baseball Library in Greenville, South Carolina.

Jackson was born in Pickens County in South Carolina in 1888. He worked in a textile mill as a child and was uneducated—reportedly nearly illiterate, which later became a factor in the Black Sox Scandal. He played baseball, and his hitting ability was evident early. In 1900, at the age of 13, he began playing for the Brando Mill baseball team. He received his nickname when he got blisters on his foot from a new pair of cleats, took off the shoes, and played in his socks. After a heckling fan called him a "shoeless son of a gun," he was called Shoeless Joe Jackson thereafter.

Jackson began his professional baseball career in 1908 with the Greenville Sinners in the minor leagues, and he then played for three major league teams during his 12-year career. He stared with the Philadelphia Athletics in 1908–1909, New Orleans Pelicans in 1910, and Cleveland Indians in 1911–1915 before being traded to the Chicago White Sox in 1915. He played left field most of the time and had a batting average of .356—which is still the third highest in the major leagues. He set the record for the highest single-season batting average for a rookie when he batted .401 in 1911, the beginning of the modern era in baseball.

The Black Sox Scandal was a terrible blow to baseball. Eight White Sox players, including Jackson, were accused of throwing the 1919 World Series to the Cincinnati Reds. Jackson was named even though he made 12 hits—a World Series record—and batted .375. In grand jury testimony, he admitted receiving $5,000 for participating in the conspiracy, but he and his seven teammates were acquitted in the court trial in 1921. However, Commissioner Landis banned all eight players from playing in the majors, which meant they could not be inducted into the Baseball Hall of Fame. He said cleaning up baseball's image took precedence over legal judgments. During the rest of his life, Jackson proclaimed his innocence, and the other seven implicated players later confirmed that he never attended any of the conspiracy meetings.

For 20 years after the ban, Jackson played and managed minor league teams. He then returned to South Carolina to run a dry-cleaning business, barbecue restaurant, and liquor store before his death in 1951. Jackson's former home in Greenville is now the site of the Shoeless Joe Jackson Museum and Baseball Library. It was moved to its present location in 2006 to serve as the museum. The museum contains memorabilia, photographs, and other information about Jackson's life and career and baseball.

Shoeless Joe Jackson Museum and Baseball Library, 356 Field St., Greenville, SC 29608 (postal address: PO Box 4755, Greenville, SC 29608-4755). Phone: 864/235-6280. E-mail: info@shoelessjoejacksonmuseum.org. Website: www.shoelessjoejackson.org. Hours: 2–3 Sat. and by appointment. Admission: free.

Roger Maris

Roger Maris Museum. Roger Maris was a right fielder for the New York Yankees who is best known for hitting 61 home runs in 1961—breaking Babe Ruth's single-season record of 60 major league home runs in 1927. Maris's record stood for 37 years before being surpassed by Mark McGwire of the St. Louis Cardinals with 70 home runs in 1998 and then by the 73 home runs by Barry Bonds of the San Francisco Giants in 2001. The Roger Maris Museum in his hometown of Fargo, North Dakota, now honors his life and baseball career.

Maris had a 12-year career with four teams in major league baseball, including six years with the New York Yankees in 1960–1966. He also played with the Cleveland Indians in 1957–1958, Kansas City Athletics in 1958–1959, and St. Louis Cardinals in 1967–1968. He was an all-star four times, member of World Series championship teams three times, American League most valuable player twice, and Gold Glove Award winner for fielding once. He also won the 1961 Hickok Belt as the top professional athlete of the year before retiring in 1968.

Maris was born in Hibbing, Minnesota, in 1934 and grew up in Grand Forks and Fargo, North Dakota. He was a gifted athlete who excelled in football in Fargo and once set a high school record of four touchdowns on kickoff returns in a game.

The Roger Maris Museum opened in the West Acres Shopping Center in Fargo in 1984 and was renovated in 2003. It is a 72-foot-long glassed-in exhibit devoted to Maris's life and career. It displays personal items, trophies, and the 1961 Hickok Belt from Maris's youth and playing days; replicas of his 1961 locker and plaque at the Yankees' Monument Park; and videos of his playing days at Yankee Stadium. More than 7 million people visit the shopping mall annually, and many stop to see the museum.

Roger Maris Museum, West Acres Shopping Center, 3902 13th Ave. S., Fargo, ND 58103. Phone: 701/282-2222 and 800/783-6450. E-mail: westacres@westacres.com. Website: www.rogermarismuseum.com. Hours: 7 a.m.–9 p.m. Mon.–Sat, 10–6 Sun.; closed Easter, Thanksgiving, and Christmas. Admission: free.

Jack Nicklaus

Jack Nicklaus Museum. Jack Nicklaus is regarded as one of the greatest professional golfers of all time. During his 25-year professional career, he had 114 wins and recorded the most victories in major championships (18). He has won the Masters six times, PGA Championship five times, U.S. Open four times, and Open Championship three times.

The Jack Nicklaus Museum on the campus of Ohio State University in Columbus tells about his life and career as well as the history and highlights of golf.

Nicklaus, who is known as "The Golden Bear," was born in Columbus in 1940 and began golfing at the age of 10. As a teenager, he won five Ohio State Junior titles, the Ohio Open, and the U.S. National Jaycees Championship and qualified for and played in the U.S. Open. He went to Ohio State University and won the U.S. Amateur Championship twice and the NCAA Championship. He also finished second in the 1960 U.S. Open, thirteenth in the Masters, and was a member of the U.S. Walker Cup teams that defeated Great Britain and Ireland in 1959 and 1961 and the victorious U.S. Eisenhower Trophy team in 1960. For his achievements, Nicklaus was named the world's top amateur golfer for three straight years by *Golf Digest* magazine.

At the age of 22, Nicklaus became a professional in 1962 and defeated Arnold Palmer for the U.S. Open Championship. It was the beginning of a long rivalry that attracted viewers to the new technology of television. The following year, he became the youngest golfer to win the Masters and third youngest winner of the PGA Championship. In the years that followed, Nicklaus dominated the golf world before a longtime painful left hip forced him to retire from the professional golf tour in 1986, although he competed in some tournaments until 2005.

Nicklaus, who began designing golf course in the 1960s, now operates one of the largest golf design practices in the world with his four sons and son-in-law. In 1992 he also founded Nicklaus Golf Equipment, which manufactures golf equipment. He also manages the annual Memorial Tournament at Muirfield Village Golf Club, which he designed in 1974. Among the many awards Nicklaus has received are PGA Tour Player of the Year five times, Bob Jones Award, Payne Stewart Award, and induction into the World Golf Hall of Fame.

The Jack Nicklaus Museum has 24,000 square feet of exhibits and a theater. Five galleries are devoted to his life and golfing career and display many of his golf clubs, golf balls, golf bags, scorecards, trophies, awards, and mementoes. Among the galleries are those on major championships, paintings of Nicklaus by noted golf artists, his golf course design work, and the Nicklaus family. The museum also has galleries on the Memorial Tournament and the history and legends of golf.

Jack Nicklaus Museum, Ohio State University, 2355 Olentangy River Rd., Columbus, OH 43210. Phone: 614/247-5959. Fax: 614/247-5906. E-mail: info@nicklausmuseum.org. Website: www.nicklausmuseum.org. Hours: 9–5 Tues.–Sat.; closed Sun.–Mon. and major holidays. Admission: adults, $10; students, $5.

The Jack Nicklaus Museum at Ohio State University, Columbus. Courtesy of the Jack Nicklaus Museum, Ohio State University.

Jesse Owens

Jesse Owens Memorial Park Museum. Jesse Owens was an American track-and-field star who achieved international fame by winning four gold medals at the 1936 Summer Olympics in Berlin, Germany. Hitler was using the games to show the world a resurgent Nazi Germany whose propaganda promoted "Aryan racial superiority" and depicted ethnic Africans as inferior. Adolf Hitler reportedly was upset by the Owens victories. He also refused to shake hands with all Olympic winners as scheduled after only congratulating the German winners on the first day of the Olympics.

Owens won the 100- and 200-meter races and the long jump and was part of the 4 x 100-meter relay team—a performance not equaled until Carl Lewis won gold medals in the same events at the 1984 Summer Olympics. The victories by Owens were cheered enthusiastically by the 110,000 people attending the Olympics, despite Hitler's feelings. After the Olympics, the American team was invited to come to Sweden to compete. But Owens decided instead to return to the United States to capitalize on some lucrative commercial offers he was receiving.

As a result, American athletic officials withdrew his amateur status, thereby ending his track career. The commercial offers never materialized, and Owens was forced to find other means of support. He tried to make a living in other ways but eventually filed for bankruptcy and was prosecuted for tax evasion. He then bounced back, serving as a "goodwill ambassador" for companies and even the United States Olympic Committee.

Owens was born in Oakville, Alabama, in 1913, moved to Cleveland with his parents when nine, did odd jobs in his spare time, developed a passion for running, and excelled on junior and technical high school teams. He attracted national attention when he tied the world record of 9.4 seconds in the 100-yard dash and long jumped 24 feet, 9.5 inches at the 1933 National High School Championships. He was recruited by Ohio State University, where he became known as "Buckeye Bullet" and won eight individual NCAA championships and set three track-and-field world records and tied another in 1935–1936 before competing in the Olympics.

Owens, who received the Presidential Medal of Freedom in 1976 and the Congressional Gold Medal post-humously in 1990, is immortalized at the Jesse Owens Memorial Park Museum in his hometown of Oakville, near Danville. A bronze statue of Owens greets visitors to the park, which opened in 1996. Museum exhibits tell about his achievements and the people who helped shaped him as an athlete and a man. Among the objects displayed are printed programs from the 1936 Olympics, replicas of track uniforms and shoes, and medals and trophies from his high school days. The museum also has large photographic panels, interactive kiosks that highlight his accomplishments, and a minitheater where Owens narrates the *Return to Berlin* movie about the 1936 Olympics.

Jesse Owens Memorial Park Museum, 7019 County Rd. 203, Danville, IL 35619. Phone: 256/974-3636. E-mail: jesseowensinfo@charter.net. Website: www.jesseowensmuseum.org. Hours: 9–5 Mon.–Sat., 1:30–5 Sun.; closed major holidays. Admission: free, but $2 per person for groups of 10 or more.

Richard Petty

Richard Petty Museum. The Richard Petty Museum in Randleman, North Carolina, is devoted to the life and career of one of racing's greatest legends. "The King," as Richard Petty is called, has won 200 races and seven NAS-CAR championships—a feat accomplished by only one other driver (Dale Earnhardt). He also has had a record number of poles (127) and over 700 top-ten finishes in his 1,185 starts, including 513 consecutive starts from 1971 to 1989. Petty, who began his racing career in 1958 and retired in 1992, was elected to the NASCAR Hall of Fame in the inaugural class in 2010.

Richard Petty comes from a family of racing drivers. He was born in Level Cross, North Carolina, in 1937 to Lee Arnold Petty, also a NASCAR driver, and Elizabeth Toomes Petty. His father won the first Daytona 500 in 1959 and was a three-time racing champion. Richard's son, Kyle Petty, also is a NASCAR driver. Richard's grandson, Adam Petty, was killed in a racing accident in New Hampshire in 2000, five weeks after the death of Lee Petty. Richard and his wife, Lynda, who have four children, still resides in his hometown of Level Cross.

The Petty family founded and operates both Richard Petty Motorsports, the two-car NASCAR Sprint Cup Series racing team, and the Richard Petty Museum, established in 1988. The museum features Petty's racing cars, awards, photographs, videos, and family and racing history, as well as personal collections of Richard and his wife. The latter includes collections of 900 dolls, 500 pocket watches, and 350 guns. The annual attendance is 25,000.

Richard Petty Museum, 142 W. Academy St., Randleman, NC 27317-1502. Phone: 336/495-1143. Fax: 336/495-1153. E-mail: bdavis@rpmuseum.com. Website: www.rpmuseum.com. Hours: 9–5 Wed.–Sat.; closed Sun.–Tues, Thanksgiving, and Christmas. Admission: adults, $10; seniors and military, $8; children, $5; children under 5, free.

Paul Robeson

See Musicians/Singers/Composers section.

Eddie G. Robinson

Eddie G. Robinson Museum. The Eddie G. Robinson Museum at Grambling State University in Grambling, Louisiana, honors the longtime football coach who won 408 games from 1941 to 1997. His teams won nine Black College National Championships and 17 Southwestern Athletic Conference titles. Robinson is the NCAA Division's all-time winningest football coach and the namesake for the Football Writers Association of America national football coach of the year award. He became the collegiate coach with the most victories in 2012 when Joe Paterno's 112 victories from 1998–2011 were vacated from his record 409 wins since 1966 at Pennsylvania State University because of the Jerry Sandusky child-sex tragedy.

Robinson's life and long career are featured in the museum, which opened in 2010 in the 18,000-square-foot women's gymnasium on the campus. In addition to exhibits and a film about the famed coach, the museum contains photographs of more than 200 of his Grambling players who became professional football players, a scale model of the Cotton Bowl scoreboard showing the final score of Grambling's victory of Alcorn State in 1985, and such other materials as oral histories, playbooks, and game plans and films.

Eddie G. Robinson Museum, Women's Memorial Gymnasium, Grambling State University, Grambling, LA 71245. Phone: 318/274-2210. Website: www.robinsonmuseum.com. Hours: 9–4:30 Tues.–Sat.; closed Sun.–Mon. and major holidays. Admission: free.

Babe Ruth

Babe Ruth Museum. George Herman "Babe" Ruth Jr. was called "The Great Bambino" and the "Sultan of Swat" for his home run ability. During his 22-year career, he hit 714 home runs, including 60 in 1927. Both were major league records until broken in more recent years. His .690 lifetime slugging percentage, however, still stands. Ruth's life and baseball achievements are the focus of the Babe Ruth Museum, located in the renovated 1856 Camden Station rail terminal in Baltimore with the Sports Legends Museum at Camden Yards.

Ruth was born in 1895 in a tiny row house in Baltimore. The upstairs bedroom where he was born is now part of the Babe Ruth Museum. He did not have a happy childhood. He often was left alone while his parents worked in a tavern they owned near the waterfront. When seven years old, Ruth was turned over to the St. Mary's Industrial School for Boys, a reformatory and orphanage. His parents rarely visited, and he became unruly and unable to adapt to the regimented and structured life of St. Mary's. Fortunately, Brother Matthias, the perfect of discipline, took interest in Ruth, gave him support, and helped improve his baseball swing on the school's baseball team, where he alternated between being a catcher and a pitcher.

When Ruth was 19, he signed a contract with Jack Dunn, owner and manager of the Baltimore Orioles, a minor league team of the Boston Red Sox at that time. When the other players saw the young Ruth, they called him "Jack's newest babe"—and that is how Ruth got to be known as Babe Ruth. He played only five months with the Orioles before being purchased by the Boston Red Sox, where he played outfield and pitched. In addition to hitting home runs, he had an impressive pitching record, including 29 and two-thirds scoreless innings in the 1918 World Series—a record that stood for 43 years.

In 1919 Ruth was sold to the New York Yankees by Harry Frazee, the new owner of the Red Sox, who needed funds. In his first season with the Yankees in 1920, Ruth hit 54 home runs. He continued his spectacular home run hitting, and baseball fans began filling the Polo Grounds, which was shared with the New York Giants, to see him play. This led to the construction of Yankee Stadium, which opened in 1923 and became known as "The House That Ruth Built." It was the beginning of a long series of American League and World Series championships for the Yankees. The rotund baseball star, who worked and played hard and lived life to the fullest, died in 1948 at the age of 53 after being diagnosed with throat cancer and losing 80 pounds.

The Babe Ruth Museum, founded in 1974, contains exhibits, photographs, and a film about his life and career and displays such memorabilia as balls and bats, other equipment like a catcher's mitt and jersey, and the hymnal book used by Ruth while attending St. Mary's Industrial School. The Sports Legends Museum at Camden Yards is located in the basement of the historic Camden Station and requires a separate admission. The annual attendance is 33,000.

Babe Ruth Museum, 216 Emory St., Baltimore, MD 21230. Phone: 410/727-1539. Fax: 410/727-1652. E-mail: info@ baberuthmuseum.com. Website: www.baberuthmuseum.com. Hours: 10–5 Tues.–Sun., but 10–7 on Orioles game days; closed Mon., New Year's Day, Thanksgiving, and Christmas. Admission: adults, $6; seniors, $4; children 3–12, $3; children under 3, free.; combination ticket with Sports Legends Museum—adults, $12; seniors, $8; children 3–12, $5.

Jim Thorpe

Jim Thorpe Historical Home. Jim Thorpe was one of the most outstanding and versatile athletes in American sports history. He won gold medals for the decathlon and pentathlon at the 1912 Summer Olympics in Stockholm and excelled in football at collegiate and professional levels and at professional baseball and basketball. In 1950 the Associated Press named him the greatest athlete of the first half of the twentieth century. His life and career now are featured at the Jim Thorpe Historical Home in Yale, Oklahoma, where he lived in 1917–1923.

Thorpe was a Native American who was born in 1888 near Prague, Oklahoma. He attended the Sac and Fox Indian Agency School in Oklahoma, Haskell Indian Junior College in Kansas, and Carlisle Indian School in Pennsylvania. It was at Carlisle, where he was coached by the legendary Glenn Scobey "Pop" Warner, that Thorpe first drew national attention for his athletic talents. In addition to competing in track and field, baseball, and lacrosse, Thorpe led the football team to 11 victories and one defeat in 1911 and to the national collegiate championship in 1912. He was named an All-American in both years.

Although he competed only sporadically in track-and-field events, Thorpe made the American team for the 1912 Summer Olympics in Stockholm and won gold medals for the decathlon and pentathlon. While presenting the medals, King Gustav V of Sweden told Thorpe that he was "the greatest athlete in the world." When he returned to New York City, Thorpe was honored with a ticker-tape parade on Broadway. But the joy was short lived. He lost his amateur status and the Olympic medals after published reports showed he was paid ($2 a game) for playing semiprofessional baseball during the summers of 1909–1910. However, Thorpe was reinstated and regained the Olympic medals in 1982 when it was determined that his disqualification violated the rules.

After losing his amateur status, Thorpe became a professional in 1913. He then played professional baseball, football, and basketball until 1928. He played baseball with the New York Giants, Milwaukee Brewers, Cincinnati Reds, and Boston Braves until 1919. As the same time, he starred in professional football with the Canton Bulldogs, which won titles in 1916, 1917, and 1919. In 1920 Thorpe was elected the first president of the newly formed American Professional Football League (now the National Football League). He served only until 1921 but continued to play football for six teams until 1928 (making the all-pro team in 1923 and the 1920s all-decade team). During that period, he also played professional basketball with the barnstorming "Jim Thorpe and His World Famous Indians."

Thorpe was inducted into the Pro Football Hall of Fame in 1963 and honored by the halls of fame for college football, U.S. Olympic athletes, and national track-and-field competition. In 1999 the U.S. House of Representatives designed Thorpe as "America's Athlete of the Century."

The Jim Thorpe Historical Home, the only house he ever owned, was founded as a museum in 1973. It is operated by the Oklahoma Historical Society and its affiliate Jim Thorpe Memorial Foundation. The house has been restored and contains 1920s furnishings and displays about Thorpe, his family, and his athletic accomplishments and awards. A replica of Thorpe's 1876 boyhood cabin also is at the site. Guided tours are offered of the museum.

Jim Thorpe Historical Home, 706 E. Boston Ave., Yale, OK 74085. Phone and fax: 918/387-2815. E-mail: jimthorpe@okhistory.org. Website: www.okhistory.org/sites/thorpehome. Hours: 9–5 Wed.–Sat.; closed Sun.–Tues. and legal holidays. Admission: free.

Ted Williams

Ted Williams Museum and Hitters Hall of Fame. The Ted Williams Museum and Hitters Hall of Fame is located behind the right-field fence at Tropicana Field, the home field of the Tampa Bay Devil Rays major league baseball team in St. Petersburg, Florida. The museum originally opened in 1994 in Hernando, Florida, a few blocks from Williams's final home but closed in 2006 because of its remote location and poor attendance. It then was moved and expanded at its new site in St. Petersburg, where it is a popular attraction.

Williams is considered one of the greatest hitters in the history of professional baseball. He was the star left fielder for the Boston Red Sox from 1939 until his retirement in 1960, except for his military service twice as a Marine fighter pilot in World War II and the Korean War. He led the American League in batting six times, had a career batting average of .344, hit 521 home runs, and was the most valuable player and the Triple Crown holder (for home runs, runs batted in, and batting average) twice. In 1941 he also was the last player in the major leagues to bat over .400 in a regular season.

Ted Williams was born Teddy Samuel Williams in 1918 in San Diego. He joined the Red Sox at the age of 21. After retiring as a player, he served as manager of the Washington Senators in 1969–1971 and was named manager of the year in 1969. He continued to manage the team when it became the Texas Rangers in 1972 and then ran a baseball school and spent much time hunting and fishing. He was inducted into the Baseball Hall of Fame in 1966 and the International Game Fishing Association Hall of Fame in 2000. Williams also was selected for the Major Leagues Baseball All-Century Team.

Williams died of a heart attack in 2002, and a court battle and much publicity followed over the disposition of his body. His will said he wanted to be cremated, but two of his children—John-Henry and Claudia—chose to have him frozen by cryonics. His other daughter, Bobby-Jo Ferrell, opposed the move. In the legal fight that followed, a paper-napkin agreement signed by Williams showed that he was willing to have his body preserved by cryonics in the hope that he later would rejoin his family. The court approved freezing the body. Unfortunately, his head was damaged by a worker during transfer to his final container.

The Ted Williams Museum and Hitters Hall of Fame was founded in Hernando by Sam Tamposi and Gerald Nash with assistance from Williams, who also wanted to recognize the great hitters in baseball. Williams selected the first group of 20 baseball legends, which included such inductees as Ty Cobb, Rogers Hornsby, Babe Ruth, Joe DiMaggio, Mickey Mantle, and Hank Aaron. Other exhibits dealt with Williams's personal life, military service, and baseball career.

At its new location at Tropicana Field in St. Petersburg, the museum has many of the memorabilia, photographs, and other aspects of the original site. But the museum has been redesigned and expanded, with a new 7,000-square-foot wing that highlights Williams's life by decades and contains the Hitters Hall of Fame, which has increased to 38 inductees. The exhibit hall has displays about each honoree; game footage and interviews with such players as Stan Musial, Bob Feller, and Joe DiMaggio; and information about such historical events as Babe Ruth's called home run in the 1932 World Series against the Chicago Cubs. The museum is open free of charge to attendees during Tampa Bay Devil Rays home games.

Ted Williams Museum and Hitters Hall of Fame, Tropicana Park, 1 Tropicana Dr., St. Petersburg, FL 33705. Phone: 838/326-7297. E-mail: info@tedwilliamsmuseum.com. Website: www.tedwilliamsmuseum.com. Hours: open two hours before and during Devil Rays home games. Admission: free with purchase of ball game ticket.

Babe Didrikson Zaharias

Babe Didrikson Zaharias Museum and Visitor Center. Mildred "Babe" Didrikson Zaharias is considered by many to be the greatest female athlete of all time. She excelled in track, basketball, golf, and other sports and won two gold medals and a silver medal at the 1932 Summer Olympics in Los Angeles and 82 women's golf tournaments, including 10 Ladies Professional Golf Association titles. She is now honored at the Babe Didrikson Zaharias Museum and Visitor Center in Beaumont, Texas.

Born in Port Arthur, Texas, in 1911, Didrikson (as she was known before her marriage to professional wrestler George Zaharias in 1938) moved to Beaumont with her parents at the age of four. She said she acquired her "Babe" nickname (after Babe Ruth) after hitting five home runs in a childhood baseball game.

Didrikson, who was an excellent roller skater, bowler, billiards player, diver, and baseball and softball player, first gained attention by leading the Golden Cyclones of the Texas Employers Casualty Insurance Company to the American Athletic Union basketball championship in 1931. This was followed in 1932 by winning eight of 10 events and the team title at the AAU track-and-field championships. That qualified her for the 1932 Olympics, where she won the javelin throw and 80-meter hurdles and would have won a third gold medal in the finals of the breaker jump, but her final jump was disallowed because she jumped over head first.

It was not until the mid-1930s that Didrikson began playing golf—the sport for which she is best known. In 1938 she entered the Los Angeles Open, a Professional Golfers' Association men's tournament, but missed the cut. She made the cut in all future PGA tournaments she entered but never came out a winner. It was a different story in women's golf tournaments. She became the leading female golfer in the 1940s and early 1950s. In 1950 she won the "Grand Slam"—the three women's majors of the day—and went on to become the fastest player to reach 10 wins and then 20 and 30 victories. In 1953 Didrikson was diagnosed with colon cancer but still won the Vare Trophy for the lowest scoring average and her tenth and final major win—the U.S. Women's Open. The cancer later reoccurred, and she died at the age of 45 in 1956.

The Babe Didrikson Zaharias Museum, founded in 1976, also serves as the visitor center for the city of Beaumont. It traces her life and athletic achievements and features Olympic medals, sports trophies, golf clubs and bags, photographs, videos, and other materials pertaining to her life and career. Annual attendance is 7,000.

Babe Didrikson Zaharias Museum and Welcome Center, Interstate 10, Exit 854, MLK Blvd., Beaumont, TX 77701 (postal address: PO Box 3827, Suite 100, Beaumont, TX 77704). Phone: 409/833-4622. Fax: 409/880-3750. E-mail: klewis@ci.beaumont.tx.us. Website: www.babedidriksonzaharias.org. Hours: 9–5 daily; closed Christmas. Admission: free.

AUTHORS/WRITERS

See also Journalists/Publishers, Playwrights, and Poets

George Ade

See Playwrights section.

Louisa May Alcott

Louisa May Alcott's Orchard House. The Orchard House in Concord, Massachusetts, was the home of the talented Alcott family and where Louisa May Alcott wrote her classic novel *Little Women* in 1868. The ca. 1690 house, one of the oldest and most authentically preserved historic houses in the nation, tells the story of the Alcotts and their legacy in the fields of literature, art, education, philosophy, and social justice.

Orchard House evolved from the purchase of two turn-of-the-seventeenth-century houses on 12 acres along Lexington Road in 1857 by Amos Bronson Alcott, a teacher and Transcendental philosopher, who had moved the family 22 times in nearly 30 years. He took the smaller tenant farmhouse and joined it to the rear of the larger manor house to form the present Orchard House, named for its apple orchard.

The Alcott family lived at Orchard House from 1858 to 1877. It now is best known as the house where one of the Alcotts' four daughters, Louisa, wrote *Little Women*. She was born in Germantown, Pennsylvania, in 1832 and started writing before the move to Concord. *Little Women* was based loosely on her childhood experiences with her three sisters.

Louisa May Alcott's first published book was *Flower Fables*, a collection of tales written for a daughter of Ralph Waldo Emerson, a family friend, in 1855. She then began writing for the *Atlantic Monthly*, followed by five other books before *Little Women* was published in 1868. The next year she wrote *Part Second* (also known as *Good Wives*), which followed the sisters into adulthood and their marriages, and then *Little Men* and *Jo's Boys* to complete the family-related series. She also wrote other novels that followed the *Little Women* line, as well as wholesome stories for children. In addition, Louisa, who was a feminist and abolitionist, wrote about women's issues.

Alcott continued to write until she died in 1888 at the age of 55. She had chronic health problems, but her death was attributed to mercury poisoning from a compound containing mercury after getting typhoid fever during the Civil War.

Orchard House, which was founded as a historic house in 1911, has changed little since the Alcott days. The rooms look much as they did when the Alcott family lived there. About 80 percent of the furnishings were owned by the Alcotts. Guided tours now point out the objects that were important to the family and introduce visitors to family members portrayed by costumed interpreters. The site also has numerous educational programs, ranging from living-history nineteenth-century classroom and theater programs to outreach visits and rental study kits. Annual attendance is nearly 50,000.

Louisa May Alcott's Orchard House, 399 Lexington Rd., Concord, MA 01742-3712 (postal address: PO Box 343, Concord, MA 01742-0343). Phone: 978/369-4118. Fax: 978/369-1367. E-mail: info@louisamayalcott.org. Website: www.louisamayalcott.org. Hours: Apr.–Oct.—10–4:30 Mon.–Sat., 1–4:30 Sun.; Nov.–Mar.—11–3 Mon.–Fri., 10–4:30 Sat., 1–4:30 Sun.; closed Jan. 1–3, Easter, Thanksgiving, and Christmas. Admission: adults, $9; seniors and college students, $8; children 6–17, $5; children under 6, free.

Parlor and dining rooms of Louisa May Alcott's Orchard House in Concord, Massachusetts. Courtesy of Louisa May Alcott's Orchard House; photograph by Herb K. Barnett.

Hans Christian Andersen

Hans Christian Andersen Museum. The life and works of Hans Christian Andersen, the Danish author and poet noted for his fairy tales, are presented at the Hans Christian Andersen Museum in Solvang, California. Solvang is a small Danish-oriented town in San Barbara County that was founded in 1911 by a group of Danish educators who came to the West to escape the Midwestern winters. Many of the community's buildings are in the Danish style, and there are Danish bakeries, shops manned by merchants in Danish costumes, smorgasbord restaurants, and such sights as a copy of the famous *Little Mermaid* statue from Copenhagen, a bust of Hans Christian Andersen, and a one-third-scale replica of the Rundetårn Observatory in Copenhagen.

The Hans Christian Andersen Museum is located in the Book Loft Building and operated by the Ugly Duckling Foundation. It contains information about Andersen's life, a model of his childhood home, copies of many first and early editions of his books and other works, poetry and correspondence in Andersen's handwriting, original letters and pictures, photographs of Andersen at various times of his life, and antique tools for making wooden shoes similar to those used by Andersen's father. The museum also offers lectures, participates in local festivals, and celebrates Andersen's birthday on April 2.

Andersen, who was born in Odense, Denmark, in 1805, published his first novel, *The Improvisatore*, in 1835, the same year he wrote the first installment of his *Fairy Tales*. He finished the second and third parts in 1836 and 1837 and published his best novel, *Only a Fiddler*, in 1837. In the ensuing years, he continued to write novels, travel books, and new installments of fairy tales until 1872, including such favorites as *The Ugly Duckling*, *The Emperor's New Clothes*, and *The Princess and the Pea*. He died in 1875.

Hans Christian Andersen Museum, 1680 Mission Dr., Solvang, CA 93463. Phone: 805/688-2052. Website: www.solvangca.com. Hours: 10–5 daily. Admission: free.

Arna Wendell Bontemps

Arna Bontemps African American Museum. Arna Wendell Bontemps was a major figure in the African American literary movement known as the Harlem Renaissance in the 1920s–1930s. Known for the volume and versatility of his work, he was the author of 25 books, including novels, children's books, biographies, histories, plays, and a collection of poems. He now is remembered at the Arna Bontemps African American Museum, located in the house of his birth in Alexandra, Louisiana.

Bontemps was born in 1902 in a simple one-story frame Queen Anne revival cottage at the edge of downtown Alexandra. He lived there until 1906 when his family moved to California, where he earned a bachelor's degree in 1923. He then moved to New York City to teach at the Harlem Academy until 1931. It was during that time that his first work was published—a poem in the *Crisis*, the National Association for the Advancement of Colored People magazine, in 1924. In 1926 and 1927 Bontemps was awarded the periodical's poetry prize. He followed in 1931 with his first novel, *God Sends Sunday*. He then worked as a teacher in Huntsville, Alabama, and Chicago.

In 1943 Bontemps received a master's degree in library science from the University of Chicago and became the head librarian at Fisk University in Nashville, Tennessee. It was a position he held until 1965. In his final years, he taught at the University of Illinois and Yale University and served as writer-in-residence at Fisk University. He died in his Nashville home in 1973.

Bontemps's childhood home in Alexandra now is listed on the National Register of Historic Places and houses the Arna Bontemps African American Museum. It contains historical information and objects related to Bontemps and his family as well as African American history and culture.

Arna Bontemps African American Museum, 1327 3rd St., Alexandra, LA 71301-8248. Phone: 318/473-4692. Fax: 318/473-4675. E-mail: admin@arnabontempsmuseum.com. Website: www.arnabontempsmuseum.com. Hours: 10–4 Tues.–Fri., 10–2 Sat.; closed Sun.–Mon. and major holidays. Admission: free.

Louis Bromfield

Malabar Farm State Park. "Malabar Farm" was the name Pulitzer Prize–winning author Louis Bromfield gave the farmlands he purchased near Lucas, Ohio, in 1939 and where he lived until he died in 1956. It now is a museum-like state park in his memory. Bromfield was a native Ohioan who wrote 30 books—all of them best sellers—and won the 1927 Pulitzer Prize for his novel *Early Autumn*. The 1,000-acre farm was his major work during his last 20 years, when he became an early proponent of organic and self-sustaining gardening and his farm was among the first to ban pesticides.

Bromfield was born in a farming family in Mansfield, Ohio, in 1896. He attended Cornell Agricultural College (now Cornell University) and Columbia University in 1915–1916 and then enlisted in the American Ambulance

Corps with the French Army in World War I. He received the Croix de Guerre and the Legion of Honor for his service in France.

After the war, Bromfield returned to New York City and worked as reporter for several news services and magazines and then became a music and play critic. In 1921 he married socialite Mary Appleton Wood. They had three daughters. In 1924 he published his first novel, *The Green Bay Tree*, which was a critical and commercial success. Bromfield and his family went for a vacation in France in 1925—and stayed 13 years. He settled in the ancient village of Senlis near Paris. There he wrote *Early Autumn*. While in Europe, he traveled to India, which inspired *The Rains Came* (1937), made into a movie as *Mrs. Parkington* (1943).

Bromfield became dissatisfied with life in France and returned to the United States with his family in the late l930s. He returned to his first interest—agriculture. In 1939 he bought three exhausted farms in Pleasant Valley near Lucas and his hometown of Mansfield, Ohio, and worked to restore the land through innovative soil and water conservation techniques. He called the property "Malabar Farm." It was named after the Malabar Coast of India, the setting of *The Rains Came*.

Bromfield continued to write novels but dedicated his life to agriculture and began writing nonfiction. He became a farmer and conservationist, and his farm was used as a government test site for soil conservation practices. Bromfield's innovative work continues to influence agricultural methodologies around the world.

Louis Bromfield died of bone cancer in 1956 at the age of 59, and the farm was opened to the public in 1958 by the Bromfield Malabar Farm Foundation, which operated it until acquired by the State of Ohio in 1972. The main attraction at the 875-acre state park is the 32-room country mansion that formerly was the home of Bromfield and his family. It still contains the family's original furnishings.

The park also has the farm's other buildings and equipment, a 6,500-volume library, and a visitor and education center with exhibits about Bromfield and the farm. Other facilities include a domestic animal zoo, songbird aviary, horse camp, fishing ponds, campgrounds, hiking trails, gift shop, picnic area, and award-winning restaurant. The park offers guided tours, nature programs, and special events. Annual attendance is over 350,000.

Malabar Farm State Park, 4050 Bromfield Rd., Lucas, OH 44843-9754. Phone: 419/892-2784. Fax: 419/892-3988. E-mail: malabar.farm.parks@dnr.state.oh.us.Website: www.malabarfarm.org. Hours: park grounds—dawn–dusk daily; house and other facilities—Memorial Day–Labor Day: 10–5 daily; Sept.–May—10–5 Sat.–Sun.; closed Mon.–Fri. and major holidays. Admission: grounds—free; house tours—adults, $4; seniors, $3; children 6–18, $2; children under 6, free.

Pearl S. Buck

Pearl S. Buck House. Pearl S. Buck was a Pulitzer Prize–winning author who was the first American woman to be awarded the Nobel Prize in Literature. She lived at the 60-acre Green Hills Farm near Perkasie, Pennsylvania, for nearly 40 years, raising her family, writing, and pursuing humanitarian interests. The Pearl S. Buck House is now a National Historic Landmark with exhibits and programs about her life and accomplishments, and it serves as the headquarters for its international adoption and child assistance programs.

Buck, who spent most of her first 42 years in China, was born to Presbyterian missionary parents in 1892 in a home owned by her grandmother in Hillsboro, West Virginia (*see* separate listing). She grew up among the traditions and customs of the Chinese, and many of her works relate to her experiences in China. She lived with her parents at their mission station in Chinkiang (present-day Zhenjiang), where she was taught by her Calvinist mother and a Confucian tutor.

Buck earned a bachelor's degree (and Phi Beta Kappa) from Randolph-Macon Woman's College in 1914 and then served as a Presbyterian missionary until 1933. In 1917 she married John Lossing Buck, a missionary agricultural economist, and moved to Nanhsuchou, China, for two and a half years. It was her memories of life in the region and her husband's land usage research that became the basis of *The Good Earth*, her best-known work, for which she received the 1931 Pulitzer Prize. From 1920 to 1933 the couple made their home in Nanking (now Nanjing) and experienced the fighting between Chiang Kai-shek's Nationalist Army and communist and warlord forces. The Bucks were divorced in 1935, and Pearl married her publisher, Richard Walsh, and settled at Green Hills Farm, close to the home where her mentally disabled daughter was located. It also is where she raised seven adopted children and cared for many others.

Pearl Buck was a humanitarian who worked to promote tolerance, human rights, intercultural understanding, and quality of life and opportunities for children. She established the Welcome House Inc., the first international interracial adoption agency, in 1949 after learning that existing adoption services considered Asian and mixed-race children unadoptable; the Pearl S. Buck Foundation in 1964 to support children not eligible for adoption; and

Opportunity House and Orphanage in Asia in 1965 to combat injustices and prejudices suffered by children. Pearl S. Buck International, which administers the international child and family development programs, has its home office at Green Hills Farm.

During her long career, Buck produced more than 1,000 works, including 120 books, over 400 short stories, 400 nonfiction articles, essays, and speeches. She wrote on a wide variety of subjects, including Asian cultures, civil and women's rights, immigration, adoption, missionary work, and war. She received the Nobel Prize for Literature in 1938. Buck died in 1973 and is buried at Green Hills Farm.

The Pearl S. Buck House is a historic house museum in a pre-1825 stone farm house with furnishings and surroundings that reflect her two hemispheres—Asian artifacts and Pennsylvania country furniture. The museum, which offers guided tours, also contains her literary and humanitarian awards, including the Nobel and Pulitzer Prizes, an 8,200-volume library featuring Buck's works, and a 1,600-square-foot space for exhibits. Multicultural education programs also are presented at the site. The annual attendance is 10,000.

Pearl S. Buck House, 520 Dublin Rd., Perkasie, PA 18944-3000. Phones: 215/249-0100 and 800/220-2825. Fax: 215/249-9657. E-mail: info@psbi.org. Website: www.psbi.org. Hours: 11–2 Tues.–Sat., 1–2 Sun.; closed Mon., Jan.–Feb., and major holidays. Admission: adults, $7; seniors and students, $6; children under 6, free.

Pearl S. Buck Birthplace Museum. The Hillsboro, West Virginia, home at which author Pearl S. Buck was born in 1892 now is a restored historic house museum called the Pearl S. Buck Birthplace Museum. Her Southern Presbyterian missionary parents, Absalom Sydenstricker and Caroline Stulting, left West Virginia for China soon after their marriage in 1880 but returned for Pearl's birth in her grandmother's house.

When Pearl was three months old, the family left for a new mission assignment in China. That was the beginning of Pearl Buck's nearly 40 years in China before returning to live the remaining 40 in the United States. Her experiences in China greatly influenced her life and writings, including *The Good Earth*, for which she received the 1931 Pulitzer Prize.

The birthplace house, founded as a museum in 1974, has been restored, and guides take visitors through period rooms containing some of the original furniture and memorabilia, as well as West Virginia crafts. The site also has a nineteenth-century barn with historic equipment and Pearl Buck's father's house, which was moved from its original location and reassembled as a cultural center, known as the Sydenstricker Museum. Annual attendance is around 2,000.

Pearl S. Buck Birthplace Museum, Rte. 293 North, Hillsboro, WV 24946 (postal address: PO Box 126, Hillsboro, WV 24946-0126). Phone: 304/653-4430. E-mail: info@pearlsbuckbirthplace.org. Website: www.pearlsbuckbirthplace.org. Hours: May–Oct.—9–4:30 Mon.–Sat.; closed Sun., Nov.–Apr., New Year's Day, Thanksgiving, and Christmas. Admission: adults, $6; seniors, $5; students, $1; children under 6, free.

John Burroughs

John Burroughs Memorial State Historic Site. John Burroughs was a naturalist and essayist who played an important role in the nation's conservation movement at the turn of the twentieth century. He was considered the most important practitioner after Henry David Thoreau of the nature essay. He wrote more than 30 books, published hundreds of nature-oriented essays and poems in magazines, and became extremely popular with his unique perceptions of the natural world as the nation took interest in nature and conservation.

Burroughs was born on a farm in the Catskill Mountains near Roxbury, New York, in 1837. He spent many hours wandering in the mountains. At the age of 17, he left school to become a teacher, continuing his studies at such places as the Hartwick Seminary near Cooperstown. It was there that he became acquainted with the works of William Wordsworth and Ralph Waldo Emerson, which greatly influenced his interest in nature. Burroughs then began teaching and in 1860 wrote his first essay, "Expression," which was published in the *Atlantic Monthly*. He continued to publish while serving as a federal bank examiner from 1864 into the 1880s.

It was during the Civil War that Burroughs grew interested in the poetry of Walt Whitman. He met Whitman in Washington and was encouraged to develop his nature writing as well as his philosophical and literary essays. Burroughs wrote the first biography and critical work on the poet, *Notes on Walt Whitman as Poet and Person*, in 1871, and four years later he published *Wake-Robin*, his first collection of nature essays.

Burroughs then bought a farm he called Riverby in West Park, New York, in 1874; moved to an Adirondack-style cabin, called Slabsides, that he and his son built in 1895; and then bought and renovated an old farmhouse near his birthplace that he named Woodchuck Lodge. He used the lodge as a summer residence until his death in 1921.

Burroughs's three historic sites—Riverby, Slabsides, and Woodchuck Lodge—still exist and have become National Historic Landmarks. Woodchuck Lodge also has been designated as the John Burroughs Memorial State Historic Site. Visitors can now tour the summer home near Roxbury and see where Burroughs is buried at the foot of a rock on which he played as a child.

John Burroughs Memorial State Historic Site, Burroughs Memorial Rd., Roxbury, NY 12474 (postal address: Mine Kill State Park, PO Box 923, North Blenheim, NY 12131-0923). Phone: 518/827-6111. Fax: 518/827-6782. E-mail: laura.tully@oprhp.state.ny.us. Website: www.nysparks.com. Hours: dawn–dusk daily. Admission: free.

John Burroughs Sanctuary/Slabsides. Following the death of naturalist/essayist John Burroughs in 1921, his nine-acre wooded and hilly tract that contained his Slabsides cabin was presented to the John Burroughs Association, which was founded to preserve his legacy. When nearby logging and development threatened the property in the 1960s, the association bought the adjoining lands and created the 170-acre John Burroughs Sanctuary at West Park, near Esopus, New York.

Slabsides, designated a National Historic Landmark in 1968, is a one-story log cabin with open living, dining, kitchen, and study areas and a bedroom on the west side of a hill in the wooded sanctuary. It can be reached only by walking up a gravel road for half a mile. The cabin, which got its name from the rough bark-covered lumber strips on its outer walls, is furnished as Burroughs left it. It is open to visitors only twice a year and by appointment, but trails through the woods around it that inspired Burroughs are open year-round. The John Burroughs Association is administered out of the American Museum of Natural History in New York City.

John Burroughs Sanctuary/Slabsides, off John Burroughs Dr., West Park, NY 12493 (postal address: John Burroughs Assn., 15 W. 77th St., New York, NY 10024). Phone: 212/769-5160. Fax: 212/313-7182. E-mail: breslof@amnh.org. Website: www.research.amnh.org/burroughs. Hours: sanctuary trails—dawn–dusk daily; cabin—12–4:30 third Sat. in May and first Sat. in Oct. and by appointment. Admission: free.

Erskine Caldwell

Erskine Caldwell Birthplace Museum. Author Erskine Caldwell was the son of Presbyterian minister whose early books sometimes were banned and seized because of their unseemly content or title. But he later became known more for extolling the simple life of the less fortunate. His life and works are featured at the Erskine Caldwell Birthplace Museum on the town square in Moreland, Georgia. The museum contains many of his books, memorabilia, photographs, art from book covers, dramatizations of his stories, and notebooks he used to jot down ideas for books.

Caldwell was born in 1903 in a house in the woods outside Morehead that later was moved into town. However, his early childhood was spent moving across the South as his minister father (with the Associate Reformed Presbyterian Church) changed positions frequently. He dropped out of Erskine College and changed jobs often before beginning his writing career, which produced such popular books as *Tobacco Road* (1932), *God's Little Acre* (1933), *Journeyman* (1935), and *Georgia Boy* (1943).

Caldwell's wrote 25 novels, 150 short stories, 12 nonfiction collections, and two books for young readers. His first books were short story collections—*Bastard* in 1929 and *Poor Fools* in 1930. *Bastard* was banned and copies were seized because of its content. In 1933 Caldwell was arrested and copies of *God's Little Acre* were seized at the instigation of the New York Literary Society (apparently incensed by the book's title) when he went to New York City for a book signing event. He was exonerated in a trial and countersued for false arrest and malicious prosecution.

Erskine Caldwell Birthplace Museum, Cap St., Moreland, GA 30259 (postal address: PO Box 207, Moreland, GA 30259-0207). Phone: 770/254-8657. E-mail: winston@newnan.com. Website: www.newnan.com/ec. Hours: 11–3 Tues.–Sat. and by appointment; closed Sun.–Mon. and major holidays. Admission: adults, $2; children, $1.

Rachel Carson

Rachel Carson Homestead. Rachel Carson was a marine biologist and writer credited with advancing the global environmental movement with her books about synthetic pesticides and the sea. Her 1962 book, *Silent Spring*, about environmental problems caused by synthetic pesticides led to the banning of DDT and other pesticides, a grassroots environmental movement, and the creation of the Environmental Protection Agency. *Silent Spring* followed three bestselling books about the oceans—*Under the Sea Wind* (1941), *The Sea Around Us* (1951), and *The Edge of the Sea* (1955).

Carson's family home in Springdale, Pennsylvania, now known as the Rachel Carson Homestead, is a historic home museum devoted to her life and career and the environment. Rachel Louise Carson was born in 1907 on the small farm outside the town of Springdale along the Allegheny River in western Pennsylvania.

Carson began writing stories mostly about animals at the age of eight and had her first story published in a children's magazine when she was 11 years old. She graduated at the head of her class from high school in nearby Parnassus in 1925 and from Pennsylvania College for Women (now Chatham University), where she switched from English to biology as her major and graduated magna cum laude in 1929.

Carson then attended a summer course at the Marine Biological Laboratory at Wood's Hole, Massachusetts, and then enrolled at Johns Hopkins University graduate school, where she had an assistantship in the laboratory and received a master's degree in zoology in 1932. She taught at Johns Hopkins and the University of Maryland for several years while working on a doctorate but was forced to drop out when her father died in 1935, and she never finished because she had to find employment to care for her aging mother and support herself.

Carson found a part-time position with the U.S. Bureau of Fisheries, serving as a science writer for radio scripts. In 1936 she was the first woman to take a civil service exam and outscored all the other applicants. She was hired as a full-time junior aquatic biologist by the Bureau of Fisheries. Carson worked on everything from cookbooks to scientific journals. She also wrote short articles for the *Baltimore Sun*. Her big break came when a division head rejected one of her writings because it was "too literary." He suggested she submit it to the *Atlantic Monthly* magazine, which published it as "Undersea" in 1937. The Simon & Schuster publishing house was impressed with the article and suggested that she expand the article into a book. The result was her well-received first book, *Under the Sea Wind*, published in 1941.

After the U.S. Bureau of Fisheries became the U.S. Fish and Wildlife Service, Carson was made editor-in-chief of all of its publications in 1949. At the same time, she was working on a second book, which was published as *The Sea Around Us* in 1951 and immediately became a best seller and won the 1952 National Book Award. It also was made into a documentary film that received an Oscar award.

In 1952 Carson resigned from her job with the Fish and Wildlife Service to concentrate on her writing, and then she and her mother moved to Southport Island, Maine. In 1955 Carson completed *The Edge of the Sea*, the third volume of her sea trilogy, which focuses on life in coastal ecosystems. The book also received favorable reviews and became a best seller. It was followed by her most famous and controversial book, *Silent Spring*. She had been concerned about the impact of synthetic pesticides and environmental poisons on the natural world since the mid-1940s.

Carson moved to Silver Spring, Maryland, and found she had breast cancer and underwent radical mastectomy in 1960. However, the cancer spread and led to her death in 1964. *Silent Spring* was published in 1962 and became a Book-of-the-Month Club selection and a best seller worldwide. The book sought to show that DDT and other synthetic pesticides had a harmful effect on the environment. Although the chemical industry and especially companies that produced such pesticides denied the charge and sought to discredit Carson's research, DDT and some other pesticides later were banned.

The 1870 five-room house in Springdale, Pennsylvania, that was Carson's birthplace and childhood home is now the Rachel Carson Homestead, a historic house museum. Founded in 1975, the museum contains Carson family period artifacts and exhibits about Carson and environmental history. It also has a library with books by and about Carson as well as environmental history and issues. Annual attendance is 2,000.

Rachel Carson Homestead, 613 Marion Ave., Springdale, PA 15144-1242 (postal address: PO Box 46, Springdale, PA 15144-0046). Phone: 724/274-5459. Fax: 724/275-1259. E-mail: info@rachelcarsonhomestead.org. Website: www.rachelcarsonhomestead.org. Hours: by appointment; closed major holidays. Admission: adults, $10; seniors and children 5–12, $5; children under 5, free.

Willa Cather

Willa Cather State Historic Site. Willa Cather was a Pulitzer Prize–winning author who spent her formative years in Red Cloud, Nebraska, and later based many of the scenes and characters in her books on the people and settings of the pioneer farming community named for the Oglala Sioux chief. Cather's childhood home and other buildings connected with her writings now are preserved as part of the Willa Cather State Historic Site.

Cather, who was one of the leading figures of the American literary modernism movement, was born near Winchester, Virginia, in 1873 and came to Red Cloud with her family when nine years old. She spent the rest of her childhood in the town that she made famous in her writings. After attending the University of Nebraska, she moved to Pittsburgh and then joined the editorial staff of *McClure's Magazine* in New York City. She was promoted to managing editor of the magazine in 1908, published her first novel, *Alexander's Bridge*, in 1912, and coauthored a critical and controversial biography of Mary Baker Eddy, founder of the Christian Science Church. Cather then returned to the prairie for inspiration and wrote such works as *O Pioneers!* in 1913 and *My Ántonia* in 1918, which became popular and critical successes. In 1923 she won the Pulitzer Prize for *One of Ours*.

The Willa Cather Pioneer Memorial and Educational Foundation (now the Willa Cather Foundation) was founded in 1955 to further study of Cather's life and works and to preserve many sites in her hometown of Red Cloud. Six of the historic structures—the Cather Childhood Home, Garber Bank Building, Grace Episcopal Church, St. Juliana Catholic Church, Burlington Depot, and Pavelka Farmstead—were given to the Nebraska State Historical Society and now form the core of the Willa Cather State Historic Site.

The Willa Cather Foundation owns and manages four other sites—the 1885 Red Cloud Opera House, Baptist Church, Harling House, and Moon Block. In addition, the foundation owns and manages the 608-acre Willa Cather Memorial Prairie five miles from Red Cloud, operates the Willa Cather Historical Center museum and gallery, and offers guided tours of the restored Cather childhood home and other historic sites in Red Cloud. Annual attendance is 10,000.

Willa Cather State Historic Site, 413 N. Webster St., Red Cloud, NE 68970-2550, and Willa Cather Foundation, 413 N. Webster St., Red Cloud, NE 68970. Phone: 402/746-2653. Fax: 402/746-2652. E-mail: info@willacather.org. Website: www.willacather.org and www.nebraskahistory.org. Hours: Apr.–Oct.—8–5 Mon.–Sat., 1–5 Sun.; Nov.–Mar.—8–5 Mon.–Fri., 9–12 and 1–5 Sat.; closed Sun. and major holidays. Admission: adults, $10; children 5–12, $4; children under 5, free.

Ralph Waldo Emerson

Ralph Waldo Emerson House. Ralph Waldo Emerson was an American lecturer, philosopher, essayist, and poet who led the transcendentalist philosophic and literary movement of the 1830s and 1840s. Transcendentalism developed in New England as a reaction against scientific rationalism and a protest against the general state of culture and society. The transcendentalists believed in an ideal spirituality that transcends the physical and empirical and can be realized only through an individual's intuition, rather than through the doctrines of established religions.

Emerson was born in Boston in 1803. He was the son of the Rev. William Emerson, a Unitarian minister, and Ruth Haskins. His father died when Ralph was seven years old, and he and four brothers were raised by his mother with the help of other women in the family. He began schooling at the Boston Latin School when he was nine and at the age of 14 enrolled at Harvard College. He was an average student, worked his way through college, and graduated in 1821. In his senior year, he decided to go by his middle name, Waldo.

Emerson became a teacher and served as schoolmaster before enrolling at Harvard Divinity School and graduating first in his class. He became junior pastor at the Old Second Church in Boston, where he resigned his pastorate in 1831 after being unable in conscience to administer the sacrament of the Lord's Supper after the death of his young wife of tuberculosis. He also disagreed with the church's methods, especially the administration of the communion service and public prayer. He then toured Europe and in England visited with William Wordsworth, Samuel Taylor Coleridge, and Thomas Carlyle, the Scottish-born writer known for his attacks on hypocrisy and materialism and belief in the power of the individual. The friendship that developed with Carlyle helped Emerson formulate his own philosophy. He became known for challenging traditional thought—and as the chief spokesman of transcendentalism.

In the 1836 essay that became Emerson's first book, *Nature*, he stated that everything is a microcosm of the universe and that everyone shares the "Supreme Mind"—thereby allowing them to disregard external authority and to rely on direct experience. He gave more than 1,500 public lectures and published dozens of essays (mostly based on the lectures).

Emerson's essays from the mid-1830s to the mid-1840s constituted his most fertile period, with his first two collections of essays—*Essays: First Series* (1841) and *Essays: Second Series* (1844)—presenting the core of his thinking. His best-known addresses were "The American Scholar" (1837) and "The Divinity School Address" to graduates of the Harvard Divinity School, in which he shocked Boston's conservative clergymen with his descriptions of the divinity of man and the humanity of Jesus. But the transcendentalism movement began to die out in the late 1840s.

After his most active transcendentalism years, Emerson began to have health problems in 1867, including loss of memory beginning in 1872. He stopped making public appearances in 1879 because of the memory problems. His house in Concord also was badly damaged in an 1872 fire and then restored with community assistance. Emerson died of pneumonia at the age of 78 in 1882.

Emerson's home became a historic house museum in 1930 and now is listed in the National Register of Historic Places. It is operated by the Ralph Waldo Emerson Memorial Association. The four-square, two-story frame structure originally was built in 1828, bought by Emerson in 1835, and rebuilt after the 1872 house fire. It became a meeting place for philosophers, idealists, and poets. The house's furnishings are much as they were when Emerson lived there. It also contains some of his memorabilia, portraits, books, and other belongings. Annual attendance is nearly 3,500.

Ralph Waldo Emerson House, 28 Cambridge Turnpike, Concord, MA 01742-1700. Phone: 978/369-2236. Hours: mid-Apr.–Oct.—10–4:30 Thurs.–Sat., 1–4:30 Sun.; closed Mon.–Wed. and Nov.–mid-Apr. Admission: adults, $8; seniors and students, $6; children under 6, free.

William Faulkner

Rowan Oak, Home of William Faulkner. Rowan Oak is the name of the large Greek revival home in Oxford, Mississippi, where author William Faulkner and his family lived from 1930 until his death in 1962. He purchased what was known as the Bailey House, built by a Tennessee colonel in the 1840s frontier settlement, because he was fascinated by its history. Faulkner then renovated and gave the house its present name.

In 1972 Faulkner's daughter, Jill Faulkner Summers, sold the house to the University of Mississippi so that the public could visit and learn about her father's work. Rowan Oak remains much as it did when Faulkner lived there and wrote most of his works. It now receives 27,000 visitors a year.

Faulkner, who won the Nobel Prize for Literature in 1949, was born in New Albany, Mississippi, in 1897. He lived most of his life in Mississippi and was greatly influenced by the history and culture of the South. Faulkner became one of the most influential writers of the twentieth century. He wrote novels, novellas, short stories, and poems, and even served as an occasional screenwriter. In addition to receiving the Nobel Prize, Faulkner was awarded two Pulitzer Prizes—for *A Fable*, a 1954 novel, and the 1962 novel *The Reivers*.

Faulkner wrote his first novel, *Soldiers' Pay*, in 1925 while living in New Orleans. From the 1920s to World War II, he largely made his reputation as a leading author by publishing 13 novels and numerous short stories, including such celebrated books as *The Sound and the Fury* (1929), *As I Lay Dying* (1930), *Sanctuary* (1931), *Light in August* (1932), and *Absalom, Absalom!* (1936). In the 1940s he served as the screenwriter for two films directed by Howard Hawks—based on Raymond Chandler's *The Big Sleep* and Ernest Hemingway's *To Have and Have Not*. But he returned to Rowan Oak to do the scripts.

Many of Faulkner's novels and short stories took place in Yoknapatawpha County, based on Lafayette County where Oxford is located. Three of his novels—*The Hamlet*, *The Town*, and *The Mansion* (known as the Snopes Trilogy)—document the town and area around Jefferson through an extended family headed by Flem Snopes. Faulkner actually wrote many more short stories than novels. They were published from 1919 to 1999—37 years after his death.

Rowan Oak, Home of William Faulkner, 916 Old Taylor Ave., Oxford, MS 38655 (postal address: University of Mississippi Museum, PO Box 1848, University, MS 38677-1848). Phone: 662/915-7073. Fax: 662/915-7035. Website: www.olemiss.edu. Hours: 10–4 Tues.–Sat., 1–4 Sun.; closed New Year's Eve and Day, Independence Day, Thanksgiving, and Christmas Eve and Day. Admission: adults, $5; children, free.

F. Scott Fitzgerald

Scott and Zelda Fitzgerald Museum. Author F. Scott Fitzgerald, who wrote novels and short stories during the jazz age (a term he gave to the roaring 1920s), is considered one of America's greatest writers of the twentieth century. He is best known for *The Great Gatsby*, which chronicled the flapper era, but he also wrote four other novels and many short stories in the 1920s–1930s and scripts for movies during the second half of the 1930s.

Fitzgerald, who was born in St. Paul, Minnesota, in 1896, had his initial literary effort published in the school newspaper when 12. A poor student, he still attended Princeton University but left to enlist in the navy during World War I and became a first lieutenant. While attending a dance at a country club in 1918, he met and fell in love with Zelda Sayre, an Alabama society girl. They were married after his first novel, *This Side of Paradise*, was published in 1920. It was followed by *The Beautiful and Damned* (1922), *The Great Gatsby* (1925), *Tender Is the Night* (1934), and *The Last Tycoon*, published posthumously in 1942.

The lives and legendary love affair of Scott and Zelda, who also wrote short stories and magazine articles, now are the focus of the F. Scott and Zelda Fitzgerald Museum in the historic Cloverdale district of Montgomery, Alabama, near the home of Zelda's parents. The couple lived in the house with their young daughter, Frances, in

1931–1932 after returning from a two-year tour of Europe gathering color for their writings and getting treatment for Zelda's breakdown.

The leased house was where Scott wrote *Tender Is the Night* about a destructive marriage in a European setting, and Zelda outlined a similar book about a marriage, titled *Save Me the Waltz*, which was published in 1932. The novels, based loosely on their marriage experiences, gave entirely different views of a stormy marriage. During their marriage, they accused each other of stealing their materials, had romances with others, and eventually became estranged.

The Montgomery museum, founded in 1989, contains various manuscripts and editions of Scott's novels, originals of Zelda's art, furniture from her childhood home, original letters, photographs, portraits, and other memorabilia related to the lives of the two writers.

F. Scott and Zelda Fitzgerald Museum, 919 Felder Ave., Montgomery, AL 36106 (postal address: PO Box 64, Montgomery, AL 36101-0064). Phone: 334/264-4222. E-mail: info@fitzgeraldmuseum.net. Website: www.fitzgeraldmuseum.net. Hours: 10–2 Wed.–Fri., 1–5 Sat.–Sun.; closed Mon.–Tues. and major holidays. Admission: adults, $5; seniors and students, $2; children under 6, free.

Theodor Seuss Geisel (Dr. Seuss)

See Artists/Sculptors section.

Zane Grey

Zane Grey Museum. Zane Grey is known as the father of the Western novel. He was one of the first authors to write extensively about the West. He authored more than 90 books with over 40 million readers and had more than 50 of his works converted into 110 movies. In the process, he became the first millionaire author.

Grey's life now is celebrated at the Zane Grey Museum in Lackawaxen, Pennsylvania, where he lived in 1914–1918 and is part of the Upper Delaware Scenic and Recreational River administered by the National Park Service. It is where Grey began his writing career, telling stories about fishing along the Upper Delaware River, and where his ashes and those of his wife are buried.

Grey was born in Zanesville, Ohio, in 1872 and moved with his parents to Columbus in 1890. It was in Ohio that he developed his interest in fishing, baseball, and writing. His baseball prowess led to a scholarship at the University of Pennsylvania, where he studied dentistry; several seasons of amateur baseball; and an 1899 dental practice in New York City. While in New York, he began his writing—a magazine article in 1902 and his first novel, *Betty Zane*, in 1903.

Grey loved to get away to the outdoors and to fish and began visiting Lackawaxen. It was there he met Lina Elise Roth while canoeing in the river and fell in love and married her in 1905. "Dolly," as Grey called her, was a teacher who played an important role in his struggle to become a successful writer, even providing inheritance funds for him to go on a hunting expedition that resulted in the 1908 book *The Last of the Plainsmen*.

After Grey left dentistry to pursue a full-time writing career, the couple moved to a farmhouse at the junction of the Lackawaxen and Delaware Rivers, where he wrote about fishing. The couple took a honeymoon trip to the Grand Canyon in Arizona, which led to his interest in Western novels. After the 1908 expedition adventure story, Grey wrote his first Western novel, *Heritage of the Desert*, in 1910 and then his most famous work, *Riders of the Purple Sage*, the following year. By 1915 he had 15 books in print, as well as many fishing and outdoor adventure articles and serialized stories.

In 1914 the Grey family moved into the house that later became the museum, and then to California in 1918 to enable Grey to work with motion picture companies on many Western films based on his novels. A prolific writer, he had one or more novels published every year and a fishing or outdoor adventure book every few years. Even after his death in 1939, he left behind more than 20 manuscripts that were published posthumously.

In 1945 Grey's widow sold the Lackawaxen house to Helen James, the daughter of a family friend, who operated an inn at the site for 25 years while collecting memorabilia and other materials associated with Grey. She and her husband then operated a Zane Grey Museum from 1973 until 1989, when it was sold to the National Park Service and included in the Upper Delaware Scenic and Recreational River site. Guided tours are now provided at the museum, which contains furnishings, artworks, photographs, books, and other objects associated with Grey and his family. The site, which is listed on the National Register of Historic Places, has an annual attendance of 8,000.

Zane Grey Museum, Scenic Dr., Lackawaxen, PA 18435 (postal address: Upper Delaware Scenic and Recreational River, 274 River Rd., Beach Lake, PA 18405). Phone: 570/685-4871. Fax: 570/685-1874. E-mail: upde_inerpretation@ nps.gov. Website: www.nps.gov/upde. Hours: Memorial Day–Labor Day—9–5 Fri.–Sun.; closed Mon.–Thurs.; Sept.–mid-Oct.—10–5 Sat.–Sun.; closed Mon.–Fri. and remainder of year. Admission: free.

National Road/Zane Grey Museum. The National Road/Zane Grey Museum in Norwich, Ohio, honors America's busiest early land route to the West and the Western author who was born in nearby Zanesville. The National Road, which was started in 1806, was the only significant land link between the East Coast and the Western frontier in the early nineteenth century. Grey, who was born in 1872 in the town that was founded by his mother's ancestors, later moved to the Atlantic and then Pacific coasts and wrote more than 90 books—mostly about the Western frontier—during the early twentieth century (*see* Zane Grey Museum).

The museum, founded in 1973, has three sections. A collection of vehicles, dioramas, and other exhibits tell the story of the National Road that stretched for 700 miles from Cumberland, Maryland, to Vandalia, Illinois, and passed through Zanesville. The Zane Grey section has his re-created study, many manuscripts, and memorabilia related to his life. The third section is devoted to the area's renowned pottery, produced from around the turn of the twentieth century through midcentury. Annual attendance is 5,000.

National Road/Zane Grey Museum, 8850 E. Pike, Norwich, OH 43767. Phones: 740/872-3143 and 800/752-2602. Fax: 740/872-3510. Website: www.ohiohistory.org. Hours: May–mid-Oct.—10–4 Wed.–Sat., 1–4 Sun.; closed Mon.– Tues., Memorial Day, Independence Day, Labor Day, and remainder of year. Admission: adults, $7; seniors and military, $6; students, $3; children under 6, free.

Alex Haley

Alex Haley Museum and Interpretive Center. Alex Haley was a prominent African American author best known for *Roots: The Saga of an American Family*, a Pulitzer Prize–winning novel based on his family's history. *Roots* was published in 37 languages and reached a record-setting 130 million viewers in a television miniseries in 1977. Haley's childhood home in Henning, Tennessee, is now the site of the Alex Haley Museum and Interpretive Center, devoted to his life and works.

Roots, which was published in 1976, tells the story of Kunta Kinte, who was kidnapped in Gambia in 1767 and taken to Maryland on the *Lord Ligonier*, a slave ship, to be sold. It then traces the life of Kinte and his family. In Haley's 10 years of research for the novel, he traveled to the African village where Kinte grew up and was captured, found the records of the slave ship, did other historical research, and interviewed relatives and others to produce the book that received a special award from the Pulitzer board in 1977. Haley claimed to be a seventh-generation descendant of Kunta Kinte.

A sequel series, *Roots: The Next Generation*, also was aired in 1979. In the late 1970s, Haley began working on a second historical novel based on another branch of his family (traced through his grandmother Queen, the daughter of a black slave woman and her white master), but he died before finishing it. The book, titled *Alex Haley's Queen*, was completed by David Stevens at his request and subsequently made into a movie in 1993.

Alex Haley was born as Alexander Murray Palmer Haley in 1921 in Ithaca, New York, where his father, Simon Haley, a World War I veteran, was an agricultural graduate student at Cornell University, and his mother, Bertha Palmer Haley, was a teacher. For the first five years of his life, he lived with his mother and grandparents in Henning, Tennessee, while his father finished his studies at Cornell. His father rejoined the family after receiving his degree and taught as a professor of agriculture at various southern universities.

Haley, who was an exceptionally bright student, graduated from his school at the age of 15. He enrolled at Alcorn A&M College in Mississippi and then transferred to Elizabeth City State Teachers College in North Carolina after a year. When he was 17 in 1939, he quit school and enlisted in the Coast Guard, where he served for 20 years. He began as a seaman and advanced to chief petty officer. He began writing short stories and articles while serving in the Pacific during World War II. He retired from the Coast Guard in 1959 and began his writing career and eventually became a senior editor for *Reader's Digest*.

Haley first became known for his series of *Playboy* magazine articles on leading African Americans, such as Martin Luther King Jr., Muhammad Ali, Sammy Davis Jr., Mils Davis, Jim Brown, Quincy Jones, and Malcolm X. He also wrote articles on such other figures as television star Johnny Carson, lawyer Melvin Belli, and American Nazi leader George Lincoln Rockwell. The Malcolm X article was followed by Haley's first book in 1965, *The Autobiography of*

Malcolm X, dealing with his life and the civil rights movement. It became an international best seller. In 1973 he also wrote his only motion picture screenplay, *Super Fly T.N.T.*

Alex Haley was married three times and had three children. He died of a heart attack in 1992 at the age of 70. He is buried in the front lawn of Alex Haley Museum and Interpretive Center in Henning, Tennessee. The museum, which began as the Alexander Haley House Museum, is located in the 10-room bungalow-style house where he lived with his grandparents during his childhood from 1921 to 1929 and some subsequent summers. The house was constructed in 1918–1919 by his material grandfather.

The house, which contains period furnishings and memorabilia, now is listed on the National Register of Historic Places. In 2010, when the museum's name was changed, a new 6,500-square-foot interpretive center with personal artifacts, mementos from Haley's career, and exhibits about his life and accomplishments was added behind the house by the Tennessee Historical Commission. Annual attendance is 4,000.

Alex Haley Museum and Interpretive Center, 200 S. Church St., Henning, TN 38041-7201. Phone: 731/7328-2240. Hours: 10–5 Tues.–Sat., Sun. by appointment; closed Mon. and major holidays. Admission: adults, $6; seniors, $5; children 5–18, $4; children under 5, free.

Nathaniel Hawthorne

Nathaniel Hawthorne's Birthplace. Nathaniel Hawthorne, a prominent novelist and short story writer in the middle of the nineteenth century, was born in 1804 in a house that now is part of the House of the Seven Gables historical complex in Salem, Massachusetts. The 1750 Georgian house was moved several blocks in 1958 to be next to the House of the Seven Gables, which inspired Hawthorne's 1851 classic, *The House of the Seven Gables.*

The House of the Seven Gables, a 1668 house that later acquired seven gables, is the oldest surviving seventeenth-century wooden mansion in New England. It once was owned by Hawthorne's cousin, Susanna Ingersoll. She sometimes entertained him there and later reportedly inspired him to write a novel about the house. The House of the Seven Gables, also known as the Turner-Ingersoll Mansion, now is a historic site with five houses, including Hawthorne's birthplace house (known as the Hooper-Hathaway House) and two colonial revival gardens.

Hawthorne lived in the birth house until he was five years of age. His father, a sea caption, died while on a voyage, and his wife was left with three small children and no support. She had to move out and seek assistance from her family. The early childhood trauma later was reflected in Hawthorne's literary works. Many of the characters in his novels suffer from the loss of one or both parents and are dependent upon the charity of others.

The Hawthorne family moved to Maine, where he was educated at Bowdoin College. Hawthorne worked as a writer and contributor to periodicals between 1825 and 1836. In 1828 he published his first novel, *Fanshawe*, at his own expense. When it did not receive much attention, he burned all the unsold copies. But it initiated a friendship with the publisher, which resulted in Hawthorne editing and writing a number of reference and children's books. In 1842 Hawthorne married Sophia Peabody, and they lived in "The Old Manse" in Concord, Massachusetts, until 1845 (*see* separate listing). While living at the historic house, Hawthorne wrote *Mosses from an Old Manse*.

A number of novels followed, including such critical and popular successes as *The Scarlet Letter* in 1850 and *The House of the Seven Gables* in 1851. He also wrote *The Blithedale Romance* in 1852 and then was appointed consul in Liverpool, England, by President Franklin Pierce after writing the campaign biography for his friend. He lived there for four years and then went to Italy and wrote *The Marble Faun*, his last completed novel, in 1860. When he returned to America, he wrote essays contained in the 1864 *Our Old Home*, written from "The Wayside," his home in Concord from 1852 until his death in 1864 (*see* separate listing).

Guided tours are given by costumed interpreters of the House of the Seven Gables historical complex, now listed on the National Register of Historic Places. The Hawthorne Birthplace House is only a few feet from the House of the Seven Gables that Hawthorne made famous in fiction. It is one of the five houses and two gardens on the complex tour. The site museum has an introductory slide and tape program and more than 2,000 artifacts and other objects, 500 photographs and glass plate negatives, more than 40 framed works, and over 650 volumes in a research and rare book library. The annual attendance is 125,000.

The House of Seven Gables, 115 Derby St., Salem, MA 01970-5640. Phone: 978/744-0991. Fax: 978/741-4350. E-mail: info@7gables.org. Website: www.7gables.org. Hours: Nov.–June—10–5 daily; July–Oct.—10–7 daily; closed New Year's Day, Thanksgiving, and Christmas. Admission: adults, $12; seniors, $11; children 5–12, $7.25; children under 5, free.

The Old Manse. The Old Manse is a historic 1770 two-story Georgian clapboard house in Concord, Massachusetts, where author Nathaniel Hawthorne and his wife, Sophia, lived in 1842–1845. The house was built by the Rev. William Emerson, grandfather of transcendentalist writer Ralph Waldo Emerson. It is where the Hawthornes spent their happiest years, with Nathaniel writing and Sophia painting, and where they etched affectionate sentiments on window panes in the upstairs room he used as a study. And it was Hawthorne who gave the house its name, the Old Manse, meaning the minister's home.

The Rev. Emerson, a fiery preacher known for his religious and political sermons, witnessed—from the house—the 1775 skirmish at the North Bridge in Concord that began the Revolutionary War. When the Continental Army took over Harvard University's campus in Cambridge in 1776, he arranged for the college to move to Concord for nine months. He also joined the army as a chaplain later that year and was assigned to Fort Ticonderoga, where he fell ill and died shortly after arrival. As a result, his wife, Phebe, who had five small children, took in boarders to help support her young family and the 22-acre working farm. One of the boarders was the new minister, the Rev. Ezra Ripley, whom she married in 1780. Ripley was the minister in Concord for 63 years.

Ralph Waldo Emerson was the son of William Emerson II, one of the surviving children of the Rev. Emerson. He often would spend a school or summer term at the Old Manse, as well as when a young man. It is where he finished the draft for his first published work, the essay *Nature*. After Ezra Riley died in 1841, the Old Manse was rented to the Hawthornes. Hawthorne wrote much about the house and surrounding landscape, which later appeared in his *American Notebooks* and in *Mosses from the Old Manse*, published in 1846.

The Emerson-Ripley descendants owned the Old Manse until 1939, when it was converted into a historic house museum by the Trustees of Reservations, a nonprofit conservation organization. It now is a National Historic Landmark. Tours are offered of the house, which contains period furniture from the Emerson-Ripley family, antiques, and memorabilia, as well as the poems that the Hawthornes etched on the upstairs windows. The Old Manse also has a re-created heirloom garden originally planted by Henry David Thoreau in honor of the Hawthornes' wedding and trails that lead to the North Bridge and a stone boathouse on the Concord River. Annual attendance is 11,400.

The Old Manse, 269 Monument St., Concord, MA 01742-1837 (postal address: PO Box 572, Concord, MA 01742-0572). Phone: 978/369-3909. Fax: 978/287-6154. E-mail: oldmanse@ttor.org. Website: www.oldmanse.org. Hours: mid-Apr.–Oct.—10–5 Mon.–Sat., 12–5 Sun. and holidays; Nov.–mid-Apr.—2–5 Thurs.–Fri., 12–4:30 Sat.–Sun.; closed Mon.–Wed. Admission: adults, $8; seniors and students, $7; children 6–12, $5; children under 6, free.

The Wayside. The Wayside in Concord, Massachusetts, is known as "the Home of Authors." Louisa May Alcott, Nathaniel Hawthorne, and Margaret Sidney (Harriett Lothrop) once lived in the seventeenth-century house now administered by the National Park Service as part of the Minute Man National Historical Park. However, the house usually is associated with Hawthorne, who named the house and lived there in 1852–1853 and 1860–1864; it was the only house he ever owned.

The Alcott family lived at the site from 1845 to 1852. Bronson Alcott, the father, bought the house and named it "Hillside," which later was changed by Hawthorne. It is where Alcott's daughter, Louisa May, and her sisters lived many of the childhood adventures described in her 1868 classic, *Little Women*. It also is where Louisa May Alcott began her literary career, writing fanciful stories that resulted in her first published story, "The Rival Painters," in 1852 and first book, *Flower Fables*, in 1855. The house was sold to Hawthorne in 1852, and the Alcotts moved next door to what became known as the Orchard House (*see* listing for Louisa May Alcott).

Nathaniel Hawthorne, his wife, Sophia, and their three young children lived in the house in two periods—1852–1853 and 1860–1864—and rented the house to family members while they were in Europe, with Hawthorne serving as American consul in Liverpool, England, and writing in Italy. When the family returned, the Hawthornes added a three-story tower (with the top floor becoming Nathaniel's study) and a second floor over the west wing of the cottage, enclosed the bay porch, and moved the barn to the east side of the house. After Nathaniel died in 1864, his wife and children moved to England, and the house was sold in 1870.

In 1883 Boston publisher Daniel Lothrop and his wife, Harriet, purchased the house. Harriet was the author of the Five Little Peppers series of 11 books featuring a family of five children prone to mischief and other children's books using the pen name Margaret Sidney. She loved Concord and worked to save the Wayside, Orchard House, and two other historic houses. Her daughter, Margaret, devoted 40 years to saving the Wayside, opening it to tours, gathering information about its history, and publishing a book that established it as the home of authors.

Today, the Wayside is a historic house museum that was designated a National Historic Landmark in 1963 and became part of the Minute Man National Historical Park in 1965. It was the first literary site to be acquired by the National Park Service. The house was restored and opened to the public in 1971. The house has guided tours and living history programs, and a visitor center in the barn has exhibits that connect the Wayside authors to one another and to fellow authors and major events in American history and literature. The visitor center also contains lifelike sculptures of Nathaniel Hawthorne, Louisa and Bronson Alcott, and Margaret Sidney, as well as an audio-visual program that brings their words and works to life.

The Wayside, 455 Lexington Rd., Concord, MA 01742, Phone: 978/318-7825. Fax: 978/315-7800. E-mail: mima. info@nps.gov. Website: www.nps.gov/archive/mima/wayside. Hours: May–Oct.—hours and days vary; closed remainder of year. Admission: visitor center and grounds—free; house tour—adults, $5; children under 17, free.

Ernest Hemingway

Hemingway Museum and Birthplace. Ernest Hemingway, who received the 1952 Pulitzer Prize for *The Old Man and the Sea* and the 1954 Nobel Prize in Literature, was a journalist and writer who had a significant influence on the development of twentieth-century fiction writing. His distinctive writing style was characterized by tightly written prose and understatement that was followed later by many novelists. Hemingway wrote seven novels, six collections of short stories, and two nonfiction works during his lifetime, and he had three novels, four collections of short stories, and three nonfiction autobiographical works published after his death in 1961.

Hemingway's life and works are now chronicled at the Hemingway Museum and Birthplace at the restored Victorian house in Oak Park, Illinois, where he was born in 1899. After serving as the editor of the high school newspaper and yearbook in Oak Park, he became a reporter for the *Kansas City Star*. It was the beginning of a journalistic career that included working for the *Toronto Star* and as a war correspondent in the Spanish Civil War, World War II, and the Greco-Turkish War. During World War I, he volunteered to be an ambulance driver for the Red Cross in Italy while only 18 and was seriously wounded by mortar fire and spent six months recovering in a hospital.

During the early 1920s, Hemingway became part of the group of expatriate artists in Paris that included Gertrude Stein, Ezra Pound, Sylvia Beach, James Joyce, Max Eastman, Lincoln Stevens, and Wyndham Lewis, as well as the artists Miró and Picasso. In 1925 Hemingway's first collection of short stories, *In Our Time*, and his first novel, *Sun Also Rises*, were published. In 1928 he visited and stayed off and on until the early 1930s at the home of his second wife, Pauline Pfeiffer, in Piggott, Arkansas (*see* separate listing), where he wrote portions of *A Farewell to Arms*, published in 1929.

Hemingway bought a house in Key West, Florida, in 1931 and lived there with his family until 1940 (*see* separate listing), during which time he traveled to Africa and made Ketchem, Idaho, near the new resort of Sun Valley, his primary summer home. When the couple divorced in 1940, Hemingway moved to Cuba, where he lived until 1960. When he left Cuba, Castro made his residence there into a museum honoring Hemingway.

In the 1930s Hemingway wrote *Green Hills of Africa* about big-game hunting after his trip to Africa and *To Have and Have Not*, his only novel set in the United States. They were followed by *For Whom the Bells Toll*, which was published in 1940; *Across the River and into the Trees* in 1950; and the prize-winning *The Old Man and the Sea* in 1952.

Hemingway, who was married four times, suffered from numerous accident injuries and ill health during most of his adult life and was bed-ridden from late 1956 to early 1957. He spent the summer of 1959 in Spain writing a series of articles and gathering photographs for *Life* magazine on bullfighting, which was his passion. It was there that his mental deterioration was noticeable. After receiving medical treatment for several illnesses, Hemingway committed suicide by shooting himself with his shotgun at his home in Ketchum in 1961. Four other members of his family—his father, sister, brother, and granddaughter—also died of suicide.

The Hemingway Museum, founded in his family's Queen Anne–style home in 1990, remains much as it did when he lived in the house. It contains such memorabilia as Hemingway's childhood diary, rare photos, early writings, letters, and other objects, as well as special exhibits on such topics as Hemingway's love of the outdoors and the arts, his childhood experiences that influenced his early writings, and his involvement in wars and the movies. The annual attendance is nearly 7,000.

Hemingway Museum and Birthplace, 200 Oak Park Ave., Oak Park, IL 60302-2128 (postal address: PO Box 2222, Oak Park, IL 60303-2222). Phone: 708/848-2222. Fax: 708/386-2952. E-mail: ehfop@sbcglobal.net. Website: www.ehfop.org. Hours: 1–5 Sun.–Fri., 10–5 Sat.; closed major holidays. Admission: adults, $8; seniors and children 6–12, $6; children under 6, free.

Ernest Hemingway Home and Museum. The 1851 Spanish colonial–style house in Key West, Florida, where Ernest Hemingway and his family lived for more than 10 years is now the Ernest Hemingway House and Museum. The eight-room house in the Old Town section was his home from 1931 to 1940. It still contains much of the original furniture, as well as the former carriage house where Hemingway's studio was located, the gardens, the swimming pool (the first residential pool in Key West), and the wall he built surrounding the grounds. More than 60 cats, some of which are descendants of Hemingway's six-toed tomcat, also roam the grounds.

Hemingway's years in Key West were his most productive. It is where he produced such books as *For Whom the Bell Tolls*, *Death in the Afternoon*, *Green Hills of Africa*, *To Have and Not Have*, and such short stories as "The Snows of Kilimanjaro" and "The Short Happy Life of Frances Mancomber." He also finished *A Farewell to Arms* while living briefly in a prior Key West residence.

Hemingway and his second wife, Pauline, divorced in 1940, and he moved to Cuba, where he lived until 1960. Pauline and their two sons remained in the house until her death in 1951. The house was purchased by Mrs. Bernice Dickson, a local businesswoman, who lived there until it opened as a museum in 1964, when she moved into the carriage house. The museum is now operated by the Dickson family.

The historic house contains European antiques from Hemingway's many trips, personal treasures, and gifts from famous friends. They include such items as trophy mounts and skins from Hemingway's African safaris and hunting expeditions, a seventeen-century carved Spanish bench and an eighteenth-century Spanish walnut dining table, a Venetian glass chandelier, a cardinal's chair used in a Hemingway play, and a replica of a ceramic cat from artist Pablo Picasso. Guided tours are given of the museum.

Ernest Hemingway Home and Museum, 907 Whitehead St., Key West, FL 33040-7473. Phone: 305/294-1136. Fax: 305/294-2755. E-mail: hemingway@bellsouth.net. Website: www.hemingwayhome.com. Hours: 9–5 daily. Admission: adults, $12; children over 5, $6; children under 6, free.

Hemingway-Pfeiffer Museum and Educational Center. Ernest Hemingway and his second wife, Pauline Pfeiffer, occasionally stayed at her parents' 14-room home in Piggott, Arkansas, from 1928 into the 1930s. It is where he wrote portions of one of his most famous novels, *A Farewell to Arms*, and several short stories. The site now is the Hemingway-Pfeiffer Museum and Educational Center, which seeks to further understanding of the 1920s and 1930s by focusing on the Pfeiffer family and Hemingway.

Hemingway initially came to Piggott to meet his in-laws and to await the birth of the couple's first child in 1928. He then stayed frequently with the prominent Piggott family on their 60,000-acre estate, where a barn loft had been converted into a studio for him to do his writing. Unfortunately, a fire in the studio in 1932 destroyed many of Hemingway's belongings. The studio was repaired, and Hemingway continued to use the space until he traveled to Africa and then settled in Key West, Florida (*see* separate listing).

The house and barn were built in 1910 and purchased by Pauline's father, Paul Pfeiffer, in 1913. After the death of the parents, the property was bought by the Tom James family in 1950 and by Arkansas State University in 1997. The house and the barn were listed on the National Register of Historic Places in 1982 and opened as a museum in 1999.

The Pfeiffer house and barn now appear as they did during Hemingway's stays in the 1920s–1930s. The house contains many of the furnishings of the Pfeiffer house and exhibits examining literature of the 1930s through the works of Hemingway and other writers of the period. An old house across the street serves as an educational center. Annual attendance is 3,000.

Hemingway-Pfeiffer Museum and Educational Center, 1021 W. Cherry St., Piggott, AR 72454-1419. Phone: 870/598-3487. Fax: 870/598-1037. Website: www.hemingway.astate.edu. Hours: 9–3 Mon.–Fri., 1–3 Sat.; closed Sun., New Year's Eve and Day, Memorial Day weekend, Independence Day, Labor Day weekend, Thanksgiving, and Christmas Eve and Day. Admission: suggested donations—adults, $5; seniors, $3; children under 12, free.

O. Henry (William Sydney Porter)

O. Henry Museum. William Sydney Porter was a master short story writer at the turn of the twentieth century who wrote under the pen name O. Henry. His stories were known for their wit, characterizations, and surprise endings. The house where he lived in Austin, Texas, in 1891 now is the site of the O. Henry Museum, which traces his life and works. Porter started using the pseudonym O. Henry in the late 1880s as he began his writing career. It is said that the pen name came from his frequent calling of "Oh, Henry" to the family cat.

Porter was born in 1862 in Greensboro, North Carolina, and moved with his father into the home of his paternal grandmother when three years old after his mother died. As a child, he was always reading and developed a lifelong love of books. In 1879 he started working at his uncle's pharmacy and became a licensed pharmacist three years later. He also was known for his sketches of townspeople. After developing a persistent cough, he left for Texas primarily for his health in 1882. He worked as a shepherd, ranch hand, and cook on a sheep ranch in La Salle County as his health improved.

In 1884 Porter moved to Austin, where he had a number of different jobs, including pharmacist, draftsman, bank teller, and journalist. While participating in musical and theater groups in Austin, he met and eloped with

Athol Estes from a wealthy family in 1887, the same year he was hired as a draftsman in the Texas General Land Office. In addition to drawing maps from surveys and field notes, he started developing plots and characters for such stories as "The Gifts of the Magi," "The Ransom of Red Chief," and "The Cop and the Anthem." He died in New York in 1910.

The O. Henry Museum, founded in 1934, is located in a house that was built around 1800 and is operated by the City of Austin. It tells the story of Porter's life while living in Austin. It contains period furnishings, memorabilia, documents, letters, and photographs and has guided tours, writing classes, special events, and a historical and library outreach program. Annual attendance is 15,000.

O. Henry Museum, 409 E. 5th St., Austin, TX 78701-3705. Phone: 512/472-1903. Fax: 517/472-7102. Website: www.ohenrymuseum.org. Hours: 12–5 Wed.–Sun.; closed Mon.–Tues., New Year's Day, Independence Day, Labor Day, Thanksgiving, and Christmas. Admission: free.

O. Henry House Museum. William Sydney Porter, the acclaimed short story writer who used the pen name O. Henry, lived in San Antonio in 1893–1895 after being accused of embezzlement at an Austin bank where he was a teller and bookkeeper. In San Antonio, he founded and served as editor of the *Rolling Stone*, a humorous weekly newspaper. When the newspaper folded, Porter and his family moved to Houston, where he wrote a column for the *Houston Post* until he was indicted and convicted in a controversial bank embezzlement trial in Austin (*see* separate listing).

The small adobe house in which Porter and his family lived in San Antonio is now the O. Henry House Museum. While in San Antonio, he used the city as the setting of some of his most intriguing short stories, including, "A Fog in Santone" and "The Higher Abdication." The house was purchased by the San Antonio Conservation Society in 1959 to save it from demolition. It then was sold and moved several times before being relocated to a parking lot and operated by the county. The restored museum, which reopened in 1999, contains period furniture, a large portrait of Porter, and items related to his life and writings.

O. Henry House Museum, 601 Dolorosa St., San Antonio, TX 78207. Hours: vary. Admission: free.

Langston Hughes

Langston Hughes House. Langston Hughes was one of the foremost figures of the Harlem Renaissance literary movement of the 1920s and 1930s, which focused on African American identity. He was an author and poet who was known as the "Poet Laureate of Harlem." He also was a social activist, playwright, and columnist and was one of the earliest innovators of the new literary art form known as "jazz poetry."

Hughes was born in Joplin, Missouri, in 1902. His father left the family early and later divorced his mother, who was a teacher. While she traveled seeking employment, Langston was raised primarily by his maternal grandmother and family friends. Hughes then lived again with his mother in Lincoln, Illinois, and Cleveland. While in grammar school, he was elected class poet, and while in high school he wrote for the school newspaper, edited the yearbook, and began writing short stories, poetry, and dramatic plays.

Hughes's professional writing career started in the 1920s as the Harlem Renaissance was beginning. In 1921 his signature poem, "The Negro Speaks of Rivers," appeared in the *Crisis* magazine, and his first book of poetry, *The Weary Blues*, was published in 1926. His life and work, as well as those of his contemporaries, were greatly influenced by the renaissance and working together to create the short-lived magazine *Fire! Devoted to Younger Negro Artists*. They criticized the older writers and divisions and prejudices based on skin color in the black community, and they wanted to show the real lives of blacks in the lower social-economic strata. In 1926 Hughes published what was considered their manifesto in the *Nation*. He also explored the black human condition, stressed the theme that "black is beautiful," and emphasized folk and jazz rhythms as the basis of his poetry.

Hughes attended Columbia University in New York City briefly and later Lincoln University, a historically black university in Chester County, Pennsylvania, where he received a bachelor's degree in 1929. He then returned to New York, where he lived in Harlem the rest of his life. His first novel, *Not Without Laughter*, won the Harmon Gold Medal for literature in 1930, and his first collection of short stories, *The Ways of White Folks*, was published in 1934. Among the works that followed were *The Big Sea* (1940), *Shakespeare in Harlem* (1942), *Fields of Wonder* (1947), *Simple Speaks His Mind* (1950), and *Simple Stakes a Claim* (1957). Hughes also cowrote the screenplay for *Way Down South* and the lyrics for the opera *Street Scene* in the 1940s.

The political views of Langston Hughes often caused him problems. He was accused of being a communist after being involved in a number of projects supported by communist organizations, but he never became a party member. Hughes died in New York City in 1967 of complications from prostate cancer. In his memory, the Langston Hughes House—an 1869 three-story Italianate-style row house in Harlem where he lived the last 20 years—was given landmark status by the New York City Preservation Committee, and East 127th Street was renamed in his honor. The house also is listed on the National Register of Historic Places. The historic house now has a performance and gallery space on the first floor and offices on the other two levels and generally is closed.

Langston Hughes House, 30 E. 127th St., New York, NY 10035. Phone: 212/927-3413. Hours: varies, but normally closed. Admission: free.

Zora Neale Hurston

Zora Neale Hurston National Museum of Fine Arts. Zora Neal Hurston was an African American author, folklorist, and anthropologist during the Harlem Renaissance in the 1920s and 1930s. She wrote four novels and more than 50 short stories, plays, and essays and is best known for her 1937 novel *Their Eyes Were Watching God*, which celebrated the lives of African Americans. Her hometown of Eatonville, Florida, the nation's oldest incorporated black municipality, founded the Zora Neale Hurston National Museum of Fine Arts in her honor.

Hurston was born in 1891 in Notasulga, Alabama. Her father was a Baptist preacher and her mother a school teacher. She was the fifth of eight children. Her family moved to Eatonville when she was three years old. Her interest in literature began in 1901 when some northern schoolteachers visited Eatonville and gave her some books.

In 1917 Hurston began attending Morgan Academy, the high school branch of Morgan College, a historically African American college in Baltimore. She graduated in 1918 and enrolled at Howard University, earning an associate's degree in 1920. Hurston received a scholarship in 1925 to Barnard College, where she was the only black student and where she conducted ethnographic research with noted anthropologist Franz Boas of Columbia University. After graduating with a Bachelor of Arts in anthropology in 1927 at the age of 36, she spent two years as a graduate student in anthropology at Columbia University. She was married and divorced twice during this period.

Hurston traveled extensively in the South and the Caribbean in the 1930s to conduct anthropological research. During her travels, she wrote "Mules and Men," a short story documenting African American folklore that is considered a folklore classic, in 1935, and the base materials for *Jonah's Gourd Vine*, published in 1934. In 1936–1937 she went to Haiti and Central America for further anthropological research on a Guggenheim Fellowship that resulted in *Tell My Horse*, on her fieldwork studying African and voudon rituals, in 1938. Hurston also lived in Honduras in 1947–1948 when she wrote much of *Seraph on the Suwanee*, noted for its focus on white characters.

Hurston also established a school of dramatic arts at Bethune-Cookman College (now University) in Daytona Beach, Florida, in 1934. And later she served on the faculty of the North Carolina College for Negroes (now North Carolina Central University) in Durham.

In 1950 Hurston moved to Florida, where she worked as a librarian in Cape Canaveral and at the Patrick Air Force Base before settling in Fort Pierce in 1957. Her last years were spent working as a freelance writer for magazines and newspapers.

Hurston died in poverty in 1960 after a period of financial and medical difficulties. Her death at the St. Lucie County Welfare Home in Fort Pierce resulted from hypertensive heart disease after suffering a stroke at the age of 69. Her remains were buried in an unmarked grave at the Garden of Heavenly Rest cemetery in Fort Pierce until 1973, when novelist Alice Walker and literary scholar Charles Hunt found the grave and gave it a name.

The Zora Neale Hurston National Museum of Fine Arts was founded in Eatonville, Florida, in 1990 by the Association to Preserve the Eatonville Community to display the works of artists of African descent who live on the continent or in the diaspora. It also honors Zora Neale Hurston, Eatonville's most famous former resident, who is celebrated at an annual festival. The museum features three-month changing exhibitions by aspiring and prominent African American artists.

Zora Neale Hurston National Museum of Fine Arts, 227 E. Kennedy Blvd., Eatonville, FL 32751-5303. Phone: 407/647-3307. Fax: 407/539-2192. E-mail: info@zorafestival.com. Website: www.zoranealehurstonmuseum.com. Hours: 9–4 Mon.–Fri., 11–1 Sat.; closed Sun. and major holidays. Admission: free.

Washington Irving

Washington Irving's Sunnyside. Washington Irving was America's first internationally famous author. He was called the father of the American short story. In addition to short stories, he wrote essays, poetry, newspaper columns, and historical, biographical, satirical, and travel books. He is best remembered for "Rip Van Winkle," about a man who slept for 20 years, published in 1819, and "The Legend of Sleepy Hollow," about a teacher chased by a headless horseman, an 1820 story.

Irving was born into a wealthy merchant's family in 1783 in New York City and early developed a passion for books. While studying for the law, he contributed whimsical letters to a newspaper edited by a brother and later became the leading figure in a group that published *Salmagundi* in 1807–1808. The following year he published the genially satirical *History of New York by Diedrich Knickerbocker*.

In 1819–1820, while in England, Irving wrote some essays under the pseudonym Geoffrey Crayon that appeared in *The Sketch Book*, which included Rip Van Winkle and Sleepy Hollow stories. It was followed by *Bracebridge Hall* on 1822. He then worked at American embassies in Madrid and London in 1826–1832 and wrote *History of Christopher Columbus*, *A Chronicle of the Conquest of Granada*, *Companions to Columbus*, and *Alhambra*.

After Irving returned to the United States, he began in 1835 to expand and change his Sunnyside country home near Tarrytown, New York, where he lived from 1836 to 1842, when he became U.S. minister to Spain. He served in the diplomatic post until 1846 and then came back to Sunnyside, where he lived until his death in 1859. It was at Sunnyside that he wrote such works as *Oliver Goldsmith*, *Mahomet and His Successors*, and *The Life of George Washington*, a five-volume study considered his greatest work.

Sunnyside originally was a two-room tenant farmhouse of pedestrian colonial architecture. Over the years, bachelor Irving transformed the cottage into an eclectic fairy-tale version of a Dutch bowery with a Spanish-style tower. The house and grounds, which have been restored to the way they were when Irving lived there, now are part of Historic Hudson Valley, a nonprofit educational and historic preservation organization overseeing a network of six historic structures along the Hudson River in the Tarrytown area.

Costumed guides in period hoop skirts and formal dress now take visitors on tours of the house and grounds. Families also can enjoy "Irving's Traveling Totes," which includes games for children, a scavenger hunt, a set of nineteenth-century-style dominoes, and a "Legend of Sleepy Hollow" picture book. The site also has a visitor center with exhibits and presents a special Sleepy Hollow program around Halloween and evening candlelight tours during the Christmas season.

Washington Irving's Sunnyside, 89 W. Sunnyside Lane, Tarrytown, NY 10591 (also contact: Historic Hudson Valley, 150 White Plains Rd., Tarrytown, NY 10591). Phones: Sunnyside—914/591-8763; Historic Hudson Valley—914/613-8200. Faxes: Sunnyside—914/591-4436; Historic Hudson Valley—914/631-0089. E-mail: mail@hudsonvalley.org. Website: www.hudsonvalley.org. Hours: Apr.–Oct.—11–5 Wed.–Mon.; closed Tues.; Nov.–late Dec.—10–4 Sat.–Sun.; closed Mon.–Fri. and late-Dec.–Mar. Admission: grounds—adults, $5; children 5–17, $3; children under 5, free; house tour—adults, $12; seniors, $10; children 5–17, $6; children under 5, free.

Washington Irving Trail Museum. The Washington Irving Trail Museum in Ripley, Oklahoma, is named in honor of the famed American writer who camped nearby in 1832 while traveling through central Oklahoma with Captain Jesse Bean and his U.S. Rangers on an exploratory trip. Irving, best known as the author of "Rip Van Winkle" and "The Legend of Sleep Hallow," described the journey through the frontier before it was settled in his book *A Tour of the Prairies*. The museum was named for Irving because it was established in 1994 at the site of his encampment. The museum is devoted to the history of the area and features Native American, pioneer, Civil War, and other historical artifacts and exhibits. Annual attendance is 7,500.

Washington Irving Trail Museum, 3918 S. Mehan Rd., Ripley, OK 74062-6278. Phone: 405/624-9130. E-mail: cchluber@aol.com. Website: www.washingtonirvingtrailmuseum.com. Hours: 10–5 Wed.–Sat., 1–5 Sun.; closed Mon.–Tues. and major holidays. Admission: free.

D. H. Lawrence

D. H. Lawrence Ranch. D. H. Lawrence was a noted English author, poet, playwright, essayist, and literary critic who came to the United States with his wife, Frieda, in 1922 and lived on a ranch near San Cristobal, New Mexico, in 1924–1925, which has become a Lawrence memorial. The couple returned to Europe in 1925, and Lawrence died of tuberculosis at the age of 44 in France in 1930. Frieda returned to the ranch after his death and lived there until she died in 1956. She bequeathed the ranch to the University of New Mexico, which now uses it as an educational and recreational retreat.

D. H. Lawrence was born David Herbert Richards Lawrence in Eastwood, England, in 1885. He suffered from bronchitis almost from birth. It was a condition that plagued him throughout his relatively short life. He was a good student, receiving a scholarship to Nottingham High School. His first novel, *The White Peacock*, was published in 1911. It was followed by *The Trespasser* in 1912, *Sons and Lovers* in 1913, and numerous short stories, articles, essays, and poetry. In 1914 he married Frieda. They planned to live in Italy, but the outbreak of World War I prevented the move.

Lawrence continued to write, with his novels dealing largely with female emancipation, class struggle, and sexual liberation. He is best known for his 1928 novel *Lady Chatterley's Lover*, which was considered shocking at the time. It became a test case in the 1960s over whether a book is literature or an obscene publication. It opened the door to a permissive society.

Lawrence and his wife came to the United States in 1922 after being invited by Mabel Dodge, a wealthy society hostess and arts patron who had taken up residence in Taos, after she had read some of his works. But after a conflict between the parties, the Lawrences returned to England. However, they came back to New Mexico as Mabel's guests in 1924, and she gave them the 160-acre Kiowa Ranch, about 20 miles northwest of Taos.

Lawrence and his wife lived on the ranch for nearly two years, during which time he worked on two novels, *St. Mawr* and *The Plumed Serpent*. He was diagnosed with tuberculosis in 1924, and the following year he and Frieda returned to Europe as his health improved and their visas were about to expire. They settled in Italy, and Lawrence died in France six years later.

After Lawrence was buried near Venice, Frieda returned to the New Mexico ranch. In 1935 Frieda had his remains exhumed, cremated, and the ashes brought to the ranch by Angelo Ravagli, whom Frieda had married in 1934. Ravagli also constructed the white plastered memorial building that honors Lawrence at the ranch.

D. H. Lawrence Ranch, State Rte. 522, San Cristobal, Taos, NM 27571. Phone: 505/271-2421. Hours: 8–5 daily. Admission: free.

Sinclair Lewis

Sinclair Lewis Boyhood Home. Sinclair Lewis was a leading novelist, short story writer, and playwright who was the first American to be awarded the Nobel Prize in Literature. He received the prize in 1930 "for his vigorous and graphic art of description and his ability to create, with wit and humor, new types of characters." Lewis, who wrote 23 novels, was known for his critical views of American society and capitalist values and his strong characterization of modern working women.

Lewis's greatest success was *Main Street*, a 1920 realistic novel about small-town life. It was followed by such other popular works as *Babbitt*, which satirized American commercial culture and boosterism (1922); *Arrowsmith*, about an idealistic doctor (1925); *Elmer Gentry*, which depicted evangelicalism as hypocritical (1927); and *Dodsworth*, about the affluent and successful leading essentially pointless lives despite their wealth and advantages (1929).

Many of Lewis's novels were based on his boyhood perceptions of small-town life in Sauk Centre, Minnesota, where he was born in 1885. The house was the center of social life in the frontier town, and he often would mimic the voices of guests. Lewis enrolled at Yale University in 1913 and began writing romantic poetry and short sketches and served as an editor of the *Yale Literary Magazine*. After graduation, Lewis moved about working for newspapers and publishing houses and writing articles for magazines.

Lewis's first published book was *Hike and the Aeroplane*, a 1912 Tom Swift–style novel written under the pseudonym Tom Graham. He then started to write serious novels under his own name, such as *Our Mr. Wrenn: The Romantic Adventures of a Gentle Man* in 1914 and *The Innocents: A Story for Lovers* in 1917. The 1920s stories that led to the Nobel Prize followed. He also won the Pulitzer Prize for his 1925 *Arrowsmith* novel but turned it down. The book later was made into a movie, as was his *Elmer Gentry*, for which Burt Lancaster won the Oscar for best acting. Lewis wrote nine more novels, including *It Can't Happen Here* in 1935, before his death in Italy in 1951.

Lewis's early life is featured at the Sinclair Lewis Boyhood Home in his hometown of Sauk Centre, Minnesota. The two-story wood-frame house where he spent his boyhood is located across the street from the home where he was born (now a private home). It contains period furnishings (some of which belonged to the Lewis family); Sinclair's small wooden bed, roll-top desk, and some of his manuscripts and books; his father's second-floor office with medical equipment; family china, photographs, and other memorabilia; and the carriage house where young Lewis began writing a diary and short stories. Guided tours are given of the site. Sauk Centre also has a Sinclair Lewis Interpretive Center (*see* separate listing) in a small building where the chamber of commerce has an office.

Sinclair Lewis Boyhood Home, 812 Sinclair Lewis Ave., Sauk Centre, MN 56378 (postal address: PO Box 25, Sauk Centre, MN 56378-0222). Phones: 320/352-5359 and 320/352-5201. Fax: 320/352-5202. E-mail: chamber@saukcentrechamber.com. Website: www.saukcentrechamber.com. Hours: June–Aug.—1–5 Tues.–Sat.; closed Sun.–Mon. and remainder of year. Admission: adults and students, $5; children 6–12, $2; children under 6, free.

The Sinclair Lewis Boyhood Home in Sauk Centre, Minnesota. Courtesy of the Sinclair Lewis Foundation, Sauk Centre Convention and Visitors Bureau.

Sinclair Lewis Interpretive Center. After Sinclair Lewis wrote his best-selling *Main Street* in 1920, the people in his home town of Sauk Centre, Minnesota, were shocked and angry because Sauk Creek was disguised as fictional Gopher Prairie and many of the residents recognized themselves as unsavory characters in the book. The book was even banned by the town library. But town got over it, and Lewis became a favorite son and celebrity that it honored.

Sauk Centre, where he was born in 1885, now has two museum-like facilities celebrating his early years in town and his literary achievements. They are the Sinclair Lewis Interpretive Center, which shares a small building with the chamber of commerce, and the Sinclair Lewis Boyhood Home (*see* separate listing) where he grew up. It also has a street and park named for him and holds an annual Sinclair Lewis Days celebration and Sinclair Lewis Writers' Conference. In addition, the street signs say "Original Main Street," and the high school athletic teams are now the "Main Streeters."

The interpretive center has exhibits about his early years in Sauk Centre and as a Nobel Prize–winning author. In addition to displays about life and career, the center has such objects on display as Lewis personal items, high school and college diplomas, family memorabilia, part of the notebook he used to collect names for characters in his novels, writing desk, death certificate, and the metal urn in which his ashes were returned to Sauk Centre from Italy, where he died. The interpretive center and the boyhood home have nearly 4,500 visitors annually.

Sinclair Lewis Interpretive Center, 1220 Main St., Sauk Centre, MN 56378 (postal address: PO Box 222, Sauk Centre, MN 56378-0222). Phone: 320/352-5201. Fax: 320/352-5202. E-mail: chamber@saukcentrechamber.com. Website: www.saukcentrechamber.com. Hours: Memorial Day–Labor Day—8:30–4:30 Mon.–Fri., 9–5 Sat.–Sun.; closed remainder of year. Admission: free.

Jack London

Jack London State Historic Park Museum. Jack London was a rugged adventurer who became the most popular and highest paid writer of the first decade of the twentieth century. He wrote more than 50 books and hundreds of short stories, articles, and letters—some of which became popular motion pictures. He based many of his stories on firsthand experiences at sea, in Alaska, and in the fields and factories of California.

London was a pioneer in the emerging field of commercial magazine fiction and one of the first Americans to make a lucrative career exclusively from writing. He is best remembered as the author of *The Call of the Wild* (1903), *Sea Wolf* (1904), and *White Fang* (1906). With his earnings, he purchased a ranch—which he called "Beauty Ranch"—in Glen Ellen, California, on the eastern slope of the Sonoma Mountains in 1905, where he and his second wife, Charmian, spent the rest of their lives and he did most of his writing. The ranch now is the site of the 1,400-acre Jack London State Historic Park, which has a museum about London's life and career.

London was born in San Francisco in 1876 and lived in Oakland most of his youth. He spent much of his time reading at the library but did not finish high school. In 1889 London began working at a cannery. This was followed by serving as an oyster pirate, becoming a member of the California Fish Patrol, and working on a sealing schooner off the coast of Japan. When he returned, the country was in the 1893 economic panic and labor unrest. London became a hobo before returning to Oakland to complete high school and begin writing articles for the school magazine.

In 1896–1897 Lewis became a socialist and attended the University of California, but he dropped out and joined the Klondike Gold Rush. His first successful stories were later set in the Yukon, including the popular "To Build a Fire." But he developed scurvy, survived the Klondike, and returned to California in 1898 and decided to pursue a writing career.

London's writing career began at the turn of the twentieth century. Many of his books and short stories dealt with adventure, brutality, murder, and suicide. London was so successful that he was able to buy the 1,000-acre ranch near Glen Ellen, California; travel widely (including a 27-month trip with his wife to the South Pacific and Australia); and build a 15,000-square-foot stone mansion called "Wolf House" on the ranch in 1911–1913. But the dream mansion was destroyed by fire as it was nearing completion.

London died on the ranch at the age of 40 in 1916. Charmian stayed at the ranch and built a new house, called the "House of Happy Walls," in 1919–1926. It is where she lived until her death in 1955. Her will directed that the House of Happy Walls be used as a memorial to Jack London and a museum housing his collection of photographs and exhibits about his life, adventures, and career.

In 1956 the ranch became the Jack London State Historic Park, with the House of Happy Walls serving as the museum. The park also contains London's cottage (where he did most of his writing), the charred remains of the Wolf House, and such ranch buildings as two barns/stables, concrete silos, a building London designed for pigs, and ruins of an old winery, In addition, the park has woodlands, a five-acre lake, a bathhouse, trails, and the grave sites of London and his wife. The house museum has some of the furniture planned for the Wolf House that burned, early manuscripts, memorabilia from London's travels, and exhibits about his life and works. Photographs and a video on London's life and adventures can be seen at the cottage, where London had his study. The annual attendance is approximately 90,000.

Jack London State Historic Park and Museum, 2400 London Ranch Rd., Glen Ellen, CA 95442-9749. Phone and fax: 707/938-5216. E-mail: jacklondonshp@gmail.com. Website: www.jacklondonpark.com. Hours: park—10–5 Sat.–Wed.; museum—10–4 Sat.–Wed.; both closed Thurs.–Fri., New Year's Day, Thanksgiving, and Christmas. Admission: $8 per car; $7 for seniors.

Herman Melville

Herman Melville House. Author Herman Melville wrote his most famous novel, *Moby-Dick*, and three other novels at the Herman Melville House, known as "Arrowhead," in Pittsfield, Massachusetts, in the Berkshire Mountains. He and his family lived in the 1783 farmhouse from 1850 to 1863. The site was called "Arrowhead" because of the great number of arrowheads dug up around the property during planting season. It also is where he wrote *Pierre*, *The Confidence Man*, and *Israel Potter*.

Melville made his first trip to Pittsfield in 1832 when he visited his Uncle Thomas. He fell in love with the uncle's farm and the view of Mount Greylock and continued to make annual visits until 1850 when he decided to move his family to Pittsfield. Despite *Moby-Dick*, which was not well received during Melville's lifetime, he did not make a living from his writing at Arrowhead and moved to New York City 13 years later to work as a customs inspector. He never wrote prose again, just poetry.

Melville was born in New York City in 1819 and went to sea as a cabin boy in 1839, sailed on a whaler in 1840, deserted the ship in the Marquesas Islands and found temporary refuge among cannibal natives, escaped on an Australian whaler, and became a seaman on the USS *United States* frigate in 1843–1844. He wrote five novels based on his experiences at sea, including *Moby-Dick*, which tells about a sailor and his voyage on a whaling ship during which a giant white sperm whale destroys Captain Ahab's ship and bites off his leg. Although not appreciated at Melville's time, it has become one of the masterpieces of American literature.

Melville's first book was published in 1846. It was *Typee: A Peep at Polynesian Life*, which describes a love affair with a beautiful native girl. It became a best seller and was followed by *Omoo: A Narrative of Adventures in the South Seas* (1847), *Mardi: And a Voyage Thither* (1849), *Redburn: His First Voyage* (1849), and *White-Jacket, or The World in a Man-of-War* (1850). Melville wrote other novels, short stories, and poems but struggled financially until his death in 1891.

Arrowhead was sold by Melville to his brother, Allan, in 1863 and remained in family ownership until 1927. It was purchased by the Berkshire County Historical Society in 1975 and restored, and now it is operated as a historic house museum. The 44-acre site, which was designated a National Historic Landmark in 1962, includes the Melville's house, a barn, and a nature trail through the woods. The house contains some of the Melville family's furnishings, clothing, and memorabilia, as well as a video about Berkshire during the time Melville lived there. The historical society, which has its office in the historic home, also presents special exhibitions on historical topics at the site. The annual attendance is 4,500.

Herman Melville House, Berkshire County Historical Society, 780 Holmes Rd., Pittsfield, MA 01201. Phone: 413/442-1793. Fax: 413/443-1449. E-mail: info@mobydick.org. Website: www.mobydick.org. Hours: Memorial Day–Oct.—10:30–4 Fri.–Wed.; closed Thurs.; remainder of year—by appointment. Admission: adults, $12; children 6–18, $8; children under 6, free.

James A. Michener

James A. Michener Art Museum. Author James A. Michener wrote more than 40 fiction and nonfiction books—most of which are best-selling sweeping historical sagas that span many generations in a particular region. But he also was an art collector and a major donor to an art museum in Doylestown, Pennsylvania, that now bears his name—the James A. Michener Art Museum. A section of the museum also is devoted to his life and career.

The James A. Michener Art Museum in Doylestown, Pennsylvania. Courtesy of the Education Department, James A. Michener Art Museum.

The museum, which opened in 1988, is located in the renovated 1884 Bucks County Prison, which was about to be torn down when the county commissioners agreed to preserve the historic landmark and lease it for an art museum dedicated to the art and culture of the region. Since then, it has been expanded twice. It now has an impressive collection of Pennsylvania impressionism and a representative works by other artists. Michener, who said the visual arts inspired his writing, dreamed of a regional art museum in the early 1960s and later gave financial support, works from his art collection, and other materials to the museum.

In 1992 the museum was renamed for Michener, Doylestown's favorite son, who lived much of his life in the area and became one of the nation's most prolific and gifted writers. The museum has a permanent exhibit about Michener titled *James A. Michener: A Living Legacy*. It re-creates his Bucks County office, where he wrote *Tales of the South Pacific*, for which he received the Pulitzer Prize in 1948 and which was adapted for the Broadway and film musical *South Pacific*. The exhibit contains the desk, chair, typewriter, dictionary, books, and other objects from his office where he lived and worked for more than 35 years. The museum archive also has original artwork created by Michener, photographs, maps, postcards, his stamp collection, and materials from his service as a NASA advisory board member.

Michener sold an estimated 75 million copies of his books worldwide. They include such early works as *The Fires of Spring* (1949), *Sayonara* (1954), and *The Drifters* (1971), as well as those historically based books for which he became best known, such as *Hawaii* (1959), *Iberia* (1968), *Centennial* (1974), *Texas* (1985), *Alaska* (1988), *Caribbean* (1989), and *Mexico* (1992).

Michener, who died in 1997, lived his final years in Texas, where he founded the Michener Center for Writers at the University of Texas. He gave away much of the money he earned, contributing more than $100 million to universities, libraries, museums, and other charitable causes.

James A. Michener Art Museum, 138 S. Pine St., Doylestown, PA 18901-4931. Phone: 215/340-9800. Fax: 215/340-9807. E-mail: jamam1@michenerartmuseum.org. Website: www.michenerartmuseum.org. Hours: Memorial Day–Labor Day—10–4:30 Tues. and Thurs.–Fri., 10–9 Wed., 10–5 Sat., 12–5 Sun.; Sept.–May—10–4:30 Tues.–Fri., 10–5 Sat., 12–5 Sun. Admission: adults, $10; seniors, $9; college students, $7.50; children 6–18, $5; children under 6, free.

Margaret Mitchell

Margaret Mitchell House and Museum. The 1899 Tudor Revival house in Atlanta where Margaret Mitchell wrote *Gone with the Wind*, one of the most popular books of all time, now is a historic house museum honoring the 1937 Pulitzer Prize winner. Mitchell and her husband, John Marsh, lived in an apartment in the single-family home that was converted into a 10-unit apartment building in 1919. They moved into the apartment in 1925. The three-story house remained an apartment building until 1978, when it was abandoned. But a group of preservationists saved the house in 1985 and restored it, with only Mitchell's apartment keeping its original architectural features. The house was damaged by two fires and then restored in the 1990s, and now it is one of the treasured landmarks in Atlanta.

Gone with the Wind, about a love/hate relationship between a manipulative woman and a roguish man in the South during the Civil War and Reconstruction, was an overnight success. But it was almost never published. Mitchell, who was born in Atlanta in 1900, dropped out of Smith College and became a newspaperwoman. In 1918 she became one of the first female columnists in the South, writing a weekly column for the *Atlanta Journal*. In the early 1920s, she wrote articles, interviews, sketches, and book reviews. Mitchell got married in 1922 and then divorced and married Marsh, who was the best man at her first wedding. He encouraged and assisted her with her writing, which was largely for her own amusement and a secret to her friends.

Between 1925 and 1930, Mitchell worked on parts of a voluminous manuscript that later became the 1,037-page *Gone with the Wind*. It was not until 1935, however, when Macmillan editor Harold Latham visited Atlanta and Mitchell agreed to escort him around the city that she returned to the book. Latham became enchanted with Mitchell and asked if she had ever written a book. If she had, he would like to see it. After some hesitation, she gathered together pieces of the huge, disjointed, and incomplete manuscript and gave it to Latham before he left. He immediately saw that the novel had great potential. She finished the manuscript in 1936, and it became a blockbuster, winning the Pulitzer Prize in 1937 and eventually selling more than 30 million copies.

Gone with the Wind was made into a motion picture staring Clark Gable and Vivien Leigh in 1939 that became the highest grossing film in history. It received a record 10 Academy of Motion Picture Arts and Sciences awards. A museum, called "Scarlett on the Square," in nearby Marietta, Georgia, is devoted to the film. It contains screenplays, costumes, and other materials from the movie.

Margaret Mitchell died in 1949 without writing another book. She was struck by a speeding car driven by a drunken driver while she crossing the street in Atlanta. For years, it was thought that she had written only one complete novel. But a second novel, *Lost Laysen*, surfaced in the 1990s. Written in two notebooks in 1916, it was found among a collection of letters Mitchell had given to a suitor, Henry Love Angel, in the early 1920s. The manuscript, a romance set in the South Pacific, was found by Angel's son, authenticated, and published in 1996.

The Margaret Mitchell Museum, which was founded in 1990, contains little, except the walls, that was original in the three-room apartment she called "the dump." The apartment has been restored with period furnishings to the way it would have been in the 1920s. The house also has displays of Mitchell family photographs, letters, and memorabilia. A visitor center, which offers guided tours, contains an introductory video and exhibits of photographs, her life, and the *Gone with the Wind* book and movie. The two-block site around the house is listed on the National Register of Historic Places. The museum has an annual attendance of 50,000.

Margaret Mitchell House, 990 Peachtree St., Atlanta, GA 30309-3964. Phone: 404/249-7015. Fax: 404/249-7118. E-mail: john@gwtw.org. Website: www.margaretmitchellhouse.com. Hours: 10–5:30 Mon.–Sat., 12–5:30 Sun.; closed New Year's Day, Thanksgiving, and Christmas Eve and Day. Admission: adults, $12; seniors and students, $9; children 4–12, $5; children under 4, free.

Edgar Allan Poe

Edgar Allan Poe National Historical Site. Edgar Allan Poe was a writer, poet, editor, and literary critic in the nineteenth century who was best known for his tales of mystery and the macabre. Part of the American romantic movement, he was one of the nation's earliest short story writers and among the first Americans to write detective and science fiction. His life and works are now celebrated at four sites, including the Edgar Allan Poe National Historic Site in Philadelphia.

Poe was one of the first prominent American writers to try to earn a living through writing. But he was always in financial difficulty and moved frequently. Many of his works are of the dark romanticism genre, dealing with death, decomposition, premature burial, the dead, and mourning. But he also wrote satires, humorous stories, and hoaxes and was best known for his literary criticism.

Poe was born in Boston in 1809. He was orphaned when his mother died shortly after his father abandoned the family. He was raised by the family of John Allan, a successful Scottish merchant in Richmond, Virginia, who took him in and gave him the name of "Edgar Allan Poe" but never formally adopted him. Poe went with the Allan family to England and Scotland in 1815–1816.

He then enrolled at the University of Virginia but dropped out after one semester after becoming estranged from his foster father over gambling debts and support (and was disowned in 1830 after frequent quarrels). Unable to support himself, Poe enlisted in the army, rose to the rank of sergeant major for artillery, and was admitted to the U.S. military academy at West Point (where he was court martialed and dismissed in 1831 for gross neglect of duty and disobedience of orders).

Poe began his writing career in 1926 with an anonymous collection of poems, *Tamerlane and Other Poems*, which received little attention. He then spent a number of years working for literary journals and periodicals, began turning from poetry to prose, and moved about to such cities as Baltimore, Philadelphia, and New York. In 1845 Poe published his most famous poem, "The Raven." It was followed by such tales as "The Fall of the House of Usher," "The Gold-Bug," "The Murders in the Rue Morgue," and "The Purloined Letter." The only complete novel he ever wrote was *The Narrative of Arthur Gordon Pym of Nantucket* in 1838.

Poe died in 1849 at the age of 40 after being found delirious on the streets of Baltimore. His death still remains a mystery, although alcoholism was among the causes suspected. His medical records were lost and he never became coherent enough to explain what happened or why he was wearing clothes that were not his own.

The Edgar Allan Poe National Historic Site is based in the only house that remains of the several where Poe lived in Philadelphia and wrote 31 stories in 1837–1844. It is believed that he, his first cousin/wife, Virginia, and aunt/mother-in-law, Maria Clemm, lived in the house for a year or less. They previously lived together in Baltimore (*see* separate listing).

The house was saved in 1933 and refurbished to look like it did in Poe's time by Richard Gimbel, son of the founder of the Gimbels department store. He left the property to the city in his will. The National Park Service was later given custody and reopened the home as a historic site in 1980. The site now includes two adjoining houses that contain exhibits, a film room, and a collection of Poe's works and criticism, as well as audio interpretations if his writings and a welcome area and store. Ranger-led tours are offered and special themed events relating to

Poe's life and works are presented. The site is affiliated with the Independence National Historical Park. The annual attendance is 18,500.

Edgar Allan Poe National Historic Site, 530-32 N. 7th St., Philadelphia, PA 19123 (postal address: 143 S. 3rd St., Philadelphia, PA 19106-2818). Phone: 215/597-8780. Fax: 215/861-4950. Website: www.nps.gov/edal. Hours: 9–5 Wed.–Sun.; closed Mon.–Tues., New Year's Day, Veterans Day, Thanksgiving, and Christmas. Admission: free.

Edgar Allan Poe House and Museum. The 1830s row house in Baltimore where the Edgar Allan Poe House and Museum is located was the writer's home during part of the decade. The small two-and-a-half-story house was rented by Poe's widowed aunt, Maria Clemm, in 1832. Poe moved in at the age of 23 in 1832. Others living in the house at the time were Clemm's 10-year-old daughter, Virginia; his invalid grandmother, Elizabeth Cairnes Poe; and possibly his brother, William Henry Leonard Poe. Edgar occupied a small room in the attic for three years, where it is believed he wrote seven stories and four poems.

In 1835 Poe left Baltimore for Richmond to become assistant editor of a literary periodical. However, he was fired within weeks for drunkenness and returned to the Clemm home in Baltimore. That same year he married Virginia, although she was his first cousin and only 13 years of age. After showing signs of tuberculosis in 1842, she died in 1847 while they were living in the "Poe Cottage" in the Bronx, New York (*see* separate listing). Poe, his wife, and her mother are now buried under a monument erected in his honor in Westminster Graveyard in downtown Baltimore.

The municipal-operated Edgar Allan Poe House and Museum was founded in 1923 in the house where Poe once lived. In the 1930s the house was saved from destruction when the area was being cleared for the Poe Homes public housing project. It became the home of the Edgar Allan Poe Society of Baltimore, which opened it to the public in 1949 and now works with the Baltimore City Preservation Commission in operating the modest museum.

The museum—now a National Historic Landmark—contains such items as a lock of Poe's hair, reproductions of a portrait of Poe's wife and other Poe-related images, original china from John Allan's family, reprints of an announcement of a new literary magazine being started by Poe, and an obituary about Poe's death from a Philadelphia newspaper in 1849. The museum and the Poe Society also offer lectures, audiovisual presentations, tours of the Poe grave and catacombs, and annual special events honoring Poe, including what is said to be the largest Poe birthday celebration, held every January at Westminster Hall and the burial ground. The museum's annual attendance is 6,000.

Edgar Allan Poe House and Museum, 203 N. Amity St., Baltimore, MD 21223-2501 (postal address: Suite 1037, 417 E. Fayette St., Baltimore, MD 21202-3431). Phone: 410/396-7932. Fax: 410/396-5662. Website: www.ci.baltimore. md.us/government/history/poehouse.htm. Hours: Jan.–Mar.—closed for renovation; Apr.–Nov.—12–3:30 Wed.–Sat.; closed Sun.–Tues., Dec.–Mar., and national holidays. Admission: adults, $3; military, their families, and children under 13, free.

Edgar Allan Poe Museum. The Edgar Allan Poe Museum in Richmond, Virginia, was founded in 1922 by a group of residents who originally urged the city council in 1909 to erect a statue of Poe on the 100th anniversary of his birth but were turned down because he was considered a disreputable person. Poe came to the city from Boston, where he was born. He became orphaned after his father abandoned the family and his mother died. He spent his childhood and youth with John Allan, a Scottish merchant, and his wife, Frances, a Richmond couple who became his guardians in the early 1800s. Allan became estranged from Poe in 1826 because of his gambling debts and disowned him in 1830 after bitter quarrels.

Poe moved to other cities but returned to Richman in 1835–1837 to work as an assistant editor at the *Southern Literary Messenger*, where he was fired for being drunk and then rehired. He became an effective staff member who published poems, book reviews, critiques, and stories before leaving Richmond. Poe then began to write prose instead of poems and published the only novel he ever finished, *The Narrative of Arthur Gordon Pym of Nantucket*, in 1838. After several other magazine editing jobs, he tried to start his own journal, *The Stylus*, in Philadelphia in 1840, but it never materialized. He continued to write dark tales and poems, including his most famous work, "The Raven," in 1845, before his death in New York City in 1849. Today, Poe is remembered for his tales of mystery and the macabre and for being among the earliest American writers of short stories and detective and science fiction.

Unlike the three other museums devoted to Poe's life and career, the Edgar Allan Poe Museum in Richmond is not located in a building where he once lived. It is housed in four buildings only blocks away from where he first lived and worked, and near where his mother, Eliza Poe, is buried in Richmond. The museum, which began at the ca. 1737–1740 Old Stone House, was saved and opened in 1922 by the Association for the Preservation of Virginia Antiquities.

The Old Stone House, now operated by the Poe Foundation, contains furniture from homes in which Poe and his sister, Rosalie Mackenzie, lived. The other buildings feature many of Poe's first and early editions, including "The Raven" and his first poetry book, *Tamerlane and Other Poems;* manuscripts and early daguerreotypes and portraits; Poe's vest, trunk, and walking stick; a lock of Poe's hair; and such memorabilia as movie posters, advertisements, and toys featuring Poe and his works. One of the buildings is used for changing special exhibitions about Poe and his works, and a courtyard has a garden inspired by Poe's poem "To One in Paradise." The annual attendance is 17,000.

Edgar Allan Poe Museum, 19-14-16 E. Main St., Richmond, VA 23223-6964. Phone: 804/648-5524. Fax: 804/648-8729. E-mail: info@poemuseum.org. Website: www.poemuseum.org. Hours: 10–5 Tues.–Sat., 11–5 Sun.; closed Mon., New Year's Day, and Christmas. Admission: adults, $6; seniors and students over 8, $5; children under 9, free.

Edgar Allan Poe Cottage. Edgar Allan Poe spent the last years of his life—from 1846 to 1849—at the "Poe Cottage" in the Bronx, New York. The small wooden farmhouse built around 1812 was located in a bucolic setting that overlooked rolling hills to the shores of Long Island. It was the last surviving house of the old village of Fordham. The cottage now is the site of a museum, founded in 1955, called the Edgar Allan Poe Cottage. It is one of four museums devoted to Poe's life and works in the cities of Richmond, Baltimore, Philadelphia, and the Bronx (*see* separate listings).

Born in Boston in 1809, Poe moved quite frequently as he pursed a writing career. He came to New York City in 1844 with his wife, Virginia, and mother-in-law, Maria Clemm, in search of international fame. In 1846 he moved to the Bronx, where he wrote such poetic works as "Annabel Lee," "The Bells," and "Eureka." But he came to the Bronx cottage primarily because his wife, Virginia, was ill with tuberculosis and he hoped the country air would help her failing health. But she died in January 1847. His death followed two years later in Baltimore.

The City of New York bought the cottage in 1913 and moved it across the street to the Poe Park, which was created in 1902. In 1917 the cottage was restored and opened as a historic house museum by the Bronx Society of Arts and Sciences. Since 1975 it has been operated by the Bronx County Historical Society, which has refurnished and restored the site to represent 1840s New York life and Poe's life at the time.

The cottage contains period furniture, including some original pieces, such as Poe's rocking chair and the bed in which Virginia died. The museum also has a film presentation and guided tours. A visitor center designed by noted architect Toshiko Mori is being developed for Poe Park. The annual attendance is 42,000.

Edgar Allan Poe Cottage, Poe Park, Grand Crossing at E. Kingsbridge Rd., Bronx, NY 10458 (postal address: Bronx County Historical Society, 3309 Bainbridge Ave., Bronx, NY 10467-2840). Phone: 718/881-8900. Fax: 718/881-4827. E-mail: kmcauley@bronxhistoricalsociety.org. Website: www.bronxhistoricalsociety.org. Hours: 10–4 Sat., 1–5 Sun.; closed Mon.–Fri., but group tours by appointment. Admission: adults, $3; seniors, students, and children, $2.

Carl Sandburg

See Poets section.

Mari Sandoz

Mari Sandoz High Plains Heritage Center. The life and literature of Mari Susette Sandoz and the culture of the High Plains region are celebrated at the Mari Sandoz High Plains Heritage Center in Chadron, Nebraska. Sandoz was a novelist and biographer who was one of Nebraska's foremost writers during the first half of the twentieth century. She is best known for her extensive writings about pioneer life and the Plains Indians.

Born in 1896 to Swiss immigrants on a farm in the Sandhills section of Nebraska, she had a hard early life. She developed snow blindness in one eye after spending a day digging the family's cattle out of a snowdrift, never went to high school, had an unhappy teenage marriage to a neighboring rancher, held a series of low-paying jobs, suffered from poor health, and initially wrote with little success—once burning more than 70 of her manuscripts in a wash tub in her backyard in frustration. Yet she overcame such obstacles and disappointments to graduate from college, become a successful teacher and lecturer, and produce some of the best early writing about pioneer life on the prairies and Plains Indians.

Sandoz's breakthrough came in the mid-1930s when *Old Jules,* a biography of her father's difficult life, leadership in a pioneer community, and friendly relations with local Indians, won a nonfiction book contest and became a

Book of the Month Club selection. It was followed by *Slogum House* in 1937 and *Capital City* in 1939—controversial books about rural Nebraskans and life in Lincoln. In 1942 she wrote a monumental biography of Crazy Horse, the great Lakota leader, *Crazy Horse: The Strange Man of the Oglalas*, which is considered her greatest work. It was followed by a series of other books about the Plains Indians, including *Cheyenne Autumn* (1953), *The Buffalo Hunters* (1954), *The Horsecatcher* (1957), *The Cattlemen* (1958), *The Story Catcher* (1963), and *The Beaver Men* (1964).

The Mari Sandoz High Plains Heritage Center, opened in 2002 by Chadron State College, traces Sandoz's life and has collections and exhibits of archival materials, records, documents, books, specimens, and artifacts of the region. The center features exhibit galleries, a preservation/preparation workroom with a digital imaging laboratory, and an archival library. Outside are an arboretum, gardens, and a hiking/biking heritage trail. Annual attendance is 8,000.

Mari Sandoz High Plains Heritage Center, Chadron State College, 1000 Main St., Chadron, NE 69337-2667. Phone: 308/432-6401. Fax: 308/432-6464. Website: www.sndozcenter.com. Hours: 8–12 and 1–4 Mon.–Fri., 9–12 and 1–4 Sat.; closed Sun. and college holidays. Admission: free.

John Steinbeck

National Steinbeck Center. The National Steinbeck Center in Salinas, California, honors John Steinbeck, a leading novelist, short story writer, and war correspondent who received the 1940 Pulitzer Prize for *The Grapes of Wrath* and the 1962 Nobel Prize in Literature for "realistic and imaginative writing, combining as it does sympathetic humor and keen social perception." During his career, he wrote 27 books, including 16 novels, six nonfiction books, and five collections of short stories. The National Steinbeck Center in Salinas is dedicated to Steinbeck and has exhibits and collections about his life and works.

Steinbeck was born in Salinas in 1902 and grew up in the culturally diverse Salinas Valley. Most of his early writings dealt with familiar subjects from his formative years in California. He later wrote about American historical conditions and events that he experienced as a journalist. Steinbeck's stories often dealt with struggling characters, such as working-class and migrant workers during the Dust Bowl and Great Depression periods of the 1930s. His later books were devoted to a wide range of other topics.

Steinbeck developed an early love for reading the written word, fostered largely by his mother, a former teacher. But his writing career did not begin until he dropped out of Stanford University in 1925 and went to New York City. When he failed to get any of his work published, he returned to California, settled in nearby Pacific Grove, and married the first of three wives.

Steinbeck's first published novel was *Cup of Gold* in 1927, followed by three other books before his first critical success, *Tortilla Flat*, a 1935 novel about a group of classless and usually homeless young men after World War I. The novel later was made into a 1942 motion picture—the first of 17 movies based on Steinbeck works.

In the next four years, Steinbeck wrote three California-oriented novels set among common people during the Dust Bowl and Great Depression—*In Dubious Battle* (1936), *Of Mice and Men* (1937), and *The Grapes of Wrath* (1939). *Of Mice and Men*, about the dreams of two migrant laborers working in California, became a Broadway play and a film, and *The Grapes of Wrath*, dealing with the plight of Dust Bowl migrants, won the Pulitzer Prize and is considered Steinbeck's best work.

During World War II, Steinbeck served as a war correspondent for the *New York Herald Tribune*, worked with the Office of Strategic Services (predecessor of the Central Intelligence Agency), and participated in some commando raids. He suffered a number of wounds from shrapnel and psychological trauma but recovered and wrote such other highly regarded works as *Cannery Row* (1945), *East of Eden* (1952), and *The Winter of Our Discontent* (1961) before his death in 1968.

The National Steinbeck Center, which opened in 1998, traces Steinbeck's life and career and seeks to further learning about literature, human nature, history, agriculture, and the arts. The center serves as a museum, archive, and educational center. It has a 12,000-square-foot exhibit space devoted to Steinbeck's life, works, and philosophy and a wing concerning the experiences of agricultural workers in the United States (a subject of great interest to Steinbeck).

The center contains 30,000 objects, manuscripts, letters, photographs, oral history tapes, screenplays, and reviews related to Steinbeck's life and writings and presents temporary exhibitions, lectures, literary programs, art activities, and an annual Steinbeck Festival. The center's annual attendance is 70,000.

National Steinbeck Center, 1 Main St., Salinas, CA 93901-3436. Phone: 831/775-4721. Fax: 831/796-3828. E-mail: info@steinbeck.org. Website: www.steinbeck.org. Hours: 10–5 daily; closed New Year's Day, Thanksgiving, and Christmas. Admission: adults, $10.95; seniors, military, and students, $8.95; youth 13–17, $7.95; children 6–12, $5.95; and children under 6, free.

Steinbeck House. The 1897 Steinbeck House in Salinas, California, was the 1902 birthplace and boyhood home of Pulitzer and Nobel Prize–winning author John Steinbeck. The Queen Anne–style Victorian house now is a luncheon restaurant that also functions as a museum with Steinbeck memorabilia, photographs, and tours. It has been operated since 1974 by the nonprofit Village Guild. The proceeds go to Salinas Valley charities and to maintain the Steinbeck House, which is located two blocks from the National Steinbeck Center (*see* separate listing).

Steinbeck House, 132 Central Ave., Salinas, CA 93901-2651. Phone: 408/424-2737. Website: www.steinbeck-house.com. Hours: by appointment. Admission: adults, $5; seniors, students, and retired military, $3; children under 6 and active military, free.

Robert Louis Stevenson

Robert Louis Stevenson Silverado Museum. Robert Louis Stevenson was a Scottish novelist, essayist, and poet who wrote such classics as *Treasure Island, Kidnapped, Dr. Jekyll and Mr. Hyde,* and *A Child's Garden of Verses.* He spent part of his career in the United States after meeting Fanny Osborne, a married woman from California, at an artists' colony in France in 1876. They fell in love, and he followed her back to the United States. They got married in 1880 and spent their summer honeymoon in an abandoned bunkhouse at the old Silverado Mine on the slopes of Mount St. Helena. Nothing remains of the old cabin, but the area now is part of the Robert Louis Stevenson State Park. Stevenson later wrote about their experiences in *The Silverado Squatters.* The Robert Louis Stevenson Silverado Museum, founded in St. Helena in 1969, is devoted to the author's life and works.

Stevenson was born in Edinburgh, Scotland, in 1850. He was a sickly person most of his life, and spent many years looking for a place that would help his health. It was believed that he had tuberculosis. As a result, Stevenson and his wife left California and searched in vain from 1880 to 1887 for a suitable place to live in Scotland, England, and Europe. It was during this period that he produced the bulk of his most famous works.

Treasure Island, a tale of piracy, buried treasure, and adventure, was published in 1883, and *Kidnapped,* a historical novel about a boy's pursuit of his inheritance and involved in the Jacobite troubles in Scotland, and the *Strange Case of Dr. Jekyll and Mr. Hyde,* a novella about a dual personality, followed in 1886. His best-known works of poetry, *A Child's Garden of Verses* (1885) and *Underwoods* (1887), also appeared during this period.

In 1887, on the advice of his physician to find a complete change of climate, Stevenson planned to go to Colorado but decided to spend the winter at Saranac Lake in the Adirondacks after arriving in New York City (*see* separate listing). The following summer, he and his family chartered a yacht and sailed from San Francisco to the eastern and central Pacific Ocean. His health improved greatly from the salt sea air and the thrill of adventure, and they wandered around the Pacific for nearly three years.

As a result, Stevenson purchased 400 acres in 1890 in Upolu, one of the Samoan islands in the South Pacific, where he and his wife lived until his death in 1894. It also is where he continued to write such works as *The Beach of Falesa, Catriona, The Ebb-Tide,* and *Vailima Letters.* He was loved and called "Tusitala" (storyteller) by the island natives, who carried his body to nearby Mount Vaea, where they buried him overlooking the sea.

The Robert Louis Stevenson Silverado Museum in St. Helena was founded in 1969 by Norman H. Strouse, a retired advertising executive who became an admirer and ardent Stevenson collector after reading *The Silverado Squatters.* The museum, now operated by the Vailima Foundation, originally was located in the Hatchery, an old stone building, and then moved to a new wing at the St. Helena Public Library Center in 1879.

The museum tells about Stevenson's life and career and contains first editions of his works, manuscripts, letters, memorabilia, paintings, photographs, and sculptures relating to Stevenson. It has guided tours and presents changing special exhibitions, lectures, and other educational programs. It has about 4,000 visitors annually.

Robert Louis Stevenson Silverado Museum, 1490 Library Lane, St. Helena, CA 94574-1143 (postal address: PO Box 409, St. Helens, CA 94574-0409). Phone: 707/963-3757. Fax: 707/963-0917. E-mail: dorothy@silveradomuseum.org. Website: www.silveradomuseum.org. Hours: 12–4 Wed.–Sun.; closed Mon.–Tues. and major holidays. Admission: free.

Robert Louis Stevenson House. The Robert Louis Stevenson House in Monterey, California, is where the Scottish writer stayed while courting Fanny Osbourne in 1879 and then marrying her in 1880. It is a 1830s two-story adobe that was a rooming house known as the French Hotel at the time. He lived there four months, waiting for his future wife's divorce to be finalized. Stevenson worked on *The Amateur Immigrant,* which dealt with the first leg of his trip to America (not published until 1895), and wrote about his stay in Monterey in *The Old and New Pacific Capitals* (1882).

The historic building was saved from destruction by two women in 1937 and presented to the State of California. It now is part of the Monterey State Historic Park. It contains period furnishings, first-edition books, manuscripts, and personal belongings of the famed novelist and offers guided tours. The annual attendance is 25,000.

Robert Louis Stevenson House, 530 Houston St., Monterey, CA 93940-3226 (postal address: 20 Customs House Plaza, Monterey, CA 93942). Phone: 831/649-7118. Fax: 831/647-6236. Website: www.historicmonterey.org. Hours: 8–4 daily; closed New Year's Day, Thanksgiving, and Christmas. Admission: free.

Robert Louis Stevenson Memorial Cottage Museum. The cottage in Saranac Lake, New York, where Scottish author Robert Louis Stevenson spent the winter of 1887–1888 is now a literary museum called the Robert Louis Stevenson Memorial Cottage Museum. Stevenson and his family arrived from Scotland, spent the winter in the Adirondacks, and planned to go to Colorado Springs in the spring. Instead, they went to San Francisco and Stevenson chartered a boat that took his family on a Pacific Ocean voyage that lasted nearly three years—and later resulted in Stevenson living the rest of his life on a Samoan island.

The decision to spend the winter in Saranac Lake was made in New York City after he heard promising reports from friends about Dr. Edward Livingston Trudeau and his progressive Adirondack Cottage Sanatorium. He decided to make the side trip to the mountains of upstate New York to find relief from a pulmonary disease. Stevenson reportedly felt better after the stay and decided to take the ocean cruise.

The cabin where Stevenson stayed—known as the Baker Cabin—was turned into a museum in 1916. The museum contains the original furniture, personal memorabilia, early photographs, letters, Stevenson's velvet smoking jacket, and books and articles by and about Stevenson. It has about 500 visitors a year.

Robert Louis Stevenson Memorial Cottage Museum, 44 Stevenson Lane, Saranac Lake, NY 12983-1975 (postal address: PO Box 607, Saranac Lake, NY 12983-0607). Phone: 518/891-1462. Website: www.n3carts.org/stevenson. Hours: July–Columbus Day—9:30–12 and 1–4:30 Tues.–Sun. and by appointment; closed Mon. and remainder of the year. Admission: adults, $5; children under 12, free.

Harriet Beecher Stowe

Harriet Beecher Stowe Center. Harriet Beecher Stowe achieved international fame with the publication of her antislavery novel *Uncle Tom's Cabin* in 1852. It was one of more than 30 books she wrote on a broad range of subjects, including homemaking, childrearing, religion, biographies, and children's books and dealing with such controversial subjects as slavery, religious reform, and gender roles. Her writing career spanned 51 years and included novels, short stories, poems, articles, and hymns. She spent the last 23 years of life in Hartford, Connecticut, where the Harriet Beecher Stowe Center now celebrates her life and works.

Stowe was born in Litchfield, Connecticut, in 1811. She grew up in a large and prolific family that included religious leaders, educators, writers, and antislavery and rights advocates. She attended the seminary operated by her sister and moved to Cincinnati in 1832 to join her father, the Rev. Lyman Beecher, who had become president of Lane Theological Seminary (*see* separate listing). She was a teacher at the seminary, where she met and married Calvin Ellis Stowe, a professor at the seminary and critic of slavery, in 1836. They later moved to Brunswick, Maine, where her husband taught at Bowdoin College, and lived there until 1853.

Stowe began to write while in Cincinnati and had her first work published, *The Mayflower: Sketches of Scenes and Characters Among the Descendants of the Pilgrims*, in 1834. When Congress passed the Fugitive Slave Law in 1850, she wrote the first installment of *Uncle Tom's Cabin*, about the hard life of African Americans under slavery and a call for freedom and equality, for an antislavery journal. After the two-part series ran in the journal, it was published as a best-selling book in 1852 and became a factor leading to the Civil War. The book sparked a national debate, galvanizing the abolition movement in the North and provoking proslavery forces in the South.

In 1853 the Stowes moved to Andover, Massachusetts, where Calvin Stowe served as professor of theology at Andover Theological Seminary until 1864. During this period, Harriet wrote such works as *Dred: A Tale of the Great Dismal Swamp*, *The Minister's Wife*, and *The Pearl of Orr's Island*.

After retirement, the Stowes moved to Hartford and built a house on Nook Farm, a neighborhood of friends and relatives. In 1873 they moved into a Victorian Gothic revival brick cottage-style house on nearby Forest Street, where Harriet lived until her death in 1896. While in Hartford, she wrote such works as *The American Woman's Home* (1868), *Lady Byron Vindicated* (1871), and *Pogunuc People* (1878).

The Stowe home became part of the Harriet Beecher Stowe Center, founded in 1941. The center preserves and interprets the home and the center's collections, promotes discussion of her life and work, and seeks to further social justice and positive change. In addition to the Stowe home, the center consists of the adjacent 1884 Katharine Seymour Day House, an 1873 visitor center, Victorian-style gardens, and the Stowes' Nook Farm neighborhood.

The center's collections include approximately 6,000 objects and over 200,000 manuscripts, pamphlets, books, and images. It also has a library collection of over 180,000 manuscripts, 12,000 books, 4,000 pamphlets, and 12,000 photographs, prints, broadsheets, posters, and drawings. The collections contain Stowe/Beecher family furnishings and Stowe manuscripts, books, paintings, drawings, letters, statuary, decorative items, and photographs. They also deal with such important themes in the nineteenth century as women's history and suffrage, abolition, African American history, and racial history and attitudes.

Guided tours are given of the Stowe family home, as well as themed tours and a living history tour with a costumed interpreter dressed as one of the Stowes' twin daughters. The center also offers lectures and other programs using Harriet Beecher Stowe's life and impact to inspire people to work for positive change. The annual center attendance is over 25,000.

Harriet Beecher Stowe Center, 77 Forest St., Hartford, CT 06105. Phone: 860/522-9258. Fax: 860/522-9259. E-mail: info@stowecenter.org. Website: www.harrietbeecherstowecenter.org. Hours: Nov.–May—9:30–4:30 Wed.–Sat., 12–4:30 Sun.; closed Mon.–Tues., New Year's Day, Easter, Thanksgiving, and Christmas Eve and Day; June–Oct.— also open Tues.; closed Mon. and Independence Day. Admission: adults, $9; seniors, $8; children 5–16, $6; children under 5, free.

Harriet Beecher Stowe House. The Harriet Beecher Stowe House in Cincinnati—a hotbed of abolitionist activity in the early 1800s—is a historic house museum that once was the residence of author Harriet Beecher Stowe and most of her brothers and sisters. The Stowe family moved from Connecticut to Cincinnati in 1832 when her activist father, the Rev. Lyman Beecher, became the first president of the newly founded Lane Theological Seminary. The 5,000-square-foot house, which was completed in 1833, was built by the seminary for the president and his family. It is where Harriet began her writing career, publishing *The Mayflower: Sketches of Scenes and Characters Among the Descendants of the Pilgrims* in 1834.

Harriet, who founded and taught with her sister at the affiliated Western Female Institute, lived in the house until 1836 when she married Calvin E. Stowe, an antislavery professor at Lane Theological Seminary. The Stowe family moved to Brunswick, Maine, when her husband was offered a teaching position at Bowdoin College. It is where she wrote the antislavery classic *Uncle Tom's Cabin*.

The Beecher house in the Walnut Hills section of Cincinnati now is a historical and cultural site owned by the Ohio Historical Society and operated by the a friends group. The house museum focuses on Harriet Beecher Stowe but also includes the Beecher/Stowe families, friends, and colleagues; Lane Seminary; the abolitionist, rights, and Underground Railroad movements in which the historical figures participated in the 1830s–1860s; and African American history as related to these movements.

Harriet Beecher Stowe House, 2950 Gilbert Ave., Cincinnati, OH 45206. Phone: 513/751-0651. Website: harriet-beecherstowehouse.org. Hours: Feb.–Apr. and Dec.—10–12 Wed., 10–2 Sat.; May–Labor Day—10–2 Tues.–Thurs. and Sat.; Sept.–Nov.—10–2 Tues.–Wed. and Sat.; other times by appointment. Closed federal holidays. Admission: free.

Harriet Beecher Stowe Slavery to Freedom Museum. The Harriett Beecher Stowe Slavery to Freedom Museum is located in an 1807 Georgian brick house in the Old Washington Historic District of Maysville, Kentucky, where the future author of *Uncle Tom's Cabin* witnessed a slave auction in 1833 and was inspired to write the antislavery book. Stove had come from Cincinnati to visit one of her Western Female Institute students, Elizabeth Key, who took Stowe to see where slaves were auctioned on the block on the courthouse lawn. Harriet was so distressed by the auction that she never forgot it—and later based some of the characters in *Uncle Tom's Cabin* on slaves in the auction.

The house has a Georgian frontispiece, curved interior stairway, and the original woodworking, mantels, doors, floors, and chair railings. Behind the house is a small brick two-level structure with vertical gun slits, known as an Indian fort. Such forts were used by settlers to ward off hostile Indians. The house chronicles Harriet Beecher Stowe's life and contains period furnishings, slave documents and shackles, and Civil War memorabilia. The site is on the Old Washington and Underground Railroad and has tours by costumed guides arranged through the Washington Visitors Center.

Harriet Beecher Stowe Slavery to Freedom Museum, 2124 Old Main St., Maysville, KY 410596 (postal address: PO Box 184, Old Washington, KY 41096). Phones: 606/564-0250 and 606/564-9419. E-mail: orioffgmiller@mac.com. Websites: www.washingtonky.com/stowe.html and www.cityofmaysville.com. Hours: 10–4 Sat., 12–4 Sun.; closed Mon.–Fri. and major holidays. Admission: adults, $3; children 6–12, $1; children under 6, free.

Henry David Thoreau

Thoreau Farm: Birthplace of Henry David Thoreau. Henry David Thoreau was an author, poet, philosopher, and naturalist who is best known for his book *Walden, or Life in the Woods*, on living simply in natural surroundings, and his essay "Civil Disobedience," on individual moral opposition to unjust government action. He also was an abolitionist, tax resister, development critic, surveyor, historian, and transcendentalist in the mid-nineteenth century.

Thoreau wrote books, articles, essays, journals, and poems that filled more than 20 volumes. Many were on natural history and philosophy. In addition to wanting better ecology, environment, and government, he was interested in such other areas as survival over hostile elements, historical change, and natural decay. As an abolitionist, he opposed the Fugitive Slave Law and spoke out in favor of civil disobedience. Many of his ideas influenced the political ideas and actions of others in future generations.

Thoreau was born in 1817 at a 1730s farmhouse near Concord, Massachusetts. His father was a pencil maker. The family moved to the Concord town center when he was only eight months old. Thoreau went to Harvard College from 1833 to 1837. After receiving his degree, he taught in the Concord public school system, only to resign after a few weeks because he was opposed to administering corporal punishment. He and his brother John then opened a grammar school called Concord Academy, which they operated until 1842 when John died from tetanus after cutting himself while shaving.

Thoreau also met Ralph Waldo Emerson after graduation from Harvard. Emerson took an interest in Thoreau, advising and introducing him to other literary figures. At Emerson's urging, Thoreau published his first essay in 1840—on the playwright Aulus Persius Flaccus—for the *Dial*, the transcendentalist quarterly. He followed with essays and poems in the next three years while living in Emerson's home and serving as tutor for Emerson's children, editorial assistant, and handyman/gardener.

In 1845 Thoreau quit working at his father's pencil factory and retreated to Concord's Walden Pond, a wilderness that later became a state park. He built a small house near the lake on land owned by Emerson and spent two years studying nature and writing *Walden, or Life in the Woods* (published in 1854). It called for the use of natural simplicity, harmony, and beauty as models for a just social and cultural society. A replica of the simple Thoreau cabin was built near the site in 2003 and now can be rented.

Thoreau wrote extensively during his life but published only one other book, *A Week on the Concord and Merrimack Rivers* in 1849—the same year as his magazine article on civil disobedience. From 1851 to his death, he was concerned primarily with natural history and travel/expedition narratives. Thoreau died of tuberculosis at the age of 44 in 1862. A collection of his journals, manuscripts, letters, and writings, published in 1906, took 20 volumes.

The five-room farmhouse where Thoreau was born is now a historic house museum on 20 acres known as Thoreau Farm: Birthplace of Henry David Thoreau. It is devoted to his life and career. The site is located two and a half miles northeast of Concord and is being preserved by the Thoreau Farm Trust. Guided tours are offered, as well as classes and workshops. Annual attendance is around 3,500. Eighteen acres of the original property also have been dedicated to Gaining Ground, a nonprofit organization that raises organic vegetables and donates them to food programs for the needy.

Thoreau Farm: Birthplace of Henry David Thoreau, 341 Virginia Rd., Concord, MA Concord, MA 01742-2727. Phone: 978/369-3091. E-mail: info@thoreaufarm.org. Website: www.thoreaufarm.dreamhosters.com. Hours: May–mid-Oct.—12–4 Sat.–Sun. and by appointment; closed Mon.–Fri. and mid-Oct.–Apr. Admission: free; guided tour, $4.

James Thurber

Thurber House. The Thurber House in Columbus, Ohio, was the home of author, humorist, and cartoonist James Thurber and his family while he was a student at Ohio State University in 1913–1917. He never graduated from Ohio State because an eye injury prevented him from completing a compulsory ROTC course. But Thurber, who lost sight in one of his eyes in a boyhood accident, did receive a posthumous degree for his later achievements. The house that Thurber's parents rented is now a historic house museum devoted to his life and works.

Thurber, who became the most outstanding American humorist of the twentieth century, was born in Columbus in 1894. He overcame the boyhood eye injury, although it eventually caused him to go blind. Thurber wrote nearly 40 books during his career, including essays, short stories, fables, and children's stories. He also did humorous drawings, many of which appeared in the *New Yorker*.

Thurber's first writing job was as a reporter for the *Columbus Dispatch* in 1920. He served as managing editor of the *New Yorker* in 1927–1930; coauthored his first book—*Is Sex Necessary?*—in 1929; and began cartooning in 1930.

His career then moved from editing to humorous writing and cartooning. Among the books that followed were *The Owl in the Attic* (1931), *The Seal in the Bedroom* (1932), *My Life and Hard Times* (1933), *The Middle-Aged Man on the Flying Trapeze* (1935), *The Secret Life of Walter Mitty* (1939), *A Thurber Carnival* (1945), and many others. In 1960 *A Thurber Carnival* was adapted for a 1960 Broadway play in which Thurber played himself. He died the following year of pneumonia.

The Thurber House, which is listed on the National Register of Historic Places, contains period furnishings, Thurber's typewriter and other memorabilia, and information about his life and career. The house is located next to the Thurber Center, a contemporary classroom, conference facility, and gallery celebrating book-related art-work. Between the two buildings are grounds that include a reading garden, statues, benches, and a foundation. The house serves as a literary center, having a writer-in-residence program, author readings, writing classes for children, Thurber events, and a bookstore.

Thurber House, 77 Jefferson Ave., Columbus, OH 43215. Phone: 614/464-1032. Fax: 614/228-7445. Website: www.thurberhouse.org. Hours: 1–4 daily; closed major holidays. Admission: free.

Mark Twain (Samuel Langhorne Clemens)

Mark Twain House and Museum. Samuel Langhorne Clemens, better known by his pen name of Mark Twain, was a nineteenth-century author and humorist of wit and incisive satire who was considered the greatest American humorist of his age. His 1874–1891 home in Hartford, Connecticut—where he wrote some of his most popular novels, including *The Adventures of Tom Sawyer* and *Adventures of Huckleberry Finn*—is now the site of the Mark Twain House and Museum, which honors his life and works.

The ornate 19-room Victorian Gothic revival house, known for its whimsy and stylistic idiosyncrasy, has bay windows that extend up to form turrets topped with porches, a steeply pitched roof, an asymmetrical bay window layout, painted brick with a diaper pattern, and exotic and provocative interiors. Twain enjoyed living and en-tertaining in the house, where he wrote many other books besides *Tom Sawyer* (1876) and *Huckleberry Finn* (1884). They included *A Tramp Abroad* (1880), *The Prince and the Pauper* (1882), *Life on the Mississippi* (1883), and *A Connecti-cut Yankee in King Arthur's Court* (1889).

Twain was born in 1835 in Florida, Missouri, and moved to Hannibal, Missouri, with his family when four years of age (*see* separate listings). When he was 12, he began working as a printer's apprentice and three years later became a typesetter and wrote articles and humorous sketches for the *Hannibal Journal* newspaper. He then was a printer in New York City, Philadelphia, St. Louis, and Cincinnati and educated himself in public libraries in the evenings.

In 1850 Twain became a steamboat pilot on the Mississippi River. When the Civil War stopped river traffic in 1861, he joined a brother who had been appointed secretary to the territorial governor of Nevada in a two-week stagecoach ride to the West. He became an unsuccessful silver miner and then worked for *Territorial Enterprise* in Virginia City, where used his pen name for the first time.

A move to California in 1864 resulted in more newspaper work and Twain's first great writing success, the hu-morous "The Celebrated Jumping Frog of Calaveras County," published in the *New York Saturday Press* in 1865. This led to newspaper-funded travelogues in the Sandwich Islands (now Hawaii) and the Mediterranean, and then a tour of Europe and the Middle East that resulted in *The Innocents Abroad* in 1869. In 1872 Twain also wrote *Roughing It*, based on his journey to Nevada and subsequent life in the West.

In 1968 Twain moved to Buffalo, New York, where he became part owner, editor, and writer for the *Buffalo Express* newspaper. Here he met and married Olivia Langdon, who came from a wealthy liberal family, in 1870. The following year the couple moved to Hartford and in 1873 began building their grand home that now houses the museum. They had three daughters in a marriage that lasted until Olivia's death in 1904. Poor financial in-vestments by Twain, however, resulted in the family moving to Europe in 1891. Twain's writings, lectures, and investment help from financier Henry Huttleston Rogers enabled him to pay off the debts and return in 1900. The Hartford house was then sold, and the family settled in Redding, Connecticut, where Twain died in 1910.

The Twain house in Hartford served as a home, school, apartment building, and library before becoming a mu-seum. The Mark Twain Memorial and Library Commission was established in 1929 to purchase and restore the house and carriage house. The house was opened as a museum in 1960, designated a National Historic Landmark in 1963, and restoration was largely completed by 1974. The museum now also has a visitor center and an 1874 house for conferences and administration. It contains Twain family furniture, books, manuscripts, decorative arts, artworks, photographs, memorabilia, and exhibits and offers guided tours and such educational programs as lectures by au-thors and artists, symposia, dramatic performances, concerts, and family activities. Annual attendance is over 60,000.

Mark Twain House and Museum, 351 Farmington Ave., Hartford, CT 06105-4498. Phone: 860/278-0998. Fax: 860/278-8148. E-mail: info@marktwainhouse.org. Website: www.marktwainhouse.org. Hours: 9:30–5:30 Mon.–Sat.,

12–5:30 Sun.; closed Tues. in Jan.–Mar., New Year's Day, Easter, Independence Day, Thanksgiving, and Christmas Eve and Day. Admission: adults, $14; seniors and military, $12; children 6–16, $8; children under 6, free.

Mark Twain Birthplace Historic Site and Museum. The two-room frame house where author/humorist Samuel Langhorne Clemens, more popularly known as Mark Twain, was born in 1835 is preserved in the museum at the Mark Twain Birthplace State Historic Site outside Florida, Missouri. The small 1830s structure was moved from the village of Florida, where a granite monument is located at the original site of the house. The state historic site is part of the 2,775-acre Mark Twain State Park.

The birthplace house, which is displayed in a 12,000-square-foot park museum, has been restored and contains period furnishings. The museum also has exhibits interpreting Twain's life and works and features first editions of Twain's works, his handwritten manuscript of *The Adventures of Tom Sawyer*, and furnishings from his 1874–1891 home in Hartford, Connecticut, that now is the Mark Twain House and Museum (*see* separate listing).

Mark Twain Museum, Mark Twain Birthplace State Historic Site, 37352 Shrine Rd., Florida, MO 65283-2127. Phones: 573/565-3449 and 800/334-6946. E-mail: moparks@dnr.mo.gov. Website: www.mostateparks.com/twain-site.htm. Hours: Apr.–Oct.—10–4:30 daily; Nov.–Mar.—10–4:30 Wed.–Sun.; closed Mon.–Tues., New Year's Day, Thanksgiving, and Christmas Day. Admission: adults, $2.50; children 6–12, $1.25; children under 6, free.

Mark Twain Boyhood Home and Museum. Author/humorist Samuel Langhorne Clemens, who later went by the pen name of Mark Twain, moved with his parents and other children from Florida, Missouri, to Hannibal, Missouri, in 1839 when he was four years old. The house in which he spent his boyhood in 1844–1853 is now part of the Mark Twain Boyhood Home and Museum in Hannibal. It was where he found inspiration for many of his stories as Mark Twain, including *The Adventures of Tom Sawyer* and *Adventures of Huckleberry Finn.*

Twain entered the workforce early in his life. After his father died in 1847, he became a printer's apprentice the following year at the age of 12. In 1851 he began working as a typesetter and contributor of articles and humorous sketches to the local newspaper, owned by his older brother, Orion. When he became 18, he left Hannibal to work as a printer in the east, where he spent his evenings at public libraries educating himself. At the age of 22, he returned to Missouri and worked as a steamboat pilot until the outbreak of the Civil War in 1961 curtailed traffic on the Mississippi River. Twain then went west with his brother, which led to his career as an author and humorist (*see* Mark Twain House and Museum).

The Mark Twain Boyhood Home and Museum in Hannibal was founded in 1936, but the site has been open as a museum since 1912. The 1844 boyhood home is a National Historic Landmark and listed on the National Register of Historic Places. The museum complex includes six additional buildings—the Interpretive Center, Becky Thatcher House, Huck Finn House, J. M. Clemens Justice of the Peace Office, Grant's Drug Store, and the Museum Gallery. The Becky Thatcher House was the home of Twain's childhood girlfriend, Laura Hawkins, and the Huck Finn House is a replica of the home of Tom Blankenship, upon whom Twain based the Huck Finn character.

A tour of the site usually begins at the Interpretive Center, which has exhibits on Twain's life and works and the steamboat era and features a video on Twain and the people on whom he later based many of his characters. It is not possible to enter the restored boyhood home or his father's justice of the peace office, but visitors can see the inside furnishings from outdoor platforms.

The other buildings can be visited, including the Museum Gallery, which has exhibits on Twain and his books and a collection of Norman Rockwell paintings of *Tom Sawyer* and *Huck Finn* scenes. The museum also has such other exhibits as replicas of a stagecoach, river raft, and steamboat pilot house, as well as scenes from *Tom Sawyer.* Among its collections are first editions of Twain's works, numerous memorabilia, and some of his personal items. Annual attendance is over 60,000.

Mark Twain Boyhood Home and Museum, 208 N. Main St., Hannibal, MO 62301-3537. (postal address: 120 N. Main St., Hannibal, MO 62301-3537). Phone: 573/221-9010. Fax: 573/221-7975. E-mail: museumoffice@marktwainmuseum.org. Website: www.marktwainmuseum.org. Hours: Mar.—9–4 Mon.–Sat., 12–4 Sun.; Apr. and Sept.–Oct.—9–5 daily; May—8–5 daily; June–Aug.—8–6 daily; Nov.–Feb.—10–4 Mon.–Sat., 12–4 Sun.; closed New Year's Day, Easter, Thanksgiving, and Christmas. Admission: adults, $8; seniors, $6.50; children 6–12, $4; children under 6, free.

Lew Wallace

General Lew Wallace Study and Museum. Lew Wallace was a Union general in the Civil War who became a lawyer, governor, diplomat, and author after the war. He was the youngest general in the war, being promoted to brigadier general and placed in command of a brigade at the age of 34 and later advancing to major general. He is best known, however, as the postwar author of the best-selling *Ben-Hur: A Tale of the Christ*, a historical novel that became an award-winning play and movie.

Wallace was born in Brookville, Indiana, in 1827. He was the son of David Wallace, a U.S. Military Academy graduate who became governor of Indiana. Lew Wallace was studying law when the Mexican-American War began in 1846. He received his first military experience when he raised a company of militia and served in the army of General Zachary Taylor, rising to the rank of first lieutenant. After leaving the service, he received his law degree and was elected prosecuting attorney in the First Congressional District of Indiana.

At the start of the Civil War in 1861, Wallace was appointed state adjutant general and helped raise troops in Indiana. He then became colonel of the 11th Indiana Infantry, served in West Virginia, and was made brigadier general. In 1862 Wallace commanded Fort Henry along the Tennessee River, checked a Confederate assault, retook lost ground at Fort Donelson, and was promoted to major general.

In the ensuing Battle of Shiloh, as commander of the 3rd Division under General Ulysses S. Grant, Wallace was blamed for confusion over orders from Grant that resulted in Union forces being pushed back. His most notable service after that was the 1864 Battle of Monocacy, where his forces delayed Confederate advances on Washington and won belated praise from Grant. Later in the war, Wallace directed American government efforts to aid Mexico in expelling French occupation forces that had seized control of the country in 1864. Wallace resigned from the U.S. Army in 1865, worked as a lawyer, served as governor of the New Mexico Territory in 1878–1881, and was minister to the Ottoman Empire (Turkey) in 1881–1885.

Wallace's writing career, which specialized in historical novels, began in the 1870s with the 1873 publication of *The Fair God* on the Spanish conquest of Mexico. In 1880, while serving as governor in New Mexico, he wrote *Ben-Hur*, a romantic tale set in the Roman Empire at the time of Christ. *The Prince of India*, on the Byzantine Empire, was published in 1893. *Ben-Hur* became the best-selling American novel of the nineteenth century. It also was made into a popular Broadway play and adapted for four motion pictures, including the 1959 version starting Charlton Heston, which won 11 Academy Awards and many other honors.

Wallace died in 1905, and the General Lew Wallace Study and Museum—initially known as the Ben-Hur Museum—was founded in Crawfordsville, Indiana, later that year. In 1910 a marble statue of Wallace in a military uniform was installed by the state in National Statuary Hall in Washington.

The museum, which is devoted to Wallace's life and career, consists of his 1906 study and the accompanying carriage house. The museum, which has been designated a National Historic Landmark, contains many of his personal belongings (such as artworks, violins, books, and inventions), items related to the *Ben-Hur* movies and Broadway play, and Civil War and World War I objects. It also has a video presentation, permanent and temporary exhibits, and educational programming in an interpretation center in the carriage house. Annual attendance is 7,000.

General Lew Wallace Study and Museum, 200 Wallace Ave., Crawfordsville, IN 47933-2546 (postal address: PO Box 662, Crawfordsville, IN 47933-0662). E-mail: study@ben-hur.com. Website: www.ben-hur.com. Hours: Feb.–mid-Dec.—10–5 Wed.–Sat., 1–5 Sun., Mon.–Tues. by appointment; closed mid-Dec.–Jan. and major holidays. Admission: adults, $3; students, $1; children under 6, free.

Robert Penn Warren

See Poets section.

Noah Webster

See Educators section.

Eudora Welty

Eudora Welty House. The Eudora Welty House in Jackson, Mississippi, was the home of Pulitzer Prize–winning author Eudora Welty for 76 years. She was known for her short stories and novels about the American South. She did all of her writing in an upstairs bedroom of the Tudor revival–style house where she lived from 1925 until her death in 2001. The house is considered one of the most intact literary houses in America in terms of its authenticity. The house and its furnishings and garden are as they were in 1986 when she made the decision to bequeath her house to the State of Mississippi.

Welty, who was born in Jackson in 1909, moved into the house with her parents in 1925. She graduated from Mississippi State College for Women (now Mississippi University for Women) and had further studies at the University of Wisconsin and Columbia University. During the 1930s, while traveling around Mississippi for the Works Progress Administration during the Great Depression, she took memorable photographs of people of all social and economic classes that resulted in two books, *One Time, One Place* (1971) and *Photographs* (1989). Her photography, which she continued to do until the 1950s, later became the basis of several short stories.

Welty's first short story, "Death of a Traveling Salesman," was published in 1936. She drew attention with her first collection of short stories, *A Curtain of Green*, in 1941. It included such stories as "Why I Live at the P.O.," "Petrified Man," and "A Worn Path." During her writing career, she wrote 10 collections of short stories and six novels as well as some nonfiction and literary criticism. She was awarded the Pulitzer Prize for Fiction in 1973 for the novel *The Optimist's Daughter*. She was 92 when she died of pneumonia in 2001.

The Eudora Welty House was listed in the National Register of Historic Places in 2002 and declared a National Historic Landmark in 2004. It opened to the public as a historic house museum in 2006. It now can be seen only as part of guided tours. The tours are conducted by the Eudora Welty Foundation, which was established in 1999 to assist the Mississippi Department of Archives and History in celebrating her legacy and encouraging reading and the efforts of young writers.

Eudora Welty House, 1119 Pinehurst St., Jackson, MS 39202-1812 (postal address: Eudora Welty Foundation, PO Box 55685, Jackson, MS 39296-5685). Phone: 601/353-7762. E-mail: weltytours@mdah.state.ms.us. Website: www.eudorawelty.org. Tour hours: 9, 11, 1, and 3 Tues.–Fri.; closed Sat.–Mon. and state holidays. Admission: adults, $5; students 6–18, $3; children under 6, free.

Edith Wharton

The Mount: Edith Wharton's Estate and Gardens. The Mount, a 1902 classical revival mansion in Lenox, Massachusetts, was the home of noted author Edith Wharton, the first woman to receive the Pulitzer Prize for Literature. She designed the house based on the principles described in her first book, *The Decoration of Houses*, coauthored in 1897 with architect Ogden Codman Jr. The house was inspired by the seventeenth-century Belton House in England, with influences from classical Italian and French architecture. As a result of her design books and the Mount, Wharton became the only woman of the 11 founders of the American Society of Landscape Architects.

Despite the size and beauty of the house and the Berkshires site, Wharton and her husband, Edward Robbins Wharton, lived in the Mount only from 1902 to 1911. They were married for 28 years. After their divorce in 1913, she lived the rest of her life in France, returning only to receive an honorary degree from Yale University in 1923. After the Whartons left, the Mount became a private residence, a girl's school dormitory, and the site of a theater company before being purchased by the Edith Wharton Restoration group, restored, and established as a historic house museum in 1979.

Edith Wharton, who was a novelist and short story writer, was born into a prominent New York City family in 1862 and began writing as a teenager. Her first work was a collection of poetry, *Verses*, in 1878. She married Wharton, from a well-established Boston family, in 1885. They traveled widely, and she began writing novels and short stories as well as nonfiction travel books. A number of her novels, including *The House of Mirth* in 1905, and short story collections, such as *Tales of Men and Ghosts* in 1910, were written while residing at the Mount.

Most of Wharton's works, known for their subtle use of dramatic irony and ghost stories, were written while she lived in France. They included *The Age of Innocence*, which described the lives of the New York upper class and their vanishing world in the early twentieth century, for which she won the Pulitzer Prize in 1920. During World War I, she worked in charitable efforts for refugees. She continued writing until her death in 1937.

The Mount: Edith Wharton's Estate and Gardens, which is located on 49 and a half acres, consists of the restored house and gardens, a Georgian revival gatehouse and stable, greenhouse, lime walk, and a large grass terrace overlooking the grounds. The house has three stories on the entry side and two stories on the garden side. The white stucco exterior features black shutters, clusters of gables and white chimneys, a balustrade and cupola, and a large stone terrace overlooking the grounds. The interior looks much as it did originally. Guided tours are given of the house and gardens, with special attention to Edith Wharton's role. Annual attendance is 30,000.

The Mount: Edith Wharton's Estate and Gardens, 2 Plunkett St., Lenox, MA 01240 (postal address: PO Box 974, Lenox, MA 01240-0974). Phones: 413/551-5100 and 413/551-5111. Fax: 413/637/0619. E-mail: info@edithwharton.org. Website: www.edithwharton.org. Hours: May–Oct.—10–5 daily; Nov.–Apr.—10–4 Fri.–Sun.; closed Mon.–Thurs. and major holidays. Admission: grounds—May–Oct.: $12; Nov.–Apr.: free; house—adults, $16; seniors, $15; students, $13; children, free.

Laura Ingalls Wilder

Laura Ingalls Wilder Museum. The Laura Ingalls Wilder Museum in Pepin, Wisconsin, honors the author who was born in the area and wrote the popular Little House series of children's books based on her childhood in a pioneer family. In addition to the museum, the Laura Ingalls Wilder Memorial Society has a replica of the cabin in which she was born at the original site, and a Laura Ingalls Wilder Days festival is held every September.

Wilder is best known for *Little House on the Prairie*, a 1935 novel that later became a popular television series. She began the Little House series with *Little House in the Big Woods* in 1932 at the age of 65. Eight more books followed with her stories about the frontier years, and she became a best-selling author.

Wilder was born to Charles and Caroline Ingalls in 1867 in the Big Woods area seven miles from Pepin. The woods, log cabin, and barn no longer exist. But a replicated cabin, called the Little House Wayside, can now be seen at the site, and items relating to Laura's life and the era are featured at the Laura Ingalls Wilder Museum in Pepin. Wilder's experiences as a child in the area was the basis of her first book *Little House in the Big Woods*.

Her father's restless spirit led to a number of moves during Laura's childhood that later resulted in Little House books. The Ingalls family left Pepin and settled on land that was in Indian Territory near Independence, Kansas. It was an experience that led to the publication of *Little House on the Prairie* in 1935.

In 1874 the family moved to Walnut Grove, Minnesota, where they lived in a dugout house along a river bank. When a grasshopper plague destroyed their crops, they moved to Burr Oak, Iowa, where Laura's father managed a hotel a year before returning to Walnut Creek. In 1879 the Ingalls family moved again to Dakota Territory to homestead in what later became De Smet, South Dakota. Five of Laura's books—*By the Shores of Silver Lake* (1939), *The Long Winter* (1940), *Little Town on the Prairie* (1941), *These Happy Golden Years* (1943), and *The First Four Years* (published posthumously in 1971)—were based on her experiences in the Dakotas.

In De Smet, the self-taught Laura worked as a teacher, married homesteader Almanzo James Wilder in 1885, and gave birth to her daughter Rose. However, after fire destroyed their home and barn and several years of severe drought, the family spent about a year in 1890 with her parents, who now had a prosperous farm in Spring Valley, Minnesota. This was followed by about a year in Westville, Florida, where they sought help for Almanzo's health from the warm climate. When he wilted in the heat and humanity, the family returned to De Smet in 1892, where Almanzo worked as a day labor and Laura as a seamstress to earn enough money to buy a farm.

Two years later, the Wilder family made its final move to Mansfield, Missouri, where they bought land that developed into a successful farm called Rocky Ridge Farm. It was where Laura did all of her writing and the couple spent the rest of their lives (*see* separate listing). She began writing magazine articles in 1911 and then books in the 1930s. She continued writing books in the Little House series until 1942. She and her husband then retired to the farm, where Laura died in 1957 at the age of 90.

Laura Ingalls Wilder Museum, 306 3rd St., Pepin, WI 54759. Phone: 715/442-2142. E-mail: info@lauraingallspepin.com. Website: www.lauraingallspepin.com. Hours: May 15–Oct. 15—10–5 daily; closed remainder of year and major holidays. Admission: free.

Laura Ingalls Wilder Museum and Tourist Center. The Laura Ingalls Wilder Museum and Tourist Center in Walnut Grove, Minnesota, is devoted primarily to the Little House books author who lived there as a child in 1874–1876. It is housed in a ca. 1894 railroad station, which also serves as a tourist information center. Another historic site near Walnut Grove is the dugout site where the Ingalls family lived while homesteading in the area.

The Ingalls family moved to Walnut Grove from Indian Territory near Independence, Kansas, in 1874 and lived in the dugout home and suffered three consecutive crop failures. Instead of completing the homestead process, they bought the land, resold it immediately for $400, and moved to Burr Oak, Iowa, to help operate a hotel. Wilder's 1937 book *On the Banks of Plum Creek* is devoted to the family stay in Walnut Creek.

Founded in 1974, the Walnut Creek museum contains Laura Ingalls Wilder exhibits and memorabilia, as well as displays on the history of Walnut Creek and collections of quilts, furniture, toys, and other objects. The museum, which has an annual attendance of 17,500, also has an 1890 house with three pre-1920s furnished rooms and a collection of over 250 dolls. In addition, Walnut Creek has an annual Wilder Pageant, an outdoor drama on the life of Laura Ingalls Wilder, in July.

Laura Ingalls Wilder Museum and Tourist Center, 330 8th St., Walnut Creek, MN 56180. Phone: 507/859-2358. Fax: 507/859-2933. E-mail: lauramuseum@walnutgrove.org. Website: www.walnutgrove.org. Hours: Apr. and Oct.—10–4 Mon.–Sat., 12–4 Sun.; May and Sept.—10–5 Mon.–Sat., 12–5 Sun.; June–Aug.—10–6 daily; closed Nov.–Mar. Admission: adults, $5; children 6–12, $2; children under 6, free.

Laura Ingalls Wilder Park and Museum. Charles Ingalls, father of Laura Ingalls Wilder, moved the family to Burr Oak, Iowa, in 1876 after experiencing the worst grasshopper plague ever in Walnut Grove, Minnesota. A friend from church, William Steadman, just bought a hotel in Burr Oak and invited the Ingalls family to help manage the hotel. The nine-year-old Laura and other members of the family were kept busy with hotel chores for a year. It is said that Laura developed her love of books and words in Burr Oak, where stories flowed from the tombstones of pioneers in the Burr Oak cemetery, which Laura and a girlfriend frequently visited on summer afternoons. In 1877 Charles Ingalls moved the family back to Walnut Grove, Minnesota.

During the early 1900s, the Masters Hotel was used as a private residence and frequently changed hands. In 1973 it was discovered that the Ingalls family had lived there. A group of residents then bought the building, renovated it, and opened the former hotel as a museum in 1976. The historic site, now known as the Laura Ingalls Wilder Park and Museum, also has been listed on the National Register of Historic Places. The restored hotel museum contains furniture of the 1800s period and has displays and memorabilia of Laura's life and days in Burr Oak. The museum also has an adjacent early building and a picnic shelter in the surrounding park. The museum has 8,000 visitors annually.

Laura Ingalls Wilder Park and Museum, 3603 236th Ave., Burr Oak, IA 52101-7889. Phone: 563/735-5916. Fax: 563/735-5464. E-mail: museum@lauraingallswilder.us. Website: www.lauraingallswilder.us. Hours: Memorial Day–Labor Day—9–5 Mon.–Sat., 12–4 Sun.; Sept. after Labor Day–Oct.—10–4 Mon.–Sat., 12–4 Sun.; Nov.–Mar.—10–3 Thurs.–Sat.; closed Sun.–Wed., New Year's Day, Thanksgiving, and Christmas Eve and Day; Apr.–late May—10–4 Tues.–Sat.; closed Sun.–Mon. Admission: adults, $7; children 6–17, $5; children under 6, free.

Laura Ingalls Wilder–Rose Wilder Lane Historic Home and Museum. Author Laura Ingalls Wilder wrote *Little House on the Prairie* and eight other books in the Little House series based on her childhood experiences on the frontier while living on Rocky Ridge Farm near Mansfield, Missouri. Laura and her husband, Almanzo Wilder, moved to the area in 1894, using their meager savings to make a down payment on 40 acres of undeveloped land that they converted into a 200-acre relatively prosperous poultry, dairy, and fruit farm with an impressive 10-room farmhouse after a difficult beginning. It now is the site of the Laura Ingalls Wilder–Rose Wilder Lane Historic Home and Museum.

Laura began writing in 1911 after being inspired by the success of her daughter, now Rose Wilder Lane, as a freelance writer (who later became a successful author). Laura wrote an article for the *Missouri Ruralist*, which led to being a columnist and editor, a position she held until the 1920s. She also wrote articles for other magazines. After the 1929 stock market crash wiped out the Wilders' savings, Laura's daughter urged her to write about her childhood experiences on the frontier. This resulted in the first of the Little House books, *Little House in the Big Woods*, in 1932 and led to eight other books, including *Little House on the Prairie*, which became a popular television series in 1974–1984.

Laura continued writing until she was 76 years old. She retired to the farm with her husband, where they lived into their 90s. Lane, who had assisted her mother in writing and lived with her parents from time to time, became a successful author, journalist, and world traveler. After Laura's death, Lane and local townspeople purchased the house and its grounds for a museum. It now contains five of the original nine handwritten manuscripts in the Little House series, translations of the books, and the family organ and photographs, the father's fiddle, clothing, and memorabilia. The life and career of Rose Wilder Lane, and re-creations of rooms from her homes and her desks, manuscripts, and souvenirs from world travels also are displayed at the museum. The annual attendance is 55,000.

Laura Ingalls Wilder–Rose Wilder Lane Historic Home and Museum, 3068 Hwy. A, Mansfield, MO 65704-8104. Phones: 417/924-3626 and 877/924-7126. Fax: 417/924-8580. E-mail: info@lauraingallswilderhome.com. Website: www.lauraingallswilderhome.com. Hours: Mar.–mid-Nov.—9–5 Mon.–Sat., 12:30–5 Sun.; mid-Nov.–mid-Dec.—by appointment; closed Easter and remainder of year. Admission: adults, $8; seniors, $6; children 6–17, $4; children under 6, free.

Tennessee Williams

See Playwrights section.

Thomas Wolfe

Thomas Wolfe Memorial. An 1883 Victorian boarding house where author Thomas Wolfe spent his childhood is the site of a memorial in his honor in Asheville, North Carolina. Wolfe, a major novelist of the twentieth century, lived in the boarding house that his mother ran from the ages of 6 to 15 in 1906–1916. Wolfe's mother, Julia, added 11 rooms and modernized the house in 1916. It became a memorial in 1949, but a suspicious fire nearly destroyed the historic house museum in 1998. However, it was reconstructed and reopened in 2003.

Wolfe was known for mixing original poetic, rhapsodic, and impressionistic prose with autobiographical writing reflecting the American culture and mores of the 1920s–1930s. He wrote four long novels and many short stories, dramatic works, and novel fragments. He burst on the literary scene with his first two novels, which fictionalized his early experiences in Asheville—*Look Homeward, Angel* (1929) and *Of Time and the River* (1935). But his career was cut short when he died at the age of 37 in 1938 after becoming ill with pneumonia and then tubercular meningitis.

Wolfe was born in Asheville in 1900. He began attending the University of North Carolina when 15 and became interested in playwriting. He wrote several plays that were performed by students and later in workshops but never on Broadway because of their excessive length. When his plays did not sell, Wolfe decided that his writing style was more suited to fiction. He then went to Europe in 1924 and later began writing the first version of a long novel, *O Lost*, which evolved into his first published book, *Look Homeward, Angel*.

Because of the volume of materials left at Wolfe's death, less than half of his works were published during his lifetime. He left two complete novels unpublished. Two other novels, *The Web and the Rock* and *You Can't Go Home Again*, resulted from his writings and were published posthumously in 1939–1940. The lengthy manuscript for *O Lost* also was reconstructed and published in 2000. Several of his novels were adapted for plays, including *Look Homeward, Angel*, which received six Tony Award nominations and won the 1958 Pulitzer Prize for Drama.

The 29-room Thomas Wolfe Memorial, a designated National Historic Landmark now operated by the State of North Carolina, was restored and reopened in 2003 after the disastrous fire. The original furnishings are much as they were when Wolfe lived there. The historic house also has memorabilia, a visitor center, guided tours, and an 18,000 annual attendance.

Thomas Wolfe Memorial, 52 N. Market St., Asheville, NC 28801-8105. Phone: 828/253-8304. Fax: 828/252-8171. E-mail: contactus@wolfememorial.com. Website: www.wolfememorial.com. Hours: Apr.–June 2—9–5 Tues.–Sat., 1–5 Sun.; Nov.–Mar.—10–4 Tues.–Sat., 1–4 Sun.; closed Mon., Thanksgiving and day after, and Christmas Eve and Day. Admission: adults, $1; children 50¢.

AVIATORS/ASTRONAUTS

Neil Armstrong

Armstrong Air and Space Museum. Neil Armstrong, the first person to set foot on the moon, is honored at the Armstrong Air and Space Museum in his hometown of Wapakoneta, Ohio. He walked on the moon while serving as mission commander of Apollo 11, landing on the moon in 1969. The museum traces the former astronaut's life and career and describes Ohio's contributions to the history of space flight.

Armstrong was a naval aviator and test pilot who became an astronaut in 1962. In his first spaceflight, he was the command pilot aboard *Gemini 8* and performed the first manned docking of two spacecraft with pilot David Scott. On the Apollo 11 lunar mission in 1969, Armstrong and Buzz Aldrin spent two and a half hours exploring the moon's surface while Michael Collins remained in orbit in the command module. Armstrong was joined by Aldrin about 15 minutes later to become the second man on the moon. They took photographs, conducted experiments, and brought back the first soil and rock samples and results from various experiments on the moon.

Armstrong began studying aerospace engineering at Purdue University in 1947, but it was interrupted when he received a navy call-up for service two years later. Armstrong underwent flight training and became a naval aviator 18 months later. After receiving jet training, he flew 78 missions in the Korean War in 1951–1952. During a low bombing run, his plane was hit by anti-aircraft fire, and a portion of the plane's right wing was sheared off by a cable strung across a valley by North Korean forces. However, he was able to eject and be picked up safely. He left the navy as a lieutenant junior grade in the naval reserve in 1952 and resigned his reserve commission in 1960.

Armstrong returned to Purdue and received an aeronautical engineering degree in 1955. He then worked as a test pilot at the National Advisory Committee for Aeronautics High-Speed Flight Station (now Dryden Flight Research Center) before joining the NASA Astronaut Corps in 1962. After making the first manned landing on the moon, he was made deputy associate administrator for aeronautics for the NASA Office of Advanced Research and Technology. In 1971 he resigned from NASA and became professor of aerospace engineering at the University of Cincinnati. After teaching for eight years, he served on the boards of a number of companies and retired as chairman of the EDO Corporation. He died in 2012 of complications from cardiovascular procedures at the age of 82.

The Armstrong Air and Space Museum, founded in 1972 and operated by the Ohio Historical Society, tells about Armstrong's life and career and contains the Gemini and Apollo space suits he wore on the missions, the *Gemini 8* spacecraft he flew, a 1946 Aeronca 7AC Champion plane he first flew, lunar landing and space shuttle landing simulators, a moon rock brought back by Armstrong and Aldrin, a portrait gallery of all Ohio astronauts, and historical items about the Soviet space program from Yuri Gagarin, the first human to go into space. The annual attendance is 50,000.

Armstrong Air and Space Museum, Interstate 75 and Bellefontaine Rd., PO Box 1978, Wapakoneta, OH 45895-0978. Phones: 419/738-8811 and 800/860-0142. Fax: 419/738-3361. E-mail: rmacwhinney@ohiohistory.org. Website: www.ohiohistory.org. Hours: 9:30–5 Tues.–Sat., 12–5 Sun.; closed Tues. and major holidays. Admission: adults, $8; children 6–12, $4; children under 6, free.

Octave Chanute

Chanute Air Museum. The Chanute Air Museum, located on the grounds of the decommissioned Chanute Air Force Base in Rantoul, Illinois, is dedicated to Octave Chanute, an innovative railroad and bridge engineer who became an aviation pioneer in the late nineteenth century. Chanute developed early hang gliders, invented the "strut-wire" braced wing structure of powered biplanes, and organized the highly successful 1893 International Conference on Aerial Navigation and the first written collection of aviation research in 1894. He also provided assistance to Wilbur and Orville Wright and helped to publicize their flying experiments.

The museum, which was founded in 1992, contains exhibits on the life and career of Chanute and the history of the former air base and aviation in Illinois. It also has more than 3,500 artifacts related to air flight, flight simulators, and over 30 American fighter, bomber, and training planes, as well as replicas of such aircraft as the 1903 Wright Flyer, JN-4D Jenny, *Spirit of St. Louis*, and Chanute Glider. The annual attendance is 17,000.

Chanute was born in Paris, France, in 1832, came to the United States in 1838, and worked as a railroad engineer in 1853–1873 and consulting engineer in bridge building in 1873–1883. He became interested in aviation during a visit to France in 1875 and decided to devote his remaining years to furthering the new field of aviation after his retirement in 1890. He first gathered all the data he could find about aviation experiments around the world, which resulted in journal articles in 1891–1893 and then publication of *Progress in Flying Machines* in 1894. He also organized the international aerial navigation conference at the 1893 World's Columbian Exhibition in Chicago.

In 1886–1897 Chanute tested hang gliders based on designs of Otto Lilienthal of Germany and his own. These experiments convinced Chanute that the best way to achieve extra lift was to stack several wings one above the other, which led to his development of the "strut-wire" braced wing design for biplanes. It was the Chanute "double-decker" approach, as the Wright brothers called it, that they used in their glider and Flyer designs at the turn of the twentieth century.

Chanute Air Museum, 1011 Pacesetter Dr., Rantoul, IL 61866-3672. Phones 217/893-1613 and 877/728-8685. Fax: 217/892-5774. E-mail: director@aeromuseum.org. Website: www.aeromuseum.org. Hours: 10–5 Mon.–Sat., 12–5 Sun.; closed New Year's Day, Easter, Thanksgiving, and Christmas. Admission: adults, $10; seniors, $8; children 4–8, $5; children under 4, free.

Glenn H. Curtiss

Glenn H. Curtiss Museum. The Glenn H. Curtiss Museum in Hammondsport, New York, is named for a builder of bicycles and motorcycles who became one of America's earliest aircraft builders and pilots in the early twentieth century. He was the founder of the Curtiss Aeroplane and Motor Company, which now is part of the Curtiss-Wright Corporation. The museum features exhibits about Curtiss's life and accomplishments and a collection of historic aircraft and displays.

Curtiss, who was born in Hammondsport in 1878, had an early interest in mechanics and inventions. He became a Western Union bicycle messenger, a bicycle racer, and then a bicycle shop owner. In 1900 Curtis formed a company to produce Hercules bicycles and then became interested in motorcycles in 1901 as internal combustion engines became more available. He started building motorcycles with his own single cylinder engines the following year. In 1903 he set a motorcycle land speed record at 64 miles per hour, followed by a world record of 136.36 miles per hour in 1907.

In 1904 Curtiss supplied an adapted motorcycle engine for the first successful dirigible in America. He then was invited by Alexander Graham Bell to join the Aerial Experiment Association and provide an engine for heavier-than-the-air flight. In 1908 he designed and flew his first flying machine, the *June Bug*, a distance of 5,000 feet to win the *Scientific American* Trophy. Curtiss then won the Gordon Bennett Trophy for speed at the world's first international aviation meet in Rheims, France, in 1909 and made the first long-distance flight in America (from Albany to New York City) in 1910.

It also was in 1910 that Curtiss began a long relationship with the U.S. Navy when he demonstrated the takeoff and successful landing of a Curtiss Pusher from a temporary platform on a navy ship. This was followed by the Curtiss development of a pontoon that enabled flyers to take off and land on water, the sale of the Curtiss A-1 seaplane with retractable wheels to the navy, and the Curtiss training of the navy's first pilots. For these contributions, Curtiss has been called the father of naval aviation.

In 1912 Curtiss produced—in partnership with John Cyril Porte, a retired English naval officer—a two-seater flying boat called *Flying Fish* and then a larger version with two engines, *America*, in 1914 for a trans-Atlantic crossing competition. Modified versions of the flying boat were used by both the British and Americans in World War I. The Curtiss company also produced the famous JN-4 Jenny two-seat trainer for the army and the N-9 seaplane version and the NC-4 long-range, four-engine flying boat for the navy.

After World War I, Curtis became known for producing racing aircraft that won numerous races. In 1929 the Wright Aeronautical Corporation, a successor to the original Wright brothers company, merged with Curtis Aeroplane and Motor Company to form the Curtiss-Wright Corporation. Curtiss died in 1930 at the age of 52 after an appendectomy.

The Glenn H. Curtiss Museum was founded and dedicated to his memory in 1961. It contains exhibits about his life and collections relating to early aviation and local history. The museum's collection of historic aircraft include reproductions of a 1912 Pusher, 1913 Model E flying boat, 1917 Jenny, 1919 Seagull flying boat, 1927 Robin, and 1931 Junior. The museum also displays a C-46 transport from World War II, motorcycles, boats, tools, fire equipment, and other collections. It also has an "Innovation Gallery" where visitors can explore the history and workings of aviation technology. About 25,000 visit the museum annually.

Glenn H. Curtiss Museum, 8419 State Rte. 54, Hammondsport, NY 14840-9795. Phone: 607/569-2160. Fax: 607/569-2040. E-mail: info@glennhcurtissmuseum.org. Website: www.glennhcurtissmuseum.org. Hours: May–Oct.—9–5 Mon.–Sat., 10–5 Sun.; Nov.–Apr.—10–4 daily; closed New Year's Day, Easter, Thanksgiving, and Christmas Eve and Day. Admission: adults, $7.50; seniors, $6; students 7–18, $4.50; children under 7, free.

John Glenn

John and Annie Glenn Historic Site. The John and Annie Glenn Historic Site in New Concord, Ohio, honors a former astronaut and senator who was the first American to orbit the earth and his wife, who has made contributions to programs for children, the elderly, and the handicapped. The historic site is located at John Glenn's boyhood home.

Glenn, who was a Marine Corps fighter pilot before joining NASA's Mercury program as a member of the original astronaut group, orbited the earth in the *Friendship 7* spaceship in 1962. After retiring from the space program, he was elected as a Democrat from Ohio in the United States Senate from 1974 to 1999. Annie Glenn, his childhood sweetheart whom he married in 1943, has been active in community service and received the first national award from the American Speech and Hearing Association for inspiring people with communicative disorders.

During World II, Glenn was a Marine Corps pilot who flew 59 combat missions in the South Pacific and was promoted to captain. When the Korean Conflict broke out, he flew 63 combat missions, including two where he had over 250 flake holes in his F9F Panther jet interceptor, and then 27 missions in a faster F-86 Sabre in a second Korean tour. After the war, he was a test pilot and completed the first supersonic transcontinental flight in a Vought F8U-1 Crusader in 1957, flying from California to New York in 3 hours, 23 minutes, and 8.4 seconds.

Glenn was assigned to the newly created National Aeronautics and Space Administration in 1959 as a member of the original Mercury team while still remaining an officer in the Marine Corps. In 1962 he became a national hero when he circled the globe three times in less than five hours aboard *Friendship 7* to become the fifth person in space and the first American to orbit the earth. Glenn resigned from the NASA astronaut corps in 1964 and from the Marines in 1965, retiring as a colonel, to run for the U.S. Senate.

Glenn was elected a senator from Ohio in 1970 and served until 1999. He also was a contender for the Democratic vice presidential nomination three times and a presidential candidate in 1984, when he lost to Walter Mondale. While still in the Senate in 1998, Glenn made his second space flight at the age of 77. He participated in a nine-day mission that provided research information on weightlessness and other aspects of space flight for the same person 36 years apart.

The John and Annie Glenn Historic Site, which opened in 2002, takes visitors back to Glenn's early days, with costumed interpreters portraying his father, mother, two brothers, and a newspaper boy during his boyhood in the Great Depression and on the home front during World War II. Guided tours also are presented of Glenn's bedroom, a toy room, and an exhibit containing childhood items and memorabilia from his military, space, and political careers. Plans are under way to add an exploration center at the site that would further public understanding of science, technology, engineering, and math.

John and Annie Glenn Historic Site, 72 W. Main St., New Concord, OH 43762 (postal address: PO Box 107, New Concord, OH 43762-0107). Phones: 740/826-3305 and 800/752-2602. Website: www.johnglennhome.org. Hours: mid-Apr.–mid-Oct.—10–4 Wed.–Sat., 1–4 Sun.; closed Mon.–Tues., Independence Day, and remainder of year. Admission: adults, $7; seniors, $6; students, $3; children under 6, free.

Amelia Earhart

Amelia Earhart Birthplace Museum. Amelia Earhart was a celebrated aviation pioneer who set numerous flying records in the late 1920s and early 1930s. She also was an author, fashion trendsetter, and an inspiration to women at that time. She disappeared over the Pacific Ocean in 1937 while trying to set another record—to be the first to fly around the world at the equator. Her life and achievements now are featured at the Amelia Earhart Birthplace Museum in her hometown of Atchison, Kansas.

Earhart was the first woman to cross the Atlantic Ocean in an airplane (1928), first woman to fly solo across the Atlantic (1932), first to fly solo from Hawaii to the mainland (1935), and first to fly from Mexico City to New York City (1935). In 1937, after Earhart and navigator Frederick Noonan flew over 22,000 miles—nearly two-thirds of the historic around-the-world flight—her Lockheed L-10E Electra took off from Lae, New Guinea, for the tiny Howland Island in the Pacific and was never heard from again. A widespread naval, air, and land search failed to find the plane or Earhart and Noonan. It was assumed that the plane ran out of fuel and crashed in the ocean.

Earhart became interested in flying after attending an air show in Toronto, Canada, in 1918 and then went for a plane ride in Long Beach, California, in 1920. She took flying lessons and saved enough to purchase a used Kinner Airster biplane in 1922. The following year she set a world record for female pilots at that time when she flew to an altitude of 14,000 feet. In 1928 she was the first woman to fly across the Atlantic as a member of a three-member team. Earhart followed with her Atlantic solo flight and other record-setting flights in the 1930s, when she set seven women's speed and distance records.

In 1931 Earhart married book publisher George P. Putnam, who was instrumental in funding, managing, and publicizing her aviation exploits. In addition to her flying career, Earhart was a writer who served as associate editor of *Cosmopolitan* magazine in 1928–1930, wrote magazine articles and newspaper columns, and authored two books about her flying experiences. In 1932 she also developed flying clothes for the Ninety-Niners, an international organization of female pilots who sought to advance the cause of women in aviation. She was one of the founders and the first president of the organization. In addition, she designed a line of women's clothing and sportswear.

The Amelia Earhart Birthplace Museum is located in the 1861 Gothic revival cottage where she was born and spent much of her childhood. It was founded in 1984 by the Ninety-Niners organization. The house has been restored and contains period furniture, personal and family memorabilia, and displays about the lives of Earhart and other women pilots. The museum has guided tours, lectures, and other educational programs and sports an annual Amelia Earhart Festival and Women in History Month. The annual attendance is 10,000.

Amelia Earhart Birthplace Museum, 223 N. Terrace St., Atchison, KS 66002-2525 (postal address: 609 Meridian Rd., Chester, NE 68327-7004). Phone: 913/367-4217. E-mail: aemuseum@lvnworth.com. Website: www.ameliaearhartmuseum.org. Hours: 9–4 daily; closed New Year's Day and Christmas. Admission: adults, $4 donation; children, $1 donation.

Virgil Grissom

Virgil Grissom Memorial at Spring Mill State Park. A museum dedicated to astronaut Virgil "Gus" Grissom is part of the Pioneer Village and Virgil Grissom Memorial at Spring Mill State Park near Mitchell, Indiana. Grissom, a native of Mitchell, was an air force pilot who was one of the original NASA Project Mercury astronauts. He was killed in 1967 with fellow astronauts Ed White and Roger Chaffee during a training exercise and prelaunch test for the Apollo 1 mission at Kennedy Space Center in Florida.

Grissom, who was born in Mitchell in 1926, flew 100 combat missions as an air force fighter pilot during the Korean Conflict. After the conflict, he became an instructor pilot and then a test pilot and was promoted to captain. In 1959 he was chosen as one of the seven Project Mercury astronauts. Grissom piloted the Mercury-Redstone 4, known as *Liberty Bell 7*, in 1961. The suborbital flight was the second American spaceflight. The flight also became known for the loss of the space capsule at sea during splashdown when explosive bolts blew the hatch off and water flooded the capsule as Grissom was rescued.

Grissom then flew with pilot John Young in the *Gemini 3* spaceship and was backup pilot for *Gemini 6A* when he was assigned as commander of the first Apollo flight in 1967. It was during a training exercise that the three-man crew died when the command module caught fire and burned on the launchpad.

The Virgil Grissom Memorial Museum was dedicated in 1971, four years after his death, as part of the Spring Mill State Park near Grissom's hometown of Mitchell, Indiana. The museum tells about his life and achievements and displays his space suit, *Gemini 3* space capsule, and memorabilia from his youth and career. The park also has a 1800s pioneer village, boat ride into a cave, pioneer cemetery, hiking trail, and rustic inn.

Virgil Grissom Memorial Museum, Pioneer Village and Virgil Grissom Memorial at Spring Mill State Park, 3333 State Rd. E., Mitchell, IN 47446 (postal address: PO Box 376, Mitchell, IN 47446-0376). Phone: 812/849-4129. Fax: 812/849-4004. E-mail: springmillstatepark@dnr.in.gov. Website: www.in.gov/dnr/parklake/6685.htm. Hours: 8:30–4 daily. Admission: free, but $5 per instate vehicle and $7 for out-of-state vehicle on Fri.–Sat.

Charles A. Lindbergh

Charles A. Lindbergh Historic Site. The Charles A. Lindbergh Historic Site in Little Falls, Minnesota, preserves the famous aviator's boyhood home and tells about his life and career. Lindbergh made aviation history in 1927 by making a nonstop solo flight across the Atlantic Ocean from New York City to Paris in a single-engine monoplane called the *Spirit of St. Louis*. He was a virtually unknown 25-year-old U.S. Air Mail pilot at the time but quickly became a national hero who used his fame to promote the rapid development of American commercial aviation.

Lindbergh also is remembered for the kidnapping and murder of his infant son, Charles Lindbergh Jr., in 1932. It was a sensational case that eventually led to the Lindbergh family moving to Europe in 1935 and not returning until the Japanese attacked Pearl Harbor in 1941. He was an outspoken advocate of keeping the United States out of World War II and was accused of being racist and having Nazi sympathies while traveling to Germany in 1936–1938 to report to the U.S. military on German aviation progress. Lindbergh became a supporter of the war after the Japanese attack and was actively involved. He served as an aviation consultant and flew about 50 combat missions in the Pacific to improve aerial performance.

In 1923 Lindbergh purchased a war-surplus Curtiss JN-4 Jenny for $500, made his first flight on his own, and barnstormed as a pilot. After several accidents, he sold the Jenny, resumed barnstorming, and then was ordered to report for a year of military flight training with the Army Air Service. He graduated first in his class in 1925 and earned his army pilot's wings and a commission as second lieutenant in the Air Service Reserve. He returned to civilian aviation as a barnstormer and flight instructor but continued to do some occasional military flying with the Missouri National Guard and was promoted to first lieutenant.

In 1925 Lindbergh was hired to plan and serve as chief pilot of a contract air mail route between St. Louis and Chicago. He successfully pioneered air mail service but was forced to bail out twice because of bad weather. Lindbergh continued to serve as chief pilot of the air mail service until mid-February in 1927, when he left for San Diego to oversee the design and construction of the *Spirit of St. Louis*, a Ryan NY-211 high-wing monoplane, which he planned to use in the competition for $25,000 Orteig Prize for the first successful nonstop flight between New York City and Paris. He used his modest savings and a $15,000 bank loan to build the plane and make the 33-and-a-half-hour solo historic flight in 1927.

In December 1927 Lindbergh met Anne Morrow, the daughter of diplomat Dwight Morrow, in Mexico City, where her father was the U.S. ambassador. The couple married in 1929 and had six children. She also became a noted aviator and author. She flew solo in 1929, became the first American woman to earn a first-class glider pilot's license in 1930, and explored and charted air routes between continents with her husband, being the first to fly from Africa to South America and to explore air routes from North America to Asia and Europe in the 1930s.

During World War II, Lindbergh served as a technical adviser to a number of American aviation companies, helping them overcome engineering and production problems. After the war, he was a consultant to the chief of staff of the air force and Pan American World Airways.

Beginning in 1960, Lindbergh became involved in the environmental movement and campaigned to protect endangered species. He also continued to write about his aviation experiences and other subjects. He wrote two bestselling books about his historic 1927 transatlantic flight—*WE*, immediately following the flight, and *The Spirit of St. Louis,* which won the Pulitzer Prize in 1954. He also wrote other books on science, technology, nationalism, war, materialism, and values until his death in Hawaii in 1974. Anne Morrow Lindbergh wrote 13 books, of which the *Gift from the Sea* became a best seller in 1955. Lindbergh died of lymphoma in 1972 at the age of 72 and his wife of a stroke in 2001 at the age of 94.

The Charles A. Lindbergh Historic Site is located adjacent to the Charles A. Lindbergh State Park in Little Falls, Minnesota. The Minnesota Historical Society preserves the 1906 home and interprets the Lindbergh history. The historic house contains the original family furnishings and many of its possessions. It also has an adjacent visitor center with exhibits and memorabilia related to Lindbergh's life and career.

Among the visitor center exhibits are a re-creation of the attic of the boyhood home filled with young Lindbergh's toys and souvenirs, a full-scale replica of the *Spirit of St. Louis* cockpit that visitors can step into, and numerous photographs and other historic objects. The center also has a small 1920s-style movie theater that shows Lindbergh's 1927 transatlantic flight. The annual attendance is 3,500.

Charles A. Lindbergh Historic Site, 2151 S. Lindbergh Dr., Little Falls, MN 56345 (postal address: 1620 Lindbergh Dr. South, Little Falls, MN 56345). Phone: 320/616-5412. Fax: 320/616-5423. E-mail: lindbergh@mnhs.org. Website: www.mnhs.org/places/sites.lh. Hours: Memorial Day weekend–Labor Day—10–5 Thurs.–Sat., 12–5 Sun.; closed Mon.–Wed.; May and Sept.–Oct.—10–4 Sat., 12–4 Sun.; closed Mon.–Fri. and remainder of year. Admission: adults, $7; seniors, $6; children 6–17, $5; children under 6, free.

Glenn L. Martin

Glenn L. Martin Maryland Aviation Museum. Glenn L. Martin was an aviation pioneer who grew up fascinated by the airplane developed by the Wright brothers at the turn of the twentieth century. In 1909, at the age of 23, he decided to build his own plane based on the Curtis *June Bug.* When it was destroyed in the first test flight, he built another one using silk and bamboo in its construction with the assistance of his mother, Minta Martin. It made a successful short flight and launched his long and successful aviation career.

In 1912 Martin built a seaplane that he flew from Newport Bay, California, to Avalon on Catalina Island and then back across the channel, which totaled 68 miles and required only 37 minutes to fly from Newport to Avalon. It broke the earlier English Channel record for over-water flight, and he received a $100 prize. That same year, Martin founded the Glenn L. Martin Aircraft Company and built an airplane factory in an old Methodist Church building in Los Angeles. To help finance his fledgling business, he did stunt flying at fairs and airfields and even played a role as a dashing pilot in a 1915 silent film starring Mary Pickford.

In 1916 Martin merged his company with the original Wright Company to form the Wright-Martin Aircraft Company. But he left the company the following year and formed a second Glenn L. Martin Company, which moved from Cleveland to Baltimore, Maryland, in 1928. Martin merged with the American Marietta Corporation in 1961 to become Martin Marietta Corporation. Another merger in 1995 with the Lockheed Corporation resulted in the formation of Lockheed Martin, a major aerospace and defense contractor.

The Martin Company produced more than 11,000 planes by 1960, including MB-1 and 2 bombers for World Wars I and II. In 1932 Martin won the Collier Trophy for his involvement with the Martin B-10 bomber. He died in 1955. A 1961 merger resulted in Martin Marietta, which produced missiles, space hardware, guidance systems, sonar, and avionics instead of airplanes. But the company returned to building airplanes after the 1995 merger with Lockheed.

The Glenn L. Martin Maryland Aviation Museum was founded in 1990 at the Martin State Airport in Middle River, near Baltimore. It traces the history of the company and of aviation in Maryland. The exhibits contain many items of Maryland and Martin Company historical significance, as well as industrial models of aircraft and rockets, wind tunnel models, restored and partly restored aircraft, and many original photographs relating to the Martin Company and its people. The museum's collections include 13 historic aircraft, thousands of original motion picture films, plans, documents, research models, aircraft tools and components, and over 200,000 aviation and company photographs.

Glenn L. Martin Maryland Aviation Museum, 701 Wilson Point Rd., Hanger 5, Ste. 531, (Middle River, MD), Baltimore, MD 21220-4238 (postal address: PO Box 5024, Baltimore, MD 21220-0024). E-mail: info@marylandaviationmuseum.org. Website: www.marylandaviationmuseum.org. Hours: 11–3 Wed.–Sat.; closed Sun.–Tues. and major holidays. Admission: free.

Christa McAuliffe and Alan Shepard

McAuliffe-Shepard Discovery Center. The McAuliffe-Shepard Discovery Center in Concord, New Hampshire, honors two NASA space heroes from the state—Christa McAuliffe, the first teacher in space, who died in the 1986 *Challenger* space shuttle disaster, and Alan B. Shepard Jr., the first American in space, who later commanded the

The McAuliffe-Shepard Discovery Center, a contemporary science center and planetarium in Concord, New Hampshire. Courtesy of the McAuliffe-Shepard Discovery Center; photograph by Kathryn Michener.

Apollo 14 mission and walked on the moon in 1971. The discovery center is an air and space museum that honors their memories and has exhibits and programs on astronomy, aviation, and Earth and space sciences.

The center originally was founded in 1990 as the Christa McAuliffe Planetarium and later changed from a planetarium to a more comprehensive science center. A new section also was added to honor of the life and career of Shepard. The center now has a full-size replica of a Redstone rocket surrounded by a multisensory exhibit in the plaza and interactive exhibits, space artifacts, planetarium shows, observatory viewing, and educational programs inside, as well as tributes to McAuliffe and Shepard. The annual attendance is more than 50,000.

Although not a member the NASA Astronaut Corps, 34-year-old McAuliffe was part of the 1986 *Challenger* space shuttle crew and was to conduct experiments and teach lessons to school children from space via closed circuit television. But when an O-ring seal design flaw caused the fuel tank to rupture and the spacecraft to break apart 73 seconds into its flight, all seven members of the crew were killed. The State of New Hampshire then built the planetarium in her memory.

Alan Shepard, a naval aviator who was part of the original group of seven Project Mercury astronauts, was the second person and the first American in space. He was scheduled to be the first person in space by piloting the *Freedom 7* space capsule in October 1960. But the flight was postponed several times. Meanwhile, Soviet cosmonaut Yuri Gagarin became the first person to orbit the earth in April 1961. Unlike Gagarin's orbital flight, Shepard made a ballistic trajectory suborbital flight to an altitude of 116 statute miles and landed in the ocean 302 miles down the Atlantic Missile Range. In 1971 he also was commander of *Apollo 14* on the nation's third successful lunar landing and walked on the surface of the moon. Shepard died in 1998 of leukemia at the age of 74.

McAuliffe-Shepard Discovery Center, 2 Institute Dr., Concord, NH 03301-7422. Phone: 603/271-7827. Fax 603/271-7832. Website: www.starhop.com. Hours: 10–5 Mon.–Thurs. and Sat.–Sun.; 10–9 Fri.; closed major holidays. Admission: adults, $9; seniors and students, $8; children 3–12, $6; children under 3, free.

Ellison S. Onizuka

Astronaut Ellison S. Onizuka Space Center. The Astronaut Ellison S. Onizuka Space Center in Kailua-Kona, Hawaii, is dedicated to the memory of the state's first astronaut, who died in the 1986 *Challenger* space shuttle disaster. Seven crew members were killed when the spaceship broke apart after the fuel tank ruptured 73 seconds after launch. The space center, located at the Keahole-Kona International Airport, tells about Onizuka's life and career, the history of manned space flight, and daily life in space. It contains such items as Onizuka's personal materials, an *Apollo 13* space suit, and a lunar sample. He was 39 years old.

Astronaut Ellison S. Onizuka Space Center, Keahole-Kona International Airport, PO Box 833, Kailua-Kona, HI 96745. Phone: 808/329-3441. Fax: 808/326-9752. E-mail: tashima@aloha.net. Hours: 8:30–4:30 daily; closed New Year's Day, Thanksgiving, and Christmas. Admission: adults, $3; students and children under 13, $1.

Wilbur and Orville Wright

Wright Brothers National Memorial. Wilbur and Orville Wright made aviation history in 1903 when they flew the first successful sustained flights in a motor-powered heavier-than-air machine at Kill Devil Hills, near Kitty Hawk, North Carolina. They made four flights from the base of the hill on December 17, including a 12-second flight that traveled 120 feet by a plane piloted by Orville, followed by Wilbur's 59-second flight covering 852 feet. The historic flights now are honored at the Wright Brothers National Memorial, established at the site in 1927.

The Wright brothers are credited with inventing, building, and flying the world's first successful airplane. In 1905, after continued improvements, they made a successful circular flight of 24 and a half miles in 38 minutes and 3 seconds near their hometown of Dayton, Ohio. Although many others worked on experimental aircraft at the turn of the century, fixed-wing powered flight did not become possible until the Wright brothers developed three-axis controls that enabled pilots to steer and maintain the equilibrium of an aircraft. The Wright brothers overcame conflicting claims and skepticism to receive a patent for their flying machine in 1906 and three years later sold a two-seater version to the U.S. Army.

Wilbur Wright was born in 1867 near Millville, Indiana, and Orville in Dayton in 1871. They developed their mechanical skills after the family moved to Dayton by starting a printing business, opening a bicycle shop, and then manufacturing their own brand of cycles. They became interested in developing a flying machine in the 1890s after reading about the pioneering aeronautical efforts of Otto Lilienthal, Samuel Langley, and Octave Chanute.

While others sought to achieve flight by increasing engine power, the Wright brothers felt better pilot control was the answer and began experimenting with a five-foot box kite and gliders. In 1900 they went to the coastal area of North Carolina with breezy ocean winds and sandy landing surfaces to begin manned flights. After building and testing three glider versions in 1900–1902, the brothers developed the powered *Wright Flyer I*, which they used in their successfully flights in 1903.

They then returned to Dayton, built *Wright Flyer II*, created an 85-acre pasture airfield at nearby Huffman Prairie, continued their experiments, and made longer flights. That airfield now is part of the Dayton Aviation Heritage National Historical Park (*see* separate listing). Wilbur died of typhoid fever in 1912 at the age of 45. Orville retired after selling his interest in the Wright aeronautical company in 1915 and making his last flight as a pilot in 1918. He served on various boards and advisory committees until his death of a heart attack in 1948 at the age of 76.

The Wright Brothers National Memorial has a 60-foot granite memorial shaft atop of Big Kill Devil Hill, reconstructed Wright camp buildings, and a visitor center with exhibits on the lives and careers of the Wright brothers, full-scale models, and tools and machines that they used during their flight experiments. The models include the 1903 *Flyer I* aircraft in which the Wright brothers made the first controlled flight and a model of the Wright brothers' 1902 glider. The center also contains a portion of the engine from the first flight, a reproduction of the wind tunnel used to test wing shapes, and portraits and photographs of other flight pioneers. The annual attendance is nearly 500,000.

Wright Brothers National Memorial, Virginia Dare Tr., U.S. 158, Kill Devil Hills, NC 27948 (postal address: 800 Colington Rd., Kill Devil Hills, NC 27948). Phone: 252/441-7430. Fax: 252/441-7730. Website: www.nps.gov/wrbr. Hours: mid-June–Labor Day—9–6 daily; remainder of year—9–5 daily; closed Christmas. Admission: adults, $4; children under 16, free.

Dayton Aviation Heritage National Historical Park. The Dayton Aviation Heritage National Historical Park in Dayton, Ohio, commemorates three outstanding turn-of-the-twentieth-century local men—aviation pioneers Wilbur and Orville Wright and poet Paul Laurence Dunbar. The Wright brothers built and flew the world's first successful power-driven heavier-than-air aircraft in 1903. Dunbar wrote novels, plays, short stories, lyrics, and over 400 published poems that largely reflected the African American experience in the nation.

The Wright brothers operated a printing business, bicycle shop, and then a bicycle manufacturing company in Dayton when they became interested in developing a flying machine. They did much of their research and experimentation before making the first successful flight at the Wright Brothers National Memorial site in Kill Devil Hills, North Carolina (*see* separate listing). After the successful flight, they returned to Dayton to continue the development and flying at a pasture airport they created at nearby Huffman Prairie. Huffman Prairie is now one of four parts of the Dayton Aviation Heritage National Historical Park, located within the eight-county National Aviation Heritage Area. The park also includes the Wright Cycle Company Complex, Wright Brothers Aviation Center at Carillon Historical Park, and the Paul Laurence Dunbar State Memorial operated by the Ohio Historical Society (*see* separate listing in Poets section).

Visitors can tour all four sites and see the Wright brothers' historically refurnished printing office, their original bicycle shop, the Wright brothers' third airplane and Huffman Prairie airport, and Dunbar's last home. Exhibits describe the lives and works of the Wright brothers and Dunbar at a visitor center/museum and two interpretive centers—the Aviation Trail Visitor Center and Museum, Wright-Dunbar Interpretive Center, and Huffman Prairie Interpretive Center.

Dayton Aviation Heritage National Historical Park, 16 S. Williams St., Dayton, OH 45402. Phones: Wright-Dunbar Interpretive Center—937/225-7705; Huffman Prairie Interpretive Center—937/222-4512. Fax: 937/222-4512. Website: www.nps.gov/daav. Hours: hours vary at different sites, but 8:30–5 daily at interpretive centers; closed New Year's Day, Thanksgiving, and Christmas. Admission: basically free, but tours at Dunbar House—adults, $6; students, $3; children under 5, free; admission at Dayton History at Carillon Park—adults, $8; seniors, $7; children 3–17, $5; children under 3, free.

Wilbur Wright Birthplace and Interpretive Center. Wilbur Wright, the oldest of the aviation pioneer Wright brothers, was born on a small farm near Millville, Indiana, in 1867. Wilbur's early life is now celebrated at the Wilbur Wright Birthplace and Interpretive Center, a re-creation in nearby Hagerstown, Indiana, of the farmhouse in which he was born.

The center tells how Wright developed early technical skills and learned critical thinking during his childhood, was injured during an ice skating game, completed high school but never received a certificate because his family moved to Dayton, and how he and his brother, Orville, began their careers and were the first to fly in a controlled, powered, and sustained heavier-an-air aircraft they developed (*see* separate listings for their careers). The center contains 1903 period furniture, a replica of the *Wright Flyer*, and an F-84F jet fighter, as well as exhibits about local history. The annual attendance is 10,000.

Wilbur Wright Birthplace and Interpretive Center, 1525 N. County Rd. 750 East, Hagerstown, IN 47346 (postal address: 15159 Hoover Rd., Hagerstown, IN 47346). Phone: 765/489-4005. E-mail: wilbur@nltc.net. Website: www.wilburwrightbirthplace.com. Hours: 10–5 Mon.–Sat., 1–5 Sun.; closed major holidays. Admission: adults, $4; seniors, $3; students, $2; families, $7.

BUSINESS/INDUSTRIAL/FINANCIAL FIGURES

Andrew Carnegie

Carnegie Museums of Pittsburgh. Andrew Carnegie was a Scottish immigrant who became the founder of the American steel industry, the world's richest man, and one of the nation's most important philanthropists in the late nineteenth century. He sold his steel interests in 1901 to J. P. Morgan, who merged them into United States Steel Company. Carnegie then gave away most of his fortune to libraries, universities, museums, science, and world peace. In the 18 years after he retired from steel, $350 million (billions in today's dollars) went to various causes in the United States, Scotland, Great Britain, and elsewhere.

Carnegie is best known for systematically funding 2,507 libraries throughout the English-speaking world, including 1,689 libraries in the United States, 600 in Great Britain, 125 in Canada, and 66 in Ireland. But he also made major contributions to such major institutions as the Carnegie Institution of Washington, Carnegie Corporation of New York, Carnegie Foundation for the Advancement of Teaching, Carnegie Endowment for International Peace, and Carnegie Hero Fund Commission, as well as such Pittsburgh educational and cultural facilities as the Carnegie Institute of Technology (now Carnegie Mellon University) and Carnegie Museums of Art and Natural History (now part of Carnegie Museums of Pittsburgh).

Carnegie believed that men who acquired great wealth should return it to the community to preserve individual initiative, a doctrine he expressed in his 1900 book, *The Gospel of Wealth*. He is quoted as saying, "The man who dies thus, dies disgraced."

He was born in Dunfermline, Scotland, in 1835 and grew up in an unorthodox political environment that influenced his later life. His father, William Carnegie, was a hand loom weaver with a background of radical idealism, and his mother, Margaret Morrison Carnegie, came from a family that sought political reform for the benefit of the working classes. The Carnegie family immigrated to the United States in 1848 as the British textile trade became industrialized and there was no demand for his father's woven linens. The family settled in Allegheny, Pennsylvania, near Pittsburgh.

Andrew soon became the chief earner in the family. At the age of 13, he worked as a bobbin-boy in a cotton factory and then went to work for a local telegraph company the following year. He quickly mastered telegraphy and was hired in 1853 as private secretary and personal telegrapher by Thomas Scott, Pittsburgh superintendent of the Pennsylvania Railroad. When Scott became general superintendent of the railroad, Carnegie replaced him at the age of 24. He remained with the Pennsylvania Railroad until 1965. During the Civil War, he went with Scott, then assistant secretary of war, to organize the Union's military telegraph department and helped open rail lines to Washington and elsewhere.

In 1864 Carnegie invested in a farm with oil wells on its property in western Pennsylvania and earned $1 million, and subsequently he joined a group in establishing a steel rolling mill. Carnegie then formed a bridge company and an ironworks; bought a sleeping car company; became a partner in an iron forging firm; invested in a steel company with a Bessemer plant that produced high-quality steel rails; and purchased iron ore lands in the Lake Superior region, ships and ore-handling facilities, and other steel mills.

Carnegie made Henry Clay Frick, president of H. C. Frick and Company, a partner in the Carnegie Company in 1884. Frick controlled most of the coal beds and coke ovens in the region. Frick later was made chairman of what became the Carnegie Steel Company and made it into the nation's largest steel company (*see* Henry Clay Frick in this section).

The Carnegie/Frick partnership cooled after Frick used 300 strikebreakers in the violent 1892 Homestead Steel Works strike in which 10 men were killed and 60 wounded. Frick and the company were widely denounced. An assassination attempt was also made on Frick's life after the confrontation. He was shot twice and stabbed four times but survived and was praised for his courage.

The partnership ended in 1899 after a quarrel between Carnegie and Frick. Carnegie's interests in the steel company were sold to J. P. Morgan in 1901 and became part of the new United States Steel Company. Carnegie retired and devoted himself to his various philanthropic efforts until his death in 1919, while Frick became involved in other industrial and financial activities and collecting art, which became the New York art museum, called the Frick Collection after his death in 1919 (*see* Frick Collection and Frick Art and Historical Center).

The Carnegie Museum of Art and the Carnegie Museum of Natural History in Pittsburgh were founded at the turn of the twentieth century by Andrew Carnegie. Today, they are part of the Carnegie Museums of Pittsburgh, which also includes two other museums added in recent years—the Carnegie Science Center, a hands-on contemporary science and technology museum, and the Andy Warhol Museum, the world's largest museum dedicated to one artist. The four museums have a total annual attendance of over 1.6 million.

The art and natural history museums were established by Carnegie at about the same time (1895–1896), are located in the same Carnegie Institute and Library complex, and one admission covers admittance to both institutions. The complex, a landmark building listed on the National Register of Historic Places, also houses the Carnegie Music Hall and the main branch of the Carnegie Library of Pittsburgh.

The Carnegie Museum of Art could be called the nation's first museum of modern art. It was founded as a contemporary art museum by Carnegie, who wanted it to be devoted to "Old Masters of tomorrow" rather than Old Masters of the past. It has a collection of over 75,000 objects (including about 35,000 artworks) and features American art from the late nineteenth century, French impressionists and postimpressionists, European and American decorative arts from the late seventeenth century to the present, and film and video works. The museum's annual attendance is 645,000.

The Carnegie Museum of Natural History is considered one of the five top natural history museums in the United States. Founded in 1996, it now covers 115,000 square feet, has a collection of 22 million specimens, displays exhibits in 20 galleries, and serves over 386,000 visitors a year. The museum is best known for its extensive dinosaur collection.

The Carnegie Science Center, which opened in 1991, evolved from the Buhl Science Center, which began as a planetarium in 1939. It is a contemporary science and technology museum with interactive exhibits, sky and laser shows, and an Omnimax big-screen theater with science and space films. Among its features are a World War II submarine, a miniature railroad and village, and the world's largest permanent robot exhibit. Annual attendance is 500,000.

The Andy Warhol Museum is the newest of the four Carnegie museums, opening in 1994. It contains 4,000 works in all media by Warhol, a Pittsburgh native. He became known for his "pop" culture art and underground films during the latter half of the twentieth century. The museum's annual attendance is over 90,000.

The Carnegie Museums of Pittsburgh, which administers the four museums, is operated by the Carnegie Institute, which also is located in the Carnegie Institute and Library complex in the Oakland section of Pittsburgh.

Carnegie Museums of Pittsburgh (central offices), 4400 Forbes Ave., Pittsburgh, PA 15213-4080. Phone: 412/622-3131. Website: www.carnegiemuseums.org.

Carnegie Museum of Art, 4400 Forbes Ave., Pittsburgh, PA 15213-4080. Phone: 412/622-3131. Fax: 412/622-3112. Website: www.cmoa.org. Hours: 10–5 Tues.–Wed. and Fri.–Sat., 10–8 Thurs., 12–5 Sun.; closed Mon., New Year's Day, Easter, Independence Day, Labor Day, Thanksgiving, and Christmas. Admission (includes art and natural history museums): adults, $15; seniors, $12; students and children, $11; children under 3, free.

Carnegie Museum of Natural History, 4400 Forbes Ave., Pittsburgh, PA 156213-4080. Phone: 412/622-3131. Fax: 412/622-8837. Website: www.carnegiemnh.org. Hours and admission: same as Carnegie Museum of Art.

Carnegie Science Center, 1 Allegheny Ave., Pittsburgh, PA 15212-5895. Phone: 412/237-3400. Fax: 412/237-1375. Website: www.carnegiesciencecenter.org. Hours: 10–5 Sun.–Thurs., 10–7 Fri.–Sat.; closed Thanksgiving, Christmas, and Pittsburgh Steelers home game days. Admission: adults, $17.95; children, $9.95.

Andy Warhol Museum, 117 Sandusky St., Pittsburgh, PA 15212-5890. Phone: 412/237-8300. Fax: 412/237-8340. Website: www.warhol.org. Hours: 10–5 Tues.–Thurs. and Sat.–Sun., 10–10 Fri.; closed Mon. and legal holidays. Admission: adults, $15; seniors, $9; students and children 3–18, $8.

Walter P. Chrysler

Walter P. Chrysler Museum. The Walter P. Chrysler Museum in Auburn Hills, Michigan, is devoted to the history and contributions of the founder of the Chrysler Corporation and the automobile manufacturing company he ran as president or chairman from 1925 to 1940. He was an automotive industry leader who made the Chrysler Corporation into one of the largest car companies in the world. He also financed the construction of the Chrysler Building, the world's tallest building in New York City at the time and was *Time* magazine's "Man of the Year" in 1929.

Chrysler, who was a railroad machinist, mechanic, and works manager, got his start in the automotive field as a works manager for Buick in 1911 and became its president in 1916–1919. He then acquired controlling interest in the ailing Maxwell Motor Company in 1921, introduced the first Chrysler car in 1924, and absorbed Maxwell into the new Chrysler Corporation in 1925. By 1936 he largely turned the running of the company over to others, and he became the semiretired head of the corporation until his death in 1940.

The Walter P. Chrysler Museum, founded in 1998 at the corporate headquarters, has 55,000 square feet of exhibits about Chrysler and the automobile company. Exhibits describe Chrysler's role in the development of the company and the corporation's design, engineering, and marketing contributions. Many of the 300 Chrysler-related vehicles in the museum's collection are displayed in a two-story atrium and three levels of exhibits. Annual attendance is 39,000.

Walter P. Chrysler Museum, 1 Chrysler Dr., Auburn Hills, MI 48326-2778. Website: www.wpchryslermuseum.org. Hours: 10–5 Tues.–Sat., 12–5 Sun.; closed Mon., New Year's Eve and Day, Easter, Independence Day, Thanksgiving and day before, and Christmas Eve and Day. Admission: adults, $8; seniors, $7; children 6–12, $4; children under 6, free.

Walter P. Chrysler Boyhood Home and Museum. The Walter P. Chrysler Boyhood Home and Museum in Ellis, Kansas, is located in the 1889 clapboard home where Chrysler lived from 1889 to 1908. In 1954 the Chrysler Corporation purchased the house, opened it as a museum honoring Chrysler, and gave the deed to the City of Ellis. A new building was built behind the house in 1994 to display many personal items from Chrysler and family members.

Chrysler was born in Wamego, Kansas, in 1875 and moved to Ellis with his parents when three years old. The museum tells about how he milked cows and sold milk door to door, worked in a grocery, sold silverware around town, shot marbles, and played softball as a boy. It also traces his life from becoming a machinist's apprentice and working on railroads before entering the automotive field in 1911 and becoming a successful automobile company founder and executive. Among the many personal items displayed are Chrysler's marbles, mechanical bank, mandolin, pen and pencil set, notebook, and books. The museum also has photographs, paintings, publications, and various collections, including eight vintage Chrysler-made vehicles.

Walter P. Chrysler Boyhood Home and Museum, 102 E. 10th St., Ellis, KS 67637 (postal address: PO Box 229, Ellis, KS 67637-0229). Phone: 785/726-3636. Fax: 785/726-3653. E-mail: chrysler55@eaglecom.net. Website: www.chryslerboyhoodhome.com. Hours: Memorial Day weekend–Labor Day—10–4 Tues.–Sat.; closed Sun.–Mon.; remainder of year—11–3 Tues.–Sat.; closed Sun.–Mon., New Year's Day, Easter, Thanksgiving, and Christmas. Admission: adults, $3; seniors, $2; children 8–15, $1; children under 8, free.

Glenn Curtiss

See Aviators/Astronauts section.

John Deere

John Deere Historic Site. The John Deere Historic Site in Grand Detour, Illinois, preserves and interprets the place where blacksmith John Deere developed and manufactured the first cast-steel plow in 1837. The self-polishing plow, which worked on tough soil, was credited with opening the Great Plains to farming and settlement. In 1868 he founded the Deere & Company, the largest agricultural and construction equipment manufacturer in the world.

Deere, who was born in Vermont, moved to Illinois and set up a blacksmith shop in the small Rock River town in 1836. When he found many farmers were discouraged by their efforts to cultivate the sticky Midwestern soil, he set out to develop a plow that would shed the soil. In 1837, he forged such a plow using a discarded saw blade and sold it to a local farmer, who told others about the success of the plow. By 1841 he was producing 75 to 100 plows a year. He then moved to nearby Moline and opened a factory that sold more than 10,000 plows by 1855. As business continued to improve, he turned the day-to-day operations over to his son, Charles, and devoted most of his time to civic and political affairs.

The John Deere Historic Site includes the 1836 home that Deere built and later expanded and an archaeological exhibit that shows the site of the original blacksmith shop. The restored six-room house is furnished as the Deere family would have done. It also has household objects that show how pioneers cooked, cleaned, bathed, and spent leisure hours. The archaeological site, which was found in 1962, is where the blacksmith shop was located and where Deere developed the historic plow. The site has been preserved in an exhibit building, which shows a simulated conversation about daily events between John and Demarius Deere, how the blacksmith shop was arranged and operated, artifacts found at the site, and a pictorial representation of the progress of Deere's business.

John Deere Historic Site, 8334 S. Clinton St., Grand Detour, IL 61021-9406. Phone: 815/652-4551. Website: www.deere.com/en_us/attractions/historicsite/index.html. Hours: May–Oct.—9–5 Wed.–Sun.; closed Mon.–Tues. and Nov.–Apr. Admission: adults and children over 11, $5; children under 12, free.

Walt Disney

See Entertainers section.

Washington Duke

Duke Homestead State Historic Site. The Duke Homestead State Historic Site in Durham, North Carolina, is where Washington Duke opened his first tobacco factory that led to the 1890 establishment of the American Tobacco Company, which was the world's largest tobacco company until broken up by an antitrust suit in 1911. Duke was a farmer who turned to the cultivation of tobacco in 1859 after his cotton crop failed and is credited with developing a market for tobacco.

After the Civil War, the Duke family turned from tobacco farming to tobacco processing. Duke opened several factories on his rural farm and then moved the operation to Durham, where the tobacco company was founded and became the leading cigarette producer in the nation. Duke and others eventually made Durham and North Carolina the international center of tobacco.

The Duke farm was purchased by Duke University in 1931, designated a National Historic Homestead in 1966, and made a National Carolina State Historic Site in 1974. The site includes the restored 1852 Duke home with four furnished rooms, tobacco barns, well house, pack house, reconstructed 1858 first factory, 1870 third factory, and a visitor center with exhibits about tobacco farming, processing, and the history of tobacco. Guided tours, participatory demonstrations, craft workshops, and other educational activities are offered. The historic site is visited by 18,000 annually.

Duke Homestead State Historic Site, 2828 Duke Homestead Rd., Durham, NC 27705-2726. Phone: 919/477-5498. Fax: 919/479-7092. E-mail: duke@neder.gov. Website: www.ibiblio.org/dukehome. Hours: 9–5 Tues.–Sat.; closed Sun.–Mon., Thanksgiving, and Christmas Eve and Day. Admission: free.

Eleuthére Irénée du Pont

Hagley Museum and Library. Eleuthére Irénée du Pont was a French-born Huguenot chemist and industrialist who immigrated with his parents to the United States in 1799 and founded the gunpowder manufacturer that became the E. I. du Pont de Nemours and Company in Wilmington, Delaware. The Hagley Museum and Library at the site of the 1802–1921 powder yards now honors his memory and collects, preserves, and interprets the history of the American enterprise.

Du Pont started his black powder mills, called Eleutherian Mills, along the banks of the Brandywine Creek in 1802. The company grew rapidly and became the largest supplier of gunpowder to the American military by the mid-1800s. The company experienced its greatest growth in the twentieth century when it became a leader in the chemical and materials science fields, resulting in the development of neoprene, nylon, Lucite, Teflon, Mylar, and other popular fiber and plastics products. It also acquired Conoco Inc., a major oil and gas producing company, in 1981. Today, Du Pont is one of the largest chemical companies in the world.

The first family home and gardens of Eleuthére Irénée du Pont at Eleutherian Mills are now among the highlights of the Hagley Museum and Library, founded in 1952 at the historic 235-acre gunpowder works site. The 1803 Georgian-style residence is furnished with antiques and memorabilia of the five generations of Du Ponts associated with the home. Adjacent to the house is the restored French-style garden created by E. I. du Pont.

The site, a National Historic Landmark, also contains the first office and barn, restored mills, storehouses, machine shop, waterwheel, workers' community, school, another historic garden, exhibits about the site and its workers, and a visitor center. Guided tours are given, as well as demonstrations of a water turbine, steam engine, power tester, and working machine shop. The library contains a major research collection of manuscripts, archives, photographs, pamphlets, and books documenting the history of American business and technology. The annual attendance is more than 63,000.

Hagley Museum and Library, 298 Buck Rd. East, PO Box 3630, Wilmington, DE 19807 (postal address: PO Box 3630, Wilmington, DE 19807-0630). Phone: 302/658-2400. Fax: 302/658-0568. Website: www.hagley.org. Hours: mid-Mar.–Jan. 3—9:30–4:30 daily; Jan. 4–mid-Mar.—visitor center open 9:30–4:30 and only two guided tours; closed Thanksgiving and Christmas. Admission: adults, $11; seniors and students, $9; children 6–14, $4; children under 6, free.

George Eastman

George Eastman House/International Museum of Photography and Film. The life and times of George Eastman, founder of the Eastman Kodak Company, are documented in his 1905 colonial revival mansion, which now is part of the of the George Eastman House/International Museum of Photography and Film in Rochester, New York. Eastman, who is considered the father of modern photography and inventor of motion picture film, lived in the 50-room house from 1905 to 1932. It is where the George Eastman Museum of Photography, the world's first photography museum and one of the oldest film archives, opened in 1949.

The George Eastman House is now as the core of a new and expanded photography and film museum called the International Museum of Photography and Film, which contains world-renowned photograph and motion picture archives and is known for preserving films, conserving photographs, and educating archivists and conservators. It also has a new facility that houses more than 400,000 photographs and negatives, 23,000 films and over 5 million film stills, 43,000 publications, and more than 25,000 pieces of technology.

The original furnishings, complex decorative interior, some bedrooms, and the formal gardens of the Eastman House have been restored; a motion picture theater has been renovated; and a lecture hall has been converted into a multimedia theater. Eastman's life and times are exhibited on the second floor, which also has a children's

Discovery Room with hands-on programs in a new wing. Eastman's extensive personal and business artifacts are made available to visitors and researchers through the George Eastman Archive and Study Center. The house and museum have an annual attendance of 155,000.

George Eastman House/International Museum of Photography and Film, 900 East Ave., Rochester, NY 14607. Phone: 585/271-3361. Fax: 585/271-3970. E-mail: info@geh.org. Website: www.eastmanhouse.org. Hours: 10–5 Tues.–Wed. and Fri.–Sat.; 10–8 Thurs.; 1–5 Sun.; closed Mon., New Year's Day, Thanksgiving, and Christmas. Admission: adults, $10; seniors, $8; students, $6; children 5–12, $4; children under 5, free.

Thomas Alva Edison

See Scientists/Engineers/Inventors section.

Edsel Ford

Edsel and Eleanor Ford House. Edsel Ford, son of pioneer auto manufacturer Henry Ford, served as president of the Ford Motor Company from 1919 until his death in 1943. He worked with his father to replace the aging Model T with the Model A, which featured a more modern body design, four-wheel mechanical brakes, and a sliding-gear transmission. In addition, he was responsible for introducing such cars as the Mercury, Lincoln Zephyr, and Lincoln Continental. He also is remembered, unfortunately, for a new line of stylish Edsel cars named in his honor and introduced by the company in 1957. The design failed to win buyer interest and was discontinued after three years.

Edsel Ford and his wife, Eleanor, lived in a large house that resembles a cluster of Cotswold village cottages with stone roofs, vine-covered walls, and lead-paned windows. It was designed by noted architect Albert Kahn on 87 acres along the shores of Lake St. Clair in Grosse Pointe Shores, Michigan. The house is listed on the National Register of Historic Places. After Ford died of stomach cancer at the age of 49 in 1943, his wife lived at the house until her death in 1976. She wished that the property be used for "the benefit of the public."

The house, which has original furnishings and collections of antiques and art, now is open for public tours and the site of classes, lectures, and special events. The site also has a pool house, power house, gate lodge, playhouse, and two exhibit buildings—a cottage with exhibits about the Fords and the estate and a garage containing four classic cars. A 1990 activities center serves as a welcome and orientation center. The property also includes gardens and the extensive grounds that combine woodlands, meadows, and wetlands. Annual attendance is 40,000.

Edsel and Eleanor Ford House, 1100 Lake Shore Rd., Gross Pointe Shores, MI 48236. Phone: 313/884-4222. Fax: 313/884-5977. E-mail: info@fordhouse.org. Website: www.fordhouse.org. Hours: Jan.–Mar.—11:30–4 Tues.–Sun.; Apr.–Dec.—9:30–6 Tues.–Sat., 11:30–6 Sun.; closed Mon., New Year's Day, Thanksgiving, and Christmas. Admission: grounds and house—adults, $12; seniors, $11; children 6–12, $8; children under 6, free; grounds only—$5.

Henry Ford

Henry Ford Estate–Fair Lane. Henry Ford, who founded the Ford Motor Company in 1901, revolutionized transportation and industry in 1908 with the inexpensive Model T automobile and the use of modern assembly lines in mass production. He made it possible for many to own cars by lowering costs, while rewarding workers with higher wages. And his mass production assembly-line approach was adopted by other automobile manufacturers and industries.

Ford, who was a prolific inventor with 161 American patents, followed the Model T with the popular Model A, which had more modern styling and mechanical improvements, in 1927 and other innovations in the years that followed as head of the company. He became one of the richest and best-known people in the world as head of the automobile company. In 1947 he died of cerebral hemorrhage at the age of 83 and left most of his fortune to the Ford Foundation, while arranging for his family to retain control of the Ford Motor Company.

The family of Henry Ford and his wife, Clara, lived on a 1,300-acre estate, which they called "Fair Lane," in Dearborn, Michigan, for more than 30 years. Their 31,000-square-foot home, made of limestone in a modified early English style, now is located on 72 acres (designated a National Historic Landmark) on the campus of the University of Michigan–Dearborn and open to guided public tours. The Ford Motor Company purchased the estate in 1957 and donated 210 acres to the University of Michigan for a Dearborn branch. The house now is administered by the Edsel and Eleanor Ford House nonprofit. In addition to the 56-room mansion, the site has a six-level hydroelectric powerhouse that still generates electricity and houses a laboratory and garage, greenhouse, staff cottages, pony barn, boathouse, and several gardens. The site is visited by 150,000 annually.

Henry Ford Estate–Fair Lane, 4901 Evergreen Rd., Dearborn, MI 48128. Phone: 313/593-5590. Fax: 313/593-5243. E-mail: grodgers@umd.umich.edu. Website: www.henryfordestate.org. Tour hours: Jan.–Mar.—1:30 Tues.–Sun.; closed Mon. and New Year's Day; Apr.–Dec.—10:30, 11:30, 12:30, 1:30, and 2:30 Tues.–Sun.; closed Mon., Easter, Thanksgiving, and Christmas. Admission: adults, $12; seniors and students, $11; children 6–12, $8; children under 6, free.

The Henry Ford. The Henry Ford, formerly the Henry Ford Museum and Greenfield Village in Dearborn, Michigan, is the largest indoor-outdoor history museum complex in the nation. It consists of the indoor Henry Ford Museum, which features a large collection of historical objects originally assembled by the pioneer automobile manufacturer, and the outdoor Greenfield Village, which contains 83 historic structures, including Ford's 1863 birthplace, as well as living history activities and a wide range of rides and other entertainment.

The museum complex was founded by Henry Ford in 1929. It originally was called the Edison Institute and named for Thomas Edison, a close friend of Ford's, on the 50th anniversary of his invention of the incandescent light bulb. The two museums later operated under their separate Henry Ford Museum and Greenfield Village names before adopting the Henry Ford as their present name.

The Henry Ford Museum began with Ford's personal collection of historical items, which he had been collecting since 1906. The present-day 12-acre indoor site consists primarily of antique machinery, automobiles, locomotives, aircraft, and pop culture items. It includes such items as George Washington's camp chair, the chair in which Abraham Lincoln was shot in Ford Theatre, Buckminster Fuller's prototype Dymaxion car, the Fokker Trimotor airplane that flew the first flight over the North Pole, the bus on which Rosa Parks refused to give up her seat and led to the Montgomery bus boycott, Igor Sikorsky's prototype helicopter, and the 1961 Lincoln Continental in which John F. Kennedy was riding when assassinated. The museum also has an Imax large-screen theater that shows historical documentaries and other films.

The adjacent Greenfield Village, which covers 80 acres, features a collection of buildings from the seventeenth century to the present—many staffed by costumed interpreters—that are grouped together in a village setting to show how Americans have lived and worked since the nation's founding. In addition to Ford's birthplace and a prototype of the garage where he built the quadricycle, they include such buildings as Noah Webster's home where he compiled the first American dictionary, the courthouse where Abraham Lincoln practiced law, the Wright brothers' bicycle shop and home, and Thomas Edison's Menlo Park laboratory.

It also is possible to go for a ride at Greenfield Village in an authentic Ford Model T and a railroad, steamboat, and carousel; see skilled artisans blow glass and make other products; and actually work on an 1880s-style farm. In addition, the village offers tours of the Ford Rouge Factory, a summer daytime Discovery Camp for young children, and numerous special events, including Memorial Day Civil War encampment and demonstrations, Motor Muster, Fourth of July holiday concerts, Ragtime Street Fair, and Old Car Festival. The Henry Ford Museum and Greenfield Village have separate entrances and fees and a combined annual attendance of 1.6 million.

The Henry Ford, 20900 Oakwood Blvd., Dearborn, MI 48124-4088. Phones: 313/982-6101 and 800/835-5237. Fax: 313/982-6250. E-mail: elainem@thehenryford.org. Website: www.thehenryford.org. Hours: Henry Ford Museum—9:30–5 daily; closed Thanksgiving and Christmas; Greenfield Village—mid-Apr.–Oct.—9:30–5 daily; closed remainder of the year except for select nights in December for Holiday Nights in Greenfield Village. Admission: Henry Ford Museum—adults, $17; seniors, $15; children 5–12, $12.50; children under 5, free; Greenfield Village—adults, $24; seniors, $22; children 5–12, $17.50; children under 5, free.

Edison and Ford Winter Estates
See Thomas Alva Edison in Scientists/Engineers/Inventors section.

Henry Clay Frick

Frick Collection. Henry Clay Frick was a leading industrialist, financier, and art patron during the late nineteenth and early twentieth centuries. He had a private art collection featuring high-quality Old Master paintings and fine furniture that later became one of the nation's most highly regarded small museums, called the Frick Collection. The collection, which Frick began in 1881 and was opened to the public in 1935, is located in his historic landmark mansion in New York City.

Frick, who achieved great success in the coal, steel, and financial fields and was vilified for his ruthlessness in business, was born to a farm family in West Overton in western Pennsylvania in 1849. He was the grandson of a wealthy miller and distiller and early showed an aptitude for business but received little formal education. With the financial backing of relatives and banker Thomas W. Mellon, he founded H. C. Frick and Company. He began buying coal lands and constructing coke ovens in the region and eventually controlled 80 percent of the coke ovens in western Pennsylvania.

Frick's abilities as a financial and industrial manager attracted the attention of steel magnate Andrew Carnegie. Carnegie made Frick a partner in the steel company and purchased a controlling interest in Frick's coke company in 1882. Frick became chairman of the Carnegie Company when Carnegie retired in 1889. Under his leadership, the company became what probably was the largest steel company in the world.

In 1892 the Homestead strike occurred at one of Carnegie's steel plants near Pittsburgh. It was one of the most bitter labor conflicts of the period. It resulted in violence, adversely affected Frick's relations with Carnegie, and nearly cost Frick his life in an assassination attempt. The Amalgamated Iron and Steel Workers Union went on strike after Frick proposed lowering the piecework wage rate to help pay for expensive new machinery in depressed business conditions.

Frick authorized the hiring of 300 strikebreakers through the Pinkerton Detective Agency. When they came down the Monongahela River in armed barges to the steel plant and attempted to land, a daylong battle ensued in which 10 men were killed and 60 wounded. Frick was widely denounced for provoking the violence. Shortly thereafter, an assassin entered Frick's office and shot him twice and stabbed him four times, but he survived and was praised for his courage in fighting off and helping capture the gunman.

Frick's partnership with Carnegie, however, was terminated in 1899, largely as a result of a dispute over the price of coke. It led to Carnegie selling his interests in 1901 to J. P. Morgan, who merged them into the United States Steel Corporation. By 1905 Frick's business, social, and artistic interests had shifted from Pittsburgh to New York. He moved the family to New York and spent most of the first 10 years living in a Vanderbilt mansion on Fifth Avenue. In 1913–1914 the Frick neoclassical mansion designed by Thomas Hastings was constructed at Fifth Avenue and 70th Street in Manhattan. It was designed to accommodate Frick's large art collection, which he began in Pittsburgh in 1881.

From 1883 to 1905, the Frick family lived in an Italianate mansion called Clayton in Pittsburgh's East End neighborhood known as Millionaires' Row. About 1885, Frick started collecting art in earnest, with much of the early purchases being focused on French landscape painters of the Barbizon school. He then greatly expanded his collection while in Pittsburgh and after the move to New York in 1905.

Frick died of a heart attack in 1919 at the age of 69. His artworks formally became known as the Frick Collection in 1920, the same year Frick's daughter Helen Clay Frick established the collection's Frick Art Reference Library. Frick's widow, Adelaide Childs Frick, and daughter Helen lived in the New York mansion until 1931. The daughter continued to add to her father's collection and later restored the Clayton family estate in Pittsburgh, where she opened the Frick Art Museum in 1970, featuring some of her father's collection and other artworks she had collected (*see* Frick Art and Historical Center).

The Frick Collection in New York opened to the public in 1935 after being bequeathed to the City of New York and altered and enlarged by architect John Russell Pope. The collection now is devoted largely to late medieval through early modern works and includes paintings, drawings, sculptures, decorative arts, and furniture. It includes such famous paintings as *Mistress and Main* by Johannes Vermeer, *The Progress of Love* by Jean-Honoré Fragonard, *St. John the Evangelist* by Piero della Francesca, *St. Francis in Ecstasy* by Giovanni Bellini, and Gilbert Stuart's portrait of George Washington.

Among the other artists represented in the collection are Rembrandt, El Greco, Thomas Gainsborough, Francisco Goya, Pierre-Auguste Renoir, J. M. W. Turner, John Constable, Titian, and Hans Holbein the Younger. The collection also includes such items as eighteenth-century French furniture, Limoges enamel, and Oriental rugs and has an adjacent building that houses the Frick Art Reference Library, with over 250,000 books, 78,000 sales catalogues, 3,650 serial titles, and 1.2 million photographs. The museum's annual attendance is nearly 270,000.

Frick Collection, 10 E. 70th St., New York, NY 10021. Phone: 212/547-0641. Fax: 212/879-2091. E-mail: info@frick.org. Website: www.frick.org. Hours: 10–6 Tues.–Sat., 11–5 Sun.; closed Mon., New Year's Day, Independence Day, Thanksgiving, and Christmas. Admission: adults, $18; seniors, $15; students, $10; children under 10 not admitted.

Frick Art and Historical Center. The Frick Art and Historical Center in Pittsburgh is located at Clayton, the primary estate of industrialist Henry Clay Frick and his family from 1883 to 1905. The estate was restored and an art museum was founded by Helen Clay Erick, a daughter who was born, spent her childhood, retained a fondness for, and returned to live there. It now features two museums and historical buildings that focus on the life and times of Henry Clay Frick.

Frick, who became a major steel figure in the nineteenth century, purchased and renamed the 11-room Italianate home, originally called "Homewood," on five acres in Pittsburgh's East End in 1881 after returning from a wedding trip with his wife, Adelaide Childs Frick. He had architect Andrew Peebles make interior and exterior modifications to the house, which he named Clayton. It is where the couple's four children were born and where Frick began accumulating his artworks—some of which still remain at the estate, The basic Frick Collection, however, is at the Frick mansion built in New York City in 1913–1914 (*see* separate listing).

Helen Clay Frick helped her father build his art collection and established the Frick Art Reference Library at the Frick Collection. When he died in 1919, she inherited the Clayton estate and its contents, the artworks at the family's summer home in Massachusetts, and $38 million, making her America's richest heiress at the time. One of her first actions was to restore the Clayton estate to its 1880s appearance.

Like her father, Helen was an art collector and established the Frick Art Museum in Pittsburgh in 1970. It was followed by the Frick Art and Historical Center in 1990. The center now also includes a car and carriage museum, with many of the early Frick automobiles and carriages; visitor center; children's playhouse; greenhouse; and café. Frick, who was born in 1888 and never married, moved back to Clayton in 1981 and lived there until her death in 1984. She left instructions for the family home to be restored and opened to the public, which it was in 1990.

The art museum contains European paintings with emphasis on Italian works of the early Renaissance, eighteenth-century French paintings and sculpture, bronzes and terracotta sculptures, tapestries, decorative arts, and Chinese porcelain. The Fricks' Clayton home features nineteenth-century art, family heirlooms, decorative arts, period furniture and furnishings, glassware, porcelain, textiles, and costumes. The center's annual attendance is nearly 130,000.

Frick Art and Historical Center, 7227 Reynolds St., Pittsburgh, PA 15208-2919. Phone: 412/371-0600. Fax: 412/371-6104. E-mail: info@thefrickpittsburgh.org. Website: www.thefrickpittsburgh.org. Hours: 10–5 Tues.–Sun.; closed Mon., New Year's Day, Independence Day, Thanksgiving, and Christmas Eve and Day. Admission: free; tours—adults, $12; seniors and students, $10.

J. Paul Getty

J. Paul Getty Museum. J. Paul Getty was the founder of Getty Oil Company, owned the controlling interest in nearly 200 businesses, and was an avid art and antiquities collector who once was ranked as the richest person in the nation and the world. In 1957 *Fortune* magazine called him the richest living American, and in 1966 the *Guinness Book of Records* named him as the world's richest private citizen with a wealth of over $2 billion.

Getty also established a major art museum: the J. Paul Getty Museum, which has two sites—a museum of European art from the Middle Ages to the twentieth century in Los Angeles and the Getty Villa, a museum and education center dedicated to the study of ancient Greek, Roman, and Etruscan arts and culture in Pacific Palisades, California. Both sites began with art and antiquities from the Getty collection.

Jean Paul Getty was one of the first persons in the world to have a fortune worth more than a billion dollars. He was born in Minneapolis in 1892 to George F. Getty and Sarah Risher Getty. His father founded the Minnehoma Oil Company. In 1904 the family moved to Los Angeles, where Jean Paul went to a private school and graduated from Polytechnic High School in 1909.

Getty then attended the University of Southern California in Los Angeles and the University of California at Berkeley and graduated from Oxford University's Magdalen College in England in 1914 with degrees in economics and political science. During the summer breaks, he worked in his father's oil fields in Oklahoma as a roustabout.

After graduation, Getty became a successful oil wildcatter in Tulsa, Oklahoma. It did not take long—just two years—for him to make his first million in 1916. He struck oil with the first well he drilled—the Nancy Tayor No. 1—near Haskell, Oklahoma. But he disappointed his father in 1917 when he decided to retire and become a playboy in Los Angeles. The retirement, however, was short lived. Getty returned to Oklahoma in 1919 and made $3 million during the 1920s. But his income suffered from his many marriages (three in the 1920s and two later) and two divorces.

Getty expanded his holdings during the 1930s depression. He acquired Pacific Western Oil Corporation and began gaining control of the Missouri Corporation, which included Tidewater Oil and Skelly Oil. They were merged into Getty Oil in 1967. Getty, who learned to speak Arabic, also began making major investments in the Middle East starting in 1949. He acquired a barren tract of land near the border of Saudi Arabia and Kuwait where his company discovered oil. It has produced 16 million barrels of oil a year since 1953 and enabled Getty to take controlling interest in nearly 200 businesses in addition to Getty Oil, which is said to be worth $2 billion to $4 billion by associates.

Getty moved to England in the 1950s. His sixteenth-century Tudor estate at Sutton Place near Guildford became the center of Getty Oil and associated companies. He lived there the rest of his life in the British Isles. In 1970 he began selling off his oil interests, starting with the sale of the company's European activities to Burmah Oil, which was bought by BP. After Getty's death in 1976, other sales were made to Texaco, Pennzoil, Lukoil Oil, and eventually (as Getty Petroleum Marketing) to a private investment group in 2011.

Getty died in 1976 of heart failure at the age of 83. His five marriages included Jeanette Demont, Allene Ashby, Adolphine Helmle, Ann Rork, and Louise Dudley. He had five sons and 15 grandchildren, one of whom was kidnapped in a sensational case in Italy in 1973. John Paul Getty III, a 16-year-old rebellious grandson, was kidnapped in Rome and $17 million was demanded as ransom. When the boy's father, J. Paul Getty II, said he did not have the money and J. Paul Getty refused to help, the ransom was lowered to $3.2 million. It was accompanied by a lock of hair, one of the boy's ears, and the threat of further mutilation unless the ransom was paid.

J. Paul Getty grudgingly paid $2.2 million of the ransom and loaned $800,000 to the boy's father at 4 percent interest for the remainder of the ransom. The boy was returned but permanently affected by the trauma. He turned into a drug addict, suffered a stroke, and became speechless, nearly blind, and partially paralyzed before dying at the age of 54. Nine persons were arrested for the kidnapping, but only two were convicted.

The J. Paul Getty Museum was founded by Getty in 1954. It began as a gallery adjacent to his house in Pacific Palisades. When he ran out of space, he built a museum, which later became the Getty Villa, on the property to house his expanding collection. It opened in 1974. Following Getty's death two years later, the museum inherited $1.2 billion, making it the richest art museum in the world. Part of the new resources then were used to develop a much larger facility designed by architect Richard Meier, called the Getty Center, which opened in 1997 on a 24-acre site in the Brentwood neighborhood of Los Angeles.

The two sites now are part of the J. Paul Getty Museum, which has an annual attendance of 1.6 million. Admission is free, but there is a $15 parking fee. The Getty Center museum contains European paintings, drawings, sculpture, illuminated manuscripts, decorative arts, and European and American photographs. Its collection of about 450 paintings from 1300 to 1900 includes such works as *Arii Matamoe* by Paul Gauguin, *Irises* by Vincent Van Gogh, and *Portrait of a Halberdier* by Jacopo Pontormo. The museum also has an orientation film with an overview of the Getty collection and activities, a selection from the special collections of the Getty's Research Library, and a 134,000-square-foot garden designed by artist Robert Irwin.

The site has four exhibit pavilions and five other buildings. Among the other facilities are the Getty Research Institute, which seeks to further knowledge and understanding of the visual arts; the Getty Conservation Institute, which advances conservation practices through research, education, applied fieldwork, and dissemination of knowledge; the Getty Foundation; and the J. Paul Getty Trust, which owns and operates the museum. The Getty Villa contains the museum's collection of Greek, Roman, and Etruscan antiquities and serves as an educational center with exhibitions, conservation, scholarship, research, and public programs.

The Getty museum has been involved in controversies with Italy and Greece about some of its ancient art and antiquities from those countries. One of its former antiquities curators and a dealer have been charged with trafficking in stolen antiquities, and the museum has been forced to return a number of artworks and antiquities said to have been dug up or stolen and shipped abroad illegally.

J. Paul Getty Museum, 1200 Getty Center Dr., Ste. 1000, Los Angeles, CA 90049-1687. Phone: 310/440-7300. Fax: 310/440-7751. E-mail: administration-museum@getty.edu. Website: www.getty.edu. Hours: 10–5:30 Tues.–Thurs. and Sun., 10–5 Fri.–Sat.; closed Mon., New Year's Day, Independence Day, Thanksgiving, and Christmas. Admission: free; parking fee, $15.

Getty Villa. The Getty Villa in Pacific Palisades, California, is part of the two-part J. Paul Getty Museum in Los Angeles. The art museum began as a gallery adjacent to Getty's home in 1954, expanded to the newly created Getty Villa in 1974, and opened a second and larger facility at Getty Center in the Brentwood section of Los Angeles in 1997 (*see* separate listing).

The Getty Villa building looks like an ancient Italian villa. Its design was inspired by the Villa of the Papyri at Herculaneum on the slope of the Vesuvius volcano in southern Italy and incorporated elements of several other ancient sites. The Papyri Villa was buried in ash in the A.D. 79 eruption of the volcano, and its remains were first excavated until 1750–1765. It got its name from the discovery of 1,785 carbonized papyrus scrolls in the house.

The Getty Villa was closed in 1997 when the Getty Center reopened in 2006 after being renovated with a new architectural plan by Machado and Silvetti Associates that shows Greek, Roman, and Etruscan antiquities within Roman-style architecture and gardens. The artworks are arranged by themes, and the architectural plan surrounding the villa is designed to simulate an archaeological dig. The villa displays approximately 1,200 works from its collection of 44,000 Greek, Roman, and Etruscan antiquities and serves as an educational center with special exhibitions, public programs, and research, conservation, and scholarship activities. The villa hosts such programs as theater performances, play readings, musical programs, and traveling exhibitions. Annual attendance at the museum is over 400,000.

Getty Villa, 17985 Pacific Coast Hwy., Pacific Palisades, CA 90272 (postal address: Visitor Services, 1200 Getty Center Dr., Ste. 1000, Los Angeles, CA 90049-1687). Phone: 310/440-7300. Fax: 310/440-7751. E-mail: visitorservices@getty.edu. Website: www.getty.edu. Hours: 10–5 Wed.–Mon.; closed Tues., New Year's Day, Independence Day, Thanksgiving, and Christmas. Admission: free; parking fee, $15 (but free for evening events).

William Randolph Hearst

See Journalists/Publishers section.

Milton S. Hershey

The Hershey Story: The Museum on Chocolate Avenue. The life and legacy of Milton S. Hershey, founder of the Hershey Company, and the firm's 150 years of operations are featured at the Hershey Story: The Museum on Chocolate Avenue in Hershey, Pennsylvania. The $23 million museum, which succeeded an earlier version, opened in 2009 and has over 90,000 visitors a year.

Hershey, who was born in nearby Derry Church in 1857, succeeded in establishing one of the largest chocolate companies in the world in 1903. He dropped out of school after the fourth grade, served as apprentice with a printer and then a candy maker, and founded a successful caramel company in Lancaster in 1883. Proceeds from the caramel factory enabled him to start the Hershey Chocolate Company in 1894, buy some farmland near his hometown, develop a popular milk chocolate, build the world's largest chocolate manufacturing plant, and create a model town around the facility.

Hershey and his wife, Catherine, founded the Hershey Industrial School for orphan boys in 1909 and formed a trust fund in 1918 that benefited the renamed Milton Hershey School (now a school for underprivileged boys and girls) and held a majority of voting shares in the Hershey Chocolate Company. In 1935 Hershey established the M. S. Hershey Foundation, which provides educational and cultural opportunities for Hershey residents. Among the many community facilities provided by Hershey are a theater, zoo, museum, gardens, ice skating rink, and community archives. It also made a $50 million contribution to a medical center built in Hershey by Pennsylvania State University.

The Hershey Story takes visitors from Milton S. Hershey's earliest entrepreneurial ventures to the development of the Hershey Company as the nation's largest chocolate manufacturer. The museum has two main exhibit sections—the Museum Experience, which contains a series of historical and interactive exhibits, and the Chocolate Lab, where visitors can engage in hands-on experiments. It also has a shop and café. Two other Hershey attractions are Hershey Chocolate World, a corporate visitor center with chocolate food, shops, and entertainment, and Hersheypark, an amusement park with over 60 rides and attractions.

The Hershey Story: The Museum on Chocolate Avenue, 63 W. Chocolate Ave., Hershey, PA 17033-1558. Phone: 717/534-3439. Fax: 717/534-8940. E-mail: info@hersheymuseum.org. Website: www.hersheymuseum.org. Hours: 9–5:30 daily; closed Thanksgiving and Christmas. Admission: adults, $10; seniors $9; children 3–12, $7.50; children under 3, free.

Glenn L. Martin

See Aviators/Astronauts section.

Cyrus H. McCormick

Cyrus H. McCormick Memorial Museum. Cyrus Hall McCormick revolutionized grain harvesting. He invented the first successful mechanical reaper, which harvested grain five times faster with much less effort than with a scythe or sickle and led to the founding of the McCormick Harvesting Machine Company. The company later became the International Harvester Company (now Navistar Corporation).

McCormick, who was born in 1809, first demonstrated the reaper in 1831 at his family's farm in Rockbridge County, Virginia, which now is the location of the Cyrus H. McCormick Memorial Museum operated by Virginia Polytechnic Institute and State University. The 632-acre farm was given to Virginia Tech by the McCormick family in 1954 and now serves primarily as an agricultural research station. The museum was established in 1956.

McCormick had a talent for mechanics and learned the skills of his father, who had experimented with farm machinery since 1816. His father patented a thresher and other farm machines, but none were commercially successful. He even tried to build a mechanical reaper, but the efforts ended in failure. When he abandoned work on the reaper, his son, Cyrus, took over the project and developed a machine that was radically different from his father's designs. He produced a machine with the gearing, reciprocating knife, projecting teeth, and rotating reel that became the basis of modern harvesting machines.

McCormick patented his reaper in 1834 and initially had limited production as he competed against a reaper developed by Obed Hussey. In 1844 he arranged for the manufacture of his machines in New York, Ohio, and other states, and three years later he had enough capital to establish his own factory in Chicago as he continued to improve his reaper and acquire the patents of others. McCormick's factory produced 800 reapers in the first year and 4,000 annually by 1858, when Hussey sold out.

In 1871 the McCormick factory was destroyed in the great Chicago fire that swept the city. He rebuilt the factory, and in 1902 the McCormick Harvesting Machine Company merged with Deering Harvester Company and three smaller manufacturers to form International Harvester Corporation. The company diversified and became a leading manufacturer of agricultural machines and equipment, light and heavy-duty trucks, and lawn and garden tractors. In the 1980s, however, a long and bitter labor dispute caused serious financial problems that resulted in the company being restructured and to change its name to the Navistar Corporation.

The historic McCormick farm still has eight of its original nine buildings, including the manor house, carriage house, grist mill, blacksmith shop, slave quarters, smoke house, school room, and housekeeper's quarters. The story of the reaper's invention and the history of grain harvesting by machines is told at the museum. The workshop/grist mill area of the farm is now a National Historic Landmark. Annual attendance is 8,000.

Cyrus H. McCormick Memorial Museum, 128 McCormick Farm Circle, Steeles Tavern, VA 24476 (postal address: PO Box 100, Steeles Tavern, VA 24476-0100). Phone: 540/377-2255. Fax: 540/377-5850. E-mail: dafiske@ vt.edu. Website: www.vaes.vt.edu/steeles/history.html. Hours: 8–5 daily. Admission: free.

J. P. Morgan

Morgan Library and Museum. John Pierpont Morgan—better known as J. P. Morgan or Pierpont Morgan—was the nation's dominant financier, banker, and banking and industrial consolidator in the late nineteenth century and early twentieth century. He also was a leading art and rare book collector during that period—which later resulted in the founding of the Morgan Library and Museum (formerly Pierpont Morgan Library) in New York City.

Morgan was both praised and criticized for his financial and industrial dealings. In the years following the Civil War, he and his financier father, Junius, had a reputation for stability and integrity. Much of their work was in funding and reorganizing railroads. Between 1890 and 1913, Pierpont worked on the consolidation of a number of industries, including the merger of Edison General Electric and Thomson-Houston Electric Company to form General Electric and the merger of Federal Steel Company, Consolidated Steel and Wire Company, and others with Carnegie Steel Company to create the United States Steel Corporation, the largest corporate enterprise in the world at that time.

Morgan was instrumental in breaking Jay Cooke's government bond monopoly in 1873, creating a private syndicate on Wall Street to provide urgently needed gold and a bond issue in the Panic of 1893, and helping to resolve the nation's financial crisis in the Panic of 1907 by rallying bankers to supply a rescue plan at a time when the United States did not have a central bank. Although hailed as a national hero, Morgan was accused of manipulating the situation for personal gain and controlling the nation's finances. He and others who had large investments in banks, railroads, and corporations were called "robber barons" by critics at the time. In the 1890–1913 period, 42 corporations were organized or their securities were underwritten in whole or part by J. P. Morgan and Company.

Morgan amassed an extraordinary collection of Old Master drawings and prints, early printed books, and illuminated, literary, and historical manuscripts. In addition, he had examples of the earliest evidence of writing in ancient seals, tablets, and papyrus fragments from Egypt and the Near East and historically significant American history manuscripts and printed materials. The collection was housed in his Pierpont Morgan Library, a private library and museum founded in 1906 and housed in a building designed by Charles McKim of McKim, Mead, and White and now a National Historic Landmark.

J. P. Morgan Jr. took over his father's business following his death in 1913 but never was as successful. In 1924 he made the Pierpont Morgan Library a public institution as a memorial to his father. It now occupies a complex of buildings, including the original library structure, at Madison Avenue and 37th Street. It functions as a museum and scholarly research center.

The library/museum underwent a major expansion designed by architect Renzo Piano, reopening in 2006 with a new name—the Morgan Library and Museum. Morgan's residence was replaced by an exhibition hall and a reading room in 1928, but an 1852 Italianate brownstone house purchased by Morgan in 1904 remains. The exhibition space has been doubled, with expansion above and below street level. A new reading room under a translucent roof structure has been added, as well as a four-story steel-and-glass atrium that links the original library building and the Morgan house.

The original collection, which still remains the focus, has been expanded and supplemented by such other materials as music manuscripts, early children's books and manuscripts, and materials from the twentieth and other centuries. The exhibitions are complemented by musical performances, lectures, readings, and video presentations. Annual attendance is over 150,000.

Morgan Library and Museum, 223 Madison Ave., New York, NY 10016-3405. Phone: 212/685-0008. Fax: 212/481-3484. E-mail: media@themorgan.org. Website: www.themorgan.org. Hours: 10:30–5 Tues.–Fri., 10:30–9 Fri., 10–6 Sat., 11–6 Sun.; closed Mon., New Year's Day, Thanksgiving, and Christmas. Admission: adults, $15; seniors, students, and children under 16, $10; free admission 7–9 p.m. Fri.

George Peabody

George Peabody House Museum. The George Peabody House Museum in Peabody, Massachusetts, is located at the restored birthplace of the international merchant, financier, and benefactor of numerous philanthropies. The building also serves as the community cultural center and visitor center for the Essex National Heritage Area.

Peabody, who is considered the father of modern philanthropy, was born in 1795 in what was then South Danvers (now Peabody) but spent most of his adult life in England. He was a partner in a wholesale dry goods firm, founded a securities firm, and served as a financier and partner in Peabody, Morgan and Co. until he retired in 1864.

Peabody founded and supported numerous causes and institutions, including helping "the deserving poor" in England, destitute children in the South after the Civil War, and such institutions named in his honor as the Peabody Institute of Johns Hopkins University, Peabody Museum of Archaeology and Ethnology at Harvard University, Peabody Museum of Natural History at Yale University, and Peabody Essex Museum in Salem.

The City of Peabody bought his birthplace in 1989 and converted it into the George Peabody House Museum, which is dedicated to preserving Peabody's history and his legacy of community interest. It also has exhibits on tanneries and the tanning process, including a small shop with leather-making artifacts. The house once was the site of such a cottage industry. Special exhibitions are also presented at the cultural center.

George Peabody House Museum, 205 Washington St., Peabody, MA 01960. Phone: 978/531-0355. Website: www.peabodymuseum.org. Hours: 10–3 Mon.–Wed. and Fri.–Sat., 10–7 Thurs.; closed Sun. and major holidays. Admission: free.

J. C. Penney

J. C. Penney Museum. James Cash Penney, who founded the J. C. Penney Company, was born on a farm near Hamilton, Missouri, in 1875 and opened his first store in Kemmerer, Wyoming, in 1902. The J. C. Penney Company became one of the largest and most successful department stores in the world. Two museums now are devoted to Penney's life and career—the J. C. Penney Museum in Hamilton and the J. C. Penney Homestead in Kemmerer (*see* separate listing).

Penney was the seventh of 12 children of a poor farmer who was a Baptist minister. Penney worked on the farm, raised cattle, and then became a clerk at a local dry goods store. When diagnosed as being susceptible to tuberculosis and told to move to a drier climate, he went to Denver in 1897. It was there he met Thomas Callahan and Guy Johnson, who invited him to work at one of their Wyoming dry goods stores, where he later opened his first store and started the J. C. Penney Company.

Hamilton civic leaders proposed starting a museum honoring Penney in 1969, but he said he did not want any memorial built in his lifetime. After his death in 1971, the museum was founded in 1974 and opened two years later. In 1988 Penney's boyhood home was saved from razing and moved to the center of town. The museum tells of Penney's life and contains such artifacts and memorabilia as his first and last desks, office chair, Masonic sword, photographs, and Penney sales literature. Annual attendance is 1,000.

J. C. Penney Museum, 312 N. Davis St., Hamilton, MO 64644-1145. Phone: 816/583-2168. Hours: 9–5 Mon., 8–6 Tues. and Thurs., 8–5 Wed. and Fri.; 8–12 Sat.; closed Sun. and major holidays. Admission: free.

J. C. Penney Homestead. The J. C. Penney Company's first store was in Kemmerer, Wyoming, which is the home of the J. C. Penney Homestead, a historic house museum about the company founder's life and career and one of the largest department stories in the world.

Penny was born on a farm in Missouri but moved to Colorado because of his health in 1897. He worked in a Denver dry goods store, opened a butcher shop that failed, and then went to work for Thomas Callahan and Guy Johnson, who owned a number of dry goods stores called the Golden Rule Stores in Colorado and Wyoming.

In 1902, after working with Johnson at the Evanston store, Penney was invited to join Callahan and Johnson as a partner for a new small store in Kemmerer. He and his new wife and child lived in the attic of the building. The store turned out be quite successful, and he was asked to manage two other stores within a year as part of the three-way partnership. The original Kemmerer building later burned and was replaced by a slightly larger store in 1929 (and is still in operation). In 1907 Penney gained full control of the Golden Rule Stores when Callahan and Johnson sold their interests.

In 1907 Penney moved the company headquarters to Salt Lake City to be closer to banks and railroads. His wife, Berta, died of pneumonia in 1910, and he later remarried twice. By 1912 Penney had 34 stores in the Rocky Mountains region. He changed the dry goods chain's name to J. C. Penney Company in 1913 and relocated it to New York City the following year to be closer to sources of merchandise. By 1917 the company had 175 stores in 22 states. It grew into a major retailer and now has over 1,100 stores in all 50 states and Puerto Rico.

Penney, who died in 1971 at the age of 95, was supportive of many causes. He was active in improving the quality of livestock, establishing a purebred Guernsey herd that he gave to the University of Missouri and a purebred Aberdeen Angus herd on the site of his father's Missouri farm. He also built a residential community for retired clergy and founded the J. C. Penney Foundation, which supports such issues as community renewal, the environment, and world peace as well as the J. C. Penney Homestead in Kemmerer.

Penney's first store still is in operation in Kemmerer, with its tin ceiling, antique cash pulley system, and other early features. The Penney home down the street now is a museum—known as the J. C. Penney Homestead. The six-room cottage, which is listed on the National Register of Historic Places, was restored in 1982 and moved to Penney Avenue on the Triangle. It contains period furnishings, personal memorabilia, and photographs.

J. C. Penney Homestead, J. C. Penney Homestead and Historical Foundation, 107 J. C. Penney Dr., Kemmerer, WY 83101-2941. Phone: 307/877-3164. E-mail: swehm@sweetwater.net. Hours: May–Sept.—9–6 Mon.–Sat., 1–6 Sun.; closed Oct.–Apr. Admission: free.

Frank Phillips

Frank Phillips Home. Frank Phillips and his brother, Lee Eldas Phillips Sr., founded Philips Petroleum Company, a major American oil firm, in 1917, which merged with Conoco Oil Company in 2002 to form ConocoPhillips. Frank Phillips was an entrepreneur who had worked as a farmer, barber, bond salesman, oil wildcatter, and banker and planned to be a big-time banker when the United States became involved in World War I. He and his brother foresaw the need for oil and consolidated their holdings to form a new major oil company—Phillips Petroleum.

Frank Phillips was born in 1873 in Scotia, Nebraska. When he was one year old, swarms of grasshoppers descended on the region and wreaked havoc among the farms, including his family's. The Phillips family moved to a small farm in southwest Iowa, where Frank Phillips got his entrepreneurial start. He worked for other farmers, digging up potatoes for 10 cents a day. When he was 14, he persuaded a barber to take him on as an apprentice, and 10 years later he owned all three barber shops in town—one of which was located in the basement of a bank in Creston. Phillips married one of the banker's daughters, and the father hired him to join him in selling bonds.

During one of his stops in St. Louis, he met an old friend, C. B. Larabee, who told him about an oil boom that was just beginning to take place in Osage County in Oklahoma. Later in 1905, Phillips and his younger brother, L. E. Phillips, went to Bartlesville and founded the Anchor Oil & Gas Company, which had a gusher after three dry holes. It was the first of 80 consecutive producing wells drilled by the company.

The Phillips brothers then established a bank in Bartlesville with $50,000 capital and acquired a rival bank to create the First National Bank of Bartlesville. Frank Phillips, who was concerned about the boom-bust instability of the oil business, planned to open a bank in Kansas City that would be the cornerstone of a group of banks throughout the Midwest. But when the nation became involved in World War I and oil prices increased from 40 cents to more than a dollar a barrel in 1917, the brothers consolidated their holdings and formed Phillips Petroleum.

Frank Phillips became president and led the Phillips Petroleum Company until he was 65 in 1939, when he company reported record profits of $24.1 million for the prior year. He became the company's first chairman, a position he held until he retired at the age of 79 in 1949, a year after his wife, Jane, died, and he died in 1950. Their house, known as the Frank Phillips Home, was donated by their granddaughter, Elizabeth Irwin, to the Oklahoma Historical Society in 1973 and is now a historic house museum.

The 26-room neoclassical mansion was built in 1909 and has been remodeled twice, but it still contains much of the Phillips family furniture, decorations, and personal effects. Annual attendance is 8,400. Frank and Jane Phillips also had a ranch retreat, known as Woolaroc, about 12 miles southwest of Bartlesville, which continues to operate as a museum and wildlife preserve (*see* separate listing).

Frank Phillips Home, 1197 S. Cherokee Ave., Bartlesville, OK 74003-5027. Phone; 918/336-2491. Fax: 918/336-3529. E-mail: fphillipshome@okhistory.org. Website: www.frankphillipshome.org. Hours: 10–5 Wed.–Sat., 1–5 second Sun. of month; closed Sun.–Tues. and major holidays. Admission: adults, $5; children 5–11, $2; children under 5, free.

Woolaroc Museum. Woolaroc was a most unusual ranch retreat owned by Frank Phillips, president of Phillips Petroleum Company, and his wife, Jane, in the Osage Hills near Bartlesville, Oklahoma, from 1925 until his death in 1950. It now is a 3,700-acre wildlife preserve with many species of native and exotic animals, a museum with a collection of Western art and artifacts, and two living history areas where visitors can experience life in an 1840s mountain-man camp and at an early oil drilling site.

The ranch got its name from a portmanteau of the words *woods*, *lakes*, and *rocks*—features of the area where it is located. The name originally was intended for the rustic ranch lodge, but it soon became the name for the entire ranch. The site is now owned and operated by the Frank Phillips Foundation, which was founded in 1937 by Mr. and Mrs. Phillips for the primary purpose of providing educational support for the employees of Phillips Petroleum Company (now ConocoPhillips) and their families.

The ranch, which originally covered 17,000 acres, is part of a historic district, listed on the National Register of Historic Places, with 18 buildings, 22 sites, 115 structures, and 17 objects. The site is regarded as a historically significant for its reflection of the time period, its role in the petroleum industry, and its landscape architecture.

Visitors can tour the ranch lodge, which is furnished as it was at the time of Frank and Jane Phillips; see the artworks, Indian artifacts, one of the largest collections of Colt firearms in the world, and the *Woolaroc*, an aircraft that won the 1927 ill-fated Dale Air Race; experience the life of a mountain man and oil pioneer; observe such animals as bison, elk, and longhorn cattle; and take a nature trail through the ranch's extensive natural environment. The artworks include the 12 miniature three-foot sculptures commissioned in 1928 by E. W. Marland, founder of the Marland Oil Company (which later became Conoco), for the 27-foot *Pioneer Woman* statue installed in Ponca City in 1930. The ranch's annual attendance is 100,000.

Woolaroc Museum, 1925 Woolaroc Ranch Rd., Bartlesville, OK 74003-7171. Phone: 918/336-0307. Fax: 918/336-0084. E-mail: lstone@woolaroc.org. Website: www.woolaroc.org. Hours: Memorial Day–Labor Day—10–5 Tues.–Sun.; closed Mon.; Sept.–May—10–5 Wed.–Sun.; closed Mon.–Tues., Thanksgiving, and Christmas. Admission: adults, $8; seniors, $6; children under 12, free.

R. J. Reynolds

Reynolda House Museum of American Art. The longtime home of the family of Richard Joshua Reynolds, founder of the R. J. Reynolds Tobacco Company, now is the site of the Reynolda House Museum of American Art in Winston-Salem, North Carolina. The museum has restored interior rooms and furnishings to reflect the nearly 50 years that the family lived there and an orientation video, oral history kiosk, and audio tours that describe the Reynolds family and the life they lived.

The Reynolds mansion was built in 1917 by Reynolds and his wife, Katharine. It was the center of a 1,067-acre estate, called Reynolda, which had 30 buildings, 28 of which still remain—most of which are now shops and restaurants in Historic Reynolda Village. It also still has formal gardens, greenhouses, and woodland walking trails.

Reynolda was the home of two generations of the Reynolds family. Mary Reynolds Babcock, the oldest daughter, acquired the estate in 1935 and lived there with her husband, Charlie, until the home opened as an arts and education institution in 1965 and then as the Reynolda House Museum of American Art in 1967. The museum, which has added a new wing, contains an impressive collection of American art ranging from the colonial period to the present, including works by such artists as Albert Bierstadt, Mary Cassatt, John Singleton Copley, Thomas Eakins, Georgia O'Keeffe, and Grant Wood. The annual attendance is over 36,000.

Reynolda House Museum of American Art, 2250 Reynolda Rd., Winston-Salem, NC 27109-5117 (postal address: PO Box 7287, Winston-Salem, NC 27109-7287). Phones: 336/758-5150 and 888/63-1149. Fax: 336/758-5704. E-mail: reynolda@reynoldahouse.org. Website: www.reynoldahouse.org. Hours: 9:30–4:30 Tues.–Sat., 1:30–4:30 Sun.; closed Mon., New Year's Day, Thanksgiving, Christmas, and January. Admission: adults, $10; seniors and teachers, $9; students and children under 19, free.

Reynolds Homestead. The Reynolds Homestead on the Commonwealth Campus of Virginia Tech in Critz, Virginia, preserves the 1850 birthplace and boyhood home of Richard Joshua Reynolds, founder of the R. J. Reynolds Tobacco Company. The 1843 two-story brick home was the home of the Hardin and Nancy Reynolds family on the 717-acre Rock Spring Plantation, which was deeded to the university and restored in 1970. Reynolds started the tobacco company in Winston-Salem after selling his share in the family's tobacco business in 1874.

The house, which has been designated a state and national historic landmark, features many of the Reynolds family's furnishings and personal possessions and offers guided tours. The homestead's original brick kitchen, milk house, icehouse, granary, and family and slave cemeteries are still located on the grounds. The historic site also serves as a continuing education center that offers music, art, lecture, film, fitness, and other programs. A 780-acre Forest Resources Research Center surrounds the former Reynolds plantation. The homestead's annual attendance is 1,500.

Reynolds Homestead, 463 Homestead Lane, Critz, VA 24082-3044. Phone: 276/694-7181. Fax: 276/694-7183. Website: www.reynoldshomestead.vt.edu. Hours Apr.–Oct.—9–4 Tues.–Fri., 1–4 Sat.–Sun.; closed Mon.; Nov.–Mar.—9–4 Tues.–Fri.; closed Sat.–Mon., New Year's Day, Thanksgiving, and Christmas. Admission: adults, $3; children, $2.

Frank. A Seiberling

Stan Hywet Hall and Gardens. Frank A. Seiberling, founder of the Goodyear Tire & Rubber Company and Seiberling Rubber Company, built Stan Hywet Hall and Gardens (Old English for stone quarry) in 1912–1915 in Akron. The 65-room estate, a Natural History Landmark, is considered one of the finest examples of Tudor revival architecture in America. It now is a historic house museum honoring the pioneer rubber and tire manufacturer.

Seiberling, who played a leading role in making Akron into the rubber center of the world, started the Goodyear company in 1898 and named it for Charles Goodyear, the discoverer of vulcanization, who died in 1860. It became the largest tire company in the world. Seiberling resigned as president of Goodyear in 1921 after it was taken over by financial interests and reorganized. He then founded Seiberling Rubber Company.

Stan Hywet Hall and Gardens, which originally covered 1,000 acres, now occupies 70 acres. Its principal feature is the 65,000-square-foot Manor House, which contains English and American period artifacts, sixteenth- to eighteenth-century European tapestries, eighteenth- to twentieth-century American and British fine art, and early glass, ceramics, textiles, and decorative arts. Among the other structures are the Gate Lodge, which was the birthplace of Alcoholics Anonymous, and the Carriage House, site of the museum offices, store, and cafe. Other facilities include landscaped gardens and grounds, tea houses, conservatory, greenhouse, and 250-seat auditorium. In 1957 the Seiberlings donated the estate to a nonprofit organization, which restored and opened it to the public. It serves 200,000 visitors a year.

Stan Hywet Hall and Gardens, 714 N. Portage Path, Akron, OH 44303-1399. Phones: 330/836-5533 and 330/315-3284. Fax: 330/836-2680. Website: www.stanhywet.org. Hours: Feb.–Mar.—10–4 Tues.–Sat., 1–4 Sun.; closed Mon.; Apr.–Dec.—10–4 daily; closed Easter, Nov. 13, Thanksgiving, and Christmas Eve and Day. Admission: mansion and gardens—adults, $12; children 6–12, $6; children under 6, free; gardens—adults, $5; children 6–12, $3; children under 6, free.

Cornelius Vanderbilt II

The Breakers. The Breakers, the grandest of the elaborate "summer cottages" in Newport, Rhode Island, was built by Cornelius Vanderbilt II, grandson of Cornelius Vanderbilt, known as the Commodore, who was founder of the family transportation and financial dynasty. Cornelius II succeeded his grandfather and father, William, as president and then chairman of the New York Central and related railroad lines in 1885.

The Breakers, a 70-room Italian Renaissance–style villa designed by Richard Morris Hunt, was built in the 1893–1895 to replace a smaller wooden-framed house that was destroyed in a fire. The five-story, 65,000-square-foot mansion, located along the cliffs overlooking the Atlantic Ocean, became the largest and most opulent house in the summer resort, which was considered the social center of the nation at the turn of the century.

The house, a National Historic Landmark, was inherited by Vanderbilt's youngest daughter, Gladys, who married a Hungarian count and lived there part-time. She opened the mansion to raise funds for the Preservation Society of Newport County in 1948, and the society purchased the property from heirs in 1972. It now is one of the society's 11 historic properties. The Breakers, which still retains its original furnishings and gardens, is open to the public and has approximately 300,000 visitors a year.

The Breakers, 44 Ochre Ave., Newport, RI 02840 (postal address: Preservation Society of Newport County, 424 Bellevue Ave., Newport, RI 02840). Phone: 401/847-1000. Website: www.newportmansions.org. Hours: Apr.–Dec.—9–6 daily; Jan.–Mar.—9–5 daily; closed Thanksgiving and Christmas. Admission: adults, $18; children 6–17, $4.50; children under 5, free.

Frederick W. Vanderbilt

Vanderbilt Mansion National Historic Site. The 1896–1899 Beaux-Arts-style country home of Frederick W. Vanderbilt on 600 acres along the Hudson River in Hyde Park, New York, became the Vanderbilt Mansion National Historic Site in 1940. It is an example of a Gilded Age country place that illustrates the political, economic, social, cultural, and demographic changes that occurred during the industrial period after the Civil War.

Vanderbilt, a director of the New York Central Railroad for 61 years, was a brother of Cornelius Vanderbilt II; a son of William Henry Vanderbilt, chairman of the New York Central; and a grandson of "Commodore" Cornelius Vanderbilt, patriarch of the transportation and financial family. Frederick and his wife, Louise, also had residences in New York City, Newport, and Bar Harbor. The Hyde Park country house contains much of its original furnishings; has a visitor center, gardens, and walking carriage trails; and offers guided house tours. The annual attendance is 360,000.

Vanderbilt Mansion National Historic Site, Rte. 9, Hyde Park, NY 12538 (postal address: 4097 Albany Post Rd., Hyde Park, NY 12538). Phones: 845/229-9115 and 845/229-9116. Fax: 845/229-0739. Website: www.nps.gov/vama. Hours: grounds—sunset–sunset daily; house—9–5 daily; closed New Year's Day, Thanksgiving, and Christmas. Admission: grounds—free; house—adults, $8; children under 16, free.

George Washington Vanderbilt II

Biltmore Estate. The largest privately owned home in the United States is the 250-room French château at the Biltmore Estate in Asheville, North Carolina. It was built in the 1890s by George Washington Vanderbilt II, a member of the prominent Vanderbilt family, which made fortunes in steamboats, railroads, and other business enterprises in the nineteenth century. Unlike many other members of the Vanderbilt family, George did not achieve great success in the business world. But he inherited a fortune that enabled him to purchase 125,000 acres and build the 175,000-square-foot mansion and live the life of a country gentleman. The architect was Richard Morris Hunt, and the grounds were designed by Frederick Law Olmstead.

Following his death in 1918, Vanderbilt's widow, Edith, sold approximately 86,000 acres to the U.S. Forest Service, which created the Pisgah National Forest. Other sales followed as finances demanded, and only 8,000 acres remain today as part of the Biltmore Estate, a historic house site founded by a descendant in 1930 that now attracts 900,000 visitors annually. The mansion still retains many of its original artworks, tapestries, furnishings, antiques, and books. Among the other site features are a welcome center, formal and informal gardens, winery, outdoor center, conservatory, carriage and trail rides, and the River Bend Farm, with craft demonstrations, farm animals, kitchen garden, antique farm equipment, creamery, and old-fashioned mercantile store. Guided tours are offered of the house, rooftop, winery, farm, grounds, and behind the scenes.

Biltmore Estate, 1 Approach Rd., Asheville, NC 28803. Phones: 828/255-1333 and 800/411-3812. Fax: 828/225-6383. Website: www.biltmore.com. Hours: 8:30–3 Mon.–Thurs., 8:30–4 Fri.–Sun.; winter—10–3 Mon.–Fri., 10–4 Sat.–Sun. Admission: varies with seasons—adults, $40 to $60; youth 10–16, free to $30; children under 10, free.

Wilbur and Orville Wright

See Aviators/Astronauts section.

EDUCATORS

Mary McLeod Bethune

Mary McLeod Bethune Home. Mary McLeod Bethune was the daughter of former slaves who grew up amid poverty and oppression in the South in the post–Civil War period. She was planning to be an African missionary, but when that was not possible, she became an innovative educator and an effective social and political activist for racial and gender equality. She founded a girls school, a college, and a national black women's organization; served as president of other leading black groups; was the first African American woman to hold a high position in the federal government; and became one of the nation's most influential African Americans at her time.

Bethune was born on a cotton and rice plantation near Mayesville, South Carolina, in 1875—the fifteenth of 17 children of Samuel and Patsy McLeod. She worked in the fields picking cotton when she was five and took an early interest in education. She was a bright student and received scholarships to further her education. She attended the local Trinity Presbyterian Mission School, Scotia Seminary (now Barber-Scotia College), and the Bible Institute for Home and Foreign Missions (later Moody Bible Institute).

She was going to be an African missionary, but when she learned that the Presbyterian Mission Board would not assign an African American to Africa, she turned to teaching and soon saw that the education of black students was the most effective way to improve conditions for African Americans. From 1895 to 1904, she taught in various mission schools in Georgia, South Carolina, and Florida. In 1898 she married Albertus Bethune, another teacher, who left her and their son in 1907 when he could not work and returned to his parents' home in South Carolina, where he died of tuberculosis in 1918.

In 1904 Bethune founded the Daytona Educational and Industrial Training School for Negro Girls (later renamed the Daytona Normal and Industrial Institute), with five young black girls and her son as pupils. The school enrollment grew to 351 by 1920 and became a coed high school after a merger with the Cookman Institute for Men of Jacksonville, Florida, in 1923. A year later, the school became affiliated with the United Methodist Church and evolved into a junior college called the Bethune-Cookman College. In 1941 it became a four-year baccalaureate program and achieved university status in 2007. Bethune retired in 1942 after 38 years directing the school, but she continued to live in the campus house she built in 1925 until her death in 1955.

Bethune's efforts in building the school attracted national attention, and she began to play a greater role in the public sector. She was in great demand as a speaker, served on numerous national committees, and was president of the National Association of Teachers in Colored Schools. In 1935 she also founded the National Council of Negro Women, where she served as president for 14 years and had the headquarters in her Washington townhouse. She also was active in the Interracial Council of America, served as director of the Division of Negro Affairs of the National Youth Administration in 1938–1944, advised the U.S. delegation involved in developing the United Nations charter, and served as adviser to Presidents Franklin D. Roosevelt and (on a more limited scale) Harry S. Truman and Dwight D. Eisenhower on matters affecting race relations.

Bethune, who died in 1955 at the age of 79, received many honors and awards, including 11 honorary degrees. The house where she lived on the Bethune-Cookman University campus now is a museum and a National Historic Landmark—known as the Mary McLeod Bethune Home—and her later townhouse that housed the National Council of Negro Women in Washington is called the Mary McLeod Bethune Council House National Historic Site (*see* separate listing). The 1925 Mary McLeod Bethune Home is a two-story frame house that has Bethune's original furnishings and memorabilia, citations, and photographs, as well as an addition that serves as an archive for her papers.

Mary McLeod Bethune Home, Bethune-Cookman University, 640 Mary McLeod Bethune Blvd., Daytona Beach, FL 32114. Phone: 386/481-2122. Hours: by appointment. Admission: free.

Mary McLeod Bethune Council House National Historic Site. The Mary McLeod Bethune Council House National Historic Site, established in 1991 in Washington, honors the African American educator and social and political activist and the national organization she founded to advance opportunities for black women, their families, and communities. Bethune became known for her efforts to further racial and gender equality as well as education. Her Washington townhouse, where she lived from 1943 until 1949 while working for the federal government and directing the National Council of Negro Women, became a center for the development of strategies and programs to advance the interests of African American women and the black community.

Bethune founded the Daytona Educational and Industrial Training School for Negro Girls (later changed to Daytona Normal and Industrial Institute) in Daytona Beach, Florida, in 1904. It merged with the Cookman Institute for Men in 1923 to form the coeducational Bethune-Cookman College, which became Bethune-Cookman University in 2007. She received national recognition for her work at the college, became politically active, and soon was involved at the national level as a spokesperson for the African American community.

Bethune served as president of the National Association of Colored Women; founded the National Council for Negro Women in 1935 (and was president for 14 years); served as director of the Division of Negro Affairs in the National Youth Administration (the first African American woman to head a federal agency) from 1936 to 1944; and was an advisor on minority affairs to President Franklin D. Roosevelt and later to Presidents Harry S. Truman and Dwight D. Eisenhower in a more limited role.

She served as the president of Bethune-Cookman College until retiring in 1942, when she moved temporarily to an 1876 three-story Victorian townhouse she bought in Washington to be close to her government work and to house the headquarters of the National Council of Negro Women. When Bethune died in 1955, she left the historic building to the women's council, which sold it to the National Park Service in 1979 for a historic site and moved to a new, larger Washington building. The council now reaches nearly 4 million women with its 28 national affiliate organizations and 200 community-based sections.

The Bethune townhouse has become the Mary McLeod Bethune Council House National Historic Site. It has two buildings—the fully restored townhouse and a carriage house. The museum/archives serves as a central library for records of Bethune and other black female leaders and displays artifacts, manuscripts, paintings, and photographs relating to the black women's rights movement. It also offers a video on Bethune's life and guided tours by park rangers. The site has been designated a National Historic Landmark and is listed on the National Register of Historic Places. Annual attendance is 8,600.

Mary McLeod Bethune Council House National Historic Site, 1318 Vermont Ave., N.W., Washington, DC 20005-3607. Phone: 202/673-2404. Fax: 202/673-2414. Website: www.nps.gov/mamc. Hours: 9–5 Mon.–Sat.; closed Sun., New Year's Day, Thanksgiving, and Christmas. Admission: free.

Prudence Crandall

Prudence Crandall Museum. Prudence Crandall is known for opening New England's first academy for black girls in 1833–1834. She began an academy in Canterbury, Connecticut, in 1832 at the request of the community to educate the daughters of wealthy local families. It became quite popular until Sarah Harris, a 20-year-old black woman was admitted, which led white parents to withdraw their children and closed the school. Crandall responded the following year by reopening the academy for "young ladies and little misses of color," and more than 20 young African American women from throughout the region enrolled.

The State of Connecticut sought to close the school by passing the "Black Law," which made it illegal for Crandall to operate her school. When she persisted, she was arrested and faced trial, but the case was dismissed. A mob then attacked and set fire to the academy in 1834 and forced the school to close. The Black Law was repealed four years later, and schools were opened to all children. The Prudence Crandall Museum, located in the 1805 Prudence Crandall house, now tells the story and features three rooms with changing exhibitions. It is operated by the Connecticut Commission of Culture and Tourism.

Prudence Crandall Museum, Routes 14 and 169, Canterbury Green, Canterbury, CT 06331 (postal address: PO Box 58, Canterbury, CT 06331-0058). Phone: 860/546-9916. Fax: 860/546-7803. E-mail: crandall.museum@ct.gov. Website: www.cultureandtourism.org/cct/cwp/view.asp?a=2127&q=302260. Hours: Apr.–mid-Dec.—10–4:30 Wed.–Sun.; closed Mon.–Tues., remainder of year, and major holidays. Admission: adults, $3; seniors and children 6–12, $2; children under 6, free.

William Holmes McGuffey

William Holmes McGuffey Museum. The William Holmes McGuffey Museum at Miami University in Oxford, Ohio, honors the developer of the McGuffey Eclectic Readers—a series of four readers published in 1836–1837 and used in schools and by the public to learn to read until recent years. More than 122 million original and revised editions have been sold since published.

McGuffey, who was born in 1800 in Claysville, Pennsylvania, was a graduate of Washington College, where he became an instructor. In 1826 he was hired as a professor at Miami University, where he taught for 10 years, was ordained a Presbyterian minister, and created the McGuffey Readers, one of the nation's first and most widely used series of textbooks. He also served as president of Cincinnati College in 1836–1839, Ohio University in 1839–1843, and Woodward College in 1843–1844 and then was professor of philosophy at the University of Virginia from 1845 until his death in 1873.

The William Holmes McGuffey Museum, which was founded in 1960, is located in the house where McGuffey lived while at Miami University. It contains collections and exhibits relating to his life, the McGuffey Readers, Miami University history, and nineteenth-century domestic life and architecture of southwest Ohio. They include memorabilia, period furniture, paintings, decorative arts, and other historical materials. The annual attendance is 2,500.

William Holmes McGuffey Museum, Miami University, 410 E. Spring St., Oxford, OH 45056-3646. Phone: 513/529-8380. Fax: 513/529-2637. E-mail: mcguffeymuseum@muohio.edu. Website: www.units.muohio.edu/mcguffeymuseum. Hours: 1–5 Tues.–Fri., 1–4 Sat.–Sun.; closed Mon. and university holidays. Admission: free.

Sequoyah

Sequoyah Cabin. Sequoyah was an American Indian scholar who developed the Cherokee syllabary, enabling the Cherokee to read and write. The one-room cabin he built in 1829 in Sallisaw, Oklahoma, is now a historic site museum operated by the Oklahoma Historical Society and designated as a National Historic Landmark by the U.S. Department of Interior.

Sequoyah was born as Nathaniel Gist in Taskigi, Tennessee, about 1770. It is believed he had a white father who left the family when Sequoyah was a young child. He was lame in one leg but became known as a skilled blacksmith, silversmith, and artist. The Cherokee did not have a written language, and he began experimenting in an effort to develop a written alphabet in 1809. In 1813–1814, he served with the U.S. Army in the Creek War and in 1818 went to operate a salt production and blacksmith works near present-day Russellville, Arkansas.

By 1821 he found that the Cherokee language is composed of a set number of recurring sounds. He gave each sound a symbol and was able to create a workable alphabet to communicate written messages. The Cherokee Council approved the system, and Sequoyah taught thousands of people to read and write.

In 1828 Sequoyah was part of a delegation sent to Washington by the Arkansas Cherokee to make a treaty to exchange their lands for sites in Indian Territory (now Oklahoma). Sequoyah also traded his land and saltworks for land located on Big Skin Bayou Creek in what became Sequoyah County, where the historic Sequoyah log cabin was built in 1829. It became part of the Oklahoma Historical Society in 1936 and was enclosed in a stone cover building constructed as part of the Works Progress Administration program. It contains historic furnishings and exhibits relating to the Cherokee and other Native Americans and the development of the syllabary. Annual attendance is 20,000.

Sequoyah Cabin, 470288 Hwy. 101, Sallisaw, OK 74955-9744 (postal address: Rural Rte. 1, PO Box 103A, Sallisaw, OK 74955-9744). Phone: 918/775-2413. E-mail: seqcabin@okhistory.org. Website: www.okhistory.org/outreach/homes/sequoyahcabin.html. Hours: 9–5 Tues.–Fri., 2–5 Sat.–Sun.; closed Mon. and major holidays. Admission: free.

Booker T. Washington

Booker T. Washington National Monument. The Booker T. Washington National Monument in Hardy, Virginia, honors the African American educator who established and headed Tuskegee Normal and Industrial Institute (now Tuskegee University) in Tuskegee, Alabama, during the late 1800s and early 1900s. The monument is located at the site of the Burroughs Plantation, a tobacco farm where Washington was born as a slave and lived during childhood. It now is a living history farm museum with plantation equipment and exhibits on black history and the life and times of Washington.

Washington was an important and controversial African American educational leader during a period of increasing racism in the nation. He was an able administrator who guided Tuskegee, founded in 1881, through difficult growing times. With an annual appropriation of only $2,000, the institute literally was built by students, who helped construct the buildings, grow the crops, and raise the livestock as they learned the trades as well as academics.

Washington was the dominant figure in the African American community in the United States from 1890 to 1915. But he was criticized for his conservative views opposing agitation for social and political purposes among African Americans. He overcame many obstacles with support from powerful whites and most African American business, education, and religious leaders; his ability to raise large amounts of funds from philanthropists; and his accommodation to the political realities in an age of Jim Crow segregation.

Washington was born in 1856 and experienced great hardships as a child on the tobacco farm. He was a graduate of Hampton Institute, where he taught in a program for Native Americans in 1879–1881. When Alabama decided to open a school for practical training of African Americans in the trades and professions, he was chosen to organize and operate the institution at Tuskegee.

Washington spearheaded the Tuskegee Institute's development and became one of the nation's leading education administrators at the turn of the century. By the time of his death of congestive heart failure at the age of 59 in 1915, Tuskegee had over 100 buildings, a faculty of about 200, around 1,500 students, and an endowment of $2 million. He told of his struggles in *Up from Slavery*, published in 1901.

The Booker T. Washington National Monument was founded in 1956. As a living history site, it has an operating farm; costumed interpreters; collections of plantation equipment and furniture, blacksmith tools, and archaeological artifacts; a multipurpose room and exhibition hall; a library with books on agriculture, slavery, and black history; and a one-and-a-half-mile trail. Annual attendance is 20,000.

Booker T. Washington National Monument, 12130 Booker T. Washington Hwy., Hardy, VA 24101-3968. Phone: 540/721-2094. Faxes: 540/721-8311 and 540/721-5128. Website: www.nps.gov/bowa. Hours: 9–5 daily; closed New Year's Day, Thanksgiving, and Christmas. Admission: free.

The Oaks. The Oaks is a historic house museum that was the first home of Booker T. Washington, who established the Tuskegee Institute in Tuskegee, Alabama, in 1881 and directed the institution for 34 years. The house now is part of the Tuskegee Institute National Historic Site, established in 1941 on the campus of Tuskegee University, one of the oldest and largest primarily African American universities in the nation.

Washington built the house adjacent to the campus in 1899 of bricks made by students and faculty of the school, which was created for the practical training African Americans in the trades and professions. The house contains the original Washington furniture and personal effects and reflects the broad interests of the Washington family. Guided tours of the historic house are offered by park rangers. The Tuskegee Institute National Historic Site has an annual attendance of over 490,000.

The Oaks, Tuskegee Institute National Historic Site, 1212 W. Montgomery Rd., Tuskegee, AL 36088 (postal address: PO Drawer 10, Tuskegee, AL 36088-0010). Phones: 334/727-6390, 334/727-3200, and 334/727-9321. Faxes: 334/727-4597 and 334/727-1448. Website: www.nps.gov/tuin. Hours: 9–5 daily; closed New Year's Day, Thanksgiving, and Christmas. Admission: free.

Noah Webster

Noah Webster House. Noah Webster was a prominent lexicographer, teacher, and author/editor in the late eighteen and early nineteenth centuries who has been called the father of American scholarship and education. He is best known for publishing the first American dictionary in 1828, his speller books that taught five generations of children how to spell and read, and his impact in making public education more secular and less religious. He also worked as a lawyer, taught school, edited newspapers and magazines, wrote books, served in the militia in the Revolutionary War, argued for a strong federal government, and founded and edited the first Federalist newspapers.

Webster was born in 1758 in a typical New England wooden-frame house of that era in West Hartford, Connecticut, that is now a historic house museum. His father was a farmer, justice of the peace, deacon of the local Congregational church, and captain in the local militia who mortgaged the family farm to enable his son to attend Yale University. Webster entered Yale at the age of 16 and spent four years studying with the learned Ezra Stiles, Yale's president. After graduation in 1778, he taught school and practiced law in Connecticut in 1779–1783 but did not find law to his liking. He published several textbooks, including the *Grammatical Institute of the English Language, Part I*, a 1783 spelling book that later became known as *Webster's Spelling Book* or the *Blue-Back Speller*, which was followed by parts two (grammar) and three (reader) in 1784–1785. They served as a major spelling guide for more than 100 years.

Webster became an ardent Federalist. His *Sketches of American Policy* in 1785 was one of the first publications to advocate strong central government. In 1793 Alexander Hamilton lent him $1,500 to move to New York City to found and edit the *American Minerva* (which became the *Commercial Advertiser*), the leading Federalist newspaper and New York's first daily paper. He also published the semiweekly *Herald: A Gazette for the Country* (later called the *New York Spectator*).

In 1806 Webster published *A Compendious Dictionary of the English Language*, which was expanded into *An American Dictionary of the English Language* in 1828 after further study and a visit to England and France in 1824–1825. Rights to Webster's dictionary were sold by his heirs in 1843—the year he died—to G. and C. Merriam Co., now Merriam-Webster Inc., part of the Encyclopaedia Britannica Company. Webster also wrote a *History of the United States* in 1832 and published a revision of the Authorized Version of English Bible in 1833.

Webster's birthplace and home, which was built around 1748, became a historic house museum in 1965. It was a typical New England wooden-frame house of that era and was later was extended to two and a half stories. It has been designated a National Historic Landmark. Webster also had a house later in New Haven, Connecticut, which has been relocated to Greenfield Village in Dearborn, Michigan.

The Noah Webster House was continuously occupied until 1962, when it was given to the town of West Hartford and developed into a historical museum. It also serves as the headquarters of the West Hartford Historical Society. The museum contains eighteenth-century period furnishings and decorative arts; early editions of Webster's dictionary, spellers, and other publications; china, glassware, desk, and two clocks that he owned; period clothing; local and regional manuscripts; paintings; and photographs. Annual attendance is 17,500.

Noah Webster House, 227 S. Main St., West Hartford, CT 06107-3430. Phone: 860/521-5362. Fax: 860/521-4036. Email: comments@noahwebsterhouse.org. Website: www.noahwebsterhouse.org. Hours: 1–4 Thurs.–Mon.; closed Tues.–Wed. and national holidays. Admission: adults, $7; seniors, $5; children 6–18, $4; children under 6, free.

Frances Willard

See Social Activists section.

ENTERTAINERS

(*See also* Actors and Musicians/Singers/Composers sections)

P. T. Barnum

Barnum Museum. Phineas Taylor Barnum, better known as P. T. Barnum, was a 1800s showman who promoted celebrated hoaxes and founded the circus that eventually became the Ringling Bros. and Barnum & Bailey Circus. Before his death in 1891, he planned, funded, and began construction of the Barnum Museum in Bridgeport, Connecticut, which opened in 1893 as the home of the local scientific and historical societies and later became more of a showplace for his life and some of his collections.

Barnum had many different careers. He was a small business owner and newspaper publisher before embarking on an entertainment career, and later he also served as a museum owner, theater operator, real estate developer, state legislator, mayor, reformer, and circus operator. He first organized a variety troupe and then purchased Scudder's American Museum in New York City and renamed the museum for himself. The museum featured hoaxes and human curiosities, such as the "Feejee" mermaid with the head of a monkey and tail of a fish and "General Tom Thumb," a 25-inch-tall dwarf who was proclaimed as the smallest person alive.

Barnum then bought Peale's Museum in Philadelphia and other museums and expanded his museum, which was destroyed in two fires of unknown origin in 1865 and 1868. At the age of 61, Barnum co-established the P. T. Barnum Grand Traveling Museum, Menagerie, Caravan, and Hippodrome in 1871. He merged with James Bailey and James L. Hutchison in 1881, and it became the Barnum & Bailey Greatest Show on Earth in 1888 and then the Barnum & Bailey Circus, which evolved into the Ringling Bros. and Barnum & Bailey Circus.

Before his death in 1891, Barnum contracted for the construction of the Barnum Institute of Science and History to house the work of the Bridgeport Scientific Society and the Fairfield County Historical Society. The museum opened in 1893 in a new three-story ornate building with Byzantine to Romanesque architectural influences that now is listed on the National Register of Historic Places.

When the two societies ceased operation in the 1930s, the City of Bridgeport assumed ownership of the building and opened it as the Barnum Museum in 1936. The Barnum Museum Foundation took over management, renovated the museum, and reopened it in 1989. The museum now is devoted to the life of Barnum and the history of Bridgeport and contains such things as a 1,000-square-foot replica of Barnum's circus, a miniature reproduction of his estate library, an exhibit on Tom Thumb, and an authentic 2,500-year-old Egyptian mummy. Annual attendance is 25,000.

Barnum Museum, 820 Main St., Bridgeport, CT 06604-4912. Phone: 203/331-1104. Fax: 203/331-0079. Website: www.barnum-museum.org. Hours: 10–4:30 Tues.–Sat., 12–4:30 Sun.; closed Mon., New Year's Day, Memorial Day, Independence Day, Labor Day, Thanksgiving, and Christmas. Admission: adults, $8; seniors and students, $6; children 4–17, $5; children under 4, free.

Buffalo Bill Cody (William F. Cody)

Buffalo Bill Historical Center/Buffalo Bill Museum. William F. Cody, who was known as "Buffalo Bill" Cody, was one of the most colorful figures of the Old West. He was a Pony Express rider, army teamster, frontier scout, buffalo hunter, and showman who got his nickname for supplying railroad workers with buffalo meat by killing 4,860 bison in eight months in 1867–1868. He is best remembered, however, as the founder of "Buffalo Bill's Wild West," a circuslike traveling show that featured cowboys and Indians, horseback parades, feats of skill, staged races, and sideshows at the turn of the twentieth century.

Cody was born near Le Claire, Iowa, in 1846 and became a Pony Express rider at the age of 14. He then worked delivering supplies to Fort Laramie, serving as an Indian scout for the army, and providing buffalo meat for western railroad workers, and he made his stage debut in a show called "The Scouts of the Plains" in Chicago in 1872. After touring for 10 years, he founded the traveling Western show, which later became the Buffalo Bill's Wild West and Congress of Rough Riders and featured such performers as sharpshooter Annie Oakley and Sioux leader Sitting Bull.

The Wild West show became so popular that it traveled to Europe in 1887–1889 and toured the nation until 1913. During that period, Cody purchased a 4,000-acre ranch near North Platte, Nebraska, and was instrumental in founding Cody, Wyoming. Upon his death in Denver in 1917, Cody was buried on nearby Lockout Mountain in Golden, where the Buffalo Bill Museum and Grave is now located (*see* separate listing).

A frontier wagon, part of the Buffalo Bill Museum at the Buffalo Bill Historical Center in Cody, Wyoming. Courtesy of the Buffalo Bill Historical Center.

The Buffalo Bill Historical Center was founded in Cody's memory in Cody, Wyoming, in 1917. The 237,000-square-foot complex is now the largest and most comprehensive site celebrating his life (*see* other listings). The center consists of five museums and a research library about the American West, including the Buffalo Bill Museum, devoted to his life and times. The other museums are the Cody Firearms Museum, Plains Indian Museum, Whitney Gallery of Western Art, and Draper Museum of Natural History. The library is the Harold McCracken Research Library.

The Buffalo Bill Museum traces Cody's life and interprets the history of the American cowboy, dude ranching, Western conservation, frontier entrepreneurship, and concepts about the American West. In addition to a wide range of artifacts, the museum has a time line that correlates Cody's life with world events. Annual attendance is 200,000.

Buffalo Bill Historical Center, 720 Sheridan Ave., Cody, WY 82414-3428. Phone: 307/587-4771. Fax: 307/578-4066. E-mail leeh@bbhc.org. Website: www.bbhc.org. Hours: Mar.–Apr. and Nov.—10–5 daily; closed Thanksgiving; May–mid-Sept.—8–6 daily; mid-Sept.–Oct.—8–5 daily; Dec.–Feb.—10–5 Thurs.–Sun.; closed Mon.–Wed. and Christmas. Admission: adults, $18; seniors and students, $13; children 6–17, $10; children under 6, free.

Buffalo Bill State Historical Park. In 1886 William F. "Buffalo Bill" Cody bought a 4,000-acre ranch, which he called Scout's Rest Ranch, near North Platte, Nebraska, with his Wild West show earnings. The site now is the Buffalo Bill State Historical Park, which celebrates the life and times of the army scout, buffalo hunter, and showman who personified the frontier spirit.

The historical park, established in 1964, features an elegant 18-room Second Empire house, a large barn, and a number of outbuildings on 25 acres. The barn contains memorabilia from Buffalo Bill's Wild West traveling show, original show posters, personal property and correspondence, photographs, and a movie made of film clips taken when the show was touring the United States and Europe in 1883–1913. The annual attendance is 20,000.

Buffalo Bill Ranch State Historic Park, 2921 Scout's Rest Ranch Rd., North Platte, NE 69101-8444. Phone: 308/535-8035. Fax: 308/535-8070. E-mail: buffalo.bill@ngpc.ne.gov. Website: www.ngpc.state.ne.us/parks. Hours: late Mar.–late May and early Sept.–late Oct.—10–4 Mon.–Fri.; closed Sat.–Sun.; late May–early Sept.—9–5 daily; closed remainder of year. Admission: $4 per car.

Buffalo Bill Museum of Le Claire, Iowa. The Buffalo Bill Museum of Le Claire, Iowa, is located a short distance from where William F. "Buffalo Bill" Cody was born in 1846. The museum chronicles his life and accomplishments and has exhibits on the steamboat era on the Mississippi River. It contains Cody and riverboat memorabilia, as well as an 1846 wooden-hull sternwheeler, pioneer and Indian artifacts, and other historical objects. The museum was founded in 1957 by the Le Claire Women's Club and has an annual attendance of 15,000.

Buffalo Bill Museum of Le Claire, Iowa, 199 N. Front St., Le Claire, IA 52753 (postal address: PO Box 284, Le Claire, IA 52753-0284). Phones: 563/289-5580 and 563/289-4603. E-mail: ahlgren@mchsi.com. Website: www.buffalobillmuseumleclaire.com. Hours: 9–5 Mon.–Sat., 12–5 Sun.; closed New Year's Day, Thanksgiving, and Christmas. Admission: adults, $5; children 5–15, $1; children under 5, free.

Buffalo Bill Cody Homestead. William F. Cody's boyhood home is located at the Buffalo Bill Cody Homestead in Princeton, Iowa. The native limestone home, which was built in 1847 by Cody's father, has been restored by the Scott County Conservation Board and contains mid-nineteenth-century furnishings, farm implements, and Indian artifacts. The homestead is located on a hillside surrounded by a prairie where buffalo and longhorn cattle are grazing. The annual attendance is 7,000.

Buffalo Bill Cody Homestead, 28050 230th Ave., Princeton, IA 52768-9713 (postal address: 14910 110th Ave., Davenport, IA 52804-9020). Phone: 563/225-2981. Fax: 563/381-2805. Website: www.scottcountyiowa.com. Hours: Apr.–Oct.—9–5 daily; closed remainder of year. Admission: adults, $2; children under 17, free.

Buffalo Bill Museum and Grave. The Buffalo Bill Museum and Grave is located where William F. Cody, known as Buffalo Bill, is buried atop Lockout Mountain in Golden, Colorado. He died in 1917 while visiting his sister in Denver. A controversy ensued after his death over the burial site. He allegedly said he wanted to be buried on the mountain overlooking Denver and the plains, although residents of Cody, Wyoming, which he helped found, claimed that he preferred Cody. His wife, who had married Buffalo Bill before he became famous, was buried next to her husband in 1921.

The museum, founded in 1921 by Johnny Baker, Cody's foster son, is devoted to the life, times, and legacy of Buffalo Bill. It has a 3,000-square-foot exhibit area with displays about his life, Wild West shows, Indian artifacts, firearms, and Western art. The exhibits feature such historical objects as the Stetson hat that Buffalo Bill worn at his last performance, a peace pipe belonging to Sitting Bull, the head of the last buffalo shot by Buffalo Bill, and early recordings of Buffalo Bill's voice introducing the Wild West show, as well as personal artifacts, posters, photographs, and archival materials. The museum has 64,000 visitors annually.

Buffalo Bill Museum and Grave, 987½ Lookout Mountain Rd., Golden, CO 80401. Phone: 303/526-0747. Fax: 303/526-0197. E-mail: buffalobill.museum@ci.denver.co.us. Website: www.buffalobill.org. Hours: May–Oct.—9–5 daily; Nov.–Apr.—9–4 Tues.–Sun.; closed Mon. and Christmas. Admission: adults, $5; seniors, $4; children 6–15, $1; children under 6, free.

Walt Disney

Walt Disney Family Museum. Walter E. Disney, better known as Walt Disney, was a film producer who became one of the nation's greatest entertainment generators. He created animated cartoons that featured such characters as Oswald the Rabbit, Mickey Mouse, and Donald Duck; made hit movies like *Snow White and the Seven Dwarfs* and *Cinderella*; produced such television shows as the *Mickey Mouse Club* and *The Wonderful World of Disney*; and founded popular theme parks like Disneyland in California and Disney World in Florida. His life and accomplishments now are the focus of the Walt Disney Family Museum, founded in San Francisco in 2009.

Born in Chicago in 1901, Disney became an innovator in motion picture animation. He produced his first animated film with sound, *Steamboat Willie*, in 1928 and his first full-length animated movie, *Snow White and the Seven Dwarfs*, in 1937. These were followed by such films as *Pinocchio* (1940), *Fantasia* (1940), *Dumbo* (1941), *Cinderella* (1950), *Alice in Wonderland* (1951), and *Peter Pan* (1953).

Disney also began to move into other fields. He produced such feature films as *Treasure Island* (1950), *Old Yeller* (1957), and *Mary Poppins* (1964), as well as television programs, music records, and theme parks. In 1955 Disney opened Disneyland, which featured his animated characters, in Anaheim, California. It was followed by the development of a more elaborate version of Disneyland, called Magic Kingdom, which later was expanded and called Disney World, in Orlando, Florida. Disney was making plans for a ski resort when he died in 1966.

The Walt Disney Family Museum, located in a historic 1904 building and 20,000-square-foot modern addition in San Francisco's Presidio complex, tells the story of Disney's life and family. It contains Disney's personal papers and belongings, family photographs and home movies, Oscar award statuettes, early drawings and posters, animation cells, films, and displays about animation development, art, and theme parks. The museum has a large-screen theater and an auditorium for film showings and programs and offers guided tours. Admission is only by timed-entry tickets obtained in advance.

Walt Disney Family Museum, 104 Montgomery St., The Presidio, San Francisco, CA 94129-1718. Phone: 415/345-6800. Fax: 415/345-6896. E-mail: info@wdfmuseum.org. Website: www.waltdisney.org. Hours: 10–6 Wed.–Mon.; closed Tues., New Year's Day, Independence Day, Thanksgiving, and Christmas. Admission: adults, $20; seniors and students, $15; children 6–17, $12.50; children under 6, free.

Walt Disney Hometown Museum. The Walt Disney Hometown Museum is located in Marceline, Missouri, where Disney lived on a farm with his parents as a child for four years and developed his interest in drawing. He was four years old when the family came to Marceline in 1906 from Chicago, where Disney was born. The family then moved to Kansas City in 1911. It is where he later began his artist career.

The Walt Disney Hometown Museum, located in the restored Santa Fe railroad depot, has exhibits that tell about Disney's childhood, family, friends, and associates who supported him in his early creative efforts. It contains such items as personal belongings from the Disney family, hundreds of letters written by family members between the early 1900s and late 1960s, family photographs, Mickey Mouse dolls, and an early midget car from Disneyland.

Walt Disney Hometown Museum, 120 E. Santa Fe Ave., Marceline, MO 64658-1144. Phone: 660/376-3343. Website: www.waltdisneymuseum.org. Hours: Apr.–Oct.—10–4 Tues.–Sat., 1–4 Sun.; closed Mon. and remainder of year. Admission: adults, $5; children 6–10, $2.50; children under 6, free.

Walt Disney's Carolwood Barn. After Walt Disney moved to a new home on five acres in the Holmby Hills district of Los Angeles in 1949, he built a miniature live steam railroad and a workshop, monitor/control, and storage barn in his backyard the following year. Disney, who loved trains, called the layout the Carolwood Pacific Railroad, named for the street on which the property was located, and the locomotive the *Lilly Belle* for his wife, Lillian. The railroad had a 46-foot-long trestle, a 90-foot tunnel, overpasses, gradients, and elevated berm.

Several years after Disney died in 1966, his wife donated the train tracks to the Los Angeles Live Steamers, a group of steam train enthusiasts of which Disney was a member. After Lillian died, the Disney property was sold and her eldest daughter, Diane Disney Miller, arranged with the City of Los Angeles and Los Angeles Live Steamers Museum to have the barn removed and reinstalled at Griffith Park. The barn, now called Walt Disney's Carolwood Barn, opened in 1999. It contains a collection of Disney and steam-related items, including Disney-built workbenches, his electronic control track switches, and pieces of his Carolwood rolling stock; memorabilia relating to the Disneyland Monorail; and samples of train and toy collections.

Walt Disney's Carolwood Barn, Griffith Park, 5202 Zoo Dr., Los Angeles, CA 90027 (postal address: Carolwood Foundation, PO Box 2208, Toluca Lake, CA 91610). Phones: 805/498-2336 and 310/213-0722. E-mail: info@carolwood.com. Website: www.carolwood.com. Hours: 11–3 third Sun. of each month. Admission: free.

Harry Houdini

Houdini Museum and Theater. Harry Houdini was a famous magician, escapologist, and stunt performer who was born in Hungary in 1874 as Ehrich Weiss, the son of a rabbi. He came to America with his parents in 1878 and started calling himself Harry Houdini when he became a professional magician. He began his career as a nine-year-old trapeze artist and then experimented with handcuff escape acts in 1893. He freed himself from jails, chains, ropes, and straitjackets, which evolved into acts with the possibility of failure and death. He became known for escaping from a locked, water-filled milk can; nailed packing crates; riveted boilers; a locked glass-and-steel cabinet filled with water while suspended upside down; and even the belly of a whale washed ashore.

Houdini, who claimed he was born in Appleton, Wisconsin, lived there when his father was serving as a rabbi. The History Museum at the Castle in Appleton has an exhibit with a collection of his performance paraphernalia and other materials, and a commercially oriented Houdini museum and shop has operated at various hotels in Las Vegas, Nevada. A Houdini museum also was destroyed in a 1995 fire in Niagara Falls.

The only remaining free-standing museum devoted to Houdini's life and exploits is the Houdini Museum and Theater in Scranton, Pennsylvania, where he performed several times. The museum, founded in 1992, displays some of his belongings, props, and posters and presents magic shows as part of a guided tour. The annual attendance is approximately 40,000.

Houdini Museum and Theater, 1433 N. Main St., Scranton, PA 18508-1822 (postal address: 229 Willow Ave. Olyphant, PA 18447-1443). Phone: 570/342-5555. Website: www.houdini.org. Hours: Memorial Day weekend–June— 1–4 Sat.–Sun.; closed Mon.–Fri.; July–Labor Day—1–4 daily; May and Sept.—open for morning group reservations; closed remainder of year. Admission: adults, $14.95; children under 12, $11.95.

Pawnee Bill

Pawnee Bill Ranch and Museum. Gordon W. Lillie, who was known as "Pawnee Bill," was a Wild West show entertainer, and his ranch in Pawnee, Oklahoma, featured bison. Lillie's traveling Wild West show closed in the early 1900s, and he died in 1942, but his ranch is still there and visitors can see the ranch, its museum, and animal herds—and even attend a Wild West show the last three Saturdays in June.

The Pawnee Bill Ranch, now operated by the Oklahoma Historical Society, has been restored and opened to the public. Lillie was a Wild West showman and performer who is best known for his brief partnership with Buffalo Bill Cody, but he also had his own traveling Wild West show during the late nineteenth and early twentieth centuries and ran a successful ranch and other businesses in the early twentieth century.

Lillie was born in Bloomington, Illinois, in 1860. He worked in Wild West shows. In 1886, he married May Manning and two years later launched his first Wild West show, called "Pawnee Bill's Historic Wild West," with May starring as the "Champion Girl Horseback Shot of the West." When the first season turned out to be a financial disaster, the show was reorganized on a smaller scale and renamed "Pawnee Bill's Historical West Indian Museum and Encampment Show." It had moderate success. Lillie then added performers from a variety of backgrounds, including Mexican cowboys, Pawnee Indians, Japanese performers, and Arab jugglers. But the show continued to struggle, and in 1908 Pawnee Bill and Buffalo Bill joined forces in a combined Wild West show, which later was foreclosed as it was about to open in Denver.

While Gordon Lillie was on tour, May ran their ranch, which sought to perpetuate and develop buffalo in Pawnee, Oklahoma. He also lobbied Congress to pass legislation to protect the bison. In 1910 work was completed on their 5,300-square-foot Tudor-style arts-and-crafts ranch house of native stone on a hill (known as Blue Hawk Peak) overlooking the 2,000-acre ranch.

In 1930 the Lillies opened "Pawnee Bill's Old Town" near the ranch, where they sold Indian and Mexican crafts and held an annual rodeo. However, a fire destroyed the site, and it never was rebuilt. Tragedy also struck the couple when returning from a 50th wedding anniversary celebration in Tulsa in 1936. The car they were driving crashed. May died of her injuries, and Pawnee Bill never recovered fully. Before his death in 1942, Lillie deeded the ranch to the Boy Scouts of America, who declined the offer but made extensive use of the property. The State of Oklahoma acquired the ranch in 1962, and it now is operated as the Pawnee Bill Ranch and Museum by the Oklahoma Historical Society.

The Pawnee Bill Ranch, which is listed on the National Register of Historic Places, now consists of 500 of the original 2,000 acres and includes a ranch house with original furnishings and other buildings constructed between 1910 and 1926, such as a three-story barn, carriage house, log cabin, blacksmith shop, and observation tower.

A museum building was added in 1970 with exhibits on ranching, Wild West shows, the American Indian experience in Wild West shows, and a collection of ranch and Wild West show photographs, early farming and ranching equipment, Indian artifacts, show billboards and posters, a calliope, and a stagecoach. Guided tours are offered of the ranch, including the pastures with bison, longhorn cattle, and horses. The ranch also has education programs and an annual reenactment of "Pawnee Bill's Historic Wild West Show" for three days in June. Annual attendance is over 47,000.

Pawnee Bill Ranch and Museum, 1141 Pawnee Bill Rd., Pawnee, OK 74058-3563 (postal address: PO Box 493, Pawnee, OK 74058-0493). E-mail: pawneebill@okhistory.org. Website: www.pawneebillranch.org. Hours: Apr.– Oct.—1–4 Sun.–Mon.; 10–5 Tues.–Sat.; Nov.–Mar.—10–5 Wed.–Sat., 1–5 Sun.; closed Mon.–Tues. and state holidays. Admission: adults, $3; seniors, $2.50; students 6–18, $1.50; children under 6, free.

John Ringling

John and Mable Ringling Museum of Art, Cá d'Zan, and Circus Museum. John Ringling was one of five brothers who founded the Ringling Brothers Circus in 1870 and then bought the Barnum & Bailey Circus in 1907 to form the giant Ringling Bros. and Barnum & Bailey Circus. As the surviving brother, he later took over the management, purchased other circuses in 1929, and became the owner of every traveling circus in America. Ringling also profited from his investments in such other businesses as railroads, oil, and real estate.

John Ringling and his wife, Mable, spent their winters in Sarasota, Florida, and decided to build their home and an art museum there in the 1920s after Sarasota had become the winter quarters for the circus. They built a waterfront 56-room Venetian Gothic mansion, which they called Cá d'Zan (Venetian for "House of John"), in 1925 and the John and Mable Ringling Museum of Art, which opened in 1931, to house their art collections.

Today, the restored mansion is filled with original furnishings and art, and the 30-room art museum features paintings and sculptures by the great Old Masters, including Rubens, van Dyck, Velázquez, Titian, Tintoretto, Veronese, El Greco, and Gainsborough. The museum's courtyard also contains casts of original antiquities and Renaissance sculptures, including a towering *David* by Michelangelo, and two large fountain replicas. In 1948 a third building—the Circus Museum—was added to honor Ringling, trace the history of circuses, and house circus memorabilia and artifacts.

The John and Mable Ringling Museum of Art, which has been designated Florida's state art museum, is now governed by Florida State University. In addition to the Circus Museum, four other buildings have been added to the courtyard in recent years—a visitors' pavilion/theater, a learning center, an education/conservation building, and an art museum wing. The mansion and the art and circus museums—as well as guided tours—are included in a single admission fee. The annual attendance is 360,000.

The court of a historic 56-room Venetian Gothic mansion built in Sarasota, Florida, in 1925 by John Ringling of Ringling Bros. and Barnum & Bailey Circus, and his wife, Mable. Courtesy of the John and Mable Ringling Museum of Art, the State Art Museum.

John and Mable Ringling Museum of Art (and Cá d'Zan and Circus Museum), 5401 Bay Shore Rd., Sarasota. FL 34243-2161. Phones: 941/351-1660 and 941/359-5700. Fax: 941/359-7704. Website: www.ringling.org. Hours: 10–5 daily, with art and circus museums open to 8 on Wed.; closed New Year's Day, Thanksgiving, and Christmas. Admission: adults, $25; seniors, $20; students, teachers, military, and children 6–17, $10; children under 6, free.

Will Rogers

Will Rogers Memorial Museum. Will Rogers was many things—Cherokee cowboy, circus rider/trick roper, comedian, humorist, social commentator, vaudeville performer, newspaper columnist, and actor. Born to a prominent Indian Territory family on a working ranch in 1879, he became a world famous entertainer who was the highest-paid movie star in the 1930s. He made 71 movies and wrote more than 4,000 nationally syndicated newspaper columns. His life was cut short when he was killed in 1935 with aviator Wiley Post when their small plane crashed near Barrow, Alaska Territory.

Rogers's life and career are featured at the Rogers Memorial Museum in Claremore, Oklahoma. The 16,652-square-foot museum, which opened in 1938, is located on a 20-acre site purchased by Rogers in 1911 for his retirement home and now contains the family tomb. The museum, which has eight galleries and an archive, traces Rogers's life and contains personal items, memorabilia, manuscripts, speeches, photographs, paintings, saddles, playbills, and other materials, and it shows movies starring Rogers in a 178-seat theater. A duplicate of Jo Davidson's classic sculpture in Washington of Rogers riding his horse, "Soapsuds," is located near his tomb. The annual attendance is 117,000. The Will Rogers Memorial Commission, which governs the museum, also operates the Will Rogers Birthplace Ranch in nearby Oologah, Oklahoma (*see* separate listing).

Will Rogers Memorial Museum, 1720 W. Will Rogers Blvd., Claremore, OK 74017-3208 (postal address: PO Box 157, Claremore, OK 74018-0157). E-mail: wrinfo@willrogers.com. Website: www.willrogers.com. Hours: 8–5 daily. Admission: donation.

Will Rogers Birthplace Ranch. The Will Rogers Birthplace Ranch is housed in the 1875 log-walled, two-story house with clapboard siding in Oologah, Oklahoma, where the famous entertainer was born in 1879. The house,

The Will Rogers Memorial Museum in Claremore, Oklahoma. Courtesy of the Will Rogers Memorial Museum, Claremore, OK.

built by Rogers's father, Clement, a Cherokee rancher, senator, and judge, was two miles east of town originally. It was moved to its present location north of the Oologah when the Verdigris River valley was flooded to create Oologah Lake. The Greek revival–style structure, once the seat of power and culture in the former Indian Territory, is one of the few surviving buildings from that period.

The Rogers ranch, which covered 60,000 acres and had 10,000 head of Texas longhorn cattle and other farming operations, now occupies 400 acres with 50 longhorn cattle. Will Rogers worked on the ranch until 1901, when he left home with a friend and went to Argentina to start a ranch, which failed. He returned to the United States and began his entertainment career as a rider and trick roper in a circus. The historic house, which has been restored with period furnishings, operates as a subsidiary of the Will Rogers Memorial Museum (*see* separate listing).

Will Rogers Birthplace Ranch, 9501 E. 380 Rd., Oologah, OK 74053. Phones: 918/275-4201 and 800/324-8218. E-mail: dwilliams@willroers.com. Website: www.willrogers.com. Hours: 8–5 daily. Admission: donation.

Will Rogers State Historic Park. The former estate of Will Rogers in Pacific Palisades, California, is now the Will Rogers State Historic Park. He bought the land in 1922 and converted it into a 186-acre ranch for his family, which included his wife, Betty, and three children. The ranch consisted of a 31-room ranch house, stable, corrals, riding ring, roping arena, polo field, golf course, and hiking trails. After Rogers died in a plane crash in 1935, his widow continued to live on the ranch until her death in 1944, when it became the Will Rogers State Historic Park.

The 1924 Rogers ranch house and landscape have been restored, and other historic structures are being restored and the maintenance facilities moved from the historic area. Guided tours are given of the ranch house, which contains family furniture, a collection of Indian rugs and baskets, and many personal belongings. The property continues to be a working ranch, and the polo field is still used for polo matches. The ranch guesthouse is now a visitor center with a film on Rogers's life and an audio tour of the grounds. The historic park is visited by 230,000 annually.

Will Rogers State Historic Park, 1501 Will Rogers State Park Rd., Pacific Palisades, CA 90272-3941. Phone: 310/454-8212. Fax: 310/459-2031. Websites: www.ugf.edu and www.parks.ca.gov/default.asp?page_id=626. Hours: park—8–sunset daily; house—11–2 Thurs.–Fri., 10–4 Sat.–Sun.; closed Mon.–Wed., New Year's Day, Thanksgiving, and Christmas. Admission: $12 per vehicle ($11 for seniors).

EXPLORERS

Juan Rodríguez Cabrillo

Cabrillo National Monument. The Cabrillo National Monument, located on the Point Loma Peninsula in San Diego, California, commemorates the landing of a Spanish expedition led by Juan Rodríguez Cabrillo in 1542. It was the first time that a European expedition set foot on the west coast of what later became part of the United States.

Cabrillo was a "conquistador"—a term applied to Spanish soldiers who explored, conquered, and settled in the New World. In 1519 he served as a captain of crossbowmen in the army of Hernán Cortés. After the defeat of the Aztecs, he joined other Spanish military expeditions in southern Mexico and what today is Guatemala and San Salvador. Cabrillo settled in Guatemala, where he became a trader, shipbuilder, and wealthy landowner in the 1530s. He was asked by the governor of Guatemala to build and supply ships to explore the Pacific and then to lead an expedition to explore the coastal region north and west of New Spain (largely Mexico).

In 1542 Cabrillo's expedition of three ships sailed out of the Mexican port of Navidad (near modern-day Manzanillo). It arrived three months later in the bay of San Diego and claimed the land for Spain. The expedition then traveled north beyond Monterey Bay before being turned back by storms. Cabrillo decided to winter in the Channel Islands, where he died of injuries suffered in a skirmish with natives in 1543. Although the expedition was considered a failure by Cabrillo's contemporaries, it produced the first written description of the West Coast and opened the way for colonizing what became California.

The Cabrillo National Monument was established by President Woodrow Wilson in 1913, but it was not until 1939 that the 14-foot statue of Cabrillo that overlooks the bay and grounds was installed. The memorial also has a visitor center/museum with exhibits and a film about the Cabrillo expedition, ranger-led programs about Cabrillo on weekends and many weekdays during the summer, and a living history program where costumed interpreters dressed in clothes worn 450 years ago sometimes stroll the grounds. An annual Cabrillo Festival Open House also is held on a Sunday every October with a reenactment of Cabrillo's landing at Ballast Point in San Diego Bay.

Among the other sights that can be seen on the memorial grounds are the restored 1880 Old Point Loma Lighthouse, a historic building that tells the history of Fort Rosecrans, former military installations such as coastal artillery batteries, and an overview of San Diego's harbor and skyline. Annual attendance is over 886,000.

Cabrillo National Monument, 1800 Cabrillo Memorial Dr., San Diego, CA 92106-3601. Phone; 619/557-5450. Fax: 619/226-6311. Website: www.nps.gov/cabr. Hours: 9–5 daily; closed Christmas. Admission: $5 per vehicle; $3 per person; seniors, disable citizens, and children under 16, free.

Francisco Vásquez de Coronado

Coronado National Memorial. The Coronado National Memorial near Sierra Vista, Arizona, commemorates the first organized expedition into the American Southwest by Spanish conquistador Francisco Vásquez de Coronado in 1540–1542. It was an expedition to find the fabled "cities of gold" reported to be in the region. Coronado did not find the treasure, but his travels helped to expand Spanish rule over large parts of the Southwest and Great Plains that later became part of the United States.

Coronado was born to a wealth family in Salamanca, Spain, in 1510 and came to Mexico in 1535 as an assistant to the viceroy of New Spain (largely Mexico). Three years later, he became the governor of New Galicia, a province of Mexico that is now Sinaloa and Nayarit. In 1539 he sent Friar Marcos de Niza to visit the area that later became the state of New Mexico. The friar returned and told Coronado about a city of gold called Cibola. That raised Coronado's interest, and he decided to organize an expedition to obtain the gold.

In 1540 he took a large expeditionary force of some 335 Spanish, 300 Indian allies, 1,000 slaves (Indians and Africans), and four Franciscan monks to look for Cibola. Coronado took the expedition north along the coast of the Gulf of California to the Sonora, then upstream and across the Gila River and found and conquered Cibola, located west of present-day New Mexico. But the so-called city of gold turned out to be a simple pueblo of the Zuni Indians without gold, and Friar Marcos was sent back to Mexico in disgrace.

Coronado also explored six other Zuni pueblos and sent out various other parties without success. One of the expeditions resulted in the first Europeans to see the Grand Canyon. Another searching party went east and found villages around the Rio Grande River, where the winter demands led to a brutal war with the Indians, resulting in the destruction of the Tiguex pueblos and the deaths of hundreds of Indians.

Coronado then met an Indian called "the Turk," who told him about Quivira, a rich region in the northeast. With the Turk as the guide, Coronado set out in 1541 to find what was believed to be an area with "seven cities of gold." While in the Texas Panhandle, Coronado felt the Turk was lying about the route and the guide was strangled. Other guides led Coronado to Quivira (near present-day Lindsborg, Kansas), which turned out to be a poor village of thatched huts. Coronado did not find the cities of gold, which apparently never existed. He was bankrupted by the expedition, returned to Mexico, was found guilty of mistreating his indigenous subjects, and was transferred to a minor position in Mexico City, where he died in 1554.

The memorial site became the Coronado National Memorial in 1952 after initially being called the Coronado International Memorial in 1941. It is located on a route believed to have been taken by Coronado on the southeastern side of the Huachuca Mountains south of Sierra Vista, Arizona. The memorial has a visitor center/museum with exhibits about Coronado's exploration of the American Southwest and mid-sixteenth-century Spanish costumes, documents, and weapons. It also has nature trails and picnic areas, although some natural areas were damaged by a monument fire in 2011. Annual attendance is 26,000.

Coronado National Memorial, 4100 E. Montezuma Canyon Rd., Hereford, AZ 85615-9376. Phone: 520/366-5515, Ext. 22. Fax: 520/366-5705. Website: www.nps.gov/coro. Hours: 9–5 daily; closed Thanksgiving and Christmas. Admission: free.

Coronado State Monument. The Coronado State Monument is located in Bernalillo, New Mexico, where Francisco Vásquez de Coronado entered the Rio Grande Valley while in search of the "seven cities of gold" in 1540 (*see* Coronado National Memorial). His expedition never found cities of gold. Instead, there were villages inhabited by prosperous native people in the area. Coronado's party camped near the Tiwa pueblo of Kuaua, originally settled in A.D. 1300, in the fertile land near the Rio Grande River and present-day Albuquerque. Kuaua eventually disappeared, but the earthen pueblo was excavated in the 1930s by WPA workers, who reconstructed new ruin walls over the reburied original ruins.

Since then, the buried pueblo has been partly rebuilt as the site of the state monument. A square kiva, excavated in the south plaza, has been reconstructed. Some of the finest examples of pre-Columbian mural art were found in the kiva, and reproductions of murals depicting pueblo life can be seen in the kiva. The Kuaua Mural Hall also contains 15 panels of original murals excavated out of one of the rectangular kivas.

A visitor center has exhibits of prehistoric and historic Indian and Spanish colonial artifacts, and a children's wing displays the history of central New Mexico. A video presents the history and lifestyles of the two cultures. Visitors also can try on conquistador armor and grind corn on a slab/metate with a two-handed mano/grinding stone. Annual attendance is 18,000.

Coronado State Monument, 485 Kuaua Rd., Rte. 44, Bernalillo, NM 87004-7099. Phones: 505/867-351 and 800/419-3738. Fax: 505/867-5872. Website: www.sandovalhisory.com. Hours: 8:30–5 Wed.–Mon.; closed Tues., New Year's Day, Easter, Thanksgiving, and Christmas. Admission: adults, $3; children under 17, free; New Mexico residents are free on Sun. and state seniors free on Wed.

Coronado-Quivira Museum. The Coronado-Quivira Museum in Lyons, Kansas, is located in the Great Plains region where Spanish conquistador Francisco Vásquez de Coronado sought the "seven cities of gold" in 1541. At the time, it was the home of the Quivira Indians, who later became the Wichita Indians. Coronado never found the cities of gold, and his expedition turned out to be a failure. The museum tells the story of his search and about the Quivira Indian culture, as well as the Santa Fe Trail from 1821 to 1872 and the settlement period that followed the closing of the trail.

The museum, operated by the Rice County Historical Society, was founded in 1927. It contains Coronado and Quivira artifacts, as well as objects related to the Santa Fe Trail and the pioneer days. Among the exhibits are a replica of a grass lodge once inhabited by the agricultural Quivira, Spanish weapons, a preserved piece of chain mail, and paintings depicting the pioneer period.

The museum also has a Victorian house with an open wall where visitors can see the inside rooms, a fire engine, a general store, and other displays of life in rural Kansas at the turn of the twentieth century. The museum is located in an old Carnegie Library and an adjacent structure. Annual attendance is 3,500.

Coronado-Quivira Museum, 105 W. Lyons St., Lyons, KS 67554-2703. Phone: 620/257-3941. Phone: 620/257-3941. E-mail: cqmdirector@yahoo.com. Hours: 9–5 Tues.–Sat.; closed Sun.–Mon. and major holidays. Admission: adults, $3; children 6–12, $2; children under 6 and county residents, free.

Hernando de Soto

De Soto National Memorial. The De Soto National Memorial near Bradenton, Florida, commemorates the 1539 landing of Spanish explorer Hernando de Soto and the first extensive European exploration of the southeastern section of what is now part of the United States. De Soto and nine ships with over 600 soldiers, 220 horses, weapons, and other supplies landed in the Tampa Bay area with an order from King Charles V to "conquer, populate, and pacify" the land. The national memorial was established in 1948 to preserve the controversial story of the exploration and interpret its significance in American history.

De Soto had accompanied Pedro Arias Dávila, captain general of Spanish lands in the New World, to Central America in 1516-20 and participated in the conquest of Nicaragua in 1523. He also served as Nicaragua's military commander and with Francisco Pizarro, conqueror of Peru, in 1531-36. After arriving in Florida in 1539, De Soto was in constant conflict with Indians as he explored sections of Alabama, Tennessee, Mississippi, Arkansas, Oklahoma, and Louisiana in search of gold and other treasures. In 1540, he discovered and crossed the Mississippi River. It also was in Louisiana that he died of a fever and his body was sunk in the river to prevent Indians from desecrating it.

The De Soto expedition landed in the Tampa Bay area and began a 4,000–mile journey through Florida and other states. The army was welcomed and opposed by the Native American tribes in four years of constant conflict. Instead of finding gold and other treasures, the expedition marched from one village to another taking food and enslaving the natives as guides and porters. The diseases brought by the De Soto expedition and other Europeans virtually wiped out all the Native American tribes in Florida at that time.

The story of the exploration is told in the visitor center/museum at the De Soto National Memorial near Bradenton. The park has a film on the expedition and exhibits that feature historic armor, weapons, and related period items. Visitors can try on helmets and armor. There also is a nature trail through several Florida ecosystems, including a mangrove forest like the one De Solo's men encountered when they landed. Guided trail walks are offered by park rangers, and the park has a Camp Uzita, a living history camp from mid-December to mid-April where rangers and volunteers dressed in period clothing present talks on historical subjects ranging from the De Soto expedition to Florida's Native Americans. Annual attendance is over 275,000.

De Soto National Memorial, 75th St., N.W., Bradenton, FL 34209 (postal address: PO Box 15390, Bradenton, FL 34280-5390). Phone: 941/792-0458, Ext. 105. Fax: 941/792-5094. E–mail: deso_ranger_activities@nps.gov. Website: www.nps.gov/deso. Hours: 9–5 daily; closed New Year's Day, Thanksgiving, and Christmas. Admission: free.

John C. Frémont

Frémont House. John C. Frémont, a U.S. Army topographer who led exploratory expeditions in the American West in the mid-1800s, was called "The Pathfinder" and "The Great Pathfinder" because of his early mapping exploits. In his career that followed, Frémont was appointed governor of territorial California and then Arizona, served as one of California's first two senators, was an 1856 presidential candidate, and fought in the Civil War as a Union major general. While Arizona's territorial governor in 1878–1881, he and his wife, author Jessie Ann Benton Frémont, lived in an 1875 Victorian-style house that now is one of the historic structures at the Sharlot Hall Museum in Prescott, Arizona.

Frémont was born as John Charles Fremon in Savannah, Georgia, in 1813 to Charles Fremon, a French immigrant and tutor, and Anne Beverley Whiting, the daughter of a socially prominent planter. He later changed his name to his father's original French name. Frémont studied topography at the College of Charleston and in 1941 married the daughter of influential U.S. senator Thomas Hart Benton, a leading proponent of the manifest destiny expansionist movement. Benton spearheaded the passage of appropriations for surveys of the Oregon Trail, the Oregon Territory, and the Great Basin and California's Sierra Mountains—and was instrumental in Frémont's appointment to head the mapping expeditions.

Frémont, who had assisted Joseph Nicollet in surveying lands between the Mississippi and Missouri rivers in 1838–1839, made three expeditions with frontiersman Kit Carson to the Oregon Territory and Trail, Sierra Nevada Mountains, and California. They resulted in a report and maps that were extremely helpful to immigrants heading westward. The objective of the third expedition was to find the source of the Arkansas River in Colorado. But when heavy snow disrupted the expedition, Frémont unexpectedly took his exploratory party to California just before the 1846–1848 Mexican-American War. It was his urging of the American settlers in California to show their patriotism that influenced the outbreak of the Bear Flag Revolt and his involvement in the fighting and eventual control of California.

In 1847 Regional Commander Robert F. Stockton appointed Frémont military governor of California. But Brigadier General Stephen W. Kearny had similar orders from the president and the secretary of war, and Frémont was asked to give up the position. When he refused, Frémont was charged with failing to obey an order of a superior officer and military misconduct. He was court-marshaled and convicted in 1848, but pleas from his wife and Senator Benton convinced President James K. Polk to remit the penalty. However, Frémont decided to resign from the army and then undertook winter expeditions in 1848–1849 and 1853–1854 to locate passes for a southern railroad route to California. In 1850–1851, he became one of the first two senators from California and in 1856 was the first presidential candidate of the new Republican Party (which he lost to James Buchanan).

When the Civil War broke out, Frémont was appointed major general and given the command of the Department of the West. He then was relieved of command and moved to the Mountain Department of Western Virginia in 1862. Later, when placed under the Brigadier General John Pope, he asked to be relieved and then resigned. After the war, he lost a fortune in railroad ventures and was saved from poverty by his wife's writings, appointment as governor of the Territory of Arizona, and restoration of his rank of major general in the U.S. Army with retirement pay. He died of peritonitis in New York at the age of 77 in 1890.

John and Jessie Frémont lived in the 1875 Victorian-style house in Arizona in 1878–1881 while he was territorial governor. The house was moved to its present location at the Sharlot Hall Museum in Prescott in 1972. The museum was founded in 1928 by Sharlot Hall, a journalist, poet, and historian who was the first woman to hold an office in the Arizona territorial government. Among the other historic structures at the museum are the 1864 governor's mansion, 1864 Fort Misery general store, 1867 schoolhouse, 1877 William C. Bashford house, and an early ranch house log cabin. Annual attendance is over 19,000.

Sharlot Hall Museum, 415 W. Gurley St., Prescott, AZ 86301-3691. Phone: 928/445-3122. Fax: 928/776-9053. E-mail: gails@sharlot.org. Website: www.sharlot.org. Hours: June–Sept.—10–5 Mon.–Sat., 12–4 Sun.; Oct.–May—10–4 Mon.–Sat., 12–4 Sun.; closed New Year's Day, Thanksgiving, and Christmas. Admission: adults, $5; children under 19, free.

Louis Jolliet

See Father Marquette National Memorial.

Meriwether Lewis and William Clark

Lewis and Clark National Historical Park. The most famous exploratory expedition in the nation's history was the Lewis and Clark Expedition from the Mississippi River to the Pacific Coast in 1804–1806. The expedition was the idea of President Thomas Jefferson, who had been fascinated for years by the virtually unknown territory west of the Mississippi River and was eager to explore the great expanse after acquiring most of the land from France in the Louisiana Purchase of 1803—the same year he announced plans to send an expeditionary party overland to the Pacific.

Jefferson chose Captains Meriwether Lewis and William Clark, two Virginia-born veterans of Indian Wars, to head what was called the "Corps of Discovery." The objectives of the exploratory party were scientific, commercial, and political. The expedition was to explore the Missouri River to its source and then establish the most direct water route to the Pacific; trade, learn more about, and establish sovereignty over the indigenous tribes along the way; gather information about the geography, resources, plants, and animals of the region; and claim the Pacific Northwest and the Oregon Territory for the United States (before European nations).

Jefferson chose Lewis as the leader of the Corps of Discovery, and Lewis selected Clark to share the responsibilities and oversee the scientific and geological observations and collections. The expeditionary party consisted of 31 men, mostly enlisted army men. An Indian guide—a Shoshone Indian woman named Sacagawea—later was added and made most of the trip (*see* separate listing).

The expedition left in 1804, reached the Pacific Coast in November 1805, and returned safely in 1806 after traveling more than 4,000 miles across the continent. Although the expedition failed to find a commercial water route to Asia, it reinforced the nation's claim in the region and returned with a vast amount of information about the geography, plant and animal life, and Indiana culture, as well as numerous plant and animal specimens.

The Lewis and Clark National Historical Park near Astoria, Oregon, and the mouth of the Columbia River is where the Corps of Discovery camped in winter of 1805. They built a log stockade, which they called Fort Clatsop, named for a the local Clatsop Indians who had befriended them. A replica of the fort now provides a look into what life was like that initial winter more than 200 years ago.

In addition to the fort, the historical park includes a visitor center with a historical exhibit about the site, the six-and-a-half-mile Fort-to-Sea Trail, and a number of sites along the Columbia River and the Pacific Coast (Dismal Nitch, Station Cam, Salt Works, Netul Landing, and Memorial to Thomas Jefferson). Among the ranger summer activities are living history demonstrations and guided Netul Trail riverbank walks, guided kayak canoe tours, and forest ranger programs. Annual attendance is 226,000.

Nearby are the Oregon state park sites of Fort Stevens State Park, Sunset Beach State Recreation Area, and Ecola State Park, as well as the Washington state parks of Cape Disappointment (which has the Lewis and Clark Interpretive Center; *see* separate listing) and Fort Columbia. A Lewis and Clark National Historic Trail system—which traces the path of the expedition over 3,700 miles through 11 states—has over 100 federal, tribal, state, local, and private sites that commemorate the Corps of Discovery achievement (*see* separate listing).

Meriwether Lewis, who was born in 1774 in Albemarle County, Virginia, managed his family's plantation briefly after his father died and then joined the Virginia militia to help put down the Whiskey Rebellion in Pennsylvania. He then continued his military career in the army, where he became a captain while serving on the frontier in Ohio and Tennessee. In 1801 President Jefferson, a family friend, appointed him his secretary and then to the Lewis and Clark Expedition. He returned a hero from his expedition exploits and was made governor of the Louisiana Territory in 1807. However, he turned out to be a poor administrator who quarreled with territorial leaders and failed to keep Washington informed of his policies and actions. In 1809 he died a mysterious death in a tavern lodge on the Natchez Trace that was never clearly proved either a murder or a suicide (*see* Meriwether Lewis National Monument).

William Clark was born in 1770 in Caroline County, Virginia. He was one of 10 children, including five bothers who were all Revolutionary War veterans. After the war, he migrated to Mulberry Hill, Kentucky, where he learned about wilderness skills and natural history from his older brother George Rogers Clark, an American Revolutionary soldier and frontier leader (*see* separate listing in Frontiersmen section).

Clark joined the Kentucky militia at the age of 19 and later the army, where he learned to build forts, draw maps, lead pack trains, and fight Indians on their ground. He also was sent to spy on the Spanish, who were exploring and building forts on the east side of the Mississippi River. By 1795 Clark had been promoted to captain, and Meriwether Lewis had been assigned to him.

The two soldiers developed a lasting friendship that led to Lewis selecting Clark for the Corps of Discovery. After the expedition, Clark received double pay and 1,600 acres of land. He resigned from the army in 1807 and served as brigadier general of militia and superintendent of Indian affairs for the Territory of Upper Louisiana until 1821 and as governor of the Missouri Territory from 1813 to 1821. When Missouri became a state in 1820, Clark was defeated in the election for governor. In 1822 he was appointed superintendent of Indian affairs by President James Monroe—a position Clark held until his death in 1838. While serving in the Indiana affairs position, he was involved in implementing President Andrew Jackson's Indian removal policy.

Lewis and Clark National Historical Park, 92343 Fort Clatsop Rd., Astoria, OR 97103-9197. Phone: 503/861-2471, Ext. 214. Fax: 503/861-2585. E-mail: deborah_s_wood@nps.gov. Website: www.nps.gov/lewi. Hours: mid-June–Labor Day—9–6 daily; Sept.–mid-June—9–5 daily; closed Christmas. Admission: adults, $3; children under 16, free.

Jefferson National Expansion Memorial. *See* Thomas Jefferson in Presidents section.

Cape Disappointment State Park Lewis and Clark Interpretive Center. Cape Disappointment State Park—a Washington state park across the Columbia River from the Lewis and Clark National Historical Park—has a Lewis and Clark Interpretive Center devoted to the historic expedition. After William Clark and other members of the Corps of Discovery visited the site in 1805, Clark wrote in his journal that "men appear much satisfied with their trip beholding with astonishment the high waves dashing against the rocks and this immense Ocean." Cape Disappointment got its name in 1788 from an English explorer, Captain John Meares, after he missed the passage over the bar to the Columbia River.

The visitor center, founded in 1976, is perched on a cliff 200 feet above the Columbia River on the Long Beach Peninsula fronted by the Pacific Ocean. It focuses largely on the Pacific Coast stay of the Lewis and Clark Expedition. It has interactive exhibits and programs that let children try to pack a canoe without tipping, follow a treasure hunt, and check on what the Corps of Discovery ate for the inaugural meal. During the winter and spring, trained volunteers help visitors spot passing gray whales on their migration. The center also tells about the 1,882-acre state park, formerly known as Fort Canby State Park; the park's history as a coastal artillery site; and the Cape Disappointment Lighthouse, the oldest operating lighthouse on the West Coast, which protects mariners from the rough and ever-changing Columbia River bar in the treacherous waters known as the Graveyard of the Pacific.

Lewis and Clark Interpretive Center, Cape Disappointment State Park, Ilwaco, WA 98624 (postal address: PO Box 488, Ilwaco, WA 98624-0488). Phone: 360/642-3029. Fax: 360/642-4216. E-mail: leic@parks.wa.gov. Website: www.capedisappointment.org. Hours: park—6:30–dusk daily; interpretive center—10–5 daily. Center admission: adults, $5; children under 7, free.

Lewis and Clark National Historic Trail Headquarters Visitor Center. The Lewis and Clark National Historic Trail is a highway route across 3,700 miles and 11 states that commemorates the Lewis and Clark Expedition of 1804–1806. It is part of the nation's National Trails System administered by the National Park Service.

The network includes more than 100 interpretive centers, museums, and related facilities operated by federal, state, local, tribal, public, and private agencies and organizations, only five of which are operated by the National Park Service. They tell about the Corps of Discovery and often provide opportunities for hiking, boating, and horseback riding. The trail, which was established in 1978, basically follows the path of the Lewis and Clark Expedition from its origin in Wood River, Illinois, to the mouth of the Columbia River in Oregon.

The headquarters for the Lewis and Clark National Historic Trail is located at the National Park Service Mid-West Regional Headquarters in Omaha. It has a visitor center with exhibits about the Lewis and Clark Expedition. Many other interpretive centers, museums, and related facilities also offer exhibits and programs along the trail. They include such places as the Lewis and Clark National Historic Trail Interpretive Center in Great Falls, Montana (*see* separate listing).

Lewis and Clark National Historic Trail Headquarters Visitor Center, 601 Riverfront Dr., Omaha, NE 68102. Phone: 402/661-1804. Fax: 402/0661-1805. Website: www.nps.gov/lecl. Hours: Memorial Day–Labor Day—8–5 Mon.–Fri., 9–5 Sat.–Sun.; remainder of year—8–4:30 Mon.–Fri.; closed Sat.–Sun., New Year's Day, and Christmas. Admission: free.

Lewis and Clark National Historic Trail Interpretive Center. The Lewis and Clark National Historic Trail Interpretive Center in Great Falls, Montana, is a 25,000-square-foot facility with nature trails operated by the U.S. Department of Agriculture's Forest Service. It is located on a bluff overlooking the Missouri River and has exhibits about the expedition and the Plains and Pacific Northwest tribes. The Great Falls center has an annual attendance of 70,000.

Lewis and Clark National Historic Trail Interpretive Center, 4201 Giant Springs Rd., Great Falls, MT 59405-0900 (postal address: PO Box 1806, Great Falls, MT 59403-1806). Phone: 406/727-8733. Fax: 406/453-6157. Hours: Memorial Day–Sept.—9–6 daily; Oct.–May—9–5 Tues.–Sat., 12–5 Sun.; closed Mon., New Year's Day, Thanksgiving, and Christmas. Admission: adults, $8; children under 16, free.

Meriwether Lewis National Monument. Meriwether Lewis, who led the 1804–1806 Lewis and Clark Expedition to the Pacific Coast and back to St. Louis, is honored at the Meriwether Lewis National Monument near Hohenwald,

Tennessee. The historic site museum at the Meriwether Lewis Park, founded in 1936, deals with the life and death of Lewis, who died in 1809 at a tavern lodge under unusual circumstances. It still is not clear whether he was murdered or committed suicide.

Lewis, who was governor of Upper Louisiana Territory at the time, was on his way to Washington when he died of gunshot wounds. He was staying at a tavern when he suffered multiple gunshot wounds and died in his room. There are two theories—he was attacked and robbed by an intruder, or he shot himself (based on what the tavern keeper's wife said about Lewis). She told of seeing him acting strangely at dinner, pacing around to room, talking to himself, and having a flush face like someone in a fit, although a number of others said the story was fabricated. It never was determined if the death was murder or suicide. Lewis was buried near the place of his death, where the museum and park are located near present-day Hohenwald, Tennessee. The museum tells about Lewis's life, career, and death. Annual attendance is 9,000.

Meriwether Lewis National Monument, 189 Meriwether Lewis Park, Hohenwald, TN 38462-5591 (postal address: National Park Service, 2680 Natchez Trace Pkwy., Tupelo, MS 38804). Website: www.nps.gov/natr. Hours: 8–5 daily. Admission: free.

Jacques Marquette

Father Marquette National Memorial. The Father Marquette National Memorial in St. Ignace, Michigan, honors the French missionary and explorer who traveled throughout the remote Great Lakes region in the 1660s–1670s to open missions among the Indians. He also founded Michigan's earliest European settlements in Sault Ste. Marie in 1668 and St. Ignace in 1671. The memorial is located in the Straits State Park at St. Ignace's lakefront.

Jacques Marquette, also known as Père Marquette, was born in Leon, France, in 1637 and entered Jesuit novitiate in 1654. He was ordained and came to New France (Canada) in 1666. He was a missionary among the Ottawa and Huron Indians in 1668 and founded the mission of St. Ignace on the north shore of the Straits of Mackinac in 1671.

Marquette lived among the Indians for nine years and became fluent in several native languages. While he was doing missionary work near the western end of Lake Superior in 1672, Comte de Frontenac, the new governor of New France, commissioned French Canadian Louis Jolliet, a fur trader and cartographer, with Marquette as missionary and five others to explore and map a large river believed to flow into the Pacific Ocean.

The exploratory team followed Lake Michigan to Green Bay and then went down the Wisconsin and Fox rivers in birch-bark canoes to the Mississippi River. They traveled on the Mississippi until they reached the confluence with the Arkansas River, where friendly Indians advised them not to go any farther because of hostile tribes. It was decided to return to the north. As a result of the expedition, it was concluded that the Mississippi River flowed south to the Gulf of Mexico and did not offer a navigable route to the Pacific.

The expedition returned to Lake Michigan by the Illinois and Chicago Rivers, during which Marquette became ill and went to Mackinac Island to recover. He then returned to the Illini tribes to establish a mission in 1675. However, his health deteriorated again, and he died of dysentery as he was returning to Mackinac. Jolliet, who was born near Quebec City in 1645, continued his explorations in Hudson Bay and Labrador and was granted the island of Anticosti in 1680 and then developed a virtual fiefdom near Quebec City. He was appointed "royal hydrographer" in 1693 but died during an exploration in 1700.

Founded in 1980, the Father Marquette National Memorial is located on a rise overlooking the Straits of Mackinac. It has an interpretive trail that tells the story of Father Marquette and the meeting of French and Native American cultures in the interior of North America in the seventeen century. The park's museum was destroyed in a fire in 2000. Annual attendance is nearly 15,000.

Father Marquette National Memorial, West of I-75 off U.S. Rte. 2, St. Ignace, MI 49781-1729 (postal address: 720 Church St., St. Ignace, MI 49781-1729). Phone: 906/643-8620. Fax: 906/643-9329. Hours: Memorial Day–Labor Day—9:30–5 daily; closed remainder of year. Admission: free, but Michigan State Parks vehicle permit required.

Marquette Mission Park. The Marquette Mission Park in St. Ignace, Michigan, is where Father Jacques Marquette established a Jesuit mission and village in 1671 and is buried. It is the oldest documented archaeological site in Michigan, a designated National Historic Landmark, and listed on the National Register of Historic Places.

Huron and Ottawa Indians lived in the area until driven from their homes by the Iroquois in the 1640s, when they moved to Chequamegon Bay near today's Ashland, Wisconsin. That is where they met Father Marquette. When hostilities developed with neighboring Lakota, the Huron and Ottawa returned to the Mackinac Straits with Marquette, who founded a mission and village near the tribes' palisaded villages in 1671. In 1701, when the French moved their fort from the village to Detroit, most of the Hurons went with them. However, the mission was maintained until 1706, when it was closed, and then reopened in 1712 and served until 1741, when it was moved to the south shore of the Straits. A second mission then was established at a different site in 1837, and the structure was moved to the park in 1954.

The St. Ignace park contains Marquette's burial site, a mission housing the Museum of Ojibwa Culture, an Ojibwa tipi, a Huron longhouse, a commemorative foundation, and interpretive panels. Marquette died in 1675 en route back to Michigan after becoming ill at a mission he founded in Illinois. His remains were moved to St. Ignace two years after his death and later discovered and reburied at the site of the St. Ignace mission chapel. The interpretive signs tell of Father Marquette's life, the work of the Jesuits in the wilderness, and the changes that took place in the region in the mid-1600s. The Museum of Ojibwa Culture features exhibits about Ojibwa culture, which became dominate in the Upper Great Lakes.

Marquette Mission Park, 500 N. State St., St. Ignace, MI 49781-1429. Phone: 906/643-9161. Fax: 906/643-9380. E-mail: mmperry@up.net. Hours: Memorial Day weekend–June—9–5:30 daily; July–Labor Day—9–8 daily; day after Labor Day–mid-Oct.—9–5 daily; closed remainder of the year. Admission: donation.

Nathaniel B. Palmer

Captain Nathaniel B. Palmer House. Captain Nathaniel B. Palmer was a seal hunter, explorer, sailing captain, and ship designer who is credited as discoverer of Antarctica. In 1820, when only 21 years old, he commanded *Hero*, a 14-meter sloop that entered Orleans Strait and came very close to the Antarctic Peninsula. He was also a skilled and fearless seal hunter and a pioneer clipper ship master and designer.

Palmer was born in Stonington, Connecticut, in 1799. He and his brother, Alexander S. Palmer, who also became a sea captain, built a 16-room Victorian mansion on a high rise overlooking the upper end of the Stonington harbor. The house still has its beautiful ornate woodwork and the octagonal cupola from which the family could identify ships arriving from distant ports.

The house, called Pine Point, is now a historic house museum known as the Captain Nathaniel B. Palmer House. Once threatened with demolition, the house was purchased in 1994 and restored by the Stonington Historical Society, opening in 1996. It contains memorabilia pertaining to Nathaniel and his discovery of Antarctica and the adventurous lives of the Palmer brothers, as well as portraits, furnishings, and artifacts of other Stonington family members. Annual attendance is 2,500.

Captain Nathaniel B. Palmer House, 40 Palmer St., Stonington, CT 96378-1014 (postal address: Stonington Historical Society Inc., PO Box 103, Stonington, CT 06378). Phone: 860/535-8445. E-mail: director@stonington.org. Website: www.stoningtonhistory.org/palmer.htm. Hours: May–Oct.—1–5 Wed.–Sun.; closed Mon.–Tues. and Nov.–Apr. Admission: adults, $9; children, $6; families, $25 (includes admission to Old Lighthouse Museum).

Robert E. Peary and Donald B. MacMillan

Peary-Macmillan Arctic Museum. The Peary-Macmillan Arctic Museum, founded in 1967 at Bowdoin College in Brunswick, Maine, is named for two Bowdoin graduates who were Arctic explorers. They gathered anthropological, historical, and natural history materials pertaining to the Inuit (Eskimo) cultures of Labrador and Greenland in their explorations in the Arctic region at the turn of the twentieth century—many of which are now displayed in the museum.

Robert E. Peary made numerous explorations of the Arctic region between 1886 and 1909 and is credited with being the first person to reach the North Pole in 1909. He was a civil engineer who served in the U.S. Navy from 1881 until he retired as a rear admiral in 1911. Donald Baxter MacMillan, who served briefly as a member of Peary's North Pole team, made over 30 expeditions to the Arctic during his 46-year career as a teacher, explorer, and researcher. He also took films and thousands of photographs of Arctic scenes, put together a dictionary of the Inuktitut language, and wrote about his and Peary's polar adventures.

The Bowdoin museum is built largely around materials donated by MacMillan, supplemented by additional Inuit artifacts and contemporary arts and crafts. Among the other highlights are natural history specimens, Arctic exploration equipment, and many of MacMillan's historic polar photographs and films. The museum has three galleries and exhibit spaces for photographs in the foyer. The college also has an Arctic Studies Center and the Hawthorne-Longfellow Library, which contains MacMillan's papers and archival materials related to Peary. The museum's annual attendance is 11,500.

Peary-MacMillan Arctic Museum, Bowdoin College, 9500 College Station, Brunswick, ME 04011-8495. Phones: 207/725-3416 and 207/725-3062. Fax: 207/725-3499. Website: www.bowdoin.edu/arctic-museum. Hours: 10–5 Tues.–Sat., 2–5 Sun.; closed Mon. and national holidays. Admission: free.

John Wesley Powell

John Wesley Powell Memorial Museum. John Wesley Powell was a soldier, geologist, explorer, and director of major scientific and cultural institutions. He is best known for the 1869 Powell Geographic Expedition that took him on a three-month trip down the Green and Colorado Rivers and first known passage through the Grand Canyon. He also made other explorations in the Rocky Mountains and the Colorado River region and later served as director of the U.S. Geological Survey and the Bureau of Ethnology at the Smithsonian Institution.

Powell, who was born in 1834, was restless as a youth and engaged in a series of adventures, walking across Wisconsin and rowing down such rivers as the Mississippi, Ohio, and Illinois. He also took an interest in the natural sciences, especially geology. He enlisted in the Union Army during the Civil War and lost most of one arm when hit by a minie ball in the Battle of Shiloh. But he stayed in the army and rose to the rank of major. Powell then became a professor of geology and curator of a natural history museum before beginning his western explorations in the Rocky Mountains and the Green and Colorado Rivers, making historic expeditions through the Grand Canyon in 1869 and 1871.

Powell served as the second director of the U.S. Geological Survey in 1881–1894 and the first head of the Bureau of Ethnology (1879–1902) at the Smithsonian Institution. He also was known for his writings, such as *Exploration of the Colorado River of the West and Its Tributaries*, a report on his exploration findings (1875); *An Introduction to the Study of Indian Languages*, the first classification of American Indian languages (1877); and *Report on the Lands of the Arid Region of the United States* (1878). When Powell died in 1902, he was buried in Arlington National Cemetery for his service to the nation.

The sketches, photos, and other memorabilia of Powell's epic Colorado River voyages are presented at the John Wesley Powell Memorial Museum, founded in Page, Arizona, in 1969. The museum also traces his life and contributions and has an extensive collection of Native American and pioneer artifacts, as well as exhibits on the geology of the canyons cut by the Colorado River and the history and development of Page. In addition, it contains films on Lake Powell, dam construction, and other subjects. The museum's annual attendance is 16,600.

John Wesley Powell Memorial Museum, 6 N. Lake Powell Blvd., Page, AZ 86040 (postal address: PO Box 547, Page, AZ 86040-0547). Phones: 928/645-9496 and 888/597-6873. Fax: 928/645-3412. E-mail: director@powell-museum.org. Website: www.powellmuseum.org. Hours: 9–5 Mon.–Fri.; closed Sat.–Sun. and Thanksgiving and Christmas. Admission: adults, $5; seniors, $3; children 5–12, $1; children under 5, free.

John Wesley Powell River History Museum. The focus of the John Wesley Powell River History Museum in Green River, Utah, is the famous western river explorer and his crew's exploration, mapping, and surveying of the Green and Colorado Rivers in 1869 and 1871–1872. The museum invites visitors to relive Powell's exciting journey down the rivers and through the Grand Canyon—said to be the last unknown area of the United States. Green River, which flows into the Colorado River, is the starting point for most boating trips down the Colorado.

The museum has artifacts, models, working displays, and full-size replicas of the boats used in Powell's river explorations. In addition to telling about the historic journeys, the museum has exhibits relating to southern Utah history, Native Americans, mountain men, local and regional artworks, and the River Rafters' Hall of Fame. A film, *Journey into the Great Unknown*, is also shown in the museum theater. The museum's annual attendance is 30,000.

John Wesley Powell River History Museum, 1765 E. Main St., Green River, UT 84525 (postal address: PO Box 620, Green River, UT 84525-0620). Phone: 435/564-3427. Fax: 435/564-3427. E-mail: director@johnwesleypowell.com. Website: www.johnwesleypowell.com. Hours: Apr.–Oct.—8–7 daily; Nov.–Mar.—9–5 Tues.–Sat.; closed Sun.–Mon., New Year's Day, Thanksgiving, and Christmas. Admission: adults, $4; children 3–12, $1; children under 3, free; families, $10.

Sacagawea

Sacajawea Interpretive Center. Sacagawea was a Lemhi Shoshone woman who had an important role in the Lewis and Clark Expedition at the beginning of the nineteenth century. She served as an interpreter and guide for the expedition from North Dakota to the Pacific Ocean between 1804 and 1806. The Sacajawea Interpretive Center at the Sacajawea State Park near Pasco, Washington, is one of the many tributes to her (Sacagewea's name is spelled in many different ways).

Not much is known about Sacagawea's life. She was the daughter of a Shoshone chief who was born around 1788 in Lemhi County, Idaho. At the age of about 12, she was captured by the Hidatsa tribe and sold to Toussaint Charbonneau, a French Canadian trapper who lived in the Indian village. He made her his wife. She was pregnant with her first child when the Corps of Discovery arrived to spend the 1804–1805 winter near the Hidatsa village close to present-day Washburn, North Dakota.

The Lewis and Clark Expedition built Fort Mandan and interviewed several trappers about interpreting and guiding the Corps of Discovery up the Missouri River in the spring. They hired Charbonneau as the interpreter and then learned that his wife, Sacagawea, spoke Shoshone. Since they knew they would need the assistance of the Shoshone tribe at the headwaters of the Missouri, they also hired her. Both then moved into the fort, where she had the baby boy, Jean Baptist Charbonneau, in February.

In April 1805 the Corps of Discovery left Fort Mandan and headed up the Missouri River. While polling up the river, Lewis and Clark nearly lost their journal, records, and some other materials that fell out of a capsized boat. The materials were saved only by the quick action of Sacagawea. She also was extremely helpful when the expedition met the Shoshone tribe. It turned out that the chief was her brother Cameahwait, who agreed to provide horses and guides to cross the Rocky Mountains. The mountains were cold and barren, and the expedition was forced to eat tallow candles to survive before reaching more temperate areas. And then Sacagawea helped find and cook camas roots so that they could regain their strength.

When the expedition approached the mouth of the Columbia River on the Pacific Coast, Sacagawea gave up her beaded belt for a fur robe made of sea otter skins that Lewis and Clark wanted to give to President Thomas Jefferson. On the way back, she suggested a better route through the Rocky Mountains. She guided the Corps of Discovery through a mountain gap—now called the Gibbons Pass—and a pass—now the Bozeman Pass—that took the expedition into the Yellowstone River basin. This later became the optimal route for the Northern Pacific Railway to cross the continental divide.

When the expedition reached North Dakota in 1806, Charbonneau and Sacagawea left the Lewis and Clark Expedition to return to the Mandan villages. However, as Clark traveled down the Missouri River, he invited them to settle in St. Louis. Three years later, they accepted the invitation and entrusted Jean Baptiste's education to Clark. The boy was enrolled in the St. Louis Academy boarding school. Sometime after 1910, Sacagawea also gave birth to a daughter, Lizette.

It is believed that Sacagawea died at Fort Manuel in South Dakota in 1812. After her death, William Clark adopted her two young children in 1813. Some Indians believe she left her husband, married a Comanche, and then returned to the Shoshone in Wyoming, where she died in 1884. It is not known where she is buried, although there are several sites that claim her grave.

Another controversy is the spelling, pronunciation, and etymology of Sacagawea's name. Lewis and Clark mention her name 17 times with eight different spellings in their original journals. "Sakakawea" and "Sacajawea" are among the other widely used spellings. The spelling depends to a large degree on how the name is pronounced. In the Hidalsa language, her name means "Bird Woman." In 1910 "Sacagawea" was established as the proper spelling by the United States Bureau of American Ethnology and later adopted by the U.S. Mint, United States Board of Geographic Names, and National Park Service.

Tributes in many forms have been made to Sacagawea, including statues, place-names, museums, and even a dollar coin. One of the earliest museum facilities was the Sacajawea Interpretive Center at the 284-acre Sacajawea State Park, founded in 1940 near Pasco, Washington, and one of the newest is the Sacajawea Interpretive, Cultural, and Educational Center, established in 2003 in Salmon, Idaho (*see* separate listing).

The Sacajawea Interpretive Center tells the story of the Lewis and Clark Expedition through the experiences of Sacagawea with the Corps of Discovery. The park is located at the confluence of the Snake and Columbia Rivers, where the expedition camped, hunted, repaired equipment, and met with some 200 Sahaptin-speaking Indians. Interactive exhibits relate what is known about Sacagawea's life before, during, and after the expedition. A traditional Wanapum native village also has been re-created at the park by the Wanapum band of Native Americans. In addition, the park contains stone and bone tools dating from 200 to 12,000 years ago of the Sahatin- and Cayuse-speaking tribes along the Columbia, Snake, Palouse, and Walla Walla Rivers. Annual attendance is 650.

Sacajawea Interpretive Center, Sacajawea State Park, 2503 Sacajawea Park Rd., Paseo, WA 99301-6413. Phone: 509/545-2361. Website: www.stateparks.com/sacajawea.html. Hours: park—Apr.–Oct.: 6:30–dusk daily, closed Nov.–Mar.; interpretive center—mid-May–Oct.: 10–5 daily; closed Nov.–mid-May. Admission: suggested donation, $1.

Sacajawea Interpretive, Cultural, and Educational Center. The Sacajawea Interpretive, Cultural, and Educational Center in Salmon, Idaho, is a city-operated museum dedicated to the Indian woman who served as the interpreter and guide for the 1804–1806 Lewis and Clark Expedition to the Pacific Coast. The center, founded in 2003, is located in the visitor center for the 71-acre park two miles east of downtown Salmon.

The Sacajawea center features exhibits about her life and role in the historic expedition and the Agaideka Shoshone perspective. The park also has a Sacagawea monument, learning center/research library, interpretive demonstrations, outdoor school, theater, outdoor amphitheater, garden, ropes challenge course, and interpretive and nature trails.

Sacajawea Interpretive, Cultural, and Educational Center, 110 Lewis and Clark Way, Salmon, ID 83467-5340 (postal address: 200 Main St., Salmon, ID 83467-4111). Phones: 208/756-1222 and 208/756-1188. E-mails: jlb.sac@gmail.com and sacajaweacenter@gmail.com. Website: www.sacajaweacenter.org. Hours: park—9–5 Mon.–Sat., 12–5 Sun.; visitor center—open May–Oct.; closed Nov.–Apr. Admission: $5 per person; families, $12.

FIRST LADIES

Abigail Adams

Abigail Adams Birthplace. The house in Weymouth, Massachusetts, where Abigail Adams, wife of John Adams, second president of the United States, was born in 1744 and lived until her marriage in 1764 now is a historic house museum known as the Abigail Adams Birthplace. It was part of the parsonage of the North Parish Congregational Church (which became Unitarian) in Weymouth, where her father, the Rev. William Smith, was the minister. Her mother was Elizabeth, and the Smith family had three daughters.

The house, which was built in 1685 and moved twice, recently was restored and largely refurbished with reproductions by the Abigail Adams Historical Society, which operates the site. The improvements included new windows, siding, heating, and air conditioning. Most of the house's artifacts have been moved to the Adams National Historical Park, which contains the birthplaces of both John Adams and son, John Quincy Adams, as well as the Peacefield estate where the family later lived. John Quincy Adams also became the sixth president of the nation.

Abigail Adams was born and raised in the historic building and was married there and kept coming back to the house until her father's death in 1783. She also wrote many of her early letters from the house and later became known for her letter writing. She and her husband exchanged 1,200 letters, largely filled with intellectual government and political discussions while he stayed in Philadelphia during the Continental Congress. When the capital was moved to Washington in 1800, Abigail Adams became the initial first lady to preside over the White House. After the presidency, the couple retired to their home in Quincy, Massachusetts, where she died of typhoid fever in 1818.

Abigail Adams Birthplace, 180 Norton St., Weymouth, MA 02191 (postal address: PO Box 147, Weymouth, MA 02191-0147). Phone: 781/335-4205. Website: www.weymouth.ma.us/history/index.asp?id=1126. Hours: closed during renovations.

Mamie Doud Eisenhower

Mamie Doud Eisenhower Birthplace. Mary Geneva Doud—who was known as Mamie—was born in Boone, Iowa, in 1896 and married Dwight D. Eisenhower of Abilene, Kansas, in 1916. He was a second lieutenant in U.S. Army who later became a general, chief of Allied forces in Western Europe in World War II, and the 34th president of the United States in 1953–1961. She was the second child of John and Elivera Doud, and her father retired as a meatpacking executive at the age of 38.

Mamie and Eisenhower met in 1915 in San Antonia, Texas, where the Doud family had a winter home and Eisenhower was stationed. They were married in 1916 in Denver, Colorado, where her parents had their home at the time. She was 19. During his military and political career, they moved frequently—28 times. Eisenhower served as president in 1953–1961 and then purchased their first permanent home on a farm in Gettysburg, Pennsylvania (*see* Eisenhower National Historic Site in the Presidents section). After her husband's death in 1969, Mamie continued to live on the farm until the late 1970s, when she took an apartment in Washington. In 1979 she suffered a stroke and died at the age of 82.

After the Doud family left the birthplace home in Iowa, it was occupied by several different families, converted into apartments, and purchased and used by a church. In 1975 the house was moved it to its present location, restored on the inside to the 1890s period, and opened to the public in 1980 as the Mamie Doud Eisenhower Birthplace. It now is operated by the Boone County Historical Society.

The historic house contains many items of family furniture, including the bed in which Mamie was born, dining room table and chairs, sideboard, platform rocker, hanging oil lamp, clock, master bedroom furniture, and a number of Mamie's personal items, such as her baptism certificate. The lower level is devoted to a museum and library. The exhibits contain such items as Mamie's awards, photographs, campaign items, and other memorabilia. Annual attendance is 6,000.

Mamie Doud Eisenhower Birthplace, 709 Carroll St., Boone, IA 50036 (postal address: Boone County Historical Society, 602 Story St., Boone, IA 50036-2832). Phones: 515/432-1896 and 515/432-1907. Fax: 515/432-1907. Hours: June–Oct.—10–5 Mon.–Sat.; other times by appointment; closed Sun. and Nov.–May. Admission: adults, $4; children 6–17, $1; children under 6, free.

Betty Ford

Betty Ford Alpine Gardens. Betty Ford, the wife of Gerald R. Ford, the 38th president of the United States, was one of the most candid and controversial of the nation's first ladies. But she received high public approval ratings despite opposition from some conservative Republicans, who objected to her more moderate and liberal positions on a range of social issues. She increased public awareness of breast cancer following her 1974 mastectomy, was pro-choice on abortion, urged the passage of the Equal Rights Amendment, was a leader in the women's movement, and cofounded the Betty Ford Center, an alcohol treatment and drug rehabilitation clinic.

Betty Ford was born Elizabeth Ann Bloomer to a traveling rubber salesman, William Stephenson Bloomer Sr., and his wife, Hortense, in Chicago in 1918. At the age of 14, she began modeling clothes and teaching children to dance. When her father died, she and her mother moved to Grand Rapids, Michigan, where she worked as a fashion coordinator in a department store and took dance lessons, which led to being part of a dance troupe that performed in Carnegie Hall in New York.

She returned to Grand Rapids and headed fashion coordination at the store and then married a longtime friend, William C. Warren, in 1942. The marriage did not work out, and she was divorced in 1947. Then she met and married Gerald R. Ford, a lawyer in Grand Rapids, in 1948. He ran for the House of Representatives and served as a leading congressman for 13 terms.

In 1973, when Vice President Spiro Agnew resigned, President Richard Nixon chose Ford, who was House minority leader, to replace him under terms of the 25th Amendment. He became president in 1974 when Nixon left office as a result of the Watergate break-in and cover-up.

In 1982 Betty Ford, who had suffered from alcohol and drug problems, cofounded with Leonard Firestone the Betty Ford Center, a residential chemical dependency recovery hospital in Rancho Mirage, California, that emphasized the needs of women. It followed her release after treatment at the Long Beach Naval Hospital. The Fords had homes in Rancho Mirage and Vail, Colorado.

In 1985 the Vail Alpine Garden Foundation was founded to inspire a passion for plants in high-altitude communities, and in 1988 the Vail gardens were named the Betty Ford Alpine Gardens for her contributions to Vail Valley and the nation. The gardens, located at an altitude of 8,200 feet, are in Ford Park, which also includes the Gerald R. Ford Amphitheater, named for the former president. The gardens have approximately 100,000 visitors a year.

Betty Ford Alpine Gardens, Ford Park, 530 S. Frontage Rd., Vail, CO 81657 (postal address: 83 Gore Creek Dr., Ste. 7, Vail, CO 81657). Phone: 970/476-0103. Fax: 970/476-1685. E-mail: info@bettyfordalpinegardens.org. Website: www.bettyfordalpinegardens.org. Hours: dawn–dusk daily. Admission: free.

Lady Bird Johnson

Lady Bird Johnson Wildflower Center. Claudia Alta Taylor Johnson, who was known simply as Lady Bird Johnson, was the wife of Lyndon Baines Johnson, the 36th president of the United States. She became the nation's first lady after her husband succeeded to the presidency following the assassination of President John F. Kennedy in 1961. He became Kennedy's vice president in 1960 after serving as a congressman from Texas in 1937–1949 and as a U. S. senator in 1949–1961, serving as majority whip, minority leader, and majority leader in the Senate. He was president from 1963 to 1969.

Lady Bird Johnson was born in Karnack, Texas, in 1912. Her father owned a general store, and her mother died when she was five years old. It is said that she received her nickname when a nursemaid said she was "as purty as a lady bird"—and it stuck for her entire life. After graduating from high school, she attended St. Mary's Episcopal School for Girls and the University of Texas at Austin, where she graduated in 1934 with a bachelor's degree in history and journalism. She met her husband when he was a congressional secretary visiting Austin on official business, and they were married in 1934, just seven weeks after their first date.

In 1943 Mrs. Johnson bought a failing low-power Austin radio station and worked to convert it to a successful AM and FM radio and television station. The Johnson family later acquired stations in Waco and Corpus Christi and a cable television system. The TV station was sold in 1972 and the cable system in the early 1990s, and the family expanded their interests in Austin to six stations.

While in Washington, Lady Bird created the First Lady's Committee for a More Beautiful Capital and then expanded the program to the entire nation. She also was active in the president's war on poverty and the Head Start project for preschool children. After leaving the White House in 1969 and her husband's death in 1973, she became an entrepreneur, creating the $150-million LBJ Holding Company. She also received the Presidential Medal for Freedom and the Congressional Gold Medal, the nation's highest civilian award, for her many achievements.

In 1982 she and actress Helen Hays founded an organization to preserve North American native plants and natural landscapes. It was first called the National Wildlife Research Center, then changed to the Lady Bird Johnson Wildflower Center to honor the former first lady. In 2006, a year before Mrs. Johnson died, the center became an organized research unit of the University of Texas at Austin.

The 279-acre wildflower center has 23 themed gardens, a nature center, outdoor sculptures, walking trails, visitors gallery, changing exhibits, online offerings, and an active research program. The collections emphasize native plants of central Texas but also have plants of south and west Texas and northern Mexico and 25,000 images of North American plants. An arboretum—which has examples of all 53 Texas oak species and other native trees—was added in 2012. The center's annual attendance is 100,000.

Lady Bird Johnson Wildflower Center, 4801 La Crosse Ave., Austin, TX 78739-1702. Phone: 512/232-0100. Fax: 512/232-0156. Website: www.wildflower.org. Hours: 9–5:30 Tues.–Sat., 12–5:30 Sun.; closed Mon., New Year's Day, Independence Day, Thanksgiving, and Christmas Eve, Day, and week. Admission: adults, $8; seniors and students over 12, $7; children through 12, $3.

Mary Todd Lincoln

Mary Todd Lincoln House. The Mary Todd Lincoln House in Lexington, Kentucky, was the family home of the wife of Abraham Lincoln, the 16th president of the United States. The three-story brick building now is a historic house museum that chronicles her life. Mary Todd was born in Lexington in 1818 (the fourth of 16 children in two marriages), but her family did not move into the ca. 1803–1806 house until 1832, when she was 14. The 14-room house was an inn and tavern before being purchased by her father, Robert Smith Todd, a banker and politician, who married Elizabeth Humphreys after Mary's mother, Elizabeth Parker Todd, died when Mary was six years old.

Mary Todd lived in the house until 1839, when she moved to Springfield, Illinois, to live with her sister, Mrs. Ninian Edwards. It was there that she met and married a young lawyer named Abraham Lincoln in 1842. Mary's father was one of the wealthiest and most prominent men in Lexington, and she moved in the highest levels of society and received an extensive education at Madame Charlotte Mentelle's boarding school.

In many ways, Mary Todd was quite different from Lincoln, who was socially awkward, came from a comparatively poor background, and was largely self-taught. Yet they had quite a few things in common, including the love of poetry, literature, and politics, and she admired his intellect and political ambition and he valued her judgment and help. However, by marrying Lincoln, Mary gave up a life of relative ease and privilege for one with a working lawyer who was often away while she did all the housework and raised four boys.

At the White House, Mary Lincoln experienced controversy and tragedy. Because she came from slave-holding Kentucky and some family members supported the South, many critics felt she had Confederate sympathies. She also felt out of place in Washington, and her behavior, such as extravagant White House expenditures and public displays of temper, also alienated some. In addition, there was the loss of Willie, her seven-year-old son, to typhoid fever in 1862 and the assassination of her husband in 1865.

Mr. Lincoln lived for 17 years after her husband's death, suffering from physical and emotional ailments and the death of Tad, her 18-year-old son. In 1875 her erratic behavior resulted in confinement in an asylum in Illinois by her son Robert. After retiring to Europe, illness forced her to return to the United States, where she lived largely in seclusion with her sister Elizabeth in Springfield, Illinois, until she died in 1882. She is entombed with her husband in Oak Ridge Cemetery in Springfield (*see* separate listing).

The Todd house in Lexington was the residence of the Todd family until the father died in 1849. As a result of a discrepancy in his will, a public auction was held and the house and entire contents were sold. The house became a museum in 1968 after a copy of the inventory list from the house sale was used to find antiques for the restored structure.

The house, operated by the Kentucky Mansions Preservation Foundation, now contains period furniture, family portraits, and furnishings from the Todd and Lincoln families. A garden also has been added, but nothing remains of the outbuildings, which included an outdoor kitchen, washhouse, smokehouse, carriage house, stables, and slave quarters. Annual attendance is 9,600.

Mary Todd Lincoln House, 578 W. Main St., Lexington, KY 40507 (postal address: PO Box 132, Lexington, KY 40588-0132). Phone: 859/233-9999. Fax: 859/252-2269. E-mail: mtlhous@windstream.net. Website: www.mtlhouse. org. Hours: Mar. 15–Nov. 30—10–4 Mon.–Sat.; closed Sun. and remainder of year. Admission: adults, $9; children 6–12, $4; children under 6, free.

Dolley Madison

Dolley Todd House. Dolley Payne Todd Madison was a famous Washington hostess while her husband, James Madison, was secretary of state (1801–1809) and fourth president of the United States (1809–1817). She charmed everyone and set standards that other American women tried to follow at the time, especially in fashions. A spirited hostess, she was known for her Parisian gowns and feathered turbans, as well as her use of snuff and rouge. Her life now is featured at the Dolley Todd House, where she once lived in Philadelphia and which now is part of the Independence National Historical Park.

Dolley Payne, one of eight children, was born to John and Mary Cole Payne at a Quaker settlement in North Carolina in 1768. The family moved back to Virginia in 1769 and then to Philadelphia in 1781. Dolley's father became a starch merchant whose business failed, and he died in 1792. She married John Todd Jr., a Quaker lawyer, in 1790 and moved into what is now the Dolley Todd House in Philadelphia. They had two children, John Payne Todd and William Temple Todd, but her husband and son William died in the yellow fever epidemic of 1793. Dolley became a widow with a young child at the age of 25. Shortly afterward, James Monroe, a lawyer and member of Congress, asked his friend, Aaron Burr, to introduce him to Dolley in 1794. After a brief romance, they were married later in the year.

Three years later, Madison, Dolley, and her son moved to the Montpelier family plantation in Virginia. He then served as minister to France and governor of Virginia before being appointed secretary of state in 1811 by President Thomas Jefferson and elected president in 1816. During the War of 1812, when the British burned the Capitol and the White House, Dolley is remembered for saving the Landsdowne portrait of George Washington from the fire.

Dolley Madison served as a popular first lady during her husband's 1817–1825 presidency and then returned to Montpelier. After President Madison's death in 1836, she ran the plantation and then moved back to Washington in 1837 and lived there until she died in 1849. When she returned to Washington, Dolley left the management of Montpelier in the hands of her wayward son, John Payne Todd, who ran up debts, and the family home had to be sold. James and Dolley Madison are now buried at Montpelier.

Dolley Payne Todd Madison's life now is featured at the 1775 Dolley Todd House, part of the Independence National Historical Park, established in 1948 in Philadelphia. The house, where Dolley and her first husband, John Todd, lived in 1791–1793, is furnished in muted Quaker fashion and reflects the middle-class lifestyle of eighteenth-century Philadelphia. The house is one of many historic buildings and sites in three square blocks of the city where the Declaration of Independence and the Constitution were written and which served as the nation's first capital in 1790–1800.

The park includes such places as the 1732–1800 Independence Hall, Liberty Bell Pavilion, 1790–1800 Congress Hall, 1773 Carpenters' Hall, 1722–1790 Franklin Court, and various historic houses and offices. It has an annual attendance of 5.5 million visitors. The Dolley Todd House is open only by tour. Admission is free but limited to tours of 10 visitors at a time, and tickets are available at the park's visitor center only on the day of the visit.

Dolley Todd House (Walnut and 4th Sts.), Independence National Historic Park, 143 S. 3rd St. (Independence Visitor Center at 525 Market St.), Philadelphia, PA 19106-2818. Phones: 215/597-8787, 800/537-7676, and 267/519-4295 (for phone audio tour). Fax: 215/597-5556. Website: www.nps.gov/inde. Hours: park—9–5 daily; sites—varies. Admission: free, but tickets required for tours.

Eleanor Roosevelt

Eleanor Roosevelt National Historic Site. The Eleanor Roosevelt National Historic Site in Hyde Park, New York, was the private retreat of the wife of Franklin Delano Roosevelt, the 32nd president of the United States. The 180-acre site, called Val-Kill (named after the nearby stream), is located two miles east of the Roosevelt family home. It is where Eleanor Roosevelt pursued here political and social interests as author, diplomat, and humanitarian and wrote her "My Day" newspaper column, the Universal Declaration of Human Rights, and other works from 1945 until her death in 1962. It is the only national historic site devoted to a first lady of the United States.

The full name of Eleanor Roosevelt, who was the first lady from 1933 to 1945, was Anna Eleanor Roosevelt, but she preferred to be called Eleanor. She was born into wealth and prestige in New York City in 1884, the daughter of Elliott and Anna Hall Roosevelt. who both died while she was a child. She was raised from early adolescence by her maternal grandmother, Mary Ludlow Hall. She received private tutoring, attended Allenswood Academy in England, and then became involved in social work in New York.

Eleanor met Franklin D. Roosevelt, a distant cousin, in 1902, and they were attracted to each other and were married in 1905, despite the opposition of Franklin's domineering mother, Sara Delano Roosevelt. The couple, who had six children, lived at the Roosevelt estate in Hyde Park and had a place in New York. Eleanor was supportive of her husband during his polio and political efforts, began a popular syndicated newspaper column called "My Day" in 1936, and worked to further New Deal programs, the founding and operations of the United Nations, and the causes of women and civil rights.

In 1924 Eleanor also developed an interest, with Roosevelt's encouragement, in Val-Kill Industries, which initially provided winter jobs for rural workers and women. After the workshop closed, Eleanor Roosevelt converted Val-Kill, a Dutch colonial cottage made of fieldstone, into living quarters in 1937. After President Roosevelt's death in 1945, the site became Eleanor's full-time home for the rest of her life. She never felt at home at the Hyde Park estate because of the contentious relationship with Sara Delano Roosevelt.

Val-Kill was made a national historic site by President Jimmy Carter in 1977. Eleanor Roosevelt died in 1962 at the age of 78. She developed aplastic anemia and reactivated tuberculosis after being struck by a car. Val-Kill contains two buildings—the original stone cottage that FDR built as his wife's retreat (now a conference center) and the Val-Kill workshop building (converted into a home by Eleanor in 1937). The cottage, which contains original and replacement furnishings, can be seen only on guided tours that include an introductory film and programs on such topics as Mrs. Roosevelt's political activities, personal challenges, home life, and international diplomatic efforts. The grounds, which have rose and cutting gardens, fields, trails, wooded areas, and a pond, can be toured by visitors on their own. Annual attendance is 58,000.

Eleanor Roosevelt National Historic Site, 4097 Albany Post Rd., Hyde Park, NY 12538-1917. Phones: 845/229-9115 and 845/229-9116. Fax: 845/229-0739. Website: www.nps.gov/elro. Hours: cottage—May–Oct.—9–5 daily; Nov.–Apr.—9–5 Thurs.–Mon.; closed Tues.–Wed., New Year's Eve and Day, Thanksgiving, and Christmas; grounds—9–sunset daily. Admission: cottage tour—adults, $8; children under 15, free; grounds—free.

FRONTIERSMEN

James Beckwourth

Jim Beckwourth Museum. James Pierson Beckwourth was an African American mountain man, fur trader, and explorer in the American West in the 1800s. He was born into slavery in Virginia in 1798 and later moved to the West and lived with the Crow Indians for many years. He is best known as the discoverer of Beckwourth Pass through the Sierra Nevada Mountains between Reno, Nevada, and Portola, California, during the Gold Rush years. It opened a lower pass than the Donner Pass to California. He also improved the Beckwourth Trail, which many of the early settlers followed to central California.

Beckwourth's life story was told in an 1856 book written by Thomas D. Bonner, an itinerant justice of the peace. It was titled *The Life and Adventures of James P. Beckwourth: Mountaineer, Scout and Pioneer, and Chief of the Crow Nation of Indiana.* The book originally was regarded as questionable folklore by early historians but since has become a source of social history, especially about life among the Crow at that time. Beckwourth now is regarded as an important African American frontiersman in the nation's Western history.

Beckwourth built a cabin and trading post in Portola now known as the Jim Beckwourth Museum. The cabin was constructed in the 1850s as a trading post and hotel. The museum records his life story and adventures.

Jim Beckwourth Museum, 1820 Rocky Point Rd., Portola, CA 96122, Phone: 830/832-4888. Hours: Memorial Day–Labor Day—1–4 Sat.–Sun. and by appointment; closed remainder of the year. Admission: free.

Daniel Boone

Daniel Boone Homestead. The Daniel Boone Homestead is an open-air museum near Birdsboro, Pennsylvania, where the famous frontiersman was born in 1734 and lived until moving to North Carolina in 1750. He became known for his wilderness exploits and Indian encounters during his lifetime and for his simulated adventures on television and in movies during the second half of the twentieth century. The homestead is located on 579 acres and is the largest site administered by the Pennsylvania Historical and Museum Commission.

Boone's father, Squire Boone, a Quaker weaver and blacksmith, emigrated from England in 1713 to join William Penn's colony of dissenters in Pennsylvania. Four years later, his parents joined him. Squire Boone married Sarah Morgan, also a Quaker, in 1720 and in 1731 purchased 250 acres in Oley Valley (near Reading) and built a one-room log cabin and spring house. Daniel, who was the sixth of 11 children, grew up as an outdoorsman and hunter with little formal education. The Boone family moved to Davie County in North Carolina in 1750 after the father was expelled from the Quaker sect because two of his children married non-Quakers.

As a young man, Daniel Boone served with the British military in 1755–1856 during the French and Indian War for control of land beyond the Appalachian Mountains. He was a wagon driver in General Edward Braddock's ill-fated attempt to drive the French out of western Pennsylvania. When he returned home, he married a neighbor, Rebecca Bryan, lived on the father's farm, and eventually had 10 children.

When a conflict developed between the settlers and the Cherokees, Boone and many other families in Yadkin Valley fled to Culpeper County in Virginia. He served in the North Carolina militia during the Cherokee uprising and then became a market hunter and trapper of deer, bear, buffalo, and other animals that would take him into the wilderness for large periods, sometimes as much as two years.

Four-story Georgian-style house and re-created pioneer village, part of the Historic Daniel Boone Home and Heritage Center operated by Lindenwood University in St. Charles, Missouri. Courtesy of the Historic Daniel Boone Home and Heritage Center, Lindenwood University.

One of the distant hunting sites was Kentucky, where he and a fellow hunter were captured in 1769 by Shawnees. The Shawnees took all their skins and told them never to return. But after the Iroquois ceded their claim to the region to the British in the Treaty of Stanwix, Boone led his family and a group of about 50 immigrants to Kentucky. On the way, the party was attacked and Boone's son, James, and Henry Russell were captured by a band of Delawares, Shawnees, and Cherokees and tortured to death. As a result, the expedition was abandoned.

Boone then traveled to Kentucky to warn others about the outbreak of war. After a brief conflict, the Shawnees gave up their claim to Kentucky, and the claims of the Cherokees also were purchased to establish a new colony called Transylvania. Boone was hired to open a path through the wilderness and the Cumberland Gap into Kentucky. In the process, he built a fort that became Boonesborough and later brought his family and other settlers to the area in 1775.

The start of the American Revolution in 1775 resulted in efforts by Indians to drive settlers and hunters out of Kentucky. Many left, but about 200 stayed, primarily at the fortified settlements of Boonesborough, Harrodsburg, and Logan's Station. In 1777 Boone was wounded when the Shawnees shattered his kneecap, and later his hunting party was captured while seeking meat and salt for an isolated Boonesborough. He escaped but was criticized, tried for surrendering, and acquitted after leading a raid against the Shawnees and defending Boonesborough against a 10-day Indian siege.

In 1780 Boone took part in George Rogers Clark's invasion of the Ohio Country, fighting in the Battle of Piqua. He then became a lieutenant colonel in the Fayette County militia, representative to the Virginia General Assembly, and county sheriff. While traveling to Richmond to take his seat in the legislature, he and several other legislators were captured by the British in 1781, but he was released on parole several days later. The British surrendered at Yorktown later that year, although the fighting continued into 1782. Boone fought in the Battle of Blue Licks in another Clark expedition into Ohio, the last major campaign of the Revolutionary War.

After the war, Boone and his family moved in Limestone, Kentucky (which later became Maysville). He operated a tavern and worked as a surveyor, horse trader, and land speculator but eventually was defrauded of his land. In 1799 Boone resettled in a frontier area controlled by the Spanish that later became the state of Missouri and part of the Louisiana Purchase. To encourage settlement, the Spanish governor gave him 850 acres and made him "syndic" (judge and jury) and military commander of the Femme Osage District (which became Defiance, Missouri), where he built a large stone house in the early 1800s (*see* Daniel Boone Home and Heritage Center listing). Boone, who spent his last years with his family and hunting and trapping, died of natural causes in the home at the age of 85 in 1820.

The Daniel Boone Homestead in Birdsboro, Pennsylvania, became a historical site and museum in 1937. It tells the story of Boone's youth in Oley Valley and the daily lives of the Boone, Maugridge, and DeTurk families who lived there at the time. The site has eight historic structures from the eighteenth and nineteenth centuries, with guided tours (often led by guides in period dress) being offered of the Boone house. Other historic buildings include a barn, smokehouse, blacksmith shop, sawmill, bakeshop, and another log house. The museum also has living history programs, nature trails, and a visitor center with exhibits and a video on Boone's life and displays of artifacts related to eighteenth-century life in the valley. Annual attendance is 90,000.

Daniel Boone Homestead, Daniel Boone Rd., Birdsboro, PA 19508-8735. Phone: 610/582-4900. Fax: 610/582-1744. E-mail: info@danielboonehomestead.org. Website: www.danielboonehomestead.org. Hours: Jan.–Feb.—10–4 Sat., 12–4 Sun.; Mar.–mid-June and Sept.–Dec.—10–4 Fri.–Sat. and 12–4 Sun.; mid-June–Aug.—10–4 Tues.–Sat., 12–4 Sun.; closed Mon. and major holidays. Admission: visitor center—free; self-guided visit—$3; guided tour—adults, $6; seniors, $5.50; children 5–11, $4; children under 5, free.

Historic Daniel Boone Home and Heritage Center. The home that Daniel Boone designed and built in 1803–1810 and a re-created pioneer village are featured at the Historic Daniel Boone Home and Heritage Center in Defiance, Missouri. The four-story Georgian-style home is where the frontiersman spent his last years and died in 1820. The historic site is now operated by Lindenwood University.

Boone and his family spent seven years building the stone structure after they moved in 1799 from Kentucky to the frontier across the Mississippi River in Spanish controlled territory that later became the state of Missouri. The Spanish were interested in attracting more settlers to the wilderness, and the governor gave Boone 850 acres and appointed him "syndic" (judge and jury) and military commander of the Femme Osage District, where the house now overlooks Femme Osage Valley. The house has seven fireplaces, a ballroom on the top floor, original family furnishings, and such other sights as Boone's writing desk, long rifles, family dishes, and restored gardens.

The historic site also has about a dozen nineteenth-century buildings that have moved to the site from within 50 miles of the local area to form a re-created pioneer community. They include such structures as a general store, a schoolhouse, a chapel, a gristmill, and a woodworker's residence—all containing period pieces. In addition to self-guided visits, the historic site offers guided tours of both the Boone house and the pioneer village. A 15-minute video on the life of Daniel Boone is played in the theater before each tour. The site's annual attendance is 50,000.

Historic Daniel Boone Home and Heritage Center, 1868 Hwy. F, Defiance, MO 63341-1908. Phones: 636/798-2005 and 636/798-2903. Fax: 636/798-2914. E-mail: boonehome@lindenwood.edu. Website: www.lindenwood.edu/boone. Hours: mid-Apr.–Oct.—9–6 daily; Nov.–mid-Apr.—9–5 daily; closed New Year's Day, Easter, Thanksgiving, and Christmas Eve and Day. Admission: self-guided tour—adults, $7; seniors, $6; children 4–11, $4; children under 4, free; guided tours of Boone house and heritage center—each for adults, $7; seniors, $6; children 4–11, $4; children under 4, free.

Jim Bowie

Jim Bowie Display and Museum. Jim Bowie was a nineteenth-century frontiersman who also was a pioneer planter, slave trader, land speculator, and controversial soldier. Born in Kentucky, he spent most of his life in Louisiana and became a legendary figure in Texas history and a folk hero in American culture. Bowie, who also was known for his large knife called the Bowie knife, met his death in the 1836 Battle of the Alamo while fighting for Texas independence from Mexico. His life is now featured at the Jim Bowie Display and Museum in a city information center in Opelousas, Louisiana.

James Bowie, who became known as Jim Bowie, was born in Logan County, Kentucky, in 1796. He was the ninth of the 10 children of John Bowie and Elve Ap-Catesby Jones Bowie. They first lived in Georgia but moved frequently. The family next settled on a farm in Kentucky, where Jim was born. His father had 11 cattle, eight horses, and eight slaves. The family then moved to the Red River area in 1797, Missouri in 1800, Rapides Parish in Louisiana in 1802, Bayou Teche in 1809, and a permanent family home in Opelousas in 1812.

The Bowie children were raised on the frontier, and they helped clear the land and plant the crops. All the children learned to read and write in English, and Jim and his elder brother Rezin also could read, write, and speak Spanish and French. The children learned to survive on the frontier and to run a farm or plantation. Jim, who excelled with guns and knives and even knew how to rope alligators, had a reputation as being fearless.

When Andrew Jackson issued a plea for volunteers to fight the British in the War of 1812, Jim and Rezin Bowie enlisted in the Louisiana militia in 1814. But they arrived in New Orleans too late to participate in the fighting. Jim then settled in Rapides Parish and in 1819 joined the Long Expedition in an attempt to free Texas from Spanish control. The expedition experienced little resistance, captured Nacogdoches, and declared Texas an independent republic. Bowie returned to Louisiana, but then Spanish troops regained control.

Jim and Rezin were given cattle, horses, and 10 slaves by their father shortly before he died in 1818 or 1819. The brothers worked together to begin developing several large estates in Lafourche Parish and Opelousas. When they needed more capital, they bought smuggled slaves from pirate Jean LaFitte and resold them at a greater market price. In this way, the brothers made $65,000 that they used in land speculation.

In 1825 Jim and Rezin and their younger brother, Stephen, bought Acadia, a plantation near Alexandria, Louisiana, on which they established the first steam mill in the state to grind sugar cane. In 1831 they sold it and 65 slaves for $90,000. Jim and Rezin then bought a plantation in Arkansas. In the late 1820s, Jim and his brother John became involved in a major land speculation court case in which the land grant documentation was forged.

Jim Bowie also had a feud with Norris Wright, the sheriff of Rapides Parish, that resulted in the sheriff's death when stabbed by Bowie's large hunting knife, which had a nine-and-a-quarter-inch blade. The feud began after Bowie supported Wright's opponent for sheriff, and Wright, a bank director, was instrumental in turning down a Bowie loan. After a confrontation one day, Wright fired a shot at Bowie. As a result, Bowie then carried his hunting knife at all times.

In 1827 Bowie and Wright were attending a duel on a sandbar near Natchez, Mississippi, that became known as the "Sandbar Fight." The duel was resolved by a handshake after both participants fired two shots that missed. But their supporters began fighting, and Bowie was shot in the hip and knocked to the ground again when hit on the head with the empty pistol. Wright then shot at and missed Bowie, who returned fire and may have hit Wright. Wright took his sword cane and impaled Bowie, who pulled Wright to the ground and disemboweled him with his hunting knife. Wright died instantly and Bowie was shot again and stabbed by another member of the group. Bowie survived, and no charges were filed because witnesses agreed that Bowie did not start the fight with Wright.

In 1830 Bowie left Louisiana to become a permanent resident of Texas and moved to San Antonio de Béxar (now simply San Antonio). He bought a textile mill as he entered into a partnership with Juan Martin de Veramendi, the chief administrator of San Antonio, who became vice governor of the province. He then began buying land and convincing others to purchase land for resale to him (which largely was outlawed by Mexico in 1834–1835).

Bowie married his business partner's daughter, 19-year-old Maria Ursula de Veramendi, in 1831. The couple built a house on land given them by Maria Ursula's father and shortly thereafter moved into the Veramendi Palace to live with her parents. They had two children. But his wife, the children, and his wife's brother and parents died in a cholera epidemic after going to Monclova to escape the epidemic in San Antonio in 1833.

Tensions between Anglo colonists and Mexican officials increased when the Mexican Congress passed a series of laws in 1830–1832 that seemed to discriminate against Anglo colonists in the province of Coahuila y Tejas. The colonists welcomed General José Antonio Mexia when he ousted commanders loyal to President Anastasio Bustamante, and Bowie and other colonists forced Mexican Army commander José de las Piedras and his soldiers in Nacogdoches to leave after demanding that all residents in the area surrender their arms.

Bowie returned to land speculation after the Mexican government passed new laws in 1834–1835 allowing land sales in Texas. But his appointment as land commissioner to promote sales in the Texas-Coahuila area ended when Mexico's new president, Antonio López de Santa Anna, abolished the Coahuila y Tejas government and ordered the arrest of all Texicans doing business in Monclova. Bowie was forced to flee, returning to the Anglo areas of Texas, where the colonists were beginning to agitate for war against Santa Anna. Stephen F. Austin also returned from imprisonment in Mexico City and began raising an armed force to march on San Antonio.

The Texas Revolution began in October 1835 with the Battle of Gonzales. It was followed later in the month by the Battle of Concepción when Austin sent a scouting party headed by Bowie to find supplies for his army. Bowie's party was attacked by a Mexican force of 300 infantry and cavalry soldiers, but the Mexicans surrendered three days later after the death and desertion of many of their soldiers.

On November 3, 1835, Texas declared itself an independent state. A provisional government was formed, with Henry Smith of Brazoria as governor. Austin resigned as commander of the army and was replaced by Sam Houston. In the "Grass Fight," Bowie led a Texas group that captured many horses and mules in a fight with Mexican soldiers outside San Antonio before the surrender of the city.

The final chapter in Jim Bowie's life was at the Battle of the Alamo in San Antonio in early 1836. After Houston learned that President and General Santa Anna was leading a large Mexican military force to San Antonio, Bowie offered to take a group of volunteers to defend the Alamo from the expected attack, but Houston said they would be unable to defend the former mission that was now a military fort. He ordered Bowie and 30 men to remove 19 heavy cannons that were left by the Mexicans and then demolish the 3-acre fort. Upon arrival, Bowie could not remove the cannons because of the lack of the necessary draft animals, and there was disagreement about destroying the fort.

Bowie found only 104 men and few weapons and supplies at the Alamo. It was clear that there were not enough men, weapons, gunpowder, and other supplies to hold the fort in a large-scale attack. But a vote was taken, and it was decided to defend the site until help arrived. When Colonel James C. Neill, the acting Alamo commander, left to see his sick family, find supplies, and recruit reinforcements, Lieutenant Colonel William B. Travis was placed in command of the regular army soldiers and volunteer cavalry, and Bowie took charge of the volunteers.

In the few days that remained before the confrontation, Travis and Bowie appealed for help and took steps to increase the number of volunteers, rifles, cannon powder, food, and other supplies. Among the new volunteers were Davy Crockett and 30 Tennesseans. But the number of defenders was estimated to be only around several hundred, while the original Mexican force of 1,500 was increased to 3,100 by the time of the battle. The Texans offered to surrender, but they were refused by Santa Anna, who demanded unconditional surrender and planned to retake Texas.

The 13-day battle began on February 23 and ended on March 6, 1836. The first 12 days were largely skirmishes with minimal casualties. On March 6 a major assault was launched by the Mexican Army, which overwhelmed the Alamo defenders in a third attack after being repulsed in two earlier attempts. It is estimated that 182 to 257 Texicans were killed at the fort (the exact number is not known because all the bodies were stacked and burned on orders from Santa Anna). The Mexicans are said to have lost 400 to 600 soldiers in the battle.

Bowie, who was ill, was shot while on a cot, and Crockett was executed after his capture. It was reported that the ashes of Bowie, Crockett, and Travis later were found in a simple coffin with their names on the box. The coffin then was buried in an orchard near the fort, but the burial site was never found. The life and achievements of Jim Bowie now are presented at the Jim Bowie Display and Museum at the city information center in Opelousas, Louisiana, where he once lived.

Jim Bowie Display and Museum, 828 E. Landry St., Opelousas, LA 70570. Phones: 337/948-6263 and 800/424-5442. Hours: 8–4:30 Mon.–Fri., 9–4 Sat.; closed Sun. and major holidays. Admission: free.

Kit Carson

Kit Carson Home and Museum. Christopher Houston "Kit" Carson was a wagon trail driver, interpreter, trapper, mountain man, guide, scout, rancher, Indian agent, and soldier born in Madison County, Kentucky, in 1809. His parents emigrated to Missouri and apprenticed him when 14 to a saddle maker, where he worked for two years and then ran away to Taos in 1826 and worked as a wagon train driver to Mexico. It was the beginning of an adventurous life that made him one of the most colorful figures in Western history. His story is told at the Kit Carson Home and Museum in the house he and his wife, Josefa Jaramillo, and eight children occupied in 1843–1865.

In his long frontier career, Carson had many different roles. He had a remarkable ability with languages and first served as a translator on the wagon train to Chihuahua along the Santa Fe Trail. He next joined an expedition to California in 1829–1831, became a trapper and mountain man, lived with Indian tribes, and served as a hunter for Bent's Fort in Colorado. He had two Indian wives (an Arapaho and a Cheyenne) before marrying the daughter of the prominent Jaramillo family in Taos, New Mexico, in 1843.

Carson's backwoods experience led U.S. Army lieutenant and explorer John C. Frémont (who later became a presidential candidate) to hire him as guide for three exploratory expeditions to California in 1842–1846, including during the Bear Flag Rebellion just before the Mexican-American War. It also was Carson who guided the forces of General Stephen W. Kearney from New Mexico to California when American occupation of Los Angeles was challenged by forces led by Andrés Pico. It was during the Mexican war that Carson began his military career, being made a lieutenant by Regional Commander Robert F. Stockton in the battle for California.

After the 1846–1848 Mexican-American War, Carson and a partner became ranchers in New Mexico and drove 6,500 sheep over the mountains to California. From 1854 to 1861, he served as federal Indian agent for northern New Mexico and was instrumental in bringing about treaties with various Indian tribes. He held the post until the Civil War, when he played a major military role in the state. Carson helped organize the New Mexico volunteer infantry that fought in the Battle of Valverde in 1862. He also was involved in forcing the hostile Navajo onto a distant reservation in 1864 by destroying their crops, orchards, and livestock. Despite his objections, the Navajo had to walk 300 miles from Arizona to Fort Sumner, New Mexico, where they remained in confinement until 1868. Carson was made a brigadier general for his meritorious service during the war.

In 1866 Carson was given command of Fort Garland in Colorado, but ill health forced him to resign from the U.S. Army the next year. He and his family, who were engaged in ranching, then moved to Boggsville, near Fort Lyon, in southeastern Colorado, where his wife died of childbirth complications in 1868. A month later, Carson died of an aortic aneurism at the fort's surgeon's quarters. The stone medical building later was moved to a nearby correctional facility and converted into a chapel, known as the Kit Carson Memorial Chapel at Fort Lyon (*see* separate listing).

Carson and his wife were buried near their former Taos home, which they owned for 25 years. The Taos home became a historic house museum called the Kit Carson Home and Museum in 1918. The site was purchased in 1910 by the Masonic Grand Lodge of New Mexico to honor Carson, a Mason since 1854. In addition to the three-room 1825 adobe home that Carson bought as a wedding present, the site also consists of an adjacent 1830–1850 adobe structure known as the Romero House, a 1951–1952 concrete block structure that was expanded in 1958, and an adjoining house built as a rental property in 1953.

Parlor room in Kit Carson's Taos, New Mexico, home, where he lived with his family from 1843 to 1865. It is now the Kit Carson Home and Museum. Courtesy of the Kit Carson Home and Museum, Taos, NM; photograph by Tomas Valerio.

The museum, which became a National Historic Landmark in 1963, tells of the history and culture of Kit Carson and his family. It contains such items as buffalo hide and sheepskin bedding, a wooden chest, a cooking fireplace, kitchen utensils, photographs, and a film on Carson's life. Annual attendance is 23,500.

Kit Carson Home and Museum, 113 Kit Carson Rd., Taos, NM 87571-5949. Phone: 575/758-4945. E-mail: directorkchm@yahoo.com. Website: www.kitcarsonhome.com. Hours: 11–5 daily; closed New Year's Day, Easter, and Christmas. Admission: adults, $5; seniors, $4; students, $3; children, $2.

Kit Carson Memorial Chapel at Fort Lyon. The Kit Carson Memorial Chapel at Fort Lyon in Colorado is where the famous frontiersman died in 1868 when the building served as the post surgeon's quarters at Fort Garland. The structure was moved in 2002 to a correctional facility on the way to the Fort Lyon National Cemetery near Las Animas. See the above Kit Carson Home and Museum listing for more about Carson's life.

Kit Carson Memorial Chapel at Fort Lyon, Fort Lyon Dept. of Corrections, Gate Rd. and Cemetery Rd., Fort Lyon, CO 81038. Phone: 710/456-2948. Hours: by appointment. Admission: free.

George Rogers Clark

George Rogers Clark National Historical Park. George Rogers Clark was a frontier military leader in the Revolutionary War who is credited with winning the "Old Northwest" for the United States. It resulted largely from the 1778–1779 march of his band of frontiersmen from Kaskaskia on the Mississippi River in midwinter and subsequent victory over the British at Fort Sackville in Vincennes, Indiana, where he now is honored at the George Rogers Clark National Historical Park.

Clark, who was the brother of William Clark of the Lewis and Clark Expedition, was born in 1752 near Charlottesville, Virginia. He became a land surveyor and in 1774 fought against the Shawnees in what was called "Lord Dunmore's War." The following year he went to Kentucky (then a part of Virginia) to conduct a survey for the Ohio Company and soon became a leader on the frontier. He was chosen as a delegate to the Virginia legislature, helped organize Kentucky as a county of Virginia, and obtained a supply of powder from Governor Patrick Henry for the settlers to use in combating Indian raids that Clark believed to be instigated and supported by the British in forts north of the Ohio River.

In 1777 Clark submitted a plan to the governor for offensive operations against the Indians and the British. It was approved in early 1778, and Clark was commissioned a lieutenant colonel, given funds, and authorized to enlist troops. By the end of May, he and about 175 men were at the falls of the Ohio River (the site of present-day Louisville). They then took Forts Kaskaskia and Cahokia in Illinois and Fort Sackville in Indiana in a daring 210-mile, 18-day march that winter. Fort Sackville later was retaken by the British, but Clark again forced the British to give up the fort and Vincennes. He also built Fort Jefferson on the Mississippi River near the mouth of the Ohio River in 1780 and destroyed the Indian villages of Chillicothe and Piqua and along the Miami River.

The 1783 Treaty of Paris ending the Revolutionary War gave the United States most of the territory west of the Appalachians and north of New Orleans, including the Old Northwest Territory. Clark was relieved of his command by Virginia the same year, but he continued to be active in Indian affairs, including negotiating the Treaty of Fort McIntosh in 1785. He also resumed his surveying career and then moved from Kentucky to a small cabin on land near where Clarksville, Indiana, is now located (across the Ohio River from Louisville). He died in 1818 after spending the final decades of his life living in comparative poverty and obscurity.

A classical memorial honoring Clark was authorized in 1928 by President Calvin Coolidge, dedicated by President Franklin D. Roosevelt in 1936, and then turned over to the State of Indiana in 1940. In 1966 Indiana transferred the site to the National Park Service, and it became the George Rogers Clark National Historical Park in 1967. It is located along the banks of the Wabash River in Vincennes at what is believed to have been the site of Fort Sackville.

The park is dominated by the Clark Memorial, which is a granite structure more than 80 feet high and 90 feet across at the base. It has 16 Doric columns with the inscription "The Conquest of the West—George Rogers Clark and The Frontiersmen of the American Revolution." Inside the rotunda are a bronze statue of Clark and seven murals, each covering 16 by 28 feet.

The park has a visitor center with exhibits about Fort Sackville, the various cultures involved in the Clark story, and other aspects of the conquest of the Northwest Territory. Among the collections are American and British frontier weapons, uniforms, clothing, accoutrements, French Canadian household items, maps, and other historical materials. The park also presents a 30-minute film on Clark's frontier campaign, a six-minute audio program relating to the murals, and periodic living history programs with costumed interpreters. Annual attendance is 130,000.

George Rogers Clark National Historical Park, 101 S. 2nd St., Vincennes, IN 47591-1001. Phone: 812/882-1776, Ext. 110. Fax: 812/882-7270. E-mail: gero_ranger_activities@nps.gov. Website: www.nps.gov/gero. Hours: 9–5 daily; closed New Year's Day, Thanksgiving, and Christmas. Admission: adults over 16, $3; children under 17, free.

Buffalo Bill Cody

See Entertainers section.

Davy Crockett

Davy Crockett Birthplace State Park. David Crockett, better known as Davy Crockett, was a celebrated 1800s folk hero who was also a frontiersman, soldier, businessman, and politician. He grew up in the backwoods of northeast Tennessee and was known for his hunting and storytelling before he joined the Tennessee militia, operated mills and a distillery, was elected a state legislator and then a congressman, took part in the Texas Revolution, and was killed in the Battle of the Alamo in 1836.

The museum at the Davy Crockett Birthplace State Park in Limestone, Tennessee, tells about Crockett's life and exploits—many of which were popularized in stage plays and publications during his lifetime and on television and in motion pictures in more recent years.

Crockett was born in 1786 in an autonomous territory then known as the state of Franklin (now Greene County, Tennessee). He was the fifth of nine children of John and Rebecca Hawkins Crockett. His father, who fought in the Battle of Kings Mountain during the American Revolutionary War, moved to Morristown, Tennessee, in 1790 and built a tavern, which now is the Crockett Tavern Museum (*see* separate listing). When Davy was eight years old, he told his father he wanted to hunt with a rifle and would make every shot count. His dad agreed, and Davy began hunting with his older brothers.

Davy was sent to school when 13 but dropped out after four days and ran away from home after beating the school bully and being fearful of his father's reaction and a reprisal beating by the boy's friends. Davy spent three years roaming the region and learning the skills of an outdoorsman, hunter, and trapper. He returned home when he was nearly 16 and helped his father pay off some debts by being hired out. On a day before his 20th birthday, he married Mary (Polly) Finley and they had two sons and a daughter. After his wife died, he married a widow named Elizabeth Patton in 1815 and they had three children.

In 1813 Crockett joined the Second Regiment of the Tennessee Volunteer Mountain Riflemen and fought against hostile Indians in the Creek War. He served as a scout and shot game to feed the starving troops. He returned home after being discharged in 1814. In 1817 Crockett moved to Lawrence County, joined he 57th Regiment of the Tennessee militia and became a lieutenant colonel, served as a justice of the peace, and established a diversified industry consisting of a powder mill, gristmill, and distillery—all of which were washed away in a 1921 flood. Financial difficulties from the flood caused him to move to West Tennessee.

In 1824 Crockett ran for the U.S. House of Representatives and lost, but he was elected in his second try in 1826 as a Jacksonian. However, he was defeated for reelection in 1830 after he opposed President Andrew Jackson's Indian Removal Act, only to be reelected in 1832. In 1834 he wrote an autobiography titled *A Narrative of the Life of David Crockett: Written by Himself*, which told of his exploits. He though it would help his reelection to Congress in 1834, but he lost. He had said he would go to Texas to fight in the revolution against Mexico if he was defeated. When he lost, Crockett left for San Antonio, Texas, in November 1835 with a group of other volunteers.

Crockett arrived in San Antonio in early February with about 30 Tennesseans, several weeks before President and General Antonio López Santa Anna and his army of 3,100 Mexican soldiers launched their 13-day attack on the Texans occupying the old mission known as the Alamo. The battle culminated with the Mexicans overwhelming and killing the defenders, including Crockett. They then burned the bodies of the defenders, leaving only ashes to be buried later by Texans in a single coffin with the names of Crockett, Jim Bowie, and Lieutenant Colonel William B. Travis of the Texas army on the box. The box was buried in a nearby peach tree grove but never recovered. Santa Anna later was defeated in the Battle of Jacinto, and Texas became an independent republic.

Crockett's life and exploits were popularized in stage plays and almanacs before and after his death, but as the years passed, memories of Crockett faded. It was not until the 1950s that he became the best-known frontiersman in American history. The transformation occurred when Walt Disney produced three television programs on Crockett's life (with Fess Parker in a coonskin cap as Crockett), followed by a motion picture on Crockett's adventures (*Davy Crockett, King of the Wild Frontier*) and the selection of "The Ballad of Davy Crockett" as one of the top songs on *Billboard*'s best-selling pop chart of 1955. These were followed by five more television programs and 25 movies on Crockett and his exploits, with such actors as John Wayne, Johnny Cash, and Billy Bob Thornton playing Crockett.

The Davy Crockett Birthplace State Park near Limestone, Tennessee, now celebrates Crockett's life. It has a replica of the log cabin where he was born and a museum with exhibits and videos on his life and career, photographs, and period furniture. The replica cabin was built in the 1950s from logs from the original cabin, which were dismantled and used to construct a small house. The footstone from the original cabin can be seen in front of the cabin.

The 105-acre state park along the Nolichucky River in Greene County is operated by the Tennessee Department of Environment and Conservation. It also has a campground, swimming pool, and playground.

Davy Crockett Birthplace State Park Museum, 1245 Davy Crockett Park Rd., Limestone, TN 37581-1804. Phone: 423/257-2167. Fax: 423/257-2430. Website: www.tn.gov/environment/park/davycrockettshp. Hours: Memorial Day–Labor Day—8–12 and 1–4:30 Mon.–Fri., 1–5 Sat.–Sun.; day after Labor Day–day before Memorial Day weekend—8–12 and 1–4:30 Mon.–Fri.; closed Sat.–Sun. and major holidays. Admission: free.

Crockett Museum. The Crockett Museum is located at the David Crockett State Park near Lawrenceburg, Tennessee. It depicts the life and times of Davy Crockett, the backwoodsman who became a soldier, industrialist, congressman, and folk hero. Established in 1959, the park also has campgrounds, a swimming pool, a 40-acre lake, sports facilities, hiking and bicycling trails, a restaurant, and milling demonstrations during the summer months.

Crockett Museum, David Crockett State Park, 1300 W. Gaines (Hwy. 64), Lawrenceburg, TN 38464 (postal address: PO Box 398, Lawrenceburg, TN 38464-0398). Phones: 615/762-2288 and 877/804-2681. Website: www.lawrenceburg.com/crockettmuseum. Hours: park—8 a.m.–10 p.m. daily; museum—10–5 Memorial Day–Labor Day; closed remainder of year. Admission: free.

David Crockett Cabin Museum. The David Crockett cabin in Rutherford, Tennessee, was the folk hero's last home. It is where he and his family lived from 1822 to the fall of 1835, when he went to Texas and was killed in the Battle of the Alamo in early 1836. The house was his home when he hunted and killed 105 bears and served three terms in Congress. It now is the David Crockett Cabin Museum, a historic house museum. It contains Crockett's letters to his family, period furniture, and the grave of his mother, as well as exhibits about his life. Annual attendance is 1,500.

David Crockett Cabin Museum, 219 N. Trenton St., Rutherford, TN 38369 (postal address: 945 S. Trenton St., Rutherford, TN 38369-9670). Phone: 731/665-7253. E-mail: jobne@msn.com. Website: www.davycrockettcabin.org. Hours: Memorial Day–Labor Day—9–5 Tues.–Sat., 1–4:30 Sun., other times by appointment; closed Mon.; day after Labor Day–day before Memorial Day—9–5 Tues.–Sat.; closed Sun.–Mon. and major holidays. Admission: adults, $2; children, $1; families, $5.

Crockett Tavern Museum. John Crockett, father of Davy Crockett, operated a 1790s tavern in Morristown, Tennessee, that also was Davy's boyhood home. It was used as a hospital during the Civil War and a smallpox hospital after the war before being destroyed in a fire. A replica of the building was opened at the site in 1958 by the Hamblen County Chapter of the Association for the Preservation of Tennessee Antiquities and opened as the Crockett Tavern Museum (after a replica of the Crockett family well was built there in 1949).

The museum was started after the 1955 Morristown city centennial celebration, which featured a large parade and pageant. Among the guests was movie actor Fess Parker, who portrayed Davy Crockett in the popular Walt Disney television series about Crockett at the time, and the movie *Davy Crockett, King of the Wild Frontier* was being shown at a downtown theater.

Davy's father struggled with hardships and debts during most of his life. After many failed attempts at business, the father finally established a successful tavern where the museum is now located. Davy often was hired out to drive cattle and perform other work to pay off his father's debts. He also worked at the tavern, hunting game for the tavern supper table and taking care of the livestock of cattle drovers and sheepherders while staying at the tavern.

The reconstructed tavern is furnished with authentic household items from the time period, and the building is made from recycled materials dating to the same period. It contains period furniture, pioneer utensils and tools, and other historical materials used in the late 1700s and early 1800s, as well exhibits about the Crockett family and the tavern. Guided tours are offered, and an annual Davy Crockett Birthday Party is given in August. The museum's annual attendance is 1,500.

Crockett Tavern Museum, 2002 Morningside Dr., Morristown, TN 37814-5459. Phone: 423/587-9900. E-mail: crockett@discoveret.org. Website: www.discoveret.org/crockett. Hours: May–Oct.—11–5 Tues.–Sat.; closed Sun.–Mon. and Nov.–Apr. Admission: adults, $5; seniors, $4.50; students 5–18, $1; children under 5, free.

Wyatt Earp

Wyatt Earp Birthplace House. Wyatt Earp was a frontiersman who gained prominence as a lawman in Western frontier towns in the late nineteenth century. He also was many other things at various times, including farmer, teamster, buffalo hunter, miner, barber, boxing referee, and saloon and gambling operator. Earp also was arrested on a number of charges and even escaped from a jail. He became best known for his role in the so-called Gunfight at the O.K. Corral in Tombstone, Arizona, in 1881, in which three outlaw cowboys were killed. Earp's life story now is told at the Wyatt Earp Birthplace Home in Monmouth, Illinois.

Wyatt Berry Stapp Earp was born in Monmouth in 1848 to Nicholas Porter Earp and Virginia Ann Cooksey Earp. His father, who was a widower, had a son, Newton, by the first marriage. Wyatt was one of five brothers (also James, Virgil, Morgan, and Warren) from the second marriage. A year after Wyatt's birth, the family moved to a 160-acre farm near Pella, Iowa. In 1856 Earp's father sold the farm and moved the family to Turtle, Illinois, where he was elected the town's constable. Three years later, he was convicted of bootlegging, was unable to pay the fine, and had his property sold at an auction, and the family returned to the Pella area.

After the Civil War began, the father (who had served in the Mexican-American War) recruited and drilled local companies, and the three oldest sons (Newton, James, and Virgil) enlisted in the Union Army in 1861. The 13-year-old Wyatt and his two younger brothers, Morgan and Warren, tended the farm. When the three older brothers returned from the war, the family joined a wagon train for California. There Wyatt worked as an assistant stage coach driver in California's Imperial Valley and then as a teamster taking cargo from Wilmington, California, to Salt Lake City in Utah Territory.

In 1870 Wyatt married Urilla Sutherland, the daughter of a hotel keeper, in Lamar, Wyoming, but she died later that year of typhoid fever when pregnant. Later that year, he was elected constable of Lamar but almost immediately started having legal problems. He was charged with pocketing license fees he was collecting for Lamar and stealing two horses. While awaiting trial, Earp escaped from jail by climbing out through the roof. He fled to Peoria, Illinois, where he reportedly was a buffalo hunter in 1871–1874. Earp also was arrested and fined three times during 1872 for "keeping and being found in a house of ill-fame." It is not known what his role was at the brothel.

Earp then moved to Wichita, Kansas, a cattle boomtown. Cattle were being driven from Texas to Wichita, where they were shipped by rail to stockyards. He joined the marshal's office as a deputy, but it ended in 1876 when he was arrested after he got into a fistfight with the former city marshal, who accused him of using his office to help hire his brothers as lawmen.

In 1876 Wyatt Earp became an assistant marshal in Dodge City, Kansas, which had become a major terminal for cattle drives from Texas along the Chisholm Trail. It is believed that he went to Deadwood, another boomtown in Dakota Territory, and throughout Texas to gamble in 1977 before returning to Dodge City in 1878 as assistant marshal. While in Texas, he may have met John Henry "Doc" Holliday, who assisted him in a barroom confrontation and became a close friend. In Dodge City, Earp also met Bat Masterson, who also became a friend, and Celia Anne "Mattie" Blaylock, who became his common-law wife until 1881. She accompanied him to Las Vegas, New Mexico Territory, and then Tombstone, Arizona Territory.

In 1879 Wyatt Earp went to Tombstone after being told about silver mining opportunities there by his older brother Virgil, who was in Prescott in Arizona Territory. Wyatt was accompanied by Mattie Blaylock, his brother James and his wife, and Doc Holliday and his common-law wife, "Big Nose" Kate. They were joined by Virgil, who was appointed deputy U.S. marshal for the Tombstone mining district.

In 1880 Wyatt went to work for Wells Fargo & Co. as a shotgun messenger on stagecoaches when transporting strongboxes, and then he became deputy sheriff in the area that included Tombstone, serving only about three months. During the summer, Morgan and Warren, the younger Earp brothers, arrived in Tombstone, and Morgan was hired by Marshal Virgil. While enforcing the law, the Earp brothers soon were having difficulties with some of the local outlaw cowboys suspected of stage robberies and murders, including Tom and Frank McLaury and Ike and Billy Clanton, who even threatened to kill the Earps. Tensions escalated in 1881 and led to what is regarded as the most famous gunfight in the Old West—the Gunfight at the O.K. Corral in Tombstone on October 26. The gunfight only lasted about 30 seconds, during which time three of the outlaws were killed and three lawmen were wounded.

Virgil, Wyatt, and Morgan Earp and Doc Holliday, who was deputized, were approaching the corral when firing broke out. Cowboys Ike Clanton and Billy Claiborne immediately ran and escaped, but Billy Clanton and the two McLaury brothers were killed. Virgil, Morgan, and Holliday were wounded but recovered. Only Wyatt was unharmed. But Virgil later was ambushed and maimed and Morgan was assassinated. In the months after the gunfight, Wyatt and Warren Earp, Holliday, and others pursued the cowboys responsible for the deaths of Virgil and Morgan. This led to more killings and retributions.

In the years that followed, Wyatt Earp traveled and lived throughout the West, serving as a lawman, mining for silver or gold, operating saloons and gambling establishments, and doing other jobs before finally settling in Los Angeles. He even ran a saloon in the Klondike Gold Rush in Alaska in 1897 and refereed another fight in California in 1902. Despite all his law enforcement services as constable, sheriff, or marshal; gunfights; and being the target in shootings, Wyatt Earp never was wounded. In 1882 he and Josephine Warren began a common-law marriage that lasted until his death 46 years later. He died in Los Angeles of chronic cystitis at the age of 80.

The public knew little about Earp and the Gunfight at the O.K. Corral until after his death. In 1931 author Stuart Lake published what has been called a largely fictionalized biography, *Wyatt Earp: Frontier Marshal*. The story was repeated in a 1940 book that was developed into a motion picture titled *My Darling Clementine* by director John Ford. It was followed by the movie *Gunfight at the O.K. Corral* in 1957—which gave the gunfight its name. Since then, Earp and the gunfight have been portrayed, with varying degrees of accuracy, in many films and books.

The home in which Earp was born in 1848 is now a historic house museum called Wyatt Earp Birthplace Home in Monmouth, Illinois. The museum was founded in 1986 in the ca. 1841 house, which is listed on the National Register of Historic Places. It contains Earp memorabilia, 1840–1880 furnishings, photographs, news stories, films and slide shows, books, and information about his life. The museum offers guided tours and sponsors an annual Earp birthday celebration. Annual attendance is 500.

Wyatt Earp Birthplace Home, 400 S. 3rd St., Monmouth, IL 61462-1435 (postal address: 13500 N. Rancho Vistoso Blvd., #252, Tucson, AZ 85755). Phones: 309/734-6771 and 641/420-4407. E-mail: wyattearpbirthplace@aol.com. Website: www.carpmorgan.com/wyattearpbirthplacewebsite.html. Hours: by appointment. Admission: adults, $3; children 6–12, $1.

JOURNALISTS/PUBLISHERS

George Ade

See Playwrights section.

William Cullen Bryant

See Poets section.

Samuel Langhorne Clemens

See Mark Twain in Authors/Writers section.

Eugene Field

See Poets section.

Benjamin Franklin

See Public Officials/Political Figures section.

Warren G. Harding

See Presidents section.

William Randolph Hearst

Hearst Castle. The Hearst Castle, once the home of newspaper and magazine publisher and politician William Randolph Hearst, is a palatial Spanish revival estate on a hillside near San Simeon along the central California coast that now is a state historical park. Construction of the huge mansion, designed by architect Julia Morgan, began in 1919 and continued until 1947 but never was completed. It was built by Hearst on a 250,000-acre family ranch he inherited from his mother, Phoebe Hearst.

Hearst was a newspaper magnate who entered publishing in 1887 by taking over the *San Francisco Examiner* from his father, George Hearst. He moved to New York City and acquired the *New York Journal* and then created a chain of nearly 30 other papers. He was a controversial publisher. Hearst was credited with inflaming public opinion leading up to war with Spain in 1898, and he engaged in a bitter circulation war with Joseph Pulitzer's *New York World* that led to sensationalized stories of questionable truth, called "yellow journalism." Heart then moved into the magazine field and became the largest newspaper and magazine publisher in the world.

Hearst also was a leader of the liberal wing of the Democratic Party from 1896 to 1935 but later became a conservative. He ran for numerous political offices. He was elected twice to the U.S. House of Representatives and ran unsuccessfully for New York City mayor and New York governor and lieutenant governor. Hearst also was in the news for his longtime affair with Marion Davies, a popular film actress and comedienne, resulting in separation from his wife, Millicent, in the mid-1920s.

The Hearst Castle, named "The Enchanted Hill" but called "The Ranch" by Hearst, is a mixture of architectural styles that he admired in his travels in Europe. The 60,645-square-foot mansion had 56 bedrooms, 61 bathrooms, and 19 sitting rooms, as well as indoor and outdoor swimming pools, tennis courts, a movie theater, a private zoo, an airfield, and 127 acres of gardens—most of which still remain. Hearst made persistent design changes, and the estate never was completed. Construction was halted in 1947 when he stopped living there because of ill health. The castle retains many of its original furnishings, antiques, and art treasures, and a visitor center contains exhibits about the site and Hearst's life and career. Five types of tours are offered to visitors, who number 860,000 annually.

Hearst Castle, 50 Hearst Castle Rd., San Simeon, CA 93452-9741. Phone: 805/927-2020. Fax: 805/927-2031. E-mail: visitorinfo@hearstcastle.com. Website: www.hearst-castle.org. Hours: tours 8:20–3:20 daily; closed New Year's Day, Thanksgiving, and Christmas. Admission: adult tours, $24–$30; children 6–17 tours, $12–$15; children under 6, free.

Jesse Helms

See Public Officials/Political Figures section.

Ernest Hemingway

See Authors/Writers section.

Robert R. McCormick

Robert R. McCormick Museum at Cantigny. Robert R. McCormick was a controversial newspaper publisher who was born into a journalistic dynasty. He was the grandson of Joseph Medill, the legendary owner of the *Chicago Tribune* and former mayor of Chicago. McCormick became president of the *Tribune* in 1911 and served as publisher and editor-in-chief from 1925 to 1955. He was an innovative, domineering, extremely conservative, and very successful newspaper baron whose life is celebrated at the Robert R. McCormick Museum at Cantigny, the former Medill-McCormick family country estate, which has become a public park in Wheaton, a suburb of Chicago.

McCormick was born in Chicago in 1880 to Robert Sanderson McCormick, a former ambassador to Austria-Hungary, Russia, and France, and Katherine Medill McCormick, the daughter of Joseph Medill. While his father was serving in a staff position at the London embassy, he attended the Ludgrove School and then Groton School in New England upon his return. He graduated from Yale University in 1903 and then received a law degree at Northwestern University.

McCormick initially worked as a law clerk and tried politics. He served two years as a city councilman and five years as president of the Chicago Sanitary District. After being admitted to the bar in 1907, he cofounded the law firm that later became Kirkland & Ellis. His legal and political careers ended when he became president of the *Chicago Tribune* in 1911 and editor and publisher with his cousin, Joseph Medill Patterson, in 1914. They shared that position until 1926, after which McCormick held the title by himself. McCormick and Patterson also founded the *New York Daily News* in 1919 and coproduced it until 1926, when Patterson became the sole editor and publisher.

Medill, who was born in 1823 and died in 1899, was a lawyer who started the *Cleveland Leader* in 1852, was one of the founders of the Republican Party in 1854, moved to Chicago and was elected mayor in 1871–1874, and gained control of the *Chicago Tribune* in 1876 and served as editor and publisher until his death at the turn of the century, when control passed to the family.

In 1915 McCormick went to Europe as a war correspondent at the beginning of World War I. When he returned, he joined the Illinois National Guard and became a major in the First Cavalry Regiment. When the United States entered the war, McCormick was sent to France as an intelligence officer on the staff of General John J. Pershing.

When he asked for more active service, he was assigned to artillery and served in the First Battery, Fifth Field Artillery Regiment, and First Infantry Division (also known as the "Big Red One"). He became a full colonel in field artillery, received the Distinguished Service Medal, and thereafter always was referred to as Colonel McCormick.

After returning home from the war, he renamed his estate in honor of the Battle of Cantigny, in which the First Division and he participated. It now is a 500-acre park open to the public with two museums, formal and informal gardens, a playground, picnic grounds, Boy Scout campgrounds, hiking trails, a golf course, restaurants, and a gift shop.

McCormick remained in the Officer Reserve Corps until 1929 and in 1960 established the First Division Museum at Cantigny, which now occupies a 1993 building with 10,000 square feet of exhibits and artifacts devoted to the division's history and service in World War I, World War II, and later wars. The museum also has a large outside display of tanks, armored vehicles, and artillery pieces ranging from World War I to the present.

As the head of the *Chicago Tribune*, McCormick built a newspaper empire that once controlled three major papers—the *Chicago Tribune*, *New York Daily News*, and *Washington Times-Herald*. In addition, the company purchased a 50,000-watt radio station that became WGN, a "superstation" heard across the nation. He controlled the company until the mid-1950s, when he experienced failing health after a pneumonia attack and died in 1955. He was buried in his military uniform at Cantigny.

In 1955 the Robert R. McCormick Museum at Cantigny was founded in the 35-room Georgian country home built in 1896 by Joseph Medill and enlarged in 1932 by McCormick on the family estate. It tells about the life and career of McCormick and contains antique furnishings, carpets, paintings, memorabilia, photographs, books, and sword and miniature cannon collections.

All visits at the museum are by guided tours. Cantigny also has a visitor center with a giant park floor map, an orientation film, a large painted collage on McCormick's life, and a room that tells about Joseph Medill. The McCormick museum also offers lectures, chamber music, and outdoor concerts and is the site of patriotic celebrations. Annual attendance is 55,000.

Robert R. McCormick Museum, 1 S. 151 Winfield Rd., Wheaton, IL 60189-3353. Phone: 630/260-8159. Fax: 630/260-8160. E-mail: mccormickmuseum@cantigny.org. Website: www.cantigny.org/museums/mccormick/default/aspx. Hours: grounds—7–sunset daily; museum—Feb.: 10–4 Fri.–Sun.; closed Mon.–Thurs.; Mar.–Apr. and Nov.–Dec.: 10–4 Tues.–Sun.; closed Mon., Thanksgiving and day after, Christmas Eve and Day, and New Year's Eve; May–Oct.: 10–5 Tues.–Sun.; closed Mon. and Jan. Admission: free, but parking fee is $5.

Margaret Mitchell

See Authors/Writers section.

William Sidney Porter

See O. Henry in Authors/Writers section.

Ernie Pyle

Ernie Pyle Museum. Ernie Pyle was a roving newspaper columnist who wrote about ordinary people in out-the-way places in a folksy style and won the Pulitzer Prize in 1944 for his articles about the life of American soldiers at the front lines during World War II. He became one of the most famous and beloved correspondents of the war with his stories about G.I.s in battle and under other difficult circumstances in Europe, Africa, and the Pacific.

After seven years traveling the country as a columnist for the Scripps Howard newspaper service and writing about people he met along the way, Pyle went to cover the Battle of Britain after the United States entered World War II in 1942. He subsequently followed the fighting into North Africa, Sicily, Italy, France, and the Pacific, writing about the lives and feelings of common soldiers before being killed by a Japanese bullet while covering the war on Ie Shima, an island near Okinawa, in 1945. His heartwarming stories about the courage and resoluteness of the grunts were carried in some 400 daily and 300 weekly newspapers at their peak and were especially revered by World War II servicemen, veterans, and their families and descendants.

Pyle was born on a tenant farm near Dana, Indiana, in 1900. The 1851 farmhouse that was his boyhood home was moved into Dana and became the Ernie Pyle State Historic Site in 1976. It contained Pyle memorabilia, photographs, and information about his life and career, as well as a visitor center and two World War II Quonset huts with uniforms, weapons, and other equipment from the war. However, the historic site was closed by the State of Indiana in an economy move in 2010 and a friends group now operates the museum by appointment.

Pyle's legacy is also preserved at Indiana University, where he began his career as a journalism student. The university's Lilly Library contains the bulk of his archives, and the School of Journalism is housed in Ernie Pyle Hall and offers scholarships in his name. Pyle's last home in Albuquerque, New Mexico, also honors him at the Ernie Pyle House/Library (*see* separate listing).

Pyle's war stories. which won the hearts of infantrymen and other soldiers, are preserved in four books—*Ernie Pyle in England*, *Here Is Your War*, *Brave Men*, and *Last Chapter*. In 1944 he was awarded the Pulitzer Prize for his war coverage. A stone monument was erected at the site where Pyle was killed and buried with his helmet on among the graves of soldiers on the Pacific island. He later was reburied at the army cemetery on Okinawa and then moved to the National Memorial Cemetery of the Pacific in Honolulu. Pyle also was among the few American civilians killed during the war to be awarded the Purple Heart.

Ernie Pyle Museum, 120 W. Briarwood Ave., Dana, IN 47847-0338 (postal address: PO Box 81, Vincennes, IN 47591-0081, and Friends of Ernie Pyle, PO Box 345, Dana, IN 47847-0345). E–mail: erniepyle@abcs.com. Hours: by appointment. Admission: donation.

Ernie Pyle House/Library. The Ernie Pyle House/Library in Albuquerque, New Mexico, is located in the last house occupied by the famous roving columnist and war correspondent. It functions as a memorial to the 1944 Pulitzer Prize–winning newspaperman and as a branch of the Albuquerque/Bernalillo County Library System. Pyle became one of the nation's most popular journalists in the 1930s–1940s with folksy human-interest stories from his travels and war experiences. The house has been designated a National Historic Landmark and is listed on the National Register of Historic Places.

Pyle was born and educated in Indiana but became a national figure as a roving columnist from 1935 until 1942, when the United States entered World War II. He then went to Europe, North Africa, Sicily, Italy, France, and the Pacific, writing about the experiences and feelings of American soldiers—for which he received the Pulitzer Prize and during which he was killed by Japanese machinegun fire on a Pacific island in 1945.

Pyle and his wife, Jerry, built the Albuquerque house in 1940, planning to make that their home. They were divorced in 1942 and remarried by proxy while he was in northern Africa in 1943. The City of Albuquerque acquired the small white house in 1948 and converted it into its first branch library. It now contains Pyle memorabilia and archives, as well as a small collection of adult and children's books.

Ernie Pyle House/Library, 900 Girard Blvd., S.E., Albuquerque, NM 87106. Phone: 505/256-2065. E-mail: erniepyle@ cabq.gov. Hours: 10–6 Tues. and Thurs.–Sat.; 11–7 Wed.; closed Sun.–Mon. and major holidays. Admission: free.

James Whitcomb Riley

See Poets section.

Carl Sandburg

See Poets section.

Lowell Thomas

Victor Lowell Thomas Museum. Lowell Thomas was a popular journalist who was a broadcaster and author who traveled around the world and talked and wrote about his travels. He appeared on radio and television, gave lectures, made travelogues and movies, and wrote more than 50 books of travel, comment, and adventure.

Thomas was born in Wooding, Ohio, in 1892 and at the age of eight moved to the gold-mining town of Victor, Colorado, with his family. When he was 10, he became a newsboy and worked at the *Victor Daily Record*, folding and delivering the morning newspaper and the *Denver Post* before going to school. He then covered prize fights, brawls, shootings, and operas in the mountain mining town. In 1912 he became editor of the competing *Victor Record* and later worked as a reporter for the *Chicago Evening Journal* while attending college. He obtained bachelor and master degrees in two years at an Indiana college and did further graduate work at Princeton.

By the time he was 24, Thomas already was well traveled. He began traveling in 1915, was a radio newscaster from 1930 to 1976, and became the first television news broadcaster in 1940. He spent 46 years on radio doing NBC's *Literary Digest*, and from 1951 to 1955 he made the first three Cinerama three-dimensional motion pictures.

From 1935 to 1952, he was the voice for *Movietone News* and starred in the *High Adventure* television series in 1957–1959 and *Lowell Thomas Remembers* in 1976–1979. He retired from broadcasting in 1976 and died at the age of 89 in New York in 1981.

The Victor Lowell Thomas Museum, founded in 1954, tells about Thomas's life in Victor and professional career, as well as local history and culture. It contains memorabilia, period furniture, mining equipment, a doll collection, and historical photographs. The museum also has gold panning and gold mine tours. Annual attendance is 8,000.

Victor Lowell Thomas Museum, 3rd St. and Victor Ave., Victor, CO 80860 (postal address: PO Box 0238, Victor, CO 80860-0238). Phone: 719/689-5509. E-mail: museum@victorcolorado.com. Website: www.victorcolorado.com/museumhistory.htm. Hours: Memorial Day–Labor Day—9:30–5:30 Wed.–Sun.; closed Mon.–Tues.; early Sept.–Columbus Day—9:30–5:30 Sat.–Sun.; closed Mon.–Fri. and to Memorial Day. Admission: adults, $4; seniors, $3; children under 13, $2.

James Thurber

See Authors/Writers section.

Noah Webster

See Educators section.

Ida B. Wells-Barnett

See Social Activists section.

William Allen White

William Allen White State Historic Site. William Allen White was a Kansas small-town newspaper editor who gained national prominence with his commonsense editorials and books and progressive movement political activities. He first attracted national attention in 1896 with an editorial titled "What's the Matter with Kansas?"—and later became known as the "Sage of Emporia" and unofficial spokesman for middle America. Although basically aimed at a small town, his messages also applied to the needs and values of an emerging urban America.

White was born in Emporia, Kansas, in 1868, but his parents moved the family to El Dorado, Kansas, when he was young, and he spent most of his childhood there. He attended the College of Emporia and the University of Kansas, which later named its School of Journalism for him (although he never received a degree). He started his newspaper career as a reporter in El Dorado and Lawrence and then became an editorial writer for the *Kansas City Star* in 1892. Three years later, he bought the weekly *Emporia Gazette* for $3,000 with borrowed funds. He served as editor and publisher until his death in 1944.

In his 1896 editorial about Kansas, White attacked William Jennings Bryan, the Democrats, and the Populists, charging that Kansas was suffering economically because of their antibusiness policies. In the years that followed, White's newspaper editorials and writings in his books were frequently reprinted by other publications. He became a leader in the progressive movement in 1912 after initiating the Kansas Republican League to oppose railroads and helping former President Theodore Roosevelt form the Progressive (Bull-Moose) Party in opposition to conservative forces surrounding incumbent Republican President William Howard Taft.

White also was a strong supporter of President Woodrow Wilson's proposal for a League of Nations, and in the 1920s he was critical of the isolationism and conservatism of the Republication Party. In 1924 he ran for governor of Kansas to stop expanding Ku Klux Klan activities in the state but lost the election. Despite his support for New Deal programs in the 1930s, White never voted for Franklin D. Roosevelt. Yet when Roosevelt asked White to help generate support for the formation of the Committee to Defend America by Aiding the Allies before the United States entered World War II in 1940–1941, White accepted and spent much of the last three years of his life working with the committee.

White wrote 22 books during his long career. They included biographies, fiction, and collections of short stories, magazine articles, and speeches. His autobiography, which was published posthumously, received a Pulitzer Prize in 1947. The *Emporia Gazette* continues to be published today by the White family.

The Emporia home of White and his wife, Sallie, from 1899 until his death in 1944 is now a National Historic Landmark and the William Allen White State Historic Site. The 11-room Tudor revival home became a state historic site in 2003. It contains period furnishings and many items that belonged to the Whites, including artworks, books, photographs, and items they collected in their world travels. The site also has a visitor center with exhibits that tell about White's life and career. The grounds include gardens and a lily pond. Annual attendance is 2,000.

William Allen White State Historic Site, 927 Exchange St., Emporia, KS 66801-3040. Phone and fax: 620/342-2800. E-mail: wawhitehouse@kshs.org. Website: www.kshs.org/p/william-allen-white-house/11953. Hours: 11–5 Thurs.–Sat.; closed Sun.–Wed. and state and national holidays. Admission: adults, $3; students, $1; children under 4, free.

Emporia Gazette and Museum. The *Emporia Gazette*, which William Allen White purchased in 1895, is still being published weekly in Emporia, Kansas, by the fourth generation of the White family. It also has a small historical museum with old newspaper equipment and materials, such as a Linotype machine, hand-fed printing press, and samples of old comics. White's old office also is still there with memorabilia. Visitors can look through the museum on their own or make an appointment for a guided tour during the *Gazette*'s weekday schedule.

Emporia Gazette and Museum, 517 Merchant St., Emporia, KS 86801. Phone: 620/342-4800. Website: www.emporiagazette.com. Hours: Mon.–Fri.—9–5 and tours by appointment; closed Sat.–Sun. and major holidays. Admission: free.

Walt Whitman

See Poets section.

John Greenleaf Whittier

See Poets section.

MEDICAL INNOVATORS

Clara Barton

Clara Barton Birthplace Museum. Clarissa Harlowe Barton—who became known as Clara Barton—was a pioneer teacher, nurse, and humanitarian who founded and served as the first president of the American Red Cross. She was born in a farmhouse on Christmas Day in 1821 in North Oxford, Massachusetts, where the Clara Barton Birthplace Museum is located, and died in 1912 at her last home in Glen Echo, Maryland, now the site of the Clara Barton National Historic Site (*see* separate listing).

Barton sought to improve people's lives by "offering a hand up, not a handout"—as she stated. In the process, she helped thousands and inspired countless teachers, medical professionals, and social workers. It all began in 1838 when she became a teacher in a one-room schoolhouse at the age of 16. She then had a year of further education and opened the only free school in Bordentown, New Jersey, where the attendance grew from six pupils to over 200 by the end of the school year because of her teaching abilities. The people of Bordentown were so impressed that they built a new school, but they hired a man rather than Barton to run the school. She resigned and moved to Washington and served as a clerk at the U.S. Patent Office.

When the Civil War began in 1861, Barton tended wounded Massachusetts soldiers in Washington. After the First Battle of Bull Run, she established the first agency to obtain and distribute supplies to the wounded. Barton then got permission to go with ambulances to the front, followed by going to the front lines to care for the wounded. She became known as "the angel of the battlefield." In 1864 Barton was appointed in charge of hospitals for the Army of the James and superintendent of all Union nurses. In 1865 President Abraham Lincoln asked her to set up a bureau to search for the missing men of the Union Army.

After the war, she went to Europe for a rest and became involved with the International Red Cross, assisting in relief work for victims of the 1870–1871 Franco-Prussian War. In 1881 she convinced President Chester Arthur to establish the American Red Cross, and she became its first president (serving until 1904). Barton also wrote the amendment to the Red Cross constitution that provided for the distribution of relief during natural disasters as well as in war, and she lobbied Congress to sign the Geneva Convention, which provided for the treatment of the sick and wounded in battle and the proper handling of prisoners of war. Barton spent the last 15 years of her life in Glen Echo, Maryland. The 38-room house where she lived also served as the early headquarters and storage area for the American Red Cross. It now is the Clara Barton National Historic Site (*see* separate listing).

The Clara Barton Birthplace Museum, which is in the National Register of Historic Places, is housed in the ca. 1818–1820 farmhouse where she was born and lived in North Oxford. Founded in 1921, the museum contains memorabilia of Clara Barton and her family, early correspondence, American Red Cross historical materials, Civil War relics, and books and correspondence by Barton. The site also serves as the home of the Barton Center for Diabetes Education. Annual attendance is 1,200.

Clara Barton Birthplace Museum, 66 Clara Barton Rd, North Oxford, MA 01537-0356 (postal address: PO Box 355, North Oxford, MA 01537-0355). E-mail: clarabartonbirthplace@bartoncenter.org. Hours: June–Aug.—10–4 Fri.–Sun.; closed Mon.–Thurs. and Independence Day; Sept.—10–4 Sat.; closed Sun.–Fri. and Oct.–May. Admission: adults, $6; children 6–12, $3; children under 6, free.

Clara Barton National Historic Site. The Clara Barton National Historic Site in Glen Echo, Maryland, interprets the life of the founder and first president of the American Red Cross. The nine-acre site, located two miles from Washington, includes Barton's 38-room former residence that also served as the early headquarters of the American Red Cross and a supply center. It is where Barton spent her last 15 years before her death in 1912.

The historic site, established in 1975, was the first national historic site dedicated to the accomplishments of a woman. It preserves the home, Victorian furnishings, and archive of the pioneer teacher, nurse, and humanitarian and the early history of the American Red Cross. The National Park Service has restored 11 rooms of the three-story structure, including Barton's bedroom, parlors, and Red Cross offices. Changing exhibitions and special programs are also presented. The house is shown only through guided tours. Annual attendance is 17,000.

Clara Barton National Historic Site, 5801 Oxford Rd., Glen Echo, MD 20812-1201. Phone: 301/320-1410. Fax: 301/320-1415. E-mail: gwmp_clara_barton_nhs@nps.gov. Website: www.nps.gov/clba. Hours: 10–5 daily with tours at 10–4 on the hour; closed New Year's Day, Thanksgiving, and Christmas. Admission: free.

Harvey Cushing

The Cushing Center. Dr. Harvey Cushing was an early twentieth-century pioneer in brain surgery who is considered the father of modern neurosurgery. In addition to developing many of the basic surgical techniques for operating on the brain, he discovered the endocrinological syndrome (caused by a malfunctioning pituitary gland) known as Cushing's disease and introduced a noninvasive way to measure blood pressure in the United States. It was under his influences that neurosurgery became a new and autonomous surgical discipline. The Cushing Center at the Harvey Cushing/John Hay Whitney Medical Library at Yale University in New Haven, Connecticut, is now devoted to his medical work and historical book collection.

Harvey Williams Cushing was born in Cleveland in 1869 to Kirke and Bessie Williams Cushing. His father was a physician whose family came to Massachusetts as Puritans in the seventeenth century. Cushing received a Bachelor of Arts from Yale University in 1891 and a degree from Harvard Medical School in 1895. After an internship at Massachusetts General Hospital and a residency in surgery at Johns Hopkins Hospital, he performed cerebral surgery under specialists in Europe and then began a private practice in Baltimore before joining the staff of Johns Hopkins Hospital at the age of 32. He married Katharine Stone Crowell, a childhood friend, in 1902, and they had five children.

At Johns Hopkins, Cushing was made associate professor of surgery and placed in charge of cases of surgery of the central nervous system. He also wrote monographs on surgery of the brain and spinal column, studied intracerebral pressure, and made advances in bacteriology, localization of the cerebral centers, operating with local anesthesia, and measuring blood pressure in surgery. In 1911 he became chief surgeon at the Peter Bent Brigham Hospital in Boston and then professor of surgery at the Harvard Medical School in 1912.

During World War I, Cushing served as director of the American base hospital attached to the British forces in France in 1917–1919, and in 1918 he was made senior consultant in neurological surgery for the American Expeditionary Forces in Europe. He resumed his academic career after the war, retiring in 1933 but working at the Yale University School of Medicine until 1937. He died in 1939 from complications of a myocardial infarction at the age of 70.

Cushing received many honors for his medical achievements, including the medical libraries at Yale and Harvard being named for him. He was awarded the Lister Medal for his contributions to surgical science and was elected into the Royal Swedish Academy of Sciences and the Royal Society of London. He also received the 1926 Pulitzer Prize for Biography for a book on the life of Sir William Osler, one of the founders of modern medicine.

Cushing's latest honor is the Cushing Center, an exhibit hall opened in 2010 in the lower level of the Cushing/Whitney Medical Library at Yale University, dedicated in 1941. The center features 400 jars of patients' brains and tumors from a brain tumor registry. It also tells about Cushing and displays memorabilia, examples of his surgical and other artworks, and books from his collection of thousands of first and second editions of every major and scientific text from the eleventh century through the eighteenth century, including those authored by Cushing. The 400,000-volume library also has a historical collection of medical books, manuscripts, prints, drawings, artifacts, and other medically related objects.

The Cushing Center, Harvey Cushing/John Hay Whitney Medical Library, Yale University, 333 Cedar St., New Haven, CT 06510-3206 (postal address: PO Box 208014, New Haven, CT 06520-8014). Phones: 203/785-5354 and 203/785-5352. Fax: 203/785-5636. E-mail: medical.history@yale.org. Website: www.historical.medicine.yale. ed. Hours: 9:30–8 Sun., 8–8 Mon.–Fri, 10–7 Sat.; closed New Year's Day, Independence Day, Thanksgiving, and Christmas. Admission: free.

Michael E. DeBakey

Michael E. DeBakey Library and Museum. The Michael E. DeBakey Library and Museum at the Baylor College of Medicine in Houston honors the pioneering cardiovascular surgeon and chronicles the history of the medical school. The library/museum traces the life and career of the world-renowned cardiac surgeon who also was an innovator, scientist, medical educator, and international medical statesman credited with inventing and perfecting scores of medical devices, techniques, and procedures that led to healthy hearts and productive lives.

Dr. DeBakey was the first to perform a successful coronary artery bypass and to insert a mechanical device into the chest to assist the heart. Among his many other medical innovations were devising the "roller pump," an essential component of the heart-lung machine; an efficient method of grafting frozen blood vessels to correct aortic aneurysms, as well as the use of plastic tubing instead of grafts; and the development of mobile army surgical hospitals (M.A.S.H. units) and specialized medical and surgical center systems to treat returning military personnel that became the Veterans Administration Medical Center System.

Dr. DeBakey was born in Lake Charles, Louisiana, in 1908 and died at the age of 99 in Houston in 2008. He received his medical degree from Tulane University and served as chair of surgery at the Baylor College of Medicine from 1948 to 1993. He became the medical school's first president, chancellor, and chancellor emeritus and director of the Methodist DeBakey Heart and Vascular Center. He performed more than 60,000 cardiovascular procedures and served as a medical advisor to nearly every American president and many heads of state throughout the world in the last 50 years.

Dr. DeBakey also trained thousands of surgeons and published more than 1,300 medical articles, chapters, and books during his career. In addition, he edited the *Yearbook of Surgery* in 1958–1970, served on many medical editorial boards, and led the movement to establish the National Library of Medicine, now the world's largest medical archives repository. Among the numerous honors he received are honorary degrees, professional awards, the National Medal of Science, and the Presidential Medal of Freedom with Distinction, the nation's highest honor for an American citizen.

The Michael E. DeBakey Library and Museum, which opened in 2010, traces his life and career and contains such exhibits as a re-creation of an operating room, his conference room table, a replica of the sewing machine he used to make the first Dacron graft, many of his awards and honors, hundreds of framed photographs, and videotapes of many of Dr. DeBakey's surgeries, speeches, and other events, which can be accessed on large-screen monitors. Other exhibits describe Baylor's medical school and its history. A bronze statue of Dr. DeBakey also stands in the courtyard in front of the building.

Michael E. DeBakey Library and Museum, Baylor University College of Medicine, 1 Baylor Plaza, Houston, TX 77030-3411. Phones: 713/798-4951 and 713/798-6194. Website: www.bcm.edu/debakeymuseum. Hours: 9–5 Mon.–Fri.; closed Sat.–Sun. and major holidays. Admission: free.

William W. Mayo

W. W. Mayo House. Dr. William Worrall Mayo was an Englishman who studied science and medicine in Manchester, Glasgow, and London and emigrated to the United States in 1845. He received a medical degree at Indiana Medical College in 1850, settled in Minnesota in 1854, and opened a private practice that evolved into the Mayo Clinic, the first integrated group medical practice.

After working in Lafayette, Indiana, Dr. Mayo and his family moved to the Le Sueur area in Minnesota, where he opened a medical practice and he and his brother, James Mayo, built a small Gothic-style house in 1859. The house, now known as the W. W. Mayo House, has become a historic house museum owned by the Minnesota Historical Society and operated by the Mayo House Interpretive Society.

Dr. Mayo established his first medical practice in Le Sueur but had to accept other types of work for financial reasons. It also was where his eldest son, Dr. William James Mayo, was born in 1861 after three daughters. A second son, Dr. Charles Horace Mayo, was born after a move to Rochester—where the three Mayo doctors and four other physicians later founded the Mayo Clinic, which became a not-for-profit medical facility in 1919.

Dr. William Worrall Mayo came to Rochester in 1863 to serve as examining surgeon for men being inducted into the Union Army during the Civil War. He then moved his family to Rochester, practiced medicine, and became an education board member, alderman, mayor, and state senator. In 1883 a tornado destroyed much of the community, and Dr. Mayo and his two sons, who had joined his practice, treated many of the injured, and the Sisters of St. Francis served as volunteer nurses. Dismayed by the lack of hospital facilities in the area, Mother Alfred Moes of the Sisters of St. Francis asked Dr. Mayo to collaborate on building and staffing a hospital. He agreed, and his sons joined him in providing the medical care at St. Mary's Hospital, which opened in 1889. Other doctors soon joined the Mayo private practice, and the concept of a multispecialty group practice evolved into the Mayo Clinic in the 1890s.

Dr. William Worrall Mayo retired in 1891 and died in 1911 following an accident, but his sons and grandsons continued to be active in the clinic. In 1919 the remaining members of the Mayo private practice created the Mayo Properties Association and established the Mayo Clinic as a not-for-profit entity. Drs. William and Charles Mayo, who retained ownership of the Mayo Clinic properties and furnishings, gave everything to the new nonprofit and continued their association with the clinic until their deaths in 1939.

The Mayo Clinic and Rochester grew into a major medical center as specialists, patients, and companies were attracted to the area. Today, the nonprofit Mayo Clinic has more than 55,000 doctors, nurses, scientists, students, and allied health staff in three metropolitan areas—Rochester, Minnesota; Jacksonville, Florida; and Scottsdale/Phoenix, Arizona—as well as the Mayo Clinic Health System, a network of clinics and hospitals serving the health needs of people in 70 communities in Iowa, Minnesota, and Wisconsin.

Ownership of the W. W. Mayo House passed to Charlotte Write Bradley, who gave the home as an 1874 wedding present to daughter Elizabeth and her husband, Carson Nesbit Cosgrove, who was involved in the founding of the Minnesota Valley Canning Company (which later became the Green Giant Company). The house was the home of three generations of Cosgroves, served as the Le Sueur Public Library from 1936 to 1967, and has been restored and furnished to the 1860 period.

The Mayoview History Center, located in a storefront south of the house, now features exhibits about the Mayo family, St. Mary's Hospital, and the Mayo Clinic and gives tours of the historic site. A bronze sculpture titled *Mothers*, by noted Minnesota sculptor Dr. Paul Granlund, stands adjacent to the house. It depicts Louise Mayo, wife of Dr. William W. Mayo, and Louise Cosgrove, wife of Edward Cosgrove, with three of their children.

W. W. Mayo House, 118 N. Main St., Le Sueur, MN 56058. Phone: 507/665-3250. Website: www.mayohouse. org. Hours: Apr.–June and Sept.–Nov.—12–4 Fri.–Sun.; closed Mon.–Thurs. and Dec.–Mar.; July–Aug.—10–4:30 Thurs.–Sat., 12–4:30 Sun.; closed Mon.–Wed. Admission: adults, $4; seniors, $3; children 6–17, $2; children under 6, free.

Walter Reed

Walter Reed Birthplace. The Walter Reed Birthplace in Gloucester County, Virginia, is where the U.S. Army physician who conquered yellow fever was born. In 1900, after the 1898 Spanish-American War, he led a team that confirmed the theory that yellow fever was transmitted by a particular mosquito species rather than by direct contact. The finding gave impetus to the new fields of epidemiology and biomedicine and enabled the United States to resume and complete work on the Panama Canal in 1904–1914.

Major Reed was born in 1851 to a Methodist minister Lemuel Reed and his wife in a small three-room frame house that once was common to rural Tidewater Virginia. The Reed family lived there while awaiting the construction of the church manse. Reed received his medical degree from the University of Virginia in 1869 and a second medical degree from the New York University Bellevue Hospital Medical College in 1870. After interning at several New York hospitals, he worked for the New York Board of Health, married Emilie Lawrence, and joined the U.S. Army Medical Corps in 1875.

Dr. Reed spent much of his career until 1893 in the American West, and then completed advanced work in pathology and bacteriology at Johns Hopkins University. It was followed by faculty appointments at George Washington University and the new Army Medical School in Washington, where he was professor of bacteriology and clinical microscopy. He also served as curator of the Army Medical Museum, which later became the National Museum of Health and Medicine.

The Spanish-American War in 1898 occurred after reports of atrocities in Cuba by Spanish soldiers and the sinking of the American battleship *Maine* with explosives while in Havana to protect American citizens and interests. The 10-week war ended with Spain giving the United States temporary custody of Cuba and indefinite custody of Puerto Rico, Guam, and the Philippines. But thousands of soldiers were affected by the topical disease of yellow fever.

Dr. Reed was sent to Cuba to study the problem at U.S. Army encampments in 1899 and to head an army board charged with examining topical diseases, including yellow fever. The research and experiments showed that transmission of yellow fever was by mosquitoes and not by clothing and bedding soiled by body fluids and excrement. In 1902 Dr. Reed suffered an appendix rupture and died of the resulting peritonitis at the age of 51. The Walter Reed Army Medical Center in Washington later was named in his honor.

The Reed house originally was acquired by the Medical Society of Virginia in 1937 and now is operated as a museum by the Association for the Preservation of Virginia Antiquities. It has been restored with mid-nineteenth-century period furniture. Annual attendance is 1,000.

Walter Reed Birthplace, 4021 Hickory Fork Rd., Gloucester County, VA 23061 (postal address: PO Box 160, Gloucester, VA 23061-0160). Phone: 804/693-3663. E-mail: ccbzanoni@aol.com. Hours: May–Oct.—by appointment; closed Nov.–Apr. and major holidays. Admission: suggested donation—adults, $5.

MILITARY FIGURES

Ethan Allen

Ethan Allen Homestead Museum. Ethan Allen was a farmer, businessman, land speculator, and politician, but he is best remembered as a Revolutionary War hero and the founder of Vermont. He and a ragtag militia known as the Green Mountain Boys—accompanied by Benedict Arnold and volunteers from Massachusetts and Connecticut—captured Fort Ticonderoga from the British in 1775. It was the first successful colonial campaign of the war. Allen also worked to have Vermont declared a state by the Continental Congress, which did not occur until two years after his death in 1789.

Allen was born in Litchfield, Connecticut, in 1738. His education was cut short when his father died in 1755 and he had to take over the family farm. He joined the militia during the French and Indian War but did not engage in any fighting. He and his brothers acquired large tracts of land in 1769 in what was called the New Hampshire Grants. But settlers from New York disputed ownership of the land, which led to a long series of legal disputes and the formation of the Green Mountain Boys to fight off the New Yorkers. With Allen as commander, the group fought a number of skirmishes on the frontier and then surprised the British at Fort Ticonderoga. But the Green Mountain Boys found Allen flamboyant and disagreeable and voted him out as commander, and they became part of the Continental Army.

Allen then was part of the ill-fated colonial army's invasion attempt in Canada in 1775. He and about 100 men crossed the St. Lawrence River and attacked Montreal, while another company did not. Allen was captured and held prisoner until exchanged for a British officer in 1778. When he returned, he met with General George Washington at Valley Forge, was made a brevetted colonel, and returned a military hero in Vermont, which declared independence in 1777. Allen then spent several years involved in Vermont's political and military matters, including appearing before the Continental Congress in 1778 in an effort to obtain recognition for Vermont as an independent state. He also wrote about his captivity during the war and such works as *Reason, the Only Oracle of Man* and *An Essay on the Universal Plenitude of Being*.

Allen's family, which had lived in Sheffield, Connecticut, moved to Sunderland, Vermont, in 1777 during his capture. Allen's first wife, Mary Bronson, died in 1783, and he married Frances Buchanan and they had three children. In 1787 Allen and family moved to Burlington to a farm on 1,400 acres he had purchased and built a small unassuming frame home that now is a historic house museum. He died two years later at the age of 50 after suffering an apoplectic fit and failing to regain consciousness.

The Allen farmhouse became the Ethan Allen Homestead Museum. The museum, which was founded in 1988 by the Ethan Allen Homestead Foundation, sits on a small promontory just above the Winooski River. It looks like a Cape Cod–style home because of its modern siding. The museum tells about Allen's life and local history and contains Native American artifacts and gardens. Annual attendance is 4,000.

Ethan Allen Homestead Museum, 1 Ethan Allen Homestead, Burlington, ME 05408-1141. Phone: 802/865-4556. Fax: 802/865-0661. E-mail: info@ethanallenhomestead.org. Website: www.ethanallenhomestead.org. Hours: mid-May–mid-Oct.—10–4 Thurs.–Mon.; closed Tues.–Wed. and mid-Oct.–mid-May. Admission: adults, $7; seniors and Vermont residents, $5; children 6–12, $3; children under 6, free.

Kit Carson

See Frontiersmen section.

George Rogers Clark

See Frontiersmen section.

George Crook

General Crook House Museum and Library/Archives Center. The General Crook House Museum and Library/Archives Center at Historic Fort Omaha (now the campus of the Metropolitan Community College in Omaha, Nebraska) is named for a U.S. Army officer with a distinguished record in the Civil War and Indian Wars in the second half of the nineteenth century. The facility was built in 1879 while General George Crook was commander of the Department of the Platte, based at the frontier fort. It now is listed on the National Register of Historic Places.

Crook was born in 1828 near Taylorsville, Ohio, and graduated from the U.S. Military Academy in 1852. He served in the Pacific Northwest in 1852–1864, during which time he became first lieutenant and then captain while fighting to bring Indian tribes under control. With the outbreak of the Civil War in 1861, he was made a lieutenant colonel in Ohio's 36th Infantry Regiment. He fought at Antietam (1862), Chickamauga (1863), and the Shenandoah Valley campaign (1864) and rose to the wartime rank of brigadier general when he commanded the cavalry of the Army of the Potomac from early 1885 until the end of the war.

After the Civil War, Crook reverted to being lieutenant colonel of the 36th Infantry, based in Boise, Idaho. He then fought in three Indian uprisings—the Snake War (1864–1868), the Great Sioux War (1876–1877), and the Apache War (where he made one of his more significant military accomplishments in 1883). He led U.S. troops and Apache scouts into Mexico in search of the Chiricahuas, Geronimo's tribe, who were raiding from sanctuaries in the Sierra Madre. After a firefight, Crook negotiated the peaceful return of the Apaches to their Arizona reservations and was promoted to brigadier general.

Crook served as commander of the Department of the Platte twice—in 1875–1882 and 1886–1888. The General Crook House was built to house the commander in 1879 when he moved the headquarters from downtown Omaha to Fort Omaha. He was the only commander to occupy the two-story Italianate house because the army's Department of the Platte was disbanded after his tenure. In 1888 Crook was made a major general and assigned to head the Division of the Missouri, based in Chicago, where he died in 1890.

The Crook House, operated by the Historical Society of Douglas County, became a historic house museum in 1956 and now also serves as a library and archives. The museum contains furnishings from the 1880 period and artifacts that interpret the lifestyle of the commanding officer of a major frontier fort, as well as fort life and the history of Douglas County. It also has permanent exhibits and changing exhibitions, a Victorian heirloom garden, 30,000 historic photographs and documents, a library with 2,000 books on county history, an archive with 6 million pieces, and guided tours. Annual attendance is 18,000.

General Crook House Museum and Library/Archives Center, 5730 N. 39th St., Ste. 11B, Omaha, NE 68111-1658. Phone: 402/453-9990. Fax: 402/453-9448. E-mail: house@omahahistory.org. Website: www.omahahistory.org. Hours: museum—10–4 Tues.–Fri., 1–4 Sat.–Sun., other times by appointment; closed Mon. and major holidays; library—10–4 Tues.–Fri.; closed Sat.–Mon. and major holidays. Admission: adults, $5 (but $6 mid-Nov. and Dec.); students, $4; children 6–12, $3; children under 6, free.

Jefferson Davis

See Public Officials/Political Figures section.

Grenville M. Dodge

Historic General Dodge House. The 14-room Historic General Dodge House in Council Bluffs, Iowa, is an 1869 Victorian home built by a civil engineer who became an army general, congressman, businessman, and builder of the transcontinental and other railroads. Grenville M. Dodge lived in the three-story mansion, which overlooks the Missouri Valley, until his death in 1916. The house has been designated a National Historic Landmark.

Dodge was born in Putnamville, Massachusetts, in 1831. His family moved frequently as his father, Sylvanus, tried different occupations. While his father was serving as postmaster of the South Danvers office and owner of a bookstore in 1844, the 14-year-old Grenville worked on a neighboring farm and met Frederick W. Lander, the owner's son, who asked him to help survey a railroad. Lander became impressed with Dodge's work and encouraged him to go to Norwich University, his alma mater, and become a civil engineer. Lander later became one of the ablest surveyors of explorations in the American West, and Dodge developed into the nation's leading railroad civil engineer and builder.

Dodge received a civil engineering degree from Norwich in 1850, and his first surveying position was with the Illinois Central Railroad. In 1852 he became the principal assistant for Peter M. Dey, a well-known surveyor, and they made the first railroad survey across Iowa for the Mississippi and Missouri Railroad. Other surveys, including work for the Union Pacific Railroad, followed as Dodge moved to Council Bluffs, where he started a banking and real estate business, became a bank president, and started buying land along railroad routes he had surveyed. The speculation turned out to be quite profitable as railroads expanded and new communities were established along the routes.

When the Civil War began in 1861, Governor Samuel Kirkwood asked Dodge to join his staff and go to Washington to secure weapons for Iowa regiments being organized for the Union Army. After returning with 6,000 muskets, he organized the Fourth Iowa Volunteer Infantry and received a commission as colonel of the regiment. The regiment forced the Confederates from northern Missouri and took part in the Battle of Pea Ridge. Dodge was made brigadier general because of his leadership and the performance of the Iowa volunteers.

The battle was followed by a number of command assignments against Confederate forces and participating in General William Tecumseh Sherman's Atlanta campaign in 1864, during which he was wounded for a third time. Following the campaign, he was promoted to major general and assigned to oversee the Indian campaign on the Plains and to protect stage and freight routes to California. He resigned from the army in 1866, was elected to the U.S. House of Representatives from Iowa, and then became chief engineer for the Union Pacific Railroad.

As the transcontinental railroad project evolved, Dodge was given responsibility for selecting and surveying the 1,186-mile route west to Promontory Point, Utah, for the link up with the western half of the route. The transcontinental railroad was completed in 1869, opening the American West to settlement and the transportation of crops, minerals, and natural resources to eastern markets. As a result, Dodge received numerous requests to serve as consultant, including for the Trans-Siberian Railway in Russia and for various government assignments.

The Historic General Dodge House, operated by the City of Council Bluffs, was founded as a historic house museum in 1964. It contains Victorian furnishings and arts, 1869–1916 artifacts, railroad and Civil War historical materials, films, and guided tours. Annual attendance is 11,000.

Historic General Dodge House, 605 3rd St., Council Bluffs, IA 51503-6614 (postal address: 621 3rd St., Council Bluffs, IA 51503-6614). Phones: 712/322-2400 and 712/322-3504. Fax: 712/322-3504. E-mail: generaldodgehouse@windstream.net. Website: www.dodgehouse.org. Hours: Feb.–Dec.—10–5 Tues.–Sat., 1–5 Sun.; closed Mon., Jan., and some major holidays. Admission: adults, $7; seniors, $5; children 6–16, $3; children under 6, free.

Dwight D. Eisenhower

See Presidents section.

John C. Frémont

See Explorers section.

James A. Garfield

See Presidents section.

Ulysses S. Grant

See Presidents section.

Nathanael Greene

General Nathanael Greene Homestead. Nathanael Greene was a Revolutionary War general whose actions in the Carolinas and Georgia made possible the surrender of the British Army under Lord Charles Cornwallis at the Battle of Yorktown. From 1770 to 1776, he lived in the historic house in Coventry, Rhode Island, that became the General Nathanael Greene Homestead in 1924 and a National Historic Landmark in 1972.

Greene, who became one of George Washington's favorite lieutenants, was born in Potowomut, Rhode Island, in 1742. He received only a slight formal education but read voraciously in a variety of subjects. As a young man, he worked in the family's iron foundry and was placed in charge of the foundry purchased by his father when the family moved to Coventry in 1770. He was elected to the Rhode Island General Assembly in the same year.

In 1774 Greene helped organize a local militia and became brigadier general of the Rhode Island Army of Observation later in the year. In 1775 he was made a brigadier in the Continental Army, and when the British evacuated Boston in 1776, George Washington gave him command of the city. He then was made major general, assigned to Long Island in New York, and fought in the Battles of Trenton, Princeton, Brandywine, Germantown, Monmouth, and Newport in 1776–1778, often commanding in Washington's absence.

In 1780 he fought at Springfield and was given command of the army in the South, where Georgia and South Carolina were in British hands and North Carolina and Virginia were exposed to invasion. The Continental Army troops in the region were demoralized, but Greene restored morale; recaptured the initiative by combining regulars, militia, and guerrillas; and made the British pay heavily even in losing. After Morgan's victory at the Battle of Cowpens in 1781, Greene fought a bitter losing engagement with Cornwallis at the Battle of Guilford Court House in North Carolina. But the British suffered so many losses that the weakened Cornwallis forces returned to Virginia and were defeated in the Battle of Yorktown to end the war.

Greene was so highly regarded that he was offered the position of secretary of war after the conflict. Instead, he retired after eight years of warfare to an estate near Savannah, Georgia. He died of sunstroke in 1885 at the age of only 43. The two-and-a-half-story house in Rhode Island where Greene lived in 1770–1776 now is a historic house museum. It was purchased by the Homestead Association in 1919 and restored and opened as a museum on 13 acres in 1924. The two main floors consist of four rooms on each side of a central hall. The house has Victorian period furnishings and contains Greene family history, memorabilia, and photographs. Tours are given of the historic house.

General Nathanael Greene Homestead, 50 Taft St., Coventry, RI 02816-5314. Phone: 401/821-8630. Website: www.nathanaelgreenehomestead.org. Hours: Apr.–Oct.—10–5 Wed. and Sat., 1–5 Sun.; other times by appointment; closed Mon.–Tues., Thurs.–Fri., and Nov.–Mar. Admission: adults, $5.

Benjamin Harrison

See Presidents section.

William Henry Harrison

See Presidents section.

Rutherford B. Hayes

See Presidents section.

Andrew Jackson

See Presidents section.

Stonewall Jackson

Stonewall Jackson House. Thomas Jonathan Jackson, better known as "Stonewall" Jackson, was a Confederate general during the Civil War who is considered by military historians as one of the most gifted tactical commanders in the nation's history. He also is remembered for being shot accidentally by his own soldiers in the 1863 Battle of Chancellorsville, losing his arm, and surviving only to die of complications from pneumonia eight days later.

His life is now celebrated at the Stonewall Jackson House, the only house he ever owned. He bought the house while living in Lexington, Virginia, in 1851–1861 with his second wife, Mary Anna Morrison, and serving as professor of natural and experimental philosophy and instructor of artillery tactics at Virginia Military Institute.

Jackson, who was born in 1824 in Clarksburg, Virginia (now West Virginia), was orphaned as a child and raised by his uncle Cummins Jackson and other extended members of his father's family. He worked as a constable and teacher before being appointed to the U.S. Military Academy. After graduating from West Point, he served in the U.S. Army, fought in the Mexican-American War, and was stationed in New York and Florida before joining the Virginia Military Institute faculty. He remarried in 1857 and bought the house in 1858.

Jackson left teaching to join the Confederate Army in 1861 when the Civil War broke out, becoming a brigadier general. He became known as "Stonewall" Jackson for his stand at the First Battle of Bull Run in 1861 and was promoted to major general later in the year. A disciplined and aggressive master of tactics, he led the Confederates in the Shenandoah Valley campaign, assisted General Robert E. Lee in the Seven Days Battles, and fought at Manassas Junction, Second Bull Run, Antietam, Fredericksburg, and Chancellorsville, where he was mortally wounded accidentally by Confederate pickets after routing Union forces.

The Stonewall Jackson House was constructed in 1802 and purchased by Jackson in 1858 for $3,000. It served as the Stonewall Jackson Memorial Hospital from 1907 to 1954, when it was converted into a historic house museum by the Stonewall Jackson Foundation. The house was restored in 1979 to its appearance at the time of Jackson's occupancy and now is on the National Register of Historic Places. It is furnished with period pieces, including many of Jackson's personal possessions, and has restored gardens. Guided tours are given of the period rooms. Annual attendance is over 20,000.

Stonewall Jackson House, 8 E. Washington St., Lexington, VA 24450-2529. Phone: 540/463-2552. Fax: 540/463-4088. E-mail: director@stonewalljackson.org. Website: www.stonewalljackson.org. Hours: Mar.–Dec.—9–5 Mon.–Sat., 1–5 Sun.; closed Jan.–Feb. (except Lee-Jackson Day on Jan. 15 and Jackson's Birthday on Jan. 21), New Year's Day, Easter, Thanksgiving, and Christmas. Admission: adults, $8; children 6–17, $6; children under 6, free.

Stonewall Jackson's Headquarters. During the winter of 1861–1862 in the Civil War, Confederate General Thomas "Stonewall" Jackson used a six-room cottage-style house in Winchester, Virginia, as his headquarters. That house now is a historic house museum known as Stonewall Jackson's Headquarters, a Virginia and National Historic Landmark operated by the Winchester-Frederick County Historical Society.

The Hudson River Gothic revival–style house was built in 1854 by William McP. Fuller and sold in 1856 to Lewis T. Moore, a lieutenant colonel in the Fourth Virginia Volunteers, who invited Jackson to use his home as his headquarters. Jackson's office is essentially the same as when he used it. The museum also has a collection of Jackson memorabilia and personal objects, including his prayer book and table.

Stonewall Jackson's Headquarters, 415 N. Braddock St., Winchester, VA 22601 (postal address: Winchester-Frederick County Historical Society, 1340 S. Pleasant Valley Rd., Winchester, VA 22601-4447). E-mail: wfchs@verizon.net. Website: www.winchesterhistory.org/stonewall_jackson.htm. Hours: Apr.–Oct.—10–4 Mon.–Sat., 12–4 Sun. closed Nov.–Mar. Admission: adults, $5; seniors, $4.50; students K–12, $2.50; families, $12.

John Paul Jones

John Paul Jones House Museum. John Paul Jones was an American naval hero known for saying, "I have not yet begun to fight," in response to a taunt about surrender from the British captain of the HMS *Serapis* during the Revolutionary War. Jones became America's most popular naval fighter and earned an international naval reputation for his daring exploits.

Jones was born in a gardener's cottage in Kirkbean, Kirkcudbright, Scotland, in 1747. He went to sea at the age of 12, became a merchant captain when 21, and made several voyages to the West Indies and the American colonies. He took the surname "Jones" to avoid prosecution after killing a mutinous sailor in self-defense in 1773—the same year he joined his brother in Virginia. In 1775 he volunteered for the newly formed Continental Navy, was made a senior lieutenant, and sailed the *Providence* along the Atlantic coast, capturing eight British ships and sinking eight others.

Jones was made a captain in 1776 and given command of the newly built *Ranger*. He made a spectacular cruise through St. George's Channel and the Irish Sea as he took a number of prizes in 1777–1778. In 1779 Jones commanded the *Bonhomme Richard* when it intercepted a British merchant fleet escorted by the HMS *Serapis* and the HMS *Countess of Scarborough*. This was where he uttered his famous rejoinder and forced both ships to surrender before his ship sank. He then sailed the British warships to the Netherlands.

In 1790 Jones retired in poor health to France. After being refused promotion to rear admiral by the U.S. Congress in 1787, a gold medal was struck in his honor. The following year he accepted a commission to command Russian naval forces against the Ottoman Empire in the Black Sea. In 1790 he returned to Paris, where he died in 1792. His remains were returned to the United States in 1905.

The John Paul Jones Home in Portsmouth, New Hampshire, is the only surviving building known to have been associated with Jones in his lifetime. He was a tenant there in 1781–1782. Built in 1758, the three-story Georgian-style house was the home of Portsmouth sea captain and merchant Gregory Purcell and his wife. When Purcell died in 1776, his widow took in boarders. Jones rented a room while he supervised construction of the 74-gun ship *America*. He was to command the ship, but it was presented instead to France as a gift for assistance during the Revolutionary War.

The house, which is a National Historic Landmark, became a historic house museum in 1920. It has been restored by the Portsmouth Historical Society; contains exhibits on John Paul Jones and Portsmouth history; and has collections of Jones artifacts, ship models, period furniture and costumes, Colonial through Victorian artifacts, and such other items as rugs, canes, glass, documents, and eighteenth- and nineteenth-century ceramics. The site also has a welcome center and gardens. Annual attendance is 4,000.

John Paul Jones House, 43 Middle St., Portsmouth, NH 03801-0728 (postal address: PO Box 728, Portsmouth, NH 03902-0728). Phone: 603/436-8420. E-mail: info@porthsmouthhistory.org. Website: www.porthsmouthhistory. org. Hours: Memorial Day–Oct.—11–5 daily; closed Nov.–late May; Admission: adults, $6; Portsmouth residents, $5; children under 13, free.

Thaddeus Kościuszko

Thaddeus Kościuszko National Memorial. Thaddeus Kościuszko was a Polish military engineer who designed successful fortifications during the American Revolution. After the war, he returned to Poland to fight for its independence. But he was wounded, imprisoned, and banished from Poland by Russia—and returned to the United States and lived in a small house in Philadelphia that now is the Thaddeus Kościuszko National Memorial.

Kościuszko was born in 1746 in Siechnowica, Poland. After attending the Cadet School in Warsaw, he left for Paris in 1770 to continue his engineering and artillery studies. While Poland was undergoing the first partition of 1772, he was exposed to the progressive ideology of the French Enlightenment. In 1776 he left for America and the struggle for independence by the colonies. He joined the Continental Army and received a commission as colonel of engineers. He was the first of the foreign officers to receive a commission from the Continental Congress to serve in George Washington's army. He organized the successful blockade of Charleston, South Carolina, which was also a decisive factor in the development of battlements in the victory at Saratoga, New York. This was followed by two years' work on fortifications at the U.S. Military Academy at West Point and other military installations, which resulted in his promotion to brigadier general in 1783.

In 1784 Kościuszko returned to Poland and helped organize the Polish Army, command troops in battles with the Russians, and lead the adoption of a new constitution. After several battle victories in 1794, the Polish forces were defeated and Kościuszko was seriously wounded and taken prisoner at Maciejowice. He was held a prisoner for two years and released on the condition he would never return to Poland.

After returning to the United States in 1796, he lived and recovered from his wounds at Mrs. Ann Relf's boarding house on Society Hill in Philadelphia. In 1798 he moved to France and continued his efforts to gain freedom for Poland until his death in Solothurn, Switzerland, in 1817. The house in Philadelphia where he lived became the Thaddeus Kościuszko National Memorial in 1972 and is administered as part of the Independence National Historical Park. The site, listed on the National Register of Historic Places, contains exhibits on Kościuszko's military career and stay in Philadelphia and artifacts on loan from Poland. An audiovisual presentation also shows monuments to him from all over the world. It is closed temporarily for renovation.

Thaddeus Kościuszko National Memorial, 301 Pine St., Philadelphia, PA 19106-9616 (contact: Independence National Historical Park, 143 S. 3rd St., Philadelphia, PA 19106-2818). Phones: 215/597-7130 and 215/597-8787. Faxes: 215/861-4950 and 215/597-5556. Hours. closed for renovation. Admission: tour ticket required.

Robert E. Lee

Arlington House, the Robert E. Lee Memorial. Robert E. Lee was an exceptional career military officer and combat engineer in the United States Army for 32 years who resigned to join the Confederate cause at the outbreak of the Civil War. President Abraham Lincoln invited Lee to take command of the Union Army when the war began, but Lee declined because his home state of Virginia had seceded from the Union. He initially commanded the Confederate Army of Northern Virginia and then became the commanding general of the Confederate Army.

Lee was respected by both the South and the North, and his home in Arlington, Virginia, was designated a national memorial—called the Arlington House, the Robert E. Lee Memorial—in 1925. The grounds of the mansion, assumed by the federal government, became the site of the Arlington National Cemetery.

Lee was born in 1807 in Stratford Hall, Virginia, the son of Lieutenant Colonel Henry Lee III, a Revolutionary War hero who was a cavalry officer known as "Light Horse Harry" for his horsemanship. Robert E. Lee's mother was Mary Anna Randolph Custis, daughter of George Washington Parke Custis, a foster son of George Washington. Henry Lee and Custis were cousins who grew up together and were married at the Curtis mansion, which became Lee's home for 30 years.

Lee graduated second in his class at the U.S. Military Academy, where he served as cadet corps adjutant. After graduation in 1829, he worked on various engineering projects and in scouting and guiding American troops in the Mexican-American War, where he won three brevets and was slightly wounded. He became superintendent at the military academy in 1852 but left three years later to be lieutenant colonel of the Second Cavalry. In 1859 he led a force of marines and militia to put an end to the Harper's Ferry raid by John Brown. Lee then served in Texas before being asked to command the Union's field forces on the day after Virginia seceded. He refused and joined Confederate forces in Virginia.

As brigadier general and then general, Lee served in a number of assignments in Virginia before being placed in charge of Southern forces in the state and then along the southern coast. After being called back as advisor to President Jefferson Davis, he was sent to help the Confederate forces in what was called the Seven Days Battles. The battles turned out to be tactical defeats, but Lee was successful in turning back General George B. McClellan's Union Army from the gates of Richmond.

After the Second Battle of Bull Run was won, McClellan was fought to a standstill at Antietam, and Lee crossed the Potomac two days later. This was followed by victories at Fredericksburg and Chancellorsville. But when Lee launched the Confederate invasion of the North, it was defeated at Gettysburg and had to return to Virginia. Lee was able to hold on to Richmond and Petersburg for nearly 10 months before beginning his retreat to Appomattox, where he was forced to surrender to General Ulysses S. Grant, ending the Civil War. Lee returned to Richmond as a

Arlington House, the home of General Robert E. Lee, in Arlington, Virginia. Courtesy of the Lee Family and Arlington House, the Robert E. Lee Memorial.

paroled prisoner of war and then became president of Washington College (now Washington and Lee University) in Lexington, where he died of heart disease at the age of 63 in 1870. He is buried in the Lee Chapel and Museum on the campus (*see* separate listing).

Arlington House, which has been restored to its 1861 appearance, was built in stages—the north and south wings between 1802 and 1804 and the large center section and the portico 13 years later. The most prominent features of the mansion are the eight massive columns of the portico, each being five feet in diameter. The national memorial also has two slave quarters. Only about 28 acres of the original 1,100 estate remain part of the memorial. The bulk of the land was converted to the Arlington National Cemetery after the two military cemeteries—Washington and Alexandria—were filled with Union dead toward the end of the Civil War.

Arlington House has an exhibit on Robert E. Lee's life and contains furnishings and memorabilia of the Lee and Custis families. The collections also include decorative arts, music, manuscripts, archives, and eighteenth- and nineteenth-century furnishings. Changing exhibitions also are presented. The historic site is now closed while undergoing renovation. Annual attendance is 500,000.

Arlington House, the Robert E. Lee Memorial, Arlington National Cemetery, Arlington, VA 22211 (postal address: National Park Service, George Washington Memorial Pkwy., Turkey Run Park, McLean, VA 22101). Phone: 703/235-1530. Fax: 703/235-1546. E-mail: gwmp-arlingtonhouse@nps.gov. Website: www.nps.gov/arho. Hours: 9:30–4:30 daily; closed New Year's Day and Christmas. Admission: free.

Lee Chapel and Museum. After the Civil War, General Robert E. Lee became president of Washington College, which now is Washington and Lee University, in Lexington, Virginia. He served as president from 1865 to 1870 and is honored in the Lee Chapel and Museum and buried in a family crypt in an addition to the chapel. The 1867–1868 chapel, which also became a museum in 1928, is a National Historic Landmark.

Construction of the chapel began at the request of Lee, and the simple Victorian design of the chapel, made of brick and native limestone, is believed to have been proposed by his son, George Washington Custis Lee. The plans were developed by Colonel Thomas Williamson, who along with Lee was an engineering professors at neighboring Virginia Military Institute. President Lee attended daily worship services with the students, and his office, and those of the treasurer and student center, were located in the lower level.

The museum is located in the lower level of the chapel. It contains Lee's office much as he left it in 1870 and exhibits of Lee family artifacts and memorabilia; Washington, Custis, and Lee portraits; and the university's history and heritage. It also presents changing exhibitions. Lee originally was buried in the chapel but now is in an 1883 addition, which also houses the memorial sculpture of Lee by Edward Valentine and a family crypt in the lower level. In addition to the general's remains, the crypt includes his wife, mother, father, children, and other relatives. Lee's beloved horse, *Traveler*, also is interred outside the museum entrance. The chapel has a 500-seat auditorium that also is used for concerts, lectures, and other university events. The chapel/museum's annual attendance is 44,000.

Lee Chapel and Museum, Washington and Lee University, Lexington, VA 24450-2116 (postal address: 11 University Pl., Lexington, VA 24450-2116). Phone: 540/458-8768. Fax: 540/458-5804. E-mail: ldonald@wlu.edu. Website: www.leechapel.wlu.edu. Hours: Apr.–Oct.—9–5 Mon.–Sat., 1–5 Sun.; Nov.–Mar.—9–4 Mon.–Sat., 1–4 Sun.; closed New Year's Eve and Day, Easter, Independence Day, Thanksgiving weekend, Christmas week, and other university holidays. Admission: suggested donations—adults, $5; children under 12, $3.

Douglas MacArthur

General Douglas MacArthur Memorial. General Douglas MacArthur, one of the most colorful and controversial men in American military history, was a key figure in the American victory in the Pacific theater during World War II. He was considered flamboyant and egotistical but also known for some brilliant examples of military strategy. At the same time, he sometimes had strong differences of opinion with the leadership.

As the supreme commander of Allied forces in the southwest Pacific, he was considered a national hero for liberating the Philippines and Pacific islands by 1945 on the way to the planned invasion of Japan. He later accepted the surrender of the Japanese and led that country's reconstruction. And after North Korea invaded South Korea in 1950, MacArthur was placed in charge of United Nations forces, drove the invaders back, and planned to follow the North Koreans and assisting Chinese forces into China in 1951.

President Harry S. Truman strongly opposed going into China, fearing that it would expand the war. When the dispute became public, MacArthur was relieved of command. He later gave his famous address to Congress, which is remembered for his saying, "Old soldiers never die; they just fade away." MacArthur then retired and was considered for the Republican nomination for president in 1948 and 1952 before his death in 1964 at the age of 84.

MacArthur was born in 1880 in Little Rock, Arkansas. He was raised in a military family and later served with his father, Lieutenant General Arthur MacArthur Jr., in the Philippines. They were the first father and son to be awarded the Medal of Honor. Douglas MacArthur graduated first in his class from the U.S. Military Academy in 1903 and then went to the Philippines and worked as an aide to his father, who was military governor.

During World War I, MacArthur served with distinction in the Battle of the Marne and was promoted to colonel. He returned to the Philippines as major general in 1922–1925 and commander of the Department of the Philippines in 1928–1930. MacArthur became Army Chief of Staff in 1930–1935, during which time he evicted the protesting Bonus Army from Washington.

In 1935 he again was sent to the Philippines—this time to organize defenses in preparation for their independence. In 1937 he retired from the Army, but when relations with Japan worsened, he was recalled. After the attack on Pearl Harbor, he was placed in charge of defending the Philippines. When the Philippines were overrun by the Japanese, MacArthur was ordered by President Franklin D. Roosevelt to withdraw to Australia. Before leaving, he made the vow, "I shall return," and he did, liberating the Philippines and recapturing strategic islands by 1945. He was promoted to General of the Army.

MacArthur now is honored at the General Douglas MacArthur Memorial, a complex of four buildings in Norfolk, Virginia, the hometown of the general's mother. The memorial, founded in 1964, is operated by the City of Norfolk. The museum is located in Norfolk's nineteenth-century city hall, which houses the marble crypts of the general and his wife, Jean, in a monumental rotunda. "I shall return" and excerpts from MacArthur's speeches are engraved on a bronze plaque at his final resting place. Nine galleries circle the rotunda and tell the story of MacArthur and others who have served in the armed forces from the Civil War to the Korean War. Among the objects on display are the general's corncob pipe, sunglasses, and other personal memorabilia. The museum also has two temporary galleries for changing exhibitions.

The memorial's theater continuously shows a 24-minute film on MacArthur's life and times. The Jean MacArthur Research Center houses the library and archives, education programs, and the administrative offices of the MacArthur Memorial and the General Douglas MacArthur Foundation. The gift shop displays MacArthur's 1950 Chrysler Imperial limousine, which he used from 1950 until the end of his life in 1964. The memorial's annual attendance is more than 37,000.

General Douglas MacArthur Memorial, MacArthur Sq. (between City Hall Ave. and Plume St.), Norfolk, VA 23510-2382. Phone: 757/441-2965. Fax: 757/441-5389. E-mail: macarthurmemorial@norfolk.gov. Website: www.macarthurmemorial.org. Hours: 10–5 Mon.–Sat., 11–5 Sun.; closed New Year's Day, Thanksgiving, and Christmas. Admission: free.

MacArthur Museum of Arkansas Military History. The MacArthur Museum of Arkansas Military History in Little Rock is named for General Douglas MacArthur, who was born in the city in 1880. The museum was founded in 2001 to interpret the state's military heritage from its territorial period to the present.

The museum is located in the historic Tower Building of the Little Rock Arsenal, birthplace of MacArthur. It preserves the contributions of Arkansas men and women who served in the armed forces and contains exhibits of artifacts, weapons, uniforms, documents, photographs, and other materials related to the state's military history. Annual attendance is 28,000.

MacArthur Museum of Arkansas Military History, Tower Bldg., Little Rock Arsenal, 503 E. 9th St., Little Rock, AR 72202-3997. Phone: 501/376-4602. Fax: 501/376-4593. E-mail: smcateer@littlerock.org. Website: www.arkmilitaryheritage.com. Hour: 9–4 Tues.–Fri., 10–4 Sat., 1–4 Sun.; closed Mon., New Year's Day, Thanksgiving, and Christmas Eve and Day. Admission: free.

George C. Marshall

George C. Marshall Museum. General George C. Marshall was a military leader, diplomat, economic rebuilder, and Nobel Peace Prize winner. He built and directed the largest army in history, was called the "organizer to victory" in World War II by British Prime Minister Winston Churchill, and was praised by many others for helping Europe recover economically after the war with the Marshall Plan he developed. He became the nation's first General of the Army in 1944 after the five-star rank was created by Congress.

Marshall was born in 1880 in Uniontown, Pennsylvania. His father owned a prosperous coal business, but George decided to become a soldier and enrolled at Virginia Military Institute. He graduated in 1901 as senior first captain of the Corps of Cadets and served in various posts in the Philippines and United States. Marshall then graduated with honors from the Infantry-Cavalry School at Fort Leavenworth in 1907 and the Army Staff College in 1908.

In World War I, Marshall was appointed to the General Staff, sent to France with the First Division, and earned a promotion for staff work in the Battles of Cantigny, Aisne-Marne, St. Mihiel, and Meuse-Argonne. It was followed by acting as aide-de-camp to General John J. Pershing in 1919–1924 and such other assignments as serving in China, assistant commandant of the Infantry School, commander of the Eighth Infantry, and commander of the Fifth Infantry, with the rank of brigadier general.

In 1938 Marshall joined the Army General Staff in Washington and the following year was named Army Chief of Staff, with the rank of general, by President Franklin D. Roosevelt. After the Japanese attack on Pearl Harbor in 1941, he became responsible for building, supplying, and in part deploying over 8 million soldiers. He also served on a policy committee that supervised the atomic studies by American and British scientists that resulted in the development of the atomic bomb and participated in the Atlantic Charter, Casablanca, Quebec, Cairo-Tehera, Yalta, Potsdam, and other such international conferences.

When World War II ended in 1945, Marshall resigned from his military career and became a full-time diplomat. He was sent to China by President Harry S. Truman in 1945–1947 in an attempt to mediate the civil war. In 1947 he was appointed secretary of state, during which he proposed the postwar European economic recovery program known as the Marshall Plan. In addition to rebuilding Europe, the plan helped contain the spread of communism and laid the foundation for today's American foreign policy. Marshall then retired but returned to serve as secretary of defense in 1950–1951 at the time of the Korean War. He received the Nobel Prize for Peace in 1953 and died in 1959.

The George C. Marshall Foundation was founded in 1953 at the urging of President Truman as the place where the values that shaped and motivated Marshall are kept alive. In addition to operating a museum, library, and archives, the foundation hosts conferences, symposia, and executive leadership workshops; offers undergraduate scholar and fellowship programs; and maintains a Marshall papers program.

The Marshall Museum opened in 1964 in conjunction with the Marshall Research Library. Both are housed in the foundation building along the parade ground at Virginia Military Institute in Lexington, Virginia. The museum traces Marshall's life, career, and times and features artifacts and such items as the Nobel Peace Prize, a 1943 Jeep, an interactive World War II map, and a video on his life. The library contains Marshall's papers, more than 300 other collections, and a 25,000-volume library of twentieth-century American military history. The annual attendance is 18,000.

George C. Marshall Museum, 1600 VMI Parade Ground, Lexington, VA 24450 (postal address: PO Box Drawer 1600, Lexington, VA 22450-1600). Phone: 540/463-7103. Fax: 540/464-5229. E-mail: marshallfoundation@marshall-foundation.org. Website: www.marshallfoundation.org/museum. Hours: 9–5 Tues.–Sat.; 1–5 Sun.; closed Mon., New Year's Day, Thanksgiving, and Christmas Eve and Day. Admission: adults, $5; seniors and students, $3; children under 13 and military, free.

George C. Marshall International Center at Dodona Manor. Dodona Manor in the historic district of Leesburg, Virginia, was the home of General George C. Marshall from 1941 until his death in 1959. The federal-style house, which is a National Historic Landmark, was built in the mid-1820s and owned by several families and possibly used as a female boarding school before being purchased by Marshall and his wife, Katherine, who named it for the Greek oracle Dodona.

After Marshall's death, the house fell into disrepair and the George C. Marshall International Center at Dodona Manor was founded in the 1990s to restore and preserve the home. The George C. Marshall Home Preservation Fund was formed to save the house and grounds from demolition. The Dodona Manor was restored in 1999–2000 and opened to the public in 2005.

The center seeks to increase awareness of the crucial role Marshall played in the twentieth century. It interprets the Marshall home and gardens and has exhibitions, education programs, lectures, outreach events, and international exchanges. Among the original Marshall belongings are furniture, art, clothes, maps, books, Chinese furniture and artwork, trunks, personal items, and ephemeral objects that support the interpretation of the home and Marshall's career. Tours are offered of Dodona Manor on weekends. Annual attendance is 4,000.

George C. Marshall International Center at Dodona Manor, 217 Edwards Ferry Rd., Leesburg, VA 20176-2305. Phones: 703/777-1880 and 703/777-1301. Fax: 703/777-2889. E-mail: dodona@georgecmarshall.org. Website: www.georgecmarshall.org. Hours: Sept.–May—10–5 Sat., 1–5 Sun.; closed Mon.–Fri. and most major holidays (but open l–5 Memorial Day, Labor Day, and Columbus Day); June–Aug.—1–5 Mon., 10–5 Sat., 1–5 Sun.; closed Tues.–Fri. Admission (by tour): adults, $10; seniors, $8; students and children 9–17, $5; children under 9, free.

Audie Murphy

Audie Murphy/American Cotton Museum. Audie Murphy was a World War II hero who became a movie star—and died in a civilian plane crash in 1971. He was one of the most highly decorated and famous soldiers of the war, receiving the Medal of Honor, the U.S. military's highest award for valor, and 32 other American and foreign decorations. After the war, he appeared in 44 motion pictures and composed country music before the plane in which he was a passenger crashed into a Virginia mountain. His life and accomplishments are now featured at the Audie Murphy/American Cotton Museum in Greenville, Texas.

Murphy tried to join the military after the Japanese attacked Pearl Harbor in 1941 but was turned down because he was underage. On his 18th birthday, he tried to enlist again but was not accepted by the Marines, army paratroopers, or navy because he was too short and underweight at five feet, five inches and 110 pounds. But the U.S. Army finally took him and sent him off to Camp Wolters in Texas for basic training. He then went to Fort Meade in Maryland for advanced infantry training and in early 1943 was shipped out to Casablanca, Morocco, as part of the Third Infantry Division. He took part in the division's training maneuvers but saw no combat action in Africa.

Murphy finally engaged in combat when he took part in the invasion of Sicily in 1943. After the Third Division invaded the Italian mainland, Murphy and his men took cover in a quarry near Salerno when attacked by German soldiers. In the fight that followed, three Germans were killed and several captured. He also distinguished himself in many other battles while in Italy, earning promotions and decorations for valor in combat at the Volturno River, Anzio beachhead, and the Italian mountains.

When his best friend was killed by a German machine gunner who feigned surrender, Murphy wiped out the German machine gun post and used the German machine gun and grenades to destroy several others nearby enemy positions. Shortly thereafter, he was wounded in the hip and spent 10 weeks recuperating. When he returned, he was made company commander and suffered further wounds from a mortar round.

Murphy received the Medal of Honor in early 1945 at the Battle of Holtzwihr when the temperature was 14 degrees with 24 inches of snow and his unit was reduced to an effective strength of 19 out of 128. He shot at the German soldiers until his rifle was out of ammunition and then climbed in an abandoned burning M10 tank destroyer and used its machine gun to cut down a full squad of German infantry and others while calling for artillery fire by using a landline telephone. He was wounded in the leg but directed artillery fire for an hour before the telephone line was cut by Germany artillery. He then organized his remaining men into a counterattack, which drove the Germans from Holtzwihr.

After the war, Murphy wrote about his war experiences in *To Hell and Back*, published in 1949. In 1955 the book was made into a popular motion picture of the same name. It opened the door to a film career that included 44 movies, including 33 Westerns in which he starred. He also became a country music composer. Murphy died at the age of 44 in a private plane crash in which he and five others were killed when the plane struck Brush Mountain near Catawbo, Virginia. He was buried with full military honors in Arlington National Cemetery.

Murphy was born near Kingston, Texas, in 1886 to poor sharecroppers Emmett Berry Murphy and Josie Bell Killian Murphy. He was the sixth of 12 children. He attended elementary school in nearby Celeste, Texas, until his father abandoned the family, dropping out in the fifth grade to help support the family, often plowing and picking cotton. He also became very skilled with the rifle, often hunting to feed the family. When his mother died in 1941, he worked at a combination general store, garage, and gas station in Greenville. Later that year, he placed three of the youngest siblings in an orphanage to ensure their care and then reclaimed them after World War II. When he became 18 in 1942, he joined the U.S. Army.

The Audie Murphy/American Cotton Museum in Greenville was founded in 1987 to honor the war hero and other veterans and preserve the history of the American cotton industry, as well as Hunt County and the northern Texas Blackland Prairie. The museum has a 10-foot statue of Murphy outside the building and features the Audie L. Murphy Hunt County Veterans' Exhibit, which tells the Audie Murphy story and contains a large collection of memorabilia from his military service and movie career, as well as materials about other Hunt County veterans. The museum also has an annual Audie Murphy Days and Cotton History Conference. The museum's annual attendance is 5,500.

Audie Murphy/American Cotton Museum, 600 Interstate 30 East, Greenville, TX 75401 (postal address: PO Box 347, Greenville, TX 75403-0347). Phone: 903/450-4502. Fax: 903/454-1990. E-mail: amacm@att.net. Website: www.cottonmuseum.com. Hours: 10–5 Tues.–Sat.; closed Sun.–Mon. and major holidays. Admission: adults, $6; seniors, veterans, and college students, $4; children 6–18, $2; children under 6, free.

George S. Patton

General George Patton Museum of Leadership. General George S. Patton, known as "Old Blood and Guts," was one of the most effective and flamboyant generals of World War II. He was known for his battle strategies and use of tanks in northern Africa and Europe but also for his eccentricities and controversial outspokenness.

Patton drove the German forces out of France toward the end the war, capturing more enemy prisoners and liberating more territory in less time than any other commander in military history. At the same time, he wore ivory-covered Colt .45 revolvers, traveled with a bull terrier at the front, slapped a hospitalized soldier (for what he believed was cowardice), and was relieved of his command of the Third Army for his critical military opinions.

Patton was born in San Gabriel, California, in 1885. He went to the Virginia Military Institute and graduated from the U.S. Military Academy in 1909. He was a cavalryman who served on the staff of General John J. Pershing during the unsuccessful pursuit of Pancho Villa in Mexico in 1916–1917. In World War I, Patton was assigned to the Tank Corps and became expert in the use of the new weapon—mobile armored tanks. In 1940 he was made commander of the Second Armored Division and in 1942 established the Desert Training Center to train American troops in desert warfare in preparation for the invasion of North Africa.

Patton went to North Africa, where he commanded American forces in Morocco in 1942 and in Tunisia in 1943. He became commander of the Seventh Army in Sicily later in 1943 and in 1944–1945 commanded the Third Army's historic sweep across France into Germany. After the Allied victory in 1945, Patton was relieved of his Third Army command, and he died in a car accident in Heidelberg, Germany, at the age of 60.

The General George Patton Museum of Leadership was founded as the Patton Museum of Cavalry and Armour in 1948 and later was called the General George Patton Museum. It now is the General George Patton Museum of Leadership, affiliated with the U.S. Army Armor Center and administered by the U.S. Army Accessions Command at Fort Knox.

The museum is devoted to the life and career of General Patton, as well as the history of the army cavalry and armored forces. In addition to many of Patton's belongings, it contains collections of tanks, armored vehicles, firearms, medals, decorations, and a library on United States and foreign fighting vehicle history and technology. The annual attendance is 358,000.

General George Patton Museum of Leadership, 4554 Fayette Ave., Fort Knox, KY 40121-0208 (postal address: PO Box 208, Fort Knox, KY 40121-0208). Phone: 505/624-3812. Fax: 502/624-2364. E-mail: knox.museum@conus.army. mil. Website: www.knox.army.mil/museum. Hours: 9–4:30 Mon.–Fri., 10–5:30 Sat.–Sun.; closed New Year's Eve and Day, Easter, Thanksgiving, and Christmas Eve and Day. Admission: free.

General George S. Patton Memorial Museum. The General George S. Patton Memorial Museum is located at the site of the Desert Training Center in Chiriaco Summit, California, which he established in 1942 to train American troops in desert warfare in preparation for fighting in North Africa during World War II. The center developed into the nation's largest military installation, stretching from Arizona to Nevada to California and eventually training 60 divisions and over a million World War II soldiers.

The museum was founded in 1988 near the entrance to Camp Young, which was the headquarters of the Desert Training Center. Patton decided to locate the training camp at the desert site where he had surveyed the area for an aqueduct system a few years earlier and after a tour led by Joe Chiriaco, a local store and gas station owner. The museum concept began when the Bureau of Land Management erected a small triangular rock monument with an American flag. It was followed by the Chiriaco family, veteran volunteers, and the land management agency working to establish a museum in honor of American veterans. The museum became a nonprofit with a large share of the artifacts being donated by veterans and their families.

The museum's exhibits are devoted to General Patton, the Desert Training Center, World War II, other eras of military history, the Colorado River Aqueduct, and the region's natural science. The Patton section contains memorabilia from his life and career. The museum also has a large tank yard with tanks ranging from World War II through the Vietnam War. The annual attendance is 73,500.

General George S. Patton Memorial Museum, 62-510 Chiriaco Rd., Chiriaco Summit, CA 92201-8203. Phone and fax: 760/227-3483. E-mail: contact@generalpattonmuseum.com. Website: www.generalpattonmuseum.com. Hours: 9:30–4:30 daily; closed Thanksgiving and Christmas. Admission: suggested donations—adults, $5; seniors, $4.50; children 7–12, $1; children under 7, military, and American Legion and Veterans of Foreign Wars members, free.

Oliver Hazard Perry

Perry's Victory and International Peace Museum. Commodore Oliver Hazard Perry was hailed as a hero for leading American forces in a decisive naval victory over the British in the Battle of Lake Erie in the War of 1812. The victory was the turning point in the battle for the American West in the war, and his leadership greatly influenced the successful outcome of all nine Lake Erie military campaign triumphs. His achievements—and the lasting peace between Great Britain, Canada, and the United States—are celebrated at what is called Perry's Victory and International Peace Museum at Put-in-Bay, Ohio.

Perry came from a naval family in Rhode Island. He was born in 1785 in South Kensington, the son of Captain Christopher Raymond Perry and Sarah Wallace Alexander. He also was the older brother of Commander Matthew Calbraith Perry, who compelled Japan to open to the West by threatening the use of force. As a boy, he sailed ships in anticipation of a future career in the U.S. Navy and at the age of 14 was appointed a midshipman in the navy in 1799. During the conflict with France, he was assigned to his father's frigate, the USS *General Greene*, and he experienced his first combat in 1800 off the coast of the French colony of Haiti, which was rebelling.

Perry served on the USS *Adams* during the First Barbary War and later commanded the USS *Nautilus* during the capture of Derna. In 1806 he was given command of the sloop USS *Revenge*, during which he engaged in patrol duties to enforce the Embargo Act and conducted a successful raid to regain an American ship held in Spanish territory in Florida. He then was given command of United States naval forces on Lake Erie during the War of 1812.

The Battle of Lake Erie was fought on September 10, 1813. When a Royal Navy task force disabled Perry's flagship, the USS *Lawrence*, he transferred his command to the USS *Niagara*, brought the other American schooners in closer, and continued to attack the British ships. The U.S. ships broke through the British line and damaged the Royal Navy ships to such an extent that they surrendered and were taken back to Presque Island. In his battle report to General William Harrison, Perry simply said, "We have met the enemy and they are ours; two ships, two brigs, one schooner, and one sloop." It was the first time an entire British naval squadron had surrendered.

The victory led to the critical Battle of the Thames, the defeat of British forces by Harrison's army, the death of Indian leader Tecumseh, and the breakup of the Indian alliance in the West. Perry actually was actively involved in nine campaigns that led to and followed the Battle of Lake Erie, for which he was promoted to captain and awarded the Congressional Gold Medal.

After President James Monroe made Perry a commodore, he sent him on a diplomatic mission to South America. In 1819 Perry died after a successful expedition to Venezuela to consult with Simon Bolivar about piracy in the Caribbean. He contracted yellow fever from mosquitoes while aboard the USS *Nonsuch*.

Perry's Victory and International Peace Memorial is located near where the Battle of Lake Erie took place close to South Bass Island in Ohio. It features a 352-foot monument—the world's most massive Doric column—which is also one of the tallest monuments in the United States. It was started by a multistate commission in 1912–1915 and completed in 1931 after the federal government assumed control and provided additional funding. It recently was renovated, and a new visitor center was added in 2002.

Visitors can take an elevator to the observation deck at the 317-foot level of the monument for a panoramic view of the Lake Erie islands and shorelines of Ohio, Michigan, and Ontario. Interred beneath the rotunda floor are the remains of three American and three British officers who were killed during the Battle of Lake Erie. The names of Perry's vessels and the Americans killed or wounded in the battle also are carved in the rotunda walls.

A film tells about the Battle of Lake Erie in the visitor center, and during the summer park rangers give interpretive talks about the battle, the War of 1812, the construction of the monument, and related topics. On weekends, rangers offer living history demonstrations dressed in War of 1812 military and civilian costumes, firing demonstrations with flintlock muskets, and sometimes 32-pounder cannonade firing demonstrations. The memorial's annual attendance is over 200,000.

Perry's Victory and International Peace Memorial, 93 Delaware Ave., Put-in-Bay, OH 43456 (postal address: PO Box 549, Put-in-Bay, OH 43456-0549). Phone: 419/285-2184. Fax: 419/285-2516. Website: www.nps.gov/pevi. Hours: Jan.–late Mar.—by appointment; late Mar.–late Apr. and late Oct.–late Nov.—10–6 Sat.–Sun.; late Apr.–late May and early Sept.–late Oct.—10–5 daily; late May–early Sept.—9–7 daily; closed late Nov. and Dec. Admission: adults, $3; children under 16, free (must be accompanied by an adult).

John J. Pershing

General John J. Pershing Boyhood Home State Historic Site. General John Joseph Pershing is best remembered as the commander-in-chief of the American Expeditionary Force in Europe during World War I. But he also was an Indian fighter on the American West frontier and fought against the Spanish in Cuba in the Spanish-American War, the Moro revolt in the Philippines, and bandit Pancho Villa in Mexico. After World War I, he was promoted to General of the Armies, served as Army Chief of Staff, and received a Pulitzer Prize in 1932 for his two-volume book on experiences during World War I.

Pershing was born in 1860 in Laclede, Missouri. He graduated from Missouri Normal School (now Truman State University) and taught in a one-room schoolhouse for a year before entering the U.S. Military Academy. In 1886 he graduated from West Point with an outstanding record and was assigned to the cavalry. He served on the American frontier against the Sioux and the Apache. From 1891 to 1895, he was a military instructor at the University of

Nebraska, where he earned a law degree. In 1898 he fought with distinction in battles around Santiago, Cuba, in the Spanish-American War. The next year he was in the Philippines helping to suppress the Moro revolt. President Theodore Roosevelt was so impressed with Pershing's performance that he promoted him to brigadier general despite his low seniority.

In 1904–1905 Pershing served as military attaché in Tokyo and as an observer of the Russo-Japanese War. He returned to the Philippines in 1906 and held several important commands before becoming commander of the Presidio military base in San Francisco in 1914. While away on special assignment in 1915, his wife and three daughters perished in a tragic fire in which only his son survived.

In 1916 Pershing was given command of the expedition to capture Pancho Villa, the Mexican bandit who made raids across the border. Villa was wounded but eluded the pursuing American forces. Pershing received praise for his command of the expedition. In 1917, when the United States entered World War I, President Woodrow Wilson and Secretary of War Newton Baker named Pershing to command the American Expeditionary Force in support of the Allies. Under Pershing's leadership, the American army served as an independent force rather than being amalgamated into the Allied forces, although sometimes American units participated in battles under French or British command. The system basically worked, with the Germans surrendering to the Allies after the Meuse-Argonne and other battles in 1918.

Pershing returned as a war hero and was elevated to General of the Armies. In 1921 he became Army Chief of Staff and made a number of important changes in the War Department. Pershing retired in 1924 but continued to be active, writing and chairing several commissions. He died in 1948 in Washington.

The General John J. Pershing Boyhood Home State Historic Site in Laclede preserves and interprets his boyhood home and the ca. 1870 Prairie Mound School where he taught after graduating from college. The Pershing family moved into the Gothic revival house in 1866 when he was six years old and stayed until 1885. The state acquired the site in 1952 and dedicated it to Pershing and the soldiers who served under him. The historic site, established in 1960, traces the life and military career of Pershing and contains personal artifacts, period furniture, a wall of honor, and a bronze statue of the general. Annual attendance is 8,500.

General John J. Pershing Boyhood Home State Historic Site, 1100 Pershing Dr., Laclede, MO 64651 (postal address: PO Box 141, Laclede, MO 64651-0141). Website: www.mostateparks.com/pershingsite.htm. Hours: Apr. 15–Oct. 15—10–4 Mon.–Sat., 12–6 Sun.; Oct. 16–Apr. 14—10–4 Mon.–Sat., 12–5 Sun.; closed New Year's Day, Easter, Thanksgiving, and Christmas. Admission: adults, $2.50; children 6–12, $1.25; children under 6, free.

Franklin Pierce

See Presidents section.

Theodore Roosevelt

See Presidents section.

Zachary Taylor

See Presidents section.

Lee Wallace

See Authors/Writers section.

George Washington

See Presidents section.

Alvin C. York

Sgt. Alvin C. York Historic Park. Sergeant Alvin C. York was a World War I soldier who became one of the most celebrated military figures in American history. He was honored for attacking a German gun position, taking 32 machine guns, killing 28 enemy soldiers, and capturing 132 others. It occurred after York and his platoon were sent behind enemy lines to take out a German machine gun nest. After half of the platoon were killed, York led a counterattack. When the platoon was pinned down, he charged the machine gunners alone, surprising and capturing the Germans.

York was awarded the Congressional Medal of Honor and other honors and became an instant celebrity. The Sgt. Alvin C. York Historic Park, a state park on his farm in his hometown of Pall Mall, Tennessee, now honors the war hero.

Alvin Cullum York was born in a two-room log cabin near Pall Mall in 1887. He was the third of 11 children of William Uriah York and Mary Elizabeth Brooks York. It was a poor farm family, with the father working as a blacksmith to supplement the family income, the mother knitted all the family clothes, and the eight sons helping their father harvest all their food. The York boys attended school for only nine months because they were needed to work on the farm and hunt small game to feed the family.

When his father died in 1911, Alvin helped his mother raise the younger siblings since his two other brothers had married and moved away. He first worked in railroad construction and then as a logger. He had a history of drinking and fighting, but he changed after becoming a member of the pacifist Church of Christ in Christian Union. He then became opposed to violence and didn't want to join the army in World War I.

At the age of 29, however, he was drafted and sought exemption as a conscientious objector (which would give him assignments that did not conflict with antiwar principles). His appeal was denied, and he was drafted and sent for training with Company G of the 328th Infantry Regiment in the 82nd Infantry Division at Camp Gordon in Georgia.

York was troubled by the conflict between his pacifism and his training for war and talked to his company commander about the dilemma. He was granted a 10-day leave to go home and think about it, and he came back convinced that God meant for him to fight and would keep him safe. York's extraordinary actions that won him the Medal of Honor occurred in 1918 during the U.S.-led portion of the Meuse-Argonne offensive in France, which was part of the broader Allied offensive to breach the Hindenburg line.

In recognition of his wartime heroism, a school, highway, bridge, church chapel, and state park in his home county were named for York. The Sgt. Alvin C. York Historic Park, located on the grounds of his farm and gristmill in Pall Mall, has York's home and general store (which also serves as the visitor center), an M247 Sergeant York tank, and an early post office, Methodist church, Bible institute, and cemetery where he and his family are buried.

The Nashville Rotary Club raised the funds to purchase the 400-acre Wright farm and to build a two-story colonial revival–style home for York in 1922. He opened a general store across from the house in 1924, published an autobiography in 1928, and funded a schoolhouse and bought the 1880 gristmill near his farm in the 1940s from proceeds from the 1941 motion picture *Sergeant York.*

After York died in 1964, his widow, Gracie Williams York (whom he married after returning from the war in 1919), sold the farm and house to the State of Tennessee, which made it into a state park. A museum with exhibits about York's life and war experiences is located on the first floor of the house. It has personal and wartime mementos, historical photographs, and family portraits. The visitor center also shows a video on York and the park. The outbuildings include a barn with two cylindrical stone silos. The farm now is a National Historic Landmark and is listed on the National Register of Historic Places.

Sgt. Alvin C. York Historic Park, Rte. 127, Pall Mall, TN 38577 (postal address: Sgt. Alvin C. York Historic Park, General Delivery, Pall Mall, TN 38577). Phone: 931/879-6456. Websites: www.state.tn.us/environment/parks/sgtyork and www.sgtyork.org. Hours: Apr.–Oct.—9–5 daily; Nov.–Mar.—9–4 daily; closed major holidays. Admission: free.

MUSICIANS/SINGERS/COMPOSERS

Rex Allen

See Actors section.

Marian Anderson

Marian Anderson Residence Museum and Birthplace. Marian Anderson was one of the most celebrated singers of the twentieth century. She was an African American contralto who spent most of her career performing in concerts and recitals in major music venues and with leading orchestras throughout the nation and Europe between 1925 and 1965. Conductor Arthuro Tuscanini said she had "a voice such as one hears only once in a hundred years." She also was an important figure in the struggle for black artists to overcome racial prejudice during the middle of the century.

Anderson was born in 1897 in Philadelphia in the same neighborhood where the Marian Anderson Residence Museum and Birthplace are now located. Her father sold ice and coal at the Reading Railroad Terminal and later operated a small liquor business. She began her singing in the choir at the Union Baptist Church, where the congregation established a special fund to enable her to obtain professional training after she showed great promise.

Anderson debuted at the New York Philharmonic in 1925 and sang for the first time at Carnegie Hall in 1928. In the early 1930s, she made concert tours through Europe, and Finnish composer Jean Sibelius dedicated his *Solitude* to her. In 1939 a racial incident occurred that made her the center of a highly publicized controversy. The Daughters of the American Republic refused to give her permission to sing to an integrated audience in Constitution Hall in Washington. President Franklin D. Roosevelt and First Lady Eleanor Roosevelt reacted by arranging for her to give a critically acclaimed open-air concert on the steps of the Lincoln Memorial attended by more than 75,000 people and a radio audience in the millions.

The DAR incident helped remove racial barriers for African American artists. Anderson also broke the color barrier at the New York Metropolitan Opera in 1955 at the age of 58, even though she no longer was in her prime vocally. She sang the part of Ulrica in Giuseppe's *Un ballo in maschera*. It was the only time she sang in an opera onstage. She also was active in the civil rights movement of the 1960s.

Anderson, who had been serving informally as goodwill ambassador of the United States, was appointed an alternate delegate to the United Nations in 1958 and was awarded the UN Peace Prize in 1972. She also received many other awards and honors, including the Presidential Medal of Freedom, National Medal of Arts, and Grammy Lifetime Achievement Award. Anderson retired from singing in 1965 and died in 1993 at the age of 93.

The two-story Philadelphia house Anderson owned since 1924 and her family's house where she was born have been preserved by the Marian Anderson Historical Society, and are now known as the Marian Anderson Residence Museum and Birthplace. The residence museum is listed on the National Register of Historic Places. After Anderson married architect Orpheus "King" Fisher, she moved to Connecticut (*see* separate listing) and put her house up for sale. Upon Anderson's death in 1993, Blanche Burton-Lyles, one of her Philadelphia protégés and the first African American woman to perform a piano recital with the New York Philharmonic in Carnegie Hall, bought the house and later purchased her birthplace home. She then founded the Marian Anderson Historical Society to preserve Anderson's legacy.

The Anderson house, across the street from the Union Baptist Church, has a collection of memorabilia, books, rare photos, paintings, and films. The house is the site of musical programs, lectures, audiovisual presentations, and even private lessons. Both the Anderson home and the birthplace house are located on what formerly was Martin Street, which has been renamed for Marian Anderson, and they can be toured by reservation.

Marian Anderson Residence Museum, 762 Marian Anderson Way, and Marian Anderson Birthplace, 1833 Marian Anderson Pl., Philadelphia, PA 19146 (postal address: Marian Anderson Historical Society, 762 Marian Anderson Way, Philadelphia, PA 19146-1822). Phone: 215/732-9505. Fax: 215/732-1247. E-mail: phyllis@mariananderson.org. Website: www.mariananderson.org. Hours: by appointment. Admission: tours—adults, $10; seniors and children under 12, $5.

Marian Anderson Studio. In the 1940s singer Marian Anderson and her husband, architect Orpheus "King" Fisher, moved from Philadelphia to what they called "Marianna Farm" near Danbury, Connecticut. One of the facilities on the farm was the Marian Anderson Studio, where the world-famous contralto rehearsed for her concerts and recitals. After the singer's death in 1993, a developer purchased the property, and the studio was about to razed when a community effort saved it.

The small studio was preserved by moving it to the Danbury Museum and Historical Society, which has a collection of historic buildings. The studio was moved in 1999 and opened to the public in 2004. It has been restored, tells the Marian Anderson story, and features her concert gowns, vintage photographs, and programs. The studio now is part of the free Saturday tours of the museum's historic houses.

The Danbury Museum and Historical Society resulted in 1947 from the merger of the Scott Fanton Museum and the Danbury Historical and Arts Center. Other buildings on the museum grounds are the 1785 John and Mary Rider House; ca. 1790 John Dodd Hat Shop; Little Red Schoolhouse, a reproduction of a late eighteenth- and early nineteenth-century one-room schoolhouse; and 1963 Huntington Hall, which houses the offices, exhibits, research library, and gift shop. The museum also has the ca. 1829 Charles Ives Birthplace at another location. Annual attendance is 4,000.

Marian Anderson Studio, Danbury Museum and Historical Society, 43 Main St., Danbury, CT 06810-8011. Phone: 203/743-5200. Fax: 203/743-1131. E-mail: info@danburymuseum.org. Website: www.danburymuseum. org. Hours: varies with events, but tours of historic houses at 10–4 Sat.; closed New Year's Day, Thanksgiving, and Christmas. Admission: free.

Louis Armstrong

Louis Armstrong House Museum. Louis Armstrong was a leading black trumpeter and singer known for his raspy singing voice who influenced the development of jazz music. He came into prominence in the 1920s and helped shift the focus of jazz music from collective improvisation to solo performance. Armstrong, who was called "Satchmo" and "Pops," was known for his deep, distinctive voice, improvisation, and charismatic stage presence as much as for his trumpet playing. In many ways, he also influenced popular music in general.

Armstrong was born in New Orleans, Louisiana, in 1901, began his professional career in 1914, and was performing until he died at the age of 69 in 1971. During his long career, he performed more than 300 concerts each year, composed dozens of songs, recorded hit songs for five decades, and appeared in over 30 motion pictures.

The house that was the home of Armstrong and his wife, Lucille, in Corona, New York, from 1943 to 1971 is now a National Historic Landmark site—the Louis Armstrong House Museum. It has an exhibit on Armstrong's life and legacy; collections of photographs, sound recordings, letters, manuscripts, instruments, and artifacts; and a Japanese-inspired garden. The house is shown only through guided tours during which audio clips from Armstrong's home-made recordings are played and visitors hear him practicing his trumpet, enjoying a meal, or talking with friends.

Louis Armstrong House Museum, 34-56 107th St., Corona, NY 11368-1226. Phones: 718/478-8274 and 718/997-3670. Website: www.louisarmstronghouse.org. Hours: 10–5 Tues.–Fri., 12–5 Sat.–Sun.; closed Mon., New Year's Eve and Day, Thanksgiving, and Christmas Eve and Day. Admission: adults, $10; seniors, students, and children, $7; children under 4, free.

Gene Autry

See Actors section.

Eubie Blake

Eubie Blake National Jazz Institute and Cultural Center. James Hubert Blake, who became known as Eubie Blake, was a black composer, lyricist, and pianist of ragtime, jazz, and popular music. He began composing as a child, played in vaudeville, and wrote with performer Noble Sissle the 1921 musical revue *Shuffle Along*, which featured many of the songs they had written and was the first Broadway musical hit written by and about African Americans.

Blake was born in Baltimore in 1887 to two former slaves. His father worked as a stevedore on the Baltimore docks for nine dollars a week. Blake was the only survivor of eight children—the others all died in infancy. His musical training began when he was four or five years old when his parents bought him a $75 pump organ, making payments of 25¢ a week. When he was seven, he started getting music lessons from a neighbor who was a church organist. And when Blake was 15, he played the piano at a bordello without the knowledge of his parents.

Blake got his first big break in 1907 when world champion boxer Joe Gans hired him to play the piano at his Goldfield Hotel, the first "black and tan club" in Baltimore. In 1912 he began playing in vaudeville, and after World War I he and Noble Sissle formed a vaudeville music duo, called the "Dixie Duo," and then collaborated on the Broadway play *Shuffle Along*.

During his musical career, Blake produced such popular compositions as "Charleston Rag," "Bandana Days," "Love Will Find a Way," "Memories of You, and "I'm Wild about Harry." He also made three films with producer Lee DeForest in 1923, and his works were featured in the Broadway play *Eubie!* in 1978.

The Eubie Blake National Jazz Institute and Cultural Center was founded in his honor in 1983, the same year he died at the age of 96. It functions more like a performing arts center than a museum but does have exhibits with photographs and memorabilia of Blake and such other Baltimore artists as Billie Holiday and Cab Calloway. The focus is on local arts and cultural events, including jazz performances, recitals, and music instruction. Annual attendance is 10,000.

Eubie Blake National Jazz Institute and Cultural Center, 847 N. Howard St., Baltimore, MD 21201-4605. Phone: 410/225-3130. Fax: 410/225-3139. E-mail: info@eubieblake.org. Website: www.eubieblake.org. Hours: 1–6 Wed.–Fri., 11–3 Sat., Sun. by appointment; closed Sun.–Tues. and federal holidays. Admission: $5.

Pablo Casals

Pablo Casals Museum. Pau Casals i DeFilló, known as Pablo Casals during his professional career, was a Spanish Catalan cellist, conductor, and composer who is regarded as one of the greatest cellists of all time. In addition to concerts, he made many recordings of solo, chamber, and orchestral music. He moved to Puerto Rico in 1956 and lived there the last 16 years of his life. His house is now the site of the Pablo Casals Museum.

Casals was born in El Vendrell, Catalonia, Spain, in 1876. His father was a parish organist and choirmaster who gave him instruction in piano, song, violin, and organ. Casals could play the violin, piano, and flute at the age of four and was able to perform in public at the age of six. He became interested in the cello when he was 11 after hearing a traveling group of musicians. In 1888 he enrolled in the Escola Municipal de Música in Barcelona, where he studied cello, theory, and piano. He gave his first public recital as a cellist in 1891 at the age of 14. After graduating with honors, he was appointed to the faculty of the music school and became principal cellist in the orchestra at Barcelona's opera house. In 1897 he appeared as a soloist with the Madrid Symphony Orchestra and was awarded the Order of Carlos III by the queen.

Casals began his international career in 1899, playing at the Crystal Palace in London and later for Queen Victoria. He then appeared as a soloist in Paris and toured Spain, the Netherlands, the United States, and South America. In 1904 he was invited to play for President Theodore Roosevelt at the White House and made his debut at Carnegie Hall. In the years that followed, he played and directed many concerts, produced compositions, taught classes, and made numerous recordings, including his memorable Bach Cello Suites from 1930 to 1939.

Casals, who was an ardent supporter of the Spanish Republican government, vowed not to return to Spain after its defeat in the 1936 Spanish Civil War until democracy was restored. He lived in several countries before settling in Puerto Rico, where his mother and wife were born. After moving there in 1956, he founded the Puerto Rico Symphony Orchestra and the Conservatory of Music of Puerto Rico. In 2009 a new symphony hall named in Casals's honor opened in San Juan. Among his many other awards and honors were decorations and medals from heads of state, a commemorative postage stamp in Spain, a Grammy Lifetime Achievement Award, and the establishment of such events as the International Pablo Casals Cello Competition and the annual Casals Festival in Puerto Rico.

Casals died in San Juan in 1973 at the age of 96 and was buried in the Puerto Rico National Cemetery. His remains later were moved to his hometown of El Vendrell, which has a museum in his honor in Spain. His eighteenth-century house in Old San Juan, which he called "El Pesebre," became the Pablo Casals Museum in 1977. The museum celebrates his life and accomplishments and contains many of his instruments, manuscripts, recordings, letters, photographs, diplomas, decorations, and medals and videos of some of his performances as a soloist and conductor. Annual attendance is 15,000.

Pablo Casals Museum, Plaza San José, 101 San Sebastian St., San Juan, PR 00901 (postal address: PO Box 41227, San Juan, PR 00940-1227). Phone: 787/723-9185. Faxes: 787/722-3338 and 787/722-5843. Hours: 9:30–5 Tues.–Sat.; closed Sun.–Mon. Admission: adults, $1; children, 50¢.

Rosemary Clooney

Rosemary Clooney House. Rosemary Clooney was a pop and jazz singer and actress who came into prominence in the early 1950s with a novelty hit song, "Come On-a My House." It was followed by such other pop songs as "Botch-a-Me," "Mambo Italiano," "Tenderly," "Half as Much," "Hey There," and "This Ole House." She became a popular movie actress and jazz vocalist, appearing in numerous films since the 1950s, giving concerts and making recordings until 2001, and receiving a Grammy Lifetime Achievement Award.

Clooney was born in Maysville, Kentucky, in 1928 and moved to Cincinnati, Ohio, in 1941. She and her sister, Betty, began singing at a Cincinnati radio station in 1945. They went on the road and made records with Tony Pastor's Orchestra, after which Betty returned home and Rosemary started making records and appearing on the Ed Sullivan and Bob Hope television shows.

Clooney made her first motion picture in 1952 and followed in 1953 with *White Christmas* (as well as marrying actor Jose Ferrer). She also had her own variety show in 1956–1958 and made other movies, but she suffered a setback with a nervous breakdown in 1968 after divorcing Ferrer (with whom she had five children). She recovered and resumed her singing and acting career, including participating in Bing Crosby's 50th anniversary in show business celebration in 1974 and performing for Queen Elizabeth of Great Britain in 1987 and President and Mrs. William J. Clinton at the White House in 1993.

Clooney, who died of cancer in 2002, moved from Beverly Hills, California, to a ca. 1830 house in Augusta, Kentucky, in 1980. It became the site of the Rosemary Clooney House museum, which opened in 2005. The museum traces the life and career of Clooney and contains family photographs, chart hits of the 1950s, motion pictures in which she appeared, costumes worn by Clooney and other actors, memorabilia from the *White Christmas* movie, and Clooney's bedroom as it was when she lived in Augusta.

Rosemary Clooney House, 106 E. Riverside Dr., Augusta, KY 41002 (postal address: PO Box 197, Augusta, KY 41002). Phone: 866/898-8091. E-mail: info@rosemaryclooney.org. Website: www.rosemaryclooneyhouse.com. Hours: 11–3 Tues.–Fri., 11–5 Sat., 1–5 Sun., Mon. by appointment; closed major holidays. Admission: $5.

Bing Crosby

See Actors section.

Stephen Foster

Stephen Foster Memorial Museum. Stephen Collins Foster, the nation's preeminent songwriter of the nineteenth century, is honored at the Stephen Foster Memorial at the University of Pittsburgh. He composed more than 200 songs in his lifetime, including such memorable works as "Oh! Susanna," "Camptown Races," "Old Folks at Home," "My Old Kentucky Home," "Old Black Joe," "Jeanie with the Light Brown Hair," and "Beautiful Dreamer." In addition to academic facilities, the memorial center houses the Stephen Foster Memorial Museum and the Center for American Music.

Foster was born in nearby Lawrenceville in 1826 and died in an accidental fall at the age of 37 in 1864. He attended several private schools, including Athens Academy where his first composition, "Tioga Walt," was performed in 1839 when he was only 14. During his teenage years, Foster was influenced by two men—a classically trained music instructor and a blackface singer in traveling circuses. Foster and his friends would often sit at a piano and write and sing minstrel songs. He later blended the two genres in some of his best-known songs.

In 1846 Foster moved to Cincinnati, worked for his brother's steamship company as a bookkeeper, and produced his first successful songs, including "Oh! Susanna." He then returned to Pennsylvania, signed a contract with the Christy Minstrels, and wrote most of his best-known compositions, including "Camptown Races," "Nelly Bly," "Old Folks at Home" (also known as "Swanee River"). and "Jeanie with the Light Brown Hair." Many of the songs were of the blackface minstrel show tradition that was popular at the time.

Foster, his wife, and daughter moved to New York City in 1860, but the wife and daughter left him and returned to Pittsburgh about a year later. His new works did not sell, and he had a difficult time making a living as a professional songwriter. He realized little financially from his earlier works because of the limited scope of music copyright and composer royalties at the time and soon became impoverished. In 1864, while suffering from persistent fever, Foster fell out of bed and struck his head while trying to call a chambermaid and died three days later.

The Stephen Foster Memorial is one of two Gothic revival buildings (the other being the Heinz Memorial Chapel) designed by architect Charles Klauder to accompany the University of Pittsburgh's skyscraper main structure, called the Cathedral of Learning. The Stephen Collins Foster Memorial, which was conceived by members of the Tuesday Musical Club as a tribute to the Pittsburgh native and composer, was dedicated in 1937. It has two theaters that serve as the home of the university's Department of Theatre Arts productions; the Stephen Foster Memorial Museum, which contains items on the composer's life; and the Center for American Music, a research library, archive, and museum on American music and its role in American life.

The Stephen Foster Memorial Museum features materials pertaining to the composer from the Foster Hall Collection, which was founded by Josiah Kirby Lilly of the Lilly pharmaceutical company. The museum has an exhibit on Foster's life and works and selections from the collection that include sound recordings, photographs, lantern slides, films, video cassettes, books, songbooks, vocal and instrumental scores, historic instruments, paintings, drawings, prints, posters, handbills, maps, catalogs, and periodicals.

Stephen Foster Memorial Museum, University of Pittsburgh, 4301 Forbes Ave., Pittsburgh, PA 15260. Phone: 412/624-4100. Website: www.pitt.edu. Hours: 9–4 Mon.–Fri.; closed Sat.–Sun. and university holidays. Admission: free.

Stephen Foster Folk Culture Center State Park. The Stephen Foster Folk Culture Center State Park—and its Stephen Foster Museum—in White Springs, Florida, resulted from Foster's song "Old Folks at Home" (also called "Swanee River"), which made the river known throughout the world. The state park was established in 1939 along the banks of the river (which is spelled Suwannee River) after being suggested in 1931 by Josiah Kirby Lilly of the

Lilly pharmaceutical company. Lilly was a Foster admirer and collector of his artifacts and memorabilia, which he donated to the University of Pittsburgh and now are featured in a campus museum. The Florida Federation of Music Clubs adopted Lilly's idea and obtained contributions of land along the river, and the Stephen Foster Memorial Committee administered the development of the park, which opened in 1950.

The Stephen Foster Museum features exhibits about Foster's most famous songs, and the park's 97-bell carillon has exhibits inside the tower about the carillon and Foster and plays his music throughout the day. The park also has a craft square with demonstrations of quilting, blacksmithing, stained glass making, and other crafts, as well as hiking, bicycling, canoeing, horseback riding, wildlife viewing, and numerous special events. Annual attendance is nearly 45,000.

Stephen Foster Folk Culture Center State Park, 11016 Lillian Saunders Dr. (U.S. 41 N.), White Springs, FL 32096-0435 (postal address: PO Drawer G, White Springs, FL 32096-0435). Phone: 386/397-2733. Fax: 386/397-4262. E-mail: morris.cook@dep.state.fl.us. Website: www.floridastateparks.org/stephenfoster. Hours: 9–5 daily. Admission: single-occupant vehicle, $4; 2–8 people per vehicle, $5; pedestrians, cyclists, and extra passengers over 8, $2 per person.

Judy Garland

See Actors section.

Woody Guthrie

Woody Guthrie Archives. Woodrow Wilson Guthrie, better known as Woody Guthrie, was a folksinger, musician, and composer who wrote over 1,000 political, traditional, and children's songs, ballads, and improvised works and traveled widely in support of union and populist causes in the mid-twentieth century. Among his best-known works are "This Is Your Land," "So Long (It's Been Good to Know Yuh)," "Union Maid," and "Hard Traveling."

Guthrie was born in 1912 in Okemah, Oklahoma, where his father, a cowboy, land speculator, and local politician, taught him Western, Indian, and Scottish folk songs. His mother was also musically inclined. He was a sensitive youth whose home life was devastated by a series of tragic personal losses, including a fire that destroyed the family home, the accidental death of his older sister, the institutionalizing and death of his mother, and the family's financial ruin.

His father went to Texas to repay his debts, while Woody and the other children stayed with their eldest brother. He worked odd jobs, begged for meals, sometimes slept in homes of friends, and showed a natural affinity for music. He learned to play the harmonica and later the guitar, playing for donations and dances. At the age of 19, he married the first of three wives, with whom he had three children, all of whom would later die prematurely.

During the Dust Bowl era in the 1930s, Guthrie joined the thousands of Okies who migrated to California looking for work. He settled in a neighborhood with a concentration of political radicals in Echo Park, a suburb of Los Angeles. He became a radio performer of commercial and traditional folk music and began to write and perform some of the protest songs for which he became known as he traveled across the nation.

After Guthrie's death in 1967, the Woody Guthrie Foundation was established to preserve and disseminate information about his cultural legacy, accumulated in the Woody Guthrie Archives, which opened in 1996. The archives contain more than 10,000 items of primary and secondary source material, including Guthrie's original song lyrics, notebooks, diaries, manuscripts, personal papers, recordings, and artworks. In addition, the archives have supporting information and documentation in photographs, printed material, film, video, and audio media. The foundation and archives also produce and circulate exhibits, programs, and publications about Guthrie's life and times in America in the twentieth century.

Woody Guthrie Foundation and Archives, 125-131 E. Main St., Ste. 200, Mount Kisco, NY 10549. Phone: 914/864-1789. Fax: 914/864-1790. E-mail: wgarchive@woodyguthrie.org. Website: www.woodyguthrie.org. Hours: 10–5 Tues.–Thurs.; closed Fri.–Mon. and major holidays. Admission: free.

W. C. Handy

W. C. Handy Museum and Library. William Christopher Handy was an African American blues musician and composer who was among the most influential of American songwriters. He was known as the father of the blues, although he was not the founder of the blues form of music. He is credited with being the first to codify and publish songs in the mode known as the blues. He transformed black folk music from a limited regional music style to one of the most dominant national forces in American music. Among his best-known works were "Memphis Blues," "St. Louis Blues," "Beale Street Blues," "Yellow Dog Blues," and "Careless Love."

Handy, the son of a pastor of a small church, was born in a log cabin in Florence, Alabama, in 1873, which today is the W. C. Handy Museum and Library. The cabin was built by his grandfather, William Wise Handy, who became an African Methodist Episcopal minister after emancipation. The composer was a deeply religious person who was influenced by church music that he sang and played as a youth. He also later used the sounds of nature in his music.

Handy was apprenticed in carpentry, shoemaking, and plastering and worked as a laborer, musician, college music instructor, band leader, music publisher, and author as well as a composer. But it was not until 1914, at the age of 40, that he established his musical style with the publication of his first hit, "Memphis Blues." His published music works were record breaking because he was among the first African Americans to be successful economically because of publishing.

In addition to composing and publishing blues music, Handy wrote five books about music and black musicians. His productivity was curtailed when he became blind in 1943 after an accidental fall from a subway platform. He then suffered a stroke in 1955 and died in 1958 of bronchial pneumonia. More than 25,000 people attended his funeral and over 150,000 gathered in the streets outside the church to pay their respects.

Handy received numerous honors and awards for his achievements. In addition to a stamp and motion picture in his honor, he received the Grammy Trustees Award for lifetime achievements and was inducted into the Alabama Music Hall of Fame, Alabama Jazz Hall of Fame, and National Academy of Popular Music Song Writers Hall of Fame.

The W. C. Handy Museum and Library, founded in 1968 and operated by the City of Florence, is devoted to the composer's life and career. It contains such personal memorabilia as his trumpet, his piano, and original manuscripts from some of his most famous works. Annual attendance is 3,500. Each year the city also has the W. C. Handy Music Festival, which features musicians from around the country for 10 days in late July or early August. It is the largest festival annually in the Shoals area.

W. C. Handy Museum and Library, 620 W. College St., Florence, AL 35630-5360 (postal address: 217 Tuscaloosa St., Florence, AL 35630-4724). Phone; 256/760-6434. Fax: 256/760-6382. E-mail: bbroach@florenceal.org. Website: www. florenceal.org. Hours: 10–4 Tues.–Sat.; closed Sun.–Mon. and major holidays. Admission: adults, $2; children, 50¢.

Buddy Holly

Buddy Holly Center. Charles Hardin Holley, known professionally as Buddy Holly, was a singer, songwriter, and rock-and-roll star whose career—which lasted only a year and a half—was cut short by an airplane crash in 1959. He was only 22 when he died, but he was one of the most creative forces in early rock and roll and influenced contemporary and later musicians such as the Beatles, the Rolling Stones, Bob Dylan, and Eric Clapton.

Holly's recordings were extraordinary for their ingenuity and high level of engineering. Before overdubbing became a common practice, he was layering his records with multiple vocal and instrumental lines. He also experimented when it fit the musical objective, such as drumming on a cardboard box, playing an electric guitar through an organ speaker, and adding a delicate celeste.

Holly was born in a musical household in Lubbock, Texas, in 1936. His mother was an excellent vocalist, and he had three brothers who played the violin, accordion, and piano (and sang). By the time he entered junior high school, he was an accomplished guitarist, banjo player, and mandolinist. He helped organize several groups that played at school and community functions and then had a local radio show. In 1955, when Elvis Presley was gaining in popularity, Holly was impressed and influenced by Presley's rhythm and actions during a personal appearance in Lubbock.

After a failed recording effort, Holly formed a new musical group, Buddy Holly and the Crickets, with a new sound built around the close interplay of his voice, open-chord guitar strumming, and syncopated drumming. They made some hit records, did a 25-day tour of England, and then disbanded as Holly concentrated on songwriting and developing a solo career. In 1958 he agreed to a three-week winter tour in the Midwest beginning in January 1959. It was during one of these stops that he chartered a plane to take him and some of the band members from Mason City, Iowa, to Fargo, North Dakota. The plane crashed and Holly was killed five minutes after taking off when the pilot was blinded by bad weather.

The City of Lubbock's Buddy Holly Center, which was established in 1999, celebrates the life and music of Holly. In addition to containing such Holly memorabilia as his music, clothing, photographs, and contracts, the center houses the Texas Musicians Hall of Fame and exhibits on contemporary visual arts and music. Holly also was among the first group of inductees to the Rock and Roll Hall of Fame in 1986.

Buddy Holly Center, 1801 Crickets Ave., Lubbock, TX 79401-5128. Phone: 806/775-3560. Fax: 806/767-0732. E-mail: info@buddyhollycenter.org. Website: www.buddyhollycenter.org. Hours: 10–5 Tues.–Sat., 1–5 Sun.; closed Mon. Admission: adults, $5; seniors, $3; students and children 7–17, $2; military and children under 7, free.

Scott Joplin

Scott Joplin House State Historic Site. Scott Joplin was an African American composer and pianist who became known as the king of ragtime. He wrote 44 original ragtime pieces, one ragtime ballet, and two operas. One of his earliest pieces, "Maple Street Rag," published in 1899, became ragtime's first and most influential works. It also brought him fame and greatly affected subsequent ragtime composers and musicians.

Joplin was born in a musical African American family of laborers near Marshall, Texas, in 1867. He showed musical talent at an early age and was able to play several instruments and compose and improvise his own music by the age of 11. In the years that followed, he mastered the formal structure of classical music and the free-flowing artistic expression of black musicians from the minstrel tradition to become the leading exponent of that new syncopated musical genre that became known as ragtime.

Joplin spent most of the late 1880s traveling around the South as an itinerant musician. In the 1890s he settled in Sedalia, Missouri, where he completed a degree in music at George R. Smith College for Negroes and experimented with intricate musical rhythms that resulted in "Maple Leaf Rag," which became a national sensation. In 1900 he moved to St. Louis with his wife. From 1900 to 1903, they lived in an apartment in a building that later became the Scott Joplin House State Historic Site. It is where he produced some of his best-known compositions, including "The Entertainer," "Elite Syncopations," "March Majestic," and "Ragtime Dance."

In 1907 Joplin moved to New York to increase national exposure and further his career. Instead, he experienced the financial failure of the most ambitious work of his life—the opera *Treemonisha*. He financed and directed the opera, and it closed after one disastrous performance. Joplin went bankrupt, suffered a breakdown, became ill, and died of dementia in 1917 at the age of 49. He was buried in a pauper's grave that remained unmarked until 1974.

The ca. 1860 Italianate house where Joplin lived in St. Louis was placed on the National Register of Historic Places in 1976 and became the Scott Joplin House State Historic Site, a historic house museum, in 1982. The house was refurnished to look the way it did in 1902. The modest second floor flat that the Joplins occupied has a turn-of-the-century appearance, with gas lights and period furnishings. A visitor center features exhibits on Joplin's life and work, St. Louis and the neighborhood as Joplin knew them, and African American cultural and ragtime history. It also has a music room where visitors can operate a player piano with rolls of ragtime music, including some that were cut by Joplin. Annual attendance is 12,500.

Scott Joplin House State Historic Site, 2658 Delmar Blvd., St. Louis, MO 63103-1404. Phone: 314/340-5790. Fax: 314/340-5793. Website: www.mostateparks.com/park/scott-joplin-house-state-historic-site. Hours: Mar.–Oct.— 10–4 Mon.–Sat., 12–4 Sun.; Nov.–Feb.—10–4 Tues.–Sat.; closed Sun., New Year's Day, Easter, Thanksgiving, and Christmas. Admission: adults, $2.50; children 6–12, $1; children under 6, free.

B. B. King

B. B. King Museum and Delta Interpretive Center. Riley B. King, who goes by the stage name of B. B. King, is an African American blues guitarist, singer, and songwriter known for his expressive singing and fluid, complex guitar playing. He gives about 250 performances a year throughout the world and has nine B. B. King's Blues Clubs featuring his style of music in nine cities from Los Angeles to New York.

King was born in 1925 in a small cabin on a cotton plantation outside Berclair, Mississippi, near Indianola, where the B. B. King Museum and Delta Interpretive Center is now located. He was raised by his maternal grandmother, grew up singing in the gospel choir at the Elkhorn Baptist Church in Kilmichael, Mississippi, and got his first guitar at the age of 12. By the late 1940s, he performed regularly on a Memphis radio station. During this time, he got the nickname "Beale Street Blues Boy," which later was shortened to "B. B."

King began making recordings in 1949 and then assembled his own band and started making tours across the nation. By 1956 he was playing 342 concerts a year and producing such hits as "3 O'Clock Blues," "You Know I Love You," and "Whole Lotta Love." His success continued through the 1970s with songs like "To Know You Is to

Love You" and "I Like to Live the Love." Since then, he has continued to tour, give concerts, appear on television and movies, and produce such recordings as "When Love Comes to Town," "Since I Met You Baby," and "When the Thrill Is Gone."

During his long career, King has received the National Medal of Arts, Presidential Medal of Freedom, Kennedy Center Honors Award, and Grammy Lifetime Achievement Award and been inducted into the Blues Hall of Fame and Rock and Roll Hall of Fame. The B. B. King Museum and Delta Interpretive Center in Indianola was opened in his honor in 2008. In addition to exhibits, recordings, and films of his life and career, the center celebrates the Delta blues heritage and local culture. It also has a guitar studio where visitors can play instruments in an interactive environment.

B. B. King Museum and Delta Interpretive Center, 400 2nd St., Indianola, MS 38751-2851. Phone: 662/887-9539. E-mail: info@bbkingmuseum.org. Website: www.bbkingmuseum.org. Hours: Apr.–Oct.—10–5 Tues.–Sat., 12–5 Sun.–Mon.; Nov.–Mar.—closed Mon., New Year's Day, Thanksgiving, and Christmas. Admission: adults, $10; seniors and students, $5.

Mario Lanza

Mario Lanza Museum. Mario Lanza was a popular tenor and motion picture actor in the 1940s and 1950s who was born Alfred Arnold Cocozza, the son of Italian immigrants. He adopted the stage name of Mario Lanza for its similarity to his mother's maiden name, Maria Lanza, while a scholarship student at the Berkshire Music Center at Tanglewood, Massachusetts, in 1942. He got his big break in 1947 after appearing at the Hollywood Bowl. Louis B. Mayer, head of MGM, saw Lanza's performance, was impressed with his singing, and signed him to seven-year contract—and he soon became a singing and acting star.

Lanza, who was born in 1921 in Philadelphia, Pennsylvania, was exposed to classical singing as a child by his parents, and his vocal talents became apparent by the age of 16. He started out in local operatic productions while still in his teens, and in 1942 came to the attention of conductor Serge Koussevitzky, who provided Lanza with a full scholarship to the Berkshire Music Center, where he studied with such conductors as Boris Goldovsky and Leonard Bernstein. In his opera debut at the music center, he won praise for his role as Fenton in *The Merry Wives of Windsor*, followed by an impressive performance as Rodolfo in *La Bohème*.

His operatic career was interrupted by World War II, when he served in Special Services in the U.S. Army Air Corps. He resumed his career after the war, singing in a concert with the NBC Symphony Orchestra and on the *Great Moments in Music* radio program on CBS in 1945. He then studied with noted teacher Enrico Rosati for 15 months, followed by a yearlong tour of the United States, Canada, and Mexico. It was during his appearance at the Hollywood Bowl that he signed with Metro-Goldwyn-Mayer and began a career that combined films, opera, concerts, and recordings. In 1949 he also made his first commercial recording with the aria "Che Gelida Manina" from *La Bohème*, which was selected as the best operatic recording of the year.

Lanza's first movie was *That Midnight Kiss* with Kathryn Grayson and Ethel Barrymore in 1949. It was followed by *The Toast of New Orleans*, which featured the song "Be My Love," the first million-selling hit. In 1951 he starred in the role of Enrico Caruso, his tenor idol, in *The Great Caruso*. After two more million-selling film recordings, Lanza engaged in a protracted battle over artistic differences with studio head Dore Schary during his next movie, *The Student Prince*, and was dismissed.

Lanza became depressed and a virtual recluse for more than a year and then made three more films that were not as successful as his earlier works. But he was still in demand for concerts, operas, and recordings. However, his health continued to decline as he suffered from advanced phlebitis, pneumonia, and acute high blood pressure. In 1959 he died of a heart attack at the age of 38.

Lanza's life and career are now featured at the Mario Lanza Museum, operated by the Mario Lanza Institute. The museum was founded in 1962 and originally was housed in the Settlement Music School. It moved in 2002 to the first floor of Columbus House near Lanza's birthplace in south Philadelphia. The museum contains such items as memorabilia, costumes, photographs, paintings, gold records, and videos of his films. The museum has an annual Mario Lanza Ball, and the nearby St. Mary Magdalen de Pazzi Church holds an annual Mario Lanza Memorial Mass in his honor. The museum's annual attendance is 2,500.

Mario Lanza Museum, Mario Lanza Institute, Columbus House, 712 Montrose St., Philadelphia, PA 19147-3944 (postal address: PO Box 54624, Philadelphia, PA 19148-0624). Phone: 215/238-9691. Fax: 215/238-9694. E-mail: mariolanzamuseum@aol.com. Website: www.mario-lanza-institute.org. Hours: 11–3 Mon.–Wed. and Fri.–Sat.; closed Thurs. and Sun. (also Sat. in July–Aug.). Admission: free.

Loretta Lynn

Coal Miner's Daughter Museum. Loretta Lynn is a country singer and songwriter whose 1976 autobiography, *Coal Miner's Daughter*, was made into an Academy Award–winning movie and became the name of her museum on a 6,500-acre ranch in Hurricane Mills, Tennessee. Her life is a rags-to-riches story that traces her accent to the top of the country music world, including 16 number-one country hits and 52 top-10 works.

Loretta Lynn was born as Loretta Webb in Butcher Holler, Kentucky, in 1932. She was the second of Ted and Clara Webb's eight children. Her family eked out a living during the Great Depression years, with her father working in a coal mine at night and farming during the day. She married Oliver Lynn when she was 14, and she was a full-time mother to four children by the time she began singing seriously and playing the guitar in 1961. Things began to change when she was seen in a televised talent show by a record producer. She started making recordings, including "I'm a Honky Took Girl," "Biggest Fool of All," and "Success" (her first top-10 hit in 1962). Along the way, she developed her own distinctive country style.

Lynn then began to write more of her own songs—often with a strong female point of view or confronting many of the social issues of her time. "Dear Uncle Sam" was one of the first recordings to recount the human costs of the Vietnam War. It was followed in the 1960s by a number of hits where a woman was not afraid to stand up for herself. In 1972 she won the Best Female Vocalist award from the Country Music Association for the second time and then became the first woman to receive the association's Entertainer of the Year award. She also won her first Vocal Duo of the Year award that year with Conway Twitty—and held on to the title through 1976.

During the next decade, Lynn had more song hits. In 1976 her *Coal Miner's Daughter* autobiography became a *New York Times* best seller and was made into a hit movie in 1980. She made her last major hit, "I Lie," in 1982. She spent most of the 1990s away from the spotlight, taking care of her husband, who died in 1996. They had established "The Dude Ranch" in Hurricane Mills in 1972, which grew into an extensive entertainment complex and includes the Coal Miner's Daughter Museum.

The complex—known as Loretta Lynn's Ranch—has four museum sites, as well as Lynn's white-pillared plantation house that dates to the 1800s, a simulated coal mine, a replica of Lynn's birthplace home, a frontier homestead, a concert stage, a working post office, a nonalcoholic saloon, and a full-service RV park with cabins to rent, a swimming pool, playgrounds, canoeing, paddle boats, and a mini-theater. Tours are offered through the plantation house, coal mine, and birthplace home.

The museum focal point is the 18,000-square-foot Coal Miner's Daughter Museum, which features a large collection of memorabilia, awards, costumes, photographs, graphics, and mementos from entertainment friends. The other museums are the Native American Artifact Museum, with over 5,000 artifacts and other Indian tribal materials; Grist Mill Museum, containing a variety of equipment used during the production of corn meal in the late 1800s; and Loretta's Fan and Doll Museum, which displays dolls and other gifts sent to Loretta Lynn by fans.

Coal Miner's Daughter Museum, 1877 Hurricane Mills Rd., Hurricane Mills, TN 37078. Phone: 931/296-1840. Websites: www.lorettalynn.com and www.lorettalynnranch.net. Hours: Apr.–Oct.—9–5 daily; closed Nov.–Mar. Admission: free; home tours—adults, $12; children 6–12, $6; children under 6, free.

Roger Miller

Roger Miller Museum. Roger Dean Miller was a singer, songwriter, and musician best known for his 1960s country/pop hits such as "King of the Road," "Dang Me," and "England Swings." He won 11 Grammy Awards and a Tony Award for writing the music and lyrics for *Big River*, which received seven Tonys, including best musical, in 1985.

Miller was born in 1936 in Fort Worth, Texas. His mother died when he was a year old, and he was sent to live with his aunt and uncle in Erick, Oklahoma. He had a lonely and unhappy childhood but developed an interest in music from listening to the *Grand Ole Opry* and the Light Crust Doughboys on the radio. When 17, he stole a guitar and turned himself in. Rather than go to jail, he joined the army and was sent to Korea in the 1950s. When he returned, he went to Nashville and began his musical career. By the late 1950s he'd written such popular songs as "Billy Bayou," his first number-one song, and "Home" for Jim Reeves and "Invitation to the Blues" for Ray Price.

In the 1960s Miller had hits ranging from humorous novelty songs with whimsical lyrics to sincere ballads, including "King of the Road" in 1965. He also had his own television show in 1966 and wrote and performed three songs in the 1973 *Robin Hood* animated movie. He was voted into the Nashville Songwriters Hall of Fame in 1973 and into the Country Music Hall of Fame posthumously in 1995. His final hit was "Old Friends," which he recorded with Willie Nelson in 1982. Miller continued to record and tour until he died of lung and throat cancer in 1992.

Miller's life and accomplishments are celebrated at the Roger Miller Museum, which opened in his hometown of Erick, Oklahoma, in 2004. The museum contains exhibits, memorabilia, musical instruments, stage costumes, and photographs related to his life and career. The city also named Roger Miller Boulevard in his name.

Roger Miller Museum, 101 E. Roger Miller Blvd., Erick, OK 73645 (postal address: PO Box 464, Erick, OK 73645-0464). Phone: 580/526-3833. Fax: 580/526-33331. Website: rogermillermuseum.com. Hours: 10–5 Wed.–Sat., 1–5 Sun., other times by appointment; closed Mon.–Tues. and major holidays. Admission: adults, $3; seniors, $2; children, $1.

Bill Monroe

Bill Monroe Homeplace. William Smith Monroe, better known simply as Bill Monroe, was a Kentucky musician who is credited with creating the style of music called bluegrass—which took its name from his popular band, the Blue Grass Boys. He grew up in a musical family in Rosine, Kentucky, where the Monroe farmhouse became a magnet for music and dancing after the farm chores were completed. His performing career covered 60 years as a singer, instrumentalist, composer, and bandleader.

Monroe was born in 1911 in a log cabin, which was destroyed by fire when he was five years old. A framed house was built at the same site around the original sandstone chimney. The five-room, white clapboard house, which now overlooks five acres of the original 1,000 acres, was restored to its 1917 appearance by the Monroe Brothers Foundation in 2001. The Bill Monroe Homeplace functions as a historic house museum and tells about Monroe's family and career and contains period furnishings, heirlooms, instruments, photographs, mementoes, and personal belongings. An annual Jerusalem Ridge Bluegrass Celebration and Festival also is held in Rosine.

Monroe was the youngest of eight children. His mother and her brother, Pendleton Vandiver, were musically talented; Bill's older brothers, Birch and Charlie, played the fiddle and guitar; and he first played the mandolin. When a teenager, his mother and then father died, and he went to live with his Uncle Pen (Vandiver). Monroe frequently accompanied his uncle when he played the fiddle at dances and later was inspired to record one of his most famous fiddle compositions, which he titled "Uncle Pen."

In 1929 Monroe moved to Indiana to work at an oil refinery with his brothers Birch and Charlie. They formed a musical group called the Monroe Brothers and played, with friend Larry Moore, at local dances and house parties. After Birch and Moore left the group, Bill and Charlie Monroe continued to perform live on the radio and ultimately recorded 60 tracts for Victor's Bluebird label, including the gospel hit "What Would You Give in Exchange for Your Soul?," between 1936 and 1938. After the Monroe Brothers disbanded in 1938, Bill Monroe formed the Kentuckians in Little Rock and then the initial Blue Grass Boys in Atlanta. The band gained a regular spot on the *Grand Ole Opry* show, made some personnel and stylistic changes, and became the Original Bluegrass Band in the 1940s. The band finally had all the bluegrass genre elements—breakneck tempos, sophisticated vocal harmony arrangements, and impressive instrumental proficiency in solos and breaks on the mandolin, banjo, and fiddle.

In 1946–1947 the band recorded 28 songs for Columbia Records, which soon became the classics in the field. They included such hits as "Toy Heart," "Blue Grass Breakdown," "Molly and Tenbrooks," "My Rose of Old Kentucky," and Monroe's most famous song, "Blue Moon of Kentucky." After several band members left to form their own groups, Monroe reorganized and produced such classics as "My Little Georgia Rose," "Uncle Pen," "Roanoke," and "Raw Hide."

The popularity of rock and roll and the Nashville sound in the 1950s caused Monroe to associate his style more with traditional folk music in the 1960s, rather than the country-and-western genre with which it had been identified. And that is when the word *bluegrass* started to be used to describe the sound of Monroe and others in the field. Bluegrass festivals began to be more common, and even Monroe founded the annual Bill Monroe Beam Blossom Bluegrass Festival in southern Indiana in 1967—now the world's oldest continuously operated annual bluegrass festival.

Monroe continued to compose, record, perform, and tour in his later years but suffered a stroke and died in 1996 at the age of 84. Among his many honors are being made an honorary Kentucky colonel; receiving the National Medal of Arts and Grammy Lifetime Achievement Award; and being inducted into the Country Music Hall of Fame, Songwriters Hall of Fame, Rock and Roll Hall of Fame, and International Bluegrass Music Hall of Honor.

Bill Monroe Homeplace, 210 Hwy. 62 E., Rosine, KY 42349. Phone: 270/274-9181. Website: www.visitohiocountyky.org/billmonroe.html. Hours: 9–5 Mon.–Sat., 1–5 Sun; closed Thanksgiving and Christmas. Admission: free.

Willie Nelson

Willie Nelson and Friends Museum and General Store. One of the largest collections of country music memorabilia is located at the Willie Nelson and Friends Museum and General Store in Nashville. It began in 1979 at a picture-framing store operated by Frank and Jeanie Oakley. Country music singing star Willie Nelson frequently came to the art shop for picture framing while visiting friends and staying at his cabin in nearly Ridgetop. As a result of the visits, the store had a large display of framed artworks and photographs of country music performers, as well as Willie Nelson memorabilia and souvenirs. The country music museum/general store was born in 1979 after Nelson received the Entertainer of the Year award.

The 10,000-square-foot Willie Nelson and Friends Museum and General Store is now the largest country museum and gift shop in Nashville. The museum contains one of the largest exhibits and collections of personal items from Willie Nelson and such friends as Johnny Cash, Patsy Cline, Waylon Jennings, George Jones, Dolly Parton, Webb Pierce, Jeannie Selley, Connie Smith, Marty Stuart, Mel Tillis, Porter Wagoner, the Wilburn Brothers, and Faron Young. Among the objects displayed are instruments, clothing, photographs, recordings, and other musical and personal items.

Willie Nelson was born during 1933 in the small farming community of Abbott, Texas. His parents were migrant farmers, and he picked cotton as a child. He was left with paternal grandparents, who were voice and piano teachers. He and his sister, Bobbie, spent considerable time on music and soon became quite proficient—she as a classical pianist and he initially in songwriting. He eventually developed into a leading country music singer and songwriter, as well as an author, poet, actor, and activist who became something of an icon in American popular culture with his distinctive dual hair braids and bandana handkerchief, which make him instantly recognizable.

Nelson began as a songwriter in the 1960s, writing such hits as "Crazy," "Funny How Time Slips Away," and "Rainy Day Blues." In the 1970s he became a leading country music singer with the critical and commercial success of "Shotgun Willie," "Red Headed Stranger," and "Stardust." Among the other popular songs that followed were "On the Road Again," "To All the Girls I've Loved Before," and "Mamas Don't Let Their Babies Grow Up to Be Cowboys." He has made over 200 albums, such as *Good Times, One for the Road, Always on My Mind*, and *Songbird*. He also was one of the main figures in the outlaw country music movement in the 1960s as a reaction to the conservative restrictions of the Nashville sound.

Nelson has appeared in more than 30 motion pictures and television shows, including such films as *The Electric Horseman, Honeysuckle Rose, Thief,* and *Barbarosa*; written poems; and coauthored several books. He also has become an activist. In 1985 he started the annual Farm Aid megaconcerts to help farmers and has worked for the use of biofuels and the legalization of marijuana. Among the many honors he has received are the Kennedy Center Honors award, induction in the Country Music Hall of Fame and National Agricultural Hall of Fame, and inclusion in the Library of Congress National Recording Registry.

Willie Nelson and Friends Museum and General Store, 2613 McGavock Pike, Nashville, TN 37214-1215. Phone: 615/885-1515. Website: www.willienelsongeneralstore.com. Hours: 8:30 a.m.–9 p.m. Mon.–Sat.; 8:30–8 Sun.; closed New Year's Day and Christmas. Admission: adults, $5; seniors, $4.50; children 6–12, $3; children under 6, free.

Elvis Presley

Graceland. One of the most visited private homes in the United States is Graceland, the former residence of Elvis Presley in Memphis, Tennessee. More than 650,000 people come to see the 14-acre estate and mansion each year where the "King of Rock and Roll" lived from 1957 until his death in 1977. Presley was one of the most popular singers and movie stars of the twentieth century and the best-selling solo artist in the history of popular music (over a billion records).

Presley, who was born to Vernon and Gladys Presley in Tupelo, Mississippi, in 1935, moved to Memphis in 1948 when he was 13. During his teenage years, he was influenced by pop and country music of the period, gospel music he heard in church and at all-night gospel sings he frequently attended, and the black music he heard on historic Beale Street. He began his singing and guitar-playing career in 1954 with legendary Sun Records, where he became—accompanied by guitarist Scotty Moore and bassist Bill Black—one of the originators of rockabilly, an up-tempo, backbeat-driven fusion of country, rhythm, and blues.

In 1955 Colonel Tom Parker, who would manage Presley for over two decades, then sold his contract to RCA Victor, where his first record was "Heartbreak Hotel," which became a number-one hit in 1956. Presley became an international sensation and the leading figure of the new sound known as rock and roll. It was followed by his uninhibited interpretations of songs in television appearances and the first of 33 movies, *Love Me Tenderly*. His energetic body gyrations also created considerable controversy and Presley being called "Elvis the Pelvis" and sometimes filmed only down to the waist.

In 1957 he produced three number-one singles—"Too Much," "All Shook Up," and "Let Me Be Your Teddy Bear"; purchased Graceland, an 18-room mansion for himself and his parents about nine miles south of downtown

Memphis; and received a draft notice that resulted in two years of service in the Army Armored Division—during which he made 10 top-40 song hits, his mother died of heart failure, he was exposed to drugs, and he met Priscilla Beaulieu, whom he later married after seven years of courtship. He resumed his musical career in 1960 after being honorably discharged with the rank of sergeant.

Upon his return to civilian life, Presley made *G.I. Blues*, a soundtrack from a movie; *His Hand in Mine*, a long-playing recording of sacred music; and *Something for Everybody*, an album that exemplified the Nashville country sound. He also gave two shows in Memphis for 24 local charities and a benefit concert for a Pearl Harbor memorial in Hawaii, which was his last public performance for seven years as he focused on making motion pictures (he made 27 movies during the 1960s). The films generally were panned but profitable and resulted in records and albums in 20 instances. Because of the rapid production (sometimes three movies a year), it affected the quality of the films and the music.

After purchasing Graceland in 1957, Presley made extensive modifications to suit his needs and tastes. The site—originally called Graceland Farms—was owned by S. C. Toof, founder of a local printing firm and named for his daughter, Grace, who inherited the property. A portion of the land, now Graceland, was given to a niece, Ruth Moore, who, with her husband, Dr. Thomas Moore, built the colonial-style mansion constructed of tan limestone with four large-columned pillars and two lions on the sides of the portico.

Graceland now has 23 rooms, including eight bedrooms and bathrooms. Presley added a fieldstone wall surrounding the grounds; wrought-iron music-themed gate; swimming pool; racquetball court; "jungle room," which features an indoor waterfall and a recording studio; mediation garden, where Presley, his parents, and grandmother are buried; and other modifications. Graceland grew from 10,266 square feet when purchased by Presley to 17,552 square feet today. The complex also has a visitor center, hotel, museum, and souvenir shops that are being replaced by new facilities over a three-year period.

Presley's father remarried after his wife died and eventually moved. Priscilla Beaulieu also lived at Graceland for five years before she and Elvis were married in 1967 and then for five more years until they were separated in 1972. The couple had a daughter, Lisa Marie Presley, in 1968. She lived with her mother in California after the couple divorced. Elvis, who had a prescription drug problem, died at Graceland in 1977 at the age of 42 reportedly of a heart attack, although there were conflicting reports as to the cause of his death. Lisa Marie inherited the estate when she turned 25 and sold 85 percent of it. She later married pop singer Michael Jackson.

Graceland, which has been designated a National Historic Landmark and is listed on the National Register of Historic Places, opened to the public in 1982 as a historic house museum. Graceland also has exhibits on Presley's life and career, his influence on pop culture, fashion trends, Elvis in the news, and a historic 1968 television event, as well as the Elvis Presley Car Museum, which contains over 33 vehicles owned by Presley and two jet airplanes—a 1958 Convair 880 and a smaller Lockheed Jet Star—formerly used by Presley in his travels. Three tour options are offered as part of the admission.

Graceland, 3764 Elvis Presley Blvd., Memphis, TN 38116-4198 (postal address: PO Box 16508, Memphis, TN 38186-0508). Phone: 901/332-3322. Fax: 901/344-3116. E-mail: graceland@elvis.com. Website: www.elvis.com. Hours: Jan.–Feb.—10–4 daily; closed Tues.; Mar.–May—9–5 Mon.–Sat., 10–4 Sun.; June–Aug.—9–5 Mon.–Sat., 9–4 Sun.; Sept.–Oct.—9–5 Mon.–Sat., 10–4 Sun.; Nov.—10–4 daily; closed Thanksgiving; Dec.—10–4 daily; closed Christmas. Admission: three tour options—adults, $31, $35, and $70; seniors and students, and youth 13–18, $27, $31.50, and $70; children 7–12, $14, $17, and $70; children under 7, free.

Elvis Presley Birthplace and Museum. The two-room shotgun house in Tupelo, Mississippi, where Elvis Presley was born in 1935 is now the Elvis Presley Birthplace and Museum. His identical twin, Jesse Garson Presley, was stillborn, and Elvis grew up as the only child of Vernon and Gladys Presley. The house was built by Elvis's father, but the family lived in it for only two years before losing it and eventually moving to Memphis in 1948 when he was 13.

Elvis was close to his parents and especially his mother and found his initial musical inspiration at the Assembly of God Church that the family attended. His father changed jobs frequently and often relied on help from neighbors and government food assistance. In 1938 the Presleys lost their home when the father was found guilty of altering a check written by the landowner. He was jailed for eight months, and Elvis and his mother moved in with relatives, and later the family lived in a largely African American neighborhood.

Elvis was regarded as an average student when he entered elementary school at East Tupelo Consolidated School. He had a good voice and made his first public performance in a contest in 1945 when 10 years old, only to place fifth. He received his first guitar for a birthday present a few months later, followed by basic guitar lessons from two of his uncles and the church pastor. When in sixth grade at Milam School, he started bringing his guitar to school and would play and sing during lunchtime. When he was 12, a classmate arranged for him to appear on his brother's local radio show.

In 1948 the Presley family moved to Memphis—first in rooming houses and then in public housing. Although he never received formal music training or learned to read music (he studied and played by ear), Elvis was influenced by his early informal training, gospel singing, the Beale Street blues scene, and his early musical experiences, which led to the 1953 breakthrough at Sun Records (*see* the listing for Graceland).

The Elvis Presley Birthplace and Museum in Tupelo opened in 1992. It consisted of the personal collection of Janelle McComb, a longtime family friend of Elvis. It was completely renovated in 2006 and a new exhibit added, titled "Remembrance of Things Past." It has Tupelo artifacts, large photographs, graphics, and two audiovisual presentations that bring to life the childhood world of Elvis in Tupelo, including his family and first music. The 15-acre site also contains a bronze statue of Elvis as a boy, a fountain, a memorial wall, and the Assembly of God Church where Presley learned to love gospel music (it has been restored and moved to the museum grounds).

Elvis Presley Birthplace and Museum, 306 Elvis Presley Dr., Tupelo, MS 38804-2812. Phone: 662/841-1245. Fax: 662/690-6623. E-mail: info@elvispresleybirthplace.com. Website: www.elvispresleybirthplace.com. Hours: May–Sept.—9–5:30 Mon.–Sat., 1–5 Sun.; Oct.–Apr.—9–5 Mon.–Sat., 1–5 Sun.; closed Thanksgiving and Christmas. Admission: adults—house, $4; museum, $8; church, $5; combo, $12; children—house, $2; museum, $4; church, $3; combo, $6.

Elvis Presley Museum. One of the largest private collections of Elvis Presley memorabilia is featured at the Elvis Presley Museum in Pigeon Forge, Tennessee. The exhibits contain examples of Presley's cars, clothing, jewelry, guns, and other items. The collection was assembled by Mike L. Moon, a Georgia entrepreneur and once owner of the Stamps Quartet. He began the collection in 1971 after receiving a black leather belt from the singer/actor as a gift following a Las Vegas performance. The collection now belongs to Moon's daughter, Lynn Moon McAllister, and her family. Live musical shows by performers are also presented in the museum complex.

Elvis Presley Museum, 2638 Parkway, Pigeon Forge, TN 37863-3246. Phones: 865/428-2001 and 866/683-5847. Website: www.elviaspresleymuseum.com. Hours: varies; closed Thanksgiving and Christmas. Admission: museum—adults, $17; seniors, $15; children 6–11, $12; children under 6, free; live show—adults, $20.

Paul Robeson

Paul Robeson House. Paul Leroy Robeson was a controversial African American bass-baritone concert singer who also was an All-American and professional athlete, film and stage actor, recording artist, human rights activist, multilingual orator, lawyer, and writer. The house where he lived in west Philadelphia, Pennsylvania, from 1966 to 1976 is now a historic house museum called the Paul Robeson House.

Robeson was an international concert star who became known for his political radicalism and activism in the civil rights movement and was blacklisted from performing on stage, screen, radio, and television during the Cold War. In the 1930s Robeson was attracted to communism, saying he found Russia to be free of racial prejudice. He was widely criticized when he failed to renounce Stalin when the Soviet leader signed a pack with Hitler and later for his acceptance of the 1952 Stalin Prize, which made him an outcast during the Cold War.

Robeson's passport was revoked in 1950 under the McCarran Act over his work in the anti-imperialism movement and what the State Department called his "frequent criticism while abroad of the treatment of blacks in the United States." Robeson's right to travel was restored in 1958, but his health was faltering, and by 1965 he was forced into retirement and spent his remaining years at his house in Philadelphia. He died in 1976 at the age of 77, unapologetic about his political views and career.

Robeson was born in 1898 in Princeton, New Jersey, the son of a minister who had been a runaway slave. He was a bright student and outstanding athlete who received a scholarship to Rutgers University, where he was elected to the Phi Beta Kappa honor society, graduated as class valedictorian in 1919, and was an All-American football player who put himself through Columbia Law School by playing professional football on weekends.

He went to work for a New York law firm but quit when a stenographer refused to take dictation from an African American. He turned to the stage and music and was praised for his performance in the title role of *Emperor Jones*. In the career that followed, Robeson became known best for his stage portrayal of William Shakespeare's *Othello* and his singing of "Ol' Man River" in stage and movie versions of *Show Boat*. He also was the first major concert star to popularize the performance of African American spirituals, and he learned more languages to be able to sing folk songs from other cultures.

In 1998 the West Philadelphia Cultural Alliance initiated a major campaign to restore his 1966–1976 house. It now is an official project of the Save America's Treasures public-private partnership between the White House Millennium Council and the National Trust of Historic Preservation. The house became a National Historic Landmark in 2000. It contains such materials as memorabilia, furnishings, paintings, and photographs about Robeson's life, family, and career.

Paul Robeson House, 4951 Walnut St., Philadelphia, PA 19139-4228 (postal address: West Philadelphia Cultural Alliance, 4949-4951 Walnut St., Philadelphia, PA 19139-4228). Phone: 215/747-4675. E-mail: wpca@paulrobesonhouse.org. Website: www.paulrobesonhouse.org. Hours: by appointment. Admission: adults, $5; children, $4.

Paul Robeson Cultural Center (Rutgers). The Paul Robeson Cultural Center at the New Brunswick campus of Rutgers University honors an alumnus who became a world-renowned concert singer known for his political and civil rights activism (*see* previous listing). The cultural center was established in 1967 to provide a supportive atmosphere to the increasing numbers of African American students entering the university, and it was renamed for Robeson in 1972.

The center, which moved to a new home adjacent to the Busch Campus Center in Piscataway in 1992, has played a vital role at Rutgers by reflecting the rich heritage of African Americans through programs that focus on their literacy, cultural, and historic contributions to society. The center now provides educational, cultural, and social programs and services that reflect the experiences and aspirations of minority students, with an emphasis on African Americans.

Paul Robeson Cultural Center, Rutgers University, New Brunswick Campus, 600 Bartholomew Rd., Piscataway, NJ 08854-8002. Phone: 732/445-3545. Fax: 732/445-3151. Website: www.prcc.rutgers.edu. Hours: Sept.–May—8:30 a.m.–11 p.m. Mon.–Thurs.; 8:30–9 p.m. Fri., 12–4 Sat.–Sun.; June–Aug.—8:30–4:30 Mon.–Fri.; closed Sat.–Sun. Admission: free.

Paul Robeson Galleries. The Paul Robeson Galleries on the Newark Campus of Rutgers University function as an artistic and cultural center that presents visual arts exhibitions and education and public programs in partnerships with community organizations. The galleries, located in the Paul Robeson Campus Center, are named for the alumnus who became an international stage and screen star. They embody Robeson's lifelong commitment to artistic freedom, cultural democracy, and transnationalism. Annual attendance is 8,500.

Paul Robeson Galleries, Rutgers University, Newark Campus, Paul Robeson Campus Center, 350 Dr. Martin Luther King Jr. Blvd., Newark, NJ 07102. Phone: 973/353-1610. Fax: 973/353-5912. E-mail: gallery@andromeda. rutgers.edu. Website: www.andromeda.rutgers.edu/artgallery. Hours: 10–5 Mon.–Thurs. and first Sat. of each month; closed Fri., other Sats., and Sun. Admission: free.

Paul Robeson Cultural Center (Penn State). Pennsylvania State University also has a Paul Robeson Cultural Center on its University Park campus in State College. It was established in the Walnut Building in 1972, replacing a student-run facility called the Black Cultural Center. The original center sought to provide cultural, educational, and social support for African American students and to serve as a place for building understanding. In 1986 the Walnut Building was remodeled, the center was given a new name, and its mission was expanded.

The Paul Robeson Cultural Center seeks to emphasize the diversity of the historic, current, and future roles of African American culture and to show how this diversity intersects, overlaps, and complements the cultures of Latino, African, Asian/Pacific Islander, Caribbean, European, and indigenous American peoples. It provides programs and services that encourage the appreciation of the diverse perspectives, experiences, and cultures of many underrepresented cultures on the campus and in the community. The students, faculty, and staff named the new center after Paul Robeson, whose achievements, dedication, and commitment in the areas of intellectual development, physical excellence, humanitarian spirit, and artistic accomplishment were to serve as a model for all students.

In 1999 the Robeson Center moved into an expanded building as part of the HUB–Robeson Center complex. The construction added more space and new facilities for both HUB (the student union originally named the Hetzel Union Building) and the connecting Robeson Center. The Robeson Center functions as a forum for the cultural enrichment, educational development, and social advancement of all students, with the emphasis on the diversity of the historic, current, and future roles of the various minority cultures. It offers programs, exhibits, films, plays, musical presentations, publications, and other activities and has a conference room (Heritage Hall), an art gallery (Robeson Gallery), and office spaces for African American, Puerto Rican, Caribbean, and other student organizations.

Paul Robeson Cultural Center, Pennsylvania State University, 21 HUB–Robeson Center, University Park, PA 16802. Phone: 814/865-3776. Websites: www.studentaffairs.psu.edu/cultural and www.sa.psu.cdu/prcc/facili-ties.shtml. Hours: 8 a.m.–10 p.m. Mon.–Fri.; varies Sat.–Sun. and June–Aug. Admission: free

Jimmie Rodgers

Jimmie Rodgers Museum. James Charles Rodgers, who was called Jimmie Rodgers, was one of the nation's first country music superstars in the early twentieth century. He is best known for his rhythmic yodeling. Rodgers's career, however, was short lived because of his health. He died of tuberculosis at the age of 35.

Rodgers was born in 1897 in Meridian, Mississippi. His mother, Eliza Rodgers, who had seven children, died when he was about six or seven years old. He was the youngest of three sons and was sent to live with various relatives in southeast Mississippi and southwest Alabama. Jimmie returned after a few years to live with his father, Aaron Rodgers, who was a railroad maintenance foreman, and his new wife.

At the age of 13, Jimmie Rodgers twice organized traveling shows, only to be brought home by his father to work on the railroad. A few years later, he became a brakeman on the New Orleans and Northeastern Railroad, where he worked until 1924. At the age of 27, he contracted tuberculosis. Once again he organized a traveling show. While performing in the Southeast, a cyclone destroyed his tent, and he returned to railroad work as a switchman for the Southern Pacific Railroad in Florida. In early 1927 he left the railroad and returned to Meridian with his wife, Carrie, and daughter, Anita.

In the summer of 1927, Rodgers performed on an Asheville, North Carolina, radio station, and then recorded two songs that received only modest success, "The Soldier's Sweetheart" and "Sleep, Baby, Sleep." He had better luck with his next recordings, which included four songs. One was "Blue Yodel," better known as "T for Texas," which sold nearly half a million copies and made Rodgers an instant country music star. He also made a movie short titled *The Singing Brakeman*, toured with humorist Will Rogers, and recorded "Blue Yodel No. 9" with jazz trumpeter Louis Armstrong. However, Rodgers's health began to fade after years of fighting tuberculosis, and he died in 1933 from a lung hemorrhage two days after recording "Mississippi Delta Blues" and "Years Ago."

Rodgers was one of the first three musicians to be inducted into the Country Museum Hall of Fame when established in 1961. He was also elected to the Songwriters Hall of Fame and the Rock and Roll Hall of Fame, was named one of the "40 Greatest Men of Country Music," had his "Blue Yodel No. 9" selected among the "500 Songs That Shaped Rock and Roll," and had a commemorative stamp issued in his honor in 1978.

The Jimmie Rodgers Memorial Museum was founded in Meridian in 1976. It contains exhibits and memorabilia related to his life and career, including his guitar used in *The Singing Brakeman* movie. The museum also displays a range of railroad equipment from the steam-engine era and works with the city in holding an annual Jimmie Rodgers Memorial Festival every May. The museum's annual attendance is 7,000.

Jimmie Rodgers Museum, 1725 Highland Park Dr., Meridian, MS 39307 (postal address: PO Box 4555, Meridian, MS 39304-4555). Phone: 601/485-1808. E-mail: jimmie_rodgers@hotmail.com. Website: www.jimmierodgers.com. Hours: 10–4 Tues.–Sat.; closed Sun.–Mon. and major holidays. Admission: adults, $8; seniors, $5; children under 19, $3; children under 8, free.

Bessie Smith

Bessie Smith Cultural Center. The Bessie Smith Cultural Center in Chattanooga, Tennessee, is named for a local black singer who was known as the "empress of the blues." She was one of the most popular blues and jazz singers in the 1920s and 1930s and—along with Louis Armstrong—greatly influenced later jazz singers.

Bessie Smith was born in Chattanooga in 1894, the daughter of a laborer who was also a part-time Baptist preacher. By the time she was nine years old, both her father and mother had died and her older sister had to care for the sisters and brothers. To earn money for their poor family, Bessie and her brother Andrew began performing on the streets—she sang and danced, and he accompanied her on guitar.

Smith's oldest brother, Clarence, ran away and joined a traveling minstrel and vaudeville show. He came back in 1912 with the troupe and got Bessie a job as a dancer and singer with Pa and Ma Rainey. Ma Rainey became Bessie's mentor and greatly influenced her showmanship. Bessie stayed with the traveling show until 1915 and then developed her own following in the South and along the eastern seaboard. She had an elegant contralto voice and mesmerizing showmanship and began to appear with the best musicians at sold-out concerts of classic blues songs, many of which she wrote or cowrote, such as "Nobody Knows You When You're Down and Out," "Empty Bed Blues," and "Backwater Blues." She also performed country blues, vaudeville, and jazz songs.

Smith recorded her first record, a coupling of "Gulf Coast Blues" and "Downhearted Blues," in 1923. It was an immediate hit, selling 750,000 copies that year. She went on to make some 160 recordings for Columbia Records, including the popular "St. Louis Blues," one of her finest recordings with Louis Armstrong. She also appeared in two Broadway plays, *How Come?* and *Pansy*, and made her only film appearance in *St. Louis Blues*.

Smith became the biggest star on the black theater booking circuit, making her the highest-paid African American entertainer of her day. However, the Great Depression, radio, and sound movies adversely affected the record companies and the sale of recordings in the 1930s. Jazz also had replaced the blues as the dominant music. Smith became a swing musician and was making a comeback when she died in an automobile accident in 1937 at the age of 43. Her recordings became part of the Grammy Hall of Fame in 1973 when a special Grammy Award was established to honor recordings of "qualitative or historical significance" at least 25 years old.

The Bessie Smith Cultural Center resulted from the merger of two community organizations—the Chattanooga African American Museum, a cultural center and museum, and the Bessie Smith Performance Hall, an educational institution that hosted concerts and other community events. The newly combined and renovated facility was established in 1983, opened in 1986, and adopted the Bessie Smith Cultural Center as its name in 2009. It functions as an interdisciplinary cultural center that promotes cultural, educational, and artistic excellence and fosters research and education of African and African American heritage, and as a venue that allows the community to celebrate through education, art, and entertainment. It features African American and African historical exhibits, photographs, and artifacts, including a section on Bessie Smith, and offers history, art, dance, music, craft, and other programs. Annual attendance is 156,000.

Bessie Smith Cultural Center, 200 Martin Luther King Blvd., Chattanooga, TN 37403 (postal address: PO Box 11493, Chattanooga, TN 37401-2493). Phones: 421/266-8658 and 421/267-1628. Fax: 423/267-1076, E-mail: info@bessiesmith.org. Website: www.bessiesmithcc.org. Hours: 10–5 Mon.–Fri., 12–4 Sat.; closed Sun. and national and legal holidays. Admission: adults, $7; seniors and students, $5; children 6–12, $3; children under 6, free.

John Philip Sousa

Sousa Archives and Center for American Music. John Philip Sousa was called "The March King" because he excelled in composing and playing military and patriotic marches during the late romantic period of the Victorian and Edwardian eras. Among his many marches were such favorites as "The Washington Post," "Semper Fidelius" (official march of the U.S. Marine Corps), and "The Stars and Stripes Forever" (national march of the United States).

Sousa, who was born in 1854 in Washington, DC, began his musical career playing violin and studying music theory and composition. In 1867, when he was 13, his father, John Antonio Sousa, a trombonist in the U.S. Marine Band, enlisted him in the Marine Band as an apprentice to keep him from joining a circus band. He left the Marine Band in 1875, learned to conduct, and then focused exclusively on writing and conducting marches from 1880 until his death in 1932.

In 1880 Sousa rejoined the Marine Band and served as director for 12 years. He led the President's Own band under five presidents from Rutherford B. Hayes to Benjamin Harrison and played at two inaugural balls. After leaving the Marine Band in 1892, Sousa organized his own band and toured until 1931, performing at 15,623 concerts and touring Europe and Australia. During World War I, he was commissioned a lieutenant commander and led the Naval Reserve Band in Illinois. He also is credited with developing the sousaphone, a modified helicon, which was a large brass instrument.

The Sousa Archives and Center for American Music began in 1994 as the Sousa Archives for Band Research at the University of Illinois at Champaign-Urbana. It contained Sousa materials obtained from a personal connection between Sousa and Albert Austin Harding, the university's first bandmaster, as well as items from Herbert L. Clarke. Since then other collections have been added, including papers, music, and instruments by composers and others. The archive/museum got its present name in 2004 when the collection was transferred to the university library. It now supports and facilitates research and education by preserving and providing access to the documentary evidence of the nation's music and fine arts heritage. Annual attendance is 2,500.

Sousa Archives and Center for American Music, University of Illinois at Urbana-Champaign, 236 Harding Band Bldg., 1103 S. 6th St., Champaign, IL 61820. Phone: 217/244-9309. Fax: 217/244-8695. E-mail: sousa@illinois.edu. Website: www.library.illinois.edu/sousa. Hours: 8:30–12 and 1–5 Mon.–Tues. and Thurs.–Fri., 10–12 and 1–5 Wed.; closed Sat.–Sun. and major holidays. Admission: free.

Fred Waring

Fred Waring Collection. Frederick Malcolm Waring was a popular musician, bandleader, and radio-television personality for nearly 70 years. Fred Waring also was known as "the man who taught America how to sing" because of his emphasis on choral music. He taught and supervised a summer workshop on choral singing for 37 years and founded one of the largest choral music publishing firms.

Waring, who was born in Tyrone, Pennsylvania, in 1900, began his musical career as a teenager when he, his brother, and a friend formed a band that evolved into Fred Waring's Banjo Orchestra. It became a local favorite, playing for parties, dances, and proms. He enrolled at Pennsylvania State University in State College and planned to major in architectural engineering. The banjo orchestra became so successful, however, that he dropped out of college and toured with the band, which later became known as Fred Waring and His Pennsylvanians.

From 1923 to 1932, Waring's orchestra was among Victor Records' best-selling bands. It also performed regularly on radio and received an exceptional reception in 1933 for its rendition of "You Gotta Be a Football Hero." Waring then added a men's singing group to his ensemble and recruited Robert Shaw, who later became the nation's preeminent conductor of serious choral music, to train the singers. During World War II, Waring composed and performed numerous patriotic songs, including "My America," and his ensemble appeared at war bond rallies and entertained troops at training camps.

In 1943 Waring also acquired the Buckwood Inn in Shawnee on Delaware, Pennsylvania, which he renamed the Shawnee Inn and used as the center of his musical activities. It was where he rehearsed and broadcast his radio programs, held his choral workshops, and started his music publishing company (Shawnee Press). It also was during the 1940s and early 1950s that Waring and His Pennsylvanians produced such hits as "Battle Hymn of the Republic," "Smoke Gets in Your Eyes," "Button Up Your Overcoat," "White Christmas," and "Dancing in the Dark."

From 1948 to 1954, *The Fred Waring Show* ran on CBS Television and was honored as the best musical program. In the 1960s and 1970s, when popular music tastes turned from choral music, Waring also changed with the times. He introduced his Young Pennsylvanians, a youthful group that featured old favorites and choral arrangements of contemporary songs. The popular touring group was traveling some 40,000 miles a year when Waring died of a stroke in 1984 at the age of 84.

Waring received many musical awards and other honors over his long career. They included the Congressional Gold Medal. He also served on Penn State's Board of Trustees and was named a distinguished alumnus of the university. The university also has a room devoted to the Waring Collection in its Alumni Library. It contains information and materials about his life and career, including his experiences in acquiring an electric blender company that produced the successful "Waring Blendor" in the 1930s.

Fred Waring Collection, Alumni Library, Pennsylvania State University, Patee Library Complex, University Park, PA 16802. Phone: 814/863-2911. E-mail: rsa4@psu.edu. Website: www.alumni.libraries.psu.edu. Hours: 7:45 a.m.–2 a.m. Mon.–Thurs., 7:45–7 Fri., 10–7 Sat., 10 a.m.–2 a.m. Sun.; closed major holidays. Admission: free.

Lawrence Welk

Lawrence Welk Museum. Lawrence Welk was an accordionist, bandleader, and television impresario who hosted a television musical program—called *The Lawrence Welk Show*—from 1955 to 1982. Welk was known for his "champagne music"—which was derived from a hotel engagement when a dancer referred to the band's sound as "light and bubby as champagne." A "bubble machine" later was used to produce streams of large soap bubbles across the bandstand.

Welk, who always had a Russian/German accent, was born in 1903 to German immigrants who came from the Ukraine (then part of Russia) to a homestead in the farming community of Strasburg, North Dakota, in 1892. The area was settled largely by Germans from Russia and Welk did not learn English until he enrolled in school. He became interested in music and convinced his father to buy him a $400 mail-order accordion with the promise that he would work on the farm until he was 21 and that any money earned doing farmwork or performing would go to the family. That's what happened. When Lawrence became 21, he left the family farm to pursue a career in music.

During the 1920s, Welk performed with other bands before starting his own orchestra. He led several big bands in North and South Dakota and served as the station band for a radio station in Yankton. He also graduated from the MacPhail School of Music in Minneapolis in 1927. During the 1930s and 1940s, Welk led a traveling big band that specialized in dance tunes and "sweet" music and played at such places as the Trianon Ballroom in Chicago and Roosevelt Hotel in New York. The orchestra also made motion picture "soundies" considered to be early versions of music videos and had its own national radio program in 1929–1952.

In 1951 Welk settled in Los Angeles and began producing *The Lawrence Welk Show* from the Aragon Ballroom in Venice Beach. It turned out to be a local hit and was picked up by ABC in 1955. The show had the bubble machine, Welk dancing with the band's female vocalist (or women from the audience) when the orchestra played a polka or waltz, and conservative music with concentrations of popular music.

A home retirement community developed by Welk still exists on some 600 acres near Escondido, California. Originally called the Lawrence Welk Village, it is now the Welk Resort and Champagne Village. It is where the

Lawrence Welk Museum is located, as well as a country club, a 331-seat theater with live Broadway and musical performances, restaurants, and shops. The museum, which is in the lobby of the theater, tells about Welk's life and career, features his champagne music, and contains memorabilia, photographs, posters, newspaper clippings, a large cutout of Welk directing his orchestra in front of a television camera, and the world's largest champagne glass, which Welk received on his 25th anniversary.

Lawrence Welk Museum, 8860 Lawrence Walk Dr., Escondido, CA 92026-6403, Phones: 760/749-3000, 760/749-3448, and 800/932/9355. E-mail: box.office@welktheatre.com. Website: www.welktheatresandiego.com. Hours: 10–5 daily. Admission: free.

Lawrence Welk Birthplace. Bandleader Lawrence Welk was born in 1903 in a sod house near the German-speaking farming community of Strasburg, North Dakota. He was the sixth of eight children of Ludwig and Christina Welk, who emigrated to America in 1892 from Odessa, Ukraine, which was part of Russia at the time. The Welks homesteaded in an area that was settled largely by Germans from Russia and spoke a combination of the two languages. Lawrence did not learn to speak English until he enrolled in school—and later was known for his German/Russian accent.

Lawrence became interested in music as a youth and asked his father to buy him a $400 mail-order accordion. His father agreed after his son pledged to work on the farm until he was 21, and he would pay for the instrument by giving the family any money he made doing farmwork or performing. Lawrence kept his promise and did not leave home until 1924 (*see* the Lawrence Welk Museum listing for information about his career and achieving musical and television fame on *The Lawrence Welk Show*).

The Welk family farm site, which now covers six acres and is leased from the Schwab family, is known today as the Lawrence Welk Birthplace, as well as the Ludwig and Christina Welk Farmstead. It opened in 1991 as a historic site and is listed on the National Register of Historic Places. It consists of a small house, summer kitchen, barn, granary, blacksmith shop, carriage house, windmill, and outhouse (as well as the Schwab sod house). A life-size cardboard cutout of Lawrence Welk greets visitors in the dining room (with his accordion nearby and his champagne music filling the house), but he never returned to the farmstead that later was restored by volunteers. However, approximately 7,000 visitors come to see the historic site each year.

Lawrence Welk Birthplace, 845 88th St., S.E., Strasburg, ND 58573. Phones: 701/336-7103, 701/336-7169, and 701/336-7353. E-mail: tsci@bektel.coml. Website: www.strasburgnd.com/historicsites. Hours: Memorial Day–Labor Day—by appointment; closed remainder of year. Admission: adults, $5; children under 12, $3.

Lawrence Welk Collection. North Dakota State University has an extensive collection of Lawrence Welk music and memorabilia in its libraries and Institute for Regional Studies and University Archives. The bandleader's collection, provided largely by the Welk family, consists of over 10,000 music arrangements, as well as scrapbooks, manuscripts, photographs, artifacts, record albums, show logs, publications, and oral histories.

Lawrence Welk Collection, North Dakota State University Libraries, Institute for Regional Studies and University Archives, Skills and Technology Training Center, Room 117, 1305 19th Ave., Fargo, ND 58108-6050 (postal address: Libraries, NDSU Dept. 2080, PO Box 6050, Fargo, ND 58108-6050). Phone: 701/232-8914. Fax: 701/231-5632. E–mail: ndsu.library.archives@ndsu.edu. Website: www.library.ndsu.edu/archives/welk-collection. Hours: by appointment. Admission: free.

Hank Williams

Hank Williams Museum. Hank Williams was one of the nation's leading country singers and songwriters in the first half of the twentieth century. He performed on radio and traveling country music shows and wrote more than 100 songs in the blues, traditional country music, and hymns. He recorded 35 singles that ranked in the top 10 of *Billboard*'s country-and-western songs, including 11 that were number one. He is best known for such works as "Lovesick Blues," "Your Cheatin' Heart," "Jambalaya," "Cold, Cold Heart," "Kaw-linga," "Half as Much," and "Hey, Good Lookin'."

Williams was born Hiram King Williams in the rural community of Mount Olive, Alabama, in 1923. His mother gave him a guitar when he was eight, but it was Rufus "Tee Tot" Payne, a local blues street singer, who taught him to play the guitar and sing the blues. In 1937 the family moved to Montgomery, his mother opened a boarding house, and Hank won a talent show at a local theater with his original tune, "WPA Blues." He then formed a band called the Drifting Cowboys and performed regularly on a local radio station in 1941, followed by a medicine show in 1944.

Williams got his first break in 1946 when Fred Rose of Acuff-Rose Publishing asked him to record two songs, "Never Again" and "Honky Tonkin," which were quite successful and Williams signed a contract with MGM Records. It was followed by such hits as "Move It on Over," "I'm a Long Gone Daddy," and "Lovesick Blues." Williams and his band continued to turn out such popular numbers as "Wedding Bells," "Crazy Heart," and "Baby, We're Really in Love" in 1949–1952.

He started to have problems in 1951, starting with a marriage separation, back surgery, taking drugs for pain, and excessive drinking. On New Year's Day in 1953, while being driven for a concert in Canton, Ohio, Williams died in the back seat of his car. He was only 29 years old.

In 1961 Hank Williams was one of the first three to be inducted into the Country Museum Hall of Fame. A life-size statue of Williams is also located in Lister Hill Park in downtown Montgomery. His life and career are featured at the Hank Williams Museum, founded in 1997 and opened two years later in Montgomery. It has 35 showcases and contains such personal items as his clothing, hats, portraits, photographs, awards, records, guitar, piano, horse saddle, and 1952 Cadillac.

Hank Williams Museum, 118 Commerce St., Montgomery, AL 36104-2538. Phone: 334/262-3600. E-mail: hankwilliamsmuseum@bellsouth.net. Website: www.thehankwilliamsmuseum.com. Hours: 9–4:30 Mon.–Fri., 10–4 Sat., 1–4 Sun. Admission: adults, $8; children 3–11, $3; children under 3, free.

OUTLAWS

Billy the Kid Bonney

Billy the Kid Museum. William H. Bonney, who was born William Henry McCarty Jr. and became known as Billy the Kid, was a youthful gunman and outlaw who is credited with killing 21 people in the American West in the second half of the 1800s. It is believed that he was born in New York City about 1859, but he lived in New Mexico from 1869 until his death in 1881. The Billy the Kid Museum in Fort Sumner, New Mexico, now tells about his life and exploits.

Billy the Kid reportedly became a killer at the age of 12 and a gunman in the "Lincoln County War" between cattle barons in New Mexico in 1878. He became involved in many of the shootings in the dispute and refused to honor the truce arranged by Governor Lew Wallace, and he eventually was shot and killed by Sheriff Pat Barrett.

The museum, founded in 1953, traces his life. It has such items as his rifle, chaps and spurs, original wanted poster, and locks of his hair. Among the other exhibits are more than 150 firearms of varying ages, the cavalry sword of frontiersman/cattleman John Chisum, and a collection of early fire trucks and automobiles. The annual attendance is 20,000.

Billy the Kid Museum, 1435 E. Sumner Ave., Fort Sumner, NM 88119-9606. Phone: 575/355-2380. Fax: 575/355-1380. E-mail: info@billythekidmuseumfortsumner.com. Website: www.billythekidmuseumfortsumner.com. Hours: mid-May–Sept.—8:30–5 daily; Oct.–mid-May—8:30–5 Mon.–Sat.; closed Sun., Easter, Thanksgiving, and Christmas. Admission: adults, $5; seniors, $4; children 7–15, $3; children under 7, free.

Dalton Brothers

Dalton Gang Hideout. The Dalton Gang was composed of former lawmen and outlaws who robbed trains and banks in the Old West in 1890–1892. They were known as the Dalton Gang because the leaders were three Dalton brothers. Grattan, Robert, and Emmett Dalton were former law enforcement officers who were related to the Younger brothers, who rode with Jesse James in the James-Younger Gang in Missouri after the Civil War.

Bob Dalton, who was born in 1867 in Missouri, was a U.S. marshal among the Osage tribe in Indian Territory (Oklahoma) in 1890 when he was accused of selling whiskey in the territory, jumped bail, and did not appear for trial. At about the same time, his older brother, Grat Dalton, was fired as a deputy marshal for conduct unbecoming of an officer. Emmett Dalton, a former lawman who had engaged in horse theft and train and bank robbery, joined them later in 1890, and all three were accused of stealing horses. Bob and Emmett fled to California, while Grat was arrested but released for lack of evidence.

The brothers then were joined by other outlaws to form the Dalton Gang, which began a series of railroad and bank robberies in the American West before being killed or captured in 1892. They had two other brothers—Frank Dalton, a deputy U.S. marshal who was killed in 1887 while trying to arrest a horse thief, and William Dalton, an outlaw who already was a member of another gang, the Wild Bunch, and did not join them. For some time, the three brothers hid from the law at their sister's small house on the outskirts of Meade, Kansas. Many people suspected Eva Dalton, who was married to J. N. Whipple, a mercantile store operator, of hiding her brothers, but no evidence was found until the Whipples moved from town in 1892 and the new owners found an underground tunnel from two rooms in the basement to the barn.

The Whipple house became a tourist attraction in 1941 known as the Dalton Gang Hideout after the WPA rebuilt the 95-foot dirt tunnel, which was replaced with a stone passageway. The Meade Chamber of Commerce took over the site in 1970, and the Meade County Historical Society assumed control in 1995. The house and barn have been restored, with the house containing period furniture and the barn being converted into a small historical museum and gift shop. Annual attendance is 9,000.

Dalton Gang Hideout, 502 S. Pearlette St., Meade, KS 67864 (postal address: PO Box 515, Meade, KS 67864-0515). Phones: 620/873-2731 and 800/354-2743. E-mail: daltonhideout@yahoo.com. Website: www.oldmeadecounty. com/hideout.htm. Hours: 9–5 Mon.–Sat., 1–5 Sun. Admission: $4.

Dalton Defenders Museum. The train and bank robberies by the Dalton Gang came to an end on October 5, 1892, when the three Dalton brothers and two other members of the gang tried to rob two banks in Coffeyville, Kansas. The gang members were either killed or captured in a gun battle with townspeople as the gang was leaving the banks with nearly $25,000. The Dalton Gang attempted the bank robberies because Bob Dalton wanted to "beat anything Jesse James ever did"—rob two banks at once, in broad daylight.

The gang members were recognized by one of the Coffeyville townspeople as they crossed the plaza to enter the C. M. Condon & Company and First National Banks. The town was alerted, and the citizens armed themselves with weapons from nearby hardware stores and confronted the robbers as they left the banks. In the ensuing gunfight, eight men were killed and four were wounded. The dead included four of the robbers—brothers Bob and Grat Dalton and the two other gang members, Bill Power and Dick Broadwell. The third brother, Emmett Dalton, was seriously wounded. The four townspeople killed included town marshal Charles Connelly. Emmett Dalton, the youngest of the Dalton brothers, had 23 gunshot wounds, but he recovered and was sentenced to life in the Kansas Penitentiary at Lansing. He served 15 years and was pardoned by the governor and moved to California and became a real estate agent, author, and actor. He was 66 when he died in 1937.

The plaza area where the robbery and gun battle took place remains much the same as it did in 1892. The Perkins building, home of the Condon Bank during the raid, has been restored and now has bronze markers in the cement indicating where the defenders fell during the gun battle. The nearby Death Alley, which contains an old jail, has a recording that tells about the bank robbery and gunfight. A single granite stone marks the graves of gang members Bob and Grat Dalton and Bill Power in the Elmwood Cemetery (the fourth robber, Dick Broadwell, is buried in Hutchinson).

The story of the bank robbery and battle is told at the Dalton Defenders Museum, operated by the Coffeyville Historical Society just east of the plaza area. It contains artifacts and memorabilia from the raid, including the safe and doors from the First National Bank, doorframe from the Condon Bank vault, three of the bank robbers' revolvers, a cartridge belt, saddles, stolen moneybags, and a mural of the defenders. The museum also has exhibits about the early history of Coffeyville; presidential candidate Wendell Willkie, who lived and taught school in Coffeyville; and Walter Johnson, hall-of-fame pitcher of the Washington Senators in 1907–1927. The museum's annual attendance is 9,000.

Dalton Defenders Museum, 113 E. 8th St., Coffeyville, KS 67337-5803 (postal address: PO Box 843, Coffeyville, KS 67337-0843). E-mail: chamber@coffeyville.com. Website: www.daltondefendersmuseum.com. Hours: 10–4 Mon.–Sat., 1–4 Sun.; closed Easter, Thanksgiving, and Christmas. Admission: adults, $3; children 7–17, $1; children under 7, free.

John Dillinger

John Dillinger Museum. The John Dillinger Museum in Hammond, Indiana, is devoted to the life and times of the noted bank robber and other gangsters during the 1930s Depression era. The museum, located in the Indiana Welcome Center, uses Dillinger and other outlaws of the period as examples of what happens to people who engage in criminal activities.

Dillinger, who was called "Public Enemy No. 1" by the FBI, was known for his many bank robberies and daring jail escapes. He was born in Indianapolis in 1902 and killed by FBI agents in Chicago in 1934. The museum shows the many advances made in crime fighting during the first 30 years of the century. It contains interactive displays, life-size wax figures, and historical and educational exhibits, including the wooden gun Dillinger used in a jail escape and the trousers he wore when killed. The museum was opened in 1999 and recently renovated by the Lake County Convention and Visitors Bureau.

John Dillinger Museum, Indiana Welcome Center, 7770 Corinne Dr., Hammond, IN 16323. Phone: 219/989-7979. E-mail: info@dillingermuseum.com. Website: www.dillingermuseum.com. Hours: 10–3 daily. Admission: adults, $4; seniors, $3; children 6–12, $2; children under 6, free.

Jesse and Frank James

Jesse James Farm and Museum. The most famous Western outlaw in the nineteenth century was Jesse James. He and his brother, Frank, were part of the notorious James-Younger Gang, which originated with a group of Confederate "bushwhackers" who fought in the bitter partisan conflict in the divided state of Missouri during the Civil War. They were members of the notorious Quantrill's Riders, a rogue force that made raids on border towns in Kansas and Missouri during the war—often in retaliation to attacks by the Kansas Jayhawks and similar Union guerrilla groups. After the war, the James brothers formed a criminal gang that later included four Younger brothers and was known as the James-Younger Gang. They robbed banks, stagecoaches, and trains and killed those who resisted.

Jesse James was born in 1847 on a farm near Kearney, Missouri, that later became the Jesse James Farm and Museum. He was one of three children of Robert S. James, a commercial hemp farmer who also was a Baptist minister. He went to California during the gold rush to minister those searching for gold and died there when Jesse was three years old. Jesse had an older brother, Frank, and a younger sister, Susan. The farm had more than 100 acres and six slaves.

Jesse's mother, Zerelda, remarried twice. Her third husband was Dr. Reuben Samuel, who moved into the James home after their 1855 marriage. They had four children, acquired seven slaves, and grew tobacco in the region of Missouri that was known as "Little Dixie" because it was settled largely by slaveholders from the South who had migrated to the border state. Clay County, where the James farm was located, experienced great turmoil after the passage of the 1854 Kansas-Nebraska Act, which led to increasing violence between pro- and antislavery militias in Kansas.

When the Civil War broke out in 1861, the James-Samuel family sided with the Confederates. After the Union victory in the Battle of Pea Ridge, Missouri became the scene of intense guerrilla warfare with civilians being killed, prisoners executed, and some dead even being scalped. Frank James became a member of a local pro-Confederate bushwhacking group at the outset and in 1863 was identified as a guerrilla fighter. It resulted in the James-Samuel farm being raided by a Union militia force with Reuben Samuel being hung from a tree briefly and young Jesse being lashed.

Frank and Jesse then joined Quantrill's Raiders, one of the most violent guerrilla groups, formed by William Clarke Quantrill. It was Quantrill who organized the 1863 massacre of Lawrence, Kansas, in which a quarter of the town's buildings were burned and at least 150 people killed.

Frank James joined the Quantrill's Raiders in 1863 and is believed to have taken part in the raid on the abolitionists' center of Lawrence. Jesse James joined him in 1864 when he returned to Clay County. Jesse suffered a serious chest wound that summer but recovered and took part in the Centralia Massacre in which about 22 unarmed Union troops were killed or wounded, with some being scalped and dismembered.

As a result of the James brothers' and other raids during the Civil War, Union military authorities made their family leave Clay County. Frank James followed Quantrill into Kentucky, and Jesse went to Texas with his bushwhacker group. On the way home as the war was ending, Jesse was shot in the chest when he tried to surrender to a Union cavalry patrol near Lexington, Missouri. But he recovered once again from a life-threatening wound. He went to his uncle's home, where he was tended to by his first cousin, Zerelda Mimms. It began a nine-year courtship that culminated in marriage in 1874.

After the Civil War, Jesse and Frank James reportedly continued to be members of their bushwhacker gang commanded by Archie Clement, which began robbing Republican-owned banks, committing the nation's first daylight peacetime armed bank robbery. It occurred at the Clay County Savings Association in Liberty, Missouri, in 1866, during which an innocent bystander was killed. When Clements later was killed, the gang survivors continued to conduct bank robberies for two years, but it is uncertain whether the James brothers were involved.

The first time Jesse James was publicly called an outlaw was in 1869 after the bank robbery and shooting death at the Daviess County Savings Association in Gallatin, Missouri. He shot the cashier in a mistaken self-proclaimed revenge slaying. It also was about this time when the James and Younger gangs merged to form the James-Younger Gang, which included the two James brothers; four Younger brothers (Cole, Jim, John, and Bob); and other former

Confederate bushwhackers. They robbed banks, stagecoaches, and railroads from Iowa to Texas and from Kansas to West Virginia.

The James-Younger Gang came to an end in 1876 when the gang attempted to rob the First National Bank of Northfield, Minnesota. Only Jesse and Frank James were alive and free after the raid. The robbery was delayed when the acting cashier told three bank robbers that he could not open the bank safe, falsely claiming that it was secured by a time lock. Meanwhile, Northfield townspeople raised the alarm when they grew suspicious of the two gunmen at the bank entrance and three others at a bridge across the adjacent square. In the shootout that followed, two of the outside robbers were killed and the other three were wounded, and the other gang members escaped. The bank robbers killed two people. The Younger brothers later were captured and another bandit killed by the militia, leaving only the James brothers.

Jesse and Frank James resurfaced in Nashville, Tennessee, under assumed names later in 1876. Jesse organized a new gang in 1879 and began a series of train and other robberies. But the gang soon turned against each other or were captured. Jesse grew paranoid and killed one gang member and frightened off another. In 1881 the brothers returned to Missouri.

Jesse rented a house in St. Joseph, while Frank moved to Virginia. Frank held several obscure jobs and teamed with Cole Younger in a Wild West show before he died in Kearney in 1915. Jesse asked Charley and Bob Ford to move in with him and his family as protection in St. Joseph.

Charley Ford was a former gang member, but his brother was a new recruit who secretly had been negotiated with Missouri Governor Thomas T. Crittenden about a reward for James. On April 3, 1882, Bob Ford killed Jesse by shooting him in the back of the head in the house (*see* Jesse James Home Museum listing). After collecting some of the reward, the Ford brothers left St. Joseph. Charley committed suicide in 1884 in Richmond, Missouri, and Bob was killed in 1892 in a tent saloon he operated in Creede, Colorado.

The James house in St. Joseph now is the Jesse James Home Museum, while the James family home near Kearney is the Jessie James Farm and Museum. The family farm was purchased by Clay County in 1978 from Jesse's grandchildren. The farmhouse consists of two parts—the original 1822 two-room log cabin and two mail-order rooms that the James family attached at the front. It also has an attic where the children slept and Jesse and Frank may have hid at times. The house has been restored and now looks like it did in the mid-nineteenth century. The house contains some of the family's personal belongings and furnishings, including the bed in which Jesse was born. Guided tours are given of the house.

The historic site also has Jesse's original grave (he later was reburied in the Mt. Olivet Cemetery in Kearney), a restored slave cabin, and a visitor center. The visitor center contains three exhibit galleries with memorabilia and artifacts, such as guns, boots, letters, and personal documents. The center also has a short film on the James brothers and their gang. Annual attendance is 12,000.

Jesse James Farm and Museum, 21216 Jesse James Farm Rd., Kearney, MO 64060-9343. Phone: 816/628-6065. Fax: 816/628-6676. Website: www.jessejames.org. Hours: May–Sept.—9–4 daily; Oct.–Apr.—9–4 Mon.–Fri., 12–4 Sat.–Sun.; closed New Year's Day, Thanksgiving, and Christmas. Admission: adults, $8; seniors, $7; children 8–15, $4.50; children under 8, free.

Jesse James Home Museum. The house in St. Joseph, Missouri, where outlaw Jesse James was living and killed in 1882 is now the Jesse James Home Museum, which is devoted to his life and death. The 34-year-old James, who had a wife and two children, rented the home after a career of bank, stagecoach, and train robberies and murders with his brother Frank and the Younger brothers (*see* Jessie James Farm and Museums listing). He was gunned down in the living room of the house for a bounty by an outlaw he had befriended.

Jesse rented a modest house under the assumed name of Tom Howard at 1318 Lafayette Street and asked Charley Ford, a former gang member, and his brother, Bob Ford, who was new to the gang, to move in with them. The Fords agreed, but Bob Ford also was negotiating with Governor Thomas T. Crittenden to bring in James and collect a reward of $10,000.

On April 3, 1882, James was killed by Ford as Jesse and the Fords were preparing to leave the house for a robbery. It occurred when James noticed a picture that needed straightening on the wall of the living room, took off his coat and gun, and stood on a chair to fix the picture. Bob Ford then shot him in the back of the head, killing James after 16 years as a criminal.

The murder of Jesse James and succeeding events made national headlines. Bob Ford wired the governor to claim the bounty. When the brothers surrendered to authorities, they were surprised to find they were charged with first degree murder. But in a single day, they were indicted, pleaded guilty, sentenced to death by hanging, and granted a full pardon by the governor, who may have known that the Ford brothers intended to kill James rather than bring him in alive.

The Fords left St. Joseph after receiving a small portion of the reward money and later starred in a reenactment of the shooting in a touring stage show. Charley Ford, who suffered from tuberculosis and a morphine addiction, committed suicide in Richmond, Missouri, in 1884. Bob Ford was shotgunned to death in his tent saloon in Creede, Colorado, in 1892.

The 1879 James house originally was located on a hill about two blocks north of its present site. In 1939 it was moved to the Belt Highway and on the grounds of the Patee House Museum, which formerly was the World's Hotel. Mr. and Mrs. Robert Keatley purchased the James house in 1977 and donated it to the Pony Express Historical Association. The house contains the James family furnishings, the bullet hole in the wall, and artifacts from James's grave, which was exhumed in 1995 for DNA tests. The latter include the coffin handles, a small tie pin James was wearing the day he was killed, a bullet removed from the lung area, and a casting of his skull that shows the bullet hole behind his right ear. Annual attendance is 18,000.

Jesse James Home Museum, 1202 Penn St., St. Joseph, MO 64503 (postal address: PO Box 1022, St. Joseph, MO 64502-1022). Phone: 816/232-8206. Fax: 816/232-3717. Website: www.ponyexpressjessejames.com. Hours: Apr.–Oct.—10–5 Mon.–Sat., 1–5 Sun.; Nov.–Mar.—10–4 Sat., 1–4 Sun.; closed Mon.–Fri., New Year's Day, Easter, Thanksgiving, and Christmas. Admission: adults, $3; seniors, $2; students, $1.50; children under 6, free.

Jesse James Bank Museum. The Clay County Savings Association in Liberty, Missouri, was robbed and a young college student killed in 1866 by outlaws believed to have included Jesse and Frank James, but their participation never could be verified. The James brothers belonged to the Archie Clement Gang, which reportedly committed the robbery, before forming their own gang. It was the first successful daylight peacetime armed bank robbery in the United States.

The Jesse James Bank Museum, founded in 1966, is now located in the 1858 former bank building on Historic Square in Liberty. The bank has been restored to look like it did at the time of the robbery. It contains period furniture, the original bank vault, an early clock set to the time of the robbery, and documents and photographs related to the James brothers, who lived on a farm in nearby Kearney. The museum, which has an annual attendance of 4,400, is operated by the Clay County Department of Parks, Recreation, and Historic Sites.

The bank robbery is reenacted annually at a fall festival in Liberty. Other historical events take place along Main Street, known as the "Living History Street," including skirmishes, military drills, mini-melodramas, and other living history programs.

Jesse James Bank Museum, 103 N. Walter St., Liberty, MO 64968-1736. Phone: 816/736-8510. Fax: 816/628-6676. Website: www.claycogov.com. Hours: 10–4 Mon.–Sat.; closed Sun. and major holidays. Admission: adults, $5.50; seniors, $5; children 8–15, $3.50; children under 8, free.

Jean Lafitte

Jean Lafitte National Historical Park and Preserve. Jean Lafitte was a French pirate, smuggler, and privateer in the Gulf of Mexico who was captured, pardoned, and helped General Andrew Jackson defend New Orleans against the British in 1815. He then returned to attacking ships around Central American ports until he was killed while raiding Spanish ships in about 1823. The Jean Lafitte National Historical Park and Preserve in southeast of New Orleans, which was established to protect the rich natural and culture resources of Louisiana's Mississippi River Delta region, is named for the nineteenth-century pirate.

Not much is known about the background of Lafitte. It is believed that he was born either in France or the French colony of Saint-Domingue (now Haiti) about 1776. He claimed his birthplace was Bordeaux, France, in 1780, but he and his elder brother, Pierre, also said they were born in Bayonne. Other documents give the birth site as St. Malo and Brest, France; Orduna, Spain; and Westchester, New York. One Lafitte biographer believes Lafitte was born to French planters on Saint-Domingue, while another claims it was in France.

Lafitte, his brother, and his widowed mother migrated in 1784 to New Orleans in Louisiana, which was claimed by France. Lafitte lived with his mother and Pedro Aubry, a merchant she married, while his brother was raised by another family. By 1805 Pierre became a privateer, and Jean is believed to have operated a warehouse and helped his brother sell or trade merchandise taken from ships.

After the United States purchased Louisiana in 1803 and passed the Embargo Act of 1807, the warehouse and smuggling operations were moved to an island in Barataria Bay. By 1810 the operations were quite successful and Jean Lafitte also turned to piracy. But in 1814 American authorities raided the new site, captured most of the Lafitte's fleet, and arrested 80 people. Jean Lafitte offered to have his men assist inadequate American forces against the British, who were about to attack New Orleans, if they were pardoned. General Andrew Jackson agreed, and the experienced pirates and smugglers helped defeat the British in the 1815 Battle of New Orleans.

Later that year, the Lafitte brothers agreed to serve as spies for Spain in the Mexican War of Independence. Jean Lafitte was sent in 1817 to Galveston Island in Spanish Texas, where several revolutionaries were located. After his arrival, the revolutionaries left, and Lafitte developed the island into a smuggling base that he called "Campeebe." In 1818 the colony suffered two serious incidents. After Lafitte's men kidnapped a Karankara Indian woman, the warriors killed five men in the colony. Most of the men in the Karankara tribe were then killed by the colonists. It was followed by a hurricane that flooded the island and destroyed most of the ships and houses.

In 1821 the USS *Enterprise* was sent to the island to remove Lafitte and his men from the Gulf of Mexico after an American ship was attacked by the pirates. Lafitte agreed to leave but destroyed most of the fortress and settlement. He and his men moved to Cuba and opened a new base but were forced to leave. Lafitte then went to Columbia, where he was welcomed, given a commission and a ship, and for the first time could legally confront Spanish ships. But in 1823 he was wounded and died in a battle with two Spanish ships and buried at sea.

The 20,020-acre Jean Lafitte National Historical Park and Preserve was founded in southern Louisiana in 1978 and named for the early nineteenth-century pirate. The park/preserve protects examples of the rich natural and cultural resources in the delta region. The park consists of six physically separate sites and a park headquarters. Three of the sites interpret the Cajun culture of the Lafayette area, which was developed after Acadians were re-settled in the region by the British after expulsion from Canada in the eighteenth century.

The other sections are the 23,000-acre Barataria Preserve (in Marrero), which focuses on the natural and cultural history of the region; the Chalmette Battlefield and National Cemetery (in Chalmette), which includes the Battle of New Orleans site, an education center, and a visitor center with a film and exhibits; and the French Quarter (in New Orleans), with a visitor center that interprets the history of New Orleans, the French Quarter, and the diverse cultures of Louisiana's Mississippi Delta region. The park headquarters is also located in New Orleans. Annual attendance is 391,000.

Jean Lafitte National Historical Park and Preserve, 419 Decatur St., New Orleans, LA 70130-1035. Phone: 504/589-3882. Fax: 504/589-3851. E-mail: kathy_lang@nps.gov. Website: www.nps.gov/jela. Hours: 9–5 daily; closed New Year's Day, Mardi Gras, and Christmas. Admission: free.

Bonnie Parker and Clyde Barrow

Bonnie and Clyde Ambush Museum. Bonnie Parker and Clyde Barrow were outlaws and lovers who robbed gas stations, stole cars, and killed policemen in the early 1930s. On May 23, 1934, they were killed on a country road eight miles from Gibsland, Louisiana, by six sheriff's deputies who fired 130 rounds into the car they were driving. The story of their rise and fall now is told in a storefront museum called the Bonnie and Clyde Ambush Museum in Gibsland.

The museum, which opened in 2005, is located in the building that formerly housed Ma Canfield's Café, the last place Bonnie and Clyde stopped before the shooting. They bought two sandwiches to go, the remains of which were found in the car after the gun battle. The museum contains some of the guns seized, swatches of Clyde's pants, Bonnie's red tam, glass from the windshield of their car, rare photographs and films, and the riddled replica car used in the 1967 *Bonnie and Clyde* film (which starred Faye Dunaway and Warren Beatty). The museum is managed by L. J. "Boots" Hinton, son of one of the deputies who participated in the 1934 shooting. Every May, a Bonnie and Clyde Festival is held in Gibsland, which features a reenactment of the death of the outlaws.

Bonnie and Clyde Ambush Museum, 2419 Main St., Gibsland, LA 71028 (postal address: PO Box 39, Gibsland, LA 71028). Phone: 318/843-1934. Website: www.bonnieandclydemuseum.com. Hours: 10–6 Sun.–Tues. and Thurs.–Fri., 12–5 Sat.; closed Wed. Admission: adults, $7; seniors, military, and children 5–12, $5; children under 5, free.

Pancho Villa

Pancho Villa State Park. Pancho Villa State Park in Columbus, New Mexico, is where guerrillas of the 1910–1920 Mexican Revolution under General Francisco "Pancho" Villa attacked and burned a small border town and military outpost and killed 18 Americans in 1916. The reason for the raid is not known, but it is believed the attack was made because of United States recognition of Villa's political opponent as Mexico's president or Villa's need for military equipment and supplies. The Columbus attack resulted in General John J. Pershing and 5,000 American troops searching in vain for Villa and his raiders in an 11-month punitive expedition in Mexico.

American forces never found Villa or his followers and were called back with the outbreak of World War I after going 400 miles into Mexico and reaching the southern city of Parral. It was the last true cavalry action by the U.S. Army—and the first time the army used mechanized vehicles, including automobiles, trucks, and airplanes, in a military operation. The 1916–1917 Mexican experience proved invaluable to General Pershing in World War I, and Villa was assassinated in 1923 after retiring in 1920.

Villa was born in 1878 as José Doroteo Arango Arámbula to Agustin Arango and Micaela Arámula at the Rancho of the Coyotada in San Juan del Rio, Mexico. He was the oldest of five children and helped his mother care for his siblings after his father died. He attended a local church-run school but dropped out after his father's death. At the age of 16, Villa moved to Chihuahua but then reportedly returned to Durango and shot and killed the owner of the hacienda, who had raped his sister. He then became a member of an outlaw gang headed by Ignacio Parra, one of Mexico's most famous bandits at the time.

In 1902 Villa was arrested for stealing mules and assault. He escaped a death sentence because of his connections to a powerful politician to whom Villa sold his stolen animals. Instead, he was forced to join the Mexican Army. But he fled after killing an army officer and stealing his horse in 1903 and became a bandit known as Francisco "Pancho" Villa. After the Mexican Revolution began in 1910, Villa joined the prodemocracy movement and helped to drive dictator Porfirio Diaz into exile.

When one of President Francisco I. Madero's military commanders started a counter rebellion, against Madero, Villa and his mounted cavalry fought with General Victoriano Huerta to support Madero. Huerta later saw Villa as an ambitious competitor and accused him of stealing a horse and insubordination. He sought to execute Villa, but the sentence was commuted to imprisonment by Madero. Villa then escaped from jail. After crushing the rebellion, Huerta conspired to assassinate Madero and proclaim himself provisional president. He was opposed by Venusiano Carranza, whose army—including Villa's forces—forced Huerta into exile in 1914.

Carranza became provisional president of Mexico, and Villa was made provisional governor of the state of Chihuahua in northern Mexico. Villa's guerrilla militia became the most powerful and feared military unit in Mexico. Villa and his supporters seized hacienda land and distributed it to peasants and soldiers. He also had the wealthy pay for the salaries, clothing, and food of his militia; printed fiat money that had to be accepted as currency; confiscated gold from some banks; and robbed and commandeered trains. Villa's rule in Chihuahua came to an end after two years when he tried to replace Carranza as provisional president and his forces were defeated in three major battles.

Carranza became the president of Mexico in 1915. Villa continued to oppose his leadership, but he no longer had an army. He went back to being a guerrilla leader in the mountains of Chihuahua who made small-scale raids. When Carranza was assassinated in 1920, Villa sought amnesty from the interim president, Jose de la Luz Herrera, who met with Villa and agreed to pay him to "retire." Villa was given a 25,000-acre hacienda in Canutillo, Chihuahua, and 50 guerrillas who remained in his cavalry were allowed to serve as his personal guards. In addition, 200 guerrillas and veterans of Villa's militia were given 500,000 gold pesos in pensions and permitted to live at the hacienda.

Villa met his death in 1923 when he and two of his bodyguards were killed by seven assassins, who fired over 40 shots as he was driving to his hacienda from a bank in Parral. The assassination was the result of a conspiracy by Villa opponents. Villa became a revolutionary hero in Mexico's history.

Villa was 45 when he died. He was married in 1911 to Maria Luz Corral. They had one child, a daughter who died shortly after birth, but his wife also took care of the other children fathered by Villa through his various extramarital affairs. After Villa's death, five other women also claimed to be his widow.

The Pancho Villa State Park is located where Camp Furlong, the small military outpost in Columbus, was when attacked by Villa's raiders in 1916. The camp was closed in 1926, but two adobe structures and the customs house and recreation hall still remain. Some of the buildings in town also survived, including the railroad depot and Hoover Hotel. The 1902 customs house now serves as a visitor center for the park, which also has a new 7,000-square-foot museum with exhibits about Villa, his 1916 raid, and Pershing's Mexican expedition. Among the objects on display are artifacts, military weapons, a 1916 Dodge touring car, and a replica of a Curtiss JN-3 Jenny airplane. The 60-acre park also has botanical gardens, walking paths, campgrounds, and picnic facilities.

Pancho Villa State Park, Hwys. 9 and 11, Columbus, NM 88029 (postal address: PO Box 450, Columbus, NM 88029-0450). Phone: 575/531-2711. Fax: 505/531-2115. E-mail: victor.trujillo@state.nm.us. Website: www.columbusnewmexico.com. Hours: 8–5 daily. Admission: $5 per vehicle.

PATRIOTIC FIGURES

Ethan Allen

See Military Figures section.

Nathan Hale

Nathan Hale Homestead Museum. Captain Nathan Hale was an officer in the Continental Army who was captured and hanged by the British while gathering information on their operations on Long Island in 1776 during the American Revolutionary War. His last words were said to be, "I only regret that I have but one life to lose for my country." The body of the 21-year-old, who was on assignment for General George Washington, never was returned or found.

The Nathan Hale Homestead Museum in Coventry, Connecticut, now honors Hale as a military hero. Despite the name of the site, Hale never lived in the house. He was born in 1755 and lived in a house at the same farm site that was razed by his parents to build a larger Georgian-style home for their family in 1776. The family did not move in until a month after Nathan's death.

Nathan, who was a graduate of Yale University and taught school for two years before entering the army, was the son of the Rev. Deacon Richard Hale, a prosperous livestock farmer and minister. It was a patriotic family, with six of the eight Hale sons serving in the Continental Army (three of whom died from war wounds). The house, which was home to 12 to 20 people at various times, was sold by the Hale family in the 1820s, but it has remained virtually intact.

The Hale house museum resulted initially from the efforts of George Dudley Seymour, a New Haven lawyer. When he learned the old Hale farm was for sale and needed repairs, he purchased the property in 1914, restored the farmhouse, and furnished it with Connecticut antiques and artifacts. He also bought the Strong-Porter House, home of Nathan's grandmother, across the road from the Hale farm. Both are now listed on the National Register of Historic Places. In the 1940s Seymour deeded the former Hale property to Connecticut Landmarks, which established the museum in 1948.

The farmhouse, outbuildings, and stone walls, as well as what remains of the original 400 acres of farm fields, now compose the historic site, which is surrounded by the Nathan Hale State Forest. The house contains Hale family and period furniture. A barn behind the house has a small statue of Nathan Hale and a short video on his life and contributions to the revolution. The site also has an eighteenth-century demonstration garden, living history and hearth cooking programs, horseback riding, hands-on activities, nature trails, summer camp program, and guided tours. Annual attendance is 8,000. Coventry also has a 45-foot Greek revival obelisk built in 1846 that honors Nathan Hale.

Nathan Hale Homestead Museum, 2299 South St., Coventry, CT 06238 (postal address: PO Box 760, Coventry, CT 06238-0760). Phone: 860/742-6917. E-mail: hale@ctlandmarks.org. Website: www.ctlandmarks.org/index.php?page=nathan-hale-homestead. Hours: Memorial Day weekend—12–4 Sat., 11–4 Sun.; June–Aug.—12–4 Wed.–Sat., 11–4 Sun.; Sept.–Oct.—12–4 Fri.–Sat., 11–4 Sun.; closed Nov.–late May. Admission: adults, $7; seniors, $6; students, $4; children under 6, free.

Patrick Henry

Red Hill Patrick Henry National Memorial. Patrick Henry was an American Revolution leader and orator who led the independence movement in Virginia in the 1770s. He headed the opposition to the Stamp Act of 1765 and is best known for his 1775 "Give me Liberty, or give me Death" speech calling for military resistance to British rule in the colonies. He was considered, along with Samuel Adams and Thomas Paine, one of the most influential exponents of the American Revolution and independence. Henry's life and contributions are now celebrated at the Red Hill Patrick Henry National Memorial, located at his last home and burial place near Brookneal, Virginia.

Henry was a successful Virginia lawyer who became an effective politician and the "voice of the American Revolution." He introduced radical resolutions in the Virginia House of Burgesses opposing King George III's Stamp Act of 1765, saying, "If this be treason, make the most of it"; initiated the intercolonial committee of correspondence with Thomas Jefferson and Richard Henry Lee in 1773; was a member of the Continental Congress in 1774–1776 and a Founding Father of the United States; served as governor of Virginia for five terms in 1776–1779 and 1784–1786; spoke out against the proposed United States Constitution in 1788 because he feared it adversely affected the rights of states and the freedom of individuals; and served as a member of Virginia's legislature for 25 years before retiring in 1790.

Henry was born on a Studley plantation near Hanover, Virginia, in 1736. He was the son of John Henry, a Scottish-born planter, and Sara Winston Syne, a young widow from a prominent gentry family. He attended a local school for a few years but received most of his formal education from his father, who had attended King's College in Aberdeen. At the age of 15, he worked briefly as a clerk for a local merchant and then opened a store with his older brother, William, that failed. When he became 18, he married 16-year-old Sara Shelton, whose dowry included a 600-acre farm, a house, and six slaves. A fire destroyed their house in 1757, followed by a second attempt at storekeeping that failed.

Henry then began reading law while helping his father-in-law at a tavern located across the road from the county courthouse in Hanover. By 1760 he decided to become a lawyer. Although self-taught and barely prepared, he was able to convince a review panel to admit him to the bar. He established a thriving practice, with his political career beginning in 1763 with the Parsons' Cause case. At that time in the tobacco-based economy in Virginia, clergymen of the established Anglican church and public officials received an annual salary in tobacco, with 16,000 pounds per year going to clergymen. When the market price of tobacco was reduced from two cents to one cent, a parson brought suit against the vestry for back pay and won. Henry was asked to appeal. In a dramatic oration, he criticized the clergy and challenged British authority, and the jury granted only token damages of one penny in a popular decision. Two years later, Henry was elected to Virginia's House of Burgesses.

Henry retired from the state's legislature in 1790 and moved to the Red Hill plantation—now known as the Red Hill Patrick Henry National Memorial—along the Staunton River near Brookneal in 1794 as his health was declining. He continued to practice law from a law office on the grounds but died at the age of 63 five years later. The site has seven historic buildings and a cemetery where he is buried with his second wife, Dorothea Dandridge Henry, and other family members.

Red Hill has the world's largest collection of Patrick Henry memorabilia, including Peter Frederick Rothermel's painting *Patrick Henry before the Virginia House of Burgesses*. The home, which has been reconstructed on the original site, is a simple one-and-a-half-story house with eighteenth-century period furnishings. The site also has Henry family furniture, jewelry, musical instruments, paintings, law books, and other memorabilia, as well as a 15-minute video on Henry's life and career. In addition to guided tours, the memorial has special exhibitions, living history demonstrations, lectures, and such annual events as Revolutionary War–era reenactments and a Living History Day for school children. Annual memorial attendance is over 9,000.

Red Hill Patrick Henry National Memorial, 1250 Red Hill Rd., Brookneal, VA 24528-3302. Phone: 434/376-2044. Fax: 434/376-2647. E-mail: redhill@redhill.org. Website: www.redhill.org. Hours: Apr.–Oct.—9–5 Mon.–Sat., 1–5 Sun.; Nov.–Mar.—9–4 Tues.–Sat., 1–4 Sun., Mon. by appointment; closed New Year's Day, Thanksgiving, and Christmas. Admission: adults, $6; children, $2.

Thomas Paine

Thomas Paine Memorial Museum. Thomas Paine was a political philosopher and author who wrote two of the most widely read and influential works during the 1770s–1780s revolutionary period in the United States—*Common Sense*, a 1776 pamphlet urging immediate declaration of independence, and *Crisis*, a periodical series of 16 issues in 1776–1783 that upheld the Colonial cause and rallied the army during the American Revolutionary War. His writings inspired passion—and frequently action and sometimes criticism. John Adams, second president of the United States, reportedly said, "Without the pen of the author of *Common Sense*, the sword of Washington would have been raised in vain."

Paine was an Englishman born in Thetford in the county of Norfolk in 1737 who emigrated to the American colonies in 1774 and supported the cause of the colonies. His father was a corsetiere who had great hopes for his son, but Thomas failed at school and as an apprentice. They were followed by going to sea briefly and working as a tax officer, during which time he wrote *The Case of the Officers of Excise*, making the argument for a pay raise for tax workers in 1774. It was the same year that he met Benjamin Franklin in London, which resulted in Franklin helping him immigrate to Philadelphia.

In 1776, Paine published *Common Sense* and joined the Continental Army when the Revolutionary War began. He spent most of the war years traveling with the army and writing the popular *Crisis* pamphlets. After the war, he returned to Europe and pursued other ventures. He even worked on a smokeless candle and an iron bridge. It also was a period when he wrote some of his most famous works—*The Rights of Man* and *The Age of Reason*.

The Rights of Man, which was written in 1791–1792 in response to criticism of the French Revolution, caused Paine to be called an outlaw in England for his anti-monarchist views. He would have been arrested if he did not flee to France. But in 1793, he was imprisoned in France for not endorsing the execution of Louis XVI. That is when he wrote and distributed the first part of *The Age of Reason*, Paine's anti-church and most famous work at the time. He was freed in 1794 with the assistance of James Monroe, who was America's minister to France.

Paine remained in France until 1802, when he returned to the United States after receiving an invitation by President Thomas Jefferson. But he found that his contributions to the American Revolution were virtually eradicated because of his religious views. He was ridiculed by the public and abandoned by his friends. Paine lived from 1802 until his death in 1809 at the age of 72 in a two-story frame house on a 320-acre farm in New

Rochelle, New York. The farm was given to him by the State of New York legislature in 1784 for his assistance during the Revolutionary War. The site now is called the Thomas Paine Cottage (*see* separate listing). The cottage has been owned by the 1886 Huguenot and New Rochelle Historical Association and operated as a historic house museum since 1910.

The other Paine museum in New Rochelle is the Thomas Paine Memorial Museum, built by the Thomas Paine National Historical Association in 1925–1926 on the edge of what originally was Paine's farm, reduced to 277 acres. It is adjacent to the Thomas Paine Cottage, an outdoor marble monument, and an 1881 bronze bust of Paine. The Paine association originally was founded in 1784 in New York City to commemorate the life and public service of Paine. The museum is devoted to Paine's life and career and features his collections and the Hufeland Library with his and other books.

Thomas Paine Memorial Museum, 983 North Ave., New Rochelle, NY 10804. Phone: 914/632-5376. Hours: Apr.–Oct.—2–5 Fri.–Sat. and by appointment; closed Sun.–Thurs., Nov.–Mar., and major holidays. Admission: free.

Thomas Paine Cottage. Thomas Paine, who wrote inspiring works and became a hero during the American Revolutionary War, lived in the Thomas Paine Cottage in New Rochelle, New York, from 1802 until his death in 1809. It now is a historic house museum honoring the English political philosopher and writer.

Paine, who was born in Thetford, England, in 1737, immigrated to the American colonies in 1774 and wrote the powerful *Common Sense*, a prorevolutionary pamphlet, in 1776 and the 16-part *Crisis* periodical series, which helped inspire the army. He served in the Continental Army and later returned to Europe and produced two of his most famous writings—*The Rights of Man* and *The Age of Reason*.

Paine then returned to the United States in 1802 and settled on a 320-acre farm (later 277 acres) in New Rochelle, which the New York legislature had given him in 1784 for his services during the Revolutionary War. Paine's first house was destroyed in a fire in 1793 and replaced with the current two-story frame saltbox structure. The house also had an addition in 1804, and Greek revival–style pillars were added in 1830. The Huguenot and New Rochelle Historical Association acquired the house in 1886, moved it 440 yards to its present location in 1908, and opened it as a historic house museum in 1910.

Paine originally was buried near the cottage and monument in 1809 after dying in Greenwich Village in New York City. In 1819 William Cobbett, an English radical, moved the remains to England to build a larger monument, but he died and the Paine's remains disappeared. Dr. Moncure D. Conway claimed to have recovered a portion of Paine's brain around 1905, and it was buried under the monument although never authenticated.

The Thomas Paine Cottage, a National Historic Landmark and listed on the National Register of Historic Places, is located on the last two acres of original 320 acres given to Paine. It is furnished in late eighteenth- and early nineteenth-century style. The museum traces Paine's life and career and contains a chair he owned and a cast-iron Franklin stove presented to him by the inventor. It also has exhibits on the history of New Rochelle, the local Siwanoy Indians, and the Huguenots. In addition, the Sophia Brewster One-Room Schoolhouse, the oldest private school in New Rochelle, has been moved to the site, where an interpreter in period clothing presents programs for school groups.

Thomas Paine Cottage, 20 Sicard Ave., New Rochelle, NY 10804. Phone: 914/633-1776. E-mail: painecottage@optonline.net. Website: www.thomaspainecottage.org. Hours: 10–5 Tues., Thurs., and Sat.–Sun.; 2–5 Fri.; closed Mon., Wed., and major holidays. Admission: suggested donations—adults, $3; children, $2.

Paul Revere

Paul Revere House. Paul Revere was a Boston silversmith during the American Revolution whose 1775 midnight ride alerted the colonial militia of approaching British forces before the battles of Lexington and Concord. The horseback ride became a legendary part of American history when dramatized in Henry Wadsworth Longfellow's poem "Paul Revere's Ride," published in 1861. The poem, which appeared in *Atlantic Monthly* magazine, transformed Revere from a relatively obscure figure in American history into a national folk hero.

Although largely known for his famous ride, Revere had a long and productive life. He was born in 1734 in Boston's North End, the son of Apollos Rivoire (later changed to Paul Revere), a French Huguenot immigrant, and Deborah Hichborn, daughter of a local artisan family. He was the eldest son of nine children and learned the art of gold and silversmithing from his father. When he was 19, his father died and he became the family's main source of income. Revere got his first experience in warfare two years later when he volunteered to fight in the French and Indiana War and served as a second lieutenant in the colonial artillery.

Revere became a prosperous and prominent goldsmith/silversmith who initially supplemented his income by working as a copper plate engraver and a dentist. He became involved in the American Revolution by providing information about British troop movements in the area, and then as a courier to the Continental Congress in Philadelphia and spreading word of the Boston Tea Party to New York and Philadelphia. On the night of April 18, 1775, he made his historic ride after receiving instructions from Dr. Joseph Warren to go to Lexington to warn John Hancock and Samuel Adams of the British approach.

When the war erupted, Revere served as a lieutenant colonel in the Massachusetts State Train of Artillery and commander of Castle Island in Boston. But his troops saw little action. They did participate in minor expeditions to Newport and Worcester, and there was a failed Penobscot expedition. After the war, Revere expanded his business interests. He also imported goods from England, ran a small hardware store, and opened a foundry that supplied equipment for shipyards, produced cannons, and cast bells. He also opened the first copper rolling mill, which became Revere Copper and Brass Inc.

Revere retired in 1811, leaving the cooper business to his sons and grandsons, and died of natural causes at the age of 83 in 1818. He was married twice and had 16 children—eight by his first wife, Sarah Orne, whom he married in 1757 and had died in 1773, and eight more by his second wife, Rachel Walker. The Revere home was built about 1680 and purchased by Revere in 1770 and sold in 1800. The house, now the oldest building in downtown Boston and a National Historic Landmark, became one of the earliest historic house museums in the nation in 1908.

The Paul Revere House, which is operated by the Revere Memorial Association, has a late seventeenth-century appearance. It features period furnishings that belonged to the Revere family and contains such items as Revere engravings, documents, silver, and other family items and memorabilia. It also has illustrated panels about Revere and the house, and the courtyard has a 900-pound bell, a small mortar, and a bolt from the USS *Constitution*, which were made by Paul Revere & Sons. Annual attendance is nearly 265,000.

Paul Revere House, 17 North Sq., Boston, MA 02113-2405. Phone: 617/523-2338. Fax: 617/523-1775. E-mail: staff@paulreverehouse.org. Website: www.paulreverehouse.org. Hours: Apr. 15–Oct.—9:30–5:15 daily; Nov.–Apr. 14—9:30–4:15 daily; closed Mon. in Jan.–Mar., New Year's Day, Thanksgiving, and Christmas. Admission: adults, $3.50; seniors and college students, $3; children 5–17, $1; children under 5, free.

Betsy Ross

Betsy Ross House. Controversy still continues over whether seamstress Betsy Ross designed and made the nation's first flag—and whether it took place in the historic house museum known as the Betsy Ross House in Philadelphia, Pennsylvania. But one thing is certain—many people do believe it, and over 315,000 people come every year to learn more about her and the house, which has become a major tourist attraction.

It is believed that Betsy Ross made the first American flag in 1776 and lived in the small house adjacent to Independence National Historical Park and located near Independence Hall and the Liberty Bell. Several surviving family members have said so, but there is no concrete evidence, and historians still debate her role and whether the flag was made in the house.

Georgian-style house in Philadelphia, where Betsy Ross is believed to have made the nation's first flag in 1776. Courtesy of the Betsy Ross House; photograph by George Widman.

The American Revolutionary War created many widows. Betsy Ross was one of them, ultimately losing three husbands. But her skills as a seamstress and furniture upholsterer enabled her to support herself and her seven children. It is believed that she made the flag after meeting with the Continental Congress's three-man Flag Committee, consisting of George Washington, who sat next to her in church and for whom she did some work; George Ross, a prominent jurist and relative; and Robert Morris, a leading colonial financier and politician. But others may have been involved in the design and production of the flag. She also lived in a number of different houses, and the Georgian-style historic house reportedly was one of them.

Betsy Ross was born Elizabeth Griscom, the eighth of 17 children of Quaker parents, in Philadelphia in 1752. She learned to sew from her great aunt, went to a Quaker public school, and was apprenticed to an upholsterer. She fell in love with John Ross, a fellow apprentice, and they eloped in 1773. The marriage caused a split from her Quaker family and resulted in her expulsion from the Society of Friends congregation. The couple started their own upholstery business and joined Christ Church, where she met Washington. When the Revolutionary War began, Ross was killed by a gunpowder explosion while guarding munitions as a member of the local militia.

During the war, Betsy Ross continued to work in the upholstery business, including repairing uniforms and making tents and blankets. In 1777 she married her second husband, mariner Joseph Ashburn. His ship was captured by a British frigate in 1780, and he was imprisoned in a jail and died of an unknown illness. Her third husband was John Claypoole, an old friend whom she convinced to give up the life of the sea to help with upholstery. They married in 1783, and he died in 1817 after two decades of poor health.

Betsy Ross continued the upholstery business for 10 more years before retiring and moving in with one of her daughters. She was completely blind by then and died in her sleep at the age of 84 in 1836. She and Claypoole are buried in the courtyard of the historic house museum.

The Betsy Ross House is believed to be where she lived with her first husband, John Ross, from 1773 until his death in 1776. The Georgian-style house was built around 1740, with the stair hall and the rear sections added 10 to 20 years later. The structure is a variation of a "bandbox" style house, with one room on each floor and a winding staircase from the cellar to the upper levels. The house served as a business and a residence for many different storekeepers and artisans for more than 150 years.

The house was restored in 1937 with funding from radio mogul A. Atwater Kent, who also purchased two adjacent properties to develop a civic garden. In 1941 the property was given to the City of Philadelphia, which added an annex building in 1966, and the courtyard was renovated and a fountain added in 1974. Historic Philadelphia Inc. has managed the historic site since 1995.

The house is furnished in the period that Ross is said to have lived there. It has seven rooms, including a parlor, kitchen, bedrooms, and an upholstery shop. They contain period antiques, eighteenth-century reproductions, and objects that belonged to Betsy Ross and her family, such as her walnut chest-on-chest, Chippendale and Sheraton side chairs, quilted petticoat, eyeglasses, and Bible. A costumed Betsy Ross and other historical storytellers often greet visitors in the courtyard. The house also is the site of concerts, playlets, and Flag and Independence Day observances each year. Annual attendance is 315,000.

Betsy Ross House, 239 Arch St., Philadelphia, PA 19106-1999. Phone: 215/686-1252. Fax: 215/686-1256. E-mail: lisa@betsyrosshouse.org. Website: www.betsyrosshouse.org. Hours: Apr.–mid-Oct.— 10 5 daily; mid-Oct.–Mar.— 10–5 Tues.–Sun.; closed Mon., Thanksgiving, Christmas, and New Year's Day. Admission: adults and seniors, $3; students and children, $2.

John Philip Sousa

See Musicians/Singers/Composers section.

PLAYWRIGHTS

(*See also* Authors/Writers section.)

George Ade

George Ade Memorial Museum. George Ade was a humorist, author, and playwright who reached prominence at the turn of the twentieth century. His former home in Brook, Indiana, is now a historic house museum. He was born in Kentland, Indiana, in 1866 and began his writing career as a newspaperman on the *Chicago Record* in 1890–1900.

In 1899 one of Ade's first books, *Fables in Slang,* was published. It was followed by such other books as *The Girl Proposition* (1902), *Breaking into Society* (1903), *Knocking the Neighbors* (1912), *Single Blessedness* (1922), and *The Old Time Saloon* (1931). While authoring books, he also was writing plays, such as *The Sultan of Sulu* (1902), *The County Chairman* (1903), *The College Widow* (1904), and *The Boys* (1907). Ade died in 1944.

The George Ade Memorial Association was founded in 1961 to honor the Indiana native in his former residence in Brook. The museum features exhibits, period furniture, mementos, artwork, and objects collected by Ade during his trips in the late nineteenth and early twentieth centuries.

George Ade Memorial Museum, Hwy. 16, Brook, IN 47922 (postal address: PO Box 221, Brook, IN 47922-0221). Phone: 219/275-6161. Hours: varies. Admission: free.

Sinclair Lewis

See Authors/Writers section.

Eugene O'Neill

Eugene O'Neill National Historic Site. Eugene O'Neill was one of America's greatest playwrights. He is the only American playwright to be awarded the Nobel Prize for Literature (in 1936), and he received the Pulitzer Prize for four plays—*Beyond the Horizon* (1920), *Anna Cristie* (1922), *Strange Interlude* (1928), and *Long Day's Journey into Night* (1957). In 1976 his secluded home in Danville, California, became the Eugene O'Neill National Historic Site.

O'Neill was born in New York City in 1988. In his early life (1907–1913), he was a seaman, wrote poetry, and was a reporter for the *New London Times*. He decided to devote himself to writing plays after being treated for tuberculosis in a sanatorium in 1912–1913. In the years that followed, O'Neill became a major force on the Broadway stage. His first performed play was *Bound East for Cardiff* in 1916, his first published play was *Beyond the Horizon* in 1920, and the first hit was *Emperor Jones* in 1921.

O'Neill wrote his final and some of his most memorable plays—*The Iceman Cometh, Long Day's Journey into Night,* and *A Moon for the Misbegotten*—at Tao House, the home in Danville where O'Neill and his wife, actress Carlotta Monterey, lived from 1937 to 1944. The house, located on a 13-acre site adjacent to the Las Trampas Regional Wilderness, was saved from demolition in the early 1970s by the Eugene O'Neill Foundation through several fundraising efforts. The house was designated a National Historic Landmark in 1971 and became a National Historic Site five years later. O'Neill, who had multiple health problems, died in 1953 at the age of 65 after being unable to write because of Parkinson-like tremors in his hands.

The house museum contains period furnishings, clothing, jewelry, paintings, manuscripts, letters, photographs, playbills, phonograph records, and autographed books. Special events sometimes include productions of O'Neill plays in an adjacent barn. The historic site has a private road, and visitor vehicles are not allowed. Access is only by advance reservations and guided tours. A free twice-daily free shuttle is provided from Danville Wednesdays through Sundays. Annual attendance is nearly 3,500.

Eugene O'Neill National Historic Site, Kuss Rd., Danville, CA 94526-0280 (postal address: PO Box 280, Danville, CA 94526-0280). Phones: 925/838-0249 and 925/943/1531. Fax: 925/838-9471. E-mail: euon_interpretation@nps.gov. Website: www.nps.gov/euon. Hours: tours—10 a.m. and 1:30 p.m. Wed.–Sun.; closed Mon.–Tues., New Year's Day, Thanksgiving, and Christmas. Admission: free shuttle and admission.

Monte Cristo Cottage. The 1840s Monte Cristo Cottage in New London, Connecticut, was the boyhood summer home of Eugene O'Neill from 1900 to 1917, when he began to support himself as a playwright. It now is a National Historic Landmark and a museum operated by the Eugene O'Neil Theater Center. The cottage is named for the dashing Edmund Dantes in *The Count of Monte Cristo*—the favorite role of the playwright's father, actor James O'Neill.

The cottage was restored and furnished in 1972 and renovated and reopened in 2005 based on Eugene O'Neill's autobiographical *Long Day's Journey Into Night.* It contains an extensive collection of artifacts and memorabilia, an O'Neill portrait and poster gallery, and an exhibit on the life and works of the playwright.

Monte Cristo Cottage, 325 Pequot Ave., New London, CT 06320. Phone: 860/443-5378, Ext. 285. Fax: 860/443-9853. Website: www.oneilltheatercenter.org/prog/monte/montprog.htm. Hours: Memorial Day–Labor Day—12–4 Thurs.–Sat., 1–3 Sun.; closed Mon.–Wed. and early Sept.–late May. Admission: adults, $7; seniors and students, $5.

William Shakespeare

Folger Shakespeare Library. William Shakespeare was a sixteenth- and seventeenth-century English poet and playwright considered the greatest writer of the English language and the preeminent dramatist. The world's most extensive collection of his printed works and the primary repository for rare materials from 1500 to 1750 are located at the Folger Shakespeare Library in Washington. The research library, which also functions as a museum, presents exhibitions, plays, music, poetry, lectures, family programs, publications, and national outreach services on Shakespeare education to classroom teachers, as well as advanced scholarly programs.

Shakespeare was born in 1564 in Stratford-upon-Avon, where he spent most of early life. He was the third child of eight of John Shakespeare, a successful glover and an alderman, and Mary Arden, daughter of an affluent land-owning farmer. He went to a free school with intense instruction in Latin grammar and the classics. He married Anne Hathaway at the age of 18 and had three children. It is not known exactly when he began writing, but it is believed to be in the mid-1580s.

Between 1585 and 1592, he began a successful career in London as an actor, writer, and part owner of a playing company. However, it was largely his later partnership in the famous Globe and Blackfriars theaters and other purchases and investments that made him a wealthy man at the turn of the century and enabled him to buy New Palace, the second largest house in Stratford, in 1597. He divided his time between London and Stratford and retired to Stratford around 1613 and died in 1616. His surviving works, including some collaborations, consist of about 38 plays, 154 sonnets, two long narrative poems, and several other poems, mostly produced between 1589 and 1613.

The Folger Shakespeare Library was founded in 1932 by Henry Clay Folger, president and then chairman of Standard Oil, an avid Shakespearean collector and an Amherst College graduate who left the library in trust with the college. It is located next to the Library of Congress on a site selected by Folger and his wife, Emily Jordan Folger, who worked with her husband on the Shakespearean collection. The white marble building, designed by architect Paul Philippe Cret, has nine street-level bas-reliefs of scenes from Shakespeare's plays, a statue of Puck, and many inscriptions selected by Henry Folger. It now is listed on the National Register of Historic Places. The grounds include an Elizabethan garden with plantings from Shakespeare's plays or that were commonly used at his time.

The Folger Shakespeare Library in Washington, DC. Courtesy of the Folger Shakespeare Library.

The library collection consists of more than 310,000 books, about 55,000 manuscripts (from Elizabeth I and John Donne to Mark Twain and Walt Whitman), 250,000 playbills, and 50,000 works on paper, including prints and photographs. It also has many paintings and sculptures that are mostly related to Shakespeare or his plays. The Folger is best known for its 82 copies of the 1623 Shakespeare First Folio and the many earlier quartos of his individual plays. In addition, the library has the world's third largest collection of English books and substantial holdings of continental and later English imprints. The library's cultural and arts programs include exhibitions, theater, poetry, concerts, and lectures. The annual attendance is 200,000.

Folger Shakespeare Library, 201 E. Capitol St., S.E., Washington, DC 20003-1094. Phone: 202/544-4600. Fax: 202/544-4623. E-mail: webmaster@folger.edu. Website: www.folger.edu. Hours: 10–5 Mon.–Sat.; closed Sun. and federal holidays. Admission: free.

Tennessee Williams

Tennessee Williams Birthplace. Tennessee Williams was a writer and playwright who wrote such award-wining plays as *A Streetcar Named Desire* (1947), *The Rose Tattoo* (1951), and *Cat on a Hot Tin Roof* (1955) and introduced the American theater to previously taboo subjects like homosexuality, nymphomania, castration, and cannibalism. He is regarded as one of the most accomplished playwrights of the English-language theater. Williams also wrote short stories, novels, poetry, essays, screenplays, and a volume of memoirs during his long career from the mid-1930s to 1983.

Williams was born as Thomas Lanier Williams III in Columbus, Mississippi, in 1911; had a younger brother and older sister; and grew up in a dysfunctional family. His father was a hard-drinking traveling shoe salesman with violent behavior; his mother sometimes was snobby, neurotic, and hysterical; and his sister developed emotional problems that later required institutional care. He also suffered from diphtheria as a child, which left him weak and confined to his house for recuperation and nearly ended his life.

When Williams was seven years old, the family moved to St. Louis when he father was promoted to a job at the home office of the shoe company. The family also moved frequently within the city as his father continued his heavy drinking and violent behavior and his socially conscious mother searched for what she considered an appropriate address. The family situation later influenced Williams's writings.

Williams showed promise in writing in high school, winning third prize with an article in a magazine and a short story published in another publication. He then enrolled in the journalism school at the University of Missouri and received honorable mention as a freshman for a play about rebelling against religious upbringings. But Williams found classes boring, and after failing military training, his father pulled him out of college and put him to work in the shoe factory. Unhappy and overworked, Williams then suffered a nervous breakdown.

In 1936 Williams attended Washington University and wrote *Me Vashya* (1937) and in 1938 received a degree from the University of Iowa, where he wrote *Spring Storm*. In 1939 he took "Tennessee Williams" as his professional name and also received a $1,000 grant from the Rockefeller Foundation in recognition of his play *Battle of Angeles*. He also moved to New Orleans to write for the Works Progress Administration.

Williams's first Broadway stage hit was *The Glass Menagerie*, a highly autobiographical 1944 drama that won the New York Drama Critics' Circle Award for the best play of the season. By 1959 he had earned three New York Drama Critics' Circle Awards, three Donaldson Awards, two Pulitzer Prizes, and a Tony Award. *The Glass Menagerie* and *A Streetcar Named Desire* were made into movies, as were such later screen adaptations as *Cat on a Hot Tin Roof*, *The Rose Tattoo*, *Orpheus Descending*, *The Night of the Iguana*, and *Summer and Smoke*.

These 1940s–1960s successes were followed by great personal turmoil and theatrical failures as his work suffered from increasing alcoholism and drug consumption and often poor choices of collaborators. Williams also was depressed by the death of a longtime homosexual lover. He never had a prize-winner again and died in 1983 at the age of 71 after choking on the cap of a bottle of eye drops.

The birthplace of Tennessee Williams in Columbus, Mississippi, now is a National Literary Landmark and a museum-like State Welcome Center. The two-story 1875 Victorian house was moved to its present location in 1995 and restored to its 1911 condition. In addition to tours of the house, an annual festival, called the Tennessee Williams Tribute and Tour of Victorian Houses, is held each year in Columbus.

Tennessee Williams Birthplace, State Welcome Center, 300 Main St., Columbus, MS 39701-4532. Phones: 662/328-0222, 662/328-5413, and 800/328-2686. E-mail: shcaradine@cableone.net. Website: www.columbus-ms.org. Hours: 10–5 daily. Admission: free.

August Wilson

August Wilson Center for African American Culture. The August Wilson Center for African American Culture in Pittsburgh presents exhibits and performing and visual arts programs that feature the contributions of African Americans in western Pennsylvania. The center was founded in the city's cultural district in 2002 and renamed for August Wilson, the Pulitzer Prize– and Tony Award–winning playwright, in 2006. It offers exhibits, theater, dance, music, history, film, literature, visual art, interactive education, and entertainment under one roof.

The 85,000-square-foot center has multiple galleries for exhibitions, a 486-seat theater for performances, an educational center for classes and lectures, and various spaces for community programs and events. The core exhibit is the multimedia "Pittsburgh: Reclaim, Renew, Remix," which focuses on the contributions of African American artists, musicians, dancers, and sports and literary figures in western Pennsylvania. It also displays works by regional and national artists in various disciplines of the visual arts. Annual attendance is 20,000.

The center also tells about August Wilson, a Pittsburgh native, who won a Pulitzer Prize and Tony Award for *Fences* in 1985 and a Pulitzer Prize and New York Drama Critics' Circle Award for *The Piano Lesson* in 1990. Among his other best-known plays are *Ma Rainey, Black Bottom,* and *Joe Turner's Come and Gone.* Wilson's most extensive work was the Pittsburgh Cycle, a series of 10 plays produced from 1990 to 2009—each set in a different decade and dealing with the black experience in the twentieth century.

Wilson was born as Frederick August Kittel Jr. in the city's Hill District in 1945. He was the fourth of six children born to a German immigrant baker and an African American cleaning woman named Daisy Wilson from North Carolina. Wilson's mother raised the children alone until he was five years old in a two-room apartment above a grocery store, and his father was mostly absent during his childhood. In the 1950s his parents divorced, and his mother remarried and moved into a white neighborhood. But the family was forced to move again because of racial hostility.

Wilson, who was the only black student in his Catholic high school in 1959, was soon driven away by threats and abuse. He transferred to a vocational school but found the curriculum unchallenging and dropped out and spent the remainder of his teen years educating himself by reading about black writers at the Carnegie Library (which later gave him a degree—the only such one it ever bestowed). About that time, he decided he wanted to be a writer and began writing poetry and submitting it to magazines.

In 1968 Wilson cofounded the Back Horizon Theater in the Hill District, where his first play, *Recycling,* was performed. His first professional play, *Sizwe Banzi Is Dead,* was presented at the Pittsburgh Public Theater in 1976. Two years later, Wilson moved to St. Paul, Minnesota, where he had a long association with the Penumbra Theatre Company, which gave the premiers of some of Wilson's plays. In 1990 he moved to Seattle, where he developed a relationship with the Seattle Repertory Theatre.

In 2005 Wilson was diagnosed with liver cancer and died three months later in Seattle and was interred in a Pittsburgh cemetery. Two weeks later, the Virginia Theatre in Broadway's theater district was renamed in his honor. Wilson also received many other theater honors and university honorary degrees during his career. In addition, his childhood home in Pittsburgh was made a historic landmark by the state in 2007.

August Wilson Center for African American Culture, 980 Liberty Ave., Pittsburgh, PA 15222-3736. Phone: 412/258-2700. Fax: 412/258-2701. E-mail: pquatchak@augustwilsoncenter.org. Website: www.augustwilsoncenter.org. Hours: 11–6 Tues.–Sat.; closed Sun.–Mon., and major holidays. Admission: adults, $10; seniors, $8; students and children, $6.

POETS

(*See also* Authors/Writers section.)

Arna Wendell Bontemps

See Authors/Writers section.

Robert and Elizabeth Barrett Browning

Armstrong Browning Library. Robert and Elizabeth Browning were two of the most prominent English poets during the nineteenth century. They began writing in the early 1800s, fell in love and married in their middle years, and continued to produce exceptional poetry the rest of their lives. The Armstrong Browning Library at Baylor

University in Waco, Texas, now houses the world's largest collection of Browning materials and other collections of rare nineteenth-century books, manuscripts, and works of art.

Robert Browning was a master of dramatic verse, especially monologues, while Elizabeth Barrett (later Browning) was known for her early sensitive poems and later work with political and social themes. Elizabeth's poetry was widely popular in England and the United States, while Robert's early monologues suffered from being too difficult or obscure, but they became more popular later in his life.

Robert was born in 1812 in Camberwell, now part of Southwark in South London. His father, Robert, was a bank clerk and his mother, Sarah Anna, a daughter of a German ship owner. His father, who had a library of around 6,000 books, encouraged Robert and his sister, Sarianna, to take an interest in literature and the arts. By the age of 12, Robert had written a book of poetry, which he destroyed when a publisher could not be found. He was educated at home by a tutor. He devoted himself to poetry and prose and lived at home until the age of 34, with his father paying for the publication of his son's poems, such as *Pauline* and *Paracelsus*. He also wrote eight plays, starting with the tragic *Stafford*, performed in 1837. He died in 1889 at the age of 77 and is buried in Poets' Corner in Westminster Abbey in London.

In 1845 Browning met Elizabeth Barrett, a poet who lived as a semi-invalid in her father's house in London. She belonged to a family whose wealth derived from 10,000 acres in Jamaica and a grandfather with sugar plantations, mills, glassworks, and ships that traded between Jamaica and Newcastle. She was born in 1806 in County Durham, the eldest of 12 children of Edward and Mary Graham Barrett. She spent her childhood on the family's 500-acre estate near Ledbury, Herefordshire, and was educated at home with a tutor. She was sickly much of her life, largely because of a spinal injury when 15 and a lung ailment in 1837. Two of her most popular works were *Sonnets from the Portuguese*, a collection of love lyrics (1850), and *Aurora Leigh*, which portrays male domination of a woman (1857). She died in 1861 at the age of 55. The Armstrong Browning Library at Baylor University is a nineteenth-century research center dedicated to the study of the lives and works of Robert and Elizabeth Barrett Browning. It houses more than 25,000 books and over 10,000 letters, manuscripts, and artifacts. It includes original letters and manuscripts, books from the poets' library, all the first and many successive editions of their poetry, and secondary works and criticisms, as well as Browning poetry set to music and such personal items as their family furniture, portraits, jewelry, and memorabilia.

The library also contains substantial book and manuscript collections of such other nineteenth-century writers as Matthew Arnold, John Ruskin, Joseph Milsand, Ralph Waldo Emerson, Charles Dickens, and other writers in other areas of nineteenth-century culture. In addition to paintings and drawings of and by the Brownings, the library has Old Masters paintings and other artwork, sculpture, and decorative arts.

The Armstrong Browning Library had its beginning in 1918 with books given to the university by Dr. A. J. Armstrong, former chairman of the English Department, and his wife, Mary Maxwell Armstrong, who dreamed of making the collection into a world-class Browning research center. The free library opened in 1951 and now has an annual attendance of over 22,000.

Armstrong Browning Library, Baylor University, 710 Speight Ave., Waco, TX 76706 (postal address: 1 Bear Pl., #97152, Waco, TX 76798-7152). Phone: 254/710-566. Fax: 254/710-3552. E-mail: avery_sharp@baylor.edu. Website: www.browninglibrary.org. Hours: 9–5 Mon.–Fri., 10–2 Sat.; closed Sun. and university and major holidays. Admission: free.

William Cullen Bryant

William Cullen Bryant Homestead. William Cullen Bryant was a major nineteenth-century romantic poet who also was a lawyer and served as editor and publisher of the *New York Evening Post* for 50 years. His 1789 boyhood home and adult summer residence in Cummington, Massachusetts, is now a historic house museum devoted to his life and career, called the William Cullen Bryant Homestead. He is known for his tender and graceful poetry, pervaded by a contemplative melancholy and a love of solitude and the silence of the woods.

Bryant was born in 1794 in a log cabin near Cummington, and he and his family moved to the nearby homestead when he was two years old. He was the second son of Dr. Peter Bryant, a doctor and later state legislator, and Sarah Snell, who traced her ancestry to passengers on the *Mayflower*. He became interested in poetry early under his father's tutelage, and wrote "The Embargo" when 13. It was an attack on President Thomas Jefferson that reflected his father's Federalist political views.

Bryant then studied law and was admitted to the bar in 1815. He practiced law in Great Barrington, Massachusetts, from 1816 to 1825, during which time he published some of his most famous works—"Thanatopsis," a meditation on death; "To a Waterfowl," about a bird he saw walking to work, in 1817; *Poems*, a collection; and "The Ages," a panorama in verse on the history of civilization, in 1821.

Bryant, who did not enjoy law work and could not support his family on poetry, became a journalist with the help of well-connected literary friends in 1825. He was hired as editor of the *New-York Review* magazine and then the *United States Review and Literary Gazette*. Two years later, he became assistant editor of the *New York Evening Post* newspaper, and then editor-in-chief and part owner. He served as editor and publisher of the paper until his death in 1878 and became wealthy and a powerful force in New York and the nation. During that time, he made the *Post* a Democratic and later Free Soil and then Republican organ. He was a strong abolitionist who helped Abraham Lincoln win the presidential election, as well as a passionate conservationist and horticulturalist who was instrumental in the establishment of Central Park.

Bryant continued to write poetry and prose during his newspaper career, including *The Fountain and Other Poems* in 1842 and *The White-Footed Doe and Other Poems* in 1844. In the last decade of his life, he did blank verse translations of Homer's works in 1871–1874 and wrote the very successful *Picturesque America*, a two-volume description of scenic places in the United States and Canada, in 1872–1874. He died in 1878 after an accidental fall while participating in a Central Park tribute to Italian patriot Giuseppe Mazzini.

The William Cullen Bryant Homestead is a National Historic Landmark located on a hillside overlooking the Westfield River Valley. It became a museum in 1928 after the original acreage was received in a bequest from Minna Godwin Goddard in 1927. The homestead's pastoral landscape is largely unchanged from the early 1800s, featuring old-growth woodlands with some trees reaching heights of 150 feet. Bryant repurchased the family homestead in 1865, 30 years after it was sold out of the family. He then used it as a summer retreat.

The homestead contains three generations of Bryant family furnishings, nineteenth-century European and Middle East exotic travel memorabilia, and rural life artifacts. The property has a visitor center, gift shop, barn, picnic areas, and two and a half miles of footpaths and carriage roads. The grounds are open year-round and the house for guided tours from the last weekend in June through Columbus Day weekend. Annual attendance is 7,000.

William Cullen Bryant Homestead, 207 Bryant Rd., Cummington, MA 01026-9639. Phone: 413/634-2244. Fax: 413/634-0376. E-mail: pvregion@ttor.org. Website: www.thetrustees.org. Hours: grounds—sunrise–sunset daily; house—1–5 Sat.–Sun. and Mon. holidays from last week in June through Columbus Day weekend; closed remainder of year. Admission: grounds—free; house guided tours—adults, $5; children 6–12, $2.50; children under 6, free.

Cedarmere. Cedarmere was the home of poet and *New York Evening Post* editor and publisher William Cullen Bryant in Roslyn Harbor, New York, from 1843 to his death in 1878. It served as a Long Island retreat where he was close to nature and wrote much of his poetry and prose during his New York years. The site now is a historic house museum operated by the Nassau County Department of Parks, Recreation, and Museums on seven and a half acres overlooking Roslyn Harbor.

Cedarmere had its beginning in 1787 when Richard Kirk, a Quaker farmer, greatly enlarged the original farmhouse. He also renovated it several times and planted numerous exotic flowers on the grounds. Bryant made further improvements in the house and grounds and added a Gothic revival mill at the bucolic pond in 1863. Following Bryant's death, Cedarmere was occupied by his daughter, Julia, and grandson, Harold Godwin. Godwin added such features as a stone bridge and sunken garden and rebuilt the house following a major fire in 1902. The estate was left to Nassau County by Godwin's daughter, Elizabeth, to be preserved as a memorial to Bryant. The house, which contains exhibits about Bryant, currently is closed for renovation, but the grounds are open to the public.

Cedarmere, Bryant Ave. (near North Blvd.), Roslyn Harbor, NY 11576. Phone: 516/571-8130. Website: www.nassaucounty.gov/agencies/park/wheretogo/museums. Hours: grounds are open daily, but house is closed for renovation. Admission: free.

Emily Dickinson

Emily Dickinson Museum: The Homestead and the Evergreens. Emily Dickinson is considered one of America's greatest poets, even though she published only seven poems during her lifetime. But she wrote nearly 1,800 poems—most of which were not revealed and published until after her death. She lived a mostly introverted and reclusive life in the family homestead, which is now part of the Emily Dickinson Museum in Amherst, Massachusetts. The museum consists of two historic houses—the birthplace and home of Dickinson (the Homestead) and the home of her brother Austin and his family next door (the Evergreens).

Emily Dickinson was born in 1830 into a prominent Amherst family that lived in a large 1813 house built by her grandfather, Samuel Dickinson, who was instrumental in the founding of Amherst College. Emily's parents, Edward and Emily Norcross Dickinson, had three children, including an older son, Austin, and a younger daughter, Lavinia Norcross. Her father was treasurer of Amherst College for nearly 40 years and also served as a state legislator and a member of Congress.

Emily received a classical education for a Victorian girl in primary school and Amherst Academy. After finishing at the academy, she began attending Mount Holyoke Female Seminary, only to drop out in less than a year. She also took an interest in religion after participating in a religious revival, but her churchgoing ended about 1852. When she became 18, a family friend introduced her to the writings of William Wordsworth and Ralph Waldo Emerson, which influenced some of her later works and resulted in her being called a transcendentalist. She also was influenced by some of her religious experiences and the contemporary popular literature she read.

Emily Dickinson began writing in the mid-1800s. In 1858, when she started withdrawing from the outside world, she began reviewing poems she had written earlier and shared with the family but had not published. She made clean copies for pieced-together manuscript booklets. During her lifetime, she made 40 such booklets with nearly 1,800 poems, as well as numerous vibrant letters. No one knew of the collection until it was discovered by her sister, Lavinia, after Emily's death.

Although Emily became withdrawn physically, she continued to write and remain active with family members and close friends. Emily died in 1886 at the age of 55. She never was recognized for her poetry during her lifetime. The first volume of her works was published posthumously in 1890, and a complete and largely unaltered collection of her poetry did not come out until 1955.

Emily Dickinson's most productive writing period was during the first half of the 1860s, after withdrawing from social life. Her poems were greatly influenced by the metaphysical poets of seventeenth-century England, the Book of Revelation, and a Calvinist, orthodox, and conservative approach to Christianity. The themes of her writings ranged from flowers and gardens, mind and spirit, and the gospel to death and immortality.

The Emily Dickinson Museum: The Homestead and the Evergreens was formed in 2003 from a transfer of the property and assets of the Martha Dickinson Bianchi Trust to the trustees of Amherst College. Bianchi, Emily's niece (daughter of her brother, Austin), had inherited the Evergreens and the Homestead and sold the latter to the Parke family after removing the Dickinson family furnishings and other belongings and moving many of them to the Evergreens, where she lived. As a memorial to her aunt, Bianchi placed Emily's manuscripts, writing desk, bureau, piano, and other materials in a first-floor room called the "Emily Room."

In 1965 Amherst College purchased the Homestead and used it as a faculty residence. Bianchi lived at the Evergreens until her death in 1943, and it was occupied by other family heirs until 1988 and remained virtually unchanged for 100 years. The Bianchi Trust was established in 1992 to develop the house into a cultural facility. Unlike the Homestead, the Evergreens remained fully furnished with Dickinson family furniture, household accoutrements, artworks, and personal items.

The museum now has approximately 8,000 objects from the Evergreens, as well as the "Emily Room." The two houses and the grounds are open to the public, with a choice of three guided tours of the Homestead and the Evergreens and a self-guided tour of the grounds. Annual attendance is 12,000.

Emily Dickinson Museum: The Homestead and the Evergreens, 280 Main St., Amherst, MA 01002-2349. Phone: 413/542-8161. Fax: 413/542-2152. E-mail: info@emilydickinsonmuseum.org. Website: www.emilydickinsonmuseum.org. Hours: Mar.–Dec.—11–4 Wed.–Sun.; closed Mon.–Tues., Thanksgiving and day before., Dec. 21–22, 24–25, 28–29, and Jan.–Feb. Admission: grounds—$6 with wand or free with guided tour; guided house tours— adults, $8 to $10; seniors and college students, $7 to $9; students 6–17, $4 to $5; children under 6 and students of Five College Consortium colleges, free.

Paul Laurence Dunbar

Paul Laurence Dunbar State Memorial. Paul Laurence Dunbar has been called the "poet laureate of African Americans." He was one of the first blacks to gain national prominence as a poet. Although he lived only 33 years, he was a prolific writer with a long list of literary achievements. He was best known for his poetry, but he also wrote short stories, novels, librettos, plays, songs, and essays.

Dunbar was born in Dayton, Ohio, in 1872 and died in 1906 of tuberculosis. He was the son of escaped slaves from Kentucky who instilled in him a love of learning and history. Paul wrote his first poem at the age of six and gave his first public recital when nine years old. His father was a Civil War veteran who had served in the 55th Massachusetts Infantry Regiment and the Fifth Massachusetts Colored Cavalry Regiment. His mother kept vigil over his belongings in the family home until her death in 1934. In 1936 the Dunbar House in Dayton became the Paul Laurence Dunbar State Memorial, the first state memorial to honor an African American.

Dunbar, who was the only black student in Dayton's Central High School, was the class president, editor of the school newspaper, and president of the school literary society. In 1890 he wrote and edited Dayton's first black newspaper, the *Tattler*. It was printed by the fledgling company of Wilbur and Orville Wright, who were Dunbar's high school classmates and friends. Dunbar published *Oak and Ivy*, his first collection of poetry, in 1893. It was followed by *Majors and Minors* in 1895 and *Lyrics of Lowly Life* (including the popular "Ode to Ethiopia"), which brought him national attention, in 1896. They were followed by a dozen books of poetry, four books of short stories, five novels, a Broadway play, essays, and poems with African American songs. Dunbar wrote in African American dialect as well as in conventional English.

Dunbar traveled to England in 1897 to recite his work on the London literary circuit; married Alice Ruth Moore in 1898 and wrote books of poetry with her as companion pieces; worked at the Library of Congress in Washington and attended Howard University in 1900; separated but not divorced in 1902; and experienced depression and declining health (he was ill much of his life from tuberculosis) and moved back to the Dunbar House in Dayton to live with his mother in 1904. He died two years later.

Dunbar House, an Italianate turn-of-the-century home, is part of the National Park Service's Dayton Aviation Heritage National Historical Park and Dayton Aviation Trail, which commemorates Wilbur Wright, Orville Wright, and Paul Laurence Dunbar. The house contains Dunbar's literary possessions, clothing, library, and recreational items and family furniture, artworks, and photographs. A new visitor center also has interpretive panels on Dunbar's life. Annual attendance is 5,000.

Paul Laurence Dunbar State Memorial, 219 N. Paul Laurence Dunbar St., Dayton, OH 45401-6502 (postal address: Dayton History, 1000 Carillon Blvd., Dayton, OH 45409). E-mail: aheckman@daytonhistory.org. Website: www.ohiohistory.org/places/dunbar. Hours: Apr.–late May and early Sept.–Oct.—9–5 Sat., 12–5 Sun.; closed Mon.–Fri. and Nov.–Mar.; Memorial Day weekend–Labor Day—9–5 Thurs.–Sun.; closed Mon.–Wed. Admission: adults, $6; children 6–12, $3; children under 6, free.

Ralph Waldo Emerson

See Authors/Writers section.

Eugene Field

Eugene Field House and St. Louis Toy Museum. Eugene Field was a newspaperman known for his children's poetry and light, humorous essays during the latter part of the 1800s. The 1845 house where he was born and spent his early childhood in St. Louis is now a National Historic Landmark, listed on the National Register of Historic Places, and the site of the Eugene Field House and St. Louis Toy Museum.

Field was born in 1850 in the St. Louis house that now is both a memorial and a museum. After his mother died in 1856, he was raised by Mary Field French, a cousin in Amherst, Massachusetts. His father was attorney Roswell Martin Field, who represented Drew Scott, the slave who sued for his freedom—and the law case that influenced the start of the Civil War.

Field attended Williams College but dropped out when his father died. He then enrolled at Knox College and after a year transferred to the University of Missouri, where his brother Roswell was a student, and he did some writing for the student newspaper. He then toured Europe and when he returned went to work for the *St. Joseph Gazette* in St. Joseph, Missouri, where he soon became the city editor. That same year he married Julia Comstock, with whom he had eight children.

In St. Joseph, Field became known for his humorous articles written in a gossipy style, which sometimes were reprinted in other newspapers around the country. It was where he wrote "Lovers Lane" about a street in St. Joseph, which became one of his most popular poems. He moved back to St. Louis in 1876 and served as editorial writer for the *Morning Journal* and subsequently the *Times-Journal*. He became managing editor of the *Kansas City Times* and later served as editor of the *Denver Tribune*.

In 1883 Field moved to Chicago, where he became a longtime and famous columnist for the *Chicago Daily News*. He wrote a humorous column called "Sharps and Flats" until his death of a heart attack at the age of 45 in 1895. The column was a mixture of whimsical narrative, children's verse, wit, and humor.

Field began publishing his poetry in 1879. He wrote over a dozen volumes of poetry, and became noted for his lighthearted poems for children, such as "Wynken, Blynken, and Nod." He also wrote a number of short stories, including "The Holy Cross" and "Daniel and the Devil."

The Field house, which now also houses the St. Louis Toy Museum, opened to the public in 1936. It was the first historic house in the city. The house originally was part of a 12-unit row house complex known as Walsh's Row. It was leased by the Field family from 1850 to 1864 and the only unit spared when the row houses were demolished by the Board of Education, which owned the property in the 1930s. The board gave the operation of the house and museum to the Eugene Field House Foundation, which has renovated the property.

The house museum contains objects owned by the Field family, a 200-volume library of Eugene Field's works, historical materials donated by others, toys and dolls dating from the 1790s, and a book collection spanning 250 years. The toy museum has permanent exhibits and presents changing exhibitions and programs. Annual attendance is 7,000.

Eugene Field House and St. Louis Toy Museum, 634 S. Broadway, St. Louis, MO 63102-1613. Phone: 314/421-4689. Fax: 314/588-9328. E-mail: info@eugenefieldhouse.org. Website: www.eugenefieldhouse.org. Hours: Mar.–Dec.—10–4 Wed.–Sat., 12–4 Sun., other times by appointment; closed Mon.–Fri., Jan.–Feb., New Year's Day, Easter, Independence Day, Thanksgiving, and Christmas. Admission: adults, $5; children under 12, $1.

Robert Frost

Robert Frost Farm. Robert Lee Frost never graduated from college, but he received more than 40 honorary degrees, including ones from Harvard, Princeton, Oxford, and Cambridge. He was a highly regarded poet known for his realistic depictions of rural life and command of American colloquial speech in the early twentieth century. His poems, which often used settings of rural life in New England in examining complex social and philosophical subjects, received four Pulitzer Prizes and other honors.

Frost was born on the West Coast but spent most of his life in New England. He was born in San Francisco in 1874—the son of William Prescott Frost Jr., a teacher and later editor of the *San Francisco Bulletin* (which later merged with the *San Francisco Examiner*), and Isabelle Moodie. After his father died in 1885, the family moved to Lawrence, Massachusetts, with the assistance of Robert's grandfather, William Frost. Sr., an overseer at a New England mill. In 1892 he graduated from Lawrence High School, where he published his first poem.

Frost attended Dartmouth College for two months but dropped out and returned home, where he helped his mother (a teacher), delivered newspapers, and worked in a factory. This also was when he felt poetry was his true calling. In 1894 he sold his first poem, "My Butterfly: An Elegy," which appeared in the *New York Independent*. The following year he married Elinor Miriam White. They had six children, only two of whom outlived their father.

Frost attended Harvard College in 1897–1899 but left because of illness. In 1900 Robert and Elinor became farmers. His paternal grandfather, who was concerned about Robert's apparent lack of ambition, bought them a farm in Derry, New Hampshire, shortly before he died. They lived on the farm until 1911, with Robert writing poetry early in the morning before the farm chores. But farming proved unsuccessful, and Frost turned to teaching from 1906 to 1911 at the Pinkerton Academy and the New Hampshire Normal School (now Plymouth State University). The farm became the Robert Frost Farm, a historic house museum and state park, in 1968.

The Frost family spent 1912–1914 in Great Britain, where his first two poetry books (*A Boy's Will* and *North of Boston*) were published. As World War I began in Europe, the Frosts returned to America and bought a farm in Franconia, New Hampshire, where they lived until 1920 and spent 19 summers there. It is where Robert launched his career of writing, teaching, and lecturing and had three of his books published. In 1976 the farm was purchased by the town of Franconia, restored, and renamed the Frost Place as a museum and poetry conference site (*see* separate listing).

Frost taught English at Amherst College in 1916–1920, 1923–1924, and 1927–1938; poetry at Harvard University in 1939–1943; and as a faculty member at Dartmouth College in 1943–1949. The Frost family lived in a historic ca. 1769 house in South Shaftsbury, Vermont, from 1920 to 1929. It became the Robert Frost Stone House Museum in 2002 (*see* separate listing). From 1921 to 1927, he also held a fellowship teaching position at the University of Michigan in Ann Arbor and lived part of the year there. The Ann Arbor house is now located in Greenfield Village at the Henry Ford Museum in Dearborn, Michigan.

Frost spent nearly every summer and fall from 1921 to 1963 teaching at the Middlebury College's Bread Loaf School of English, which he cofounded, at its mountain campus in Ripton, Vermont. In 1938, after the death of his wife, he purchased the nearby Homer Noble Farm to have a place to stay while participating in the summer program. He lived and worked in a small cabin, which served as his summer home for 39 years. The cabin, now owned by Middlebury College, is open only on special occasions.

Robert Frost, who died in 1963 at the age of 88 of complications from prostate surgery, received the four Pulitzer Prizes in poetry in 1924, 1931, 1937, and 1943. Among his many works were *Mountain Interval* (1916), *New Hampshire* (1923), *West-Running Brook* (1928), *A Way Out* (1929), *A Further Range* (1936), *From Snow to Snow* (1936), *A Witness Tree* (1942), *Steeple Bush* (1947), *In the Clearing* (1962), and verse plays *A Masque of Reason* (1945) and *A Masque of Mercy* (1947).

One of the largest collections of Frost materials is located in the special collections at Jones Library, the public library in Amherst, Massachusetts. It consists of about 12,000 items, including original manuscript poems and letters, correspondence, photographs, and audio and visual recordings. Amherst College also has a collection of his papers in its archives and special collections.

The Robert Frost Farm, the first of five farms once owned by Frost, has become a National Historic Landmark and is listed on the National Register of Historic Places. It functions as a historic house museum and a New Hampshire state park. The site, with its simple two-story clapboard farmhouse, was the setting for 43 of Frost's poems. It is where the majority of the poems in his first two books were written and many from his third book. The museum tells about Frost's life and career, contains early 1900s furniture and some Frost family belongings, and has a nature/poetry walk, poetry readings, a young poet program, a lecture series, and guided tours. Annual attendance is 6,500.

Robert Frost Farm, 122 Rockingham Rd., Rte. 28, Derry, NH 03038 (postal address: PO Box 1075, Derry, NH 03038-1075). Phone: 603/432-3091. E-mail: info@robertfrostfarm.org. Website: www.robertfrostfarm.org. Hours: May–late June and early Sept.–Oct. 10—10-5 Wed.–Sun.; closed Mon.–Tues.; late June–early Sept.—10-5 daily; closed Oct. 11–Apr. Admission: adults, $7; children 6–17, $3; children under 6 and state residents. free.

The Frost Place. The Frost Place in Franconia, New Hampshire, is where the Robert Frost family lived in 1915–1920 while he launched his career of writing, teaching, and lecturing. The poet had three books published there and returned for 19 summers with his family after a teaching position at Amherst College took him away in 1916.

In 1976 the town of Franconia purchased the farm, restored the facilities, and opened it as a historic house museum and educational center for poetry programs and events. It contains Frost personal belongings, memorabilia, and first editions and has a half-mile Poetry Nature Trail with signage containing poems written during the poet's Franconia years. Among the poetry-related activities are an annual poetry festival with seminars and workshops, a teachers' conference on poetry and teaching, a conference for young poets, a summer fellowship for an emerging American poet, and an annual Frost Day celebration.

The Frost Place, Ridge Rd., Franconia, NH 03580 (postal address: PO Box 74, Franconia, NH 03580-0074). Phone: 603/828-5510. E-mail: frost@frostplace.org. Website: www.frostplace.org. Hours: Memorial Day–June—1-5 Sat.–Sun.; closed Mon.–Fri.; July–mid-Oct.—1-5 Wed.–Mon.; closed Tues. and mid-Oct.–late May. Admission: suggested donations—adults, $5; seniors, $4; children, $3.

Robert Frost Stone House Museum. The ca. 1769 house where Robert Frost and his family lived in South Shaftsbury, Vermont, from 1920 to 1929 now is a museum—the Robert Frost Stone House Museum. It is where Frost wrote many of the pieces that became part of his fourth book and first Pulitzer Prize–winning collection—*New Hampshire*—which included "Stopping by Woods on a Snowy Evening." He received the prize in 1924, and it was followed by three other Pulitzers in 1931, 1937, and 1943.

The historic house is a rare example of colonial architecture made of native stone and timber. The museum was founded in 2002. An entire room is devoted to the prize-winning book. The museum also has Frost personal items and hanging exhibitions on his life and works. The central hallway is dedicated to J. J. Lankes, who decorated Frost's books in the 1920s with woodcut prints. The grounds, which cover seven acres, contain many of the images in his poetry, including stone walls, birch trees, fields, woods, and some of Frost's original apple trees.

Robert Frost Stone House Museum, 121 Historic Rte. 7A, Shaftsbury, VT 05262. Phone: 802/447-6200. E-mail: friends@sover.net. Website: www.frostfriends.org/stonehouse.html. Hours: May–Aug.—10-5 daily; Sept.–Nov.—10-4 Wed.–Sun.; closed Mon.–Tues., Dec.–Apr., and major holidays. Admission: adults, $5; students under 18, $2.50; children under 6, free.

Langston Hughes

See Authors/Writers section.

Henry Wadsworth Longfellow

Longfellow National Historic Site. Henry Wadsworth Longfellow was the most dominant and beloved American poet of the nineteenth century. He became a leading national literary figure by the 1850s and a world-famous personality by the time of his death in 1882. Nearly everyone read his poems at the time, especially the myths and classic epics he created from American historical events and materials. His lyric poems were known for their musicality. Among his most popular works were *Evangeline: A Tale of Acadie*, "Paul Revere's Ride," *The Courtship of Miles Standish*, and *The Song of Hiawatha*.

In 1973 the Longfellow National Historic Site was established in his honor at his former home in Cambridge, Massachusetts. The house also served as the headquarters for General George Washington during the British siege of Boston in 1775–1776. Longfellow originally rented space in the building, known as Craigie House, in 1837. However, when Longfellow married Frances "Fanny" Appleton in 1843, the bride's father, Nathan, made a gift of the house to the couple, who later had six children.

Longfellow was born in 1807 to Stephen and Zilpah Wadsworth Longfellow in Portland, Maine (then part of Massachusetts). His father was a lawyer, and his maternal grandfather, Peleg Wadsworth, was a general in the Continental Army and a member of Congress. Henry, who was the second of eight children, grew up in what was known as the Wadsworth-Longfellow House (*see* separate listing). He went to the private Portland Academy until the age of 14 and had his first poem—a patriotic and historical poem called "The Battle of Lovell's Pond"—printed in the *Portland Gazette* in 1820.

In 1822 he and his brother Stephen enrolled at Bowdoin College, where his grandfather was a founder and his father a trustee. There he met writer Nathaniel Hawthorne, who became his lifelong friend. In his senior year, Henry began to submit his poetry and prose to various newspapers and magazines. Between the start of 1824 and graduation in 1825, he published nearly 40 minor poems. He also was elected to Phi Beta Kappa and gave the student commencement address.

After graduating from college in 1825, he traveled in Europe for three years studying French, Spanish, Italian, German, and other languages and then became professor of modern languages at Bowdoin from 1829 to 1835, during which he published his first book, a translation of the poetry of medieval Spanish poet Jorge Manrique in 1833, and a travel book, *Outre-Mer: A Pilgrimage Beyond the Sea*, in 1835. In 1831 he married a childhood friend, Mary Storer Potter, who died after a miscarriage in 1835. That same year he was offered and accepted the position of Smith Professorship of Modern Languages at Harvard College, with the stipulation that he spend a year or so in Europe studying German, Dutch, Danish, Swedish, Finnish, and Icelandic.

Longfellow remained on the faculty at Harvard until 1854, when he retired from teaching and decided to devote himself wholly to writing. While at Harvard, he published *Voices of the Night*, a collection that included translations, nine original poems, and seven poems he wrote as a teenager (1839); *Ballads and Other Poems* (1841); *Evangeline: A Tale of Acadie* (1847); *The Seaside and the Fireside* (1850); and *The Golden Legend* (1851).

In his later years, Longfellow published such works as *The Song of Hiawatha* (1855), *The Courtship of Miles Standish* (1858), *Tales of a Wayside Inn* (including "Paul Revere's Ride") (1863), and *The Divine Comedy of Dante Alighieri*, a three-volume translation (1867). In 1861 Longfellow suffered a tragic loss when his wife, Fanny, died when her clothes caught fire while melting sealing wax. He died in 1882 at the age of 75 after experiencing severe stomach pains.

The Longfellow National Historic Site preserves the 1759 Cambridge house where the poet lived from 1837 to 1882—and which served as General George Washington's headquarters during one stage of the Revolutionary War. It was a cosmopolitan home and still contains many of the objects that reflected Longfellow's interest in other cultures. The house contains European and Asian artworks, furniture, and decorative objects, as well as Longfellow's personal library, manuscripts, and family materials. The site also has a visitor center, gardens, and bookstore. Admission to the house is only by guided tour. Annual attendance is 38,000.

Longfellow National Historic Site, 105 Brattle St., Cambridge, MA 02138-3499. Phone: 612/876-4491. Fax: 617/497-8718. Website: www.nps.gov/long. Hours: June–Oct.—10–4 Wed.–Sun.; closed Mon.–Tues. and Nov.–May; grounds and gardens—dawn–dusk daily. Admission: house tours—adults, $3; children under 16, free; grounds and gardens—free.

Wadsworth-Longfellow House. The 1785–1786 boyhood home of poet Henry Wadsworth Longfellow is now a historic house museum in Portland, Maine. The site—called the Wadsworth-Longfellow House—is where three generations of one family made significant contributions to the literary, cultural, and political life of New England and the United States. The house, which is the oldest standing structure on the Portland peninsula, was opened in 1901 as the state's first historic house museum.

The first completely brick house in Portland, the Wadsworth-Longfellow House was built by Henry's grandfather, General Peleg Wadsworth, who retired with his wife, Elizabeth, to a farm in Hiram, Maine, in 1807. They had 10 children, including daughter Zilah, who married Stephen Longfellow and was Henry's mother. Henry moved to Cambridge, Massachusetts, when he became a faculty member at Harvard in 1835, but his younger sister, Anne Longfellow Pierce, widowed at an early age, continued to live in the house until her death in 1901.

The house and the family furnishings were willed to the Maine Historical Society by Mrs. Pierce in 1895 to be preserved as a museum dedicated to her brother and his family. The house originally was a two-story structure with a pitched roof, but a third story was added in 1815 after a roof fire the prior year. Virtually all of the furnishings, household items, and artifacts are original to the Wadsworth and Longfellow families. The furnishings from the three generations illustrate the changes in style, technology, and attitude over the nineteenth century.

The house also has a colonial revival garden (created by the Longfellow Garden Club in 1926), and the historical society's headquarters, museum, and library are located adjacent to the historic house. A combination admission can be purchased for the house and the Maine History Museum.

Wadsworth-Longfellow House, 485 Congress St., Portland, ME 04101-3414. Phones: 207/772-1807 and 207/774-1822. Fax: 207/775-4301. E-mail: info@mainehistory.org. Website: www.mainehistory.com. Hours: May–Oct.—10–5 Mon.–Sat., 12–5 Sun.; Nov.—10–5 Sat.; closed Sun.–Fri.; Dec.—10–5 Mon.–Sat., 12–5 Sun.; closed Jan.–Apr. and state and federal holidays. Admission: adults, $8; seniors, $7; children, $3; children under 6, free; combination admission with history museum: adults, $12; seniors, $10; children, $3; children under 6, free.

Longfellow-Evangeline State Historic Site. Henry Wadsworth Longfellow's 1840 epic poem *Evangeline: A Tale of Acadie* resulted in the founding of the Longfellow-Evangeline State Historic Site in St. Martinville, Louisiana, which makes the public more aware of the 1755 expulsion of the Acadians from Nova Scotia to Louisiana and a local novel based on the poem. The reproduced farmstead along the Bayou Teche became the first park in the state park system in 1934 and a National Historic Landmark in 1974.

The Longfellow poem is a story of loss and devotion set against the deportation of the Acadian people. In 1907 Judge Felix Voorhies wrote a story, *Acadian Reminiscences: The True Story of Evangeline,* that told of two ill-fated lovers, Evangeline and Gabriel, and their legendary meeting place at nearby Evangeline Oak and interpreted the history of French-speaking people of the state. The 157-acre state park, features the ca. 1815 Maison Olivier plantation home built by Pierre Olivier Duclozel de Vezin, a wealthy Creole at the time. The site also has a ca. 1790 Acadian cabin, blacksmith shop, barn, outdoor and bread ovens, privy, and visitor center. The park offers living history demonstrations, educational programs, and guided tours. Annual attendance is 27,000.

Longfellow-Evangeline State Historic Site, 1200 N. Main St., St. Martinville, LA 70582-3516. Phones: 337/394-3754 and 888/677-2900. Fax: 337/394-3553. E-mail: longfellow@crt.la.gov. Website: www.crt.state.la.us/parks.longfell.aspx. Hours: 9–5 Tues.–Sat.; closed Sun.–Mon., New Year's Day, Thanksgiving, and Christmas. Admission: adults, $4; seniors and children under 13, free.

John G. Neihardt

John G. Neihardt State Historic Site. John C. Neihardt, poet laureate of Nebraska, is best known as the author of *Black Elk Speaks,* the 1932 biography of the visionary Oglala Lakota holy man. But he also was the author of poetry and prose that told stories of mountain men, explorers, settlers, frontier wars, and the mystical world of the Sioux on the Great Plains. He wrote to preserve and express elements of the pioneer past in books ranging from travelogues to epic poetry.

Neihardt was born in 1881 in Sharpsburg, Illinois. His mother, Alice, moved the family to Nebraska in 1891 when he was 10, and he wrote his first poem when 12. At the age of 13, he enrolled at Wayne Normal College in Wayne, Nebraska, and received a degree in science in 1897. In 1900 he published *The Divine Enchantment,* a long mystic poem, which was the first of 25 volumes of poetry, fiction, and philosophy published during his lifetime—more than half produced while living in Bancroft. They include such diverse works as the *Bundle of Myrrh,* a collection of lyrics; *The River and I,* a travel adventure; and *The Cycle of the West,* a five-part epic history of the American West. In 1921 Neihardt was made poet laureate of Nebraska—the first time a state legislature conferred such an honor.

Neihardt met Black Elk, the Lakota elder, on the Pine Ridge Reservation in South Dakota in 1930 while researching the Plains Indian wars. *Black Elk Speaks,* the holy man's life story and prayer for the future of his people, came out of the relationship. In the process, Neihardt and his two daughters were spiritually adopted into Black Elk's world.

Neihardt became a professor of poetry at the University of Nebraska in 1923, literary editor of the *St. Louis Post Dispatch* in 1926–1938, director and field representative of the Bureau of Indian Affairs in 1943–1948; and poet in residence and lecturer in English at the University of Missouri in 1948–1966. He died in 1973 at the age of 92 in Columbia, Missouri.

The John G. Neihardt State Historic Site was established in Bancroft in 1976 in the house where the poet wrote many of his works in 1911–1921. It is a Nebraska State Historical Society facility operated by the John G. Neihardt Foundation. The site features Neihardt's restored study, a memorial room with items given to Neihardt by Black Elk and memorabilia, a library featuring Neihardt's works, and a Sioux Sacred Hoop Prayer Garden that was planted under the direction of Neihardt. Annual attendance is 2,600.

John G. Neihardt State Historic Site, 306 W. Elm St., Bancroft, NE 68004-4127 (postal address: PO Box 344, Bancroft, NE 68004-0344). Phones: 402/648-3388 and 888/777-4667. Fax: 402/648-3388. E-mail: neihardt@gpeom.net. Website: www.neihardtcenter.org. Hours: Mar.–Nov.—9–5 Mon.–Sat., 1:30–5 Sun.; closed major holidays; Dec.–Feb.—9–5 Mon.–Fri.; closed Sat.–Sun. and New Year's Day. Admission: free.

James Whitcomb Riley

James Whitcomb Riley Birthplace and Museum. James Whitcomb Riley was a best-selling poet and author known as the "Hoosier Poet" and the "Children's Poet" because of his dialect works and children's poetry. His works tended to be humorous or sentimental and reflect the homespun language of everyday midwesterners. He published approximately 1,000 poems, over half in dialect. His most famous works were "Little Orphant Annie" and "The Raggedy Man" at the turn of the twentieth century. His life and career are now the focus of two historic house museums in Indiana—the James Whitcomb Riley Birthplace and Museum in Greenfield and the James Whitcomb Riley Museum Home in Indianapolis (*see* separate listing).

Riley was born in 1849, the third of six children of attorney Reuben Andrew Riley and Elizabeth Marine Riley. His mother, a poet and storyteller, taught him to write at home before sending him to the local school. He found school difficult and often was absent and punished. He dropped out when 16, and he and some friends started a company that painted signs, houses, and ornamental pictures. Riley began writing verses as part of signs he created and started submitting poems to newspapers. He left the company after one of his poems was published and then started traveling with a medicine show, painting, and reciting his poems. Riley developed an early interest in poetry from an uncle who sometimes wrote verses for local newspapers. His last teacher also noticed Riley's interest in poetry and urged him to pursue it. Riley called his poems simple statements that came from the heart.

During the 1870s, Riley had a series of jobs with Indiana newspapers and gradually gained prominence through poetry readings and lecturing tours in the 1880s—first in the Midwest and then nationally. In 1879 he was hired as a columnist at the *Indianapolis Journal*, where he often included his poetry. He remained with the paper until his first book, *The Old Swimming Hole and 'Leven More Poems*, was published in 1883.

Riley followed with other dialect and children's books of simple life with kindly humor, pathos, sincerity, and naturalness. They included *Old Fashioned Roses* (1888), *Rhymes of Children* (1890), *Green Fields and Running Brooks* (1892), *A Child-World* (1896), *Home Folks* (1900), *The Raggedy Man* (1907), *The Little Orphant Annie Book* (1908), *When the Frost Is on the Punkin* (1911), and *Old Times* (1915). He also wrote one play, *Flying Islands of the Night*, in 1891.

Riley died of complications from a stroke at the age of 66 in 1916 in Indianapolis, where he spent the last 23 years of his life. The 1849 house in which he was born is located along the old National Road (now U.S. Route 40) and was sold by his father in 1870 after his law practice suffered following the Civil War. But James Whitcomb Riley bought the house in 1893, and it was purchased by the City of Greenfield in 1936 and became the James Whitcomb Riley Birthplace and Museum in 1937.

The Riley house is now operated by the Riley Old Home Society and the city's Department of Parks and Recreation. The museum contains exhibits on the life and career of James Whitcomb Riley and has memorabilia, manuscripts, scrapbooks, furniture, books, paintings, and other historical materials. The city also holds an annual festival honoring Riley and presents a Christmas program at the house. The museum's annual attendance is over 4,000.

James Whitcomb Riley Birthplace and Museum, 250 W. Main St., Greenfield, IN 46140 (postal address: Greenfield Parks and Recreation Dept., 280 N. Apple St., Greenfield, IN 46140-2656). Phones: 317/462-8539 and 317/477-4340. Fax: 317/477-4341. Hours: Apr.–early Nov.—10–4 Mon.–Sat.; closed Sun. and early-Nov.–Mar. Admission: adults, $3.50; children 6–18, $1.25; children under 6, free.

James Whitcomb Riley Museum Home. Poet James Whitcomb Riley lived the last 23 years of his life (from 1893 to 1916) in a late Victorian home in Indianapolis that now is a historic home museum—the James Whitcomb Riley Museum Home. He moved into the house after his poetry books started being published and as he was receiving national recognition as a major poet of dialect and children's works.

The two-story brick Italianate home was built in 1872 by John R. Nickum, an Indianapolis baker. Nickum's daughter, Magdalena, and her husband, Charles Holstein, a lawyer, lived in the house in 1893 when they invited Riley to live with them as a means of helping with expenses. After Riley and the Holsteins died, William Fortune bought the house in 1916 and transferred it to the James Whitcomb Riley Memorial Association (now the Riley Children's Foundation). It was established as a museum in 1922 and listed on the National Register of Historic Places in 1962.

The house, located in the Lockerbie Square Historic District, contains most of the household items of Riley's days, including furnishings, memorabilia, artworks, and books. Among Riley's belongings at the house are his writing deck, his top hat and cane, and a portrait of his beloved dog. Guided tours are offered. Annual attendance is 7,500.

James Whitcomb Riley Museum Home, 528 Lockerbie St., Indianapolis, IN 46202-3617. Phone: 317/631-5885. Fax: 317/955-0619. E-mail: rileyhome@rileykids.org. Website: www.rileykids.org/about/riley_museum. Hours: 10–3:30 Tues.–Sat.; closed Sun.–Mon. and major holidays. Admission: free.

Carl Sandburg

Carl Sandburg Home National Historic Site. Carl Sandburg was a Pulitzer Prize–winning poet who also wrote history, biographies, novels, children's literature, and newspaper stories in the first half of the twentieth century. He received three Pulitzers—two for poetry and another for a biography of Abraham Lincoln. His birthplace in Galesburg, Illinois, is now a state historic site (*see* separate listing), and his final home in Flat Rock, North Carolina, is the site of the Carl Sandburg Home National Historic Site.

Sandburg was born to Swedish immigrants August and Clara Sandburg in a three-room cottage in Galesburg in 1878. He was the second of seven children. His father, a railroad blacksmith helper, purchased the modest house in 1873 and sold it for a larger residence a year after Carl's birth. Carl quit school after his graduation from eighth grade at the age of 13 in 1891 and spent the next few years working at such odd jobs as barbershop porter, milk wagon driver, bricklayer, and farm laborer to help support the family. At 17, he traveled west to Kansas as a hobo and then enlisted in the U.S. Army during the Spanish-American War and was stationed in Puerto Rico for eight months.

The final home of Carl Sandburg, located in Flat Rock, North Carolina. Courtesy of the National Park Service, Carl Sandburg Home National Historic Site.

After the war, Sandburg worked his way through Lombard College in Galesburg but did not receive a degree. However, Professor Philip Green Wright was so impressed with Sandburg's writing potential that he paid for the publication of his first volume of poetry, *Reckless Ecstasy*, in 1904 and published two other volumes printed on Wright's basement in 1907–1908.

After college, Sandburg moved to Milwaukee, where he worked as an advertising writer, contributed articles to newspapers, worked as an organizer for the Social-Democrat Party in Wisconsin, served as secretary to the first socialist mayor of Milwaukee, and met and married his wife, Lillian Steichen (and later had three daughters).

Sandburg moved to Chicago in 1912 and met Harriet Monroe, who had recently founded *Poetry* magazine. She liked his plain-speaking free-verse style, which was reminiscent of Walt Whitman, and published a number of his poems in 1914. They were followed by *Chicago Poems* (1916); *Cornhuskers* (1918), for which he received his first Pulitzer Prize; and *Smoke and Steel* (1920)—all of which established Sandburg as a major figure in contemporary literature. He became known for free-verse poems that celebrated American common people, industry and agriculture, and geography and landscapes.

Sandburg also worked as a journalist during this period. He served as a reporter for the *Day Book*, which took no advertisements, in 1913–1917 and the *Chicago Daily News* from 1917 to 1930. While at the *Daily News*, he reported on the Chicago race riots in 1919 and served as film critic in 1920–1927. It also was during the 1920s that Sandburg wrote *Rootabaga*, a book of fanciful children's tales in 1922; *The American Songbag*, a collection of folk songs in 1927; and the first of his two-volume biography of Lincoln—*Abraham Lincoln: The Prairie Years* (1926). The second volume, *Abraham Lincoln: The War Years*, won the Pulitzer Prize in 1940. The third Pulitzer Prize was for *The Complete Poems of Carl Sandburg* in 1950.

The Sandburg family moved to Harbert, Michigan, in 1930 and then purchased the 1838 Connemara Farms in Flat Rock, North Carolina, in 1945. Sandburg updated the historic farm and spent his last 22 year at the site, which provided the solitude he sought for writing and the more than 30 acres wanted for his wife's champion Chikaming dairy goats. He wrote over one-third of his works while living there, including the novel *Remembrance Rock* (1948), the prize-wining *Complete Poems* and *New American Songbag* (1950), the autobiographical *Always the Young Stranger* (1953), *Wing Song* (1960), and *Honey and Salt* (1963). Sandburg died of natural causes at the age of 79 in 1967, and his wife sold the farm to the federal government to preserve it as a memorial to Sandburg. It became the Carl Sandburg Home National Historic Site in 1968 and opened to the public in 1974. Since then, the site has been expanded to 264 acres, and a visitor center has been added.

The historic site has 32 structures. Among the site's features are the Sandburg residence, a dairy farm with about 15 prized goats, a barn, sheds, rolling pastures, mountainside woods, hiking trails, two small lakes, several ponds, flower and vegetable gardens, and an apple orchard. Guided tours are offered of the house, which is furnished the way it was during the 1950s. It has over 65,000 objects on display, including Sandburg's working library, books, letters, papers, and photographs. The site also has exhibits on Sandburg's life and career, live performances are given of Sandburg's *Rootabaga Stories*, and excerpts from the Broadway play *The World of Carl Sandburg* are presented at the amphitheater from June to mid-August. The historic site's annual attendance is 100,000.

Carl Sandburg Home National Historic Site, 81 Carl Sandburg Lane, Flat Rock, NC 28731-8635. Phone: 828/693-4178. Fax: 828/693-4179. E-mail: carl_administration@nps.gov. Website: www.nps.gov/carl. Hours: 9–5 daily; closed Christmas. Admission: grounds—free; house tour—adults, $5; seniors, $3; children under 16, free.

Carl Sandburg State Historic Site. The three-room home where poet and author Carl Sandburg was born in 1878 and an adjacent small park and garden are a state historic site in Galesburg, Illinois. The cottage contains Sandburg family and period furnishings, memorabilia, and the writer's works and has a visitor center with artifacts, exhibits, and videos about Sandburg. The flowers in the garden surround "Remembrance Rock," where the ashes of Carl Sandburg; his wife, Lillian; and two daughters, Margaret and Janet, are buried.

The historic site is supported by the State of Illinois and the nonprofit Carl Sandburg Historic Site Association. The association, which planned and funded the garden, also sponsors the "Penny Parade," which brings school children to the site; offers band and folk music concerts on the grounds and in the visitor center; and is a participating sponsor of the Sandburg Day Festival every April. The site's annual attendance is 16,000.

Carl Sandburg State Historic Site, 313 E. 3rd St., Galesburg, IL 61401-6021 (postal address: PO Box 108, Galesburg, IL 61401). Phone: 309/342-2361. Fax: 309/342-2141. E-mail: carl@sandburg.org. Website: www.sandburg.org. Hours: May–Oct.—9–5 Thurs.–Sun.; closed Mon.–Wed. and Nov.–Apr. Admission: suggested donations—adults, $4; children, $2; families, $10.

William Shakespeare

See Playwrights section.

Anne Spencer

Anne Spencer House and Garden. Anne Bethel Spencer was a poet of the Harlem Renaissance in the 1920s–1930s and an activist for equal civil and educational rights. Her house served as a political center in Lynchburg, Virginia. She was the first Virginian and the first African American to have her poetry included in the *Norton Anthology of American Poetry*. Her home from 1903 to her death in 1975 is now a historic house museum called the Anne Spencer House Museum and Garden.

The two-story Queen Anne–style clapboard home was built in 1903 with a large garden and a one-room retreat, called "Edankraal," where the poet did much of her writing. The local NAACP chapter was founded and centered at the house for many years.

Anne Spencer was born Annie Bethel Bannister in Henry County, Virginia, in 1882. She was the only child of Joel Cephus Bannister and Sarah Louise Scales. When her parents separated, she moved with her mother to West Virginia. Her mother enrolled her at the Virginia Theological Seminary and College to further her skills after noticing her daughter's abilities with the English language. When she graduated in 1899, Anne gave the valedictory address. She married Edward Spencer in 1901, and they built the house in Lynchburg. James Weldon Johnson, who later became a celebrated Harlem Renaissance poet, helped discover Anne's poetry talent and suggested that she use Anne Spencer as her pen name.

As Spencer's poetry became more popular, she assumed a more important role in the Harlem Renaissance and the civil rights movement. Although most of her poems were reflections of her own thoughts, her works were also influenced by other African American leaders. Among her notable works were "At the Carnival," "Before the Feast of Shushan," and "Translation."

Spencer died in 1975, and the house became a museum in 1977. The house, which is listed on the National Register of Historic Places, is operated by the Anne Spencer Memorial Foundation. It has Victorian furnishings, stained glass windows, writings by Spencer, artworks, photographs, and other historical materials. Annual attendance is 1,000.

Anne Spencer House and Garden, 1313 Pierce St., Lynchburg, VA 24501-1935. Phone: 434/845-1313. Hours: by appointment. Admission: adults, $5; seniors, $4; college students, $3; children under 12, $2.

Henry David Thoreau

See Authors/Writers section.

Robert Penn Warren

Robert Penn Warren Birthplace Museum. Robert Penn Warren was a university professor, poet, novelist, and literary critic who became the first poet laureate of the United States in 1938 and a three-time winner of the Pulitzer Prize. He is the only person to have won Pulitzers for both poetry and fiction. His life and works are featured at the Robert Penn Warren Birthplace Museum in Guthrie, Kentucky.

Warren is best known for his Pulitzer Prize–winning novel *All the King's Men*, which was inspired by the life and death of Governor Huey Long of Louisiana. He also published 16 volumes of poetry, two of which—*Promises: Poems, 1954–1956* and *Now and Then: Poems, 1976–1978*—won Pulitzer Prizes. In addition to poetry and novels, he published such other works as a book of short stories, two selections of critical essays, three historical essays, two studies of race relations in America, a biography, textbooks, and studies of Melville, Dreiser, and Whittier. He served as the nation's first poet laureate in 1986–1987.

Warren was born in 1905 in the small brick cottage in Guthrie that houses the Warren museum today. He was the oldest of three children of banker Robert Franklin Warren and schoolteacher Anna Ruth Penn Warren. He graduated from high school in 1921—the same year he suffered an injury to his left eye from a rock thrown by a younger brother that eventually led to removal of his eye. That summer he had his first poem, "Prophecy," published while taking part in a summer military training program at Fort Knox. However, his appointment to the U.S. Naval Academy was cancelled because of the eye injury.

Warren enrolled at Vanderbilt University in 1921 at the age of 16 and became the youngest member of a group of southern poets called the Fugitives who were advocates of the rural southern agrarian tradition and based their poetry and perspectives on classical aesthetic ideals. His poems were published in the group's magazine, *The Fugitive*. He then obtained a master's degree at the University of California, a fellowship to Yale University, and a degree as a Rhodes Scholar at Oxford University.

In the years that followed, he produced a wide range of literary works as he taught at Vanderbilt University, Southwestern College, the University of Minnesota, Yale University, and Louisiana State University. While at LSU, he cofounded and edited *The Southern Review*. He also was one of the leading representatives of New Criticism, featuring works that helped revolutionize the teaching of literature.

From the 1950s until his death from bone cancer in 1989, Warren lived in Fairfield, Connecticut, and at his summer home in Stratton, Vermont. Among the many honors he received, in addition to being the nation's first poet laureate and receiving three Pulitzer Prizes, were the National Medal for Literature, the Presidential Medal of Freedom, the National Medal of Arts, and the Bollingen Prize.

Warren's 1905 home in Guthrie, Kentucky, is now the site of the Robert Penn Warren Birthplace Museum. It contains family and period furnishings, many of Warren's childhood possessions, first editions and other copies of his books, family photographs, and artifacts related to the history of the town.

Robert Penn Warren Birthplace Museum, 3rd and Cherry Sts., Guthrie, KY 42234. Phone: 270/483-2683. Website: www.robertpennwarren.com. Hours: 11:30–3:30 Tues.–Sat., 2–4 Sun.; other times by appointment; closed Mon. and major holidays. Admission: free.

Walt Whitman

Walt Whitman Birthplace State Historic Site and Interpretive Center. Walt Whitman was one of the nation's most influential and controversial poets, essayists, journalists, and humanists in the nineteenth century. He was considered the "father of free verse" and represented the transition from transcendentalism to realism. He now is remembered at two state historic sites—the Walt Whitman Birthplace State Historic Site and Interpretive Center in Huntington, New York, and the Walt Whitman House Museum and Library in Camden, New Jersey (*see* separate listing).

Whitman was one of the first American poets to gain international attention. He is best known for *Leaves of Grass*, a collection of free-verse poems that was a celebration of nature and the self, first published in 1855 and revised and enlarged in eight more editions until his death in 1892. It was described as the first expression of a distinctly American voice. The poems in *Leaves of Grass* were written without rhyme or traditional meter and dealt with the beauty of the human body, physical health, and sexuality. They included some offensive sexual themes that resulted in the book being called too frank and "trashy, profane, and obscene" by some critics.

Whitman was born in 1819 in a farmhouse built by his father in Huntington on Long Island in New York. He was the second of nine children of Walter Whitman, a house builder, and Louise Van Veisor. The family moved to Brooklyn, where Walt dropped out of school when 12 and became a printer's apprentice. He worked as a printer/typesetter in New York City until a major printing district fire made such jobs scarce. He then taught intermittently at various schools for several years and published some of his early poetry anonymously in the *New York Mirror*.

In 1838 Whitman began his journalistic career. He started a weekly newspaper, the *Long-Islander*, on Long Island but sold it the following year. In 1841 he went to work for the *New World* in New York and then became editor of the *Aurora* in 1842, the *Brooklyn Daily Eagle* in 1846–1848, and the *New Orleans Crescent* in 1848. He returned to Brooklyn and founded the *Brooklyn Freeman*, a Free Soil newspaper, and continued to develop his unique style of poetry into part of *Leaves of Grass*, which contained 12 untitled poems in the privately published first edition in 1855.

It was then that Whitman decided to become a poet, and he wanted to do something different. Addressing a range of subjects, he used free verse with cadences based on the Bible. He sent a copy of the book to Ralph Waldo Emerson, who wrote a supportive letter that Whitman used to promote the book. It received mixed reviews, with many of the comments focusing on the offensive sexual themes. Whitman revised and expanded the content with 20 additional poems in the second edition in 1856 and continued to make changes in future editions of what he considered his masterpiece. He also experienced financial difficulties during the early editions of the book and returned to newspaper work as an editor with Brooklyn's *Daily Times* in 1857–1859. Although the book did not sell well at the beginning, it eventually became popular nationally and internationally.

With the outbreak of the Civil War, Whitman wrote "Beat! Beat! Drums!" in patriotic support of the North in 1861 and later *Memoranda During the War* after seeing the number of wounded and amputees while searching for his wounded brother. He became so moved by the casualties of war that he became a volunteer nurse in army hospitals and a part-time clerk in the army paymaster's office in Washington. After the war, he worked as a clerk for two federal agencies until 1873, when he was stricken with paralysis from a stroke while visiting his dying mother in Camden, New Jersey.

Whitman stayed with his brother George in Trenton until 1882, when sales from the sixth edition of *Leaves of Grass* enabled him to buy a house in Trenton that became the Walt Whitman House Museum and Library in 1946. Whitman spent his declining years working on additions and revisions to a new addition of the book and preparing his final volume of poems and prose, *Good-Bye, My Fancy* (1891). He died the following year at the age of 72.

The Walt Whitman Birthplace State Historic Site and Interpretative Center is located at the farmhouse in the West Hills section of Huntington on Long Island, New York, where Walt Whitman was born in 1819 and spent his early years. It contains original letters and manuscripts, artifacts, Whitman's school desk and memorabilia, first editions of his works, 130 portraits of Whitman, period furnishings, a library, literary materials, and a visitor center with exhibits and an audiovisual show on his life and career. Guided tours are offered of the house, which is listed on the National Register of Historic Places. The site also has a poet-in-residence program, an annual poetry contest for local grade school children, and special events. Annual attendance is 16,500.

Walt Whitman Birthplace State Historic State and Interpretive Center, 246 Old Walt Whitman Rd., Huntington Station, NY 11746-4148. Phone: 631/427-5240. Fax: 631/427-5247. E-mail: director@waltwhitman.org. Website: www.waltwhitman.org. Hours: June 15–Labor Day—11–4 Mon.–Fri., 11–5 Sat.–Sun.; remainder of year—1–4 Wed.–Fri., 11–4 Sat.–Sun.; closed Mon.–Tues. Admission: adults, $5; seniors and students, $4; children, free.

Walt Whitman House Museum and Library. The Walt Whitman House Museum and Library in Camden, New Jersey, is a state historic site that honors the famous nineteenth-century poet. It is located at the house where he lived from 1884 until his death in 1892. It is the only house that he ever owned. Whitman had come from Washington to see his dying mother in 1973 when he suffered a stroke that paralyzed him, and he never left Camden. He lived with his brother and wife until they moved to rural Burlington. Walt stayed in Camden and purchased a house with income from the sixth edition of *Leaves of Grass*. He lived there until his death in 1892 and is buried in a tomb he designed in Harleigh Cemetery.

The Walt Whitman House Museum and Library, which has been designated a National Historic Landmark, was established by the State of New Jersey in 1946. It contains his letters, manuscripts, library, rare books, furniture, photographs, memorabilia, and other personal belongings. The museum has guided tours and offers such programs as public lectures, poetry readings, teacher workshops, and symposia and seminars. Annual attendance is 3,000.

Walt Whitman House Museum and Library, 330 Mickle Blvd., Camden, NJ 08103-1126. Phone: 856/964-5383. Fax: 856/964-1088. Website: www.nj.gov/dep/parksandforests/historic/whitman/index.html. Hours: June 15–Labor Day—11–4 Mon.–Fri., 12–5 Sat.–Sun.; remainder of year—1–4 Wed.–Fri., 11–4 Sat.–Sun.; closed Mon.–Tues., New Year's Day, Thanksgiving, and Christmas. Admission: adults, $4; seniors, $3; children, free.

John Greenleaf Whittier

John Greenleaf Whittier Homestead. The John Greenleaf Whittier Homestead in Haverhill, Massachusetts, is where the deeply religious Quaker poet, editor, and abolitionist was born in 1807 and lived for 29 years. The farmhouse was built in 1688 by Thomas Whittier, his great-great-grandfather, on 148 original acres that became the Whittier family homestead for five generations. The homestead, which remains essentially the same as it was at the poet's time, has served as the setting for Whittier's best-known narrative poem *Snow-Bound* in 1866 and such other poems as "Fernside Brook," "The Barefoot Boy," and "The Sycamores." Whittier moved to Amesbury, Massachusetts, in 1836 and lived there until his death in 1892. That site also has become a historic house museum, called the John Greenleaf Whittier Home (*see* separate listing).

Whittier, the son of devout Quakers John and Abigail Whittier, became a prominent poet and editor despite little formal schooling. He attended Haverhill Academy briefly but was largely self-educated. He became interested in poetry after a teacher introduced him to the poetry of Robert Burns. By the time he was 20, Whittier had published enough verse to attract the attention of editors and readers in the antislavery cause. He published his first poem, "The Exile's Departure," in William Lloyd Garrison's *Newburyport Free Press* in 1828.

Whittier became devoted to social causes and reform and worked for a number of abolitionist newspapers and magazines during his career. He edited the *American Manufacturer* and the *Essex Gazette* and then served as editor of the influential *New England Weekly Review* in 1830–1832. His first book, *Legends of New England in Prose and Verse*, was published in 1831. It was followed by *Justice and Experience* in 1833, which urged immediate abolition. From the 1830s to the Civil War, he wrote essays, articles, and poems that mostly concerned abolition.

John Greenleaf Whittier also was involved politically, supporting Republican candidates and running for office. He was a delegate to the 1831 Republican national convention. supporting Henry Clay, and in 1834 he was elected as a Whig to one term for the Massachusetts legislature. He was not always popular because of his views, being mobbed and stoned in Concord, New Hampshire, in 1835, and the offices of the *Pennsylvania Freeman* were burned to the ground and sacked when he was editor in 1838.

Whittier founded the antislavery Liberty Party in 1840 and ran for Congress unsuccessfully in 1842. In the mid-1850s, he worked to form the Republican Party and for the election of presidential candidate John C. Frémont. He also helped start the *Atlantic Monthly* magazine in 1857. The Civil War inspired his famous *Barbara Frietchie* poem, and from 1865 until his death in 1892 he wrote of religion, nature, and rural life—and experienced his greatest popularity.

James Carleton, a boyhood friend of Whittier and former mayor of Haverhill, bought the Whittier farm after the poet's death and donated it to the Haverhill Whittier Club, which opened it in 1893. The club still holds the deed in trust, which calls for the house and grounds to be maintained for visitors who love and cherish the memory of Whittier. It features many of the original aspects of the homestead.

John Greenleaf Whittier Homestead, Amesbury Rd. (Rte. 110), Haverhill, MA 01830 (postal address: 305 Whittier Rd., Haverhill, MA 01830-1738). Phone: 978/373-3979. Website: www.johngreenleafwhittier.com. Hours: May–Nov.—11–4 Wed.–Fri., 10–4 Sat., 1–4 Sun.; closed Mon.–Tues. and Dec.–Apr. Admission: adults, $5; seniors and students over 17, $3; students under 18, $2.

John Greenleaf Whittier Home. In 1836 poet John Greenleaf Whittier moved from his homestead in Haverhill to Amesbury, Massachusetts, where the abolitionist lived until his death in 1892. The home now is a historic house museum called the John Greenleaf Whittier Home. His birthplace and boyhood home in Haverhill also has become a museum (*see* John Greenleaf Whittier Homestead listing).

Whittier moved with his mother, aunt, and sister to Amesbury and wrote most of his poetry and prose in the house during his 56 years of residence, including his classic *Snow-Bound*. He also enlarged the 1820 house several times, raising the left side and adding a section and another story. The house and the furnishings now are basically unchanged from when Whittier lived there.

The Whittier home was acquired by his niece, Lizzie, upon Whittier's death, but she was not interested in living in it. The Whittier Home Association was formed in 1898 and acted as the caretaker, while Lizzie's husband and son occupied the house for a number of years. In 1918 the association became the owner and still operates the home as a historic house museum.

The Whittier home has been designated a National Historic Landmark and is listed on the National Register of Historic Places. The house and its furnishings—including the living rooms, bedroom, and writing study—are essentially the way they were when Whittier died in 1892. The house, which has guided tours, contains manuscripts, books, photographs, and exhibits on Whittier's life and career. Annual attendance is 400.

John Greenleaf Whittier Home, 86 Friend St., Amesbury, MA 01913 (postal address: PO Box 632, Amesbury, MA 01913-0014). E-mail: whittierhome@verizon.net. Website: www.whittierhome.org. Hours: May–Oct.—11–4 Wed. and Sat., other times by appointment; closed remainder of week and year. Admission: adults, $6; seniors and students, $5; children 7–17, $3; children under 7, free.

PRESIDENTS

George Washington

Mount Vernon: George Washington's Estate and Gardens. George Washington was a national hero known as the father of his country because of his vital role as commander-in-chief of the Continental Army during the 1775–1783 American Revolutionary War. He was also the first president of the United States from 1789 to 1797. His home in Virginia—known as Mount Vernon—is now the most popular historic estate in the nation, with an annual attendance of over 1.1 million.

George Washington was born in 1732 on a tobacco plantation near Colonial Beach, Virginia, to Augustine and Mary Ball Washington, prosperous plantation owners who were members of the Virginia gentry. He was the first of four siblings from his father's second marriage. He also had two half-brothers, Lawrence and Augustine, from the first marriage to Jane Butler. His father died when George was 11, and Lawrence became his surrogate father and role model.

George and Lawrence both inherited property—Lawrence received a plantation on the Potomac River, which he later named Mount Vernon, and George got Ferry Farm, where he spent much of his boyhood. He later acquired Mount Vernon after Lawrence's death in 1752. As a result of Lawrence's connections, George was appointed to the well-paid position of county surveyor at the age of 17 in 1749. This enabled him to purchase land in the Shenandoah Valley—the first of his many land investments in western Virginia. However, Lawrence, who suffered from tuberculosis, died in 1752.

In 1753 Washington was appointed a major in the Virginia militia by Governor Robert Dinwiddie and became involved in a number of frontier confrontations regarding British and French claims to the Ohio Country, which evolved into the French and Indian War in 1754–1762. These included Washington being captured and released by the French after being sent to protect a British fort under construction at present-day Pittsburgh, and rallying British troops retreating in disarray after Major General Edward Braddock was mortally wounded in a 1755 Ohio Country expedition. Washington was made commander of the Virginia Regiment, the first full-time American militia. He led the militia in more than 20 battles against Indians in the West, and in 1758 he participated in the British recapture of Fort Duquesne in Pittsburgh. He then retired from the Virginia Regiment to Mount Vernon.

Washington became one of the wealthiest men in Virginia in 1759 when he married Martha Dandridge Custis, a wealthy widow. The compatible couple never had any children together but raised two of her children from the previous marriage and later two of her grandchildren. Washington became a leading plantation owner and political figure and lived an aristocratic lifestyle. He doubled the size of Mount Vernon, switched from tobacco to other crops, expanded the facilities, and increased the number of slaves to over 100. He also held local office and was elected to the Virginia provincial legislature. At the same time, he became increasingly resentful of British economic forces in his personal finances and those of the colonies.

In 1774 Washington was one of seven Virginia delegates who traveled to Philadelphia for the First Continental Congress, created by the 13 colonies. When the Revolutionary War began in 1775, Washington was the unanimous choice of the Second Continental Congress as commander-in-chief of the Continental Army, which he led until the war ended and he retired in 1783. Washington did not win many battles, but he never let the British destroy his army and was victorious at the end.

The Revolutionary War already was under way when Washington arrived in Cambridge, Massachusetts, to take charge of the Continental Army. Battles already had been fought at Lexington and Concord, and the British were occupying Boston. This was followed by the British capturing New York and New Jersey. The only encouraging sign was Washington's 1776 Christmas night crossing of the Delaware River and winning the Battle of Trenton (*see* separate listing). But Washington was unsuccessful in defending Philadelphia, and his troops spent the cold winter of 1777–1778 at Valley Forge. The army barely survived the winter, but it did and even won some engagements. The decisive battle came at Yorktown, Virginia, in 1781 when British troops under Major General Charles Cornwallis surrendered.

After victory was finalized in 1783, Washington resigned and returned to Mount Vernon with the expectation that his days of public service were over. However, he became dissatisfied with the weak state of the union in the Articles of Confederation and presided over the Constitutional Convention that drafted the nation's Constitution in 1787. Two years later, he was elected the first president of the United States, and then reelected for a second term in 1793. He helped shape the role of the president in the first term by appointing the cabinet, supported programs to pay off all state and national debts, implemented an effective tax system, created a national bank, and selected a site for the nation's new capital. In the second term, he proclaimed the nation's neutrality in European wars, avoided war with Great Britain, dealt firmly with a tax protest, and expressed his opposition to the emerging political party system.

Washington refused a third term and returned to Mount Vernon in 1797. He died in 1799 after developing a severe throat infection. Washington was hailed as the nation's hero who was "first in war, first in peace, and first in the hearts of his countrymen." His will provided for the freeing of the slaves on the plantation after his and his wife's deaths. The remains of George and Marsha Washington, as well as other family members, are entombed on the grounds.

Ownership of Mount Vernon passed through a series of relatives until it was offered for sale in 1848 by John Augustine Washington, who tried unsuccessfully for five years to restore the estate. When the United States and Commonwealth of Virginia governments declined to purchase the property, the Mount Vernon Ladies Association of the Union, under the leadership of Ann Pamela Cunningham, bought the estate in 1854 and restored it. The 500-acre estate on the banks of the Potomac River now is a designated National Historic Landmark and listed on the National Register of Historic Places.

Mount Vernon consists of the Georgian-style mansion with period furniture and décor, a dozen historic structures, the Washington Tomb, and nearly 50 acres, which include gardens and restored landscapes. In addition, the estate has a working blacksmith shop, a pioneer farm site with a reconstructed slave cabin, and a 16-sided treading barn. Three miles from the mansion are the reconstructed George Washington distillery and gristmill. Guided tours are offered of a number of the sites.

Two additional major facilities are the Ford Orientation Center, which features a historic film and a miniature replica of Washington's home, and the Donald W. Reynolds Museum and Education Center, home to 25 theaters and galleries that tell the story of Washington's life with more than 500 artifacts, 11 video presentations, and an immersion theater.

Mount Vernon: George Washington's Estate and Gardens, South End of George Washington Memorial Pkwy., Mount Vernon, VA 22309 (postal address: George Washington's Mount Vernon, PO Box 110, Mount Vernon, VA 22121-0110). Phone: 703/780-2000. Fax: 703/799-8654. E-mail: info@mountvernon.org. Website: www.mountvernon.org. Hours: Apr.–Aug.—8–5 daily; Mar., Sept., and Oct.—9–5 daily; Nov.–Feb.—9–4 daily. Admission: adults, $15; seniors, $14; children 6–11, $7; children under 6, free.

George Washington Birthplace National Monument. The George Washington Birthplace National Monument is located at the site where Washington was born in 1732. It was on a tobacco plantation operated by his parents, Augustine and Mary Ball Washington, where Popes Creek joins the Potomac River near Colonial Beach, Virginia. The actual house no longer exists because of a fire and flood in 1779, but a memorial house has been built that represents a typical upper-class house of the period. The future president of the United States lived at the plantation until he was three years old and often returned later in his boyhood.

The site, which was settled by Washington's great-grandfather, John Washington, is representative of eighteenth-century Virginia tobacco farms. It contains farm buildings, groves of trees, livestock, gardens, and crops of tobacco and wheat as it did when George was a child. The memorial house has eighteenth-century period furnishings A memorial shaft obelisk, made of Vermont marble and one-tenth the size of the Washington Monument, is located at the entrance.

The birthplace house was built before 1718 and enlarged by Washington's father in 1722–1726. It became a 10-room mansion in the mid-1770s. On Christmas Day in 1779, the house was destroyed by fire and flood and never rebuilt. The house was located adjacent to the memorial house, and its foundation is outlined in the ground by crushed oyster shells. The family plot in the nearby Bridges Creek cemetery contains the graves of 32 members of the Washington family, including George's half-brother, father, grandfather, and great-grandfather.

The national monument was created in 1930, and the memorial house was built in 1930–1931. The house, which has a central hallway and four rooms on each floor, is furnished in 1730–1750 style by the Wakefield National Memorial Association. The site also has a visitor center with exhibits and a film depicting Washington family life, costumed reenactors who demonstrate candle and soap making, ranger talks, guided tours, hiking trails, and picnic grounds. Annual attendance is 131,000.

George Washington Birthplace National Monument, 1732 Popes Creek Rd., Colonial Beach, VA 22443-5115. Phone: 804/224-1732. Fax: 804/224-2142. Website: www.nps.gov/gewa. Hours: 9–5 daily; closed New Year's Day, Thanksgiving, and Christmas. Admission: free.

George Washington's Ferry Farm. Ferry Farm near Fredericksburg, Virginia, was George Washington's boyhood home. It was one of several farms owned by his father, Augustine Washington, and later was it inherited by George. In 1738, when George was six years old, his family moved from his birthplace on a plantation near Colonial Beach, Virginia, to this farm along the Rappahannock River. The farm became known as the Ferry Farm because people crossed the river on a ferry from the farm to the town of Fredericksburg. The farm was the setting for some of the best-known childhood stories about Washington, such as admitting to cutting down the cherry tree and tossing a silver dollar across the wide river.

When his father died in 1743, George was 11 years old. The will provided a parcel of land to each of the sons, leaving Ferry Farm and 10 slaves to George to be inherited when he turned 21. George's mother, Mary Ball Washington, who brought several properties, including Ferry Farm, to the marriage as her dowry, managed the farm until George came of age. It is where he received his formal education and forged friendships that lasted the rest of his life. In 1754 he moved to Mount Vernon. His mother continued to live at the farm until 1772, when she moved to Fredericksburg to live closer to her daughter, Betty.

Washington's house at Ferry Farm no longer exists, but its site was found on a bluff overlooking the river in 2008 by archaeologists, who discovered the foundation and cellars with thousands of fragmented artifacts. The house was a large one-and-a-half-story clapboard-covered wooden structure that suffered fire damage in 1840, served as a Union camp and was virtually destroyed during the Civil War, and lost its remaining wood to later builders in the Reconstruction period. Among the artifacts are such items as pieces of pottery and other ceramics, glass shards, wig curlers, and toothbrush handles made of bone.

Ferry Farm, which covers approximately 80 acres, has a visitor center with exhibits on the history of the farm and displays some of the colonial and Civil War artifacts found on the property. Visitors also often can see archaeologists working on artifacts in the archaeology laboratory in the visitor center. The archaeological dig site normally is open May through August.

Ferry Farm is operated by the George Washington Foundation, which acquired the site in 1996 to save it from commercial development. The nonprofit foundation also operates the Historic Kenmore Plantation, a 1775 Georgian-style brick mansion in Fredericksburg built by George Washington's sister, Betty, and her merchant husband, Colonel Fielding Lewis. A combination ticket is available for those who wish to visit both historic sites. The annual attendance for the two sites is 29,000.

George Washington's Ferry Farm, 268 Kings Hwy., Fredericksburg, VA 22405 (postal address: George Washington Foundation, 1201 Washington Ave, Fredericksburg, VA 22401). Phone: 540/371-3363. Fax: 540/371-3398. E-mail: mailroom@kenmore.org. Website: www.kenmore.org. Hours: Mar.–Oct.—10–5 daily; Nov.–Dec.—10–4 daily; closed Jan.–Feb., Easter, Thanksgiving, Christmas Eve and Day, and New Year's Eve. Admission: adults, $8; students, $4; children under 6, free; combination ticket for two sites—adults, $15; students, $8; children under 6, free.

George Washington's Office Museum. Colonel George Washington used a little log cabin as a military office from September 1755 to December 1756 while he directed the construction of Fort Loudoun in Winchester, Virginia. The fort was one of a series of frontier military outposts being constructed by the British prior to the French and Indian War. Washington planned the fort and supervised the work. The fort, which covered half an acre, was a redoubt with four bastions, 14 mounted cannons, and barracks for 450 men. The fort was never attacked, and only the well remains of the fort today.

The log cabin is now the middle room of George Washington's Office Museum, operated by the Winchester-Frederick County Historical Society. The museum contains some of Washington's personal effects, surveying equipment, and a scale model of the town of Winchester in 1755. A statue of Washington as a young surveyor is located outside the museum, as well as a cannon left in Alexandria by British General Edward Braddock, for whom Washington was senior aide at the time.

George Washington's Office Museum, 32 W. Cork and Braddock Sts., Winchester, VA 22601 (postal address: Winchester-Frederick County Historical Society, 1340 S. Pleasant Valley Rd., Winchester, VA 22601-4442). E-mail: wfchs@verizon.net. Website: www.winchesterhistory.org/george_washington.htm. Hours; Apr.–Oct.—10–4 Mon.–Sat., 12–4 Sun.; closed Nov.–Mar. Admission: adults, $5; seniors, $4.50; students, $2.50; families, $12.

George Washington's Headquarters. A log cabin in Cumberland, Maryland, served as headquarters for George Washington on two occasions—while he was a colonel in the French and Indian War in 1755–1758 and briefly while commander-in-chief reviewing troops gathered to put down the Whiskey Rebellion in 1794. The cabin, now a historic site called George Washington's Headquarters, is said to be his first headquarters.

The one-room cabin was part of Fort Cumberland during the French and Indian War and now is its only remaining structure. The building, which has been moved to Riverside Park, was built by British General Edward Braddock for Washington, who was serving as senior aide to the general at the time. The cabin is not open to the public, but the inside can be viewed through a window with an audio description. It is operated by the city and the Cresap Chapter of the Daughters of the American Revolution.

George Washington's Headquarters, Greene St., Cumberland, MD 21502 (postal address: Parks/Recreation Dept., City Hall, PO Box 1702, Cumberland, MD 21501-1701). Phone: 301/759-6636. Fax: 301/759-3223. E-mail: djohnson@cumberland.md.us. Hours: by appointment. Admission: free.

Washington Crossing Historical Park. One of the most memorable events of the American Revolutionary War was the surprise crossing of the Delaware River on Christmas night 1776 by General George Washington and men of the Continental Army and militia who attacked and defeated Britain's Hessian troops in and around Trenton, New Jersey. The triumph set the stage for Washington's subsequent victories at the Second Battle of Trenton and Princeton. The crossing was immortalized by artist Emanuel Gottlieb Leutze's famous painting *Washington Crossing the Delaware*.

The crossing of the Delaware River occurred after a series of Continental Army defeats. In the Battle of Long Island, the British outmaneuvered the colonists and captured New York City. Washington and his ragged army were forced to retreat across the Hudson River and New Jersey to Pennsylvania. With the arrival of a harsh winter, morale was low as soldiers lacked warm clothing, food, and adequate equipment, and the army lost men through desertions and expired enlistments. A victory was desperately needed to turn the tide.

Washington proposed crossing the icy Delaware River in a surprise attack on British forces consisting of hired Hessian (German) troops stationed around Trenton. The original plan called for three divisions to cross the river under the cover of darkness. But the two planned crossings south of Trenton in support of the operation were either called off or ineffective because of an abrupt change in the weather. Despite the icy river, sleet, and blinding snowstorm, Washington and 2,400 men took to their heavy Durham pig iron and other boats near McConkey's Ferry and successfully completed the Christmas night crossing.

The next day, Washington's troops marched into Trenton and routed the surprised Hessians under Johann Rall, capturing and taking approximately 900 prisoners back to Pennsylvania. On January 2 and 3, the colonial forces defeated British reinforcements under Lord Charles Cornwallis and then his rear guard at Princeton before settling in winter quarters in Morristown, New Jersey. The victories rejuvenated the Continental Army and gave new life to the American Revolution.

Two state historical parks now honor Washington's crossing of the Delaware River and victories and make up the Washington's Crossing National Historic Landmark—the Washington Crossing Historical Park in Pennsylvania and the Washington Crossing State Park in New Jersey (*see* separate listing). The Pennsylvania site is a 500-acre park founded in 1917 and operated by the Pennsylvania Historical and Museum Commission. It is headquartered in Washington Crossing, named for its proximity to Washington's crossing of the Delaware. The park has two sections—the Washington Crossing section and the Thompson Mill section.

The Washington Crossing section includes the site where Washington crossed the Delaware River; McConkey Ferry Inn, where Washington is believed to have been prior to the crossing; Taylor House, home of the influential businessman Mahlon Taylor; and Memorial Building, which contains a copy of the famous painting of Washington crossing the Delaware. The Thompson Mill section contains Bowman's Hill Tower, a 110-foot tower dedicated to Washington and the Continental Army; Thompson-Neely House, site of many conferences before the Battle of Trenton; and Memorial Flagstaff, which has graves of Continental Army troops who were the first of the nation's unknown soldiers. The park's estimated annual attendance is 350,000.

Washington Crossing Historical Park, 1112 River Rd., Washington Crossing, PA 18977-1202 (postal address: PO Box 103, Washington Crossing, PA 18977-0103). Phone: 215/493-4076. Fax: 215/493-4820. Website: www.ushistory.org/washingtoncrossing. Hours: 9–5 Tues.–Sat., 12–5 Sun.; closed Mon. and most major holidays. Admission: adults, $7; seniors, $6; children 3–11, $4; children under 3, free.

Washington Crossing State Park. The 3,126-acre Washington Crossing State Park in New Jersey is located where General George Washington and 2,400 men of the Continental Army and militia crossed the icy Delaware River from Pennsylvania in a surprise attack on British forces in Trenton on Christmas night in 1776 during the American Revolutionary War. The victory over Hessian troops at Trenton was followed by the defeat of British reinforcements at the Second Battle of Trenton and Battle of Princeton on January 2 and 3, providing new hope for the struggling Continental Army.

The park is a combination historical, cultural, and nature park operated by the New Jersey Division of Parks and Forestry. The site first began as a historic house museum in 1912 with the establishment of the Johnson Ferry House, an early eighteenth-century farmhouse and tavern near a ferry landing where Washington and the boatloads of troops crossed the Delaware. It also is believed that Washington and other officers used the building that Christmas night.

The house was owned by Garret Johnson, who ran a 490-acre colonial plantation and a ferry service across the river. The bed-chamber, textile, and storage rooms are furnished with local period pieces. The site also has an eighteenth-century kitchen garden, and living history demonstrations frequently are given on weekends.

Among the other historical aspects are the Washington Crossing Visitor Center Museum and the Swan Historical Foundation Collection. The visitor center contains exhibits on the Revolutionary War, and the Swan Collection is a living military history laboratory of the American Revolution with over 700 historical objects that interpret the 1745–1789 era. In addition, the park administers the Trenton Battle Monument, which marks the site where the American artillery emplacement controlled the streets of Trenton, leading to the defeat of the three Hessian divisions at the Battle of Trenton.

The park also is the site of such cultural offerings as the Washington Crossing Open Air Theater, which presents performing arts programs May through September, and the John W. H. Simpson Observatory, with Friday night programs April through October. The nature facilities include the Nature Center, with nature education programs Wednesday through Sunday; a 140-acre Natural Area with an interpretive center, a mature mixed oak-hardwood forest, other woods and fields, and a nature blind where birds and animals can be observed; walking trails; and camping and picnicking facilities.

Washington Crossing State Park, 355 Washington Crossing, Pennington Rd., Titusville, NJ 08560-1517. Phones: park—609/737-0623; Johnson Ferry House—609/737-2515; visitor center museum—609/737-9303. Website: www. state.nj.us/dep/parksandforests/parks/washcros.html. Hours: park—8–6 daily; Johnson Ferry House—10–12 and 1–4 Wed.–Sat., 1–4 Sun.; closed Mon.–Tues.; visitor center museum—9–4 daily. Admission: Memorial Day–Labor Day—$5 per car on Sat.–Sun.; free other times.

Washington Headquarters State Historic Site. The house that served as the headquarters for General George Washington the longest during the Revolutionary War was the Hasbrouck House, now part of the Washington Headquarters State Historic Site in Newburgh, New York. Washington used the house as his headquarters for more than 15 months—from April 1782 until August 1783. It was acquired by the State of New York in 1850 and became the first publicly operated historic site in the country in 1884.

The historic site is where Washington issued his order for "cessation of hostilities," which formally ended the Revolutionary War. It also is where he rejected the idea that he should be king after the war, spoke out against military control of the government, defused a mutiny threat among officers over pay and pensions, wrote a letter to state governors that influenced the writing of the Constitution, and created the Badge of Military Merit, which was the forerunner of the Purple Heart.

The Newburgh site was chosen by Washington because of its comparatively safe location north of the strategically important West Point. The house was built in 1750 by Jonathan and Catherine Hasbrouck and underwent two enlargements before being completed in 1770. The historic site covers three acres and has three buildings, a monument, and a statue. They include the Hasbrouck House, a museum added in 1910, a maintenance shed/garage built in 1942, an 1890 monument called the Tower of Victory, and a 1924 statue titled *The Minuteman*. The historic site, which is a National Historic Landmark, has an annual attendance of 21,000.

Washington's Headquarters State Historic Site, Liberty and Washington Sts., Newburgh, NY 12551-1476 (postal address: PO Box 1783, Newburgh, NY 12551-1783). Phone: 845/562-1195. Fax: 845/561-1789. Website: www. nysparks.state.ny.us/historic-sites/17/details.aspx. Hours: mid-Apr.–Oct.—10–5 Wed.–Sat., 1–5 Sun.; closed Mon.–Tues.; Nov.–Mar.—by appointment; closed early Apr. Admission: adults, $4; seniors and students, $3; children under 13, free.

Washington Monument (Washington). In recognition of George Washington's service to the nation, the United States built the 555-foot, 5¼ inch Washington Monument, the world's tallest obelisk, in Washington. The actual construction began in 1848 but was not completed until 1884 because of the Civil War, lack of funds, and political differences. More than 460,000 people now visit the monument each year. Views of over 30 miles can be seen from the top.

The obelisk, located at the west end of the National Mall, was designed by architect Robert Mills. It is made of marble, granite, and bluestone gneiss, with a slight difference in the shading of the marble where construction was halted for a number of years. It once was the tallest structure in the world. The cornerstone was laid in 1848, the capstone was set in 1884, the obelisk was dedicated in 1885, and the monument officially opened in 1888. It was closed temporarily in 2011–2013 because of damage from an earthquake.

Washington Monument, National Mall, 15th St., Washington, DC (postal address: National Mall and Memorial Parks, 900 Ohio Dr., S.W., Washington, DC 20024. Phone: 202/426-6841. Website: www.nps.gov/wamo. Hours: Memorial Day weekend–Labor Day—9 a.m.–10 p.m. daily; remainder of year—9–5 daily; closed Independence Day and Christmas. Admission: free, but it is necessary to obtain a timed ticket at the Washington Monument Lodge on 15th St.

Washington Monument (Baltimore). The first architectural monument planned to honor George Washington was the Washington Monument in Baltimore, Maryland. A monument initially was proposed in Baltimore in 1809, and a committee was formed to commission and fund the monument. The first of six lotteries authorized by the Maryland General Assembly was held in 1811, and they eventually raised enough funds to build the tribute for the nation's first president. The design submitted by architect Robert Mills, who later designed the Washington Monument in the nation's capital, was selected, and construction began in 1815. The monument was completed in 1829.

The Washington Monument in Baltimore is a 178-foot Doric white marble column in a historic neighborhood. The site consists of three main elements—a museum devoted to Washington and the construction of the monument on a rectangular base on the ground floor; a plain, unfluted column with 228 steps to a viewing area at the top; and a standing statue of Washington atop the monument. Although work began on the Baltimore monument earlier, the first Washington monument to be completed was at the Washington Monument State Park near Boonsboro, Maryland, in 1827 (*see* separate listing).

Washington Monument, 699 N. Charles St., Baltimore, MD 21201. Phones: 410/396-0929 and 410/396-1049. Hours: 10–4 Wed.–Fri., 10–5 Sun.; closed Mon.–Tues. Admission: suggested donation—$5.

Washington Monument State Park. The first monument honoring George Washington to be completed was built by the citizens of Boonsboro, Maryland, near the summit of South Mountain's 1,540-foot monument knob in 1827. Most of the town's 500 residents gathered at the public square and then marched to the music of a fife and drum corps several miles to the site and built and dedicated the 30-foot rugged stone memorial. The day ended with the reading of the Declaration of Independence and a three-round salute fired by three Revolutionary War veterans.

The 30-foot monument became a popular meeting place, but it suffered weather and vandalism damage over the years and needed to be restored by 1882. A canopy was added and a roadway was built up the mountainside to the site. In 1934 the monument was rebuilt in its present form by the Civilian Conservation Corps, and the site became the Washington Monument State Park. A museum with artifacts related to the history of the monument and the Battle of South Mountain is now part of the monument.

Washington Monument State Park, 6620 Zittlestown Rd., Middletown, MD 21769. Phone: 301/791-4767. Website: www.dnr.state.md.us/publiclands.western/washington.asp. Hours: 8–sunset daily. Admission: free.

Mount Rushmore National Memorial. George Washington and three other American presidents—Thomas Jefferson, Abraham Lincoln, and Theodore Roosevelt—are honored at the Mount Rushmore National Monument near Keystone, South Dakota. Sixty-foot sculptures of their faces were carved into the granite of Mount Rushmore by Gutzon Borglum and his son, Lincoln Borglum, between 1927 and 1941. The site, which became a national memorial in 1933, covers 1,278 acres.

Historian Doane Robinson is credited with the idea of carving the likenesses of famous people into the Black Hills region to promote South Dakota tourism. Gutzon Borglum, the noted Danish American sculptor, was selected for the project. Robinson's initial proposal in 1923 was to sculpt granite pillars known as the "Needles," but it was rejected because of the poor quality of the granite and opposition from environmentalists and Native American groups. Mount Rushmore, the highest mountain in the region at 5,725 feet, was then selected. It also was decided to give the sculpture a more national focus. Borglum selected the four presidents to be carved into the mountain because of their role in founding and preserving the republic during its first 150 years.

Congress approved the project in 1925, and Borglum and 400 workers began carving the sculpture in 1927. The original plan was to sculpt the figures from head to waist, but this was changed to just the facial likeness because of insufficient funds. Borglum directed the project until the late 1930s and died in 1941 of embolism. His son, Lincoln, who also was a sculptor and his assistant, finished the work. The National Park Service, which operates the site today, took control of the project in 1933.

A canyon behind the sculpture features a chamber with a vault with 16 porcelain enamel panels that contain the Declaration of Independence, the Constitution, biographies of the four presidents and Borglum, and the history of the site. The memorial also has an information center, the Lincoln Borglum Visitor Center, the Sculptor's Studio, and a Presidential Trail. The facilities include 5,200 square feet of exhibits, a library with historic papers and journals, and a 1,500-seat outdoor amphitheater for programming. Among the memorial's collections are 40,000 pieces of archival materials, 3,500 tools and equipment used in the construction of the sculpture, and 2,000 historic photographs and negatives. Annual attendance is over 2.7 million.

Mount Rushmore National Memorial, 13000 Hwy. 244, Bldg. 31, Ste. 1, Keystone, SD 57751-0268. Phone: 605/574-2523. Fax: 605/574-2307. E-mail: bruce_weisman@nps.gov. Website: www.nps.gov/moru. Hours: information center—Memorial Day weekend–mid-Aug.: 8 a.m.–10 p.m. daily; mid-Aug.–Sept.: 8 a.m.–9 p.m. daily; Oct.–late May: 8–5 daily. Admission: free, but $11 parking fee.

George Washington Masonic National Memorial. The Masonic building in Alexandria, Virginia, is dedicated to George Washington, the nation's first president and a Mason. The building—called the George Washington

Masonic National Memorial—is a 333-foot neoclassical tower designed after the ancient lighthouse of Alexandria in Egypt. Construction of the building, which is located on Shooter's Hill, began in 1922, it was dedicated in 1932, and the interior was finally completed in 1970.

A memorial for a statue of Washington originally was proposed in 1852 by Masonic Lodge 4 in Fredericksburg, Virginia, with funding from state Masonic lodges. Enough funds were raised for a life-size bronze statue of Washington in Masonic regalia that was displayed in Alexandria until the summer of 1863, when it was moved to Richmond and destroyed in a fire when the South surrendered to the Union Army in 1865.

In 1909 it was proposed that a Masonic memorial be constructed on Shooter's Hill in Alexandria. Instead, a citizens' committee converted the land to the George Washington Memorial Park. Construction of the park sparked renewed Masonic interest in building its own memorial. Alexandria-Washington Lodge 22 proposed a national Masonic Washington memorial and was successful in buying a portion of the city park for a Masonic temple honoring Washington in 1915. They then received national Masonic support to construct the memorial. The designs started with a three-story memorial structure and eventually grew to the 333-foot granite tower.

The memorial consists of nine floors. The first floor features the Grand Masonic Hall with 12 dioramas depicting Masonic events in Washington's life in a semicircle surrounding a bust of Washington. Three rooms also contain exhibits on the history and activities of the Shriners. Memorial Hall on the second floor contains a 17-foot-high bronze statue of Washington in Masonic regalia, murals of Washington, a replica of the Alexandria-Washington lodge room at the time Washington presided over the lodge, and a theater.

Among the other sights in the building are exhibits about the Mystic Order of Veiled Prophets of the Enchanted Realm and the organization's archives; a George Washington Museum with exhibits, artifacts, and a statue; a 20,000-volume library; various spots dedicated to Masonry; a chapel; and the Tall Cedars Room and observation platform. Guided tours are offered. Annual attendance is 76,000.

George Washington Masonic Memorial, 101 Callahan Dr., Alexandria, VA 22301-2751. Phone: 703/683-2007. Fax: 703/519-9270. E-mail: gseghers@gwmemorial.org. Website: www.gwmemorial.org. Hours: Apr.–Sept.—9–4 Mon.–Sat., 12–4 Sun.; Oct.–Mar.—10–4 Mon.–Sat.; 12–4 Sun.; closed major holidays. Admission: first and second floors, free; tower exhibits and observation platform—adults, $5; families of 5 or more, $20; children under 13, free.

George Washington Masonic Museum. George Washington became a Mason when he lived at Ferry Farm near Fredericksburg, Virginia, in 1752. Today, the George Washington Masonic Museum in Fredericksburg is named for the first president of the United States in recognition of service to the lodge and the nation. The Fredericksburg Masonic Lodge 4 museum contains memorabilia and artifacts relating to his membership, including an original Gilbert Stuart portrait, as well as other eighteenth- and nineteenth-century Masonic and American historical items. The museum is housed in the lodge's historic 1816 temple building.

George Washington Masonic Museum, Fredericksburg Masonic Lodge 4, 803 Princess Annex St., Fredericksburg, VA 22401-5819 (postal address: PO Box 702, Fredericksburg, VA 22404-0702). Phone: 540/373-5885. Website: www.qwashington1999.org. Hours: varies. Admission: free.

John Adams and John Quincy Adams

Adams National Historical Park. The Adams National Historical Park in Quincy, Massachusetts, honors two early presidents of the United States—John Adams and his son, John Quincy Adams—and tells the story of five generations of the distinguished New England family from 1720 to 1927. John Adams served as the first vice president and second president of the nation in 1797–1801 and John Quincy Adams was the sixth president in 1825–1829.

The historical park, founded in 1927, consists of 11 buildings on 13 acres that trace the lives of the former presidents and others who were first ladies, foreign ministers, historians, writers, and family members who supported and contributed to their success. Among the historic structures are the 1731 "Peacefield," home to four generations of the Adams family; John Adams's birthplace; John Quincy Adams's birthplace; the 1870 Stone Library, with more than 14,000 historic volumes (believed to be the first presidential library); and an 1873 carriage house.

The park also provides access to the adjacent United First Parish Church, where both presidents and their first ladies are entombed in the Adams family crypt. All park tours begin at an off-site visitor center, which has exhibits, runs a trolley bus service, and offers guided tours on the two presidents and the Adams family. The park contains approximately 100,000 objects, including original furnishings, books, archival materials, and archaeological items donated by the family in 1946. Annual attendance is 185,000.

John Adams was a lawyer, statesman, diplomat, and political theorist who was one of the principal Founding Fathers of the United States. He was born in 1735 in a section of Braintree (now Quincy), Massachusetts, to John

John Adams and his son, John Quincy Adams, are honored at the Adams National Historical Park in Quincy, Massachusetts. Courtesy of the National Park Service, Adams National Historical Park.

Adams Sr. and Susanne Boylston Adams—a family that traced its history to Puritan emigrants who came to Massachusetts Bay Colony from England in 1638. His father was a farmer, a Puritan deacon, a militia lieutenant, and a town councilman who was educated at Harvard College. John Adams attended the Latin School, received tutoring, and graduated from Harvard in 1755. He earned a law degree and was admitted to the Massachusetts bar in 1758.

In 1764 Adams married Abigail Smith, a third cousin, and they had four children. She turned out to be invaluable in assisting and advising her husband and teaching and guiding her son, who later became President John Quincy Adams (*see* Abigail Adams in First Ladies section).

John Adams was an influential constitutional lawyer and Federalist politician. He first came to prominence in the early stages of the American Revolution when, as a delegate from Massachusetts to the Continental Congress, he was instrumental in persuading Congress to declare independence. In 1775 he nominated George Washington as commander-in-chief of the Continental Army. He also assigned Thomas Jefferson to drafting the United States Declaration of Independence in 1776 and largely wrote the long-standing Massachusetts State Constitution in 1780, which led to the ending of slavery in that state.

Adams demonstrated his diplomatic skills while representing Congress in Europe. He was chiefly responsible for obtaining important loans from Dutch bankers and with Benjamin Franklin and John Jay negotiated the eventual Revolutionary War peace treaty with Great Britain in 1782. Adams also served as minister to Great Britain in 1785–1788.

He was elected vice president for two terms during George Washington's presidency and was chosen president in 1796 when Washington decided against a third term. He was not an especially popular president and was defeated by Thomas Jefferson for reelection.

After his presidency, Adams returned to Massachusetts and spent most of his later years learning, corresponding with old friends, and mending relations with Thomas Jefferson and other rivals. He died at the age of 90 on Independence Day in 1826, the same day as Jefferson.

John Quincy Adams, the eldest son of John and Abigail Adams, was a diplomat, senator, congressman, and the first president of the United States whose father also was president (the second was George W. Bush). He was born in 1767 on a farm in Braintree, Massachusetts, like his father. In many respects, John Quincy also was similar to his father in temperament, viewpoints, and career.

John Quincy spent much of his early years in Europe. At the age of 14, he served as a secretary on a mission to Russia and then as secretary to his father when posted as American envoy to France and the Netherlands in 1778–1782. In 1779 he started a diary that he kept until just before he died in 1848. It totaled 50 volumes and became one of the most extensive and valuable collections of firsthand information about the early days of the republic.

Adams graduated from Harvard College in 1787 with Phi Beta Kappa honors, received a master's degree in 1790, and became a lawyer in Boston the next year. He then was appointed minister to the Netherlands and served in Germany from 1796 to 1801. He married Louisa Catherine Johnson in 1797, and they had four children.

In 1802 Adams was elected to the U.S. Senate, serving from 1803 to 1808, when he was named minister to Russia by President James Madison. He also served as one of the negotiators for the 1814 Treaty of Ghent that ended the War of 1812 with Great Britain, and then he became minister to Great Britain in 1815–1817. He was secretary of state under President Monroe in 1817–1825, during which he settled the Oregon Territory boundary with Britain in 1818, purchased Florida from Spain, and largely formulated the Monroe Doctrine in 1823.

As president, Adams initiated a program of highways and canals to bring the nation's sections together and urged the development of the arts and sciences by establishing a national university, financing scientific expenditures, and building an observatory. But his critics charged him with corruption and public plunder, and he lost reelection to Andrew Jackson. However, he was elected to the House of Representatives from the Plymouth district in 1830 and served in Congress until his death of a heart attack in 1848 when 80 years old.

Adams National Historical Park, 135 Adams St., Quincy, MA 02169-1749. Phone: 617/770-1175. Fax: 617/472-7562. E-mail: adams_visitor_center@nps.gov. Website: www.nps.gov/adams. Hours: mid-Apr.–mid-Nov.—9–5 daily; closed remainder of year. Admission: adults, $5; children under 16, free.

Abigail Adams Birthplace. *See* Abigail Adams in First Ladies section.

Thomas Jefferson

Monticello: Home of Thomas Jefferson. Thomas Jefferson, one of the principal Founding Fathers of the nation, was the third president of the United States, serving from 1801 to 1809. He was a major Virginia tobacco planter who was a leading member of the Continental Congress, principal author of the Declaration of Independence, governor and originator of the Virginia statute for freedom of religion, founder of the University of Virginia, and initiator of the Louisiana Purchase from France and the Lewis and Clark Expedition that explored the American West during his presidency.

Jefferson's plantation home—which he called Monticello (from the Italian "little mountain") because it is on the summit of an 850-foot peak—celebrates his life and career in Charlottesville, Virginia. It has been owned and operated by the Thomas Jefferson Foundation since 1923. The 11,000-square-foot house, which Jefferson designed and rebuilt over 40 years, originally was built in 1772 and is based on the neoclassical principles described in the books of Andrea Palladio, an Italian Renaissance architect. It has been designated a National Historic Landmark and listed in the National Register of Historic Places. It also is the only private home in the United States that has been chosen a UNESCO World Heritage Site.

Jefferson was born in 1743 in Goochland (now Albemarle County), Virginia, to Peter Jefferson, a planter and major slaveholder, and June Randolph, a member of one of Virginia's most distinguished families. Thomas was the third of 10 children. When Colonel William Randolph, an old friend of Peter Jefferson, died in 1745, Peter became executor and in charge of Randolph's estate in Tuckahoe, as well as his infant son. When his father died in 1757, Thomas Jefferson inherited the 5,000-acre estate with about 50 slaves.

Thomas started his schooling in 1752 at a local school headed by a Scottish Presbyterian minister, and began studying Latin, Greek, and French at the age of nine. He then followed with instruction in history, science, classics, mathematics, metaphysics, philosophy, and violin. He also had an introduction to the writings of John Locke, Francis Bacon, and Isaac Newton. Jefferson graduated from William and Mary College with the highest honors in 1762, read law while working as a law clerk, and was admitted to the Virginia bar in 1767.

As a youth, Jefferson became an avid reader and eventually collected thousands of books, which played an important role in his life. He actually had three libraries—the first was burned in a plantation fire, the second was sold to Congress after the British burned the Capitol in 1814 and it became the nucleus of the Library of Congress, and the third is now in the south wing of his mansion.

Jefferson actively practiced law from 1768 to 1773 and served in local government as a magistrate, county lieutenant, and member of the Virginia's House of Burgesses (1769–1775) in his early professional life. In 1772, at the age of 28, he married Martha Wayles Skelton, a 23-year-old widow. They had six children, but only two survived to adulthood. His wife died after childbirth in 1782, and he never remarried. But it is believed that he had six children by Sally Hemings, a mixed-race slave. Her family was the only slave family Jefferson ever freed. The Jefferson family denied the relationship, but a 1998 DNA study showed a match between the Jefferson male line and a Hemings descendant.

In 1773 Jefferson, R. H. Lee, and Patrick Henry improved communications among the colonies by forming an intercolonial committee that exchanged information regularly, and the following year he wrote the widely circulated *Summary View of the Rights of British America*. Jefferson became a delegate to the Continental Congress in 1776 and was appointed chairman of the committee that prepared the Declaration of Independence. He wrote and presented the first draft of the declaration and became known as the author of the Declaration of Independence. He also was the author of Virginia's 1777 statute on religious freedom and wrote *Notes on the State of Virginia* in 1785, which included contemporary scientific knowledge and Virginia's history, politics, and ethnography.

Jefferson served as governor of Virginia in 1779–1781; on the Continental Congress, 1783–1785; as minister to France, 1785–1789; and as secretary of state, 1790–1793. In 1796 Jefferson ran to succeed Washington as president but lost to John Adams by three electoral votes and served as vice president (1797–1801). Four years later, he defeated Adams and became the third president of the United States.

As president, Jefferson purchased the vast Louisiana Territory from France in 1803, sent the Lewis and Clark Expedition to explore the West in 1804–1806, and became a leading opponent of the international slave trade and presided over its abolition in 1807. Yet he remained a planter with hundreds of slaves on his various plantations.

Jefferson's second term suffered from the failed Aaron Burr treason trial and difficulties with Britain. Burr, who lost to Jefferson and served as vice president in the 1801–1805 presidency, conspired with General James Wilkinson and others to seize territory from Mexico and the Southwest to create a new republic. He was charged with treason but was acquitted in 1807.

After serving as president in 1801–1809, Jefferson continued to be active in public affairs. In 1819 he founded the University of Virginia, the first American university centered on a library rather than a church. Jefferson spearheaded the legislative campaign for its charter, secured its location, designed the buildings, planned the curriculum, and served as the first rector (president). The university opened in 1825—the same year his health began to deteriorate. He died the following year at the age of 83 from a combination of illnesses, including uremia, severe diarrhea, and pneumonia, on July 4—the 50th anniversary of the Declaration of Independence and on the same day as second president John Adams. He is buried in the family cemetery at Monticello.

Monticello was inherited by Jefferson's surviving daughter, Martha Jefferson Randolph. The estate was encumbered with debt, and she had financial problems, resulting in the sale of the plantation in 1831. Navy Admiral Uriah P. Levy purchased the estate three years later and restored Monticello, but the Confederates seized the property during the Civil War and then sold it.

Levy's nephew, Jefferson Monroe Levy, settled lawsuits and took control of the estate in 1879 and commissioned repairs and restoration. In 1923 the Thomas Jefferson Foundation bought the land. It has operated Monticello as a historic house museum since then. The foundation also has acquired 2,500 of the original 5,000 acres of the plantation; restored the mansion, gardens, and other facilities; and made such additions as the 15,500-square-foot Jefferson Library, Smith International Center for Jefferson Studies, Thomas Jefferson Center for Historic Plants, Sanders-Monticello Trail, and a visitor center.

Visitors can view rooms on the ground floor and in the cellar of the 11,000 square-foot mansion (and the third floor dome only during one of the tours). Among the other buildings on the plantation are a dairy, a small nail factory, a joinery, washhouses, storehouses, and slave dwellings known as "Mulberry Row." Monticello also has collections of Jeffersonian furniture, memorabilia, art objects, slavery artifacts, personal items, and books. Annual attendance is 450,000.

Monticello: Home of Thomas Jefferson, 931 Thomas Jefferson Pkwy., Charlottesville, VA 22902-7148 (postal address: PO Box 316, Charlottesville, VA 22902-0316). Phone: 434/984-9822. Fax: 434/977-7751. E-mail: info@monticello.org. Website: www.monticello.org. Hours: Mar.–Oct.—8–5 daily; Nov.–Feb.—9–4:30 daily; closed Christmas. Admission: adults, $15–$20; children 6–11, $8; children under 6, free.

Thomas Jefferson's Poplar Forest. The Poplar Forest in Forest, Virginia (near Lynchburg), was a 4,819-acre plantation that Thomas Jefferson used as a source of income and a retreat where he could pursue his passion for reading, writing, studying, and gardening after serving as president of the United States. He used the remote location as a place to escape the many visitors he received at Monticello in Charlottesville.

Jefferson and his wife, Martha, inherited the estate, known as Poplar Forest, from her father, John Wayles, in 1773. In the early years of ownership, Jefferson merely managed the plantation from Monticello, except for two months in 1781 when the family left Monticello for Poplar Forest to avoid being captured by the British in the American Revolutionary War.

During his presidency in 1806, Jefferson supervised the laying of the foundation for the Poplar Forest's octagonal house, which still exists today. He also oversaw the ornamentation of the house and grounds and the planning of his vegetable garden. In his visits to the estate, he frequently was accompanied by family members, usually grandchildren. He made his last trip to Poplar Forest in 1823 because of health reasons.

Jefferson originally intended to give Poplar Forest to his youngest daughter, Mary Jefferson Eppes, and her family, but she died at the age of 26. In 1823 he gave the property to her only surviving son, Francis, and his bride upon their marriage. They sold the plantation in 1828 and moved to Florida.

The octagonal house was built according to Palladian principles, like Monticello, and included a central cube room, with porticos to the north and south and a service wing to the east. Although the design of the house worked for Jefferson, subsequent owners of the property found it difficult to inhabit and made changes to suit their needs. The house also was damaged in a fire in 1845 and converted into a more typical farmhouse.

In 1983 the nonprofit Corporation for Jefferson's Poplar Forest acquired and began to restore and preserve the house and 50 acres of what remained of the plantation. Since then, the house has been undergoing restoration to how it was when Jefferson owned it, and over 600 acres of the original plantation have been purchased to provide a landscape easement for the house. The house now is a historic house museum, and the site has been designated a National Historic Landmark. Admission includes a guided house tour and access to the grounds and exhibits. Annual attendance is nearly 22,500.

Thomas Jefferson's Poplar Forest, 1008 Poplar Forest Dr., Forest, VA 24551 (postal address: PO Box 419, Forest, VA 24551-0419). Phone: 434/525-1806. Fax: 434/525-7252. Hours: Mar.–Dec. 15—10–4 daily; closed Thanksgiving and Dec. 16–Feb. Admission: adults, $14; seniors and military, $12; college students, $7; children 12–18, $6; children 6–11, $2; children under 6, free.

Thomas Jefferson Memorial. The Thomas Jefferson Memorial along the Tidal Basin of the Potomac River in Washington, DC, honors the third president of the United States. The neoclassical building was designed by John Russell Pope, with construction beginning in 1939 and completed in 1943. It was dedicated on the 200th anniversary of Jefferson's birthday and was one of the last American public monuments in the Beaux-Arts tradition.

The national memorial, which is listed on the National Register of Historic Places, features a 19-foot bronze statue of Jefferson by sculptor Rudolph Evans in a building that is open to the elements. The sculpture, which shows Jefferson looking out toward the White House, was added four years after the dedication. The monument has circular marble steps, a portico, a circular colonnade of Ionic columns, and a shallow dome.

The interior walls are engraved with passages from Jefferson's writings. The most prominent words are in the frieze below the dome and say, "I have sworn upon the altar of God eternal hostility against every form of tyranny over the mind of man." The southwest interior wall has excerpts from the Declaration of Independence, the northwest interior wall contains quotations from Jefferson's 1777 Virginia bill about freedom of religion, and the northeast interior wall features quotes from some of his other writings.

The imposing Jefferson Memorial, which is open 24 hours every day, is a popular site for special programs and rallies and has an annual attendance of over 2.3 million. It is managed by the National Mall and Memorial Parks division of the National Park Service.

Thomas Jefferson Memorial, Tidal Basin, South Bank, 15th St., N.W., Washington, DC (postal address: National Mall and Memorial Parks, National Park Service, 900 Ohio Dr., S.W., Washington, DC 20024). Phone: 202/426-6841. Website: www.nps.gov/thje. Hours: open 24 hours. Admission: free.

Jefferson National Expansion Memorial. The Jefferson National Expansion Memorial in St. Louis was established in 1935 to honor the westward movement of American explorers and pioneers and the role of President Thomas Jefferson in the Louisiana Purchase and the Lewis and Clark Expedition in the nation's westward expansion. The memorial consists of a 91-acre park along the Mississippi River that includes the spectacular 630-foot tall Gateway Arch, the Museum of Westward Expansion, and the historic 1839 Old Courthouse where the 1847 and 1850 trials of the Dred Scott slavery case were held, which hastened the start of the Civil War.

The memorial was developed largely through the efforts of Luther Ely Smith, a St. Louis civic booster who first proposed the idea in 1933 while the federal government was looking for a suitable memorial for Jefferson. He was the chairman of the local committee that convinced St. Louis to pass a bond issue to begin the project, selected the site, convinced President Franklin D. Roosevelt to make it a national park in 1935, and partly financed the 1947 architectural competition that selected the Gateway Arch as the memorial's focal point. Smith, who became chairman of the Jefferson National Expansion Memorial Association, felt the memorial should be on a location that was symbolic of one of Jefferson's greatest accomplishments—the 1803 Louisiana Purchase.

Eero Saarinen, the noted Finnish American architect, won the 1947 memorial competition with the huge stainless steel catenary arch called the Gateway Arch, which is 630 feet tall and wide at its base and located along the Mississippi River. In addition to a grand staircase, it has a unique tram system that carries the public to an observation room at the top of the arch for a panoramic view of the St. Louis area.

A visitor center and the 45,000-square-foot Museum of Westward Expansion are housed underneath the arch. The museum has permanent exhibits and changing exhibitions on the history of the St. Louis riverfront, nineteenth-century westward movement, Indian tipi and artifacts, mounted animal specimens, the Lewis and Clark Expedition, and Jefferson's role, as well as three theaters with films on the construction of the Gateway Arch and western exploration, settlement, and history.

Entrance to the Museum of Westward Expansion at the Jefferson National Expansion Memorial in St. Louis, Missouri. Courtesy of the National Park Service, Jefferson National Expansion Museum.

Among the museum's collections are objects, images, and books about the history of the park and St. Louis, western expansion, and the Lewis and Clark Expedition. Riverboat rides also are available on the adjoining Mississippi River. Among the summer events are Fair St. Louis, Live on the Levee, and the Free Family Junior Ranger Experience. The memorial's annual attendance is 2.5 million.

The Old Courthouse, located two blocks from the arch, is one of the oldest buildings in St. Louis. The courthouse has restored courtrooms and museum exhibits on the history of St. Louis. It was the site of the first two Dred Scott trials. In 1847 Scott and his wife, Harriet, sued for and were granted their freedom. After many appeals, the Supreme Court ruled that slaves were property and had no right to sue.

Jefferson National Expansion Memorial, 11 N. 4th St., St. Louis, MO 63102-1810. Phones 314/655-1700 and 314/655-1600. Fax: 314/655-1639. E-mail: jeff_superintendent@nps.gov. Website: www.nps.gov/jeff. Hours: Gateway Arch and museum—Memorial Day–Labor Day: 8 a.m.–10 p.m. daily; early Sept.–late May: 9–6 daily; closed New Year's Day, Thanksgiving, and Christmas; courthouse—8–4:30 daily; closed New Year's Day, Thanksgiving, and Christmas. Admissions: tram—adults, $10; children 3–15, $5; children under 3, free; 70 mm movie—adults, $7; children 3–15, $2.50; children under 3, free; riverboat—adults, $14; children 3–15, $8; children under 3, free.

Mount Rushmore National Memorial. *See* Mount Rushmore National Memorial under George Washington in Presidents section.

James Madison

James Madison's Montpelier. James Madison was a Virginia statesman and political theorist who was the primary author of the United States Constitution, key author of the nation's Bill of Rights, and fourth president of the United States in 1809–1817. During the Constitutional Convention, he was praised as having the intellectual depth of a scholar and the practical wisdom of a politician. Madison became known as the "father of the Constitution."

It was at Montpelier, the Madison family plantation in the Blue Ridge Mountains in Orange, Virginia, that Madison studied the principles and ideas of government, conceived the foundation of democracy upon which the nation evolved, and began a political career that led to his election as president of the nation. Today, the 2,650-acre plantation is the site of James Madison's Montpelier, a historic house museum that honors his memory.

Madison was the oldest of 12 children born to James Madison Sr., a leading tobacco planter, and Nelly Conway Madison, daughter of another prominent planter. He was born in 1751 in Fort Conway, Virginia, and grew up on a plantation his father inherited and expanded to 5,000 acres to become the largest landowner in Orange County.

Young Madison, who was called "Jemmy," studied mathematics, geography, and modern and ancient languages from ages 11 to 16 under a Scottish teacher. This was followed by two years of tutoring and enrollment at the College of New Jersey (which later became Princeton University). He graduated in 1771.

Madison worked with preacher Elijah Craig on constitutional guarantees for religious liberty in Virginia after witnessing the persecution of Baptist preachers arrested for ministering without a license from the established Anglican Church. And while serving in the Virginia legislature in 1776–1779, he helped Thomas Jefferson draft the state statute on religious freedom. Madison also was among the first to recognize that the initial attempt to govern by the Continental Congress (under the 1781–1788 Articles of Confederation) required a stronger central government with more powers.

At the Constitutional Convention in 1787, Madison proposed the "Virginia Plan," where the interests of individuals, states, and the national authority were balanced and mixed into what was called "an extended republic." He then got such leaders as George Washington, Benjamin Franklin, and Edmund Randolph to endorse the idea, and Madison, Alexander Hamilton, and John Jay wrote a series of 85 newspaper articles that became the *Federalist Papers*, explaining how the proposed constitution would work. Patrick Henry and some others opposed the proposed constitution on the grounds that it took away the independence of the states and the rights of citizens, but the Madison-developed constitution was ratified.

Madison was elected and reelected to the U.S. House of Representatives from Virginia in 1789–1797 despite the opposition of Governor Patrick Henry, who gerrymandered Madison's home district. He became an important leader in Congress. In 1798 he drafted the Virginia Resolutions, which were inspired by resentment at the Federalist Alien and Sedition Acts.

It was also in the 1790s that Madison married Dolley Payne Todd, a widow, and adopted her surviving son, John Payne Todd (1794). For marrying Madison, a non-Quaker, Dolley Madison was expelled from the Society of Friends. However, she became one of the most popular first ladies to occupy the White House when Madison was elected president (*see* Dolley Madison in First Ladies section).

Madison served as secretary of state during the presidency of Thomas Jefferson in 1801–1809. During that period, he played an important role in arranging the Louisiana Purchase from the French in 1803 and the Lewis and Clark Expedition to the Pacific in 1804–1806. Madison was elected to succeed Jefferson as president in 1808 and served during the War of 1812.

When Madison's second term as president ended in 1817, he and Dolley retired to Montpelier. Madison continued to stay active. In 1819 he founded the American Colonization Society, which was dedicated to freeing slaves and transporting them to the west coast of Africa, and attended the 1829 Virginia Constitutional Convention. He also followed Thomas Jefferson as the second rector of the University of Virginia from 1826 until his death in 1836. He died at the age of 85 and was buried with Dolley Madison, who died in 1849, in the family cemetery at Montpelier.

Montpelier, which has been designated a National Historic Landmark, was established as a museum in 1976 by the James Madison Memorial Foundation and has undergone a $25 million restoration. It offers guided tours of the 1820s Madison mansion, which contains family furnishings, portraits, and possessions.

Among the other historical sites are the original Mount Pleasant homestead site, Madison's "Temple" over the icehouse, formal gardens, an archaeological dig and laboratory, a restored 1910 train depot, a freeman's cabin and farm, a 200-acre old-growth forest and demonstration trail, Civil War encampment sites and huts, and historic family and slave cemeteries. Montpelier also has a visitor center with an interactive model of the estate, a visual presentation, and exhibits; a hands-on tent where period chores and crafts are demonstrated; an outdoor kitchen with cooking demonstrations; and an exhibit on Dolley Madison's clothes. Annual attendance is 4,500.

James Madison's Montpelier, 129 Caroline St., Orange, VA 22960-1532 (postal address: PO Box 911, Orange, VA 22960-0911). Phone: 540/672-1776. Fax: 540/672-0231. E-mail: info@montpelier.org. Website: www.montpelier.org. Hours: Apr.–Oct.—9–5 daily; Nov.–Mar.—9–4 daily; closed Thanksgiving and Christmas. Admission (includes guided tour of the house): adults, $16; children 6–14, $8; children under 6, free.

Todd House. *See* Dolley Madison in First Ladies section.

James Monroe

Ash Lawn–Highland. James Monroe, a Virginia lawyer and governor, was the last of the nation's Founding Fathers and last of the Virginia dynasty to become president of the United States. He was elected the fifth president and served two terms from 1817 to 1825. Two museums now are devoted to his life and career—Ash Lawn–Highland, his home from 1899 to 1823 in Charlottesville, and the James Monroe Museum and Memorial Library, in Fredericksburg, where he practiced law from 1786 to 1789 (*see* separate listing).

Monroe was born in 1758 in Westmoreland County to planter Spence Monroe and Elizabeth Jones Monroe. He attended Campbelltown Academy between the ages of 11 and 16, and excelled as a student. When 16, as the eldest son, he inherited his father's fortune and became financially responsible for the other siblings. In 1774 Monroe enrolled at the College of William and Mary, where most of the students, including Monroe, had patriotic fervor and considered rebelling against King George.

After the battles of Lexington and Concord in 1775, Monroe and 24 others raided the arsenal at the governor's palace and made off with 200 muskets and 300 swords that they turned over to the Williamsburg militia. Monroe dropped out of college the following spring and joined the Third Virginia Regiment in the Continental Army. He served as an officer in the army and took part in Washington's crossing of the Delaware River and the Battle of Trenton, where he was shot in his left shoulder.

Monroe studied law under Thomas Jefferson from 1780 to 1783, when he sold his small inherited plantation to enter law and politics. He was elected to the Virginia House of Delegates in 1782 and to the Fourth Continental Congress in 1783, as well as the Fifth and Sixth Congresses. Monroe married Elizabeth Kortright of New York City in 1786. They had three children and owned the Highland estate from 1793 to 1826. After their deaths, the site's name was changed to Ash Lawn–Highland.

After the ratification of the Constitution, Monroe ran for the House of Representatives in the first Congress but lost to James Madison. However, he was elected to the U.S. Senate in 1790 and then joined the Democratic-Republican faction led by Thomas Jefferson and Madison. He became party leader in the Senate by 1791 and then resigned his senatorial seat in 1794 to serve as minister to France. He obtained the release of Thomas Paine, who had been arrested for opposing the execution of Louis XVI, and also managed to free all Americans held in French prisons. But President George Washington replaced Monroe as French ambassador in 1795 largely because of his outspoken support of the French Revolution and opposition to the 1794 Jay Treaty with Great Britain.

Monroe returned to practicing law in Virginia until elected governor as a Republican, serving his first term from 1799 to 1802 (he later was reelected governor four times). President Thomas Jefferson then sent Monroe to France to assist in negotiating the Louisiana Purchase, followed by Monroe's appointment as minister to Britain from 1803 to 1807. When Madison was elected president, Monroe returned to Virginia and served in the House of Delegates and was elected to another term as governor in 1811, serving only four months before being named secretary of state by Madison.

After the British invaded Washington and burned the U.S. Capitol and the White House in the War of 1812, Monroe was appointed secretary of war and served until the 1815 peace treaty. He then was reappointed secretary of state and stayed until he became president in 1817.

Monroe, who was reelected unopposed in 1820, reduced political tensions by ignoring party lines in making appointments to lower federal posts and by making two long cross-country tours to build national trust. But the administration suffered before resolving the Panic of 1819 and the dispute over the Missouri Territory as a slave state in 1820. Monroe's greatest success was the proclamation of the Monroe Doctrine in 1823, stating that the United States would not tolerate further European intervention in the Americas.

By 1815 Monroe was beginning to sell some of his Highland plantation to pay for operating expenses and personal debt. He sold part of the land in 1817 for the new University of Virginia being developed by Thomas Jefferson, and then the remainder of the estate in 1825. James and Elizabeth Monroe moved to near the University of Virginia campus in Oak Hill, Virginia, in 1830, but Elizabeth died that year.

Monroe then lived with his daughter, Maria Hester Monroe Gouverneur, in New York City, where he died on July 4, 1831, of a heart attack and tuberculosis at the age of 73. He was the third president who was a Founding Father to die on Independence Day (after John Adams and Thomas Jefferson). His tomb in Richmond, Virginia, is now a National Historic Landmark.

In 1837 the plantation was sold to Alexander Garrett, who gave the site its present name of Ash Lawn–Highland. It then was purchased in 1867 by John Massey, who expanded the property. The estate was sold for the last time in 1930 to philanthropist Jay Winston Johns, who opened the house to tours in 1931 and willed the property in 1974 to the College of William and Mary, where James Monroe went to college.

Today, the college operates Ash Lawn–Highland as a 535-acre working farm, historic house museum, and performance site for the arts. The 1799 Monroe house has been restored and provides a look at nineteenth-century life with early American and Victorian architecture and decorative arts from those periods. The site also has a garden pavilion and outbuildings; house and farm tours; craft demonstrations; hands-on educational workshops; a spring wine festival; and summer festival of operas, plays, chamber music, and family entertainment. Annual attendance is 68,000.

Ash Lawn–Highland, 1000 James Monroe Pkwy., Charlottesville, VA 22902-7505. Phone: 434/293-8000. Fax: 434/979-9181. E-mail: info@al-h.us. Website: www.ashlawnhighland.org. Hours: Apr.–Oct.—9–6 daily; Nov.–Mar.—11–5; closed Thanksgiving, Christmas, and New Year's Day. Admission: adults, $10; seniors, $9; children 6–11 and local residents, $5; children under 6, free.

James Monroe Museum and Memorial Library. The James Monroe Museum and Memorial Library in downtown Fredericksburg, Virginia, has the largest collection of artifacts and documents related to the fifth president of the United States (1817–1825). The museum contains over 1,600 objects, including personal items, costumes, memorabilia, and decorative items; the archives houses more than 10,000 documents; and the library contains over 3,000 volumes of rare and historic books.

Monroe practiced law in Fredericksburg from 1786 until his move to Charlottesville in 1789. The museum was opened in 1927 by Monroe descendants as a place to house personal collections handed down through generations of the family. It is located in a building that the descendants believed was Monroe's law office. However, the Monroe office building no longer exists, although it was located at the site.

The present museum/library structure actually consists of three connected historic buildings that housed a schoolhouse, warehouses, and restaurants following the Civil War. It has three exhibition galleries, a library, and memorial garden. The museum offers guided tours, long-term and changing exhibitions relating to Monroe's life and career, and such special events as an annual Monroe lecture, Monroe birthday celebration, Christmas program, and Welsh Festival. The museum/library now is owned by the Commonwealth of Virginia and administered by the University of Mary Washington. Annual attendance is 10,000.

James Monroe Museum and Memorial Library, 908 Charles St., Fredericksburg, VA 22401-5801. Phone: 540/654-1043. Fax: 540/654-1106. E-mail: jmmuseum@umw.edu. Website: www.umw.edu/jamesmonroemuseum. Hours: Mar.–Nov.—10–5 Mon.–Sat., 1–5 Sun.; Dec.–Feb.—10–4 daily; closed New Year's Eve and Day, Thanksgiving, and Christmas Eve and Day. Admission: adults, $5; children 6–18, $1; children under 6, free.

Andrew Jackson

The Heritage: Home of President Andrew Jackson. Andrew Jackson was a country lawyer on the frontier who became a politician, an army general, and the seventh president of the United States (1829–1837). He defeated the Creek Indians in Georgia and Alabama, the British in New Orleans, the Seminole Indians in Georgia, and the Spanish in Florida. His nickname was "Old Hickory" because of his toughness and aggressive personality. His followers created the modern Democratic Party, and the 1830–1850 period became known as the era of Jacksonian democracy.

Jackson was born in 1767 in the Waxhaw region backcountry of South and North Carolina to Andrew and Elizabeth Hutchinson Jackson, who had emigrated from Ireland two years earlier. His father died in an accident a few days before he was born on an uncle's farm. Jackson received a sporadic education in the local "old-field" school and joined a local militia as a courier at the age of 13 during the American Revolutionary War.

Jackson's eldest brother, Hugh, died in the Battle of Stone Ferry in 1779, and Jackson and his brother Robert were captured by the British and nearly starved to death in captivity. They also contracted smallpox, and Andrew was slashed with a sword that left scars when he refused to clean the boots of a British officer. In 1781 Robert died of smallpox and their mother, Elizabeth, died of cholera while caring for prisoners of war on ships in the Charleston harbor. Jackson blamed the British for his family's losses.

Jackson then worked in a saddle maker's shop and later taught school and studied law in Salisbury, North Carolina. He was admitted to the bar in 1787 and moved to Jonesborough, North Carolina (which later became Tennessee), where he began his legal career working largely on disputed land claims and assaults. He was appointed district prosecutor in 1788 and elected as a delegate to the Tennessee constitutional convention in 1796. When Tennessee became a state that year, Jackson was elected to the U.S. House of Representatives and then to the U.S. Senate in 1797, only to resign within a year and become a judge on the Tennessee Supreme Court until 1804.

It was during this period that Jackson also married and prospered as a planter and merchant. Actually, he married Rachel Donelson Robards twice—in 1790 when they thought she was divorced and in 1794 after she obtained the divorce from an abusive husband. They had two adopted sons and became the guardians of eight other children of relatives and friends.

In 1803 Jackson built a home and the first general store in Gallatin, Tennessee. The following year he acquired what he called "The Hermitage," a 640-acre plantation in Davidson County, near Nashville, which he expanded to 1,050 acres. The principal crop was cotton, and the workers were slaves. He started with nine slaves and eventually had as many as 150. Jackson also became a major land speculator in western Tennessee after negotiating the sale of Chickasaw Nation land in 1818 and being one of three original investors who founded Memphis in 1819.

Jackson's military career really began in 1801 when he was appointed commander of the Tennessee militia with the rank of colonel. He became a major general the next year but did not really become active until the outbreak of the War of 1812. In 1814 he commanded the American forces in the Battle of Horseshoe Bend, defeating the "Red Stick" Creek Indians who had killed 400 settlers in the Fort Mims massacre. In the 1815 Battle of New Orleans, he led American forces to a decisive victory over invading British troops and became a national hero.

In the First Seminole War, Jackson was ordered by President James Monroe to stop Spanish Florida from becoming a refuge for runaway slaves. He led a campaign in 1817 that burned the houses and crops of the Seminoles and Creeks, and when he found letters implicating the Spanish and British, he captured Pensacola, deposed the Spanish governor, and tried and executed two British men who had been assisting the Indians. Secretary of State John Quincy Adams used Jackson's conquest in getting Spain to cede Florida to the United States in 1821.

Jackson was reelected to the U.S. Senate and nominated for president in 1822, but he lost the presidential bid. In 1824 he received the most votes for president in a close election, However, since none of the candidates had a majority, the president was selected by a vote of the House of Representatives. Again, Jackson lost when House Speaker Henry Clay threw his support behind John Quincy Adams, who was chosen as president. Jackson resigned from the Senate in 1825, reorganized and attracted new support, and ran in the 1828 election as a Democrat and defeated Adams.

Jackson appealed to common people and fought against what he denounced as a closed, undemocratic aristocracy. Although he supported a small and limited federal government, he strengthened the power of the presidency and expanded the spoils system. He was criticized for such controversial actions as his aggressive enforcement of the Indian Removal Act, which relocated most Indian tribes from the Southeast to Indian Territory (now Oklahoma); vetoing the renewal of the national bank's charter and ensuring its collapse; and sending troops to South Carolina when it sought to nullify a high protective tariff. Many also were critical because he continued to be a slaveholder.

Guided tour of The Hermitage: Home of President Andrew Jackson in Tennessee. Courtesy of the Hermitage, Nashville, TN.

When Jackson completed his presidency in 1837, he retired to his plantation, the Hermitage, where he died in 1845 at the age of 78 of chronic tuberculosis, dropsy, and heart failure. He and his wife are buried in tombs in the garden of the estate.

The Hermitage now is a historic house museum—and National Historic Landmark—that was opened to the public in 1889. It is owned and operated by the nonprofit Ladies Heritage Association. When Jackson and his wife moved there in 1804, their home was a two-story log blockhouse, built to resist Indian attacks. He replaced it with an eight-room federal-style brick house in 1819–1821, but it was seriously damaged in an 1834 chimney fire. The Hermitage mansion then was rebuilt in its present Greek revival style in 1836.

The historic site now has 1,120 acres, 32 historic buildings, two gardens, archaeological sites, two springs, and a cotton patch. The mansion contains Jackson furnishings, costumes, manuscripts, and other family possessions. Among the other historic buildings on the grounds are the 1804 log cabin, 1821–1836 slave quarters and other out-buildings, and 1833 Old Hermitage Church. Annual attendance is over 235,000.

The Hermitage: Home of President Andrew Jackson, 4580 Rachel's Lane, Hermitage, TN 37076-1331. Phone: 615/889-2941. Fax: 615/889-9909. E-mail: info@thehermitage.com. Website: www.thehermitage.com. Hours: Apr.–Oct. 15—8:30–5 daily; Oct. 16–Mar.—9–4:30 daily; closed Thanksgiving, Christmas, and third week in Jan. Admission: adults, $18; seniors, $15; students 13–18, $12; children 6–12, $8; military and children under 6, free.

Andrew Jackson Museum. The Andrew Jackson Museum at the Andrew Jackson State Park near Lancaster, South Carolina, tells of his boyhood in South Carolina and life in the state's backcountry from his 1767 birth until he left South Carolina in 1784. The 360-acre park and the museum were established in 1952 to honor the seventh president of the United States.

Jackson was born in the Waxhaw region backcountry along the South Carolina–North Carolina state line to Scotch Irish immigrants Andrew and Elizabeth Jackson. His father died shortly after his birth, and his mother raised the family in the home of her sister, Jane, and her husband, James Crawford. The park now includes the property that once belonged to the Crawfords. The museum features Jackson's early years in the area and has four rooms that show colonial life in South Carolina's backcountry (dining room, bedroom, textile room, and early implements).

The museum grounds also have a bronze statue of the young Andrew Jackson astride a horse (titled *Andrew Jackson, a Boy of the Waxhaws*) by Anna Hyatt Huntington, a Daughters of the American Revolution marker at what is said to be his birthplace, a replica of a late eighteenth-century one-room schoolhouse, and an amphitheater.

Andrew Jackson Museum, Andrew Jackson State Park, 196 Andrew Jackson Park Rd., Lancaster, SC 29720-6404. Phone: 803/285-3344. Website: www.southcarolinaparks.com/park-finder/state-park/1797.aspx. Hours: museum—1–5 Sat.–Sun., by appointment Mon.–Fri.; park—Apr.–Oct.: 9 a.m.–9 p.m. daily; Nov.–Mar.: 8–6 daily. Admission: park—adults, $2; seniors, $1.25; children under 16, free; museum—free with park admission.

Museum of the Waxhaws and Andrew Jackson Memorial. Both North and South Carolina claim President Andrew Jackson as one of their own since he was born in the backcountry of the Waxhaw region near the state line. In Waxhaw, North Carolina, the Museum of the Waxhaws and Andrew Jackson Memorial is devoted to both the history of the region (named for the Waxhaw Indians) and the seventh president of the United States.

The museum, founded in 1996 and operated by the Andrew Jackson Historical Foundation, has exhibits about the Waxhaws, early explorers and settlers, the American Revolution, the Civil War, life in the region around 1900, and the boyhood and presidency of Andrew Jackson. Guided tours are given of the 8,500 square feet of exhibits. The museum also has theater programs, craft workshops, lectures, and such annual events as living history days and summer outdoor dramas. Annual attendance is 3,000.

Museum of the Waxhaws and Andrew Jackson Memorial, 8215 Waxhaw Hwy., Waxhaw, NC 28171 (postal address: PO Box 7, Waxhaw, NC 28173-1038). Phone and fax: 704/843-1832. E-mail: mwaxhaw@museumofthewaxhaws.org. Website: www.museumofthewaxhaws.com. Hours: 10–5 Fri.–Sat., 2–5 Sun.; closed New Year's Day, Thanksgiving, and Christmas. Admission: adults, $5; seniors, $4; children 6–12, $2; children under 6, free.

Martin Van Buren

Martin Van Buren National Historic Site. The Martin Van Buren National Historic Site, which honors the eighth president of the United States (1837–1841), is located at his Lindenwald estate near Kinderhook, New York. Van Buren, a founder of the Democratic Party, purchased the 36-room mansion on 126 acres when elected to the presidency, and it became his home and farm until his death in 1862. He was the first American president born as a citizen of the United States (all the prior presidents were born as British subjects before the American Revolution).

Van Buren was born in the village of Kinderhook in upstate New York in 1782 to Abraham Van Buren, a farmer and tavern keeper, and Maria Van Alen Van Buren. His parents were of Dutch ancestry, and Van Buren was the only U.S. president who spoke English as a second language. He received an elementary education at the local schoolhouse and studied Latin at the Kinderhook Academy and Washington Seminary in Claverack. At the age of 14, he began studying law, spending six years with a Kinderhook attorney and a final year in the office of William P. Van Ness, a political lieutenant of Aaron Burr. He was admitted to the bar in 1803 and married Hannah Hoes, a childhood sweetheart, in 1807. The Van Burens had six children. Hannah died of tuberculosis in 1819, and Martin never remarried.

Van Buren became active in politics at an early age. When 17, he attended a party convention in Troy, New York, and worked to get Van Ness the congressional nomination. He was an early supporter of Aaron Burr and the Clintonian faction of the Democratic-Republican Party. From 1808 to 1813, he was surrogate of Columbia County. He then joined the opposition party in 1813 and served as a state senator in 1812–1820 and state attorney general in 1815–1819. In 1817 he created and became the leading figure in the first political machine encompassing all of New York.

Van Buren was elected U.S. senator from New York in 1821 and reelected in 1827, and then he was elected governor of New York in 1828. He also served as one of the principal managers of the Andrew Jackson's presidential campaign. After Jackson's election, Van Buren was appointed secretary of state in 1829. He resigned two years later and was named minister to Great Britain by Jackson but not confirmed by the Senate, largely because of the opposition of Vice President John Calhoun. But in the 1832 election, Jackson selected Van Buren as his vice president, and they won in a landslide because of Jackson's popularity.

Van Buren was the first real politician to run for the presidency, using grassroots campaigning and working to unite the different sections of the country in a political party. He was called the "Little Magician" because of his political skills. Van Buren was elected president for the 1837–1841 term but lost his 1844 Democratic reelection bid and lost again as a third-party candidate (Free Soil Party) in 1848.

As president, he advocated lower tariffs and free trade, set up a system of bonds for the national debt, opposed the renewal of the national bank's charter, and favored an "independent treasury" system that gave the Treasury control of all federal funds and required all payments be made in specie. Van Buren became unpopular mainly because of the Panic of 1837, which was followed by five years of depression, marked by bank failures and record unemployment.

After his presidency, Van Buren spent most of his time at his Kinderhook home and farm, from where he ran the unsuccessful 1844 and 1848 presidential campaigns and engaged in other political activities. It is where he died in 1862 at the age of 79 of bronchial asthma and heart failure.

Lindenwald became the Martin Van Buren National Historic Site in 1974. The 36-room federal/Gothic revival–style mansion contains the furnishings and personal effects of the former president. Rangers provide tours of the house. The historic site, which is a National Historic Landmark, also has a visitor center and offers special events during the summer. The annual attendance is 21,000.

Martin Van Buren National Historic Site, Rte. 9H, Kinderhook, NY 12106-3605 (postal address: 1013 Old Post Rd., Kinderhook, NY 12106-3605). Phone: 518/758-9689. Fax: 518/758-6986. Website: www.nps.gov/mava. Hours: grounds—7–dusk daily; house—9–4 daily mid-May–Oct.; closed Nov.–mid-May. Admission: grounds—free; house tour—adults, $5; children under 16, free; families, $12.

William Henry Harrison

Grouseland, William Henry Harrison Mansion. William Henry Harrison was a frontier military hero and politician who was the ninth president of the United States and the first president to die in office. He served the shortest tenure in U.S. presidential history—only to his 32nd day in office. He was 68 years and 23 days old when elected to office in 1841, making him the oldest president chosen until Ronald Reagan in 1980. He died of complications from pneumonia.

Harrison's death caused a brief constitutional crisis that ultimately was resolved by the passage of the 25th Amendment. The crisis arose over the succession process. Meanwhile, Vice President John Tyler moved into the White House, took the oath of office, and assumed full presidential powers. It set a precedent that governed future successions and was codified in the constitutional amendment that followed.

Harrison was born in 1771 on the Berkeley Plantation in Charles City County, Virginia, but spent most of adult life in the old Northwest Territory. He was the youngest of seven children of Benjamin Harrison V and Elizabeth Bassett Harrison and the last president born as a British subject before American independence. His father was a planter, a delegate to the Continental Congress in 1774–1777, a signer of the Declaration of Independence, and the governor of Virginia in 1781–1784.

At the age of 14, Harrison entered Presbyterian Hampden-Sydney College and studied Latin, French, and other subjects from 1787 to 1790. He then briefly attended an academy in Southampton County, where he became involved with antislavery Quakers and Methodists. Harrison's father moved him to Philadelphia, where he boarded with Robert Morris and enrolled at the University of Pennsylvania to study medicine. Shortly after arriving in 1791, his father died and left him without funds for further schooling.

Virginia Governor Henry Lee, a friend of Harrison's father, heard of William's financial situation and persuaded him to join the army. Harrison was commissioned an ensign in the U.S. Army infantry and assigned to Cincinnati in the Northwest Territory, where the army was fighting hostile Indians. He impressed General "Mad Anthony" Wayne, who promoted him to lieutenant and then to aide-de-camp. He took part in Wayne's Battle of Fallen Timbers victory in 1794 and was one of the signatories of the Treaty of Greenville in 1795, which opened much of present-day Ohio to settlement.

It also was in 1795 that Harrison eloped with Anna Symmes of North Bend, Ohio, after her father, a judge and former representative to the Congress of the Confederation, refused to give her permission to marry because of his concern that Harrison could not provide for his daughter. However, after the marriage, Judge John Cleves Symmes sold the couple 160 acres of land. The Harrisons had 10 children, and Anna frequently was in poor health, primary because of the many pregnancies. But she outlived her husband by 23 years, dying at the age of 88 in 1864.

Harrison resigned from the U.S. Army in 1797 to enter politics and to run a horse-breeding enterprise. He was appointed secretary in the Northwest Territorial government and in 1799 was elected as the first delegate of the territory in Congress. He was successful in getting the Harrison Land Act passed, which made it easier for average settlers to buy land in the Northwest Territory. Shortly thereafter, Harrison was appointed governor of the new territory by President John Adams.

In 1801 Harrison moved to Vincennes, which became the capital of the Indiana Territory (consisting of the future states of Indiana, Illinois, Michigan, Wisconsin, and the eastern portion of Minnesota). There he built Grouseland, a plantation-style home named for the many grouse in the area, which is now a historic house museum honoring Harrison. The governor's primary job was to obtain lands from Indian tribes that would allow European American settlement and enable the region to gain statehood.

Harrison oversaw the development of 13 treaties in which 60 million acres of land were obtained from the Native Americans—often greatly opposed by some Indian leaders, who sought to have the treaties nullified. The Indian resistance movement expanded under the leadership of the Shawnee brothers Tecumseh and Tenskwatawa (The Prophet) and resulted in what was called "Tecumseh's War." The war climaxed in the 1811 Battle of Tippecanoe at Prophetstown, along the Wabash and Tippecanoe rivers in Indiana. Harrison led an army of more than 1,000 men in a show of force to intimidate the Shawnee into making peace. The Shawnee responded by staging a surprise attack, but they were defeated. As a result of the victory, Harrison earned the "Old Tippecanoe" nickname and became a national hero.

In the War of 1812 against the British, Harrison recaptured Detroit and then defeated the British and their Indian allies at the 1813 Battle of the Thames, in which Tecumseh was killed. After the war, he served in the U.S. House of Representatives (1816–1819), Ohio state senate (1819–1821), U.S. Senate (1824–1828), and as minister to Columbia (1828–1829).

Harrison ran for president as the Whig Party candidate in 1836 but lost a close election to Martin Van Buren. He was nominated again by the Whigs in 1840, and this time he was elected, with John Tyler as vice president. They had one of the most famous campaign slogans—"Tippecanoe and Tyler Too." Harrison was in office only a month when he died in 1841.

Grouseland, the 1804 Harrison mansion in Vincennes, was established as a historic house museum in the president's honor in 1911. It is a large two-story brick structure that was the official and social center of the Northwest Territory. It is where Harrison met with Indian leaders and negotiated treaties.

The Daughters of the American Revolution saved the building from destruction, and the Grouseland Foundation now operates the site, which is a National Historic Landmark. Other state historic buildings, including the Territorial Capitol, have been moved to the grounds. The mansion contains early nineteenth-century furniture and personal artifacts. It has guided tours, temporary exhibitions, and living history events. Annual attendance is 10,500.

Grouseland, William Henry Harrison Mansion, 3 W. Scott St., Vincennes, IN 47591-1433. Phone: 812/882-2096. Fax: 812/882-7626. E-mail: grouseland@sbcglobal.net. Website: www.grouselandfoundation.org. Hours: Jan.–Feb.—11–4 Tues.–Sun.; closed Mon.; Mar.–Dec.—10–5 daily; closed Thanksgiving, Christmas, and New Year's Day. Admission: adults, $5; seniors, $4; students and children, $3.

Berkeley Plantation. The Berkeley Plantation in Charles City, Virginia, was the birthplace of William Henry Harrison, the ninth president of the United States. It also is one of the oldest great estates of America. The original site on the north bank of the James River (20 miles upstream from Jamestown) was settled in 1619 by 38 English settlers. In the Indian massacre of 1622, nine of the settlers at Berkeley Hundred were killed, as well as about one-third of the entire population of the Virginia Colony. One of the survivors was Benjamin Harrison IV, who founded the Berkeley Plantation and built the Georgian-style three-story brick mansion (built of brick fired on the plantation) that became the ancestral home of President Harrison.

The grandfather's son, Benjamin Harrison V, who was a signer of the Declaration of Independence and a governor of Virginia, was William's father. William lived at the approximately 1,000-acre Berkeley Plantation until his father died. He then dropped out of medical school for financial reasons and joined the U.S. Army in 1791, being assigned to the Northwest Territory. When his mother died in 1793, he inherited her 3,000-acre Wanut Grove Plantation. He sold part of the land to his brother, Carter, and 1,600 acres to John Tyler, who later succeeded him as president (*see* Sherwood Forest Plantation listing under John Tyler).

During the Civil War, Union troops occupied Berkeley Plantation, and President Abraham Lincoln twice came there in 1862 to confer with General George H. McClellan. The Harrison family could not regain possession of the plantation after the war, and it fell into disrepair after several owners. The plantation was purchased in 1907 by John Jamieson, who was a Union drummer boy during the Civil War. It was inherited by his son, Malcolm Jamieson, and wife, Grace, in 1927, and they restored the mansion.

The mansion now features a collection of eighteenth-century antiques and has 10 acres of formal gardens and parterres. Guides in period costumes give tours, which include an audiovisual program and a collection of Civil War artifacts and paintings by Sydney King.

Berkeley Plantation, 12602 Harrison Landing Rd., Charles City, VA 23030-3339. Phone: 804/820-6018. Fax: 804/820-6757. E-mail: info@berkeleyplantation.com. Website: www.berkeleyplantation.com. Hours: Jan.–mid-Mar.—10:30–3:30 daily; mid-Mar.–Dec.—9:30–4:30 daily; closed Thanksgiving and Christmas. Admission: adults, $11; students 13–16, $7.50; children 6–12, $6; children under 6, free.

John Tyler

Sherwood Forest Plantation. John Tyler, the 10th president of the United States, was the first to become the president following the death of a predecessor. When William Henry Harrison died after only a month in office, Vice President Tyler immediately occupied the White House, took the oath of office, and assumed presidential powers, even though there was no constitutional policy on succession. Tyler set the precedent on succession that later was incorporated in the 25th Amendment to the Constitution. Tyler was called "his accidency" by some because of the way he became president.

Tyler had several other distinctions. He was the first president to take a stand against his party's platform and to be expelled from the party (the Whigs). All but one of his cabinet members resigned. Tyler also favored states' rights and joined the Confederate Congress in the Civil War after leaving the presidency. As a result of these and other actions, Tyler became the only U.S. president whose death was not officially recognized in Washington.

Tyler was born to an aristocratic Virginia family in Charles City County in 1790. The family, which traced its lineage to colonial Williamsburg in the mid-1600s, lived on the 1,200-acre Greenway Plantation with a six-room mansion Tyler's father built. Tyler was one of eight children of John Tyler Sr. and Mary Armistead Tyler. His father was a member of the Virginia House of Delegates who later became the house's speaker, a state court judge, governor, and a federal district judge. His mother, who was the daughter of a prominent plantation owner, died when young Tyler was seven years old, and he was raised with his two brothers and five sisters on the plantation, which grew wheat, corn, and tobacco.

At the age of 12, Tyler entered the preparatory branch of the College of William and Mary. He graduated in 1807 when 17 and went on to study law with his father, who was a state judge at the time. He was admitted to the bar at the age of 19 and began practicing law in Richmond. Two years later, he was elected to the Virginia House of Delegates and served five successive one-year terms. Tyler became known for his strong support of states' rights and opposition to a national bank. During the War of 1812, he organized a small militia in 1813 to defend Richmond from the British, but the attack never came. It also was in 1813 that he married Letitia Christian and that his father died, and Tyler inherited his estate and 13 slaves. While he regarded slavery as evil, he never attempted to justify it, free any slaves, or support national emancipation.

In 1817–1821 Tyler was elected to the U.S. House of Representatives. He then served as governor of Virginia in 1825–1827 and U.S. senator from 1827 to 1836, when he was nominated for vice president by the Whig Party. He left the Democratic-Republican Party after President Andrew Jackson threatened to use federal troops to enforce a tariff in South Carolina after the state passed a bill nullifying the federal tax and when Jackson moved to dissolve the national bank (on which Tyler changed his position). The Whig Party then nominated him for vice president—with William Henry Harrison as the presidential candidate—to draw support from Virginia and the South in the 1840 election.

Harrison and Tyler were elected, but Harrison died a month after inauguration and Tyler succeeded him for the remainder of the term. However, he had a rocky four years, with neither the Whigs nor the Democrats supporting many of his programs. Numerous initial supporters did not share his strict constructionist ideals. He also acted against his party's platform, vetoed some of its proposals, lost most of his cabinet by resignation, and was dropped from the Whig Party. Yet he had a number significant achievements, such as the Webster-Ashburton Treaty with Britain and the Treaty of Wanghia with China, settlement of the Second Seminole War, and the 1845 annexation of the Republic of Texas.

Tyler's wife, Letitia, died in the White House in 1842, and he later married Julia Gardiner. He had 15 children (eight with his first wife and seven with his second wife)—more than any other U.S. president.

Because of the political opposition, Tyler decided not to seek nomination for a second term. He retired to his new residence, the Sherwood Forest Plantation, near his birthplace at Greenway Plantation along the north bank of the James River in Charles City County. He purchased the 1,600-acre plantation in 1842. It formerly was part of the 3,000-acre Walnut Grove Plantation, which William Henry Harrison inherited from his mother in 1793. The site has the distinction of being the only private residence in the United States to have been owned by two unrelated American presidents.

Tyler spent the rest of his life on the Sherwood Forest Plantation. He likened himself to Robin Hood when he renamed the Walnut Grove Plantation to signify that he had been "outlawed" by the Whig Party. He lived there with his wife and some of his children. He continued to be active in politics as regional hostilities escalated. Tyler sided with the South and was elected to the Confederacy's House of Representatives. He organized the Virginia Peace Convention in 1861 in an attempt to resolve the North-South differences and avoid a war, but it was unsuccessful. He died in 1862 of a heart attack at the age of 71.

The Tyler house is said to be the longest frame house in America, extending over 300 feet. It features a long ballroom that Tyler added in 1845 to accommodate the style of dancing popular at the time—called the "Virginia reel" then and now known as line dancing. The Greek revival–style house contains original family furniture, silver and china of President Tyler, and other items; an Oriental rug collection; and early paintings. The grounds include 25 acres of terraced gardens, woodlands, and lawn and such original outbuildings as milk, smoke, garden, slave, overseer, and kitchen/laundry/wine houses. Annual attendance is 5,000.

Sherwood Forest Plantation, 14501 John Tyler Memorial Hwy., Charles City, VA 23030 (postal address: PO Box 8, Charles City, VA 23030-0008). Phone: 804/829-5377. Fax: 804/829-2947. E-mail: ktyler@sherwoodforest.org. Website: www.sherwoodforest.org. Hours: 9–5 daily; closed Thanksgiving and Christmas. Admission: adults, $10; children under 15, free.

James K. Polk

President James K. Polk State Historic Site. James Knox Polk was a Tennessee politician who was a "dark horse" Democratic candidate elected the 11th president of the United States (1845–1849). In an election upset, he defeated Henry Clay of the Whig Party to become the last strong pre–Civil War president and was noted for his foreign policy successes. He set out to accomplish certain objectives and promised to serve only one term—and that is what he did.

Among Polk's achievements as president were returning to the independent treasury system (where federal funds were held in the Treasury rather than banks or other financial institutions), reducing high tariffs, resolving the Oregon boundary dispute with Britain, admitting Texas as a state, and acquiring lands in the Southwest and California in the Mexican-American War of 1846–1848. Polk also created the new Department of the Interior and oversaw the opening of the U.S. Naval Academy and the Smithsonian Institution, the groundbreaking for the Washington Monument, and the issuance of the first United States postage stamp.

Polk was born in 1795 in what is now Pineville, North Carolina. He was the first of 10 children of Samuel and Jane Knox Polk. His father was a successful farmer and surveyor, and his mother was a relative of Scottish religious reformer John Knox. In 1806 the Polk family moved to the Duck River area in what is now Maury County, where his father turned to land speculation and became a county judge. Polk was largely homeschooled and graduated with honors from the University of North Carolina. He then went to Nashville to study law under noted trial attorney Felix Grundy and was admitted to the bar in 1820. In 1819 he entered politics and was elected clerk for the Tennessee state senate. This was followed by being elected to the state legislature in 1823 and marrying Sarah Childress in 1824. She played an active role in his campaigns the rest of his life.

In 1825 Polk was elected to the House of Representatives at the age of 29. After being reelected five times, he was made chairman of the House Ways and Means Committee in 1833 and then chosen speaker of the House in 1835. He left Congress in 1839 when elected governor of Tennessee, but he lost two reelection campaigns. However, Polk was nominated as the compromise Democratic candidate for president in 1844 in a tight race after eight ballots. Two of the main campaign issues were the annexation of the Republic of Texas and settlement of the Oregon Territory claims with the British—both of which Polk favored and resolved.

The war with Mexico had its origin with the admittance of Texas as a state in 1845. Mexico, which had lost Texas in 1836, opposed the move. Polk had tried to purchase California from Mexico, which refused to negotiate. Polk then sent troops under General Zachary Taylor into the area between the Nueces River and the Rio Grande River, an area that both nations claimed. Taylor also crossed the Rio Grande and briefly occupied Matamoros, Tamaulipas, and the Mexicans crossed the Rio Grande and killed 11 American soldiers.

War was declared, and Polk assumed control of the conflict. Forces under Generals Taylor and Winfield Scott captured Mexico City and had victories in northern Mexico, General Stephen W. Kearny took control of New Mexico, and Captain John C. Frémont led settlers in Northern California to overthrow Mexican forces. The Treaty of Guadalupe gave the United States 1.2 million square miles of territory, including California, Nevada, Utah, most of Arizona, and parts of New Mexico, Colorado, and Wyoming (which increased the country by one-third).

Polk kept his promise and did not run for reelection. He was exhausted by his years of public service, the presidency, and the war. He died in his new home, called "Polk Place," in Nashville three months after leaving office in 1849. He was the youngest former president to die in retirement at the age of 53 and had the shortest retirement of all presidents at 103 days. It is believed that he contracted cholera during a goodwill tour in New Orleans just before leaving office three months earlier. He and his wife are buried in a tomb on the grounds of the Tennessee State Capitol in Nashville.

The President James K. Polk State Historic Site, established in 1968 in Pineville, North Carolina, honors Polk. The site, located on land once owned by his parents, is the area where Polk was born and spent his youth. It commemorates significant events in Polk's presidency, such as the Mexican-American War, the settlement of the Oregon boundary dispute, and the annexation of Texas and California. It features reconstructions of typical buildings of the homestead period, including log houses, a separate kitchen, and a barn. All are authentically furnished. The site also has a visitor center with exhibits about the Polk family and a film on his life and career. Annual attendance is 13,000.

President James K. Polk State Historic Site, 12031 Lancaster Hwy., Pineville, NC 28134 (postal address: PO Box 475, Pineville, NC 28134-0475). Phone: 704/889-7145. Fax: 704/889-3057. E-mail: polk@ncder.gov. Website: www.nchistoricsites.org/polk.htm. Hours: 9–5 Tues.–Sat.; closed Sun.–Mon., and major state holidays. Admission: free.

James K. Polk Ancestral Home. The James K. Polk Ancestral Home in Columbus, Tennessee, is an 1816 federal-style brick house that Polk's father, Samuel, built while his son, James, was attending the University of North Carolina. It is the only surviving residence (besides the White House) of the 11th president of the United States. After graduating in 1818, Polk returned to Tennessee and stayed with his parents until he married Sarah Childress in 1824. While living in the family home, he practiced law and started his political career by being elected to the state legislature.

The historic house museum, established in 1924, features such items as furniture, paintings, and White House china from Polk's years in Tennessee and Washington. The site also contains the family's detached kitchen building, reconstructed in 1946, which has period cooking and household materials. Early nineteenth-century crafts and chores also are demonstrated in the building occasionally.

Another historic structure, the adjacent ca. 1820 house where two of Polk's married sisters lived at different times, has a 12-minute orientation video, a museum room, temporary exhibits, and a sales shop. The museum room displays such historic items as White House mementos and gifts, 1844 presidential campaign memorabilia, daguerreotypes of President and Mrs. Polk, and miniature portraits of the first 11 presidents.

The cast iron fountain from President Polk's final mansion, which was located in downtown Columbus before being torn down in 1901, now can be seen in the courtyard, which also has formal boxwood, white azalea, and wildflower gardens. The historic site has an annual attendance of over 10,000.

James K. Polk Ancestral Home, 301 W. 7th St., Columbus, TN 38401-3132 (postal address: PO Box 741, Columbus, TN 38402-0741). Phone: 931/388-2354. Fax: 931/388-5971. E-mail: jameskpolk@bellsouth.net. Website: www.jameskpolk.com. Hours: Apr.–Oct.—9–5 Mon.–Sat., 1–5 Sun.; Nov.–Mar.—9–4 Mon.–Sat., 1–5 Sun.; closed Thanksgiving, Christmas Eve and Day, and New Year's Day. Admission: adults, $7; seniors, $6; children 6–18, $4; children under 6, free; families, $20.

Zachary Taylor

President Zachary Taylor's Mausoleum and Monument. Zachary Taylor was an American military leader who became the 12th president of the United States (1849–1850) after initially expressing little interest in politics. The general, who was known as "Old Rough and Ready," was nominated for president by the Whig Party after playing a critical role in the 1846–1848 Mexican-American War victory. But Taylor died after serving just 16 months of his presidential term and was succeeded by Vice President Millard Fillmore. Only William Henry Harrison and James Garfield served less time than Taylor as president.

Zachary Taylor, a career military officer, never voted until his presidential election. He also was the last president to hold slaves while in office and the last Whig candidate to win a presidential election. He had a 40-year career in the U.S. Army, serving at many military forts and in the Northwest Territory Indian wars, the War of 1812, the Black Hawk War, and the Second Seminole War, as well as the Mexican-American War.

Taylor was born on a farm in Montebello, Virginia, in 1784. He was one of six sons and three daughters born to Richard and Sarah Dabney Taylor. His father had served as a lieutenant colonel in the American Revolution. The family moved to a 400-acre farm on the frontier near present-day Louisville, Kentucky, when Zachary was young, and he spent most of his childhood living in a log cabin before moving into a larger brick house (which was called "Springfield") as the area boomed and the family was more prosperous.

Taylor's father became the owner of 10,000 acres throughout Kentucky, property in Lexington, and 26 slaves by 1800. There was no formal schooling on the frontier at the time, and Zachary's early education was sporadic with tutors. He joined the Kentucky militia as a teenager and enlisted in the U.S. Army and was commissioned a first lieutenant in 1808. He spent most of 1809 in camps in the New Orleans area and returned to Louisville in 1810 and married Margaret Mackall Smith. Five of their six children were born at his Springfield boyhood home. He was promoted to captain and in 1811 was sent to Indiana Territory to assume control of Fort Knox.

During the War of 1812, Taylor successfully defended Fort Harrison in Indiana Territory from an attack by Shawnee Chief Tecumseh and was given the temporary rank of major. He then served as aide to General Samuel Hopkins on expeditions into the Illinois Territory and to the Tippecanoe battle site, established two military forts, and commanded four others. When the War of 1812 ended, he resigned from the army only to return a year later. He was promoted to colonel in 1832 and devoted much of the year pursuing and fighting Chief Black Hawk, until Indian resistance ended in the region.

In 1837 Taylor fought in one of the largest U.S.-Indian battles of the nineteenth century. His forces defeated the Seminole Indians in the Battle of Lake Okeechobee in Florida. He was made a brigadier general and given command of all American troops in Florida. He was then made commander of the Second Department of the U.S. Army's Western Division.

In 1844 Taylor was sent to Fort Jesup in Louisiana in anticipation of the annexation of the Republic of Texas—to guard against any attempts by Mexico to reclaim the territory lost in 1836. He remained there until mid-1845, when annexation became imminent and President James K. Polk ordered him to occupy the disputed territory on the Texas-Mexico border. The American troops encamped there until the following spring in anticipation of a Mexican attack and then advanced to the Rio Grande River in March 1846. When negotiation efforts failed and Mexican forces attacked American units near the river, President Polk asked Congress to declare war against Mexico.

In May Taylor led U.S. Army forces that defeated the Mexican Army at the Battle of Palo Alto and the nearby Battle of Resaca de la Palma at the border. He followed in September with a victory in the Battle of Monterrey and in 1847 inflicted heavy losses on Santa Anna's Mexican forces, forcing them to withdraw at the Battle of Buena Vista. When he returned to his command of the U.S. Army's Western Division, he received a hero's welcome in New Orleans and Baton Rouge and was being urged to run for president.

Taylor considered himself an independent, but a Whig in principle and a Jeffersonian-Democrat in other ways. Political clubs were formed that supported Taylor for president. Despite opposition from antislavery elements because he was a slave owner, Taylor was nominated by the Whigs and was elected president in 1848, with Millard Fillmore of New York as his vice presidential running mate.

During the brief time he served as president, Taylor took a moderate position on slavery and opposed extension of slavery into the territories acquired from Mexico, threatened to use military force against secessionists to preserve the Union, and agreed to share with Great Britain any canal that might be built in Nicaragua (which never was constructed but led to the later development of an Anglo-American alliance).

Taylor died in 1850 of gastroenteritis at the age of 65 and was buried in the family cemetery. In 1883 the State of Kentucky erected a 50-foot granite monument topped with a life-size figure of President Taylor at the site. The federal government moved the remains of Taylor and his wife, Margaret, who died in 1852, to a new limestone and marble neoclassical mausoleum—known as President Zachary Taylor's Mausoleum and Monument—in 1926, and two years later Congress made the family cemetery the Zachary Taylor National Cemetery. The state also increased the size of the cemetery from a half acre to 16 acres, and a memorial sundial was added in 1930. Every year on Taylor's birthday (November 24), military personnel from Fort Knox conduct a wreath-laying ceremony in his honor.

President Zachary Taylor's Mausoleum and Monument, Zachary Taylor National Cemetery, 4701 Brownboro Rd., Louisville, KY 40207. Phones: 502/892-3852 and 502/893-3852. Fax: 502/893-6612. Website: www.cem.va.gov/cems/nchp/zacharytaylor.asp. Hours: grounds—sunrise–sunset daily; office—8–4:30 Mon.–Fri.; closed Sat.–Sun. and federal holidays except for Memorial Day and Veterans Day. Admission: free.

Millard Fillmore

Millard Fillmore House. Vice President Millard Fillmore became the 13th president of the United States (1850–1853) following the midterm death of Zachary Taylor. He was the last Whig Party member to hold the office of president, and his support of the Compromise of 1850 and insistence on the enforcement of the Fugitive Slave Act alienated the North and led to the dissolution of the Whig Party as many Whigs joining the new Republican Party, including Abraham Lincoln. Fillmore refused to be part of the Republican Party, but he did become the presidential nominee of the American Party, part of the Know-Nothing movement, in 1856 after being refused the Whig reelection nomination in 1852.

Fillmore was born in a log cabin in the Finger Lakes region of New York in 1800 to Nathaniel and Phoebe Millard Fillmore. He was the second of nine children. At the age of 14, he was sent by his father to apprentice with a cloth maker in Sparta, New York. After four months, he left and later apprenticed in the same trade in New Hope, New York. Fillmore received little schooling on the frontier, although he did spend six months at the New Hope Academy in 1819 before clerking for a judge and starting to study law. At the academy, he met Abigail Powers, whom he married in 1826 and later had two children with.

Fillmore moved to Buffalo, New York, where he continued his studies in law offices and was admitted to the bar in 1823. He began his law practice in East Aurora, where he built his home in 1825 that later became a historic house museum (the Millard Fillmore House). In 1834 he formed the prominent law partnership of Fillmore and Hall with Nathan K. Hall (who later served in Fillmore's cabinet as postmaster general).

Fillmore also became involved in politics in the 1820s. He was elected to the New York state assembly on the Anti-Masonic ticket in 1828 and served three one-year terms. This was followed by election to Congress as a Whig in 1832, serving from 1833 to 1843. He ran for governor of New York as a Whig in 1844 but lost. In 1846 Fillmore was one of the founders of the University of Buffalo and served as its first chancellor. He then was elected New York state comptroller for 1848–1849 and developed a new state banking system that served as a model for the future national banking system.

Fillmore was selected as the vice presidential nominee by the Whig Party in 1848, and when Taylor died he became president. However, the entire cabinet resigned after Fillmore came out in support of the Compromise of 1850 and signed the Fugitive Slave Act, which permitted slaveholders to seek escapees. It split the Whig Party and contributed to its disintegration by 1856.

Among other Fillmore actions as president were sending Commodore Matthew C. Perry to Japan to establish trade and diplomatic relations, opposing France's Napoleon III in his attempt to annex Hawaii, making federal land grants that encouraged the construction of new railroads, and helping to restore good will lost in Latin America because of the Mexican-American War.

Because of the slavery issue, Fillmore did not receive the Whig Party reelection nomination for president in 1852. As a result, he joined the American Party, part of the anti-immigrant, anti-Catholic Know-Nothing movement, and became its nominee for president in 1856—and lost. Many other Whigs also left the party but joined the new Republican Party.

In 1858 Fillmore's first wife, Abigail, died, and he married Caroline McIntosh, a wealthy widow, and moved to a large house in Buffalo, where he lived until he died in 1874 of the aftereffects of a stroke at the age of 74. Fillmore kept active during in his postpresidential years, including being one of the founders of the Buffalo Historical Society in 1862. During the Civil War, he was critical of the policies of President Lincoln, and after the war he supported the Reconstruction efforts of President Andrew Johnson.

The house that Fillmore built in East Aurora, New York, in 1826 became a historic house museum in 1975 devoted to his life and career. He and his first wife lived there four years, during which time his son, Millard, was born and Fillmore began his political career. The house, which originally was on Main Street, has had many owners and changes over the years. It was moved to the rear of the lot for the construction of a theater and stood in disrepair for many years until purchased in 1930 by artist Margaret Evans Price, who moved it to its present location and remodeled it for her studio.

In 1975 the Aurora Historical Society brought the house and restored it as a museum with period furnishings, including some Fillmore pieces. The site now contains his bed and antique toys, an original pantry with tin ware and pottery, a restored fireplace, a barn, and rose and herb gardens. The house is a National Historic Landmark and is listed on the National Register of Historic Places. Annual attendance is 1,500.

Millard Fillmore House, 24 Shearer Ave., East Aurora, NY 14052 (postal address: Aurora Historical Society, PO Box 472, East Aurora, NY 14052-0472). Phones: 716/652-8875 and 716/652-4735. E-mail: ahs1951@verizon.net. Website: www.aurorahistoricalsociety.com. Hours: June–Oct.—1–4 Wed. and Sat.–Sun.; closed remainder of week and year. Admission: adults, $10; children 13–18, $5; children under 13, free.

Franklin Pierce

Franklin Pierce Homestead. Franklin Pierce was a Democrat from New Hampshire who was elected the 14th president of the United States (1853–1857). He was a lawyer and a former general, congressman, and senator who became known as a "doughface," a Northerner with Southern sympathies. He came out in favor of the Kansas-Nebraska Act of 1854 (which allowed individual states to decide for themselves whether to allow slavery). It replaced the Missouri Compromise of 1820, which was declared unconstitutional by the U.S. Supreme Court. The action renewed the debate over expanding slavery in the American West.

Pierce was not renominated because of his support of the Kansas-Nebraska Act, which reopened the question of slavery in the West, and the Ostend Manifesto, a proposal to purchase Cuba from Spain and to seize it if the offer was refused. His political career was destroyed during the Civil War when he gave his support to the Confederacy and his personal correspondence with Confederate President Jefferson Davis was leaked to the press.

Franklin Pierce was born in a log cabin in Hillsborough, New Hampshire, in 1804. He was the fifth of eight children of Benjamin Pierce, a frontier farmer, and Anna. B. Kendrick. His father was a Revolutionary War soldier, a state militia general, and a two-time Democratic-Republican governor of New Hampshire. Franklin initially attended school at Hillsborough Center and then transferred to Hancock and Francetown academies before enrolling at Phillips Exeter Academy. In 1820 he enrolled at Bowdoin College, where he joined literary, political, and debating clubs. He graduated in 1824 and two years later entered law school in Northampton, Massachusetts, and studied under two judges in Amherst. He was admitted to the bar and began a law practice in Concord, New Hampshire, in 1827.

After graduating from college, Pierce entered politics. He became a member of the Democratic leadership group and was elected to the New Hampshire House of Representatives in 1828 and served as speaker in 1832–1833. This was followed by election to Congress from 1833 to 1837. In 1834 he married Jane Means Appleton, daughter of the former president of Bowdoin College. They had three children, all of whom died in childhood, including Benjamin, who was decapitated in a train accident when he was 11 years old. This sent Pierce's religious wife, who never was happy with her husband's involvement in politics, into despair. She regarded the death of their last child as God's punishment for her husband's pursuit and acceptance of the presidency. She was overcome with melancholia during his inauguration, distanced herself during his presidency, and became known as "the shadow of the White House."

From 1837 to 1842, Pierce served in the U.S. Senate. He then tired of politics and resumed his law practice and was U.S. attorney for New Hampshire in 1845–1847. When the Mexican-American War of 1846–1848 broke out, Pierce enlisted in the volunteer services and rose to the rank of colonel. In 1847 he was made a brigadier general and was given command of reinforcements for General Winfield Scott's forces preparing to attack Mexico City. In the Battle of Contreras, he suffered serious leg wounds when he fell from his horse, but he returned to lead his brigade in the U.S. capture of Mexico City.

After the war, he served as president of the New Hampshire state constitutional convention in 1850. In 1852 he attended the Democratic National Convention in Baltimore but was not considered a serious candidate for president. However, when the four major contenders for the nomination were still deadlocked after 35 ballots, Pierce's name was put forward as a compromise candidate and was nominated unanimously on the 49th ballot. In the election, he defeated General Winfield Scott of Virginia, the Whig Party candidate. It was the last presidential election in which the Whigs entered a candidate.

When Pierce took office, the nation was enjoying relative tranquility after the Compromise of 1850 calmed the debate over slavery. But the slavery issue reemerged with the 1854 passage of the Kansas-Nebraska Act, which Pierce supported, reopening the question of slavery in the American West. He sought to oppose antislavery agitation for the sake of harmony and business prosperity, but he was accused of favoring the South's position.

Another controversial issue for the Pierce administration was the promotion of territorial expansion. In 1853, 30,000 square miles of an area south of New Mexico and Arizona was bought from Mexico in the Gadsden Purchase for a southern railroad route to the Pacific Coast. The United States also pressured Great Britain to relinquish its interest along part of the Central American coast. The expansion issue came to a head with the Ostend Manifesto, a proposal drafted by three American diplomats in Europe (on instructions from Secretary of State William L. Marcy) to purchase Cuba from Spain for $120 million and to justify "wrestling" it from Spain if the offer was refused. The proposal never was acted upon, but it weakened the Pierce administration and support for Manifest Destiny.

These policies brought public and political criticism that resulted in Pierce failing to be renominated for president in 1856. He retired from politics to his home in Concord. During the Civil War, however, he was critical of President Lincoln, his correspondence with Confederacy President Jefferson Davis became public, and he expressed support for the Southern cause. He died in 1869 from cirrhosis of the liver at the age of 64 after his wife, Jane, died of tuberculosis in 1863. Two historic house museums now are devoted to Pierce's life and career—the Franklin Pierce Homestead, his boyhood home in Hillsborough, and the Pierce Manse, where he and his family lived in Concord in 1842–1848 (*see* separate listing).

Pierce lived at the Franklin Pierce Homestead from 1804 to 1834, except for seven years while he was away for schooling and law study. It is not certain whether Franklin was born there or in one of the houses now beneath the nearby impoundment of Franklin Pierce Lake. The house, which was built by his father, remained in the family until 1925, when it was acquired by the State of New Hampshire. It is now a state historic site, and the museum is operated by the Hillsborough Historical Society. The house has been designated a National Historic Landmark and is listed on the National Register of Historic Places.

The museum contains Pierce furniture, clothing, photographs, and campaign posters, as well as period furniture and household and farm equipment. It has 5,000 square feet of exhibit space, a 70-seat auditorium, educational programs, and guided and walking tours. Annual attendance is nearly 5,000.

Franklin Pierce Homestead, Rtes. 31 and 9, Hillsborough, NH 03244 (postal address: Hillsborough Historical Society, PO Box 896, Hillsborough, NH 03244-0896). Phone: 603/478-3165. Fax: 603/478-5500. E-mail: c_chadwick@ conknet.com. Website: www.franklinpierce.ws/homestead/homestead.html. Hours: June and Sept.—10–4 Sat., 1–4 Sun.; closed Mon.–Fri.; July–Aug.—10–4 Mon.–Sat., 1–4 Sun.; other times by appointment. Admission: adults, $5; children 6–17, $1; children under 6, state seniors, and Hillsborough residents, free.

Pierce Manse. The Pierce Manse in Concord, New Hampshire, was the home of President Franklin Pierce and his family from 1842 to 1848. The large Greek revival house is the only home owned and lived in by Pierce. It now is a historic house museum and a National Historic Site. The house was saved from demolition in 1971 and now is operated by a volunteer civic group known as the Pierce Brigade. The museum contains furniture and memorabilia of President Pierce and his family. Annual attendance is 1,100.

Pierce Manse, 14 Horseshoe Pond Lane, Concord, NH 03301-5028 (postal address: Pierce Brigade, PO Box 212, Concord, NH 03302-0425). Phone: 603/225-4555. Fax: 603/22-0540. E-mail: camport@politicallibrary.org. Website: www.politicallibrary.org. Hours: mid-June–Aug.—11–3 Tues.–Sat.; other times by appointment; closed Sun.–Mon., Sept.–mid-June, and holidays. Admission: adults, $7; seniors, $6; students and children, $3; families, $15.

James Buchanan

President James Buchanan's Wheatland. The United States began to fall apart before the Civil War when James Buchanan was elected the 15th president of the United States (1857–61)—and he did not know how to stop the increasing hostilities and secessions by the states. He thought secession from the Union was unconstitutional but that the federal government had no authority to stop it. The result was a splintered, angry country, and he decided not to seek reelection as tensions and criticisms increased.

Buchanan was a successful attorney and popular politician from Pennsylvania who was the last president born in the eighteenth century and the only one that remained a lifelong bachelor. He was a Democrat who was seen as a compromise presidential candidate by both sides of the slavery question. He thought secession was illegal, and that going to war to stop it also was illegal. But his efforts to maintain peace alienated both the North and the South as seven states seceded from the Union during his presidential term.

Buchanan was born in a log cabin in Cove Gap, near Mercersburg, Pennsylvania, in 1791 to businessman James Buchanan and Elizabeth Speer Buchanan. He was the second of 11 children born to the Buchanans. James Jr. attended the village academy and later Dickinson College, where he graduated with honors in 1809. He then moved to Lancaster, where he studied law and was admitted to the bar in 1812.

When the War of 1812 began, Buchanan opposed the war on the grounds that it was an unnecessary conflict. But he joined the light dragoon volunteers in defense of Baltimore when the British invaded nearby Maryland. He began his political career as a Federalist when elected to the Pennsylvania House of Representatives in 1814–1816. He then was elected to the 17th U.S. Congress and four succeeding terms in 1821–1831, followed by serving as minister to Russia in 1832–1834.

In 1834 Buchanan was elected to the U.S. Senate as a Democrat and served until 1845, when he was chosen as secretary of state by President James K. Polk. In his new role, he helped negotiate the 1846 Oregon Treaty that established the 49th parallel as the northern boundary of the western United States. From 1853 to 1856, Buchanan served as minister to Great Britain. It was during this period that he was one of three American diplomats in Europe to draft the controversial Ostend Manifesto, which called for offering to purchase Cuba from Spain and (against Buchanan's recommendation) "wresting" it if Spain refused to accept the offer. The offer was never made, partly because of Northern concerns that Cuba would become another Southern slave state.

Upon his return from Britain, Buchanan attended the 1856 Democratic Party presidential nominating convention in Cincinnati. He was not a candidate but was aware that he might be nominated since he was in England during the passage of the Kansas-Nebraska Act and was not tainted by the slavery issue. The Democrats turned to Buchanan after the convention could not agree on a candidate—and he was elected over former Democratic President

PresidentsMillard Fillmore, who became the Know-Nothing Party candidate, and John C. Frémont, the explorer, army officer, and politician who was the first Republican Party candidate.

Buchanan expressed concern about the growing schism in the country, and said he intended to restore harmony to the Union under a national and conservative government. In his inaugural address, he said the Supreme Court would settle the territorial question in the 1858 Dred Scott case, which it did not. The court ruled that African Americans were not citizens and had no inherent rights, that Congress had no constitutional power to exclude slavery in the territories, and that the Missouri Compromise of 1820 was unconstitutional.

Buchanan supported the Kansas-Nebraska Act of 1854, which permitted states to decide for themselves whether to have slavery, only to be opposed by Senator Stephen A. Douglas, the Democratic leader in the Senate, who rallied the popular base and reversed the decision. This enabled Kansas to become a free state in 1861. Buchanan never did find a legal solution to the nation's slavery problem.

Although the slavery question dominated Buchanan's presidency, he also dealt with other matters. They included the short-lived Mormon War, which occurred over a dispute when the Mormon-dominated Territory of Utah sought to become a state; the Panic of 1857, brought about by the overconsumption of goods from Europe and the drain of Union specie; establishment of diplomatic relations with Japan; expansion of American influence in Central and South America and discouraging of intervention by European powers; and continued efforts to purchase Cuba from Spain.

By the election of 1860, Buchanan was tired of the presidency and did not seek reelection. In 1861 he retired to his home, called Wheatland, in rural Lancaster, Pennsylvania. It is where he died in 1868 at the age of 77. His funeral was attended by 20,000 people because of his popularity.

The Wheatland estate now is a historic house museum called President James Buchanan's Wheatland. It is a 17-room federal-style mansion built in 1828 by William Jenkins, a lawyer and banker. He called it the Wheatlands, either because it was surrounded by wheat fields or because the site used to be a wheat field. Jenkins sold the house and 17 acres in 1841 to his son-in-law, William M. Meredith, a Philadelphia lawyer. It was used primarily as a summer house. When it proved to be too far from his work, he sold the estate to Buchanan in 1848. After Buchanan's death in 1868, the house was inherited by several relatives before being acquired in 1886 by the James Buchanan Foundation for the Preservation of Wheatland, which merged with the Lancaster County Historical Society in 2009 to form LancasterHistory.org.

The two-and-a-half-story restored mansion is furnished as it would have been in the mid-nineteenth century. The grounds, which total 10 acres, also contain a carriage house, a smokehouse, and a privy. The carriage house serves as the Wheatland visitor center. Guided tours of the house are given. The site now is a National Historic Landmark and is listed on the National Register of Historic Places. Annual attendance is 34,000.

President James Buchanan's Wheatland, 230 N. President Ave., Lancaster, PA 17603-3125. Phone: 717/392-4633. Fax: 717/293-2739. E-mail: info@lancasterhistory.org. Website: www.lancasterhistory.org. Hours: 9:30 a.m.–9:30 p.m. Tues. and Thurs., 9:30–4:30 Wed. and Fri.–Sat.; closed Sun.–Mon. and national holidays. Admission: adults, $5; students and children, free; tours—adults, $8.30; seniors, $7.50; students over 11, $6; children 6–11, $4.

Buchanan's Birthplace State Park. Buchanan's Birthplace State Park near Cove Gap, Pennsylvania, is located where President James Buchanan was born in a log cabin in 1791. A native stone pyramid monument that is 38 feet square and 31 feet high now marks the site of the cabin in the state park dedicated to the 15th president of the United States (1857–1861).

Harriet Lane Johnson, Buchanan's niece, who never married and served as his first lady, led the effort to create a memorial to her uncle. She was unsuccessful in attempts to purchase his birthplace at his father's general store complex known as "Stony Batter." After her death, a lawyer was able to buy the property in 1907 and constructed the pyramid monument by late winter. The memorial was accepted from the Harriet Lane Johnson Trust by the Pennsylvania General Assembly in 1911, and the state park was established honoring the only Pennsylvanian to serve as president. The 18-and-a-half-acre park is nestled in the gap of Tuscarora Mountain in Franklin County between McConnellsburg and Mercersburg.

Buchanan's Birthplace State Park, State Rte. 16, Cove Gap, PA 17236 (postal address: Buchanan's Birthplace State Park, c/o Cowans Gap, Fort Loudon, PA 17224-9801). Phone: 717/485-3948. Hours. sunrise–sunset daily. Admission: free.

Abraham Lincoln

Abraham Lincoln Presidential Library and Museum. President Abraham Lincoln is remembered primarily for preserving the Union, winning the Civil War, and freeing the slaves—at the cost of his life. He was elected as the 16th president of the United States and led the nation through a great constitutional, military, and moral crisis in

1861–1865 before being assassinated. He was the first Republican to be elected president and the first president to be killed while in office.

Lincoln came from a humble frontier background and overcame many obstacles to become and serve as president as the United States was undergoing turmoil. His life and career are presented at the Abraham Lincoln Presidential Library and Museum in Springfield, Illinois, and celebrated at more museums, historic sites, and memorials than any other American president, including George Washington.

Abraham Lincoln was born in a one-room log cabin to Thomas and Nancy Hanks Lincoln on a farm in Hardin County near Hodgenville, Kentucky, a slave state in 1809. He was one of three children that included an older sister, Sarah, and a younger brother, Thomas, who died in infancy. His paternal grandfather and namesake, Abraham, brought his family from Virginia to Jefferson County, Kentucky, where he was ambushed and killed in a 1786 Indian raid witnessed by his children, including Thomas (Lincoln's father). His mother came to Kentucky with her mother from the section of Virginia that later became part of West Virginia.

Abraham Lincoln's father bought and sold several farms, including the Sinking Spring Farm, where Abraham was born, and owned two 600-acre farms, several town lots, livestock, and horses by the time of his son's birth. However, he lost all his land because of faulty property titles by 1816 and moved the family across the Ohio River to public land in Perry County in nonslave Indiana in 1817 when Abraham was seven years old. His mother died two years later, and his sister (who later died in her 20s during childbirth) cared for Abraham until their father remarried in 1819. His father married Sarah Bush Johnson, a widow with three children. Lincoln later became very close to his stepmother.

Lincoln, an avid reader, was largely self-educated. He had a very limited formal education of about a year of classes by itinerant teachers. As a youth, he became an adept axman in building rail fences and had a reputation as a very competitive wrestler.

As was the custom at the time, he gave his father all his earnings outside the home until he was 21. But he grew increasing distant from his father, partly because of his father's lack of education.

In 1830 the Lincoln family moved west along the Ohio River and settled on public land in Macon County, Illinois, another free state. Thomas Lincoln then relocated the family to a new homestead near present-day Charleston in Coles County. That was when the 22-year-old Abraham decided to leave home and seek a better life. He canoed down the Sangamon River to New Salem, Illinois, where he and some friends were hired in 1831 by a local businessman to take goods down the Sangamon, Illinois, and Mississippi Rivers to New Orleans. There he witnessed slavery firsthand and then walked back home.

Upon his return to New Salem, Lincoln studied law from 1831 to 1837. When the Black Hawk War began in 1832, he was elected captain in the Illinois militia but never had combat. He then became a shopkeeper, postmaster, general store owner, and county surveyor in New Salem. He worked with the public and acquired the social skills and storytelling talent that made him popular with local residents.

Lincoln began his political career by losing an 1832 election to the Illinois state legislature as a member of the Whig Party. But he won the next election in 1834 and served until 1841. He moved to Springfield to practice with the John T. Stuart law firm after being admitted to the bar in 1837. In 1844 Lincoln became a partner with lawyer William Herndon. Since he did not have enough work in Springfield, Lincoln supplemented his income starting in 1849 by following the court as it made its rounds on the circuit to various county seats in Illinois. He also was elected as a congressman in the U.S. House of Representatives for one term in 1847–1849.

His personal life also was changing during this period. He first became romantically involved with Anne Rutledge and planned to marry her. But she died of typhoid fever in 1835. Lincoln became engaged in 1840 to Mary Todd, who was from a wealthy slave-holding family in Lexington, Kentucky. A wedding was scheduled and then canceled in 1841 at Lincoln's initiative. However, they got together again and were married in 1842 at Mary's married sister's mansion in Springfield. In 1844 the couple brought a house in Springfield near Lincoln's law office (*see* Lincoln Home National Historic Site listing). They had four boys with only one reaching adulthood, Robert Todd Lincoln.

In the 1850s, Lincoln returned to practicing law in Springfield. He handled all types of cases, serving railroads, banks, insurance companies, and manufacturing firms, as well as criminal trials. When the U.S. Supreme Court approved the Kansas-Nebraska Act of 1957, which said African American were not citizens and had no inherent rights and states could decide for themselves whether to permit slavery, Lincoln decided to oppose Illinois Senator Stephen A. Douglas, who supported the act.

The two candidates engaged in seven debates across the state. Douglas was reelected senator by the state legislature, but the exposure vaulted Lincoln into national politics. Lincoln was nominated for president at the Republican Party national convention and was elected largely because of his moderate views on slavery and support for improving the national infrastructure and the protective tariff.

Seven Southern states had seceded from the Union before the presidential inauguration, and the U.S. military installation at Fort Sumter in the Charleston, South Carolina, harbor was attacked and other military posts in the

South were taken over by Confederate soldiers shortly thereafter. Without declaring war, Lincoln initially distributed $2 million for war supplies without an appropriation from Congress, called for 75,000 volunteers for military service, and suspended the writ of habeas corpus and began jailing suspected Confederate sympathizers without warrant. Although he faced criticism and defiance from all directions, Lincoln took steps he believed were necessary to preserve the Union—and later to free the slaves.

The Union Army suffered battlefield defeats during the first year and a half of the Civil War. It was not until after the victory at Antietam in 1862 that Lincoln felt confident enough to include the abolishment of slavery with the preservation of the Union as the goals of the war. The war effort gradually improved for the North, partly because of the attrition of Southern forces, which began to rely more on guerilla fighting. In the 1864 presidential election, Lincoln was reelected as he defeated George B. McClellan, the former commander of the Army of the Potomac. The Civil War ended for all practical purposes on March 28, 1865, when Confederate General Robert E. Lee, commander of the Army of Virginia, surrendered to General Ulysses S. Grant.

Lincoln favored rapid reunification with as little retribution as possible. Reconstruction actually began as early as 1863 in areas firmly under Union military control. A group of Republican congressmen opposed the Reconstruction, wanting complete allegiance and repentance from former Confederates before getting assistance.

As the political battle was about to begin, Lincoln was assassinated by John Wilkes Booth, a well-known actor and Southern sympathizer, while attending a performance at Ford's Theatre in Washington on April 14, 1865. Lincoln died of gunshot wounds the next morning after being taken across the street to the Petersen House (*see* Ford's Theatre National Historic Site listing). His body lay in state at the Capitol and then was taken by funeral train to Springfield, Illinois, for burial (*see* Lincoln Tomb State Historic Site listing). Lincoln was 56 years old when he died.

The Abraham Lincoln Presidential Library and Museum in Springfield now is devoted to the life and accomplishments of the 16th president. The library/museum was founded in 2005 by the State of Illinois and is operated by the Illinois Historic Preservation Agency. The museum has 10 exhibit areas and two theaters that include life-size dioramas of Lincoln's boyhood home, areas of the White House, the presidential box at Ford's Theatre, and settings of key events in Lincoln's life. The museum has two special effects theater shows—*Lincoln's Eyes* and *Ghosts of the Library*.

The library's Lincoln Collection consists of over 12,000 books and pamphlet, more than 3,000 Lincoln-related prints and photographs, and over 1,000 broadsides from the 1830s to the 2010s. Other materials include 1,600 original letters and manuscripts written or signed by Lincoln; approximately 320 pieces of Mary Lincoln's correspondence; more than 280 artifacts associated with the president and his family; over 2,000 Lincoln fine art, ephemera, and popular art and crafts that reflect evolving notions of Lincoln and his legacy; and the entire 20,000 pages of the letterpress books of Lincoln's son, Robert Lincoln, as well as hundreds of letters by his wife, children, and grandchildren. Outdoor performances and events are presented at Union Square Park. The library/museum's annual attendance is 600,000.

Abraham Lincoln Presidential Library and Museum, 212 N. 6th St., Springfield, IL 62701-1004. Phones: 217/782-5764 and 800/610-2094. E-mail: hpa.info@illinois.gov. Hours: museum—9–5 daily; library—9–5 Mon.–Fri.; closed Sat.–Sun.; both closed New Year's Day, Thanksgiving, and Christmas. Admission: library—free; museum—adults, $12; seniors and students, $9; military, $7; children 5–15, $6; children under 5, free.

Abraham Lincoln Birthplace National Historical Park. The Abraham Lincoln Birthplace National Historical Park in Hodgenville, Kentucky, preserves the two farm sites where Lincoln was born and lived as a child. Lincoln was born to Thomas and Nancy Lincoln in 1809 in a one-room log cabin on Sinking Spring Farm. The family shortly thereafter moved to 30 rented acres a few miles to the northeast along Knob Creek, where Lincoln lived when two to seven years old. The historical park includes both locations, but the original buildings no longer exist and have been replaced with structures with similar early logs.

A Beaux-Arts neoclassical memorial building was dedicated at the birthplace site at the 116-acre Sinking Spring Farm in 1911. It contains a log cabin similar to the one in which Lincoln was born. The original log cabin was reputed to have been dismantled before 1865 to construct a nearby house and later used in other house construction. The Knob Creek site contains a log cabin and a historic tavern. The cabin is not original to the site but may have belonged to a neighbor and moved to the site of the Lincoln home. The original memorial was constructed by the Lincoln Farm Association and was donated to the federal government for the Abraham Lincoln National Park in 1916. It became a national historic site in 1959 and a national historical park in 2009.

The historical park has a visitor center with the Lincoln family Bible, exhibits on the Lincoln family's frontier cabin life, and a 15-minute film on Lincoln's early years in Kentucky. During the summer, a pioneer garden containing corn, pumpkin, and various period herbs can be seen at the Knob Creek site. Annual attendance at the historical park is 235,000.

Abraham Lincoln Birthplace National Historical Park, 2995 Lincoln Farm Rd., Hodgenville, KY 42748-9707. Phones: 270/358-3137 and 270/358-3138. Fax: 270/358-3874. E-mail: abli_superintendent@nps.gov. Website: www. nps.gov/abli. Hours: Sinking Spring—Memorial Day–Labor Day: 8–6:45 daily; early Sept.–late May: 8–4:45 daily; Knob Creek—daylight hours daily; closed New Year's Day, Thanksgiving, and Christmas. Admission: free.

Lincoln Homestead State Park. The 120-acre Lincoln Homestead State Park near Springfield, Kentucky, features a historic building and two reconstructions associated with Abraham Lincoln's father. Thomas Lincoln. Captain Abraham Lincoln, the president's grandfather, moved to the site in 1781–1782 with his wife, Beersheba, and children from Virginia following the American Revolutionary War. He was killed in an Indian attack in 1786, but Thomas was saved by his oldest brother, Mordecai, who shot the Indian attacker.

One of the three buildings associated with Thomas Lincoln is the two-story Francis Berry House, where Nancy Hanks, Abraham's mother, was living and working as a seamstress when courted by Thomas Lincoln. It also was where Thomas proposed to Nancy by the cabin's fireplace. The two reconstructed 1782 buildings are the workshop where Thomas learned blacksmithing and carpentry and the Lincoln log cabin where the Lincoln family and Abraham lived as a boy.

The state park was established in 1936. It has a museum with exhibits on the houses and the Lincoln family. The park also has a lake, picnic facilities, a children's playground, and an 18-hole golf course. Across the road from the park is the historic house built by Mordecai Lincoln as an adult. The park's annual attendance is 4,000.

Lincoln Homestead State Park, 5079 Lincoln Park Rd., Springfield, KY 40069-9504. Phone: 859/336-7461. Fax: 859/336-0659. E-mail: lincolnhomestead@ky.gov. Website: www.stateparks.com/lincoln_homestead.html. Hours: May–Sept.—10–5:30 daily; closed Oct.–Apr. Admission: adults, $2; children, $1.50.

Lincoln Boyhood National Memorial. The southern Indiana farm site where Abraham Lincoln lived with his family from 1816 to 1830 is now the Lincoln Boyhood National Memorial. It is where he grew from a seven-year-old boy to a 21-year-old man and where his mother, Nancy, died and is buried in the Pioneer Cemetery. It also is where his father got remarried to Sarah Bush of Kentucky in 1819. The 14 years Lincoln spent on the Pigeon Creek Farm had a profound influence on his life, including his sense of honesty, belief in the importance of education and learning, respect for hard work, compassion for fellow man, and moral convictions about right and wrong.

The centerpiece of the memorial is the 1944 memorial building, which features five sculpted panels portraying different phases of Lincoln's life. It has exhibits, artifacts, a 15-minute film about Lincoln's life in Indiana, and a gallery displaying Lincoln-related artwork. The site of the original Lincoln cabin is located nearby, as well as a living history farm with a replica of the farmhouse and rangers in period clothing who work the 1820s-style farm. The annual attendance is 150,000.

Lincoln Boyhood National Memorial, 3027 E. South St., Lincoln City, IN 47552 (postal address: PO Box 1816, Lincoln City, IN 47552-1816). Phone: 812/937-4541. Fax: 812/937-9929. E-mail: libo.superintendent@nps.gov. Website: www.nps.gov/libo. Hours: visitor center—early Apr.–late Oct.: 8–5 daily; late Oct.–early Apr.: 8–4:30 daily; grounds—dawn–dusk daily; living history farm—open early Apr.–late Sept.; site closed New Year's Day, Thanksgiving, and Christmas. Admission: adults, $3; children under 17, free; families, $5.

Lincoln State Park and Colonel Jones Home. The 1,747-acre Lincoln State Park and Colonel Jones Home in Lincoln City, Indiana, was established in 1932 as a memorial to Abraham Lincoln's mother, Nancy Hanks Lincoln. The Lincoln family lived on an adjacent farm, now the Lincoln Boyhood National Memorial, from 1816 to 1830.

Lincoln's mother died in 1819 and is buried on the memorial grounds. His sister, Sarah Lincoln Woods, died during childbirth and is buried in the Little Pigeon Baptist Church cemetery at the state park. The park also contains a 100-acre forest that includes the restored 1834 federal-style home of Colonel William Jones, who was Lincoln's merchant employer and later a Civil War officer.

The park honors President Lincoln with the Abraham Lincoln Bicentennial Plaza, which has a twice-life-size bronze bust of the president and limestone pedestals describing milestones in his formative years in Indiana. The park also contains the Lincoln Amphitheater for outdoor programming and the Sarah Lincoln Woods Nature Preserve, which features early species of prairie plants, exhibits, a live animal area, and bird-watching and audiovisual programming rooms. The recreational facilities of the park include a lake and beach, hiking trails, cottages and cabins, and boating and camping facilities. Annual attendance is 2,000.

Lincoln State Park and Colonel Jones Home, Hwy. 162, Lincoln City, IN 47552 (postal address: PO Box 216, Lincoln City, IN 47552-0216). Phones: 812/937-4710 and 812/937-2802. E-mail: mcrews@dnr.in.gov. Website: www.in.gov/dnr/parklake/2979.htm. Hours: early May–Oct.—11–4 Sat.–Sun.; other times by appointment. Admission: suggested donation—adults, $2; children, free.

Lincoln Trail Homestead State Memorial. In 1830 Thomas Lincoln and 12 members of his extended family, including Abraham, moved from Indiana to Illinois by oxcart. They traveled to an area along the Sangamon River near present-day Harristown and Decatur, where they built a log cabin on a 10-acre farm but lived only one year because of a poor corn crop, harsh winter weather, and some family members developing severe cases of malaria associated with the wetlands. That winter brought subzero weather and six feet of snow, and the family faced hunger and Abraham reportedly sought food from neighbors. The site now is the Lincoln Trail Homestead State Memorial.

Abraham's father and stepmother, Sarah Bush Lincoln, moved to Coles County with the families of the two daughters and sons-in-law of the stepmother and built a new farmstead near Charleston, which later became the Lincoln Log Cabin State Historic Site (*see* separate listing). Abraham, who worked as a rail splitter for fences while living on the farm, went down the Sangamon River in a flatboat to New Salem, where he lived for about six years (*see* Lincoln's New Salem State Historic Site). The abandoned Lincoln family cabin later was used as a schoolhouse and a farm building, and then it was dismantled after the president's death in 1865 and circulated for public viewing in Chicago, Boston, and New York, where it eventually became part of showman P. T. Barnum's museum.

After the Lincoln family left the farm site, it was settled later by the Whitley family, who lived there for several generations and built a dam across the Sangamon River to power a small flower mill. The state memorial was created in 1938 and formally dedicated in 1957. The park contains a memorial commemorating the beginning of Lincoln's life in Illinois, but archaeologists still have not found the exact site of the Lincoln family's 1830–1831 cabin.

The park, which now covers 1,023 acres, has a 146-acre lake, beech-maple forest, wildflowers, and such recreational activities as boating, camping, fishing, hiking, and winter sports. The Lincoln Heritage Trail, which has 3,000 highway markers, now shows the 1,000-mile path traveled by Abraham Lincoln from his birthplace in Kentucky, through Indiana and Illinois, to the memorial site from 1816 to 1830.

Lincoln Trail Homestead State Memorial, Lincoln Travel Memorial Pkwy., County Rd. 30, Harristown, IL 62537 (postal address: Lincoln Trail Homestead State Memorial, c/o Spitler Woods State Natural Area, 705 Spitler Park Dr., Mount Zion, IL 62549). Website: www.dnr.state.il.us/lands/landng/parks/r3/lincoln.htm. Hours: sunrise–sunset daily. Admission: free.

Lincoln Log Cabin State Historic Site. The Lincoln Log Cabin State Historic Site near present-day Lerna and Charleston, Illinois, was the site of the last home of Thomas and Sarah Bush Lincoln, Abraham's father and stepmother. The Lincoln family, except for Abraham, wandered for a number of years from their failed farm near Decatur after a wretched winter in 1830–1831. Instead of going with the family, Abraham, who was 22 at the time, went down the Sangamon River to find work in New Salem and never rejoined the family. He visited occasionally, provided financial aid, and saw that the farm was maintained for his stepmother after his father died in 1851.

Thomas Lincoln eventually bought a small plot near the Embarras River in Pleasant Grove Township in Coles County in 1840 and built a saddlebag cabin in the Goosenest Prairie with two rooms and additional sleeping and storage space in a loft. The cabin was home to as many as 18 members of the Thomas and Sarah Lincoln extended family. The original Thomas Lincoln log cabin was disassembled and exhibited at the World's Columbian Exposition in Chicago in 1893 and then lost after the exposition. A replica of the cabin and a visitor center now are located at the historic site.

The historic site, which was established in 1929, is operated by the Illinois Historic Preservation Agency. It is interpreted to the mid-1840s and includes cornfields, gardens, orchards, livestock, outbuildings, and house furnishings that would be found on a farm of that period. The site also has historical exhibits and guided tours and offers living history programs in the summer. Annual attendance is 126,000.

Lincoln Log Cabin State Historic State, 402 S. Lincoln Hwy. Rd., Lerna, IL 625440. Phone: 217/345-1845. Fax: 217/345-6472. E-mail: hps.lincolnlog@illinois.gov. Website: www.lincolncabin.org. Hours: Nov.–late Mar.—9–4 Wed.–Sun.; closed Mon.–Tues., New Year's Day, Thanksgiving, and Christmas; Memorial Day–Oct.—9–5 Wed.–Sun. and Veterans Day; closed Mon.–Tues. Admission: free.

Lincoln's New Salem State Historic Site. The pioneer village where Abraham Lincoln lived and worked in 1831–1837 as a boatman, shopkeeper, general store owner, postmaster, land surveyor, and where he was first elected to a political office, has been re-created as Lincoln's New Salem State Historic Site near Petersburg, Illinois. Lincoln came down the Sangamon River on a flatboat after his father's farm failed and was abandoned near Decatur and the family moved to a new homestead in Coles County (*see* Lincoln Trail Homestead State Memorial).

Salem was founded in 1828 by James Rutledge and John Cameron, who built a gristmill on the Sangamon River two miles south of Petersburg and 20 miles northwest of Springfield. The village grew rapidly the first few years and then was abandoned in 1840 after the river was found not to be well suited for steamboat travel and the county seat was located in Petersburg instead of Salem.

Lincoln, who was 22 years old at the time, arrived in New Salem on a flatboat and initially worked at odd jobs, such as a boatman and a rail splitter, and often slept in a tavern or general store and took his meals with a nearby family. New Salem was a small commercial village with about 20 to 25 families, most of whom were young businessmen and craftsmen. Lincoln soon found a variety of jobs and decided to try politics. He ran for the Illinois General Assembly in 1832, winning the local votes but losing the county election. After he ran again in 1834, he moved to Springfield in 1837 and became a lawyer and politician.

The current New Salem was founded in 1917 and rebuilt as a historic park on the foundations of the original village by the Civilian Conservation Corps during the 1930s. It features one original and 22 reconstructed buildings—mostly log cabins—and costumed interpreters of the Lincoln residency era. They include 10 shops and a schoolhouse, a tavern, stores, industries, and homes with period furnishings, artifacts, and farm tools. The site also has exhibits, guided tours, and summer outdoor dramas. The site is listed on the National Register of Historic Places. Annual attendance is 400,000.

Lincoln's New Salem State Historic Site, 15588 History Lane, Petersburg, IL 62675-6010. Phone: 217/632-4000. Fax: 217/632-4010. E-mail: hpa.newsalem@illinois.gov. Website: www.lincolnnewsalem.com. Hours: Nov.–Feb.—8–4 Wed.–Sun.; closed Mon.–Tues.; closed Thanksgiving, Christmas, and New Year's Day; Mar.–mid-Apr.—9–5 Wed.–Sun.; closed Mon.–Tues.; mid-Apr.–mid-Sept.—9–5 daily; mid-Sept.–Oct.—9–5 Wed.–Sun.; closed Mon.–Tues. Admission: donation.

Lincoln Home National Historic Site. The Lincoln Home National Historic Site preserves the home of Abraham Lincoln and his family when he lived in Springfield, Illinois, from 1844 to 1861 before becoming president. The house, which was the only home Lincoln ever owned, was purchased by Lincoln and his wife, Mary Todd Lincoln, in 1844. The historic site now is the focus of a four-block historic district that surrounds the home, a visitor center, and several other historic structures.

The house, located on the corner of 8th and Jackson streets, contains 12 rooms over two floors. While loving in the house, Lincoln worked as a lawyer, served in the House of Representatives, and was elected the 16th president of the United States. The house became a National Historic Site operated by the National Park Service in 1971 after being designated a National Historic Landmark in 1960 and listed on the National Register of Historic Places in 1966.

The house and the other buildings in the 12-acre historic district have been restored to their appearance during the time Lincoln lived in the neighborhood. Two of the structures—the Dean House and the Arnold House—house exhibits on the life and times of Lincoln and his neighbors. The Lincoln house contains house furnishings and artifacts relating to the Lincoln family. Robert Todd Lincoln, Lincoln's son, gave the family home to the State of Illinois in 1887 under the condition that it would be maintained forever and open to public at no charge. The site has free guided tours, dramatizations, and audiovisual, lecture, educational, costumed interpretive, and street theater programs. The annual attendance is 277,000.

Lincoln Home National Historic Site, 413 S. 8th St., Springfield, IL 62701-1905. Phone: 217/492-4241. Fax: 217/492-4673. E-mail: liho_superintendent@nps.gov. Website: www.nps.gov/liho. Hours: 8:30–5 daily; closed New Year's Day, Thanksgiving, and Christmas. Admission: free.

Lincoln-Herndon Law Offices State Historic Site. An 1841 Greek revival–style building in Springfield, Illinois, where Abraham Lincoln and his law partner, William H. Herndon, had their offices from 1844 to 1852 has been preserved as the Lincoln-Herndon Law Offices State Historic Site. The building and the Lincoln and Herndon law offices at 6th and Adams Streets became a state historic site in 1985. The building and the Lincoln and Herndon offices have been restored and are operated by the Illinois Historic Preservation Agency.

The structure is the surviving portion of the Tinsley Block, an 1840–1841 brick office complex constructed by Seth M. Tinsley, a local developer, to provide office space for a growing number of professionals working in the newly designated state capital city. The Illinois legislature moved the capital from Vandalia to Springfield in late 1839, and a new limestone state house was being built just north of the Tinsley offices (it now is the Old State Capitol

State Historic Site). The Illinois Supreme Court, where the partners often had cases, met in the state Capitol across the street, and the U.S. District Court occupied space on the second floor of the Tinsley Block.

Lincoln originally moved into the third floor offices in 1843 with his first partner, Stephen T. Logan. When the firm broke up in 1844, Lincoln took in Herndon, a young lawyer, as a junior partner. It was during this period that Lincoln spent much of his time riding the judicial circuit in central Illinois and trying cases in more than a dozen county courthouses. He also served one term in the U.S. House of Representatives in 1847–1849.

Lincoln and Herndon moved from the Tinsley Block to a new office site on the west side of the Old State Capitol Square about 1852. Most of the Tinsley Block, except for the building where the Lincoln and Herndon offices were located, was torn down in 1872. The site underwent many changes before it became a state-owned building in 1985 and was restored. It now is listed on the National Register of Historic Places as part of the Central Springfield Historic District.

A visitor center is now located on the first floor of the building. It contains an exhibit gallery, an audiovisual theater, and a room re-created as an 1840s post office. The second floor has rooms representing those used by the federal court. The third floor, which housed the Lincoln and Herndon offices, features three lawyers' offices and a common room. Visitors see an orientation video in the visitor center and then are taken on a guided tour of the building. Annual attendance is 30,000.

Lincoln-Herndon Law Offices State Historic Site, 112 N. 6th St., Springfield, IL 62701 (postal address: Old State Capital Complex, Springfield, IL 62701). Phone: 217/785-7289. Fax: 217/557-0282. Website: www.illinoishistory. gov/hs/lincoln_herndon.htm. Hours: 9–4 Sat; closed Sun.–Fri. and major holidays. Admission: suggested donations—adults, $2; children, $1.

Lincoln-Douglas Debate Museum. The Lincoln-Douglas Debate Museum in Charleston, Illinois, is the only site devoted to the 1858 senatorial debates of Abraham Lincoln and Stephen A. Douglas. The fourth of the seven debates was held on September 18 at the Coles County Fairgrounds and was attended by more than 12,000 people, many of whom came by train and wagon. The debates focused on the issue of slavery, particularly on how the nation's territories should be accepted into statehood.

Lincoln opposed the extension of slavery, while Douglas favored what he called a doctrine of "popular sovereignty," with residents of the territories deciding whether slavery should be permitted. Lincoln won the popular vote, but Douglas was reelected senator by the Democrat-controlled state senate (state legislatures elected U.S. senators at that time). Although Douglas was returned to the U.S. Senate, Lincoln made such an impression in the debates that it positioned him to win the American presidency two years later.

The Lincoln-Douglas Debate Museum, located at the fairgrounds, describes the debates and tells of their significance, the issues debated, and how the debates affected the nation. It tells the story with exhibits, artifacts, photographs, and audio presentations. The museum also has a model of what the Charleston debate may have looked like, a hands-on children's area, and life-size sculptures of Lincoln and Douglas.

Lincoln-Douglas Debate Museum, Coles County Fairgrounds, 416 W. Madison Ave., Charleston, IL 61920. Phone: 217/348-0430. Hours: 9–4 daily; closed major holidays. Admission: free.

Lincoln Depot. The Lincoln Depot is a historic railroad station where President-Elect Abraham Lincoln gave his farewell address as he left Springfield, Illinois, on February 11, 1861, for Washington to be inaugurated as the 16th president of the United States. The old brick building has been restored and now is a museum commemorating his departure, where he said, "I now leave, not knowing when, or whether ever, I may return, with a task before me greater than that which rested upon Washington." A crowd of 1,000 stood in the rain to see him off.

The depot was constructed in 1852 by the Great Western Railroad and damaged by an 1857 fire and rebuilt. The railroad then merged with several other small railroads to form the Toledo, Wabash, and Western Railroad. It later became the Wabash Railroad, which moved the passenger operations to another location and operated the old building as a freight house and added a second story in 1900. The depot was sold when the Wabash Railroad consolidated its operations in Decatur.

The building was used as a warehouse or storage space until the 1960s, when a local group operated it as a historic site and museum from 1965 to 1970. The former depot survived another fire in 1968 and was restored and used for training historic site management and interpretation by Sangamon State University from 1977 to 1980. The historic structure now is owned by Copley Press Inc., publisher of the *State-Journal Register*, with the Lincoln Home National Historic Site providing National Park Service ranger interpretation.

The depot still contains the separate waiting rooms for men and women. It also has exhibits, and on the second floor is a video that describes Lincoln's 12-day trip to Washington for the inauguration.

Lincoln Depot, 930 E. Monroe St., Springfield, IL 62701. Phones: 217/544-8695 and 217/788-1356. Hours: Apr.–Aug.—10–4 daily; closed Sept.–Mar. Admission: free.

President Lincoln's Cottage. President Lincoln's Cottage is a national monument on the grounds of the Armed Forces Retirement Home (formerly Soldiers' Home) in Washington, where President Abraham Lincoln and his family spent three summers to escape the heat and political pressure of downtown Washington. The cottage functioned as the summer White House, serving as a quiet setting for important meetings and a place for solitary reflection on national issues, as well as a site for family relaxation. Lincoln lived there from June to November in 1862–1864, and it is where he wrote the preliminary draft of the Emancipation Proclamation.

The historic Gothic revival–style cottage, formerly known as the Anderson Cottage, was built in 1842–1843 as the home of George Washington Riggs, who established the Riggs National Bank in Washington. It was first used as a seasonal presidential site by President James Buchanan (1857–1861) and later by Presidents Rutherford B. Hayes (1877–1881) and Chester A. Arthur (1881–1885).

The cottage was made a national monument by President Bill Clinton in 2000. Restoration was completed by the National Trust for Historic Preservation in 2007 and opened to the public in 2008. It now is managed by the National Trust and the Armed Forces Retirement Home, which has been designated a National Historic Landmark. The cottage contains period furnishings, including a replica of the desk on which Lincoln wrote the Emancipation Proclamation (the original is in the Lincoln Bedroom at the White House). The adjacent Robert H. Smith Visitor Education Center contains exhibits about Lincoln as the commander-in-chief during the Civil War, as well as exhibits on the Soldiers' Home and wartime Washington, temporary exhibitions, public programs, and guided tours.

President Lincoln's Cottage, Rock Creek Church Rd., N.W. (at Upshur St., N.W.), Washington, DC 20011 (postal address: AFRH-W 1315, 3700 N. Capitol St., N.W., Washington, DC 20011-8400). Phone: 202/829-0436, Ext. 31231. Fax: 202/829-0437. Website: www.lincolncottage.org. Hours: visitor center/cottage—9:30–4:30 Mon.–Sat., 11:30–5:30 Sun.; closed New Year's Day, Thanksgiving, and Christmas. Admission/tour: adults, $12; children 6–12, $5; children under 6, free.

Ford's Theatre National Historic Site. Ford's Theatre in Washington is where President Abraham Lincoln was assassinated by John Wilkes Booth, an actor and Southern sympathizer, in 1865—just five days after Confederate General Robert E. Lee surrendered as the Civil War was drawing to a close. Lincoln was shot while attending a play in the theater on April 14, and the fatally wounded president died the following day in the Petersen House across the street. A museum at the theater tells the story of the assassination conspiracy that led to the president's death, as well as of Lincoln's presidency and the Civil War.

President Lincoln and his wife, Mary Todd Lincoln, were attending a performance of *Our American Cousin* at Ford's Theatre when Booth entered the box occupied by the president's party and shot Lincoln, jumped onto the stage, and escaped through the back of the theater. The wounded president was carried across the street to the Petersen House, a boarding house, where he died the next morning. He was the first American president to be assassinated. An unsuccessful attempt was made on the life of Andrew Jackson in 1835.

Booth, a well-known stage actor and a member of a prominent Maryland theatrical family, planned and carried out the attack as part of an elaborate conspiracy to simultaneously kill President Lincoln, Vice President Andrew Johnson, and Secretary of State William Seward. to help the Confederate cause by creating Union government chaos. Despite General Lee's surrender, Booth believed the war was not over because Confederate General Joseph E. Johnson's army was still fighting Union forces.

Booth was successful in his assassination of Lincoln, but his coconspirators were not. Seward was wounded by Lewis Powell and David Herold and recovered, and George Atzerodt, who was to kill Johnson, lost his nerve and fled Washington. Booth was tracked to southern Maryland and then to a farm in northern Virginia, where he was shot and killed by a Union soldier 12 days later. Eight others were tried and convicted, and four of the conspirators were hanged. Lincoln's body was taken by special train and buried in his hometown of Springfield, Illinois (*see* Lincoln Tomb State Historic Site).

Ford's Theatre and the Petersen House now are part of Ford's Theatre National Historic Site, established in 1932. The theater building began as a house of worship in 1833. When the church moved to a new structure in 1861, John T. Ford bought the building and converted it into a theater. It was damaged in a 1862 fire and rebuilt with 2,400 seats in 1863. After the assassination, the federal government purchased the building and prohibited its use for public entertainment. It served as a facility for War Department record keeping, a medical library, and an army medical museum until 1887, when it became a War Department clerk's office.

In 1893 the front part of the building collapsed, killing 22 clerks and injuring 58. The building was repaired and used for a warehouse until 1911 and then remained unused for a number of years. In 1932 the theater building and the Petersen House were preserved together as the Ford's Theatre National Historic Site, with Petersen's House opening in 1933 as a historic house museum furnished to appear as it did on the day of Lincoln's death.

In 1955 Congress approved an engineering study for the restoration of the building and the funds for its restoration in 1964. The theater reopened in 1968 with a gala performance. The building again was renovated in the 2000s and reopened in 2009, which commemorated Lincoln's 200th birthday.

Ford's Theatre is a working theater again, presenting professional performances. However, visitors can see the 661-seat theater when it is not being used for matinees, rehearsals, and special events. Free timed-entry ticket tours are offered of the theater and Petersen House.

The Lincoln Museum, formerly located in the basement of the theater, now is housed in a 10-story building adjacent to the Peterson House and across the street from the theater. It tells the story of Lincoln's presidency with artifacts, photographs, and interactive exhibits about Lincoln and his life in the White House, the assassination, and the Civil War.

Among the historical objects on display are the clothing and boots Lincoln wore the night of the assassination; Lincoln family possessions; John Wilkes Booth's pistol, knife, diary, and compass; weapons and other belongings of assassination conspirators; Lincoln campaign buttons and office items; statues and large portraits of the president; and Ford's Theatre playbills, tickets, and posters. The Ford's Theatre historic site has more than 1 million visitors annually.

Ford's Theatre National Historic Site, 511 10th St., N.W., Washington, DC 20004. Phones: 202/426-6924 and 202/426-1845. Fax: 202/426-1845. Website: www.nps.gov/foth. Hours: theater—9–5 daily; Petersen House—9:30–5:30 daily; closed Christmas. Admission: free for those with same-day time-entry tickets (but $2.50 for advance tickets).

Lincoln Tomb State Historic Site. After President Abraham Lincoln's assassination, his body was viewed in the East Room of the White House and the Capitol Rotunda in Washington and then placed on a chartered funeral train that returned to his hometown of Springfield, Illinois, for burial. The funeral train essentially retraced the 1,654-mile route the president-elect took from Springfield to Washington for the inauguration in 1861. The train stopped in 12 cities from April 21 to May 3 for the public to honor and sometimes to view the body in state capitols and historic sites.

Lincoln's funeral train was the first national commemoration of a president's death by rail. He was observed, mourned, and honored by citizens in such cities as Baltimore, Philadelphia, New York City, Buffalo, Cleveland, Indianapolis, and Chicago, as well as Washington and Springfield. The nine-car train carried about 300 mourners, including relatives, governors, military officers, federal officials, and other dignitaries. It also had the remains of Willy Lincoln, the son who had died in 1862 at the age of 11 and had been disinterred to be buried with his father in Springfield. Lincoln's wife, Mary Todd Lincoln, remained at the White House because she was too distraught to make the trip. She made the trip a month later.

In Springfield, Lincoln's body lay in state at the Old State House and then was buried in the Lincoln Tomb State Historic Site at Oak Ridge Cemetery, which now also contains his wife and three of their four children. The tomb, located in the center of a 12-and-a-half-acre plot, has a 117-foot-high obelisk on a rectangular base with a semicircular entryway, which features a bronze replica of the sculpture of Lincoln's head in the U.S. Capitol on a pedestal. A full-length statue of Lincoln also stands in front of the obelisk and above the entrance.

The interior of the memorial contains a rotunda, a burial room, and connecting corridors. A replica of the statue of Lincoln by Daniel Chester French in the Lincoln Memorial in Washington dominates the entrance foyer. The rotunda walls are decorated with 16 marble pilasters that symbolize Lincoln and the 15 presidents that preceded him. The burial room is at the rear of the memorial. A seven-ton block of reddish marble in the center of the room is located 10 feet over Lincoln's burial vault. Four crypts containing the remains of Mrs. Lincoln and three of their children are along the south wall.

On the day Lincoln died in 1865, a group of Springfield citizens formed the National Lincoln Monument Association for the purpose of constructing a memorial or tomb. After Lincoln laid in state in the state Capitol for one night, his body was placed in the receiving vault at Oak Ridge Cemetery, the site requested for burial by Mrs. Lincoln. The association raised the necessary funds for the memorial tomb and completed it in 1874. The State of Illinois acquired the memorial in 1895 and rebuilt and restored the site in 1899–1901. The tomb was designated a National Historic Landmark and listed on the National Registry of Historic Places in the 1960s. The historic site now receives 345,000 visitors annually.

Lincoln Tomb State Historic Site, Oak Ridge Cemetery, 1500 Monument Ave., Springfield, IL 62702-2500). Phone: 217/782-2717. Fax: 217/524-5738. Website: lincolntomb.org. Hours: May–Labor Day—9–5 daily; early Sept.–Oct.—9–5 Tues.–Sat.; Nov.–Feb.—9–4 Tues.–Sat.; Mar.–Apr.—9–5 Tues.–Sat.; closed major holidays. Admission: free.

Lincoln Memorial Garden and Nature Center. The Lincoln Memorial Garden and Nature Center in Springfield, Illinois, is a living memorial to Abraham Lincoln. All the plants in the 100-plus-acre garden are native to the three states where he once lived—Kentucky, Indiana, and Illinois.

The garden was founded in 1936 by Harriet Knudson, a member of the Springfield Civic Garden Club, as a living tribute to the 16th president of the United States. The City of Springfield donated the land along Lake Springfield for the garden, the Garden Clubs of Illinois agreed to sponsor the project, and noted landscape architect Jens Jenson designed the garden. The Abraham Lincoln Memorial Garden Foundation was formed in 1952 to operate the memorial garden.

The basic garden design plan was to provide a series of interconnected paths bordered by various arrangements of native plants that would have been familiar to Lincoln. The path lanes are held together by eight council rings (circular benches of stone designed to foster friendly gatherings within the garden). The memorial garden now also includes the 29-acre Ostermeier Prairie Center, a nearby farm acquired in 1995 that contains an early farmhouse, barn, pasture, cropland, and prairie typical of the pioneer days in central Illinois. Annual attendance is 50,000.

Lincoln Memorial Garden and Nature Center, 2301 E. Lake Dr., Springfield, IL 62712-8908. Phone: 217/529-1111. Fax: 217/529-0134. E-mail: lmg2301@comcast.net. Website: www.lincolnmemorialgarden.org. Hours: garden—sunrise–sunset daily; nature center—10–4 Tues.–Sat., 1–4 Sun.; closed Mon. (building closed on Easter, Independence Day, Thanksgiving, and Christmas week). Admission: donation.

Lincoln Memorial. The Lincoln Memorial on the National Mall in Washington honors the 16th president of the United States. The memorial, built in 1914–1922, takes the form of a Greek Doric temple with a 19-foot marble sculpture of a seated Abraham Lincoln by Daniel Chester French. The architect of the memorial was Henry Bacon, and the interior murals were the work of artist Jules Guerin. Inscriptions of two of Lincoln's speeches—"The Gettysburg Address" and his "Second Inaugural Address"—are featured in the memorial.

The memorial has 5.5 million visitors a year. It has been the site of a number of historic events, especially during the civil rights movement. In 1939 Eleanor Roosevelt, wife of President Franklin D. Roosevelt, arranged for African American contralto Marian Anderson to sing at the Lincoln Memorial after the Daughters of the American Revolution refused to allow her to perform before an integrated audience at its Constitution Hall. It is also where the Rev. Martin Luther King Jr. gave his famous "I Have a Dream" address before 250,000 at the 1963 March on Washington for Jobs and Freedom.

Lincoln Memorial, 2 Lincoln Memorial Circle, N.W., Washington, DC 20024 (postal address: National Mall and Memorial Park, 900 Ohio Dr., S.W., Washington, DC 20024). Phones: 202/426-6841 and 202/485-9880. Website: www.nps.gov/linc. Hours: open 24 hours daily, with a ranger on duty from 9:30 a.m. to 11:30 p.m. Admission: free.

Mount Rushmore National Memorial. *See* Mount Rushmore National Memorial under George Washington in Presidents section.

The Lincoln Museum. Twelve dioramas depicting Abraham Lincoln's life are featured at the Lincoln Museum in Hodgenville, Kentucky, three miles from the Abraham Lincoln's birthplace The scenes range from his formative years in Kentucky to his assassination at Ford's Theatre in Washington. The museum also has an art gallery with paintings, drawings, and other artworks related to the Lincoln era, as well as exhibits of memorabilia, campaign posters, and newspaper clippings. Annual attendance is 30,000.

The Lincoln Museum, 66 Lincoln St., Hodgenville, KY 42748-1551. Phone: 270/358-3163. E-mail: abe@lincolnmuseum-ky.org. Website: www.lincolnmuseum-ky.org. Hours: 8:30–4:30 Mon.–Sat., 12:30–4:30 Sun., Admission: adults, $3.

Lincoln Heritage Museum. The Lincoln Heritage Museum at Lincoln College in Lincoln, Illinois, features collections and exhibits of Abraham Lincoln and Civil War–related artifacts. The town, located 30 miles north of Springfield, was the first to be named for Lincoln before his election to the presidency. He christened the town in 1853 in a ceremony in which he took a watermelon from a wagon, broke it open, and poured the juice on the ground.

The museum began in 1942 when Judge Lawrence Stringer, an 1887 alumnus, willed his extensive collection about Lincoln and the area to the college. The collection initially was displayed in the Lincoln Room, and then it was moved to the McKinstry Memorial Building when it became part of the Lincoln College Museum in 1971. The collection continued to grow with donations from Robert Todd Lincoln Beckwith, the last surviving direct descendant of Lincoln, and others. The name of the museum was changed to the Lincoln Heritage Museum in 2008 to better reflect the museum's mission and content. Plans now call for the museum to be moved to the new Lincoln Center being developed.

Among the many Lincoln-related materials at the museum are artist Sacha Newly's depiction of a young Lincoln in front of words of the Gettysburg Address; the rocker of Tad Lincoln, the youngest of Lincoln's four children; a canvas campaign banner; and William Cogswell's portrait of Lincoln. The museum also has numerous Civil War artifacts, including a Union drum, rifles, recruiting broadsides, diaries, and soldiers' personal effects, as well as historical materials about the college, city, and county. The museum's annual attendance is 4,000.

Lincoln Heritage Museum, Lincoln College, 300 Kekuk St., Lincoln, IL 62656-1699. Phone: 217/732-3155, Ext. 295. E-mail: rkeller@lincolncollege.edu. Website: www.lincolncollege.edu/museum. Hours: 9–4 Mon.–Fri., 1–4 Sat.; closed Sun. and all federal holidays and weekends except Lincoln's birthday. Admission: free.

Abraham Lincoln Library and Museum. The Abraham Lincoln Library and Museum at Lincoln Memorial University in Harrogate, Tennessee, has one of the largest and most diverse collections of Lincoln-related materials in the world. It contains such items as the cane Lincoln carried the night he was assassinated at Ford's Theatre, two life masks, the tea set used in the Lincoln home in Springfield, and approximately 30,000 books, pamphlets, photographs, paintings, and sculptures related to Lincoln and the Civil War period.

The library/museum, which was founded in 1897, includes rare books and other publications, Civil War sheet music, military histories and rosters, manuscripts, photographs, newspapers, broadsides, and commemorative objects pertaining to the 16th president and the war between the states. Its prized music collection consists of approximately 2,012 pieces of mid-nineteenth- and early twentieth-century sheet museum.

From its earliest days, the library/museum received and displayed Abraham Lincoln and Civil War memorabilia. From 1929 to the early 1970s, a room in the Duke Hall of Citizenship was dedicated to the growing collection. A separate building to house the library/museum was opened in 1977 and now receives 14,000 visitors annually.

Abraham Lincoln Library and Museum, 6965 Cumberland Gap Pkwy., Harrogate, TN 37752 (postal address: PO Box 2006, Harrogate, TN 37752-2006). E-mail: thomas.mackie@lmunet.edu. Website: www.lmunet.edu/museum. Hours: 10–5 Mon.–Fri., 12–5 Sat., 1–5 Sun.; closed New Year's Day, Easter, Thanksgiving, and Christmas. Admission: adults, $5; seniors, $3.50; children 6–12, $3; children under 6, free.

Lincoln Memorial Shrine. The Lincoln Memorial Shrine in Redlands, California, is the only museum and archive west of the Mississippi River dedicated to Abraham Lincoln. It was established in 1932 by Robert Watchorn, an English immigrant coal miner who became an oil executive and developed a fascination with the life and times of Abraham Lincoln. He founded the shrine as a memorial to his son, an early American military pilot who died after serving in World War I.

Watchorn, who became a winter Redlands resident, was born in England in 1858 and was forced to work in coal mines at the age of 11 because of his family's poverty. He immigrated to America in 1880 and was working in Pennsylvania coal mines when he was attracted to Lincoln, who had died 15 years earlier. He saw Lincoln's life as a personification of the "American dream," the ability to advance one's circumstances by studying, working diligently, and applying oneself.

Watchorn was elected the first secretary of the United Mine Workers union and in 1891 was appointed Pennsylvania's state inspector of factories and mines and ended child labor in the state. In 1905 President Theodore Roosevelt named him commissioner of immigration at Ellis Island in New York's harbor. Watchorn then became treasurer of Union Oil Company, followed by successful wildcatting and making a fortune with Watchorn Oil and Gas Company. That's when he began collecting artifacts, manuscripts, and books related to Lincoln's life and times.

Watchorn and his wife, Alma Jessica Simpson, had two sons. One of the sons, Emory, also developed an interest in Lincoln. He was an army pilot during World War I who died two years after the war, and his parents built the Lincoln Memorial Shrine in Redlands in his honor. It opened in 1932 in a one-room octagonal building and featured Watchorn's Lincoln collection. Fountains and limestone walls with Lincoln quotations were added in 1937, and two wings were built in 1998 to house a growing number of acquisitions.

The shrine now is a unit of the Special Collections Division of the A. K. Smiley Public Library. It contains artifacts of Lincoln and the Civil War period; rare manuscripts and documents of Lincoln and leading Civil War generals, soldiers, and citizens; and collections of sculpture, murals, and paintings. The shrine also offers guided tours, lectures, education programs, and changing exhibitions. Annual attendance is 14,000.

Lincoln Memorial Shrine, 125 W. Vine St., Redlands, CA 92373-4761. Phones: 909/798-7632 and 909/798-7636. Fax: 909/798-7566. E-mail: archives@akspl.org. Website: www.lincolnshrine.org. Hours: 1–5 Tues.–Sun.; closed Mon. and major holidays. Admission: free.

Andrew Johnson

Andrew Johnson National Historic Site. Vice President Andrew Johnson became the 17th president of the United States (1865–1869) after the assassination of President Abraham Lincoln in 1865. He presided over the initial Reconstruction period following the Civil War, which was contentious and resulted in Johnson being the first American president to face impeachment.

Johnson was impeached by the U.S. House of Representatives in a political battle with radical Republicans, who objected to his Reconstruction policies and his violating the Tenure of Office Act by firing Secretary of War Edwin M. Stanton without Senate approval. But he was acquitted by one vote when the Senate did not have the necessary two-thirds majority necessary for passage. Two sites in Greeneville, Tennessee, are now devoted to his life and career—the Andrew Johnson National Historic Site and the President Andrew Johnson Museum and Library (*see* separate listing).

Johnson was born in Raleigh, North Carolina, to Jacob and Mary McDonough Johnson, who also had another son and daughter. His father was the town constable who died suddenly after rescuing three drowning men, leaving his family in poverty when Andrew was three years of age. His mother did spinning and weaving to support the family before getting remarried to Turner Doughtry. Andrew then was bound over as an apprentice tailor. He received no formal education but taught himself to read and write with some help from his masters as part of his apprenticeship. When he was 16 or 17, he left the apprenticeship and ran away with his brother.

Johnson worked as a tailor for two years in Laurens, South Carolina; learned to tailor frock suits in Mooresville, Alabama; and then returned to Raleigh and traveled with his mother, stepfather, and brother to Greenville, Tennessee, where he established a very successful tailoring business. This also is where he, at the age of 18, married 16-year-old Eliza McCardle in 1827. They were married for 50 years and had five children. She also taught him basic algebra and helped him improve his literacy, reading, and writing skills. In the process, he read about famous oratory and became interested in politics and debates. He started debating, cofounded a debating society, and then ran for public offices and was elected town alderman and later mayor. He gained statewide exposure when he campaigned for a new state constitution that disenfranchised freedmen and reformed real estate tax rates.

Johnson then was elected to virtually every major state and federal government position. In 1835 he became a member of the Tennessee House of Representatives, and in 1843–53 he served five terms in the U.S. House of Representatives. He was a two-term governor of Tennessee in 1853–1857 and a U.S. senator in 1857–1862. From 1862 to 1864 during the Civil War, Johnson was military governor of Tennessee with the rank of brigadier general. In the 1864 presidential election, the longtime Democrat was elected vice president as a Republican. Abraham Lincoln selected Johnson as his vice presidential running mate largely because he was one of the few Southern leaders who was pro-Union, and Lincoln felt it would help unify the divided nation.

Johnson was vice president for less than six weeks before succeeding Lincoln as president after the assassination in April 1865. Wide differences developed between Johnson and Congress over control of the Reconstruction policies and other matters. As a result, the House of Representatives passed an 11-count resolution for his impeachment in 1868. Radical Republicans who wanted hardline policies of protection for newly freed slaves and punishment of former slave owners and government and military officials were opposed to his more moderate approach.

President Johnson offered amnesty for most former Confederates and watered down harsher plans for high-ranking government and military officials. He also vetoed legislation that extended civil rights and financial support to former slaves and other issues favored by the Republican activists. Congress was only able to override a few of Johnson's vetoes. But the midterm elections led to veto-proof Republican majorities in Congress, and the radicals were able to pass civil rights legislation and take control of the Reconstruction efforts.

In 1867 Congress passed the Tenure of Office Act over Johnson's veto, which restricted the president from relieving any member of his cabinet without the concurrence of the Senate. Johnson called the act unconstitutional and replaced Secretary of War Edward M. Stanton with General Ulysses S. Grant, the commanding general of the U.S.

Army, on an interim basis without seeking Senate approval. Because of the controversy, Grant resigned shortly thereafter and Lorenzo Thomas was named secretary of war.

The House of Representatives then impeached Johnson for "high crimes and misdemeanors," primarily for violating the recently instituted Tenure of Office Act. The act was designed to give Congress control over cabinet appointees and specifically to protect Stanton's position. The House of Representatives voted to impeach Johnson, but the measure failed in the Senate by a single vote. The Tenure of Office Act was repealed by Congress in 1887, and subsequent U.S. Supreme Court rulings seem to support Johnson's position that the president can replace cabinet members without Senate approval.

Among the successes of the Johnson administration were the purchase of Alaska from Russia, the annexation of Midway Island, pushing France out of Mexico by sending an army force to the border, and communication with Europe after completion of the transatlantic cable.

After the presidency, Johnson ran for and election to the Senate in 1869 and to House of Representatives in 1872. He was elected to the Senate in 1874, becoming the only former president of the United States to serve in the Senate. He died of a stroke at the age of 82 in 1875 and is buried in the Andrew Johnson National Cemetery, now part of the Andrew Johnson National Historic Site in Greeneville, Tennessee. His body is wrapped in an American Flag with a copy of the U.S. Constitution under his head, as he requested.

The 16-acre Andrew Johnson National Historic Site began as a national monument in 1935 and was redesignated a national historic site in 1963. It consists of such historic facilities as the 1820–1875 Andrew Johnson National Cemetery, 1830s–1840s Johnson House, 1851–1875 Johnson Tailor Shop, and 1851–1875 Andrew Johnson Homestead. The Johnson family owned the homestead 24 years, and his descendants continued to live there until 1956. The two-story Greek revival house is furnished extensively with original furnishings and belongings. The site also has a visitor center, which contains an orientation film, exhibits, collections, and the tailor shop. Annual attendance is 44,000.

Andrew Johnson National Historic Site, 101 N. College St., Greeneville, TN 37743-5607 (postal address: 121 Monument Ave., Greeneville, TN 37743-5552). Phones: 423/638-3551 and 423/639-3711. Faxes: 423/638-9194 and 423/798-0754. Website: www.nps.gov/anjo. Hours: 9–5 daily; closed New Year's Day, Thanksgiving, and Christmas. Admission: free.

President Andrew Johnson Museum and Library. The President Andrew Johnson Museum and Library is located in the 1841 Old College building at Tusculum College in Greeneville, Tennessee. The historic building is one of 10 structures on the campus listed on the National Register of Historic Places. The museum/library contains Johnson family papers, books, and artifacts, as well as political memorabilia, sheet music, manuscripts, pamphlets, books, photographs, newspapers, and college history items. Johnson served as a trustee of the college from 1844 to 1875. Annual attendance is 2,800.

President Andrew Johnson Museum and Library, Tusculum College, Old College Bldg., Greeneville, TN 37743 (postal address: PO Box 5026, Greeneville, TN 37743-5026. Phone: 423/636-7348. Fax: 423/638-7166. E-mail: gcollins@tusculum.edu. Website: www.ajmuseum.tusculum.edu. Hours: 9–5 Mon.–Fri.; closed Sat.–Sun. and major holidays. Admission: free.

Ulysses S. Grant

Ulysses S. Grant National Historic Site. General Ulysses S. Grant is best known as the Union general who won the Civil War—and saved the nation—with his battle victories and military leadership. Largely because of his wartime role, he was elected the 18th president of the United States (1869–1877) and helped to restore the nation during the Reconstruction period.

Grant succeeded where other Union military leaders had failed—stopping the Confederate forces and regaining the initiative in the war between the states. President Abraham Lincoln made him the commanding general of the Union Army after defeating Confederate forces in such battles as Shiloh, Chattanooga, and Vicksburg. He then coordinated the devastating Southern campaigns of William Tecumseh Sherman, Philip Sheridan, and George H. Thomas and caused Confederate General Robert E. Lee to surrender at Appomattox, which led to the end of the war in 1865.

Grant was born in Point Pleasant, Ohio, in 1822. His father, Jesse Root Grant, was a self-reliant tanner and businessman, and his mother was Hannah Simpson Grant. In 1823 the family moved to Georgetown, Ohio. At the age of 17, Grant was nominated to the U.S. Military Academy by Congressman Thomas L. Hamer, with help from his father. But the congressman mistakenly got his name wrong—Ulysses S. Grant instead of Hiram Ulysses Grant. So he adopted the new name.

At West Point, Grant was an average student, ranking 21st in a class of 39, but a superb horseman. He set an equestrian high jump record that lasted nearly 25 years. Although naturally suited for cavalry, he was assigned as a regimental quartermaster after graduation. He was not happy with a military life and planned to resign his commission after serving the minimum obligated duty time.

During the Mexican-American War of 1846–1848, Lieutenant Grant served under Generals Zachary Taylor and Winfield Scott. He became discontented with his quartermaster duties, went to the front lines, and participated as a de-facto cavalryman in four battles. At Monterrey, he carried a dispatch through sniper-lined streets on horseback while mounted in one stirrup. Grant also was brevetted for bravery—at Molino del Rey and Chapultepec.

In 1848 Grant married Julia Boggs Dent, daughter of a Missouri plantation and slave owner and sister of his West Point roommate, Fred Dent. They had four children, and she managed their household accounts for them until her death in 1902. During the next six years, the couple went to such places as Detroit; Sackets Harbor, New York; San Francisco; Fort Vancouver, Oregon; and Fort Humbolt, California. In 1953 Grant was promoted to captain and assigned to command an infantry unit at Fort Humbolt. However, he resigned from the U.S. Army in 1854 after reports of heavy drinking.

From 1854 to 1858, the Grants lived and worked at White Haven, his wife's family farm about 10 miles southwest of downtown St. Louis, now the Ulysses S. Grant National Historic Site. In 1856 Grant built a house on the grounds, but they left the farm when they met with no farming success and their fourth child was born in 1858. The family moved to St. Louis, where Grant worked briefly in 1859 and then returned to Galena, where he helped his father in the tannery in 1860.

With the outbreak of the Civil War in 1861, Grant rejoined the military service. Two days after Confederate troops attacked Fort Sumter in the Charleston harbor in South Carolina, President Lincoln issued a call for 75,000 volunteers, and Grant helped recruit a company of volunteers in Illinois. He then was made a colonel by Illinois Governor Richard Yates and assigned to train and head the 21st Illinois Volunteer Regiment. His first battles during the Civil War began in the Cairo, Illinois, area, where the Ohio River flows into the Mississippi River. They were followed by a series of battles and promotions that led to General Lee's surrender at Appomattox on April 9, 1865. Shortly thereafter, Confederate President Jefferson Davis officially ended the Civil War—and President Lincoln was assassinated.

Grant became a national hero and was promoted to the new rank of General of the Army in 1866 and served for a short time as interim secretary of war in 1867 under President Andrew Johnson. He was a Republican who was elected president in 1868 and reelected in 1872. He basically continued the radical Republication approach to the postwar Reconstruction efforts. He signed and enforced civil rights laws, fought Ku Klux Clan violence, helped rebuild the Republican Party in the South and elect African Americans to Congress and state governments for the first time, established the first national park at Yellowstone, implemented international arbitration, settled Alabama claims with Britain, and kept the United States out of war with Spain over the *Virginius* Incident.

Although Grant personally was honest and had successes, his administration had economic, corruption, and scandal problems, including the Economic Panic of 1873 and depression that followed, corruption and bribery in seven government departments, low standards on cabinet and government appointments, whisky graft trials, an attempt to corner the gold market, and a Republican Party split in 1872.

After leaving office, Grant went on a two-year world tour. In 1880 he made an unsuccessful bid for a third presidency. He became a partner in a New York financial firm in 1881 that went bankrupt. Four years later, while insolvent and dying of cancer, he wrote his memoirs to raise funds. The *Personal Memoirs of U.S. Grant* turned out to be quite successful, but Grant died before the book was published. Throat cancer caused his death at the age of 63 in 1885. His remains are in the General Grant National Memorial in New York City (*see* separate listing).

The 18th president of the United States is honored at the Ulysses S. Grant National Historic Site in Grantwood Village, Missouri, the site of his wife's White Haven family farm, where Grant and his family lived in 1854–1858. A nonprofit group was formed in 1985 to preserve White Haven as a historic site. It was designated a National Historic Landmark in 1989, turned over to the National Park Service in 1990, and restored and opened to the public the following year.

The 9.65-acre site was part of the 1,100-acre plantation of Colonel Frederick Dent, father of Grant's wife. After they were married, the Grants moved to White Haven and planned to retire there after Grant's presidency, but they never did. Guided tours now are given of the main house at the site, which has five historic structures. A visitor center in the former stables contains exhibits about Ulysses and Julia Dent Grant and the role he played in the nation's past. It also shows an introductory film on White Haven. Annual attendance is nearly 25,000.

Ulysses S. Grant National Historic Site, 7400 Grant Rd., Grantwood Village, MO 63123 (postal address: 7400 Grant Rd., St. Louis, MO 63123). Phone: 314/842-1867. Fax: 314/842-1650. Website: www.nps.gov/ulsg. Hours: 9–5 daily; closed New Year's Day, Thanksgiving, and Christmas. Admission: free.

Grant's Birthplace State Memorial. The house where President Ulysses S. Grant was born in 1822 is now a state memorial in a historic district in Point Pleasant, Ohio. Grant's Birthplace State Memorial is operated as a historic house museum by the Ohio Historical Society and features items once owned by Grant and period pieces.

The 1817 three-room cottage, which is listed on the National Register of Historic Places, is located on four acres next to the tannery site where Grant's father worked in the picturesque Ohio River town. It has been restored and once was toured nationwide on a railroad flatcar. It now receives 6,000 visitors annually.

Grant's Birthplace State Memorial, 1551 State Rte. 232, Point Pleasant, OH 45157 (postal address: PO Box 2, Richmond, OH 45152-0002). Phones: 513/553-4911 and 800/283-8932. Fax: 614/297-2352. Website: www.ohiohistory.org/places/grantbir. Hours: 9:30–5 Wed.–Sat., 1–5 Sun.; closed Mon.–Tues. and major holidays. Admission: adults, $3; seniors, $2; children 6–12, $1.50; children under 6, free.

U. S. Grant Home State Historic Site. If Ulysses S. Grant, who lived many places, had a hometown, it probably was Galena, Illinois. He moved there from Ohio with his parents as a youth, returned to work at his father's tannery, recruited and commanded Illinois volunteers there at the outbreak of the Civil War, and returned as a hero after the war. The residents of Galena were so proud of Grant that they gave him a home upon his return from the Civil War in 1865. That house is now the U. S Grant Home State Historic Site.

The gift house—a two-story 1860 Italianate bracketed-style brick structure—was purchased for Grant by a group of prominent local Republicans to show the community's gratitude for his wartime accomplishments. Grant used the house as his official political and voting address and lived there with his family during his 1868 presidential campaign, as well as for a few brief periods during his 1869–1877 presidency and retirement.

The house is decorated and furnished to represent the mid-1860s, with many of the furnishings being from the Grant family. The first floor has an entry hall, parlor, dining room, library, kitchen, pantry, and staff room, while the second floor consists of five bedrooms. The house, which has been designated a National Historic Landmark and is listed on the National Register of Historic Places, is part of a three-block historic district. Guided tours are provided, with interpreters in period costumes from April through October. An adjacent building has exhibits on Grant's life and the history of the home. A statue of Grant's wife, Julia, was added to the grounds of the house in 2000. Following Grant's death, his children donated the house to the City of Galena in 1904 to be used as a memorial, and the city transferred ownership to the State of Illinois in 1931. It was established as a state historic site in 1932. Annual attendance is nearly 85,000.

U. S. Grant's Home State Historic Site, 500 Bouthillier Sr., Galena, IL 61036-2704 (postal address: 307 Decatur St., PO Box 333, Galena, IL 61036-0333). Phone and fax: 815/777-3310. E-mail: granthome@granthome.com. Website: www.granthome.com. Hours: Mar.–Oct.—9–5 Wed.–Sun.; Nov.–Feb.—9–4 Wed.–Sun.; closed Mon.–Tues. and major holidays. Admission: suggested donations—adults, $4; children under 18, $2.

Ulysses S. Grant Cottage State Historic Site. The Adirondack cottage where former President Ulysses S. Grant died in 1885 became a state historic site in 1957. Grant went to Joseph W. Drexel's 1878 cottage in Wilton, New York, to complete work on his memoirs and died of throat cancer four days after completing the proofreading. The cottage now is the Ulysses S. Grant Cottage State Historic Site.

Grant, suffering from ill health, arrived at the cottage on June 16 with a large entourage, consisting of his family, friends, servants, and physicians, and died on July 23. He wanted to complete the memoirs to pay outstanding debts and to provide funds for his wife and children after his death. The book was a success and helped resolve the family's financial problems.

The 1878 four-room cottage and its furnishings remain essentially the way they were during the six-week stay of the Grant family. Visitors can tour the downstairs of the cottage and see the original furnishings and decorations, personal items belonging to the Grant family, the bed where Grant died, and some floral arrangements that remain from his funeral. The historic site, which also has a visitor center, is owned by the State of New York and operated by the Friends of the Ulysses S. Grant Cottage. Annual attendance is 2,500.

Ulysses S. Grant Cottage State Historic Center, Mount McGregor, Wilton, NY 12831 (postal address: PO Box 2294, Wilton, NY 12831-2294). Phone: 518/587-8277. E-mail: info@grantcottage.org. Website: www.grantcottage.org. Hours: Memorial Day weekend–Labor Day—10–4 Wed.–Sun.; closed Mon.–Tues.; Labor Day–Columbus Day—10–4 Sat.–Sun.; closed Mon.–Fri. and remainder of year. Admission: adults, $5; seniors and students 6–18, $4; children under 6, free.

General Grant National Memorial. The General Grant National Memorial in New York City, also known as Grant's Tomb, honors the Civil War military hero who became the 18th president of the United States. It is a mausoleum and memorial in Riverside Park, which overlooks the Hudson River and contains the bodies of Grant and his wife, Julia Dent Grant, and tributes to Grant's life and accomplishments.

The memorial, which is the largest mausoleum in North America, is an eclectic neoclassical structure reminiscent of the Pantheon. It was located in New York rather than Washington or West Point because the city originated the proposal, offered to raise the necessary funds, and agreed to include Grant's wife in the mausoleum upon her death (which Grant insisted upon and was against the policies of both Arlington Cemetery and West Point). Over 90,000 people from around the country and world donated more than $600,000 toward the construction. It was the largest public fundraising ever at the time. Over 1 million people attended the parade and dedication ceremony of the tomb.

Groundbreaking for the granite and marble memorial, designed by architect John Hemenway Duncan, was in 1891. The dramatic building, which has 150-foot soaring domed ceilings, was completed in 1897 and became a national monument in 1958. It was restored in the 1930s by the Works Progress Administration, and again by the federal government in the 1990s.

In addition to the black granite tombs of Ulysses and Julia Grant, the memorial has exhibits depicting Grant's life and accomplishments. It contains statues that depict Grant's childhood, military service, presidency, and death, with exhibits about his career and the construction of the monument. In the tomb, a mural features General Grant accepting the surrender from Confederate General Robert E. Lee at Appomattox, which led to the end of the Civil War. The busts of five Civil War Union generals (William T. Sherman, Philip H. Sheridan, George H. Thomas, James B. McPherson, and Edward Ord) are in the crypt around the sarcophagi. The memorial also has ranger-guided tours and costumed interpreters who explain Grant's role during the Civil War and his presidency. The annual attendance is 118,000.

General Grant National Memorial, W. 122nd St. and Riverside Dr., New York, NY 10027-2522 (postal address: 26 Wall St., New York, NY 10005). Phones: 212/6666-1640 and 212/666-1668. Fax: 212/932-9631. Hours: 9–5 daily; closed New Year's Day, Thanksgiving, and Christmas. Admission: free.

Ulysses S. Grant Presidential Library. The Ulysses S. Grant Collection at the Mitchell Memorial Library at Mississippi State University in Starkville was designated as the Ulysses S. Grant Presidential Library in 2012 by the Ulysses S. Grant Association. The Grant Presidential Collection now includes approximately 15,000 linear feet of correspondence, research notes, artifacts, photographs, scrapbooks, and memorabilia, as well as information on Grant's childhood, military career, presidency, and later life until his death in 1885. The collection also contains about 4,000 monographs on various aspects of his life and times.

Ulysses S. Grant Presidential Library, Mitchell Memorial Library, Mississippi State University, 395 Hardy Rd., Mississippi State, MS 39762-7668 (postal address: PO Box 5408, Mississippi State, MS 39763-7668). Website: www.library.msstate.edu/usgrant. Phones: library—662/325-7668; collection—662/325-4552. Hours: 8–4:30 Mon.–Fri.; closed Sat.–Sun. and major holidays. Admission: free.

Rutherford B. Hayes

Rutherford B. Hayes Presidential Center. One of the earliest presidential libraries and museums in the United States opened in 1916. It honored Rutherford B. Hayes, the 19th president, who oversaw the end of the Reconstruction and the nation's entry into the Second Industrial Revolution during his 1877–1881 presidency. The Hayes Commemorative Library and Museum, now called the Rutherford B. Hayes Presidential Center, is located at Rutherford's former estate, Spiegel Grove, in Fremont, Ohio.

Haynes, a Republican, became president even though he apparently lost the popular vote in one of the most contentious and hotly disputed elections in American history. He defeated Democrat Samuel J. Tilden for the presidency when a congressional commission awarded him 20 disputed electoral votes in what was called the Compromise of 1877. The Democrats accepted Hayes's election when he agreed to end the military occupation of the South and pledged not to run for reelection.

Hayes's second son Webb Cook Hayes and his siblings initiated the museum tribute to Hayes shortly after the turn of the twentieth century and convinced the State of Ohio to undertake the project. They deeded over to the state the president's estate and all of its holdings and agreed to share in the funding of the facility. Ground was broken for the building in 1912. It opened four years later, and major additions were made in 1922 and 1968, increasing the size to 52,640 square feet. In 1981 the Rutherford B. Haynes Presidential Center was adopted as the name of the library/museum. It is now funded by the Rutherford B. Hayes–Lucy Webb Hayes Foundation and an annual appropriation through the Ohio Historical Society.

Rutherford Birchard Hayes was born in Delaware, Ohio, in 1822. He was the son of Rutherford Hayes, a Vermont storekeeper who took the family to Ohio in 1817 and died 10 weeks before his son's birth. His mother, Sophia Birchard Hayes, brought up Rutherford and his sister, Fanny, with the assistance of a younger brother, Sardis Birchard, who lived with the family for a time.

After attending local schools, Hayes transferred to a preparatory school in Middletown, Connecticut. He then enrolled at Kenyon College, where he graduated with highest honors and gave the valedictorian address in 1842. A law degree from Harvard Law School followed, and he was admitted to the Ohio bar in 1845. He first opened a law office in Lower Sandusky (now Fremont) and then moved to Cincinnati in 1850. It was in Cincinnati that Hayes met Lucy Webb, and they were married in 1852. The couple had four sons.

Hayes began his law practice dealing mainly with commercial cases but later became known as a criminal defense attorney. He was an abolitionist and specialized in defending escaped slaves accused under the 1850 Fugitive Slave Act. It brought his work to the attention of the newly formed Republican Party, resulting in Hayes being chosen by the city council to fill a vacancy as city solicitor and then being elected to the position in 1859. But he was defeated for reelection in 1861 after voters turned against the Republican Party because of the secession of Southern states and the threat of civil war.

When the Civil War started, Hayes joined a Union volunteer company, and later he was made a major in the 23rd Regiment of Ohio Volunteer Infantry. The regiment became part of the Kanawha Division and engaged in such battles as Carnifex Ferry, South Mountain, Buffington Island, Cloyd's Mountain, Opequon Creek, and Cedar Creek. Hayes was cited for conspicuous gallantry and promoted to lieutenant colonel, colonel, brevet brigadier general, and brevet major general. He was wounded five times, including once seriously.

While serving in the Army of the Shenandoah in 1864, Hayes was elected to the U.S. House of Representatives from Cincinnati without campaigning. He voted with other Republicans against President Andrew Johnson's Reconstruction plan and for the Civil Rights Act of 1866. He resigned his congressional seat in 1867 to run for governor of Ohio and was elected to two terms, serving to 1871. He resumed his law practice but was elected to a third term as governor in 1875, followed by becoming president in the fiercely disputed 1876 election.

Hayes believed in government advancement by merit, equal treatment without regard to race, and improvement through education. During his presidency, he ordered federal troops out of Southern state capitals as Reconstruction ended, initiated civil service reforms that led to further reforms in the 1880s and 1890s, fought against inflation, used troops to quell the 1877 railroad strike, sought to alleviate the plight of American Indians, and vetoed the controversial Chinese Immigration Exclusion Act.

After serving one term, as promised, Hayes retired to his Spiegel Grove estate in Fremont in 1881, but he continued to stay active in local affairs and in veterans' issues, prison reform, and education at the national level. He died of a heart attack in 1893 at the age of 70. The 25-acre Hayes Presidential Center at Siegel Grove now includes the home, library, museum, other buildings, gardens, walking trails, and tombs of Rutherford and Lucy Hayes. In addition to the 1859 Hayes residence, the other structures include the 1873 Dillon House, 1870s carriage house, 1873 White House gates, and service buildings.

The library consists of 70,000 books and other materials on American history, while the museum collections include 13,000 artifacts, of which nearly 1,800 are displayed in the galleries. Among the center's collections are 75,000 photographs from 1840 to the present, Hayes family memorabilia and portraits, Mrs. Hayes's wedding and reception gowns, the president's carriage, Civil War relics, manuscripts, White House china, weapons, Indian artifacts, and two doll houses. Annual attendance is over 41,000.

Rutherford B. Hayes Presidential Center, Spiegel Grove, Fremont, OH 43420-2796. Phone: 419/332-2081. Fax: 419/332-4952. Website: tcullbertson@rbhayes.org. Website: www.rbhayes.org. Hours: 9–5 Tues.–Sat., Sun. and holidays 12–5; closed Mon., New Year's Day, Easter, Thanksgiving, and Christmas. Admission: adults, $13; children 6–12, $5; children under 6, free.

James A. Garfield

James A. Garfield National Historic Site. James A. Garfield, the 20th president of the United States, was the second president to be assassinated. He served for just 200 days in 1881 before being shot and killed by a deranged political office seeker at a Washington train station. Garfield now is honored at the James A. Garfield National Historic Site at his home in Mentor, Ohio, which began as the Garfield Memorial Library in 1886—a forerunner to today's presidential libraries and museums.

Garfield was the last president to be born in a log cabin and the first to be elected in a front-porch campaign (not actively campaigning but receiving delegations and making pronouncements from his hometown). He became president after serving nine consecutive terms in the U.S. House of Representatives. During the short time he was president, Garfield regained presidential authority from the Senate in executive appointments, purged corruption in the Post Office Department, and took steps to update U.S. naval power and reform the civil service system.

Garfield, who was born in Orange Township (now Moreland Hills) in Ohio in 1831, was the youngest of five children of Abram and Eliza Ballou Garfield. His father, who was a wrestler, died when he was 17 months old, and he was raised by his mother. He received a rudimentary education at the village school and began going to the Disciples of Christ Church with his family. At the age of 16, he worked as a canal driver near Cleveland. After being forced to return home by illness, he enrolled at the Geauga Seminary, where he became interested in learning and teaching and worked as a carpenter to support himself. In 1849 he became a teacher, and the following year he resumed going to church and was baptized.

In 1851–1854 Garfield attended Western Reserve Eclectic Institute (now Hiram College). He also was hired as a teacher at the college and developed a regular preaching circuit at nearby churches. He then attended Williams College in Massachusetts and graduated in 1856 as an outstanding student. After preaching at Franklin Circle Christian Church for several years, he decided to give up preaching. He returned to teaching and taught classical languages at Western Reserve Eclectic and served as principal from 1857 to 1860. In 1858 he married Lucretia Rudolph, a bright student in his Greek class. They had seven children, one of whom, James R. Garfield, later became secretary of the interior under President Theodore Roosevelt.

It also was during this period that James A. Garfield became interested in politics. He was against slavery and began giving speeches in support of the Republican Party and its antislavery position. He also decided to study law and passed the bar in 1859—the same year he was elected as an Ohio state senator. When the Civil War began in 1861, he joined the Ohio volunteers and was commissioned a colonel and given command of the 42nd Ohio Volunteers Infantry.

In his first engagement, Garfield led Union troops to a victory over the Confederates in eastern Kentucky and was promoted to brigadier general. He later commanded the 20th Brigade under General Don Carlos Buell at the Battle of Shiloh; worked under General Thomas J. Wood at the Siege of Corinth; served as chief of staff for General William S. Rosecrans, commander of the Army of the Cumberland; and was promoted to major general after the Battle of Chickamauga. In 1862, while still in the army, he was elected to the U.S. House of Representatives for the 19th Ohio Congressional District and resigned his military commission in 1863 to serve the first of nine consecutive terms.

In 1880 the Ohio legislature elected Garfield to the U.S. Senate. In the same year, the leading Republican presidential contenders—Ulysses S. Grant, James G. Blaine, and John Sherman—failed to have enough support to be nominated for president. Garfield became the party's compromise nominee and defeated Democrat Winfield Hancock for president. He served only 200 days before dying at the age of 49 of the gunshot wound by assassin Charles J. Guiteau.

The James A. Garfield National Historic Site now honors the 20th president of the United States and preserves his home, called Lawnfield, in Mentor, Ohio. He purchased the country estate in 1876 and enlarged the small farmhouse from one and a half to two and a half stories, added a porch, and refinished the interior for his young and active family, which included six children. After he died, his wife built an addition for his books and papers—called the Garfield Memorial Library—in 1886 it was the first of its kind established for former presidents.

In 1936 Garfield's children donated the house and its contents for use as a museum at the Western Reserve Historical Society. The Garfield home became a National Historic Site in 1980 and was restored in the 1990s. The site was operated jointly with the National Park Service until 2008, when the historic site was transferred to the park service. It contains the Garfield library, furnishings, memorabilia, photographs, campaign office, and horse barn and has a visitor center and education facility. Guided tours are offered. Annual attendance is over 22,000.

James A. Garfield National Historic Site, 8095 Mentor Ave., Mentor, OH 44060-5753. Phone: 440/255-8722. Fax: 440/205-3849. E-mail: sherda_williams@nps.gov. Website: www.nps.gov/jaga. Hours: May–Oct.—10–5 Mon.–Sat., 12–5 Sun.; Nov.–Apr.—12–5 Sat.–Sun.; closed Mon.–Fri., New Year's Day, Thanksgiving, and Christmas. Admission: adults, $5; children under 16, free.

James A. Garfield Memorial. The James A. Garfield Memorial is a 180-foot-tall cylindrical monument built in 1885–1890 that combines Romanesque Gothic and Byzantine styles of architecture at the Lake View Cemetery in Cleveland. The crypt contains the caskets of the assassinated 20th president of the United States and his wife, Lucretia, as well as the urns with ashes of their daughter and her husband.

The memorial, designed by architect George Keller with exterior sculptures by Caspar Buberl, was funded by public contributions. A 12-foot marble statue of President Garfield by Alexander Doyle is on the main floor. The exterior of the balcony contains five terra cotta panels with over 110 life-size figures depicting various aspects of Garfield's life and death, such as teacher, general, orator, taking the oath of office, and laying in state in the Capitol rotunda.

The Memorial Hall features gold mosaics, colored marble, stained glass windows, and deep red granite columns. The window panes represent the 13 original colonies, plus the state of Ohio. On a clear day, visitors can see downtown Cleveland and 40 miles of the Lake Erie shore from an outdoor balcony, located 64 steps from the lobby. The memorial, which has interpretive guides, is listed on the National Register of Historic Places.

James A. Garfield Memorial, Lake View Cemetery, 12316 Euclid Ave., Cleveland, OH 44106-4393. Phone: 216/421-2665. Fax: 216/421-2415. E-mail: info@lakeviewcemetery.com. Website: www.lakeviewcemetery.com. Hours: Apr.–mid-Nov.—9–4 daily; closed mid-Nov.–Mar. Admission: free.

Chester A. Arthur

President Chester A. Arthur State Historic Site. Chester Alan Arthur was a Vermont native who became a part of the Republican political machine in New York City and surprised nearly everyone by embracing the cause of civil service reform when he became the 21st president of the United States (1881–1885) after the assassination of President James A. Garfield. Today, his life and achievements are featured at the President Chester A. Arthur State Historic Site in Fairfield, Vermont, the city of his birth.

Arthur was born in the small Vermont farming community of Fairfield in 1829 to William and Malvina Stone Arthur. His parents met while his father was teaching in Dunham, Canada. He changed jobs frequently, moving to Burlington, Jericho, and Waterville, where he joined the Free Will Baptists and became a minister in that sect. In 1828 the family moved to Fairfield, where Arthur was born in a small temporary parsonage the following year. They lived in Fairfield until 1832, when his father moved the family to several towns in Vermont and upstate New York before settling in the Schenectady area.

After schooling in Perry and Greenwich, New York, Arthur enrolled in Union College in 1845 and studied the traditional classical curriculum, was elected to the Phi Beta Kappa honor society, and served as president of the debate society. After graduating in 1848, he taught school in Schaghticoke and North Pownal, Vermont, and then became principal in Cohoes, New York. At the same time, he began studying law and decided to move to New York City, where he read law in the office of Erastus D. Culver, an abolitionist lawyer and family friend. After being admitted to the bar in 1854, he joined the firm, which was renamed Culver, Parker, and Arthur.

Arthur became involved with the Republican Party in New York City and was appointed collector of the port of New York and enlisted thousands of port employees under his supervision to support Roscoe Conkling's Stalwart faction of the Republican Party. However, he was ousted in 1878 by President Rutherford B. Hayes, who was attempting to reform the Customs House and civil service system. With Conkling's machine assistance, Arthur was nominated by the Republicans as vice president. After being elected, he stood firmly with Conkling in his patronage struggle with President Garfield.

After Arthur succeeded Garfield as president, he was eager to prove he was above machine politics and placed great emphasis on civil service reform and the merit system. In 1883 Congress passed the Pendleton Act, which established the bipartisan Civil Service Commission, outlawed political assessments against office holders, required competitive examinations for certain government positions, and protected employees from removal for political reasons. Arthur vigorously defended the law. Among his other achievements were updating the U.S. Navy, enacting the first general federal immigration law, and vetoing the Rivers and Harbors Act, which called for excessive federal appropriations.

Arthur did not run for reelection because of health problems, suffering from a fatal kidney disease. He died in 1886 at the age of 57. His life and career are presented at the President Chester A. Arthur State Historic Site, established in 1953 and housed in the re-created second house in which Arthur lived as an infant in Fairfield, Vermont. A primitive cabin where he was born (and which no longer exists) was hastily built to house the pastor's family until the permanent parsonage was completed by the Baptist congregation for his father, who had been appointed the minister. The site also contains the North Fairfield Baptist Church, a ca. 1820 brick building. It was donated to the state in 1970 by the Vermont Baptist State Convention and is open at the same time as the state historic site. The historic site has an annual attendance of 3,000.

President Chester A. Arthur State Historic Site, 4588 Chester Arthur Rd., Fairfield, VT 05455 (postal address: Historic Preservation, National Life Bldg., 2nd Floor, Montpelier, VT 05633). Phone: 802/828-3051. Fax: 802/828-3206. E-mail: john_dumville@state.vt.us. Website: www.historicvermont.org/arthur. Hours: July–mid-Oct.—11–5 Wed.–Sun.; closed Mon.–Tues. and mid-Oct.–June. Admission: suggested donation—adults, $5; children, free.

Grover Cleveland

Grover Cleveland Birthplace. Stephen Grover Cleveland—who rarely used his first name—is the only president of the United States to serve two nonconsecutive terms (1885–1889 and 1893–1897). He was the 22nd and 24th president and the only Democrat to be elected to the presidency during a period of Republican political domination from 1860 to 1912. Cleveland was the leader of the probusiness Bourbon Democrats, who opposed high tariffs, the silver standard, inflation, imperialism, and subsidies to businesses, farmers, and veterans. He was a conservative who fought for political reform and fiscal conservatism, and a reformer who battled political corruption, patronage, and bossism. Even the reform wing of the Republican Party—called the Mugwumps—largely came out in his support in 1884.

Stephen Grover Cleveland was born in Caldwell, New Jersey, in 1817 to Richard Faley Cleveland, a Presbyterian minister, and Ann Neal Cleveland. He was the fifth of nine children. As the father was transferred, the family relocated to Clinton and Holland Patent, New York, where he died in 1853. Grover went to elementary school at the Fayetteville Academy and Clinton Liberal Academy and then dropped out to help support the family.

After his brother William went to work as a teacher at the New York Institute for the Blind in New York City, Grover was hired as an assistant teacher. In 1895 he moved to Buffalo, where his uncle gave him a clerical job and introduced him to the partners of the Rogers, Bowen, and Rogers law firm. He later served a clerkship with the firm, was admitted to the bar in 1859, and worked for the Rogers law firm as a lawyer for three years before opening his own law office. He became an assistant district attorney, lost a close race for district attorney as a Democrat, and then was elected Erie County sheriff in 1870.

In 1881 Grove Cleveland was elected mayor of Buffalo. He developed an impressive record fighting entrenched interests and was nominated for governor of New York State in 1882. Cleveland won again and became known as an honest public official who opposed unnecessary spending. He then was nominated by the Democratic Party for president in 1884 and was elected—despite opposition by New York City's Tammany Hall political organization and the disclosure that he fathered an illegitimate child while a lawyer in Buffalo and was paying child support.

During his 1885–1889 presidency, he made appointments based on merit rather than politics, established the Interstate Commerce Commission to regulate railroads for the first time, created the Department of Labor to provide arbitration in labor disputes, modernized the U.S. Navy, took back lands given to railroads that they did not develop as agreed, and vetoed controversial bills giving free seed to Texas farmers and fraudulent pension claims by Civil War veterans.

Cleveland, a bachelor, also married a 21-year-old woman, Frances Clara Folsom, the daughter of a deceased law partner, in the first marriage by a president in the White House in 1886. They turned out to be an affectionate couple, and she was a popular first lady. They had five children.

Cleveland ran for reelection in 1888 but lost to Benjamin Harrison, an Indiana Republican senator and lawyer, and he returned to New York to practice law. The two candidates met again in a rematch in 1892 when Harrison ran for reelection and Cleveland was nominated by the Democrats. This time, Cleveland won and again sought to change from the silver to the gold standard and to reduce tariff rates. He was successful in replacing the silver coinage system, but the new import tax was more than he sought because of opposition by northern industrial states. Cleveland's 1893–1897 term also was affected adversely by the Panic of 1893 depression, the Pullman railroad strike, and other labor problems.

Cleveland retired to his estate, Westland Mansion, in Princeton, New Jersey. He served as a trustee of Princeton University, worked to reform the country's insurance industry, and kept active in political matters. He died in 1908 of a heart attack at the age of 71. Cleveland now is memorialized in a historic house museum where he was born—the Grover Cleveland Birthplace in Caldwell, New Jersey. The 1832 building also is known as the Caldwell Presbyterian Church Manse, which served as the parsonage for Grover's father while he was the pastor.

The museum, which is listed on the National Register of Historic Places, was founded in 1913 by a group of supportive citizens. It now is a state historic site operated by the New Jersey Department of Environmental Protection. The historic house, located on a two-and-a-half-acre site, contains the furnishings and memorabilia of President Cleveland at the turn of the twentieth century. Among its Cleveland artifacts are such items as his cradle, clothes, White House chair, and fishing equipment. Annual attendance is 6,000.

Grover Cleveland Birthplace, 2107 Bloomfield Ave., Caldwell, NY 07006-5115. Phone: 973/226-0001. Fax: 973/226-1810. E-mail: gcmuseum@gmail.com. Website: www.clevelandbirthplace.org. Hours: 10–12 Wed.–Sat., 1–4 Sun.; closed Mon.–Tues. and state and federal holidays. Admission: free.

Benjamin Harrison

Benjamin Harrison Presidential Site. Benjamin Harrison, grandson of President William Henry Harrison, was the 23rd president of the United States (1889–1891). He was a Republican politician, lawyer, and Civil War brigadier general who was appointed U.S. senator and defeated Democratic incumbent Grover Cleveland in the 1888 presidential election, and then lost to Cleveland in an 1892 rematch.

Harrison's administration was known for its economic legislation, which included the McKinley tariff and Sherman antitrust acts and annual federal spending that reached 1 billion dollars for the first time. Democrats used the high tariff and the record expenditures to defeat the Republicans in the 1890 midterm elections and in Harrison's reelection in 1892.

The Harrison family traced its history to Jamestown, Virginia, in 1630 with the arrival of an earlier Englishman with the Benjamin Harrison name. The future president, however, was born in North Bend, Ohio, in 1833, the second of eight children of John Scott Harrison and Elizabeth Ramsey Irwin. His father was a farmer with modest income who later became a U.S. congressman. In addition to being a grandson of President William Henry Harrison, Benjamin was the great-grandson of Benjamin Harrison V, a Virginia governor and signer of the Declaration of Independence.

Harrison's early education was in a one-room schoolhouse. He later was tutored with college preparatory studies. He enrolled in Farmer's College near Cincinnati in 1847 and then transferred to Miami University in Oxford, Ohio. At Farmer's College, he met Caroline Lavinia Scott, daughter of the college's president, whom he married in 1853. They had two children. After graduating from Miami University, Harrison studied law at a Cincinnati law firm, lived on the family farm, passed the bar, and began practicing law in Indianapolis.

In Indianapolis, Harrison joined the Republican Party shortly after its formation in 1856, campaigned for presidential candidate John C. Frémont, and was elected city clerk. In 1858 he entered into a law partnership, and in 1860 he was elected reporter of the Indiana Supreme Court. In 1862 Harrison was asked by Governor Oliver Morton to recruit a regiment in response to President Abraham Lincoln's call for more volunteers. Harrison did raise the regiment, but he turned down the governor's offer for him to be the commander because of his lack of military experience. He was made a second lieutenant in the new 70th Indiana Infantry and then promoted to colonel.

After spending most of the first two years performing reconnaissance duty and guarding railroads in Kentucky and Tennessee, the regiment joined General William T. Sherman's Atlanta campaign and moved to the front lines. Harrison was placed in command of the First Brigade of the First Division of the XX Corps, which saw action from the Battle of Resaca to Atlanta and then in the Battle of Nashville. He was made a brigadier general and marched in the Grand Review in Washington before being mustered out in mid-1865.

While serving in the army in 1864, Harrison was reelected reporter of the Supreme Court of Indiana and served four more years. He did not receive the Republication nomination for governor of Indiana in 1872 and was defeated when nominated in 1876. But when Republicans retook control of the state legislature, Harrison was chosen as U.S. senator and served from 1881 to 1887. In 1888 Harrison was nominated for president by the Republicans and defeated President Grover Cleveland in a front-porch campaign by turning out protectionist voters in the industrial states of the North. Harrison had 90,000 fewer votes than Cleveland, but he carried the Electoral College 233 to 168.

When Harrison began his presidency, the federal government had a billion-dollar surplus (due largely to high import tariffs), but it evaporated by end of his term. Substantial appropriations went for such expenditures as internal improvements, naval expansion, and steamship line subsidies. The Sherman Antitrust Act to protect trade and commerce against unlawful restraints and monopolies was passed, but attempts to reduce tariffs and to annex Hawaii were defeated.

Harrison was nominated for reelection in 1892, but he was defeated by Cleveland this time. Although urged to run again in 1896, he decided against it and endorsed William McKinley, who was elected. He got remarried in 1896 to Mary Scott Lord Dimmick, niece of his deceased wife (Caroline died in the White House in 1892). He also attended the 1893 World's Columbian Exhibition in Chicago, taught at Stanford University, represented Venezuela in the border dispute with British Guiana, and attended the 1899 Hague Peace Conference. He died in 1901 of influenza and pneumonia at the age of 67.

Harrison's 1874–1875 home in Indianapolis now is a historic house museum, called the Benjamin Harrison Presidential Site (formerly the President Benjamin Harrison Home). It is a 16-room Italianate home with a carriage house. The house features an annual exhibition and contains Harrison papers, furnishings, books, election campaign items, inaugural Bible, gifts to the president, and other memorabilia, as well as a women's suffrage collection. Visitations are by guided tours. The house was designated a National Historic Landmark in 1964 and established as a museum in 1966. It is operated by the President Benjamin Harrison Foundation, which was created by the Jordan Foundation. Annual attendance is 26,000.

Benjamin Harrison Presidential Site, 1230 N. Delaware St., Indianapolis, IN 46202-2531. Phone: 317/631-1888. Fax: 317/632-5488. E-mail: harrison@pbhh.org. Website: www.presidentbenjaminharrison.org. Hours: Feb.–May and Aug.–Dec.—10–3:30 Mon.–Sat.; June–July—10–3:30 Mon.–Sat., 12:30–3:30 Sun.; closed Memorial Day, Labor Day, Thanksgiving, Christmas Eve and Day, and first three weeks of Jan. Admission: tours—adults, $8; seniors, $6; students 5–17, $3; children under 5, free.

William McKinley

William McKinley Presidential Library and Museum. William McKinley, the 25th president of the United States (1897–1901), was the third American president to be assassinated. He was mortally wounded by an anarchist while attending the 1901 Pan-American Exposition in Buffalo, New York. He now is honored at the William McKinley Presidential Library and Museum and the McKinley National Memorial in Canton, Ohio, and the McKinley Birthplace Home in Niles, Ohio (*see* separate listings).

McKinley, a staunch Republication, was elected an Ohio congressman at the age of 34 and advanced rapidly in the political world. He served 14 years in the U.S. House of Representatives and was elected to two terms as governor of Ohio before becoming president. He was best known for supporting the gold standard and higher tariffs, and for forging a Republican coalition that largely dominated national politics until the 1930s.

McKinley was born in 1843 in Niles, Ohio. When he was 10 years old, his family moved to Poland, Ohio, where he graduated from Poland Academy. He attended Allegheny College for only one term before illness forced him to return home. He then became a part-time student while working to pay the tuition.

When the Civil War began in 1861, McKinley was teaching in a country school. He enlisted in the Union Army and became a private in the 23rd Ohio Infantry. McKinley was promoted a number of times for bravery. He was made a commissary sergeant for serving the regiment during a battle in western Virginia, a first lieutenant for driving a mule team delivering rations under enemy fire at Antietam, and a then captain and brevet major of volunteers before being mustered out in 1865.

After being discharged from the service, McKinley attended Albany Law School and was admitted to the bar in 1867. He established a law practice in Canton and became involved in politics. He soon became Republican county chairman, was active in the temperance movement, and became president of the YMCA. He campaigned for Ulysses S. Grant in his presidential bid and was elected Stark County prosecutor in 1869–1871.

In 1873 McKinley married Ida Saxton, the daughter of a local banker. They had two daughters. Both died in childhood—the second after a difficult delivery. Mrs. McKinley's mother also died, causing her severe depression. She then began suffering crippling phlebitis, epileptic seizures, and other disorders, and McKinley became a virtual caretaker for her physical and psychiatric problems.

McKinley was elected to the U.S. House of Representatives in 1876. He served 14 years—in 1877–1882 and 1885–1891. He became chairman of the powerful Committee on Ways and Means and authored the McKinley tariff, which raised import rates to the highest in history, largely to protect Ohio industry. In general, however, he supported public over private interests. After losing in the 1890 Democratic landslide, he ran for governor of Ohio and was elected to two terms in 1891 and 1893.

In 1896 the Republican Party nominated McKinley for president, and he defeated Democrat William Jennings Bryan in a front-porch campaign with the help of Mark Hanna, a wealthy Cleveland businessman, who served as political manager. McKinley supported the current gold standard, while Bryan advocated the free and unlimited coinage of silver and gold. Hanna introduced revolutionary advertising techniques that helped elect McKinley, who presided over a return to prosperity after the Panic of 1893 and led the nation to a more active role in world affairs.

The Spanish-American War of 1898 resulted from two factors. Many Americans and the press felt the United States should have a more vigorous foreign policy, especially in Latin American and the Caribbean, and reports that Spanish forces had killed nearly a quarter of Cuba's population and that others were suffering acutely in the struggle for the island's independence. The McKinley administration pressured Spain to end its repression but was rebuffed. And then the visiting USS *Maine* battleship exploded in the Havana harbor, killing 260. The American press blamed the Spanish, and unsuccessful diplomatic relations were followed by a declaration of war.

It turned out to be a 100-day war. The U.S. Pacific fleet under Commodore George Dewey defeated the Spanish fleet in the Battle of Manila in the Philippines, which also was a Spanish colonial possession and fighting for independence. In Cuba, Theodore Roosevelt, who later became president, led American troops to victory in the Battle of San Juan Hill, and the U.S. Navy destroyed the Spanish warships in a sea battle. In the Treaty of Paris, Spain gave Cuba independence and the United States possession of the former Spanish colonies of Puerto Rico, Guam, and the Philippines (which later was given its freedom). McKinley also annexed the Republic of Hawaii in 1898.

In the 1900 presidential election, McKinley again faced William Jennings Bryan. He focused on the return of prosperity and foreign policy in the election, while Bryan spoke against McKinley's imperialism. McKinley's second term came to a tragic end in 1901 while he was standing in line to shake hands with ordinary citizens in the Temple of Music at the Pan-American Exposition in Buffalo. He was shot twice by Leon Czolgosz, an anarchist, on September 6 and died a week later.

President McKinley was succeeded by Vice President Theodore Roosevelt. McKinley, who was 58 years old when he died, is entombed with his wife and two daughters at the McKinley National Memorial in Canton. The City of Buffalo also erected a 98-foot monument in a downtown square following McKinley's assassination.

The William McKinley Presidential Library and Museum in his hometown of Canton honors the 25th president of the United States. It was founded in 1946 and is operated by the Stark County Historical Society. The library/museum has the largest collection of McKinley artifacts, a gallery devoted to his life and career, and a library with 5,000 volumes on McKinley. The museum section also has an exhibit gallery on Stark County history, a life-size historical street with early shops, and a temporary exhibition gallery. The library/museum is located adjacent to the McKinley National Memorial, which the museum manages. The library/museum annual attendance is 45,000.

William McKinley Presidential Library and Museum, 800 McKinley Memorial Dr., N.W., Canton, OH 44708-4832 (postal address: PO Box 20070, Canton, OH 44701-0070). Phone: 330/455-7043. Fax: 330/455-1137. E-mail: mmuseum@neo.rr.com. Website: www.mckinleymuseum.org. Hours: 9–4 Mon.–Sat., 12–4 Sun.; closed New Year's Day, Easter, Memorial Day, Labor Day, Thanksgiving, and Christmas. Admission: adults, $8; seniors, $7; children 3–18, $6; children under 3, free.

McKinley National Memorial. The McKinley National Memorial in Canton, Ohio, contains the tomb of William McKinley, the 25th president of the United States, as well as those of his wife, Ida Saxton McCormick, and two daughters, Katherine and Ida. The monument was designed by Harold Van Buren Magonigle to combine the cross of a martyr with the sword of a president who had served as commander-in-chief during wartime (the 1898 Spanish-American War).

The mausoleum towers 77 feet over four long terraces (originally a reflecting pool) leading to 108 steps to the memorial, which contains the tombs. A nine-and-a-half-foot bronze statue of President McKinley delivering his final public address at the Pan-American Exposition in Buffalo, New York, where he was assassinated, is located on the steps to the memorial.

The memorial was founded by the McKinley National Memorial Association, formed by the president's closest advisers immediately following the funeral in 1901. After a $600,000 fundraising drive, construction begin in 1905, and the memorial was dedicated in 1907. The monument was transferred to the Ohio State Archaeological and Historical Society (now Ohio Historical Society) in 1943, which founded the McKinley museum on the memorial grounds (*see* separate listing) in 1946 and rehabilitated the site in 1951. In 1973 the administration was turned over to the Stark County Historical Society, which manages the site through the museum. The memorial now is a National Historic Landmark and is listed on the National Registry of Historic Places.

McKinley National Memorial, 800 McKinley Monument Dr., N.W., Canton, OH 44708-4832 (postal address: PO Box 20070, Canton, OH 44701-0070). Phone: 330/455-7043. Fax: 330/455-7043. E-mail: mmuseum@neo.rr.com. Website: www.mckinleymuseum.org. Hours: 9–8 Mon.–Thurs., 9–5:30 Fri.–Sat., 1–5 Sun.; closed major holidays. Admission: free.

National McKinley Birthplace Memorial. President William McKinley was born in Niles, Ohio, where two sites now memorialize the 25th president of the United States—the National McKinley Birthplace Memorial and the McKinley Birthplace Home and Research Center (*see* separate listing).

McKinley was born to William McKinley Sr. and Nancy Allison Campbell McKinley in 1843. He was the seventh of nine children. His father worked in mining and the manufacturing of pig iron. After the family moved to Poland, Ohio, the house became a general store and later a birthplace memorial that closed and was destroyed in a fire in 1937.

In 1909 initial congressional funding for a national memorial honoring McKinley in Niles was authorized, and in 1911 the National McKinley Birthplace Association was founded. The town of Niles donated an entire city block for the memorial. A fundraising drive began in 1912, followed by a design competition. A Beaux-Arts design by the firm of McKim, Mead, and White was selected in 1915, and the building was dedicated in 1917.

The memorial is a classic Greek structure of Georgia marble with two wings—one for a public library and the other for a museum and auditorium. A 12-foot marble statue of McKinley is also in the center of the "Court of Honor," surrounded by busts and tablets of prominent men closely associated with McKinley. The museum contains memorabilia from McKinley's early life in Niles, political campaign materials, presidential items, and artifacts from the Civil War and Spanish-American War. The site, which is listed on the National Registry of Historic Places, is operated by the McKinley Memorial Library.

National McKinley Birthplace Memorial, 40 N. Main St., Niles, OH 44446-5012. Phone: 330/652-1704. Fax: 330/652-5788. E-mail: mckinley@mcklib.org. Website: www.mckinley.lib.oh.us. Hours: 9–8 Mon.–Tues. and Thurs., 9–5 Wed. and Fri.–Sat.; closed Sun. and major holidays. Admission: free.

McKinley Birthplace Home and Research Center. President William McKinley was born in a small wood-plank-sided home in Niles, Ohio, in 1843. It was a two-story home with eight rooms that covered only 924 square feet. The McKinley family lived there for 10 years. It became a general store and then was moved and made into a memorial to McKinley, but it closed and the building was burned in a 1937 fire.

A bank building was built on the original site and donated to the City of Niles in 1994 and demolished in 1999. The McKinley Memorial Library, which operates the McKinley Memorial, was granted the site in 2001. An adjacent lot where a schoolhouse McKinley attended was located also was acquired by the library. A larger replica of the birthplace house then was built on the expanded grounds for the McKinley Birthplace Home and Research Center. Opened in 2003, the house is furnished like a typical home in the 1840s and contains a library of McKinley materials, a computer laboratory, meeting space, and a gift shop. Annual attendance is 8,000.

McKinley Birthplace Home and Research Center, 40 S. Main St., Niles, OH 44446-5012. Phone: 330/652-5788. Fax: 330/652-5788. E-mail: mckinley@mcklib.org. Website: www.mckinley.lib.oh.us. Hours: 9–5 Wed.–Sat., 1–5 Sun.; closed Mon.–Tues. and major holidays. Admission: free.

Theodore Roosevelt

Theodore Roosevelt Birthplace National Historic Site. Theodore Roosevelt became the 26th president of the United States (1901–1909) after the assassination of William McKinley. He served two terms as a Republican, founded the short-lived Progressive (Bull Moose) Party in 1912, and lost his bid for a third term in 1816. He also became known for his exuberant personality and wide range of interests and achievements as a naturalist, explorer, hunter, author, and soldier.

Roosevelt was born into a wealthy family in a three-story brownstone in New York City in 1858 that now is the Theodore Roosevelt Birthplace National Historic Site. He was the second of four children born to Theodore and Martha Bulloch Roosevelt. His father was a philanthropist, merchant, and partner in the family glass-importing firm, and his mother was a Southern belle from a slave-owning family in Georgia who still maintained Confederate sympathies. The family was strongly Democratic until the mid-1850s, when it joined the new Republican Party.

Roosevelt was a sickly child who suffered from asthma and was mostly homeschooled by tutors and his parents. His lifelong interest in zoology began when he was seven years old and saw a dead seal at a local market. After obtaining the seal's head, he studied natural history and with two cousins formed the makeshift "Roosevelt Museum of Natural History." He learned the rudiments of taxidermy and filled the so-called museum with animals he killed or caught and then studied and prepared for display. When nine years old, he wrote a paper on the natural history of insects. Encouraged by his father, Theodore also began exercising and boxing to overcome his poor physical condition. He also made two trips abroad with the family that had a lasting impact, traveling to Europe in 1869–1870 and Egypt in 1872–1873.

In 1876 Roosevelt enrolled at Harvard, where he did well in science, philosophy, and rhetoric but poorly in Latin and Greek. He had a photographic memory and memorized much of the books he read. He also was an eloquent conversationalist and could engage in several conversations or tasks at the same time. While at Harvard, Roosevelt made a study of the U.S. Navy's role in the War of 1812, which resulted in the highly praised *The Naval War of 1812*. His father's death in 1878 came as a major blow, but he graduated Phi Beta Kappa in 1880 with a Bachelor of Arts degree magna cum laude.

Roosevelt then went to Columbia Law School but dropped out when offered a chance to run for New York state assemblyman. He subsequently was elected to his first political post as the youngest member of the New York Assembly. He also was married in 1880 to Alice Hathaway Lee, who died of kidney failure in 1884. Roosevelt's mother also died on the same day in the same house. He was married a second time to his childhood sweetheart, Edith Kermit Carow, in 1886, and they had five children.

In 1884 Roosevelt moved to the Dakota Territory and operated a cattle ranch. He then served as U.S. Civil Service commissioner from 1889 to 1895, president of the New York City Police Commissioners in 1895–1897, and assistant secretary of the navy in 1897–1898. With the outbreak of the Spanish-American War in 1898, Roosevelt joined the U.S. Volunteer Cavalry Regiment, which became known as the Rough Riders, and led it to victory in the Battle of San Juan Hill in Cuba.

After the 100-day war, Roosevelt was governor of New York in 1898–1900. The Republican Party then nominated him for vice president and William McKinley as president. They were elected, and when McKinley was assassinated in 1901, Roosevelt succeeded him as president. At the age of 42, he became the youngest man to hold the presidency.

Roosevelt was one of the nation's most productive presidents. He moved the country from a tradition of isolation into an international world power and changed the traditional laissez-faire federal policy on the domestic scene. In the process, he expanded the powers and responsibilities of the presidential office. He called his domestic program the "Square Deal" because it sought to give the average citizen a fair share under his policies. He also was called the "Trust Buster" for using antitrust laws to fight corruption in the railroad, oil, and other industries.

One of his most important accomplishments was in conservation. He provided federal protection to almost 230 million acres and designated 150 national forests, the first 51 federal bird reservations, 21 reclamation projects, 18 national monuments, five national parks, and four national game preserves. He also began the Panama Canal and helped Panama gain independence; established the Department of Commerce and Labor; instituted the "Big Stick" policy as part of the Monroe Doctrine to prevent foreign encroachment in Latin America; reduced the national debt by over $90 million; and secured the passage of the Elkins and Hepburn Acts to regulate railroads, the Meat Inspection and Pure Food and Drug Acts to protect consumers, and the Federal Employers' Liability Act for labor.

President Roosevelt also was active in foreign affairs. He was awarded the Nobel Peace Prize for negotiating the end to the Russo-Japanese War. He also successfully mediated international disputes over Venezuela, the Dominican Republic, and Morocco. In addition, Roosevelt was the first world leader to submit a dispute to the Court of Arbitration at the Hague and the initial head of state to call for the Second Hague Peace Conference, which obtained equal status for Latin American countries and outlawed the use of force in the collection of foreign debts.

Roosevelt was a leader in such other fields as history, natural history, and literature. He was the author of 35 books; served as president of the American Historical Association; was one of the original members of the American Institute of Arts and Letters; was one of the first 15 mw=embers elected to the American Academy of Arts and Letters; and was one of the founders of the Boone and Crocket Club, the National Collegiate Athletic Association, and the Long Island Bird Club. He also led two major scientific expeditions for major American museums—one to Africa and another to South America.

After serving nearly eight years as president, Roosevelt declined to run for reelection in 1908. He went on an expedition to Africa and a tour of Europe. When he returned, a bitter rift developed with President William Howard Taft, who succeeded him and was expected to be the Republican candidate again. When he decided to seek the 1912 nomination and failed, Roosevelt started the Progressive Party and ran for president as a third-party candidate.

The Progressive Party also was called the "Bull Moose Party" after Roosevelt told a reporter, "I'm as fit as a bull moose." The decision split the Republican Party and Democrat Woodrow Wilson was elected, with Roosevelt coming in second and Taft third. Roosevelt was shot in the chest while campaigning in Milwaukee in 1912 but felt well enough to give a 90-minute speech before seeking medical attention. He recovered without serious harm. The would-be assassin, John Nepomuk Schrank, was found insane and later died in a state hospital.

After the election, Roosevelt returned to his Sagamore Hill home in Cove Neck, New York (*see* Sagamore Hill National Historic Site listing). He then made the expedition to South America, where a river on which he traveled is now named for him. During the trip, he contracted malaria, which affected his health. During the World War I era, he was a major force for military preparedness. He died in 1919 of a heart attack at the age of 60.

The Theodore Roosevelt Birthplace National Historic Site in New York City celebrates the 26th president's life and career. It is a re-created three-story Gothic revival–style brownstone where Roosevelt was born in 1858. The original building was demolished in 1916, and the present replica was built in 1919–1923 by the Women's Roosevelt Association, which later merged with the Roosevelt Memorial Association in 1953 to form the Theodore Roosevelt Association. The association donated the reconstructed house to the National Park Service in 1963. Annual attendance is 40,000.

The Roosevelt home originally was built in 1848 and purchased by the Roosevelt family in 1854. The Roosevelts lived there until 1872, when the neighborhood became more commercial and the family moved uptown to West 57th Street. The reconstructed house—rebuilt as it was in 1865—was dedicated in 1923 and subsequently refurnished with many of the furnishings from the original house by the president's widow, Edith, and his two sisters.

The house, which is listed on the National Register of Historic Places, has five period rooms, two museum galleries, and a bookstore. Hundreds of items from Roosevelt's life are displayed in the ground-floor gallery. Annual attendance is 40,000.

The collection of publications, photographs, ephemera, and other archival materials relating to Theodore Roosevelt was assembled by the Theodore Roosevelt Association and opened at the Roosevelt Memorial Library at the historic site in 1923. The collection was donated two decades later to Harvard University, where it is a special collection of the Harvard College Library (*see* Theodore Roosevelt Collection). The collection is housed in the Houghton and Widener libraries, with a gallery displaying some of the materials in the adjacent Pusey Library.

Theodore Roosevelt Birthday National Historic Site, 28 E. 20th St., New York, NY 10003-3311. Phone: 212/260-1616. Fax: 212/677-3587. Website: www.nps.gov/thrb. Hours: 9–5 Tues.–Sat.; closed Sun.–Mon., New Year's Day, Independence Day, Thanksgiving, and Christmas. Admission: free.

Sagamore Hill National Historic Site. Sagamore Hill in Cove Neck, New York, was the home of President Theodore Roosevelt and his family from 1885 until his death in 1919. As a youth, he spent many summers on extended vacations with family in the Oyster Bay area on Long Island. He bought the land in 1880, the same year he married Alice Hathaway Lee.

Roosevelt planned to name the home "Leeholm" for his first wife, but when she died in 1834 before the house was completed, he chose the Sagamore Hill name. Roosevelt married Edith Kermit Carow in 1886, and it became their primarily residence for the rest of their lives and where they raised their five children. In 1963 the 80-acre site was made the Sagamore Hill National Historic Site.

The 22-room Queen Anne house was expanded to 23 rooms with the addition of a large room (40 by 30 feet) in 1905. It became the "Summer White House" during the seven summers when Roosevelt was president in 1901–1909, and it was where he died in 1919. Nearly all the furnishings in the house are original. The Theodore Roosevelt Museum, which is devoted to the 26th president's life and achievements, is located in the Old Orchard Building on the grounds in the former residence of his son Theodore Roosevelt Jr. and his family. The site also has a visitor center and bookstore. The Sagamore Hill home of the Roosevelts can be seen only by guided tour. Annual attendance is 65,000.

Sagamore Hill National Historic Site, 20 Sagamore Hill Rd., Oyster Bay, NY 11771-1899. Phone: 516/922-4788. Fax: 516/922-4792. E-mail: sahi_information@nps,gov. Website: www.nps.gov/sahi. Hours: Memorial Day–Labor Day—9:30–5 daily; remainder of year—9:30–5 Wed.–Sun.; closed Mon.–Tues., New Year's Day, Thanksgiving, and Christmas. Admission: adults, $5; children under 16, free.

Theodore Roosevelt Inaugural National Historic Site. The Theodore Roosevelt Inaugural National Historic Site in Buffalo, New York, preserves the house where Theodore Roosevelt took the oath of office as president after the assassination of President William McKinley in 1901. It was decided to conduct the inauguration immediately in Buffalo because of the politically charged circumstances of the president's death.

The historic building is the lone surviving structure of the Buffalo Barracks compound, a ca. 1838 military post constructed to ensure border security during tensions between the United States and Anglo-Canada. The building originally was built as the officers' quarters in 1840. After the post was disbanded in 1845, the structure became a private residence. Subsequent owners continued to modify the building.

President McKinley was attending the Pan-American Exposition in Buffalo when he was shot by an anarchist. As his condition worsened, Vice President Theodore Roosevelt rushed to Buffalo, only to arrive after McKinley had died. Because of the tragic circumstances, it was decided to hold the inauguration as soon as possible, and the former army officers' quarters, which became the renovated home of Ansley and Mary Grace Wilcox, was selected as the most appropriate site. A federal judge administered the oath of office in the home's library with approximately 50 dignitaries attending. The Wilcoxes lived in the house until their deaths in the 1930s, when the property became a restaurant and then a historic site in 1966 and opened to the public in 1971.

The historic house now has a museum devoted to the 1901 Pan-American Exposition, the Wilcox house, McKinley's death, Roosevelt's life, and the inauguration. Among the exhibits is a re-creation of the Oval Office as it appeared during Roosevelt's presidency. The site also offers changing exhibitions and such special events as an inauguration reenactment, Victorian tea and Christmas programs, and family and children's events. Visits are by guided tour only. Annual attendance is 17,600.

Theodore Roosevelt Inaugural National Historic Site, 641 Delaware Ave., Buffalo, NY 14202-1079. Phone: 716/884-0095. Fax: 716/884-0330. E-mail: thri_administration@nps.gov. Website: www.nps.gov/thri. Hours: 9:30–4:30 Mon.–Fri.; 9:30–4:30 Sat.–Sun.; closed major holidays. Admission: adults, $10; seniors and students, $7; children 6–18, $5; children under 6, free; families, $25.

Theodore Roosevelt Collection. Manuscripts, printed works, pictures, ephemera, and archival resources related to the personal and professional life of Theodore Roosevelt are located in a special collection at the Harvard College Library in Cambridge, Massachusetts. The Theodore Roosevelt Collection was started by the Roosevelt Memorial Association in 1923 and given to Harvard, his alma mater, in 1943. It now is a major resource for the study of the life and times of the 26th president of the United States.

The collection is located in the Hough and Widener Libraries, with some materials displayed in the adjacent Pusey Library. The collection includes 27,000 personal papers; 14,000 printed volumes; 11,000 photographs and artworks; such ephemera as campaign literature, broadsides, and newspaper clippings; and such archival resources as speeches, interviews, research notes, and correspondence. Among the 35 books Roosevelt wrote were *The Naval War of 1812* (1882), *Ranch Life and the Hunting Trail* (1888), *Essays on Practical Politics* (1888), *The Winning of the West* (1889–1896), *The Rough Riders* (1899), *Hunting the Grizzly Bear* (1905), and *America and the World War* (1915).

Theodore Roosevelt Collection, Houghton Library, Harvard University, Cambridge, MA 02138. Phone: 617/384-7938. Fax: 617/495-1376. E-mail: wfdaiey@fas.harvard.edu. Website: www.lib.harvard.edu/houghton/collection/roosevelt.html. Hours: 9–7 Mon.–Thurs., 9–5 Fri.–Sat.; closed Sun. and major holidays. Admission: free.

Mount Rushmore National Memorial. *See* Mount Rushmore National Memorial under George Washington in Presidents section.

William Howard Taft

William Howard Taft National Historic Site. William Howard Taft was the 27th president of the United States (1909–1913) and the only American president who served as both the nation's president and the chief justice of the U.S. Supreme Court. He was handpicked by President Theodore Roosevelt as his successor but opposed for reelected by Roosevelt, who left the Republican Party and ran against Taft in the 1912 election as the candidate of the short-lived Progressive Party (also known as the Bull Moose Party)—and they both lost to Woodrow Wilson of the Democratic Party.

Taft served as secretary of war under President Roosevelt in 1904–1908, and Roosevelt felt Taft was "progressive" and supported him for the presidential nomination. However, after being elected in 1908, he made a number of pro–big business appointments, raised tariffs, named Roosevelt in an antitrust suit, and took other actions that angered Roosevelt and progressives. They also differed over the powers of the president. Roosevelt felt that the president had a duty to do anything demanded by the needs of the nation unless forbidden by the Constitution or federal law, while Taft believed that the president can exercise no power that cannot be traced fairly to a grant of power in the Constitution or an act of Congress.

As a result of these philosophical and political differences, a rift developed between the two men, and Roosevelt changed his mind about running again for president. When he lost the Republication nomination to Taft, Roosevelt ran as the Progressive Party nominee in 1912. Roosevelt received more votes than Taft in the election, but Woodrow Wilson was elected president. Taft, a lawyer, often said he was more interested in becoming chief justice of the Supreme Court than being president. In 1921, it happened—he was appointed chief justice by President Warren G. Harding and served until shortly before his death in 1930.

Taft now is honored at the William Howard Taft National Historic Site in the house in which he was born in 1857 and spent his boyhood in upper-class Mount Auburn, Ohio (now part of Cincinnati). His parents were Alphonso and Louisa Torrey Taft. William was the seventh of nine children—five (including three who died earlier) by Fanny Phelps Taft (Alphonso's first wife who died) and four by Louisa (the second wife and William's mother). His father was a lawyer who became a prominent Republican and served as secretary of war and attorney general under President Ulysses S. Grant. William attended Woodward High School and later laid the cornerstone for the new high school, which became the site of the School for Creative and Performing Arts. Like other family members, he attended Yale College, where he was a member of the literary and debating society, intramural heavyweight wrestling champion, and ranked second in his graduating class in 1878. He was called "Big Bill" because of his size. As an adult, he eventually weighed more than 300 pounds—which probably makes him the largest U.S. president.

After college, Taft went to Cincinnati Law School and graduated with a law degree in 1880. While in law school, he worked on the *Cincinnati Commercial* newspaper. After admission to the bar, Taft was appointed collector of internal revenue in the area. In 1886 he married Helen Herron, and the following year he was appointed a judge in the Ohio Supreme Court. This was followed in 1890 by being named the youngest-ever solicitor general at the age of 32. In 1891 he was appointed to the newly created United States Court of Appeals for the Sixth Circuit.

From 1896 to 1900, Taft also served as dean and professor of constitutional law at the University of Cincinnati in addition to his judgeship.

In 1900 President William McKinley named Taft chairman of a commission to organize a civilian government in the Philippines, which the United States received from Spain as part of the 1898 Spanish-American War treaty. He served as the first civilian governor general of the Philippines in 1901–1903, and then President Theodore Roosevelt appointed him secretary of war in 1904. Roosevelt had such confidence in Taft that he had him continue his involvement in the Philippines, supervise the beginning of construction on the Panama Canal, and oversee other developments when Roosevelt was away. When Roosevelt decided not to run for reelection in 1908, he thought Taft was a genuine "progressive" and helped nominate him for the presidency and defeat Democrat William Jennings Bryan.

During his presidency, Taft alienated many liberal Republicans, who later formed the Progressive Party. This included defending the Payne-Aldrich Act, which continued high tariff rates. On the other hand, little attention was given to such other actions as initiating 80 antitrust suits, establishment of a postal savings system, directing the Interstate Commerce Commission to set railroad rates, and congressional proposals submitted to states for a federal income tax and direct election of senators. When Taft's presidency disappointed Roosevelt, the former president changed his position about running again. After losing the Republican nomination, Roosevelt ran unsuccessfully as the Progressive Party candidate.

After his presidency, Taft served as professor of law at Yale University, engaged in arbitration, and sought to further world peace through the League to Enforce Peace, which he founded. In 1921 President Warren G. Harding made him what he always wanted to be—chief justice of the U.S. Supreme Court. He served until five weeks before his death in 1930 at the age 72. In addition to being the only president to be chief justice of the court, he was the only chief justice to serve with associate justices he had appointed to the court. He was buried in a special grave site in Arlington National Cemetery with his wife, Helen Harron Taft, who died in 1943 at the age of 83. Taft was the first of only two presidents to be buried in the cemetery, and Mrs. Taft is the only first lady buried in the cemetery.

President Taft was born and lived most of his first 25 years in what is now the William Howard Taft National Historic Site in Cincinnati. The historic house museum, established in 1969, is a two-story Greek revival house. It was built in the 1840s and purchased by Taft's father in 1851. He lived there until he went to Yale University in 1874. A fire damaged the second floor and roof in 1878, and William's parents moved to California for health reasons in 1889. After William's father died, his mother sold the house in 1899. In the 1950s, the William Howard Taft Memorial Association acquired the house and transferred it to the National Park Service in 1969.

The historic site, which is a National Historic Landmark and is listed on the National Register of Historic Places, has two main buildings. The house now is restored to the way it looked when William lived there, including family portraits and book. The first floor has William's birthplace and four rooms with period furniture, and the second floor contains exhibits on his life and accomplishments. The other building is a visitor center with a short biographical film on Taft, an audio-animatronic exhibit of Charles Phelps Taft II fishing and telling stories about his father and other members of the family, a gift shop, and offices. Annual attendance is 17,000.

William Howard Taft National Historic Site, 2038 Auburn Ave., Cincinnati, OH 45219-3025. Phone: 513/684-1262. Fax: 513/684-3627. Website: www.nps.gov/wiho. Hours: 8–4 daily; closed New Year's Day, Thanksgiving, and Christmas. Admission: free.

Woodrow Wilson

Woodrow Wilson Presidential Library and Museum. Woodrow Wilson, the 28th president of the United States (1913–1921), is best remembered as the American president during World War I and for his role in founding the League of Nations (for which he received the Nobel Peace Prize in 1919). He was much more, including being a leader in the progressive movement, president of Princeton University, governor of New Jersey, and the only president to have a Ph.D. He persuaded Congress to pass such major progressive reforms as the Federal Reserve Act, the Federal Trade Commission Act, the Clayton Antitrust Act, the Federal Farm Loan Act, the Adamson Act imposing an eight-hour workday for railroads, and an income tax. He also was an advocate for women's suffrage and sought to restrict child labor.

Wilson was born in Staunton, Virginia, in 1856, the third of four children of Dr. Joseph Ruggles Wilson and Jessie Janet Woodrow. His birthplace now is part of the Woodrow Wilson Presidential Library and Museum. His father was one of the founders of the Southern Presbyterian Church, which split from the northern Presbyterians in 1861, and his mother was the daughter of a Presbyterian minister. Woodrow spent the majority of his childhood up to age 14 in Augusta, Georgia, where his father taught at a seminary and served as a minister. The Boyhood Home of President Woodrow Wilson is now located in Augusta (*see* separate listing).

Wilson had a difficult time learning to read as a child. He was over 10 years of age before he could read, which may have been the result of dyslexia. As a teenager, he taught himself shorthand to compensate, and he studied at home with his father and took classes in a small school in Augusta. In 1873–1874 he attended Davidson College, until medical ailments kept him from returning. When his father took a teaching position at Princeton University, Woodrow transferred to Princeton and graduated in 1879. He also took an interest in politics, read widely in political philosophy and history, and organized a Liberal Debating Society. In 1879 Wilson attended the University of Virginia Law School and became president of the Jefferson Literary and Debating Society, but illness again forced him to drop out. He then continued his studies at home in Wilmington, North Carolina.

In 1882 he passed the bar and began his law practice in Atlanta, but he decided in 1883 to enroll at Johns Hopkins University and study for a doctorate in history and political science, He received his Doctor of Philosophy degree three years later. In 1885 he married Ellen Louise Axson, the daughter of a Savannah, Georgia, minister. They had three daughters. When she died in 1914, Wilson married Edith Galt, who later was instrumental in concealing the seriousness of his stroke from his cabinet, Congress, and the public in 1919–1921.

After receiving his doctorate, Wilson had faculty appointments at Bryn Mawr College, Wesleyan University, and Princeton University, where he became professor of jurisprudence and political economy in 1890. He developed a reputation as a lecturer, scholar, and reformer and was made president of Princeton University in 1902. He headed the university until 1910, when he was elected governor of New Jersey as a Democrat and served from 1911 to 1913.

Wilson was nominated as the Democratic Party nominee for president of the United States in 1912. He was elected when William Howard Taft and Theodore Roosevelt split the Republican vote. He began instituting many of the changes he descried in his book *The New Freedom*. They included such actions as revising the banking system, changing the tariff, acting against unfair business practices, and controlling monopolies and fraudulent advertising. Many of the reforms were as progressive as those of Roosevelt's Progressive Party.

Wilson was determined to maintain neutrality when World War I broke out in Europe. He offered to mediate a settlement, but both sides refused. When Germany began its unrestricted submarine warfare and started sinking American ships, Wilson asked Congress to declare war in 1917, and he mobilized the nation to help defeat the Germans. Wilson also was involved in negotiating the peace treaty and developing the conception of the League of Nations. However, he failed to convince the Senate of American acceptance of the league, which eventually led to its demise.

While in Pueblo, Colorado, in 1919 trying to raise public support for ratification of the league covenant, Wilson collapsed and later suffered a cerebral hemorrhage and then a stroke that paralyzed his left side and blinded his left eye. He was bedridden for weeks and never fully recovered. But he continued to serve as president until his term ended in 1921. The debilitating effects of the stroke were kept from the cabinet, Congress, and the public as his wife, Edith, served as his steward and selected issues for his attention and action. When his term ended, President and Mrs. Wilson moved to a Georgian revival–style house in Washington, where he died in 1924 at the age of 67. Mrs. Wilson continued to live in the house until her death in 1961 and left it to the National Trust for Historic Preservation to be made into a museum honoring her husband (*see* Woodrow Wilson House listing).

The Woodrow Wilson Presidential Library and Museum was founded in 1938 at the site where Wilson was born in Staunton, Virginia, in 1856. It has been designated a National Historic Landmark and is listed on the National Register of Historic Places. The birthplace structure is a restored 1846 Greek revival house that was a Presbyterian manse, the home of the Rev. Wilson and his family from 1855 to 1858. It contains the Wilsons' household belongings and period furniture.

The museum and library are in an adjacent renovated château-style mansion. The museum has seven galleries on the first floor with exhibits of historical photographs, documents, and objects on Wilson's life and achievements. One of the highlights is his 1919 Pierce Arrow limousine. The second floor contains a research library and archives, educational program space, and meeting rooms, while the third floor provides storage for the collections and archives. Only the first floor is open to the public. It has guided interpretation. A 1930s boxwood garden, a restoration project of the Garden Club of Virginia, also is located at the site. Admission includes a guided tour of the manse and entrance to the museum. Annual attendance is 21,500.

Woodrow Wilson Presidential Library and Museum, 18 N. Coalter St., Staunton, VA 24401-4332 (postal address: PO Box 24, Staunton, VA 24402-0024). Phone: 540/885-0897. Fax: 540/886-9874. E-mail: info@woodrowwilson.org. Website: www.woodrowwilson.org. Hours: 10–5 Mon.–Sat., 12–5 Sun.; closed New Year's Day, Easter, Thanksgiving, and Christmas Eve and Day. Admission: adults, $14; seniors and military, $12; students over 12, $7; children 6–12, $5; children under 6, free.

Boyhood Home of President Woodrow Wilson. As a child, President Woodrow Wilson lived in several Presbyterian manses as his minister father moved from one congregation to another. The place where he spent the most time—his formative years from 1860 to 1870—was in Augusta, Georgia. The manse now is a historic house museum—the Boyhood Home of President Woodrow Wilson—operated by Historic Atlanta Inc.

The historic house, purchased in 1991 and opened in 2001, has been designated a National Historic Landmark and is listed in the National Register of Historic Places. It contains biographical materials, original and period furniture, and 1860 decorative arts. The site also has a 200-volume Wilson library, a historic carriage house, and a detached kitchen and service building. Annual attendance is 3,500.

Boyhood Home of President Woodrow Wilson, 419 7th St., Augusta, GA 30901-2317 (postal address: PO Box 37, Augusta, GA 30903-0037). Phone: 706/722-9828. Fax: 706/724-3083. E-mail: erick@historicaugusta.org. Website: www.wilsonboyhoodhome.org. Hours: 10–4 Tues.–Sat.; closed Sun.–Mon., New Year's Day, Thanksgiving, and Christmas. Admission: adults, $5; seniors, $4; students, $3; children under 5, free.

Woodrow Wilson Family Home. The only house that the parents of Woodrow Wilson ever built and owned was in Columbia, South Carolina. The Wilson family lived in the Victorian house until 1875, when Dr. Joseph Ruggles Wilson, who taught at the Presbyterian Theological Seminary and was a minister at the First Presbyterian Church, left Columbia to teach at Princeton University. Woodrow was 16 to 19 years of age during the stay. His parents later chose Columbia's First Presbyterian Church yard for burial.

The house, built in the mode of a Tuscan villa, contains Wilson family memorabilia, the bed in which the future president was born, and exhibits on the life and accomplishments of President Wilson. The garden features magnolias planted by Woodrow's mother over 100 years ago. The site, which recently was rehabilitated, is managed by the Historic Columbia Foundation.

Woodrow Wilson Boyhood Home, 1705 Hampton St., Columbia, SC 29201. Phone: 803/252-7742. Website: www.columbiasouthcarolina.com/historic-homes.html. Hours: normally 10:15–3:15 Tues.–Sat., 1:15–4:15 Sun.; closed Mon. and major holidays; but site currently is closed for renovation. Admission: adults, $6; seniors and military, $5; children 6–17, $3; children under 6, free.

Woodrow Wilson House. When Woodrow Wilson's term as president ended in 1921, he was so stricken in body and spirit that he did not attend the inauguration of his successor, Warren G. Harding. Instead, he and his wife, Edith, went directly to the Washington home they purchased and remodeled, and he spent the last three years of his life there. He died in the house in 1924 at the age of 67, and Mrs. Wilson continued to live in the home until her death in 1961. The site was founded as a historic house museum in 1963.

The 1915 Georgian revival–style house remains as it was when the Wilsons lived there. Mrs. Wilson left the house to the National Trust for Historic Preservation, to be made into a museum honoring her husband. The three-story home has been restored to reflect the era when the president and his wife lived there in the early 1920s.

The historic site contains many aspects of the period, such as silent films, flapper dresses, and zinc sinks. Among the items on display are the original furniture, White House objects, family belongings, memorabilia, historical photographs, and gifts from heads of state around the world. The house also presents changing exhibitions and has a period garden. Most tours are preceded by a video presentation. Annual attendance is nearly 11,700.

Woodrow Wilson House, 2340 S St., N.W., Washington, DC 20008-4016. Phone: 202/387-4062. Fax: 202//483-1466. E-mail: faucella@woodrowwilsonhouse.org. Website: www.woodrowwilsonhouse.org. Hours: 10–4 Tues.–Sun.; closed Mon. and major holidays. Admission: adults, $10; seniors, $8; students, $5; children under 12, free.

Warren G. Harding

Harding Home and Museum. Warren G. Harding was an influential newspaper publisher and the first incumbent senator to be elected president of the United States. He served as the 29th president in 1921–23. He never finished his term in office, dying in 1923 of congestive heart failure after he collapsed in California on a return trip from Alaska. He made some important advances, but his administration was plagued by corruption and scandals, including the notorious Teapot Dome scandal in which one of his cabinet members and several appointees were convicted of bribery or defrauding the federal government.

Harding was an affable conservative newspaperman-turned-politician who ran a "make no enemies" campaign to be chosen the Republican compromise presidential nominee in 1920. He promised to return the nation to normalcy after World War I by encouraging industrialization and a strong economy without foreign influence. And he won the election by the largest presidential landslide in the nation's history since popular vote totals were first recorded in 1824. Harding received more than 60 percent of the vote to 34 percent for the Democratic candidate, James M. Cox. The unemployment rate dropped by half, but the administration had other problems, including helping friends and political contributors with financially rewarding positions that sometimes involved corruption and scandals.

Harding was born in 1865 in Corsica (now Blooming Grove), Ohio. He was the eldest of eight children of Dr. George Tryon Harding Sr. and Phoebe Elizabeth Dickerson Harding. His father owned a farm and also taught at a rural school and started a doctor's practice after obtaining a medical degree, while his mother was a midwife who later obtained her medical license. The Harding family eventually moved to Caledonia, Ohio, where his father acquired the *Argus*, a local weekly newspaper and Warren learned the basics of newspapers.

When he enrolled at Ohio Central College, he also worked on the *Union Register* in Mount Gilead and became an accomplished cornet player. After graduating in 1884, Harding raised $300 and in partnership with others bought the failing *Marion Daily Star*. He became complete owner of the *Star* by 1886, gave the Republican Party its editorial support, and made the *Marian Daily Star* one of the most popular newspapers in the county. Harding then ran for his first political office, the race for county auditor. It was followed in 1899 by being elected Ohio state senator for the 13th District. In his second term, he was chosen Republican floor leader.

In 1901 Harding married Florence Kling De Wolfe, a divorcee and daughter of Amos Hall Kling, one of Marion's wealthiest real estate speculators and a political foe. She turned the *Marian Daily Star* into a profitable business in her management of the circulation and was invaluable as the first lady when Harding was president. In 1893 the *Star* also became the official paper for Marion's government notices. Amos Kling then remarried and made up with his daughter and her husband, and they went on a European cruise together.

When Harding returned, he reorganized the newspaper into Harding Publishing Co. and issued stock in the company, taking two-thirds and allowing the employees to purchase the remainder, which was the first profit-sharing arrangement of its kind in Ohio. Harding continued to be involved in the *Star* until the last year of his presidency, when he sold the paper for $550,000 because he did not plan to resume his newspaper career.

In 1903 Harding ran for governor of Ohio but had to settle for lieutenant governor in an intraparty agreement. He was elected and became the Republican nominee for governor of Ohio in 1909. The party was divided between progressives and conservatives, and he lost to the united Democrats. But in 1914 he became the first senator from Ohio to be elected to the U.S. Senate—and later the nation's first sitting senator to be elected president.

Harding served as the chairman and keynote speaker of the 1916 Republican convention and in 1920 was chosen as the party's nominee for president. He staged a front-porch campaign to defeat James M. Cox, promising a "return to normalcy" from the "progressive ideology" of Woodrow Wilson and the laissez-faire policies of the William McKinley era.

President Harding established the Bureau of the Budget, General Accounting Office, and Veterans Bureau; spurned the League of Nations and signed separate peace treaties with Germany and Austria; passed legislation to help agriculture; increased tariffs; reduced taxes; created a national system of nearly 3,000 child and health centers; dealt with striking workers in the mining and railroad industries; and organized an international conference to reduce arms.

The Harding administration also became known for corruption and scandals. Harding had what was called the "Ohio Gang," a group of political allies and campaign contributors who were appointed to financially powerful posts—and some used their new powers for personal gain. The biggest scandal was the 1922–1923 Teapot Dome bribery scandal in which Secretary of the Interior Albert B. Fall leased three navy petroleum reserves—including the Teapot Dome site in Wyoming—to private oil companies at low rates without competitive bidding. Fall later was convicted of accepting bribes from the oil companies.

Harding's Victorian home in Marion, Ohio, now is a historic house museum, called the Harding Home and Museum. Harding and his future wife, Florence Kling DeWolfe, designed the Queen Anne–style home in 1890, a year before they were married. They lived there for 30 years before his presidency. The restored house, which contains the original furniture and furnishings, has an expansive porch from which Harding ran his 1920 front-porch presidential campaign.

Mrs. Harding bequeath the house to the Harding Memorial Association. The museum, founded in 1925, now is operated by the Ohio Historical Society. The site also has a one-story clapboard house that served as the Harding campaign headquarters. It now contains exhibits about the lives of President and Mrs. Harding, with memorabilia from Harding's boyhood to presidency. Annual attendance is 6,000.

Harding Home and Museum, 380 Mt. Vernon Ave., Marion, OH 43302-4120. Phones: 740/387-9630 and 800/600-6894. Fax: 740/387-9630 (call first). E-mail: shall@hardinghome.org. Website: www.ohiohistory.org. Hours: Memorial Day weekend–Labor Day—12–5 Wed.–Sun., closed Mon.–Tues.; Sept.–Oct.—12–5 Sat.–Sun., Mon.–Fri. by appointment; Apr.–May and Nov.–Mar.—by appointment; closed Mon. holidays, New Year's Day, Labor Day, Thanksgiving, and Christmas. Admission: adults, $6; children 6–12, $3; children under 6, free.

Calvin Coolidge

Calvin Coolidge State Historic Site. Vice President Calvin Coolidge became the 30th president of the United States (1923–1929) upon the sudden death of President Warren G. Harding in 1923. He was a Vermont lawyer who worked his way up the Republican political ladder in Massachusetts to the vice presidency and assumption of the presidency. He took the oath of office from his father—a local notary public—in the family homestead after the untimely death of Harding. As president, Coolidge helped restore public confidence in the White House after the scandals of the previous administration and developed a reputation as a small-government conservative and a man who said very little.

Coolidge was born John Calvin Coolidge Jr. in 1872 in Plymouth Notch, Vermont—where the Calvin Coolidge State Historic Site and President Calvin Coolidge Museum and Education Center (*see* separate listing) are now located. He was the eldest of two children of John Calvin Coolidge Sr. and Victoria Josephine Moor. His father was a prosperous farmer, storekeeper, and public official who served at various times as justice of the peace, tax collector, and state legislator. Calvin attended Black River Academy and then Amherst College. After graduating from Amherst, he apprenticed and read law with a local law firm. He was admitted to the bar in 1897 and became a country lawyer, opening a law practice in Northampton in 1898. In 1905 Coolidge met and married Grace Ann Goodhue, a teacher at a school for the deaf. They were opposites in personality. He was quiet and serious, while she was talkative and fun loving. But they had a happy marriage and two sons.

Coolidge became involved in Republican politics early in his law career, campaigning for presidential candidate William McKinley in 1896 and being selected as a member of the Republican city committee the next year. He was elected a city councilman in Northampton in 1898 and city solicitor in 1900, followed by appointment as clerk of the county courts. In 1904 Coolidge met with his only election defeat while running for school board.

In 1906 Coolidge was elected to the Massachusetts House of Representatives and then as mayor of Northampton in 1909. He became a state senator in 1911 and was chosen president of the senate in 1914. Coolidge next was elected lieutenant governor in 1915 and governor in 1918. While governor, he gained national attention by taking action to stop a police strike in Boston. It was suggested that he run for president in 1920, but he was nominated and won election as vice president. When President Harding died suddenly in 1923, Coolidge was vacationing in Vermont. After an urgent message from Washington, he took the oath of office from his father, a local public official and notary, in his boyhood home in Plymouth Notch.

Coolidge believed in preserving the old moral and economic perspectives in a period of relative prosperity—and doing and saying little. He would not use federal economic power to restrict growth or to help the depressed state of agriculture or some other industries. He also favored isolation in foreign policy and worked to maintain the status quo. He was quite popular during the early period of prosperity, but support began to change as the economy suffered later. He decided not to run for a second full-term presidency in the 1928 election and retired to his home in Northampton, Massachusetts, where he died of a heart attack in 1933 at the age of 60.

Coolidge's birthplace cabin and boyhood home—part of what is known as the Coolidge Homestead—are located in the Calvin Coolidge State Historic Site, as is the new President Calvin Coolidge Museum and Education Center. The historic site was established in 1947 and is operated by Vermont's Division for Historic Preservation. The Coolidge family house, which contains furnishings from the night Coolidge was sworn in as president by his father, was his home from the age of four in 1876 to when he went to the Black River Academy in 1887.

The state historic site includes 26 historic structures scattered over 580 acres in Plymouth Notch, including such other early buildings as historic houses, a farm shop, a horse barn, a general store, a cheese factory, a church, and a one-room schoolhouse. The buildings have been returned to the way they were when Coolidge was president. A video and photo exhibit of his life are presented in the barn, and the rooms in Coolidge Hall that he used as a Summer White House in 1924 have been restored and a contemporary video added. The new museum serves as the historic site's visitor center. Annual attendance is 40,000.

Calvin Coolidge State Historic Site, 1780 Rte. 100A, Plymouth Notch, VT 05056 (postal address: PO Box 247, Plymouth Notch, VT 05056-0247). Phone: 802/672-3773. Fax: 802/828-3206. E-mail: william.jenney@state.vt.us. Website: www.historicvermont.org/coolidge. Hours: mid-May–mid-Oct.—9:30–5:30 daily; closed mid-Oct.–mid-May. Admission: adults, $7.50; children 6–14, $2; children under 6, free; families, $20.

President Calvin Coolidge Museum and Education Center. The newest museum honoring the 30th president of the United States is the President Calvin Coolidge Museum and Education Center at the Calvin Coolidge State Historic Site in Plymouth Notch, Vermont. The museum, which was opened by the state in 2010, is devoted to the life and accomplishments of the Vermont native, who was born and lived his early years in what is called the Coolidge Homestead.

The museum features a permanent exhibit, titled "Calvin Coolidge: His Life and Legacy," and presents changing exhibitions and programs relating to Vermont's native son who served as president in 1923–1929. The building also serves as the visitor center for the state historic site, which includes 26 historic structures, including Coolidge's birthplace and boyhood home. In addition, the building has a large special-function room, a classroom, and the offices and library of the Calvin Coolidge Memorial Foundation, which assisted in raising funds for the new facility.

President Calvin Coolidge Museum and Education Center, 1780 Rte. 100A, Plymouth Notch, VT 05056 (postal address: PO Box 247, Plymouth Notch, VT 05056-0247). Phone: 802/672-3773. Fax: 802/828-3206. E-mail: william. jenney@state.vt.us. Website: www.historicvermont.org/Coolidge. Hours: mid-May–mid-Oct.—9:30–5:30 daily; closed mid-Oct.–mid-May. Admission: included in admission to historic site (adults, $7.50; children 6–14, $2; children under 6, free; families, $20).

Calvin Coolidge Presidential Library and Museum. The Calvin Coolidge Presidential Library and Museum began as a special collections room at Forbes Library in Northampton, Massachusetts, in 1920. That is when Coolidge began donating documents and memorabilia to the library (and continued to do so the remainder of his life). The collection was expanded in 1956 when Massachusetts established the Calvin Coolidge Memorial Room as a separate entity within the library at the behest of his wife, Grace Goodhue Coolidge. In 2000 the collection was given its present name.

The materials document the life of the 30th president of the United States, who lived and worked in Northampton. They include manuscripts, letters, presidential papers, photographs, artifacts, recordings, videos, and other materials and exhibits relating to his birth and formative years in Vermont, student days at Amherst College, years as a lawyer in Northampton, political career, presidential service, and retirement in Northampton. The library/museum also includes materials about the life of his wife, as well as a 4,000-volume library of books associated with Calvin Coolidge, guided tours, and lectures.

Calvin Coolidge Presidential Library and Museum, Forbes Library, 20 West St., Northampton, MA 01060-3713. Phones: 413/587-1014, 413/587-1012, and 413/587-1011. Fax: 413/587-1015. E-mail: ccolidge@forbeslibrary.org. Website: www.forbeslibrary.org. Hours: 3–9 Mon. and Wed., 1–5 Tues. and Thurs., Sat. by appointment; closed Fri., Sun., and major holidays. Admission: free.

Herbert Hoover

Herbert Hoover Presidential Library-Museum. Herbert Clark Hoover became the 31st president of the United States (1929–1933) just before the Wall Street Crash of 1929 and the Great Depression that followed in the 1930s—and lost his reelection bid largely because he did not produce an economic recovery. He was a successful mining engineer and humanitarian who served as secretary of commerce under Presidents Warren G. Harding and Calvin Coolidge, and he made the Commerce Department into an effective cabinet post. He was elected president in a landslide, but he failed to recognize the all-encompassing nature of the Great Depression and used constitutional restraint as a reason not to act more forcefully in assisting millions who were unemployed and suffering.

Hoover tried to combat the Great Depression with public works like the Hoover Dam, volunteer efforts, higher tariffs, and increases in the corporate and higher tax brackets, but nothing worked economically—although some ideas were adapted by President Franklin D. Roosevelt and were more productive. After his defeat at the polls, Hoover opposed Roosevelt's New Deal policies but continued his humanitarian work and even was called back later to help make the federal bureaucracy more efficient through the Hoover Commission.

Hoover was the first American president from west of the Mississippi River. He was born in West Branch, Iowa, in 1874 to Jessie and Hulda Minthorn Hoover, both of whom were Quakers. His parents died by 1884, leaving Herbert an orphan at the age of nine. Lawrie Tatum, a fellow Quaker, was appointed Hoover's guardian. Hoover stayed briefly with his grandmother and then an uncle in Iowa before going to Oregon to live with another uncle, Dr. John Minthorn, a frontier physician and businessman whose son had died.

Hoover attended Friends Pacific Academy and worked as an assistant in his uncle's real estate office while going to night school and learning bookkeeping, typing, and math. He then became one of the first students enrolled at new Stanford University in 1891. Hoover graduated with a degree in geology in 1895 and was hired by Bewick, Moreing & Co. as a geologist and mining engineer to work in western Australian minefields. He became mine manager at the age of 23 and led a major program of expansion.

In 1899 Hoover married Lou Henry, his Stanford sweetheart, and they had two sons, Hoover and his family then went to China, where he was lead engineer on a mining project. The Hoovers were trapped in Tianjin with other foreigners for almost a month before being rescued by U.S. marines during the Boxer Rebellion in 1900. Hoover was made a Bewick, Moreing & Co. partner in 1901 and given responsibility for various Australian operations, where he devised a practical and profitable way to use the new froth flotation process to treat tailings and recover the zinc.

Hoover then cofounded the Zinc Corporation and later became an independent mining consultant in 1908, traveling throughout the world until the outbreak of World War I in 1914. He gave lectures on mining at Columbia and Stanford Universities, which were published in 1909 as *Principles of Mining*, a standard textbook in the field. He and his wife also published an English translation of the 1556 Latin mining classic *De re metallica* by Renaissance author Georgius Agricola in 1912.

When the war began, Hoover helped organize the return of 120,000 Americans from Europe, directing 500 volunteers in the distribution of food, clothing, steamship tickets, and funds. This was followed by a food crisis in Belgium after it was invaded by Germany. Hoover organized a relief effort to feed the entire nation for the duration of the war and administered the distribution of over 2 million tons of food to 9 million war victims. When the United States entered the war in 1917, President Woodrow Wilson appointed Hoover head of the U.S. Food Administration, which helped reduce public consumption of foodstuffs needed overseas, thereby avoiding food rationing.

After the war, Hoover headed the American Relief Administration and organized food shipments for millions of starving people in Europe. He was hailed by the *New York Times* as one of the "10 most important living Americans" for his efforts. In 1919 Hoover established the Hoover War Collection at Stanford University, which consisted of all the files of his relief efforts, as well as documents and other materials related to the war and postwar revolutions collected by scholars he sent to Europe. The collection later became the Hoover War Library and now is known as the Hoover Institution.

In 1920 Hoover placed his name on the ballot for president in the California state primary. After he lost in his home state, he endorsed Warren G. Harding, who appointed him secretary of commerce. Although the Commerce Department was considered a minor cabinet post at the time, Hoover sought to make it the center of the nation's growth and stability. He set out to coordinate economic activities throughout the government and sought to change the adversarial relationship with business into a partnership. Many of his efforts were aimed at eliminating waste and increasing efficiency in business and industry. He also promoted such areas as product standardization, international trade, and single-family home ownership.

In 1928, when Calvin Coolidge decided not to run for reelection, Hoover became the Republican nominee for president. He defeated Alfred E. Smith, the Democratic candidate, by a large majority. During the first few months, Hoover asked Congress to fund such programs as more national park land, prison reform, better education on American Indian reservations, and an agricultural marketing act that would help farms establish cooperatives, control surpluses, and stabilize the food supply. But the stock market crashed after eight months in office, due largely to excessive stock market speculation. Hoover was slow to react and then ordered federal agencies to speed up construction projects and increase expenditures for public works. He also appealed to the private sector and volunteers to come to the aid of others in the depression.

By 1933, 25 percent of the nation's workers were without jobs and one-quarter of the banks had failed. Some 17,000 World War I veterans were so desperate that they staged a "Bonus March" in Washington in 1932 for payment of bonuses granted by Congress in 1924. Instead, they were turned away and their camp was destroyed by army troops led by General Douglas MacArthur. Hoover, who would not exceed a balanced budget, was criticized for the way the protest was handled and for refusing to authorize large-scale relief programs for the needy and hungry in what was the most severe economic crisis in the nation's history. As a result, Hoover was defeated for reelection and replaced by President Franklin D. Roosevelt and his New Deal programs.

Hoover retired to his home in Palo Alto, California, but continued to be quite active for more than 31 years. He spent much time at the Hoover Institution and served as coordinator of the Food Supply for World Famine (1946–1947) and chairman of the Commission on Organization on Government Operations (1947–1949) and the Commission on Government Operations (1953–1955), which sought ways to streamline government. He died in 1964 at the age of 90 following massive internal bleeding.

The Herbert Hoover National Historic Site in West Branch, Iowa, now commemorates Hoover's life, and the adjoining Herbert Hoover Presidential Library and Museum contains volumes and exhibits about the former president (*see* separate listing). The 187-acre national historic site was established in 1965 in his hometown. It contains the 1871 small cottage where Hoover was born in 1874, a blacksmith shop similar to the one owned by his father, the 1853 first West Branch schoolhouse, the 1856 Quaker meetinghouse where the Hoover family worshipped, the graves of Herbert Hoover and his wife, and an 81-acre tallgrass prairie. The site has guided tours, historic library materials, exhibits, lectures, concerts, education programs, and an annual "Hooverfest" festival every August. The historic site's annual attendance is 125,000.

Herbert Hoover National Historic Site, 110 Parkside Dr., West Branch, IA 52358 (postal address: PO Box 607, West Branch, IA 52358-0607). Phone: 319/643-2541. Fax: 319/643-7863. Website: www.nps.gov/heho. Hours: 9–5 daily; closed New Year's Day, Thanksgiving, and Christmas. Admission: free.

Herbert Hoover Presidential Library and Museum. The Herbert Hoover Presidential Library and Museum was founded in 1962 in West Branch, Iowa, where the 31st president of the United States was born in 1874. It is located on the grounds of the Herbert Hoover National Historic Site (*see* separate listing) and one of the 13 presidential libraries/museums operated by the National Archives and Records Administration.

The library/museum was rededicated in 1992 by President Ronald Reagan as the result of a major renovation that expanded the library/museum from 32,000 to 44,500 square feet with new and additional library materials and museum exhibits. The exhibits trace Hoover's life and achievements, with displays depicting his experiences in the Australian outback and China at the turn of the century, a Belgian relief warehouse during World War I, and the 1929 inaugural platform, as well as his fishing cabin and an exhibit of Mrs. Hoover's dresses.

The 25,000-volume library has Hoover's papers and more than 150 other collections, including the manuscript holdings of Clark Mollenhoff, Felix Morley, Gerald P. Nye, Westbrook Pegler, Lewis Strauss, Laura Ingalls Wilder, and Robert E. Wood. The flat white marble gravestones of President and First Lady Hoover are located several hundred feet behind the building. Annual attendance is 70,000.

Herbert Hoover Presidential Library and Museum, 210 Parkside Dr., West Branch, IA 52358-9685 (postal address: PO Box 488, West Branch, IA 52358-0488). E-mail: hooverlibrary@nara.gov. Website: www.hoover.archives. gov. Hours: 9–5 daily; closed New Year's Day, Thanksgiving, and Christmas. Admission: adults, $6; seniors, $3; children under 16, free.

Franklin D. Roosevelt

Home of Franklin D. Roosevelt National Historic Site. Franklin Delano Roosevelt served as the 32nd president of the United States for 12 years (1933–1945) during some of the nation's darkest hours. He was elected to four terms as president—more than any other president—to lead the nation out of the Great Depression in the 1930s and to victory in World War II in the 1940s. His life and service now are the focus of the Home of Franklin D. Roosevelt National Historic Site and the Franklin D. Roosevelt Presidential Library and Museum (*see* separate listing) in Hyde Park, New York.

Roosevelt, a liberal Democrat, became the central figure in the nation's economic recovery with his New Deal policies, which followed an ineffective response by incumbent Republican President Herbert Hoover to the 1929 stock market crash and ensuing depression. Among Roosevelt's work programs were the Works Projects Administration, Civilian Conservation Corps, National Youth Administration, National Recovery Act, and Public Works Administration. Other important actions were the Federal Emergency Relief Administration to assist those in desperate need, the Social Security Act for a national system of old-age pensions, a coordinated system of federal and state action to assist the unemployed, and such other legislation as the Agricultural Adjustment Act, National Housing Act, and Federal Securities Act.

After the Japanese invaded China and the German aggression in Europe in 1938, Roosevelt sought to keep the United States officially neutral while providing diplomatic and other support to China and Britain. In 1941 Roosevelt obtained congressional approval to provide lend-lease aid to the countries fighting the Germans. After the Japanese attacked Pearl Harbor in 1941, he mobilized the American economy to assist the Allied war effort and implemented an overall war strategy on two fronts that resulted in victory. In the process, he worked closely with Winston Churchill and Joseph Stalin as the Allies defeated the Axis powers. But he never saw the end of the war or the founding of the United Nations (which he helped initiate as a replacement for the ineffective League of Nations), dying in 1945, shortly before the surrender of Germany and Japan and the establishment of the UN.

Roosevelt came from a wealthy New York family and grew up in an atmosphere of privilege. He was born in 1882 in Hyde Park, New York, the only child of James and Sara Ann Delano Roosevelt, who were sixth cousins. His mother was the dominant influence in Franklin's early years—and a problem for his wife, Eleanor, after he married and they lived together. Roosevelt, who learned to ride, shoot, and play polo, tennis, and golf as a youth, was conversant in German and French from frequent family trips to Europe. He attended Groton School, an Episcopal boarding school, where he was greatly influenced by the headmaster, Endicott Peabody, to enter public service and help the less fortunate.

Roosevelt enrolled at Harvard College, where he served as editor of the *Harvard Crimson* daily newspaper and graduated in 1903. While at Harvard, his fifth cousin, Theodore Roosevelt, became president and his role model and hero, largely because of his vigorous leadership style and reforming zeal. He also met his future wife, Eleanor Roosevelt, who was Theodore's niece and his fifth cousin, once removed, at a 1902 White House reception.

Roosevelt entered Columbia Law School in 1904, then dropped out after passing the New York state bar exam in 1907 and went to work for a law firm. In 1905 Roosevelt married Eleanor, despite strong opposition from his mother. Since both of her parents had died by the time she was 10, Eleanor's uncle, President Theodore Roosevelt, stood in at the wedding for her deceased father, Elliott. The young couple moved to the family estate, called Springwood, in Hyde Park. It was owned by Franklin's mother until her death in 1941. Franklin was outgoing and socially active, while Eleanor was shy and did not enjoy socializing. They had six children—five boys and a daughter—between 1906 and 1916.

Roosevelt first entered politics in 1910 when he was elected to the New York state senate. He was elected to a second term in 1912 and became known for his opposition to Tammany Hall, the powerful New York Democratic machine, which he later befriended. After coming out in support of Woodrow Wilson for president, he was appointed assistant secretary of the navy by Wilson in 1913. During his seven years in that position, he founded the U.S. Navy Reserve and sought to upgrade the naval forces during World War I. In 1914 he ran for the U. S. Senate from New York but lost.

After resigning as the navy secretary in 1920, Roosevelt was nominated as vice president at the age of 38, with Governor James M. Cox of Ohio as the Democratic candidate for president in another unsuccessful election. After the defeat, he returned to his New York law practice.

In 1921, while vacationing at Campobello Island at the Canadian border off the coast of Maine (*see* separate listing), Roosevelt contracted polio, which disabled him the remainder of his life. It resulted in permanent paralysis from the waist down, and he never again could use his legs fully. In the search for treatment, he found the warm waters in Warm Springs, Georgia, helpful and in 1926 founded the Roosevelt Warm Springs Institute for Rehabilitation to assist others. He later helped establish the National Foundation for Infantile Paralysis (now the March of Dimes).

Roosevelt learned to walk short distances with braces and a cane and could drive a car adapted with specially designed hand controls. But he usually was assisted in public and used a wheelchair at home. Roosevelt's difficulty in walking and reliance on a wheelchair was not publicized during his life because it was seen as a sign of weakness and instability at the time.

In 1928 Roosevelt was elected governor of New York, with the help of Tammany Hall, and served two productive terms. As the nation struggled in the Grand Depression, he was nominated by the Democrats in 1932 to face Herbert Hoover, who sought reelection as president. Roosevelt was elected and promised prompt and vigorous action in his inaugural address, saying the often quoted, "The only thing we have to fear is fear itself." He then took a series of banking, emergency relief, agricultural, public works, industrial, retirement, and other actions that became known as New Deal policies. The economy grew 58 percent and unemployment was reduced from 25 to 14.3 percent between 1932 and 1940. During the 1940–1945 war years, unemployment declined ever further—to 1.9 percent.

Roosevelt broke the unwritten two-term presidential rule with his four elections (1931, 1936, 1940, and 1944). There is no constitutional ban on more than two terms, but nearly all presidents followed George Washington's two-term decision. Several presidents ran for third terms, but all were defeated.

President Roosevelt died of a stroke at the age of 63 and is buried with his wife, Eleanor, and their dog, Fala, in the Rose Garden at their home in Hyde Park. The three-story colonial revival–style house, which dates to the early 1800s and was more than doubled in size by Roosevelt and his mother in 1915, became the Home of Franklin D. Roosevelt National Historic Site in 1945. The historic site includes the Springwood home, the Franklin D. Roosevelt Presidential Library and Museum, the Henry A. Wallace Visitor and Education Center, Top Cottage (FDR's retreat), gardens, grave site, grounds, and trails on the 300-acre site.

The Roosevelt home, which can been seen only by guided tours, has an entrance hall, a living room/library, a music room, three bedrooms, a dressing room, and a work space used by Roosevelt's mother, Sara. The visitor/education center shows a film that introduces visitors to the Roosevelt experience and provides tickets for tours of the home, and the Top Cottage is a 1938–1939 wheelchair-accessible cottage that Roosevelt designed to relax in and receive notable guests. The annual attendance is 105,000.

Home of Franklin D. Roosevelt National Historic Site, Rte. 9, Hyde Park, NY 12538 (postal address: 4097 Albany Post Rd., Hyde Park, NY 12538-1997). Phones: 845/229-9115, 845/229-9116, and 800/337-8474. Fax: 845/486-0739.

Website: www.nps.gov/hofr. Hours: 9–5 daily; closed New Year's Day, Thanksgiving, and Christmas. Admission (includes museum visit): adults, $14; children under 16, free.

Franklin D. Roosevelt Presidential Library and Museum. The Franklin D. Roosevelt Presidential Library and Museum at the Roosevelt historic home in Hyde Park, New York, is devoted to the life and achievements of the 32nd president. It was established in 1940—the first of 13 presidential libraries and museums now operated by the National Archives and Records Administration.

The federal library/museum concept originated with Roosevelt, who felt there was a need to preserve important presidential papers. Prior to his presidency, the disposition of such papers, books, and memorabilia was left to chance. The papers of presidents were considered private property, which they took with them after serving their terms. Some remained with families, while others were scattered, sold, or destroyed. The presidential libraries/museums now are built by supporters of the presidents and then turned over to the National Archives for operation.

The Roosevelt library has over 17 million pages of documents, 150,000 audiovisual items, and 50,000 books. They include the personal papers of Franklin and Eleanor Roosevelt, as well as those of various individuals and organizations associated with them. The museum also has more than 34,000 items in its collection, including Roosevelt's personal collections and materials that reflect the political, social, military, diplomatic, and cultural life in America in the 1930s and 1940s. Roosevelt amassed collections of such items as naval art, Hudson River Valley art, historical prints, and arts and crafts produced by the WPA and other government agencies. Personal items, clothing, furniture, and other materials connected to the president and first lady were added later, including millions of pages of Eleanor Roosevelt's papers.

The museum's galleries feature permanent exhibits where visitors can experience the lives of the Roosevelts and the dramatic events of the Great Depression, the New Deal, and World War II. They deal with such topics as the president's early life, his presidential years, his oval office, his private study, his life of Eleanor Roosevelt, and Roosevelt's 1936 Ford Phaeton with specially outfitted hand controls. The museum also presents traveling, joint, and online exhibitions. Annual attendance is 110,000.

Franklin D. Roosevelt Presidential Library and Museum, 4079 Albany Post Rd., Hyde Park, NY 12538—1999. Phones: 845/486-7770 and 800/337-8474. Fax: 845/486-1147. Hours: Apr.–Oct.—9–6 daily; Nov.–Mar.—9–5 daily; closed New Year's Day, Thanksgiving, and Christmas. Admission (includes home tour): adults, $14; children under 16, free.

Eleanor Roosevelt National Historic Site. *See* Eleanor Roosevelt in First Ladies section.

Roosevelt Campobello International Park. Franklin Delano Roosevelt was vacationing on Campobello Island in New Brunswick, Canada (off the coast of Lubec, Maine) during the summer of 1921 when he suddenly was taken ill with polio that crippled him for life. It paralyzed him from the waist down, and it was only through therapeutic treatment and the use of braces and a cane or a wheelchair that he later was able to get around. The southern end of the island at the Canadian border where he was stricken was established as the Roosevelt Campobello International Park in 1964 in an agreement signed by President Lyndon B. Johnson and Prime Minister Lester B. Pearson. The park is owned and administered by a joint United States and Canadian commission.

The 2,800-acre park is connected to Lubec by the FDR International Bridge. The park includes the cottage and the grounds where Roosevelt and his wife, Eleanor, were vacationing, as well as the waters where he sailed and the woods, bogs, and beaches he experienced. Tours are offered of the cottage, and a visitor center has exhibits about Roosevelt and a video about the island. Among the cottage rooms on display are the office, bedrooms, nursery, writing room, living room, dining room, kitchen, and laundry. The park has eight miles of walking trails and nearly eight and a half miles of driving.

Roosevelt Campobello International Park, Campobello Island, New Brunswick, Canada (postal address: Executive Secretary, Roosevelt Campobello International Park, PO Box 97, Lubec, ME 04652). Phone: 506/752-2922. Fax: 506/752-6000. Website: www.nps.gov/roca. Hours: grounds—open daily a half hour before sunrise to a half hour after sunset; Roosevelt cottage and visitor center—10–6 daily from the Sat. prior to Memorial Day through Columbus Day; closed remainder of year. Admission: free.

Roosevelt's Little White House State Historic Site. After being stricken with polio in 1921, Franklin Delano Roosevelt found the strength to resume his political career in the therapeutic warm waters in Warm Springs, Georgia. It also is where he established an institute to treat those afflicted with polio and built a retreat that became known as the "Little White House." He stayed there during his frequent trips to Warm Springs for treatment and rest and died there in 1945. The retreat is now preserved as Roosevelt's Little White House State Historic Site.

Roosevelt first went to Warm Springs in 1924 for treatment at a resort—and hopefully a cure for poliomyelitis. There was no cure, but the warm waters did ease the pain and made it possible to move his legs somewhat. Two years later, he bought the resort and founded a nonprofit rehabilitation institute to help others. In 1932 he had a modest one-story, six-room cottage built overlooking a heavily wooded ravine, which became the Little White House. He spent time there every year except 1942.

Important national figures and cabinet members often accompanied Roosevelt to Warm Springs so that he could meet with institute board members while continuing to run the government and receive personal physical therapy. Roosevelt said some conditions in the area—such as the high electric rates in Warm Springs—also inspired certain New Deal programs, such as the Rural Electrification Administration, which brought electric power to rural areas at reasonable rates.

After Roosevelt died of a stroke in the Little White House in 1945, the Roosevelt Warm Springs Institute Foundation gave the property to the State of Georgia. The Little White House was opened to the public in 1948. It remains the same as it was the day the president died. In 1980 the house and historic pools and springs became part of the Georgia Department of Natural Resources State Parks and Historic Sites. The Roosevelt Warm Springs Institute, located adjacent to the house, now is managed by the Department of Labor as a vocational rehabilitation center that treats persons with post-polio syndrome and a wide range of other illnesses and injuries.

The complex is located in the Warm Springs Historic District, which is a National Historic Landmark and listed in the National Registry of Historic Places. It is now known as Roosevelt's Little White House Historic Site. In addition to Roosevelt's house, it includes the FDR Memorial Museum, with exhibits and a film on the president; Memorial Fountain; the Walk of the States; two of Roosevelt's cars; and the original bump gate that opened with an automobile bump. The historic therapy pools and springs also are open daily for free tours. The historic site has an annual attendance of 100,000.

Roosevelt's Little White House State Historic Site, State Hwy. 85-U.S. Hwy. 27, Warm Springs, GA 31830-2157. Phone: 706/655-5870. Fax: 706/655-5872. Website: www.gastateparks.org. Hours: 9–4:45 daily; closed New Year's Day, Thanksgiving, and Christmas. Admission: adults, $7; seniors, $6; children 6–18, $4; children under 6, free.

Franklin Delano Roosevelt Memorial. The Franklin Delano Roosevelt Memorial in Washington honors the 32nd president of the United States in a sequence of four outdoor "rooms"—one for each of his record four terms of office. The monument, which is spread over seven and a half acres, is located along the cherry tree walk along the Potomac River Tidal Basin at the National Mall. The winning design was selected in a 1974 competition, but it was not until 1997 that the memorial was established because of delays in funding by Congress.

The memorial, designed by Lawrence Haiprin with sculptures and works by five others, makes use of running water and waterfalls in the outdoor spaces to show how the presidency becomes more complex during Roosevelt's 12 years in the White House. The waterfalls grow larger and more complex as the water moves from his first to last term as president.

The statue showing Roosevelt in a chair with a cloak obscuring the chair and, at his side, his dog, Fala was controversial. Some wanted his polio disability to be shown by having him in a wheelchair, but their concerns were initially overridden. The National Organization on Disability later raised enough funds to add a sculpture of him in a wheelchair. There also is a bronze statue of First Lady Eleanor Roosevelt standing in from of a United Nations emblem. Other sculptures depict scenes from different periods, such as the Great Depression, where people are listening to a fireside chat on the radio and waiting in a bread line. Interpretive programs are presented by rangers every hour from 10 a.m. to 11 p.m. More than 2.8 million people visit the memorial each year.

Franklin Delano Roosevelt Memorial, West Basin Dr. and Ohio Dr., Washington, DC 20024 (postal address: National Mall and Memorial Parks, 900 Ohio Dr., S.W., Washington, DC 20024). Phones: 202/426-6841 and 202/485-9880. Website: www.nps.gov/frde. Hours: open 24 hours, with rangers on duty 9:30 a.m.–11:30 p.m. Admission: free.

Franklin D. Roosevelt Four Freedoms Park. The Franklin D. Roosevelt Four Freedoms Park in New York City is the newest memorial honoring the 32nd president of the United States. It opened in 2012 at the southernmost point of Roosevelt Island in the East River between Manhattan and Queens. Roosevelt Island was named for the former president in 1973, with plans calling for a memorial at the southern tip. The Franklin and Eleanor Roosevelt Institute raised funds for the park and the project.

The park memorializes Roosevelt's famous "Four Freedoms" speech to Congress in 1941. The noted architect Louis Kahn was asked to design the monument in 1972, two years before his own death. He was carrying the finished designs when he died in Penn Station in 1974. The designs for Four Freedoms Park were continued by Mitchell/Giurgola Architects, who followed Kahn's original intentions.

The monument is a simplified, roofless version of a Greek temple in granite, with excerpts from Roosevelt's "Four Freedoms" speech carved on the walls. The memorial has four rooms, representing his four terms in office. (1933–1945). The first room features a life-size statue of a poor Appalachian couple, the second a bread line, the third a person listening to Roosevelt's fireside chats, and the fourth a statue of Roosevelt's wife, Eleanor. A mural also depicts the 54 social programs—in images, writing, and Braille— that were implemented while Roosevelt was president. In addition, a courtyard contains a bust of Roosevelt, sculpted in 1933 by Jo Davidson. The site is a New York state park.

Franklin D. Roosevelt Four Freedoms Park, Roosevelt Island, New York, NY. Phone: 212/204-8831. Hours: 8 a.m.–11:45 p.m. daily. Admission: free.

Harry S. Truman

Harry S. Truman National Historic Site. Vice President Harry S. Truman succeeded President Franklin D. Roosevelt as the 33rd president of the United States (1945–1953) when Roosevelt died less than three months after beginning his unprecedented fourth term in 1945. It was during Truman's tenure that some of the most important events of the century occurred—Germany surrendered, the atomic bomb was used against Japan, the United Nations was founded, the Marshall Plan to rebuild Europe was initiated, the Truman Doctrine to contain communism began, the Cold War started, the Berlin Airlift took place, the North Atlantic Treaty Organization was created, and the United States became involved in the Korean War.

Truman, a World War I artillery captain and a senator from Missouri, was selected by Roosevelt to replace Vice President Henry A. Wallace as his running mate in 1944. He was a folksy, unassuming president who relied heavily on his cabinet in decision making, unlike Roosevelt, who kept personal control of all major decisions. In many cases, Truman's decisions were controversial, and he became one of the most unpopular presidents to leave the White House. But assessments of his presidency after his retirement became much more positive, and he now is considered one of the nation's most praised presidents.

Truman's family farm in Grandview, Missouri, and his longtime home in Independence, Missouri, now are preserved at the Harry S. Truman National Historic Site, and his life and career are presented at the Harry S. Truman Library and Museum in Independence (*see* separate listing). He was born on a farm in Lamar, Missouri, in 1884, the eldest of three children of John Anderson Truman, a farmer and livestock dealer, and Martha Ellen Young Truman. The family lived in Lamar until Harry was 10 months old then moved to Harrisonville, Belton, and his grandparents' farm in Grandview. When he was six, Harry's parents moved to Independence so he could attend the Presbyterian Church Sunday School. He did not attend a traditional school until two years later. He graduated from Independence High School in 1901 and then worked as a railroad timekeeper, clerk, and newspaper mailroom worker before returning to the Grandview farm in 1906.

Truman enlisted in the Missouri National Guard in 1905 and served until 1911. He remained on the farm until the United States entered World War I in 1917 when he rejoined the National Guard. While on the farm, he met and courted Bess Wallace, who turned him down when he proposed.

Truman became an officer and then battery commander of an artillery regiment in France during the war. As captain, he turned out to be an effective leader and later was promoted to major and then colonel in the Army Reserves. His war record proved invaluable in his political career.

After the war, Truman returned to Independence and married Bess Wallace in 1919. They later had one child, Mary Margaret. He briefly attended a business school and then took night courses at the Kansas City Law School. Truman was the only president who served after 1897 who did not have a college degree.

Truman and Edward Jacobson, who ran the Camp Doniphan canteen with Truman before going overseas, opened a haberdashery in downtown Kansas City in 1919, but it failed during the 1921 recession. In 1922 Truman was elected as an administrative judge in the Jackson County Court with the help of the Kansas City Democratic machine led by Thomas Pendergast. In 1926 he was elected the presiding judge and reelected in 1930. Truman was appointed Missouri's director for the Federal Re-Employment Program in 1933 and was elected a U.S. senator from Missouri with Pendergast's support.

In his first senatorial term, Truman spoke out against corporate greed and the dangers of moneyed special interests getting too much influence in national affairs. During the second term, he gained further attention by chairing the war investigating committee, which was called the "Truman Committee." It sought out waste and mismanagement in the war effort and reportedly saved $15 billion.

Truman was elected vice president in the 1944 election with President Roosevelt but scarcely saw Roosevelt and received little or no briefing on the issues that he faced shortly thereafter. After the victory in Europe, he asked Japan to surrender only to be rejected. He then authorized dropping atomic bombs on two Japanese cities devoted to war work—Hiroshima and Nagasaki—that ended the war. It also was in 1945 that the United Nations charter was signed.

Truman followed with a 21-point program to expand Social Security, a full-employment program, a permanent Fair Employment Practices Act, and public housing and slum-clearance programs. Among the other Truman actions were the Marshall Plan to help restore Europe, the Truman Doctrine when Russia threatened Turkey and Greece, the Berlin Airlift to ferry supplies to the encircled German city, and the development of the North Atlantic Treaty Organization military alliance. When North Korea attacked South Korea in 1950, the United States and United Nations responded by helping South Korean forces against the Northern army.

Truman decided not to run for reelection in 1952 and retired to his home in Independence. He died of multiple organ failure in 1972 at the age of 88. Unlike most historic sites, the Harry S. Truman National Historic Site includes two locations—his home in Independence, Missouri, and his grandparents' farm in Grandview, Missouri, where he lived as a youth. Truman lived at the home in Independence after his marriage to Bess Wallace in 1919 until his death in 1972. The house was built by Bess's maternal grandfather, George Porterfield Gates, over a period of years (1867 to 1885). Harry and Bess initially could not afford a new home, so they moved in with her mother and grandparents and later inherited the house.

The Independence house, which was established as a national historic site in 1983, shows the simple life the Trumans lived before and after the presidency. The Victorian-style house contains the furnishings, clothing, and personal possessions of the president and first lady, as well as items from Bess's mother and grandparents. Guided tours are given of the house during the summer, as well as the Truman neighborhood and historic Independence on Fridays and Sundays. A visitor center features an audiovisual program on President and Mrs. Truman. The site also has two adjacent houses—one of the home of Mrs. Truman's brother and another where the president's favorite aunt and cousins lived.

The Truman farmhouse in Grandview is located 15 miles from Independence. It was built in 1894 by Harry Truman's maternal grandmother and became part of the national historic site in 1994. It has been designated a National Historic Landmark. The two-story farmhouse is located on 5.25 acres that remain from the former 600-acre farm owned by the president's grandparents and later operated by his father. Other structures at the site include a reconstructed smokehouse, a garage, a restored box wagon, and other original and reconstructed buildings. Truman worked on the farm as a youth from 1906 to 1917. Guided tours are given on Friday, Saturday, and Sunday during the summer. Annual attendance is 5,000.

Harry S. Truman National Historic Site, Truman Home, 223 N. Main St., Independence, MO 64050-2804. Phones: 816/254-9929 and 816/254-2720. Fax: 816/254-4491. E-mail: larry_villalva@nps.gov. Website: www.nps.gov/hstr. Hours: Memorial Day–Oct.—8:30–5 daily; Nov.–Memorial Day—8:30–5 Tues.–Sun.; closed Mon., New Year's Day, Thanksgiving, and Christmas. Admission: adults, $4; children under 16, free.

Harry S. Truman National Historic Site, Truman Farm Home, 12301 Blue Ridge Blvd., Grandview, MO 64030-1159 (postal address: 223 N. Main St., Independence, MO 64050-2804). Phones: 816/254-9929 and 816/254-2720. Fax: 816/254-4491. E-mail: larry_villalva@nps.gov. Website: www.nps.gov/hstr. Hours: Memorial Day–Labor Day—9:30–4 Fri.–Sun.; closed Mon.–Thurs. and day after Labor Day to Memorial Day. Admission: adults, $4; children under 16, free.

Harry S. Truman Library and Museum. The Harry S. Truman Library and Museum in Independence, Missouri, tells of the life and achievements of the 33rd president of the United States (1945–1953) and preserves his papers, books, and other historical materials. Established in 1957, the library/museum was the first presidential library/museum to be created under the 1955 Presidential Libraries Act administered by the National Archives and Records Administration.

The library/museum was designed by architect Edward F. Neild, who died while working on the design. It is located on a hill in Independence overlooking the Kansas City skyline. Truman maintained a working office in the building and often arrived at the library/museum before the employees—and sometimes surprised early telephone callers by picking up the phone and giving directions and answering questions. It is where he wrote letters, speeches, articles, and his book, *Mr. Citizen*, until his death in 1972.

The museum has two floors of exhibits relating to Truman's life and presidency. They contain artifacts, documents, photographs, film clips, memorabilia, and a full-scale replica of the Oval Office. The Truman museum was the first presidential museum to include the president's office, which has become a feature of many other presidential museums. The two ongoing exhibits are devoted to Truman's life and times and his presidential years. The lobby entrance also features the mural *Independence and the Opening of the West* by Thomas Hart Benton.

The funeral services for President Truman were held in the building's auditorium, and he was buried in the courtyard in 1972. His wife, Bess, was buried next to him in 1982. The cremated remains of their daughter, Margaret, and her husband, Clifton Daniel, also are interred in the courtyard.

The library/museum has guided tours, temporary and traveling exhibitions, lectures, and organized educational programs. In the White House Decision Center educational program, students take on the roles of the president and his advisers in facing real-life historical decisions in a re-creation of the White House West Wing. The library/ museum annual attendance is 90,000.

Harry S. Truman Library and Museum, 500 W. U.S. Hwy. 24, Independence, MO 64050-1798. Phones: 816/268-8200 and 800/833-1225. Fax: 816/268-8295. E-mail: truman.library@nara.gov. Website: www.trumanlibrary.org. Hours: May–Sept.—9–5 Mon.–Wed. and Fri.–Sat., 9 a.m.–9 p.m. Thurs., 12–5 Sun.; Oct.–Apr.—9–5 Mon.–Sat., 12–5 Sun.; closed New Year's Day, Thanksgiving, and Christmas. Admission: adults, $8; seniors, $7; children 6–15, $3; children under 6, free.

Harry S. Truman Birthplace State Historic Site. The small house where President Harry S. Truman was born in Lamar, Missouri, in 1884 is now a historic house museum and a state historic site. The six-room house was purchased by Truman's father, John A. Truman, a livestock dealer who primarily sold horses and mules, in 1882. Harry was only 10 months old when the livestock business was sold and the family moved to Harrisonville and eventually settled in Independence in 1890.

The United Auto Workers of America bought the Lamar property in 1957 and gave it to the people of Missouri. The house has been restored and redecorated to the period of ownership and occupancy by the Truman family. It is furnished with the type of furniture used in modest homes in the 1880s. Guided tours are offered.

The last time Truman returned to Lamar was in 1944 to give his vice presidential nomination acceptance speech. The Harry S. Truman Birthplace State Historic Site, which is listed on the National Register of Historic Places, is maintained by the Missouri Department of Natural Resources. Annual attendance is 26,600.

Harry S. Truman Birthplace State Historic Site, 1009 Truman Ave., Lamar, MO 04759-1543. Phone: 417682-2279. Fax: 417/682-6304. E-mail: moparks@dnr.mo.gov. Website: www.mostateparks.com/trumansite.htm. Hours: Mar.–Oct.—10–4 Wed.–Sat., 12–4 Sun.; Nov.–Feb.—10–4 Wed.–Sat.; closed Sun.–Tues. and major holidays. Admission: free.

Harry S. Truman Little White House. The Harry S. Truman Little White House in Key West, Florida, was the winter retreat for the 33rd president of the United States from 1946 to 1952. Truman initially came to the historic site when he was physically exhausted after the first 19 months in office and his doctor recommended taking a vacation in a warm climate to recuperate. A naval base in Florida was recommended, and he enjoyed the experience so much that he returned whenever he felt the need for rest—making 11 visits totaling 175 days while in office.

Truman stayed in an 1890 building at a submarine naval base along the Key West waterfront. The site became known as the "Truman Annex." It was part of a wooden duplex that originally contained quarters for the base commander and the paymaster. In 1911 the building was converted into a single-family dwelling for the base commander and the land between the house and the sea was filled in. Later, the waterfront view was blocked by a new building. The house served as the naval station commandant's home until 1974, when the submarine base was closed. In 1987 the historic building was deeded to the State of Florida, and the house was restored to its 1949 appearance. It opened in 1991 as a state historic site and museum.

In addition to being a place of rest, the Winter White House was the site of important meetings and decision making. It also has been used by other presidents and senior government officials over the years. James Forrestal met there with the Joint Chiefs of Staff in 1947, and Dwight D. Eisenhower held a series of meetings there in 1948–1949 leading to the creation of the Department of Defense. Eisenhower also returned in 1955–1956 as president to recuperate from a heart attack.

In 1961 President John F. Kennedy and British Prime Minister Harold Macmillan held a summit meeting in the house, and Kennedy made a second visit in 1962 immediately following the Cuban Missile Crisis. Former President Jimmy Carter and family held a reunion at the house in 1996, and former President Bill Clinton and his wife, then Senator Hillary Rodham Clinton, spent a weekend at the site.

Guided tours now are given of the Winter White House, which is surrounded by a botanical garden. Annual attendance is 63,000.

Harry S. Truman Little White House, 111 Front St., Key West, FL 33040-8311 (postal address: PO Box 6443, Key West, FL 33041-6443). Phone: 305/294-9911. Fax: 305/294-9988. E-mail: bwolz@trumanlittlewhitehouse.com. Website: www.trumanlittlewhitehouse.com. Hours: 9–5 daily; Admission: adults, $16.13; seniors, $13.98; children 5–12, $5.58; children under 5 and local residents, free.

Dwight D. Eisenhower

Eisenhower National Historic Site. Dwight D. Eisenhower was the commanding general of Allied forces in Europe in World War II and became the 34th president of the United States (1953–1961). He was a moderate Republican who won the presidency by a landslide, defeating Democrat Adlai Stevenson and ending two decades of the New Deal in the 1952 postwar election. He entered the presidential race to counter the nonintervention position of Senator Robert A. Taft, a fellow Republican, and to overcome "communism, Korea, and corruption."

As the supreme commander of Allied forces in Europe, Eisenhower planned and supervised the invasion of North Africa in 1942–1943 and then the invasion of France and Germany in 1944, which led to the successful end of World War II. After the war, he became president of Columbia University and in 1951 was named the first supreme commander of the North Atlantic Treaty Organization. He entered politics reluctantly, but he quickly adapted to his new role, which included the cold war with the Soviet Union.

Eisenhower was born in 1890 in Denison, Texas, but he grew up in a large family in Kansas. He was the third of seven boys of David Jacob Eisenhower and Ida Elizabeth Stover Eisenhower. His father owned a general store in Hope, Kansas, that failed, and the Eisenhowers went to Texas in 1889. In 1892 they moved to Abilene, Kansas, which they considered their hometown and where their father worked as a railroad mechanic and later with a creamery.

Dwight, who was called "Ike," became interested in military history from reading books in his mother's collection. His parents were members of the River Brethren sect of the Mennonites, and the family did daily Bible readings at breakfast and dinner. His mother later joined the International Bible Students Association, which became the Jehovah's Witnesses, and the Eisenhower home served as the local meeting hall from 1896 to 1915. Dwight was quite religious but never joined any sect or religion.

After graduation from Abilene High School, Eisenhower and his brother Edgar were going to take alternate years at college because they lacked the funds for full-time enrollment. When he learned that the military and naval academies required no tuition, he sought the senatorial appointment and passed the entrance exam for West Point in 1911. His decision to attend the military academy saddened his pacifist mother, but she did not overrule him. He turned out to be an average student and was a starting running back and linebacker on the academy football team until he broke a leg in making a tackle. He later served as junior varsity football coach and yell leader.

After graduation from West Point in 1915, Lieutenant Eisenhower served with the infantry at various camps in Texas and Georgia until 1918. While in Texas, he met and fell in love with Mamie Geneva Doud while she was visiting from Boone, Iowa. They were married in July 1916. In their first 35 years of marriage, they moved 35 times. They had two sons—Doud, who died of scarlet fever in 1921 at the age of three, and John, who became a brigadier general, author, and ambassador to Belgium. Dwight also began to paint after watching his wife's portraits being made. During the last 20 years of his life, he created 260 oils, mostly landscapes and some portraits.

When World War I began, Eisenhower was sent to Fort Leavenworth, Kansas; transferred to Camp Meade in Maryland with the 65th Engineers; and then assigned to the new tank corps. He rose to the temporary rank of lieutenant colonel and trained tank crews at the Civil War battleground in Gettysburg, Pennsylvania. His units were about to go overseas when the armistice was signed.

In the 1920s Eisenhower returned to Fort Meade to command a battalion of tanks, collaborating with George S. Patton and other senior tank leaders. Eisenhower then became executive officer to General Fox Conner in the Panama Canal Zone and attended the Command and General Staff College at Fort Leavenworth, where he graduated first in a class of 248 officers in 1926. This was followed by assignment to the American Battle Monuments Commission, directed by General John J. Pershing, and then graduation from the Army War College in 1928.

After a year's assignment in France, Eisenhower was made executive officer to General George V. Mosely, assistant secretary of war, and was involved in war planning from 1929 to 1933. He then became chief military aide to General Douglas MacArthur, army chief of staff, and participated in the clearing of the "Bonus March" encampment of World War I veterans in Washington. In 1935 he accompanied MacArthur to the Philippines and served as assistant military adviser to the Philippine government. After returning to the United States, Eisenhower held a series of staff positions in Washington, California, and Texas.

In 1941 Eisenhower was appointed chief of staff to General Walter Krueger, commander of the Third Army at Fort Sam Houston in San Antonio, and was promoted to brigadier general later that year. After the Japanese attack on Pearl Harbor on December 7, 1941, he was assigned to the General Staff in Washington and was involved in creating major war plans to defeat Japan and Germany.

In 1942 Eisenhower became assistant chief of staff in charge of the new Operations Division under General George C. Marshall. Later that year he went to England with General Henry H. Arnold, commanding general of the Army Air Forces, to inspect the effectiveness of the European Theater of Operations and then was appointed commanding general for European operations.

In November 1942, Eisenhower became the supreme commander of the Allied forces in the North Africa Theater of Operations. After victories in North Africa and Italy, he was named supreme Allied commander in Europe in December 1943 and directed the D-Day landing in France on June 6, 1944, which led to the surrender of Germany on May 8, 1945. He then served as military governor of the United States occupation zone in Germany before returning to Washington as army chief of staff and overseeing the demobilization.

In 1948 Eisenhower became president of Columbia University and served until 1953. He was given leave in 1951 to serve as supreme commander of the newly created North Atlantic Treaty Organization. When he returned and retired from the service and the university, he was approached by both the Republican and Democratic parties about running for president of the United States. He accepted the Republican nomination and was elected president in 1952 and reelected in 1956.

As president, Eisenhower believed in negotiating and cooperation and tried to avoid confrontations. He became best known for construction of the interstate highway system, obtaining an armistice in the Korean War, and atomic bomb and other negotiations with the Soviet Union during the cold war. He also sent federal troops to enforce a federal desegregation order at Central High School in Little Rock, Arkansas, and the first military advisors to South Vietnam. After denouncing New Deal policies in the campaign, he continued most of the programs and even expanded Social Security. Eisenhower also was criticized for not doing more for the space program or the civil rights movement, for not coming out against McCarthyism, for his handling of the U-2 plane incident, and for failing to further the goals of the right.

Several changes also took place regarding the presidency while Eisenhower was in office. In the 22nd Amendment to the U.S. Constitution, presidential terms were limited to two terms. Eisenhower also became the first president to benefit from the new Former Presidents Act, which provided a pension, state-provided staff, and Secret Service protection for presidents after their terms.

After serving two terms as president, Eisenhower retired to his working farm adjacent to the Gettysburg battlefield in 1961. While he was president, the farm served as a weekend retreat for Eisenhower and a meeting place for world leaders. It also was a successful cattle operation, with a show herd of black Angus cattle. In 1955 he suffered a heart attack while in Denver and spent seven months in a hospital while recuperating, but he was reelected in 1956. He died in 1969 of congestive heart failure at the age of 78.

The Eisenhowers donated their farm to the National Park Service in 1967. It became the Eisenhower National Historic Site, which was opened to the public in 1980, a year after Mrs. Eisenhower died. The Eisenhowers had purchased the farm in 1950 and expanded it from 189 to 230 acres, rebuilt the old farmhouse, started the cattle herd, and added a putting green and skeet range.

The historic site now covers 690 acres, with the home, grounds, barns, and cattle operation being open to public tours. Visits can be made only by shuttle bus service from the adjacent Gettysburg National Military Park Visitor Center. Two films cover the grounds and Eisenhower's life and accomplishments. The house contains nearly all the original furnishings. The site also has the Eisenhowers' farm equipment, vehicles, and personal possessions, as well as presidential and World War II memorabilia. The site is a National Historic Landmark and is listed on the National Register of Historic Places. Annual attendance is 70,000.

Eisenhower National Historic Site, 1195 Baltimore Pike, Suite 100, Gettysburg, PA 17325-7034. Phone: 717/338-9114. Fax: 717/338-0821. E-mail: eise_site_manager@nps.gov. Website: www.nps.gov/eise. Hours: visitor center—8–5 daily; site—9–4 daily (visits only by shuttle bus); closed New Year's Day, Thanksgiving, and Christmas. Admission: adults, $7.50; children 6–12, $5; children under 6, free (fees cover the shuttle bus and access to the home, grounds, reception center, and all programs on the site).

Dwight D. Eisenhower Presidential Library and Museum. The Dwight D. Eisenhower Presidential Library and Museum in Abilene, Kansas, is dedicated to the life and achievements of the 34th president of the United States. Founded in 1945, the presidential library/museum also contains Eisenhower's boyhood home, a statue of the president, a meditation building that is the burial site of President and Mrs. Eisenhower and their firstborn son, and a visitor center.

Abilene is where Eisenhower grew up and lived from 1892 when three years old until graduating from the U.S. Military Academy at West Point. The library contains 25,000 volumes and historical materials about Eisenhower, while the museum has exhibits, materials, and objects related to his life in 30,000 square feet of gallery space. There are five major galleries (introductory, military, presidential, Mrs. Eisenhower, and temporary exhibition). They present an overview of Eisenhower's early life and career, his military career and World War II, his 1953–1961 presidential administration, and Mrs. Eisenhower's life as first lady.

Eisenhower's six-room boyhood home was occupied by his family from 1898 until his mother's death in 1946. It is furnished as it was at the time of Mrs. Ida Eisenhower. The bronze statue of Eisenhower in his military uniform by Robert L. Dean Jr. has a granite base with quotations from his career.

The grave sites are in the Place of Meditation, a small limestone building where it was hoped that visitors would reflect upon the ideals that made the nation great and that they would continue to be loyal to those ideals. A visitor center is located on the site of the former Lincoln School, where Eisenhower first enrolled in elementary school. It features a film on Eisenhower and houses a gift shop. The presidential library/museum has an annual attendance of nearly 160,000.

Dwight D. Eisenhower Presidential Library and Museum, 200 S.E. 4th St., Abilene, KS 67410-2900 (postal address: PO Box 339, Abilene, KS 67410-0339). Phones: 785/263-6700 and 877/746-4453. Fax: 785/263-6715. E-mail: eisenhower.library@nara.gov. Website: www.eisenhower.archives.gov. Hours: Memorial Day weekend–Labor Day—8–5:45 daily; day after Labor Day–late May—9–4:45 daily; closed New Year's Day, Thanksgiving Day, and Christmas. Admission: adults, $10; seniors, $8; children 8–15, $1; active military and children under 8, free.

Eisenhower Birthplace State Historic Site. The Eisenhower Birthplace State Historic Site is located at a modest 1881 two-story frame house in the Texas railroad town of Denison where the 34th president of the United States was born in 1890. The house originally was purchased by the City of Denison in the late 1940s and restored to its 1890 appearance by the Eisenhower Birthplace Foundation. It is now operated by the Texas Historical Commission. It has a visitor center with items related to Eisenhower and his role in history. A state park named for Eisenhower is also located northwest of Denison. The birthplace site has an annual attendance of 15,000.

Eisenhower Birthplace State Historic Site, 609 S. Lamar Ave., Denison, TX 75021-1821. Phone: 903/465-8908. Fax: 903/465-8988. Website: www.eisenhowerbirthplace.com. Hours: 9–5 Tues.–Sat., 1–5 Sun.; closed Mon., New Year's Day, Thanksgiving, and Christmas Eve and Day. Admission: adults, $3; children 12–18, $2; children under 12, free.

Mamie Doud Eisenhower Birthplace. *See* Mamie Doud Eisenhower in First Ladies section.

John F. Kennedy

John Fitzgerald Kennedy National Historic Site. John Fitzgerald Kennedy, the 35th president of the United States, was fatally shot while riding in a motorcade in Dallas, Texas, in 1963. He was the fourth and last American president to be assassinated. Kennedy was in office less than three years, but they were filled with such far-reaching historical events as the Bay of Pigs invasion, the Cuban Missile Crisis, the building of the Berlin Wall, the Soviet-U.S. space race, the birth of the civil rights movement, the early stages of the Vietnam War, and the conspiracy controversy surrounding his assassination.

Kennedy, the first president to be born in the twentieth century, was elected in 1960 at the age of 43. He was the second youngest to ascend to the presidency (after Theodore Roosevelt). He also is the only Catholic to be elected president and to win a Pulitzer Prize (for *Profiles in Courage* in 1956). Kennedy's debate with Richard Nixon during the 1960 election also was the first televised presidential debate and influenced the election outcome. Kennedy's presidency was called "The Camelot Years"—a term first used by Jacqueline Kennedy—because it was a period of optimism and hope; the young were energetic and confident, the economy was in good shape, and the nation was helping the rest of the world and was widely admired.

John F. Kennedy was born in Brookline, Massachusetts, in 1917. He was one of the nine children of wealthy businessman Joseph P. Kennedy Sr. and Rose Fitzgerald Kennedy, daughter of John Fitzgerald, mayor of Boston and three-time member of Congress. John, who was a sickly child, lived in Brookline for 10 years and went to schools there through the fourth grade.

In 1927 the Kennedy family moved to the Bronx and then Bronxville when business interests took the father to New York City. John attended Riverdale Country School and Canterbury School, private schools for boys, before finishing the ninth through twelfth grades at the Choate School in Wallingford, Connecticut. While at Choate in 1934, Kennedy had an emergency hospitalization, with the problem being diagnosed as colitis.

In 1935 Kennedy spent six weeks at Princeton University. He then was hospitalized for two months of observation for possible leukemia and convalesced further at the family winter home in Palm Beach, Florida. This was followed by working on a ranch near Benson, Arizona, in the spring of 1936. In the fall, he enrolled at Harvard College. He toured Europe during the summers of 1937 and 1939 and worked with his brother Joe during the summer of 1938 at the American Embassy in London, where his father was ambassador.

At Harvard, Kennedy developed an interest in political philosophy and wrote his thesis about British participation in the Munich Agreement, which became the best seller *Why England Slept*. He graduated from Harvard with a Bachelor of Science cum laude in international affairs in 1940. In early 1941, he helped his father write a memoir of his three years as an American ambassador and then went on a tour of South America.

In September 1941, Kennedy joined the U.S. Navy after being turned down by the army because of chronic lower back problems. After attending the Motor Torpedo Boat Squadron Training Center, he was assigned to Panama and later to the Pacific Theater. He was made a lieutenant and given command of a PT-109 patrol torpedo boat. In August 1943, Kennedy's boat and two others were on night patrol near New Georgia in the Solomon Islands when his boat was rammed by a Japanese destroyer.

The crew swam to a small nearby island, and despite reinjuring his back, Kennedy towed a badly burned crewman through the water to the island. They subsequently were rescued, and Kennedy received the Navy and Marine Corps Medal for his actions and was given command of another boat—a PT boat converted into a gunboat (PT-59). He was honorably discharged from the service with five additional decorations in early 1945, just prior to the Japanese surrender.

When John was still in service, his older brother, Joseph, was killed in action, and he was expected to replace him as the family's political standard-bearer. The opportunity came in 1946 when Representative James Michael Curley vacated his seat in the strongly Democratic 10th Congressional District in Massachusetts to become mayor of Boston. Kennedy was elected and served as congressman for six years. He then ran for U.S. senator in 1952 and defeated Republican incumbent Henry Cabot Lodge Jr. This also was the year that he married Jacqueline L. Bouvier, a New York book editor who became an elegant first lady. She became a fashion icon and oversaw the restoration of the White House. They had four children. Arabella was stillborn in 1956, and Patrick died several days after birth of respiratory distress syndrome in 1963. Another son, John, and his wife died in a plane crash in 1999. The surviving daughter, Caroline, was born in 1957.

Kennedy underwent several spinal operations in 1953–1954. He often was absent from the Senate, largely because he was critically ill at times. It was during one of his convalescences in 1956 that he wrote the Pulitzer Prize–winning *Profiles in Courage*, which was about senators who risked their careers for their personal beliefs. At the 1956 Democratic National Convention, Kennedy was nominated for vice president to run with presidential nominee Adlai Stevenson but finished second in the balloting to Senator Estes Kefauver.

In 1958 Kennedy was reelected senator from Massachusetts and began to prepare for the 1960 presidential election. At the Democratic National Convention, he was nominated over Senator Lyndon B. Johnson, and then he selected Johnson as his vice presidential running mate. The Republican candidate was Vice President Richard Nixon, and the major campaign issues were the economy, Cuba, Soviet space and missile programs, and Kennedy's Roman Catholicism. It was a close race that many believe was decided by the first televised presidential debate. Nixon had a "five o'clock shadow" and was tense, perspiring, and uncomfortable, while Kennedy used makeup services, appeared relaxed, and made a better impression. Although both made effective arguments, the large television audience favored Kennedy as the winner, which is believed to have influenced the election outcome.

In his inaugural address, Kennedy made his often-quoted statement, "Ask not what your country can do for you; ask what you can do for your country." In some ways, he was better known for his inspiring speeches than his legislative actions. But he did increase minimum wages, improve Social Security benefits, pass urban renewal, create the Peace Corps, and set the space goal of landing on the moon by the end of the 1960s. He did not enact any civil rights legislation, but he used executive orders and personal appeals to assist the civil rights movement.

Kennedy's foreign affairs policies suffered a defeat in 1961 when he did not stop an attempt by a small force of Cuban exiles to overthrow the Cuban communist government in the Bay of Pigs invasion. The attack failed and the invaders were captured. However, Kennedy was successful in convincing the Russians to remove their missiles from Cuba by agreeing the United States would not invade Cuba.

Kennedy also agreed to a nuclear test ban treaty in 1963 with the Soviet Union and Great Britain in an attempt to halt the spread of nuclear weapons. Aid to Latin American countries was provided through the Alliance for

Progress program, and advisory military assistance went to South Vietnam, where North Vietnam was sending troops through Laos to fight in what evolved into the Vietnam War.

Kennedy was assassinated on November 22, 1963, while in Dallas. He was traveling in a motorcade with his wife and Texas Governor John Connally and his wife when shot by Lee Harvey Oswald, who was killed by Jack Ruby, a Kennedy supporter, while in police custody after his capture. For years there was a controversy over whether Kennedy was killed in a conspiracy. But a 10-month investigation by the Warren Commission concluded that Kennedy was killed by Oswald acting alone and that Ruby acted alone. Kennedy, who was 46 when he died, was buried in Arlington National Cemetery. His wife, Jacqueline, and two of their children, Arabella and Patrick, also are interred there. Mrs. Kennedy, who returned to book editing, married Aristotle Onassis, a Greek shipping magnate, in 1968 and died in 1994.

Kennedy's birthplace and childhood home in Brookline, Massachusetts, is now the John Fitzgerald Kennedy National Historic Site. The 1909 house was purchased by Kennedy's father in 1914, and the family lived there until 1920, when they moved to a larger house a few blocks away. The Kennedy family repurchased the home in 1966, and Kennedy's mother, Rose, restored it to look as it did when John was born in 1917. The three-story house was donated by Mrs. Kennedy to the National Park Service for the American people in 1967 as a memorial to her son. It contains many of the original furnishings and artifacts, as well as exhibits and photographs in a lower-level visitor center. Ranger-led tours are given of the house and the neighborhood. Annual attendance is nearly 10,000.

John Fitzgerald Kennedy National Historic Site, 83 Beals St., Brookline, MA 02446-6010. Phone: 617/566-7037. Fax: 617/730-9884. E-mail: frla_kennedy_nhs@nps.gov. Website: www.nps.gov/jofi. Hours: grounds—sunrise–sunset daily; house—late May–Oct.: 9:30–5 Wed.–Sun.; closed Mon.–Tues. and Nov.–late May. Admission: free.

John F. Kennedy Presidential Library and Museum. The life, achievements, and death of the 35th president of the United States are presented at the John F. Kennedy Presidential Library and Museum in Boston, Massachusetts. The library/museum, established in 1979, is located at Columbia Point in the Dorchester neighborhood, adjacent to the Boston campus of the University of Massachusetts and the Massachusetts Archives. Over 30 million people contributed to the $20 million construction cost.

The building, which was designed by architect I. M. Pei, holds the original papers and correspondence of the Kennedy administration, as well as exhibits and other materials about his life and times. The library contains 32 million documents, 150,000 photographs, 70,000 volumes, 11,000 serial papers, and such other items as personal papers, government records, tape recordings, and political campaign materials. An audiovisual archive also has more than 400,000 still photographs taken from 1863 to 1984, over 7.5 million feet of film from 1910–1983, and 11,000 reels of audio recordings from 1910–1985.

The 38,000-square-foot museum offers an orientation film on Kennedy and a documentary on the Cuban Missile Crisis and exhibits on such subjects as Kennedy's family, the first lady, talks Kennedy gave, his presidential campaign, and the Project Mercury space program. The museum also has partial replicas of the president's Oval Office and the office of his brother, Robert F. Kennedy, while he served as attorney general. In addition, it presents temporary exhibitions and displays Kennedy's sailboat, *Victura*, outside the building from spring through fall.

The museum also has a collection of some 20,000 three-dimensional objects and works of art. They include such items as Kennedy's scrimshaw and ship model collection, gifts from heads of state, the first lady's clothing collection, and paintings and sculpture. In addition to temporary exhibitions, the museum offers formal education programs, public forum series, teacher education institutes, lectures, and an essay contest. The annual library/museum attendance is 220,000.

John Fitzgerald Kennedy Presidential Library and Museum, Columbus Point, Boston, MA 02125. Phones: 617/514-1600 and 866/535-1960. Website: www.jfklibrary.org. Hours: 9–5 daily; closed New Year's Day, Thanksgiving, and Christmas. Admission: adults, $12; seniors and college students, $10; children 13–17, $9; children under 13, free.

John F. Kennedy Hyannis Museum. President John F. Kennedy loved Cape Cod off the coast of Massachusetts. The Kennedy family had a summer home in Hyannis, and he spent many happy days at the beach, playing football with friends, and boating along the coast. The Hyannis Area Chamber of Commerce now has a museum dedicated to him—the John F. Kennedy Hyannis Museum.

The museum, located in the former town hall, was founded in 1992. It features a multimedia exhibit devoted to the days Kennedy spent on Cape Cod relaxing with his family and friends. It has over 80 photographs spanning the 1934–1963 years. They are arranged to reflect Kennedy, his family and friends, and Cape Cod. The museum also has a video narrated by Walter Cronkite that depicts some of the president's experiences on the cape.

John F. Kennedy Hyannis Museum, 397 Main St., Hyannis, MA 02601-3914 (postal address: PO Box 100, 02601-3914). Phone: 508/790-3077. E-mail: info@jfkhyannismuseum.org. Website: www.hyannis.com. Hours: mid-Feb.–mid-Apr. and Nov.–Dec.—9–5 Mon.–Sat., 12–5 Sun.; mid-Apr.–Memorial Day and day after Columbus Day–Oct.—10–4 Mon.–Sat., 12–4 Sun.; late May–Columbus Day—9–5 Mon.–Sat., 12–5 Sun.; closed Jan.–mid-Feb. Admission: adults, $5; children 10–17, $2.50; children under 10, free.

Lyndon B. Johnson

Lyndon B. Johnson National Historical Park. Vice President Lyndon Baines Johnson became the 36th president of the United States when President John F. Kennedy was assassinated in 1963. The Texas senator was asked by Kennedy to be his Democratic running mate after Johnson lost the Democratic nomination for president to Kennedy in the 1960 election. He was sworn in as president on an airplane after the fatal shooting in Dallas and served from 1963 to 1969.

Johnson, who was majority leader in the U.S. Senate, was one of the most powerful public officials in Washington during a long political career. He was one of only four people who served in all four of the major elected federal offices of representative, senator, vice president, and president. After succeeding Kennedy, Johnson was elected president in his own right in 1964 but decided not to run for a second term after he escalated American involvement in the Vietnam War, which resulted in an antiwar movement. He retired to his Texas ranch, which became the Lyndon B. Johnson National Historic Site in 1969 and was redesignated a national historical park in 1980.

Johnson was born in 1908 in a small farmhouse in Stonewall, Texas. The nearest town was Johnson City, which was named for a relative who settled in Texas. Lyndon was the oldest of five children of Samuel Ealy Johnson Jr. and Rebekah Baines. He was president of his 11th grade class and graduated from Johnson City High School in 1924. He then worked his way through Southwestern Texas State Teachers' College (now Texas State University–San Marcos), where he participated in debate and campus politics, edited the campus newspaper, and graduated in 1930.

Johnson taught debating and public speaking at schools in Pearsall and Houston, and became active in politics. His father had served five terms in the Texas legislature and was a close friend of Congressman Sam Rayburn, a rising political figure in the state. After campaigning for state Senator Welly Hopkins in his congressional race, Hopkins recommended Johnson to Congressman Richard M. Kleberg, who appointed him as his legislative secretary. While in that position, Johnson was elected speaker of the "Little Congress," composed of congressional aides, where he cultivated congressmen, newsmen, and lobbyists. He became a surrogate son to Texan Sam Rayburn, and his friends included aides to President Franklin D. Roosevelt and Vice President John Nance Garner of Texas.

In 1934 Johnson and Claudia Alta Taylor, daughter of a wealthy general store owner in Karnack, Texas, were married after eloping. They met during one of his business trips to Austin while he was a congressional secretary and she was earning degrees in history and journalism at the University of Texas. She became known as "Lady Bird" Johnson, a nickname she received as a child when a nursemaid said she was "purty as a bird."

In 1942 Mrs. Johnson bought a financially troubled radio station in Austin, made it profitable, and used the station to develop a successful communications company that later became the $150 million LBJ Holding Company. The Johnsons had two daughters, Lynda Bird Johnson in 1944 and Luci Baines Johnson, born in 1947.

After her husband became president, Mrs. Johnson became active in beautification programs to improve urban and high environments and promoted the Head Start program for preschool children. In 1982 she and actress Helen Hayes founded the Lady Bird Johnson Wildflower Center in Austin to increase the sustainable use and conservation of native wildflower, plants, and landscapes (*see* separate listing in First Ladies section).

In 1935 President Roosevelt named Johnson head of the National Youth Administration in Texas, which created education and job opportunities for young people. Two years later, he ran for Congress in the 10th Congressional District in Texas and was elected. He served from 1937 to 1949. In 1941 he ran for U.S. Senate in a special selection but lost.

After the United States entered World War II in 1941, Johnson was the first congressman to volunteer for active duty. He served for two years in the navy as a lieutenant commander. He asked for a combat assignment but was sent to inspect ships and facilities in Texas and on the West Coast. President Roosevelt, who wanted his own reports on war conditions, then assigned Johnson to a three-man survey team on conditions in the Southwest Pacific. He reported that conditions were deplorable and needed a higher priority, which the region received.

In 1948 Johnson sought a U.S. senatorial seat a second time, and this time he won. In 1953 he became the youngest minority leader in Senate history. The next year he was reelected as senator and served as majority leader when the Democrats won control. Johnson was a skillful Senate leader who was willing to compromise when necessary.

He had a fairly conservative record and developed a friendly working relationship with Republican president Dwight D. Eisenhower.

Johnson decided to run for president in the 1960 election. Northern Democrats, however, initially considered him largely a sectional candidate and too close to Southwestern oil and gas interests. As a result, he lost the Democratic nomination for president to John F. Kennedy, a young Massachusetts senator who was opposed by some because he was a Roman Catholic. When Kennedy asked Johnson to be his running mate, he accepted and was elected vice president as Kennedy defeated Richard Nixon to become president. As vice president, Johnson headed the President's Committee on Equal Employment Opportunities and undertook a number of missions abroad.

After Kennedy was assassinated and Johnson became president in 1963, he used his political skills to obtain passage of the Equal Opportunity Act, which launched the War on Poverty program, and a strong Civil Rights Act—both initiated during the Kennedy administration. Johnson followed with what he called the Great Society program. In 1964 he urged the nation "to build a great society, a place where the meaning of man's life matches the marvels of man's labor."

Johnson then proposed programs in education, health, poverty, urban renewal, beautification, conservation, crime and punishment, depressed areas, and voting rights. Improvements were made in many of the areas, including a Medicare amendment to the Social Security Act that provided health care for the elderly in his second term. It also was during Johnson's tenure that American astronauts orbited the moon in 1968. As a result, Johnson was reelected as president in 1964, overwhelming Republican Barry Goldwater.

Despite the advances, two problems continued to plague the Johnson administration—unrest and rioting in black ghettos and the escalating Vietnam War. Racial tensions increased and resulted in widespread destructive riots in major cities.

At the same time, protests against the war were mounting. The United States was providing military assistance to South Vietnam to prevent a communist takeover of the region. But escalation in troops and bombings was not ending the drawn-out struggle.

When Johnson became president in 1963, the number of American military personnel in Vietnam was 16,000. The number increased to 180,000 by the end of 1963 and to 500,000 by the 1968 election. The cost and the casualties were adversely affecting public support and Great Society programs. As a result, Johnson stopped the bombings and sought to negotiate the end of the war. He also withdrew from running for reelection in 1968 and retired to his ranch in Texas when his term ended. There he died of a heart attack in 1973 at the age of 64, five days before the conclusion of the treaty by which the United States withdrew from Vietnam.

The LBJ Ranch now is part of the 1,570-acre Lyndon B. Johnson National Historical Park (674 acres of which are federal) in Blanco and Gillespie Counties in central Texas. The historical park, founded in 1969, has two distinct visitor areas. The ranch site is near Stonewall, and the other part is in Johnson City, 14 miles to the east. The park includes the birthplace, home, ranch, and final resting place of the 36th president.

The Johnson City section contains the 1901 boyhood home of Johnson and his grandparents' 1867 log cabin settlement, as well as the visitor center for the park and a nature trail. The reconstructed 1888 birthplace, Johnson's one-room schoolhouse, the ranch house where the Johnsons lived (which functioned as the Texas White House during the presidency), the Show Barn and grazing cattle, and the Johnson Family Cemetery are on the Johnson ranch along the Pedernales River.

To see the LBJ Ranch, visitors must take a guided bus tour or obtain a permit for a self-guided auto tour from the visitor center at the adjacent Lyndon B. Johnson State Park and Historic Site (*see* separate listing). The visitor center contains exhibits on Johnson's life and accomplishments, his Great Society, and Mrs. Johnson. Video presentations also are shown on the Johnson administration and Mrs. Johnson's life and achievements. Guided tours are offered of the boyhood home. In addition to self-guided driving tours of the Johnson ranch site, guided tours are offered of the Johnson ranch house, known as the Texas White House. Annual attendance at the historical park is 98,000.

Lyndon B. Johnson National Historical Park, 100 Ladybird Lane, Johnson City, TX 76636, and LBJ Ranch, Stonewall, TX 78671 (postal address: PO Box 329, Johnson City, TX 78636-0329). Phone: 830/868-7128. Faxes: 830/868-0810 and 830/868-7863. E-mail: lyjo_superintendent@nps.gov. Website: www.nps.gov/lyjo. Hours: Johnson City unit—9–5 daily; LBJ Ranch unit—9–4:30 daily; closed New Year's Day, Thanksgiving, and Christmas. Admission: Johnson City unit—free; guided tour of boyhood home, free; LBJ Ranch unit—free; Texas White House tour: adults, $2; children under 18, free.

Lyndon B. Johnson State Park and Historic Site. The 718-acre Lyndon B. Johnson State Park and Historic Site is located across the Pedernales River from the LBJ Ranch (now the Lyndon B. Johnson National Historical Park) in Gillespie County, Texas, west of Johnson City and east of Fredericksburg. It was made possible by friends of

President Johnson who raised the necessary funds to buy the initial 269 acres for the state park in 1965. The park was dedicated in 1970 and later expanded to its present size.

In addition to being located in the heart of the former president's home country, the area has been influenced by three major cultures—Native American, Spanish, and German. The Hill Country was home to Indians first; then came the Spanish conquistadors, followed by German immigrant settlers. All three cultures have had a major impact on the development of the region and the park. Park visitors can study history and nature and engage in picnicking, fishing, swimming, and viewing Texas longhorn cattle, buffalo, white-tailed deer, wild turkey, and other wildlife.

The focal point of the park is the visitor center and its exhibits. It has memorabilia from Johnson's presidency and interactive displays about the land and people that shaped the president. Visitors to the LBJ Ranch also must stop at the visitor center to obtain a permit to drive their cars for a tour. Guided bus tours of the ranch also begin at the visitor center. The Behrens Cabin, a two-room dogtrot cabin built by German immigrant H. C. Behrens in the 1870s, is attached to the visitor center. It has furnishings typical of the period.

Another historic cabin located nearby is the 1860s Danz family log cabin, and just east of the center is the Sauer-Beckmann Farmstead, a living history farm that depicts rural Texas life as it was around 1918. The farm originally was settled by Johann and Christine Sauer and family in the 1860s and then by Herman Beckmann and his sons in the early 1900s. Costumed park employees now do the farm and household chores using period tools and techniques. Guided tours are given of the site.

Lyndon B. Johnson State Park and Historic Site, PO Box 238, Stonewall, TX 78671. Phones: 830/644-2252 and 899/792-1112. Website: www.twd.state.tx.us/spdest/findadest/parks/lyndon_b_johnson. Hours: 8–dusk daily. Admission: free, but fees for activities.

LBJ Presidential Library. The papers, life, and times of President Lyndon B. Johnson are the focus of the LBJ Presidential Library, located on the University of Texas campus in Austin. It is one of the nation's 13 presidential libraries/museums operated by the National Archives and Records Administration.

The Johnson library (formerly the Lyndon Baines Johnson Library and Museum), which was dedicated in 1971, contains 45 million pages of historical documents, including the papers of the 1963–1969 president and those of his close associates and others. The library also has 15,000 volumes and 3,900 serials. The museum collection consists of more than 54,000 objects, with the core being personal items owned, used, bought, or worn by President and Mrs. Johnson. They include clothing worn at the 1964 inauguration, the desk used for the signing of the 1965 Voting Rights Act, chairs from the Oval Office, and thousands of other objects related to their daily lives, official duties, and political events.

Permanent exhibits range from the life and times of President Johnson to displays about the White House and the first lady. A replica of the Oval Office also is located on the top floor of the library. In addition, changing and traveling exhibitions are presented on the Johnson years and American history.

The Johnson library/museum is located on 14 acres adjacent to the LBJ School of Public Affairs, but it is operated independently from the University of Texas. It has guided tours, education programs, lectures, symposia, films, and special events. Annual attendance is 240,000.

LBJ Presidential Library, 2313 Red River St., Austin, TX 78705-5737. Phone: 512/721-0200. Faxes: 512/721-0171 and 512/721-0170. E-mail: johnson.library@nara.gov. Websites: www.lbjlibrary.org and www.lbjlib.utexas.edu. Hours: 9–5 daily; closed Christmas. Admission: free.

LBJ Museum of San Marcos. The LBJ Museum of San Marcos in Texas presents changing exhibitions that usually relate to President Lyndon B. Johnson, a 1930 graduate of Southwest Texas State Teachers College (now Texas State University–San Marcos). Among the exhibitions was a 2012 display on how the 36th president's early life and being a student in San Marcos influenced his later actions in education and civil rights.

The museum, founded in 1997, focuses on Johnson's experiences at the college, his teaching experiences in southern Texas, and their impact in the development of his education and civil rights legislation. As a student at the college, Johnson was a debater, active in campus politics, and editor of the student newspaper. After graduation, he taught public speaking briefly in Texas elementary schools and learned firsthand of the impact of poverty and discrimination on the lives of young school children.

The storefront museum features a collection of about 150 Johnson-related items, including campaign and presidential memorabilia, photographs, newspaper clippings, books, artworks, speeches, and pens he used to sign some education and other important legislation. Other Johnson-related exhibitions have dealt with such topics as LBJ on the election trail, Johnson in Cotulla in 1928–1929, and Lady Bird Johnson's doll collection.

LBJ Museum of San Marcos, 131 N. Guadalupe St., San Marcos, TX 78666-5606 (postal address: PO Box 3, San Marcus, TX 78667-0003). Phone: 512/353-3300. Hours: 10–5 Thurs.–Sat.; closed Sun.–Wed. and major holidays. Admission: free.

Lady Bird Johnson Wildflower Garden. *See* Lady Bird Johnson in First Ladies section.

Richard Nixon

Richard Nixon Presidential Library and Museum. Richard Milhous Nixon, the 37th president of the United States (1969–1974), is the only American president to resign his office. Faced with imminent impeachment, he resigned in 1974 after the FBI determined that some of his aids had spied upon and sabotaged Democratic candidates as part of the infamous Watergate scandal (when five burglars were arrested in 1972 after breaking into Democratic Party headquarters at the Watergate office complex in Washington). The incident was one of a series of major scandals involving Nixon's Committee to Re-elect the President, including a White House "enemies list" and various "dirty tricks."

Despite the scandals and resignation, Nixon has been praised by some for his diplomatic efforts, especially with the Soviet Union and China; for his efforts to end the Vietnam War; and for combining conservative rhetoric with liberal action in some environmental policies. When he was vice president, Nixon also redefined the office by making it a highly visible platform and base for a presidential candidate. He is the only person to have been elected twice as vice president and twice as president.

As president, Nixon created the Environmental Protection Agency and the Occupational Safety and Health Administration, implemented the first federal affirmative action program, imposed wage and price controls, indexed Social Security for inflation, created Supplemental Security Income, eliminated the gold standard, reduced speed limits, began the space shuttle program, started normal diplomatic relations with China, and turned the fighting in the Vietnam War over to the South Vietnamese people.

Because of his impending impeachment and resignation, Nixon initially did not qualify for the federal presidential library and museum program administered by the National Archives and Records Administration. As a result, the Richard Nixon Library and Birthplace in Yorba Linda, California, was built (at the birthplace site) and operated by the private Richard Nixon Foundation in 1990. However, the facility became part of the federal program in 2007 and is now jointly operated, and the name has been changed to the Richard Nixon Presidential Library and Museum. Some 46 million pages of White House records and other materials from the Nixon administration also have been transferred from the National Archives to the Nixon library/museum.

Nixon was born in Yorba Linda in 1913 in a house his father built from a Sears, Roebuck & Co. kit and where Richard spent his childhood. His parents were Francis A. Nixon and Hannah Milhous Nixon, who raised him as a conservative evangelical Quaker. He attended Fullerton and Whittier High Schools, graduating first in his class and showing a penchant for Shakespeare and Latin.

Nixon received a full-tuition scholarship to Harvard University, but his family could not afford to send him because it did not cover living expenses. He attended Whittier College, a local Quaker college, where he was elected student body president and finished second in his class in 1934. He then received a full scholarship from Duke University and graduated from the School of Law. Nixon returned to California, passed the bar exam, and began working in a small law office in nearby La Mirada. There he met Patricia Ryan, a high school teacher, whom he married in 1940. They had two daughters, Tricia and Julie.

During World War II, Nixon served in the navy, becoming a lieutenant commander. He was in the supply corps in the South Pacific after training at Quonset Point, Rhode Island, and Ottumwa, Iowa. Nixon was an excellent poker player and accumulated enough winnings while in the service to finance his first political campaign for Congress. He was elected to the U.S. House of Representatives in California's 12th Congressional District in 1946 and then reelected to a second term. He became known as a member of the House Un-American Activities Committee and for his leading role in the Alger Hiss case.

In 1952 Nixon was nominated by the Republicans as vice president and was elected with President Dwight D. Eisenhower. He was the first vice president to actually run the government temporarily. He did so three times when President Eisenhower was ill in 1955 and 1956 and suffered a stroke in 1957. He ran for president in 1960, only to lose to Senator John F. Kennedy in an extremely close race. It didn't help Nixon when Eisenhower was asked what policy decisions Nixon had helped make and he replied, "Give me a week and I might think of one."

Nixon relied heavily on television in his political campaigns, although this sometimes backfired. When he was accused of misappropriating money out of a business fund for personal use, he defended himself in an emotional speech by providing a personal summary of his finances and giving his "Checkers" speech—saying he would not return the gift of a cocker spaniel named Checkers because his daughter loved it. In this case, it worked to his advantage, resulting in public support and prompting Eisenhower to keep him on the ticket.

Nixon's loss to Kennedy in the presidential election, however, was attributed partly to his "5 o'clock shadow" and sweaty, uncomfortable appearance, as opposed to Kennedy's more relaxed look, in a television debate. In 1962, after Nixon lost the California governor's race, he accused media—including television—of favoring his opponent, Pat Brown. He said it was his last press conference and "you don't have Dick Nixon to kick around any more."

But it was not true. Nixon had a difficult time with television and the press the remainder of his life—and especially after Watergate. After the loss in California, he moved to New York City, where he became a senior partner in a leading law firm. During the congressional elections in 1966, he traveled around the country in support of Republican candidates. And he made a remarkable political comeback in the 1968 presidential election when he was nominated by the Republican Party and defeated Democrat nominee Hubert H. Humphrey and independent candidate George Wallace.

The Nixon administration came to an end in 1974 when Nixon resigned amid the Watergate scandal. He was given a blanket pardon by Gerald R. Ford, the vice president who succeeded him as president. The pardon hurt Ford politically and was cited as one of the reasons for his defeat in the 1976 election.

In the years that followed, Nixon worked to rehabilitate his public image with some success. He became an elder statesman in foreign affairs. He also wrote eight books on world affairs after his departure from the White House. He died in 1994 of a major heart attack at his home in Park Ridge, New Jersey. He and his wife, Pat Nixon, who died 10 months earlier of lung cancer, now are buried on the grounds of the Richard Nixon Presidential Library and Museum in Yorba Linda, California, where Nixon was born.

The 52,000-square-foot Nixon library/museum was founded in 1990 by the Richard Nixon Foundation as the Richard Nixon Library and Birthplace. The grounds include Nixon's birth house as well as the 38,000-square-foot Loker and Annenberg centers with a replica of the White House East Room and a special events room. It became part of the federal system of presidential libraries and museums administered by the National Archives and Records Administration in 2007.

The library houses Nixon presidential materials (texts, photographs, sound, and movie images). They include the 46 million pages of White House records and other materials received from the National Archives, which has duplicates of White House tapes in the Nixon Library at the archives in College Park, Maryland.

Tours of the Nixon museum began in the auditorium, which contains vintage campaign films, news footage, and historically significant television appearances by President Nixon. This leads to galleries that trace Nixon's life, achievements, and times, with exhibits that display a 12-foot section of the Berlin Wall, Nixon's private study, the presidential helicopter used in 1961–1976, the 1967 Lincoln Continental limousine used by Nixon and two other presidents, life-size papier-mâché statues of 10 world leaders, and re-creations of the Lincoln Sitting Room and East Room of the White House. The museum also has an exhibit on First Lady Pat Nixon, and the house in which Nixon was born is located on the grounds near the museum. Annual attendance has averaged about 70,000.

Richard Nixon Presidential Library and Museum, 18001 Yorba Linda Blvd., Yorba Linda, CA 92886-3949. Phone: 714/993-5075. Fax: 714/528-0544. E-mail: rexjht@msn.com. Website: www.nixonlibrary.gov. Hours: 10–5 Mon.–Sat., 11–5 Sun.; closed New Year's Day, Thanksgiving, and Christmas. Admission: adults, $11; seniors, $8.50; college students and active military, $6.95; children 7–11, $4.75; children under 7, free.

Gerald R. Ford

Gerald R. Ford Presidential Museum. Vice President Gerald R. Ford became president of the United States after Richard Nixon resigned in 1974. He was the 38th president and served only from 1974 to 1977. He was the only person who served as vice president and president who had not been elected to either office. Ford, Republican minority leader of the U.S. House of Representatives, was the first person appointed vice president under the 25th Amendment after Spiro Agnew, who had been elected with Nixon, resigned in 1973 after pleading no contest to income tax evasion. After serving only nine months as vice president, Ford filled the remaining three years of Nixon's second term as president. When he ran for president in 1976, he lost to Democrat Jimmy Carter in a close election.

Ford actually was born with a different name—Leslie Lynch King Jr. He was born in Omaha in 1913, the son of Leslie Lynch King and Dorothy Ayer Gardner, who separated two weeks after his birth and divorced later that year. He and his mother moved to Grand Rapids, Michigan, where her parents lived. In 1916 Dorothy King married Gerald R. Ford, a paint salesman, and the couple began calling her son Gerald R. Ford Jr., although his name was not changed legally until 1935.

Ford grew up in a close-knit family that included three younger half-brothers, Thomas, Richard, and James. He went to South High School in Grand Rapids, where he made the honor society and was an all-city and all-state football player. He also was an Eagle Scout and worked in the family paint business and at a local restaurant. In 1931–1935 Ford attended the University of Michigan, where he majored in economics and received a Bachelor of Arts degree.

Ford was a gifted athlete, playing on the university's national championship football teams in 1932 and 1933. He was voted the most valuable player in 1934 and played in two all-star games. He received offers from several professional football teams but became boxing coach and assistant football coach at Yale University, where he earned a law degree in 1941.

Ford's first involvement in politics was in 1940 when he worked on Wendell Willkie's presidential campaign. He returned to Grand Rapids, passed the bar exam, formed a law partnership, and became active in Republican political activities as the United States entered World War II. He joined the U.S. Naval Reserve as an ensign in 1942 and was assigned to the USS *Monterey*, a light aircraft carrier.

Ford initially was athletic director and gunnery officer, and then assistant navigator. The carrier took part in most of the major operations in the South Pacific, and Ford was nearly swept overboard in a typhoon in the Philippine Sea in 1944. The ship was badly damaged in the storm and resulting fire and had to be taken out of service. Ford spent the rest of the war ashore and left the service as a lieutenant commander in 1946.

When Ford returned to Grand Rapids, he became a partner in a prestigious local law firm. His experiences during the war also caused him to change his previous isolationist leanings to an international outlook, and he decided to challenge the Republican isolationist incumbent in the U.S. House of Representatives in the 1948 election. He won the nomination and the election.

While campaigning, Ford married Elizabeth Anne Bloomer Warren, a department store fashion consultant. They had four children. Mrs. Ford, better known as Betty Ford, became a politically active first lady. She was noted for raising breast cancer awareness after a mastectomy, cofounding the Betty Ford Center (a substance abuse and alcohol addiction treatment center primarily serving women), and supporting other women's issues, including the Equal Rights Amendment.

Gerald R. Ford served in the House of Representatives from 1949 to 1973, being reelected 12 times. He described himself as a moderate in domestic affairs, an internationalist in foreign affairs, and a conservative in fiscal policy. As his reputation as a legislator grew, he declined offers to run for the U.S. Senate and governorship of Michigan.

In 1961 Ford was part of the House revolt by the "Young Turks," a group of progressive Republicans who felt the older leadership was stagnating. He defeated Charles Hoeven of Iowa as chairman of the House Republication Conference. This was followed in 1965 by replacing Charles Halleck as House minority leader, a position he held for eight years. Ford led the Republican opposition to many of President Lyndon B. Johnson's programs, ranging from social welfare to Vietnam War escalation.

In the 1968 and 1972 elections, Ford was a loyal supporter of Richard Nixon and was considered for vice president but not nominated. His ultimate goal was to become speaker of the House of Representatives. However, the Republicans never did obtain a majority in the House during his tenure.

In 1973 Ford was appointed to an even more important position by President Nixon after Spiro Agnew resigned as vice president after being charged with income tax evasion and pleading no contest. It was followed by President Nixon's Watergate scandals, his resignation, and Ford succeeding Nixon as president in 1974. Ford then granted Nixon a pardon prior to the filing of any formal criminal charges, which many opposed and hurt Ford politically when he sought election as president and lost in 1976.

As president, Ford was faced with a Congress that was increasing assertive of its rights and powers and a Democratic congressional majority. But he was able through frequent use of the veto to control spending and compromise to pass legislation that cut taxes, decontrolled energy, reformed antitrust law, and deregulated railroads and securities.

In foreign affairs, the policies of detente with the Soviet Union, "shuttle diplomacy" in the Middle East, and the phasing out of the Vietnam War continued. Among the other developments were the Helsinki human rights agreements, East European national boundary settlements, trade and arms negotiations, an international economic summit meeting, and the Apollo-Soyuz joint manned space flight. Two unsuccessful assassination attempts were made by women in California.

After leaving the White House in 1977, President and Mrs. Ford moved to California and built a house in Rancho Mirage. He wrote his memoir, gave speeches, and continued to be active in political activities. Betty Ford, who was one of the most candid first ladies in history, continued to be active in women's and other issues. She founded the Betty Ford Center for substance abuse and alcohol addiction in 1982 and spoke out on such topics as feminism, equal pay, sex, drugs, abortion, gun control, and the Equal Rights Amendment.

President and Mrs. Ford both died in Rancho Mirage when they were 93. The president suffered a heart attack in 2006, and Mrs. Ford died of natural causes in 2011. Both are buried on the grounds of the Gerald R. Ford Museum in Grand Rapids. They both received the Congressional Gold Medal in 1998, and she also was presented the Presidential Medal of Freedom in 1991.

Ford is the only U.S. president to have his federally operated presidential library and museum in two locations—the Gerald E. Ford Library on the campus of the University of Michigan in Ann Arbor (*see* separate listing) and the Gerald R. Ford Presidential Museum in Grand Rapids. All the presidential libraries and museums now must be located at one site.

The Ford museum, which opened to the public in 1981, has hands-on, interactive, video, and holographic exhibits on President Ford's life and presidency. Visitors can take a holographic tour of the White House, experience a day in the Oval Office through a sound and light show, and travel around the world with the president and Secretary of State Henry Kissinger by video.

The museum also has a Watergate gallery with a multiscreen historical presentation and some of the actual burglary tools, and an interactive Cabinet Room where visitors can take part in presidential decision making. Other exhibits focus on lives and achievements of President and Mrs. Ford. The museum also presents temporary exhibitions, guided tours, and programs and special events that range from a 1940s fashion show to activities for school children. Annual attendance is 204,000.

Gerald R. Ford Presidential Museum, 303 Pearl St., N.W., Grand Rapids, MI 49504-5353. Phones: 616/254-0400 and 616/254-0367. Fax: 616/254-0386. E-mail: ford.museum@nara.gov. Website: www.fordlibrarymuseum.gov. Hours: 9–5 daily; closed New Year's Day, Thanksgiving, and Christmas. Admission: adults, $7; seniors and military, $6; college students, $5; youth 6–18, $3; children under 6, free.

Gerald R. Ford Library. Unlike other federally operated presidential libraries and museums, the Gerald R. Ford Library is located at a different location than the Ford museum. The library is on the campus of the University of Michigan in Ann Arbor, where Ford went to college, while the Gerald R. Ford Presidential Museum is 130 miles away in his hometown of Grand Rapids, Michigan. All presidential libraries and museums operated by the National Archives and Records Administration now must be at the same site.

When he was a congressman, Ford began donating his papers to the Bentley Historical Library at the university in 1961. As he was finishing his presidential term, he offered to give his White House materials to a presidential library that would be built at the university and administered by the National Archives. The library was founded in 1977 and dedicated in 1981, the same year the museum opened in Grand Rapids. The library and the museum have the same director.

The 50,000-square-foot library has 25 million pages of materials. The core consists of the 1974–1977 presidential papers of President Ford and his White House staff. The library also has President Ford's pre- and postpresidential papers and the papers of Betty Ford, as well as collections of federal records, personal papers of former government officials, interviews of researchers of the period, and materials of private individuals associated with various issues. The annual attendance is 750.

Gerald R. Ford Library, 1000 Beal Ave., Ann Arbor, MI 48109-2114. Phone: 734/205-0555. Fax: 734/205-0573. Website: www.fordlibrarymuseum.gov. Hours: 8:45–4:45 Mon.–Fri.; closed Sat.–Sun. and major holidays. Admission: free.

Gerald R. Ford Conservation Center. The Nebraska State Historical Society has a conservation laboratory in Omaha named in honor of President Gerald R. Ford, with an exhibit gallery on the life and accomplishments of the 37th president. It is located adjacent to the birth site of the only American president born in the state.

The center, which opened in 1995, was made possible by businessman and philanthropist James M. Paxson. In 1974 he purchased the site in Hanscom Park where Ford was born and converted it into a park dedicated to President Ford. Paxson then provided funds to the historical society foundation for the construction and operation of a conservation center in Ford's name adjoining the park. The center conserves and preserves museum artifacts, textiles, paper, rare books, manuscripts, and photographs for the historical society and other museums, libraries, and facilities.

Gerald R. Ford Conservation Center, Nebraska State Historical Society, 1326 S. 32nd St., Omaha, NE 68105-2044. Phone: 402/595-1180. Fax: 402/595-1178. E-mail: naha.grfcc@nebraska.gov. Website: www.nebraskahistory.org. Hours: by appointment; closed major holidays. Admission: free.

Betty Ford Alpine Garden. *See* Betty Ford in First Ladies section.

Jimmy Carter

Jimmy Carter National Historic Site. James Earl Carter Jr., who preferred to be called Jimmy, was a Georgia peanut farmer who became a state senator, governor, and the 39th president of the United States (1977–1981). He defeated Gerald R. Ford for the presidency in 1976 after Ford succeeded President Richard Nixon, who resigned as a result of the Watergate scandal. Carter also became the only American president to receive the Nobel Peace Prize after leaving office.

While president, Carter emphasized human rights and worked to promote peace in the Camp David Accords, Panama Canal treaties, Strategic Arms Limitation Talks with the Soviet Union (SALT II), diplomatic relations with China, and treaty of peace between Egypt and Israel.

After losing his reelection bid to Ronald Reagan in 1980, Carter and his wife, Rosalynn, founded the Carter Center, a nonprofit organization to advance human rights, resolve conflicts, promote democracy, and overcome disease. He also has traveled widely to conduct peace negotiations, observe elections, and improve health in developing nations. In addition, the Carters volunteer one week a year for Habitat for Humanity, which helps needy people to renovate and build homes for themselves.

Among Carter's other actions as president were the return of the Panama Canal Zone to Panama; a national energy policy that included conservation, price control, and new technology; major environmental protection legislation; deregulation of energy, transportation, communications, and finance; and new cabinet-level Departments of Energy and Education. But his tenure also was marked by the 1979–1981 Iran hostage crisis and the U.S. boycott of the Moscow Olympics, as well as such other events as the Three Mile Island nuclear accident, 1980 eruption of Mount St. Helens, and Soviet invasion of Afghanistan.

Carter was the first U.S. president born in a hospital. He was born in 1924 in the small Georgia town of Plains. He was the eldest of four children of James Earl Carter, a prominent farmer and businessman, and Bessie Lillian Gordy Carter, a registered nurse. Jimmy was a gifted student who also became a basketball star at Plains High School. He went to Georgia Southwestern College after high school and in 1943 was admitted to the U.S. Naval Academy. In 1946 he married his longtime acquaintance Eleanor Rosalynn Smith, who was known as Rosalynn. She later became his partner in operating the family's peanut farm and seed and farm supply warehouse and closest adviser when he became president. They had four children.

After receiving a Bachelor of Science degree at the academy, Carter served on surface ships and diesel-electric submarines in the Atlantic and Pacific fleets. He liked the navy and planned to make it a career, joining the fledgling nuclear submarine program. In 1952 he led an American team that helped the Canadians control an experimental reactor partial meltdown at the Clark River nuclear laboratory. Carter's father died the following year, and he resigned his naval commission because he was needed to run the family peanut farm and seed and farm supply company in Plains.

Carter found the family business had financial problems and was forced to live in public housing, becoming the only president who ever lived in subsidized housing for the poor. But he gradually expanded the peanut and farm supply business and became quite wealthy. In the 1960s Carter started serving on school, hospital, and library boards, and in 1961 he was elected a state senator. He served two terms and then ran for governor of Georgia in 1966, only to lose in a three-man race.

When Carter ran again in 1970, he was elected governor and served in 1971–1974. While in office, he told Georgians, "The time for racial discrimination is over. No poor, rural, weak, or black person should ever have to bear the additional burden of being deprived of the opportunity of an education, a job, or simple justice."

In 1976 Carter sought the Democratic Party nomination but was given little chance. Originally considered only a sectional candidate, his campaigning and speeches convinced the Democratic Convention to nominate him on the first ballot and enough voters to elect him as president. He served from 1977 to 1981 but lost the 1980 reelection to Ronald Reagan.

President Carter returned to Plains, Georgia, after leaving the White House. In 1982 he became a university distinguished professor at Emory University and founded the Carter Center with his wife in Atlanta. The permanent facilities of the center, including the Jimmy Carter Library and Museum, were dedicated in 1986. The Jimmy Carter National Historic Site, operated by the National Park Service, also was established in Carter's birthplace and hometown of Plains.

The national historic site includes the Carter residence, boyhood farm, the school he attended, the town railroad depot that served as his campaign headquarters during the 1976 presidential race, and the current home and compound of the Carters. A museum and visitor center are located in the former 1921–1979 Plains High School. It contains exhibits on the lives of Jimmy and Rosalynn Carter and a video on the life and accomplishments of the former president. One of the school's classrooms, the principal's office, and the auditorium also have been restored to look as they did when Carter attended in the 1930s.

Carter's boyhood home from the age of four in 1928 until he went to college in 1941 also has been restored to the way it looked before electricity was installed in 1938, and the train depot has been converted to a museum with exhibits on Carter's campaign for president. The Cutler home and compound, where the family has lived since 1961, is not open to the public. The historic site also will be the future grave site for the President and Mrs. Carter.

Jimmy Carter National Historic Site, 300 N. Bond St., Plains, GA 31780-5562. Phone: 229/824-4104. Fax: 229/824-3441. Website: www.nps.gov/jica. Hours: high school museum/visitor center—9–5 daily; depot museum—9–4:30 daily; boyhood farm—10–5 daily; Carter home—closed to public; all facilities closed New Year's Day, Thanksgiving, and Christmas. Admission: free.

Jimmy Carter Library and Museum. The Jimmy Carter Library and Museum at the Carter Center in Atlanta, Georgia, is the presidential library and museum of the 39th president, administered by the National Archives and Records Administration. Founded in 1986, the 69,750-square-foot library/museum has approximately 27 million pages of White House material and papers of administration associates and 15,269 square feet of exhibits on the life and achievements of President Carter.

The library materials include documents, memoranda, correspondence, and other papers, as well as approximately 500,000 photographs and hundreds of hours of films and audio and video tapes. The exhibits include a replica of the Oval Office, gifts received from foreign heads of state and others, and exhibits of significant events occurring during Carter's life and political career, including such other activities as the Carter Center peace, human rights, and health efforts; Habitat for Humanity house building; and 2002 Nobel Peace Prize. President Carter also is the author of 25 books. Annual attendance is 82,000.

Jimmy Carter Library and Museum, 441 Freedom Pkwy., Atlanta, GA 30307-1497. Phone: 404/865-7100. Fax: 404/865-7102. E-mail: carter.library@nara.gov. Website: www.jimmycarterlibrary.gov. Hours 9–4:45 Mon.–Sat., 12–4:45 Sun.; closed New Year's Day, Thanksgiving, and Christmas. Admission: adults, $8; seniors, military, and students, $6; children under 17, free.

Ronald Reagan

Ronald Reagan Presidential Library and Museum. Ronald Wilson Reagan, a motion picture, radio, and television actor, was elected the 40th president of the United States in 1980. He was a Democrat who became a Republican and defeated incumbent Jimmy Carter after serving as president of the Screen Actors Guild and governor of California. The 69-year-old Reagan, who became the oldest person elected president, served from 1981 to 1989, surviving an assassination attempt after only 69 days in office.

During his first term as president, Reagan sought to jump-start a stagnant economy with new political and economic initiatives. He advocated supply-side economic policies, which were called "Reaganomics." They reduced tax rates to increase economic growth, controlled the money supply to reduce inflation, deregulated the economy, and reduced government spending. The nation suffered economically in 1981–1982, but then the economy bounced back, with the unemployment rate dropping from 7.5 to 5.3 percent, poverty decreasing from 14 to 12.8 percent, and inflation falling from 13.6 to 4.1 percent. At the same time, the United States went from the world's largest creditor to the largest debtor nation as the debt rose to $2.6 trillion.

Reagan's second term focused on foreign affairs. He sought to achieve "peace through strength." He took a hard line with the Soviet Union, which he called an "evil empire." Reagan replaced the cold war détente approach of three prior presidents with an anticommunist program that included limiting high technology trade with the Soviet Union, increasing American military expenditures, and assisting anti-Soviet factions around the world, including Afghanistan and Poland. Relations with the Soviets improved as a Russian reformer, Mikhail Gorbachev, became the Soviet general secretary. After a number of meetings, Reagan and Gorbachev agree to a nuclear weapons decrease.

Among the other military actions during Reagan's tenure were the bombing of Libya after a terrorist attack, the invasion of Grenada to free medical students, a bombing in which 240 U.S. soldiers were killed during the 1993 Lebanese civil war, and the illegal Iran-Contra arms shipments to Nicaragua. In legislation, he expanded Social Security, extended voter rights, overhauled civil rights, and reformed the tax structure. He also fired airport flight controllers for endangering air travel by going on strike, and it was during his tenure that seven astronauts died in the 1986 *Challenger* space shuttle explosion.

Ronald Wilson Reagan was born in a second-floor apartment above a commercial building in Tampico, Illinois, in 1911 to Jack Reagan, a salesman, and Nellie Wilson Reagan. He had an older brother, Neil, who became an advertising executive. The family moved frequently, going to Monmouth, Galesburg, and Chicago before returning to Tampico in 1919 and living above a variety store. After the store closed in 1920, the Reagans moved to Dixon, where he attended Dixon High School and developed an interest in acting, sports, and storytelling. It also is where he had his first job as a lifeguard and reportedly made 77 rescues.

Reagan enrolled at Eureka College and majored in economics and sociology. He was active in campus politics, sports, and theater. Reagan played on the football team, served as captain of the swim team, and was elected student body president. While student president, he led a student revolt against the college president when he tried to cut back the faculty. After graduating in 1932, he was hired to broadcast home football games at the University of Iowa. A staff announcer's job in Davenport followed, and then he broadcast Chicago Cubs baseball games from a Des Moines radio station, re-creating play-by-play accounts of games received by wire.

In 1937 Reagan joined the Army Enlisted Reserve and took a screen test while traveling with the Cubs in California. The screen test led to a seven-year contract with Warner Brothers studios. He spent the first few years in "B films," appearing in 19 films by 1939. He first attracted attention playing the role of George "The Gipper" Gipp in the *Knute Rockne, All American* film. His favorite role was as a double amputee in *King's Row* in 1942.

It also was in the 1930s that Reagan met and married actress Jane Wyman. They were married in 1940 and had three children—one died in infancy and one was adopted. They were divorced in 1949 after arguments about his political ambitions while president of the Screen Actors Guild, an actors' union. In 1952 Reagan was remarried to actress Nancy Davis, who contacted him at the actors' guild after her name appeared on a Hollywood communist blacklist (she had been mistaken for another Nancy Davis). They had two children, Patti and Ron, and a long, happy life together.

After the Japanese attack on Pearl Harbor, Reagan was among the army reservists called up in 1942. Because of his nearsightedness, he was classified for limited service only and not sent overseas. He spent World War II working in the First Motion Picture Unit and was promoted to first lieutenant and then captain. After the war, he acted in many motion pictures but never regained his "star" status. His last film was in 1964.

In 1941 Reagan was elected to the Screen Actors Guild board of directors. After the war, he became a vice president and was elected president in a special election in 1947 after the president and six board members resigned following a dispute over adoption of conflict-of-interest bylaws. He served seven additional one-year terms from 1947 to 1952 and in 1959. He led the actors' union during troublesome and controversial years marked by labor-management disputes, the Taft-Harley Act, House un-American Activities Committee hearings, and a Hollywood blacklist. A fervent anticommunist, Reagan provided names of actors he believed to be communists to the FBI and testified before the House Un-American Activities Committee in the late 1940s. When Reagan began to receive fewer motion picture roles in the 1950s, he turned to television, serving as host of *General Electric Theater*, a popular weekly drama series, and then host and performer on *Death Valley Days*.

Reagan was a liberal Democrat during the early part of his life and a great admirer of Franklin D. Roosevelt and supporter of New Deal policies. He began to change his views in the 1940s after becoming embroiled in disputes over communism in the film industry. His conservative views grew in the 1950s after meeting actress Nancy Davis, a Republican whom he later married, and while serving as General Electric's goodwill ambassador from 1954 to 1962 with a conservative, probusiness message as part of his television relationship. He formally became a Republican in the 1960s and gave a rousing endorsement for Republican presidential candidate Barry Goldwater at the 1964 Republican Convention. As a result, he was urged to run for governor of California, which he reluctantly agreed to do.

In 1966 Reagan became the Republican candidate for governor of California and was elected and then reelected in 1970. In 1980 he received the Republican nomination for president and selected George Bush, former Texas congressman and United Nations ambassador, as has running mate. Reagan was elected by voters who were troubled by unemployment, inflation, and the 444-day confinement of 52 Americans in Iran. As it turned out, the hostages were being freed as Reagan was being inaugurated. But only 69 days after becoming president, he and three others (his press secretary, a Secret Service agent, and a policeman) were shot and seriously wounded by John Hinckley Jr. outside a downtown Washington hotel. Reagan is the only president to survive after being shot in an assassination attempt.

After Reagan left the White House in 1989, he and his wife returned to California, where they had a ranch in Santa Barbara, and purchased a home in Bel Air. He continued to keep active in politics with speeches and endorsements but was diagnosed with Alzheimer's disease in 1994. Reagan died of pneumonia at the age of 93 at his Bel Air home in 2004. He is buried in a tomb on the grounds of the Ronald Reagan Presidential Library and Museum in Simi Valley, California.

The Reagan library/museum was dedicated in 1991 by the Ronald Reagan Presidential Foundation. It now has the largest annual attendance of the 13 federal presidential libraries and museums administered by the National Archives and Records Administration, with over 300,000 visitors. It also is the largest of the presidential libraries and museums, covering 243,000 square feet. The complex originally was 153,000 square feet, and then expanded 90,000 square feet in 2005 for the Air Force One Pavilion that houses the Boeing 707 plane used by seven presidents from 1973 to 2001.

The library holds 50 million pages of presidential documents, over 1.6 million photographs, 500,000 feet of motion picture film, and tens of thousands of audio and video tapes. It also houses Reagan's personal papers, which include materials from his eight years as governor of California. The museum has exhibits on Reagan's life and accomplishments, ranging from his childhood, film career, and military service to his marriage to Nancy Davis, political career, and presidency. It also presents changing temporary exhibitions. Among the objects displayed in the museum are Reagan's 1965 Ford Mustang, the desk he used as governor, campaign materials, his inauguration suit, the table from the White House Situation Room, a full-scale replica of the Oval Office, news footage of the 1981 assassination attempt, and information on the proposed Strategic Defense Initiative (known as the "Star Wars" program). In addition to Air Force One in the new wing, the museum has an F-14 Tomcat on the grounds. The Reagan tomb memorial is located near a section of the Berlin Wall that Reagan helped bring down and a replica of the White House South Lawn.

Ronald Reagan Presidential Library and Museum, 40 President Dr., Simi Valley, CA 93065-0699. Phone: 800/410-8354. Fax: 805/577-4074. Websites: www.reagan.utexas.edu and www.reganfoundation.org. Hours: 10–5 daily; closed New Year's Day, Thanksgiving, and Christmas. Admission: adults, $15; seniors, $12; youth, 11–17, $9; children under 11, free.

Ronald Reagan Birthplace and Museum. The commercial building in Tampico, Illinois, where President Ronald Reagan was born in 1911 now is the Ronald Reagan Birthplace and Museum. The Reagan family lived in an apartment on the second floor of the two-story brick building, which had a tavern on the first floor. The Reagans moved to a house a few months later, and the building was used for other purposes over the years. The building has been restored and is located in the Main Street Historic District in Tampico. The museum is operated by the Tampico Historical Society.

The Graham Building, which was constructed in 1896, was the home of Ronald's parents, Jack and Nellie Reagan, from 1906 to 1911. They had two sons, Ronald and an older brother, John, while living in the apartment. The father worked as a salesman in a variety store across the street from the apartment. The family moved to a house when the store closed, and then to Dixon, Illinois, in 1920. The commercial building housed the tavern on the first floor from 1896 to 1915, when it became a bakery, and then a bank from 1919 to 1931. The first floor has been restored as the First National Bank, and the second floor to the 1911 period when Ronald Regan was born there. The apartment contains displays, photographs, and artifacts related to the Reagans. The historic district is listed on the National Register of Historic Places. The museum's annual attendance is 2,500.

Ronald Reagan Birthplace and Museum, 111 S. Main St., Tampico, IL 61283 (postal address: PO Box 344, Tampico, IL 61283-0344). Phones: 815/622-8705 and 815/438-2130. E-mails: reaganbirthplace@thewisp.net and garytjoan@thewisp.net. Website: www.tampicohistoricsociety.com/r_reagan_birthplace_museum. Hours: Apr.–Oct.—10–4 Mon.–Sat., 1–4 Sun., and by appointment; Mar.—10–4 Sat.–Sun. and by appointment; closed Mon.–Fri. in Mar., Nov.–Feb. (except. Feb. 6), Easter, and Mother's Day. Admission: free.

Ronald Reagan Boyhood Home and Visitors Center. The house in Dixon, Illinois, where Ronald Reagan and his parents and brother lived from 1920 to 1923 is now the Ronald Reagan Boyhood Home and Visitors Center. The Reagan family moved from Tampico, Illinois, when Ronald was nine years old after his father lost his job as a salesman at a variety store that closed. The Reagans rented the house for $15 a month for three years before moving to another site in Dixon. The Reagan family rented every home they lived in until Ronald bought them their first home in California.

The home, which also serves as a visitor center for the community, was built in 1891. It became a historic house museum in 1980 after being restored with furnishings of the 1920s period. Admission includes a video presentation, guided tour of the house, and access to the visitor center and gift shop. Annual attendance is over 7,000.

Ronald Reagan Boyhood Home and Visitors Center, 816 S. Hennepin Ave., Dixon, IL 61021-3646 (postal address: Ronald Reagan Home Foundation, PO Box 816, Dixon, Il 61021-0816). Phone: 815/288-5176. Fax: 815/288-3642. E-mail: reagan1@gries.net. Website: www.ronaldreaganhome.com. Hours: Apr.–Nov. 15—10–4 Mon.–Sat., 1–4 Sun.; closed mid-Nov.–Mar. and Easter. Admission: adults, $5; children under 12, free.

Ronald W. Reagan Museum at Eureka College. The Ronald W. Reagan Museum at Eureka College in Eureka, Illinois, has approximately 10,000 personal and public objects relating to Reagan's college days, movie and television career, and service as governor of California and president of the United States. It is the largest collection of Reagan materials outside of the Ronald Reagan Presidential Library and Museum (*see* separate listing). Reagan was a 1932 graduate of Eureka College.

Nearly 1,000 pieces relating to Reagan's life and career are displayed at any one time in the museum, housed in the Donald B. Cerf Center. The Reagan family made the two largest donations of items in 1975 and 1980. The museum has Reagan quotations on the walls, and plaques near the ceiling offer a time line of life events. The Ronald Reagan Peace Garden with a bust of Reagan by Lonnie Stewart also is located at the college. The garden was a gift of Mr. and Mrs. David J. Vaughan in 2000 on the 18th anniversary of Reagan's speech about world peace at Eureka College. A section of the Berlin Wall also is located in the garden.

Ronald W. Reagan Museum at Eureka College, 300 E. College Ave., Eureka, IL 61530. Phones: 309/467-6407 and 309/467-6477. E-mail: jmorris@eureka.edu. Website: www.reagan.eureka.edu. Hours: late Aug.–May—8 a.m.–8 p.m. Mon.–Fri., 10–6 Sat., 12–8 Sun.; closed major holidays; June–late Aug.—8–4 Mon.–Fri., 10–2 Sat.; closed Sun. and major holidays. Admission: free.

George H. W. Bush

George Bush Presidential Library and Museum. George Herbert Walker Bush, the 41st president of the United States, was a member of a family that was a political dynasty in New England. His father was a powerful U.S. senator, and one of his sons became president and another was elected governor of Florida. He served as president in 1989–1993 after a political career as a congressman, ambassador, director of central intelligence, and vice president.

Bush became involved in politics in 1967 after founding his own oil company and ran for president unsuccessfully in 1980 after holding various federal government positions. He lost the Republican nomination to movie actor Ronald Reagan but was chosen by Reagan to be the vice presidential nominee. They won the election, and Bush served as vice president for two terms in the Reagan administration. As the Republican candidate for president in 1988, he defeated Michael Dukakis, his Democratic opponent, but served only one term. He lost the 1992 reelection to Bill Clinton, largely because of the nation's economic problems and reneging on a 1988 campaign promise not to raise taxes.

Bush was president during a period when the Soviet Union was dissolving. The Berlin Wall fell in 1989, and the USSR underwent major changes two years later and new nations began to evolve from former Soviet territories. In other foreign affairs, Bush sent American troops to Panama to overthrow General Manuel Noriega, who was threatening the security of the Panama Canal and Americans living there, and he rallied allied nations to help defeat Saddam Hussein's Iraqi forces in Desert Storm after Hussein invaded Kuwait and threatened Saudi Arabia. Despite these successes, Bush was not able to overcome voter discontent about a faltering economy, inner-city violence, and high deficit spending, leading to his reelection defeat in 1992.

George Herbert Walker Bush was born in 1924 in Milton, Massachusetts, to Senator Prescott Sheldon Bush and Dorothy Walker Bush. Shortly after George's birth, the family moved to Greenwich, Connecticut, where he began his formal education at the Greenwich Country Day School. In 1936 he enrolled at the Phillips Academy in Andover, Massachusetts, where he was president of the senior class and a community fund-raising group, on the school newspaper editorial board, and captain of the varsity baseball and soccer teams.

After Japan attacked Pearl Harbor in 1941, Bush decided to join the U.S. Navy after graduation from Phillips Academy in 1942. He became a naval aviator at the age of 18. He was commissioned an ensign in the U.S. Naval Reserve after completing training and assigned to a torpedo squadron as a photographic officer in 1943. The squadron was based on the USS *San Jacinto* as a member of a task force that was victorious in the Battle of the Philippine Sea, one of the largest air battles of World War II.

Bush was promoted to lieutenant (junior grade) and then took part in operations against the Japanese in the Bonin Islands in 1944. He piloted one of four Grumman TBM Avengers that attacked the Japanese installations on Chichijima. The plane was hit by intense antiaircraft fire while completing its bombing, and Bush bailed out over water several miles from the island. He was rescued by the USS *Finback* submarine. He returned to the *San Jacinto* and participated in other Philippine operations until his squadron was replaced and sent home. Bush, who flew in 58 combat missions, received the Distinguished Flying Cross, three Air Medals, and the Presidential Unit Citation awarded to the *San Jacinto*. He was reassigned to Norfolk Navy Base in Virginia to train torpedo pilots and then moved to the Naval Air Station Grosse Ile in Michigan before being honorably discharged after the Japanese surrender in 1945.

While he was at the air station in Michigan, Bush married Barbara Pierce, with whom he had five children, including George W. Bush, who became the 43rd president, and Jeb Bush, who was elected governor of Florida. After leaving the service, he became a student at Yale University, where he was enrolled in an accelerated program that allowed him to graduate in two and a half years instead of four. He was president of his fraternity and captain of the baseball team. He graduated in 1948 with a degree in economics and moved his family to West Texas, where his father's connections enabled him to enter the oil business.

Bush started as a sales clerk with Dresser Industries, a subsidiary of Brown Brothers Harriman, a company where his father had served on the board for 22 years. He then began the Bush Overby Oil Development Company in 1951 and cofounded the Zapata Petroleum Corporation two years later. In 1954 he was named president of Zapata Offshore Company, a subsidiary that became independent in 1958. He moved the company from Midland to Houston and served as president until 1964 and chairman until 1966.

Bush became interested in politics in the 1960s and was chosen chairman of the Republican Party in Harris County in 1964. He also decided to run for the U.S. Senate that year. He was nominated by the Republicans but lost the election. He ran again in 1966, this time for the U.S. House of Representatives from the Seventh Congressional District, and was elected. He was reelected in 1968, but Richard Nixon convinced him to try again for a Senate seat. He was defeated in 1970—this time by former Democratic Congressman Lloyd Bentsen. In 1971 he was appointed United States ambassador to the United Nations, followed by being chairman of the Republican National Committee, chief of the U.S. Liaison Office in the People's Republic of China, and director of the Central Intelligence Agency.

In 1980 Bush sought the Republican nomination for president, only to be passed over. Instead, the Republicans selected Ronald Reagan, and Reagan chose Bush as his vice presidential running mate. Bush spent eight years as vice president before being elected president in 1988. As vice president, he had responsibility for such domestic areas as federal deregulation and antidrug programs. He also went on missions to scores of foreign countries.

After losing the reelection in 1992, President and Mrs. Bush returned to their Houston home and he retired from public service. However, when his son George W. Bush ran for president in 2000, he made many supportive appearances and speeches. He also joined with former President Bill Clinton to raise funds for victims of the tsunami that hit Thailand in 2004; Hurricane Katrina in the Gulf Coast region, especially Louisiana and Mississippi, in 2005; and the Haiti earthquake in 2010.

The George Bush Presidential Library and Museum, located at Texas A&M University in College Station, Texas, holds Bush's papers and has exhibits tracing his life and career. The library/museum, which opened in 1997, is one of the 13 federal presidential centers administered by the National Archives and Records Administration. It is on a 90-acre site on the west campus of the university adjoining the Presidential Conference Center and the George Bush School of Government and Public Service.

The facility's archive contains over 38 million pages of personal papers and official documents from Bush's vice presidency and presidency, as well as records from associates associated with President Bush during his government career. In addition to reports, memoranda, and speeches in the textual collection, the archive has approximately 1 million photographs and thousands of hours of audio and visual tapes.

The museum has 23,000 square feet of permanent exhibits and temporary exhibitions. The permanent exhibits feature materials from the museum's collection related to President Bush's life and career, as well as historical events during his life and presidency, and show the influences and challenges that shaped his life and presidency. The temporary exhibitions explore topics on the Bush administration. The museum has an orientation film featuring an interview with George and Barbara Bush and exhibits on American history; the Bush family; President Bush's early life, military and industrial careers, political activities, presidency, and achievements; and such other topics as Camp David, the Berlin Wall, and the Thousand Points of Light program.

The museum also has a replica of the Oval Office where visitors can sit behind the president's desk (and have a picture taken) and a White House Situation Room where the public can learn about the events leading up to the Persian Gulf War. Among the other museum highlights are an Avenger torpedo bomber similar to the plane Bush flew during World War II, a 1947 Studebaker like the car he drove from Connecticut to Texas, a section of the Berlin War, and replicas of Bush's Camp David and Air Force One offices. The library/museum's annual attendance is 138,000.

George Bush Presidential Library and Museum, 1000 George Bush Dr. W., College Station, TX 77845-3906. Phone: 979/691-4000. Fax: 979/691-4050. E-mail: reservations.bush@nara.gov. Website: www.bushlibrary.tamu.edu. Hours: 9:30–5 Mon.–Sat., 12–5 Sun.; closed New Year's Day, Thanksgiving, and Christmas. Admission: adults, $7; seniors and retired military, $6; children 6–17, $3; active military, children under 6, and Texas A&M and Blinn students, free (other college students, $3).

William J. Clinton

William J. Clinton Presidential Library and Museum. William Jefferson Clinton, the Democratic governor of Arkansas, was the nation's first president of the baby boomer generation. At the age of 46, he was elected the 42nd president of the United States (1993–2001) by defeating Republican incumbent George H. W. Bush in 1992. He had the highest end-of-the-office approval rating of any American president since World War II but was impeached and almost forced to resign his office because of a sexual scandal.

Clinton, who was the third youngest president, took office at the end of the cold war. He presided over the longest period of peacetime economic expansion in American history. During Clinton's presidency, the nation had its lowest unemployment rate in modern times, lowest inflation rate in 30 years, highest home ownership rates in history, improved economic equality, reduced welfare rolls, and a budget surplus. Yet he had his setbacks, including the failure to enact his health care reform program and the impeachment trial involving personal indiscretions with a White House intern.

William Jefferson Clinton was born William Jefferson Blythe III in Hope, Arkansas, in 1946. His father, William Jefferson Blythe Jr., was a traveling salesman who died in an automobile accident three months before Bill was born. His mother, Virginia Dell Cassidy, a registered nurse, went to New Orleans to obtain her certificate as a nurse anesthetist in 1948 and left him with his grandparents, Eldridge and Edith Cassidy, who ran a small grocery. His mother returned in 1950 and married Robert Clinton Sr., an automobile dealer in Hot Springs, Arkansas.

Bill Blythe, who later took his stepfather's Clinton surname, attended St. John's Catholic Elementary School, Ramble Elementary School, and Hot Springs High School. He was an active student leader who sang in the chorus and played the tenor saxophone. He was so good as a musician that he won the first chair in the state band's saxophone section.

When 16 years old, Clinton considered devoting his life to music but knew he was not good enough and decided on public service as an elected official. He said he was largely influenced by two events in 1963—meeting President John F. Kennedy at the White House while serving as a Boys Nation senator and listening to Martin Luther King's "I Have a Dream" speech. With the assistance of scholarships, he received a bachelor's degree in foreign service at Georgetown University in 1968. He became Phi Beta Kappa and received a Rhodes Scholarship to Oxford University, where he participated in Vietnam War protests and organized an October 1969 Moratorium event.

After Oxford, Clinton earned a law degree at Yale Law School in 1973. There he met and began dating another law student, Hillary Rodham. They became inseparable and moved in together and were married in 1975. In 1980 they had their only child, Chelsea, who became a television reporter.

Clinton began his political career in 1972, working in Texas for the George McGovern campaign in the Democrat's presidential campaign. After graduation from Yale, he returned to Arkansas and taught law at the University of Arkansas. In 1974 Clinton ran for the U.S. House of Representatives but lost to the incumbent Republican congressman. Two years later, he was elected Arkansas attorney general and then governor of the state in 1978. He was the youngest governor in the nation at the age of 32. He was defeated in reelection but came back to serve as governor for 10 more years. He helped transform Arkansas's economy and made major improvements in the state's educational system.

Clinton chaired the National Governors Association, headed the Democratic Leadership Council in 1990 and 1991, and decided to run for president in 1992. Although originally considered only a regional candidate, he beat Governor Jerry Brown of California for the Democratic presidential nomination. Tennessee Senator Albert Gore Jr. was chosen the vice presidential nominee. The election became a three candidate rate, with Clinton running against President George H. W. Bush, who was seeking reelection, and Ross Perot, a billionaire independent businessman. Clinton was elected president with less than a majority. He received 43 percent of the vote, while Bush had 37.4 percent and Perot 18.9 percent. He became the first Democratic president in 12 years and in 20 of the previous 24 years.

During his two terms as president, Clinton enacted such legislation as the North American Free Trade Agreement, which increased foreign trade; Family and Medical Leave Act, granting time off for health reasons; State Children's Health Insurance Program, providing insurance for millions of children; and Violent Crime Control and Law Enforcement Act, adding policemen and increasing punishment for certain crimes. He also implemented the "Don't ask, don't tell" policy, the controversial intermediate step to full gay military integration.

On the international front, Clinton presided over the 1993 signing of the Oslo Accords between Israel and the Palestine Liberation Organization; stabilized war-torn Bosnia through the Dayton Peace Accords; helped end Serbia's ethnic cleansing of Albanians in Kosovo; bombed Iraq when Saddam Hussein stopped United Nations inspectors from checking for evidence of nuclear, chemical, and biological weapons; worked to expand NATO; and engaged in a worldwide campaign against drug trafficking.

Clinton also suffered a scandal in his personal life that almost removed him from office. He was impeached for perjury and obstruction of justice by the U.S. House of Representatives after charges of having sexual relations with a 22-year-old White House intern. He first denied and then admitted the relationship. Congress appointed an independent investigator who produced a report that resulted in Clinton's impeachment. But he was acquitted of all charges by the U.S. Senate and served the remainder of his second term.

Since ending his presidential term in 2001, Clinton has continued to be involved in politics, giving speeches and raising funds in support of Democratic candidates, including his wife, Hillary Rodham Clinton, who was elected senator, ran for president in 2010, and served as secretary of state in the Obama administration. He also founded the William J. Clinton Foundation in 1997, which seeks to alleviate poverty, improve global health, strengthen economies, and protect the environment, and has funded such activities as AIDS and global warming studies, assistance to Haitian earthquake victims, and an annual meeting of world leaders to discuss global issues. Clinton and Bush also have worked together to provide aid to victims in the 2005 Thailand tsunami, 2005 Katrina Gulf Coast hurricane, and 2010 Haitian earthquake.

The William J. Clinton Presidential Library and Museum opened in 2004 on a 17-acre site next to the Arkansas River in Little Rock, Arkansas. It is part of a 30-acre complex known as the Clinton Presidential Park, which also houses the Clinton Foundation, the University of Arkansas Clinton School of Public Service, and an arboretum, amphitheater, gardens, and children's play area. The main building is the 68,698-square-foot library/museum, which cantilevers over the Arkansas River. The archives and National Archives facilities are located in a building connected to the main structure.

The 13,200-square-foot Choctaw Station, a restored historic train station, contains the university's School of Public Service, Clinton Public Policy Institute, and Clinton Foundation. The 1899 Rock Island Railroad Bridge, which crosses the Arkansas River and leads to Choctaw Station, has been converted to a pedestrian bridge.

The Clinton library/museum has the largest archival collection of the 13 federal presidential facilities administered by the National Archives and Records Administration. It contains 80 million documents, 21 million e-mail messages, 2 million photographs, and 79,000 artifacts from the Clinton presidency.

The museum has 20,000 square feet of exhibit space, featuring exhibits on the life, career, and achievements of President Clinton and American history at the turn of the twenty-first century. These include an interactive 110-foot time line of the Clinton presidency, 13 policy alcoves, an exhibit on life in the White House, a reconstruction of the Cabinet Room, and a full-scale replica of the Oval Office. The museum also has temporary exhibitions, guided tours, and educational programs. Annual attendance approaches 300,000.

William J. Clinton Presidential Library and Museum, 1200 President Clinton Ave., Little Rock, AR 72201-1749. Phone: 501/372-4242. Fax: 501/244-2883. E-mail: clinton.library@nara.gov. Website: www.clintonlibrary.gov. Hours: 9–5 Mon.–Sat., 1–5 Sun.; closed New Year's Day, Thanksgiving, and Christmas. Admission: adults, $7; seniors, retired military, and college students, $5; children 6–17, $3; children under 6, free.

Clinton Birthplace Home. The Clinton Birthplace Home in Hope, Arkansas, is where President William J. Clinton spent the first four years of his life. The house is called the "birthplace" house even though he actually was born in the Julia Chester Hospital in Hope in 1946. Clinton's mother, Virginia Cassidy Blythe, a registered nurse, moved into her parents' house after the death of her husband in a car accident while she was expecting their only child.

After Bill's birth, his grandparents, Eldridge and Edith Cassidy, cared for him while their daughter went to New Orleans in 1948 to enroll in a nurse anesthetist program. She returned in 1950 and married Roger Clinton Sr., an automobile dealer in Hot Springs. The new family moved to a house in Hope and then to Hot Springs in 1953. Bill later took his stepfather's surname.

The grandparents, who operated a small grocery, moved into the 1917 six-room house in 1938, purchased it in 1946, and owned it until 1956. The house then passed through other owners and was vacant after 1992, when it was damaged by an electrical fire. After Clinton became president, a foundation was formed that raised enough funds to buy, restore, and operate the house as a historic house museum.

The house now contains furnishings of the late 1940s, family memorabilia, photographs, and a memorial garden. The site, which opened to the public in 1997, also has a visitor center with exhibits on Clinton's childhood, personal and political life, family history, and friends from Hope. The house has been designated a National Historic Site and is listed on the National Register of Historic Places.

Clinton Birthplace Home, 117 S. Hervey St., Hope, AR 71801-4208 (postal address: PO Box 1925, Hope, AR 71802-1925). Phone: 870/777-4455. Fax: 870/722-6929. E-mail: clinton@arkansas.net. Website: www.clintonbirthplace.com. Hours: grounds—dawn–dusk daily; house museum—10–5 Mon.–Sat. and by appointment; closed Sun. and major holidays. Admission: adults, $5; seniors, $4; children 7–18, $3; children under 7, free.

George W. Bush

George W. Bush Presidential Library and Museum. The newest federal presidential library and museum is devoted to the life and career of one of the nation's most controversial presidents. The George W. Bush Presidential Library and Museum in Dallas opened in 2013 on the campus of Southern Methodist University. The 43rd president of the United States (2001–2009) was the second George Bush to hold the office. His father, George H. W. Bush, served as the 41st president in 1989–1993.

Bush was the president in 2001 when four coordinated suicide attacks upon the United States by 19 Islamic terrorists occurred in New York City and Washington, DC. Nearly 3,000 persons died. He also was a controversial Republican president during the greatest recession since World War II and led the nation into new wars in Afghanistan and Iraq.

During his eight years as president, Bush approved broad tax cuts, initiated educational reforms, provided prescription benefits for seniors, recast intelligence gathering and analysis, reformed the military, banned partial-birth abortions, and withdrew from a number of international treaty processes, including the Kyoto Protocol on global warning. It also was a period of debate over such other issues as immigration, electronic surveillance, interrogation techniques, and Social Security. But Bush's most controversial actions were initiating the longest war in American history in Afghanistan in 2001 and a war against Saddam Hussein in Iraq in 2003.

George Walker Bush was born in New Haven, Connecticut, in 1946 but was raised in Midland and Houston, Texas, by George H. W. Bush and Barbara Pierce Bush, who also had five other children—Jeb, Neil, Marvin, Dorothy, and Robin, who died from leukemia when three years old. It was a political family. George's grandfather was Prescott Bush, a U.S. senator from Connecticut; his father was vice president in 1981–1989 and president in 1989–1993; and his brother, Jeb, was governor of Florida in 1999–2007. George Bush was also governor of Texas in 1995–2000.

Bush attended public schools in Midland until the family moved to Houston when he completed seventh grade. He then went to the Kinkaid School, a prep school in Houston, for two years and finished at Philips Academy in Andover, Massachusetts. He went to Yale University and received a Bachelor of Arts degree in history in 1968, followed by a Master of Business Administration degree from Harvard Business School. He is the only U.S. president to have earned an M.B.A.

Bush joined the Texas Air National Guard in 1968 and flew Convair F-102s while serving with the 147th Reconnaissance Wing out of Ellington Field Joint Reserve Base in Houston, but he did not see active duty in the Vietnam War. In 1973 he transferred to the Air Force Reserve and was honorably discharged the next year. However, Bush started having multiple episodes of alcohol abuse and had his driver's license suspended in 1976. In 1977 he met Laura Welch, a school teacher and librarian, whom he married after a three-month courtship. She had a stabilizing effect on his life. They had fraternal twin daughters, Jenna and Barbara, in 1981.

Bush ran for his first political office in 1978, only to lose a close race for the U.S. House of Representatives from the 19th Congressional District in Texas. He returned to the oil industry and began a series of small independent oil exploration companies. He founded Arbusto Energy, which later became Bush Exploration. It merged with Spectrum 7 and Bush became chairman. When the company was hurt by falling oil prices, it was folded into HKN Inc., and Bush was named to the board of directors.

In 1988 Bush moved his family to Washington to work on his father's campaign for the U.S. presidency. He served as campaign advisor and media liaison and campaigned across the nation. After his father was elected president, he returned to Texas and purchased a share of the Texas Rangers baseball team in 1989. He served as managing general partner for five years and assisted his father when he ran for reelection in 1992 and lost. When he sold his Rangers shares in 1998, his $800,000 investment was worth $15 million.

In 1994 Bush ran for governor of Texas, facing popular Democratic incumbent Ann Richards. He won the race after she was accused of appointing avowed homosexuals to state jobs. As governor, he had a budget surplus and gave Texans their largest tax cut, sought to increase teacher salaries and educational test scores, and extended funding of organizations that warned against the dangers of alcohol and drug use and abuse and helped reduce domestic violence. In 1998 he won reelection with a record 69 percent of the vote and became the first governor in Texas history to serve two terms.

In 1999, while governor of Texas, Bush announced his candidacy for president. Calling himself a "compassionate conservative," he was selected as the Republican nominee over 11 other candidates. He chose Richard B. Chaney, a former White House chief of staff and secretary of defense, as his running mate. He defeated Vice President Al Gore, the Democratic nominee, in an election that was not decided until the U.S. Supreme Court ruled against a Florida county recount.

Bush won the presidency with 271 electoral college votes, as opposed to 266 for Gore—even though Gore had 543,895 more individual votes than Bush. In the 2004 reelection, Bush defeated Massachusetts Democratic Senator John Kerry. Kerry attacked Bush on the Iraq War and failing to stimulate the economy and job growth in the recession, while Bush called Kerry a liberal who would raise taxes and increase the size of the government and said he lacked the decisiveness and vision needed in the war on terror.

Bush sent American forces into Afghanistan in 2001 to combat Al Qaeda, a movement under Osama bin Laden that trained and financed terrorists who were exported to other countries. Al Qaeda attacks were disrupted and Bin Laden escaped capture for a decade (but was killed by the U.S. in Pakistan in 2011). The war still continues, although American forces are scheduled to be withdrawn in 2014 as the fighting is turned over to the Afghans.

A more controversial act during Bush's presidency was invading Iraq in 2005 after what appeared to be threats posed by Saddam Hussein to the United States and other countries. Hussein had refused to permit United Nations inspectors to search for nuclear, chemical, and biological weapons (which were never found). It was not until 2011 that U.S. forces were withdrawn and a democratic government assumed control in Iraq.

President and Mrs. Bush returned to Texas after leaving the White House. They purchased a home in a suburban area of Dallas. He has written a book about his life, given speeches, and been involved in plans for the George W. Bush Presidential Library, a Georgian-style building designed by Robert A. M. Stern. It is the 13th of the federal presidential libraries and museums administered by the National Archives and Records Administration. The library/museum opened in 2013 in a complex called the George W. Bush Presidential Center on a 24-acre site on the east side of the Southern Methodist University campus.

The library archives have more than 60 million pages of paper records; over 4 million photographs; more than 42,000 artifacts; 80 terabytes of electronic information, including over 200 million e-mails; and recordings and transcripts of interviews with senior Bush administration officials. The library also has a Freedom Collection, which contains the papers and oral histories of political dissidents who have sought to bring freedom and opportunity to their nations.

The museum features exhibits with historical documents, artifacts, and gifts of state related to the life, times, and accomplishments of President Bush. The exhibits have four themes—freedom, opportunity, compassion, and responsibility. Another part of the center is the Bush Institute, a policy study center that focuses on four areas—education reform, global health, human freedom, and economic growth.

George W. Bush Presidential Library and Museum, Southern Methodist University, 2943 SMU Blvd., Dallas, TX 75205. Phone: 214/346-1557. Fax: 214/346-1558. E-mail: gwbush.library@nara.gov. Website: www.georgewbush-library.smu.edu. Hours: 9–5 Mon.–Sat., 12–5 Sun.; closed New Year's Day, Thanksgiving, and Christmas. Admission: seniors, $13; adults, $16; youth 13–17, $14; youth 5–12, $10; children under 5, free; retired military, $10; non-SMU college students, $13.

PUBLIC OFFICIALS/POLITICAL FIGURES

Stephen F. Austin

San Felipe de Austin State Historic Site and **Stephen F. Austin State Park.** Stephen Fuller Austin was known as the "father of Texas" because he led the first legal and successful colonization of the region that became independent of Mexico, a republic, and then the state of Texas. He brought the first 297 families from the United States in 1821 to settle in the San Felipe area and served as secretary of state for the Republic of Texas in 1836.

The original commercial plaza near the Brazos River ferry crossing now is the center of the 13-acre San Felipe de Austin State Historic Site, formerly a part of the adjacent 463.3-acre Stephen F. Austin State Park. A small museum in the historic park's visitor center tells about Austin, the colony, and the historic site.

From 1824 to 1836, San Felipe de Austin was the social, economic, and political center of the region and the capital of the American colonies in Mexico. It was called "The Cradle of the Texas Liberty" because of the many historic events that occurred there, including the conventions of 1832 and 1833 and the consultation of 1835, which led to the Texas Declaration of Independence. It also was the home of Austin and other famous early Texans and where the first Anglo newspaper in Texas was published, the Texas postal system originated, and the Texas Rangers were started.

Austin was born in 1793 in Austinville in the mining region of southwestern Virginia. He was the second child of Moses Austin and Mary Brown Austin. When he was four years old, his family moved to the lead mining region in present-day Potosi, Missouri, where his father received a permit from the Spanish government for a mining site established by French colonists. When 11 years old, Stephen was sent to be educated at Bacon Academy in Connecticut and then to Transylvania University in Kentucky. He graduated in 1810 and began studying to be a lawyer.

At the age of 21, Austin served in the legislature of the Missouri Territory. When he was left penniless after the Panic of 1819, he moved south to what became Little Rock in the new Arkansas Territory and then to Hempstead County, where he became a circuit court judge. He also ran for the U.S. House of Representatives but placed second because of a late entry. Austin then moved to New Orleans and resumed his study of law with a former congressman.

While Austin was in Arkansas, his father traveled to Spanish Texas and obtained an empresarial grant that would allow him to take 300 American families to Texas for settlement. On the way back to Missouri, he was attacked and is believed to have died of pneumonia. He left the grant to Stephen, who left for New Orleans to meet with Spanish officials when he learned that Mexico had declared its independence from Spain and Texas was now a Mexican province rather than a Spanish territory. Austin went to San Antonio and Mexico City and convinced officials to reauthorize the grant and gave him a contract to bring 300 families into Texas.

In 1824 Mexican states were given the right to administer public lands and open them to settlement. The Mexican state of Coahuila y Tejas approved the impresario system and agreed to give 4,428 acres to each married settler, with the requirement that the settler pay the state $30 within six years. Austin brought nearly 300 settlers to what was called the Austin Colony along the Brazos River in the first year and obtained contracts to settle an additional 900 families. He provided the civil and military authority and organized small armed groups to protect colonists, which evolved into the Texas Rangers.

By 1832 the population of the American colony had grown to 11,000, and the Mexican government became concerned about the increasing number and demands of the settlers and stopped immigration. The colony sought resumption of immigration, tariff exemption, separation from Coahuila, and a new state government for Texas. Mexican President Antonio López de Santa Anna lifted the immigration ban and made other reforms in 1835, but separate statehood was turned down because the Texans did not meet the required population of at least 80,000 for a state, and they had only 30,000.

While Austin was negotiating in Mexico City, the colonists became engaged in a number of confrontations with the Mexican government. Disturbances occurred at Anahuac and Velasco in the summer of 1835, causing Santa Anna to have the Mexican Army take steps to remove all the Anglo settlers from Texas. The war began in October at Gonzales, with Austin taking temporary command of the Texan forces during the Siege of Béxar in late 1835. Sam Houston later was placed in charge of the Texans' military operations and defeated Santa Anna and the Mexican Army at the Battle of San Jacinto to win independence for Texas in 1836.

Austin was in New Orleans when the war ended but returned to run for the first presidency against Sam Houston. Houston was elected president, and he appointed Austin secretary of state. But he was in office only two months when he caught a severe cold and died of pneumonia at the age of 43.

Austin is now honored at two state parks in Felipe, Texas—the 663.3-acre Stephen F. Austin State Park, founded in 1940, and the adjacent 13-acre San Felipe de Austin Historic Site, which was transferred in 2008 from the Austin State Park to the historic site, operated by the Texas Historical Commission. It has a visitor center museum with exhibits about Austin, the original settlement, and the historic park, and it features a diorama of the ca. 1830 colonial capital. The visitor center is located in the restored 1847 J. J. Josey General Store, which displays merchandise from the pioneer era.

The historic site also has a bronze statue of Austin, a replica of an early colony log cabin, and a commemorative obelisk, as well as campgrounds, a group dining hall, a picnic pavilion, and hiking trails. Historical and nature programs and tours are given on weekends. The Stephen F. Austin State Park has campgrounds, picnic sites, hiking and nature trails, a dining hall, a playground, woodlands, fishing, and an 18-hole golf course.

San Felipe de Austin State Historic Site, 15945 FM 1458, San Felipe, TX 77473 (postal address: PO Box 17, San Felipe, TX 77473-0017). Phones: 979/885-2181 and 979/798-2202. E-mail: san-felipe@the.state.tx.us. Website: www.visitsanfelipedeaustin.com. Hours: 9–5 Tues.–Sun.; closed Mon., New Year's Eve and Day, Thanksgiving, and Christmas Eve and Day. Admission: free.

Stephen F. Austin State Park, Park Rd. 38, San Felipe, TX 77473 (postal address: PO Box 125, San Felipe, TX 77473-0125). Phone: 979/885-3613. Website: www.tpwd.state.tx.us/spdest/findadest/parks/stephen_f_austin. Hours: 8 a.m.–10 p.m. daily; closed Christmas. Admission: adults, $4; Texas seniors, $2; children under 13, free.

Alben W. Barkley

Alben W. Barkley Museum. Alben W. Barkley was vice president of the United States under President Harry S. Truman in 1949–53. He was a lawyer and former U.S. congressman and senator who was an unsuccessful candidate in the 1952 presidential election. His life and career are chronicled at the Alben W. Barkley Museum in Paducah, Kentucky, where he spent much of his life. The museum is housed in the one of the oldest buildings in the city—the 1852 Captain William Smedley historic house.

Barkley was born Willie Alben Barkley in a log cabin in 1877 near Lowes in Graves County, Kentucky. His parents were John Wilson Barkley and Electra Eliza Smith Barkley, deeply religious tenant farmers. He attended public schools and worked his way through Marvin College as a janitor. He graduated from college in 1897 after excelling in speech and debate. He then received a degree from Emory College in Oxford, Georgia, in 1900 and attended the University of Virginia School of Law. Here he legally changed his name from "Willie Alben" to "Alben William" Barkley.

Barkley was admitted to the Kentucky bar in 1901 and began practicing law in Paducah. In 1903 he married Dorothy Brower, and they had three children. She died in 1947 and he later remarried. In Paducah, Barkley served as prosecuting attorney in 1905–1909 and county judge in 1909–1913. He became a powerful Democratic Party leader with his folksy campaigning and strong oratorical skills. In 1912 he was elected to the U.S. House of Representatives from the First Kentucky Congressional District. He was reelected six times and served from 1913 to 1927.

In 1923 Barkley narrowly lost the Democratic nomination for governor, but in 1926 he was elected to the U.S. Senate and reelected three times. He served from 1927 to 1949. He was Senate majority leader from 1937 to 1947 and minority leader in 1947–1949 and received the Congressional Gold Medal, the highest congressional award bestowed to a civilian. He saw that President Franklin D. Roosevelt's domestic and war proposals, including war financing and the lend-lease bill, passed the Senate.

Barkley was nominated for vice president at the 1948 Democratic National Convention and became the oldest person to hold that office at that date when elected at the age of 71. He also was the only vice president to marry while in office. He married Jane Hadley, a widow from St. Louis who was 34 years younger at the age of 37. In 1952 Barkley announced his candidacy for president but withdrew shortly thereafter when unions refused to support him because of his advanced age.

After serving as vice president, Barkley retired and then decided to run for the Senate again in 1954. He was elected and became majority leader again in 1955 and died the next year of a heart attack at the age of 78 while giving a speech at the 1956 mock Democratic Convention.

The Alben W. Barkley Museum in Paducah now tells about his life and long political career. The museum has Barkley memorabilia and Kentucky historical materials, a genealogy section, and a large exhibit of political and election items. Some of Barkley's memorabilia also is displayed at Whitehaven, a mansion that has been turned into a welcome center off Interstate 24.

Alben W. Barkley Museum, 533 Madison St., Paducah, KY 42002-0252. Phone: 270/443-0512. Fax: 270/442-6000. E-mail: wcrouch@apx.net. Website: www.aboutpaducah.com/articles/alben-w-barkley-museum.html. Hours: 1–4 Sat.–Sun. and by appointment; closed Mon.–Fri. and major holidays. Admission: adults, $3; students under 13, $1.

John C. Calhoun

Fort Hill (The John C. Calhoun Home). John Caldwell Calhoun was a leading politician, political theorist, and states' rights advocate from South Carolina who served as a congressman, senator, secretary of war, secretary of state, and vice president during the first half of the nineteenth century. He is best known for his defense of slavery, his theory of minority rights in a democracy, and being among the first to suggest that the only solution to the North/South governing differences may be secession from the Union. He now is honored at Fort Hill, his home, which he named for nearby Fort Rutledge in 1825. It has become a historic home museum on the campus of Clemson University in Clemson, South Carolina.

Calhoun began his political career as a supporter of a strong national government, with wide powers and protective tariffs on imports. By 1840 he changed his views. He now favored states' rights, limited government, and free trade. He felt it was the right of a state to veto any federal bill it considered unconstitutional. He redefined republicanism to include approval of slavery and minority rights, with the white South being the minority because it was outnumbered by the Northern states with greater populations. He called for a "concurrent majority" where the minority could block offensive proposals.

Calhoun was born in 1782 in Granville County (now Abbeville District), South Carolina. He was the fourth child of Scotch-Irish settlers Patrick Calhoun and Martha Caldwell Calhoun. His father became a member of the colonial legislature and then state legislature and took part in the war of independence. At the age of 17, John quit school to work on the family farm when his father became ill. But he studied with his brother-in-law, the Rev. Moses Waddell, a Presbyterian minister who later became president of the University of Georgia. In 1802 he entered Yale

University as a junior and graduated with distinction in 1804. Calhoun then studied law at the Tapping Reeve Law School in Litchfield, Connecticut, and afterward in a law office in Charleston. He was admitted to the South Carolina bar in 1807.

Calhoun began his law practice in the Abbeville District and soon became a leading figure in the area and profession. He was elected to the South Carolina legislature and served in 1808–1809. In 1810 he was elected a member of the U.S. House of Representatives, serving from 1811 to 1817. He became one of the "War Hawks," who included Speaker Henry Clay and two other South Carolina congressmen. They demanded that the United States declare war against Britain to preserve honor and republic values. The War of 1812 followed. It also was during this period that Calhoun got married. In 1811 he married Floride Bonneau, a first cousin once removed. They had 10 children, with three dying in infancy.

President James Monroe appointed Calhoun as secretary of war in 1817, and he served in that capacity until 1925, during which he made major reforms in the War Department and the U.S. Military Academy. He also was a candidate for president in 1924 but withdrew when he lacked the support of South Carolina party leaders. He then served as vice president from 1825 to 1832, initially with President John Quincy Adams and during most of the first administration of President Andrew Jackson. Calhoun resigned after speaking and writing against the higher tariffs and antislavery bills that were enacted and being considered. He argued that states had a constitutional right to nullify federal legislation. Calhoun was not an enemy of the Union, but he believed that its preservation depended on rights guaranteed to states by the Constitution being recognized. Otherwise, he said, the only remedy left to the South is secession.

After leaving the vice presidency, Calhoun was elected to the U.S. Senate in 1832 and served until his death of tuberculosis in 1850 at the age of 68. As senator, he fought against the "spoils system" started by President Andrew Jackson, opposed the removal of government deposits from the Bank of the United States, and helped settle the Oregon dispute agreement with Britain and the territory to be acquired in the war with Mexico.

Calhoun was considered for the presidency in 1844 but declined to be a candidate. He was appointed secretary of state by President John Tyler in 1844 and served for a year, during which he largely worked to admit Texas as a state.

Calhoun is regarded as one of the nation's best senators. He was one of the three 1800s congressional leaders considered as the "Great Triumvirate." The other two were Henry Clay and Daniel Webster. He also was one of the five greatest senators selected by a Senate committee in 1957 (the others being Clay, Webster, Robert La Follette, and Robert Taft).

Calhoun retired to his 1,100-acre plantation in South Carolina. Fort Hill, once the home of John C. Calhoun and his family, is now a National Historic Landmark on the Clemson University campus in Clemson, South Carolina. The house originally was built around 1803 as a four-room manse, known as Clergy Hall, for Old Stone Church, a Presbyterian church. It was purchased by Calhoun and his wife, Floride, in 1825.

Calhoun enlarged the house to 14 rooms and renamed it Fort Hill for the nearby historic Fort Rutledge, which was built in 1776. The house's architectural style is Greek revival, with federal detailing and simple interior design. It contains the original Calhoun/Clemson furnishings, Flemish and family portraits, personal artifacts, and government documents. It has functioned as a historic house museum since 1889.

After Calhoun's death in 1850, his wife and three children inherited the property. It was auctioned off in 1872 and divided among the surviving heirs. Daughter Anna Maria Calhoun Clemson received the residence with about 814 acres and moved in with her husband, Thomas Green Clemson. After her death in 1875, her husband bequeathed the estate to the State of South Carolina for an agricultural college in his 1881 will with the stipulation that it be kept in repair with all its articles of furniture and vesture and always be open to visitors (which has been done by Clemson University, which evolved from the initial agricultural college). The annual attendance is over 23,500.

Fort Hill (The John C. Calhoun House), Clemson University, Fort Hill St., Clemson, SC 29634-5615 (postal address: Trustee House, Clemson University, PO Box 345615, Clemson, SC 29634-5615). Phone: 864/656-2475. Fax: 864/650-1020. E-mail: hiottw@clemson.edu. Website: www.clemson.edu/about/history/properties/fort-hill. Hours: 10–12 and 1–4:30 Mon.–Sat., 2–4:30 Sun.; closed university holidays. Admission: suggested donations— adults, $5; seniors and students, $4; children, $2.

Winston Churchill

National Winston Churchill Museum and **Winston Churchill Memorial and Library.** In 1946 Prime Minister Winston Churchill of the United Kingdom gave his famous "Sinews of Peace" speech at Westminster College in Fulton, Missouri. It was in that address that he said "an Iron Curtain has descended across the continent." The speech, which came to be known as the "Iron Curtain" speech, has become one of Churchill's most celebrated speeches and marked the beginning of the cold war. The college now pays tribute to the great English leader and his historic speech at the Winston Churchill Memorial and Library, which includes the National Winston Churchill Museum.

Winston Churchill is regarded as one of the greatest wartime leaders of the twentieth century. He was at the forefront of British politics for 50 years. He was a noted statesman and orator who served as British prime minister twice—in 1940–1945 and 1951–1955. Churchill, who also was a military officer, historian, author, journalist, and artist, is the only British prime minister to have received the Nobel Prize in Literature and the first person to be made an honorary citizen of the United States.

Churchill was born as Winston Leonard Spencer-Churchill in 1874 into the aristocratic family of the Dukes of Marlborough. His birth came two months premature and took place in the Blenheim Palace in Woodstock, Oxford-shire. His father, Lord Randolph Churchill, was a charismatic politician who served as chancellor of the exchequer. Like his father, Winston used the Churchill surname in public life. His mother, Jennie Jerome, was the daughter of an American millionaire, Leonard Jerome. She became Lady Randolph Churchill.

From the ages of two to six, Winston lived with his parents in Dublin, where his grandfather served as viceroy and employed his father as his private secretary. But he had limited contact with his parents. He became close to his nanny, who served as his confidante and tried to teach him reading, writing, and arithmetic. He then attended three independent schools—St. George's School, Berkshire Brunswick School, and Harrow School. He generally did poorly but earned high marks in English and history at Harrow. He had a speech impediment in those early years, which he later corrected. After leaving Harrow in 1893, Churchill enrolled in the cavalry program at the Royal Military College. He graduated eighth in the class in 1895 and was commissioned a cornet (second lieuten-ant) in the Fourth Queen's Own Hussars.

Churchill always was running short on funds and did not intend to follow a conventional promotional career. He used his family's influence to get posted to active military campaigns, and his writings started to get noticed and bring him additional income. He also served as a war correspondent for several London newspapers and wrote books about the campaigns. In 1895 he went to Cuba to see and write about the Spanish fighting the Cuban guerrillas. It was followed by British military engagements in India, Sudan, and South Africa in 1897–1899.

Churchill resigned from the British Army in 1899 and entered politics. He ran for Parliament as the Con-servative candidate from Oldham but lost his first election. He then became a war correspondent, only to be captured and imprisoned in the 1899–1900 Second Boer War. However, he escaped and joined the army as it took the prison. He returned to Oldham in 1900 and this time he was elected to Parliament. He also rejoined the Queen's Own Hussars as captain in 1902 and was promoted to major in 1905 and commanded the Henley Squadron until 1916.

In 1904 Churchill met his future wife, Clementine Hozier, at a ball, and they married in 1908. They had five chil-dren. He also joined the Liberal Party in 1904, only to return to the Conservatives in 1925. Before World War I, he served as president of the Board of Trade, home secretary, and First Lord of the Admiralty, where he is credited with supporting the development of tanks and larger naval ships. He continued to serve in the Admiralty during the war until the disastrous Gallipoli Campaign. Churchill then served briefly at the front as lieutenant colonel of the Royal Scots Fusiliers Battalion before returning to the government as minister of munitions in 1917, secretary of state for war and secretary of state for air in 1919, and chancellor of the exchequer in 1924. He held various other positions in the 1920s and 1930s, during which he approved of a free Ireland, returned the pound sterling to the gold standard, opposed increased home rule for India, resisted the abdication of Edward VIII, and was among the first to recognize the growing threat of Hitler and call for rearmament.

After the outbreak of World War II, Churchill again was appointed First Lord of the Admiralty, the same post he held in 1911–1915. After Neville Chamberlain resigned in May 1940, he became prime minister and minister of defense. Churchill served until 1945 and then again in 1951–1955. It was his leadership, speeches, and radio broadcasts that helped inspire the British during the war years. He was Britain's voice at such wartime meetings with Allied leaders as Roosevelt, Stalin, Chiang Kai-shek, and Truman in Washington, Casablanca, Quebec, Cairo, Tehran, Yalta, and Potsdam. He became prime minister again in 1951 when the Conservatives won control of the government. Churchill resigned in 1955 but continued to serve as a member of Parliament until retiring in 1964. He died the next year of a severe stroke at the age of 90.

Churchill received many honors during his life. Queen Elizabeth conferred on him a knighthood, made him part of the Order of the Garter, and gave him a state funeral. President John F. Kennedy made Churchill an honorary citizen of the United States.

Churchill also was a highly respected author and painter who received the Nobel Prize for Literature in 1953. He began his literary career with military campaign reports, such as *The Story of the Malakand Field Force* (1898) and *The River War* (1899).

Among Churchill's books were *Lord Randolph Churchill* (1906), *My African Journey* (1908), *The World Crisis* (four volumes, 1923–1929), *Marlborough: His Life and Times* (four volumes, 1933–1938), *The Second World War* (six volumes, 1948–1954), and *History of the English-Speaking Peoples* (four volumes, 1956–1958). His speeches also are featured in a dozen volumes, including such wartime works as *The Unrelenting Struggle* (1942), *The Dawn of Liberation* (1945), and *Victory* (1946).

The Westminster College museum is part of a three-part Churchill memorial that also includes the historic Church of St. Mary the Virgin, Aldermanbury, from London and eight sections of the Berlin Wall. The sixteenth-century church was moved stone-by-stone from London and re-created. It was designed by noted architect Christopher Wren after the 1666 Great Fire of London destroyed the original twelfth-century church.

During World War II, the church was one of 13 Wren-designed churches destroyed in a massive German air raid in 1940, and it was not one of those to be rebuilt immediately. It was soon to be demolished when Westminster College offered to rebuild the church and use it as a Churchill memorial and college chapel. London agreed, and the college raised the funds to make the move and rebuild the church, which opened in 1969.

The National Winston Churchill Museum and the Clementine-Spencer Churchill Reading Room are located beneath the church. The museum, founded in 1962, explores the life and times of Churchill, and the reading room has an extensive research collection about Churchill and his era. Eight sections of the Berlin Wall are outside the church. Edwina Sandy, granddaughter of Winston Churchill, and her husband, Richard Kaplan, obtained the large wall sections (11 feet high and 32 feet long) as a gift from East Germany in 1990. It marked the close of the cold war 44 years after Churchill warned of the creation of the "iron curtain."

The museum tells the story of Churchill's life with three-dimensional interactive experiences. The exhibits cover the major events of his life and examine the critical events of the twentieth century. In addition to his role in World War II, the museum examines his life as a politician, soldier, journalist, family man, and artist. It has rooms devoted to a World War I trench and his contributions to the technology of warfare; Churchill's suspicions of Hitler and the Nazi movement in 1929–1939; World War II and Churchill's role; the "Sinews of Peace" speech and why Churchill came to the college; and a simulated British club with an audio presentation of Churchill stories and a database of his most famous quotations and quips. Annual attendance at the memorial/library is 25,000.

National Winston Churchill Museum, Winston Churchill Memorial and Library, Westminster College, 513 Westminster Ave., Fulton, MO 65251-1299. Phone: 573/592-5334. Fax: 573/592-5222. E-mail: sara.winingear@westminster-mo.edu. Website: www.churchillmemorial.org. Hours: 10–4:30 daily; closed New Year's Day, Thanksgiving, and Christmas. Admission: adults, $6; seniors, $5; college students and youth 12–18, $4; children 6–11, $3; children under 6, free.

Henry Clay

Ashland, the Henry Clay Estate. Henry Clay, a Kentucky lawyer, politician, and skilled orator, was a dominant figure in America's first and second political party systems in the early 1800s. He is considered one of the nation's great senators. Clay also served three different terms as speaker of the U.S. House of Representatives and was secretary of state from 1825 to 1829. He wanted to be president but was an unsuccessful candidate three times with three different political parties. His home in Lexington, Kentucky, now is a historic house museum called Ashland, the Henry Clay Estate.

Clay was born in 1777 on the family homestead in Hanover County, Virginia. He was the seventh of nine children born to the Rev. John Clay and Elizabeth Hudson Clay. His father, a Baptist minister who had over 22 slaves, died four years after Henry's birth. He left Henry and his brothers two slaves each and his wife 18 slaves and 464 acres of land. His mother then married Captain Henry Watkins, who was an affectionate stepfather. Watkins moved the family to Richmond, Virginia, where Elizabeth had seven more children with Watkins, bringing the number of children to 16.

In Richmond, Clay initially worked as a shop assistant. His stepfather then found a position for him in the Court of Chancery office, where he showed an aptitude in law. He became secretary for George Wythe, chancellor of the Commonwealth of Virginia, who took an interest in him and got him a job with Virginia Attorney General Robert Brooks. Clay became a lawyer by reading the law with Wythe (who also was a mentor to Thomas Jefferson, John Marshall, and others) and Brooks and was admitted to practice law in 1797.

In 1797 Clay moved to Lexington, Kentucky, which was near where his family then lived. He developed a successful law practice with his legal skills and courtroom oratory. Payment often took the form of horses, land, and even a hotel. One of his clients was former Vice President Aaron Burr in 1806. Clay and his law partner, John Allen, successfully defended Burr, who was indicted for planning an expedition into Spanish Territory west of the Mississippi River. Thomas Jefferson later convinced Clay that Burr was guilty of the charges.

Clay married Lucretia Hart in 1799. They had 11 children—six daughters and five sons. In 1803 he entered politics and was elected Fayette County representative in the Kentucky General Assembly. Clay also began to acquire land for a farm and a more substantial home on the outskirts of town for his growing family, but it was not until 1809 that they were completed. He called the new home Ashland because of the many ash trees on the property. By 1812 Clay had a 600-acre plantation and numerous slaves (exceeding 60 at the peak). It is believed he produced tobacco and hemp.

In 1806 Clay became a U.S. senator for less than a year when the Kentucky legislature chose him to complete the term of John Breckinridge, who was appointed U.S. attorney general. He then was elected speaker of the Kentucky General Assembly in 1807. After he introduced a resolution to require members to wear homespun suits rather than those made of British broadcloth, he nearly came to blows with one of the assemblymen, Humphrey Marshall, an aristocratic lawyer, who opposed the measure. Clay challenged him to a duel, and both were wounded but recovered.

In 1810 Clay was appointed to the U.S. Senate a second time. He was named to replace Senator Buckner Thruston, who resigned to be a judge on the U.S. Circuit Court. In 1811 Clay was elected as a Democratic Republican to the U.S. House of Representatives, where he was speaker of the House most years until 1825, when he served four years as secretary of state for President John Quincy Adams. In 1831 he was elected to the U.S. Senate, and he was reelected as a Whig in 1836, serving to 1842, when he resigned.

Clay was an unsuccessful candidate for president three times, with the Democratic Republican Party in 1824, National Republican Party in 1832, and Whig Party in 1844. He returned to the Senate in 1849 and served until his death of tuberculosis in 1852 at the age of 75. He freed all his slaves in his will. Clay also became the first person to lie in state in the U.S. Capitol.

Clay was one of the three congressional leaders known as the "Great Triumvirate." The others were John C. Calhoun and Daniel Webster. He was called the "Great Compromiser" for brokering important compromises during the nullification crisis and on the slavery issue. He also was instrumental in formulating the Missouri Compromise of 1820 and the Compromise of 1850 on slavery in the Western territories.

Clay was a leading "War Hawk" who played a major role in leading the nation to war with Britain in 1812. He also fought for an increase in tariffs to foster American industry, using federal funds to build and maintain infrastructure, and having a strong national bank. In addition to opposing the Mexican-American War and the Manifest Destiny policy of Democrats, he fought against the annexation of Texas on the grounds that it would inject the slavery issue into politics. In 1957 a Senate committee selected Clay as one of the five greatest U.S. senators. The others were John C. Calhoun, Robert La Follette, Robert Taft, and Daniel Webster.

When Clay died, he left the Ashland estate to his wife, Lucretia, who moved to live with her son John and sold the property to another son, James. He found the mansion in serious need of repair and decided to raze the house and rebuild it as a memorial to his father, following his original floor plan but incorporating certain Italianate, Greek revival, and Victorian details to bring it more into current style. James Clay lived at Ashland until the Civil War in 1862, when he left Lexington for fear of retribution because of his strong Confederate leanings.

In 1866 the house was sold and became part of the new Kentucky University (which later splint into Transylvania University and the University of Kentucky). It returned to family ownership in 1882 when Anne Clay McDowell, Henry Clay's granddaughter, and her husband, Henry Clay McDowell, purchased the estate. They did some updating and lived there until their deaths. Their daughter, Nannette McDowell Bullock, and her family then resided there, and it was through her efforts that the Henry Clay Memorial Foundation was created and the legacy of Henry Clay, the house, and 17 remaining acres were preserved in 1926.

Ashland, the Estate of Henry Clay opened as a historic house museum in 1950 and became a National Historic Landmark in 1961. The 18-room house has family furnishings and an exhibit room featuring a video about Clay's life and career. The site also has a formal garden, outbuildings, walking trails, guided tours, a museum store, and a café. Annual attendance is 12,000.

Ashland, the Henry Clay Estate, 120 Sycamore Rd., Lexington, KY 40502-1842. Phone: 859/266-8581. Fax: 859/268-7266. E-mail: ahmichael@henryclay.org. Website: www.henryclay.org. Hours: Mar.–Dec.—10–4 Tues.–Sat., 1–4 Sun.; closed Mon., Jan., and major holidays; Feb.—open only by appointment for groups of 10 or more. Admission: adults, $9; children 6–18, $5; children under 6, free.

David Crockett

See Frontiersmen section.

Jefferson Davis

Beauvoir, the Jefferson Davis Home and Presidential Library. Jefferson Davis was an American military officer, congressman, senator, secretary of war, and secretary of state who became the president of the Confederate States of America during the Civil War. As a senator, he argued against secession but believed that each state was sovereign and had the right to secede from the Union. As the head of the Confederacy, he lacked the political and war skills of his counterpart Abraham Lincoln and did not have a successful military strategy against the much larger and more industrially developed Union.

As the war was coming to a close, Davis was captured, imprisoned, and indicted for treason but never prosecuted. Despite his shortcomings and the war defeat, Davis eventually was regarded as a Civil War hero by many southerners. His postwar home, called Beauvoir, in Biloxi, Mississippi, is now devoted to his life and career and the history of the retirement site.

Jefferson Finis Davis was born on a farm in Christian County (now Fairview), Kentucky, in 1808. He was the last of 10 children of Samuel Emory Davis and Jane Cook Davis. His father and older brothers had served in the Continental Army during the American Revolutionary War. The family moved to St. Mary Parish in Louisiana in 1811 and to Wilkinson County in Mississippi in 1812. Jefferson began his education at Wilkinson Academy in Woodville in 1813 and two years later entered St. Thomas School at St. Rose Priory in Washington County. He then attended Jefferson College in Washington, Mississippi, in 1818 and Transylvania University in Lexington, Kentucky, in 1821. In 1824 he enrolled at the U.S. Military Academy at West Point and graduated as a commissioned second lieutenant in 1828.

In 1829 Davis was assigned to the First Infantry Regiment at Fort Crawford, Wisconsin, where he supervised the cutting of timber for repair and expansion of the fort. An assignment to Fort Winnebago followed in 1831 to direct the construction and management of a sawmill. In 1832 he was sent to Galena, Illinois, to head a detachment to remove miners from lands claimed by American Indians. He then was assigned by Colonel Zachary Taylor to escort Indian warrior Black Hawk to prison at Jefferson Barracks in Missouri during the Black Hawk War.

That same year that Taylor, who became president in 1849, brought his family to join him at Fort Crawford, where Davis met his daughter, Sarah Knox Taylor. The young couple fell in love and were married in 1835 after he resigned from the army. Davis planned to become a cotton planter with his brother Joseph in Mississippi. But the marriage turned out to be short lived. While visiting Jefferson's oldest sister in Louisiana three months later, both contracted malaria and Sara died.

Joseph Davis gave Jefferson 900 acres of land adjoining his property. It was called Brierfield Plantation. Davis had only one slave at the time. But by early 1836 he purchased 16 more, and the number of slaves increased to 74 by 1845. Davis was a virtual recluse for eight years as he studied government and history and discussed politics with his brother Joseph. Things changed in 1840 when he attended a Democratic meeting in Vicksburg and was chosen a delegate to the state convention. He served as a delegate the next year and in 1843 ran unsuccessfully for the Mississippi House of Representatives. In 1844 he was selected as one of six presidential electors and campaigned throughout the state for Democratic candidate James K. Polk. That same year he met and married Varina Howell. Three of their six children died before reaching adulthood.

In 1845 Davis was elected to one of the at-large seats in the U.S. House of Representatives. When the Mexican-American War began in 1846, he resigned from Congress and raised a volunteer regiment called the Mississippi Rifles. The regiment took part in the successful siege of Monterrey, and he was shot in the foot in the Battle of Buena Vista. President Polk offered him a commission as a brigadier general and command of a brigade of militia, but he declined the appointment, saying the Constitution gave the power of appointing militia officers to the states and not the federal government.

Because of his war service, Davis was appointed by the governor of Mississippi to serve the remainder of the term of a U.S. senator who died in 1847. He then was elected senator in 1848 but resigned in 1851 to run for governor. He lost the election and then took part in a convention on states' rights in Jackson, Mississippi. He also campaigned for Franklin Pierce, the Democratic candidate for president. Pierce was elected, and he appointed Davis as secretary of war in 1853. Davis served until 1857, when he was reelected to the Senate.

When South Carolina adopted an ordinance of secession in 1860 and Mississippi followed in 1861, Davis resigned as senator and returned to Mississippi. He was made major general of the army of Mississippi and then elected unanimously as president of the Confederate States of America. The Civil War began when Fort Sumter in the Charleston harbor refused to surrender to Confederate General P. G. T. Beauregard and Davis approved the bombing of the fort.

Davis took control of the Confederate military strategy and refused to appoint a general to direct the military operations until the closing days of the four-year war. The Civil War came to an end in 1865 after the Union Army's sweep through the South, General Robert E. Lee's surrender, and the capture of the Confederate capital of Richmond, Virginia, and President Davis in Georgia.

After his release from prison in 1667, Davis became president of the Carolina Life Insurance Company in Memphis in 1869. He remained silent during the Reconstruction period. In 1877 he accepted an invitation from Sarah Anne Ellis Dorsey, a novelist and intellectual from Natchez, to move with his wife, Varina, into the Library Pavilion at her 608-acre compound, called Beauvoir (for beautiful view), in Biloxi, Mississippi, to write his memoir, *The Rise and Fall of the Confederate Government* (published in 1881).

Davis liked the beautiful site and arranged to purchase the property in 1879 for $5,500 in three installments. Six months after the first payment, Dorsey died and left the compound to Davis. He and his wife lived in the 1848 main house until his death in 1889 at the age of 81. He also wrote *A Short History of the Confederate States of America,* published in 1889. Varina Davis continued to live on the property with her daughter Winnie until they moved to New York City in 1891.

In 1902 Mrs. Davis sold much of Beauvoir to the Mississippi Division of the Sons of Confederate Veterans for use as a memorial to her husband and the Confederate soldier and the location of a home for Confederate veterans and widows. A dozen barracks, a hospital, and a chapel were built behind the home for veterans and widows. Between 1903 and 1959, about 2,500 veterans and their families lived at the site at one time or another.

The main house opened to tours in 1941, and other facilities were added later, including a Confederate Museum, the Jefferson Davis Gallery, the Tomb of the Unknown Confederate Soldier, and the Jefferson Davis Presidential Library and Museum. In 1969 Beauvoir experienced a little damage from Hurricane Camille, but major loss resulted from the 2005 Hurricane Katrina. A number of houses were destroyed, as well as the Confederate Museum and the first floor of the Davis Presidential Library (resulting in the loss of 35 percent of the collections). The main house and other buildings also suffered damage. Most of the hurricane-damaged facilities have been restored or replaced, including the library and museum, with federal, state, individual, and private organization support.

Beauvoir has been designated a National Historic Landmark and is listed on the National Register of Historic Places. It now consists of 52 acres. The former Davis home contains nineteenth century period furniture and decorations and Davis family materials. The Jefferson Davis Home and Presidential Library includes the main house and a new building for the library and museum. The library features over 6,000 historical books, as well as photographs, letters, manuscripts, newspaper clippings, and records of Confederate heritage organizations. The museum is devoted to Davis, Confederate history, and the site. The annual site attendance is 31,000.

Beauvoir, the Jefferson Davis Home and Library, 2244 Beach Blvd., Biloxi, MS 39531-5002. Phone: 228/388-4400. Fax: 228/388-7800. Website: www.beauvoir.org. Hours: 9–4 daily; closed Thanksgiving and Christmas. Admission: adults, $9; seniors and active military, $7.50; children, $5.

Jefferson Davis State Historic Site. The Jefferson Davis State Historic Site in Fairview, Kentucky, honors the Confederacy president, who was born in the area in 1808. At 351 feet, the monument at the site is the largest unreinforced concrete obelisk in the world. The concrete walls are eight and a half feet thick at the base and taper to two and a half feet at the top. Davis was born on a farm in the isolated western Kentucky area and rose to be a military officer, congressman, senator, secretary of war, and secretary of state in the Union before becoming the leader of the Confederate States of America in the 1861–1865 Civil War.

The monument was first proposed by General Simon Bolivar Buckner Sr. at a reunion of the Orphan Brigade of the Confederate Army in 1907. Construction began in 1917, stopped during World War I because of building material rationing, resumed in 1922, and was completed in 1924. An elevator takes visitors to an observation platform at the top. The 19-acre state park also has a new visitor center with a video on Davis's life and the construction of the obelisk, as well as a shop with books and memorabilia about Davis and Kentucky handcrafts. Guided elevator tours of the monument also are offered. Annual attendance is 25,000.

Jefferson Davis State Historic Site, 258 Pembroke-Fairview Rd., Fairview, KY 42221 (postal address: Box 157, Fairview, KY 42221-0157). Phone: 270/889-6100. Fax: 270/889-6102. E-mail: ron.sydnor@ky.gov. Hours: May–Oct.—9–5 daily; closed Nov.–Apr. Admission (includes guided tour): adults, $5; seniors and military, $4; children under 13, $3.

Jefferson Davis Memorial Historic Site. The Jefferson Davis Memorial Historic Site near Fitzgerald, Georgia, is where Confederate President Jefferson Davis was captured in 1865 by the Union Army. Davis and a few members of his staff crossed the Savannah River into Georgia as Northern forces gained control of the region. Davis was on his way to the western theater of the Civil War, where he planned to unite Southern forces and continue fighting.

The Davis group camped in a pine forest nine miles east of Fitzgerald, Georgia, on May 9, not knowing that they were being pursued and that Union troops were close. At dawn, Davis and his staff members were surrounded by two groups of cavalry who were not aware of each other's presence. The two units began firing at each other until they realized their mistake. Two Union soldiers died in the exchange of gunfire. Davis and the others were captured, and he was charged with treason and imprisoned in Virginia for two years but never prosecuted. After being released, he became the president of an insurance company, spoke and wrote about his life and Confederate history, and retired to the Beauvoir compound in Biloxi, Mississippi. He died in 1889 at the age of 81.

The site of Davis's capture is now a 13-acre Georgia state park operated by Owns County with a monument where Davis was captured and a Civil War museum with a film and artifacts related to the war and capture. The park also has a gift shop, nature trail, group shelter, picnic site, and playground.

Jefferson Davis Memorial Historic Site, 338 Jeff Davis Park Rd., Fitzgerald, GA 31750. Phone: 229/831-2335. Website: www.gastateparks.org. Hours: 9–5 Wed.–Sun.; closed Mon.–Tues. and holidays. Admission: $2.75 to $4 plus tax.

Robert J. Dole

Robert J. Dole Institute of Politics. Robert J. Dole is a Kansas lawyer and politician who served in the U.S. Senate from 1969 to 1996 and was the Republican Party nominee for vice president against Walter Mondale in 1976 and ran for president against Bill Clinton in 1996. He set a record as the longest serving Republican leader. He also was Senate majority leader in 1985–1987 and minority leader in 1995–1996. Dole now is an attorney in Washington. The Robert J. Dole Institute of Politics was established in his honor at the University of Kansas in Lawrence after the 1996 election. It is dedicated to public service, training for leadership, and promoting politics as an honorable profession.

Dole was born in Russell, Kansas, in 1923. He was the son of Doran Ray Dole and Bina M. Talbott Dole. His father ran a small creamery. As a boy, Bob Dole worked at many odd jobs, including serving as a soda jerk in a local drug store. He graduated from Russell High School in 1941 and enrolled at the University of Kansas, where he played on the basketball, football, and track teams.

Dole was studying law at Kansas when the United States entered World War II in 1942. He joined the U.S. Army Enlisted Reserve and became a second lieutenant in the 10th Mountain Division. In 1944 he was badly wounded while engaged in combat in the mountains near Bologna, Italy. He was hit by German machine gun fire in his upper right back, and his right arm was badly injured.

Dole was taken to the 15th Evacuation Hospital and then the Percy Jones Army Hospital in Battle Creek, Michigan, until 1948. Although he recovered from his wounds, his right arm was paralyzed. At the Battle Creek hospital he met future fellow politicians Daniel Inouye and Philip Hart, who also later became senators. The Battle Creek Sanitarium where the three recovered from their wounds has been renamed the Hart-Dole-Inouye Federal Center in their honor.

In 1948 Dole married Phyllis Holden, an occupational therapist at the veterans hospital in Battle Creek. They divorced in 1972. Dole's second marriage was to Elizabeth Dole, a lawyer and government official, in 1975. They became a Washington "power couple." While he was senator and ran for vice president and president, she served as secretary of transportation, secretary of labor, and other government positions and was unsuccessful in receiving the Republican presidential nomination in 2000. She also was the former head of the American Red Cross. They did not have any children, but he had a daughter from the first marriage.

Bob Dole ran for political office for the first time in 1950 and was elected to a two-year term in the Kansas House of Representatives. At the same time, he received a law degree at Washburn University in Topeka, was admitted to the bar, and began a law practice in his hometown of Russell in 1952. He also became the county attorney in Russell County and served for eight years. In 1960 he was elected to the U.S. House of Representatives in the Sixth Congressional District in central Kansas. The district was merged with the Third District in western Kansas in 1962 to form the huge First Congressional District, which included 60 counties. Dale was reelected that year and two more times.

In 1968 Dole was elected to the U.S. Senate. He was reelected as senator four more times, during which he was the leader of the Senate Republicans from 1985 to 1996, when he resigned to run for president. He served as majority leader in 1985–1987 and minority leader in 1995–1996. While in the Senate, he also served as chairman of the Republican National Committee in 1971–1973.

In 1976 Dole was chosen as the Republican vice presidential candidate when incumbent Vice President Nelson Rockefeller withdrew on the ticket headed by President Gerald R. Ford. He lost to Democrat Walter Mondale. He then ran for the 1980 Republican presidential nomination, which eventually went to Ronald Reagan. In 1996 the Republicans nominated him for president but he lost to President Bill Clinton, who was reelected to a second term. Dole resigned from the Senate and became special counsel at a Washington law firm.

After the 1996 election, the University of Kansas approached Dole about obtaining his congressional papers and developing a political education institute in his name. He agreed, and a 28,000-square-foot institute was opened in 2003 that seeks to promote political and civic participation and civil discourse in a bipartisan, balanced manner. It provides a forum for discussion of political and economic issues, fosters public service leadership, and encourages participation in the political process. In the process, the institute emphasizes that politics is an honorable profession and that the course of the nation can be redirected only through political and civic participation.

Among the institute's program features are a Presidential Lecture Series, with presentations by leading scholars, historians, journalists, government officials, and others; an annual Dole Lecture that brings a nationally prominent figure to the campus to address some aspect of contemporary politics or policy; and an annual Dole Leadership Prize, which provides a $25,000 award.

The institute houses the largest collection of Dole's congressional papers for future research and has exhibits related to the senator's life and career. The exhibit area, which has 29 exhibits and six videos, includes a Memory Wall with a photo montage and a computer kiosk with access to over 4,000 photos of Kansas World War II veterans, two large columns salvaged from the New York City Twin Towers disaster, and a 12-foot replica of the U.S. Capitol Dome with a multiscreen video tour of the legislative process narrated by Dole. Public tours of the Dole Archives are scheduled monthly.

Robert J. Dole Institute of Politics, University of Kansas, 2350 Petefish Dr., Lawrence, KS 66045-7555. Phone: 785/684-4900. Fax: 785/684-1414. E-mail: doleinstitute@ku.edu. Fax: www.doleinstitute.org/visitors.html. Hours: 9–5 Mon., 12–5 Sun.; closed New Year's Day, Easter, Thanksgiving, and Christmas Eve and Day. Admission: free.

Stephen A. Douglas

Stephen A. Douglas Tomb and Memorial. Stephen A. Douglas was a U.S. senator from Illinois who is remembered largely because of his senatorial campaign debates over slavery with Abraham Lincoln in 1858 and loss to Lincoln in the 1860 presidential election. He was known as the "Little Giant" because he was only four and a half feet tall but a forceful and dominant figure in politics. He defeated Lincoln for the Senate seat, only to lose to him for the presidency two years later. He is buried and honored at the Stephen A. Douglas Tomb and Memorial in Chicago.

Douglas was a skillful and effective Democratic Party leader who believed in the principle of "popular sovereignty" and that the majority of citizens should decide contentious issues such as slavery and territorial expansion. As chairman of the Senate Committee on Territories, he was largely responsible for the Compromise of 1850, which defined whether a new state would permit slavery. However, he reopened the slavery question in 1854 with the Kansas-Nebraska Act, which would allow a territory to decide for itself whether to permit slavery. He argued that such a move could be negated by the people of the territory, which he called "popular sovereignty." Opposition to the act led to the formation of the Republican Party and in 1860 split the Democratic Party, which resulted in Lincoln's election as president.

Douglas was born in Brandon, Vermont, in 1813 as Stephen Arnold Douglass (he later dropped the second *s* in Douglass). His parents were Dr. Stephen Arnold Douglass and Sallie Fiske Douglass. He went to Brandon Academy and then Canandaigua Academy. In 1833, when 20 years old, he moved to Winchester, Illinois. Douglas worked as a teacher and then opened a school that provided three months of instruction for three dollars. He also studied law, passed the bar, and became a lawyer in Jacksonville, Illinois.

In 1934 he was appointed state's attorney of Morgan County. He served until 1836, when he was elected to the Illinois House of Representatives. Douglas then was named registrar of the Springfield Land Office, became Illinois secretary of state, and was appointed associate justice of the Illinois Supreme Court in 1841 at the age of 27. In 1842 Douglas was elected to the U.S. House of Representatives. He was reelected in 1844 and supported territorial expansion and the Mexican-American War. He was elected a U.S. senator in 1846 and quickly became a key player.

In 1947 Douglas married Martha Denny Martin, daughter of the wealthy Colonel and Mrs. Robert Martin of North Carolina. When his wife's father died the next year, he left her a 2,500-acre cotton plantation with 100 slaves in Mississippi. Douglas was named property manager but hired a manager to run the plantation and made only brief emergency trips thereafter to avoid political difficulties. The newlyweds moved from Springfield to Chicago later in 1847. They had two sons, and his wife died in 1956 after giving birth to a daughter, who also died in several weeks. Later that year, Douglas married Rose Adele Cutts, daughter of a nephew of President James Madison. She had one daughter, who died after a few weeks, and Adele became weakened by childbirth, but lived to 1856.

Douglas helped resolve the Compromise of 1850 by dividing the compromise into separate bills to overcome opposition, and by 1852 he was considered one of the Democrats' national leaders. He was reelected senator in 1853 and had become one of the leading promoters of railroad expansion. He devised a land-grant system as a way to fund the Illinois Central Railroad's expansion from Chicago to the Gulf of Mexico, which was not completed until after the Civil War.

In 1854 Douglas obtained the passage of the Kansas-Nebraska Act, which allowed the territories to choose slave or free status when becoming states. The North was unhappy with the act, which was seen as a victory for Southern slaveholders. Douglas defended the right of people to decide such issues for themselves, saying it was consistent with American democratic tradition. In 1857 the U.S. Supreme Court ruled in the Dred Scott case that neither Congress nor a territorial legislature had the power to prohibit slavery in a territory. The decision struck down the principal parts of the Missouri and 1850 compromises, curtailed the Kansas-Nebraska Act, and denied the basis for popular sovereignty.

Slavery became the focus of the series of seven Lincoln-Douglas debates in the 1858 senatorial race. Douglas tried to show that Lincoln was a dangerous radical who was advocating racial equality, while Lincoln emphasized the immorality of slavery and sought to limit its growth. Douglas defeated Lincoln for Senate reelection, but the Democratic Party was split in the 1860 presidential election when Northern delegates nominated Douglas for president and Southern delegates left the convention and nominated Vice President John C. Breckinridge. As a result, Lincoln was elected as the first Republican president.

After the election, Douglas denounced the talk of Southern secession as criminal. When Fort Sumter was bombed, he endorsed Lincoln's proclamation and offered his services. At Lincoln's request, he toured the border states to develop support for the Union cause. Two months after the 1861 Fort Sumter attack, Douglas contracted typhoid fever and then died of pneumonia in Chicago at the age of 48. He was buried on the shore of Lake Michigan, near the site of what became Camp Douglas, a Union Army and prisoner-of-war camp during the Civil War.

Friends of Douglas formed the Douglas Monument Association in 1861 to build a suitable memorial at the grave site. In 1864 the association adopted the design of sculptor Leonard W. Volk, which included a 96-foot granite column—with a nine-foot statue of Douglas gazing over Lake Michigan—over a grave site with three circular bases topped by a 20-foot-diameter octagonal mausoleum. The memorial was constructed in 1866–1881 and still stands at the grave site, which now is operated by the Illinois Historic Preservation Agency.

In the mausoleum, a marble sarcophagus holds the remains of Douglas, surmounted by a marble bust of the senator. Four large bronze allegorical figures (portraying Illinois, History, Justice, and Eloquence) are on pedestals at the four corners of the mausoleum. Four bronze bas reliefs, representing stages in "the advance of American civilization," are above the main base of the column. Numerous trees and flower beds surround the tomb. The memorial has guided tours and lectures. Annual attendance is 15,000.

Stephen A. Douglas Tomb and Memorial, 636 E. 35th St., Chicago, IL 60616-4196. Phone: 312/225-2620. Fax: 312/225-7855. Website: www.illinoishistory.gov/hs/douglas_tomb.htm. Hours: 9–5 Wed.–Sun.; closed Mon.–Tues., New Year's Day, Thanksgiving, and Christmas. Admission: free.

Brandon Museum at Stephen A. Douglas Birthplace. The life and career of Senator and 1850 presidential candidate Stephen A. Douglas are featured at the house in which he was born in Brandon, Vermont, in 1813. The historic house has been restored and now serves as the home for the Brandon Museum at Stephen A. Douglas Birthplace and the Brandon Visitor Center. The museum, which opened in 2010, celebrates the history and lives of early Brandon residents and traces the development of the town during the mid-1800s and the antislavery movement. It contains hundreds of historical photographs, personal artifacts, and items manufactured in Brandon.

Brandon Museum at Stephen A. Douglas Birthplace, 4 Grove St. (Rte. 7), Brandon, VT 05733. Phone: 802/242-6401. Website: www.brandon.org. Hours: mid-May–mid-Oct.—11–4 daily and by appointment; closed mid-Oct.–mid-May. Admission: free.

Lincoln-Douglas Debate Museum. *See* Abraham Lincoln in Presidents section.

Queen Emma Kaleleokalani

Queen Emma Summer Palace. Queen Emma was the queen consort of King Kamehameha IV of the Kingdom of Hawaii from 1856 to his death in 1863. They were a popular couple, and she became known for her humanitarian efforts. When the 29-year-old king died, he expected her to succeed him on the throne. But he did not make the necessary legal pronouncement that would have made her the reigning sovereign queen. As a result, she had to run in the constitutionally mandated royal election and lost to future King David Kalākaua. After the election, she retired from public life. The retreat in Honolulu where the young royal couple and later Emma went to escape the summer heat now is a historic house museum called Queen Emma's Summer Palace.

Queen Emma was born in Honolulu in 1836 to High Chief George Na'ea and High Chiefess Fanny Kekelaoka-lani Young. She was the great-granddaughter of Keliimaikai, a half-brother of Kamehamela the Great. As was the Hawaiian tradition of *hānai* at the time, Emma was adopted at birth by her childless maternal aunt, Chiefess Grace Kama'iku'i Young Rooke, and her husband, Dr. Thomas C. H. Rooke, a young English court physician. She grew up at her foster parents' English mansion, with Dr. Rooke raising Emma to be very British, while her aunt also raised her to be Hawaiian.

In 1856 she married 23-year-old Alexander Liholiho, who ascended to the Hawaiian throne as King Kamehameha IV. Inspired by her adoptive father's medical work, Queen Emma encouraged her husband to establish a public hospital to help native Hawaiians who were in decline from foreign-borne diseases. In his first speech as king, Kamehameha IV called for such a hospital, pointing out that the native population had declined from 350,000 to 70,000 since Captain Cook's arrival and that extinction was a real possibility because of the introduction of foreign diseases.

The young king said the treasury was empty, but that he and the queen would raise funds for a hospital in Honolulu. Within a month, enough support was raised to build a hospital with 18 beds in 1859 and then a much larger building with 124 beds the following year. The hospital, which was located where the Queen's Medical Center stands today, was named Queen's Hospital in her honor and in recognition of her assistance.

In 1858 a son named Albert Edward Kauikeaouli Leiopapa a Kamehameha was born. The birth was celebrated throughout the kingdom, but then tragedy struck four years later. Prince Albert died suddenly of what was called "brain fever." Fifteen months later, the king, weakened by asthma and a broken heart, died at the age of 29. In her grief, Queen Emma took a new name—Kaleleonalani—which means "flight of the heavenly chiefs."

Queen Emma then devoted herself to numerous worthy causes. They included organizing a women's hospital auxiliary to assist those who are ill, helping to establish three schools, and assisting in raising funds for the St. Andrews Anglican Cathedral in Hawaii. Queen Emma died in 1885 at the age of 49 after several small strokes.

Queen Emma's Summer Palace became a historic house museum in 1915. The Greek revival–style house originally was built by John Lewis in Boston in 1848 and shipped to Hawaii via Cape Horn. It was purchased by Queen Emma's uncle, missionary John Young II, in 1895. The house became known as the Queen Emma Summer Palace because it was left to her by Young and she used it as a summer retreat with her husband from 1857 to 1863 and then as a widow until 1885.

The historic house has six rooms, with the one across the back added in 1865 to accommodate the visit of the Duke of Edinburgh. After her death in 1885, the house was bought by the Hawaiian Monarchy and was scheduled to be demolished for a park when it was acquired, restored, and converted into a museum by the Daughters of Hawaii.

The house has a collection of Queen Emma's furnishings, belongings, and memorabilia. It contains such things as an early round mission-style dining table, a baby grand piano from a European tour, a four-posted bed of Koa wood, a sleigh bed with a crown, a cradle in the shape of a canoe, a Gothic curved glass cabinet that was a wedding gift from Queen Victoria, and such symbols of royalty as a woman's feather cape and a chief's helmet made of roots. The house museum, which is listed on the National Register of Historic Places, has an annual attendance of 14,000.

Queen Emma Summer Palace, 2913 Pali Hwy., Honolulu, HI 96817-1417. Phone: 808/595-3167. Fax: 808/595-4395. E-mail: doh1903@hawaii.rr.com. Website: www.daughtersofhawaii.org. Hours: 9–4 daily; closed major holidays. Admission: adults, $6; seniors, $4; children under 18, $1.

Samuel J. Ervin

Senator Sam J. Ervin Jr. Library and Museum. Samuel J. Ervin, who liked to call himself a "country lawyer," was a folksy North Carolina politician who had great impact in Congress during the second half of the twentieth century. He served as Democratic senator from North Carolina from 1954 to 1974. His work on two Senate committees helped to bring down Senator Joseph McCarthy in 1954 and President Richard Nixon in 1974. He also was the South's constitutional expert during congressional debates on civil rights. Ervin defended Jim Crow laws and racial segregation but supported civil liberties legislation. The Senator Sam J. Ervin Jr. Library and Museum at Western Piedmont Community College in Morganton, North Carolina, is now devoted to his life and career.

Ervin was born in 1896 in Morganton. He graduated from the University of North Carolina in 1917 and Harvard Law School in 1922. He was admitted to the bar in 1919 before completing law school. During World War I, Ervin served in the U.S. Army in France and twice was cited for bravery. He was awarded the Distinguished Service Cross, the Silver Star, and two Purple Hearts. He entered politics while still a law student at Harvard.

Ervin was nominated in absentia by the Democratic Part and elected for the North Carolina House of Representatives in 1922 and then reelected in 1924 and 1930. He was elected as a county judge in 1935 and then served as a state judge from 1937 to 1943. In 1946 he was appointed to fill the U.S. House of Representatives vacancy left by the death of his brother, Joseph W. Ervin, and in 1948 was appointed to the North Carolina Supreme Court and served until 1954 when he became a U.S. senator.

In 1954 Ervin was appointed by the governor to fill the seat of Clyde Hoey, who died in office. Later that year, he was elected to the Senate and served until he retired in 1974. He was an authority on the American Constitution who sat on the Senate committee that censured Senator Joseph McCarthy of Wisconsin for his wild accusations about communists and Soviet spies in the federal government and elsewhere, and he served as chairman of the Senate committee that investigated the Watergate scandal that led to the resignation of President Richard Nixon. He also became known for helping to investigate labor racketeering and leading Southern filibusters against civil rights legislation while acting as a champion of civil liberties.

After retiring in 1974, he returned to Morganton to practice law. He also wrote his version of Watergate and an autobiography. Ervin died in 1985 at the age of 88 of complications of emphysema. In 1990 the Senator Sam J. Ervin Jr. Library and Museum was founded at Western Piedmont Community College in his hometown of Morganton.

The library/museum, which is housed in the Phifer Learning Resource Center, is devoted to Ervin's life and career and features a replica of his home library and objects from his collection of personal and political memorabilia. They include nearly 10,000 books, correspondence, photographs, and public and private documents representing his personal, professional, and intellectual life.

Senator Sam J. Ervin Jr. Library and Museum, Western Piedmont Community College, 1001 Burkemont Ave., Morganton, NC 28655. Phone: 828/448-6195. Fax: 828/448-6173. E-mail: dsmith@wpcc.edu. Website: www.samervinlibrary.org. Hours: 8–5 Mon.–Fri.; closed Sat.–Sun. and major holidays. Admission: free.

Benjamin Franklin

Benjamin Franklin National Memorial. Benjamin Franklin was one of the nation's Founding Fathers in the eighteenth century. He has been called the most accomplished American of his age and the most influential in the development of the society that American would become. Franklin was a man of many talents. In addition to serving his country as a politician, statesman, diplomat, postmaster, and political theorist, he was a printer, newspaper editor, publisher, author, scientist, inventor, merchant, musician, philosopher, satirist, abolitionist, civic activist, and philanthropist. He is honored at the Benjamin Franklin National Memorial, located at the Franklin Institute in Philadelphia.

Franklin, who was known for his curiosity, ingenuity, generosity, and diversity of interests, served as an inspiration to many early Americans and helped unite the people of the colonies into an independent nation. As a scientist and inventor, he was a major figure in the American Enlightenment and in physics for his discoveries and theories in electricity and such inventions as the lightning rod, bifocals, Franklin stove, carriage odometer, medical catheter, and glass harmonica. Franklin also charted and codified the Gulf Stream and is credited with founding the first public library, hospital, academy, and volunteer firefighting company in America.

Benjamin Franklin was born in Boston in 1706. His father, Josiah Franklin, a tallow chandler and soap and candle maker, was married twice and had 17 children—seven with his first wife, Anne Child, who later died, and 10 with the second, Abiah Folger, who was Franklin's mother. He was the 15th child and the eighth from the second marriage. Franklin attended Latin School, but had to drop out when 10 because he lacked the money to finish. He continued his education by voracious reading. He then worked for his father until he was 12, when he became an apprentice to his brother James, who taught him about printing.

When he was 15, Franklin's brother founded the *New-England Courant*, the first really independent newspaper in the colonies. When not allowed to write a letter to the paper for publication, Franklin wrote a number of letters with the pseudonym "Mrs. Silence Dogood," which were published and caused some conversation. When his brother learned of the ruse, he let Franklin know he was unhappy about it. Shortly thereafter, Ben left the apprenticeship without permission and was considered a fugitive.

At the age of 17, Franklin ran away to Philadelphia to get a new start. After working at several printing shops, he was convinced by Sir William Keith, Pennsylvania's governor, to go to England to acquire the printing equipment needed to start another newspaper in Philadelphia. He made the trip to London, but plans for the paper fell through. He got a job as a typesetter and then returned to Philadelphia in 1726 by working as a clerk, shopkeeper, and book-keeper for a merchant.

When Franklin was 17, he proposed to 15-year-old Deborah Read while he was a boarder in her family's home. Her mother would not permit her daughter to marry Franklin, and that is when he went to England. While he was there, Deborah got married to a man who ran off to Barbados to avoid paying his debts and prosecution. When Franklin returned from Europe, he had an illegitimate son named William with an unknown woman and then established a common-law marriage with Deborah since she was not free to remarry under bigamy laws. They had two children, as well as William, who became part of the family. William later was the last loyalist governor of New Jersey and eventually left for England with the British troops and never returned.

In 1727, 21-year-old Franklin created the Junto, a group of artisans and tradesmen who sought to better themselves by reading and meeting periodically to discuss issues of the day. It gave rise to many similar organizations and in 1731 became the Library Company of Philadelphia, which grew to be a major scholarly and research library with rare books, manuscripts, and graphic items. In addition to composing the charter for the facility, Franklin hired the first librarian in America. The Junto also developed into the American Philosophical Society in 1844 to help scientists discuss their discoveries.

Franklin returned to printing in 1728, opening a printing house with a partner and then became publisher of the *Pennsylvania Gazette* the following year. In 1732 Franklin began to publish his popular *Poor Richard's Almanack*, which contained witty aphorisms and moral precepts, under the pseudonym Richard Saunders. He stopped writing for the *Almanack* in 1758—the same year he printed "Father Abraham's Sermon," also known as "The Way to Wealth." He retired from printing in 1748 as he became more interested in public affairs and the natural sciences.

In addition to his numerous inventions, Franklin played a leading role in the establishment of electricity as a field in physical science and also made contributions in meteorology, oceanography, and other fields. He began his experiments with electricity in 1746 and found that an electric charge is not created by rubbing substances but merely transferred (known as the principle of conservation of charge). His most famous experiment was when he used a kit to extract sparks from a cloud in 1752. In meteorology, he showed that storms do not always travel in the direction of the prevailing wind, leading to the use of synoptic charts of dynamic meteorology, which replaced sole dependence upon charts of climatology. In oceanography, he charted and codified the Gulf Stream for the first time.

Franklin served as clerk of the Pennsylvania legislature in 1736–1751, deputy postmaster in Philadelphia in 1737–1753, and then deputy postmaster general for the colonies in 1753–1774 (during which he reformed the postal service). In 1749 he established the first American academy—the Academy of Philadelphia—with classes beginning in 1751. It eventually evolved into the University of Pennsylvania. Franklin and Dr. Thomas Bond then obtained a charter from the Pennsylvania legislature to establish the Pennsylvania Hospital, which became the first hospital in the colonies and the nation.

In 1754 Franklin led the Pennsylvania delegation to a meeting of several colonies at the Albany Congress, a meeting requested by the Board of Trade in England to improve relations with Indians and defense against the French. It is when Franklin proposed that the colonies work together as a union. The plan, which was one of the earliest calls for unity among the colonies, was not adopted. But parts of the proposal later were incorporated into the Articles of Confederation and the Constitution of the United States.

In 1757 the Pennsylvania Assembly sent Franklin to England to protest the influence of the Penn family in the government of Pennsylvania and to enforce taxes on proprietary estates. He remained there until 1762, pleading the case with the people and the ministry of the United Kingdom. While in England, he was awarded a doctor's degree for his scientific accomplishments and was known as "Doctor Franklin" thereafter. In 1764 he returned to England to serve as the agent for Pennsylvania—and later Georgia, New Jersey, and Massachusetts. In 1767 he crossed the channel to France, where he was received with honors before returning home. In 1771 he began writing his *Autobiography*, which is considered the greatest autobiography written in colonial America.

Franklin was made a member of the Second Continental Congress and served on the committee to draft the Declaration of Independence in 1775. In 1776 he was sent to France as commissioner for the United States. He remained in France until 1785, during which time he secured a critical military alliance and negotiated the Treaty of Paris (with John Jay and John Adams), which settled the American Revolutionary War with Britain in 1783. When he returned home he was considered second only to George Washington as the champion of American independence. He also became active in the abolitionist movement, freeing his two slaves and serving as president of the Society for the Relief of Free Negroes Unlawfully Held in Bondage.

Franklin retired but in 1787 was a delegate at a meeting that produced the United States Constitution to replace the Articles of Confederation. He is the only Founding Father who signed the three major documents in the founding of the United States—the Declaration of Independence, the Treaty of Paris, and the Constitution. In 1788 he finished *The Autobiography of Benjamin Franklin*, which he began in 1771. It was first published in Paris in French in 1790, but it was not until 1868 that the complete book was printed.

Franklin died in 1790 at the age of 84. He made a number of philanthropic gifts near the end of his life and in his will, including 200 pounds to help establish Franklin College in Lancaster, Pennsylvania, in 1787. It merged with Marshall College in 1853 to become Franklin and Marshall College. Franklin also bequeathed 1,000 pounds (about $4,400 then, worth around $55,000 in today's dollars) to the cities of Boston and Philadelphia to be held in trust for 200 years. The bequests grew to $2 million in Philadelphia and $5 million in Boston. Much of the interest has been used for such purposes as home loans, scholarships, and a trade school.

Franklin is now honored at the Benjamin Franklin National Memorial, which was established in 1972 at the Franklin Institute, a major science museum in Philadelphia that initially dedicated the statue of Franklin in 1938. The memorial is an affiliated area of the Independence National Historical Park.

A 20-foot-tall sculpture of a seated Franklin dominates the memorial hall at the entrance to the museum. The huge statue, which stands on a pedestal of white marble, was sculpted by James Earl Fraser between 1906 and 1911. It is located in a rotunda designed after the Pantheon by John T. Windrim in 1938. In 2008 a restoration of the memorial included the addition of a multimedia presentation about Franklin. Quotations from Franklin are projected onto the walls, and graphic panels highlight his life and accomplishments.

The Franklin Institute also has a Frankliniana Collection that is shown in a rotating display in the museum's Pendulum Staircase. It includes such items as the 1777 Nini Medallion, the maquette of Franklin's bust from Franklin's statue in the memorial, the figurehead of Franklin's bust from the USS *Franklin*, Franklin's ceremonial sword used in the court of King Louis XVI, and the odometer that Franklin used to measure the postal routes in Philadelphia. The Electricity Exhibit also has one of Franklin's lightning rods, his electricity tube, a Franklin electrostatic generator, Franklin's 1751 publication *Observations and Experiments on Electricity*, and Thornton Oakley's two 1940 historical murals of Franklin and the "Kite and Key" experiment. The museum and memorial annual attendance is 1 million.

Benjamin Franklin National Memorial, Franklin Institute, 222 N. 20th St., Philadelphia, PA 19103-1190. Phone: 215/448-1200. Fax: 215/448-1109. E-mail: dwint@fi.edu. Website: www.nps.gov/inde/benjamin-franklin-national-memorial.htm. Hours: 9:30–5 daily; closed New Year's Day, Thanksgiving, and Christmas Eve and Day. Admission: memorial—free; museum—adults, $16.50; seniors, students, and military, $15.50; children 3–11, $12.50; children under 3, free.

Franklin Court. Franklin Court in Philadelphia is where Benjamin Franklin's impressive home was located while he served in the Continental Congress and the Constitutional Convention and later died in 1790. The actual house, which no longer exists, was torn down in 1812. But a huge steel structure outlining the spot where the house stood is located there, as well as an underground museum, an eighteenth-century printing office, an operating post office, a postal museum, and an architectural/archaeological exhibit with artifacts.

Franklin Court, designed by architect Robert Ventura, was opened in 1976 as part of the nation's bicentennial observance. It is part of the 55-acre Independence National Historical Park, which covers 20 city blocks in downtown Philadelphia and serves over 5 million visitors a year. The park also includes such historic sites as Independence Hall, Congress Hall, the Carpenters' Hall, Old City Hall, the Liberty Bell, and the First and Second Banks of the United States. Admission is free, but tour tickets must be obtained on the day of the visit at the Independence Visitor Center.

Franklin Court has become one of the most popular sites in the national park. Franklin lived with his family in small row houses in the neighborhood before his large house was built. He planned much of the interior of the three-story house, but he was a colonial emissary in England and then France while it was being built. His wife, Deborah, actually oversaw the construction. Although no plans remain of the 10-room house, the steel structure indicates its dimensions and those of the adjacent smaller print shop. Excavations also have turned up parts of the foundation and walls and outdoor privy wells.

Nearby are restorations of five buildings, three of which Franklin built shortly after his return from France to be used as rental properties. They now contain a demonstration of eighteenth-century printing, an operating post office and postal museum in a replica of Franklin's post office, and an architectural/archaeological exhibit about Franklin's interest in fire-resistant buildings and a collection of early pottery and glassware recovered from his privy pits.

The historic site also has an underground museum that features an 18-minute film and exhibits of paintings, objects, and inventions associated with Franklin. Among the inventions on display are his glass harmonica, Franklin stove, and swim fin (he was a champion swimmer in his day). The museum also has a portrait and furniture gallery, a room devoted to Franklin's various roles, and a phone bank with testimonies about Franklin based on the words of Washington, Mozart, D. H. Lawrence, and others.

Franklin Court, Independence National Historical Park, 314-22 Market St., Philadelphia, PA 19106 (postal address: Independence Visitor Center, Independence National Historical Park, 143 S. 3rd St., Philadelphia, PA 19106-2818). Phone: 215/965-2305 and 215/965-2065. Fax: 215/597-5556. Hours: visitor center—Memorial Day–Labor Day: 8:30–7 daily; day after Labor Day–day before Memorial Day: 8:30–5 daily; Franklin Court—9–5 daily, although some buildings may be closed for renovation.

John Nance Garner

Briscoe-Garner Museum. John Nance Garner was one of the most powerful vice presidents in the nation's history. Garner, who had served in the U.S. House of Representatives from 1903 to 1933, was vice president in 1933–1941 during the Great Depression and New Deal years of President Franklin D. Roosevelt. His life and historical significance are presented in his former home, now the Briscoe-Garner Museum, in Uvalde, Texas. The museum is part of the Congressional History Collection of the Dolph Briscoe Center for American History at the University of Texas at Austin.

Garner, who was known as "Cactus Jack," served as the minority leader in the House of Representatives in 1929–1931 and as speaker in 1931–1933. He was a powerful congressional leader who was popular with House members of both parties. In 1932 he sought the Democratic nomination for president, but when it became evident he did not have sufficient support from the delegates, Garner agreed to be Roosevelt's running mate. He was reelected to Congress at the same time he was elected vice president, making him the only person to serve as both speaker of the House and president of the Senate at the same time.

During his first term as vice president, Garner helped Roosevelt pass much of the New Deal legislation, although he did not agree with all of it. He supported a balanced budget and federal breaking up of the Flint automobile sit-down strike but opposed packing the Supreme Court with additional judges, more New Deal proposals, executive interferences with congressional internal business, and Roosevelt's decision to run for an unprecedented third term.

Garner ran for president in 1940 but lost the Democratic nomination to Roosevelt. Garner appealed to conservatives but not liberals. Roosevelt replaced Garner with Henry A. Wallace as the vice presidency nominee. Garner retired from politics in 1941 after stepping down as vice president and ending 46 years in public life. He returned to his home in Uvalde and spent the next 26 years managing his extensive real estate holdings, advising politicians, enjoying his grandchildren, and fishing. He died in 1967 at the age of 98, making him the longest-living vice president.

Garner was born in 1868 near the village of Detroit in East Texas to John Nance Garner III and Sarah Jane Guest Garner. He attended Vanderbilt University for one semester and then dropped out. Garner later studied law, was admitted to the bar in 1890, and opened his law practice in Uvalde. He was county judge in Uvalde County in 1893–1896. His 1893 Democratic primary opponent was Mariette Rheiner, a rancher's daughter, whom he married a week after meeting her. They had one child.

Garner served in the Texas House of Representatives from 1898 to 1902. He received his "Cactus Jack" nickname after fervently supporting the prickly pear cactus while the legislature was selecting a state flower (the bluebonnet). In 1902 he was elected as a Democrat to the U.S. House of Representatives in the newly created 15th Congressional District in rural South Texas. He was reelected to the congressional seat 14 times and served until 1933. His wife was his private secretary throughout that period.

John and Ettie Garner lived in the two-story H-shaped brick home that became the museum from 1920 until Mrs. Garner's death in 1948. He continued to stay there until 1952, when he moved to a small cottage on the property and donated the house to the City of Uvalde. It served as a city library, historical museum, and community meeting facility before opening as the Garner Memorial Museum in 1973. The museum name later was changed to the John Nance Garner Museum. In 1999 operation of the house was transferred to the University of Texas's Center for American History, and in 2011 the museum was renamed the Briscoe-Garner Museum to honor two former Uvalde residents—Garner and the late Governor Dolph Briscoe.

The museum, which recently was renovated, has exhibits with photographs, cartoons, documents, paintings, sculptures, and artifacts relating to Garner's life and career on the first floor and similar displays about Briscoe on the second floor. The Center for American History archives in Austin also contain the extensive Garner scrapbook collection of papers and other materials and Briscoe's personal and gubernatorial papers. The Garner house, which has been designated a National Historic Landmark and is listed on the National Register of Historic Places, has an annual attendance of 3,500.

Garner-Briscoe Museum, 333 N. Park St., Uvalde, TX 78801-4658. Phone: 830/278-5018. Fax: 830/279-0512. E-mail: bbhadley@austin.utexas.edu. Website: www.cah.utexas.edu. Hours: 9–5 Tues.–Sat.; closed Sun.–Mon. and major holidays. Admission: free.

Alexander Hamilton

Hamilton Grange National Memorial. Alexander Hamilton was one of the nation's Founding Fathers, an early constitutional lawyer, and the first secretary of the treasury. He was the primary author of the economic policies of the George Washington administration, which included funding state debts by the federal government and establishing a national bank, a system of tariffs, and friendly trade relations with Britain. Hamilton, who became the leader of the Federalist Party, was mortally wounded by Aaron Burr in a duel after he prevented Burr from being elected governor of the state of New York in 1804. Hamilton's home in New York City now is the Hamilton Grange National Memorial.

Hamilton was born out of wedlock in Charlestown, capital of the island of Nevis in the Leeward Islands in the British West Indies. It is not certain whether he was born in 1755 or 1757 (Hamilton used both dates later). His mother was Rachel Faucette Buck, a married woman of partial French Huguenot descent who left her husband and a son in an unhappy marriage in 1850 and went to St. Kitts. Alexander's father was James A. Hamilton, a poor itinerant Scottish merchant of aristocratic descent. They had two sons (also James) in a common-law marriage (because of the prior marriage).

In 1765 Hamilton's father moved the family to St. Croix in the Virgin Islands and abandoned them, allegedly to avoid having Rachel charged with bigamy after her first husband threatened to divorce her on grounds of adultery and desertion. The mother and sons moved to Nevis, where she had been born and had inherited property from her father. She ran a small store in Christiansted, and Alexander received tutoring and went to a private school. In 1868 his mother died after a severe fever, and Alexander was effectively left a 13-year-old orphan. Her first husband seized her estate in probate court, and the boys were left penniless.

Alexander became a clerk at a local import/export firm, and then the boys were adopted by a cousin, Peter Lytton. But when Lytton committed suicide, the brothers were separated—Alexander was adopted by Thomas Stevens, a Nevis merchant, and James was apprenticed with a local carpenter. Alexander developed an interest in writing and published an essay about a hurricane that impressed community leaders, who collected a fund to send him to the American colonies for his education. He attended Elizabethtown Academy, a grammar school in Elizabethtown, New Jersey, and King's College (now Columbia University) in New York City in the early 1770s. While a college student, he did his first political writings, which supported the American revolutionary cause.

In 1775 Hamilton joined a New York volunteer militia company, consisting of King's College students. He studied military history and tactics on his own, became a lieutenant, and led a successful raid that captured a cannon during a British shelling of New York. As a result, his unit became an artillery company. He became a captain in the New York Provincial Company of Artillery and took part in the Battle of White Plains and the Battle of Trenton. He was promoted to lieutenant colonel and served for four years as George Washington's chief of staff.

In 1780 Hamilton married Elizabeth Schuyler, daughter of Philip Schuyler, a general and wealthy landowner from one of the most prominent families in the state of New York. In 1802 the Hamilton family moved into the Grange, a palatial country home he had built in a rural area just north of New York City. He lived in the house only two years before his death in a duel in 1804. The mansion now is a national memorial and a historic house museum.

While on Washington's staff, Hamilton sought field command in active combat. Washington finally relented in 1781, assigning Hamilton as commander of a New York light infantry battalion. In the assault on Yorktown, Hamilton was given command of three battalions that were to fight in conjunction with French troops in taking two redoubts of the British fortifications. Hamilton and his men took Redoubt No. 10 with bayonets, and the French successfully overcame Redoubt No. 9—which contributed to the surrender of British troops at Yorktown and ended major British military operations in America.

After the Battle of Yorktown, Hamilton resigned his commission, read law in Albany, and established a law practice (one of the first in constitutional law). In 1782–1783 he was elected as a delegate to the Continental Congress, established a law office in New York City, and collaborated with John Jay and James Madison on *The Federalist Papers*. He again was elected to the Continental Congress in 1787. In 1789 he became secretary of the treasury as the new national government got underway and began to place the nation's disorganized finances on a sound footing. Among his efforts were establishing a national bank, funding the national debt, assuming state war debts, encouraging manufacturing, and improving relations with Britain.

Hamilton's policies brought him in conflict with Madison and Thomas Jefferson, who opposed his probusiness economic program, better relations with Britain, and opposition to the principles and excesses of the French Revolution—which they saw as distain for the common man. This led to the establishment of the first American party system, with Jefferson, Madison, and the Democratic Republicans against Hamilton and the Federalists. However, while George Washington was president, most of Hamilton's policies were followed.

In 1795 Hamilton's low salary as a cabinet officer and the cost of living in New York and Washington forced him to resign and resume his law career. But he still had a powerful impact on New York and national politics. He sought to prevent John Adams, a fellow Federalist, from becoming president in 1796 but failed. He was more successful in blocking Aaron Burr from becoming president when he tied with Jefferson in 1800. Hamilton threw his support to Jefferson and helped him win the presidency.

Hamilton also opposed Burr when he ran for governor of New York in 1804. This time Burr took offense at remarks he believed came from Hamilton and challenged him to a duel. In the duel in Weehawken, New Jersey, Hamilton was mortally wounded and died the next day. He was either 49 or 51 years old.

The Grange National Memorial in St. Nicholas Park in New York City was Hamilton's home from 1802 until his death in 1804. He commissioned architect John McComb Jr. to design the two-story federal-style country home on his 32 acres in upper Manhattan. The house was named the Grange after Hamilton's grandfather's estate in Scotland. It was the only home Hamilton ever owned and remained in the family for 30 years after his death. It has been moved twice from its original site. It was moved four blocks in 1889 to conform to a new street pattern and to nearby St. Nicholas Park in 2008 to permit restoration of features lost in the first move.

The house opened as a public museum operated by the American Scenic and Historic Preservation Society in 1924 and became a National Historic Landmark in 1960 and was listed on the National Register of Historic Places in 1966. It has early nineteenth-century furnishings, Hamilton memorabilia, and a visitor center with interpretive exhibits about Hamilton and the house. The memorial also offers guided tours. Annual attendance is 11,500.

Hamilton Grange National Memorial, 414 W. 141st St., New York, NY 10031 (postal address: 5 Federal Hall NM, 26 Wall St., New York, NY 10005). Phone: 646/548-2310. Fax: 646/548-9366. E-mail: shirley_mckinney@nps.gov. Website: www.nps.gov/hagr. Hours: 9–5 Wed.–Sun.; closed Mon.–Tues., Thanksgiving, and Christmas. Admission: free.

H. John Heinz III

Senator John Heinz Pittsburgh History Center. Henry John Heinz III was a senator from Pennsylvania who was killed with six other people when a helicopter collided with his private plane in 1991. The Senator John Heinz Pittsburgh History Center in his hometown of Pittsburgh opened in 1996 in his honor. The 275,000-square-foot museum preserves and presents the regional history of western Pennsylvania.

Heinz entered politics in 1971 when he was elected a Republican congressman in the U.S. House of Representatives in a special election to fill a vacancy caused by the death of Robert Corbett and then was reelected twice. He became a senator in 1976 when he defeated seven-term Democratic congressman Bill Green, charging that he was soft on military issues because he voted against various defense appropriations in the Vietnam War era.

Heinz became one of the leaders in the Senate on the issue of American economic competitiveness. He said the nation's economic health and competitiveness were in rapid decline and that the George H. W. Bush administration's policies accelerated the decline. Heinz organized a group of Republican senators who met regularly for lunch and sought to have the administration adopt some of President Ronald Reagan's programs for rebuilding U.S. competitiveness. The group ceased to meet after Heinz's death.

The plane crash occurred in 1991 when a Bell 412 helicopter was sent to check on a landing gear problem while he was flying his Piper Aerostar plane. As the helicopter was moving in for a closer look at the landing gear, its rotor blades struck the bottom of the plane, causing both aircraft to crash. All aboard the two aircraft and two first-grade girls playing outside the Merion Elementary School in Lower Merion Township near Philadelphia were killed.

Heinz was born in Pittsburgh in 1938 to H. J. Heinz II (heir to the H. J. Heinz Company) and Joan Diehl Heinz. When his parents divorced, John moved to San Francisco with his mother and his stepfather, navy Captain Clayton C. McCauley. He graduated from the Town School, Phillips Exeter Academy, in 1956, Yale University in 1960, and Harvard Business School in 1963.

After getting an M.B.A., he enlisted in the U.S. Air Force in 1963 and was sent to the Lackland Air Force Base. He then served with the 911th Troop Carrier Group as a member of the U.S. Air Force Reserve based at the Greater Pittsburgh Airport. As a businessman, he worked as an analyst in the controller division and various other positions in the marketing division of H. J. Heinz Company. In 1970–1971 Heinz was on the faculty at the Tepper School of Business at Carnegie Mellon University.

The Senator John Heinz Pittsburgh History Center, located in the historic Strip District near downtown Pittsburgh, is the largest history museum in the state. It covers six floors in the century-old Chautauqua Lake Ice Company Building and a Smithsonian Institution addition. Among the exhibits are permanent displays on Pittsburgh and western Pennsylvania's history of significant contributions, Senator John Heinz's life and legacy, Pittsburgh as a center of glass production, the history of the H. J. Heinz Company, and a Special Collections Gallery with more than 3,000 artifacts illustrating the rich ethnic history and corporate fabric of the region. The museum also has a 7,000-square-foot Children's Discovery Hall.

Among the other facilities is a 35,000 library and archive of regional books, manuscripts, photographs, maps, atlases, newspapers, films, recordings, and other memorabilia. The Meadowcroft Rockshelter and Museum of Rural Life, a world-renowned 16,000-year-old archaeological site and a village recreating rural life in the nineteenth century south of Pittsburgh, also are part of the history center. In addition, the independent Western Pennsylvania Sports Museum is housed in the Heinz historical center complex, and the Fort Pitt Museum is located nearby at historic Point State Park downtown. The history center's annual attendance is 160,000.

Senator John Heinz History Center, 1212 Smallman St., Pittsburgh, PA 15222-4200. Phone: 412/454-6000. Fax: 412/454-6031. E-mail: hswp@hswp.org. Website: www.heinzhistorycenter.org. Hours: 10–5 daily; closed New Year's Day, Easter, Thanksgiving, and Christmas. Admission: adults, $10; seniors, $9; children 4–17, $5; children under 4, free.

Jesse Helms

Jesse Helms Center. Jesse Helms was a former Democrat who became a five-term Republican ultra-conservative senator from North Carolina. He helped organize and fund the conservative resurgence in the 1970s and assisted Ronald Reagan's run for the presidency and many local and regional candidates. His official papers are now at the Jesse Helms Center at Wingate University—a small school in Wingate, North Carolina, that opened its doors to him as a junior college when he did not have the money to go to college during the Great Depression in the 1930s.

The center, located in the A. J. Fletcher Building at the entrance to Wingate University, seeks to preserve and promote what it calls the traditional values upon which the United States was founded. The center is known for its lectures for the public, seminars for teachers, training programs for those embarking on careers in government, citizen seminars on government issues, and character education essay competition for middle and high schools. It also has exhibits and tributes to Helms.

Jesse Alexander Helms Jr. was born in Monroe, North Carolina, in 1921. His father, "Big Jesse" Helms, served as both the fire chief and chief of police, and his mother, Ethel Mae Helms, was a homemaker. He went to public schools and then attended Wingate Junior College and Wake Forest College. He dropped out of college after a year to work as a newspaper and radio reporter for 11 years. Helms's first job after college was at the *Raleigh Times*, where he served as sports reporter and then news reporter, assistant city editor, and city editor. He also worked at the *News and Observer*, where he was a sports and news reporter. While at the *News & Observer*, Helms met Dorothy Coble, society editor, whom he married in 1942. They had three children—Jane, Nancy, and Charles.

During World War II, Helms was a navy recruiter. After the war, he returned to journalism and entered politics. He became city news editor at the *Raleigh Times* and later a radio and television newscaster and commentator. In the 1950s he also served as publicity director for Willis Smith, a conservative Democrat running for U.S. senator. Smith was elected and hired Helms as an administrative assistant. In 1952 Helms worked on the presidential campaign of Senator Richard Russell until he dropped out of the race. Helms returned to work for Smith, but Smith died in 1953 and Helms returned to Raleigh. From 1953 to 1960, Helms was executive director of the North Carolina Bankers Association. He also settled in a home in Raleigh's Hayes Barton Historic District, where he lived until his death in 2008.

In 1957 Helms entered and won his first political election. He ran as a Democrat when many white southern politicians favored racial segregation. He was elected to the Raleigh city council and served two terms, earning a reputation as a conservative gadfly who opposed most proposals. In 1960 he worked on the unsuccessful primary gubernatorial campaign of I. Beverly Lake Sr., who advocated racial segregation.

It also was in 1960 that Helms became executive vice president, vice chairman, and assistant chief executive officer of the Raleigh-based Capitol Broadcasting Company. He made daily editorial comments on the firm's nightly newscasts and gained attention as a conservative commentator throughout eastern North Carolina with his attacks on the civil rights movement, liberal news media, antiwar churches, and the University of North Carolina. Helms, who switched to the Republican Party in 1970, remained with the broadcasting company until he was elected to the Senate in 1972. He was the first Republican senator from the state since 1903 and became the longest-serving elected senator in North Carolina history (serving 30 years from 1973 to 2003).

Helms rapidly became a leader in the conservative movement, being the most conservative politician of the post-1960s period. He opposed federal intervention into what he considered state affairs, such as the Civil Rights Act and the Voting Rights Act. He even tried to stop Senate approval of a federal holiday to honor Martin Luther King Jr. with a 16-day filibuster. Helms also opposed abortion, disability rights, feminism, gay rights, and contemporary art with graphic sexuality. As the longtime chairman of the Senate Foreign Relations Committee, he demanded a staunchly anticommunist foreign policy. He also blocked many presidential appointments and sought lower taxes and fewer labor unions to attract more companies to relocate to North Carolina and the South.

Helms, who did not run for reelection in 2002 for health reasons, died of vascular dementia in 2008 at the age of 86. The Jesse Helms Center was founded at Wingate University in 1987. It contains archives with his 1973–2003 congressional papers, as well as personal papers that document his pre-Senate career from the 1950s to 1970s. The center also has a number of interactive exhibits on Helms's life and career and about United States presidents, the United Nations, entrepreneurs from North Carolina, and the business and industry of the state.

The center's programs include a multiday program for young professionals and college students; a five-day residential conference that exposes high school students to free-market principles, character education, and leadership training; presentations on critical topics related to the center's mission; the "Laws of Life" character education essay contest; lecture series; and teacher workshops.

Jesse Helms Center, Wingate University, A. J. Fletcher Bldg., 3910 U.S. Hwy. 74 East, Wingate, NC 28174-0247 (postal address: PO Box 247, Wingate, NC 28174-0247). Phone: 704/233-1776. Fax: 704/233-1787. Website: www.jessehelmscenter.org. Hours: 9–5 Mon.–Fri., and by appointment on Sat.–Sun.; closed major holidays. Admission: free.

Samuel Houston

Sam Houston Memorial Museum. Sam Houston was one of the most important, colorful, and controversial figures in Texas history. He was a leader in gaining independence for Texas from Mexico and was the first and third president of the Republic of Texas, a U.S. senator from Texas, and the first and third governor of Texas. He also is the only person to serve as governor of two different states (he also was elected governor of Tennessee before settling in Texas). His life and times now are featured at the Sam Houston Memorial Museum in Huntsville, Texas.

Samuel Houston was born on a plantation in Rockbridge County in the Shenandoah Valley of Virginia in 1793. He was the fifth of nine children of Major Samuel Houston and Elizabeth Paxton Houston. Major Houston, who inherited the family farm, was commissioned a major in Morgan's Rifle Brigade during the American Revolutionary War. But he got into debt and decided to move the family to Tennessee near relatives and leave the debts behind, as frequently occurred on the frontier. However, he died in 1807 before the move, and Mrs. Houston moved her five sons and three daughters to a farm along Baker's Creek in Maryville, Tennessee. Sam was 14 at the time. Two years later, he ran away from home because he didn't like working on the family farm or general store and owed some debts.

Houston went southwest and lived with the Cherokee tribe led by Ahuludegi (also spelled Oolooteka and known as John Jolly to European Americans) on Hiwassee Island on the Hiwassee River near its confluence with the Tennessee River. The Cherokee chief became an adoptive father to Houston, who was given the Cherokee name of Colonneh (the Raven).

Houston returned to his family in Maryville in 1812 at the age of 19 and decided to teach school, much to everyone's surprise (*see* Sam Houston Schoolhouse listing). He had only six months of formal schooling, but he taught himself, including reading Latin and Greek. The one-room school—the first school built in Tennessee—turned out to be quite successful, increasing from eight to 35 students. He earned enough (at eight dollars per student) to pay his debts and to continue his own studies.

After the classes ended in the fall of 1812, he joined the 39th Infantry Regiment to fight the British in the War of 1812. By the end of the year, he had risen from private to third lieutenant. In 1814 he was wounded by an arrow at the Battle of Horseshoe Bend but returned to the battle after being bandaged. When Andrew Jackson called for volunteers to dislodge Red Sticks from a breastwork, Houston responded and suffered shoulder and arm bullet wounds and later underwent corrective surgery as a disabled veteran at a New Orleans hospital. Jackson was impressed with Houston and appointed him subagent in managing the removal of the Cherokees from East Tennessee to an Arkansas reservation. But when an inquiry was launched in 1818 into charges related to Houston's administration of supplies for the Indians, he was offended and resigned.

Houston then studied with a judge in Nashville, passed the bar examination, and opened a law practice in Lebanon, Tennessee. In 1818 he was appointed the local prosecutor in Nashville and a commander in the state militia. Houston was elected to the U.S. House of Representatives in 1822 and reelected in 1824. He was a staunch supporter of Democrat Andrew Jackson, although they differed on the treatment of Indians.

In 1827 Houston was elected governor of Tennessee. He planned to run for reelection in 1829 but resigned in embarrassment after the dissolution of his first marriage to Eliza Allen, a 19-year-old who reportedly fell out of love and left him shortly after the marriage. It was not until 1837 that he divorced her.

Houston then went with the Cherokees to the Arkansas Territory (now Oklahoma), where he was adopted as a citizen of the Cherokee nation. For several years, he lived with Tiana Rogers Gentry, a part-Cherokee widow. Although he was still married under civil law, he married her under Cherokee law. When Houston went to Texas in 1832, she did not go along and later married another man and died of pneumonia in 1838. After Houston officially divorced Eliza Allen in 1837, she remarried in 1840.

While living with the Cherokee, he went to Washington in 1830 and 1832 to complain about the frauds government agents committed against the tribe. In the process, he was accused by Congressman William Stanbery of Ohio of being in league with two others to supply rations to the various Indian tribes. When Stanberry refused to answer Houston's letters about the accusation, Houston denied the accusation, confronted him on the street, and beat him with a hickory cane. Stanbery drew a pistol and fired, but the gun misfired. Houston was charged for the attack and pleaded self-defense but was found guilty in a high-profile trial and fined $500, which he never paid.

After the 1832 trial, Houston left for Texas, which was still part of Mexico at the time. He settled in Coahuila y Tejas, and quickly became involved in the independence movement. He attended the Convention of 1833 as the representative of Nacogdoches and supported the more radical position of independence among the American settlers and Tejanos in Texas. In 1835, as Mexican General Antonio López de Santa Anna, now president, assumed dictatorial powers in Mexico, Houston was made major general of the Texas Army. In 1836 Houston negotiated a peace settlement with the Cherokee of East Texas to allay their fears about independence and was named commander-in-chief at the convention to declare Texas independence and establish a provisional government.

After the independence declaration, the Battle of the Alamo followed on March 6 at a 1718 Spanish mission occupied by Texans in San Antonio. The Alamo defenders held out for 13 days against nearly 4,000 Mexican soldiers under General Santa Anna. In the heroic stand, the defending Texans were killed, but it gave Houston time to organize his forces and defeat Santa Anna in the Battle of San Jacinto 46 days later. In the Treaty of Velasco, Santa Anna granted Texas its independence.

Houston was wounded in the ankle by a stray bullet at San Jacinto but recovered and was elected president of the Republic of Texas in 1836 and reelected in 1840. The settlement of Houston was founded and named for the Texas president in 1836. Houston also was married for a third time in 1840. The 47-year-old president married Margaret Moffette Lea, a 21-year-old from Marion, Alabama. They had eight children.

In 1845 the Republic of Texas was annexed by the United States, which triggered war with Mexico. It began after a dispute over the border, with the United States using the Rio Grande River as the border while Mexico claimed the land to the more northerly Nueces River. When Mexican troops attacked American forces in the disputed area, President James K. Polk asked Congress to declare war in 1846. The war spread to the West and into Mexico. After Mexico City was captured, the Treaty of Guadalupe Hidalgo in 1848 ceded the territories of Texas, California, and what later became Arizona, Colorado, Nevada, and Utah, and the United States agreed to pay Mexico about $18 million.

Houston served as a U.S. senator from 1846 to 1859 and governor of Texas in 1859–1861. When Texas seceded from the Union in 1861 at the outbreak of the Civil War, Houston refused to swear loyalty to the Confederacy and was removed from office. He retired to Huntsville, Texas, where he died in 1863 of pneumonia at the age of 70.

The Sam Houston Memorial Museum was founded in 1927 at Sam Houston State University in Huntsville, Texas, where he lived from 1840 to 1863. The museum contains of exhibits and objects related to Houston's life and times. It has personal possessions of Houston and his family, materials from General Santa Anna of Mexico, and objects related to Texas history. They include such things as his law office, a period kitchen, and a blacksmith shop. The museum is located on a 15-acre site with a park and pond. Annual attendance is 46,000.

The Woodland Home, where Sam Houston and his wife, Margaret, lived from 1847 to 1859, located at the Sam Houston Memorial Museum operated by the Sam Houston State University in Huntsville, Texas. Courtesy of the Sam Houston Memorial Museum, Huntsville, TX.

Sam Houston Memorial Museum, 1836 San Houston Ave., Huntsville, TX 77341 (postal address: PO Box 2057, Sam Houston State University, Huntsville, TX 77341-2057). Phones: 936/294-1832 and 936/294-1831. Fax: 936/294-3670. E-mail: smm_pbn@shsu.edu. Website: www.samhoustonmemorialmuseum.com. Hours: 9–4:30 Tues.–Sat., 12–4 Sun.; closed Mon., New Year's Day, Thanksgiving, and Christmas. Admission: adults, $4; seniors and SHSU faculty and staff, $3; children 6–18, $2; children under 6 and SHSU students, free.

Sam Houston Schoolhouse. The one-room schoolhouse where Sam Houston taught classes in 1812 is now a state historic site in Maryville, Tennessee, operated by the Sam Houston Memorial Association. Houston was 16 years old when he ran away from home in 1809 because he didn't like working on the family farm and at its general store. When he came back three years later, he wanted to teach and opened a school despite having only six months of formal schooling. He was self-taught. Much to everyone's surprise, the school was quite successful, and he was able to pay off his debts at the end of its one year of operation.

When Houston ran away, he moved to the Cherokee village on Hiwassee Island on the Hiwassee River at the confluence with the Tennessee River southwest of Maryville. He spent three years living with Chief Ahuludegi, who gave him the Cherokee name of Colonneh, meaning "the Raven." Houston learned to speak fluent Cherokee, did considerable reading, and visited his family every several months. He finally returned home in 1812 and opened the school in a 1794 log building after planting time in May.

The school began with eight students, but by the end of June it had 35 and was turning away others for lack of space. Classes continued until the corn harvest in November. At eight dollars per student, Houston earned enough to pay off his debts and continue his own studies. After the school year, he enlisted to fight the British in the War of 1812. The historic building served as a school, church, and tenant house before it was purchased by the state in 1945, with care of the structure entrusted to the San Houston Memorial Association.

The school building, which was established as a museum in 1965, has been restored and contains artifacts of the early school and Houston family. It also is the site of such annual events as a Houston birthday celebration, fall festival, Christmas open house, and pioneer and colonial encampments. The structure is a Tennessee historic site and is listed on the National Register of Historic Places. Annual attendance is 8,000.

Sam Houston Schoolhouse, Sam Houston Memorial Assn., 3650 Old Sam Houston School Rd., Maryville, TN 37804-5644. Phone: 865/983-1550. E-mail: samhoustonsch@aol.com. Website: www.samhoustonhistoricschoolhouse.org. Hours: Feb.–Dec.—10–5 Tues.–Sat., 1–5 Sun.; closed Jan., New Year's Day, Easter, Thanksgiving, and Christmas week. Admission: adults, $1; children under 10, free.

Cordell Hull

Cordell Hull Birthplace and Museum State Park. Cordell Hull, who received the Nobel Peace Prize in 1945 for his role in establishing the United Nations, was the nation's longest serving secretary of state. He served for 11 years, from 1933 to 1944 in the administration of President Franklin D. Roosevelt, after serving as a congressman and senator for 25 years. The Cordell Hull Birthplace and Museum State Park near Byrdstown, Tennessee, features the refinished log cabin where he was born and a museum devoted to his life and accomplishments.

Hull was born in Olympus, Tennessee, in 1871. He was the third of five sons born to William Paschal Hull and Mary Elizabeth Riley Hull. He attended college in 1889–1890 and graduated from Cumberland University School of Law in 1891, when he was admitted to the bar. Hull entered politics early and became chairman of the Clay County Democratic Party at the age of 19. He served in the Tennessee House of Representatives from 1893 to 1897 and then fought in the Spanish-American War, serving as a captain in the Fourth Regiment of the Tennessee Volunteer Infantry.

Hull's military service was followed by 11 terms in the U.S. House of Representatives (1907–1921 and 1923–1931), during which he authored the federal income tax laws of 1913 and 1916 and the inheritance tax of 1916. In 1917 Hull, at the age of 46, married Rose Frances Witz. They had no children. In 1920 he became chairman of the Democratic National Committee. Hull was elected to the U.S. Senate in 1930 but served only to 1933, when he was appointed secretary of state by President Franklin D. Roosevelt. He served in that position until 1944, when he resigned for health reasons.

As secretary of state, Hull was named to lead the American delegation to the London Economic Conference in 1933; tried unsuccessfully in 1938 to obtain payment of compensation for Americans from Mexico for farmlands lost during agrarian reforms in the late 1920s; was credited with preventing Nazi subterfuge in Latin America with his "Good Neighbor" policy in the 1930s; was negotiating with the Japanese ambassador and special envoy when the Pearl Harbor attack occurred in 1941; and became the underlying force and architect in the creation of the United Nations in 1941–1944, for which he received the Nobel Peace Prize in 1945.

Hull died in 1955 at the age of 83 after suffering several strokes and a heart attack. In 1997 the 45-acre Cordell Hull Birthplace and Museum State Park opened. It contains the refurbished log cabin in which Hull was born and a museum about his life and accomplishments. The museum houses Hull's papers, documents, books, photographs, and memorabilia, as well as the Nobel Prize. The park also has a scenic trail and the Bunkum Cave, where Hull's father made moonshine. A biennial Cordell Hull Folk Festival also is held in September.

Cordell Hull Birthplace and Museum State Park, 13400 Cordell Hull Memorial Dr., Byrdstown, TN 38549-4627. Phone: 931/864-3247. E-mails: david.delk@tn.gov and robin.peeler@state.tn.us. Website: www.cordellhullmuseum.com. Hours: Apr.–Oct.—9–5 daily; Nov.–Mar.—9–4 daily; closed major holidays. Admission: free.

John Jay

John Jay Homestead State Historic Site. John Jay was one of the Founding Fathers of the United States and became the first chief justice of the U.S. Supreme Court in 1789–1795. He served as president of the Continental Congress in 1778–1779; wrote *The Federalist Papers* in 1787 with Alexander Hamilton and James Madison, which supported the ratification of the U.S. Constitution; negotiated (along with John Adams, Benjamin Franklin, and Henry Laurens) the Treaty of Paris with Britain in 1782 to end the American Revolutionary War; and secured favorable terms from Great Britain on the western border and in commercial relations (Jay's Treaty of 1794). He later became a leader of the new Federalist Party and governor of New York and worked to free all the slaves in the state before his death in 1829.

Jay was born in 1745 into a wealthy family of merchants and government officials in New York City. His father, Peter Jay, was a trader of furs, wheat, timber, and other commodities. His mother, Mary Van Cortlandt, was the daughter of a state assemblyman and two-time mayor of New York City. They had 10 children. John Jay grew up in Rye, New York. He showed promise of an extraordinary life at an early age. He was tutored until he was eight years old, when he attended an exclusive boarding school in New Rochelle. Three years later, he returned to homeschooling under the tutelage of George Murray. In 1760 Jay enrolled at King's College (the forerunner to Columbia University), where he graduated with highest honors in 1764.

He then became a law clerk, studied under Benjamin Kissam, and was admitted to the bar in New York in 1768. After several years of legal practice, he created his own law office in 1771 and became a member of the New York Committee of Correspondence in 1774—the same year he was married to Sarah Van Brugh Livingston, eldest daughter of New Jersey Governor William Livingston. They had six children.

Jay was chosen secretary of the correspondence committee, which sought to protect property rights and preserve the rule of law while resisting what was regarded as British violation of American rights. He believed British tax measures were wrong and Americans were justified in resisting them. However, as a delegate to the First Continental Congress in 1774, he favored conciliation with Parliament and retired from the Congress rather than sign the Declaration of Independence in 1776.

Jay then became deeply involved in the development of a new state government in New York. The burning of Norfolk, Virginia, by British troops later in 1776 and other events convinced him to support independence. After the American Revolutionary War began, he worked tirelessly in support of the colonists' cause.

In 1778 Jay again was elected to the Continental Congress and served as president of the Congress. The following year he was appointed minister to Spain to seek recognition of colonial independence, financial aid, and commercial treaties. While in Europe, he was a member of the American negotiating party that signed the peace treaty with Britain, ending the revolutionary war in 1782. When he returned to Congress, he served as secretary of foreign affairs in 1784–1789 and coauthored with Hamilton and Madison *The Federalist Papers*, containing 85 articles explaining the new U.S. Constitution in 1787–1788.

Jay served as the first chief justice of the U.S. Supreme Court from 1789 to 1895 and negotiated Jay's Treaty with Great Britain to settle outstanding disputes in 1794–1795. He then became governor of the state of New York in 1795–1801 and enacted a 1799 bill (after his 1777 and 1785 bills for immediate freedom were defeated) that provided for the gradual emancipation of all slaves in the state by 1827. Jay was a deeply religious opponent of slavery who founded the New York Manumission Society and later served as president of the American Bible Society.

Jay was a popular governor who undertook many road and canal projects to improve the economy and fought for such political reforms as judicial and penal changes as well as abolition of slavery. He retired in 1801 and died in 1829 at the age of 83 after being stricken with palsy.

Jay retired to his farm estate near Bedford, New York. It became the John Jay Homestead State Historic Site in 1958 and later was designated a National Historic Landmark and listed on the National Register of Historic Places. The farmland was originally bought in 1703 by Jay's maternal grandfather, Jacobus Van Cortlandt. By 1800 Jay had acquired 750 acres by inheritance and purchase. He built a 24-room farmhouse and moved in with his family after retiring in 1801. His wife, Sarah, died only months after moving to their new home, and Jay spent his remaining years with his children and grandchildren on the estate. His descendants continued to live at the site until the 1950s, when a portion of the original acreage was purchased by Westchester County with the help of local residents and then transferred to the State of New York in 1958 and made a state historic site.

The site now consists of 62 acres with the 24-room house, which has been restored in the style of John Jay's lifetime; historic outbuildings; four formal gardens; an 1820s schoolhouse; rolling meadows; a pond; and wooded trails. The house contains Jay family artifacts, a 4,000-volume historic family library, personal papers, and manuscripts; ca. 1800–1833 American art, furniture, and decorations; and permanent and changing exhibits relating to Jay, his family, and the historic period. Annual attendance is over 60,000.

John Jay Homestead State Historic Site, 400 Rte. 22, Katonah, NY 10536 (postal address: PO Box 832, Katonah, NY 10536-0832). Phone: 914/232-5651. Fax: 914/232-8085. E-mail: heather.iannucci@oprhp.state.ny.us. Website: www.nyparks.com/historic-sites. Hours: house—Apr.–Nov.—10–4 Tues.–Sat., 11–4 Sun.; closed Dec.–Mar.; grounds—8–dusk daily. Admission: adults, $7; seniors, $5; children under 13, free.

Robert S. Kerr

Robert S. Kerr Conference Center and Museum. Robert Samuel Kerr was the founder of a petroleum company who became governor of Oklahoma and was elected a U.S. senator three times. He was called "the uncrowned king of the Senate" by the *Saturday Evening Post* because of his effectiveness. He was best known for enacting a series of water projects and dams that made the Arkansas River into a navigable inland waterway system, stretching from the Tulsa port of Catoosa to the Gulf of Mexico.

Kerr was born in a log cabin in 1896 near what is now Ada, Oklahoma, but was then part of Indian Territory. He was the son of William Samuel Kerr, a farmer, clerk, and politician, and Margaret Eloda Wright. He was brought up as a Southern Baptist, taught Sunday school, and enrolled in Oklahoma Baptist University as a junior in high school. He later attended East Central State College in Ada and briefly studied law at the University of Oklahoma but had to drop out for financial reasons in 1916.

Kerr was commissioned a second lieutenant in the U.S. Army when the United States entered World War I in 1917, but he did not see any combat. After the war, he became active in the Oklahoma National Guard and the American Legion. He also returned to studying law with an Ada judge and then passed the bar in 1922. Two years earlier, he married Reba Shelton, who died in labor, as did their twin daughters. Kerr then married Grayce Breene, the youngest daughter of a wealthy Tulsa family, and they had four children.

Kerr entered the oil business with James K. Anderson, his brother-in-law. They formed the Anderson-Kerr Drilling Company, which became so successful that Kerr gave up his law practice to concentrate on oil. When Anderson retired in 1936, Dean A. McGee, former chief geologist for Phillips Petroleum, joined the firm, and its name was changed to Kerr-McGee Oil Industries Inc. in 1940. The company expanded into global petroleum drilling and processing other fuels and minerals.

Kerr became a powerful figure in Democratic politics in Oklahoma and was elected governor in 1942. He was most effective in attracting wartime industries and military training facilities to the state during World War II. In 1948 he was elected to the U.S. Senate and then sought to win the Democratic nomination for president in 1952. When he lost the nomination to Adlai Stevenson, he built alliances with southern and western Democrats to dominate the Senate and further their special interests and economic development, such as the Arkansas River navigation system and petroleum and natural gas interests. He served three terms in the Senate, during which his support was pivotal to President John F. Kennedy's programs. Kerr died of a heart attack at the age of 66 in 1963.

The Carl Albert Center at the University of Oklahoma houses Kerr's papers, which cover his Senate career and include some of his gubernatorial papers and political speeches. Kerr's former home in Poteau, Oklahoma, is now the site of the Robert S. Kerr Museum, which is devoted to his life and career and Oklahoma history. The museum, founded in 1968, is located next to the mansion, which now is a bed and breakfast and conference center.

The museum contains Kerr exhibits, photographs, mementoes, farm and home implements, pioneer artifacts, barbed wire, east Oklahoma geological specimens, Spiro Mounds and Choctaw Indian artifacts, and Viking rune stones. Guided tours also are offered of the mansion. Annual attendance is over 3,500.

Robert S. Kerr Museum, 23009 Kerr Mansion Rd., Poteau, OK 74953-8119. Phone: 918/647-8221. Fax: 918/647-3952. E-mail: churleigh@carlalbert.edu. Website: www.case.co.ok.us/kerr_center. Hours: museum—by appointment; closed major holidays; mansion tours—8–4 daily; closed major holidays. Admission: museum—free; mansion tour—$2.

John Marshall

John Marshall House. John Marshall was the longest serving chief justice of the U.S. Supreme Court (34 years—from 1801 to 1835). His court opinions helped lay the basis for American constitutional law. He also made the Supreme Court an equal branch of the government with the legislative and executive branches. Marshall dominated the Supreme Court for over three decades and played a major role in the development of the American legal system. His longtime home in Richmond, Virginia—now known as the John Marshall House—is a historic house museum.

Marshall was born in a log cabin in a rural community on the Virginia frontier near Germantown (now Midland) in 1755. He was the oldest of 15 children of Thomas Marshall and Mary Isham Keith Marshall. His father was a surveyor and land agent. In the early 1760s the Marshall family moved to Leeds Manor on the eastern slope of the Blue Ridge Mountains and built a four-room cabin there, where they lived for 10 years. It was where John Marshall spent his formative years.

The Marshall family moved again in 1773, and John's father bought a 1,700-acre nearby farm and built a more imposing seven-room home as his fortunes improved. When his father moved to Kentucky in 1785, John inherited the Fauquier County property, which he kept until his death, even though he later lived in Richmond and Washington.

Since there were no schools in the area, John Marshall was largely homeschooled by his father. It gave him an interest in history and poetry. He also was able to utilize the extensive classical and contemporary literature resources of his father's employer, Lord Fairfax. By the time he was 12, John had transcribed Alexander Pope's *Essay on Man* and parts of his *Moral Essays*. When he was 14, John was sent to Campbell's academy in Washington. John's father then arranged for the Rev. James Thomson, a recently ordained Scottish minister, to serve as the teacher for local children. He lived with the Marshall family and tutored the children in Latin in return for his room and board. When he left at the end of the year, John was reading and transcribing Horace and Livy.

During the American Revolutionary War, John Marshall served in the Continental Army. He was a lieutenant with the Culpeper Minutemen in 1775–1776, a lieutenant and then a captain in the 11th Virginia Continental Regiment in 1776–1780 (serving as a judge advocate in 1777–1778), and spent the brutal winter of 1777–1778 at Valley Forge. After the war, Marshall read law under Chancellor George Wythe at the College of William and Mary and was admitted to the bar in 1880. He then practiced law in Fauquier County and was married in 1782 to Mary Willis Ambler, the daughter of the treasurer of Virginia. They had 10 children, six of whom grew to adulthood.

Marshall's political career also began in the 1780s. He quickly became a leader in the Federalist Party, which believed in a strong federal government. He served in the Virginia House of Delegates from 1782 to 1789, the Council of State in 1782–1784, and the U.S. House of Representatives in 1799–1800. In 1788 he also was a member of the three-member committee that convinced the Virginia Convention to ratify the United States Constitution. In 1800 President John Adams named him secretary of state and then chief justice of the U.S. Supreme Court in 1801. He served on the court until his death in 1835 at the age of 79. During his 34 years as chief justice, he participated in more than 1,000 decisions, writing 519 himself.

Marshall made the Supreme Court the third branch of the federal government, together with Congress and the president. He established the American judiciary as an independent and important part of government, and he was the principal founder of the system of constitutional law. The Supreme Court became the final authority on the meaning of the Constitution on all cases and controversies in which the decisions must be made by federal courts.

Among the most significant cases during Marshall's tenure were *Marbury v. Madison*, which established judicial review in which the court could declare invalid any act of Congress that was in conflict with the U.S. Constitution; *McCullock v. Maryland*, affirming the constitutional doctrine of implied powers; *Dartmouth College v. Woodward*, which protected private companies from excessive government regulation; and *Gibbons v. Ogden*, establishing that states cannot interfere with Congress's right to regulate commerce.

In 1807 Marshall also acquitted former Vice President Aaron Burr of treason and high misdemeanors in a conspiracy case in which Burr was accused of trying to seize land in the Spanish Orleans Territory and create a new republic in the Southwest. It also was while Marshall was chief justice (in 1801–1806) that he wrote the five-volume history (later shortened to two volumes) of George Washington, his close friend who died in 1799.

Marshall's wife's death in 1831 greatly affected him. He also was severely hurt in a stagecoach accident in 1835. His health rapidly declined, and he died when he returned to Philadelphia for medical assistance. A bronze statue of Marshall sitting in his judicial robe now is located on the lower west terrace of the Capitol as a tribute to his judicial service. His 1790 federal-style brick home in Richmond has become a historic house museum, called the John Marshall House. It also has been designated a National Historic Landmark and is listed on the National Register of Historic Places.

The house was located in the fashionable residential neighborhood known as Court End. It once was surrounded by Marshall's law office and such outbuildings as a kitchen, laundry, carriage house, stable, and garden and occupied a square (like a city block). The house has a dining room, parlor, and large parlor/dining room on the first floor and three bedrooms on the second. It contains furnishings associated with the Marshall family, including late 1700s and early 1800s glass, textiles, porcelain, paintings, silver, musical instruments, writing materials, and Marshall's judicial robe.

The house remained in the Marshall family until 1911 when it was sold to the City of Richmond. It has been open to the public since 1913 and now is managed by Preservation Virginia. Guided tours are offered, and special events include a spring garden party, Marshall birthday celebration, and Christmas program. Annual attendance is 4,000.

John Marshall House, 818 E. Marshall St., Richmond, VA 23219-1917 (postal address: PO Box 1098, Richmond, VA 23218-1098). Phone: 804/648-7998. Fax: 804/648-5880. E-mail: johnmarshallhouse@preservationvirginia.org. Website: www.preservationvirginia.org. Hours: Mar.–Dec.—10–5 Fri.–Sat., 12–5 Sun.; closed Mon.–Thurs.; Jan.–Feb.—by appointment. Admission: adults, $8; seniors, $7; children under 18 and students, $4; children under 4, free.

Thurgood Marshall

Thurgood Marshall Center. Thurgood Marshall was a civil rights lawyer who argued more cases before the United State Supreme Court than anyone else in history—and then became the first African American justice of the

Supreme Court. He was an associate justice of the Supreme Court from 1967 to 1991 after serving as chief counsel of the National Association for the Advancement of Colored People, a member of the U.S. Court of Appeals, and the nation's solicitor general. He became known as an advocate for the rights of minorities and the poor and had a great effect on race relations in America. The Thurgood Marshall Center in Washington is a community center and museum with exhibits about the lives and accomplishments of Marshall and other prominent African Americans from the Shaw neighborhood.

Marshall was born Thoroughgood Marshall in Baltimore in 1908, but he convinced his mother to shorten his first name to Thurgood when in the second grade because he disliked spelling it. His parents were William Marshall, who worked as a railroad porter, butler, and yacht club steward, and Norma Marshall, an elementary teacher. They instilled in him an appreciation for the United States Constitution and the rule of law. He was the youngest of two sons. He attended the Henry Highland Garnet Elementary School and graduated from the Frederick Douglass High School in 1925 and Lincoln University in Pennsylvania in 1930.

Marshall wanted to go to the University of Maryland School of Law but was told not to apply by the dean because of the school's segregation policy. So he went to Howard University's School of Law, finished first in the 1933 class, and went into private practice, specializing in civil rights. Three years later, in his first major civil rights case, Marshall ended the segregation policy at the University of Maryland by winning a suit for Donald Gaines Murray, a black Amherst College graduate with excellent credentials who was denied admission because of the policy.

In 1929 Marshall married Vivian Burey, who died in 1955. He then married Cecilia Suyat later that year. They were married until his death in 1993. They had two sons—Thurgood Marshall Jr., a former top aide to President Bill Clinton, and John W. Marshall, a former U.S. Marshals Service director and Virginia secretary of public safety.

Marshall won his first U.S. Supreme Court case (*Chambers v. Florida*) in 1940 when only 32 years old. That same year he was appointed chief counsel for the NAACP. Over the years, he argued many cases before the Supreme Court. His most famous case was *Brown v. Board of Education of Topeka* in 1954. The court ruled that "separate but equal" public education, as established in *Plessy v. Ferguson*, was not applicable to public education because it could never be truly equal. Marshall won 29 of the 32 cases he argued before the Supreme Court.

In 1961 President John F. Kennedy appointed Marshall to the U.S. Second Circuit Court of Appeals, and in 1965 President Lyndon B. Johnson named him solicitor general and then appointed him to the Supreme Court in 1967 following the retirement of Justice Tom C. Clark. He became the first African American on the court and served for 24 years.

Marshall had a liberal record that included strong support for constitutional protection of individual rights, including abortion rights. He opposed the death penalty, which was ruled constitutional in some circumstances. Although known primarily for his rulings in civil rights and criminal procedure cases, Marshall also made significant contributions to such other areas of law as member jury trials against a labor union, the standard of materiality in securities law, and savings and loan deductions for a loss in the exchange of mortgage participation interests.

Marshall retired from the Supreme Court in 1991 and died of heart failure in 1993 at the age of 84. He is buried in Arlington National Cemetery. He left all of his personal papers to the Library of Congress. Among the memorials to Marshall are an eight-foot statue in Lawyer Hall adjacent to the Maryland State House, the primary office building for the federal court system in Washington, the new Thurgood Marshall Law Library at the University of Maryland, and the Thurgood Marshall Center, a community center and museum located in the historic 12th Street YMCA building in the Shaw neighborhood of Baltimore. The 1912 five-story building, built largely by black artisans, was the nation's first full-service YMCA for African Americans. It has been designated a National Historic Landmark. The 35,000-square-foot building was restored and reopened in 2000.

The center's museum has exhibits on such African American leaders affiliated with the building as Thurgood Marshall; Dr. Charles Drew, discoverer of blood plasma; Langston Hughes, poet; Duke Ellington, jazz musician; and many others who grew up in the neighborhood and went on to careers in many fields. The center also has a tour; cultural, health, and family support; a school fund; and other programs.

Thurgood Marshall Center, 1816 12th St., N.W., Washington, DC 20009. Phone: 202/462-8314. Fax: 202/462-8365. E-mail: info@tmcsh.org. Website: www.thurgoodmarshallcenter.org. Hours: 8:30–5 Mon.–Fri., 9–5 Sat.; closed Sun. and national holidays. Admission: free.

Golda Meir

Golda Meir House Museum. Gold Meir was born in Russia, grew up and was educated in the United States, and served as prime minister and one of the founders of Israel. She became the first woman in Israel and the third woman in the world to be prime minister. She was prime minister from 1969 to 1974 and was the first female prime minister to be called the "Iron Lady" because of her strong will and straight-talking reputation. The house where she once lived in Denver, Colorado, now is a historic house museum on the campus of the Metropolitan State College of Denver.

Golda Meir, who adopted the Hebrew name in 1956, was born Golda Mabovitch in Kiev, Russia (now Ukraine), in 1898 to Mosher Mabovitch, a carpenter, and Blume Neiditch Mabovitch. In 1903 her father left to find work in America, first in New York City and then Milwaukee. He was hired at a Milwaukee railroad yard workshop, and when he saved enough money, he sent for his family the following year. After they arrived, the mother ran a grocery store and eight-year-old Golda was placed in charge when her mother went to the market for supplies.

Golda attended Fourth Street Grade School (which later was named the Golda Meir School) from 1906 to 1912. Golda became a school leader, forming the American Young Sisters Society, organizing a fund-raiser so that poor children could buy books, and graduating as valedictorian of her class, despite not knowing English when she started school.

At the age of 14, Golda went to North Division High School and worked part-time. Her mother wanted her to quit school and get married (her parents already had picked a husband for her, but she did not want to marry and was planning to be a teacher). Golda rebelled and bought a train ticket to Denver in 1913 to live with her married elder sister Sheyna Korngold, brother-in-law Sam, and niece Judith, who lived in a modest duplex, which later became the Golda Meir House Museum.

She attended North High School for nearly two years and worked part-time as a presser at her brother-in-law's dry-cleaning shop. The Korngold home was considered a social and intellectual center, where Meir was exposed to such topics as debates on Zionism, literature, women's suffrage, and trade unionism. It is where Meir discussed politics, met her future husband, Morris Meyerson (a sign painter), and developed her political philosophy. She also became deeply involved in Zionism and planned to emigrate to Israel.

Meir then returned to North Division High School in Milwaukee and graduated in 1915. She became an active member of the Young Poale Zion, which evolved into Habonim, the Labor Zionist youth movement. She also attended Milwaukee State Normal School (now the University of Wisconsin–Milwaukee) and after graduation taught in Milwaukee public schools and then joined the Yiddish-speaking Folks Schule in Milwaukee, where she became a committed Labor Zionist.

She also began dating Morris Meyerson, who was a dedicated socialist. When they were married in 1917, Meir's precondition was that they would move to Palestine. In 1921 they emigrated with her sister Shayna to the Merhavia kibbutz in the British mandate of Palestine, where she was chosen the kibbutz's representative to the Histadrut, the general federation of labor.

In 1924 Meir and her husband moved to Tel Aviv and then settled in Jerusalem. They had two children. In 1928 she was elected secretary of the Working Women's Council, which required her to spend two years as an emissary in the United States. The children went with her, but her husband did not and they grew apart but never divorced.

When she returned in 1834, Meir joined the executive committee of the Histadrut and later was made the head of the political bureau of the Jewish Agency. It was a position she held until the establishment of the state of Israel in 1948. When the British cracked down on the Zionist movement in Palestine in 1946, she became the principal negotiator between the Jews in Palestine and the British authorities.

In 1948 Meir was one of 24 people who signed the Declaration of the Establishment of the State of Israel, which created the nation. She served as Israel's first minister to the Soviet Union in 1948–1949 and as a member of the Knesset (parliament) from 1948 to 1974, labor minister in 1949–1956, and foreign minister in 1956–1966. Meir became secretary general of Mapai (Israeli Workers Party) in 1966, and when it became part of the Israel Labor Party, she was chosen its secretary. She became prime minister in 1969 when Levi Eshkol died and the political parties could not agree on a successor and selected her as a compromise choice.

Meir was a forceful leader, serving as prime minister until 1974, when she resigned after cabinet and political differences arose over the occupied Arab territories from the 1967 Six-Day War and readiness in the 20-day Yom Kippur War in 1973, which ended with a United Nations ceasefire. She died in 1978 of lymphatic cancer at the age of 80 and is buried on Mount Herzl in Jerusalem.

The 1911 house in Denver where Golda Meir lived for nearly two years with her elder sister during her youth is now the Golda Meir House Museum on the campus of Metropolitan State College. The small duplex house was nearly lost to a fire, tornado, vandalism, and repeated demolition attempts by the city. It was saved by a group of concerned citizens and was moved twice (from its original location at 1606–8 Julian Street) before being relocated by the Auraria Foundation to the college campus in 1988. It became a historic landmark in 1995 and has been restored to the way it looked when Golda Meir lived there in 1913–1914. It contains some of the original furnishings and historic objects. The house now serves as a museum, conference center, and home of the Golda Meir Center for Political Leadership, a Metropolitan State College academic program.

Golda Meir House Museum, Metropolitan State College of Denver, Auraria Campus, Denver, CO 82117 (postal address: Golda Meir Center, Dept. of Political Science, Metropolitan State College of Denver, Campus Box 43, Denver, CO 80217-3362). Phone: 303/556-3220. Website: www.mscd.edu/golda/house. Hours: by appointment; closed major holidays. Admission: free.

George W. Norris

George Norris State Historic Site. George William Norris was a Nebraska politician who served five terms in the U.S. House of Representatives and five terms in the Senate between 1903 and 1943. He was a leader of progressive and liberal causes in Congress, believing in the wisdom of the common people and in the progress of civilization. He was a Republican until 1936, when he became an independent. His home in McCook, Nebraska, is now a historic house museum at the George Norris State Historic Site.

Norris was born on a farm in 1861 near Clyde in Sandusky County, Ohio. He was the eleventh child in a poor farming family. He attended public schools and then Baldwin University in Berea, Ohio, and received a law degree at Northern Indiana Normal School (later Valparaiso University) in 1883. He moved to Beaver City, Nebraska, where he practiced law. In 1889 Norris married Pluma Lashley, who died in 1901. They had three daughters. He then married Ellie Leonard in 1903. They did not have any children.

In 1900 Norris moved to McCook, Nebraska, where he became active in politics and was elected to the U.S. House of Representatives as a Republican in the Fifth Congressional District in 1902. Although originally backed by the railroads, he supported Theodore Roosevelt's plans to regulate rates for the benefit of shippers, such as the merchants in his district.

After 1908, Norris became and insurgent, leading a revolt against Speaker Joseph G. Cannon in 1910 that changed the seniority system so that congressmen automatically moved ahead, even when opposed by the leadership. In 1911 Norris helped create the National Progressive Republican League, of which he was elected vice president. He initially supported Robert M. La Follette Sr. for president but later switched his support to Roosevelt.

In 1913 Norris was elected a senator, a position he held for 30 years. He supported direct election of senators and worked to convert all state legislatures to the unicameral system. Senators did get elected directly, but all the states except Nebraska retained their two-house systems. Nebraska changed to the one-house system in 1934. Norris also became an isolationist. He was one of only six senators who voted against declaring war on Germany in World War I in 1917, saying it would only benefit "munition manufacturers, stockholders, and bond dealers." He also voted against the Treaty of Versailles and the League of Nations, which were defeated in 1919.

Norris became a leader in the farm bloc and advocated the rights of labor. He and Representative Fiorello H. La Guardia of New York were successful in outlawing the practice of requiring prospective employees to be nonunion as a condition of employment and limiting the use of court injunctions against strikes. He also frequently criticized and voted against Republican administrations and came out in support of such Democratic presidential candidates as Al Smith in 1928 and Franklin D. Roosevelt in 1932.

Norris also supported the New Deal programs, supported the Tennessee Valley Authority Act (and was called the "father of TVA"), and was the prime mover of the Rural Electrification Act, which brought electrical service to unserved and underserved rural areas. At the same time, he spoke out against corrupt patronage and opposed Roosevelt's Judiciary Reorganization Bill to pack the Supreme Court.

Norris left the Republican Party in 1936 and was reelected as an independent but lost his Senate seat in 1942 to Republican Kenneth S. Wherry and retired from public life. He died in 1944 at the age of 83. His 1899 two-story house in McCook is now a historic house museum at the George Norris State Historic Site. It is operated by the Nebraska State Historical Society and has been designated a National Historic Landmark and is listed on the National Register of Historic Places. The museum contains period furnishings, George Norris artifacts, and a video on his life and career. Annual attendance is about 500.

George Norris State Historic Site, 706 Norris Ave., McCook, NE 69001-3142. Phone and fax: 308/345-8484. E-mail: norris@mccooknet.com. Website: www.nebraskahistory.org. Hours: 1–5 Tues.; closed Wed.–Mon. and state holidays. Admission: adults, $3; children with adults, free.

Charles Pinckney

Charles Pinckney National Historic Site. The Charles Pinckney National Historic Site in Mount Pleasant, South Carolina, honors a southern plantation owner and politician who became a member of the Continental Congress, a signer of the United States Constitution, and a state legislator, governor, congressman, senator, and ambassador during the nation's formative years. He introduced more than 30 provisions that were incorporated into the Constitution, including the controversial Fugitive Slave Clause, which required states to return escaped slaves to their owners. It was not until slavery was abolished by the 13th Amendment that the practice was eliminated.

Pinckney was born in 1757 to wealthy parents on a plantation outside Charleston, South Carolina. His father was Colonel Charles Pinckney, a prominent lawyer and planter, who left the 715-acre rice plantation, known as Snee Farm, to his son after his death in 1782. It became Charles's favorite among the seven plantations he eventually owned and where the national historic site is now located.

Pinckney received his education in Charleston, where he began practicing law and his political career in 1779. At the age of 21, he was elected to the South Carolina General Assembly. He also enlisted in the militia in the American Revolutionary War that year. He became a lieutenant, participated in the 1779 siege of Savannah, and was captured when Charleston fell to the British and held as a prisoner until 1781.

After serving in the Continental Congress in 1784–1787, Pinckney worked on the ratification of the Constitution in South Carolina in 1788, the year he married Mary Eleanor Laurens, daughter of Henry Laurens, a wealthy and politically powerful merchant. They had three children. Pinckney also was elected to the South Carolina legislature in 1786–1789 and 1792–1796 and to four terms as governor of the state (1789–1792, 1796–1798, and 1806–1808). He was appointed minister to Spain by President Thomas Jefferson (1801–1805) and ended his long career of public service by being elected to the U.S. House of Representatives in 1819–1821. He died in 1824 at the age of 67.

No standing structures remain from the time Pinckney lived at Snee Farm. The present house of native cypress and pine was built on the farm in Mount Pleasant, South Carolina, in the 1820s. Most of his papers were destroyed by the 1861 fire in Charleston, where he lived most of the year. The farm continued to be a working plantation into the twentieth century. The Charles Pinckney National Historic Site, established in 1988, now occupies 28 acres of the former 715-acre Snee Farm. It has been designated a National Historic Landmark and is listed on the National Register of Historic Places. It contains interpretive exhibits about Pinckney's life and political career, the U.S. Constitution, the history of the farm, and the contributions of African Americans to the development of the plantation. Annual attendance is 35,000.

Charles Pinckney National Historic Site, 1254 Long Point Rd., Mount Pleasant, SC 29464 (postal address: 1214 Middle St., Sullivans Island, SC 29482-9717). Phone: 843/881-5516. Fax: 843/881-7070. Website: www.nps.gov/chpi. Hours: 9–5 daily; closed New Year's Day, Thanksgiving, and Christmas. Admission: free.

Dan Quayle

Dan Quayle Center and United States Vice Presidential Museum. The Dan Quayle Center and United States Vice Presidential Museum in Huntington, Indiana, has a dual purpose—to tell the public about the life and career of Dan Quayle, the 44th vice president, and the history of the office of the vice president of the United States. The museum is located in a renovated church building in Quayle's hometown.

Dan Quayle was born James Danforth Quayle in Indianapolis in 1947 to James Cline Quayle and Martha Corinne Pulliam Quayle. He spent much of his youth in Arizona, where his father moved the family in 1955 to run a branch of Central Newspapers Inc., founded by Dan Quayle's maternal grandfather, Eugene C. Pulliam. The publishing company includes the *Arizona Republic* and the *Indianapolis Star*. The Quayles then moved to Huntington, where Dan's father ran the family newspaper, the *Huntington Herald-Press*, and where Dan graduated from Huntington High School in 1965.

Quayle enrolled at DePauw University, where he received a bachelor's degree in political science in 1969. After graduation, he joined the Indiana Army National Guard, attained the rank of sergeant, and served until 1975, during which he earned a law degree from Indiana University in 1974. It was at the law school that he met his future wife, Marilyn Tucker, who was taking night classes at the time. They were married in 1972 and now have three grown children.

In the early 1970s, Quayle held a number of state jobs before running for elective office, including investigator for the Consumer Protection Division of the Office of the Indiana Attorney General, administrative assistant to Governor Edgar Whitcomb, and director of the Inheritance Tax Division of the Indiana Department of Revenue. After receiving the law degree, he became associate publisher of the Huntington newspaper and practiced law with his wife.

Quayle's political life began in 1976 when he was elected as the Republican candidate to the U.S. House of Representatives from Indiana's Fourth Congressional District and then reelected in 1978. This was followed by election to the U.S. Senate in 1980. After being reelected as senator in 1986, he was selected by George H. W. Bush at the Republican Convention to be his vice presidential running mate in the 1988 presidential election. During the campaign, he seemed rattled at times and uncertain or evasive other times about his military service, a golfing trip, and whether he had enough experience to be vice president. When the subject in a television debate turned to his limited congressional experience and he compared it in length with that of former President John F. Kennedy, Democratic candidate Lloyd Bentsen replied, "Senator, you're no Jack Kennedy"—which subsequently became part of the political lexicon.

After the Bush/Quayle ticket was elected, he continued to be ridiculed in the media and by many voters because of his tendency to make statements that were self-contradictory, confused, or incorrect. For example, during the 1992 campaign, he misspelled "potato" as "potatoe" at an elementary school spelling bee, and while discussing a decay of moral values and family structure in American society was criticized for citing a single-mother title character in the *Murphy Brown* television series as an example of how popular culture contributes to a "poverty of values." The unfavorable perception contributed to the defeat of Bush and Quayle in their 1992 reelection bid, despite his work at the head of the Council on Competitiveness, first chairman of the National Space Council, and official trips to 47 countries.

In 1999 Quayle announced his candidacy for the 2000 Republican presidential nomination but withdrew after finishing eighth in a public opinion poll. He authored three books about his life and political philosophy in the 1990s, wrote a nationally syndicated newspaper column, served on a number of corporate boards, and became involved in a number of business ventures, such as serving as chairman of the Global Investment Division of Cerberus Capital Management, a private equity firm. The Quayles now live in Paradise Valley, Arizona, where he is president of Quayle and Associates and works as an investment banker in Phoenix. His son, Ben Quayle, was elected to the U.S. House of Representatives from Arizona's Third Congressional District in 2010.

In 1990 the Dan Quayle Commemorative Foundation was organized to honor the former vice president. It initially presented a display of Quayle memorabilia at the Huntington County Public Library. The public response resulted in the establishment of a the dual-function museum, called the United States Vice Presidential Museum at the Dan Quayle Center, in the 1919 former Christian Science building in 1993. In 2002 the name was changed to the Dan Quayle Center and United States Vice Presidential Museum.

The museum has 4,000 square feet of exhibits. The first floor is devoted to the role of the vice president and all who have served as vice president, with each one having a display column featuring political materials, letters, and other memorabilia. The second floor focuses on Quayle's life and career and contains such items as his law degree, clothing, gifts from foreign visits, and political artifacts. The annual attendance is 6,000.

Dan Quayle Center and United States Vice President Museum, 815 Warren St. Huntington, IN 45750-2151 (postal address: PO Box 856, Huntington, IN 46750-0856). Phone: 260/356-6356. Fax: 260/356-1455. E-mail: info@qualyemuseum.org. Website: www.quaylemuseum.org. Hours: 9:30–4:30 Mon.–Fri.; closed Sat.–Sun., New Year's Day, Independence Day, Thanksgiving, and Christmas Eve and Day. Admission: adults, $3; children 7–17, $1; children under 7, free.

Samuel T. Rayburn

Sam Rayburn Museum. Sam Rayburn was a Texas Democratic congressman who served in the U.S. House of Representatives for nearly 49 years and was House speaker for 17 years—the longest in American history. His life and career are now the focus of two museums in his hometown of Bonham—the Sam Rayburn Museum, part of the Dolph Briscoe Center for American History at the University of Texas at Austin, and the Sam Rayburn House Museum, a historic house museum where he lived from 1916 until his death in 1961 (*see* separate listing).

Samuel Taliaferro Rayburn was born in 1882 in a rural area of Roane County, Tennessee. When he was five, his family moved with seven siblings to a 40-acre cotton farm (on which three other children were born) in Flag Springs, Texas, in 1887. He graduated from East Texas Normal College (now Texas A&M University–Commerce) with a commerce degree in 1903 and then attended the University of Texas School of Law while teaching. After being admitted to the bar in 1908, he was elected to the Texas House of Representatives for two terms. He was chosen speaker of the House in his second term at the age of 29. In 1913 Rayburn was elected the first of 24 terms as a member of the U.S. House of Representatives.

Rayburn, who was serving as majority leader of the House, became speaker in 1940 following the death of speaker William Bankhead. He held that position until he died of pancreatic cancer at the age of 79 in 1961. The only years he was not speaker during this span were 1947–1949 and 1953–1955, when the Republicans controlled the House. He served as speaker twice as long as any of his predecessors.

Rayburn became a powerful congressional figure known for his fairness and integrity. He was largely responsible for the passage of much of President Franklin D. Roosevelt's New Deal program and was instrumental in the adoption of bills establishing the Securities and Exchange Commission and Federal Communications Commission and the approval of the Rural Electrification Act, Public Utilities Holding Company Act, and Emergency Railroad Transportation Act.

In addition, Rayburn helped Lyndon B. Johnson in his rapid rise to power and served as chairman of the Democratic National Convention in 1948, 1952, and 1956. He married Metze Jones, sister of Texas congressman Marvin Jones, but the marriage ended rather quickly, reportedly because of his work schedule and long bachelorhood.

Rayburn founded the Sam Rayburn Museum in 1957 as a tribute to the people of Bonham and Fannin County. He wanted his many books and papers to be kept together and available in the community where he had served as congressman for nearly a half century. The museum, which was operated by the Sam Rayburn Foundation, became a division of the Dolph Briscoe Center for American History at the University of Texas at Austin in 1991.

The museum contains exhibits on Rayburn's life and career and features memorabilia, papers, paintings, and a replica of the speaker's office during his tenure with original furniture. The museum also houses Rayburn's personal library and an extensive collection of books relating to his career and to the people, issues, and events in his years of public service. The archive has more than 100 oral histories of friends, relatives, and colleagues; over 40 films of Rayburn's interviews and speeches; and a collection of tape recordings and typewritten speeches. The museum is a Texas Historical Landmark. Annual attendance is 7,500.

Sam Rayburn Museum, 800 W. Sam Rayburn Dr., Bonham, TX 75418-4103 (postal address: PO Box 309, Bonham, TX 75418-0309). Phone: 903/583-2455. Fax: 903/583-7394. Website: www.cah.utexas.edu/museums/rayburn. Hours: 9–5 Mon.–Fri., 10–2 Sat.; closed Sun. and major holidays. Admission: free.

Sam Rayburn House Museum. The Sam Rayburn House Museum in Bonham, Texas, was the home of one of the most powerful and influential members of Congress in the twentieth century. He served in Congress for nearly 49 years and was speaker of the U.S. House of Representatives for a record 17 years. The 1916 home, where the politician known as "Mr. Sam" to his congressional colleagues and friends lived until his death in 1961, is now a historic house museum that celebrates his life and career.

The museum was established in 1975 and is operated by the Texas Historical Commission. All the furnishings are original and remain as they were when Rayburn lived there. The site also contains personal belongings and his 1947 Cadillac, as well as such other structures as a smokehouse, barn, and garage. Guided tours and programs are offered of the two-story house, which has been designated a National Historic Landmark and is listed on the National Register of Historic Places. Annual attendance is 7,500.

Sam Rayburn House Museum, 890 W. Hwy. 56, Bonham, TX 75418 (postal address: PO Box 308, Bonham, TX 75418-0308). Phone: 903/583-5558. Fax: 903/640-0800. E-mail: historic-site@the.state.tx.us. Websites: www.visit-samrayburnhouse.com. and www.the.state.tx.us/samrayhouse/srhoefault.html. Hours: 9–4:30 Tues.–Sun.; closed Mon., New Year's Eve and Day, Thanksgiving, and Christmas Eve and Day. Admission: adults, $4; students 6–18, $3; children under 6, free.

Margaret Chase Smith

Margaret Chase Smith Library. Margaret Chase Smith was a prominent political figure in the U.S. House of Representatives and Senate from 1940 to 1973. She was the first woman to represent Maine in Congress and the first woman to serve in both the House of Representatives (1940–1949) and the Senate (1949–1973). Smith also was the first woman to be placed in nomination for president at a major party's convention—at the 1964 Republican National Convention. She came in second to Senator Barry Goldwater. She retired to her home in Sowhegan, Maine, in 1972 after serving 32 years in Congress and established the Margaret Chase Smith Library to house her papers, memorabilia, and honors.

Smith was a moderate Republican who first achieved national attention in 1950 with her "Declaration of Conscience" speech, in which she became the first senator to denounce the tactics of Senator Joseph McCarthy in his anticommunist witch hunts. It was speculated that she might become the Republican vice presidential candidate in 1952, but it never materialized. When she left the office in 1972, she was the longest-serving female senator in history, which was not surpassed until 2011 when Senator Barbara Mikulski began her fifth term.

Smith was born to George Emery Chase and Carrie Matilda Murray Chase in Skowhegan in 1897. She was the eldest of six children, only four of whom survived to adulthood. Her father was a barber, and her mother worked as a waitress, store clerk, and at a shoe factory. She attended Lincoln and Garfield Elementary Schools and graduated from Skowhegan High School in 1916. She played on the girls' basketball team in high school and served as captain of the team in her senior year.

Margaret began working early in her youth. At the age of 12, she worked at a five-and-dime store and then served as a substitute telephone operator and part-time assistant to the tax assessor. After high school, she briefly taught at a one-room school near Skowhegan and coached the girls' basketball team at Skowhegan High School.

From 1917 to 1930, she had a variety of jobs, including working as a business executive for the telephone company, circulation manager for a weekly newspaper, treasurer of a waste process company, and office worker at a textile mill. She also became active in women's organizations, cofounding and serving as magazine editor of the Skowhegan chapter of the Business and Professional Women's Club and serving as president of the Maine Federation of Business and Professional Women's Clubs.

In 1930 Margaret married Clyde Smith and soon became involved in politics. She was elected to the Maine Republican State Committee that year and served until 1936. In 1937 her husband was elected to the U.S. House of Representatives, and she became his secretary. She managed his office, handled correspondence, conducted research, and assisted with speeches. She also served as treasurer of the Congressional Club, consisting of the wives of congressmen and cabinet members.

In the spring of 1940, Congressman Smith suffered a heart attack, and he asked his wife to run for his House seat in the fall election. When he died in April, she was elected to replace him in a special election, becoming the first woman elected to Congress from Maine. Three months later, she was elected to a full two-year term and then to three more terms. She developed a strong interest in the military and national security. In addition to serving on several military-related committees, she introduced legislation that established the WAVES for women in the navy and sponsored the Women's Armed Services Integration Act, which regularized the status of women in the armed forces. As a Republican moderate, she often supported legislation by Democratic Presidents Franklin D. Roosevelt and Harry S. Truman.

In 1948 Margaret Chase Smith was elected senator, becoming the first woman to represent Maine in the Senate and the first woman to serve in both houses of Congress. After her condemnation of McCarthyism, the Wisconsin senator removed her from one of the Senate committees and actively opposed her reelection to the Senate in 1954, the year he was censured. While in the Senate, she served on the Senate Armed Services Committee and the Senate Aeronautical and Space Committee, and supported the Vietnam War and the space program and moon landing. She also supported civil rights legislation, Medicare, and increased educational funding.

In 1964 Smith sought the Republican nomination for president but did not receive the national convention nomination. But she became the only woman to chair the Senate Republican Conference in 1967, serving to 1972. It also was in 1972 that she was defeated for reelection as senator by Democrat Congressman Bill Hathaway in the only election she ever lost in Maine. She retired to Skowhegan, where she died of a stroke in 1995 at the age of 97.

Smith received many awards for her contributions, including being selected the most influential Mainer of the twentieth century, 95 honorary university and college degrees, the Presidential Medal of Freedom, and selection to the National Women's Hall of Fame and Maine Women's Hall of Fame.

The Margaret Chase Smith Library was established at Northwood University in Midland, Michigan, in 1982 and moved in 2012 to her former residence on 15 acres in Skowhegan, Maine, where it is administered by the University of Maine. It functions as an archive, museum, and educational and public policy center. The library contains Smith's papers, memorabilia, photographs, correspondence, awards, and citations. Annual attendance is 2,500.

Margaret Chase Smith Library, 56 Norridgewock Ave., Skowhegan, ME 04976-1204. Phone: 207/474-7133. E-mail: mcsl@mcslibrary.org. Website: www.mcslibrary.org. Hours: 10–4 Mon.–Fri.; closed Sat.–Sun. and major holidays. Admission: free.

Strom Thurmond

Strom Thurmond Institute of Governmental and Public Affairs. The late Senator Strom Thurmond from South Carolina was the longest-serving U.S. senator until recently (48 years—from 1954 to 2003) and the oldest serving senator in the nation's history (to the age of 100). He was a Democrat who became a Republican—and also ran for president as the States' Rights Democratic Party candidate in 1948. The party, also known as the Dixiecrat Party, split from the Democrats over the issue of segregation. Thurmond's papers and memorabilia spanning 65 years of public service are now the heart of the Strom Thurmond Institute of Government and Public Affairs at Clemson University in Clemson, South Carolina.

Thurmond was a segregationist who conducted the longest filibuster ever by a lone senator in opposition to the Civil Rights Act of 1957, lasting 24 nonstop hours and 11 minutes. He also continued to oppose civic rights legislation in the years that followed but always claimed he was not a racist and was simply against excessive federal authority. He moderated his position on race starting in the 1970s, defending his earlier statements on the basis of states' rights.

The Thurmond Institute at Clemson University originated with the senator's 1981 decision to place all his papers and memorabilia from his political career at his alma mater. The institute now conducts applied research and service in public policy areas and offers public and academic programs in the field. It also has a small museum on Thurmond's life and career with memorabilia and houses the university's special collections.

Strom Thurmond was born as James Strom Thurmond in 1902 in Edgefield, South Carolina. He was the son of John William Thurmond, a lawyer, and Eleanor Gertrude Strom Thurmond. He attended Clemson Agricultural College of South Carolina (now Clemson University) and graduated with a degree in horticulture in 1923. He was a farmer, teacher, and athletic coach until 1929, when he was appointed Edgefield County's superintendent of education and served to 1933. He studied law with his father and was admitted to the bar in 1930. He was the Edgefield town and county attorney from 1930 to 1938, during which he was elected to the South Carolina Senate in 1933 and then to the 11th Circuit Court judgeship.

In 1942 Thurmond resigned from the bench and joined the U.S. Army. He became a lieutenant colonel and received 18 decorations for his service, including landing in a 82nd Airborne Division glider in the 1944 Battle of Normandy. He later served as president of the Reserve Officers Association (1954–1955) and retired from the U.S. Army Reserves as a major general.

Thurmond was elected governor of South Carolina as a Democrat in 1946. Two years later, he became the 1948 presidential candidate for the States' Rights Democratic Party after President Harry S. Truman desegregated the U.S. Army, proposed creating a permanent Fair Employment Practices Commission, and supported federal antilynching laws and the elimination of state poll taxes. The split from the Democratic Party came as a result of what was perceived as federal intervention in the segregation practices of the southern states, which had largely disenfranchised most African Americans and many poor whites. Thurmond received only 2.4 percent of the vote.

Thurmond stayed in the Democratic Party until 1964 and then switched to the Republican Party. He ran for the U.S. Senate in 1950 but lost in the primary election. In 1952, after endorsing Republican Dwight D. Eisenhower for President, the Democrats blocked Thurmond from running for the Senate as a Democrat, and he was forced to be a write-in candidate—and became the first person to be elected to the Senate as a write-in candidate against ballot-listed opponents. It was the beginning of his 48 years in the Senate. But when he became increasingly at odds with the Democrats, he switched to the Republican Party in 1964.

In 1957 Thurmond made his record-breaking filibuster by a single senator. Speaking for 24 hours and 18 minutes, he vehemently supported racial segregation in an unsuccessful attempt to defeat the Civil Rights Act. He also set several other U.S. Senate records—as the oldest serving senator (100 years of age), the longest-serving senator at 48 years (which was later surpassed by Robert C. Byrd), and longest-serving dean of the Senate (14 years).

Thurmond died of heart failure in 2003 shortly after leaving the Senate at the age of 100. He had been married twice. In 1947 he married Jean Crouch, who died 13 years later. They had no children. His second wife was Nancy Janice Moore, whom he married in 1965 when she was 23 and he was 66. She was Miss South Carolina of 1965. They separated in 1991 but never divorced. They had four children.

Six months after Thurmond's death, it was revealed that he had fathered an African American daughter, Essie Mae Washington, when he was 22 years old. She was the daughter of his family's maid. Although he never acknowledged the birth, he paid for her college education and assisted in other financial ways.

Strom Thurmond Institute of Government and Public Affairs, Clemson University, 230 S. Palmetto Blvd., Clemson, SC 29631. Phone: 864/656-4700. Website: www.sti.clemson.edu. Hours: varies. Admission: free.

Daniel Webster

Daniel Webster Birthplace State Historic Site. Daniel Webster was a leading lawyer, statesman, senator, and orator during the first half of the nineteenth century. His nationalistic views and effectiveness as a speaker made him one of the most famous orators and influential Whig political leaders in the period leading up to the Civil War. During his 40 years in national politics, he served in the U.S. Senate for 19 years, U.S. House of Representatives for 10 years, and as secretary of state under three presidents. He also participated in several U.S. Supreme Court cases that established important constitutional precedents that strengthened the authority of the federal government.

Webster's life and career are now presented at the Daniel Webster Birthplace State Historic Site in Franklin, New Hampshire, and two Massachusetts locations. He was born in 1782 in West Salisbury (now Franklin) to Ebenezer Webster and Abigail Eastman Webster. He grew up with nine siblings on the family's small farm. He attended district schools and Phillips Exeter Academy, a preparatory school in Exeter, New Hampshire, and graduated from Dartmouth College in 1801.

Webster then was apprenticed to lawyer Thomas W. Thompson in Salisbury and in 1804 moved to Boston and clerked for attorney Christopher Gore, who was involved in state, national, and international politics. He learned much about legal and political subjects and met many New England politicians. After being accepted into the bar in 1805, Webster returned to New Hampshire to be near his ailing father, an ardent Federalist, and established a law practice in Boscawen. He also became involved in politics, speaking in support of Federalist causes and candidates. After his father's death in 1806, Webster turned his law practice over to his older brother, Ezekiel, who also had become a lawyer.

In 1807 Webster moved to Portsmouth and opened a practice as the Napoleonic Wars began to affect Americans and Britain started to induct American sailors into its navy. President Thomas Jefferson retaliated with the Embargo Act of 1807, which stopped all trade to Britain and France—two nations with whom New England had extensive trade. Webster wrote an anonymous pamphlet attacking the embargo. When the trouble with Britain escalated into the War of 1812, Webster gave an address to the Washington Benevolent Society that condemned the war and said it violated New England's shipping rights, while denouncing those New Englanders who called for the region's secession from the Union.

Webster's speech was widely circulated in New Hampshire, and he was invited to take part in the Rockingham Convention, which sought to formally declare the state's grievances with President James Madison and the federal government. He became a member of the drafting committee and was asked to compose the statement known as the Rockingham Memorial.

Webster's efforts for New England federalism, shipping interests, and war opposition resulted in his election to the U.S. House of Representatives in 1812 and reelection in 1814. Instead of seeking a third term, Webster chose to return to his law practice and moved to Boston to obtain greater financial income for his family. In 1808 he married Grace Fletcher, with whom he had four children. She died in 1828, and Webster married Caroline LeRoy in 1829.

In his private practice, Webster became the leading constitutional lawyer and scholar. He probably had more influence than any other attorney on the U.S. Supreme Court headed by Chief Justice John Marshall. He argued 223 cases before the court and won approximately half of them. He had an important role in eight of the most celebrated cases decided by the court between 1801 and 1824. In many instances, including the 1818 *Dartmouth College v. Woodward*, 1819 *McCullough v. Maryland*, and 1824 *Gibbons v. Ogden* cases, the Supreme Court made decisions based largely on Webster's arguments. Webster also helped many of the justices interpret matters of constitutional law.

In 1823 Webster returned to Congress. He was elected to the U.S. House of Representatives from Massachusetts and served three terms. In 1827 he ran for the U.S. Senate and was reelected in 1833 and 1839. He was a key figure in what was called the Senate's "golden days." He was the Northern member of the "Great Triumvirate," which also included Henry Clay from the West (Kentucky) and John C. Calhoun from the South (South Carolina).

As the Senate's most prominent conservative, Webster led the Whig opposition to the economic policies of President Andrew Jackson and the Democratic Party, and he worked with Clay for compromise in an attempt to prevent sectionalism and the Civil War. It was said that Webster gave the most eloquent speech ever delivered in Congress when he defended the Union and opposed the nullification efforts of Senators Robert Y. Hayne, John C. Calhoun of South Carolina, and others.

Webster ran unsuccessfully for president three times and served as secretary of state in three administrations. He left the Senate in 1841 when appointed secretary of state by President William Henry Harrison and then served to 1843 under President John Tyler after Harrison's sudden death. He negotiated the 1842 Webster-Ashburton Treaty, which settled the eastern border between the United States and Canada. In 1845 Webster was reelected to the Senate, during which he opposed the annexation of Texas and the war with Mexico. In 1850 President Millard Fillmore made Webster secretary of state for the third time. He died in 1852 of a cerebral hemorrhage at the age of 70. In 1957 a Senate committee selected Webster as one of the five greatest senators—the others being Henry Clay, John C. Calhoun, Robert La Follette, and Robert Taft.

Webster's life and career are now celebrated at the Daniel Webster Birthplace State Historic Site in Franklin, New Hampshire. The two-room frame house at the site is where he was born in 1782 and spent the first few years of his life. It replaced a log cabin where the family lived before the American Revolutionary War. Webster's father, Ebenezer Webster, who operated a mill and farm, organized and captained a company of local volunteers. He built the house when he came home in the winter until the fighting resumed in the spring.

Around 1785, Ebenezer Webster sold the farm and the mill and moved the growing family, which eventually had 10 children, to more fertile land near the Merrimack River. The farm's new owner built a large farmhouse across the road and attached the small Webster house as a shed. The property was sold several times until it was acquired by the Webster Birthday Association in 1910. The frame house then was moved back to the original site, and in 1917 the restored house and 155 of the farm's original acres were donated to the State of New Hampshire.

The house now contains period furniture typical of a rustic farm in the late 1700s, as well as other items that belonged to Daniel Webster. The foundation of the old mill can be seen behind the house near Punch Creek. The Webster farm has become a state historic site operated by the New Hampshire Division of Parks and Recreation.

Daniel Webster Birthplace State Historic Site, North Rd., off Rte. 127, Franklin, NH 03235 (postal address: PO Box 1856, Concord, NH 03302-1856). Website: www.nhstateparks.com/danielwebster.html. Hours: June 21–Sept. 1—9–5 Sat.–Sun.; closed Mon.–Fri. and remainder of year. Admission: adults, $7; children 6–11, $3; children under 6 and New Hampshire residents, free.

Daniel Webster Estate and Heritage Center. Daniel Webster lived and farmed on the land where the Daniel Webster Estate and Heritage Center is now located in Marshfield, Massachusetts. But he never did live in the mansion that is called the "Webster House," even though it is on the same foundation. He died in Marshfield in 1852, and his house was destroyed in a fire in 1878.

The replacement home was built by Webster's daughter-in-law, Caroline White Webster, wife of his son, Fletcher, who died in the Civil War. The Queen Anne–style house, which contains an exhibit about Webster's life and career, is now rented out for private gatherings and small public functions.

Daniel Webster bought the Green Harbor estate in 1832 and farmed the land and lived in the original house for 20 years. A short distance from the mansion, he built a small building that he used as his law office and natural history library and where he sometimes met and entertained guests. It later was moved to an adjacent estate that Webster purchased (*see* Daniel Webster Law Office listing). It was on the estate that Webster bred cattle, improved the soil, and planted many species of trees from all over the world (many of which still stand). It was his agricultural interests that inspired the townspeople to organize what became the Marshfield Fair. The estate is listed on the National Register of Historic Places.

Daniel Webster Estate and Heritage Center, 238 Webster St., Marshfield, MA 02050. Phone: 781/834-0548. E-mail: danielwebsterestate@yahoo.com. Website: www.danielwebsterestate.org. House tour hours: July–Sept.—1–4 Thurs.; May–June and Aug.–Oct.—1–4 first Sun. of month; not offered Dec.–Apr. Tour fee: donation.

Daniel Webster Law Office. When Daniel Webster bought his estate in Marshfield, Massachusetts, in 1832, he built a small building nearby that he used as his law office, natural history library, and site to meet and entertain guests. The one-room clapboard building, which now is a National Historic Landmark and is listed on the National Register of Historic Places, is located on the grounds of the adjacent Isaac Winslow House, a 1699 historic house museum. Webster purchased the Winslow property in 1848, and it became part of his estate. The historic law office now can be visited as part of Winslow House tours offered by the Winslow House Association.

Webster's law office is where he met with most visiting dignitaries, such as British Lord Ashburton (Alexander Baring), with whom he established the boundary along the Maine border between the United States and Canada in the Webster-Ashburton Treaty in 1842. The office contains some of Webster's letters, possessions, and artifacts relating to his life at the Marshfield estate.

The Winslow House, which is listed on the National Register of Historic Places, is the ancestral home of the founding family of Marshfield. Webster bought the house from Dr. Isaac Winslow, a physician and grandson of Edward Winslow, three-time governor of Plymouth Colony. The Winslow House features period furnishings and artifacts. The estate also has a carriage house with Webster's one-horse phaeton, the Concord coach once used to transport passengers from Marshfield to Hingham, and a brougham carriage formerly owned by a railroad magnate; a blacksmith shop; and the 1857 Winslow schoolhouse.

The property was acquired by the nonprofit Winslow House Association in 1920 and restored and opened to the public. In addition to house tours, the association hosts dinners, lectures, concerts, and other community events.

Daniel Webster Law Office, Historic 1699 Winslow House, 634 Carswell St., Marshfield, MA 02050-5623 (postal address: PO Box 531, Marshfield, MA 02050-0531). Phone: 781/837-5753. E-mail: mark_schmidt@winslowhouse.org. Website: www.winslowhouse.org. Hours: mid-May–late Oct.—10:30–5 Fri.–Sun. and by appointment; closed Mon.–Thurs., late Oct.–mid-May, Memorial Day, Independence Day, and Labor Day. Admission: adults, $3; children, $1.

Roger Williams

See Religious Leaders section.

RELIGIOUS LEADERS

Mary Baker Eddy

Longyear Museum. In 1879 Mary Baker Eddy pioneered a system of prayer-based healing that led to the founding of the Church of Christ, Scientist, which now includes 1,700 churches in 76 countries. She was the author of *Science and Health with Key to the Scriptures*, the fundamental doctrinal textbook that sold more than 10 million copies, and founded the Massachusetts Metaphysical College and the Christian Science Publishing Society, which publishes the *Christian Science Monitor* newspaper. The Longyear Museum in Chestnut Hill, Massachusetts, is now devoted to her life, and the Mary Baker Eddy Library in Boston traces her career (*see* separate listing).

Eddy established Christian Science during the second half of the nineteenth century when women could not vote or generally serve as pastors or practice medicine. She founded the church partly as a result of her search to overcome years of poor health. And when she found healing methods that helped her, she sought to share the information with others through the church and her teachings, speeches, and publications.

Mary Baker Eddy was a fragile child born Mary Morse Baker in Bow, New Hampshire, in 1821. She was the youngest of six children of Mark and Abigail Ambrose Baker. The children were raised as Congregationalists with Puritan values, daily Bible reading, and talk of God's healing power, although Mary later rejected such church teachings as predestination and original sin. She suffered most of her childhood from chronic illnesses and took great interest in biblical accounts of early Christian healing. She found that healing the sick was an integral part of Christian service, and it was said that she developed an ability to heal at an early age.

Mary was homeschooled in her early years, with the assistance of one of her brothers, Albert Baker, a Dartmouth College graduate. After the family moved to Tilton when Mary was 15, she attended the private school of Professor H. Dyer Sanborn. It was under his instruction and the guidance of the Rev. Enoch Corser of the Tifton Congregational Church that she started to develop her intellectual and spiritual maturity.

Mary was married three times. The first marriage was in 1843 when she was 22 to George Washington Glover, a brother-in-law and businessman who died the next year of yellow fever. She returned to her parents' home and gave birth to a boy she named after her husband. But Mary's father said young George could not stay at the home, and he was raised largely by relatives. Her second marriage was in 1853 to Dr. Daniel Patterson, a dentist and relative of her father's second wife (Mary's mother died in 1849). It turned out to be an unhappy marriage. Patterson deserted Mary after 13 years, and she obtained a divorce on grounds of adultery seven years later. In 1877 she married Asa G. Eddy, who came to her for treatment. He died in 1882, reportedly of heart disease. She then took the name Mary Baker Eddy.

From childhood, Eddy suffered from a number of physical complaints that never were clearly understood. From the age of eight, she also had spiritual experiences when she heard her name being called by an unseen voice. As an adult, she experimented with allopathic medicine and alternative therapies such as homeopathy—none of which brought lasting health. At the same time, she continued her study of the Bible and the healing powers of Jesus.

In 1862 Eddy received hypnotic treatment for her nervous and physical conditions from Phineas P. Quimby, a mental healer in Portland, Maine. It helped with her problems and influenced her belief in Christian Science, especially after she suffered a spinal injury in a fall on an icy sidewalk and became well after reading about Jesus's healing in the Bible. As a result, she spent the next nine years in intensive scriptural study, healing activities, and teaching. In 1875 she published the *Science and Health* book, which stated that "science" was behind Jesus's healing method.

When Christian churches did not accept her beliefs, Eddy devoted the rest of her life to the establishment of the Christian Science Church. She wrote the bylaws (*The Manual of the Mother Church*), revised *Science and Health*, and in 1879 established the Church of Christ, Scientist. In 1881 she founded the Massachusetts Metaphysical College in Boston, where she taught approximately 800 students between 1882 and 1889 (when the school was closed) and sent them across the country to practice healing and instruct others in the beliefs. The students were listed as "practitioners" in the *Christian Science Journal*, a monthly magazine founded in 1883.

In 1888 a reading room selling Bibles, her writings, and other publications was opened in Boston and later was replicated in branch churches. In 1892 Eddy reorganized the church as the First Church of Christ, Scientist. She also founded the *Christian Science Sentinel*, a weekly magazine about healing and testimonies of healing, and kept revising *Science and Health*, which has six major revisions and over 400 printings.

In 1894 an edifice for the First Church of Christ, Scientist (called the Mother Church) was completed in Boston. Eddy served as the pastor in the early years and was succeeded by several others until 1895, when Eddy ordained the Bible and *Science and Health* as the church pastor. The Sunday sermons now consist of readings from the two books, with church attendees participating by sharing accounts of healing and spiritual insights. It also was in 1895 that the first edition of a church manual with guidelines was published. Eddy founded the Christian Science Publishing Society in 1898, which became the home of the *Christian Science Journal*, *Christian Science Sentinel*, *Herald of Christian Science*, and *Christian Science Monitor*.

Mary Baker Eddy died in 1810 at her home in the Chestnut Hill section of Newton, Massachusetts. She did most of her work in establishing Christian Science in Lynn, Boston, and Chestnut Hill and frequently moved. The Longyear Museum in Chestnut Hill now offers tours at eight historic homes where she once lived (Amesbury, Chestnut Hill, Lynn, Stoughton, and Swampscott, Massachusetts, and Concord, North Groton, and Rumney, New Hampshire).

The museum contains exhibits, manuscripts, photographs, art, artifacts, and a documentary film relating to the life and achievements of Eddy. It also has displays about others who assisted her in founding the Christian Science religion. The museum was founded in 1923 and opened in 1937 in the former home of philanthropist Mary Beecher Longyear in Brookline. It moved to its present location in nearby Chestnut Hill in 1999 and opened in 2001. Annual attendance is 6,000.

Longyear Museum, 1125 Boylston St., Chestnut Hill, MA 02467-1811. Phones: 617/278-9000 and 800/277-8943. Fax: 617/278-9003. E-mail: letters@longyear.org. Website: www.longyear.org. Hours: museum—10–4 Mon. and Thurs.–Sat., 1–4 Sun.; closed Tues.–Wed. and major holidays; houses—varies. Admission: free.

Mary Baker Eddy Library. The Mary Baker Eddy Library in Boston is devoted to the life, ideas, and achievements of the founder of the Christian Science Church. It contains a 12,000-volume library and a museum with 13,500 square feet of exhibits relating to Eddy and the church. The library, which opened in 2002, formerly was known as the Mary Baker Eddy Library for the Betterment of Humanity.

One of the main attractions at the library/museum is the "Mapparium," a 1935 three-story painted glass globe of the world. A complimentary exhibit, called "The Mapparium: An Inside Visit," features public letters, documents, and artifacts on the construction, history, and significance of the huge globe, which contains a 1935 map of the world that has never been updated. Among the other exhibits are the "Quest Gallery," describing Eddy's life and accomplishments; "Impressions on Paper," which focuses on her writings and reproduces her study with its desk, clock, and rocking chair; and the "Hall of Ideas," describing great ideas that have inspired individuals and transformed society throughout the ages. A number of temporary exhibitions also are presented. Annual attendance is 100,000.

Mary Baker Eddy Library, 200 Massachusetts Ave., Boston, MA 02115-3017. Phones: 617/450-7000 and 888/222-3711. Fax: 617/450-7048. E-mail: librarymail@mbelibrary.org. Website: www.marybakereddylibrary.org. Hours: 10–4 Tues.–Sun.; closed Mon. and major holidays. Admission: adults, $6; seniors and children 6–17, $4; children under 6, free.

Billy Graham

Billy Graham Center Museum. Billy Graham is an evangelical Christian minister who came to national prominent through his sermons on radio and television and huge revival meetings. It is reported that his broadcasts reached more than 2.2 billion people and that he has preached the gospel in person to more people than anyone in history (nearly 215 million in over 185 countries). More than 3.2 million people have accepted Jesus Christ as their personal savior at Billy Graham Crusades.

The Billy Graham Center Museum at Wheaton College in Wheaton, Illinois, and the Billy Graham Library at the Billy Graham Evangelistic Association headquarters in Charlotte, North Carolina (*see* separate listing), are devoted to Christian evangelism and Billy Graham's life and work.

Billy Graham was born as William Franklin Graham Jr. on a dairy farm near Charlotte, North Carolina, in 1918 to William Franklin Graham and Morrow Coffey Graham. He was raised in the Associate Reformed Presbyterian Church but was converted in 1934 at the age of 16 during revival meetings in Charlotte led by evangelist Mordecai Ham.

After graduating from Sharon High School in 1936, Graham attended Bob Jones College in Cleveland, Tennessee, and then transferred to Florida Bible Institute (now Trinity College of Florida). In 1939 Graham became a Southern Baptist minister and attended Wheaton College, where he graduated with a degree in anthropology in 1943.

It was at Wheaton College that Graham decided to take the Bible as the infallible word of God and later accepted it as the truth while at the Forest Home Christian Camp (now Forest Home Ministries) in Southern California. While attending Wheaton College, he served as pastor of the United Gospel Tabernacle and did other preaching. He also met Ruth McCue Bell, whose parents were Presbyterian missionaries in China. They were married two months after graduation in 1943 and had a long and productive life together. They had five children. She died in 2007 at the age of 87.

In 1943–1944 Graham was pastor of the Village Church in Western Springs, Illinois, and then became the first full-time evangelist for the new Youth for Christ International and traveled throughout the United States and Europe holding revival meetings. These included huge meetings in Los Angeles in 1949 that made him a national religious figure. The meetings evolved into what was called "Billy Graham Crusades." Graham also served as president of Northwestern Bible College in St. Paul, Minnesota, from 1947 to 1952.

Graham's evangelistic crusades attracted thousands. He would rent a stadium, park, or street; arrange for a large choir (as many as 5,000 singers); preach the gospel; and invite attendees to come forward to speak and pray with a counselor. These meetings sometimes lasted for weeks, such as 16 weeks at Madison Square Garden in New York City in 1957 and in London for 12 weeks in 1959. The crusade attendance could be enormous. More than 1 million attended a service in Seoul, South Korea, 250,000 in Central Park in New York City in 1991, and 155,000 at a Moscow crusade in 1992.

The Billy Graham Evangelistic Association was founded in 1950 with the headquarters in Minneapolis (later relocated to Charlotte). It added a new and expanded dimension to Graham's efforts with a weekly radio program, television specials, a syndicated newspaper column, two magazines, a website for a children's program, and a motion picture company that produced and distributed 130 films. In 2005 groundbreaking was held in Charlotte for a major new facility—the Billy Graham Library—which also houses the Billy Graham Evangelical Association headquarters. In recent years, Graham has suffered from Parkinson's disease and other illnesses. His wife is buried at the Billy Graham Library.

Graham has received many honors for his evangelistic and humanitarian work, including the Presidential Medal of Freedom and Congressional Gold Medal, as well as such special awards as the Templeton Foundation Prize for Progress in Religion and the Sylvanus Thayer Award for his commitment to duty, honor, and country.

The Billy Graham Center Museum at Wheaton College in Illinois tells the story of evangelism in North America and the life and ministry of Billy Graham. The 20,000-square-foot museum was founded in 1975 and opened in 1980. It is housed in the Billy Graham Center, a collaborative effort of the college and the Billy Graham Evangelical Association for strategic planning, inspiration, and preparation of leaders to further the evangelical mission of the church in the world.

The exhibit on Graham traces his life and achievements; contains such personal belongings as his college papers, medals, and gifts; and shows videos of his 1949 Los Angeles, 1954 London, and 1957 New York crusades. Other exhibits are devoted to the history of evangelism in America; a three-dimensional presentation of the gospel message; statements by religious witnesses; a transparent cross that celebrates the birth, death, and resurrection of Christ; and a gallery featuring changing exhibitions. Annual attendance is more than 35,000.

Billy Graham Center Museum, Wheaton College, 500 E. College Ave., Wheaton, IL 60187-5534. Phone 630/752-5909. Fax: 630/752-5916. E-mail: bgcmus@wheaton.edu. Website: www.billygrahamcenter.org/museum. Hours: 9:30–5:30 Mon.–Sat., 1–5 Sun.; closed Thanksgiving and between Christmas and New Year's. Admission: free but suggested donation—adults, $4; seniors and students, $3; children under 13, $1; families, $10.

Billy Graham Library. The Billy Graham Library is a library and museum devoted to the life and ministry of the Christian evangelist on the grounds of the international headquarters of the Billy Graham Evangelistic Association in Charlotte, North Carolina. It traces Graham's journey from a farm boy to an international ambassador of the gospel a few miles from where he was born and grew up.

The 40,000-square-foot library/museum opened in 2007 in a building that is designed after a barn to reflect Graham's rural childhood. Visitors enter the building through doors at the base of a 40-foot glass cross. Graham's historic childhood home—where he lived from the age of nine until he went to college—also has been restored and moved to the grounds. His wife, Ruth McCue Graham, is buried in the library's Memorial Prayer Garden, where he also will be interred upon his death. Another person buried on the library grounds is Mrs. Wilma Barrows, wife of Cliff Barrows, Graham's longtime music director.

The library has an extensive archive, and the museum contains exhibits, photographs, artifacts, memorabilia, films, and multimedia presentations about Graham's life and ministry. Visitors also can call up historical photographs and videos relating to Graham's life and evangelistic activities. In addition, a bookstore and a dairy bar are located in the library/museum building.

Billy Graham Library, 4330 Westmont Dr., Charlotte, NC 28217-1001. Phone: 704/401-3200. Website: www.billygrahamlibrary.org/library. Hours: 9:30–5 Mon.–Sat.; closed Sun., New Year's Day, Thanksgiving, and Christmas. Admission: free.

Martin Luther King Jr.

Martin Luther King Jr. National Historic Site. Dr. Martin Luther King Jr. was a Baptist minister who became a major figure in the African American civil rights movement in the 1950s and 1960s. He was an activist known for his nonviolent methods and inspiring speeches and writings, which advanced civil rights in the United States and around the world. His efforts led to the passage of the Civil Rights Act of 1964 and the Voting Rights Act of 1965. His assassination in 1968 shocked the nation and accelerated the advancement of civil rights.

For his role in ending racial segregation and discrimination, King received the Nobel Prize for Peace in 1964, and Martin Luther King Jr. Day was established as a federal holiday in 1986. He now also is honored at the Martin Luther King Jr. National Historic Site and the Martin Luther King Jr. Center for Nonviolent Social Change in Atlanta, Georgia, and the new Martin Luther King Jr. Memorial in Washington (*see* separate listings).

King was born Michael King Jr. in Atlanta in 1929 to the Rev. Michael King Sr. and Alberta Williams King. He was the middle of three children, having an older sister, Willie Christine, and a younger brother, Albert Williams. The family moved from a poor farming community to the Atlanta home of his mother's father, the Rev. A. D. Williams, who had developed the small Ebenezer Baptist Church into a large, forceful congregation. When the Rev. Williams died in 1931, Michael's father became pastor of the church and adopted the Martin Luther King Sr. name in honor of the German Protestant religious leader. His son Michael later followed with the name change, becoming Martin Luther King Jr.

The Rev. King Sr. fought against racial prejudice because blacks suffered and he considered racism and segregation to be against God's will. He also discouraged any sense of class superiority in his three children. It left a lasting impression on Martin Jr. He attended Atlanta's public schools, graduating from Booker T. Washington High School (after skipping the ninth and 11th grades). In 1944 he entered Morehead College in Atlanta at the age of 15 and graduated with a degree in sociology in 1948. While at Morehead, he made the decision to enter the ministry. He enrolled at Crozer Theological Seminary in Chester, Pennsylvania, where he was the student body president and class valedictorian and received a Bachelor of Divinity degree in 1951.

King then went to Boston University to earn a Doctor of Philosophy degree in 1955. While in Boston, he met Coretta Scott, an aspiring singer and musician attending the New England Conservatory. They were married on the lawn at her parents' home in Heiberger, Alabama, in 1953. They had four children—two sons and two daughters.

In 1954 King became the pastor of the Dexter Avenue Baptist Church in Montgomery, Alabama. Here he became a leader in the 1955–1956 Montgomery bus boycott to force integration of the city's bus lines—the first major step in the civil rights movement.

The protest began after Rosa Parks refused to give up her seat in the "colored section" of a bus to a white man. She was arrested and fined. The head of the NAACP chapter asked King to serve as the spokesman for the boycott, which lasted 382 days before the city agreed to remove the law requiring segregated public transportation. It drew nationwide attention and led to protests elsewhere.

In 1957 King, the Rev. Ralph Abernathy, and 60 ministers and civil rights activists founded the Southern Christian Leadership Conference to harness moral authority and organize the power of black churches. King was elected president, giving him a base of operation throughout the South and enabling him to meet with religious and civil rights leaders in the nation on race-related issues. In 1958 the SCLC held over 20 mass meetings to further voter registration and numerous projects seeking civil rights reforms.

King, who was influenced by Mahatma Gandhi's nonviolent activism in India, visited Gandhi's birthplace in 1959. He was impressed with Gandhi's peaceful teachings and protest effectiveness. The trip increased his commitment to America's civil rights struggle.

By 1960 King was gaining national attention. He returned to Atlanta to be copastor with his father at the Ebenezer Baptist Church and led a group of 75 students in a protest at a department store lunch counter that did not serve blacks. When 36 students sat at the counter and refused to leave, King and the students were arrested. However, the charges were dropped after an inquiry by John F. Kennedy, the Democratic candidate for president, who expressed concern about the arrests.

In 1963 King organized a campaign by a coalition of civil rights groups in Birmingham, Alabama, which was regarded as the most segregated city in America at the time. It included a boycott, sit-ins, and a march in which participants were attacked by police with dogs and water hoses in an assault shown on national television that caused a national outrage and calls for legislation. It was during this campaign that King drafted his "Letter from a Birmingham Jail," the manifesto of his philosophy and tactics.

Later in 1963, the "March for Jobs and Freedom" was held in Washington, and King gave his famous "I Have a Dream" speech at the Lincoln Memorial, which was attended by more than 200,000 people. In the address, he emphasized his belief that someday all men could be brothers. The address caused many Americans to question Jim Crow laws and influenced the passage of the Civil Rights Act of 1964 outlawing discrimination in public accommodations and publicly owned facilities. It also resulted in Dr. Martin Luther King Jr. receiving the Nobel Peace Prize in 1964 and being named the "Man of the Year" by *Time* magazine.

In 1965 King organized the three Selma-to-Montgomery protest marches, which grew out of the voting rights campaign in Selma. The marchers initially were attacked by state and local police with billy clubs and tear gas in what was called "Bloody Sunday" and in the third march were protected by federal troops and agents. The marches were the political and emotional peak of the civil rights movement and helped win support for the passage of the Voting Rights Act of 1965, which eliminated the remaining barriers to voting for African Americans.

From 1965 to 1968, King sought to broaden the scope of his activities by holding protest marches in large cities like Chicago and Los Angeles, coming out against United States involvement in the Vietnam War because it discriminated against the poor, and forming multirace coalitions to address problems of the disadvantages. While he was planning a "Poor People's Marsh" in Washington in 1968, he went to Memphis, Tennessee, to support striking sanitation workers.

On April 4, as he stood on the balcony of a motel, he was shot and killed by James Earl Ray, a career criminal, who was convicted and died in prison in 1998. The King family brought and won a wrongful-death judgment against Lloyd Jowers, who claimed he arranged the murder for a Mafia figure, but the Justice Department later concluded there was no evidence of an assassination plot.

Later in 1968, King's wife, Coretta Scott King, founded the Martin Luther King Jr. Center for Nonviolent Social Change, a museum dedicated to his life and achievements. In 1980 the Martin Luther King Jr. National Historic Site was established in the preservation district surrounding King's birthplace and boyhood home in Atlanta. The most recent honor is the Martin Luther King Jr. Memorial, an outdoor memorial on the National Mall in Washington, which opened in 2011.

The 35-acre national historic site in Atlanta includes the 1895 house in which Dr. King was born in 1928 and lived until 1941, his and Coretta Scott King's tomb, Ebenezer Baptist Church, the Atlanta Baptist Preparatory Institute, Our Lady of Lourdes Catholic Colored Mission, the Alexander Hamilton House, the Triangle Building, the 1894 Fire Station No. 6, various Victorian and shotgun row houses, and a visitor center. The visitor center has exhibits

The 35-acre historic site's visitor center at the Martin Luther King Jr. National Historic Site in Atlanta, Georgia. Courtesy of the National Park Service, Martin Luther King Jr. National Historic Site.

about the civil rights movement and King's life and accomplishments and features the "Courage to Lead" multimedia presentation, a stylized "Freedom Road," and the children-oriented "Children of Courage" exhibit.

The historic district also contains the family operated Martin Luther King Jr. Center for Nonviolent Social Change, a memorial tribute to Mahatma Gandhi, the International Civil Rights Walk of Fame, a Peace Plaza, and the International World Peace Rose Garden. Some of the facilities are operated by the National Park Service in partnership with the Ebenezer Baptist Church and King Center for Nonviolent Social Change. Tours are offered from mid-June to mid-August. The site's annual attendance is more than 900,000.

Martin Luther King Jr. National Historic Site, 450 Auburn Ave., N.E., Atlanta, GA 30312-4501. Phones: 404/3331-5190 and 404/331-6923. Fax: 404/730-3112. Website: www.nps.gov/malu. Hours: Memorial Day weekend–Labor Day 9–6 daily; day after Labor Day–day before Memorial Day weekend—9–5 daily; closed New Year's Day, Thanksgiving, and Christmas. Admission: free.

Martin Luther King Jr. Center for Nonviolent Social Change. In 1968 Coretta Scott King founded the Martin Luther King Jr. Center for Nonviolent Social Change as a "living memorial" to her husband and his work on important social ills around the world. The center began in the basement of their home and in 1981 was moved to the Martin Luther King Jr. National Historic Site. It is located near the house where King was born and grew up; the Ebenezer Baptist Church, where he preached from 1960 until his death in 1968; the tomb of Dr. and Mrs. King; and a reflecting pool.

The center, located in Freedom Hall, now is dedicated to research, education, and training in the principles, philosophy, and methods of nonviolence used by King. It contains a library and archive on King, black history, and the civil rights movement and materials pertaining to King, such as King family furnishings and personal effects, artwork, manuscripts, memorabilia, and works created by artists in memory of King. Annual attendance is 900,000.

Martin Luther King Jr. Center for Nonviolent Social Change, 449 Auburn Ave., N.E., Atlanta, GA 30312-1503. Phone: 404/526-8900. Fax: 404/526-8932. E-mail: information@thekingcenter.org. Website: www.thekingcenter.org. Hours: summer—9–6 Mon.–Fri.; winter—9–5 Mon.–Fri.; closed Sat.–Sun. and legal holidays. Admission: free.

Martin Luther King Jr. Memorial. The Martin Luther King Jr. Memorial is a monumental memorial honoring the civil rights leader in the West Potomac Park of the National Mall in Washington. The memorial, which opened to the public in 2011, covers four acres at the northwest corner of the Tidal Basin near the Franklin Delano Roosevelt Memorial. The memorial is the first to honor a nonpresident and the first devoted to a man of color on the mall.

The memorial resulted from an early effort by the Alpha Phi Alpha fraternity, of which King was a member while a doctoral student at Boston University in the 1950s. Plans for a permanent memorial gained momentum in 1986 after King's birthday became a national holiday. In 1998 Congress authorized the fraternity to form a foundation to establish a memorial on the mall.

The centerpiece of the memorial is a 30-foot relief of King by sculptor Lei Yixin. It is called the *Stone of Hope*, based on a line from King's "I Have a Dream" speech, saying "out of a mountain of despair, a stone of hope." It stands past two other pieces of granite symbolizing the *Mountain of Despair* and features words from the 1963 speech. The memorial also has a 450-foot crescent-shaped inscription wall with excerpts from many of King's sermons and speeches.

Martin Luther King Jr. Memorial, 1964 Independence Ave., S.W., Washington, DC 20024. Phone: 888/484-3373. Websites: www.nps.gov/mlkm and www.mlkmemorial.org. Hours: open 24 hours; park ranger at site 8 a.m.–12 midnight. Admission: free.

Joseph Priestley

See Scientists/Engineers/Inventors section.

Joseph Smith

Joseph Smith Historic Site. Joseph Smith was a nineteenth-century religious leader who founded the Latter-day Saints movement. He became a dynamic, charismatic, and controversial figure regarded as a prophet by Mormons. Beginning in the early 1820s, Smith had visions, including one in which an angel directed him to a buried book of golden plates inscribed in an early language. In 1830 he published a translation of the plates as the *Book of Mormon* and organized what became the Church of Jesus Christ of Latter-day Saints. Today, the church has over 14 million members in nearly 30,000 congregations and more than 130 temples worldwide.

The Mormon Church now is headquartered in Salt Lake City, Utah, but it once was based in Nauvoo, Illinois, where Smith was the mayor of the town and a candidate for president of the United States in addition to being the founder of the church. And it was in nearby Carthage, Illinois, that he was shot and killed by a mob in 1844 at the age of 38 while jailed on charges of ordering the destruction of a local newspaper that had claimed he was practicing polygamy and intended to become a theocratic king. Nauvoo now has a Joseph Smith Historic Site that celebrates his life.

Smith was born in Sharon, Vermont, in 1805. He was the fourth child of Joseph Smith Sr. and Lucy Mack Smith. His father was a merchant and farmer. In 1816 the family moved to a farm in the western New York village of Palmyra—and then to a 100-acre farm in nearby Manchester—after an ill-fated business venture and three years of crop failures.

The region was a hotbed of religious enthusiasm, with a number of camp meetings and revivals being held in the Palmyra area between 1817 and 1825. The Smith family and the young son became caught up in the excitement. At the age of 12, young Joseph started to show interest in religion. He read the Bible, attended church classes, took part in religious folk magic with his family that was typical of the era, and reportedly showed interest in Methodism.

Many people at that time, including Joseph's parents and maternal grandfather, had visions or dreams that they believed were messages from God. In 1832 he wrote that he had a vision in about 1820 that his sins were forgiven and the world had turned away from the gospel. This account, which later was known as Smith's "First Vision," became important to the Mormon faith by the end of the century.

In 1823, while praying for forgiveness for his sins, Smith said he was visited at night by an angel named Moroni. The angel told him where to find a buried book of golden plates and other artifacts, including a breastplate and a set of silver spectacles with lenses composed of seer stones in a hill near his home. The Smith family supplemented its farm income by digging for seer stones. Smith said he used the stones to locate lost items and buried treasure by putting a stone in a white stovepipe hat and the reflections on the stone displayed the information. He said he returned to the hill site the next morning and made annual visits the next four years but could not remove the plates because the angel prevented him.

In 1826, while traveling in western New York and Pennsylvania as a treasure seeker and farmhand, Smith was tried and released by a county court near Colesville, New York, on a charge of pretending to find lost treasure in what was called "glass-looking." He also stayed at a boarding house in Harmony, Pennsylvania, and began courting Emma Hale, daughter of the owners. Smith proposed to Emma, but her father objected to the marriage because he was a stranger and had no means of support except treasure hunting. Despite the opposition, the couple eloped, were married in 1827, and lived with his parents.

While at home, Smith made his annual visit to the hill and was able to retrieve the plates. He said the angel commanded him not to show the plates to anyone but to publish their translation, reputed to be the religious record of indigenous Americans. In October Smith and his pregnant wife returned to Harmony (now Oakland) and lived near her parents, and he transcribed some of the engraved characters (which he called "reformed Egyptian") and dictated a partial translation to his wife. But the translations were lost, and Smith resumed translating with Oliver Cowdery as his scribe in 1829. They then moved to Fayette, New York, and completed the translation.

When the translation spoke of an institutional church and requirement for baptism, Smith and Cowdery baptized each other. They later said that John the Baptist had appeared and ordained them to priesthood. Moroni, the angel, took back the plates after Smith was finished using them, according to Smith.

The translation, called the *Book of Mormon*, was published in 1830, and the Church of Christ was organized shortly thereafter with small branches in Palmyra, Fayette, and Colesville, New York. The *Book of Mormon* brought Smith regional notoriety, as well as strong opposition from those who remember his money-digging and the 1826 trial for pretending to find lost treasures. Smith and Cowdery had to flee Colesville to escape a gathering mob.

New Mormon centers were then established at two sites—Kirtland, Ohio, where Sidney Rigdon and over 100 members of his Disciples of Christ congregation were converted and Rigdon became second in command of the Mormon Church, and a new community that Smith called "New Jerusalem" in Jackson County, Missouri. The Kirtland church grew rapidly in 1831–1838, built a temple, and served briefly as the center of the Latter-day Saints movement. Jackson County residents felt neglected and unhappy with Smith's communism system and his political power, resulting in former church members beating Smith and Rigdon unconscious and tarring and feathering them.

The communal system was dropped, and Smith was unsuccessful in improving conditions in Jackson County. It resulted in the church—which changed its name to the Church of Latter Day Saints—leaving Jackson County in 1838 to establish a new Missouri town of "Far West," which became the new Mormon "Zion." The church name also was changed to Church of Jesus Christ of Latter-day Saints.

The settlement soon expanded beyond Caldwell County to form the village of Adam-ondi-Ahman. Smith now believed that greater militancy was required to survive against anti-Mormons and church traitors. The 1838 "Mormon War" began when non-Mormons sought to prevent Mormons from voting. The election-day scuffles escalated as non-Mormon vigilantes raided and burned Mormon farms, and Mormons responded with similar raids.

When the Mormons attacked the Missouri state militia at the Battle of Crooked River in an attempt to rescue captured Mormons, Governor Lilburn Boggs ordered that all Mormons be killed or driven from the state. The war ended when vigilantes killed about 18 Mormons in the Haun's Mill massacre. The Mormon colony surrendered and agreed to forfeit their property and leave the state.

Smith was court-martialed for treason and nearly executed. He was saved on the grounds that he was a civilian. Smith was jailed but escaped while being escorted back from a grand jury hearing. He fled to Illinois, which refused to return him to Missouri. While Smith was imprisoned, Brigham Young, one of the Mormon church leaders, and the Quorum of the Twelve Apostles (one of the church's governing bodies), helped 14,000 Mormons make their way to Illinois, which accepted them.

Smith then purchased some land along the Mississippi River near Quincy and established a new town, which he called "Nauvoo" (meaning "beautiful" in Hebrew). He urged followers to settle there, and they came in large numbers. But the soggy site produced mosquitoes, and many of the Mormons died from malaria in 1839–1841. To attack more settlers, Smith sent Brigham Young and other members of the Quorum of the Twelve Apostles to Britain as missionaries. They were quite successful in their recruiting, and the colony grew rapidly, built a temple in 1841–1846, and became the largest town in the state. At the same time, Smith made changes in the Mormon doctrines and performed a number of secret plural marriages, which later led to the polygamy controversy.

Smith became the second mayor of Nauvoo and in 1844 announced his candidacy for president of the United States after deserting both the Whig and Democratic parties. He sent out apostles to promote his campaign, which included calling for the abolishment of slavery by compensating slaveholders with funds from the sale of public lands and favoring a "theodemocratic" government of the Kingdom of God over a secular government. But the election bid failed.

Smith also was experiencing opposition among former supporters in Nauvoo. This included a dispute in 1844 over managing Nauvoo's economy and proposals of marriage to other wives by Smith. Charges of polygamy and other crimes were brought against him. When a new community newspaper, the *Nauvoo Expositor*, called for church reform, criticized Smith for polygamy, opposed his new doctrines, and sought the repeal of Nauvoo's charter, the city council denounced the paper as a public nuisance and ordered the Nauvoo militia to destroy it—and the publication was demolished.

A riot followed, and Smith and his brother, Hyrum, were arrested for inciting it. They were taken to the county jail in Carthage for trial, where the charges were increased to treason against the state. On June 27, 1844, an armed mob stormed the jail and shot and killed both Smith and his brother. Five men were tried for murder but were acquitted in a sham trial.

After Smith's death, county residents expected the Mormons to leave Nauvoo. When they did not, they were attacked and many left. It was followed by what was called the Battle of Nauvoo, marked by gun battles in which locals tried to evict the Mormons. The remaining Mormons decided to leave as a result of the confrontations. Under the leadership of Brigham Young and the Quorum of the Twelve Apostles, the Mormons left and made the long journey to Great Salt Lake Valley in Utah, where they settled in what became Salt Lake City and the headquarters of the Mormon church, now known as the Church of Jesus Christ of Latter-day Saints. Meanwhile, their Greek revival–style temple in Nauvoo was burned in a mysterious fire in 1848 and further damaged by tornado-strength winds in 1850 (and replaced by a replica temple in 2002).

Much of Nauvoo is now preserved as part of the Joseph Smith Historic Site, founded in 1918 and operated by the Community of Christ, based in Independence, Missouri. The church is part of the Latter-day Saints movement but separate from the Utah-based church. It traces its founding to 1830 and was known as the Reorganized Church of Jesus Christ of Latter Day Saints from 1872 to 2001.

The Nauvoo historic site now includes the 1839 Joseph Smith Homestead, the first home of Joseph and Emma Smith; the 1843 Mansion House, the 1839 house that Joseph Smith built and lived in; the Nauvoo House, a hotel and the home of Emma Smith and her second husband, Lewis Bidamon; the Red Brick Store, the reconstructed 1841 building where Smith had a store, his office, and a meeting space; the Smith Family Cemetery, containing the burial sites of Joseph and Emma Smith and other Smith family members; and a visitor center, with a film on Joseph Smith's life, exhibits and artifacts of the Smith family and close associates, and original paintings by David Hyrum Smith. Guided tours are offered. During the summer, demonstrations are given of 1840s daily living activities such as cooking, carding wool, spinning, candle making, and herb gardening, and games. Annual attendance is 90,000.

The Church of Jesus Christ of Latter-day Saints has replaced the Mormon temple in Nauvoo that was destroyed in the mid-1800s. It now is one of the sights in historic Nauvoo, which has about two dozen historic row houses, shops, and religious buildings, as well as a visitor center with an 1846 relief map, video, and exhibits and artifacts about early Nauvoo.

Joseph Smith Historic Site, 805 Water St., Nauvoo, IL 62354 (postal address: PO Box 138 Nauvoo, IL 62354-0338). Phone: 217/453-2246. Fax: 217/453-6416. E-mail: jshs@frontiernet.net. Websites: www.cofchrist.org/js and www.historicnauvoo.net. Hours: May–Oct.—9–5 Mon.–Sat., 1–5 Sun.; closed Sept. 2; Nov.–Dec.—10–4 Tues.–Sat.; closed Sun.–Mon., Christmas Eve and Day, Dec. 16, and Dec. 31; Jan.–Feb.—only groups by appointment; Mar.–Apr.—10–4 Mon.–Sat.; closed Sun. Admission: free; tours, $3.

Joseph Smith Birthplace Memorial. A 50-foot granite obelisk honors Joseph Smith, founder of the Church of Jesus Christ of Latter-day Saints, in the White River Valley near Sharon and South Royalton in Vermont. Smith, who was the founder and first president of the church, was born at the site on the town line between Sharon and South Royalton in 1805. The 40-ton shaft of the obelisk is 38 and a half feet long—one for each year of Smith's life. It is one of the largest polished shafts in the world.

The 350-acre site also contains a visitor center with exhibits on Smith's family and his life and career and a Mormon church meetinghouse. The memorial was conceived by church leader Junius F. Wells during a visit to the birthplace site in 1884. He oversaw the construction of the memorial, which was completed in 1905—on the 100th anniversary of Smith's birth.

Joseph Smith Birthplace Memorial, 357 LDS Lane, South Royalton, VT 05068. Phone: 802/763-7742. E-mail: hsjs-memorial@ldschurch.org. Website: www.lds.org/placestovisit/historical-sites/joseph-smith-birthplace. Hours: May–Oct.—9–7 Mon.–Sat., 1:30–7 Sun.; Nov.–Apr.—9–5 Mon.–Sat., 1:30–5 Sun. Admission: free.

Smith Family Farm. The Smith Family Farm in Palmyra, New York, is where Joseph Smith, first prophet and president of the Church of Jesus Christ of Latter-day Saints, spent his boyhood, experienced his first vision in 1820, and was visited in 1823 by the angel Moroni. The angel told him about the golden plates on a nearby hill that led to the founding of the Mormon Church. The farm now contains a replica of the 1818 log cabin and grove where he had the visions and a larger frame house built in 1825.

Joseph Smith Sr. and his wife, Lucy Mack Smith, and their eight children moved to Palmyra from Vermont in 1816. In 1817 Mr. Smith took out a mortgage on 100 acres of farmland in adjacent Manchester, where he and his sons built a small log cabin in 1818 and then the frame house five years later. When the father could not meet the mortgage payments, the family moved back to the log cabin in 1829. The next year, the Smiths left the area.

The log cabin no longer was standing when the Mormon Church purchased the property in 1930. It was not until 1982 that the cabin's location was found in an archaeological excavation. A reconstruction of the structure was erected in 1997–1998. The historic site also contains a welcome center that tells about the importance of the Smith family farm.

Smith Family Farm, 843 Stafford Rd., Palmyra, NY 14522. Phone: 315/597-383. E-mail: vchcumorah@ldchurch.org. Website: www.lds.org/placestovisit/eng/historical-site/smith-farm. Hours: summer—9–6 daily; winter—9–5 daily. Admission: free.

Roger Williams

Roger Williams National Memorial. Roger Williams was an English theologian who was an early proponent of religious freedom and the separation of church and state. He came to America in 1631 because he felt the Church of England was corrupt and a new church must be established for the true and pure worship of God. In 1636 Williams founded the colony of Providence Plantations (which became present-day Rhode Island), where refugees could come to worship as their conscience dictated without interference from the state. He also befriended Indian tribes, learned their languages, and became an advocate for fair dealings with Native Americans. The Roger Williams National Memorial in Providence now commemorates his life.

Williams was born in London about 1603 (the record of his birth was destroyed in the Great London Fire of 1666). He was the son of James Williams, a merchant tailor, and Alice Pemberton Williams. He spent his youth in the parish of St. Sepulchre's without Newgate. It was a period of numerous burnings of so-called Puritans or heretics at the stake that took place in nearby Springfield. This may have influenced his later beliefs about religious freedom and the separation of church and state.

As a teenager, Williams apprenticed with Sir Edward Coke, the noted jurist, and attended Charterhouse and Pembroke College at Cambridge, where he received his bachelor's degree in 1627. He had a gift for languages and became familiar with Latin, Hebrew, Greek, Dutch, and French. He took his Holy Orders in the Church of England, but he became a Puritan at Cambridge. It removed his chances of preference in the Anglican Church.

Williams became the chaplain to Sir William Macham, a Puritan lord. In 1629 he married Mary Barnard at the Church of High Lever in Essex. They had six children. All were born in America. In 1630 Williams became a separatist, and he and his wife left for America when he decided they could not remain in England under what he considered the corrupt and false Church of England headed by Archbishop William Laud.

Upon arrival in the colonies in early 1631, he turned down an offer to be the teacher (assistant minister) of the church in Boston. He said the civil magistrate could not punish any breach of the first table of the Ten Commandments, such as idolatry, Sabbath breaking, false worship, and blasphemy. He stated that every person should be free to follow his own convictions in religious matters. From the very beginning, Williams stood for three principles that marked his career in America—separatism, freedom of religion, and separation of church and state.

Later in 1631, Williams was invited to become the teacher at the Salem church, which was more favorable to separatism. But the offer was withdrawn when Boston leaders learned of the offer. Williams then moved from Salem to Plymouth Colony, where he informally assisted the minister, preached regularly, and was well received. However, he later felt the Plymouth church was not sufficiently separated from the Church of England. His study of Indian tribes in the area also caused him to doubt the validity of the colonial charters. In 1632 Williams wrote a tract that condemned the king's charters and questioned the right of Plymouth and Massachusetts to the land without first buying it from the Native Americans. When Massachusetts authorities learned of the treatise, they summoned Williams to the General Court of Massachusetts in Boston. However, the issue was settled when Williams promised not to raise the issue again and the tract disappeared.

In the fall of 1633, Williams moved back to Salem, where the Rev. Samuel Skelton made him an unofficial assistant in the church. When the minister died in 1634, Williams became the acting pastor of the church. He became embroiled in controversies again when he raised the issue of the charter and questioned the new oath of allegiance to the colonial government. He was ordered to appear before the General Court again, and the court declared that he should be removed from his church position.

The latest court order came as the town of Salem petitioned the court to annex some land on Marblehead Neck. The court would not act on the request until the Salem church removed Williams, but the church felt the order violated its independence and a letter of protest was sent to other churches (but not read). When the court refused to seat delegates from Salem in the next session, Williams lost support. And when he demanded that the Salem church separate from other churches, the request was rejected and he resigned.

In 1635 he was tried by the General Court and convicted of sedition and heresy and ordered to be banished (the order was repealed by Massachusetts in 1636). When he delayed leaving and continued his agitation, the sheriff was sent for him and found that Williams left for the head of Narragansett Bay in the deep snow three days earlier. The Wampanoags found him and took him to the winter camp of Massasoit, their sachem (chief).

In 1636 Williams and a number of followers from Salem bought land from Massasoit. But when they found that it was within Plymouth's land grant, they crossed the Seekonk River to Narragansett territory and obtained land from Canonicus and Miantonomi, sachems of the Narragansetts, and established a settlement called Providence. Williams said the settlement was to be a haven for those "distressed of conscience." It soon attracted dissenters and like-minded people and became a place of religious liberty and separation of church and state. Williams is credited with being the cofounder with John Clarke of the Baptist Church in America in Newport in 1638, but his involvement was limited. In 1639 Williams withdrew from all church connections.

In 1643 Williams returned to England to obtain a charter for his colony to forestall an attempt by neighboring colonies to take over Providence. His efforts were helped by the publication of his first book, *A Key Into the Language of America*, the first dictionary of any Indian tongue in the English language. He received the charter for Providence Plantations (which included Providence, Newport, and Portsmouth) from Parliament in 1644—the same year his most famous book, *The Bloudy Tenent of Persecution for Cause of Conscience*, was published.

When Williams returned, he opened a trading post at Cocumscussoc (now North Kingstown). He traded with the Indians, learned their language and customs, and became known for his peacemaking between neighboring colonists and the Indians. In 1851 he sold the trading post to pay for a return to England with Newport preacher John Clarke to have the charter confirmed because of a conflicting charter for "Rhode Island" obtained by William Coddington. The other charter was rescinded, and Williams returned home in 1954, while Clarke stayed and obtained a new royal charter from Charles II in 1663.

Williams served as president of the colony in 1654–1658 and then became less involved in the colony's affairs. He suffered his biggest disappointment when King Philip's War broke out in New England in 1675, which turned out to be one of the bloodiest and costliest in North American history. The war is named for the main leader of the

Indians, Metacomet, who was known to the English as King Philip. In a little more than a year, 12 of the region's towns were destroyed and many others damaged. Almost all of Providence was burned, including Williams's house. King Philip was killed by Puritan rangers in 1676, but it was not until 1678 that a truce was signed.

Roger Williams died in 1683. He was buried on his property in Providence, but his body never was found. The grave was forgotten when his house collapsed into the cellar 50 years later. Dirt from what was believed to be the burial site was later put in an urn, which now is located at the Rhode Island Historical Society.

The Roger Williams National Memorial in downtown Providence was established in 1965 to honor the founder of Rhode Island, who stood for religious freedom and separation of church and state. The four-and-a-half-acre memorial park, which is listed on the National Register of Historic Places, has a visitor center with exhibits on the life of Williams and the history of Rhode Island. Annual attendance is nearly 122,000.

Roger Williams National Memorial, 282 N. Main St., Providence, RI 02903-1240. Phone: 401/521-7266. Fax: 401/521-7239. Website: www.nps.gov/row. Hours: 9–4:30 daily; closed New Year's Day, Thanksgiving, and Christmas. Admission: free.

Brigham Young

Beehive House. Brigham Young was a Mormon leader who succeeded founder Joseph Smith as president of the Church of Jesus Christ of Latter-day Saints in 1847, serving for a record 29 years. He and the Quorum of the Twelve Apostles (a council in charge of church affairs) led the Mormon migration from Nauvoo, Illinois, to the Rocky Mountain West, where he founded Salt Lake City and served as the first governor of Utah. He was an effective and pragmatic organizer who greatly expanded the Mormon Church. Two of his homes now are historic sites—Beehive House in Salt Lake City and a winter home in St. George, Utah.

Brigham Young was born in a farming family in 1801 in Whittingham, Vermont. He was the ninth of 11 children of John Young and Abigail Howe Young. His father worked as a traveling carpenter and blacksmith. The family moved frequently throughout upstate New York during a period of religious fervor. Brigham had a limited formal education and was apprenticed to be a carpenter, painter, and glazier—trades he used to support himself in the early years.

Young was brought up in a strict, moralistic family, but he was slow to become involved with any specific religious denomination until he joined the Methodist Church in 1823. In 1824 he met and married Miriam Works, with whom he had two daughters. She died in 1832. Young became a polygamist who reportedly had 55 wives and fathered 57 children by 16 of the women.

Young became interested in Mormonism in 1830 after reading the *Book of Mormon*, Joseph Smith's translation of the golden plates. He joined the new church in 1832 and traveled to Upper Canada as a missionary and then to Kirtland, Ohio, to join other Mormons in establishing the colony. He was impressed with Smith and found Mormonism appealing in its emphasis on Christian primitivism and its millennialistic orientation, authoritarianism, and certain Puritan beliefs. Young also saw the church's lay priesthood as a way to achieve status and recognition. He then devoted all his efforts into promoting Mormonism and rose rapidly through the church ranks. By 1835 he was appointed to one of the church's governing councils, the Quorum of the Twelve Apostles. In 1838, when the Mormons were expelled from Missouri, Young took charge of the move as the senior member of the council.

Brigham Young became the church's principal leader after the murder of Joseph Smith in 1844. He felt the church followers no longer could remain in Nauvoo, Illinois, after the extreme anti-Mormon violence and organized with the Quorum of the Twelve Apostles to lead a mass Mormon migration to the West. It became the largest and best organized westward movement of pioneers in the nation's history. When the Mormons reached the Great Salt Lake Valley in what became Utah, he decided to make that their home. Young also oversaw Mormon settlement throughout Utah, as well as in other western states. He was made president of the Mormon Church in December 1847, a position he held until his death in August 1877.

Young made temple building a priority throughout his membership in the Church of Jesus Christ of Latter-day Saints—and one of his first efforts in the Great Salt Lake Valley was a temple. He was involved in the construction of temples in the Mormon colonies of Kirtland, Ohio, and Nauvoo, Illinois, and immediately built a temporary temple while breaking ground for the permanent Salt Lake Temple in 1853. He also oversaw the construction of the Salt Lake Tabernacle and later announced plans for other temples in Utah—at St. George (1871), Manti (1875), and Logan (1877).

The Mormon Church became known for polygamy during Young's presidency. The practice was started by Joseph Smith, but it was under Young's leadership that it became widespread and was acknowledged by the church in 1852. It is believed that he was one of the leading polygamists with 55 wives. Another issue involving Young was the revoking of priesthood and temple blessings from black members of the Mormon Church. He announced the racial restriction after settling in the Great Salt Lake Valley in 1846, and it was not rescinded by the church until 1978.

The Mormons experienced a number of conflicts following their settlement in the Great Salt Lake Valley. The new Mormon colony became part of the United States following the 1846–1848 Mexican-American War, when a large part of the Mexican-controlled American West, including the Salt Lake area, was ceded to the U.S. federal government. Young petitioned Congress to create the state of Deseret, but the Compromise of 1850 made it the Utah Territory. Brigham Young was named the governor of the territory, making him the head of both the church and the territorial government.

Governor Young spearheaded the development of new communities, but his leadership style was considered autocratic. His relations with the federal government also deteriorated, especially after the Mormon Church acknowledged polygamy and there were reports of widespread obstruction of federal officials. In 1857 President James Buchanan decided to install a non-Mormon as governor and sent federal troops to accompany him and man garrison forts in the territory.

When Young heard that federal troops were on their way to Utah with his replacement, he refused to step down and had his militia ambush the federal soldiers. It resulted in a brief encounters called the "Utah War." The Mormons held off the troops for a winter by taking their cattle and burning supply wagons. After considering burning Salt Lake City and moving his followers to Mexico, Young resigned as governor and was given a pardon.

Another incident that caused federal action was the Mountain Meadows massacre in which over 120 men, women, and children from Arkansas were killed by Mormons for passing through the Utah Territory in 1857. When Governor Brigham Young learned about the attack planned on the Fancher party of immigrants by church members in Parowan and Cedar City, he sent a letter to allow the wagon train to pass unmolested. But the letter is said to have arrived too late to stop the massacre.

Relations between Young and the federal government remained tense for a number of years. Federal officials sent another armed force (composed of California volunteers) to Salt Lake City in 1862. The Morrell Anti-bigamy Act, which outlawed "plural marriages," also was passed in 1962, and the Poland Act, which ended Mormon Church control over Utah's judicial system, was enacted in 1874. In 1872 Young was placed under house arrest for several weeks for "lewd and improper cohabitation" and jailed briefly in 1875 for failing to pay alimony to one of his wives. Both cases later were dismissed.

Brigham Young died in 1877 of peritonitis from a ruptured appendix at the age of 76. His funeral was held in the Salt Lake Tabernacle with an estimated 12,000 to 15,000 in attendance. He is buried on the grounds of the Mormon Pioneer Memorial Monument in Salt Lake City. A marble statue of Young, representing the state of Utah, is located in National Statuary Hall at the U.S. Capitol.

Young had two official residences in Salt Lake City—Beehive House and the adjacent Lion House. The Beehive House is connected by a suite of rooms to the Lion House. They are one block from the Salt Lake Temple and Temple Square in downtown Salt Lake City. The Beehive House was Brigham Young's home from 1854 until his death in 1877, and the rooms leading to the Lion House were his offices and private bedroom. It also served as the executive mansion of the Utah Territory from 1852 to 1855 when Young was governor. The 1854 adobe and sandstone Beehive House was built to accommodate Young and his wives and children, and the Lion House was added as his family grew. The house, which has a wooden beehive atop it, was called the Beehive House because bees symbolize the strong work ethic and value of industriousness among Mormons.

After much dispute and some litigation by Young's heirs, the Beehive House went to the heirs, who sold it to the church. It was used as the home of succeeding presidents of the church and then as the home economics wing of the Latter-day Saints University and later as a dormitory for young women. The Beehive House became a historic house museum in 1961. It has been restored and furnished to show what life was like for the Young family in the 1850s. Free tours are given of the historic house, including the sitting room, kitchen, play room, family store, fairy castle, and Young's room and office. Annual attendance is 200,000.

Beehive House, 67 East South Temple, Salt Lake City, UT 84111-9719. Phone: 801/240-2681. Fax: 801/240-2695. Website: www.lds.org/church/places-to-visit/historic-beehive-house. Hours: 9:30–8:30 daily; closed New Year's Day, Thanksgiving, and Christmas. Admission: free.

Brigham Young's Winter Home. The Brigham Young's Winter Home in St. George, Utah, is where the president of the Church of Jesus Christ of Latter-day Saints spent the last winters of his life in the 1870s. He began spending the winters in St. George as he aged and started suffering from arthritis. He found the warm, dry, and snowless winters eased his discomfort. The original portion of the two-story adobe/rock house was built in 1869–1871, and the front addition—the main part of the house—was completed in 1873. He died in 1877.

St. George, located in the hot red-rock desert in southern Utah, was settled in 1861 by Mormons sent there by the church leadership. Brigham Young launched a public works project in a food-for-labor program. While Young set the residents to work on public projects, Mormons from northern Utah donated food and living supplies. Over a 13-year period, the town constructed its tabernacle, courthouse, and Mormon temple. Brigham Young moved into the first part of his winter home in 1869. The finished home had three or more bedrooms with an office in the master bedroom, a vegetable storage room in the basement, an ingenious ventilation system where the warm air flowed out through the ceiling, large wrap-around porches, and orchards and gardens surrounding the house on three sides.

The house passed through several ownerships before it was purchased by the Mormon Church. It was founded as a historic house museum in 1975. The house has some original furnishings, as well as other period pieces typical of the 1870s. Free guided tours are offered of the house, which is located in a neighborhood of pioneer homes, many of which have been restored. More than two dozen historic houses can also be seen in a walking tour of downtown St. George. The museum's annual attendance is nearly 40,000.

Brigham Young's Winter Home, 67 West 200 North, St. George, UT 84770 (postal address: St. George Temple Visitor's Center and Historic Sites, 490 South 300 East, St. George, UT 84770-3665). E-mail: vcsgeorge@idschurch. org. Website: www.stgeorgetemplevisitorcenter.org/byounghome.html. Hours: summer—10–7 daily; winter—10–5 daily; closed New Year's Day, Thanksgiving, and Christmas. Admission: free.

SCIENTISTS/ENGINEERS/INVENTORS

Benjamin Banneker

Benjamin Banneker Park and Museum. Benjamin Banneker was one of the nation's earliest African American scientists and inventors in the eighteenth century. He was an astronomer, mathematician, surveyor, almanac author, farmer, and antislavery publicist. Banneker was born a free man and was largely self-educated. He became known for such accomplishments as building one of the first watches in America, predicting solar and lunar eclipses, assisted in surveying the federal territory that became the District of Columbia, producing some of the earliest farmers' almanacs, and opposing slavery and racial inequality. The Benjamin Banneker Park and Museum in Baltimore and the Banneker-Douglass Museum in Annapolis, Maryland (*see* separate listing), now honor Banneker.

Banneker was born on a farm near Ellicott, Maryland, in 1731. His parents were Robert and Mary Banneker. Not much is known about his early years. One of Banneker's biographers believes he was the grandson of an African slave named Banneker and Molly Welsh, a European woman who came to America as an indentured servant. She reportedly purchased Banneker to help establish a farm, and he cleared the land, solved some irrigation problems, and instituted crop rotation. Molly then freed and married Banneker.

Benjamin's mother, Mary, was the daughter of the Bannekers. His father, Robert, was a slave who fled his owner. Benjamin may have learned to read from his grandmother, Molly, but as a teenager he also briefly attended a school operated by Peter Heinrich, a Quaker farmer near the Banneker farm, who made available his personal library to Benjamin. Banneker never went to college or married and spent most of the rest of his life on the family farm with his mother and sisters. His father died in 1759, and Benjamin took over the running of the farm.

At the age of 22 in 1753, Banneker borrowed a pocket watch from a neighbor, took it apart, made a drawing of each component, reassembled the watch, and returned it to the owner. He then carved enlarged replicas of each part, and made a working wooden clock that kept accurate time and struck the hours for over 50 years.

In 1771 the Ellicott family moved into the area and built mills along the Patapsco River. Banneker supplied food for the workers and studied the mills. In 1788 he started studying astronomy with books and a telescope George Ellicott lent him. As a result, he soon was predicting future solar and lunar eclipses.

Major Andrew Ellicott, a member of the same family, hired Banneker to assist in the initial survey of the boundaries of the 100 square miles of land that Maryland and Virginia would cede to the federal government for the nation's capitol in the Territory of Columbia (later called the District of Columbia). Banneker primarily made astronomical observations to ascertain the location of the starting points on Earth to the positions of stars at specific times. In 1791, however, he left the survey team and returned home because of illness and to work his ephemeris, a table based on astronomical calculations that predicts when and where solar and lunar eclipses will occur. It was such calculations that enabled him to forecast the 1789 solar eclipse.

In 1792 through 1797, Banneker produced a series of farmers' almanacs that contained such information as weather forecasts and dates, solar and lunar eclipses, rising and setting times of the sun and moon, places and aspects of the planets, tide tables, home treatments for illnesses, court schedules, dates of yearly festivals, poetry, and essays. The 1793 almanac contained the letters exchanged by Banneker and Secretary of State Thomas Jefferson on slavery, racial equality, and Banneker's idea for a "secretary of peace."

The almanacs, which were supported by Andrew, George, and Elias Ellicott and heavily promoted by the Society for the Promotion of the Abolition of Slavery, were printed and sold in six cities in four states (Baltimore, Maryland; Philadelphia, Pennsylvania; Wilmington, Delaware; and Alexandria, Petersburg, and Richmond, Virginia). He also kept journals that contained his diary and notebooks for astronomical observations.

Benjamin Banneker died in his log cabin in 1806 at the age of 74 after selling much of his farm to the Ellicotts and others. The Banneker home was burned on the day of his burial, and the actual site was not found until the 1990s. A commemorative obelisk that the Maryland Bicentennial Commission and the State Committee on Afro American History and Culture erected in 1977 is located near Banneker's unmarked grave in an Oella, Maryland, churchyard.

In 1998 the 138-acre Benjamin Banneker Park and Museum was established in the Patapsco River Valley of Baltimore on land purchased by Robert and Mary Banneker in 1737. It tells about the life and accomplishments of Banneker, as well as the cultural and natural history of early American times. The park also seeks to conserve the wildlife habitat and archaeological sites of the former farm.

The museum contains an extensive collection of historical and archaeological objects from Banneker's era, including his work table, candle molds, and candlesticks and such other items as instruments, pieces of lenses and lead pencils, and books on African American history. The park also has living history areas that recreate the colonial farm and life of the Bannekers and presents historical special events, science and environmental programs, and visual and performing arts activities. Annual attendance is 40,000.

Benjamin Banneker Park and Museum, 300 Oella Ave., Baltimore, MD 21228-5416. Phone: 410/887-1081. Fax: 410/203-2747. E-mail: bannekermuseum-rp@baltimorecountymd.gov. Website: www.bannekermuseum.com. Hours: park—sunrise–sunset daily; museum—10–4 Tues.–Sat.; closed Sun.–Mon. and major holidays. Admission: free.

Banneker-Douglass Museum. The Banneker-Douglass Museum in Annapolis, Maryland, is dedicated to preserving and interpreting the state's African American heritage. It is located in the 1875 former Mt. Moriah African Methodist Episcopal Church in the heart of historic Baltimore and named for two of the state's leading African American historical figures—mathematician and astronomer Benjamin Banneker and abolitionist and writer Frederick Douglass.

The museum, which opened in the historic Gothic revival–style church in 1984, serves as the state's official repository of African American material culture. In addition to Banneker and Douglass, it has displays about Kunta Kinte, James Pennington, Harriet Tubman, Matthew Henson, and Thurgood Marshall. It also has a library and archives and offers lectures, workshops, performances, and educational programs relating to African American history and culture. The museum, which is listed in the National Register of Historic Places, is operated by the Governor's Office of Community Initiatives and the Maryland Commission on African American History and Culture.

Banneker-Douglass Museum, 84 Franklin St., Annapolis, MD 21401-2738. Phone: 410/216-6180. Fax: 410/974-2553. E-mail: bdmprograms@goci.state.md.us. Website: www.bdmuseum.com. Hours: Memorial Day–Labor Day—10–4 Tues.–Sat., 1–5 first Sun. of May–Aug.; closed remaining Sun.–Mon.; day after Labor Day–day before Memorial Day—10–4 Tues.–Sat.; closed Sun.–Mon. and major holidays. Admission: free.

Luther Burbank

Luther Burbank Home and Garden. Luther Burbank was a world-renowned horticulturalist and botanist who developed more than 800 strains and varieties of plants over a 55-year career. They included vegetables, fruits, flowers, grains, and grasses. Among his most successful products have been the Russet Burbank potato, Shasta daisy, fire poppy, July Elberta peach, Santa Rosa plum, Flaming Gold nectarine, Wickson plum, Freestone peach, and white blackberry. He also developed such specialty plants as a spineless cactus (useful in cattle feeding) and the plumcot and spurred the passage of the 1930 Plant Patent Act, which made it possible to patent new varieties of plants.

Burbank was born in Lancaster, Massachusetts, in 1849. He was the 13th of 15 children born to Samuel Walton Burbank and Olive Ross Burbank. His father was a farmer who also made bricks and pottery. Luther went to district public schools until 15 and then took some courses at Lancaster Academy, but he never went to college. However, he did spend a lot time reading books from the public library. Luther enjoyed the plants in his mother's large garden and became interested in developing new plant species and varieties after reading Charles Darwin's *Variations of Animals and Plants under Domestication* in 1838.

When his father died in 1870 and Luther was 21, he used his inheritance to buy a 17-acre plot of land, where he began experimenting with plants. It was there that he developed the Burbank potato, his first major success. He sold the potato rights for $150 and used the money to move to Santa Rosa, California, where he bought a four-acre site and established a greenhouse, nursery, and experimental fields for crossbreeding of plants. This land now is a city park. He later purchased 18 acres in the nearby town of Sebastopol and called it the Gold Ridge Farm.

Burbank created hundreds of new varieties of fruits, vegetables, ornamental flowers, and other plants using such techniques as grafting, hybridization, and crossbreeding, including a natural genetic variation of the Burbank potato with russet-colored skin that became known as the Russet Burbank potato, the world's predominant potato in food processing.

In 1893 Burbank published his first catalog, entitled *Creations of Fruits and Plants*, which featured some of his best varieties. He followed it with a number of books on his life, methods, and results, including the 12-volume *Luther Burbank: His Methods and Discoveries and Their Practical Application* (1914–1915), eight-volume *How Plants Are Trained to Work for Man* (1921), *Harvest of the Years* (with Wilbur Hall, 1927), and *Partner of Nature* (1927).

Luther Burbank was married twice. An 1890 marriage to Helen Coleman ended in divorce in 1896, and in 1916 he married Elizabeth Jane Waters. He had no children. Burbank died in 1926 at the age of 77 after suffering a heart attack and becoming ill with gastrointestinal complications. He is buried near the greenhouse at the Luther Burbank Home and Gardens in downtown Santa Rosa.

The Luther Burbank Home and Gardens has been designated a National Historic Landmark, and the Gold Ridge Experiment Farm is listed on the National Register of Historic Places. Luther's birthplace in Massachusetts and his California garden office also have been moved to Greenfield Village, a part of the Henry Ford museum in Dearborn, Michigan.

Burbank's home in Santa Rosa became a historic house museum in 1979. The house was left to Burbank's widow, Elizabeth Burbank, who left it to the City of Santa Rosa upon her death in 1977. The property includes the modified Greek revival house where Burbank lived from 1884 to 1906, when he moved to another home across Tupper Street (which was removed in the late 1960s for another development); a carriage house that was renovated in 1986 to serve as a museum and gift shop; the 1889 greenhouse designed and built by Burbank that now houses a replica of Burbank's office and changing exhibitions; demonstration gardens; and Burbank's grave near the greenhouse. The house features the original furnishings and memorabilia of the Burbanks, and the museum contains exhibits about the life and work of Burbank. The historic site has guided tours and plant sales. Annual attendance is 75,000.

Luther Burbank Home and Gardens, Santa Rosa Ave. at Sonoma Ave., Santa Rosa, CA 95402 (postal address: 100 Santa Rosa Ave., Room 10, Santa Rosa, CA 95404-4957). Phone: 707/524-5445. Fax: 707/524-5827. E-mail: burbankhome@lutherburbank.org. Website: www.lutherburbank.org. Hours: grounds and gardens—8–dusk daily; house and museum—Apr.–Oct.: 10–3:30 Tues.–Sun.; closed Mon. and Nov.–Mar. Admission: grounds—gardens, and museum, free; guided tours of house, gardens, and greenhouse—adults, $7; children under 12, free.

Rachel Carson

See Authors/Writers section.

George Washington Carver

George Washington Carver Museum. George Washington Carver was an African American botanist, educator, and inventor at Tuskegee Institute in Alabama who is best known for his research that produced more than 100 products made from peanuts, including cosmetics, dyes, paints, plastics, gasoline, and nitroglycerin. He made the innovations while developing peanuts, soybeans, and sweet potatoes as alternative crops to cotton in the South while at Tuskegee Institute. Carver's old laboratory building now houses the George Washington Carver Museum, which is part of the Tuskegee Institute National Historic Site on the campus of Tuskegee University.

It is believed that Carver was born into slavery in 1864 in Diamond Grove, near Crystal Place (now Diamond) in Missouri. The exact date is not known. His parents were Giles and Mary (who did not have a last name) and were purchased as slaves for $700 in 1855. George had 10 sisters and a brother, all of whom died prematurely. When he was only a week old, George was kidnapped with a sister and their mother by Arkansas night raiders, who sold them in Kentucky. Moses Carver, who owned the slaves, tried to buy them back but was able only to get the boy's return. After slavery was abolished, Moses and his wife, Susan, raised George and his older brother, James, as their own children.

George was encouraged by Mr. and Mrs. Carver to get an education. He learned reading and writing from an "Aunt Susan" since black children were not allowed in the local public school and the school for African American children was 10 miles away in Neosho. George decided to go to Neosho, where he met a kind woman, Mariah Walkins, from whom he rented a room. When he introduced himself as "Carver's George," she told him he should call himself "George Carver," which he continued to use until he later modified it to "George Washington Carver." She also urged him to get a good education and then "give your learning back to the people"—which greatly impressed him.

At the age of 13, Carver moved to Fort Scott, Kansas, where he planned to attend the academy there. But he left the city after seeing a group of whites kill a black man. Carver then was accepted at Highland College in Highland, Kansas, but was rejected because of his race when he arrived. So he homesteaded a claim near Beeler, Kansas, and manually plowed 17 acres for rice, corn, Indian corn, garden produce, and fruit and other trees and shrubs. He also did odd jobs and worked as a ranch hand.

In 1888, he obtained a $300 loan for education from the Bank of Ness City and later left the area and enrolled at Simpson College in Indianola, Iowa, where an art teacher recognized his talent for painting flowers and plants and encouraged him to study botany at Iowa State Agricultural College (now Iowa State University). He became the first black student at Iowa State in 1891 (receiving a Bachelor of Science degree in 1894 and a Master of Science degree in bacterial botany and agriculture in 1897. He later became the first black faculty member at the college.

In 1896 Booker T. Washington, founder and first principal and president of Tuskegee Normal and Industrial Institute for Negroes, convinced Carver to head the Agriculture Department. There Carver taught and did research for 47 years. He developed the department into a strong research center where he taught crop rotation, initiated research into crop products, trained students to be self-sufficient farmers, and introduced farmers to alternative crops that improved soil heavily cultivated in cotton and served as a source of their own food and improved their quality of life.

In addition to researching and promoting such alternative crops as peanuts, soybeans, and sweet potatoes, he produced 44 practical bulletins for farmers, with the most popular ones being those with 105 food recipes using peanuts. He also started an extension service that featured a mobile classroom he designed, administered the government's agricultural experiment station, and wrote articles and gave talks about such topics as Tuskegee, peanuts, and racial harmony.

George Washington Carver, who never married, died in 1943 at the age of 78 of anemia complications after falling down stairs at his home. He was buried next to Booker T. Washington in the Tuskegee campus cemetery. Carver received many honors for his achievements. In 1941 *Time* magazine called him a "Black Leonardo" because of his many talents and accomplishments like Leonardo da Vinci.

Among his many honors were a national monument dedicated to his achievements, an honorary doctorate degree from Simpson College, the Spingarn Medal for outstanding achievement from the National Association for the Advancement of Colored People, the Roosevelt Medal for outstanding contributions to southern agriculture, and an honorary membership in the Royal Society of Arts in England. A replica of the cabin in which he was born also was built and is displayed in Greenfield Village at the Henry Ford museum in Dearborn, Michigan.

In 1938, when Carver was in his 70s, he created a museum on his work at the request of the university's president in a remodeled building that formerly was the school laundry. He also founded the George Washington Carver Foundation at Tuskegee to help support the museum. The museum, which opened in 1941, featured Carver's extensive collection of native plants, minerals, birds, and vegetables; his peanut and other products; and his paintings, drawings, and textile art. The museum was dedicated to Mr. and Mrs. Henry Ford for their support.

In 1947 a fire damaged part of the museum collection, mainly paintings affected by smoke and water. The building was renovated and the museum expanded to 13,000 square feet in 1951 to include a basement exhibit area. It became more of a general historical museum with objects donated to the university or moved from other campus buildings, such as a collection of African crafts and artifacts, over 300 bound volumes and rare pamphlets of Africa, and more than 1,000 photographs of life in Ghana and Nigeria.

In 1977 the museum and "The Oaks" (the 1899 home of Booker T. Washington) were included in the newly authorized Tuskegee Institute National Historic Site, which preserves the university's early buildings. The exterior of the museum building was restored and the interior gutted and rebuilt to house exhibits, artifact storage, staff offices, and an auditorium where films on Carver and Washington are presented.

The exhibit area is divided into two parts. The main area is devoted to Carver's career and his laboratory equipment, research activities (including samples of peanut and sweet potato products), artworks, and awards and artistic works created in tribute to Carver. The second section traces the history of the Tuskegee Institute (and Washington's role) with exhibits, photographs, and artifacts. Annual attendance is over 490,000.

George Washington Carver Museum, Tuskegee Institute National Historic Site, 1212 W. Montgomery Rd., Tuskegee Institute, AL 36088-1923. Phones: 334/727-6390, 334/727-3200, and 334/727-9321. Faxes: 334/727-4597,

334/727-3448, and 334/727-1178. Website: www.nps.gov/tuin. Hours: 9–4 daily; closed New Year's Day, Thanksgiving, and Christmas. Admission: free.

George Washington Carver National Monument. The George Washington Carver National Monument near Diamond, Missouri, is located at the birthplace and boyhood home of a slave who became a noted African American agronomist known for his peanut innovations, crop rotation, and finding of alternative crops for cotton in the South. The monument was established in 1943 on 210 acres, which contain a museum, a discovery center, a statue of George as a boy, the ca. 1881 house of slaveholder Moses Carver, a nature trail, and the Carver family cemetery.

George was born to Giles and Mary (who did not have a last name) on Moses Carver's farm in 1864. When only a week old, he was kidnapped with a sister and their mother by night raiders, who were going to sell them as slaves. Moses tried to buy them back, but he could only retrieve George because his sister and mother were already sold. After the abolition of slavery, Moses and his wife, Susan, raised George and his older brother with their children. George was known simply as "Carver's George," but he changed it to "George Carver" when he enrolled in school and added Washington later.

The museum contains exhibits and a film about the life and career of George Washington Carver. The monument also has a science center, temporary exhibitions, living history programs, and guided tours. Annual attendance is 50,000.

George Washington Carver National Monument, 5646 Carver Rd., Diamond, MO 64840-8314. Phone: 417/325-4151. Fax: 417/325-4231. E-mail: gwca_superintendent@nps.gov. Website: www.nps.gov/gwea. Hours: 9–5 daily; closed New Year's Day, Thanksgiving, and Christmas. Admission: free.

George Washington Carver Memorial and Culture Center. The George Washington Carver Memorial and Culture Center in Fulton, Missouri, is located in a 1937 elementary school building that formerly served black students. The school was integrated in 1968 and finally closed in 1982. In 1989 the first floor was converted into an African American cultural center and tribute to Carver, who was born and spent his boyhood in nearby Diamond, Missouri. The center has exhibits on the history and activities of the black community and the life and career of Carver, who came to Fulton for the dedication of the school in 1937, six years before he died.

George Washington Carver Memorial and Culture Center, 906 Westminster Ave., Fulton, MO 65251-1183 (postal address: PO Box 344, Fulton, MO 65251-0344). Phone: 573/642-2619. E-mail: carvermemorial@yahoo.com. Website: www.callaway.dbrl.org/george-washington-carver-memorial-and-culture-center. Hours: varies. Admission: free.

Thomas Alva Edison

Thomas Edison National Historical Park. Thomas Alva Edison has been called America's greatest inventor. He developed many of the devices that influenced life around the world, especially in electricity, telecommunications, and mass communications. He was the inventor of such advances as the practical light bulb, phonograph, motion picture camera, mimeograph, microphone, alkaline storage battery, electric typewriter, printing telegraph, improved stock ticker tape, and many other things. Two of his most important developments were the central power station and the industrial research laboratory. He now is honored at a number of museums and historic sites, including his early sites of innovation—the Thomas Edison National Historical Park in West Orange, New Jersey, and Thomas Alva Edison Memorial Tower and Museum in Edison (formerly Menlo Park), New Jersey.

Edison was a prolific inventor with 1,093 American patents in his name, as well as many patents in the United Kingdom, France, and Germany. He also founded 14 companies, including one of the nation's largest and most successful industrial firms, General Electric Company. Although homeschooled and almost entirely deaf, he began his inventive career as a teenager and never stopped coming up with new ideas and products. When called a genius, Edison made his famous reply, "Genius is 1 percent inspiration and 99 percent perspiration."

Edison was born in 1847 in Milan, Ohio. He was the youngest of seven children of Samuel Ogden Edison Jr. and Nancy Mathews Elliott Edison. Three of his siblings died in childhood. His father had to flee from Canada because he took part in the unsuccessful Mackenzie Rebellion of 1837.

Thomas's mother withdrew him from a one-room schoolhouse after three months because his mind wandered and the teacher said he seemed to be confused. It turned out Edison had a congenital hearing problem that became worse after having scarlet fever. His mother homeschooled Thomas, who became an avid reader of the Bible, classics, world history, and English. Around the age of 12, he began to show interest in science and chemistry, and especially the works of Isaac Newton. And when he started to ask complex questions about physics and science concepts, his parents hired a tutor for him. Edison had a very inquisitive mind and an exceptional memory and ability to understand complex concepts.

Edison became an entrepreneur as a child. After his family moved to Port Huron, Michigan, in 1854, he sold newspapers and candy on Grand Trunk Railway trains from Port Huron to Detroit and supplemented his income with vegetable sales. He was thrown off the train with his equipment after a fire began in a boxcar where he was conducting chemical experiments.

In 1860, when 13, he published his own profitable newspaper, the *Weekly Herald*, which focused on political news, such as the presidential debates between Abraham Lincoln and Senator Stephen A. Douglas. He liked Lincoln's position on emancipation and worked for his campaign, distributing supportive literature.

When Edison was 15, he became a telegraph operator after saving a three-year-old boy from being struck by a runaway train. The grateful father taught him Morse code, and Edison's first job away from Port Huron was at Stratford Junction, Ontario, on the Grand Trunk Railway.

In 1866 Edison moved to Louisville, Kentucky, to work for the Western Union Company. He was serving as a Western Union employee at the Associated Press bureau news wire when his experimenting cost him his job. He worked nights because it gave him time to read and work on his experiments. But one night in 1867, he spilled sulfuric acid from a lead-acid battery onto the floor and the spill ran between the floorboards and onto his boss's desk below, resulting in his firing.

Edison then relocated to the East Coast. He worked for Western Union in Boston during the day and on his inventions at night. He developed an automatic vote recording machine for which he received his first patent in 1869, when he moved to the New York City area. The invention worked well, but the market was not ready to use the electric machine.

In New York, Edison worked as a repairman of automated devices for a financial firm and continued to tinker and experiment with mechanical devices. He made a number of inventions that he sold, including a stock ticker for which he received $40,000. He used the money to establish a small laboratory in Newark, New Jersey, develop more inventions, and get married.

In 1871 Edison married 16-year-old Mary Stilwell, an employee at one of his shops. They lived in Newark and had three children. She died in 1884 of unknown causes, possibly a brain tumor. He remarried in 1886 when 39 to Mina Miller, the 20-year-old daughter of inventor Lewis Miller, cofounder of the Chautauqua Institution and a benefactor of Methodist charities. They also had three children. Charles, who took over the company after his father's death, became secretary of the navy and governor of New Jersey, while Theodore was an inventor with more than 80 patents.

In 1876 Edison moved from Newark to Menlo Park, New Jersey, where he established the first industrial research laboratory with funds from the sale of his quadruple telegraph. There he developed the first phonograph to record and reproduce sound in 1877, the carbon microphone once used in all telephones and radio broadcasting in 1877–1878, and the first practical incandescent electric bulb in 1879.

Within a decade, the Menlo Park laboratory expanded to occupy two city blocks and Edison became known as "The Wizard of Menlo Park" because of his many inventions.

In 1878 Edison formed the Edison Electric Light Company in New York City with such financiers as J. P. Morgan and several members of the Vanderbilt family. By 1882 he established the first commercial power station (Pearl Street Station) to provide light and power to customers. He also built and operated an experimental electric railroad and developed a superior storage battery made of iron and nickel with an alkaline electrolyte.

Thomas Edison moved his industrial laboratory from Menlo Park to West Orange, New Jersey, in 1887. Both locations now are historic sites with museums. The Menlo Park site has become the Thomas Alva Edison Memorial Tower and Museum, and the West Orange complex is called the Thomas Edison National Historical Park. With the move, Edison evolved into more of a major manufacturer and business entrepreneur than an entrepreneurial inventor. He delegated much of the laboratory supervision to his most trusted assistants, while he spent most of his time on managing and expanding the business.

Edison established his electric lighting system in Great Britain and Europe, moved many of the Edison factories to Schenectady, New York, and consolidated the operations of the new and diverse General Electric Company. But he still devoted some of his time to new developments, such as patenting the kinetoscope (an early motion picture exhibition device) and the vitascope (an early film projector), purchasing the patent for a projector invented by Thomas Armat, and making the first commercial showing of motion pictures (in New York City) in 1896.

With the outbreak of World War I, Edison had his laboratory focus on military projects. It found substitutes for drugs, dyes, and chemicals previously imported from Germany; developed a process to make synthetic carbolic acid and coal-tar products needed to make explosives; and produced many safety devices. After the war, Edison, who also served as head of the Navy Consulting Board, was awarded the Congressional Medal of Honor for his services.

Edison continued to work until his death from complications of diabetes in 1931 at the age of 84. He was buried behind his home, which he called Glenmont, in West Orange. The major Edison historical site and museum is the 21-acre Thomas Edison National Historical Park in West Orange. It preserves his laboratory and home. Glenmont was designated the Edison Home National Historic Site in 1955, the laboratory became the Edison Laboratory National Monument in 1956, and together they were made the Edison National Historic Site in 1962 and then the Thomas Edison National Historical Park in 2009.

The Edison laboratory is located in a group of red brick buildings at Main Street and Lakeside Avenue in West Orange, with the Glenmont home a short distance away. Both sites have visitor centers and offer audio tours of the buildings, with the laboratory visitor center featuring a 20-minute orientation film and *The Great Train Robbery*, a 1903 silent film.

The West Orange site consists of 20 buildings from the 1880–1887 period. Among the site highlights are the three floors of the main laboratory building, the chemistry building, and the 29-room Queen Anne–style mansion where Edison lived. The site has a massive collection of over 4.5 million documents, 400,000 artifacts, 60,00 photographs, 48,000 sound recordings, 10,000 rare books, and 3,000 lab books. Annual attendance is 60,000.

Thomas Edison National Historical Park, 211 Main St., West Orange, NJ 07052-5612. Phone: 973/736-0550. Fax: 973/243-7172. E-mail: edis_superintendent@nps.gov. Website: www.nps.gov/edis. Hours: laboratory—9–5 Wed.–Sun.; closed Mon.–Tues.; Glenmont grounds—11:30–5 Fri.–Sun.; closed Mon.–Thurs.; Glenmont house ticketed tours—12–4 Fri.–Sun.; closed Mon.–Thurs. Admission: adults, $7; children under 16, free.

Thomas Alva Edison Memorial Tower and Museum. In 1876 Thomas Alva Edison moved his small laboratory from Newark to a larger facility in Menlo Park, New Jersey, that became the nation's first industrial research laboratory. For 11 years, he developed new inventions that resulted in more than 400 patents. They included such innovations as the first practical incandescent light bulb, a phonograph that recorded and reproduced sound, the carbon microphone that made telephone communication and radio broadcasting possible, and the first central electric power station, which brought electricity to the home, industry, and businesses. For such developments, Edison was called "The Wizard of Menlo Park" in the 1880s, and the Thomas Alva Edison Memorial Tower and Museum was established in Menlo Park in 1937 to honor the nation's greatest inventor.

The Thomas Alva Edison Memorial Tower and Museum is located in the Menlo Park section of Edison, adjacent to Edison State Park (Edison's former 36-acre estate). It consists of a 130-foot art deco tower and a small museum, which was added in 1947, where the Edison laboratory was located. Most of the original buildings collapsed or burned by 1926. Only two laboratory buildings remained, and Henry Ford used the remains to build a replica at Greenfield Village, a reconstructed historic village that opened in Dearborn, Michigan, in 1929.

The concrete tower has a giant incandescent light bulb—the largest in the world—at the top, and the museum tells the story of Edison and his laboratory and inventions. The museum contains examples of Edison's inventions and memorabilia. However, both the tower and the museum have deteriorated with age and are scheduled to be closed for a major tower restoration, museum updating and expansion, and the addition of a visitor center.

The Thomas Edison center at Menlo Park and Edison State Park are jointly administered by the Edison Memorial Tower Corporation, Township of Edison, and New Jersey Department of Environmental Protection's Division of Parks and Forestry.

Thomas Alva Edison Memorial Tower and Museum, 37 Christie St., Edison, NJ 08820-3860 (postal address: Edison Memorial Tower Corp., PO Box 656, Edison, NJ 08818-0656). Phone: 732/494-4194. E-mail: kccarlucci@menloparkmuseum.org. Website: www.menloparkmuseum.org. Hours: 10–4 Thurs.–Sat.; closed Sun.–Wed. and major holidays. Admission: suggested donation—$2.

Thomas Edison Birthplace Museum. The birthplace and home of Thomas Alva Edison in Milan, Ohio, now is a historic house museum. The Thomas Edison Birthplace Museum was founded in 1947—100 years after his birth in 1847. The 1841 three-story brick house planned by his father has been restored and furnished as it was at Edison's birth. In addition to family furnishings from 1780–1870, the museum has inventions, personal memorabilia, photographs, and documents. Guided tours are offered. The museum is operated by an association headed by family members. Annual attendance is nearly 8,000.

Thomas Edison Birthplace Museum, 9 N. Edison Dr., Milan, OH 44845-9321 (postal address: PO Box 451, Milan, OH 44846-0451). Phone and fax: 419/499-2135. E-mail: director@tomedison.org. Website: www.tomedison.org.

Hours: Feb. and Dec.—1–4 Sat.–Sun.; Mar. and Nov.—1–4 Wed.–Sun.; Apr.–May and Sept.–Oct.—1–5 Tues.–Sun.; closed Jan., June–Aug., New Year's Day, Easter, Labor Day, Thanksgiving, and Christmas. Admission: adults, $7; seniors, $6; children, $4; military and their families, free.

Thomas Edison House. Thomas Edison worked as a 19-year-old telegrapher for Western Union in Louisville, Kentucky, in 1866–1867 and lodged in a house that became a historic house museum, known as the Thomas Edison House, in 1978. The house is a ca. 1850 shotgun duplex in the Butchertown neighborhood of Louisville.

Edison's stay in Louisville was brief because of a chemical accident while working for Western Union at the Associated Press bureau news wire. While at the bureau one night, Edison also was experimenting with a battery when he spilled sulfuric acid on the floor and it dripped on his boss's desk on the floor below. It resulted in Edison being fired and his move to Boston. The historic house, operated by the Historic Homes Foundation, has displays about Edison and his inventions and offers guided tours. Annual attendance is 5,500.

Thomas Edison House, 729–31 E. Washington St., Louisville, KY 40202-1050. Phone: 502/585-5247. Fax: 502/585-5231. E-mail: edisonhouse@historichomes.org. Website: www.historichomes.org. Hours: 10–2 Tues.–Sat. and by appointment; closed Sun.–Mon., New Year's Day, Thanksgiving, and Christmas Eve and Day. Admission: adults, $5; seniors, $4; students, $3; children under 5, free.

Edison and Ford Winter Estates. Thomas Edison and Henry Ford, the automobile manufacturer, were good friends who had adjacent winter homes along the Caloosahatchee River in Fort Myers, Florida. In 1885 Edison visited Florida and purchased the land for a vacation home. He built the house, which he called Seminole Lodge, in 1887, and it became his winter retreat and place of relaxation. After Ford visited Edison at the site, he decided to purchase the adjoining property, known as the Mangoes, in 1916.

When Edison died in 1931, his widow, Mina Edison, deeded the Edison house to the City of Fort Myers in memory of her husband. It was opened for public tours in 1950. Ford died in 1947, but his adjacent winter estate did not become available until 1988, when the city purchased it and began offering tours in 1990. In 2003 the two properties were transferred to a nonprofit historic home corporation, the Thomas Edison and Henry Ford Winter Estates. A $10 million restoration was completed in 2006 for what became known as the Edison and Ford Winter Estates.

The site contains nine historic buildings and a botanical garden, as well as historic and scientific artifacts, including inventions, manuscripts, and memorabilia; a prototype Model T and other period cars; and exhibits about Edison and Ford in Florida. Edison's botanical garden, which originally was an experimental garden for industrial products, now has roses, orchids, bromeliads, and some 1,000 other varieties of plants from around the world. Among the trees are such unusual specimens as African sausage trees and a banyan tree that extends 400 feet around the trunk.

Among the historic buildings on the property is the rubber laboratory. Edison's winter home was the site of an unusual research project. During World War I, he became concerned that the cost of rubber was going to increase greatly. In 1926 Edison, Ford, and Harvey Firestone formed the Edison Botanic Research Corporation to find a crop that could grow quickly and contain enough latex to support the research. Exotic plants were grown and the research largely conducted by Edison in Florida, with the findings being sent to the Edison industrial laboratory in West Orange, New Jersey, for analysis. But the research was not able to produce rubber on a large enough scale to be successful. The project ended in the mid-1930s, and the office and laboratory in Fort Myers were closed. But the building recently was restored and opened to visitors. The Edison and Ford Winter Estates has an annual attendance of 200,000.

Edison and Ford Winter Estates, 2350 McGregor Blvd., Fort Myers, FL 33901-3315 (postal address: PO Box 2368, Fort Myers, FL 33901-2368). Phone: 238/334-7419. Fax: 239/461-2688. E-mail: info@edisonfordwinterestates.org. Website: www.edisonfordwinterestates.org. Hours: 9–5:30 daily; closed Thanksgiving and Christmas. Admission: adults, $20; children 7–12, $11 children under 7, free.

Edison Museum. The Edison Museum in Beaumont, Texas, is devoted to Thomas Alva Edison and his inventions and innovations. It features interactive exhibits and more than 60 historic objects. It also has over 1,400 artifacts in its study collection and a reference library. Founded in 1980, the museum is housed in the historic Travis Street Substation, the first substation to distribute electric power in southeast Texas. The museum, which is operated by Entergy/Texas, has an annual attendance of nearly 3,400.

Edison Museum, 350 Pine St., Beaumont, TX 77701-2437. Phone: 409/981-3089. Fax: 409/838-2361. Hours: 9–5 Mon.–Fri.; closed Sat.–Sun. and major holidays. Admission: free.

Henry Ford

See Edison and Ford Winter Estates and Business/Industrial/Financial Figures section.

Benjamin Franklin

See Public Officials/Political Figures section.

Robert Fulton

Robert Fulton Birthplace. Robert Fulton was an imaginative engineer and inventor best known for developing the first commercially successful steamboat. But most people do not know that he also designed the first practical submarine, the first steam-powered warship, and some of the earliest naval torpedoes—or that he began his career as a respected painter of portraits and landscapes, while also drawing houses and machinery and experimenting with mechanical inventions. His birthplace near Quarryville, Pennsylvania, is now a historic house museum devoted to his life and accomplishments.

Fulton was born in 1765 on a farm in Little Britain in Lancaster County, Pennsylvania. His parents were Robert and Mary Smith Fulton, and he had a younger brother and three sisters. The family moved to Lancaster, where he attended a Quaker elementary school. Fulton learned to sketch early and show an interest in mechanical things.

As a teenager, Fulton invented paddle wheels to go alongside his father's fishing boat, offered helpful suggestions to gunsmiths, built rockets, and experimented with mercury and bullets. At the age of 17, Fulton decided to become an artist and went to Philadelphia to study and practice art.

In Philadelphia in 1782–1786, he made enough money painting portraits and landscapes that he could send some home to help support his mother (and to buy a farm for the family in Hopewell in 1785). His father, who died when his son was eight, had been a close friend of the father of Benjamin West, the noted artist (whom Fulton did not meet until later in England). He did meet Benjamin Franklin and other Revolutionary War figures while in Philadelphia.

At the age of 23, Fulton went to England in 1786 with letters of introduction to a number of Americans living abroad. He also met with Benjamin West, with whom he had been corresponding. West, who had become a well-known artist, invited him to stay at his home, where Fulton lived for several years. He was an apprentice of West's until about 1793. West also introduced him to many others, which helped Fulton obtain commissions for portraits and landscapes while he experimented with his mechanical inventions, published a pamphlet about canals, and patented machines for dredging, sawing marble, spinning flax, and twisting hemp into rope.

In 1797 Fulton went to Paris, where he studied French, German, mathematics, and chemistry and invented the first panorama shown in Paris. He also designed the first underwater submarine for the French in 1793–1797 and built a steamboat with U.S. Ambassador Robert R. Livingston that was tested in the River Seine in 1803. Fulton then returned to England and developed the first modern naval torpedoes and several other inventions for the British in 1804–1806.

Fulton returned to the United States in 1806. He married Harriet Livingston, the niece of Robert R. Livingston. They had four children. In 1807 Fulton and Livingston built the first commercial steamboat, the *North River Steamboat*, which later became known as the *Clermont*. The steamboat, which carried passengers between New York City and Albany, made the 150-mile trip in 32 hours in 1807. Fulton's final invention was the *Demologos*, the first steam-driven warship for the U.S. Navy, which was launched in 1814. He died in 1815 from consumption after he caught pneumonia when he got soaked with icy water during an attempt to rescue a friend who fell through the ice on the Hudson River. He was 49 years old.

The stone house where Fulton was born in 1765 is now a historic house museum called the Robert Fulton Birthplace. It is located about eight miles south of Quarryville, Pennsylvania. The Commonwealth of Pennsylvania acquired the site in 1965, and the Pennsylvania Historical and Museum Commission restored and furnished the house to represent its appearance during Fulton's lifetime. The house contains exhibits about Fulton's life and accomplishments. The Southern Lancaster Historical Society gives weekend tours from Memorial Day through Labor Day.

Robert Fulton Birthplace, 1932 Robert Fulton Hwy. (Rte. 222), Fulton Township, Quarryville, PA 17566. Phone: 717/548-2679. Website: www.padutchcountry.com/members/robert_fulton_birthplace. Hours: Memorial Day–Labor Day—11–4 Sat., 1–5 Sun.; closed Mon.–Fri. and day after Labor Day–day before Memorial Day. Admission: adults, $4; children under 12, $2.

Samuel F. B. Morse

Locust Grove, the Samuel Morse Historic Site. Samuel F. B. Morse was an artist who became an inventor. He began painting portraits while a student at Yale University, attended the Royal Academy of Arts in London, opened a studio in Boston in 1815, and was known for his portraits of members of Congress. Morse became interested in developing fast long-distance communication in 1825 after receiving late word of his young wife's death while he was doing a portrait in Washington. By the time he arrived home, she already had been buried. In 1832 he got the idea of electromagnetism as a means of communication, which resulted in his development of the telegraph and later Morse code. Locust Grove, his home in Poughkeepsie, New York, now is a historic house museum that explores his two careers.

Morse was born in 1791 in Charlestown, Massachusetts. He was the first child of Pastor Jedidiah Morse, a geographer, and Elizabeth Ann Finley Breese. His father gave him a belief in the Calvinist faith and preserving Puritan traditions. Morse entered Phillips Academy in Andover, Massachusetts, at the age of nine and went to Yale College (now University) when 14. Although interested in art, he studied religious philosophy, mathematics, and the science of horses (and attended lectures on electricity by Benjamin Silliman and Jeremiah Day) and supported himself by painting. He graduated from Yale with Phi Beta Kappa honors in 1810.

Morse wanted to continue his career as a painter, but his father opposed the idea, saying he should become a bookseller's apprentice and later a book publisher. But his parents relented in 1811 after noted artist Washington Allston was impressed with Morse's Calvinist painting *Landing of the Pilgrims* and offered to take Samuel with him to England to meet American artist Benjamin West, who was living in London, and arrange for a three-year stay for painting study.

In England, Allston worked with Morse to perfect his painting techniques, resulting in Morse being admitted into the Royal Academy of Arts. Two of his best works, *Dying Hercules* and *Judgment of Jupiter*, were produced during this period. Morse returned to the United States in 1815 and enjoyed considerable success as a painter through 1825. This included such works as the *Hall of Congress* and portraits of Presidents John Adams, James Madison, and James Monroe. In 1825 he was painting the portrait of the Marquis de Lafayette, the leading French supporter of the American Revolution, when his 25-year-old wife, Susan Walker Morse, died at home in New Haven, Connecticut, and he was not able to get back in time for the funeral.

Morse was devastated by the death and the inability of current message systems to inform him sooner. He then started thinking about creating a fast long-distance way of communicating. He continued to paint until about 1837, during which time he became a founder and first president of the National Academy of Design and a professor at New York University.

Morse got the idea of using electromagnetism as a means of communication in 1832 after a chance meeting aboard a ship while returning home from Europe. It came to him after talking with Charles Thomas Jackson, a Boston scientist, who described some of the properties of electromagnetism. Morse later witnessed various experiments with Jackson's electromagnet.

After finding out that information sent great distances over copper cables travels instantaneously, he started devising a single-wire telegraph and filed a caveat at the U.S. Patent Office in 1837. It was followed by the development of Morse code—with the technical and financial assistance of Alfred Vail—which became the primary language of telegraphy in the world and still is the standard for rhythmic transmission of data.

Morse had difficulty in getting a telegraphic signal to carry more than a few hundred yards and then a few miles. He gave the first telegraphic public demonstration (that went two miles) at the Speedwell Ironworks in Morristown, New Jersey, in 1838. But it was not until 1844 that a telegraphic message—"What hath God wrought"—was sent 36 miles between Washington and Baltimore (in a $30,000 project funded by Congress) and telegraph lines began to appear between major American cities. The Morse telegraphic system was adopted as the standard for Europe (except for the United Kingdom) in 1851, and Morse introduced wired communication in Latin America in 1858.

While Morse developed the telegraph in America, others designed competing telegraphic systems here and abroad (including William Cooke and Charles Wheatstone in England), and Morse spent the rest of his life struggling to obtain telegraph patent rights and official recognition as the inventor of the telegraph (even though he received the patent in 1847). He died in 1872 of pneumonia at the age of 80, leaving his second wife, Sarah Elizabeth Griswold Morse.

The Morse summer home, located on a bluff overlooking the Hudson River in Poughkeepsie, New York, is now the site of a historic house museum, known as Locust Grove, the Samuel Morse Historic Site. The Morse family spent summers at the 200-acre estate and winters in a townhouse in New York City. The museum is located in a

1851–1852 Italianate villa designed by architect Alexander Jackson Davis and patterned after similar villas Morse saw in Italy. The estate also has landscaped grounds, miles of carriage roads, and a nature preserve. The museum was established by Annette Innis Young, a later owner who established a foundation at her death in 1975 to preserve the estate as a museum and nature center.

The house was rented and then purchased by Ms. Young's parents, William and Martha Young, a wealthy couple from Poughkeepsie, at the turn of the century. They then renovated, furnished, and expanded the house as a year-round house for their daughter, Annette, and son, Innis. After her brother died in 1953, Annette inherited the Locust Grove estate and other family properties and began donating the art, land, and historic houses to museums so that they would be protected in perpetuity. When she died 22 years later, she established the foundation to ensure that Locust Grover, her home for 80 years, and its collections would be preserved as a museum and nature center. Selections from the Young family's collection of 15,000 pieces of furniture, art, and antiques can now be seen in the mansion's 25 rooms.

The museum features a permanent exhibit devoted to Morse's life and his careers as an artist and an inventor. It contains original works of his art, including portraits, landscapes, drawings, and sculpture, and information about electromagnetic telegraphy and reproductions of Morse's early telegraph models. The exhibit also traces the development of telegraph equipment through the early twentieth century. In addition, the estate has a 3,000-volume library, visitor center, gardens, farm and farmhouse, wildlife sanctuary, and hiking trails, as well as guided tours, temporary exhibitions, educational programs, and special events. Annual attendance is 20,000.

Locust Grove, the Samuel Morse Historic Site, 2683 South Rd., Poughkeepsie, NY 12601-5275. Phone: 845/454-4500. Fax: 845/485-7122. E-mail: info@lgny.org. Website: www.lgny.org. Hours: gardens and grounds—8–dusk daily; visitor center—Jan. 3–early Apr.—10–5 Mon.–Fri.; early Apr.–Dec.—10–5 daily; mansion tours—May–Nov.—daily; Apr. and Dec.—Sat.–Sun. only; Locust Lawn Farm and Terwilliger House—open only to tours of 10 or more by appointment; closed New Year's Day, Easter, Thanksgiving, and Christmas Eve and Day. Admission: adults, $10; youth 6–18, $6; children under 6, free.

Joseph Priestley

Joseph Priestley House. Joseph Priestley was an English clergyman and chemist who came to America in 1794 and became one of the nation's leading scientists. He is credited with the discovery of oxygen, having isolated it from its gaseous state—although Carl Wilhelm Scheele and Antoine-Laurent Lavoisier also claimed the discovery. In addition to his work in the church and the laboratory, Priestley was a nature philosopher, educator, and political theorist who wrote more than 150 works, invented soda water, and discovered several other gases. But he was isolated within the scientific community for defending phlogiston theory and rejecting what eventually became the chemical revolution. The Joseph Priestley House, where he lived in Northumberland, Pennsylvania, is now devoted to his life and career in theology and science.

Priestley was born in 1733 in Birstall, near Yorkshire, England. He was the oldest of six children of Jonas Priestley, a finisher of cloth, and Mary Swift Priestley. When he was six years old, his mother died, and his father remarried in 1741. Priestley went to live with his wealthy and childless aunt and uncle, Sarah and John Keighley, near Fieldhead. His aunt had strong nonconformist religious views.

Priestley was a precocious child. At the age of four, he could recite all 107 questions and answers of the Westminster Shorter Catechism. As a result, his aunt sought to prepare him for the Calvinist ministry and emphasized education. Priestley went to the local grammar school, but ill health forced him to drop out in 1749 after three years in which he learned Greek, Latin, and Hebrew, as well as physics, philosophy, algebra, and mathematics. When he became seriously ill, he questioned his theological upbringing and was refused admission to his home church, the Independent Upper Chapel of Heckmondwike, by the church elders.

Priestley gave up plans to enter the ministry after he began to stutter during his illness. As his health improved, he prepared to join a relative in trade in Lisbon and studied French, Italian, German, Chaldean, Syrian, and Arabic. He also was introduced to higher mathematics, natural philosophy, logic, and metaphysics. Then he decided to return to theological studies and in 1752 enrolled at the new nonconformist Daventry Academy, a "dissenting" school in Northamptonshire that did not follow the Church of England. He was impressed by David Hartley's *Observations of Man*, which emphasized free will and human perfectibility through good education. In his third year, Priestley committed himself to the ministry and became a "rational dissenter" who emphasized rational analysis of the natural world and the Bible.

In 1755 Priestley became minister of a small rural Presbyterian parish in Needham Market, Suffolk, where he wrote *The Scripture Doctrine of Remission*. Three years later, he moved to Nantwich, Cheshire, where he opened a school at the church, where he taught natural philosophy and bought scientific instruments for the students. In 1761 he became a tutor of modern languages and rhetoric at the Warrington Academy in Lancashire, the largest of the dissenting academies in England. He was ordained in 1762, the same year he married Mary Wilkinson of Wrexham. They had a daughter in 1763 and three sons later.

In 1765 Priestley's *Chart of Biography* brought an honorary doctorate of laws from the University of Edinburgh, and his electricity experiments resulted in induction into the Royal Society in 1766. Among his other books during this period were *Course of Liberal Education for Civil and Active Life* (1765), *The History and Present State of Electricity* (1767), and *The History of the Present State of the Discoveries Relating to Vision, Light and Colours* (1772). Priestley was among the earliest to say electrical force followed an inverse-square law, similar to Newton's law on universal gravitation.

Priestley moved to Leeds in 1767 to become minister at Mill Hill Chapel, one of the oldest and most respected dissenting congregations in England. There he founded the *Theological Repository*, a journal devoted to an open and rational inquiry of theological questions, in 1768 and published *Institutes of Natural and Revealed Religion* (1772–1774), the fourth part of which became so long that it was published separately as *An History of the Corruption of Christianity* in 1782. They outlined his theories of religious instruction and explained his belief in Socinianism, an antecedent of Unitarianism. The doctrines said only revealed religious truths could be accepted, which became the standard for Unitarians in Britain.

Priestley began his most famous scientific research on the nature and properties of gases in the 1770s while living in Leeds. His house was located next to a brewery, and he became fascinated with the layer of dense gas (carbon dioxide) that hung over the large vats of fermenting beer. Priestley placed a bowl of water over a vat, and the carbon dioxide dissolved in the water, producing soda water. In 1773 he published an article on the carbonation of water (soda water) that won the Copley Medal from the Royal Society.

He then started examining all the "airs" that might be released from different substances. At the time, it was believed that there was only one "air." In 1772 Priestley presented the paper "On Different Kinds of Air" to the Royal Society. It was followed in 1774 by isolating and characterizing eight gases, including oxygen, through his unique design and clever operation of the research apparatus. For his innovations and writings, he received honors from other countries, such as election to the French Academy of Sciences in 1772 and the St. Petersburg Academy in Russia in 1780.

From 1772 to 1979, Priestley lived in Calne, where he was personal librarian to Lord Shelburne and tutor to his children. It was here that he conducted most of his chemical research, including the discovery of various gases, such as oxygen in 1774. His concept of the newly found "air" (gas), which supported and enhanced combustion, was based on the phlogiston theory generally held at the time—and which he supported. Phlogiston was believed to be a substance that gave materials their ability to burn, but Lavoisier correctly found the gas (which he called oxygen) to be one of the causes of combustion rather than the recipient of the supposed phlogiston. Priestley refused to accept Lavoisier's discovery and never abandoned his support for the outdated phlogiston theory, which hurt his scientific reputation.

Priestley spent 1780–1791 in Birmingham, where he served as minister of the New Meeting parish, published seven of his papers (including major works on metaphysics), and served as liaison with dissenters. At the same time, church leaders were becoming increasingly concerned about Priestley's religious views, and his political beliefs were making him unpopular with the British government. His books *The History of the Corruptions of Christianity* (1782) and *History of Early Opinions Concerning Jesus Christ* (1786) contained attacks on such doctrines as the virgin birth and the Holy Trinity, causing religious leaders to consider him an atheist. His 1768 book *The First Principles of Government and the Nature of Political, Civil and Religious Liberty*, which called for a political system that maximized civil liberty, upset the government, and his support of the American and French revolutions was seen as seditious by English authorities.

Hostility against Priestly increased in 1791 when he wrote a pamphlet that defended the French Revolution. He upset King George III and his supporters by saying it heralded a change in the role of the monarchy and that royal rulers now will be "first servants of the people and accountable to them." When Priestley expressed political views in his *General Principles of Government* that were similar to those of Tom Paine in his *Rights of Man*, Tories in Birmingham made inflammatory speeches attacking Priestley and mobs burned his house and laboratory, destroying most of his papers, books, and scientific equipment. The New Meeting and Old Meeting churches and the homes of other followers in Birmingham also were burned.

Priestley then moved to London, taught history and natural philosophy at the dissenting New College in Hackney, Middlesex, and served as minister for the Gravil Pit Meeting congregation. The protests followed him, however, as he was burned in effigy. After the war with France and the execution of Louis XVI in 1793, the 61-year-old Priestley and his family decided to emigrate to America in 1794.

Priestley planned to start a model community on undeveloped land in Pennsylvania with his sons, but it never materialized. Instead, he and his wife, Mary, built a 5,052-square-foot Georgian-style home and laboratory with federalist accents for their family in Northumberland, far up the Susquehanna River in Pennsylvania. It was located there because Mrs. Priestley wanted to be near their sons, who earlier settled in the area. Priestley would have preferred a more cosmopolitan location with greater access to other scientists and new developments.

Priestley was known in Europe primarily as a scientist, but most Americans considered him mainly a defender of religious freedom and an advocate for American independence. In the United States, he was mainly concerned with conducting experiments and writing about the results, but he had difficulty in keeping abreast of developments in England and Europe because of the distance.

It was in England that he met Benjamin Franklin, who encouraged him to write *The History of Electricity*, published in 1767. But Franklin died in 1790, and Priestley did not have an opportunity to renew their friendship. He did became friends with former President John Adams and President Thomas Jefferson, who called him "one of the few lives precious to mankind." Priestley also dedicated the *General History of the Christian Church* to Jefferson. In addition, he wrote 45 papers and four pamphlets while in the United States.

Priestley continued his scientific investigations with the support of the American Philosophical Association, stimulated interest in chemistry in the United States, and helped establish the Northumberland Academy. He also gave sermons to promote the spread of Unitarianism in America but did not resume regular preaching or become an American citizen, nor involve himself in the nation's political affairs.

Priestley became so ill in 1801 that he could no longer write or conduct experiments effectively. He recovered, only to die in 1804 at the age of 70. His wife passed away in 1796. Since then, Priestley has received many honors here and abroad, including the highest honor from the American Chemical Society, which established the Priestley Medal for distinguished service in the field of chemistry in 1922.

The Priestley home has become a historic house museum. The two-and-a-half-story frame house, which was completed in 1798, covered 5,052 square feet, with the laboratory in the north wing. After Priestley's death, his eldest son, Joseph Priestley Jr., and his family lived in the house until 1811, when they returned to England. The house then was sold to several subsequent owners and was acquired in a public auction in 1919 by Dr. George Gilbert Pond, professor of chemistry and dean of the School of Natural Sciences at Pennsylvania State University.

Dr. Pond planned to move the house to the campus for use by the chemistry department. But he died shortly after the purchase, and the university operated the site as a museum with hired caretakers until 1955, when it gave the property to the Borough of Northumberland, which maintained the house as the borough hall and a museum until 1959. The Commonwealth of Pennsylvania obtained the house in 1960, and the Pennsylvania Historical and Museum Commission restored and opened the site in 1970 as a museum, called the Joseph Priestley House. Guided tours now are offered by a friends organization.

The house, a designated National Historic Landmark and National Historic Chemical Landmark listed in the National Register of Historic Places, preserves and interprets the scientific, religious, and educational contributions of Priestley to American history. It features scientific equipment, decorative art, and historic furniture from the late 1700s period. A visitor center tells about his life and accomplishments in exhibits and a 10-minute orientation film. Annual attendance is 900.

Joseph Priestley House, 472 Priestley Ave., Northumberland, PA 17857-1226 (postal address: Friends of Joseph Priestley House, PO Box 346, Lewisburg, PA 17837). Phone: 570/473-9474. E-mail: info@josephpriestleyhouse. org. Website: www.josephpriestleyhouse.org. Hours: mid-Mar.–Nov.—1–4 Sat.–Sun.; closed Mon.–Fri., Dec.–mid-Mar., and Easter. Admission: adults, $6; seniors, $5.50; children 3–11, $4; children under 3 and active military and family, free.

Benjamin Thompson

Benjamin Thompson House. Sir Benjamin Thompson—also known as Count Rumford—was an American-born British physicist and inventor who was part of the nineteenth-century thermodynamics revolution. He was a prolific designer who challenged established physical theory at the time. Thomson also served in the loyalist forces during the American Revolutionary War, became a British colonel, and was knighted in the United Kingdom. He then was appointed minister of the Bavarian Army and made a count in Austria in the late 1700s. His birthplace in North Woburn, Massachusetts, is now a historic house museum known as the Benjamin Thompson House (also the Count Rumford Birthplace).

Thompson had the distinction of being knighted and made a count for his military and scientific advances in two countries, as well as going by two different names. He became Sir Thompson after Britain's King George III bestowed knighthood in 1784 and Count Rumford of the Holy Roman Empire following being honored by Prince Maximilian of Bavaria in 1791. He is known by two different names because he chose to be named for Rumford, New Hampshire, the town where he was married and which was the home of his wife.

Benjamin Thompson Jr. was born in rural Woburn in 1753. His family lived with his grandparents in a house built by his grandfather, Captain Ebenezer Thompson. When he has one year old, his father died, and he and his mother continued to live there until she remarried. Benjamin went to the village school and sometimes walked to Harvard College in Cambridge for lectures by Professor John Winthrop, the noted astronomer and physicist. In 1766 he was apprenticed to John Appleton, a merchant in nearby Salem, where he also found time to do chemical and mechanical experiments.

When 14 years old, Thompson knew enough about algebra, geometry, astronomy, and higher mathematics to calculate a solar eclipse to within four seconds. In 1769 he conducted experiments concerning the nature of heat and began corresponding about them with friends. Later that year, he worked for a shopkeeper in Boston and then studied medicine briefly with a doctor in Woburn. This was followed by several years working in the dry goods business in Boston and attending classes in philosophy at Harvard, as well as teaching in Bradford, Massachusetts, and Rumford, New Hampshire.

Thompson's future did not look bright until 1772, when he met and married a wealthy and influential heiress, Sarah Rolfe (née Walker). Her father was a minister, and her late husband left her property in Rumford (now Concord), New Hampshire. After moving to Portsmouth, New Hampshire, he became acquainted with Governor Benning Westworth, and as a result of his wife's influence, he was appointed a major in the New Hampshire militia. But when the American Revolutionary War began, he fought with the British.

After the marriage, Thompson became a man of property and standing in New England. When the American revolution began, he opposed the rebelling colonists and started recruiting loyalists to fight the rebels. As a result, a mob attacked the Thompson home, and he fled to the British lines in 1774, leaving his wife behind. He worked with British forces and became an adviser to General Thomas Gage and Lord George Germain. Thompson also conducted experiments on gunnery and explosives, with the results later being published in the *Philosophical Transactions of the Royal Society*.

When the British left Boston in 1776, Thompson went with them to England, where he became a clerk in Lord Germain's secretary of state office. After a few months, he was appointed secretary of the province of Georgia. Four years later, he was under-secretary of state. Thompson continued his scientific work and was elected to the Royal Society in 1779. When the British administrations changed, Thompson was named to a cavalry command and then left the British Army with the rank of lieutenant colonel. He also was honored for his services with a knighthood by King George III.

In 1785 Thompson joined the Austrian Army in its fight against the Turks. In Strasbourg, he met Prince Maximilian, elector of Bavaria, who invited him to assist with the state's civil and military matters. He agreed and spent 11 years reorganizing the army, establishing workhouses for the poor, founding the Englischer Garten in Munich, and performing other functions in Bavaria. He also continued his scientific research and writings for the Royal Society's journal. Thompson was rewarded for his services in Bavaria by being made a count in 1791.

Thompson returned to England in 1795 and resumed his scientific investigations dealing with heat. After studying the manufacture of cannon barrels, he concluded that the drilling heat was caused by the mechanical action of the drill and not the contemporary theory that it was from a fluid released from the metal. He then sought to calculate how much heat is produced by a given amount of mechanical energy and established what is called a "mechanical equivalent of heat." This led to the founding of a new branch of physics that concentrates on the nature and effects of heat, called thermodynamics.

Thompson next examined the insulating properties of such materials as furs, wool, and feathers. He found that the insulating qualities of such natural materials arise because they inhibit the convection of air. But he incorrectly inferred that gases and liquids were perfect nonconductors of heat. A prolific inventor, he also developed improvements for chimneys, fireplaces, and industrial furnaces, as well as inventing such products as thermal underwear, the double boiler, a kitchen range, and percolating and drip coffee pots.

In 1799 Thompson and Sir Joseph Banks proposed the establishment of the Royal Institution of Great Britain, which was chartered by King George III in 1800 and has become world famous for its research and lectures. Thompson also endowed the Rumford Medals, which were awarded by the Royal Society and the American Academy of Arts and Sciences, and established a professorship at Harvard University.

Thompson, whose wife had died, moved to Paris and married Marie-Anne Lavoisier, the widow of the French chemist Antoine Lavoisier, in 1804. But they separated after a year, and he stayed in Paris and continued his scientific work until his death in 1814 at the age of 61. He is buried in the small cemetery of Auteuil in Paris. A statue of Thompson is located in Munich, where he developed the huge park, with a copy in his hometown of Woburn, Massachusetts. The Benjamin Thompson House (also known as the Count Rumford Birthplace), a historic house museum, also is located in Woburn. It has been designated a National Historic Landmark and is listed on the National Register of Historic Places.

Thompson was born in the house in 1753 and spent part of his childhood there. The museum was founded in 1877 by the Rumford Historical Association, which still owns and operates the historic site. It contains information about Thompson's life and career, reconstructed models of his scientific experiments and inventions, and a library of Thompson biographies and essays.

Benjamin Thompson House, 90 Elm St., North Woburn, MA 01891-1855 (postal address: Rumford Historical Assn., 11 Lowell St., Woburn, MA 01801-2334). Phone: 781/933-4976. E-mail: ladygarak@butter.toast.net. Website: www.members.toast.net/willycw/rumford_museum. Hours: 1–4:30 Sat.–Sun. and by appointment; closed Mon.–Fri., New Year's Day, and Christmas. Admission: free.

Eli Whitney

Eli Whitney Museum. Eli Whitney was the inventor of the cotton gin—one of the principal inventions of the Industrial Revolution of the nineteenth century. The cotton gin shaped the economy of the antebellum South by removing seeds from upland short cotton and making it a profitable crop. It also had the effect of strengthening the economic foundation of slavery, whether or not Whitney had intended that. Whitney also was known for his advocacy and use of interchangeable parts, which revolutionized the manufacturing industry and helped Union forces in their victory in the Civil War. His life and inventions now are featured at the Eli Whitney Museum in Hamden, Connecticut.

Whitney was born in Westborough, Massachusetts, in 1765. He was the eldest child of Eli Whitney Sr., a prosperous farmer, and Elizabeth Fay Whitney. His mother died when he was 11, and when 14 he operated a profitable nail manufacturing operation in his father's workshop during the American Revolutionary War. He then worked as a farm laborer and schoolteacher to save money for college, even though his stepmother opposed having him go to college. He first attended Leicester Academy (now Becker College) and then entered Yale in 1789 and graduated as Phi Beta Kappa in 1792.

Whitney intended to study law but was short on funds and accepted an offer to serve as a private tutor in South Carolina. On the way there, he was invited by Mrs. Nathanael Greene, widow of the Revolutionary War general, to visit her Georgia plantation. It was there that he met Phineas Miller, her plantation manager, who was a Connecticut migrant and Yale graduate. A chance suggestion led Whitney to experiment with a machine for removing the seeds from cotton fibers, which was extremely labor intensive.

After numerous attempts, he developed an effective seed-removing machine in 1793, for which he received a patent in 1794 (but it was not validated until 1807). He entered into a partnership with Phineas Miller to manufacture cotton gins and charge farmers for cleaning their cotton, rather than selling the machines. A single cotton gin could generate as much as 55 pounds of cleaned cotton daily, and they were charging two-fifths of the value paid in cotton.

The invention of the labor-saving cotton gin resulted in a tremendous increase in cotton production that transformed southern agriculture and the national economy, with ready markets at textile mills in New England and Europe. Cotton exports increased from 500,000 pounds in 1793 to 93 million pounds in 1810 and represented over half of the value of American exports from 1820 to 1860. But Whitney and Miller did not earn a fortune because of patent infringements, long litigation, and farmer opposition to their pricing system. The cotton gin, however, may have helped preserve southern slavery by providing cotton picking jobs. Before the 1790s, it was too difficult to remove seeds from cotton and slave labor was used primarily in growing rice, tobacco, and indigo, and they were not especially profitable.

In 1798 Whitney was on the verge of bankruptcy after his New Haven cotton gin factory burned and the cotton gin litigation was taking time and money. He was saved by a government contract to produce muskets—even though he had never made a gun. The U.S. government decided to rearm after the French Revolution caused conflicts between Great Britain, France, and the United States. After receiving the contract to produce 10,000 muskets, Whitney used interchangeable parts—a new idea at the time.

Whitney was incorrectly credited with inventing the interchangeable parts concept, but it was his promotion and popularizing of the system and the impact of Union weapons during the Civil War that led to the misconception. Whitney also was credited by some historians with inventing the first milling machine. Others believe he was one of a group of inventors who developed milling machines in 1814–1818.

Whitney frequently made use of his Yale, social, and political connections to further his business interests. For example, he took advantage of being a Yale alumnus for access to Secretary of the Treasury Oliver Wolcott Jr., a Yale graduate, in the 1798 musket negotiations. His 1817 marriage to Henrietta Edwards also was helpful. She was the daughter of Pierpont Edwards, head of the Democratic Party in Connecticut; granddaughter of the famed evangelist Jonathan Edwards; and first cousin of Timothy Dwight, Yale president and the state's leading Federalist.

Eli Whitney's career was cut short when he died of prostate cancer in 1825, a month after his 59th birthday. He left his widow and four children at his home in New Haven, Connecticut. The Eli Whitney Museum is now devoted to his life and career in adjacent Hamden, where he had his arms factory. The manufacturing village, which was called Whitneyville, was a company town with production facilities and living quarters for employees. The armory and many of the other buildings are gone, but the site still contains an 1816 barn, the coal storage shed, and one of the boarding houses, as well as Whitney's dam on Mill River, which provided the power, and a reconstruction of the innovative lattice-truss covered bridge that serviced the armory.

In addition to exhibits about Whitney, the museum has displays on the cotton gin, the historic site, and A. C. Gilbert, the inventor and toy maker best known for the erector set. It also features water tables with canal locks and a design workshop that specializes in building projects for children blending science and invention.

The museum's collections include Whitney armory and period firearms, Gilbert toys and artifacts, photographs, maps, and materials on the history of manufacturing and the effect of technology on American society. The museum/workshop also offers temporary exhibitions, tours, educational programs, lectures, experimental learning, and children's programs. Annual attendance is 48,000.

Eli Whitney Museum, 915 Whitney Ave., Hamden, CT 06517-4036. Phone: 203/777-1833. Fax: 203/777-1229. E-mail: kl@eliwhitney.org. Website: www.eliwhitney.org. Hours: Memorial Day–Labor Day—11–4 daily; Sept.–May—12–5 Wed.–Fri., 10–3 Sat., 12–5 Sun.; closed Mon.–Tues., Easter, and Christmas. Admission: free.

Wilbur and Orville Wright

See Aviators/Astronauts section.

SOCIAL ACTIVISTS

Jane Addams

Jane Addams Hull-House Museum. Jane Addams was a social reformer who changed the lives of immigrant women and national and international public policies at the turn of the twentieth century—and was the first American woman to receive the Nobel Prize. She was the founder of a settlement house who also became a leader in woman suffrage and world peace. The site of the settlement house in Chicago, Illinois, is now the location of the Jane Addams Hull-House Museum, which tells about the settlement house and her accomplishments.

Jane Addams was born in Cedarville, Illinois, in 1860. She was the youngest of eight children of John Huey Addams, a bank president, agricultural businessman, and political leader, and Sarah Weber Addams, who died in childbirth when Jane was two years old. Three of her siblings also died in infancy and another when 16. Her father remarried in 1868, taking Anna Hostetter Haldeman, a Freeport widow, as his second wife when Jane was eight years old.

When in her teens, Addams hoped to do something useful in the world. She decided she wanted to be a doctor so she could live and work among the poor. She became interested in assisting poor people after her reading of Dickens and seeing her stepmother's kindness to the poor in their hometown. She graduated from nearby Rockford Female Seminary (now Rockford College) in 1881 and was planning to attend Smith College, the new women's college in Massachusetts, when her father died from an appendicitis that summer. Jane and the siblings each inherited around $50,000 (about $1.2 million today).

In the fall of 1881, Jane, her sister Alice and husband Harry, and their stepmother went to Philadelphia so that the three young people could attend medical school. But Jane suffered health problems after she and her sister completed the first year at the Woman's Medical College of Philadelphia. Jane had a spinal operation and a nervous breakdown, and the entire family returned to Cedarville without completing the degree program.

In 1883, after back surgery, Jane and her stepmother took a two-year tour of Europe. When they returned, she became fascinated with early Christianity in her readings and became baptized at the Cedarville Presbyterian Church in 1886. She then read in 1887 about a new idea—the settlement house—and decided to visit the first such facility in London. Toynbee Hall was established by Samuel and Henrietta Barnett as part of what was called the social Christian movement, with religious faith being the central motive in founding the settlement.

After the visit, Addams wanted to start a settlement house and told a college friend, Ellen Gates Starr, who joined her in the effort. In 1889 Addams and Starr cofounded Hull-House, the first settlement house in the United States, in a run-down 1856 Chicago mansion built by Charles J. Hull. Unlike the London facility, the Chicago settlement house was not religious and did not attempt to convert anyone to Christianity.

At first, Addams paid for all the needed repairs, upgrading, and operating expenses. Contributions from others later helped with expenses. Hull-House immediately opened to recently arrived European immigrants and began programs especially for women and children. Addams and Starr were the first occupants of the house, which later had 25 women residents and served several thousand people a week.

Hull-House eventually had a night school for adults, kindergarten classes, clubs for older children and girls, and such facilities as a public kitchen, coffee shop, gym, bathhouse, book bindery, music school, drama group, library, playground, summer camp, art gallery, and labor museum. By 1911 Hull-House had grown to 13 buildings. The settlement house movement also continued to grow, with the number of such houses totaling nearly 500 nationally by 1920.

Addams and the residents of Hull-House helped pass critical legislation and influenced public policy on such issues as public health and education, free speech, fair labor practices, immigrant rights, recreation and public space, arts, and philanthropy. The settlement house also affected Chicago's political and cultural life by establishing the city's first public playground and public art gallery, assisting in the desegregation of the public school system, documenting social illnesses, helping to pass the city's first tenement code and factory laws, and furthering philanthropy and culture.

In addition to the settlement house movement, Addams was active in such other areas as education, politics, suffrage, and the peace movement. She was the founder and 1911–1935 president of the National Federation of Settlements, 1915 national chairman of the Woman's Peace Party, 1919–1935 president of the Women's International League for Peace and Freedom and helped found the American Civil Liberties Union in 1920. For her efforts to further world peace, she shared the Nobel Peace Prize in 1931. She also became the role model for many women who volunteered to improve their communities.

Jane Addams suffered a heart attack in 1926 and never fully recovered. She died in 1935 at the age of 74. Hull-House also was gradually phased out as societal needs changed and the University of Illinois located its Chicago campus on the city's west-side neighborhood in 1963. All the settlement buildings were demolished, except two original structures—the 1856 Hull mansion, which is a National Historic Landmark and listed in the National Register of Historic Places, and the Residents' Dining Hall, the beautiful arts and crafts–style building. They became the Jane Addams Hull-House Museum, founded in 1967 and now administered by the university's College of Architecture and the Arts.

The museum tells the story of Jane Addams and Hull-House and serves as a memorial to Addams. The museum and its many programs make connections between the work of Hull-House residents and important contemporary social issues. Among the new exhibits are a scale model of the Hull-House settlement as it looked in 1907, Jane Addams's bedroom and her personal artifacts, art by 10 artists who lived and worked at the settlement, stories of the immigrant families who settled in Chicago neighborhoods, an exploration of childhood life in the neighborhood and Hull-House programs for children, and photographs of Hull-House by documentary photographer Wallace Kirkland. In addition to individual visits, the museum offers free guide tours at 1 p.m. on Wednesdays and Sundays. The museum's annual attendance is 13,000.

Jane Addams Hull-House Museum, University of Illinois at Chicago, 800 S. Halstead St., M/C 051, Chicago, IL 60607-7017. Phone: 312/413-5353. Fax: 312/413-2092. E-mail: jahh@uic.edu. Website: www.uic.edu/jaddams/hull. Hours: 10–4 Tues.–Fri., 1–4 Sun.; closed Mon., Sat., and major holidays. Admission: free.

Susan B. Anthony

Susan B. Anthony Museum and House. Susan B. Anthony was a major civil rights leader in the American women's rights movement in the second half of the nineteenth century. She cofounded the first women's temperance movement, published the women's rights journal *The Revolution*, and was one of the leading advocates for women's rights in American government. She gave from 75 to 100 speeches a year across the United States and Europe to further women's rights. Her house in Rochester, New York, now tells the story of Anthony's lifelong struggle to gain voting rights for women and equal rights for all.

Susan Brownell Anthony grew up in an activist family. She was born in Adams, Massachusetts, in 1820, the second oldest of seven children of Daniel and Lucy Read Anthony. Her father was a stern but open-minded Quaker who became a cotton manufacturer and abolitionist, and her mother attended the 1848 Rochester women's rights convention and signed the convention's Declaration of Sentiments. Two of Susan's siblings also were activists. Her brother Daniel became a publisher who was involved in the antislavery movement in Kansas, and her sister Mary became a teacher and a woman's rights activist.

Anthony learned to read and write by the time she was three years old. When she was six, the family moved to Battenville, New York, and she attended a local school where a teacher refused to teach her long division because she was a girl. Her father then placed her in a group home school, where he taught her himself. In 1837 she enrolled at the Deborah Moulson's Female Seminary, a Quaker boarding school in Philadelphia, but did not stay long because her family was ruined financially by the Panic of 1837. Susan's parents tried to sell everything to raise funds, and her uncle, Joshua Read, bought everything and restored it to the family. It also was in 1837, at the age of 17, that she took part in the New York antislavery and temperance movements by distributing petitions against slavery.

In 1839 the family moved to Hardscrabble, New York, and Susan left home to teach and help pay off her father's debts. She first taught at Eunice Kenyon's Friends Seminary and then at the Canajoharie Academy in 1846. She became the headmistress of the Female Department, and when she learned that the male teachers earned about four times more than women for the same duties, she fought unsuccessfully for equivalent wages. As a result, she quit teaching in 1849, moved to the family farm in Rochester, New York, and became secretary of the Daughters of Temperance in the temperance movement.

In Rochester, Anthony also began to distance herself from the Quakers and attended the local Unitarian Church. As she got older, Anthony moved further away from organized religion, and by the 1880s she had become agnostic. She also committed her life to women's rights in 1850 after reading Horace Greeley's article in the *New York Tribune* about the first National Woman's Rights Convention in Worcester, Massachusetts, and the remarks by Lucy Stone.

More than 1,000 people attended the women's rights convention, which demanded that women have the right to vote, own property, and be admitted to higher education, medicine, ministry, and other professions. Anthony also met activist Elizabeth Cady Stanton in 1851, and Greeley and Stone in 1852, in Seneca Falls, New York, where Stanton largely organized the first woman's rights convention in 1848. It also was in Seneca Falls that the National Women's Hall of Fame was founded in 1969.

Anthony joined Stanton in organizing the first women's state temperance society in America after being refused admission to a previous convention because of her sex in 1851. She also was invited to speak at the third annual National Woman's Rights Convention in 1852 and quickly gained notice as a powerful advocate of women's rights. She participated in every subsequent annual National Woman's Rights Convention, serving as convention president in 1858. Over the years, Anthony and Stanton traveled across the nation giving hundreds of speeches calling for men and women to be treated equally.

Anthony and Stanton became good friends for the rest of their lives. They worked together in many efforts, such as founding the National Equal Rights Association in 1866, as well producing *The Revolution*, a women's rights weekly journal. However, they alienated abolitionist members and the association president when they accepted help from a known racist in failed Kansas suffrage referenda seeking to grant voting rights to blacks and women.

In the publishing venture, Anthony was the founder and publisher and Stanton served as editor of *The Revolution*. The journal failed to attract enough support, went into debt, and was sold for one dollar in 1869. Anthony assumed its $10,000 debt (equal to $184,000 today), which she struggled to pay off in six years with her speaking fees.

It also was in 1869 that Anthony and Stanton founded the National Woman Suffrage Association, dedicated to obtaining voting rights for women. In 1872 Anthony sought to test the law that permitted only men to vote. She was arrested by U.S. marshals for voting in the presidential election. Anthony was tried and convicted by a judge who fined her $100. She refused to pay, and the government took no action to collect the fine.

The trial gave her an opportunity to give speeches about women's rights and to talk about the recently adopted 14th Amendment to the U.S. Constitution, pointing out that it had no gender qualification and gave all citizens the constitutional right to vote in federal elections. After the trial, Anthony toured Europe and visited many charitable organizations.

In 1884–1887 Anthony published, in collaboration with Stanton, Matilda Joslyn Gage, and Ida Husted Harper, four volumes of the *History of Western Suffrage*. And in 1890 she orchestrated the merger of the National Woman Suffrage Association and Lucy Stone's more moderate American Woman Suffrage Association, forming the National American Woman Suffrage Association. The creation of the NAWSA marginalized the more radical elements within the women's movement, including Stanton. Anthony served as the president of the new association until retiring to her Rochester home in 1900.

Anthony died in 1906 of heart disease and pneumonia at the age of 86—14 years before the 1920 passage of the 19th Amendment to the Constitution giving women the right to vote. The New York state senate passed a resolution honoring her for "unceasing labor, undaunted courage, and unselfish devotion to many philanthropic purposes and to the cause of equal political rights for women."

The Susan B. Anthony Museum and House, a National Historic Landmark listed on the National Register of Historic Places, became a historic house museum in 1946. The museum seeks to keep Anthony's vision alive and relevant. It contains her personal belongings, photographs, and writings of famous women associated with Anthony. A visitor center and museum shop are located in the historic carriage house. The museum has guided tours, special exhibitions, lectures, educational programs, teas and lunches, and special events, such as on Anthony's birthday and the anniversary of the 19th Amendment. Annual attendance is 7,000.

Susan B. Anthony Museum and House, 17 Madison St., Rochester, NY 14608-1928. Phone: 585/235-6124. Fax: 585/235-6212. E-mail: czarcone@susanbanthonyhouse.org. Website: www.susanbanthonyhouse.org. Hours: 11–5 Tues.–Sun.; closed Mon. and major holidays. Admission: adults, $10; seniors, $8; students and children under 13, $5.

Mary McLeod Bethune

See Educators section.

John Brown

Harpers Ferry National Historical Park. John Brown was an obsessed revolutionary abolitionist who was considered a fanatical outlaw by some and a martyr by others. He eventually was tried for treason and hanged for attempting an armed insurrection to eliminate slavery in the 1850s. He left a trail of murders as he moved about the country and tried to start a liberation movement among enslaved African Americans. He eventually was captured in an unsuccessful raid on a federal armory and arsenal in Harpers Ferry, Virginia (now West Virginia), in 1859, which escalated tensions and led to secession and the Civil War. He left a series of historic sites that became museums, as well as the Harpers Ferry National Historical Park.

John Brown was born into a deeply religious family in Torrington, Connecticut, in 1800. He was one of 16 children that his father, Owen Brown, had with three wives. He was the fourth of eight children of Brown and his first wife, Ruth Mills Brown. His father vehemently opposed slavery, and passed the feeling along to his son. In 1805 the family moved to Hudson, Ohio, where his father opened a tannery, when John was five years old. Owen Brown became a supporter of Oberlin Institute (now Oberlin College) but later was critical of the school's "perfectionist" leanings and preaching and left the Congregational Church and never joined another church. But John and his father were fairly conventional evangelicals for the period, pursuing personal righteousness.

At the age of 16, John Brown enrolled in a preparatory program in Plainfield, Massachusetts, and shortly thereafter transferred to the Morris Academy in Litchfield, Connecticut. He was planning to become a Congregationalist minister but dropped out when his money ran out and he suffered from an eye inflammation. He returned to his home in Ohio and worked briefly in his father's tannery before opening his own successful tannery with a brother outside of town.

John Brown was married twice and had 20 children. In 1820 he married Dianthe Lusk. Five years later, they moved with their family to New Richmond, Pennsylvania, where he bought 200 acres and opened a tannery, raised cattle, and did surveying. The couple had seven children. In 1831 one of his sons died, Brown became ill, and his various businesses suffered, leaving him in debt. His wife died in 1832, and the following year he married 16-year-old Mary Ann Day, with whom he had 13 children.

The Browns moved to Franklin Mills, Ohio (now Kent), in 1835 and entered into a partnership with Zenas B. Kent in a tannery along the Cuyahoga River. When it did not work out, he borrowed large sums of money, bought 95 acres, and waited for an industrial boom that never developed. Brown suffered great financial loss in the economic crisis of 1839 and went bankrupt in 1842. This was followed by the death of four of his children from dysentery in 1843.

Meanwhile, Brown became engaged in horse and sheep breeding and developed into an expert in fine sheep and wool. This led to a partnership with Simon Perkins Jr. of Akron, Ohio, and a move to a two-room cottage across the street from Perkins. The cottage later became a historic house museum (*see* separate listing). In 1846 Brown, Perkins, and their families moved to Springfield, Massachusetts, where the community was greatly involved in the antislavery movement. It is where African American abolitionists founded the Sanford Street Free Church (now the St. John's Congregational Church), which became one of the nation's most prominent sites for abolitionist speeches. Brown became a parishioner at the church and involved in making the city a major center of abolitionism and one of the safest and most significant stops on the Underground Railroad for fleeing slaves.

The wool partnership failed, and Brown left Springfield in 1850. The wool commission that Brown and Perkins established in Springfield closed in 1849 with a loss of $40,000 ($980,000 today) when manufacturers refused to pay their higher prices. Fortunately, Perkins covered most of the loss. The antislavery efforts also suffered when the United States passed the Fugitive Slave Act, which mandated that free-state authorities must return escaped slaves and imposed penalties on those who helped in the escapes. In response, Brown helped establish the League of Gileadites, a militant group in Springfield to prevent the capture of slaves.

In 1848 Brown bought some land in the Adirondacks near North Elba, New York, and planned to move his family there after learning that philanthropist Gerrit Smith was making 50-acre land grants to poor black families willing to clear and farm the land. He proposed to establish a farm and provide guidance and assistance to those attempting to create a community in the area, and Smith agreed to sell him enough land for a farm at one dollar an acre. Brown moved his family to the farm but spent little time there while being distracted by events in Springfield, Kansas, and Harpers Ferry. His widow, however, had his body buried on the farm after his execution in 1859. The site now is the John Brown Farm State Historic Site (*see* separate listing).

Brown went to the Kansas Territory in 1855 with a wagon full of weapons after five of his sons reported that they were unprepared for attacks from militant proslavery forces in what became known as "Bleeding Kansas." In the confrontations that followed, about 56 people were killed before both sides agreed to stop the violence. The fighting escalated in 1856—the same year Brown's father died—when the Brown family homestead was destroyed and two of Brown's sons taken captive by a Missouri proslavery force.

The raid was followed in May by a Missouri proslavery attack on Lawrence, Kansas, a center of antislavery activities in the territory. The raid included wrecking the newspapers, robbing the banks, and burning the hotel and the home of the Free Soil governor. During the Civil War, Lawrence was attacked again in 1863 by William Quantrill and his raiders in what was called the Lawrence Massacre.

Brown was outraged by the 1856 violent attack on Lawrence by proslavery forces and the weak response of antislavery partisans and other settlers. Four days after the sacking of Lawrence, Brown and four of his sons took five proslavery settlers from their cabins in Pottawatomie Creek and hacked them to death with broadswords in the Pottawatomie Massacre. Brown later claimed he did not participate in the killings but approved of the action. When a Missouri proslavery force attacked Palmyra in June, an antislavery Kansas group led by John Brown defended the town, took 23 prisoners, and exchanged the men for his two sons.

In August, a company of 300 Missourians led by Major General John W. Reid attacked Brown and a small group of his followers in Osawatomie, Kansas. Five men, including one of Brown's sons, were killed and the town burned. The John Brown Museum State Historic Site is now located in Osawatomie. It is in the former log cabin of the Rev. Samuel Adair and his wife, Florella, whose half-brother was John Brown.

The Adairs moved to the area in 1855, the same year Brown came to Kansas. They became intensively involved in the Bleeding Kansas conflict, as their cabin became a stop on the Underground Railroad and was used as a headquarters by Brown in 1855–1858. The Rev. Adair worked as chaplain at Fort Leavenworth. The Adair cabin was moved to its present location in an Osawatomie park in 1928 and enclosed within a building as a historic museum devoted largely to John Brown.

John Brown, who had obtained support from other Northern abolitionists, moved to Chambersburg, Pennsylvania, in 1859 while he formulated his plan and secured the weapons and tools for an attack on the federal armory and arsenal in Harpers Ferry, Virginia. He stayed in a boarding house during the summer under the assumed name of Dr. Isaac Smith and claimed to be scouting the area as an iron mine developer. The boarding house was opened as a historic house museum in 2009 as part of the 150th anniversary of the Harpers Ferry raid (*see* separate listing).

The plan Brown developed was to make a sudden raid at the United States Armory and Arsenal at Harpers Ferry, escape to the mountains, and use the seized weapons and others he had collected to equip rebellious slaves to strike terror in attacks on slaveholders in Virginia. He then would send agents to nearby plantations to arm the slaves and enlist white and black volunteers to free other slaves and obtain more supplies across the South.

John Brown rented the Kennedy Farmhouse, seven miles from the armory/arsenal, to train and prepare for the Harpers Ferry raid (*see* separate listing). On October 16, 19 members of Brown's band left for the raid and three stayed behind as a rear guard. The key to success was taking over the site, seizing the weapons, and leaving before military reinforcements could arrive in Harpers Ferry. The raiders captured several watchmen, cut the telegraph lines, stopped a train passing through the area, and killed an African American baggage handler who confronted the raiders. But the train was allowed to continue to Baltimore after five hours.

When the train arrived in Baltimore, the conductor contacted authorities, and Colonel Robert E. Lee was sent to Harpers Ferry with U.S. Marines. Another problem was that local slaves did not rise up against their owners and take up arms as Brown expected. Instead, Harpers Ferry townspeople began shooting at the raiders and the local militia surrounded the armory building taken over by the raiders. Three citizens were killed, but the escape route of the raiders was cut off.

Brown then took nine prisoners and moved to the small fire engine house, which became known as "John Brown's Fort." The next day, Colonel Lee ordered Lieutenant Israel Green and the Marines to storm the firehouse. They broke down the door, fought the raiders, and freed the prisoners.

Ten of Brown's original party of 22 were killed, and Brown suffered a serious sword wound from Green. Seven raiders escaped during the several days of fighting, with two being captured and tried in the Jefferson County Courthouse in Charles Town (now Charleston) with Brown and the survivors. Brown was charged with treason against the Commonwealth of Virginia, found guilty, and hanged. He was 59 years old. Six other raid members were tried later and executed. The firehouse that was used as a fort has been restored and relocated near its original site in what has become a national historical park.

The Harpers Ferry National Historical Park, which was established in 1944, tells the story of the United States Armory and Arsenal and John Brown's raid at Harpers Ferry in 1859. The rebuilt firehouse that became John Brown's Fort is only one of the sights at the park, as are some of the other historic armory/arsenal structures. The park, which covers almost 4,000 acres, is located at the confluence of the Potomac and Shenandoah rivers in and around Harpers Ferry. The U.S. armory/arsenal was located at Harpers Ferry by George Washington after visiting the area in 1785 and using the waterpower from the rivers for manufacturing purposes.

The Harpers Ferry park is best known for where John Brown attempted to seize the armory/arsenal in 1859 to obtain weapons for slaves to overthrow slavery. But the site also is where Robert Harper began a ferry service after obtaining a 1751 patent; Thomas Jefferson visited and marveled at its natural wonders in 1783; Meriwether Lewis obtained the weapons and the boats made for the Lewis and Clark Expedition; John H. Hall worked to perfect the production of interchangeable parts; James H. Burton developed the modern bullet to replace the round lead slug in 1855; and Confederate General Stonewall Jackson captured 12,500 Union troops in the 1862 Battle of Harpers Ferry—the largest number of prisoners taken at one time during the Civil War.

In addition to the firehouse, the park has such historic buildings as the 1775 Harper House, 1826 Stagecoach Inn, and 1858 Master Armorer's House; exhibits relating to archaeology, restoration, industry, wetlands, and Jefferson Rock; artifact collections pertaining to Harpers Ferry, John Brown, arms, nineteenth-century African American education, the Civil War, and nineteenth-century water-powered technology; and a research library on John Brown, the Civil War, African American history, American history, Harpers Ferry, and industrial transportation. The park also has a visitor center, guided tours, hiking trails, educational programs, special events, and seasonal living history programs. Annual attendance is 350,000.

Harpers Ferry National Historical Park, Fillmore St., Harpers Ferry, WV 25425 (postal address: PO Box 65, Harpers Ferry, WV 25425-0065). Phone: 535/535-6224. Fax: 304/535-6244. Website: www.nps.gov/hafe. Hours: 8–5 daily; closed New Year's Day, Thanksgiving, and Christmas. Admission: vehicle—$10; individual arriving on foot or bicycle—$5.

John Brown House (Akron, OH). The John Brown House in Akron, Ohio, is where the antislavery activist lived in 1844–1846. He moved to Akron from Franklin Mills (now Kent), Ohio, to join Simon Perkins Jr. of Akron in a wool trade partnership after suffering a great financial loss in the 1839 economic crisis and going bankrupt in 1842.

It was in the early 1840s that Brown became involved in horse and sheep breeding and developed into a specialist in fine sheep and wool. That's when he met Perkins, entered into a wool trade partnership with him, and moved to Akron. Brown and his family lived in a two-room cottage across the street from Perkins's large home. Two years later, he and Perkins moved to Springfield, Massachusetts, to pursue their wool trade, which failed in 1849.

The former two-room Brown cottage in Akron has been expanded by other owners over the years and now is a historic house museum operated by the Summit County Historical Society since 1942. It features an exhibit on Brown's life and can be seen only during open houses the fourth Thursday of the month between May and September.

John Brown House, 514 Copley Rd., Akron, OH 44320-2398 (postal address: Summit County Historical Society, 550 Copley Rd., Akron, OH 44320-2398). Phone: 330/535-1120. Fax: 330/535-0250. E-mail: schs@summithistory.org. Website: www.summithistory.org. Hours: May–Sept.—4–6 fourth Thurs. of month; closed Oct.–Apr. Admission: free.

John Brown Farm State Historic Site. The Adirondack Mountains farm where abolitionist John Brown and his family lived in the mid-1800s now is the John Brown Farm State Historic Site. He bought the farm for one dollar an acre from philanthropist Gerrit Smith in 1848 after hearing that Smith was giving 50-acre plots to poor black families who would clear and farm the land near North Elba, New York. Brown proposed establishing a farm to provide guidance and assistance to those attempting to create communities in the area, but he actually spent little time on the farm because he was away in his antislavery efforts in Kansas and Harpers Ferry, Virginia.

The Brown farmhouse was completed in 1855. Brown made only occasional visits to the farm, but his family lived there and ran the farm. However, Brown's wife returned his body to the farm for burial after his execution for treason in 1859 after the raid on the armory and arsenal at Harpers Ferry.

The Brown sons who died at Harpers Ferry also are buried on the farm. And there is a tombstone of Captain John Brown, an ancestor with the same name. In later years, the bodies of 12 of Brown's men from the raiding party were moved to the grave site, which also includes a heroic statue of Brown with his arm around a young African American boy, an inscribed boulder, plaques, and photographs of the Brown raiders.

The Brown farm, located on the edge of Lake Placid, has been owned by the State of New York since 1895. The site still has the original farmhouse and barn, with the house being restored to its ca. 1859 condition and maintained by the New York State Office of Parks, Recreation, and Historic Preservation. The farmhouse still contains some of its original furnishings and possessions of the Brown family. Annual attendance is 37,000.

John Brown Farm State Historic Site, 115 John Brown Rd., Lake Placid, NY 12946-3248. Phone: 518/523-3900. Fax: 518/523-3951. E-mail: brendan.mills@oprhp.state.ny.us. Website: www.nyparks.state.ny.us/info.asp?siteid=14. Hours: grounds—dawn–dusk daily; house—May–Oct.: 10–5 Wed.–Mon.; closed Tues. Admission: adults, $2; seniors and students, $1; children under 13, free.

John Brown Museum State Historic Site. The John Brown Museum State Historic Site in Osawatomie, Kansas, contains a historic log cabin that John Brown used as his headquarters and that served as a stop on the Underground Railroad for escaping Southern slaves. It was in Osawatomie that 300 proslavery Missourians attacked and burned the town in 1856 after Brown and four sons hacked five proslavery settlers to death in the Pottawatomie Massacre.

The cabin was the home of the Rev. Samuel Adair, the chaplain at Fort Leavenworth, and his wife, Florella, whose half-brother was John Brown. The cabin was moved in 1928 from the outskirts to the John Brown Memorial Park in the center of Osawatomi where the 1856 battle between pro- and antislavers took place. A pavilion was erected around the historic cabin to protect the museum. The museum contains family furniture and belongings, photographs, weapons, and other items from that period. Annual attendance is 38,000.

John Brown Museum State Historic Site, 10th and Main Sts., Osawatomie, KS 66064 (postal address: PO Box 37, Osawatomie, KS 66064-0037). Phone: 913/755-4384. Fax: 913/755-4164. E-mail: adaircabin@kshs.org. Website: www.kshs.org/p/john-brown-museum. Hours: 10–5 Tues.–Sat., 1–5 Sun.; closed Mon. and state holidays. Admission: suggested donations—adults, $3; students, $1.

John Brown House (Chambersburg, PA). When John Brown left Kansas in 1859, he went to Chambersburg, Pennsylvania, to formulate his plan and to obtain the weapons and tools for an attack on the United States Armory and Arsenal in Harpers Ferry, Virginia (now West Virginia). He occupied an upstairs bedroom while staying at Mary Ritner's boarding house during the summer, which has become a historic house museum—the John Brown House. The house is a two-story, three-bay-wide, hewn-log building covered in clapboard.

Because of his notoriety, Brown assumed the name of Dr. Isaac Smith. He said he was scouting the area as an iron mine developer. He purchased weapons and tools from local stores and other sources and stored them in a warehouse until they were transported to the Kennedy Farm near Harpers Ferry, which he rented to complete the planning and training for the 1859 armory/arsenal raid. Four members of Brown's raiding party at Harpers Ferry fled to Chambersburg and hid in the boarding house after the failed armory/arsenal takeover.

The historic house, which is listed on the National Register of Historic Places, is operated by the Franklin County Historical Society–Kittochtinny. The society rededicated the house as part of the 150th anniversary of the Harpers Ferry raid in 2009 after acquiring the house from the Pennsylvania Historical and Museum Commission in 2002.

John Brown House, 225 E. King St., Chambersburg, PA 17201-1808. Phones: 717/263-2870 and 717/264-1667. Website: www.johnbrownhouse.tripod.com. Hours: 10–4 Tues.–Sat.; closed Sun.–Mon. and major holidays. Admission: adults, $4; children 6–12, $3; children under 6, free.

Kennedy Farm House Museum. The Kennedy Farm, located about seven miles from Harpers Ferry, served as the staging area for John Brown and his band of 21 antislavery raiders for the attack at the United States Armory and Arsenal in Harpers Ferry, Virginia (now West Virginia). Brown and his followers spent three months at the farmhouse training and planning for the October 16, 1859, ill-fated Harpers Ferry assault, which resulted in Brown's execution after being convicted of treason.

The 194-acre farm was bought by Dr. Booth Kennedy in 1852. He expanded the original cottage to the two-and-a-half-story farmhouse used by Brown and his followers. Kennedy died earlier in 1859, and the property was being managed by an estate trustee when Brown—with the "Isaac Smith" name he used when acquiring the weapons and tools in Chambersburg—rented the farmhouse for nine months for $35 in gold. The farmhouse is made of log, stone, and brick with a stucco overlay. The four-bay house has three rooms on the first and second floors and two in the attic, with a double-tiered porch at the front and a small shed addition at the rear.

The site, which now is a National Historic Landmark and is listed on the National Register of Historic Places, has been restored by the Maryland Historical Trust and contains period furnishings and various artifacts. Tours are offered by appointment.

Kennedy Farm House Museum, 2406 Chestnut Grove Rd., Sharpsburg, MD 21782. Phone: 202/537-8900. Website: www.johnbrown.org. Hours: tours by appointment. Admission: donation.

César. E. Chávez

César E. Chávez National Monument and National Chávez Center. César Estrada Chávez was a farmworker, labor leader, and civil rights activist who led a reform movement in the second half of the 1900s that greatly improved working and living conditions and wages for America's farmworkers. The movement grew from a farmworkers' union to a national voice for the poor and disenfranchised. In 2012 the César E. Chávez National Monument was established at the National Chávez Center, site of the United Farm Workers of America headquarters in Keene, California, to honor the union leader.

The farmworkers' union was founded as the National Farm Workers Association in 1962 by Chávez, a farmworker who became a civil rights activist and union organizer, and Dolores Huerta, a former teacher who sought to improve social and economic conditions for farmworkers. They formed the NFW when the Community Service Organization, a Latino civil rights organization where they worked, refused to organize farmworkers.

In 1965 the Agricultural Workers Organizing Committee, led by Filipino organizer Larry Itliong, merged with the National Farm Workers Association, which changed its name to the United Farm Workers of America. The organization also changed from a workers' rights organization to a union of farmworkers and added thousands of lettuce and vegetable workers in California and orange workers in Florida.

The UFW first went on strike in support of grape workers in California in 1965 and were about to launch a major lettuce campaign in 1970, but its efforts were rebuffed when the growers signed contracts with the International Brotherhood of Teamsters to represent workers in those fields. The UFW, which lost members recruited by the Teamsters, responded with strikes, law suits, and boycotts. Chávez preached nonviolence and civil disobedience.

The battles sometimes became violent, including a number of UFW members being killed on the picket line. This led to the 1975 passage of the California Agricultural Labor Relations Act to oversee labor elections, unfair labor practices, bargaining in good faith, and discrimination against activists. Growers eventually were forced to recognize the UFW as a bargaining agent for some 50,000 field workers in California and Florida. In 2005 the UFW joined the Change to Win Federation, a coalition of labor unions functioning as an alternative to the AFL-CIO.

Chávez was born in a Mexican-American family in Yuma, Arizona, in 1927. His parents were Librado and Juana Estrada Chávez. He grew up in a small adobe house with five brothers and sisters. His family owned a grocery and a ranch but lost everything during the Great Depression in the 1930s. They moved to California and became migrant workers. Chávez dropped out of school after the eighth grade to work full-time as a farm migrant worker to help support the family. He married his high school sweetheart, Helen Fabela, and they had seven children. He worked in the farm fields of California until 1952, when he became an organizer for the Community Service Organization.

Chávez died of natural causes in 1993 at the age of 66 and is buried in the Memorial Gardens on the grounds of the 187-acre United Farm Workers headquarters, known as the National Chávez Center, in Keene, California. It is where he lived and worked since the 1970s and the site of the new César Chávez National Monument. The center has a 7,000-square-foot visitor center that displays Chávez's office and library and has exhibits about his life and career. Another building is the 17,000-square-foot Villa La Paz Conference and Education Center, used for UFW planning, training, and other programs.

César E. Chávez National Monument/National Chávez Center, 29700 Woodford Tehachapi Rd., Keene, CA 93531 (postal address: PO Box 62, Keene, CA 29700-0062). Phone: 661/823-6134. Fax: 661/823-6246. Websites: www.nps.gov/cech and www.cesarechavezfoundation.org. Hours: 10–4 daily; closed major holidays and special occasions. Admission: $3.

Prudence Crandall

See Educators section.

Crazy Horse

Crazy Horse Memorial. Crazy Horse was a Native American war leader of the Oglala Lakota tribe who was considered one of the greatest Indian warriors of the nineteenth century. He fought against federal government encroachments on the Lakota territories and way of life and was instrumental to the victory over George A. Custer and the Seventh Cavalry in the Battle of the Little Bighorn in 1876. He died the following year after surrendering and being bayoneted by a prison guard. He is now the subject of the Crazy Horse Memorial near Berne, South Dakota. The memorial, which is still under construction, features the largest mountain sculpture in the world.

It is not known exactly when and where Crazy Horse was born, but it is believed to be in 1840 along the South Cheyenne River. He was named Chas-O-Ha, meaning "In the Wilderness" or "Among the Trees." It is said that he received the name Tasunke Witko (Crazy Horse) after a vision or when he reached maturity and his father gave him his name and took the name Waglula (Worm). Crazy Horse was the third in his male line to have that name. His parents came from two tribes of the Lakota division of the Sioux. The father (Crazy Horse) was an Oglala, and his mother (Rattling Blanket Woman) was a Miniconjou.

Crazy Horse was married twice and shot in another love affair. As a young brave, he fell in love with and courted Black Buffalo Woman. But she married another man named No Water. In 1867 Crazy Horse persuaded Black Buffalo Woman to go on a buffalo hunt with him while her husband was away. When No Water returned, he came after them and shot Crazy Horse in the face, which left a noticeable scar and nearly cost him his life. Elders convinced the two men not to shed any more blood, and No Water gave Crazy Horse three horses as compensation for the shooting. In 1871 Crazy Horse married Black Shawl, who the elders sent to heal him after being shot by No Water. They had a daughter who died when three years old. His second wife was Nellie Larrabee, the daughter of a French trader and a Cheyenne woman, who was sent to live in Crazy Horse's lodge by Red Cloud.

Crazy Horse lived in the Lakota camps with his younger brother, High Horse, and a cousin, Little Hawk. There 29 U.S. troopers were killed in what was called the Grattan Massacre when they came to arrest a man for stealing a cow. Crazy Horse began having visions after witnessing the death of Conquering Bear, the Lakota leader.

Crazy Horse's father took him to Sylvan Lake in the Black Hills of South Dakota, and they both did a *hemblecha* (vision quest). During this, he learned of his animal protectors who would give him extended life (according to Lakota spirituality). He also was shown his "face paint" for battle, given a sacred song that is still sung by the Oglala people, and told he would be the protector of his people and not be hurt in combat (he never was hurt by an enemy before being killed by the prison guard in 1877).

Crazy Horse's reputation as a warrior grew in the late 1850s and early 1860s, resulting in his being named war leader of the Lakota Ogala in 1865. His first kill was a Shoshone raider who had killed a Lakota woman while she was washing buffalo meat along the Powder River. He also fought in numerous battles between the Lakota and their traditional Plains enemies—the Crow, Shoshone, Pawnee, Blackfeet, and Arikara.

Crazy Horse spent the last years of his life fighting the U.S. Cavalry. After the 1864 Sand Creek Massacre of Northern Cheyenne elderly, women, and children by the Third Colorado Cavalry, the Lakota Oglala and Mineconjou tribes joined the Cheyennes in combating the U.S. military. In 1866 Crazy Horse and nearly 1,000 Lakota and Cheyenne warriors ambushed and killed 80 U.S. infantry and cavalry troops in the Fetterman Massacre near Fort Phil Kearny in Wyoming. Crazy Horse and the Lakota also attacked a wood-cutting crew near Fort Phil Kearny in 1867 in what was called the Wagon Box Fight. This time the troopers had new breech-loading, fast-firing rifles that inflicted between 50 and 120 Lakota casualties, while the troopers suffered only five dead and two wounded.

In 1876 Crazy Horse led approximately 1,500 Lakota and Cheyenne in a surprise attack against Brigadier General George Crook with 1,000 cavalry and infantry and 300 Crow and Shoshone warriors in the Battle of the Rosebud. The battle delayed Crook's forces from joining the Seventh Cavalry under George A. Custer and contributed to his defeat at the Battle of the Little Bighorn.

On June 25, Custer's cavalry attacked a large encampment of Cheyenne and Lakota along the Little Bighorn River. Chief Gall and his Hunkpapa warriors led the counterattack, which drove Custer and the troopers to a nearby hill. Crazy Horse also was in the midst of the fighting, where it is believed his flanking assault ensured the death of Custer and his men.

That fall, Crazy Horse was unsuccessful in an attempt to rescue the camp of American Horse and his Miniconjou village in the Battle of Slim Buttes in South Dakota. American Horse and much of his family were killed after being holed up in a cave for several hours. Crazy Horse and his warriors fought their last major battle at Wolf Mountain in Montana Territory in the winter of 1876–1877. His people were weakened by the cold and hunger, and Crazy Horse decided to surrender in exchange for the promise of a reservation for his people near Powder River. He and other northern Oglala leaders—such as He Dog, Little Big Man, and Iron Crow—turned themselves in at the Red Cloud Agency near Fort Robinson in Nebraska in May 1977 as the first step in a formal surrender.

For the next four months, the Lakota and allies lived in a village established next to the Red Cloud Agency while awaiting settlement of the agreement. But a misunderstanding developed when Crazy Horse and others were asked to assist in capturing Chief Joseph of the Nez Perce, who left their reservation and were fleeing to Canada. Crazy Horse and Touch the Clouds, the Miniconjou leader, objected, saying they promised to remain at peace when they surrendered.

General George Crook was sent to Fort Robinson to resolve the growing problem. He was scheduled to meet with Crazy Horse but canceled the meeting and ordered Crazy Horse's arrest when he was told incorrectly that Crazy Horse said he intended to kill the general during the meeting. When Crazy Horse heard about the arrest order, he and his wife left his village and then agreed to return to Fort Robinson.

Crazy Horse was taken to the post guardhouse, where he reportedly resisted imprisonment, attempted to escape, and was stabbed with a bayonet by one of the military guards. He died of the wounding that night (September 5, 1877) at the age of 36. His body was turned over to his elderly parents, who initially placed it on a burial scaffold at Camp Sheridan, and then moved it to an undisclosed location, which still remains unknown.

Today, the famed warrior is a Lakota hero and the subject of the Crazy Horse Memorial in South Dakota, which contains the world's largest mountain sculpture. The sculpture, which is still under construction, shows Crazy Horse riding a horse and pointing into the distance. It will be 641 feet wide and 563 feet high when completed. The head will be more than 87 feet high, or about the height of a 22-story building. It will be even larger than the 60-foot heads of the four U.S. presidents at Mount Rushmore, which is only 17 miles away. The sculpture is being carved out of Thunderhead Mountain on land considered sacred by some Oglala Lakota. The memorial is operated by the Crazy Horse Memorial Foundation.

The huge sculpture was created by noted sculptor Korczak Ziolkowski, who worked on the project from the 1930s until his death in 1982. Since then, the work has been carried on by his wife, his children, and an engineering team. The project was commissioned by Lakota Chief Henry Standing Bear on behalf of fellow elders in 1929. Construction of the monument has been in progress since 1948.

The site has an educational/cultural center that includes the Indian Museum of North America, an educational center, and a visitor center and eventually will have a satellite campus of the University of South Dakota. The museum, which was founded in 1972, contains artifacts, crafts, and art representing the diverse cultures and histories of the American Indian people, and a 14,000-volume library of books on Indian history and two theaters. The annual attendance is 1 million.

Crazy Horse Memorial, 12151 Avenue of the Chiefs (off Hwy. 16/385), Crazy Horse, SD 57730-8900. Phone: 605/673-681. Fax: 605/673-2185. E-mail: memorial@crazyhorse.org. Website: www.crazyhorsememorial.org. Hours: mid-May–mid-Oct.—8–dusk; mid-Oct.–mid-May—8–5 daily. Admission: adults, $10 per person or $27 per car; walkers, cyclists, motorcyclists, $5; Native Americans, active military, Boy and Girl Scouts, Custer County residents, and children under 6, free.

Eugene V. Debs

Eugene V. Debs Home. Eugene V. Debs was a union leader who organized one of the nation's first industrial unions, a founding member of the Industrial Workers of the World, and a major socialist who ran for president of the United States five times in the early 1900s. He was known as a charismatic speaker with the oratorical style of evangelicalism, although generally disdainful of organized religion. But Debs also had his problems. He lost the presidential elections and his citizenship and was imprisoned for urging resistance to the military draft in World War I and for mail obstruction in the Pullman railroad car strike. His home in Terre Haute, Indiana, is now a historic house museum devoted to his life and career.

Eugene Victor Debs was born in 1855 to a prosperous family in Terre Haute. He was the son of Jean Daniel Debs and Marguerite Mari Bettrich Debs, who both emigrated from France. He was named for French authors Eugene Sue and Victor Hugo. His father owned a textile mill and a meat market. Debs attended public school but dropped out at the age of 14 and went to work in the railroad industry.

Debs initially was a painter and car cleaner in the Vandalia railroad car shops and then became a locomotive fireman on the railways for the same company in 1871–1875. During the next four years, he worked at a wholesale grocery house—and attended night classes at a local business school.

In 1875 Debs joined the Brotherhood of Locomotive Firemen. He quickly became involved in the fraternal benefit organization's activities, serving as a Terre Haute lodge delegate to the organization's national convention, associate editor of its magazine, and grand secretary, treasurer, and magazine editor from 1880 to early 1890s. At the same time, he served as city clerk in Terre Haute in 1879–1883 and was elected to the Indiana General Assembly as a Democrat in 1884–1885. He married Kate Metzel in 1885. They did not have any children.

In 1893 Debs organized the American Railway Union, one of the first industrial unions. It went on strike at the Great Northern Railway in 1894 and won most of its demands. Debs also became involved in the Pullman rail car strike in 1894. The strike began after the Pullman Palace Car Company cut the pay of its workers by 28 percent, citing reduced revenue after the economic Panic of 1893. When American Railway Union members joined in support of Pullman employees, Debs became the head of the strike and the object of much criticism and legal action.

The strikers refused to handle Pullman cars and any other railroad cars attached to them. The U.S. government obtained an injunction against the strike, and Debs was found guilty of violating the injunction and sentenced to federal prison. The U.S. Army also was sent to enforce the court order, which was upheld by the Supreme Court. The entrance by army troops ended the strike, in which 13 strikers were killed and thousands blacklisted.

While serving his six-month term in prison, Debs read about socialism and met with socialist representatives who visited him in prison. He emerged from prison as a socialist and spent the rest of his life promoting socialism and running for president. He persuaded the American Railway Union to join with the Brotherhood of the Cooperative Commonwealth to establish the Social Democracy of America, a socialist-oriented political organization. Debs ran for president of the United States in 1900 for the Social Democratic Party and received less than 1 percent of the popular vote. The party split after the election, resulting in the formation of the Socialist Party of America, with Debs being the unsuccessful Socialist candidate in 1904, 1908, 1912, and 1920.

Besides being a socialist and politician, he was still a labor organizer. In 1905 Debs and other influential union leaders formed the International Workers of the World (also known as the IWW or Wobblies). The objective was to give labor more power by uniting workers of industry. But it resulted in a split between two factions of the IWW—the Socialist Party and Bill Haywood, leader of the Western Federation of Miners.

The IWW and the Socialist Party were hurt when Haywood was removed from the national executive committee by passage of an amendment that focused on the direct action and sabotage tactics advocated by the IWW. Membership dropped dramatically after the dispute and never recovered, with the Socialists who had been elected to public office also failing to win reelection.

During World War I, Debs came out against the Wilson administration and the war—urging resistance to the military draft. He was arrested in 1918 and charged with 10 counts of wartime sedition. Debs was found guilty and sentences to 10 years in prison and disenfranchised for life (but his citizenship was restored in 1976). Wilson refused to reduce his sentence, but President Warren G. Harding commuted the sentence to time served in 1921, partly because of Debs's health. Debs was in federal prison when he ran for president on the Socialist Party ticket in 1920 and received 3.4 percent of the vote.

A crowd of 50,000, cheers, and band music greeted Debs at his home in Terre Haute when he was released from the Atlanta Penitentiary. In addition to his efforts to obtain fair pay and better working conditions for workers and his socialist involvement, Debs was known for his personal integrity, sincerity, and oratory. He died of a heart attack in 1926 at the age of 70. His home now is a historic house museum that is a National Historic Landmark, listed on the National Register of Historic Places, and located on the campus of Indiana State University in Terre Haute.

The two-story frame home, now known as the Eugene V. Debs Home, was built in 1890 by Eugene and Kate Debs after their fifth wedding anniversary. He was criticized for not building a more modest house with a working-class lifestyle. The more affluent house was made possible by his wife's inheritance from a wealthy aunt. It was acquired by the Eugene V. Debs Foundation in 1962 after it had been the home of a professor, converted into apartments, and used as a fraternity house from 1948 to 1961.

The house contains much of the original furnishings, as well as Debs union and political mementos, some of his personal library, historical photographs, and exhibits on his life and accomplishments. One room also has murals depicting Debs's life. Annual attendance is 1,300.

Eugene V. Debs Home, 451 N. 8th St., Terra Haute, IN 47807-3006 (postal address: PO Box 9454, Terra Haute, IN 47808-9454). Phones: 812/232-2163 and 812/237-3443. E-mail: charles.king@indiana.edu. Website: www.debsfoundation.org. Hours: 1–4:30 Tues.–Sat.; closed Sun.–Mon., national holidays, New Year's Eve and Day, and Christmas Eve and Day. Admission: free.

Frederick Douglass

Frederick Douglass National Historic Site. Frederick Douglass was one of the most prominent African Americans of the nineteenth century. He was a social reformer, orator, writer, and statesman who escaped from slavery and became a leader of the abolitionist movement. He was a living example that slaves had the intellectual capacity to function as independent American citizens, counter to the claims of slaveholders at that time. He is honored at the Frederick Douglass National Historic Site in Washington, DC, and four other museums named for him.

Frederick Douglass was born Frederick Augustus Washington Bailey in 1818 as a slave near Eaton in Talbot County, Maryland. But the exact date and place are not known. It is believed that it was in his maternal grandmother's shack east of Tappers Corner, between Hillsboro and Cordova.

Douglass said he and his mother were separated when he was only a few weeks old, and he assumed that the plantation owner was his father. After the separation, he lived with his maternal grandmother, Betty Bailey, until nearly seven years old, when she left him at the master's plantation. The plantation owner then sent Douglass to Baltimore to live as a houseboy with Hugh and Sophia Auld, relatives of his master. His mother died when he was about 10.

When Douglass was about 12, Auld's wife began to help him learn the alphabet—despite the fact that it was against the law to teach slaves to read. Her husband, however, put a stop to the teaching, saying that slaves would only become dissatisfied and seek freedom if they learned to read. Douglass then learned to read and write from white children in the neighborhood in exchange for food and by observing the writings of the men with whom he worked.

Douglass made further advances by buying a copy of *The Columbian Orator*, a popular schoolbook at the time, and by reading newspapers, political materials, and books, which led him to question and condemn slavery. When Douglass was hired out to William Freeland, he ran informal classes with about 40 slaves who wanted to know how to read. But when plantation owners learned that slaves were being educated, they broke up the class with clubs and stones. Douglass tried to escape from Freeland but was unsuccessful.

Douglass returned to the eastern shore when about 15 and became a field hand. In 1833 he was sent to work for Edward Covey, a poor farmer known as a "slave breaker." He whipped Douglass regularly until the 16-year-old finally rebelled and fought back. Covey stopped the beatings after a confrontation with Douglass. While with Covey, Douglass failed in an 1836 attempt to flee. He then was sent back to Baltimore to live with the Auld family, who leased him to a shipyard owner to work as a caulker. He tried to run away in 1837 but failed again. But he did manage to escape in 1838 at the age of 20.

Douglass made the escape with the assistance of Anna Murray, a free black woman he met in Baltimore and later married. He ran away in a sailor's uniform provided by Murray, who also gave him travel money from her savings. Using identification papers obtained from a free black seaman, Douglass made it to Philadelphia and continued to the safe house of abolitionist David Ruggles in New York City. He then sent for Murray, and they were married 11 days later by an African American Presbyterian minister in New York. The couple had five children and were married until her death in 1882. They moved to New Bedford, Massachusetts, where they stayed with Nathan and Mary Johnson, and where they adopted "Douglass" as their married name.

Douglass joined a black church, attended abolitionist meetings, and subscribed to William Lloyd Garrison's weekly journal, *The Liberator*. In 1841 he heard Garrison speak at a meeting of the Bristol Anti-Slavery Society and was unexpectedly invited to speak at one of the later meetings. After he told of his experiences as a slave, he was encouraged to become an antislavery lecturer. The 23-year-old Douglass gave his first speech at the Massachusetts Anti-Slavery Society's annual convention in Nantucket. He and Garrison were inspired by each other, and they became colleagues on the speaking circuit. Douglass also became known for his outstanding oratory.

The early successful talks led Douglass into public speaking and writing. He published his own newspapers, including the *North Star* and three others; participated in the first women's rights convention in Seneca Falls, New York, in 1848; and wrote three autobiographies—each expanding on the previous one. His first book, *Narrative of the Life of Frederick Douglass, an American Slave*, was published in 1845 and became an immediate best seller. The other two followed in 1855 and 1881.

In 1845–1846 Douglass spent two years touring Ireland and Britain and giving lectures in churches and chapels. He was urged to go abroad partly because there was concern that the publicity might cause his former owner, Hugh Auld, to try to reclaim his property—the escaped slave Frederick Bailey (now Frederick Douglass).

When he returned, Douglass published the abolitionist newspapers, gave a supporting statement that was helpful in passing the suffrage resolution at the women's rights convention in 1848, reversed his earlier agreement with Garrison that the U.S. Constitution was proslavery, stated that education and desegregation were the keys for African Americans to improve their lives, and opposed John Brown's plan to start an armed slave rebellion to achieve freedom in the South.

During the Civil War, Douglass and his family lived in Rochester, New York. At the outbreak of the war, he helped recruit blacks for the Union Army. He also served as consultant to President Abraham Lincoln. After the war, he moved to Washington and served as U.S. marshal for the District of Columbia in 1877–1881, recorder of deeds for the district in 1881–1886, and U.S. minister to Haiti in 1889–1891. He was the vice president nominee of the small Equal Rights Party, which ran suffragette Victoria Woodhull as the first woman candidate for president of the United States in 1872. After his first wife died in 1882, Douglass married Helen Pitts, a white woman who was the daughter of an abolitionist colleague.

Frederick Douglass died in 1895 of a heart attack at the age of 77. His final home in Washington became the Frederick Douglass National Historic Site in 1988. Douglass lived in the two-story frame house, which he called Cedar Hill, from 1877 until his death. The house originally was built around 1855 by John Van Hook in what became the Anacostia neighborhood in southeast Washington. Douglass expanded the L-shaped historic house from 14 to 21 rooms, including two-story library and kitchen wings. Also on the nine-acre hilltop site are a visitor center and Douglass's "Growlery," a small stone building where he did his studying and writing.

After Douglass's death, his widow established the Frederick Douglass Memorial and Historical Association in 1900 to honor Douglass and preserve the house. The National Association of Colored Women's Clubs joined the association in the effort until 1962, when the National Park Service took over the house to restore and prepare it as a historic site. The house now contains the furnishings, documents, library, personal possessions, and gifts given Douglass by such contemporaries as Mary Todd Lincoln and Harriet Beecher Stowe. The site also has guided tours, films, and special interpretive programs. The house can be seen only by ticketed guided tours. Annual attendance is 33,000.

Frederick Douglass National Historic Site, 1411 W St., S.E., Washington, DC 20020-4813. Phone: 202/426-5961. Fax: 202/426-0880. E-mail: cathy_ingram@nps.gov. Website: www.nps.gov/frdo. Hours: Apr.–Oct.—9–5 daily; Nov.–Mar.—9–4 daily; closed New Year's Day, Thanksgiving, and Christmas. Admission: free; guided tour, $2.

Frederick Douglass Museum and Caring Hall of Fame. The Frederick Douglass Museum and Caring Hall of Fame is located in the African American leader's first home in Washington, DC. He purchased the three-story townhouse in 1871 and two years later added an adjoining house before moving in 1877 to the larger Cedar Hill home in the Anacostia neighborhood. The historic property has been restored and reopened as a tribute to caring people as well as Douglass, an escaped slave who became a leading reformer, abolitionist, and statesman in the nineteenth century.

The Douglass home—which now includes two adjoining townhouses—has been restored to the period when he and his family lived there in 1871–1877. It contains Douglass furniture and memorabilia. The Caring Hall of Fame honors people of his spirit who have received a Caring Award, which is presented annually by the Caring Institute to the world's most caring adults and young people committed to doing the right thing on behalf of justice, equality, and human rights. It contains photographs and biographies of the honorees.

Frederick Douglass Museum and Caring Hall of Fame, 320 A St., N.E., Washington, DC 20002. Phone: 202/547-4273. Fax: 202/547-4510. E-mail: gb@nahc.org. Website: www3.nahc.org/fd/index.html. Hours: Mon.–Fri. by appointment; closed Sat.–Sun. and major holidays. Admission: free.

Frederick Douglass Museum and Cultural Center. The Frederick Douglass Museum and Cultural Center is located in Highland Beach, Maryland, a community founded in 1893 by one of Douglass's sons and his wife after being refused admission to a nearby resort because of their race. Charles and Laura Douglass then bought a 40-acre tract with 500 feet of beachfront on Chesapeake Bay and turned it into a summer enclave for their family and friends. The site became a gathering place for upper-class blacks, including such well-known personages at the time as singer Paul Robeson, educator Booker T. Washington, and poet Langston Hughes. When Highland Beach was incorporated in 1922, it became the first African American municipality in Maryland.

Although founded as a summer resort, Highland Beach now is a small town with about 60 homes of year-round residents—many of them descendants of the original settlers. The history of the town is featured at the Frederick Douglass Museum and Cultural Center, which also honors the prominent African American leader whose son founded the community. The museum/cultural center is housed in Twin Oaks, a summer cottage built in 1895 for Frederick Douglass. The property was purchased and restored by the state and county in the 1980s–1990s and deeded to the town in 1995. Annual attendance is 2,500.

Frederick Douglass Museum and Cultural Center, 3200 Wayman Ave., Highland Beach, MD 21403 (postal address: Highland Beach Historical Commission, 3200 Wayman Ave., Highland Beach, MD 21403). Phones: 410/268-2956 and 410/267-6960. Fax: 410/267-0091. E-mail: jeanw57@aol.com. Website: www.highlandbeachmd.org. Hours: by appointment. Admission: free.

Frederick Douglass–Isaac Myers Maritime Park. The Frederick Douglass–Isaac Myers Maritime Park along the Baltimore, Maryland, waterfront honors two African American leaders who had great impact in the 1800s. Douglass, who was born a slave and became a prominent social reformer and abolitionist, worked on Baltimore's docks when he lived in Baltimore. Myers, a free-born black, became a union leader and later founded and headed a shipyard and railway company at the waterfront.

Douglass lived near the waterfront and worked as a ship caulker in 1836–1837. He was one of the slaves in Baltimore at that time who were leased to shipyards by their owners. Some blacks worked as caulkers, who applied pitch and gum to seal seams between planks and beams on wooden-hull vessels. Most worked in semiskilled or skilled jobs. Douglass was hired by Myers, who was in charge of a crew that caulked large clipper ships.

Myers learned the caulking trade as an apprentice when 16 and worked in the field for about a decade. He then opened a grocery business in the early 1860s (while keeping in close touch with his colleagues in construction and maintenance at the port). After the Civil War, white workers staged a successful strike in 1865 that forced shipyards to fire approximately 1,000 black dock workers.

In response, Myers organized a group of black and white businessmen to establish a new shipyard—the Chesapeake Marine Railway and Dry Dock Company—that employed 300 black and a few white tradesmen. It was highly successful, but the firm stopped operations in 1884 when its 20-year lease ran out and requests for renewal were turned down.

In 1868 Myers, as president of the Colored Caulker's Trades Union Society, sought to have black unions admitted to the all-industry National Labor Union, which was founded two years earlier. When the issue remained unresolved, he and other African American labor leaders formed the Colored National Labor Union. But both unions disintegrated during the Depression of 1873, as Douglass assumed leadership of the black union and created the Colored Men's Progressive and Cooperative Union, which admitted women and men regardless of race (despite the name). It became a true industrial union with members from all occupational backgrounds.

In the 1870s, Myers became more involved in Republican politics and worked as a customs service agent and then postal inspector in the South. He returned to Baltimore in 1880, operated a coal yard, served as editor of a black weekly newspaper, and organized black industrial, businessmen's, building and loan, and aged ministerial organizations. He died in 1891 at the age of 56. He was married twice and had several children.

The Frederick Douglass–Isaac Myers Marine Park, operated by the Living Classrooms Foundation, opened in 2006 at Fells Pont, where the Chesapeake Marine Railway and Dry Dock Company once operated. It occupies 5,000 square feet in a new gallery building and the historic Sugar House, the oldest remaining industrial building on the Inner Harbor, which has been restored and contains the Alex Brown Maritime Education Center.

In addition to exhibits about the lives and accomplishments of Douglass and Myer, the museum tells of the contributions of African Americans to the development of Baltimore and its maritime industry. It contains artifacts, historic images and maps, archaeological findings, artistic renderings, and audio components. Among the education center offerings are programs that teach shipbuilding and skills to at-risk youths. Guided tours are offered by docents.

Frederick Douglass–Isaac Myers Maritime Park, 1417 Thames St., Baltimore, MD 21231. Phone: 410/685-0295. Fax: 410/276-6347. Website: www.douglassmyers.org. Hours: 10–5 Tues.–Sun.; closed Mon. and major holidays. Admission: adults, $5; seniors, $4; students 6–18, $2; children under 6, free.

Banneker-Douglass Museum. *See* Benjamin Banneker in Scientists/Engineers/Inventors section.

Katherine Dunham

Katherine Dunham Dynamic Museum. Katherine Dunham was a pace-setting African American dancer, choreographer, and company director who also was an educator, writer, and social activist. She was an innovator in African American modern dancer who was called the "matriarch and queen mother of black dance." She choreographed more than 90 individual dances and was known throughout the United States, Europe, and Latin American in the mid-twentieth century for her creative dances. She also became a social activist, fighting segregation in hotels, restaurants, and theaters with public condemnations and lawsuits. Her home and school in East St. Louis, Illinois, is now the Katherine Dunham Dynamic Museum.

Katherine Mary Dunham was born in a Chicago hospital in 1909 and then taken to her parents' home in suburban Glen Ellyn. Her father was Albert Millard Dunham, a descendant of West Africa and Madagascar, and her mother was Fanny June Taylor Dunham, whose heritage was French Canadian and Native American. Her mother died when Katherine was four years old, and her father remarried several years later. The family then moved to Joliet, Illinois, where her father ran a dry-cleaning shop.

As a young girl, Dunham showed interest and talent in two fields—dance and writing. She joined the Terpsichorean Club and began to learn modern dance based on the ideas of Jacques-Dalcroze and Rudolf von Laban. When 15 years old, she gave her first public dance performance at a fund-raising cabaret she organized for Brown's Methodist Church in Joliet. And when in high school, she opened a private dance school for young black children.

After Dunham graduated from Joliet Junior College, she moved to Chicago to join her brother Albert, who was a student at the University of Chicago. It was there that she learned in an anthropology lecture that much of American black culture originated in Africa. She decided to major in anthropology and studied under leading anthropologists on the faculty. While an undergraduate, she also began studying ballet with Ludmilla Speranzeva, a Russian dancer who settled in Chicago; Mark Turbyfill; and Ruth Page, prima ballerina of the Chicago Opera.

In 1930 Dunham formed a group called the Ballets Nègres, one of the first black ballet companies in the nation, which she disbanded after one well-received performance. She married Jordis W. McCoo, a postal worker, in 1931, but they divorced in 1938. She opened a dance school in 1933 and formed a modern dance group, called the Negro Dance Group, to teach the young black dancers about their African heritage. In 1934–1936 Dunham performed as a guest artist with the ballet company of the Chicago Opera. Page danced in the title role in an opera about the West Indies the first year, and Dunham succeeded her the next year, with Dunham's Negro Dance Group in the ensemble.

Dunham was trying to balance her busy life as a dancer and a college student. She also was showing great promise in her ethnographic studies of dance and was awarded travel fellowships from the Julius Rosenwald and Guggenheim Foundations to do ethnographic studies of Caribbean dance forms, especially in Haiti. Her 1935–1936 studies took her to Jamaica, Martinique, Trinidad, Tobago, and Haiti.

Dunham returned to Chicago and received her bachelor's degree in 1936. She then worked on her master's degree in anthropology and submitted "The Dances of Haiti: A Study of Their Material Aspect, Organization, Form, and Function" in partial fulfillment of the requirements for the degree. But she never received the graduate degree. When faced with a career decision, she gave up her anthropology research studies to become a professional dancer and choreographer.

In 1937 Dunham revived her dance ensemble, which performed West Indies dances and a ballet in New York City in "A Negro Dance Evening." It was the beginning of a long career in which she danced and served as choreographer. She created *Rare Tonga* and *Woman with a Cigar*, two of her well-known works characterized by exotic sexuality. She then became dance director of the Chicago Negro Theater of the Federal Theater Project, choreographed the Chicago production of *Run Li'l Chil'lun*, and produced such choreography as *The Emperor Jones* and *Barrelhouse*. This also is when she became associated with white designer John Pratt. They worked together and were married in 1951. He designed many of her sets and managed her affairs until his death in 1986.

In 1940 Dunham's entire company performed in *Cabin in the Sky*, the Broadway production staged by George Balanchine, with Dunham in the sultry role of temptress Georgia Brown. After a successful reception in New York City, the show made a national tour, and while on the West Coast the Dunham company appeared in the 1941 movie *Carnival of Rhythm*. Dunham came back to perform in such films as *Star Spangled Rhythm*, *Pardon My Sarong*, *Stormy Weather*, and *Cashbah* in the 1940s. She also returned to Broadway for a revue entitled *Bal Nègre*, choreographed the *Windy City* musical in Chicago, and opened a cabaret show in Las Vegas.

In 1948 she opened *A Caribbean Rhapsody* with her company in London and then Paris. This began nearly 20 years of performances largely abroad, during which time she developed many new productions. They included performances in 33 countries in Europe, North Africa, South America, Australia, and East Asia. The world travels ended in 1960, and Dunham's last performance on Broadway was in *Bamboche!* in 1962. The following year, she choreographed dances for a new production of *Aida* at the New York Metropolitan Opera. Her final show before retiring in 1967 was at the Apollo Theater in Harlem.

Throughout her career, Dunham was active in combating segregation in public statements and law suits, especially in areas that affected the entertainment field, such as restaurants, hotels, and theaters. She also was outraged by the lack of cultural and artistic activities in the ghettos of East St. Louis, Illinois, after she settled there while an artist in residence at Southern Illinois University in nearby Edwardsville in the 1960s. She opened the Performing Arts Training Center, a cultural program and school for neighborhood children and youth with programs in dance, drama, martial arts, and humanities. She later expanded the program to include senior citizens.

Even during her active years as a performer and choreographer, Dunham was involved in teaching and writing. In 1945 she opened and directed the Katherine Dunham School of Dance and Theatre in New York City after she was provided studio space for three years by an admirer. Among the future celebrities who attended the school were Eartha Kitt, James Dean, Sidney Poitier, Gregory Peck, Shirley MacLaine, and Warren Beatty. In 1957 Dunham also worked on writing autobiographies of her youth while taking a year off living in Kyoto, Japan. She also wrote a fictional work based on her African experiences.

Dunham and her husband moved to East St. Louis in 1969, where she became artist in residence on the Edwardsville campus of Southern Illinois University. In 1977 she converted her two-story English regency townhouse into the Katherine Dunham Dynamic Museum (she earlier had a museum in Alton, Illinois). She died in 2006 at the age of 96.

The museum contains costumes, photographs, programs, letters, awards, furniture, and mementos from her career as a dancer, choreographer, teacher, writer, and dance company owner and producer. It also has Dunham's collection of symbolic and functional art, including more than 250 African and Caribbean art objects from more than 50 countries. Annual attendance is 500.

Katherine Dunham Dynamic Museum, 1000 Pennsylvania Ave., East St. Louis, IL 62201-1407 (postal address: PO Box 6, East St. Louis, IL 62202-0006). Phone: 618/874-8560. Fax: 618/874-8562. E-mail: kdcahgloria@sbcglobal. net. Website: www.kdcah.com. Hours: 10–4 Mon.–Tues. and Thurs.–Sat.; closed Sun., Wed., and major holidays. Admission: free.

Langston Hughes

See Authors/Writers section.

Helen Keller

Ivy Green, Birthplace of Helen Keller. Helen Keller is best known as the blind, deaf, and mute person who overcame her disabilities, learned to speak, and inspired many others in speeches and lectures around the world. She also was a political activist who campaigned for women's suffrage, labor rights, socialism, and other causes in early twentieth century. Her life and achievements are now featured at Ivy Green, Birthplace of Helen Keller in Tuscumbia, Alabama.

Helen Adams Keller could see and hear normally when born in the cottage of the Ivy Green estate in Tuscumbia in 1880. But when 19 months old, she contracted a severe illness believed to have been scarlet fever or meningitis, which left her blind and deaf. Her father was Arthur H. Keller, a cotton plantation owner and weekly newspaper editor and publisher who had served as a captain in the Confederate Army during the Civil War. Her mother was Kate Adams, daughter of Charles Adams, who was a Confederate brigadier general during the war. Helen had a sister and two stepbrothers from her father's first marriage.

By the age of seven, Helen Keller had developed over 60 home signs to communicate with her family. But her mother was inspired by Charles Dickens's account in *American Notes* of Laura Bridgman, another blind and deaf woman, who had a successful education. As a result, Keller's father took her to see an eye, ear, nose, and throat specialist in Baltimore. He put them in touch with Alexander Graham Bell, the inventor and educator, who was working with deaf children at the time. The half-wild young girl was taken to see Bell, who advised them to contact the Perkins Institute for the Blind, where Bridgman had been educated. It was at the school in South Boston, Massachusetts, that director Michael Anaganos arranged for Anne Mansfield Sullivan, a 20-year-old who was visually impaired, to be Keller's instructor.

Sullivan evolved into governess and eventually companion in a 49-year relationship. Her work later was featured in the play and motion picture *The Miracle Worker*. Upon arrival in 1887, Sullivan began to teach Keller to communicate by spelling words in her hand. Keller initially was frustrated because she did not understand that every object had a word identifying it.

The breakthrough in communication came one day at a well-pump in the yard. Sullivan was running cool water in one of Keller's hands while repeatedly tapping out an alphabet code of five letters in the other hand, and Keller realized that Sullivan was symbolizing "water." She then wanted to know the names of other familiar objects.

Keller began attending the Perkins Institute for the Blind in 1888 and enrolled at the Wright-Humason School for the Deaf and Horace Mann School for the Deaf in New York City in 1896. She then returned to the Boston area to go to the Cambridge School for Young Ladies and attend Radcliffe College, where she graduated cum laude with a Bachelor of Arts degree in 1904. She became the first blind and deaf person to earn a B.A. college degree. Her education was paid for by Standard Oil magnate Henry Huttleston Rogers and his wife, Abbie—who were introduced to her by Mark Twain, an admirer.

Keller also learned to speak—and spent much of her time giving speeches and lectures. Her sense of touch became extremely supple, and she "heard" people speak by reading their lips with her hands. Keller also learned to use Braille, read sign language with her hands, and experience close-by music by placing her fingers on a resonant tabletop.

Keller spent much of her adult life raising funds for the American Foundation for the Blind and giving speeches, lecturing, and writing—frequently for such causes as women's suffrage, labor rights, socialism, peace, birth control, and rights for people with disabilities. She gave lectures in more than 25 countries on five continents. She was a pacifist who campaigned to give women voting rights, participated in antiwar rallies, and was a member of the Socialist Party of America and Industrial Workers of the World. She also was an author who wrote 12 books and a number of articles. Among the books were *The Story of My Life* (1902), *The World I Live In* (1908), *Out of the Dark* (1913), *My Religion* (1927), and *The Open Door* (1957).

Anne Sullivan, who was Keller's companion for most of her life, married John Macy in 1905. When her health began to fail around 1914, Polly Thompson, a young woman from Scotland, was hired to assist with the duties. Thompson later became Keller's secretary and then constant companion. Keller, Thompson, Sullivan, and John Macy then moved to Forest Hills, Queens, New York, which became the base of her efforts on behalf of the American Foundation for the Blind.

After Sullivan died in 1936, Keller and Thompson moved to Arcan Ridge in Easton, Connecticut, and traveled worldwide raising funds for the blind. Thompson suffered a stroke in 1957 and died in 1960. Winnie Corbally, a nurse who was brought in to care for Thompson, remained as Keller's companion for the rest of her life. Keller died at her home in 1968 at the age of 87 after a series of strokes.

The Helen Keller story now is told at Ivy Green, Birthplace of Helen Keller, which contains the main family home, the birthplace cottage, and other facilities on a 640-acre estate. The family home originally was built in 1820 by her grandparents. It is a seven-room white clapboard house typical of southern architecture. Helen was born in the adjacent one-room cottage that once served as the plantation office. It was refurnished and fitted as a bridal suite for Keller's parents when they were married and used by Helen Keller and Anne Sullivan when they lived together before leaving for further schooling.

Ivy Green, which received its name from its extensive English ivy and boxwoods, was founded as a historic house museum in 1952 and was made a permanent shrine by the State of Alabama and the Helen Keller Property Board in 1954. The historic site also is listed on the National Register of Historic Places. The main house is decorated with much of the original furniture of the Keller family and contains Helen's personal mementos, books, and gifts from her lectures and travels. Among the objects are her complete library of Braille books and her original Braille typewriter.

The grounds have an outdoor kitchen, carriage house, Lions Club memorial, New Zealand gate, well-pump, and rose, herb, butterfly, and Japanese gardens. *The Miracle Worker* is staged on the grounds in June and July, and an annual Helen Keller Festival and Historic Tour is sponsored by the property board. The museum's annual attendance is 15,000.

Ivy Green, Birthplace of Helen Keller, 300 N. Commons St., West, Tuscumbia, AL 35674-1134. Phone: 256/383-4066. Fax: 256/383-4068. E-mail: helenkellerbirthplace@comcast.net. Website: www.helenkellerbirthplace.org. Hours: 8:30–4 Mon.–Sat.; closed Sun., New Year's Day, Easter, Labor Day, Thanksgiving, and Dec. 24–26. Admission: adults, $6; seniors and military, $5; children 5–18, $2; children under 5, free.

Martin Luther King Jr.

See Religious Leaders section.

John L. Lewis

John L. Lewis Memorial Museum of Mining and Labor. John L. Lewis was the powerful leader of the United Mine Workers of America for 40 years and became one of the most effective, innovative, and controversial leaders in the history of labor. He was instrumental in the founding of the Congress of Industrial Organizations (CIO) as a rival to the American Federation of Labor (AFL) in the 1930s and was widely hated for calling nationwide coal strikes that adversely affected the American economy in the middle of World War II. The John L. Lewis Memorial Museum of Mining and Labor in his hometown of Lucas, Iowa, now celebrates his life and career.

Lewis was an aggressive union leader who obtained high wages, pensions, medical benefits, and better working conditions for miners and other union members, frequently in brutal negotiations with companies and federal agencies. He was a leading liberal who helped elect President Franklin D. Roosevelt in 1936 but broke with him on foreign policy in 1940. Lewis also became known for his massive leonine head, bushy eyebrows, powerful voice, and persistent scowl—and was a favorite subject of cartoonists.

John Llewellyn Lewis was born in 1880 in Cleveland, Iowa, a company town built around a coal mine near Lucas. He was the son of Thomas H. and Ann Watkins Lewis. He attended high school in Des Moines for three years and then went to work in the Bill Hill Mine in 1897 at the age of 17. Ten years later, he started a feed and grain distributorship and ran for mayor in Lucas, but both efforts were unsuccessful.

Lewis returned to working in coal mines and in 1906 was elected a delegate to the United Mine Workers national convention. He moved to Panama, Illinois, and then Springfield with other members of the Lewis family, and was elected president of the UMW local in 1909.

In 1911 Samuel Gompers, the head of the American Federation of Labor, hired Lewis as a union organizer, and he traveled throughout Pennsylvania and the Midwest as a union organizer and troubleshooter in coal and steel areas. He then advanced from statistician to vice president of the United Mine Workers and became the acting president in 1919, when he called the union's first major strike and 400,000 miners walked off their jobs. Lewis told the miners to return to work after President Woodrow Wilson obtained an injunction to halt the strike. He was elected UMW president in 1920—a position he held until 1960.

Lewis became the dominant labor official in what was the largest and most influential trade union in the nation at the time. He fought off others who tried to seize control of the union and its locals. That included the communists, who began to take over some locals, and political rivals who wanted to assume the UMW leadership. He placed the once-autonomous districts under centralized trusteeship control, packed the leadership positions, discredited opponents, hired some of the communist and other radical organizers, and banned or expelled others who sought to replace him. He was denounced by opponents as being despotic, but he maintained control of the union.

Lewis also challenged Gompers for the presidency of the American Federation of Labor. However, Gompers, who had led the AFL for nearly 40 years, defeated Lewis, only to die three years later and be succeeded by William Green, one of Lewis's subordinates. In 1934 Lewis obtained AFL endorsement of industrial unionism, and then with the support of the mine workers and nine other unions formed the Congress of Industrial Organizations (CIO) in 1935, with Lewis as president. The CIO included workers from such other industries as steel, automobiles, rubber, meat, glass, and electrical equipment. The CIO and AFL then began to compete for unions and contracts, resulting in the AFL expelling the entire CIO group from membership in 1938.

Although a liberal, Lewis supported Republican Herbert Hooper for president in 1928 and officially backed Hoover in 1932 while quietly supporting Democrat Franklin D. Roosevelt during the Great Depression. After Roosevelt was elected, Lewis was appointed to the Labor Advisory Board and the National Labor Board of the National Recovery Administration in 1933 and helped obtain the passage of the 1935 and 1937 Guffey Coal Acts, which were favorable to miners, and the 1935 National Labor Relations Act (known as the Wagner Act), which enabled unions to expand.

Despite his prior support, Lewis came out against Roosevelt and supported Wendell Wilkie, the Republican candidate, in the 1940 presidential election. But when 85 percent of the CIO members rejected his position and voted for Roosevelt, Lewis resigned as president of the CIO. He remained the head of the UMW but withdrew the union from the CIO and rejoined the AFL in 1944.

After the Japanese attacked Pearl Harbor and the United States entered World War II, the UMW came out in support of the war effort with a no-strike pledge. But Lewis repeatedly violated the pledge, such as in 1943 when a half million miners went on strike. President Roosevelt had to seize the mines after some steel mills closed and production was crippled by the power shortage.

Even after the war, miners went on strikes or work stoppages (in 1945, 1945, 1948, and 1949–1950) in what President Harry S. Truman called a threat to national security. It hurt the coal industry and resulted in mining job losses as many industries, railroads, and homeowners switched from coal to oil. The UMW actions also influenced the passage of the Taft-Hartley Act in 1947, which adversely affected unions.

A period of peaceful negotiations followed that brought wage increases and new medical and other benefits and the passage of the first Federal Mine Safety Act in 1952. The mechanization of mining also was beginning to eliminate jobs and reduce union membership. In addition, union operations were changing. The Landrum-Griffin Act of 1959, for example, forced UMW to discontinue district trusteeships where officers were appointed rather than being elected by the membership.

John L. Lewis retired in 1960 after four decades as president of the United Mine Workers union. He was awarded the Presidential Medal of Freedom in 1964 from President Lyndon B. Johnson for being "an eloquent spokesman of labor" and giving a "voice to the aspirations of the industrial workers of the country." He retired to his family home in Alexandria, Virginia, where he had lived with his wife and daughter since 1937. He died in 1969 at the age of 89.

The John L. Lewis Memorial Museum of Mining and Labor, founded in 1990 in Lucas, Iowa, tells of his life and career, his family history, and coal mining and labor history. It has a life-size bronze statue of Lewis and personal photographs, speeches, letters, documents, and memorabilia. The museum also contains a cartoon gallery, historical photographs, coal miners' memorabilia, period coal mining equipment, and a library with books, records, photographs, and other materials on Lewis, mining, and the labor movement. Annual attendance is 1,000.

John L. Lewis Memorial Museum of Mining and Labor, 102 Division St., Lucas, IA 50501-7700 (postal address: PO Box 3, Lucas, IA 50101-0003). Phone and fax: 641/766-6831. E-mail: danallen@coalmininglabormuseum.org. Website: www.coalmininglabormuseum.com. Hours: Apr. 15–Oct. 15—9–3 Mon.–Sat.; closed Sun., holidays, and Oct. 16–Apr. 14. Admission: adults, $2; students over 10, $1; children under 11, free.

Juliette Gordon Low

Juliette Gordon Low Birthplace. Juliette Gordon Low was a youth leader who founded the Girl Scouts of the United States of America in 1912. She wanted to bring girls of all backgrounds out of their sheltered home environments to experience the out-of-doors, develop self-reliance and resourcefulness, and serve their communities. She encouraged girls—including those with disabilities who usually were excluded—to prepare for active citizenship and lives ranging from traditional homemakers to professional women in the arts, sciences, and business. Her family home in Savannah, Georgia, is now the Juliette Gordon Low Birthplace, a historic house museum devoted to her life and the Girl Scouts.

Juliette Gordon Low was born Juliette Magill Kinzie Gordon in Savannah in 1860. She was the second of six children. Her father was William Washington Gordon II, who was a Confederate captain in the Civil War and whose family members were early settlers in Georgia. Her mother was Eleanor Kinzie Gordon, whose family was involved in the founding of Chicago. After the South's 1864 surrender to Union General William T. Sherman, the families of Confederate officers were required to leave Savannah, Mrs. Gordon took Juliette and two sisters to the home of her parents, John and Juliette Kinzie, in Chicago, and later returned to their large home in Savannah.

Low was a sensitive and talented youngster who wrote poems, sketched, wrote and acted in plays, and excelled in swimming, tennis, and rowing. She later became a skilled painter and sculptor. She was educated at such boarding schools as the Virginia Female Institute (now Stuart Hall School) in Staunton, Virginia, and Mesdemoiselles Charbonniers, a French finishing school in New York City. After her schooling, she traveled extensively in the United States and Europe.

Gordon lost most of her hearing in one after suffering an ear infection when she was 25. She then lost the hearing in her other ear when 26 after a grain of rice thrown at her wedding punctured her eardrum, which became infected and resulted in the loss of hearing. She used hearing horns and various hearing aids the rest of her life.

Gordon married William Mackay Low, the son of a wealthy cotton merchant in Savannah and England, in 1886. The couple moved to England and settled in Wellesbourne House in Warwickshire. However, the marriage did not go well, and a divorce was pending when he died from a stroke in 1905. Low returned to the United States during the 1898 Spanish-American War to help her mother organize a convalescent hospital for soldiers wounded in Cuba. Her father was commissioned a brigadier general in the U.S. Army and served on the Puerto Rican Peace Commission.

Low then returned to England, where she met Sir Robert Baden-Powell, founder of the girls guiding movement, in England in 1911. She became interested in the program and organized a troop in Scotland and two in London. Her experience resulted in wanting to do "something for all the girls" in the United States and the world. When she returned to Savannah, she met with her cousin, Nina Anderson Pape, who founded the Pape School, and told her about her interest in starting a program for girls. They recruited 18 girls who became the first troop of American Girl Guides in 1912, and a nearby carriage house was converted to club rooms and served as the early headquarters.

The organization's original name was Girl Guides of America, but it was changed to the Girl Scouts of the United States in 1913 and when incorporated in 1915 (and to Girl Scouts of the United States of America in 1947). Low served as president of the new organization until 1920, when she her title was changed to founder. She then turned her attention to the worldwide movement. She maintained contact with overseas Girl Guides and Scouts during World War I and helped lay the foundation for the World Association of Girl Guides and Girl Scouts after the war. At the same time, the Girls Scouts of the USA continued to expand its operations and the number of girls participating.

The Girl Scout program seeks to empower girls and to teach such values as honesty fairness, courage, compassion, character, sisterhood, confidence, and citizenship through such activities as camping, community service, first aid, and other practical skills—and have the achievements recognized by rank advancement and special awards. Today, the Girl Scouts organization has 3.7 million members and is the largest educational organization for girls in the world. It also has influenced more than 59 million girls, women, and men who have been associated with it.

Juliette Gordon Low developed breast cancer in 1923, continued working, and died from cancer in 1927 at the age of 66. She was buried in her Girls Scout uniform. In 1953 the Girl Scouts of the USA purchased and restored the

1821 English regency home where she was born and lived in Savannah. It was opened as a historic house museum called the Juliette Gordon Low Birthplace in 1956.

The house has been restored to reflect the 1880s and contains many pieces of the original family furniture, Juliette's artworks, and exhibits about her life and the Girl Scouts. The museum also offers educational programs and guided tours. Annual attendance is 65,000.

Juliette Gordon Low Birthplace, 10 E. Oglethorpe Ave., Savannah, GA 31401-3707. Phone: 912/233-4501. Fax: 912/233-4659. E-mail: info@juliettegordonlowbirthplace.org. Website: www.girlscouts.org/birthplace. Hours: Mar.–Oct.—10–4 Mon.–Sat., 11–4 Sun.; closed St. Patrick's Day, Easter, and Independence Day; Nov.–Feb.—10–4 Mon.–Tues. and Thurs.–Sat., 1–4 Sun.; closed Wed., Nov. 5, Thanksgiving, Dec. 24–26, New Year's Eve, and the first two weeks in Jan. Admission: adults, $8; Girl Scout adults and students 6–20, $7; Girl Scouts 6–18, $6; children under 6, free.

Thurgood Marshall

See Public Officials/Political Figures section.

John Muir

John Muir National Historic Site. John Muir was one of the nation's earliest and most influential naturalists and conservationists. He stimulated interest in conserving and protecting the environment, worked to establish the Sierra Club, and helped save such wilderness areas as Yosemite Valley and Sequoia National Park in the United States. He was a Scottish-born American whose travels, enthusiasm, and writings inspired the public, congressmen, and U.S. presidents to preserve large nature areas in the late 1800s and early 1900s. Muir's home in Martinez, California, is now the John Muir National Historic Site.

John Muir was born in 1838 in Dunbar, East Lothian, Scotland. He was the third of eight children of Daniel Muir and Ann Gilrye Muir. It is believed that his interest in nature may have been a reaction to his strict religious upbringing. His father felt that anything that distracted from Bible studies was frivolous and punishable. The family, which belonged to the Church of Scotland, joined the Disciples of Christ Church when it moved to America because his father did not believe the Scottish Presbyterian church was sufficiently strict in faith and practice. John never became that religious, but he did express deep spiritual feelings in his writings as an adult.

The Muirs immigrated to the United States in 1849 when John was 11. The family settled in a wilderness area near Portage, Wisconsin, where they started a farm called Fountain Lake Farm, which has been designated a National Historic Landmark. In 1860, when he was 22, John worked in a machine shop and enrolled at the University of Wisconsin in Madison, but he never received a degree. He went to college for about two years, during which he was stimulated by geology and botany classes and developed a lifelong interest in chemistry and the sciences.

In 1864 John went to Canada to join a brother. While in Canada, he spent most of his time wondering around the Great Lakes studying plants—and even discovered a new species of orchid. Muir returned to the United States in 1866 and worked as a sawyer in a factory that made wagon wheels. While there he had an accident that changed the course of his life—a tool he was using slipped and struck him in the eye.

Muir was confined to a darkened room for six weeks, lost sight in both eyes for a time, and became concerned about losing his eyesight. When he recovered, he decided to devote himself to botany. He then took a 1,000-mile walk from Louisville, Kentucky, to Savannah, Georgia and was planning to walk through the Southern states and then to South America. But he contracted malaria, and when Muir recovered, he decided to go to California instead of South America.

When he arrived in San Francisco in 1868, Muir went to see Yosemite Valley. He was captivated, calling Yosemite "the grandest of all special temples of Nature." After his eight-day visit, he returned to the Sierra foothills and became a ferry operator, sheepherder, and bronco buster. He spent the summer of 1869 caring for sheep in the Yosemite mountains and exploring the area, which gave him a better idea of how the area developed and the ecosystem functioned. Muir then worked at a Yosemite Valley sawmill, where he developed a water-powered mill and built himself a small cabin.

Muir theorized that glaciers created many aspects of Yosemite Valley and the surrounding area. This was counter to the prevailing theory that the valley was formed by a catastrophic earthquake. In 1871 he discovered an active alpine glacier below Merced Peak, which helped support his theory. Muir then wrote a large number of essays and magazine articles about his geologic findings and ideas that were well received. This was followed by studies of the Yosemite area's flora and fauna and a scientific journal article on the distribution and ecology of giant sequoia along the western slope of the Sierra Mountains.

In 1880 Muir married Louisa Wanda Strentzel, whose parents owned a 2,600-acre ranch and fruit orchards in Martinez, a small town northeast of San Francisco. For the next 10 years, he managed the family ranch. It became very successful, and when he died he left an estate of $250,000. The couple had two daughters. The Muir home and part of the ranch are now the John Muir National Historic Site.

After a decade on the ranch, Muir became concerned about the increasing threats to the Yosemite area and the Sierras. Private parties were claiming ownership in Kings Canyon in the Yosemite area, ancient giant sequoias were being cut down south of present-day Sequoia National Park, and livestock, especially sheep, were damaging grasslands in the Yosemite area and the Sierras. As a result, Muir decided to devote himself to conservation work.

In 1890 Muir wrote two articles in *Century* magazine describing the problem and calling for congressional action. Later that year, Congress passed the bill creating Yosemite National Park, but it left Yosemite Valley in state control. In 1892 Muir helped establish the Sierra Club, a major environmental conservation organization for which he was elected the first president—a position he held for 22 years until his death in 1914.

Largely through the Sierra Club's efforts, Congress transferred the state-controlled Yosemite Valley and Mariposa Grove to the national park in 1905. The actions came after Muir convinced President Theodore Roosevelt during a visit to Yosemite National Park in 1903 that the best way to protect Yosemite Valley was through federal control and management. Muir showed Roosevelt around the park and they camped in the backcountry. He also influenced Roosevelt's setting aside 148 million acres of additional forest reserves, and the establishment of a number of other national parks.

In 1894 Muir published his first book, *The Mountains of California*. Among the other books that followed were *Our National Parks* (1901), *My First Summer in the Sierra* (1911), and *The Yosemite* (1912). In 1896 Muir became good friends with Gifford Pinchot, another leader in the conservation movement. The friendship came to an end and the conservation movement split in 1897 when Pinchot announced support for sheep grazing in forest reserves. Both opposed reckless exploitation of natural resources, but Muir felt resources should be preserved for their spiritual and uplifting values, while Pinchot saw conservation merely as intelligent managing of resources.

John Muir, whose work led to the founding of the national park system in 1916, died of pneumonia in 1914 at the age of 76. His legacy lives on in his many books, which are still widely read, the lands that he helped conserve, and the John Muir National Historic Site, where he lived. In addition to Muir's 14-room Italianate Victorian mansion, carriage house, and orchards, the site includes the newly added Mount Wanda Nature Preserve, consisting of 325 acres of nearby woodlands and grasslands historically owned by the family and named for Muir's wife, Louisa Wanda Strentzel Muir. It is where Muir took frequent walks with his daughters and features the John Muir Nature Trail.

The Muir house was built in 1883 by Dr. John Strentzel, Louisa's father. It was made a national historic site in 1964 and later was designated a National Historic Landmark and listed on the National Register of Historic Places. The house still contains Muir's study and desk where he wrote many of his articles and books on conservation. It also has many Muir personal belongings, specimens he collected, period furnishings, and photographs and portraits of Muir and his family. The site also has a bookstore and offers guided tours, films, lectures, and special events. Annual attendance is 31,000.

John Muir National Historic Site, 4202 Alhambra Ave., Martinez, CA 94553-3826. Phone: 925/228-8860. Fax: 925/228-8192. E-mail: jomu_interpretation@nps.gov. Website: www.nps.gov/jomu. Hours: 10–5 daily; closed New Year's Day, Thanksgiving, and Christmas. Admission: free.

Carrie A. Nation

Carry A. Nation Home Memorial. Carrie Nation was a radical member of the temperance movement known for using a hatchet to wreck saloons serving alcohol during the preprohibition days. She began her crusade after marrying an alcoholic, starting a branch of the Women's Christian Temperance Union, leading a group of women to sing hymns and pray in bars, and then attacking the saloons with rocks and later a hatchet after having a vision that told her to destroy the alcohol stock of saloons. Her home in Medicine Lodge, Kansas, is now a historic house museum called the Carry A. Nation House Memorial (she spelled her first name at various times as Carry and Carrie).

Carrie Nation was born as Carrie Amelia Moore in Garrard County, Kentucky, in 1846 to George and Mary Campbell Moore, who were slave owners. During much of her early life, she had poor health and only informal learning. Her family also had financial difficulties and moved several times before settling in Belton, Missouri. A number of members of the family suffered from mental illnesses, and her mother experienced delusions at times. Carrie often sought refuge in the slave quarters.

During the Civil War, the Moore family moved several times. They returned to a farm in Cass County, Missouri, and then moved to Kansas City when the Union Army ordered them to evacuate the farm. After a Confederate raid in nearby Independence, Missouri, Carrie nursed wounded soldiers. In 1865 she met Dr. Charles Gloyd, a young physician who had served in the Union Army. They were married in 1867 but separated shortly before the birth of their daughter, Charlien, in 1868. Gloyd died of alcoholism the following year, and Carrie began considering ways to eliminate liquor.

With proceeds from her husband's estate and the sale of land she received from her father, Carrie built a small house in Holden, Missouri, and moved there with her daughter and mother-in-law. She enrolled at the Normal Institute in Warrensburg, Missouri, and received a teaching certificate in 1872. She then taught school in Holden for four years. In 1874 she married David A. Nation, an attorney, minister, and newspaperman, who also had a daughter, Lola.

They bought a 1,700-acre cotton plantation in Brazoria County, Texas, but it turned out to be an unsuccessful venture since neither knew anything about farming. As a result, Nation practiced law in Brazoria and Carrie moved to Columbia (with the two daughters and Carrie's first mother-in-law) to operate a hotel. They all got together again in Richmond, Texas, where Carrie managed a hotel. In 1889 the family moved to Medicine Lodge, Kansas. Nation worked as a preacher in a Christian church and Carrie ran a hotel.

It was in Medicine Lodge that Carrie started a branch of the Woman's Christian Temperance Union and began campaigning for the enforcement of Kansas's ban on the sale of liquor. It started with simple protests and escalated to the singing of hymns accompanied by a hand organ, praying, and pointed remarks. Carrie then had a heavenly vision which she said told her to destroy the alcohol stock of saloons. She began smashing liquor bottles in saloons with rocks and switched to a hatchet after a raid in Wichita when her husband jokingly said she should use a hatchet the next time for maximum damage. She thought that was an excellent idea and did so. It did not prevent the couple from divorcing in 1901.

Carrie then intensified her anti-alcohol campaign and took it to nearby states. She alone or accompanied by a hymn-singing woman would march into a bar and sing and pray while breaking bar fixtures and stock with a hatchet. She was arrested more than 30 times between 1900 and 1910 and paid her fines from lecture fees and sales of photographs and miniature souvenir hatchets. The hatchet raids received nationwide attention. She also published a newspaper and a biweekly newsletter. Later in life, she exploited her name by appearing in vaudeville in the United States and music halls in Great Britain.

Carrie moved to Eureka Springs, Arkansas, near the end of her life. She founded the home known as Hatchet Hall. And while giving a speech in a Eureka Springs park in 1911, she collapsed and died later in a hospital in Leavenworth, Kansas. She was buried in an unmarked grave in the Belton City Cemetery in Missouri, but the Woman's Christian Temperance Union later erected a stone with an inscription that said, "Faithful to the Cause of Prohibition. She Hath Done What She Could."

The WCTU also bought her home in Medicine Lodge in 1950, which is now operated as a historic house museum in her honor by the city. Carrie lived in the house from 1889 to 1902, then sold it and used the proceeds to open a home in Kansas City for the wives of drunkards. Carrie's brick house in Medicine Lodge has been designated a National Historic Landmark and is listed in the National Register of Historic Places. It contains such items as her pump organ, suitcase, bed, dresser, valise, hat, purse, a hatchet, and several of her souvenir hatchets. The museum is entered through the adjacent Medicine Lodge Stockade Museum. Annual attendance is 500.

Carry A. Nation House Memorial, 209 W. Fowler Ave., Medicine Lodge, KS 67104-1536 (postal address: 104 Lisa Circle, Medicine Lodge, KS 67104-1605). Phone: 620/886-3553. Hours: May–Oct.—10:30–5 daily; Nov.–Apr.—1–4 daily; closed major holidays. Admission: adults, $5; seniors, $4; children 8–16, $3; children under 8, free.

Willie Nelson

See Musicians/Singers/Composers section.

Rosa Parks

Rosa Parks Library and Museum. Rosa Parks is credited with having started the African American civil rights movement in 1955 by refusing to give up her seat on a Montgomery, Alabama, bus to a white man. She was not the first black to resist bus segregation, but the National Association for the Advancement of Colored People believed she was the best candidate for a court challenge after her arrest for civil disobedience. The action initiated the heralded Montgomery bus boycott, which lasted 382 days and resulted in a U.S. Supreme Court decision that outlawed racial segregation on public transportation and overturned her conviction. The story is now told as part of the Rosa Parks Library and Museum on the Montgomery campus of Troy University.

Rosa Parks was born Rosa Louise McCauley in Tuskegee, Alabama, in 1913 to James and Leona Edwards McCauley. Her father was a carpenter and her mother a teacher. She suffered from poor health as a child, with chronic tonsillitis. When her parents separated, she moved with her mother and younger brother to her maternal grandparents' farm in Pine Level, near Montgomery, where she began her lifelong membership in the African Methodist Episcopal Church. Rosa attended rural schools until she was 11, when she enrolled at the Industrial School for Girls in Montgomery. She then went to a laboratory school established by the Alabama State Teachers College for Negroes, until she dropped out to take care of her ill grandmother and later her mother.

At the turn of the century, southern states adopted new constitutions and election laws that largely disenfranchised black voters—and also poor white voters in Alabama. Under the Jim Crow laws, racial segregation also was imposed in public transportation, retail stores, and other public facilities. Buses and trains had separate seating sections for blacks and whites, and there was no school bus transportation for African Americans. Black students had to walk to school, and their education was always underfunded.

In 1932 Rosa married Raymond Parks, a Montgomery barber. At her husband's urging, she finished high school in 1933 at a time when less than 7 percent of African Americans had a high school diploma. She also managed to register to vote on her third try, despite the antiblack laws and discrimination by election officials. Rosa worked in a variety of jobs, ranging from domestic worker to hospital aide. She and her husband also joined the local chapter of the National Association for the Advancement of Colored People and worked for many years to improve circumstances for African Americans. In 1943 she became secretary to Edgar Nixon, president of the Montgomery chapter of the NAACP.

In 1955 a politically liberal white couple for whom she worked as a housekeeper and seamstress sponsored her attendance at the Highlander Folk School, an education center for workers' rights and racial equality in Monteagle, Tennessee. That same year she attended a mass meeting in Montgomery following the murder of Emmett Till, a 15-year-old black boy from Chicago who was killed when he violated local discrimination rules—and shortly after activists George W. Lee and Lamar Smith were killed.

On December 1, 1955, after Rosa Parks had worked all day, she boarded a bus in downtown Montgomery and sat in the back section reserved for blacks. When she was told by the bus driver to give up her seat to a white man because the white section up front was full, she refused and was arrested, found guilty, and fined. This led to the formation of the Montgomery Improvement Association and a boycott of the city-owned buses, led by Dr. Martin Luther King Jr., the young pastor of the Dexter Avenue Baptist Church.

The NAACP threw its support behind efforts to overturn the discriminatory laws and the Parks conviction on constitutional grounds, and the U.S. Supreme Court agreed. The court struck down the Montgomery ordinance under which Parks was fined and outlawed racial segregation on public transportation.

Rosa and Raymond Parks moved to Detroit in 1957, and she joined the staff of Congressman John Conyers. The Southern Christian Leadership Conference also established an annual Rosa Parks Freedom Award in her honor. After her husband died in 1977, she founded the Rosa and Raymond Parks Institute for Self-Determination, which takes young people across the country on bus tours to learn more about the history of the nation and the civil rights movement.

Rosa Parks died in 2005 of natural causes in Detroit at the age of 92, and her casket was placed in the rotunda of the United States Capitol in Washington for two days—being the only woman and the second African American to lie in state at the Capitol. She received many honors, including the NAACP's Spingarn Award, Martin Luther King Jr. Award, and two dozen honorary degrees, as well as the Presidential Medal of Freedom in 1998 and Congressional Gold Medal in 1999.

The Rosa Parks Library and Museum, which was founded in 2000 on the Troy University campus in Montgomery, tells of her life and the civil rights movement. It occupies 7,000 square feet on the first floor of a three-story building that includes the university's Montgomery library. It is located at the spot that gave birth to the 1955 Montgomery bus boycott. An introductory film depicts the plight of African Americans during the segregation period. It leads to a reconstructed street corner containing a replica of the bus on which Rosa Parks was arrested for refusing to give up her seat. Visitors hear about Parks's experience and the personal testimonials of many participants in the bus boycott.

The museum also has six exhibit areas devoted to Parks and the civil rights movement. Among the objects on display are a 1955 station wagon that represents the Rolling Church bus used in the boycott and such historical items as the fingerprint machine and police report from when Parks was arrested and reports on others who were persecuted or injured during the boycott.

The museum has a children's wing, which features an exaggerated version of a 1955 Montgomery bus that functions as a time machine. It shows scenes ranging from waiting for a Montgomery bus in 1955 to segregation and the social and legal challenges. In addition, the second floor has a research center where visitors can learn more about the legal and social challenges that helped bring about changes in discrimination and segregation in the twentieth century. The museum's annual attendance is 50,000.

Rosa Parks Library and Museum, Troy State University, 252 Montgomery St., Montgomery, AL 36104-3527. Phones: 334/241-8661 and 334/241-8615. Fax: 334/241-5435. Website: www.montgomery.troy.edu/rosaparks/museum. Hours: 9–5 Mon.–Fri., 9–3 Sat.; closed Sun. and major holidays. Admission: Adults and children over 12, $7.50; children under 13, $5.50.

Paul Robeson

See Musicians/Singers/Composers section.

Anne Spencer

See Poets section.

Elizabeth Cady Stanton

Elizabeth Cady Stanton House. Elizabeth Cady Stanton was a social activist, abolitionist, and leading figure in the women's rights movement in the nineteenth century. She is best known for initiating the first organized women's rights and suffrage effort in the United States, but she also worked to free slaves, support the temperance movement, and furthered such other women's concerns as parental, custody, property, employment, and income rights, as well as divorce laws, birth control, and economic health of the family. Her home in Seneca Falls, New York, is now the Elizabeth Cady Stanton House, a historic house museum that is part of the Women's Rights National Historical Park.

Stanton was born in Johnstown, New York, in 1815. She was the eighth of 11 children born to Daniel Cady and Margaret Livingston Cady. Five of her siblings died in infancy or early childhood, and her eldest brother, Eleazar, died at the age of 20. Her father was a prominent Federalist attorney and served one term as a congressman and later became a circuit court judge and then a New York supreme court judge. It was her father and her brother-in-law, Edward Bayard, who led her into a life of legal and social activism. She enjoyed exploring her father's law library and debating legal issues with his law clerks. It also was this early exposure to law that showed her how the law favored men over women, especially married women. Women had virtually no property, income, employment, or custody rights over children.

Elizabeth's mother was the daughter of Colonel James Livingston, an officer in the Continental Army in the American Revolution. She was unusually tall for her time and had a commanding presence but was depressed by the death of six of her children. Elizabeth's father, who also was affected by the loss of the children, especially the oldest son, immersed himself in his work. As a result, many of the child-rearing responsibilities fell to Elizabeth's oldest sister, Tryphena, and her husband, Edward Bayard, the son of a U.S. senator and an apprentice in her father's law office. He was instrumental in furthering Elizabeth's understanding of the explicit and implicit gender differences in the legal system.

Elizabeth also was exposed to slavery at an early age. Like many men at the time, her father was a slaveholder. He had at least one slave, Peter Teabout. One of Teabout's responsibilities was looking after Elizabeth and her sister, Margaret. Elizabeth, who enjoyed his company as a young girl, was born in 1815, and slavery did not end in New York State until 1827 and in the nation until the Civil War. She learned about the abolitionist movement during visits with her cousin, Gerri Smith, in Peterboro, New York, and soon developed strong sentiments about the freeing of slaves.

Elizabeth attended the coeducational Johnstown Academy until she was 16. She studied such subjects as Latin, Greek, mathematics, religion, science, French, and writing and won several academic awards, including for Greek language. In 1830 she enrolled at the Troy Female Seminary (later renamed the Emma Willard School for the founder) in Troy, New York. During her early involvement in the temperance and abolition movements, she met Henry Brewster Stanton, a journalist, antislavery orator, and acquaintance of Elizabeth's cousin, Gerrit Smith.

Smith had become an abolitionist and one of the "Secret Six" funders of John Brown's raid at Harpers Ferry. Elizabeth and Henry married in 1840 and went to Europe for their honeymoon.

When they returned, the Stantons lived in the Cady home in Johnstown, and Henry studied law with his father-in-law until 1843. The Stantons then moved to Boston, and Henry joined a law firm. They became active in the abolitionist movement and associated with such abolition figures as Frederick Douglass, William Lloyd Garrison, Louisa May Alcott, and Ralph Waldo Emerson. However, the couple did not always agree on everything. Henry, like Elizabeth's father, opposed female suffrage, and they tended to live apart rather than together on certain issues. But both considered their marriage a success, and the marriage lasted for 47 years until Henry died in 1887.

In 1847 the Stantons moved to Seneca Falls, New York, on the northern end of Cayuga Lake in upstate New York because of the effect of New England's winters on Henry's fragile health. The house was deeded to them by Elizabeth's father. There they had the last four of their seven children and lived until 1862, when the family moved to New York City.

Although she enjoyed motherhood and had become involved in community activities, Elizabeth felt the need for intellectual companionship and stimulation. It was in the summer of 1848 when she again met Lucretia Mott, a Quaker minister, feminist, and abolitionist, at the home of Jane Hunt, a fellow Quaker in Seneca Falls. Elizabeth and Mott initially became acquainted in London during the Stantons' honeymoon in 1840.

Both were attending the World Anti-Slavery Convention, where Henry Stanton and Mott were delegates and Elizabeth accompanied her husband. Mott and Elizabeth became friends when the male delegates voted against having the women delegates participate in the proceedings, and women were required to sit in a roped-off section hidden from the view of the male attendees. Mott was so upset that she discussed with Elizabeth the need for a convention on women's rights, but no action was taken at the time.

This time, Mott and Stanton acted. They organized the first women's rights convention with Mott's sister, Martha Coffin Wright, Mary Ann McClintock, and a few other Seneca Falls women. The convention was held in Seneca Falls and attended by about 300 women and 40 men on July 19 and 20 in 1848. Stanton drafted and read a "Declaration of Sentiments" that was modeled after the nation's Declaration of Independence. It proclaimed that men and women were created equal and made a number of proposals, including voting rights for women. The resolution was passed after supporting remarks by Frederick Douglass, who attended and spoke informally at the convention.

Stanton, who was gaining a reputation as an activist and reformer, was invited to speak at a second women's rights convention—the first National Women's Rights Convention—in 1850. She accepted but because of pregnancy decided to lend her name as a sponsor and have the speech read for her.

In 1851 Stanton met Susan B. Anthony, who was visiting Seneca Falls. It began a friendship and working relationship that lasted the rest of their lives. They are best known for their joint work on behalf of women's suffrage, but they initially cooperated in the temperance movement. They were instrumental in founding the short-lived Woman's State Temperance Society in 1852. Stanton became president and shocked many supporters by saying drunkenness should be made sufficient cause for divorce. The society folded after its second year, as Stanton and Anthony shifted their interests to female suffrage and women's rights.

Anthony and Stanton complemented each other. Anthony was single, had no children, and had the time and energy to travel and do the speaking, while Stanton, who was a better speaker and writer, was married, had children, was limited in travel, and was effective in scripting many of Anthony's speeches. Anthony became the organizer and tactician, while Stanton was better at crystallizing and expressing the issues. Later, when her children were older, Stanton spent much of her time writing and speaking in promoting women's suffrage. During the Civil War, she also worked to free the slaves as an abolitionist.

Stanton fought for women's rights in many states and ways. She even ran unsuccessfully for Congress from New York in 1868. She and Anthony also broke with their abolitionist allies when they opposed the ratification of the 14th and 15th Amendments to the U.S. Constitution, which defined citizenship and granted African American men the right to vote after the war. They argued that the amendments also should give black women—and hopefully all women—the right to vote. They were joined by Sojourner Truth, a leading feminist former slave, in opposing the amendments unless it included women. But black leader Frederick Douglass supported the amendments.

The proposed "all or nothing" approach caused a major schism in the women's rights movement. It gave rise to two separate women's suffrage organizations—the National Woman Suffrage Association, founded in 1869 by Anthony and Stanton (for which Stanton served as president for 21 years), and the American Woman Suffrage Association, established later in 1869 by Lucy Stone, Elizabeth Blackwell, and Julia Ward Howe, who supported the amendments.

While the latter focused only on voter rights, Stanton voiced support for such other issues as gender-neutral divorce laws, overcoming religious sexism, a woman's right to refuse her husband sexually, the right of women to serve on juries, interracial marriage, and increased economic opportunities. The two suffrage associations finally merged in 1890, with Stanton becoming the president, largely as a result of Anthony's efforts.

Stanton also wrote some of the most influential books, documents, and speeches on the woman's rights movement, such as the two-part *The Woman's Bible* (1895 and 1898), *Eighty Years & More: Reminiscences 1815–1897* (1898), and *The Solitude of Self* (first delivered as a presentation at a congressional suffrage hearing in 1892). She also co-authored with Anthony and Matilda Joslyn Gage the first three volumes of the six-volume *History of Woman Suffrage* (1884–1887). In 1868 Stanton, Anthony, and Parker Pittsbury, a leading male feminist at the time, also began publishing a militant weekly newspaper, *The Revolution*, which featured editorials by Stanton on a wide range of women's issues.

Stanton died of heart failure at the age of 86 in 1902—18 years before women were granted the right to vote in the United States. She is regarded as one of the major driving forces in obtaining equal rights for women in the United States and many parts of the world. A statue of Stanton, Anthony, and Mott is now housed in the U.S. Capitol in Washington.

The Elizabeth Cady Stanton House, where the Stanton family lived in Seneca Falls, New York, from 1847 to 1862, is now a restored historic house museum that is part of the Women's Right National Historical Park. It is a National Historic Landmark and listed on the National Register of Historic Places. The 6.8-acre park, which was established in 1980, consists of four historic buildings, a visitor center, and an educational and cultural center, which houses the Suffrage Press Printshop.

In addition to the Stanton House, the historic properties include the Wesley Chapel, where the first women's rights convention was held in 1848, and two other historic houses of women involved in the suffrage convention—the Hunt House, where the historic convention was initiated, and the McClintock House, where the women's convention was planned. The latter two houses are located in nearby Waterloo. The National Women's Hall of Fame, which is not part of the national historical park, also is located in Seneca Falls.

The Stanton House is a large farmhouse that has been restored and offers ranger-guided tours (11:15 and 2:15 daily). The park's visitor center contains exhibits that trace the women's rights movement through the 1990s and features a film, *Dreams of Equality*, and a statue exhibit, titled "The First Wave," which depicts the planners of the first women's rights convention.

Elizabeth Cady Stanton House, Women's Rights National Historical Park, 32 Washington St., Seneca Falls, NY 13148 (postal address: Women's Rights National Historical Park, 136 Fall St., Seneca Falls, NY, 13148). Phones: 315/568-2991 and 315/568-0024. Fax: 315/568-2141. Website: www.nps.gov/wori. Hours: grounds—sunrise–sunset daily; visitor center—9–5 daily; Stanton House—9–5 daily; closed New Year's Day, Thanksgiving, and Christmas. Admission: free.

Harriet Tubman

Harriet Tubman Home. Harriet Tubman was an escaped slave who became an African American abolitionist, humanitarian, and Union armed scout and spy during the Civil War. She is best remembered for her 13 missions to rescue more than 70 slaves using the Underground Railroad. She also helped John Brown recruit men for his raid on Harpers Ferry and later founded a home for elderly blacks and worked to achieve women's suffrage.

Tubman's home in Auburn, New York, is now a historic house museum, and the Harriet Tubman Museum in Cambridge, Maryland, near her birthplace, is devoted to her life (*see* separate listing). In 2013 the site in Dorchester County where she was born and escaped from slavery to help other slaves to freedom was made a national monument—the Harriet Tubman Underground Railroad National Monument—by President Barack Obama

Harriet Tubman was born as a slave named Araminta Harriet Ross in 1820. Her parents were Ben and Harriet Green Ross. Her mother was owned by Mary Pattison Brodess, and later by her son, Edward, while her father was held by Anthony Thompson, who became Brodess's second husband. Her mother served as a cook, while her father was a skilled woodsman who managed the timber on the plantation.

The Thompsons were married around 1808 and had nine children. They had difficulty in keeping the family together. After three of the daughters were sold off by Edward Brodess, Harriet's mother told the plantation owner and a trader who had come to the slave quarters to buy her youngest son that she would "split your head open" if the boy was taken. Brodess canceled the sale, and the incident influenced the family's thinking about future resistance.

Harriet was only five or six years old when she was hired out as a nursemaid and to keep watch of a baby as it slept. If the child awoke and cried, Harriet was whipped, sometimes as much as five times a night. She also worked for a planter, checking muskrat traps in nearby marshes, even after contracting measles. As she got older, she was assigned to such work as plowing, driving oxen, and hauling logs. One day, she was hit in the head accidentally when an overseer threw a two-pound weight at a fleeing slave and missed. It caused permanent damage, resulting in seizures and unconsciousness without warning, a condition she suffered for the rest of her life.

In about 1844, Harried married John Tubman, a free black man, and changed her birth name to Harriet Tubman. But she still legally remained a slave under such free and enslaved marriages. In 1849 Harriet became ill again, and Edward Brodess tried to sell her. He could not find a buyer. She also began praying for him to change his ways, and then for his death. A week later, Brodess died. As his widow planned to sell the slaves to settle the estate, Tubman and two brothers, Ben and Henry, escaped from a plantation where they were hired out. After a runaway reward of $100 for each was posted, the brothers decided to return and forced Harriet also to come back.

Tubman then ran away again, leaving behind her husband and Ross family members. For her escape, she used the Underground Railroad—an informal network of free and enslaved blacks, white abolitionists, and other activists who helped the runaways to reach freedom in the North. It is believed that she went from Maryland through Delaware to Philadelphia with help of members of the Religious Society of Friends, known as Quakers.

After finding work in Philadelphia, Tubman began thinking about helping her husband, parents, brothers, and sisters to escape—despite the 1850 passage of the Fugitive Slave Law by Congress, which required all states to assist in the capture and return of runaway slaves. But when some of her relatives were going to be sold, she returned to Maryland and rescued her family with the assistance of antislavery activists and safe houses along the Underground Railroad. Her husband, John Tubman, had remarried and decided not to join her. He and his new wife, Caroline, raised a family together until he was killed 16 years later in an argument with a white man.

Harriet Tubman became a "conductor" on the Underground Railroad as she made numerous trips to free others out of slavery. A bounty was placed on her head as she made at least 13 rescue trips to take more than 70 slaves to freedom in Northern states and Canada, which prohibited slavery. She eluded bounty hunters who were being offered as much as $40,000 for her capture. No one ever betrayed her, and she never lost a fugitive. Because of her success, she was called "Moses" by abolitionist William Lloyd Garrison.

Tubman, who settled in Auburn, New York, also helped John Brown recruit men for the 1859 Harpers Ferry armory/arsenal raid and was invited to accompany him on the raid. It is said she planned to be present but was ill at the time. During the Civil War, she served as a Union scout, spy, and nurse. She made a number of scouting and spying trips in rebel territory, identifying locations of ammunition depots, cotton warehouses, and where slaves were waiting to be freed. She even guided an armed expedition that liberated over 700 slaves in the Combahee River area of South Carolina. In addition, she worked for three years as a nurse, caring for white and black soldiers who were ill or wounded.

After the war, Tubman cared for her parents and other needy relatives at her Auburn home and then turned her residence into the Home for Indigent and Aged Negroes. She also donated land to the African Methodist Episcopal Zion Church to establish a home for black elderly and indigent people, called the Harriet Tubman Home for the Aged.

In 1869 Tubman married Nelson Davis, a local bricklayer who was a Civil War veteran. She also became active in the women's suffrage movement and gave the keynote address at the first meeting of the National Association of Colored Women in Washington in 1896. She died of pneumonia in 1913 when she was believed to be 93.

Tubman's house in Auburn, New York, is now the Harriet Tubman Home, a historic house museum. She moved to the outskirts of Auburn in 1857 after a friend, William H. Seward, who later became a U.S. senator, provided her with a two-story brick house, which he then sold to her at a modest price. When the 25-acre site was auctioned in 1896, Tubman bought the land for $1,480. Unable to raise sufficient funds on her own to build a house, she deeded the property to the African Methodist Episcopal Zion Church in 1903.

The church built the frame house that became Tubman's home in 1908. Twelve to 15 people lived in the house during the remaining years of Tubman's life. After being vacant from 1928 until 1944, the AME Zion Church raised the funds to restore the house and open it as a memorial to Tubman's life and work. Since then, a library and a large assembly hall have been constructed by the church on the site. The resident manager of the Tubman home now lives in the old brick house. The Harriet Tubman Home contains some of her original furniture and personal items. Special events commemorating Tubman also are held every Memorial Day weekend.

Harriet Tubman Home, 180 South St., Auburn, NY 13301-5636. Phone: 315/252-2081. E-mail: khill@harriethouse. org. Website: www.harriethouse.org. Hours: 12–4 Tues.–Fri., 10–3 Sat.; closed Sun.–Mon. and major holidays. Admission: adults, $4.50; seniors, $3; children 6–17, $1.50.

Harriet Tubman Museum. The Harriet Tubman Museum in Cambridge, Maryland, is devoted to the life and accomplishments of the celebrated former slave, who was born and spent her early years in the county. Tubman became known for helping to free other slaves through the Underground Railroad in the middle of the nineteenth century. The storefront museum has exhibits and programs on her life and offers tours of places in Dorchester County where Tubman once lived and worked as a slave. The museum also is known as the Harriet Tubman Organization and Education Center.

Harriet Tubman Museum, 424 Race St., Cambridge, MD 21613. Phones: 410/228-0401 and 410/228-3106. Fax: 410/228-5641. E-mail: wajjrchoptank@comcast.net. Website: www.harriettubmanorganization.org. Hours: 10–3 Tues.–Fri., 12–4 Sat.; closed Sun.–Mon. and major holidays. Admission: donation.

Tubman African American Museum. The Tubman African American Museum in Macon, Georgia, is named in honor of Harriet Tubman, who was known as the "Moses of her people" for her role in freeing slaves through the Underground Railroad in the mid-1800s. The museum, founded in 1981, has become the largest museum in the Southeast devoted to African American history, art, and culture.

The museum has permanent exhibits on such subjects as Middle Georgia history, African American folk art, and black inventors, and offers special exhibitions on other aspects of African American history, art, and culture. The objective is to document the history of black art and artists, confront and explore cultural assumptions, and provide opportunities for intellectual, social, and civic engagement between the museum and the diverse community it serves.

The museum also has a history and art collection, children's art classes, history and art outreach programs, teacher and student workshops, summer heritage camps, a computer learning center, and such special events as a weeklong Pan African Festival. Annual attendance is 57,000.

Tubman African American Museum, 340 Walnut St., Macon, GA 31201-0515 (postal address: PO Box 6671, Macon, GA 31201-6671). Phone: 478/743-8544. Fax: 478/743-9063. E-mail: guestservices@tubmanmuseum.com. Website: tubmanmuseum.com. Hours: 9–5 Tues.–Fri., 11–5 Sat.; closed Sun.–Mon., New Year's Day, Memorial Day, Independence Day, Thanksgiving, and Christmas. Admission: adults, $8; seniors, $6; military and college students, $5; children 3–17, $4; children under 3, free.

Ida B. Wells-Barnett

Ida B. Wells-Barnett Museum. Ida B. Wells was an African American journalist, activist, and early leader in the civil rights movement. She also was involved in the women's rights and suffrage movements, founded several women's organizations, spearheaded an antilynching campaign, and was one of the most fearless and articulate women of her time. Her life is now the focus of the Ida B. Wells-Barnett Museum in her hometown of Holly Springs, Mississippi.

Wells was born in Holly Springs in 1862—just before President Abraham Lincoln issued the Emancipation Proclamation. Her parents were James Wells, a carpenter, and Elizabeth Warrenton Wells, a cook in the Bolling household. They were slaves until freed by Lincoln's proclamation. It was a religious and strict family that wanted their children to have a good education. Ida attended a school for freed people called Shaw University (now Rust College) in Holly Springs until she was suspended for rebellious behavior and temper after confronting the college president.

In 1878, when she was 16, she lost both of her parents and a 10-month-old brother in a yellow fever epidemic. Ida dropped out of school and worked as a teacher in a black elementary school to keep the remaining six children together, while her grandmother and other relatives and friends cared for the siblings. She resented that white teachers were being paid $80 a month while she was receiving only $30 per month. As a result of the discrimination, she became more interested in politics and improving the education of blacks.

In 1883 Wells took three of her younger siblings to Memphis to live with her aunt and closer to relatives. When she found out she could earn more teaching there, she moved to Memphis and taught in Woodstock for the Shelby County school system. During the summers, she attended Fisk University in Nashville and also took classes at the LeMoyne Institute.

In 1884 she experienced what Rosa Parks went through 71 years later when a Chesapeake and Ohio Railroad conductor told Wells to give up her seat on the train to a white passenger and move to a smoking car. When she refused, the conductor and two men dragged her out of the car. She sued and won the 1884 case, but it was reversed and she was ordered to pay court costs.

Shortly thereafter, Wells accepted an offer to join the editorial staff of the *Memphis Evening Star* and wrote weekly articles for the *Living Way* weekly newspaper, using a pen name. She soon became known for writing about racial issues In 1889 she became co-owner and editor of an antisegregationist newspaper called *Free Speech and Headlight*, which published articles about racial injustices.

Racial tensions were rising in Memphis in 1892 when three of her black friends who started a successful grocery across the street from a white-owned grocery were lynched by a white mob after their store was attacked. In the raid, three white men were wounded by gunshots, and the three store blacks were jailed. A large white mob then stormed the jail and killed the African Americans. The death of the three men caused her to write in her newspaper that blacks should leave Memphis, and over 6,000 did and others boycotted white-owned businesses. After she was threatened, Wells bought a pistol, which she never had to use.

After the murders, Wells began an investigation of lynchings and their causes and published her findings, gave talks on the subject, and launched an antilynching campaign. She found that blacks were lynched primarily for not paying debts, competing with whites economically, not giving way to whites, and being drunk in public—and not mainly for sexually attacking white women, as believed.

When she was away in Philadelphia three months after the lynching of her three friends, a mob responded to her controversial articles by destroying her *Free Speech and Headlight* offices. As a result, Wells went to New York City, where she continued to write antilynching articles in the *New York Age* newspaper, give speeches on the subject, and organize a black boycott of the 1893 World's Columbian Exposition in Chicago with Frederick Douglass and other black leaders for not working with the black community to develop an exhibit on black life.

She then decided to move to Chicago, where she went to work for the *Chicago Conservator*, the oldest African American newspaper in the city. In 1895 she married the editor of the paper, Ferdinand L. Barnett. She was one of the first married American women to keep her own last name along with her husband's. The couple had four children, and she gave up the newspaper job after the second child.

Wells continued her antilynching campaign and became active in women's rights and suffrage efforts. In 1892 she published a pamphlet, *Southern Horrors: Lynch Law in All Its Phases*, followed by *A Red Record*, which described lynching in the United States since the Emancipation Proclamation.

Wells even took her antilynching campaign to Europe in 1893 and 1894, which resulted in the formation of the British Anti-Lynching Committee. The committee included such notables as the archbishop of Canterbury, the Duke of Argyll, members of Parliament, and the editors of the *Manchester Guardian*. Wells also became the first black woman to be a paid correspondent for a mainstream newspaper when she was hired by William Penn Nixon, editor of Chicago's *Daily Inter-Ocean*, to write about her European trip in 1894.

Wells founded a number of important African American organizations in the United States. They included the National Association of Colored Women, National Afro-American Council, and Women's Era Club, the first civic organization for African American women.

After traveling in Great Britain and the United States lecturing and teaching about the lynching problem, she spent the last 30 years of her life working on urban reform and trying to improve conditions for Chicago's rapidly growing black population. In what was called the Great Migration, people were starting to move from the South to northern industrial cities. Social tensions were increasing because of competition with rural immigrants from Europe. It was in Chicago in 1931 that she died of uremia at the age of 68.

The Ida B. Wells-Barnett Museum was founded in Holly Springs, Mississippi, in 1996 to honor the African American journalist/activist and to inspire and enrich the lives of Mississippians by sharing the history, art, and culture of Africans and African Americans. The museum is located in the Spires Bolling House, a Greek revival–style house that is one of the city's best-preserved antebellum homes.

Wells's father worked as a carpenter on the construction of the house, and Ida was born in 1862 on the grounds of the site. The museum features works by African and African American artists, including Dr. David Stratmon's 1948–1978 African art collection, and has exhibits and collections on black history and culture. Annual attendance is 13,500.

Ida B. Wells-Barnett Museum, 220 N. Randolph St., Holly Springs, MS 38635-2412 (postal address: PO Box 5033, Holly Springs, MS 38635-5033). Phone and fax: 662/252-3232. Website: www.idabwells.org. Hours: 10–5 Mon.–Fri., 12–5 Sat.; closed Sun., New Year's Day, Easter, Thanksgiving, and Christmas. Admission: adults: $4; children under 13, $3.

Frances Willard

Frances Willard House Museum. Frances Willard was a nineteenth-century educator, temperance reformer, and women's suffragist who was instrumental in the passage of the 18th Amendment on prohibition and 19th Amendment on women's suffrage in the U.S. Constitution. She also worked to provide federal aid to education, free school lunches, unions for workers, eight-hour work days, work relief for the poor, protection against child abuse, strong antirape laws, prison reform, local sanitation and health boards, and national transportation. The Frances Willard

House Museum in Evanston, Illinois, was her longtime home and the headquarters of the Woman's Christian Temperance Union.

Frances Elizabeth Caroline Willard was born in 1839 in Churchville, New York, to Joseph Flint Willard and Mary Thompson Hill Willard. She was one of four children, one of whom had died the previous year. Her father was a farmer, naturalist, and legislator, and her mother was a teacher. The family spent most of Frances's childhood in Janesville, Wisconsin, where it converted from Congregationalism to Methodism, which placed emphasis on social justice and service to the world. Frances had three years of education at Milwaukee Normal Institute when the Willard family moved to Illinois in 1858 so that Frances and her sister, Mary, could attend college and their brother, Oliver, could enroll at the Garrett Biblical Institute.

Frances Willard attended North Western Female College in Evanston, Illinois, and became a teacher. She held several teaching positions before becoming involved in the 1869 founding of the Evanston College for Ladies and then served as president in 1871–1873. She became the first dean of women at Northwestern University's Women's College when the Evanston College for Ladies merged with Northwestern in 1873. But she resigned in 1874 after confrontations with President Charles Henry Fowler over governance of the Women's College. She previously was engaged to Fowler.

In 1874 Willard participated in the founding of the Woman's Christian Temperance Union and was elected the first corresponding secretary and president of the Chicago WCTU chapter. She spent 50 days on an East Coast speaking tour that year. In 1879 she became president of the national WCTU, a position she held until her death in 1898, and gave an average of 400 lectures a year while traveling 30,000 miles annually over a 10-year period.

She also conducted prayer groups on streets and in saloons and founded WCTU's *The Union Signal* magazine, for which she served as editor in 1892–1898. In addition, she was the first president of the National Council of Women of the United States in 1888–1890 and president of the World's Christian Temperance Union in 1891–1898.

Willard used "home protection" as one of the arguments for female suffrage, saying it is one way for women to protect their homes from the devastation caused by the legalized traffic in alcohol. She also assisted in organizing the Prohibition Party in 1882 and circulated a petition against the international drug trade in 1883. In her later years, she became a socialist and called for government ownership and control of all factories, railroads, and theaters.

Willard died of influenza in New York City while preparing to sail to England and France for a visit. She was 58 years old. She was the first woman to be represented among America's leaders in Statuary Hall in the U.S. Capitol. On the 50th anniversary of her election as WCTU president, the National Women's Christian Temperance Union also commissioned a *Frances Elizabeth Willard* relief by Lorado Taft that is in the Indiana Statehouse in Indianapolis.

Willard bequeathed her Evanston home to the WCTU. It was founded as a historic house museum in 1900 and was designated a National Historic Landmark in 1965 and is listed on the National Register of Historic Places. The house's Gothic revival–style south half was built in 1865 by Willard's father and enlarged in 1878. It has a collection of original furnishings and objects, including furniture, artworks, textiles, costumes, family photographs, books, and Willard's bicycle. Guided tours are offered from 1 to 4 p.m. on the first and third Sundays of every month.

A two-story memorial library and archives was added in 1940 to the WCTU's 1922 administration building, located behind the house. It contains such historical items as letters, documents, images, serial publications, and scrapbooks. The museum's annual attendance is 400.

Frances Willard House Museum, 1730 Chicago Ave., Evanston, IL 60201-4502. Phone and fax: 847/38-7500. E-mail: info@franceswillardhouse.org. Website: www.franceswillardhouse.org. Hours: guided tours—1–4 first and third Sun. of every month and by appointment; closed Mon.–Sat. and holidays. Admission: guide tours—adults, $10; children under 13, $5.

SOCIALITES

Margaret Brown

Molly Brown House Museum. Margaret Tobin Brown was a Colorado socialite, philanthropist, and activist who survived the 1912 sinking of the RMS *Titanic* and later became famous as "The Unsinkable Molly Brown" as a result of a Broadway play and a Hollywood movie that were largely based on her experiences at the time. After the *Titanic* struck an iceberg and was sinking, she helped others board lifeboats in the ship's evacuation, helped to row her lifeboat, and exhorted the crew to return to the sinking ship to look for survivors. Her life is now the focus of the Molly Brown Home Museum in Denver.

Although she became quite wealthy, Margaret Brown was not born into wealth, nor was she called Molly. She was born as Margaret Tobin, the daughter of Irish immigrants John and Johanna Collins Tobin in 1867 in Hannibal, Missouri. She had a brother, a sister, and two half-sisters. Both parents had been widowed when young and each has a daughter from the first marriage. Margaret went to elementary school in Hannibal and in 1901 attended the Carnegie Institute in Pittsburgh, where she studied languages and literature.

At the age of 18, she moved to Leadville, Colorado, with her sister, Helen, and brother, Daniel. Margaret got a job in a mercantile store, and her brother worked in the mines. She was hoping to marry a rich man but fell in love with James J. Brown, an enterprising, self-educated Irishman, and married him in Leadville in 1886. They later had two children, a son and a daughter.

The Browns moved to neighboring Stumpftown, where they operated a soup kitchen for mining families. It was here that Margaret first became involved with the women's suffrage movement, and she helped to establish the Colorado chapter of the National American Woman Suffrage Association.

Mr. Brown, who was known as "J. J.," began working as a miner and advanced to superintendent for the Ibex Mining Company, where he developed a method to reach the gold at the bottom of mines. For the innovation, Brown received 12,500 shares of stock and a seat on the company's board. As a result of the newly acquired fortune, the Browns moved to Denver in 1894 and bought the 1887 Queen Anne–style mansion that now is the Molly Brown House Museum.

Margaret became deeply involved in the social and political affairs of Denver, as well as the arts, education, women's suffrage, and philanthropy. She became a charter member of the Denver Woman's Club, took courses at the Carnegie Institute, learned foreign languages, helped destitute children and to establish the nation's first juvenile court, and ran unsuccessfully for the U.S. Senate twice (1909 and 1914). She and her family also did considerable traveling.

In 1909 Margaret and her husband privately signed a separation agreement that gave her a cash settlement, the house, and a substantial monthly allowance. They never reconciled, but they continued to communicate and care for each other. In 1912 she was vacationing in Egypt when she learned that her grandson was ill, and she booked passage on the *Titanic*, which was leaving from Southampton, England, for New York. It was the newest, largest, and reportedly safest ocean liner on its maiden voyage to America.

However, the ship struck an iceberg and sank off the coast of Newfoundland, Canada, taking 1,514 people with it. Margaret Brown was one of the 710 survivors, becoming a heroine by helping other passengers board lifeboats and later searching for survivors while in Lifeboat No. 6. She was praised as "The Unsinkable Molly Brown," even though she was always called "Maggie" by her friends. *The Unsinkable Molly Brown* became the title of a 1960 Broadway musical and a 1964 motion picture about the *Titanic* sinking.

Margaret Brown became a well-known survivor of the *Titanic* disaster, which helped promote her various causes, such as the rights of workers and women, education and literacy for children, historic preservation, and commemoration of the bravery and chivalry by the crew aboard the *Titanic*.

In 1914 she helped settle the Ludlow coal miners' strike in Colorado, in which 20 people were killed. She also became involved in the National Women's Trade Union and traveled in support of a minimum wage and an eight-hour workday for women. When World War I broke out, Margaret shifted her efforts to war relief. She worked with the American Committee for Devastated France to help rebuild areas behind the front lines and assisted wounded French and American soldiers.

Margaret's husband died in 1922 without leaving a will, but the court divided the $277,694 (equivalent to about $3.3 million now) estate between Margaret and her son and daughter. After the passage of women's suffrage in 1920 and J. J.'s death, she joined the 1920s cultural renaissance in New York, exploring music, art, and theater to a greater degree. She became an actress and even starred in a number of Broadway stage productions.

Margaret's life and finances changed during the Great Depression. She was forced to convert her Colorado home into a boarding house. In 1932 she died in her sleep at the age of 65 at the Barbizon Hotel, the New York hotel known for housing aspiring actresses at the time. She was awarded the French Legion of Honour for her war assistance, activism, and philanthropy.

After Margaret's death, the Colorado mansion, which was in disrepair, was sold by her son and daughter in 1932 for $6,000 (now about $107,000). It was drastically remodeled by the new owners to house 12 roomers. The house continued to deteriorate and was about to be demolished in 1970 when it was purchased by a group of concerned citizens who formed Historic Denver Inc. The preservation group restored the mansion to its 1910 appearance and opened it as a historic house museum.

The historic house now has exhibits on Margaret Brown's life and the *Titanic* experience as well as on Victorian Denver and the mansion's architectural preservation. It also has collections of furnishings and fashions of the period. The museum, which is listed on the National Register of Historic Places, offers guided tours, educational programs, lectures, outreach programs, and Victorian eating experiences. Annual attendance is 47,000.

Molly Brown House Museum, 340 Pennsylvania St., Denver, CO 80203-2417. Phone: 303/832-4092. Fax: 303/832-2340. E-mail: admn@mollybrown.org. Website: www.mollybrown.org. Hours: 10–3:30 Tues.–Sat., 12–3:30 Sun.; closed Mon. and major holidays. Admission: adults, $8; seniors and military, $6; children 6–12, $4; children under 6, free.

Doris Duke

Shangri La. Doris Duke was a tobacco heiress and philanthropist who was called "the million-dollar baby" and "the richest little girl in the world" when born in 1912, and the most reluctant of celebrities as an adult. She was part of the Duke family, which made a fortune from the tobacco fields of North Carolina. Her father, James Duke, was the founder of the American Tobacco Company, and when he died in 1925 he left the bulk of his vast estate to his only child, 12-year-old Doris. His wife received only a modest trust fund, which made for a strained relationship with the daughter. During her lifetime, Doris increased her father's fortune fourfold and left an estimated $1.3 billion when she died in 1993, which went largely to her foundation, the Doris Duke Charitable Foundation, and other charities.

Doris Duke was a socialite who lived a life of world travels, the arts, garden creation, wildlife conservation, historic preservation, writing, philanthropy, and love interests—always trying to avoid the press. She had a staff of 200 who cared for her and managed her five homes, one of which was a Hawaiian retreat in Honolulu that she called Shangri La and which now is a museum of Islamic art and culture.

Doris was born in New York City to tobacco and energy executive James Buchanan Duke and Nanaline Duke, his second wife. The family fortune began with Doris's grandfather, Washington Duke, who created a tobacco cartel with other local farmers at the end of the Civil War. Doris spent her early childhood at Duke Farms, her father's 2,700-acre estate in Hillsborough Township, New Jersey.

At the age of 14, Doris had to sue her mother and other executors to prevent the sale of the farm and other properties, such as a Manhattan mansion that later housed the Institute of Fine Arts at New York University. Doris wanted to go to college, but her mother forbade it and took her on a grand tour of Europe, presenting her to society as a debutante in London and at the family residence in Newport, Rhode Island, in 1930.

Duke was married and divorced twice. At the age of 22, she married James H. R. Cromwell, who was 16 years older, in 1935. He used her fortune in his political career and became U.S. ambassador to Canada in 1940. They took a two-year honeymoon cruise around the world and settled in Hawaii, where they built Shangri La in an Islamic architectural style filled with art and cultural objects of the Muslim world. They were divorced in 1943. They had one child, a daughter named Arden who died hours after birth, and Duke was told she could not have any more children.

Duke's second marriage was to Porfirio Rubirosa, a Dominican Republic diplomat and playboy, in 1947. It was reported that she paid his wife $1 million to agree to an uncontested divorce. The marriage lasted only one year, with Duke giving him several million dollars in gifts, including a stable of polo ponies, sports cars, a converted B-25 bomber, and a seventeenth-century house in Paris. She never married again but was involved with a number of others, including a movie star, a World War II general, a Pulitzer Prize–winning author, and an Olympic swimmer.

During World War II, Duke worked at a canteen for sailors in Egypt, and then she served as a foreign correspondent for International News Service in war-ravaged Europe in 1945–1946. She then moved to Paris and wrote for *Harper's Bazaar* magazine after the war. One of her main passions was the arts. Her interests ranged from collecting priceless Islamic treasures at Shangri La in Hawaii to a complete Thai village in her New Jersey home.

Duke also took great interest in creating beautiful gardens and preserving historic structures. In 1958 she established the Duke Gardens Foundation to endow public display gardens to honor her father at Duke Farms, the family home in New Jersey, and in 1968 she created the Newport Restoration Foundation in Rhode Island to preserve more than 80 colonial buildings (five of which are now museums) in the area where she had a summer home. Her philanthropic work took many other forms, ranging from being a major benefactor of medical research and child welfare programs to providing wildlife refuge and environmental conservation support.

Among Doris Duke's many other interests were jazz, belly dancing, singing in a black gospel choir, and participating in surfing competitions. In her world travels, she communed with the likes of Indian mystics and African witch doctors. And in her later years, she died with a cast of characters around her, including Chandi Heffner, a 32-year-old Hari Krishna devotee she adopted; James Burns, Heffner's boyfriend who became Duke's bodyguard; and Bernard Lafferty, a poor Irishman who became her butler and almost inherited her estate.

Duke met Heffner in 1985 and came to believe that she was the reincarnation of her daughter who died at birth 40 years earlier. She bought her a million-dollar ranch in Hawaii and legally adopted her in 1988. Burns and Lafferty were brought into the Duke household by Heffner. Duke became mysteriously ill at her home in Hawaii during the winter of 1990, and then she later fell and was knocked unconscious. Lafferty told Duke that Heffner and Burns were conspiring against her, and Duke fled with Lafferty to her home in Beverly Hills, California. Duke sank into a deep depression, cut ties with Heffner, and gave Lafferty total control over the household.

Lafferty encouraged Duke to have a series of operations, which were unsuccessful and left her in a wheelchair. In 1993, as she became increasingly frail and disoriented, Lafferty had her sign a will that gave her fortune to him. Duke then was hospitalized a number of times and was heavily sedated with painkillers when she came home. She died in October at the age of 80. But the court ruled that Lafferty was unfit to manage such a large charity as the Duke foundation. Lafferty gave up his position, moved to Los Angeles, and died three years later. An investigation concluded that Duke's death was not a case of murder. The Duke estate now is managed by the Doris Duke Charitable Foundation, which is dedicated to medical research, the performing arts, wildlife, ecology, and the prevention of cruelty to children and animals.

Shangri La, the seasonal home that Duke built in Honolulu in 1936–1938, houses one of the nation's most extensive collections of Islamic art and culture. The museum, located on five acres overlooking the Pacific Ocean, is owned and operated by the Doris Duke Foundation of Islamic Art, created by Duke in her will to promote the study, understanding, and preservation of Islamic art and culture. She began the collection after being captivated by Islamic cultures during her 1935 round-the-world honeymoon trip. The Islamic art foundation is one of three operating foundations supported by the Doris Duke Charitable Foundation.

The museum has a collection of approximately 3,500 Islamic objects, including art, household furnishings, and other objects from Iran, Syria, Morocco, Turkey, and India. The building contains massive painted ceilings, elaborately carved doorways, intricate mosaic tile panels, colorful textiles, and other art forms. The site also contains exotic gardens, a 75-foot saltwater pool, a playhouse, and a caretaker's cottage.

The museum is open to visitors only as part of guided group tours that begin at the Honolulu Museum of Art with a viewing of the "Arts of the Islamic World" exhibition and a short video on Shangri La. In addition to exhibits, Shangri La offers lectures, classes, workshops, films, and performances on Islamic art and culture. Annual attendance is 13,300.

Shangri La, 4055 Papu Circle, Honolulu, HI 96816. Phone: 808/734-1941. Fax: 808/732-4361 (tours begin at the Honolulu Museum of Art, 900 S. Beretania St., Honolulu, HI 98814. Phones: 808/532-3621 and 800/532-8700). Website: www.shangrilahawaii.org. Hours: Wed.–Sat. by appointment; closed Sun.–Tues. and major holidays. Admission: guided tours—out-of-state visitors, $25; Hawaii residents, $20.

Isabella Stewart Gardner

Isabella Stewart Gardner Museum. Isabella Stewart Gardner was a turn-of-the-twentieth-century art collector, philanthropist, and patron of the arts who was known for her stylish tastes and unconventional eccentricities. After her husband's death in 1898, she established an art museum in 1903 that evolved into today's Isabella Stewart Gardner Museum in Boston.

The museum has become known for its exceptional art collection, which includes European, Asian, and American artworks ranging from paintings and sculpture to tapestries and decorative arts. It is housed in a building designed as a fifteenth-century Venetian palace that also served as her home.

Isabella Stewart was born in 1840 in New York City. She was the daughter of David and Adelia Smith Stewart. Her father made his fortune in the Irish linen trade and later in mining investments. Isabella was educated at private schools in New York and Paris. One of her schoolmates in Paris was Julia Gardner, whose friendship eventually led to Isabella's marriage to her older brother, John Lowell Gardner. They were married in New York City in 1860 and moved to Boston.

"Jack," as Gardner was known, attended Harvard and then entered his father's East Indies trading business with many ships. He later also had financial interests in railroads and mining and became quite wealthy. The couple had one child, John Lowell Stewart III, who died of pneumonia when two years old. However, when Jack's brother, Joseph, died in 1875 and left three young sons, Jack and Isabella raised them.

Isabella had a zest for life, as well as an intellectual curiosity and great interest in travel. In the 1880s, she and her husband traveled throughout the United States and visited Paris and such places as the Middle East, Central Europe, and Asia and learned more about foreign culture and art around the world. Her favorite foreign destination was Venice, Italy, a major artistic center for American and English expatriates. While in Venice, they usually stayed at the Palazzo Barbaro—whose architecture influenced Isabella later when planning her museum.

Jack and Isabella Stewart were active socialites who supported the arts and other causes, entertained frequently, corresponded with many, and often bought works from artists, dealers, and in their travels. She became a patron and friend of many of the leading artists and writers of the time, including John Singer Sargent, James McNeill Whistler, and Henry James. Isabella also was supportive of community social services and such cultural enrichment as music, literature, dance, and creative thinking across artistic disciplines.

The Stewarts amassed a remarkable collection of master and decorative arts with the assistance of art patrons and advisors and were starting to plan a museum when Jack died in 1898. Isabella went ahead with development of the museum and designed a building with architect William T. Sears in the Fenway area of Boston modeled after the Renaissance palaces of Venice. The building still completely surrounds a glass-covered garden courtyard, with the first three floors being galleries and the fourth floor serving as Isabella's living quarters.

Isabella called the museum Fenway Court, but it later was renamed the Isabella Stewart Gardner Museum in her honor. She ran the museum until her death in 1924 at the age of 84 after suffering a series of strokes. She created an endowment of $1 million and left a number of stipulations, including that the museum's permanent collection never be significantly altered.

The museum has remained much as Isabella Stewart Gardner left it, with a world-class collection of paintings and statues as well as tapestries, photographs, silver, ceramics, manuscripts, and architectural elements. The collection includes works by some of Europe's most important artists, such as Botticelli's *Madonna and Child with an Angel*, Titan's *Europa*, and Raphael's *The Colonna Altarpiece*. Thirteen works, however, are no longer there as a result of a major theft in 1990. The missing pieces—including *The Concert* by Vermeer, five sketches by Degas, and three works by Rembrandt—were stolen by thieves dressed as policemen who tied up the night security guards and made off with the works.

In addition to its exhibit program, the museum has guided tours, temporary exhibitions, concerts, lectures, symposia, educational programming, and an artist-in-residence program. Annual attendance is 170,000.

Isabella Stewart Gardner Museum, 280 The Fenway, Boston, MA 02115-5809 (postal address: 2 Palace Rd., Boston, MA 02115-5807). Phones: 617/566-1401 and 617/278-5156. Fax: 617/264-6096. E-mail: information@isgm.org. Website: www.gardnermuseum.org. Hours: 11–5 Tues.–Sun.; closed Mon., Independence Day, Thanksgiving, and Christmas. Admission: adults, $12; seniors, $10; college students, $5; children under 18 with parent or guardian, free.

Marjorie Merriweather Post

Hillwood Estate, Museum, and Gardens. Socialite and businesswoman Marjorie Merriweather Post once was the wealthiest woman in America, with a worth of $250 million. She was the daughter of the founder of a leading cereal company who inherited the firm and led its expansion. She also became known for her elaborate residence in Washington, which became Hillwood Estate, Museum, and Gardens, a major decorative arts museum with an extensive French and Russian collection.

Marjorie was the only child of Charles William Post and Ella Merriweather Post. She was born in 1887 in Springfield, Illinois. Her father, who was known as C. W. Post, accumulated one of the largest fortunes of the early twentieth century by his inventions of a coffee substitute and two popular breakfast cereals—Grape-Nuts and Post Toasties. C. W. founded the Postum Cereal Company, a highly successful food manufacturing firm, and trained his daughter in every aspect of the company's operations—and also exposed her to art through trips abroad and his own collecting.

When her father died in 1914, he left the company to his Marjorie, who moved to New York to oversee the company's operations and to expand her collection of decorative arts. She bought decorative objects for her New York home and became especially knowledgeable in French furnishings with help of museum classes and art dealer Sir Joseph Duveen. She later sought to share her collection with the public when she moved to a historic estate in Washington.

Marjorie was married four times. The first marriage was in 1905 to Edward Bennett Close, an investment banker from Greenwich, Connecticut. They had two daughters before divorcing in 1919. The following year, she married Edward Francis Hutton, who became chairman of Postum Cereal Company, and they developed a larger variety of food products and changed the company name to General Foods Corporation. They had one daughter, who became a movie actress named Dina Merrill.

Her second marriage ended in divorce in 1935, and that same year she married her third husband, Joseph E. Davies, a Washington lawyer. When he became American ambassador to the Soviet Union in 1937–1938, she accompanied him and acquired many Russian decorative and liturgical arts, including icons, textiles, porcelains, and silver—many of which the Soviets seized from the Romanov royal family and others during the Russian Revolution. Marjorie was divorced in 1955, and her final marriage was to Herbert A. May, a wealthy Pittsburgh businessman, in 1958. It ended in divorce in 1964, and she then reclaimed her maiden name of Marjorie Merriweather Post.

After her third divorce in 1955, Post looked for a stately home with high ceilings and a wooded site. She purchased Arbremont, a 36-room Georgian colonial estate on 25 acres along Rock Creek Park in northwest Washington in 1920. She then had its interior gutted and rebuilt. The renovations were completed in 1956 for her new home, which she called Hillwood—the same name she used for her former home in Brookville, Long Island, which became part of the C. W. Post Campus of Long Island University. The estate quickly became a major social center, featuring French, Asian, and Russian art and religious objects.

Post became concerned about the fate of Hillwood after her death and bequeath the estate with a $10 million endowment to the Smithsonian Institution in 1962. She continued to reside at the estate until her death in 1973 at the age of 86. When the endowment did not cover the cost to convert the estate into a museum and maintain it, the Smithsonian returned Hillwood to the Post Foundation in 1976. It now is operated as the Hillwood Estate, Museum, and Gardens by a foundation created for that purpose.

Hillwood has more than 16,000 objects, including such eighteenth- and nineteenth-century French and Russian works as Fabergé imperial Easter eggs, Sèvres porcelain, French furniture, Russian Orthodox icons and liturgical vessels, 1730s tapestries, and paintings, such as a full-length portrait of Catherine the Great of Russia.

It also contains 13 acres of formal gardens, and such other structures as greenhouses, a Russian whole-log dacha (which houses changing exhibitions), an Adirondack building that serves as a museum programming venue, a café, and a visitor center. The estate also has a 32,000-volume library relating to French and Russian decorative arts, a collection of costumes and accessories worn by Mrs. Post and her family, an archive, a theater, a gift shop, and a "Four Seasons Overlook" with four statues representing the seasons. The site offers guided tours and public programs. Annual attendance is 64,000.

Hillwood Estate, Museum, and Gardens, 4155 Linnean Ave., N.W., Washington, DC 20008-3806. Phones: 202/686-5807 and 202/686-8500. Fax: 202/966-7846. E-mail: kphelan@hillwoodmuseum.org. Website: www.hillwoodmuseum.org. Hours: 10–5 Tues.–Sat. (and some 1–5 Sun.); closed Sun.–Mon., Jan., and national holidays. Admission: suggested donations—adults, $15; seniors, $12; college students, $10; children 6–18, $5; children under 6, free.

Geographical Guide to "Famous" Sites

Alabama

F. Scott ad Zelda Fitzgerald Museum, Montgomery
George Washington Carver Museum, Tuskegee Institute
Hank Aaron Childhood Hoe and Museum, Mobile
Hank Williams Museum, Montgomery
Ivy Green, Birthplace of Helen Keller, Tuscumbia
The Oaks, Tuskegee (Booker T. Washington)
Paul W. Bryant Museum, Tuscaloosa
Rosa Parks Library and Museum, Montgomery
W. C. Handy Museum and Library, Florence

Arizona

Coronado National Memorial, Hereford (Francisco Vásquez de Coronado)
Frémont House, Prescott (John C. Frémont)
John Wesley Powell Memorial Museum, Page
Rex Allen Arizona Cowboy Museum, Willcox

Arkansas

Clinton Birthplace Home, Hope (William J. Clinton)
Hemingway-Pfeiffer Museum and Educational Center, Piggott (Ernest Hemingway)
MacArthur Museum of Arkansas Military History, Little Rock (Douglas MacArthur)
William J. Clinton Presidential Library and Museum, Little Rock

California

Autry National Center of the American West, Los Angeles (Gene Autry)
Cabrillo National Monument, San Diego (Juan Rodríguez Cabrillo)
César E. Chávez National Monument and National Chávez Center, Keene
Charles M. Schulz Museum and Research Center, Santa Rosa
Eugene O'Neill National Historic Site, Danville
General Patton Memorial Museum, Chiriaco Summit (George Patton)
Getty Villa, Pacific Palisades (J. Paul Getty)
Hans Christian Andersen Museum, Solvang
Hearst Castle, San Simeon (William Randolph Hearst)
J. Paul Getty Museum, Los Angeles
Jack London State Historic Park and Museum, Glen Ellen
Jim Beckwourth Museum, Portola

John Muir National Historic Site, Martinez
Lawrence Welk Museum, Escondido
Lincoln Memorial Shrine, Redlands (Abraham Lincoln)
Luther Burbank Home and Gardens, Santa Rosa
Mary Pickford Museum, Cathedral City
National Steinbeck Center, Salinas (John Steinbeck)
Richard Nixon Presidential Library and Museum, Yorba Linda
Robert Louis Stevenson House, Monterey
Ronald Reagan Presidential Library and Museum, Simi Valley
Silverado Museum, St. Helena (Robert Louis Stevenson)
Steinbeck House, Salinas (John Steinbeck)
Walt Disney Family Museum, San Francisco
Walt Disney's Carolwood Barn, Los Angeles
William S. Hart Museum, Newhall
Will Rogers State Historic Park, Pacific Palisades

Colorado

Betty Ford Alpine Gardens, Vale
Buffalo Bill Museum and Grave, Golden (William F. Cody)
Golda Meir House Museum, Denver
Jack Dempsey Museum and Park, Manassa
Kit Carson Memorial Chapel at Fort Lyon, Fort Lyon
Molly Brown House Museum, Denver
Victor Lowell Thomas Museum, Victor

Connecticut

Barnum Museum, Bridgeport (P. T. Barnum)
Captain Nathaniel B. Palmer House, Stonington
The Cushing Center, New Haven (Harvey Cushing)
Eli Whitney Museum, Hamden
Harriet Beecher Stowe Center, Hartford
Katharine Hepburn Museum, Old Saybrook
Marian Anderson Studio, Danbury
Mark Twain Home and Museum, Hartford (Samuel Langhorne Clemens)
Monte Cristo Cottage, New London (Eugene O'Neill)
Nathan Hale Homestead Museum, Coventry
Noah Webster House, West Hartford
Prudence Crandall Museum, Canterbury

Delaware

Hagley Museum and Library, Wilmington (Eleuthére Irénée du Pont)

District of Columbia

Folger Shakespeare Library, Washington (William Shakespeare)
Ford Theatre National Historic Site, Washington (Abraham Lincoln)
Franklin Delano Roosevelt Memorial, Washington
Frederick Douglass Museum and Caring Hall of Fame, Washington
Frederick Douglass National Historic Site, Washington
Hillwood Estate Museum and Gardens, Washington (Marjorie Merriweather Post)
Lincoln Memorial, Washington (Abraham Lincoln)
Martin Luther King Jr. Memorial, Washington

Mary McLeod Bethune Council House National Historic Site, Washington
President Lincoln's Cottage, Washington (Abraham Lincoln)
Thomas Jefferson Memorial, Washington
Thurgood Marshall Center, Washington
Washington Monument, Washington (George Washington)
Woodrow Wilson House, Washington

Florida

Audubon Home and Tropical Gardens, Key West (John James Audubon)
Burt Reynolds and Friends Museum, Jupiter
De Soto National Monument, Bradenton (Hernando de Soto)
Edison and Ford Winter Estates, Fort Myers (Thomas Edison and Henry Ford)
Ernest Hemingway Home and Museum, Key West
Harry S. Truman Little White House Museum, Key West
John and Mable Ringling Museum of Art, Cá d'Zan, and Circus Museum, Sarasota
Mary McLeod Bethune Home, Daytona Beach
Salvador Dali Museum, St. Petersburg
Stephen Foster Folk Culture Center State Park, White Springs
Ted Williams Museum and Hitters Hall of Fame, St. Petersburg
Zora Neale Hurston National Museum of Fine Arts, Eatonville

Georgia

Erskine Caldwell Birthplace Museum, Moreland
Jimmy Carter Library and Museum, Atlanta
Jimmy Carter National Historic Site, Plains
Juliette Gordon Low Birthplace, Savannah
Margaret Mitchell House and Museum, Atlanta
Martin Luther King Jr. Center for Nonviolent Social Change, Atlanta
Martin Luther King Jr. National Historic Site, Atlanta
Roosevelt's Little White House State Historic Site, Warm Springs (Franklin D. Roosevelt)
Tubman African American Museum, Macon (Harriet Tubman)
Ty Cobb Museum, Royston

Hawaii

Astronaut Ellison S. Onizuka Space Center, Kailua-Kona
Shangri La, Honolulu (Doris Duke)
Queen Emma Summer Palace, Honolulu

Idaho

Sacajawea Interpretive, Cultural, and Educational Center, Salmon

Illinois

Abraham Lincoln Presidential Library and Museum, Springfield
Billy Graham Center Museum, Wheaton
Carl Sandburg State Historic Site, Galesburg
Chanute Air Museum, Rantoul (Octave Chanute)
Frances Willard House Museum, Evanston
Frank Lloyd Wright Home and Studio, Oak Park
Hemingway Museum and Birthplace, Oak Park (Ernest Hemingway)
Jane Addams Hull-House Museum, Chicago

Jesse Owens Memorial Park Museum, Danville
John Deere Historic Site, Grant Detour
Joseph Smith Historic Site, Nauvoo
Katherine Dunham Dynamic Museum, East St. Louis
Lincoln Depot, Springfield (Abraham Lincoln)
Lincoln-Douglas Debate Museum, Charleston
Lincoln Heritage Museum, Lincoln
Lincoln Herndon Law Offices State Historic Site, Springfield
Lincoln Home National Historic Site, Springfield
Lincoln Log Cabin State Historic Site, Lerna
Lincoln Memorial Garden and Nature Center, Springfield
Lincoln Tomb State Historic Site, Springfield
Lincoln Trail Homestead State Memorial, Harristown
Robert R. McCormick Museum at Contigny, Wheaton
Ronald Reagan Birthplace and Museum, Tampico
Ronald Reagan Boyhood Home and Visitors Center, Dixon
Ronald R. Reagan Museum at Eureka College, Eureka
Sousa Archives and Center for American Music, Champaign (John Philip Sousa)
Stephen A. Douglas Tomb and Memorial, Chicago
U. S. Grant Home State Historic Site, Galena
Wyatt Earp Birthplace House, Monmouth

Indiana

Benjamin Harrison Presidential Site, Indianapolis
Dan Quayle Center and U.S. Vice President Museum, Huntington
Ernie Pyle Museum, Dana
Eugene V. Debs Home, Terre Haute
General Lewis H. Hershey Museum, Angola
General Lew Wallace Study and Museum, Crawfordsville
George Ade Memorial Museum, Brook
George Rogers Clark National Historical Park, Vincennes
Grouseland, William Henry Harrison Mansion, Vincennes
James Dean Memorial Gallery, Fairmount
James Whitcomb Riley Birthplace and Museum, Greenfield
James Whitmore Riley Museum Home, Indianapolis
John Dillinger Museum, Hammond
Lincoln Boyhood National Memorial, Lincoln City (Abraham Lincoln)
Lincoln State Park and Colonel Jones Home, Lincoln City
Virgil Grissom Memorial at Spring Mill State Park, Mitchell
Wilbur Wright Birthplace and Interpretive Center, Hagerstown

Iowa

Birthplace of John Wayne, Winterset
Bob Feller Museum, Van Meter
Buffalo Bill Cody Homestead, Princeton (William F. Cody)
Buffalo Bill Museum of Le Claire, Iowa, Le Claire
Herbert Hoover National Historic Site, West Branch
Herbert Hoover Presidential Library-Museum, West Branch
Historic General Dodge House, Council Bluffs
John L. Lewis Mining and Labor Museum, Lucas
Laura Ingalls Wilder Park and Museum, Burr Oak
Mamie Doud Eisenhower Birthplace, Boone

Kansas

Amelia Earhart Birthplace, Atchison
Carrie A. Nation Home Memorial, Medicine Lodge
Coronado Quivira Museum, Lyons (Francisco Vásquez de Coronado)
Dalton Defenders Museum, Coffeyville (Gratan, Robert, and Emmet Dalton)
Dalton Gang Hideout, Meade
Dwight D. Eisenhower Library and Museum, Abilene
Emporia Gazette and Museum, Emporia (William Allen White)
John Brown Museum State Historic Site, Osawatomie
Robert J. Dole Institute of Politics, Lawrence
Walter P. Chrysler Boyhood Home and Museum, Ellis
William Allen White State Historic Site, Emporia

Kentucky

Abraham Lincoln Birthplace National Historic Site, Hodgenville
Alben W. Barkley Museum, Paducah
Ashland, the Henry Clay Estate, Lexington
Bill Monroe Homeplace, Rosine
General George Patton Museum of Leadership, Fort Knox
Harriet Beecher Stowe Slavery to Freedom Museum, Maysville
Jefferson Davis State Historic Site, Fairview
John James Audubon State Park and Museum, Henderson
Lincoln Homestead State Park, Springfield (Abraham Lincoln)
The Lincoln Museum, Hodgenville
Mary Todd Lincoln House, Lexington
Muhammad Ali Center, Louisville
President Zachary Taylor's Mausoleum and Monument, Louisville
Robert Penn Warren Birthplace Museum, Guthrie
Rosemary Clooney House, Augusta
Thomas Edison House, Louisville

Louisiana

Arna Bontemps African American Museum, Alexandra
Audubon State Historic Site, St. Francisville (John James Audubon)
Bonnie and Clyde Ambush Museum, Gibsland (Bonnie Parker and Clyde Barrow)
Eddie G. Robinson Museum, Grambling
Jean Lafitte National Historical Park and Preserve, New Orleans
Jim Bowie Display and Museum, Opelousas
Longfellow-Evangeline State Historic Site, St. Martinville (Henry Wadsworth Longfellow)

Maine

Ethan Allen Homestead Museum, Burlington
Margaret Chase Smith Library, Skowhegan
Peary-Macmillan Arctic Museum, Brunswick (Robert E. Peary and Donald B. Macmillan)
Roosevelt Campobello International Park, Lubee (Franklin D. Roosevelt)
Wadsworth-Longfellow House, Portland (Henry Wadsworth Longfellow)

Maryland

Babe Ruth Museum, Baltimore
Banneker-Douglass Museum, Annapolis (Benjamin Banneker and Frederick Douglass)

Benjamin Banneker Park and Museum, Baltimore
Clara Barton National Historic Site, Echo
Edgar Allan Poe House and Museum, Baltimore
Eubie Blake National Jazz Institute and Cultural Center, Baltimore
Frederick Douglass–Isaac Myers Maritime Park, Baltimore
Frederick Douglass Museum and Cultural Center, Highland Beach
George Washington's Headquarters, Cumberland
Glenn L. Martin Maryland Aviation Museum, Baltimore
Harriet Tubman Museum, Cambridge
Kennedy Farm House Museum, Sharpsburg (John Brown)
Washington Monument, Baltimore (George Washington)
Washington Monument State Park, Boonsboro (George Washington)

Massachusetts

Abigail Adams Birthplace, Weymouth
Adams National Historical Park, Quincy (John Adams and John Quincy Adams)
Benjamin Thompson House, Woburn
Calvin Coolidge Presidential Library and Museum, Northampton
Clara Barton Birthplace Museum, North Oxford
Daniel Webster Estate and Heritage Center, Marshfield
Daniel Webster Law Office and Library, Marshfield
Dr. Seuss National Memorial Sculpture Gardens, Springfield (Theodor Seuss Geisel)
Emily Dickinson Museum: The Homestead and the Evergreens, Amherst
Frederick Law Olmsted National Historic Site, Brookline
George Peabody House Museum, Peabody
Gropius House, Lincoln (Walter Gropius)
Herman Melville House, Pittsfield
Isabella Stewart Gardner Museum, Boston
John Fitzgerald Kennedy National Historic Site, Brookline
John F. Kennedy Hyannis Museum, Hyannis
John F. Kennedy Presidential Library and Museum, Boston
John Greenleaf Whittier Home, Amesbury
John Greenleaf Whittier Homestead, Haverhill
Longyear Museum, Chestnut Hill (Mary Baker Eddy)
Louisa May Alcott's Orchard House, Concord
Longfellow National Historic Site, Cambridge (Henry Wadsworth Longfellow)
Mary Baker Eddy Library, Boston
The Mount: Edith Wharton's Estate and Gardens, Lenox
Nathaniel Hawthorne's Birthplace, Salem
Norman Rockwell Museum, Stockbridge
The Old Manse, Concord (Nathaniel Hawthorne)
Paul Revere House, Boston
Ralph Waldo Emerson House, Concord
Theodore Roosevelt Collection, Harvard College Library, Cambridge
Thoreau Farm: Birthplace of Henry David Thoreau, Concord
The Wayside, Concord (Nathaniel Hawthorne)
Whistler House Museum of Art, Lowell (James A. M. Whistler)
William Cullen Bryant Homestead, Cummington

Michigan

Edsel and Eleanor Ford House, Gross Pointe Shores
Father Marquette National Memorial, St. Ignace (Jacques Marquette)
Gerald Ford Library, Ann Arbor
Gerald R. Ford Presidential Museum, Grand Rapids

The Henry Ford, Dearborn
Henry Ford Estate—Fair Lane, Dearborn
Ida B. Wells-Barnett Museum, Holly Springs
Marquette Mission Park, St. Ignace (Jacques Marquette)
Walter P. Chrysler Museum, Auburn Hills

Minnesota

Charles A Lindbergh Historic Site, Little Falls
Judy Garland Museum of Art, Grand Rapids
Laura Ingalls Wilder Museum and Tourist Center, Walnut Grove
Sinclair Lewis Boyhood Home, Sauk Centre
Sinclair Lewis Interpretive Center, Sauk Centre
W. W. Mayo House, Le Sueur

Mississippi

B. B. King Museum and Delta Interpretive Center, Indianola
Beauvoir, the Jefferson Davis Home and Presidential Library, Biloxi
Elvis Presley Birthplace and Museum, Tupelo
Eudora Welty House, Jackson
Jimmie Rodgers Museum, Meridian
Rowan Oak, Oxford (William Faulkner)
Tennessee Williams Birthplace State Welcome Center, Columbus
Ulysses S. Grant Presidential Library, Starkville

Missouri

Daniel Boone Home and Heritage Center, Defiance
Eugene Field House and St. Louis Toy Museum, St. Louis
General John J. Pershing Boyhood Home State Historic Site, Laclede
George Washington Carver Memorial and Culture Center. Fulton
George Washington Carver National Monument, Diamond
Harry S. Truman Birthplace State Historic Site, Lamar
Harry S. Truman Library and Museum, Independence
Harry S. Truman National Historic Site, Independence and Grandview
Harry S. Truman Office and Courtroom, Independence
J. C. Penney Museum, Hamilton
Jefferson National Expansion Memorial, St. Louis (Thomas Jefferson)
Jesse James Bank Museum, Liberty
Jesse James Farm and Museum, Kearney
Jesse James Home Museum, St. Joseph
Laura Ingalls Wilder–Rose Wilder Lane Historic Home and Museum, Mansfield
Mark Twain Birthplace Historic Site and Museum, Florida (Samuel Langhorne Clemens)
Mark Twain Boyhood House and Museum, Hannibal
National Winston Churchill Museum and Winston Churchill Memorial and Library, Fulton
Scott Joplin House State Historic Site, St. Louis
Thomas Hart Benton Home and Studio State Historic Site, Kansas City
Ulysses S. Grant National Historic Site, St. Louis
Walt Disney Hometown Museum, Marceline

Montana

C. M. Russell Museum, Great Falls
Lewis and Clark National Historic Trail Interpretive Center, Great Falls (Meriwether Lewis and William Clark)

Nebraska

Buffalo Bill State Historical Park, North Platte (William F. Cody)
General Crook House Museum and Library/Archives Center, Omaha (George Crook)
George W. Norris State Historic House, McCook
Gerald R. Ford Conservation Center, Omaha
John G. Neihardt State Historic Site, Bancroft
Lewis and Clark National Historic Trail Headquarters Visitor Center, Omaha (Meriwether Lewis and William Clark)
Mari Sandoz High Plains Heritage Center, Chadron
Willa Cather State Historic Site, Red Cloud

New Hampshire

Daniel Webster Birthplace State Historic Site, Franklin
Franklin Pierce Homestead, Hillsborough
The Frost Place, Franconia (Robert Frost)
John Paul Jones House, Portsmouth
McAuliffe-Shepard Discovery Center, Concord (Christa McAuliffe and Alan Shepard)
The Pierce Manse, Concord (Franklin Pierce)
Robert Frost Farm, Derry
Saint-Gaudens National Historic Site, Cornish (Augustus Saint-Gaudens)

New Jersey

Grover Cleveland Birthplace, Caldwell
Paul Robeson Cultural Center, New Brunswick
Paul Robeson Galleries, Newark
Thomas Alva Edison Memorial Tower and Museum, Menlo Park
Thomas Edison National Historical Park, West Orange
Walt Whitman House and Library, Camden
Washington Crossing State Park, Titusville (George Washington)
Yogi Berra Museum and Learning Center, Little Falls

New Mexico

Billy the Kid Museum, Fort Sumner (William Bonney)
Coronado State Monument, Bernalillo (Francisco Vásquez de Coronado)
D. H. Lawrence Ranch and Memorial, Taos
E. L. Blumenshein Home and Museum, Taos
Ernie Pyle House/Library, Albuquerque
Georgia O'Keeffe Home and Studio, Abiquiu
Georgia O'Keeffe Museum, Santa Fe
Kit Carson Home and Museum, Taos
Pancho Villa State Park, Columbus

New York

Cedarmere, Roslyn Harbor (William Cullen Bryant)
Edward Hopper House Art Center, Nyack
Eleanor Roosevelt National Historic Site, Hyde Park
Elizabeth Cady Stanton House, Seneca Falls
Franklin D. Roosevelt Four Freedoms Park, New York City
Franklin D. Roosevelt Presidential Library and Museum, Hyde Park
Frederic Remington Art Museum, Ogdensburg
Frick Collection, New York City (Henry Clay Frick)

General Grant National Memorial, New York City (Ulysses S. Grant)
George Eastman House/International Museum of Photography and Film, Rochester
Glenn H. Curtiss Museum, Hammondsport
Hamilton Grange National Memorial, New York City (Alexander Hamilton)
Harriet Tubman Home, Auburn
Home of Franklin D. Roosevelt National Historic Site, Hyde Park
John Brown Farm State Historic Site, Lake Placid
John Burroughs Memorial State Historic Site, Roxbury
John Burroughs Sanctuary/Slabsides, West Park
John Jay Homestead State Historic Site, Katonah
Joseph Priestley House, Northumberland
Langston Hughes House, New York City
Locust Grove, the Samuel Morse Historic Site, Poughkeepsie
Louis Armstrong House Museum, Corona
Lucy-Desi Museum, Jamestown (Lucille Ball and Desi Arnaz)
Martin Van Buren National Historic Site, Kinderhook
Millard Fillmore House, East Aurora
Morgan Library and Museum, New York City (John Pierpont Morgan)
Noguchi Museum, Long Island City (Isamu Noguchi)
Robert Louis Stevenson Memorial Cottage Museum, Saranac Lake
Sagamore Hill National Historic Site, Oyster Bay (Theodore Roosevelt)
Smith Family Farm, Palmyra (Joseph Smith)
Susan B. Anthony Museum and House, Rochester
Theodore Roosevelt Birthplace National Historic Site, New York City
Theodore Roosevelt Inaugural National Historic Site, Buffalo
Thomas Cole National Historic Site, Catskill
Thomas Paine Memorial Museum, New Rochelle
Thomas Payne Cottage, New Rochelle
Ulysses S. Grant Cottage State Historic Site, Wilton
Vanderbilt Mansion National Historic Site, Hyde Park (Frederick Vanderbilt)
Walt Whitman Birthplace State Historic Site and Interpretive Center, Huntington
Washington Irving's Sunnyside, Tarrytown
Washington's Headquarters State Historic Site, Newburgh (George Washington)
Woody Guthrie Archives, Mount Kisco

North Carolina

Billy Graham Library, Charlotte
Biltmore Estate, Asheville (George Vanderbilt II)
Carl Sandburg Home National Historic Site, Flat Rock
Duke Homestead State Historic Site, Durham (Doris Duke)
Jesse Helms Center, Wingate
Museum of the Waxhaws and Andrew Jackson, Waxhaw
President James K. Polk State Historic Site, Pineville
Reynolds Home Museum, Winston-Salem (R. J. Reynolds)
Richard Petty Museum, Randleman
Senator Sam J. Ervin Jr. Library and Museum, Morganton
Thomas Wolfe Memorial, Asheville
Wright Brothers National Memorial, Kill Devil Hills (Wilbur and Orville Wright)

North Dakota

Lawrence Welk Birthplace, Strasburg
Lawrence Welk Collection, Fargo
Roger Maris Museum, Fargo

Ohio

Armstrong Air and Space Museum, Wapakoneta
Clark Gable Birth Home and Museum, Cadiz
Dayton Aviation Heritage National Historical Park, Dayton (Wilbur and Orville Wright)
Grant's Birthplace State Memorial, Point Pleasant (Ulysses S. Grant)
Harding Home and Museum, Marion (Warren G. Harding)
Harriett Beecher Stowe House, Cincinnati
Jack Nicklaus Museum, Columbus
James A. Garfield Monument, Cleveland
James A. Garfield National Historic Site, Mentor
John and Annie Glenn Historic Site and Exploration Center, New Concord
John Brown House, Akron
Lawrence Dunbar State Memorial, Dayton
Malabar Farm State Park, Lucas (Louis Bromfield)
McKinley Birthplace Home and Research Center, Niles (William McKinley)
McKinley National Memorial, Canton
National McKinley Birthplace Memorial Library and Museum, Niles
National Road/Zane Grey Museum, Norwich
Paul Laurence Dunbar State Memorial, Dayton
Perry's Victory and International Peace Museum, Put-in-Bay (Oliver Hazard Perry)
Rutherford B. Hays Presidential Center, Fremont
Stan Hywet Hall and Gardens, Akron (Frank A. Seiberling)
Thomas Edison Birthplace Museum, Milan
Thurber House, Columbus (James Thurber)
William Holmes McGuffey Museum, Oxford
William Howard Taft National Historic Site, Cincinnati
William McKinley Presidential Library and Museum, Canton
Wright-Dunbar Interpretive Center, Dayton (Wilbur and Orville Wright and Lawrence Dunbar)

Oklahoma

Frank Phillips Home, Bartlesville
Gene Autry Oklahoma Museum, Autry
Jim Thorpe Historical Home, Yale
Pawnee Bill Ranch Site and Museum, Pawnee
Robert S. Kerr Conference Center and Museum, Poteau
Roger Miller Museum, Erick
Sequoyah Cabin, Sallisaw
Tom Mix Museum, Dewey
Washington Irving Trail Museum, Ripley
Will Rogers Birthplace Ranch, Oologah
Will Rogers Memorial Museum, Claremore
Woolaroc Museum, Bartlesville (Frank Phillips)

Oregon

Lewis and Clark National Historical Park, Astoria (Meriwether Lewis and William Clark)

Pennsylvania

Andy Warhol Museum, Pittsburgh
August Wilson Center for African American Culture, Pittsburgh
Benjamin Franklin National Memorial, Philadelphia
Betsy Ross House, Philadelphia
Buchanan Birthplace State Park, Cove Gap (James Buchanan)
Carnegie Museums of Pittsburgh, Pittsburgh (Andrew Carnegie)

Daniel Boone Homestead, Birdsboro
Dolley Todd House, Philadelphia (Dolley Madison)
Edgar Allan Poe National Historic Site, Philadelphia
Eisenhower National Historic Site, Gettysburg (Dwight D. Eisenhower)
Franklin Court, Philadelphia (Benjamin Franklin)
Fred Waring Collection, State College
Frick Art and Historical Center, Pittsburgh (Henry Clay Frick)
The Hershey Story: The Museum on Chocolate Avenue, Hershey (Milton S. Hershey)
Houdini Museum and Theater, Scranton (Harry Houdini)
James A. Michener Art Museum, Doylestown
Jimmy Stewart Museum, Indiana
John Brown House, Chambersburg
John James Audubon Center at Mill Grove, Mill Grove
Marian Anderson Residence Museum and Birthplace, Philadelphia
Mario Lanza Museum, Philadelphia
N. C. Wyeth House and Studio, Chadds Ford Township
Paul Robeson Cultural Center, State College
Paul Robeson House, Philadelphia
Pearl S. Buck House, Perkasie
President James Buchanan's Wheatland, Lancaster
Rachel Carson Homestead, Springdale
Robert Fulton Birthplace, Quarryville
Roberto Clemente Museum. Pittsburgh
Rodin Museum, Philadelphia (Auguste Rodin)
Senator John Heinz History Center, Pittsburgh
Stephen Foster Memorial Museum, Pittsburgh
Thaddeus Kościuszko National Memorial, Philadelphia
Washington Crossing Historical Park, Washington Crossing (George Washington)
Zane Grey Museum, Lackawaxen

Puerto Rico

Pablo Casals Museum, San Juan

Rhode Island

The Breakers, Newport (Cornelius Vanderbilt II)
General Nathanael Greene Homestead, Coventry
Gilbert Stuart Birthplace and Museum, Saundertown
Roger Williams National Memorial, Providence

South Carolina

Andrew Jackson Museum, Lancaster
Charles Pinckney National Historic Site, Mount Pleasant
Fort Hill (The John C. Calhoun Home), Clemson
Shoeless Joe Jackson Museum and Baseball Library, Greenville
Strom Thurmond Institute of Government and Public Affairs, Clemson
Woodrow Wilson Boyhood Home, Columbia
Woodrow Wilson Family Home, Columbia

South Dakota

Crazy Horse Memorial, Crazy Horse
Mount Rushmore National Memorial, Keystone

Tennessee

Abraham Lincoln Library and Museum, Harrogate
Alex Haley Museum and Interpretive Center, Henning
Andrew Johnson National Historic Site, Greeneville
Bessie Smith Cultural Center, Chattanooga
Coal Miner's Daughter Museum, Hurricane Mills (Loretta Lynn)
Cordell Hull Birthplace State Park and Museum, Byrdstown
Crockett Museum, Lawrenceburg (Davy Crockett)
Crockett Tavern Museum, Morristown
David Crockett Cabin Museum, Rutherford
Davy Crockett Birthplace State Park Museum, Limestone
Elvis Presley Museum, Pigeon Forge
Graceland, Memphis (Elvis Presley)
The Hermitage: Home of President Andrew Jackson, Hermitage
James K. Polk Ancestral Home, Columbus
President Andrew Johnson Museum and Library, Greenville
Sam Houston Schoolhouse, Maryville
Sgt. Alvin C. York Historic Park, Pall Mall
Willie Nelson and Friends Museum and General Store, Nashville

Texas

Armstrong Browning Library, Waco (Robert and Elizabeth Barrett Browning)
Audie Murphy / American Cotton Museum, Greenville
Babe Didrikson Zaharias Museum and Welcome Center, Beaumont
Briscoe-Garner Museum, Uvalde (John Nance Garner)
Buddy Holly Center, Lubbock
Edison Museum, Beaumont (Thomas Edison)
Eisenhower Birthplace State Historic Site, Denison (Dwight D. Eisenhower)
George Bush Presidential Library and Museum, College Station
George W. Bush Presidential Library and Museum, Dallas
Lady Bird Johnson Wildflower Center, Austin
LBJ Museum of San Marcos, San Marcos (Lyndon B. Johnson)
LBJ Presidential Library, Austin
Lyndon B. Johnson National Historical Park, Johnson City
Lyndon B. Johnson State Park and Historic Site, Johnson City
Michael F. DeBakey Library and Museum, Houston
O. Henry House Museum, San Antonio (William Sidney Porter)
O. Henry Museum, Austin
Sam Houston Memorial Museum, Huntsville
Sam Rayburn Library and Museum, Bonham
Samuel J. Rayburn House Museum, Bonham
San Felipi de Austin State Historic Site, San Felipi (Stephen F. Austin)
Stephen F. Austin State Park, San Felipi

Utah

Beehive House, Salt Lake City (Brigham Young)
Brigham Young's Winter Home, St. George
John Wesley Powell River History Museum, Green River

Vermont

Brandon Museum at Stephen A. Douglas Birthplace, Brandon
Calvin Coolidge State Historic Site, Plymouth Notch

Ethan Allen Homestead Museum, Burlington
Joseph Smith Birthplace Memorial, South Royalton
Norman Rockwell Museum of Vermont, Rutland
President Calvin Coolidge Museum and Education Center, Plymouth Notch
President Chester A. Arthur Historic Site, Fairfield
Robert Frost Stone House Museum, Shaftsbury

Virginia

Anne Spenser House and Garden, Lynchburg
Arlington House, Arlington (Robert E. Lee)
Ash Lawn–Highland, Charlottesville (James Monroe)
Berkeley Plantation, Charles City (William Henry Harrison)
Booker T. Washington National Monument, Hardy
Cyrus H. McCormick Memorial Museum, Steeles Tavern
Edgar Allan Poe Museum, Richmond
General Douglas MacArthur Memorial, Norfolk
George C. Marshall International Center at Dodona Manor, Leesburg
George C. Marshall Museum, Lexington
George Washington Birthplace National Monument, Colonial Beach
George Washington Masonic Museum, Fredericksburg
George Washington Masonic National Memorial, Alexandria
George Washington's Ferry Farm, Fredericksburg
George Washington's Office Museum, Winchester
James Madison's Montpelier, Orange
James Monroe Museum and Memorial Library, Fredericksburg
Lee Chapel and Museum, Lexington (Robert E. Lee)
Monticello: Home of Thomas Jefferson, Charlottesville
Mount Vernon: George Washington's Estate and Gardens, Mount Vernon
Red Hill–Patrick Henry National Memorial, Brookneal
Reynolds Homestead, Critz (R. J. Reynolds)
Sherwood Forest Plantation: Home of John Tyler, Charles City
Stonewall Jackson Headquarters, Winchester
Stonewall Jackson House, Lexington
Thomas Jefferson's Poplar Forest, Forest
Walter Reed Birthplace, Gloucester County
Woodrow Wilson Presidential Library and Museum, Staunton

Washington

Cape Disappointment State Park and Clark Interpretive Center, Ilwaco (Meriwether Lewis and William Clark)
Crosby Museum, Tacoma (Bing Crosby)
Sacajawea Interpretive Center, Sacajawea State Park, Paseo

West Virginia

Harpers Ferry National Historical Park, Harpers Ferry (John Brown)
Pearl S. Buck Birthplace Museum, Hillsboro

Wisconsin

Laura Ingalls Wilder Museum, Pepin
Taliesin, Spring Green (Frank Lloyd Wright)
Ten Chimneys—Home of Alfred Lunt and Lynn Fontaine, Genesee Depot

Wyoming

Buffalo Bill Historical Center, Cody (William F. Cody)
J. C. Penney Homestead, Kemmerer

Bibliography

Alderson, William T., and Shirley Payne Low. *Interpretation of Historic Sites*. 2nd ed. Nashville: American Association of State and Local History, 1985.

American Heritage Guide: Historic Houses of America. New York: American Heritage Publishing, 1971.

American Historylands: Touring Our Landmarks of Liberty. Washington, DC: National Geographic Society, 1967.

Anderson, Jay, ed. *Time Machines: The World of Living History*. Nashville: American Association for State and Local History, 1984.

Benson, Susan Porter, et al., eds. *Presenting the Past: Essays on History and the Past*. Philadelphia: Temple University Press, 1986.

Burke, Michelle Prater. *Ideals Guide to Literary Place in the U.S.* Nashville: Ideals Publications, 1998.

Coleman, Laurence Vail. *Historic House Museums*. Washington, DC: American Association of Museums, 1928 (reproduced by Nabu Press in 2011).

Danilov, Victor J. *Museums and Historic Sites of the American West*. Westport, CT: Greenwood Press, 2002.

———. *Living History Museums and Historic Sites in the United States*. Jefferson, NC: McFarland & Co., 2010.

Donnelly, Jessica Foy. *Interpreting Historic House Museums*. Nashville: American Association for State and Local History, 2002.

Gutek, Gerald Lee, and Patricia Gutek. *Plantations and Outdoor Museums in America's Historic South*. Columbia: University of South Carolina Press, 1996.

Hosmer, Charles B., Jr. *Presence of the Past: A History of the Preservation Movement in the United States before Williamsburg*. New York: G. P. Putnam's Sons, 1965.

Hufbauer, Benjamin. *Presidential Temples: How Memorials and Libraries Shape Public Memory*. Lawrence: University Press of Kansas, 2006.

Hyland, Pat. *Presidential Libraries and Museums: An Illustrated Guide*. Washington, DC: CQ Press, 1995.

King, Grace. *Mount Vernon on the Potomac: History of the Mount Vernon Ladies' Association of the Union*. New York: Macmillan, 1929.

Lamb, Brian. *Who's Buried in Grant's Tomb? A Tour of Presidential Gravesites*. New York: PublicAffairs, 2010.

Leon, Warren, and Roy Rosenzweig, eds. *History Museums in the United States: A Critical Assessment*. Urbana: University of Illinois Press, 1989.

Living History in the National Park System. Washington, DC: National Park System, 1976.

Lowenthal, David. *Possessed by the Past: The Heritage Crusade and the Spoils of History*. New York: Free Press, 1996.

Mageissen, Scott. *Living History Museums: Undoing History through Performance*. Lanham, MD: Scarecrow Press, 2007.

Murtagh, William J. *Keeping Time: The History and Theory of Preservation in America*. Pittstown, NJ: Main Street Press, 1988.

The Official Museum Directory. Berkeley Heights, NJ: National Register Publishing/American Association of Museums, 2012.

Schick, Frank L. *Records of the Presidency: Presidential Papers and Libraries from Washington to Reagan*. Phoenix: Oryx Press, 1989.

Thane, Elswyth. *Mount Vernon Is Ours. The Story of Its Preservation*. New York: Duel, Sloan, and Pearce, 1966.

Tilden, Freeman. *Interpreting Our Heritage*. 4th ed. Chapel Hill: University of North Carolina Press, 2008.

Trubek, Anne. *A Skeptic's Guide to Writers' Houses*. Philadelphia: University of Pennsylvania Press, 2010.

Veit, Fritz. *Presidential Libraries and Collections*. Westport, CT: Greenwood Press, 1987.

Visiting Our Past: America's Historylands. Washington, DC: National Geographic Society, 1977.

Walker, Patricia Chambers, and Thomas Graham. *Directory of Historic House Museums in the United States*. Lanham, MD: AltaMira Press, 1999.

Wallace, Michael. *Mickey Mouse History and Other Essays on American Memory*. Philadelphia: Temple University Press, 1996.

Webster's New Biographical Dictionary. Springfield, MA: Merriam-Webster Inc., 1995.

Welborn. B. J. *America's Best Historic Places to Take the Family*. Chicago: Chicago Review Press, 1998.

———. *Traveling Literary America: A Complete Guide to Literary Landmarks*. Lookout Mountain, TN: Jefferson Press, 2005.

Index

Post, Marjorie Merriweather, 389–90, 392
Powell, John Wesley, xvi, 114, 391, 402
President Andrew Johnson Museum and Library, 242, 402
President Calvin Coolidge Museum and Education Center, 261–62, 403
President Chester A. Arthur State Historic Site, 248, 403
President James Buchanan's Wheatland, 229–30, 401
President James K. Polk State Historic Site, 224–25, 399
President Lincoln's Cottage, xiii, 237, 393
President Zachary Taylor's Mausoleum and Monument, 226, 395
Presidential Records Act of 1978, xi
presidents, xi–xv, 202–92
Presley, Elvis, viii, ix, xxx, xxxii, xxxiii, xxxiv, 164–66, 397, 402
Priestley, Joseph, xxvii, xxviii, 351–53, 399
Prudence Crandall Museum, xxiv, xxvii, 96, 392
public officials/political figures, xix–xx, 292–328
Pulitzer, Joseph, 131
Pyle, Ernie, 132–33, 394, 398
Pyle, Howard, 23

Quayle, Dan, 323–24, 394
Queen Emma Summer Palace, xx, 303–4, 393

Rachel Carson Homestead, xxxi, 38–39, 401
"Rags to Riches" Museum, xi
Ralph Waldo Emerson House, xxxi, 40–41
Randolph, William, 211
Rayburn, Samuel T., viii, xix, 276, 323–24, 402
Reagan, Ronald, xii, 221, 283, 284–87, 288, 310, 392, 394
Red Hill Patrick Henry National Memorial, xviii, 179–80, 403
Reed, Walter, xxviii, xxix, 138–39, 403
religious leaders, xxiii–xxiv, 329–41
Remington, Frederic, 18, 398
Reneker Museum of Winona History, xi
Republic of Texas, 223, 224, 226, 292, 312, 313
Revere, Paul, xviii, 181–82, 396
Rex Allen Arizona Cowboy Museum, xxxiv, 1, 391
Reynolda House Museum of American Art, 92
Reynolds, Burt, 7, 393
Reynolds, Richard Joshua (R. J.), 92–93, 403
Reynolds Homestead, xxii, 93, 399, 403
Richard Nixon Library and Birthplace, xi, 279
Richard Nixon Presidential Library and Museum, xi, xiii, 279–80, 392
Richard Petty Museum, xxvi, 30, 399
Riley, James Whitcomb, xxxi, 196–97
Ringling, John, xxxiii, 99, 103–5, 393
Ringling, Mable, xxxiii, 104, 393
Ringling Bros. and Barnum & Bailey Circus, xxxiii, 99, 103–4
Ringling Bros. Circus, xxxiii
Ringling Brothers Circus, 103
Robert E. Lee Memorial, xx
Robert Frost Farm, 192–93, 398
Robert Frost Stone House Museum, xxxi, 193, 403
Robert Fulton Birthplace, xxviii, 349, 401
Robert J. Dole Institute of Politics, xx, 301–2, 395
Robert Louis Stevenson House, xxxi, 60–61, 392
Robert Louis Stevenson Memorial Cottage Museum, xxxi, 61, 399

Robert Louis Stevenson Silverado Museum, ix, xxxi, 60, 392
Robert Penn Warren Birthplace Museum, 199–200, 395
Robert R. McCormick Museum, xxiii, 131–32, 394
Robert S. Kerr Museum, 316–17, 400
Roberto Clemente Museum, xxvi, 25, 401
Robeson, Paul, viii, xxxiv, 166–68, 398, 401
Robinson, Eddie G., xxvi, 30, 395
Robinson, Jackie, x
Rockwell, Norman, 18–20, 396, 403
Rodgers, Jimmie, xxxiv, 168, 397
Rodin, Auguste, xxx, 20, 401
Rodin Museum, ix, xxx, 20, 401
Roger Maris Museum, xxvi, 28, 399
Roger Miller Museum, 162–63, 400
Roger Williams National Memorial, xxiii, 337–39, 401
Rogers, Will, viii, xxxii, xxxiii, 105–6, 168, 392, 400
Ronald Reagan Birthplace and Museum, 286, 394
Ronald Reagan Boyhood Home and Visitors Center, 286, 394
Ronald Reagan Presidential Library and Museum, ix, xii, *xiii*, 284–86, 392
Ronald W. Reagan Museum at Eureka College, 287, 394
Roosevelt, Eleanor, xv, 119–20, 154, 239, 264, 265, 398
Roosevelt, Franklin Delano, viii, xi, xv, xix, xxv, xxvii, 134, 154, 262, 264–68, 276, 285, 308, 315, 373, 393, 395, 398, 399; advisors, 95, 126; New Deal, 285, 308, 323–24
Roosevelt, Theodore, viii, xiii, 134, 152, 247, 253–56, 258, 265, 396, 399; Spanish-American War and, 251–52, 254
Roosevelt Campobello International Park, 266, 395
Roosevelt Warm Springs Institute for Rehabilitation, 265, 267
Roosevelt's Little White House State Historic Site, 266–67, 393
Rosa Parks Library and Museum, xxv, 377–79, 391
Rosemary Clooney House, xxxii, xxxiv, 156–57, 395
Ross, Betsy, xviii, *182*, 182–83, 400
Rowan Oak, Home of William Faulkner, 41, 397
Russell, Charles M., 20, 397
Ruth, Babe, xxvi, 31, 395
Rutherford B. Hayes Presidential Center, 245–46, 400

Sacagawea, xvi, 110, 114–16, 393
Sacajawea Interpretive, Cultural, and Educational Center, xvi, 115–16, 393
Sacajawea Interpretive Center, xvi, 114–15, 403
Sagamore Hill National Historic Site, xiii–xiv, 255, 399
Saint-Gaudens, Augustus, xxx, 20–21, 398
Saint-Gaudens National Historic Site, xxx, 20–21, 398
Salvador Dali Museum, ix, xxx, 14–15, 393
Sam Houston Memorial Museum, 312–14, *314*, 402
Sam Houston Schoolhouse, 314–15, 402
Sam Rayburn House Museum, 324
Sam Rayburn Library and Museum, xix
Sam Rayburn Museum, 323–24
Samuel J. Rayburn House Museum, xix, 402
San Felipe de Austin State Historic Site, 292–93, 402
Sandburg, Carl, xxxi, 197–98, 393, 399
Sandoz, Mari Susette, 58–59, 398
Santa Anna, Antonio López de, 127, 226, 293, 313
Santa Anna, Antonio López de, xviii, 123
Schulz, Charles M., 21, 391
scientists/engineers/inventors, xxvii–xxix, 341–56
Scott, Winfield, 228
Scott Joplin House State Historic Site, viii, xxxiv, 160, 397